A New South Dakota History

D1567246

A New South Dakota History

General Editor
Harry F. Thompson

THE CENTER FOR WESTERN STUDIES
AUGUSTANA COLLEGE   2005

Contributors

Herbert T. Hoover, University of South Dakota
John E. Miller, South Dakota State University

Ruth Ann Alexander, South Dakota State University
Vine Deloria, Jr., University of Colorado
Edward P. Hogan, South Dakota State University
Carol Goss Hoover, Colorado Technical University and Mount Marty College
Arthur R. Huseboe, Center for Western Studies
Bob Lee, Sturgis, South Dakota
Michael J. Mullin, Augustana College
Rex C. Myers, Northwest College
Gary D. Olson, Augustana College
Lynwood E. Oyos, Augustana College
Ron Robinson, Augustana College
Virginia Driving Hawk Sneve, Rapid City, South Dakota
Betti C. VanEpps-Taylor, Buhl, Idaho
David A. Wolff, Black Hills State University

Published by The Center for Western Studies
Mailing address: Box 727, Augustana College, Sioux Falls, SD 57197
Building address: Augustana College, 2201 S. Summit Ave., Sioux Falls, SD 57197
E-mail address: cws@augie.edu
Copies of the current book catalog are available upon request at 605-274-4007 or visit
http://www.augie.edu/CWS.

The Center for Western Studies is an archives, library, museum, publishing house, and educational agency concerned principally with collecting, preserving, and interpreting prehistoric, historic, and contemporary materials that document native and immigrant cultures on the
northern prairie-plains. The Center promotes understanding of the region through exhibits,
publications, art shows, conferences, and academic programs. It is committed, ultimately, to
defining the contribution of the region to American civilization.

Library of Congress Cataloging-in-Publication Data
A new South Dakota history / contributors, Herbert T. Hoover ... [et al.].
    p. cm.
Includes bibliographical references and index.
ISBN 0-931170-83-4 (soft) -- ISBN 0-931170-84-2
1. South Dakota--History. I. Hoover, Herbert T. II. Title.

F651.N49 2005
978.3--dc22

                                    2005051320

Front cover images: Courtesy © Paul Horsted/dakotaphoto.com and Yankton County
                    Historical Society
Back cover image: Courtesy USGS EROS Data Center
Title page image: Courtesy © Paul Horsted/dakotaphoto.com

Publication made possible by grants and gifts from Howard and Eunice Hovland, Elmen
Family Foundation, Sheldon F. Reese Foundation, Sioux Falls Area Community Foundation,
South Dakota Community Foundation, Jerry Johnson, and Herbert T. Hoover, and with the
assistance of Pine Hill Press.

Printed in the United States of America by Pine Hill Press, Sioux Falls, SD

Contents

General Editor's Preface

Planning for *A New South Dakota History* began in 2001 with the recognition on the part of the staff of the Center for Western Studies, a regional studies agency of Augustana College, that the state was entering the new millennium without the benefit of a fresh interpretation of its past. As South Dakota's sole academic press, the Center had published several books of state-wide interest, including *The Geography of South Dakota, Sioux Country: A History of Indian-white Relations, An Illustrated History of the Arts in South Dakota*, and *What It Took: A History of the USGS EROS Data Center*, so it seemed appropriate that the Center consider undertaking a new state history. Upon the recommendation of the the the Center's Publications Committee, chaired by Dr. Lynwood E. Oyos, the Board of Directors of the Center for Western Studies, chaired by Dr. Tom Kilian, authorized the staff in September 2001 to explore the feasibility of a new state history.

Others had also been thinking along these lines, for within a few months two of the state's eminent historians—Dr. Herbert T. Hoover, of the University of South Dakota, and Dr. John E. Miller, of South Dakota State University—independently submitted proposals for a new history of the state. After meeting with Professors Hoover and Miller, the Publications Committee recommended combining the acknowledged strengths of these historians, along with chapters by other historians, to produce a collaborative interpretation of the state's past, one that emphasized the cultural and geographic diversity of the state through multiple authorship.

To this end, the committee elected to commission a group of sixteen authors to research and write a cultural history of South Dakota suitable for a general audience, including school teachers, students, political and business leaders, and the news media. The consensus of the committee was that the history should not attempt to be comprehensive but treat a selection of events and themes of fundamental importance and, by the inclusion of a recommended readings list, point toward available resources for further study. Further, the committee wished the history to address, through personal essays, spiritual and social aspects of the state's Native American culture, myth and reality of small-town life, and contributions of women writers.

The project received its first airing in South Dakota in May 2002 at the Thirty-fifth Annual Dakota Conference on Northern Plains History, Literature, Art, and Archaeology, at which a session was devoted to public comment. This was followed by a news release to the media in October 2002, announcing the project and the names of contributing authors. To encourage broad participation in the study of the state's history during the course of this project, the Dakota Conference, for the years 2003 through 2005, proposed to examine the cultural and geographic identities of which South Dakota is comprised: the prairie, plains, and Black Hills.

Since publication projects are financed outside of the Center's operating budget, fund-raising efforts on behalf of the project began almost immediately. The first proposal, to a local bank, met with failure. Seeking confirmation of the vision of the Center's board, the staff continued to write grant proposals throughout 2002. To provide funding in the interim, Professor Hoover asked that honoraria he had earned as a consultant on two other projects be donated to this project. In December 2002, having learned of the need for funding, professional educators Howard and Eunice Hovland, of Baltic, provided a major financial gift, which made it possible for the project to proceed with certainty. Shortly thereafter, the Center was notified that three foundations had approved small grant proposals: the Sheldon F. Reese Foundation, Sioux Falls Area Community Foundation, and South Dakota Community Foundation. In 2003 the Elmen Family Foundation offered to match the Hovlands' gift—and the project became fully funded.

During this time, the contributors were hard at work researching and writing, and by the summer of 2004 all chapters and essays had been submitted. At the request of faculty members at both South Dakota State University and the University of South Dakota who wanted to use the new history as a classroom text on a trial basis, the staff of the Center produced a preliminary custom-text version for the exclusive use of classes at the two universities during the fall semester of 2004. Comments by the faculty members, Dr. Jon Lauck and Dr. Herbert Hoover, and their students were helpful in revising the final edition of the new history. This custom-text version, which also functioned as an advance copy, was peer-reviewed by two scholars in the fall of 2004.

A *New South Dakota History* is truly a collaborative effort. In addition to the contributors and financial supporters already noted, I would like to acknowledge the following: Dr. Arthur R. Huseboe, executive director of the Center for Western Studies, whose idea it was to publish a new history and who provided valuable editorial assistance throughout the project; interns Antonia Dauster and Elizabeth Thrond, who assisted in several crucial areas; the many individuals and institutions who supplied photographs, as acknowledged elsewhere in the text, especially the South Dakota State Historical Society—State Archives, University of South Dakota Archives and Special Collections, Karl E. Mundt Historical and Educational Foundation and Archives, Dakota State University Archives, Adams Museum and House, South Dakota Art Museum, Dakota Indian Foundation, Yankton County Historical Society, Sacred Heart Monastery Archives, USGS EROS Data Center, South Dakota Tourism, Institute for Regional Studies (North Dakota State University), *Sioux Falls Argus Leader, Rapid City Journal*, and professional photographers Joel Strasser and Paul Horsted; Augustana College's Mikkelsen Library for scanning photographs; Center colleagues Dean A. Schueler and Lisa Hollaar for their support; and the printer, Pine Hill Press, who demonstrated extraordinary patience and care throughout the project. I would also like to extend a personal note of appreciation to my wife, Ronelle Thompson, and my children, Clarissa and Hal.

HARRY F. THOMPSON
Director of Research Collections and Publications
The Center for Western Studies, Augustana College

Introduction
South Dakota's Histories

This volume describes the past in South Dakota from prehistory to the outset of the twenty-first century. Some chapters provide new interpretations for topics already evaluated in the historical literature while others present themes not previously addressed in any publications. Sixteen authors include men and women who have earned the greatest recognition for their cultural and historical studies of the northern Great Plains. Accordingly, at the time of publication, the aggregate of their contributions must be regarded as a definitive study.

The need for this book is obvious. In the past, only three general histories of the state have appeared in book form that have received approval by professional peer review, each written with restrictive characteristics and all of them out of print. University of South Dakota Professor of History Herbert S. Schell published *History of South Dakota* through the University of Nebraska Press in three editions, the last during the year 1975. His was a pioneering effort to condense a limited variety of sources into a chronological narrative history that dealt mainly with political and economic themes. Its restrictive design is well known in the profession of history as "Paxsonian"—so-called because Schell's mentor was Frederick Logan Paxson, author of the first general history of the American West. Initially at the University of Wisconsin (where Schell took graduate training under his supervision), then at the University of California, Paxson advised graduate students that the charge of a professional historian was mainly to deal with political and economic subjects.

In Paxson's view, additional topics should be left to scholars in other disciplines—sociology, literature, anthropology, archaeology, etc. A plethora of historical themes missing in the Paxsonian model included many of importance in the history of South Dakota—Indian-white relations, tribal cultures, varied non-Indian ethnic characteristics that grew out of protracted immigration, the special roles of women and African Americans, intrastate sectional sociological differences, Christian denominational histories, artistic developments, health care delivery, the development of the Missouri River, tourism, road construction, change in the nature of urban communities—the list runs on. All of them received little if any attention in the seminal work by Professor Schell not only because he wrote an exemplary Paxson model, but also because he finished his work before the evolution since the 1960s of interdisciplinary scholarship and availability of documentary sources by their organization for use. In light of recent scholarship, even Schell's narrative history of political and economic themes is flawed because of the limited variety of sources available at the time he wrote and the absence of insights drawn from oral history. By professional standards at the outset of the twenty-first century, his Paxsonian history should be relegated to the reference shelves, with respect, for use as a source of selective details that remain reliable because of the author's integrity. A welcome revision of Schell's history, with a preface and new chapters by Professor John E. Miller, was published by the South Dakota State Historical Society Press in 2004.

A second general study to appear in book form was an extraordinary contribution by University of South Dakota Professor of English John R. Milton entitled *South Dakota: A Bicentennial History*, which appeared in *The States and the Nation* series published by the W. W. Norton & Company to celebrate the bicentennial of the United States. Members of an editorial advisory board searched for authors not to prepare the histories of the fifty states but rather to write analytical studies about the states. Board member A. Russell Mortensen, the assistant director of the National Park Service, sought commitments by prospective authors for states in the northern Great Plains with an intention wherever possible to contract services from the discipline of literature. As Mortensen's liaison, I first discussed the project with the distinguished novelist Frederick Manfred. He declined in the belief that such a study was beyond the scope of his literary interests. Manfred recommended Milton, who twice declined when I presented the opportunity— partly because he wrote fiction and also because he had not written for publication in book form. Finally, Milton agreed and, two years later, presented an early copy with this inscription above his signature, dated June 4, 1977: "For Herbert Hoover, my friend and colleague, who talked me into doing this book and must now accept the consequences. Thanks, Herb, for trusting me." Anyone familiar with the work of John Milton understands how professionally trustworthy he was and why his contribution to the bicentennial series has been received by scholars as a treasure. Milton wrote a fascinating volume about South Dakota history but not a history of the state.

The third and only other study of the general history of South Dakota in book form that gained wide recognition under peer review bore the primary title of *South Dakota Leaders*, published and distributed by University Publishing Associates, Inc., from offices in Maryland and London. The National Endowment of the Humanities funded its composition and publication as a feature in the celebration of the state centennial during the year 1989. University of South Dakota professors Herbert T. Hoover and Larry J. Zimmerman served as editors while they invited twenty-nine other authors to join them in addressing the history of the state through the lives of approximately fifty South Dakotans who had distinguished themselves. Frederick Manfred wrote a preface. The editors composed an introduction. This volume gained recognition in Europe as well as in the United States because authors of the biographies were the writers best qualified to address contributions by their exemplary subjects.

In the absence of another general history that accommodates professional standards, readers have been able to peruse thousands of books, chapters, and articles that address special features in the history of the state. Every major general encyclopedia contains a carefully edited chapter about South Dakota, each frequently revised to bring it up to date. An interesting volume, edited by James H. Madison and published by Indiana University Press in 1988 under the title *Heartland*, includes a chapter on South Dakota in a comparative study about the histories of midwestern states. Similarly, the *Encyclopedia of the Great Plains*, edited by David Wishart and published by the University of Nebraska Press in 2004, and the *Encyclopedia of the Midwest*, scheduled for release by Indiana University Press in 2005, provide the reader with an opportunity to compare South Dakota history to the histories of other central states.

Special monographic studies have appeared, many of them professionally reviewed for accuracy and published by the Center for Western Studies. For example, the current Executive Director, Professor Arthur R. Huseboe, composed *An Illustrated History of the Arts in South Dakota* (1989), assisted by Dr. Arthur Amiotte. The former Director,

Professor Sven G. Froiland, wrote the pioneering *Natural History of the Black Hills and Badlands* (1990). Professors Herbert T. Hoover and Carol Goss Hoover consolidated the complex history of Indian-white relations into a custom textbook entitled *Sioux Country: A History of Indian-white Relations* (2000). Authors associated with the Center also contributed to an anthology of essays published by the University of South Dakota Press entitled *From Idea to Institution: Higher Education in South Dakota* (1989), for which eighteen authors wrote the histories of all higher educational institutions that survived in the state to the centennial year 1989.

Thousands of other books and articles address particular aspects of South Dakota history, anthropology, sociology, art forms, and ethnic studies—a large number about Indian-white relations and central features in tribal cultures. The most recent bibliography designed with annotations for use as a readers' guide is a two-volume publication current to the year 1993 compiled by Herbert T. Hoover and Karen P. Zimmerman and issued by Greenwood Press (1993). University of South Dakota archivist/historian Karen Zimmerman contributed an extraordinary chapter on publications about prehistory and a description of primary source collections within the state. Hoover added evaluations of the most useful collections outside of the state and composed extensive lists of annotated entries for a chronological sequence of chapters that included books, articles, and documents of greatest value on a plethora of subjects from early historical times to the date of publication. The German scholar Ditmar Forst contributed an evaluation of Indian-white relations publications by European writers. Together, the editors added lists of useful periodicals, newspapers, newsletters, and public broadcasting sources. After perusing the complete manuscript, the managing editor of Greenwood Press ordered a division of entries into two volumes: *South Dakota History: An Annotated Bibliography* in the *Bibliographies of the States of the United States* series, and *The Sioux and Other Native American Cultures of the Dakotas: An Annotated Bibliography* in the *Bibliographies and Indexes in Anthropology* series. For the users' convenience, the two volumes contain a common index. Any reader or scholar who examines the index for these two volumes and explores electronic sources for the period since 1993 will easily identify most of the literature about the past in South Dakota.

General readers as well as scholars might be interested in several titles with narrow focus. Yale University Professor of History Howard Lamar published *Dakota Territory* through Yale University Press in 1956. This was the first territorial history written in the United States for publication by the standards of a major press and a book well received by scholars as an accurate expression of federal documents. Without professional review, Doane Robinson wrote two volumes of interest soon after statehood from the perspective of a newspaper editor and publisher: *History of South Dakota*, printed by B. F. Bowen and Company in 1904, and *History of the Dakota or Sioux Indians,* issued in 1904 and reprinted by Ross and Haines, Inc., as recently as 1974. Mr. Robinson came to the task with formal education no higher than the eighth grade but gained respect for his capacity to gather information, an attribute that led to his appointment as state historian in 1901. Readers must understand that Robinson's works contain obvious errors, but they provide interesting perceptions during the period of their publication by an author neither trained nor recognized as a professional scholar.

A similar evaluation might be expressed about the interesting *Challenge: The South Dakota Story*, printed by Brevet Press in 1975. Written by the journalist Robert F.

Karolevitz, it is not a history but a volume about South Dakota's past, a readable, novelistic expression of features in the history of the state to the time of publication.

Few if any other states have been better served by authors in the past—amateurs, journalists, and public officials as well as academic experts. *A New South Dakota History* consolidates a great mass of fragmented information, drawn from original sources as well as previous publications, into nearly all central themes in the history of the state. Its readers may be assured that the authors have drawn upon thousands of books, articles, and documents as well as their own research materials to create a definitive study current at the outset of the twenty-first century. It will replace dated volumes issued in the past and should be perceived as the standard history until a future generation of scholars expands the text to include historical developments during several early decades of this century.

The design represents complexity in the history of the state. Any attempt to consolidate information from previous publications and literally boxcar loads of original documents into a chronological narrative history would end in failure. For this reason, the governing board at the Center for Western Studies approved an anthology that overlooks very few themes. Perhaps the only one of obvious importance is the history of law and jurisprudence, for which there exist no descriptive publications or even documentary evaluations. An obvious reason is that the operation of local, state, and federal systems has been very complicated, and the state and local systems of jurisprudence have dramatically changed through reorganization during the 1970s. Such a gap exists in literature about any state with a history that spans little more than a century. Because of a large amount of research and publication about the history of South Dakota, however, nearly all other central themes about South Dakota since prehistoric times are included.

As background, several opening chapters approximate chronological descriptions of main developments prior to statehood, all of which recognize the prevailing influence of Native Americans who asserted ancestral claims to land contained within the boundaries of the state. Notably, this new history begins with an essay by a leading Native American author born in South Dakota, Vine Deloria, Jr. The reader is then introduced to the physical environment by Professor Edward Hogan. Herbert Hoover devotes a chapter to tribal inhabitants in the region during the prehistoric and early historic periods. Professor Rex Myers recounts the course of exploration, including the Lewis and Clark Expedition, and describes the influence of the fur trade. Hoover includes an evaluation of tribal influences in the formation of the first permanent non-Indian population, situated along the Missouri River Valley. He continues with chapters about central themes during the territorial period. One describes the military defense of land claims by Indians, the replacement of ancestral tribes by modern reservation societies, and the cession of tribal land that was essential to the creation of a state in 1889. Another traces the history of territorial governance, which explains critical legislative and administrative functions as well as the evolution of local governments.

Texts about previous conditions and developments prepare a reader for the contents of all other chapters, which explore the most important historical themes that have fashioned the unique character of the state since 1889. A stellar group of authors with capabilities proven by previous teaching, writing, or publication provide evaluations of the formation of a non-Indian population composed of more than two-dozen ethnic groups. Professor Gary Olson describes how Yankee adventurers preceded the waves of European immigrants, and Betti VanEpps-Taylor demonstrates the persistence of African

American culture. A mosaic of enclaves brought the population of the state to approximately 630,000 residents by the year 1930, a number elevated to only about 754,000 by the year 2000. Gary Olson examines the enlargement of Missouri Valley urban centers into South Dakota towns and cities, and Professor John Miller reflects on the small town in South Dakota before turning to an examination of the political dispositions of South Dakotans through the twentieth century.

Professor Lynwood Oyos and journalist Bob Lee describe how the composite of farmers and ranchers sustained agribusiness as the principal economic force in the state for more than a century. Professor David Wolff adds an evaluation of Black Hills culture and its changing roles in the economic and demographic characteristics of West River society.

Two chapters explain Christian belief systems and educational experiences for both tribal and non-Indian residents. Carol Goss Hoover deals with the Roman Catholic influence, which has stood out for its work with Native Americans and has been second only to the aggregate of Lutherans in denominational size. Lynwood Oyos condenses the complex influences of Protestant forces into an evaluation of their effects in the population of the state.

Four chapters review the literature and the art of the state from the pre-settlement period to the present. Professor Arthur Huseboe opens his chapter on literature with a glance at two of the most famous early writers associated with South Dakota, Pulitzer Prize-winning Hamlin Garland and the creator of the Wonderful World of Oz, L. Frank Baum, both of whom lived a relatively short time in the state. A section on Ole E. Rölvaag as the master of the novel of the farming frontier is followed by sections on Sioux Indian writers and twentieth-century writers who have achieved a degree of fame and recognition for the state. Professor Ruth Ann Alexander emphasizes a particular dimension with an essay about women who have added substance to the literature of the state. Professor Ron Robinson addresses the visual arts and Huseboe the performing arts as dynamic influences in the history of South Dakota.

A chapter that explains the recent relegation of agribusiness to second place in the economy of the state includes subjects little addressed in the past. Herbert Hoover describes a complex network of health care delivery systems that has evolved into a major economic influence while it has matured adequately to meet the needs of both East River and West River non-Indian residents as well as Native Americans on tribal reservations. Two chapters explore the new economies of South Dakota. Professor Ron Robinson traces the growth of the main elements of communication—printing, mail service, telecommunications, photography, and data storage. A chapter by Rex Myers evaluates transportation and tourism and how they have effected change in the entire society.

In a personal essay, award-winning author Virginia Driving Hawk Sneve demonstrates how the traditional Native American family persists into the twenty-first century Herbert Hoover supplies insights regarding the survival and change in modern reservation societies. As nine segregated groups of federally recognized Indians, the aggregate population of enrolled tribal members exists as a political as well as a cultural force that makes up approximately ten percent of the population. This chapter explains eight trust responsibility benefits sustained by the federal government that account for the survival of tribalism with growth in total enrollment since the 1960s.

Professor Michael Mullin summarizes themes and addresses changes in the state while he assesses future probabilities. His insightful analysis serves as a capstone for the entire text. It is followed by endnotes to support chapters written by the authors, a bibliography of recommended readings, and an extensive index for use by general readers as well as scholars.

A New South Dakota History should evoke interest in a great variety of readers. Those situated in Europe as well as in other states long have demonstrated a desire to learn about South Dakota because of several features in its past, including Indian tribes, a multi-ethnic population gathered in East River settlements, extraordinary characteristics in West River populations related to the Black Hills, and the history of the Missouri River. Readers within the state will receive an enlarged understanding about many developments of the past that affect their lives. Board members at the Augustana College Center for Western Studies have inspired the issue of a book comprising as many dimensions as a publisher should include under the cover of a single volume.

HERBERT T. HOOVER
Professor of History, University of South Dakota

Chapter 1
Spirits and the South Dakota Land

An introductory essay by Vine Deloria, Jr.

The plains of the Dakotas are both hospitable and hostile to people. You must welcome their bounty but ensure that they do not sweep you up, taking your life, and making you a part of their restless spirit. The Sioux Indian people knew that they must be ever vigilant to the changes in weather, and they learned to read the clouds and winds and follow the trails used by other creatures when they moved camp or sought the buffalo herds when hunting. Thus their spirituality came from continuous occupation of the land and establishing relationships with the various creatures the land was supporting. Ultimately, this adjustment required that the people become reconciled to the other creatures that lived in the region. The land presented the place to live, and the animals helped to define the manner of living.

Religion, like other aspects of our human life, is a set of beliefs and practices developed over thousands, perhaps hundreds of thousands, of years. The religious experiences and expressions of any particular group of people vary in accordance with their situation and the immediate historical memories that are recalled as precedents to solve contemporary problems. So it is with the Dakota/Lakota people of our state. In order to understand the modern expressions of spirituality, we must look back as far as tribal memories can be extended to discover how the people arrived here and what this land meant to them.

The very earliest stories of the people must take place near the Gulf of Mexico and even, perhaps, in Central America. According to Black Elk, as recorded in *When the Tree Flowered*, there was a time when the people did not have fire, lacked relatives, and lived in amorphous social groupings without laws and customs save those that prevented continuous social discord. From the description of their condition, it seems likely that they were survivors of a major climatic catastrophe that had destroyed their previous social organizations and religious beliefs. During this stay in the far south they discovered fire, and one of their medicine men had a dream about a location he designated as the mysterious island hill. This site became the focus and destination of later migrations as the people moved out of the coastal plain in search of a land meant for them alone.

The migrations must have taken thousands of years because we have reference to a time when they appear to have lived in Central America in a land of many volcanoes. In later years when the Dakota/Lakota occupied the Dakotas, the people would camp along the White River, where there were columns of white smoke rising into the air from underground burning lignite. It was along this river that elders taught the people that the columns of smoke meant that a massive fire existed somewhere in the earth. By pointing out the many smokes, they were able to explain a land in the south where they had once lived. Actually, as late as the 1860s, there were columns of smoke rising in the Black Hills and along the Little Missouri in Montana, but the people, by then confined to reservations, were unable to pass along these stories because they were denied the chance to visit these locations.

There is also a story of primeval times in the traditions remembered by James Walker's group of elders, when the Seven Council Fires lived in the far north as small hunting bands that covered a large area and spoke the same language. Eventually, the seven largest bands became loosely confederated as the Seven Fires, or allies, for protection against more numerous and hostile neighbors. One day a powerful spirit appeared to them and warned of an impending climatic catastrophe. He urged them to go south until they found a land where the leaves of the trees were different. The northern sojourn may have happened during a time when large men and animals inhabited the continent because a related story, found also in the Cheyenne traditions, suggested that a major change occurred during which animals and people were downsized to their present stature. This disaster created the conditions whereby, to establish primacy in the new world, the two-leggeds and four-leggeds held their legendary race around the Black Hills. Since they appeared to have fire in this story, it must be later than the sojourn at the Gulf of Mexico.

We do know that the Dakota/Lakota traveled over most of the North American continent in search of the mysterious island hill because we find small groups with languages closely related to the Dakota language scattered up and down the Atlantic seaboard that are thought to have broken away from the main body as it wandered northwards from the Gulf of Mexico. The Dakota migrants seem to have gotten as far north as Pennsylvania before they turned westward into the Great Lakes area. Pressures from the Indians east and north of them forced these Great Lakes inhabitants to continue moving westward. Perhaps at this time the people divided into the historic tribes that we know today, such as the Winnebagos, Osages, Omahas, Poncas, and Iowas. At some point, however, at least one legend of the Dakota people relates that they lived on the shores of the "Western Sea" where they received the Sacred Pipe. Could they have meant the Pacific Ocean? Perhaps Lake Bonneville in Utah or Lake Lahonton in Nevada would have been impressive enough to convince them that these were vast inland seas. Unfortunately, so much of the oral tradition has been lost that we can only sketch out the possible migratory routes and offer a tentative "before-and-after" chronology that, although it is almost whimsical, gives us some sense of their historical journeys.

During the course of their migrations, the Dakota/Lakotas developed a ceremonial religious life that provided a relationship with the higher spiritual powers. We cannot guess the order in which these rituals developed, but a listing of them will prove useful in understanding the Indian people we meet in American history. In *The Sacred Pipe*, Joseph Epes Brown identified seven rites of the Oglala Sioux and compared them with Roman Catholic doctrines, hoping, one suspects, to validate them as religious practices. His identifications, however, make many Indians uncomfortable, particularly when he suggests that the White Buffalo Calf Woman is an Indian counterpart of the Virgin Mary, thereby affirming the reality of the Virgin and preempting the Dakota experience altogether. His list of rituals included the following:

1) *Waki Cagapi*—the keeping of the soul
2) *Inipi*—the rite of purification
3) *Hanblecheyapi*—crying for a vision
4) *Wiwanyag Wachipi*—the sun dance
5) *Hunkapi*—the making of relatives
6) *Ishna Ta Awi Cha Lowan*—preparing a girl for womanhood
7) *Tapa Wanka Yap*—the throwing of the ball

So popular has Brown's identification been that several generations of Indians have come to believe that the number *seven* has a special status in Dakota/Lakota heritage as *three, seven*, and *twelve* do in the Christian tradition. But Brown's list is neither exhaustive nor definitive of the actual number of rituals performed by the Indian spiritual leaders. He appears to have talked only with Black Elk, who would probably know only the stories passed down in his *tiospaye,* (also spelled *tiyospaye*) or family network.

Ella Deloria, a Yankton linguist working with Franz Boas of Columbia University, was asked to verify the accuracy of reports sent to the American Museum of Natural History by James Walker at the turn of the century. She went to many old people on the Pine Ridge reservation in the late 1930s, including, wherever possible, some of Walker's original informants or their children. She discovered that there were originally three basic rituals: the Sun Dance, Making of Relatives, and Preparation of Girls for womanhood, called the Buffalo Dance because womanhood and the earth were represented by the buffalo. These rites seemed to be universal among the Teton Lakota.

Closely related to these three were five more rituals, making eight major ceremonies and thus precluding Brown's later symmetry:

1) sun-gazing
2) making relatives
3) the buffalo ceremony (girl's puberty)
4) keeping the ghost
5) the virgin's fire
6) anti-natural feast (*Heyoka-wozepi*)
7) double-woman
8) the peace-pipe

She also found that the different bands of the Dakotas had ceremonies specific to their people. The Oglala, for example, also conducted these ceremonies:

9) killing the first fox
10) ritual before butchering
11) sitting down Omaha-style
12) throwing the challenge sticks
13) warrior training for young boys
14) fasting routine
15) sweat lodge routine
16) killing a spider

Most of these rituals were so old that only the elders could remember them and describe how they were conducted; they did not know why or when the rites would have been used.

There were probably more ceremonies practiced by the Dakota/Lakota peoples hundreds or thousands of years ago that eventually became victims of the passage of time and changing conditions. Thus the practices of today, which stress the sun dance, the Yuwipi, or ceremony of the stone dreamers, and the sweat lodge, and neglect the other rites identified by Brown and Deloria, would certainly be regarded by future observers as fundamental to the exercise of the tribal religion. Even Brown admitted that no one knew what "throwing the ball" was supposed to represent. We can suggest, therefore, that as the Dakota/Lakota people completed their migrations and moved into the Dakota region, they brought with them a set of ceremonies that had served them well in previous places.

A major task in adjusting to the prairie lands of the Dakotas required close observation of the unusual features of the landscape. People noticed the gathering of birds at Spirit Mound near Vermillion, visited later by Lewis and Clark, and, knowing that the

The Black Hills of western South Dakota, called *Paha Sapa* by the Lakota, who consider them sacred, were once the home of the world's largest gold mine, Homestake, and are today a national tourist destination. *Center for Western Studies.*

spirits often took the physical form of birds to perform their tasks as messengers of the higher powers, set aside the Mound as a special place. They already knew about the Pipestone Quarry, having visited there since time before memory seeking stone for their pipes. There was a special ritual performed before entering the Quarry seeking permission from the spirits of the site to remove the stone for pipes. If the petition to enter was granted, a small rainstorm would occur and then the suppliants would be free to enter the site.

Moving up and down along the shores of the Missouri River, the people encountered the monster Unktehi who lived in the river with his glaring eye and sawtooth-shaped back. People avoided looking directly at him on the few occasions when he was seen, for it was noted that men and women often went insane and suffered bad luck if they saw him eye-to-eye. He seemed to be the last remaining creature from a previous world, although they could find skeletons of even larger creatures after intense rains when the stream banks gave way under the rush of waters and revealed what was buried in the earth. Even today some people claim to know the location of the last sighting of this monster. He figures in some of the complex legends of the early days and other worlds.

The White River surprised and pleased people. As noted, columns of smoke rose from its banks, and people remembered the long-ago times when their ancestors had fought against a people from the western mountains, probably the Salish who were on a hunting expedition into the territory of the Dakotas. In the midst of the struggle came a great earthquake, rolling the ground as if it was a rug being shaken, destroying the beautiful prairie and leaving only the burned-out stretches of riverbank. General Alfred Sully, looking at the North Dakota Badlands in the 1860s, a similar location where smokes rose, observed that it looked like hell with the fires almost burned out. Until very late in the people's experience, there were also smokes rising from mountains in the Black

Hills, and they speculated that the Hills might be part of another world. Thus the Hills were approached with true humility when the people entered to make new lodge poles.

When they did come to the Black Hills, the sacred island hill located in the center of the immense grasslands, they knew immediately that it was the site seen in a vision by Red Thunder eons ago when they lived on the Gulf of Mexico. Spiritual leaders further pointed out the great racetrack, the geological hogback formation that surrounds the Hills that had been the site of the great contest to determine the relationship of the two-leggeds and four-leggeds for this world. The race settled the question of who would be dominant in the new world in which they found themselves after the great catastrophe. Since that race, some elders have said, the Black Hills have been reserved for the birds and animals, and while the people could go there for tipi poles, vision quests, and short visits, they could not live there permanently.

Close examination of the Hills revealed many portals to other worlds, worlds that could only be reached by spiritual leaders who had been accepted by the spirits of the Hills. Thus Bear Butte, Bear's Lodge, and Inyan Kara, the heart of the world, became important locations for holding special kinds of ceremonies. It is said by the Holy Men that there is a cave in Bear Butte that can be visited during a ritual at a certain time of the year. Spirits in the cave instruct the people in many things and sometimes give prophecies about the future. An old story says that beneath the Bear's Lodge is found another world, with lakes and mountains just as in our world, but no one has known how to enter that world in many generations. Inyan Kara also has hidden places that only powerful medicine men can enter. Mountains in the Black Hills can be entered during the course of the ceremonies, suggesting that in some instances the spirit world and the world we live in are separated primarily by the way we understand the world.

During these journeys of exploration, the people found the sacred places either through vision quests or in dreams and visions thrust upon them during the course of

A point of entrance into the spiritual world for many Lakota, Bear Butte, *Mato Paha* to the Lakota, rises 1,200 feet in a cone-like projection from the plains floor northeast of the Black Hills. *Center for Western Studies.*

their daily life. Foremost in these experiences was the discovery and confrontation with the sacred stones that offered unusual powers to the spiritual leaders. On the top of certain buttes, the people found small, round stones that they said had been created by the thunders when the lightning struck the buttes during a storm. Medicine men usually had several stones to perform tasks for them. They were allowed to take a stone if it cried out to them that it would become their helper. But the stones had to be lying freely on the ground. One could not dig them out of the earth. If a stone were partially buried, that was a sign that it was not yet willing to align itself with a human. Some credence must be given to the belief that the Thunders made the stones. It seems most likely that in a few years of gathering stones the supply would be exhausted. Yet each generation of spiritual leaders found stones lying freely on the ground and ready to work with the human beings.

The stones could perform marvelous tasks. They could predict the future, heal serious and unusual illnesses, and secure the people in their villages by acting as sentinels. Some stones could also bring material things to the medicine men. Others could provide a special vision to view distant places. Frances Densmore, in *Teton Sioux Music and Culture*, relates many stories of the use of these powerful stones. In one reported incident, Goose, a Lakota medicine man, took a small stone and viewed the bottom of the Missouri when looking for a rifle that had been dropped into the river. He reported that when he looked at the river through the stone, the usually muddy water became clear—enabling him to find the rifle immediately. She also records incidents in which stones were sent to bring back certain physical objects and did so, to the surprise of the people observing the event.

Another kind of stone impressed itself on the people and these were called "picture rocks." Usually they were great granite boulders mostly sunken into the ground. Some people believed they had been brought to the plains by the ancient glaciers or gigantic floods. Early in the morning, just as the sun was rising, medicine men would consult these stones and discover that there were pictures on them predicting some event in the immediate future. People said the Night People imprinted them on the stones, although no clear definition of these people was ever given. Sometimes the pictures would appear on the face of cliffs such as the Deer Rocks in Montana or the prophetic Wall in the Black Hills. Aaron McGaffey Beede, an Episcopal missionary in North Dakota, related how these rocks one day predicted a severe thunderstorm and a lightning strike on a woman during a church service. Sadly, the pictures proved accurate and invoked great respect in him for the old ways of the spiritual elders.

If we look at the names the people gave themselves, we can easily determine the animals that were important to the people. Three animals come immediately to mind: the buffalo, the bear, and the wolf. Taken together, these three animals are found represented in the names of the people about sixty-five percent of the time. We can assume, therefore, that the spiritual relationship between the people and these animals was profound and long lasting. In character, personality, and emotional life, these animals behave in a manner very close to that of humans. They are very social, have great concern for their families, and can be fierce in defense of their own, but retain a sense of humor and penchant for recreation matched perhaps only by the beaver.

The Indian people depended upon the buffalo as the major source of their food supply both before they had horses and during the great decades of horse-mobility. People noticed that when a buffalo was injured the immediate buffalo family would gather around to help him. They were willing to sacrifice themselves during a time of danger by rallying near the wounded animal. But they also loved to wander into the sun-

Emblematic of the resiliency of life on the plains, the bison is today raised by ranchers in numbers approaching the vast herds that once roamed the Dakota plains. *Center for Western Studies.*

flower fields and toss the plants up in the air, catching them with their horns and adorning themselves with decorations. Most critical, from our perspective, was the manner in which the buffalo grazed and moved. Two elder bison would go ahead of the family group as scouts. The bulls would graze on the outside of the family group, with the cows and young calves in the center. They would rotate in case of bad weather so that everyone shared the hardships. Indians copied this mode of travel; a band, moving from one hunting place to another, would virtually duplicate the formation used by the buffalo.

The bear was an unusual animal and had a diet somewhat akin to that of the people. He could eat meat or berries and the combination seemed to suit him fine. We do not realize today how populous the bears were on the original plains landscape. Early reports tell us that great packs of white bears roamed the land, often bringing down the old bison that wandered away from the herd. James Pattie, an early explorer of the plains, recorded that in one day, while traveling some thirty miles along the Arkansas River, he counted over three hundred bears. There was thus a good chance that one would meet a bear before one met a buffalo or deer.

The bear had great medicine powers, and his knowledge of beneficial roots that could cure human ailments meant that he was highly revered by the people. The bear would appear in dreams and visions to bestow great healing powers on chosen individuals. The bear also had some prophetic powers, rarely exercised since the stones performed this function also, but greatly in demand during times of crisis. We can gauge the scope of the bear's influence on the people by simply noting the variants in people's names: Standing Bear, Conquering Bear, Black Bear, Bull Bear, and so forth. Humans displaying positive personality traits often were described in bear terms, demonstrating that the animal had a high status with the people.

The wolf had much the same profile as the bear. Large wolf packs roamed the western plains, competitors with the Indians for food. In some instances, it was a contest between wolf and human for buffalo meat, although the wolves generally took the aged and young while the Indians hunted the adult buffalo. Surprisingly, when not in direct competition for the buffalo, wolves were often friendly with the people. There are several stories of people who lived with the wolves or who were rescued by wolves that came to them in a blizzard and slept next to them, providing the human with sufficient warmth to survive.

The wolf's power to travel quickly and almost invisibly through the wilderness was the envy of the people. Almost universally the tribes of the plains called their scouts "wolves" because they were trained to move quickly without attracting attention. The survival of every hunting band was dependent on their scouts, who were responsible for locating both food and foe. Scouts were expected to give quick and accurate information. If a scout lied about or exaggerated what he saw, he might place the whole village in danger. So scouts—wolves—set standards for accurate observation and reporting. Some scouts were as legendary as the holy men. Standing Bear said that the Brûlé scout Roan Horse could travel fast at night because he could tell what the landscape was by the feeling of the wind blowing on his bare skin.

Other Indian names describe the relationship of these creatures with some tribal members. If we wished to examine the whole biotic scheme of the plains, we would need do little more than examine the names of the people and learn the stories of how animals and birds became friends with some of the humans, giving them mysterious powers. These relationships were always oriented toward the practical ways of living in this particular geographic region. People could understand the cycles of nature and the behavior of other creatures because of a deep apprehension of the world in which they lived. Although each tribe had its own name, the most common concept they shared was that the world was not physical but ultimately composed of spirit—*woniya* in the Dakota. This spirit, a superior intelligence, created the complexities of the world's organic growth and geological change. Indeed, it pervaded and supported everything.

Through understanding the relationships of man and earth and man and animals, the spiritual leaders looked for a path of action to describe the personal behavior necessary to keep people balanced and in tune with the rhythms of nature. Thus it was that the dances came about. Noticing that the birds and animals expressed themselves through dancing, the people celebrated their good fortune in the same manner. Dances can be classified as those of thanksgiving, petitioning, and celebration. Of course, there were no hard-and-fast distinctions made among the dance expressions since everything was intertwined in the minds of the people. Thus one might perform the sun dance as thanksgiving for benefits received, while another might be petitioning for good luck and assistance.

The buffalo dance and the war dance were held to seek good luck in war and hunting. These dances were public occasions in which the whole village participated. Some of the secular dances, if we would trace them back to the philosophical roots of the people, were probably originally thanksgiving and petitioning activities, although they have changed into a purely secular activity over the course of time. Participating in the dances meant creating a community mind through the melding of individual motives and energies. Thus people saw themselves as the co-creators of the future in the world in which they lived.

Revelations came to individuals, even though a heavy emphasis was placed on community religious cohesion. Young people were encouraged to undertake vision quests in order to discover the future pattern of their lives and to receive special powers through relationships with birds and animals that could benefit the community. Dreams could also provide a person with information and powers that could not be obtained by either experimentation or logical reasoning. There was no question that a person receiving a dream in which medicines were revealed, songs of power taught, or the future revealed, was a special individual in the eyes of the spirits. Dreams were an unexpected gift that was cherished and remembered. They could not be invoked or faked, which made them more valuable.

Visions were unique experiences in which people found themselves suddenly transported from their immediate physical surroundings and thrust into a strange, yet physical, world in which birds and animals conversed easily with them and frequently changed shapes to demonstrate the unity of entities in the world of spirit. Again they might receive a song to use to call a spirit helper or might be told about an herb that would be useful for a specific purpose, such as treating a wound or sickness, healing a horse, making a person invisible to the game and so forth. Sometimes the person experiencing a vision would return with a physical object he had received during the course of the vision.

So important were the messages from the spirits that the tribes devised a way to invoke visions, and since these experiences were similar to the dream scenarios, they called these invited experiences dreams or visions also. In *Teton Sioux Music and Culture,* the old men describing their religious experiences were careful to distinguish between visions and special dreams. Although they used the general term "dreaming," they readily distinguished the means by which their information and experience had come.

The most commonly used path to make contact with the higher powers was called, of course, the vision quest or *hanblechi*. In this practice, a person, usually a man, would offer himself by fasting on a high hill for four days or until he received a vision that would tell him something of his future life or enable him to make contact with some bird or animal that would take pity on him and be his friend. To ensure success, or at least enhance the promise of a favorable outcome, the person seeking the vision would ask a spiritual elder to supervise his quest. After receiving instructions from the elder and participating in a sweat lodge ritual to ensure his cleanliness, he would go to the top of a high hill and begin praying to the Great Mysterious, announcing that he was lamenting, with the hope that pity would be shown him by the spirits.

Some remarkable experiences occurred in these vision quests, and the supervising elder would always know what the lamenter was experiencing on the hill as the quest continued. Birds and animals might approach the person and encourage him with short cries of gladness. Insects might relate that the spirits were pleased with the effort being made by the person. Out-of-body episodes or psychological disconnects that changed the ability to see or hear might occur. A person might be taken to another place, sometimes into a location that would be important in his future, sometimes across the world to see distant lands or into the structure of the cosmos to see the breadth of life being infused into every living creature. Indians were not surprised to learn about the large oceans far from the prairies because they had flown over them or walked along their shores in these visions. After a vision had occurred or the four days had been completed, the person would come down from the hill, participate in another sweat lodge for cleansing, eat, and then relate parts of his experience to the supervising elder.

The distinguishing characteristic of the vision quest was that it represented the initiative of the human being in seeking the approval of the higher powers and consequently differed from the spontaneous dreams that others received. People might go on a vision quest several times during their lives, and they might also be enabled to undergo variations of this ritual based on the powers they had received in their initial contact. Indeed, the effort by individuals to separate themselves from the camp circle and go into

Erosion by wind and rain over countless millennia produced the stark beauty characteristic of the Badlands. *Center for Western Studies.*

the wilderness seeking counsel and advice through the medium of solitude and contemplation might well be considered a formal vision quest since many revelations came from these kinds of experiences.

Many young men sought to avoid the formal vision quest ritual because they knew that the life of a spiritual leader had many pitfalls and required a person of great moral strength to perform the tasks required. Sometimes the person was called to a vision quest by voices that continually sought his attention and directed him to offer himself in the ritual. One of the great contemporary medicine men at Rosebud said that he resisted doing this ritual for many years, but over that time period voices would remind him of the eventual need to undertake the experience. The great fear was that the person receiving a vision might be asked to undertake a life of poverty and humility or to sacrifice himself for the people without thought of reward. For the average person, these burdens were hardly welcome. Thus the commitment to the vision became a serious task.

One requirement of both the vision quest and the dream was the practice of enacting part of the vision or performing some feat that displayed the powers received in the sacred experience. That is to say, one could not merely speak of receiving an herb or medicine, but a person had to produce the herb and demonstrate its potency. Black Elk had a vision of dancing horses and later had to organize a dance wherein the people, symbolizing the horses, reenacted part of the scenario of his vision. Unlike faith healers and evangelists of today, Dakotas receiving powers had to display those gifts in front of the whole community. Healings had to be permanent; prophecies had to be fulfilled. No one could make claims that could not be demonstrated when the need arose.

The sweat lodge had an all-purpose function in that it was used as a means of cleansing oneself prior to undertaking another ritual such as the sun dance or vision quest, and it also produced powerful experiences when done for its own sake. A special hut was built in the shape of a hemisphere and covered with hides. In the center would be a hole dug in the earth into which people placed red-hot rocks. During the ceremony they threw water on these rocks four times as the ritual progressed. Medicine men would seek out specific rocks and find people who agreed that they would participate in the ritual. Participants say that when the spirits came into the lodge they could hear them as they encountered the hide coverings. The sweat lodge is the most popular and frequently conducted ritual today and, unfortunately, the ritual most often copied by non-Indian imitators.

A ritual not mentioned by either Joseph Brown or Ella Deloria is the Yuwipi. This ceremony goes far back in Dakota/Lakota history and has been performed over the years by many people who also have other powers. It follows a unique format not found in any other ritual and is performed at night. The practitioner's hands and fingers are bound tightly with rawhide or leather thongs until they are immobile. He is then completely wrapped in quilts, originally buffalo hides, which are also bound with leather straps all around him. He sings his songs in total darkness and the spirits come, manifesting themselves usually in little blue lights. Sometimes the spirits form circles and dance; other times they move rapidly around the room.

The spirits then converse with the spiritual leader, answer questions, and provide information requested by people at the ceremony. He can heal illnesses or give directions on what medicines to take, locate lost objects, or give advice about the future. When the purpose of the Yuwipi is fulfilled, the helpers light the room and the practitioner is seen sitting calmly with the quilts nicely folded, the leather thongs and straps neatly coiled in piles. Yuwipis are also popular today and conducted on reservations and in cities, performed by Yuwipi men from the reservations. Since healing is a major concern, descriptions of this ritual are often found in medical literature.

A major emphasis of Dakota/Lakota spirituality has always been establishing a proper relationship with the spiritual powers of the world. Birds and animals play an important role in every ceremony, if only because they are represented by the use of their physical body parts, the part representing the whole creature. Unlike Western religions, which exclude the living creatures of the world in ceremonies, the Dakota/Lakota religious traditions always seek to include the invisible powers of the natural world so that a ceremony becomes an expression by living things of their relationship to the earth.

During the 1920s, Indian people began embracing another indigenous religious tradition when practitioners of ceremonies using the peyote cactus plant fruit came into the northern plains. In some ways it was a response to the forced conversion of people once they were confined to reservations, although some of the southern plains tribes had traditions of using the plant in ceremonies long before that. In prolonged nighttime rituals involving the ingestion of the "button" or drinking a broth brewed with these fruits, people prayed before a traditional Indian altar and sought healings and prophesy. While missionaries and traditional practitioners opposed the spread of this religion, known as the Native American Church, it came to be seen as a valid indigenous expression of religious devotion, and in visions, when a person was offered a path to follow, it was included as a worthy vocation.

The Native American Church of South Dakota has been incorporated and has its own rituals and doctrines similar to those of other tribes in adjoining states. Today some traditional spiritual leaders also practice this faith just as they adhere to Roman Catholic and Protestant teachings and attend Christian services. The motto of many Dakota/Lakota people has been to accept whatever is good in other traditions and to find the path best suited for them to follow. Federal recognition of the church has meant protection from unnecessary harassment under the drug and narcotic laws. The Native American Church has been successful notably in combating alcoholism and domestic problems, although some religious conflict has occurred in families over membership in the church.

Chapter 2
Physical Environment

The great American portrait and landscape artist George Catlin, known for his depictions of Sioux and other plains Indians, in 1832 painted a verbal picture of the physical geography of a portion of eastern South Dakota when he described it as "undoubtedly the noblest mound of its kind in the world: it gradually and gracefully rises on each side, by swell after swell, without tree or bush . . . and is everywhere covered with green grass, affording the traveler, from its highest elevations, the most unbounded and sublime views of nothing at all, save the blue and boundless ocean of prairies that lie beneath and all around him, vanishing into azure in the distance, without a speck or spot to break their softness." Catlin's description of the Coteau des Prairies gives a sense of the beauty of the landscape known as South Dakota.

Verbal landscapes could be painted of each of the major physiographic regions of South Dakota. The scenes would vary from flat, dry ancient lake beds, to massive erosional plateaus scoured by ice and water, to deeply incised valleys bounded by rounded hills, to step-like tablelands rising in elevation like a staircase, to the majestic peaks of the Black Hills. The landscape would also reflect the climate, soils, flora, fauna, and water features of each physiographic scene. Actually, the intellectual artist would discover thousands of opportunities to paint scenic views of the major and minor landforms that comprise the landscapes of what is sometimes called "The Land of Infinite Variety."

South Dakota was formed over four billion years ago by major earth-building forces. It first broke through the earth's water surface between 1.6 billion and 600 million years ago. The first land area of present-day South Dakota parent material to emerge from the sea was the Black Hills. Later on, the eastern sections of the state emerged. The parent material that forms the foundation upon which the state's geologic structure is built includes granites, schists, and quartzites.

South Dakota lies on the Missouri Plateau at the center of North America. The Missouri Plateau is an extensive interior landform that gently slopes southeastward from the north, northwest, and west. Its topography includes low-lying river valleys carved by ancient streams; flat plains that are the floors of former glacial lakes; hills built of windblown soils and sands; hills shaped by water erosion; castellated badlands; plateaus interspersed with mesas and buttes; and the spectacular Black Hills. (See Map 1.)

Relief is the difference in elevation between the highest and lowest point in a landscape. The highest point in South Dakota is Harney Peak in the Black Hills at 7,242 feet in elevation. The lowest place is Big Stone Lake in northeastern South Dakota at 966 feet above sea level. Thus the relief of South Dakota is 6,276 feet. Interestingly, the average elevation of the state's landscape is about the same as the earth as a whole, 2,200 feet. In reality, the state's landscape can best be described as being gentle to rolling. Of course there are exceptions, such as the Black Hills and Badlands areas, but they cover less than fifteen percent of the land surface.

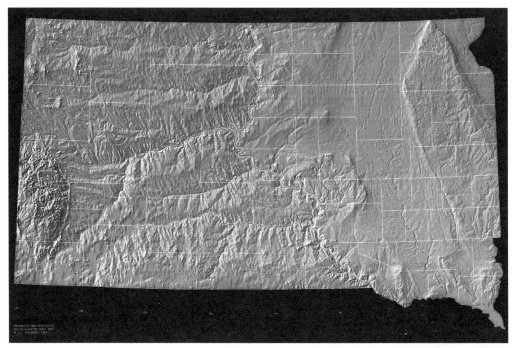

Map 1. A mosaic of remotely sensed satellite images of a physiologically dynamic South Dakota showing the Coteau des Prairies rising in the east out of Minnesota, the Missouri River flowing out of North Dakota and bisecting the state, the semi-arid plains lying to the west, including the Badlands arching just above Nebraska, and the Black Hills thrusting up from the plains on the Wyoming border. *Courtesy USGS EROS Data Center.*

■ Subsurface Geology of South Dakota

The ancient granite and quartzite base of eastern South Dakota is over 600 million years old. More recently, it was covered by water and debris, and occupied by various forms of sea and animal life. Among those types were the dinosaurs that disappeared from here about 100 million years ago. During this long period, deposits of sandstones and shales were built upon the bedrock.

Almost one million years ago, the Ice Age arrived in this area. Over time, the extensive ice sheets of four glacial periods covered the surface, shaped the landscape, and deposited debris as each retreated. The last glacier melted from the area about 10,000 years ago, leaving a thick covering of glacial drift consisting mainly of sandstones and shales.

The most recent glacial period is known as the Wisconsin Period. It lasted from 75,000 to 10,000 years ago and covered most of what is now eastern South Dakota. The limits of glaciation are generally defined by the course of the Missouri River. When the glacier retreated, it essentially left the visible terrain still found in eastern South Dakota. It should be noted, however, that streams further modified portions of the landscape.

Ice sheets dozed, crushed, cut, ground, and polished weak sedimentary rocks in their path. After the ice melted, the landscape was covered with glacial drift (rock debris) and till (dissimilar rock mixture). Finer materials were carried away by melting waters. Where the ice melt was trapped, interior drainage occurred and stratified drift (layers of silt, sand, and gravel) accumulated.

During the last 10,000 years, forces other than ice have shaped the state's landscape. It has been shaped by weathering, erosion, mass wasting, transportation, and deposition. The combined impact of these forces of nature is a landscape comprised of a variety of geographic features that make eastern South Dakota unique.

Western South Dakota is also part of the Missouri Plateau. It is more commonly referred to as the Great Plains. Located mainly west of the Missouri River, the landscape was not appreciably affected by Wisconsin glaciation. As a result, its landscape is very different from eastern South Dakota.

Western South Dakota is built of ancient sedimentary limestone, sandstone, and shale deposits, having emerged from the seas hundreds of millions of years ago. The most impressive limestone formation is the plateau portion of the Black Hills. Western South Dakota is also covered by sedimentary rock layers of sandstone and shale. These include Dakota sandstone, the principal artesian aquifer of western South Dakota, mixed sedimentary rocks, and a zone of limestone, chalk, and shale, which outcrops in places. Much of western South Dakota is overlain by the dark gray Pierre shale. Pierre shale was deposited on the bottom of a Cretaceous sea over sixty million years ago. When dry, the shale is weak and flaky and when wet, it is a thick and sticky, or "gumbo," substance. More recent sedimentary deposits are in the Big Badlands along the White River. There, fine sands, clays, and volcanic ash from the Black Hills and Rocky Mountains were deposited over Pierre shale by ancient streams.

The terrain of western South Dakota has been shaped by water cutting and carving weak Pierre shale into river valleys. Older and more resistant valley floors of gravel and sands withstood erosion and became highlands. Erosional forces also produced land-forms such as buttes, mesas, hills, and terraces. Streams flow eastward and have carved deeply into the shale areas.

The Black Hills are a miniature version of the Rocky Mountains. The Black Hills were thrust up through the Missouri Plateau about the same time as the Rocky Mountains, and by the same tectonic earth building forces. Combined, these forces caused the uplift, faulting, folding, and warping of the landscape. The result was a 300-mile-long buckle in the earth surface that extended upwards of three miles in elevation. Over time, natural forces have carved this massive block into the nearly elliptical-shaped Black Hills. The hills are comprised of four subregions: the Crystalline Core; the Limestone Plateau; the Red Valley; and the Hogbacks.

The rocks of the Black Hills are up to 1.6 billion years old. Metamorphosed ancient slates and quartzites are believed to be the oldest rocks found there. Included with these ancient rocks are the famous Black Hills gold deposits, which once supplied the largest gold mine in America. Granite is the principal rock of the crystalline core. Other rocks in the Black Hills include red sandstones and Paha Sapa limestones.

■ Physiographic Provinces of South Dakota

Located on the Missouri Plateau, South Dakota is composed of three main physiographic provinces or subdivisions of land based on topography. The three physiographic regions are the Central Lowlands of eastern South Dakota, the Great Plains of western South Dakota, and the Black Hills. Each of these regions extends beyond South Dakota's border and into other parts of the United States. Each major physiographic region is also divided into several subregions, which give us an even greater understanding and appreciation of the state's environment or physical geography. (See Map 2.)

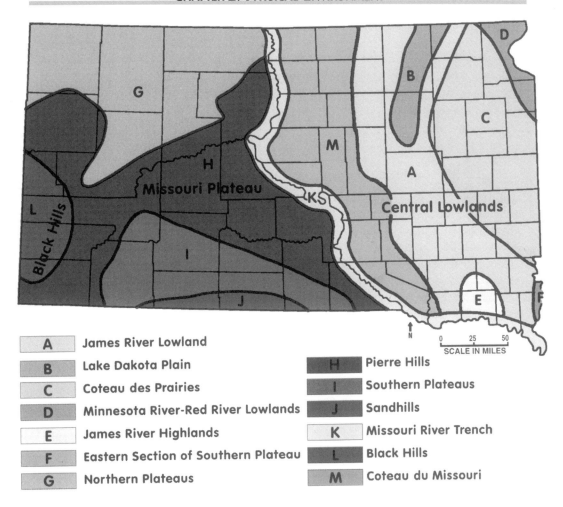

A	James River Lowland
B	Lake Dakota Plain
C	Coteau des Prairies
D	Minnesota River-Red River Lowlands
E	James River Highlands
F	Eastern Section of Southern Plateau
G	Northern Plateaus

H	Pierre Hills
I	Southern Plateaus
J	Sandhills
K	Missouri River Trench
L	Black Hills
M	Coteau du Missouri

Map 2. Physiographic Provinces of South Dakota. *From The Geography of South Dakota, Hogan and Fouberg.*

Central Lowlands

The Central Lowlands constitute the eastern third of South Dakota. This region extends eastward into Minnesota, Iowa, and other neighboring states and comprises part of the American Corn Belt. The major topographic features of the Central Lowlands are a result of glaciation. The landscape of this region is composed of gently rolling hills, with water-filled depressions, all resulting from the movement, scraping, scouring, and melting of ice. The Central Lowlands are composed of seven subregions each with unique landscapes and characteristics: the Minnesota River-Red River Lowlands; the Coteau des Prairies; the James River Lowland; the Lake Dakota Plain; the James River Highlands; the Eastern Section of the Southern Plateau; and the Southern Section of the Missouri River Trench.

The Minnesota River-Red River Lowlands were formed by an ancient northward flowing river. Later the area was attacked by glacial erosion. In South Dakota, this region is dominated by a narrow trench that was a spillway for the ancient glacial Lake Agassiz. Today, this trench is occupied by Lake Traverse on the north and Big Stone

15

Lake to the south. Between the two elongated lakes is a continental divide, near Browns Valley, Minnesota.

There the divide separates the waters of Lake Traverse, which flow into the Boise de Sioux, then the Red River of the north, and finally into Hudson's Bay and the Arctic Ocean, and Big Stone Lake, which flow into the Minnesota River, the Mississippi River, and the Gulf of Mexico. The continental divide here is so low that minor rises in the water level of one or both lakes can result in the two lakes flowing together into a single body of water and actually draining into both the Arctic Ocean and the Gulf of Mexico at the same time. The land is covered with ground and end moraine. The relief here is hardly noticeable, averaging less than twenty feet per mile.

The most conspicuous feature in the Minnesota River-Red River Lowlands is located in Grant County and is known as Mount Tom. It is a gravel end moraine about 100 feet high and about one-half mile wide at its base. The moraine runs eastward into Minnesota where it is known locally as the Antelope Hills.

The waters of Big Stone Lake and Lake Traverse cover extensive areas of the Lowlands. They are long and narrow in shape, and shallow in depth. Big Stone Lake is the largest. It runs from Ortonville, Minnesota, northwest to Browns Valley, Minnesota. It is twenty-five miles long and about one and one-half miles wide, and from fifteen to eighteen feet deep. Lake Traverse runs essentially north-northeast from Browns Valley for about fifteen miles. It is about one mile wide at its widest point, and has an average depth of ten feet.

The bedrock of the Minnesota River-Red River Lowlands is Pre-Cambrian granite. Just southeast of Milbank, South Dakota, is a small, unique area of extensive granite outcrops. The granite rock in this area is believed to be several thousand feet deep. It is a high quality granite that is today commercially quarried for monument and building stone. Throughout the rest of the region, the granite bedrock is covered by ascending layers of sandstone, shale, and limestone.

Glaciation played a major role in the shaping of the surface of this region. It left some very distinct physiographic features in the Lowlands. One is a series of very low beach ridges formed by ancient Lake Agassiz. The ridges can be seen in a ten-mile-long band at the South Dakota-North Dakota border. The old floor of Lake Agassiz to the north is today very flat and partially occupied by Mud Lake. Other glacial features are two moraines, the Big Stone Moraine and the Gary-Altamont Moraine. The former begins at the south end of Big Stone Lake and extends northwest. The latter parallels the east edge of the Coteau des Prairies. The western edge of the Lowland subregion is marked by a highland that stands about 800 feet higher in elevation. This highland subregion is the Coteau des Prairies. The Coteau is the most conspicuous landform in eastern South Dakota.

The Coteau des Prairies subregion is a flatiron-shaped plateau about 200 miles long and ranging from 1,700 feet to 2,000 feet above sea level. The point of the iron is in Sargent County, North Dakota, about fifteen miles north of the South Dakota border. On the southern end or heel of the iron, the Coteau merges into the general upland areas of Minnesota and Iowa. At its maximum, the Coteau des Prairies is about seventy miles wide.

The Coteau des Prairies reaches its highest elevation in the northeast near Roberts and Grant counties where its elevation surpasses 2,000 feet. The Coteau decreases in elevation as it slopes to the southeast, finally merging into the land near the South Dakota, Minnesota, and Iowa border just southeast of Sioux Falls.

The Coteau des Prairies is actually an erosional remnant of an ancient plateau. The northern escarpment of the Coteau is striking on its eastern side, rising over 800 feet above the Minnesota River-Red River Lowlands. The western edge is less noticeable than the eastern slope standing only 200 to 300 feet above the James River Lowlands.

Geologic evidence indicates that the bedrock of this glaciated subregion is buried some 100 to 400 feet below the Coteau's surface. The bedrock formation is primarily Pierre shale, which underlies all of the subregion except for a small area composed of Sioux Quartzite located in Minnehaha, Moody, and Lincoln counties. (See Map 3.)

Pierre shale is primarily clay with small amounts of quartz and bentonite. It is poorly consolidated and highly subject to erosion. If the Pierre shale is dry, it remains very firm and compact. However, when exposed to moisture, the bentonite within the shale absorbs water easily and makes the material highly plastic. The constant swelling and drying decomposes the material, breaking it up into flaky substances that can be easily transported by water, wind, and ice.

It is believed that the Coteau des Prairies exists because of ancient stream valleys that gave it its flatiron shape. During the glacial periods, drift was deposited around the edges of the Coteau, which impeded the advances of the most recent ice sheet movements. The Wisconsin glacial sheet attacked the Coteau des Prairies in stages leaving stratified drift, moraines (such as the Altamont), outwash deposits along its borders, and thin deposits of till, ground moraine, and end moraine across the landscape. Glacial drift, varying in thickness from 100 to 400 feet, covers the Coteau. Both margins of the Coteau contain nearly parallel recessional moraines or ridges of dumped debris left by retreating glaciers.

The Coteau des Prairies is drained by the Big Sioux River which virtually divides the subregion in half. The course of the river appears to be a result of the melting of two

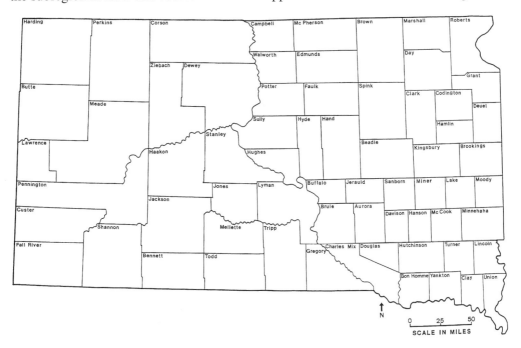

Map 3. Three-quarters of a million residents, 70,000 of whom are Native Americans, live in the sixty-six counties that comprise South Dakota. *From* The Geography of South Dakota, *Hogan and Fouberg.*

ice lobes that flanked the Coteau. While both lobes drained into the Big Sioux River, the lobe to the east melted faster than the western lobe. This resulted in the eastern tributaries of the Big Sioux carving valleys. The slower melt of the western lobe resulted in glacial drift blocking off former valleys. This resulted in the area west of the Big Sioux River being dotted with perennial and intermittent lakes and sloughs. The largest of these lakes are five to ten miles in length.

Traveling to the western edge of the Coteau des Prairies, one can see that the land is about to drop some 200 to 300 feet in elevation as one moves down the escarpment (steep slope) into the next subregion of the Central Lowlands.

The James River Lowland is a broad lowland situated between the Coteau des Prairies to the east and the Coteau du Missouri to the west. The James River Lowland is about fifty miles wide and 200 miles long from north to south. The lowland ranges in elevation from about 1,300 to 1,400 feet above sea level. The James River Lowland is about 200 to 300 feet lower in elevation than the Coteau des Prairies to the east. It is about 300 to 800 feet lower in elevation than the Coteau du Missouri to the west.

More erosion occurred in the James River Lowland than in other portions of eastern South Dakota. In the geologic past, two ancient streams drained northward through this area carving broad valleys below the neighboring coteaus. During the Wisconsin Glacial Stage, ice widened and united the two ancient valleys. As the ice retreated deposition occurred. Because ancient streams had already eroded the land below the adjacent coteaus, there was far less resistance to glaciation. Indeed, the glaciers were thickest in this subregion resulting in far more erosion.

Virtually every visible landscape feature of the James River Lowland is a result of glaciation. Ice widened and filled in valleys, deposited till and drift, and left recessional and end moraines. The result is a smooth, rolling area covered with glacial drift with some recessional moraines forming low west-to-east ridges. The glacial drift consists of numerous layers of stratified drift, till, and loess and indicates successive glacial retreats and advances. There are also three areas of isolated hills of drift-covered shale near Mitchell, Redfield, and Doland that stand sixty to eighty feet above the surrounding landscape.

The James River Lowland is underlaid by Pierre shale that resulted from ancient inland seas that deposited a thick layer of clays on their floors. Glaciers later entered the region from the north and northeast and deposited drift that ranges from fifty to 300 feet thick in places.

Today this region is a gently rolling plain incised by the James River and the other streams located in the subregion. The relief of the Lowland averages ten to thirty feet. The highest elevations in the subregion are end moraines, and the lowest elevations are stream valleys.

This subregion is drained by the James River, which flows through the central axis of the area. The Jim River, as it is also called, is often referred to as the longest non-navigable stream in the world. Its gradient is only five inches per mile. The river is so flat that, at flood stage, its tributaries may cause it to experience reverse flow. The river may also go temporarily dry during drought years.

The James River Lowland is also drained by two other rivers. The Big Sioux River exits the Coteau des Prairies and forms the extreme eastern edge of the subregion south of Sioux Falls. The Vermillion River drains through the southeastern portion of the region. Aside from the rivers, local drainage is poorly developed, with interior drainage dominating the surface. The James River Lowland contains numerous lakes, ponds, and marshes, which fluctuate greatly depending upon precipitation, snow melt, evaporation, or drought.

The Lake Dakota Plain subregion is situated in the middle of the northern portion of the James River Lowland. It is physically distinct from the lowland because it is the floor of an abandoned glacial lake or lacustrine plain. The Lake Dakota Plain extends from south of Redfield northward for over one hundred miles. Some ninety percent of it is in South Dakota, the rest in North Dakota. It is about twenty-five miles wide. It is remarkably flat with a local relief of less than ten feet. Indeed, the elevation of the plain is 1,300 feet above sea level at the North Dakota-South Dakota border and remains at almost 1,300 feet at the southern end of the lake bed.

This lacustrine plain is composed of alternating layers of fine and coarser silts, sands, and clays. The finer materials were deposited when the lake was frozen, and the coarser materials during open periods. The movement of water at the bottom of the lake spread out the materials producing an extremely flat floor.

The Lake Dakota Plain is dissected by a steep trench carved by the James River and its tributaries. The trench varies from thirty feet deep at the border area to one hundred feet deep at the south end. In the northeastern part of the subregion are patches of low, rounded hills of wind-blown sand that are termed hummocks.

The James River Highlands are located adjacent to the southern end of the James River Lowland and are the result of drainage changes that occurred during the last glacial period. The highlands consist of three ridges of drift-covered chalk or limestone bedrock.

Turkey Ridge is the largest of the three, rising over 300 feet above the surrounding land. It is about ten miles wide and forty miles long. Turkey Creek, an interlobate stream, divides the ridge flowing almost twenty miles through a 200-foot-deep narrow canyon. The James Ridge parallels Turkey Ridge. It is the smallest of the three ridges. It reaches about 260 feet above the surrounding landscape and is one mile wide and nine miles long. The Yankton Ridge is the third highland. It forms the northern border of the Missouri River Trench. The Yankton Ridge is about 500 feet above the Missouri River and extends from Yankton westward for about sixteen miles. All three ridges are composed of Pierre shale covered with thick glacial drift.

Along the South Dakota-Iowa border, in Lincoln and Union counties, is a very small subregion known as the Eastern Section of the Southern Plateau. It is basically a loessial highlands (windblown soil) that has been dissected by streams. Loess is windblown surface materials deposited over time along streams. The land here varies in elevation from 1,200 feet to 1,500 feet above sea level.

The extreme southern boundary of South Dakota is formed by the Southern Section of the Missouri River Trench. This unglaciated, flat river valley is that portion of the Missouri River that extends southeast and southward from Gavin's Point. The river lies about 100 feet below most of the surrounding sections of South Dakota, and 200 to 400 feet below the Nebraska and Iowa uplands. The Trench varies in width from two to three miles and contains extensive marshland, natural levees, and the lower portions of the James, Vermillion, and Big Sioux rivers.

Great Plains Province

The Great Plains Province is composed of six subregions: the Coteau du Missouri, the Missouri River Trench, the Northern Plateau, the Pierre Hills, the Southern Plateau, and the Sand Hills. This province encompasses the western two-thirds of South Dakota except for the Black Hills.

The easternmost subregion of the Great Plains is the Coteau du Missouri. This sub-region actually lies east of the Missouri River. The Coteau du Missouri is the western version of the Coteau des Prairies. It is an extensive remnant of a plateau that has been carved by ancient major streams. The bedrock is Pierre shale that is inclined toward the river and covered by glacial drift. Indeed, before the glaciers, the Coteau was a nearly flat bedrock region carved by major streams draining to the east and northeast. In portions of the Coteau du Missouri, the Pierre shale bedrock is overlaid by a more resistant sandstone caprock. Examples of this include the Ree Hills and the Bijou Hills.

The eastern edge of the Coteau du Missouri is composed of a variety of features. In the northern part of the subregion, glacial moraine forms the 2,000-foot-high Bowdle and Lebanon Hills. To the south of these hills there exists a thirty-mile gap where the Coteau and James River Lowland gently blend. Then a seventy-five-mile long escarpment rises 200 feet above the lowland, clearly reflecting the Coteau's eastern edge. The northern edge is the Ree Hills and the southern end is called the Wessington Hills. The entire course of the western edge of the Coteau is marked by the Missouri River Trench. Here it simply blends into "the Missouri Breaks." One of the principal effects of glaciation on this area has been to reduce the local relief.

A very significant feature of the Coteau du Missouri are landforms known as sags. Sags are lowland areas consisting of abandoned west-east-running ancient stream valleys that are now covered with glacial drift. The Great Ree Valley is the most conspicuous sag and is some 450 feet lower in elevation than the Ree Hills that parallel the sag's southern edge. There are four other sags that extend across portions of the Coteau du Missouri. These sags are not as clearly defined as the Great Ree Valley because they have been covered with drift during several periods of glacial action.

No major stream drains the Coteau du Missouri. The eastern edge of the Coteau is marked by short, parallel streams that drain into the James River. The western edge is highly irregular and runs into the breaks of the Missouri River. The Coteau is dominated by symmetrical interior drainage. The northern portion is marked by many local depressions that are filled by runoff and then dry up. The historical drainage pattern of the Coteau du Missouri has been very complex. Before glaciation, streams drained to the east and north. Today drainage is to the interior or to the west and south.

A second subregion of the Great Plains is the Missouri River Trench. This subregion extends from the North Dakota border to Gavin's Point. The Missouri River Trench is a deeply cut landform carved by and containing the Missouri River and its reservoirs. The Trench is a very steep cut into the Missouri Plateau, which results in a narrow river valley forming a barrier to east-west travel.

In its natural state, the floor of the trench is narrow, normally about one mile wide. The sides of the trench are very steep, extending 300 to 700 feet down from the plateau to the floor. The weak bedrock of Pierre shale exposed all along the Missouri River Trench has experienced excessive slumping and dissecting.

The Missouri River has been rejuvenated several times. This is a result of land being uplifted by various tectonic forces. As the region is uplifted, the stream again starts to reduce the land surface to sea level. Terraces along the valley walls provide evidence that each rejuvenation has resulted in more downward cutting of the valley.

The trench is bordered on both sides by steep-sided ravines extending several miles into the surrounding subregions and locally termed "the Missouri Breaks" or "the Breaks." They are an indication that this portion of the Missouri River is again in its youthful stage since these short tributaries have not had time to develop longer, gentler valleys.

The Missouri River drops in elevation about one foot per mile. At about the time the dams and reservoirs were constructed, the Missouri River was at equilibrium. That is, the amount of debris entering the stream was equal to its ability to carry it out. The dams of course changed this and today silting is a problem.

It should be noted that the present course of the Missouri River is a result of glaciation. The last ice sheet sealed off former streams that flowed across South Dakota from west to northeast. As a result of ice blockage, the Missouri River developed its present course.

West of the Missouri River, the Great Plains Province is composed of four more subregions. The Northern Plateaus encompass the northwestern portion of the state. The Northern Plateaus can be pictured as a staircase. The area increases in elevation in a series of step-like terraces from the Missouri River to the state's western border.

Each terrace is actually a broad, rolling sandstone plain that has been eroded by water and wind. This region was at least one thousand feet higher in elevation in the geologic past. From east to west, the steps increase in elevation. Looking back eastward from each step, the observer can see across the rolling landscape that multi-colored sandstone buttes litter the edge of each step below.

A butte is an erosional remnant resulting from the wearing away of softer sands and clays below a sandstone caprock. The sandstone caprock is part of a sandy rock blanket deposited by the ancient Cretaceous Sea. The largest and most famous buttes in the subregion are the Cave Hills, Slim Buttes, and the Short Pine Hills. The Cave Hills are salmon color, and the Short Pine Hills are especially beautiful areas with white caprocks accentuated by dark evergreens.

The Pierre Hills are a subregion comprised of smooth rounded contour hills that occupy the center of western South Dakota. The rounded hills are a result of the erosion of dark Pierre shale bedrock, which breaks down into a sticky clay called "gumbo." When wet, the clay resists water absorption; when dry, it tends to cake, flake, and decompose easily.

During wet periods, water rapidly runs off the hills and cuts deep into the weaker zones. Intermittent pools of water collect the runoff in the valleys. Alkali spots caused by a salt in the soil creates surface areas devoid of vegetation. Eastward flowing streams have cut trenches some 200 to 300 feet below the hills. In other places, prominent buttes stand above the surrounding hills. The buttes are capped with white or gray sandstones, and the highest rise some 400 feet above the surrounding lands. In the western portion of the Pierre Hills, low symmetrical cones called tipi buttes can be found.

The Southern Plateaus are another subregion of table lands composed of young rock debris deposited by the wind and water erosion of the Black Hills and Rocky Mountains. The plateaus are wide, flat areas of land between streams and contrasting deep, narrow stream valleys and canyons. It is also a region of badlands, buttes, and tables. The Southern Plateaus are dominated by colorful rocks of sands and clays. Streams have cut deep into landscape exposing the sub-surface rocks.

The northern part of the Southern Plateaus is noted for its areas of badlands topography. The largest and most famous is the Big Badlands, which follow the White River for over one hundred miles. Badlands result from combinations of factors including precipitation; running water; the weak soil and rock materials; and an elevation that produces rapid cutting by streams. The name "badlands" is given the region because it is a very rugged landscape that lacks water and vegetation.

Land in the northern part of this subregion consists of grass-covered level plains. Along the northern side of the White River Valley is an extensive physiographic feature known as the Great Wall. This badlands feature and barrier extends some sixty miles and contains numerous valleys, gullies, and passes including Big Foot Pass and Cedar Pass. The southern section of the subregion is locally known as the "Tables." It is comprised of large wide-topped buttes and mesas with some standing over 400 feet above the landscape below.

The smallest subregion of the Great Plains Province in South Dakota is the Sandhills. They are actually an extension of the Nebraska Sandhills. Here fixed sand dunes, now covered for the most part with grasses, form a topography of moderate rounded hills, dotted with some lakes and low swampy areas.

The sand dunes are the principal features of the subregion. The Sandhills are an eolian formation that was worked by wind into a succession of dunes in the Post-Pleistocene Era. Across the region three types of dunes are found: broad-massive-elongated dunes; narrow-linear dune ridges; and relatively small multi-shaped dunes. Over time, as a result of climatic change, the massive dunes stabilized and soil and vegetation developed. '

The lands between the Sandhills are essentially flat valleys. They tend to run from northwest to southeast parallel to the broad, massive, elongated dunes. These valleys vary in size and are dotted with intermittent marshes and lakes.

Black Hills

The Black Hills are the third major physiographic province of South Dakota. They are a miniature version of the Rocky Mountains formed at the same time and by the same earth-building forces. Diastrophic forces caused the surface to buckle and thrust a great earth block upward some three miles in the center of a long fold. The dome-like block extended from present-day northwestern Nebraska to Glendive, Montana.

Time and erosion have worn this great block called the Black Hills into an elliptical shaped region about sixty miles wide and 125 miles in length. The Hills rise almost four thousand feet above the nearby Missouri Plateau to the east. About two-thirds of the Black Hills lies in South Dakota, and the rest in Wyoming and Nebraska. The Black Hills are composed of four subregions, each quite different in appearance and size: the Great Hogbacks, the Red Valley, the Limestone Plateau, and the Central Crystalline Core. (See Map 4.)

The Great Hogbacks form the outer limits of the Hills. The Hogbacks are a residual monoclinal ridge resulting from sandstone bedrock that was upturned as the Black Hills broke through the earth's surface. As a result, it resembles the sharp back of a razorback hog, and that gives the region its name.

The hogback ridge of sandstone overlies weaker clays and shale. The hogbacks rise out of the Great Plains at an angle of about ten degrees and generally stand 300 to 600 feet above the surrounding land. The interior or Black Hills side of the hogbacks are much steeper, descending quickly into the Red Valley. At a few points, streams have cut water gaps through the hogbacks. These gaps may be as much as a hundred feet deep and are the main passes into the rest of the Black Hills area.

Inside the hogbacks, appearing like an elliptical course on a map, is the second subregion of the Black Hills. This impressive subsequent valley is known as the Red Valley. It gets its name from the deeply colored red sandstone of the Spearfish Red Beds.

The Red Valley lies several hundred feet below the hogbacks and averages two miles in width. It actually ranges from one-fourth mile to six miles in width. The Red Valley is generally devoid of streams. However, the rocks of this region are very weak and offer

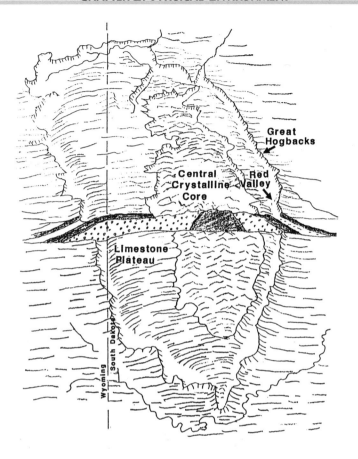

Map 4. Black Hills Province of South Dakota. *From* The Geography of South Dakota, *Hogan and Fouberg.*

little resistance to any of the agents of erosion, especially rainfall. The Red Valley nearly encircles the main section of the Black Hills and is sometimes called "the Racecourse."

The Limestone Plateau is the third major subregion of the Hills. This area also encircles the central portion of the Black Hills. However, the bulk of the Limestone Plateau lies on the west side of the Central Core with a much narrower limestone formation on the east. As a result, the western portion of the Limestone Plateau is indeed a true plateau area. It reaches 7,100 feet in elevation and is actually higher than all but the highest peak in the Hills. From the top of the plateau on the west, one can actually look down on the mountains in the Central Core. The eastern limestone area ranges up to 6,000 feet in elevation and appears more as a ridge than a plateau.

This subregion is also canyon and cave country. Streams have cut 1,000-foot-deep canyons into the limestone. Spearfish Canyon in the north is the most famous of the scenic canyons. It follows Spearfish Creek for twenty miles in a canyon so narrow that the sun cannot shine on much of the canyon floor. Several small caves also dot the Limestone Plateau. Among the more notable are Wind Cave and Jewel Cave.

The fourth subregion of the Black Hills is the Central Crystalline Core. This area is the very heart of the Black Hills. It is an area of mountain peaks and gulches filling the landscape without any semblance of order. The Central Crystalline Core is also referred to as a basin because most is lower in elevation than the western portion of the Limestone Plateau. In reality, it is a true highland area. Many peaks exceed 6,000 feet in elevation, the most notable being Harney Peak at 7,242 feet, Terry Peak at 7,071 feet, and Bald Mountain at 6,613 feet. Harney Peak is the continent's highest landform east of the Rocky Mountains.

This subregion has been carved from a crystalline rock core originally formed deep within the earth. As the mountains were thrust up, the rock was altered resulting in some exceptionally strong quartzite and granite and some soft shining mica. The more resistant granite formed the mountain tops while weaker mica and schist became eroded into the valleys.

The Black Hills also contain an area known as "the Needles," where erosion in vertical cracks has resulted in long spires of granite as much as sixty feet high. The scenic area is especially popular today with tourists.

The landscape of South Dakota reflects its physiographic diversity, ranging from river valleys to ancient lake beds, from plateaus to badlands to mountains. This landscape is the basic foundation upon which South Dakota exists. The variety of its topography contributes to the diversity of uses to which the people of South Dakota put the land.

■ Climate of South Dakota

Perhaps the geographic uniqueness of South Dakota is more obvious in its climate than in any other of its physical characteristics. Its geographic importance is so great that it extends into almost every aspect of one's daily life.

Weather is the atmospheric condition at any given moment. Climate is simply weather averaged over a long period of time. Weather and climate are of tremendous importance to South Dakotans. They affect the way people feel, the way they dress, and the way they play. They influence the growing season, crop types, and crop yields. On occasion agricultural production is destroyed by flooding, hail, drought, or wind. At other times atmospheric conditions result in bumper crops.

South Dakota's climate has four well-defined seasons: spring, summer, fall, and winter. Seasonal variations provide an important understanding of the expected weather and climate patterns over time.

Spring is a short, transitional season in South Dakota. It is marked by a rapid change in the weather. Cold winter temperatures begin to moderate, first changing to cool and eventually to warm. By mid-May, nighttime temperatures have warmed to the point that they could be described as cool. Daytime temperatures in mid-May can even be hot, reaching the mid-eighties. In May frost gradually disappears, generally being absent statewide by the end of the month. The single most important atmospheric factor in spring is a very marked increase in precipitation. Spring rains are vital to the success of the state's agricultural economy. They add moisture to the ground and provide life-giving sustenance to plant and animal life as they begin their seasons of growth. Over forty percent of the total yearly precipitation falls from April through June.

Summer in South Dakota is the season of growth. Summers are pleasant with a maximum amount of sunshine. In fact South Dakota receives seventy percent or more of possible summer sunshine. Daytime summer temperatures range from warm to hot. Nights are normally warm to cool and comfortable.

Daily high temperatures will exceed 100° F several times during a normal summer. This is especially true for the central portion of the state. However, low humidity and brisk winds keep things pleasant. The diurnal (daily) temperature range is great as a result of rapid cooling at night, caused by a lack of cloud cover to hold in the heat.

Autumn is marked by changes that include mild daytime temperatures, cool evenings, ample amounts of sunshine, and a decline in the occurrence and amount of precipitation. Autumn precipitation can be quite forceful with cold rains and chilling winds, alerting inhabitants to the pending arrival of winter.

Normally, the first fall frost occurs about September 15. However, in a given year, the first frost can occur in late August or as late as October. By the middle of October, normal night-time temperatures will be at or near the freezing level. By late October, the temperature at night will reach the 20° F range.

Winter is generally cold, dry, and long. Storms are frequent but of short duration. Occasionally, winters may be open and relatively storm free. In a normal winter, one to three heavy snow storms occur. Many more are possible. Winter landscapes can range from bare ground to three or four feet of snow cover.

By late December winter temperatures reach well below zero. This can last off and on until mid-February. Nighttime winter temperatures can reach -30° F to -40° F or more. The combination of low temperatures and strong winds produces the wind-chill factor, which measures the combined effect of cold and wind on the exposed surface bodies of human beings and livestock. It was during a South Dakota winter that the greatest temperature variation in a limited time period occurred. On January 22, 1943, the temperature at Spearfish at 7:30 a.m. was -4° F. Two minutes later it increased to 45°F, a change of 49°. This freak weather event is known as the Spearfish Chinook.

While the seasons provide a vital understanding of a portion of the total climatic picture, such weather events as thunderstorms, tornadoes, winds, blizzards, and snowfalls provide the rest.

Two very important aspects of spring and summer in South Dakota are thunderstorms and tornadoes. Thunderstorms are frequent with the greatest occurrence in early evening and early morning, from mid-May through July. The most severe thunderstorms are generally accompanied by lightning and very strong winds, and occasionally hail or even tornadoes. These storm features occur as cold fronts or squall lines sweep southeast or eastward across South Dakota. Hail is most likely to occur with a thunderstorm in late May and June.

Tornadoes can and do occur in South Dakota. Tornado watches and warnings generally begin in mid-May and can last all summer. The period of greatest intensity, however, is in June and July. A tornado is a small, intense cyclonic storm. It is relatively rare outside of the United States and Australia. It appears as a dark grey-to-black funnel cloud suspended from a cumulonimbus cloud. Winds inside a funnel cloud can reach 250 mph. The clouds contain moisture, dirt, and debris. While the path of a tornado is narrow, destruction is often tremendous as a result of wind stress and reduced air pressure. South Dakota can experience from a few to dozens of tornadoes during a normal year.

The town of Spencer, South Dakota, was devastated by a tornado in May 1998. Tornadoes, like all forces of nature, tend to take the path of least resistance. If one touches down in open country, it is more likely to go around a town than through it. The greatest destruction occurs when a tornado touches down in an open urban area such as a park or school ground. Then the storm must travel through surrounding structures in its path.

Fall marks the time of year when wind patterns shift. During summer, winds are from the south. In the fall, wind direction shifts to the east and then to the north and northwest for the winter. Winter brings blasts of Arctic and sub-Arctic temperatures and winds to the state. South Dakota has an average wind velocity of eleven to twelve mph. However, it should be understood that winds can reach seventy to ninety mph at any time of the year. Indeed winds of over 100 mph have been clocked in the state.

Two other winter phenomena common to South Dakota are snowfall and blizzards. Snowfall can occur from early October until the first part of May, although most snowfall is in the intervening months. Blizzards in the state average three a year. Some years there are none and in other years there may be four or more. South Dakota usually experiences three or four severe cold waves a year. During these cold waves, temperatures at night can reach -30° F or more. Snowfall may occur during cold waves. When low temperatures are accompanied by strong winds and heavy snowfall a blizzard can develop. Some eight to twelve inches of snowfall can occur within a twenty-four-hour period. In fact, on occasion over twenty inches of snowfall has occurred in South Dakota in a day's time. During storms and blizzards, snowfall is accompanied by drifting. When this occurs, people and livestock must obtain shelter, or perish.

■ Climate Types

Because of South Dakota's interior location, its climate is called Continental. Several climate zones also converge in South Dakota. Climate zones are idealized areas that in reality can shift in a given year.

The climate of South Dakota is composed of four climatic types or zones: Humid Continental Type "A"; Humid Continental Type "B"; Dry Continental; and Unclassified Continental. (See Map 5.) In South Dakota, the Humid Continental Type "A" climate runs roughly from the 100th° meridian west, northward to about 44° north latitude at Big Bend Dam. From there the line runs east-southeast to just south of Dell Rapids to Luverne, Minnesota. Historically, that line has been known as the crop line. The "A" climate includes everything south of this line and the "B" climate everything to the north. These are idealized lines and in reality are movable from year to year. The Dry Continental zone encompasses everything west of the 100th° meridian (roughly from Winner to Blunt to Herreid), with the exception of the Black Hills, which are Unclassified. The Humid Continental "A" possesses narrower seasonal temperature variations, receives more precipitation, and exhibits a greater evaporation rate than the other types.

In the "A" climate there are four well-defined seasons, with a longer summer and a short, milder winter. Rainfall is well distributed. South Dakota's portion of the "A" climate is in the extreme northwestern portion of the belt for the United States and is really a transition zone with greater extremes.

As previously mentioned, it runs from Luverne, Minnesota, northwest to Big Bend Dam, and southward along the 100th° meridian. The average temperature for this zone ranges from 45° F in Minnehaha County to near 50° F along the southern border of the state. The winter temperatures range from 18° F in the north to near 26° F in southern Tripp County, while the average summer mean temperatures range from 71° F in the north to near 75° F in the southern limit of the state.

In the fall the first freeze occurs from September 18 in Minnehaha County to September 29 along the Nebraska border. The last freeze in the south is May 6 and in Minnehaha County about May 15. As a result, the annual average growing season for

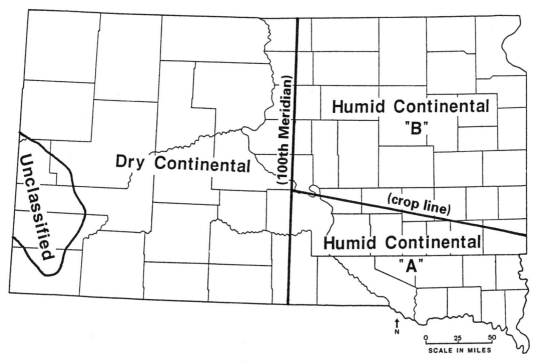

Map 5. Climate Zones of South Dakota. *From* The Geography of South Dakota, *Hogan and Fouberg.*

the Humid Continental "A" climate in South Dakota ranges from 130 days in the north to 150 days along the Missouri River Trench.

During the growing season, this zone receives forty to sixty percent of its yearly rainfall. The May-to-September rainfall averages from eleven inches in the west to near eighteen inches in the southeast portion of the zone. Annual average precipitation ranges from eighteen inches near Big Bend Dam to almost twenty-six inches in Union County. Snowfall at Big Bend averages about twenty-six inches while in Union County it approaches forty inches a year. In Todd, Tripp, and Gregory counties, snowfall averages fifty-two inches or more because it is outside the effect of the high Black Hills, which pirates moisture from the rest of the state.

The Humid Continental "B" climate also has four seasons. Summers are warm to hot and winters are long and cold. Precipitation is moderate and both rainfall and snowfall are well distributed. The Humid Continental "B" climate covers northeast South Dakota north of the crop line. The mean temperature in this zone ranges from 43° F in the north to near 47° F in the south. The winter temperatures range from 13° F in the northeast to 19° F at the crop line. Summer averages range from 68° F in Campbell County to 72° F at the crop line.

The average date of the first fall freeze varies from September 13 in McPherson County to September 23 in the south. The last spring freeze extends from May 12 in the southeast to May 27 in McPherson County. This gives the region a growing season of from 133 days in the southeast to 118 days in the north. The annual growing season precipitation from May to September ranges from eleven to fifteen inches. The annual average precipitation ranges from sixteen inches in the northwest to twenty-four inches in Minnehaha County. Snowfall amounts vary in the region. Average snowfall along the crop line is thirty-eight inches, dropping to twenty-eight inches in the central area, then increasing to thirty-nine inches along the northern border. The decrease in the central portion is a shadow effect caused by the Black Hills.

The Dry Continental is very much like the two Humid Continental types in temperature. Summers are hot. Since the atmosphere is dry, and clouds and fog are rare, sunny days prevail. The relative humidity and sensible temperatures are low. Winters can be bitterly cold. Wind is changeable all year. The diurnal temperatures are great. Annual temperature variations are tremendous and can be as much as 150° F. In the Dry Zone precipitation everywhere is less than twenty inches a year. About eighty percent of the precipitation falls as thunderstorms and cloudbursts resulting from the rapid rise of heated air. Hence rainfall in western South Dakota is highly localized, erratic, and can be unreliable.

The Dry Continental Climate of western South Dakota covers all of the state west of the 100th° meridian except for the Black Hills. Here the annual average temperature ranges from a low of 42° F near Lemmon to 48° F in Shannon and Bennett counties. The mean daily temperature for winter is 16° F in Campbell County and increases to 26° F in Todd and Bennett counties. The average summer temperature ranges from 65° F in the north to 74° F in the south.

The average date of the first fall freeze is September 17 in the north and September 25 in the south. The last spring freeze occurs from May 12 in the south to May 28 in the north. This results in a growing season of 118 days in the north to 140 days in the southeast. The Black Hills provide extra frost protection for the Rapid City area and give it a 143-day growing season and the nickname "the Banana Belt."

During the growing season, precipitation ranges from ten to twelve inches. The normal yearly precipitation for the region ranges from thirteen inches in the northwest to twenty inches in Tripp County. Snowfall ranges from twenty-eight inches in the north to fifty-two inches in Tripp County.

It should be noted that the record low temperature for South Dakota occurred in this region when it reached -58° F at McIntosh on February 17, 1936. The record high temperature was in the "A" zone at Gann Valley, where it reached 120° F, also in 1936.

The Unclassified Climate is located in the upper elevations of the Black Hills. It is an area with twenty to twenty-four inches of precipitation. Here the normal lapse rate and the adiabatic rates come into play. Under normal conditions air temperature drops 3.5° F for every 1,000-foot increase in elevation. This is the normal lapse rate. The adiabatic rate applies to clouds. The temperature in clouds will drop faster where no condensation is occurring. The elevation of the Black Hills results in temperature differences and precipitation amounts that distinguish it from the surrounding Dry Continental zone.

In South Dakota, the Unclassified Continental climate is found only in the Black Hills. Here the annual average temperature ranges from 40° F in the higher elevations to 47° F in the lower. Winter averages range from 22° F to 27° F. Summer temperatures range from 65° F in the higher areas to 71° F in the lower elevations.

The date range of the first fall freeze is September 13-20. The last spring freeze is May 15-24. The annual average growing season runs from 101 days in the higher elevations to 130 in other portions of the Hills. Precipitation is ten to twelve inches during the growing season. The annual average precipitation varies from fourteen to twenty-four inches in the Central Core area. One notable variation in the Hills is average snowfall, ranging from thirty-two inches in Butte County to over 140 inches in the mountains proper.

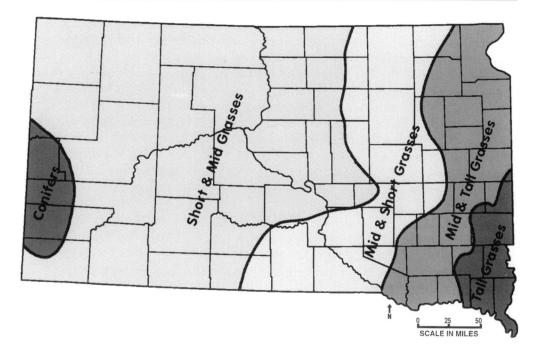

Map 6. Vegetative Zones of South Dakota. *From* The Geography of South Dakota, *Hogan and Fouberg.*

From the examination of the weather and climate of South Dakota, it is apparent that tremendous variation exists in the state's atmospheric conditions. South Dakota indeed has its beautiful weather. It also has extremely cold days. On occasion, for some people, it is too hot, or too windy, or has too much snow. In summary, climatic variations have necessitated cultural responses to make residents' lives better.

■ Plant, Animal, and Soil Geography

Plant life, animal life, and soil qualities are ever-changing aspects of South Dakota's physical geography. By understanding these changes over time, one can appreciate the impact and unique diversity of nature. People have adapted to the unique natural landscape of South Dakota and depend on its fertile soils and abundant plant and animal resources for their livelihood. The soils provide the nutrients that enable the plants and animal life of the region to form its biosphere.

Although the changing nature of plant and animal life are not always evident to the observer, in South Dakota, five ecosystems, or vegetation regions, are recognized by geographers and other scientists. From east to west across the state, these regions are the Tall Grass Prairies in the southeast corner, the Mid and Tall Grasses Region, and the Mid and Short Grasses Region, all in the eastern third of the state. (See Map 6.) The western two-thirds of South Dakota is composed of the Short and Mid Grasses or Mixed Prairie Region and the Conifers Region of the Black Hills. A very close relationship exists in these five ecosystems between the flora and fauna as influenced by terrain, climate, and soils.

29

The Tall Grass Prairies in southeastern South Dakota are made of a tall grass turf ranging from three to six feet in height. The vegetative surface also contains low shrubs and herbs. Because of its southeastern location, this region has the highest precipitation levels of the state. It also has groundwater available at all times, and the land is susceptible to spring flooding.

The Tall Grass Prairies are dominated by big bluestem, little bluestem, sand dropseed, switchgrass, Indian grass, and other varieties of tall prairie grass. The flood plains of the lower Missouri River and the Big Sioux River are covered with grasses such as wild rye, panicgrass, and bluejoint. Buck bush and wild roses are the principal shrubs. The shrubs provide the shade needed to establish the few trees that grow in the region to get seedling starts. Herbs in the region include milkweed, cinquifoil, sunflowers, and goldenrod.

Small animals dominate the animal life of the Tall Grass Prairies. Among the most common fauna are jackrabbits, cottontail rabbits, and meadow mice. The region was once home to buffalo and antelope. Today it has only one large wild animal, the deer, which is numerous. This area lacks burrowing animals because groundwater and flood waters would drown them. Birds include the marsh hawk, bobolink, short-eared owl, and short-billed marsh.

The Mid and Tall Grasses Region lies to the southeast of an undulating line running from northeastern Marshall County to southern Charles Mix County. Precipitation in this region averages eighteen to twenty-two inches a year. The natural vegetation ranges in height from one to three feet. The flora and fauna of the region reflects the characteristics and types found in the zones to the east and west.

In this vegetative zone, the height of grasses decreases from east to west. This region gradually merges into the Mid and Short Grasses Region to the west. The major grass types are needlegrass and needle-and-thread grass. The eastern portion of the region and the river valleys are similar to the Tall Grass Region, and the western portion of the region and the better drained areas are like the Mid and Short Grasses Region.

The Mid and Short Grasses Region is located east of a line from central McPherson County in the north to central Todd County in the south. Precipitation in this zone is reliable and well distributed. Plants average six inches in height but can also reach one foot or more. Mid grasses prevail in the lowlands, while short grasses dominate the better drained areas.

Major grasses are the western wheatgrass, porcupine grass, needlegrass, and prairie June grass. Other medium-height grasses also can be found in the region. Shrubs include the prairie rose and the lead plant. Herbs and seasonals include the prairie clover, goldenrod, pasque flower (the state flower), and pineapple flower.

The fauna of this region has changed over time. Once bison and antelope dominated the landscape. Now jackrabbit, badger, skunk, weasel, pocket gopher, and deer dominate the land. Reptiles have also changed over time. The once numerous prairie rattler has been replaced by the bull snake and the blue racer. Birds include lark, sparrow, owl, hawk, duck, goose, and pheasant.

Steppe grasslands cover most of the landscape of the western two-thirds of the state. This zone is known as the Short and Mid Grasses Region. It is an area of mixed prairie grasses. Here blue grama, buffalograss, little bluestem, wheatgrass, bunchgrass, and green needleleaf dominate the vegetative landscape. Blazing star, goldenrod, aster, and sunflower are also common. Legumes include prairie clover, buffalo bean, and wild alfalfas. Other plants of note are wild onions, prairie lilies, and evening primroses.

This is a region of severe climate, irregular precipitation, and often violent thunderstorms, hail, and blizzards. The region receives only thirteen to eighteen inches of precipitation a year. Physiographically, it is in the early maturity stage of erosion. As a result, the land surface offers little protection for plants or animal life.

Animal life in this region is dominated by speed animals. The antelope, which can run up to thirty-two mph, is the fastest animal in the region. The jackrabbit at twenty-eight mph is generally able to outrun the coyote which travels at twenty-four mph. Surprisingly, buffalo can reach almost twenty-five mph when running at full speed. The kit fox and grey wolf can reach speeds of twenty mph. Speed is important to survival in this region because the animals must be able not only to outrun or run down other species but also cover a great expanse of land in order to eat. Other fauna include the rattlesnake, the bull snake, and the blue racer. Birds include the lark, sparrow, blackbird, owl, hawk, turkey buzzard, falcon, duck, and goose.

The fifth natural region, the Conifers, is comprised of the Black Hills area which, because of its higher elevation, stands as an "island" above the surrounding grassy plains, hills, and ridges. The flora and fauna of this zone vary greatly with changes in elevation, weather, and climate.

The Black Hills are dominated by forests of coniferous evergreens. The principal tree of the region is the western yellow pine, or ponderosa pine. White pine, lodgepole pine, timber pine, Black Hills spruce (the state tree), and the western red cedar are also important. The yellow pine is the most important lumber tree in the region.

It is estimated that only four percent of the state's land is forest. The forests are essentially limited to two million acres of land in the Black Hills. Two-thirds of the commercial forests in the state are in National Forests and are controlled from headquarters in Custer. As a result of sustained-yield forestry, there are three times more trees in the Black Hills now than when the Custer Expedition visited in 1874.

The forests are cut for sawtimber, roundwood, and pulpwood. Sawtimber is utilized in the construction and mining industries. Roundwood is utilized for poles, posts, and pulpwood. Sawtimber, poles, and posts are milled in Custer, Hill City, and other Black Hills communities. Large amounts of ponderosa pine are shipped to out-of-state pulp mills for processing. As a resource-based industry, forest products rank after agriculture and mining in importance.

Plant life in the Conifers also includes various other grasses, shrubs, herbs, and leaves. Bluejoint and bluegrass are the major types of grasses. They are found in the Red Valley. The major shrubs are wild plum, chokecherry, and Juneberry. Herbs include horse mint, thistles, and violets. The region also contains three prominent vines: woodbine, bittersweet, and wild grape. The wild grape is famous as the pattern for all Black Hills gold jewelry.

Animal life in the Conifers Region has changed greatly over time. Once the white tailed deer, puma, black bear, and grizzly bear roamed the Black Hills. Today, except for the mountain lion, these larger animals have been forced out by development. Rabbit, squirrel, raccoon, chipmunk, and porcupine are common to the area. Mountain goat, mountain sheep, buffalo, elk, wild burro, and bobcat are also found in the Conifers. Some of these survive primarily through efforts of habitat enhancement and species protection. Birds are varied and include the woodpecker, wren, bobwhite, jay, sparrow, and robin.

Although not a part of the natural vegetation, the Deciduous Zones are distinct vegetative patterns. These zones are a result of human occupation. They are found scattered across the state, in shelter belts, tree farms, parks, towns, and river valleys. The major species in these zones vary greatly from one to another. Western cottonwood and green ash are found along the flood plains of many streams. The ash is also found on forested buttes. The Burr oak is limited primarily to portions of Tripp and Gregory counties. Elm, ash, linden, boxelder, poplar, oak, cottonwood, and other deciduous species are found in cities and towns.

They are supplemented by a wide variety of conifers including the Black Hills spruce, Colorado blue spruce, pine, and junipers. The coniferous western red cedar is found on the tops and sides of buttes and mesas in western South Dakota and along the bluffs of the Missouri River. Numerous species of shrubs, herbs, and flowers have been introduced into parks and residential areas. Some exist very nicely on their own in this natural environment, while others require watering and tending.

By comparing vegetation regions, one can see clearly that moisture is the primary factor in determining the state's patterns of natural vegetation. Taller grasses dominate the more humid eastern portion of the state. The farther west one travels the drier conditions become, and the grasses become increasingly shorter and less dense in surface cover. This pattern is broken only in such places as the Black Hills and other upland areas, which receive more moisture, or river bottomlands where available soil moisture supports thick stands of cottonwood, willow, and other broadleaf deciduous trees.

South Dakota is blessed with a considerable variety and abundance of animal life. Deer are common to all areas of the state. Herds of bison and antelope still roam large areas of the west. Smaller animals, such as jackrabbits and cottontails, squirrels, and prairie dogs, also abound. These are herbivores, or grazing animals. They are preyed upon by carnivores, or meat-eating animals, such as the coyote, fox, and mountain lion. Wolves and bears were once common in the state. Today, the hunting of game animals brings considerable revenue to the state.

Pheasants, ducks, geese, and doves are among the common game birds in South Dakota. In the spring and fall, the Missouri flyway and the state's lakes and prairie potholes and wetlands serve as temporary refuges for hundreds of thousands of ducks and geese during their seasonal migrations.

The state's lakes and streams abound with fish of many types. Anglers from throughout the nation are attracted to the state's waters in hope of taking their limit of the state fish, the walleye. Walleye, salmon, trout, pike, and other game fish are regularly stocked in the recreational water bodies.

Some types of animal life create problems. Insects such as flies and mosquitoes are a nuisance, but others, such as the grasshopper, are pests that can cause millions of dollars in crop damage. An adult hopper eats many times its own body weight each day, and swarms numbering millions of insects can strip a field bare in a matter of hours, then move on to inflict damage elsewhere.

The natural vegetation and animal life of South Dakota, the flora and fauna of the biosphere, are everyone's to enjoy, use, and share with others who are drawn to the subtle beauty of the prairie and to the forest-clad Black Hills, to the lakes and streams teeming with game fish, and to the varied wildlife. The fertile soils have long been one of South Dakota's most important economic resources, supporting both crop and livestock farming.

South Dakota's ecological and economic vitality is influenced by the three principal soil types that dominate the surface zone. Soil formation in the state was influenced by six factors: parent materials, terrain, time, vegetation, biological activity, and climate. The state is part of a vast grassland zone that extended from the Appalachian Mountains west to the Rocky Mountains. This grassland covered all of the land within the present borders of South Dakota except for the Black Hills. Parent materials provided the source from which the soils were to develop. Terrain and time acted as agents that inhibited or facilitated the processes. Vegetation, biological activities, and climate exerted the most significant influences on the development of the soils.

Soil formation starts with the parent materials from which soils develop. In South Dakota the parent materials vary from place to place. In the Black Hills, parent materials are made of crystalline rocks and sedimentary rocks, including limestone, sandstone, and shale. Sedimentary rocks developed from sands, clay, and silts that were deposited on the floors of ancient inland seas. This also includes the Pierre shale, Cretaceous and Tertiary sandstone, and siltstones that comprise most of the Missouri Plateau. The soils of eastern South Dakota are more recent and result from glaciation. During the Pleistocene, ice sheets scoured the land topping hills and filling valleys.

Glacial activity left deposits of till, outwash, lacustrine material, and stratified drift. Till is the most common deposit. It is simply a mixture of various size rock particles deposited under the ice. Outwash is primarily sand and gravel deposited by melting waters. Lacustrine deposits are parallel bands of silt and clay on the bottom of ancient lakes and ponds. Finally, drift accumulated against melting ice. The result was numerous small, convex hills that dot the Central Lowlands.

Other parent materials include wind-blown loess. Silts, sands, and clays were blown in from the west and deposited along the east side of streams. Depth varies but some impressive loessial bluffs are found in southeastern South Dakota. Stream-laid mixed materials of gravel, sand, silt, and clay are found along stream beds.

The relief of the land and time are also important to soil formation. The relief of the landscape varies greatly across the state. The terrain may be flat, rolling, mountainous, glaciated, or unglaciated. Relief can vary greatly from acre to acre, or from one's front yard to back yard. Time allows the biological and chemical activities required for soil formation to occur.

Vegetation, biological activity, and climate, interacting with the parent materials, terrain, and time, have resulted in the formation of three soil regions within South Dakota. These three regions, from east to west, are the Chernozem, Chestnut, and Gray Wooded. (See Map 7.)

The name Chernozem comes from the Russian language. It means "black earth." The Chernozem Region is composed of a soil group with a very dark brown or black color. The soil is very rich in decayed organic matter, having developed in mid-tall and tall prairie grass regions with a cool Humid Continental climate.

The Chernozem Region is located east of a line that extends from McPherson County on the north, southward to Jerauld County, then west to central Mellette, and south through Todd County to the Nebraska border. From place to place, there are some variations within the Chernozem soils. The variations are primarily a result of temperature averages and organic matter found in the soil. Chernozem soils developed in temperature averages of 43° F to 48° F, with eighteen to twenty-six inches of precipitation. The upper horizon of the Chernozem zone ranges from five to eight inches in thickness. This of course gives plants a deep, rich zone from which to extract minerals and moisture.

The Chestnut Region includes all of South Dakota west of the Chernozem Region except for the Gray Wooded Region of the Black Hills. Chestnut soils have developed in areas of short grasses or steppe vegetation with a drier climate. In this zone, precipitation ranges from thirteen to eighteen inches a year. Temperatures are also cooler, ranging from 40° F to 48° F over the years. They are similar to Chernozem soils but contain less humus (decayed vegetative matter).

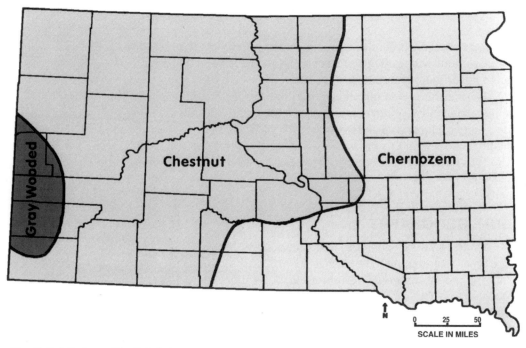

Map 7. Soil Regions of South Dakota. *From* The Geography of South Dakota, *Hogan and Fouberg.*

In South Dakota, cooler soil temperatures and lower evaporation rates in the northern portion of the zone supported more luxuriant grasses. This in turn left more organic materials to decay in the soil, resulting in a darker surface color. Southern Chestnut soils are dark brown in color. The upper horizon of Chestnut soils is thin, generally two to four inches in depth. Soils are fertile with sufficient precipitation or irrigation. However, they are located in a marginal area for crop production and must be closely monitored, utilizing special cultivation and conservation measures to protect the delicate balance of nature.

The Gray Wooded soils in South Dakota are primarily found in the Black Hills. Gray Wooded soils developed in a more humid climate than the semi-arid Chestnut soils. Here the climate is modified by altitudinal zoning and increased precipitation. The annual average temperature for the region is from 40° F to 47° F. Precipitation ranges from eighteen to twenty-five inches a year.

These soils have developed in a region with a native vegetation of coniferous evergreens. Parent materials are essentially a core of igneous and metamorphic rocks, surrounded by sedimentary limestones, sandstone, and alluvium. The soil horizon is very thin, ranging from none to one-half inch to two inches thick. Like most forest region soils, the Gray Wooded soils tend to be acidic. As a result, they are not important for crop production.

These precious environmental resources must not be taken for granted. Everyone must work to ensure that the land and abundant floral, faunal, and soil resources are used wisely and protected. This is the practice of conservation. Through the study of ecology, one learns more about the relationships that exist between plants and animals, and the habitats that they occupy. From geography, one knows the patterns of plant and animal distributions now and in the past, and how humans have used and benefitted from these important resources. Geography also enables one to learn those ways in which humans have changed the floral and faunal landscape through time. As living things, plants and animals are renewable resources, so too are the soils. If properly cared for, they will be everyone's to use and enjoy.

■ Water Resources

Water is the planet's most precious renewable resource and constitutes the earth's hydrosphere. Water, the source of life, is essential to the survival and success of South Dakota's agriculture, industry, recreation, and people. When water has been plentiful, the state's economy has generally been very prosperous. Likewise, when water supplies have been depleted, as occurred during the Dust Bowl and when drought diminished surface and groundwater supplies, the economy and the population declined. Obviously, much of South Dakota's past, present, and future is directly related to the availability and use of the state's water resources. South Dakota receives its water supply from two principal sources, surface water and groundwater, which, when combined, provide South Dakota with among the most extensive water supplies of any state.

Geographically, in order to understand properly the importance and situation of South Dakota's water resources, three questions must be examined. First, where does South Dakota's water come from? Second, where is it distributed within the state? Third, how has it affected the state's settlement and land use patterns? In examining these three geographic questions, one also learns of the many ways in which this vital resource is used, and of the major problems associated with South Dakota's water resources.

Understanding South Dakota's and indeed the earth's fresh water supply begins with the Hydrologic Cycle. It is an endless cycle in which water from the sea evaporates, is carried over land as water vapor, is precipitated on the land in fresh water form, and eventually returns to the sea by runoff from the land surface.

Over ninety-seven percent of this planet's water is contained within the vast global sea that covers about seventy percent of the earth's surface. Through evaporation, saline sea water is changed into salt-free water vapor, or moisture. This change in form from liquid to vapor constitutes the first of four stages of the Hydrologic Cycle. In the second stage, moisture-bearing air is carried by wind to and over the land. Precipitation constitutes the third stage of the cycle. In this stage, moisture is changed from the gaseous to liquid or frozen state where it falls in the form of rain, snow, hail, or sleet. Finally, during the fourth or runoff stage of the cycle, fresh water on and beneath the earth's surface is available for human use.

At any given moment only a small fraction of one percent of the earth's total water is in fresh liquid form and accessible for use on the surface as rivers, lakes, or reservoirs. In South Dakota, actual surface runoff, that is, water carried by streams and eventually returning to the sea, averages about three million acre-feet per year. Much of this water is only "passing through" the state from the Upper Missouri River drainage system en route to the Gulf of Mexico via the Mississippi River system. This water is contained for a short period of time in the four large reservoirs built along the Missouri and by thousands of smaller dams that dot the state's landscape.

Some of the surface moisture seeps into the earth and becomes groundwater. This water may be stored beneath the surface for tens of thousands of years in aquifers or water-holding beds of gravel, sand, and porous rock. It is estimated that of South Dakota's huge groundwater storage capacity, only about seventy-two million acre-feet, or less than one fifth of the total, can be easily recovered using standard pumping meth-

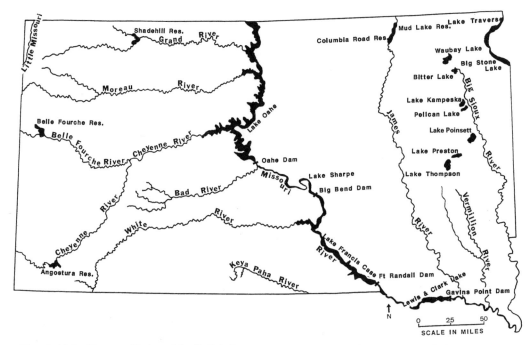

Map 8. Major Rivers and Lakes of South Dakota. *From* The Geography of South Dakota, *Hogan and Fouberg.*

ods. However, even this relatively small amount of groundwater is enough to cover the entire state to a depth of about one and one-half feet.

Geographic aspects of South Dakota's water features are reflected in the streams, lakes, wetlands, and groundwater resources of the state. By understanding these features, one is in a position to appreciate better the importance of water and how to utilize it for the needs of present and future generations of residents. (See Map 8.)

South Dakota's river and drainage basin pattern resembles a tree with the Missouri River forming the trunk and essentially all the tree branches connecting to the Missouri trunk. The exception is again the Lake Traverse drainage area. The land east of the Missouri River generally decreases in elevation from north to south. Essentially, all the land is inclined gently toward the southeastern corner of the state near Sioux City, Iowa. Three rivers—the Big Sioux, Vermillion, and James—follow the gradient flowing into the Missouri in the southeastern corner of the state. The general relief of western South Dakota drops from west to east, from the Black Hills and other upland features of this region toward the Missouri River Trench. Here the rivers flow in a generally eastward direction to join the Missouri.

The Missouri River divides South Dakota almost in half. Its present course results from past glaciation and the paths the stream has followed in more recent history. Sometimes called the "King of Rivers," "Big Muddy," or the "Mighty Mo," it begins in the northern Rocky Mountains and flows through South Dakota en route to its juncture with the Mississippi River. It is the only river in the state with a large sustained flow and thus the greatest source of surface water. It drains through the state gently, dropping in elevation about one foot per mile along its course. In 1942, as plans to develop the four reservoirs were being developed, it is said that the Missouri River had reached equilibrium. That is, the amount of debris and materials being carried into the river from its tributaries was equal to the amount it was able to carry away.

During the mid-1900s, a series of four large dams were constructed along the Missouri River in South Dakota under the federal Pick-Sloan Plan. The dams are the Oahe, Big Bend, Fort Randall, and Gavin's Point. Behind these dams four huge reservoirs were formed. They are Lake Oahe, Lake Sharpe, Lake Francis Case, and Lewis and Clark Lake. The dams and reservoirs now control the flow of the Missouri River providing flood control, power generation, recreation, and water for irrigation, municipal, and industrial uses.

Oahe Dam, with Lake Oahe, is the largest water development in the state. The dam itself is 3,500 feet wide at its base and rises to a height of 245 feet above the river bed. Lake Oahe at maximum pool level covers over 375,000 acres of land. The dam itself generates almost 600,000 kilowatts of electrical power.

Big Bend Dam and its reservoir, Lake Sharpe, are second in the chain from north to south. Big Bend Dam rises ninety-five feet above the river bottom and is 1,200 feet wide. Its waters cover up to 60,000 acres of land. Big Bend Dam generates 468,000 kilowatts of electrical power.

Fort Randall Dam and Lake Francis Case are the third link in the lake chain. Fort Randall Dam is the second largest dam. It reaches 165 feet above the valley floor and is 4,300 feet wide at its base. Lake Francis Case is the second largest of the four reservoirs covering over 100,000 acres of land. Fort Randall Dam generates 320,000 kilowatts of power.

Gavin's Point Dam and Lewis and Clark Lake complete the chain. They are the smallest dam and the smallest reservoir. Gavin's Point Dam reaches a height of eighty-five feet above the river bed. It is 850 feet wide at its base. Lewis and Clark Lake covers only 33,000 acres of land. Gavin's Point Dam's power-generation capacity is 100,000 kilowatts.

The Missouri River generally contains good quality water. Communities along its course utilize the river for municipal supply. It does face some potential problems as a result of the dams. The river was at equilibrium before the dams were built. Over time much of the debris that would have been carried away naturally by the river builds up silting in the reservoirs and interfering with the dams. This is a problem that will need continual attention in the future.

The Big Sioux River begins north of Watertown and flows down the middle of the Coteau des Prairies. South of Sioux Falls, it forms the boundary between South Dakota and Iowa. It has a drainage basin of over 9,500 square miles, of which seventy percent is in South Dakota.

Water quality of the Big Sioux River is good because its basin usually receives sufficient precipitation. From Watertown north, it generally does not flow for periods in fall and winter. Too much flow in certain years results in extensive flooding and accompanying damage.

Between the Big Sioux and James rivers is the smaller Vermillion River. It begins in the north as two separate forks, the North and the South, that join together near Parker. The Vermillion River drains the southwestern margin of the Coteau des Prairies and flows into the Missouri River near the city of Vermillion. Both the water quality of this stream and the stream flow are erratic.

The James River is the only stream other than the Missouri to flow all the way across the state. It begins in North Dakota, enters the state northeast of Aberdeen and flows south to the Missouri just east of Yankton. The gradient of the James is extremely low, dropping about six inches per mile as it flows through the state. The river and its tributaries are very susceptible to both flooding and drying up. Water quality varies with stream flow.

The Grand River is the northernmost of the major rivers of western South Dakota. The North and South forks of the Grand join just south of the city of Lemmon at Shadehill Reservoir. Its principal source of water is runoff from snow melt. Unfortunately, the Grand River is high in sodium content and is not as valuable for irrigation as one would like.

The Moreau River begins as the North and South forks and as Sand Creek. The Moreau River was formerly called the Owl River. The river and its tributaries have very erratic stream flow. They are dry much of the time since they depend on runoff from snowfall and thunderstorms. The water quality of this river is generally poor because of high mineral content.

The largest of the western tributaries of the Missouri River is the Cheyenne River, which has part of its headwater drainage in Wyoming. The Cheyenne flows through the Black Hills and Pierre Hills region. The largest of its several tributaries is the Belle Fourche River, which enters South Dakota from Wyoming. The Belle Fourche River provides water for the state's largest irrigation project.

Waters from the Black Hills' snow melt are the principal source for the Cheyenne River. However, water quality is poor because the river is higher in dissolved mineral content than any other river in the state. Before water quality regulations, mining in the Black Hills deposited significant amounts of cyanide, arsenic, and zinc in the river.

South of the Cheyenne, the Bad River drains a small area of the Pierre Hills and Southern Plateaus. Historically, this stream was known as the Teton River. It is located between the Cheyenne River and the White River. Water quality is hard and poor.

The Southern Plateaus, including the Badlands and southern Pierre Hills, are drained by the White River. It originates in Nebraska and drains into South Dakota and enters the Missouri west of Chamberlain. It is subject to periods of no flow in its Badlands and prairie portions. Likewise intense thunderstorms can cause it to become a torrential and destructive stream. The White River has essentially good water quality.

The Keya Paha River drains a small portion of south-central South Dakota. It begins near Mission and flows in a southeastward direction into Nebraska, where it joins the Niobrara River, which joins the Missouri west of Yankton. The Keya Paha, though small in volume, generally flows all year except for periods of winter freeze. It is noted for having high water quality.

About ninety percent of all the world's natural lakes are located in areas that have been glaciated. The same holds true in South Dakota where the lakes are tightly clustered in the extensively glaciated Coteau des Prairies physiographic region. The quality of the state's lakes varies greatly. Some lakes are deep and clear, while others are shallow and lined with reeds, having poor water quality. Still other lakes have shriveled in areal extent and depth and are now called "wetlands" or "sloughs." From the mid-1970s through the 1980s, wet years increased lake levels well beyond their historic banks. They consumed farm land and lake cottages. Lake Poinsett, the state's largest natural lake, became the second largest when the nearly dry Lake Thompson received enough water to surpass it in size.

Groundwater is found beneath the surface in water-holding strata called aquifers. There is storage capacity for over ten times the amount of water that exists in South Dakota's lakes, reservoirs, rivers, and streams. The groundwater supply is pumped from its reserve to the surface by wells or by free artesian flow. Groundwater provides nearly all of the state's urban and domestic water supply, as well as much of the water used in irrigation.

Although conservation of water as a resource might appear to be a sufficient response to South Dakota's semiarid climate, persistent droughts, diminished snowpacks, and growing urban populations have provoked concern in the region. In 2005 South Dakota Governor Mike Rounds hosted a meeting of seven other Missouri River governors to discuss possible cooperative responses to the declining water levels on the Missouri River. The issue of water flow on the river, controlled by the U.S. Army Corps of Engineers, has been a source of contention for many years among upstream and downstream states, and the difficulty of the Missouri River Summit to reach a consensus indicates that a balance of interests may not be achieved in the near future.

The increasing water needs of the eastern half of South Dakota were thought to be addressed by the Lewis and Clark Rural Water System, a regional pipeline designed to carry water from the Missouri River to Sioux Falls, Madison, Vermillion, and other cities in South Dakota and to cities in Minnesota and Iowa. But reductions in federal appropriations and revised projections of Sioux Falls's water needs in ten to fifteen years indicate that the pipeline will fall short of its goal within five years of its anticipated completion in 2012. More stringent conservation measures, increased utility fees, and funding for a larger pipeline with increased capacity, or the addition of a dedicated pipeline for Sioux Falls, are likely. Water from the Big Sioux River and its aquifers will not be sufficient to meet the water needs of South Dakota's largest city, whose population is expected to exceed 200,000 in less than twenty-five years.

Chapter 3
Native Peoples

Archaeologists identify six groups of Native Americans that asserted claims to land and resources within the boundaries of South Dakota before it became the central component of Dakota Territory in the year 1861.[1] Because most of them vanished before the composition of written sighting reports or official records, information about their cultures is restricted to archaeological evidence. Knowledge regarding causes for the disappearance of four of the groups derives mainly from speculation. Although their prehistoric presence left no measurable impact on life in the state, they merit attention in a general history because they were original South Dakotans.

The first identified by archaeological research as Native American residents have been labeled Paleo-Indians, who lived here as family bands managed by proficient hunters from about 12,000 to 6000 B.C. They were nomadic, mainly big-game hunters who moved on foot to kill large prey at close range with spear points of stone. Evidently, they also hunted some small game and gathered berries and vegetables.

Next came Archaic foragers, who were present from about 6000 to 1000 B.C. Because herds of big game had dwindled while the population of Indians increased, they pursued bison and smaller animals while they foraged for food, collected plants, and fished with primitive equipment and practical techniques. Their lifestyle required the production of some new tools and also the manufacture of throwing sticks that could bring down prey from greater distances. Like Paleo-Indians, Archaic peoples were mainly nomadic, but their weaponry was more effective and their subsistence patterns were more diffuse.

After them came Woodland villagers, who were the predominant residents from about 1000 B.C. to A.D. 800, when they began to share resources with Middle Missouri villagers. With bows and arrows, the Woodlanders carried on the hunt for bison and smaller game while they gathered natural bounty, fished the rivers and lakes, and farmed corn, beans, and squash. The manufacture of pottery and use of burial mounds indicated more sedentary behavior. They dwelled mainly along the Missouri River, where some occupied permanent housing and fashioned stone scrapers and knives to process hides and meat. After the Middle Missouri villagers evolved into the predominant society in South Dakota, Woodland villagers persisted mainly in the eastern part of the state.

Middle Missouri villagers entered by the year 800 and sustained settlements concentrated in the Missouri River valley from about 1050 to 1600. One interesting artifact of this culture was an open hearth, which was revealed in 1984 by the erosion of the north bank of the Missouri River in lower Bon Homme County. Archaeologist Larry Zimmerman named it the Robert Monfore Hearth Site after a rancher who reported the discovery and estimated that it had been in use between 750 and 1,000 years ago. A cross-section measured more than four feet in diameter and approximately six feet deep, and it contained debris that suggested its use as a place to process meat taken during organized hunting expeditions. (This hearth disappeared because of continued erosion along the Missouri River.) A more elaborate representation is preserved for public inspection as a fortified village site near the northwest edge of the city of Mitchell, occupied during the period 1000-1100. Evidently, these villagers came from Minnesota

Chronology

12,000 to 6000 B.C. – Paleo-Indians
6000 to 1000 B.C. – Archaic foragers
1000 B.C. to A.D. 800 – Woodland villagers
800 to 1600 – Middle Missouri villagers
1300 to 1833 – Coalescent Caddoan Arikaras
1642-1643 – The term "Sioux" adopted by Jesuits as a contraction of *Nadouessioux*
1742 – First recorded visit by non-Indians (Francois and Louis-Joseph La Verendrye) in present-day South Dakota

and Iowa. Some settled along the Big Sioux and James rivers. Others moved into the Missouri River valley, gathering mainly north of the Big Bend of the river. In North Dakota their culture gave rise to the Mandan Tribe. They raised corn, beans, squash, and sunflowers in sufficient quantities to trade with neighboring tribes for products taken during hunting expeditions. They gathered nuts as well as seeds from goosefoot, smart-weed, clover, hackberry, and pondweeds. Collections of bones at their village sites and debris in their cooking hearths sug-gest that they lived as large village groups through most of the year but traveled in the summertime to hunt bison and to garden on some plots located at a distance from village sites. They also hunted deer in the winter, fished through the warm seasons, and preyed on various species of fowl. Their era was marked by moderating temperatures and rainfall sufficient to sustain both wildlife and crops. Ample supplies of food released members of the society to refine techniques for the production of better tools and pottery.

After the Middle Missouri, came the society of Coalescent people in about 1300 — the first group with an experience recorded in non-Indian sighting reports and chronicles. They were relocated Caddoan Indians who came up from the Louisiana-Texas border area for reasons never determined by historians. Because they arrived after stronger tribes had occupied or claimed rights of use to most of the land on the Great Plains, the Caddoans found unoccupied space only along a central corridor that reached from the Red River of the south to present south-central North Dakota. One group of Caddoans settled near the center of the corridor, in northern Nebraska, where it took the name of Pawnee. A second formed villages to the south, west of the Cross Timbers, where members were known to immigrant Spaniards as *Los Humanos*, to immigrant French as Black Pawnees, and to British as *Wichitas*. A third settled mainly along the east bank of the Missouri River near the center of present-day South Dakota and took the name of Arikara, or Ree. By about 1400, this group began a process of expansion that eventually populated the area between the mouths of the White and Grand rivers.

In earthen lodging facilities above the flood plain, Arikaras thrived on a diversified economy that included some hunting but mainly the production of corn, squash, beans, pumpkins, a form of indigenous tobacco, and other crops. From ample production, they stored surplus products in elaborate caches, not only to sustain themselves, but also to market in trade with neighboring tribes. Through their heyday in the eighteenth century, Arikaras produced the only marketable agricultural surplus available between the upper Mississippi River valley and the foothills of the Rocky Mountains. By the time non-Indians appeared, more than a dozen initial villages situated along the Missouri River valley might have accommodated an aggregate of 10,000 people, who lived in sturdy, round earth houses.

■ The Arikaras

Arikaras comprised the first noteworthy group of South Dakotans recognized in contemporary written records, and theirs was the first to demonstrate that land along

41

the middle Missouri River basin was a suitable place for intensive agriculture. Well into the nineteenth century, they lived in relative comfort, trading agricultural products with neighboring tribal hunters as well as immigrant fur traders. With Northern Cheyenne and Sioux, the Arikaras, or Rees, bartered garden products for horses, meat, and hides. With fur traders, they exchanged hides and vegetables for manufactured goods. Thus they assisted Cheyennes, Sioux, and immigrant traders with adjustments to conditions on the northern Great Plains, while their flourishing economy facilitated an increase in population that occupied more than one hundred sites between the estuaries of the White and Cannonball rivers.

Growth in the society of Arikaras coincided in point of time with the arrival of non-Indians. Some trade goods entered their villages near the mouth of the Bad River as early as 1600—at a time when goods could have reached them only through tribal intermediaries. Thereafter, from neighboring tribes, the Rees acquired European guns and iron kettles with other metal goods that they worked into jewelry, knives, and arrowheads.

The first Europeans to make direct contact with them were the Verendryes, in 1742. Steadily, through the last half of the eighteenth century, non-Indians appeared in ever increasing numbers. Although Arikaras enjoyed a flourishing economy due to the barter of agricultural products, their independence diminished because of settlement by other tribes, especially Sioux. By the end of the eighteenth century, the Rees were forced into a territorial retreat. Early in the nineteenth century, they abandoned villages south of the confluence of the Cheyenne with the Missouri River and fortified larger villages near the mouths of the Cheyenne and Grand rivers, where they lived in close proximity with the Mandans.

Meriwether Lewis and William Clark found them in this area in 1804 and 1806. Other explorers regarded them as peaceful people until 1822, when Arikaras attacked a party of fur traders led by William Ashley. In retaliation, U.S. Army troops, reinforced by several hundred Sioux, won a military victory in 1823. No sighting reports described a retreat of the Rees over the ensuing decade, but the German explorer Maximilian of Wied-Neuwied found no remaining occupants in 1833. Most of them had moved into present-day North Dakota to settle beside Mandans and Hidatsas, where soon they endured a population loss to smallpox epidemics and eventually joined Mandans and Hidatsas as members of the Affiliated Tribes at the Fort Berthold Agency jurisdiction. No Arikaras appeared in records as native South Dakotans after the year 1833.[2] Understandably, because of Sioux involvement in the 1823 war and its aftermath the Rees were prominent in the scouting force of General George Custer during maneuvers that led to his battle against the Sioux at the Little Bighorn River in 1876.

■ The Sioux

To replace them came Sioux—members of fourteen among thirty-seven Native American tribes that occupied the Great Plains when non-Indians arrived. From prehistoric times to the last half of the eighteenth century, their permanent place of residence had been the vicinity of Mille Lacs, in eastern Minnesota, where no more than 32,000 moved freely about the area as they thrived on hunting, fishing, and gathering natural bounty, which included wild rice as a grain staple. Once or twice each year, members of several Sioux tribes also ranged west on hunting expeditions across the Missouri River to the foothills of the Rocky Mountains.

While the Sioux retained their place of permanent residence in the vicinity of Mille Lacs, immigrant non-Indians began to identify the composition of their tribal federation, which took its name from the pejorative Chippewa (Ojibwa) term *Nadouessioux* (meaning snake). In their earliest mission records, Jesuits spelled it *Naduesiu* and *Nadouessi* as well as *Nadouessioux*. Finally, in accounts for the years 1642-1643, Jesuits adopted the contraction Sioux, and none ever created a suitable euphemism. Despite its pejorative origin, Sioux remained in use as a term no less essential than Scandinavian and Celtic, for example, to identify groups of related tribes in Western Europe.

During the second quarter of the eighteenth century, all Sioux (except Assiniboines, who lived in Canada) initiated a withdrawal from the Mille Lacs area as a place of permanent residence to settle as distinctive divisions in villages across the province they long had used for hunting and fishing—Dakotas to the east, Nakotas in the middle, and Lakotas at the west end. Evidently they scattered for several reasons. One was a voluntary retreat from continuous competition with neighboring Ojibwas for natural bounty, which led to frequent border conflict. A second was an effort to gain direct access to trade with non-Indian merchants, who entered the region from several directions. A third might have been a need for space to accommodate a growing population. A final cause should have been a desire to withdraw from harsh weather conditions in the Mille Lacs area by settling in a more comfortable climate. South of the Canadian border, members of the fourteen tribes of Sioux scattered to mark ancestral claims across approximately 100 million acres—every *ospaye* (band) in each tribe a territory roughly defined by rivers, lakes, trails, and other landmarks.

Gradually, through the nineteenth century, observers identified these tribes and their bands and recorded terminology with which to identify them. By the outset of the twentieth century, no entire ancestral tribe lived alone on a single jurisdiction marked by boundaries surrounding a reservation. Modern Sioux gained new tribal definitions but, as individuals, they retained identifications according to prehistoric tribal affiliations.

Since missionaries began to transform their dialects into a written language, beginning in the 1840s, then to translate phonetic spellings into English, there has been no standard dictionary for any of the dialects or a comparative dictionary to identify differences and similarities among the dialects. Even if such reference works were to appear, they could not serve as practical tools during historical investigations. Those spellings and translations most likely to appear in historical records are included below, as they were recorded by anthropologists James Howard and William Powers, linguist Robert Bunge, and nineteenth-century missionary/ethnologist Stephen Return Riggs.

The first two terms italicized in the following section merit special attention to avoid confusion regarding the evolution of modern tribes that assembled on U.S. Agency jurisdictions and became permanent entities as federally recognized tribes on reservations. Other terms italicized represent individual ancestral tribes or combinations of tribes—in every instance with Anglicized spellings most evident in historical documents plus translations provided by credible ethnologists. Additional spellings in parentheses represent the phonetic perceptions of modern tribal linguists.

■ Siouan

Siouan encompasses all fourteen ancestral tribes of Sioux plus many other tribes with similar linguistic origins but separate cultural and historical experiences, such as Crow, Hidatsa, Missouri, Oto, and Quapaw—twenty-five tribes indigenous to the Great Plains alone.

Oceti-sakowin, translated as "Council Fire," is a controversial word that identifies prehistoric groups within the Sioux federation. Ethnologists who subscribe to its use suppose there were seven: one for each of the Dakota tribes (Mdewakanton, Wahpekute,

Sisseton, and Wahpeton); one for the Yankton Tribe; one for the Yanktonai Tribe; and one that encompassed all seven Lakota tribes. (See Sioux Federation illustration below.)

Dakota (from the eastern Sioux dialect) includes the four eastern Sioux tribes (Mdewakanton, Wahpekute, Sisseton, and Wahpeton) and identifies their common dialect.

Nakota and *Wiciyela* (from the middle dialect), translated as "Those who speak like men," include the three middle Sioux tribes (Yankton, Yanktonai, and Assiniboine) and identify the common origin of their respective dialects.

Lakota (from the western dialect) and the alternative *Teton* include the seven western Sioux tribes (Oglala, Brûlé, Minneconjou, Sans Arc, Two Kettle, Blackfoot Sioux, and Hunkpapa) and identify their common dialect.

Saone appeared in nineteenth-century literature to identify all Lakotas except Oglalas and Brûlés (the five northern Lakota tribal groups), and *Teton* sometimes was used to identify only Oglalas and Brûlés (the two southern Lakota tribes). During the formation of modern agency jurisdictions and the assembly of groups identified on their rolls as modern tribes, the terms *Saone* and *Teton* disappeared from the records of Indian-white relations.

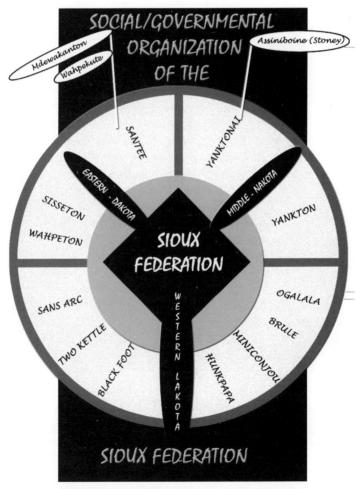

Social/Governmental Organization of the Sioux Federation. *From* Sioux Country: A History of Indian-white Relations, *Hoover and Hoover.*

Assiniboine (with such synonyms as *Stoney, Stony, Stone, Hohe, Hoheh, and Hoha*) represents the group that withdrew from the Nakota Yanktonai Tribe and, by the time non-Indians approached its members, established itself as the northern tribe in the federation. A report by Albert Gallatin in 1836 indicated that other Sioux used the term *Hoha* to identify Assiniboines as "rebels," and that Algonquins (perhaps Ojibwas) assigned the label *Stone*. Other sources suggest that the term *Stoney* might have originated with British traders to identify Assiniboines camped close to the Rocky (or Stoney) Mountains. Obviously, the origin of the term *Stoney* remains a mystery.

Mdewakanton (*Mdewakantonwan, Bdewakatuwa*) translates as "Spirit Lake [Mille Lacs] people," and "Holy water town people." The missionary/ethnologist Stephen Riggs' translation was "village of the Spirit Lake."

Wahpekute translates as "Shooters among the leaves" and "Leaves they shoot through." Riggs' translation was "Leaf shooters."

Sisseton (*Sisitonwan, Sissituwa*) translates as "People of the boggy ground" and "Fish scale village." Riggs' translation was "Village in the leaves."

Wahpeton (*Wahpetonwan, Wahpetu*) translates as "Dwellers among the leaves" and "Town of tea leaves." Riggs' translation was "Village in the leaves."

Santee (*Isanyata, Isayeti*) translates as "Dwellers at the knife lake" and "River shaped like a knife." In most historical literature, as well as in modern tribal names, the term Santee identifies only the Mdewakanton and Wahpekute Dakotas. In some historical records pertaining to communities or groups in Minnesota since the 1880s, federal officials used only Mdewakanton as a synonym for Santee and ignored the inclusion of Wahpekute as a component in Santee.

Yankton (*Ihanktonwan, Ihaktuwa*) translates as "Dwellers at the End (village)" and "Those who camp on the outside of the camp." Stephen Riggs translated the tribal name as "Village at the end" and as "First nation." Earliest reports, such as those by William Clark for his 1804 journal and by Jervis Cutler for his 1810 publication about Louisiana, identified this tribe as Yankton Ahnah to distinguish it from the Yanktonai, which observers properly identified as Yanktons of the North. Stephen Riggs wrote in his 1841 journal that "by some it [the Yankton] is thought to be the oldest band of" Sioux. In the opinion of Riggs, the dialect of the Yanktons was regarded as "the best" of the four in use by the tribes of Sioux.

Yanktonai (*Ihanktonwana, Ihaktuwala*) translates as "Little dwellers at the end" and "Little Yanktons." Riggs perceived it to mean "End village." It comprised several subdivisions known as Cut Head Yanktonai; Upper Yanktonai; and Lower Yanktonai, also identified as Hunkpatina, which Riggs recorded as the Hunkpatindan led by Waanatan.

"Little Yanktons" should not be confused as a demographic expression. When non-Indians first compiled population estimates in the United States, the aggregate census of Yanktonais substantially exceeded that of Yanktons and even that of Oglala Lakotas. According to most early estimates, the Yanktonai was the largest of all the tribes in the Sioux federation.

A comparison of its census with that of the Yankton Tribe and even a casual observation of the geographic relationships between their respective ancestral lands clearly indicate that in early records the ones called Yankton Ahnah were Yanktons and those called Yanktons of the North were Yanktonais. Although the term Ahnah suggests otherwise, both size and location indicate its use to identify the Yankton Tribe.

Teton (*Tetonwan, Tituwa, Titunwan*) is used interchangeably with Lakota in many documents and in literature. It translates as "Dwellers on the Plains" and by this usage comprises all seven tribes now commonly called Lakota, listed below. The term Teton is used in some records, however, as a term to include only the Oglalas and Brûlés. In any event, the listing of Lakota tribes by approximate location on reservations from south to north in no way implies either population size or relative importance.

Oglala translates as "They scatter their own" and "Scatter his own."

Brûlé (*Sicangu, Sicagu*) translates as "Burnt Thighs" and "People who ran through prairie fire." Riggs called them both *Sicangu* and *Yakora* and used the translation "Titonwans of the burnt wood." In the nineteenth century, two branches appeared: Highland or Upper (*Heyata Wicasa*) and Lowland or Lower (*Kul Wicasa*), translated as "People farther down the river."

Minneconjou (*Miniconjou, Minikowaju*) translates as "Planters beside the water" and "They plant beside the stream."

Sans Arc (*Itazipco*) translates as "Those without bows" and "no bows."

Two Kettle (*Oohenonpa, Oohenunpa*) translates as "Two kettles" and "Two (boilings) kettle." Riggs recognized the same name, but he also called the tribe *Shunkayutexni*, which he translated, "Those who do not eat dog meat."

Blackfoot Sioux (*Sihasapa*) translates as "Black moccasin people." (They should not be confused with those in the Algonquin-speaking Blackfoot Tribe.)

Hunkpapa translates as "Campers at the horn," "Those who camp on the horn entrance," "End of the camp circle," and "End village people."

Other variations exist in literature, documents, and oral traditions. While reading alternative spellings and translations, a careful observer can imagine historical conditions from which the terms derived.

In the United States, this federation of fourteen tribes defended rights of use on at least 100 million acres against unauthorized encroachments by neighboring tribes; claimed exclusive access to enormous quantities of robes and pelts; occupied terrain that attracted attention by scientists, ethnologists, cartographers, artists, missionaries, federal employees, and others; defended itself against intrusions by non-Indians with arms for forty-nine years; thereafter retained the largest percentage of ancestral land of any Great Plains group, except the Crow and Blackfoot; and came to settle by significant numbers on many reservations—nine of them in South Dakota. For these reasons, historical developments among the member tribes and their relationships with neighboring Indians, as well as with white people since 1634, have generated thousands of books, articles, and reports; more than a thousand recorded oral history accounts; and literally boxcar loads of original sources.

Because South Dakota was established near the center of the great province claimed as ancestral land by the fourteen tribes of Sioux and remains near the center of seventeen U.S. Agency jurisdictions created to accommodate them as modern tribes, people who descend from this federation of tribes must be regarded as the first permanent residents of the state. The Sioux tribes must also be acknowledged as abiding forces during the analysis of any aspect of South Dakota history.

Chapter 4
Exploration and the Fur Trade

■ Early Exploration

Blank maps invite speculation and exploration. European cartographers and governments knew little or nothing about central North America in the sixteenth and seventeenth centuries, admitting their ignorance with phrases like "terra incognita" and "parts unknown" sprawled across space that now reads "South Dakota." Yet surely as empty paper invited lines, unexplored territory drew interest. Indeed, what is now South Dakota served as a crossroads in trans-national rivalries for empire and economic gain. The Missouri River provided access.

Spain, France, and England coveted the region variously and simultaneously. After independence in 1783, the United States also lusted after this land. Spain made the first European claim in the sweep of Christopher Columbus's arm, taking all of the hemisphere he "discovered" for Isabella and Ferdinand. The *entrada de conquista* for gold and silver drove explorer Francisco Vasquez de Coronado north from Mexico toward the Great Plains in 1529 and Hernando de Soto across the Mississippi River twelve years later—both without profit. For the remainder of the century, Spain contented itself with largess from rich mines south of the Rio Grande River.[1]

England and France came to North America with the intent of staying by the late sixteenth century. English colonies clung to the Atlantic coast from Newfoundland to Georgia. French interests flowed upstream into the St. Lawrence watershed of opportune rivers and large lakes, driven by the enthusiasm and organization of Samuel de Champlain. "Champlain's Young Men" pushed west, and in 1634 Jean Nicolet found Lake Michigan, Green Bay, and the Fox River, which led him to within a day's portage of the Mississippi. Voyageurs in search of furs and Jesuits in search of souls combed the western Great Lakes for their respective prizes.[2]

Eager to realize opportunities based on trading French brandy and firearms (*fusils*) for furs, the government of Louis XIV authorized further exploration. At the vanguard of this effort, Father Jacques Marquette and Louis Jolliet reached the Mississippi River on June 17, 1673. Floating downstream, they realized in disappointment that the river emptied into the Gulf of Mexico (Spanish domain) instead of the Pacific as a northwest passage. En route, they passed the mouth of the Missouri River, *la rivere Pekitaunoui*, with the hope "by means of it to make the discovery of the Vermillion Sea or California."[3]

Father Marquette's speculation focused on the nexus of assumptions that made South Dakota's Missouri River heartland so interesting. Modern maps, satellites, and global positioning make it difficult for twenty-first century travelers to understand the wonderful possibilities of geographic ignorance. If the Missouri, Columbia (River of the West), Colorado, and Rio Grande shared headwaters, travel on one meant access to others. Through this region, then, any country controlling the Great Lakes and the Mississippi-Missouri rivers might also find the fabled "northwest passage" to the Pacific and trade with Asia, as well as easy access to Spain's Mexican mines. The land itself also portended profitable trafficking with natives. France held that geographic key in the late 1600s and set out to unlock its possibilities.

Chronology

1529 – Coronado explores north from Mexico in search of silver for Spain

1541 – de Soto explores west of Mississippi River in search of silver for Spain

1634 – Nicolet explores around Great Lakes and Wisconsin

1673 – Marquette and Joliet explore area around Mississippi River

1678-80 – Hennepin and LaSalle explore Mississippi River

1701 – French map Mississippi River and Big Sioux River, see the Missouri River

1713 – Treaty of Utrecht

1714 – de Bourgmont reaches mouth of Platte River

1727 – La Verendrye and family dominate trade in region

1730 – French government gives La Verendrye regional monopoly

1738 – La Verendrye explores Upper Missouri River

1741-43 – La Verendrye's sons explore South Dakota

1758 – duPratz publishes book on Louisiana Territory and Missouri River

1763 – French lose Seven Years War and their influence in North America

1764 – St. Louis founded (northernmost extent of Spanish influence)

1767-68 – Carver winters with Sioux in South Dakota

1778 – Carver publishes *Travels Through the Interior Parts of North America*

1783 – United States achieves independence

1787 – Garreau reports English in South Dakota

1794 – Truteau ascends Missouri River to White River

1795-96 – Truteau winters at Grand River

1796-97 – Evans extends Spanish influence in South Dakota

1800 – Loisel builds Fort Aux Cedres south of Pierre

1803 – Louisiana Purchase

1804 – Lewis and Clark leave St. Louis and pass through South Dakota

1805 – Lewis and Clark send keelboat back to St. Louis

Another priest, Father Louis Hennepin, explored the Mississippi with René-Robert Cavelier, Sieur de La Salle, from 1678 to 1680, then published his observations severally. Hennepin's 1697 *Nouvelle Decourverle* described the Missouri as a stream so muddy "you can scarcely drink it," going on to retell Indian accounts of a water course lined with "a great number of villages" flowing through "lands and prairies and a great hunt of wild bulls and beavers."[4] Better yet, only ten or twelve days' travel brought one to mountains that looked out on the Pacific.

To Louis-Armand de Lom d'Arce, Baron de Lahontan, goes credit for the most thoroughly *faked* exploration of the Dakotas. From the warmth of Fort Mackinac during the winter of 1688-89, the baron fabricated a trip with twenty-five men across Lake Michigan, via the Fox and Wisconsin rivers to the Mississippi, and then up to the "Long River." He spent the winter "exploring" this counterfeit waterway—clearly meant to be a Missouri look-alike. He provided detailed information on tribes such as Essanpes and Mozemleks (who looked Spanish), as well as a large salty lake and easy Pacific access. On January 25, 1689, he engraved the "Arms of France done upon a Plate of Lead" to mark the extent of his exploration, then returned to Mackinac. Concluding his narrative, the baron recommended that anyone exploring the upper plains employ young men "of dry constitution, of peaceable Temper, of an active and bold Spirit, and inur'd to the fatigues of Voyages." Furthermore, he thought any expedition leader should hire "Trumpeters and Fidlers, both for animating his Retinue and raising the admiration of the Savages." Lahontan drew maps and published results of his hoax.[5] The impact is important for the Dakotas because Long River, various tribes, and a large lake appeared on maps of the region for nearly one hundred years. Only as true exploration replaced Lahontan's illusions with real topographic details did his deception gradually fade away.

Real exploration attached itself to French fur trading efforts. Pierre Charles Le Seuer worked the Minnesota River from the mid-1680s on.[6] Undoubtedly, his voyageurs roamed the Big Sioux seeking trapping or trading opportunities. They left no confirming records; nonetheless, by 1701, French maps outlined the Big Sioux's course with some accuracy. Crowded south by Britain's Hudson's Bay Company (1670) and harassed globally as they jockeyed with England for colonial empire, the French were unable truly to focus attention on upper Mississippi and Missouri river territory until the Treaty of Utrecht (1713) opened a thirty-year window of opportunity.

Moving up the Missouri, Etienne Veniard de Bourgmont reached the mouth of the Platte River by 1714. He may or may not have personally traveled north of that point, but he carefully questioned Indians, including Omahas, "the most handsome tribe of all these continents," and his *Exact Description of Louisiana* detailed the Missouri to the Niobrara.[7] Credit for exploring the Dakota plains from the north, as well as securing the

Chronology (cont'd)

1806 – Lewis and Clark return to St. Louis

1807 – Traders leave St. Louis up Missouri River in search of furs and goods

1809-12 – Missouri Fur Company trades and explores in region

1815 – Hudson's Bay Company fur trade booms in South Dakota

1822-23 – Rocky Mountain Fur Company head up north, attacked by Native Americans

1823 – Overland Trail established, corporation fur trade drops, independent traders boom

1832 – Fort Pierre christened by Chouteau

1834 – Astor pulls out of furs to concentrate on other business

1836-40 – End of fur trade in South Dakota

1836-37 – Nicollet explores Mississippi headwaters

1838 – Nicollet moves into Missouri headwaters

1839 – Nicollet maps region

1855 – Fort Pierre sold to U.S. government

region for France, belonged to Pierre Gaultier de Varennes, the Sieur de La Verendrye. Beginning in 1727, Verendrye and his family dominated trade and exploration in a triangle of land marked by the tip of Lake Superior, the Mandan villages, and Lake Winnipeg. A mixture of fur trade profits, patriotism, and curiosity motivated him.[8] Starting from the Nipigon River, Verendrye extended a line of forts between Lake of the Woods and Lake Winnipeg. In 1730 the French government gave him a regional monopoly. He put it to good advantage, weaning Indians away from their Hudson's Bay Company trading, diverting the flow of peltry east through the Great Lakes to Quebec. This change gratified French interests, but alarmed the British, who saw a line of forts and Indian trading partnerships dividing their holdings in northern Canada from the growing economic importance of the thirteen Atlantic seaboard colonies.

Undaunted, Verendrye used profits from his endeavors to finance personal exploration of the Upper Missouri for possible access to the "River of the West" and Pacific. For several years he questioned Indians who visited his posts about rivers, fur resources, and possibilities of a northwest passage. Out of Fort La Reine, just west of Lake Winnipeg, in October 1738, Verendrye led a party of fifty-two that included his sons Louis-Joseph and Francois. They struggled southwest across bleak prairies, finally arriving at Mandan villages on December 3. These efforts marked the first-known European contact with the Mandan and, likewise, first documented presence on the Upper Missouri. Mandans impressed the French trader with their sedentary agricultural community and stories of Spanish colonies to the southwest, glowing mountains, rich silver, and dwarf Indians. The stay proved fleeting, for Verendrye returned to Fort La Reine in mid-February, 1739, his appetite whetted to know what lay west of the Missouri.

The father intended to return in 1741, but never did. The next year, he sent sons Louis-Joseph and Francois in his stead. The brothers traveled light, accompanied only by two veteran voyageurs (La Londette and Amiotte or A. Miotte). Perhaps, influenced by maps suggesting Missouri, Rio Grande, and River of the West headwaters interlinked at a mythic point somewhere south and west of the Mandan villages, and inspired by earlier stories of silver and magical mountains, they set out to satisfy the elder Verendrye's curiosity. The four left Fort La Reine in late April. They lingered among the Mandan for two months, cemented relations with native villagers (ever mindful of trading opportunities), and gathered information on what lay beyond.

On July 23, 1742, the four Frenchmen departed their Mandan hosts and did not return for nearly a year. Inauspiciously, the ring on their astrolabe broke early on so they never documented precise locations. Equally unfortunate, their descriptions of physical features proved inexact. Optimistically, they explored as far west as Powder River in what is now eastern Wyoming and Montana, captivated finally by snow-capped Bighorn Mountains. More conservative historians suggest the party devoted most of its time inside the present bounds of South Dakota, traveling slowly, spending extended periods with native bands, and seeing the Black Hills on New Year's Day, 1743, as "Shining Mountains," and then at some distance.

Louis-Joseph, Francois, and their voyageurs may not have known their precise locations, but they had clear intentions to document their advance in the name of France. In 1741 the elder Verendrye had made in Quebec at least one thin eight-and-one-half by six-and-one-half-inch lead plate. Carefully engraved in Latin on one side, it read, "Pierre Gaultier de La Verendrye places this in the 26th year of the reign of the most illustrious Louis XV, with the Lord Marquis de Beauharnois being his representative, in 1741."[9] Better late than never, the brothers took it (or them) along.

Apparently, Amiotte did some marking on his own when Louis-Joseph sent him to look for Arikara around the first of March. Two hundred and fifty-two years later, in May 1995, a black Labrador named Ben dug up a six-by-seven-inch plate on a hill overlooking the juncture of the Belle Fourche and Cheyenne rivers. Amiotte scratched his name and a March 7, 1743 date on it, then probably buried it under a rock cairn—first physical evidence of Europeans in South Dakota. Twenty-three days later, Louis-Joseph used his father's official plate to mark a spot where the Teton (Bad) River joined the Missouri and the Verendrye party camped with Little Cherries' band of Arikara. La Londette and Amiotte witnessed the event, for Louis-Joseph scratched all three names on the back of the plate—again using a rock cairn to mark the spot. The March 7 plate provoked a controversy over ownership, so in the fall of 1995, Ben's master, Dr. Max Rittgers, returned it to the Cheyenne River where no one is apt to find it. The March 30 plate has a happier

The La Verendryes claimed the region that would become South Dakota with lead plates, two of which have been recovered. This one, signed by expedition member A. Miotte, was discovered in 1995 by a black Labrador, Ben, near the confluence of the Belle Fourche and Cheyenne rivers. *Courtesy Max Rittgers.*

ending. School children found it in 1913, and the artifact now resides at the South Dakota State Historical Society museum in Pierre—not far from where the Verendryes left it.[10] If there are other plates, time has kept them hidden.

Among the Arikara, the Verendrye brothers met a man who spoke Spanish and told them of Mexican settlements three weeks away. Three days to the west, he also said, lived a French trader who had been in residence several years—perhaps a figment of campfire storytelling; perhaps South Dakota's first European settler. Either are reasonable possibilities. Regardless of the accuracy of such stories, or imprecision about where the Verendryes explored, the expedition is noteworthy for its presence in South Dakota. Their work filled map voids, replaced Lahontan's fabrications with real Indians along equally real rivers, and extended French fur trading influence as far west as it ever got. They also brought into question existing assumptions that key river headwaters interlocked and that a water route to the Pacific would prove easy.

Antoine-Simon Le Page du Pratz had the last word on French political presence in upper Louisiana. Resident along the lower Mississippi with Natchez Indians, he gathered information from traders and natives who came downriver. Returning to France, he began a series of articles about the territory in 1751, turning them into a 1758 publication that enjoyed an English translation entitled *The History of Louisiana, or of the Western Parts of Virginia and Carolina.* Du Pratz's remarkably accurate map depicted the lower Missouri, which he described as terribly muddy. Veracity diminished as the cartographer moved upstream. Instead of mapping the river's correct northerly route, he drew it flowing unimpeded due west between the fortieth and forty-second parallels. Based on the best information he had, du Pratz estimated the Missouri length at 2,400 miles; the actual distance from the mouth to its three forks origin is 2,547 miles.[11]

French defeat in the Seven Years' War (1763) removed the tri-color flag from interior North America. French culture was another matter. The Hudson's Bay Company quickly absorbed French trappers who chose to remain. They lived among native tribes and extended their influence wandering far afield. Interest in the region rose from another area about the same time. Colonialists, notably Virginians, looked west. The Loyal Land Company approached Dr. Thomas Walker in 1753 to explore Louisiana and see if the Missouri "had any communication with the Pacific." Alas, the French and Indian War stifled this effort, but not the interest of at least one participant—James Maury, young Thomas Jefferson's school master from 1758 to 1760.[12]

Spain inherited Louisiana in the political arrangements of 1763. Modern readers should understand that nationality meant more to governments than to individual trappers—French names continued to appear opportunistically. Likewise, borders meant little. In theory, the Spanish flag now flew over everything between the Mississippi River and the Pacific, and north to encompass all lands that drained into the Gulf of Mexico. Spanish officials had no illusions—actual control above New Orleans proved tenuous. In August of 1763, the government dispatched Pierre Laclede, Auguste Chouteau, and a small force of men up the Mississippi to a point where they could establish a post to control fur trade on both the Missouri and upper Mississippi. On February 15, 1764, the group founded St. Louis where the two rivers joined. That community, indeed, came to dominate upriver fur trade and commerce on both streams. For the next twenty years, however, the Spanish made no effort to extend beyond St. Louis, content to let trade and information float down to them.

Colonial Americans exhibited no such reticence. Robert Rogers, fresh from French and Indian War campaigns around Detroit, petitioned Parliament in 1765 to fund a Pacific expedition. Unsuccessful, he returned to Fort Michilimackinac as Western Indian Agent and Governor, in which capacity he directed Captain James Tute to command a party for the "discovery of the North West Passage from the Atlantick to the Passifick . . . or for the discovery of the great Rerevier Ourigan."[13] Tute dispatched himself to Prairie du Chien where Jonathan Carver joined on as cartographer. Between 1766 and 1768, Carver traveled "upwards of three thousand miles" exploring west of the Mississippi.

Precisely where Carver went, he never quite made clear, but he claimed to have spent the winter of 1767-68 with prairie Sioux, perhaps in South Dakota. "Perhaps" is a significant cautionary, for Carver described the region as "a most delightful country, abounding with all the necessities of life, that grow spontaneously . . . and every part is filled with trees bending under their loads of fruits . . .; the meadows are covered with hops and many sorts of vegetables; while the ground is stored with useful roots." But like the Verendryes, Carver listened well to what Indians told him, although in transcription he did not always draw a clear line between what he heard and what he actually saw. Sioux reported trading with western Indians who, in turn, parlayed with bearded men in large boats on the Pacific. Mandans grew and traded corn with partners who reported crystal-studded mountains toward the setting sun. Cheyenne also knew of a great western river that emptied into the Pacific—Carver mapped this as the "River of the West" to please his superiors, then repeated his understanding that all great western rivers had their headwaters in close proximity. Finally, on plains east of the Missouri, he reported "a large mountain of red marble where all neighboring nations resort for stone to make pipes of."[14] He got that location right.

Carver's *Travels though the Interior Parts of North America* sold briskly for years after its first publication in 1778. His map improved on du Pratz's version of the Missouri but still reflected indefinite headwater links to other rivers. While preparing the book for publication, Carver, in league with Parliament member Richard Whitworth, concocted a plan to establish a post on the Pacific and explore Louisiana from west to east, but "troubles in America" broke out and ended the scheme.

Following the American Revolution, new national leaders looked covetously westward, chief among them, Thomas Jefferson. As governor of Virginia in 1780, Jefferson amassed information about the Mississippi and its tributaries for his *Notes on the State of Virginia* (1785). He reported the Missouri "remarkably cold, muddy and rapid," surmising that its headwaters lay north of and at a substantially higher elevation than its mouth. He pondered possibilities that volcanoes existed along the river, sources of pumice seen floating by St. Louis. The governor also expressed amazement that the wooly mammoth "still exists in the northern and western part of America."[15] Jefferson pressed his interest in December 1783, asking George Rogers Clark to lead a western expedition before the British did. Clark declined but suggested such an effort would take several years and be an "Expence worthey the attention of Congress."[16] Unwilling to abandon his idea, Jefferson took it with him as Ambassador to France in the mid-1780s and there interested John Ledyard in a scheme worthy of Jonathan Carver. Ledyard, a former marine on Captain Cook's 1778 Pacific Coast exploration, became smitten with the economic potential in sea otter pelts. Jefferson convinced Ledyard to traverse Russia, hail a ship on the Pacific for transit to North America, then walk west to east through Oregon and Louisiana. Russian objections ended the enterprise in 1788, but not before Ledyard reached Yakutsk in eastern Siberia.[17]

Spain woke up to Louisiana's potential after 1785. The new governor, Estaban Rodrigues Miro, took inventory of his domain in a report to his superiors, acknowledged his country's inattention to the region, and admitted a willingness to let trade just float out of the Mississippi drainage. In truth, he possessed no information more current than mid-1750s' French data. Miro obviously did his homework, for he accurately described the Missouri as far as the Big Sioux and Niobrara, then carefully assumed a speculative voice to retell stories of singing falls and interlocking rivers.[18]

English and American economic pressure changed Spain's perspectives. British trappers probed into Mandan villages. The dribble of Yankee settlers through Appalachian mountain gaps became a steady stream, threatening to flood. Trapper Joseph Garreau went up the Missouri from St. Louis in 1787 returning with good news about fur trade potential and bad news that Englishmen already exploited it. Jacques d'Eglise reached the Mandan villages in 1790, found a French-Canadian who had been living there for fourteen years, and raised an alarm.[19] St. Louis merchant Manuel Perez warned that "loss of the Missouri country . . . would inaugurate an epoch of vagabonds penetrating the province of New Mexico and pillaging the mines."[20] To make matters worse, in 1790, Spain and England confronted each other at Nootka Sound. It became obvious to Miro that pressure on his province now came from three sides. Declining profits added worry. In the 1780s, St. Louis merchants enjoyed trade profits of 133 percent; by the early 1790s, those shrank to twenty-five percent.[21] Spain had to exert itself.

Jacques Clamorgan, a glib and experienced St. Louis entrepreneur, led Spain's counterattack forming the Company of Discoverers and Explorers of the Missouri, more commonly known as the Missouri Company. The syndicate of St. Louis traders pledged themselves to five objectives: ousting the British; capturing Indian trade; discovering a route to the Pacific; linking Spanish holdings in California, New Mexico and Louisiana; and defending it all. For their efforts, Spain eventually granted the Missouri Company a trade monopoly. Also at stake was a $3,000 reward offered to the first Spanish citizen who reached the Pacific via the Missouri. Less visibly, individual Spanish traders (usually with French names) moved north, particularly into Arikara country, and began trading.[22] In 1804 Lewis and Clark encountered them, long-resident among Indians living in what is now South Dakota.

On June 7, 1794, Jean Baptiste Truteau, St. Louis's first school teacher, left the community with eight men in a pirogue to ascend the Missouri on the Company's behalf. He had ambitious objectives: trade with the Mandan; tell the British to leave; contact Shoshone (Snake) Indians; cross the Rocky Mountains; and identify a river to the Pacific. Travel proved slow. In early August, Jacques d'Eglise overtook Truteau near the mouth of the Platte, also bound for Mandan trading. D'Eglise declined to join the larger party (he actually refused to join the Missouri Company altogether), but agreed to wait for Truteau at the Arikara villages. Truteau made little progress. He knew that, if tribes along the Missouri discovered his well-stocked expedition, they would hold it ransom for their own benefit. Truteau moved cautiously past the Big Sioux toward the mouth of the Niobrara and a Ponca village. His stealth proved fruitless when, near White River, he encountered Teton and Yankton Sioux who recognized him from earlier trading contacts. They would not let him pass, helping themselves liberally to trade goods and determined the Arikara would not enjoy them. In desperation, Truteau cached remaining merchandise, hid his pirogue, and proceeded on foot to the Cheyenne River where he found Arikara had abandoned their village and moved upstream. Retreating now, the party retrieved both cache and boat, then floated down the Missouri to a point near present-day Fort Randall Dam. On November 11, they built a modest cabin and wintered—ostensibly erecting the first European structure in South Dakota.

When spring came, Truteau sent what furs he had collected back to St. Louis in the pirogue. With a few men in dugout canoes constructed over the winter, he continued up the Missouri as far as Grand River, where he traded with Arikaras and spent the winter of 1795-96. He never reached the Mandans, but made contact with the Cheyenne and may have actually visited western South Dakota as far as the Black Hills. Cheyenne confirmed for Truteau that a "River of the West" existed. He gained little more for his efforts. His expedition cost the Missouri Fur Company $47,000 and realized little profit.[23]

In April 1795, the company dispatched a second party to support the first, also under instructions to reach the Pacific. Bankrolled with $54,000 in trade goods and commanded by a man named Lecuyer, this effort met with even less success, losing nearly everything to the Ponca band Truteau had avoided. In truth, Lecuyer sought out that band, with whom his two wives lived, and squandered the expedition Clamorgan entrusted him to lead.[24]

A third and final Missouri Company sortie left St. Louis in August 1795 under John Mackay, a Scottish highlander and fifteen-year North Western Fur Company veteran, who moved to St. Louis and became a Spanish subject. Clamorgan and his associates invested $50,000, thirty-three men, and four pirogues in this effort, with grand instructions to drive the British out of the Mandan trade, explore to the Pacific, and establish a line of forts to hold back English advances. Mackay expected to spend upwards of six years in the effort.[25]

Most curious in the expedition was Welsh adventurer John Evans, convinced that the Mandan tribe held descendants of three hundred Welshmen under Prince Madoc, who discovered America in 1170. The legend of Welsh-speaking Indians enjoyed popularity in Wales, and percolated actively in the American-Welsh community for more than a century. Evans became Mackay's lieutenant and, ultimately, the most successful part of the Missouri Company's multi-year exploration and trade efforts.[26]

Mackay's late start meant he reached only the Platte by winter, where he erected a block house and named the post Fort Charles, after Spanish monarch Carlos IV. He traded so successfully among the Omaha that he decided to continue no farther, but in January dispatched Evans and a small party to reach the Mandan and undertake westward exploration. Mackay drafted detailed instructions for his lieutenant, asking that he keep a journal of "all that will be remarkable in the country that you will traverse," including route, distances, and weather. In another journal, Evans was to record data on "minerals; vegetables; timber; rocks; flint-stone; territory; animals; game; reptiles; lakes; rivers; mountains; portages; . . . fish and shellfish . . . ." Mackay also wanted information on Indians, admonishing Evans to "take care that no offense is committed against the nations through which you pass. . . ." In particular Mackay desired the Welshman to look for one animal—the unicorn. Once at the Pacific, Evans should mark the extent of his explorations. Perhaps he had a lead plate, just in case. Mackay understood the broadest significance any Pacific expedition held for the Spanish monarch and "even to the universe since it ought to open communications of intercourse through this continent. . . ." He asked Evans to act boldly.[27]

Evans departed Fort Charles in early February 1796, but hostile Sioux near the Teton River turned him back. On June 8, he tried again and ascended the Missouri without incident arriving at the Mandan villages on September 23. To his great disappointment, no one spoke Welsh nor had any legendary memory of Prince Madoc. In residence among the Mandan, Evans did find a British trader named Jusseaume. Well-stocked with flags, medals, and presents, the Welshman won Mandan support and almost came to fisticuffs with Jusseaume, eventually forcing him to lower the Union Jack, after which Evans raised the Spanish banner in its stead.

Spain's flag flew over Mandan villages until May 9, 1797, when Evans retreated to St. Louis. The crown's $3,000 prize for reaching the Pacific went unclaimed. Evans did, nonetheless, what so many Europeans had done before him: ask questions and gather information. Some fancy sifted into his reports: elk whose antlers curved forward and grew so large they could not graze and starved to death; leopards, but no unicorns. Topographical facts he transcribed onto a map that became the most authoritative one produced during the eighteenth century. When Thomas Jefferson procured a map for Lewis and Clark, it was John Evans' handiwork, "said to be very accurate."[28]

Officially, Evans deserves credit as the high-water mark of Spanish exploration and influence on Dakota's prairies. That said, Jacques d'Eglise merits one more mention. He, too, struggled to trade with Mandans, suffered frustrations with Sioux and Arikara, but persisted, also determined to claim the $3,000 Pacific prize. He repeatedly disappeared from official view for long periods. St. Louis officials believed d'Eglise "seems determined to make this discovery, and since he is full of courage and ambition, he is capable of so dangerous an undertaking . . . ."[29] Most likely, this one Spanish adventurer traversed what is now South Dakota more than any other of his countrymen during the 1790s—exactly where and when is less certain.

The year 1797 also did not mark the official end of Spanish presence. Outside the financial shambles of Missouri Company's expensive expeditions, other St. Louis trading firms regularly worked the Missouri. In 1800, Regis Loisel built fort *Aux Cedres* thirty-five miles below South Dakota's present capital. From that point, he dispatched Pierre-Antoine Tabeau upriver to explore and trade in 1803, unaware that Spain had secretly given Louisiana back to France three years earlier. Tabeau discovered that the United States had also become a player in the region while descending the Missouri in May 1804. He encountered the men of the Lewis and Clark Expedition on their ascent.[30]

In retrospect, Spanish procedures had a fatal flaw. Combining exploration and trade frustrated both. An expedition heavy-laden with trade goods could not pass by native bands with ease. Eager, even greedy to obtain items of European manufacture and also politically anxious to make sure upriver rivals did not enjoy the same benefits, Poncas, Sioux, and Arikara along South Dakota's stretch of the Missouri repeatedly waylaid Spanish parties. The richness of Mandan commerce proved a final deterrent—a trader could make more in a good season than the $3,000 prize he might realize by pushing west as an explorer.

Britain dominated the lucrative Mandan trade from its posts near Lake Winnipeg, but little official pressure existed to follow the Missouri west. All the same, curiosity fired imaginations beyond simple trading profits. Alexander Mackenzie arrived at the North Western Fur Company's Athabaska post in 1787, listened to American Peter Pond's speculations on a northwest passage, and two years later set out to try a possible river to the Pacific only to discover it flowed into the Arctic Ocean instead. The river now bears his name. In 1793 Mackenzie tried another route with a small party of ten. They reached the Pacific on July 20 and spent three days exploring and meeting Indians. Mackenzie mixed a paint of vermillion and grease, wrote his accomplishment on the southeast face of a rock, then retraced his steps. Mackenzie's effort earned him credit for being the first European to cross the continent north of Mexico and provided both inspiration and methodology for Thomas Jefferson when he found out about it in 1797.[31]

■ Lewis and Clark Expedition

Jefferson's long-term fascination with the Missouri River, its potential as an access route to the Pacific, as well as its resources in trade and science finally came to fruition between 1803 and 1806. What he learned as a young man from James Maury in 1758 fed his 1780 research on "western" Virginia, and became a near obsession when he occupied positions of political power in the new U.S. government. He tried to interest George Rogers Clark in 1783; inspired John Ledyard to cross Russia in 1786-88; and, in early 1790, had Secretary of War Henry Knox promote a project that sent Lieutenant John Armstrong as far west as St. Louis. Armstrong turned back for lack of funding and to avoid Indians. Jefferson's personal library contained the works of Hennepin, LaSalle, Lahontan, du Pratz, Carver, and Mackenzie, among other explorers. Louisiana preyed on his mind.[32]

In 1792 Jefferson worked through the American Philosophical Society in Philadelphia, attempting, unsuccessfully, to interest the city's leading physician/botanist, Dr. Moses Marshall, to undertake a trip. Undaunted, Jefferson turned to French explorer and botanist Andre Michaux. With financial backing from President George Washington, John Adams, James Madison, Alexander Hamilton, seven members of the Constitutional Convention, and most of America's leading scholars and scientists, Jefferson got Michaux to agree.

Jefferson drew up detailed instructions: follow the Missouri; find "the shortest and most convenient route" to the Pacific; avoid Spanish detection; and make detailed notes on terrain, plants, minerals, Indians and animals—particularly wooly mammoths and furry alpacas. Unfortunately, Michaux became involved in political intrigues surrounding Citizen Edmond Genet. Michaux's small party advanced into Kentucky, but looked like it might be a prong in Genet's efforts to organize an American filibuster on New Orleans. The French government recalled Genet and Michaux. Jefferson felt disappointment, and so did nineteen-year-old army officer Meriwether Lewis, who volunteered to join the adventure before it aborted.[33]

Jefferson's campaign promises for the 1800 presidency did not include Louisiana. Promises to himself were another matter. In January 1801, three months before taking office, the president-elect hired Meriwether Lewis as his personal secretary, primarily for his knowledge of the "western country."[34] A year later, Jefferson asked Spain for permission to undertake a "literary pursuit" in Louisiana, only to discover Spain had surreptitiously transferred control to France. In equally secret fashion, the president sent Congress a message on January 18, 1803, asking for $2,500 to fund ten or twelve men under the command of an "intelligent officer" to "explore the whole line, even to the Western Ocean, [and] have conferences with natives on the subject of commercial intercourse . . . ."[35]

Jefferson had long since identified the "intelligent officer." Meriwether Lewis began crash preparation to lead this expedition, amassing material and scientific information to fulfill the president's purposes. At the same time, Jefferson began political blustering with two objectives: convince Spain, still in physical control west of the Mississippi, to reopen New Orleans as a point of egress for western United States produce; pressure France, Louisiana's legal proprietors, to sell the port city and enough of West Florida so that no one could choke off future river commerce. Spanish officials backed down first and reopened New Orleans. Napoleon Bonaparte looked at his options. The possibility loomed of a new war with England pregnant with potential attacks on Louisiana; Spain never realized a profit administering this sprawling territory; plans for a Caribbean empire vanished with the defeat of French forces in Santo Domingo; and American frontiersmen exhibited obnoxiously threatening designs on everything.

James Monroe and Robert Livingston sat poised in Paris ready to purchase New Orleans. Napoleon made up his mind. On April 11, 1803, French foreign minister Charles-Maurice de Talleyrand asked Livingston, "What would you give for all of Louisiana?" Terms fell quickly into place. The last day of April, the United States and France agreed on the territory's value: $15,000,000. Sold. Jefferson would not know until July 14, but it mattered not. For months, Lewis had schooled himself in science and navigation, gathered supplies, and supervised construction of a self-designed fifty-five-foot keelboat in Pittsburgh. On August 31, Lewis, the loaded vessel, and an equally packed forty-one-foot red pirogue started down the Ohio. On October 12, William Clark joined on in Lewis's eyes as an equal captain (although his official rank remained lieutenant). On December 12, the expedition went into winter quarters at Camp Dubois, opposite St. Louis.

Jefferson drafted instructions for the project, not unlike ones for Michaux ten years earlier—*sans* references to mammoths and alpacas. First and still foremost: find a route to the Pacific using the Missouri, portages, and the River of the West; map it accurately; and return safely so the government had concrete results. Make extensive notes on a variety of subjects: weather, geographic features, plants, animals, and natural resources (particularly those of economic value). Also important, establish friendly relations with Indians, especially the Sioux. Native peoples must understand, Jefferson proposed, that the United States now controlled their land, destinies, and commerce and demanded that they give up allegiances to British and Spanish traders. A good supply of friendship medals and trinkets went along to cement that understanding.

Lewis and Clark filled their roster with "good hunters, stout, healthy, unmarried men, accustomed to the woods, and capable of bearing bodily fatigue in a pretty considerable degree." In addition to the captains, five members kept journals. When they began their trek on May 14, 1804, there were forty-five men, including nine *engages* (boatmen) and seven soldiers hired only to get the party to the Mandan villages, provide military protection, and assist in moving what had become an impressive amount of cargo. The expedition departed with over fifteen tons of supplies, half in food, including thirty half-barrels of flour (3,400 pounds), fifty kegs of salt pork (3,705 pounds), one bag of coffee (fifty pounds), two bags of sugar (112 pounds), 600 pounds of grease, and 193 pounds of concentrated soup mix. They also took 100 gallons of whiskey for the men and an additional twenty for Indian negotiations. Also carefully packed were Lewis's ten books: several about classification of plants and animals, one on mineralogy, two on astronomy/navigation, plus the published journals of du Pratz and Mackenzie.

Everything lay packed in the bottom of the keelboat, the red pirogue, and a thirty-five-foot-long white pirogue purchased in St. Louis. Each craft had sails as well as oars, and the keelboat design permitted men to pole the craft in shallow water. On shore, horses accommodated mounted hunters to supply meat. Patience marked their advance against the Missouri's steady current—ten miles of progress marked a successful day. Deliberation in scientific observations and note taking slowed them more, as did occasional parlays (sometimes days at a time) with Indians.

In 1804 expedition members retraced territory familiar to Europeans. They met fur traders bound downriver, and hired one, Pierre Dorion, for his fluency in the Sioux language. In day-to-day trudging up the Missouri, corps members resembled a military unit, which they were, with routines, watches, and courts-martial for dereliction of duty. William Clark took his personal slave, York; Meriwether Lewis brought his large

Newfoundland dog, Seaman. Each morning hunters, like George Drouillard, left to scour ahead for game. Men ate one to three pounds of meat a day—fresh if possible, dried when necessary. Salt pork in combination with corn and flour became staple food; fresh meat and whatever seasonal berries they harvested along river banks provided welcome breaks in diet monotony. Catfish joined the menu above Council Bluffs. Cooking took place morning and evening only. Whatever game hunters killed, a sergeant distributed once men secured boats and made camp. Each man also received a four-ounce "gill" of whiskey from time to time—a standard military ration of the period.

All went smoothly until August, when one of the three sergeants, Charles Floyd, a man of "firmness and Deturmined resolution," became ill. Lewis's limited medical expertise proved useless and, on August 20, Floyd died. Modern historians suspect he suffered from a burst appendix, a condition that would have killed him even under the care of noted Philadelphia physician Dr. Benjamin Rush, who trained Lewis. Floyd's loss—the expedition's only death—cast a pall over the corps who buried their comrade with full military honors on a bluff overlooking the Missouri, then camped at the mouth of an adjacent river they named in his honor. A one-hundred-foot-tall obelisk at Sioux City, Iowa, dedicated in 1901, commemorates Floyd's death; it is the first U.S. National Historic Landmark.

On August 22 the corps entered what is now South Dakota and remained along this 545-mile Missouri stretch until October 13—fifty-four days at forty-two different camp sites. They paused long enough for enlisted men to vote on Patrick Gass as their new sergeant—probably the first United States election west of the Mississippi River. In a fur trade sense, this constituted "no man's land," between former Spanish influence from St. Louis and British interests extended south from Mandan villages. Here, too, Ponca, Sioux, and Arikara traditionally played havoc with traders headed upstream. Lewis and Clark understood the region's strategic importance and the political challenges necessary to convert native allegiances. They also knew its history and, at the mouth of the Vermillion River, took an all-day trek to Spirit Mound, remembering native stories of little spirits (eighteen-inch-tall dwarfs) who lived there—a tale Pierre Verendrye had heard sixty years earlier.

In August 1804, Meriwether Lewis, with his dog, Seaman, along with William Clark and members of the Corps of Discovery, walked across the grasslands to Spirit Mound, which an Oto Indian had told them was inhabited by small warriors. *Courtesy South Dakota Tourism.*

On August 23 Private Joseph Field killed the expedition's first buffalo. Hunters also killed deer that day, then saw elk and prairie wolves. A week later came an all-important meeting with Yankton Sioux, very close to the city named after them. This band of forty lodges was home to Pierre Dorion, his native wife, and their two sons. Lewis and Clark sent iron kettles and tobacco as presents and then held a council "under an Oak tree near where we had a flag flying on a high flag Staff." Clark took detailed notes of speeches and information on Sioux bands and customs, then declared the meeting a success. He added Bon Homme Island and White Bear Cliff to his maps. On the Missouri's south side, the explorers mistook natural sandstone shapes for remnants of ancient fortifications.

Past the Niobrara River, they came on an abandoned Ponca village and remains of Truteau's 1794 cabin. Confused again, they named the spot "Pawnee house." They proceeded on, eating wild plums, turkeys, and ample game, making the first scientific discovery of prairie dogs. Men paused long enough to dig six feet deep trying to find the end of one tunnel and pour five barrels of water down another in a vain effort to drown out the *petite chien*. During the next two weeks, expedition members also first identified pronghorn (repeatedly called a "goat,"), magpies ("a beautiful bird"), and jackrabbits—their first specimen had ears three inches wide and six inches long.

Abandoned Indian camps lined the river; former occupants engaged in early fall hunting on adjacent prairies. Clark filled his map with names: White River, Corvus Creek (for the magpie), American Creek, Prickly Pear Creek, Big Bend, Loiselle Creek (after Regis Loisel's 1800 post, which Patrick Gass and John Ordway measured in detail). Finally, on September 23, they encountered Teton Sioux, named the next river in their honor, and camped awaiting a council.

The Sioux had no reason to consider Lewis and Clark's expedition anything more than a replica Missouri Company trading party, nor to expect anything less than continued success raiding and thwarting it. They started by stealing John Colter's horse. There followed five days of blustering on both sides, weapons pointed, trade goods offered in good faith, tow ropes grabbed without permission. The Teton attempted unsuccessfully to waylay progress, but they guessed wrong on two accounts: the expedition meant to explore, not trade; Americans defied intimidation. Clark felt "treated badly" and happily continued out of Teton territory. Their river became Bad River.

Above the Cheyenne River, they met yet another Spaniard, Jean Valle, who spoke English and occupied a sparsely supplied cabin with two other men. Of great interest, he reported trading in the Black Hills: pine covered with plentiful game including bighorn sheep and grizzly bears and the home of Cheyenne Indians who obtained horses by raiding Spanish settlements.

On October 5 expedition members awoke to their first frost. Snow geese migrated overhead. Clark "refreshed" the men that evening with a glass of whiskey. Signs of Arikara became more common, and three days later, near Grand River, the party encountered their first occupied village, surrounded with gardens of corn, tobacco, and beans. Lewis entered the camp. He returned with Joseph Gravelines (a Regis Loisel employee who claimed to have lived among the Arikara since the early 1790s) and Joseph Garreau (an "old Spaniard" who had lived with the tribe nearly as long). The expedition waited for weather to improve for a council meeting. On October 9 Pierre-Antoine Tabeau appeared. A Montreal-born, naturalized United States citizen, he had been trading for Loisel since 1795. Tabeau translated and shared valuable information about Upper Missouri River tribes.

Staying with Arikara was everything staying with Sioux was not—relaxing, pleasant, and productive. Both York and Lewis's air gun astonished tribal members; in turn, their refusal to accept trade whiskey amazed Clark. York enjoyed the attention "and made himself more turibal than we wished him to doe" with tall tales of eating children. A band of Cheyenne appeared and added to Clark's store of information on lands to the west. Unpleasantness came internally when Private John Newman "uttered repeated expressions of a highly criminal and mutinous nature . . . ." On October 13 ten enlisted men presided over a court-martial, sentenced Newman to seventy-five lashes, and discharged him from the corps. Newman received his lashes the next day, much to the distress of visiting Indian chief Eagle Feather, who explained to Clark that Arikara never whipped anyone. More humanely, Lewis and Clark did not abandon Newman in the wilderness, but took him to the Mandan villages under sentence of heavy labor, then shipped him back to St. Louis come spring. In any case, the incident provided South Dakota's first legal proceeding.

On October 14 the explorers moved out of South Dakota headed for Mandan villages where they wintered. Diplomatic efforts included patching friendship between Arikara and Mandan, as well as sending word to Britain, via resident trappers, that the United States expected to control future Missouri River fur trade. On November 2 construction began on Fort Mandan "in honour of our Neighbours." In the months ahead, Lewis and Clark focused attention on cementing strong relations with the tribe, gathered information and scientific specimens for return to Jefferson, and collected even more data about what lay ahead. Two noteworthy additions to the party happened quickly. On November 3 Clark hired Jean Baptiste Lepage to replace Private Newman. Lepage, who had lived among the Cheyenne, brought first-hand knowledge of the Little Missouri and Black Hills. Clark found the Frenchman useful when preparing maps over the winter; Lewis thought Lepage had "no particular merit." One day later, Toussaint Charbonneau appeared with his two young Shoshone wives. Lewis and Clark engaged him, stipulating that he bring only one wife.

On April 7, 1805, Lewis and Clark sent the keelboat back to St. Louis, its most important cargo being official reports and myriad scientific specimens (living and dead) for Thomas Jefferson's edification—only a prairie dog and a magpie survived. The boat stopped at Arikara villages and picked up chief Too ne (Whippoorwill) whom Dorion agreed to escort to Washington, D.C. The rest of the expedition, thirty-two adults and one two-month old infant, packed themselves and supplies into two pirogues and six dugout canoes, then headed into the unmapped West and modern imagination. Wet, cold, and miserable for most of the trip, they found the Missouri River headwaters in the rugged Bitterroot Mountains. Technically, the Columbia's watershed began a stone's throw from the uppermost Missouri, but traverse proved nowhere near as easy as two centuries of adventurers and cartographers wished. Everyone survived mountain snow, a rainy Pacific coast winter, and a return trip that produced the only violent encounter with Indians. Lewis's party killed two Blackfeet in what is now northern Montana. Charbonneau, his wife, Sacagawea, and son departed the corps (collecting $500.33, one-half in pay) as it returned through the Mandan villages. Other expedition members also left so they could join fur trappers already headed into virgin territory. Chief Sheheke (Big White) agreed to come along for a meeting with Jefferson.

Back among the Arikara, Clark spent a day mending relations with the Mandan, amiability that unraveled since the expedition's 1804 efforts. Ominously, Clark also learned that Too ne, who had gone east in 1804 to Washington, D.C., died and the tribe nurtured growing doubts about their friendship with Americans. Mosquitoes and rain plagued the travelers, but they found game and fruit in abundance. Some days the expedition progressed thirty or forty miles with the current, so they spent only fifteen days in South Dakota. Near Big Bend, on August 30, Teton Sioux appeared—Black Buffalo's band that Clark so despised two years earlier. He did not mince words: "I told those Indians that they had been deef to our councils and ill treated us as we assended this river . . ., [and] I believed them to be bad people. . . ." The party wasted no time in discussion, but a day later delighted in recontacting the Yankton near Bon Homme Island. Clark called the Yankton "faithful Children" for listening to his council and he tied a ribbon on each man's hair. He also mapped sandstone "fortifications" he saw two years earlier. On September 2 near the mouth of the James, they found evidence of Robert McClellan's trading post built since the expedition first passed this point.

On September 3 expedition members encountered Briton James Aird who had come from Prairie du Chien via St. Louis. He and partner Robert Dickson had been trading among the Sioux for years. Aird generously shared information on what had happened in America during the expedition's absence, plus tobacco and flour, all of which the men craved. Next day, the expedition floated past the Big Sioux, then paused to rebuild Sergeant Floyd's grave. The Corps of Discovery returned to St. Louis on September 23, 1806, enjoying huzzas of praise and formal dinners, having traveled over 7,000 miles and written nearly one million words to document their accomplishments. They filled in blank map space with remarkable detail, dispelled the stubborn notion of an easy "northwest passage," set a tone for future relationships with Indians, and extended United States presence from St. Louis to the Pacific. For South Dakotans, it is nearly impossible physically to re-imagine the trip—dams constructed during the 1950s and resultant reservoirs destroyed nearly all corps camp sites within the state. A final footnote on the federal government's first South Dakota project: Congress originally allocated $2,500 for the trip; its final cost came in closer to $50,000 in material, pay, bonuses, and land warrants for each member.

In terms of public relations, the project largely failed—initially. Fur trappers before and after the expedition did more to expand knowledge of and provide access to the region's resources. Zebulon Pike got better press for his simultaneous efforts to find the Mississippi's source. While an edition of Patrick Gass's journal came out in 1807 and provoked interest, publication of the corps' official journals did not take place until 1814 and then only in Nicholas Biddle's heavily edited two volumes, which sold poorly. Real fascination came between 1893 and 1904-05 with more extensive editions of the journals and the enterprise's centennial. Gary E. Moulton's recent well-edited effort (thirteen volumes, 1983-2001) includes maps, scientific data, and journals of four other expedition members—everything necessary to understand the enterprise. Moulton's work has not and will not prevent many other efforts at interpretation, grown out of scholarly inquiry, tourism hype, and public imagination.

Modern Americans have become enamored of Lewis and Clark more than any other government-sponsored probe into the West. It contains the stuff of adventure and wonder. Meriwether Lewis's enigmatic death in 1809 started it; fascination with Clark's slave, York, and Charbonneau's Shoshone wife—Sacagawea—fed it. Clark inherited the African-American in 1799. A large man, York participated as a full expedition member, carried a gun to hunt, and often attracted native attention. Clark did not free York until after 1811. Some accounts indicated he then ran a freighting business, others that he went west and lived among the Crow. He died in the early 1830s.

Sacagawea—corps members never used a "j" when spelling her name—looms larger. She was born a Lemhi Shoshone, perhaps in 1788. Raiding Hidatsas captured

"Bird Woman" when she was twelve. Four years later, Charbonneau purchased her as his second wife. The captains jumped at a chance to have a Shoshone (Snake) interpreter because they knew that tribe had horses necessary for their mountain crossing. Sacagawea's name went on the roster as "interpreter" not guide, although familiarity with upper reaches of the Missouri proved useful. Fortuitous coincidence brought explorers into contact with the particular Lemhi band headed by Cameawait, Sacagawea's brother. She also served the expedition when her clumsy husband dumped a canoe and as a peace emissary when Columbia River tribes understood her presence to indicate Lewis and Clark were not a war party. She cast the first woman's vote in the West with her ballot helping choose a winter camp site along the Pacific. (York voted, too.) Beyond that, her life typified native wives of fur trapper/traders: drudgery, food gathering and cooking, sewing garments, taking care of his needs and those of their infant son, Jean Baptiste ("Pomp" as Clark called him, born February 11, 1805). Sacagawea experienced brief visibility from 1805 to 1806, then disappeared into obscurity until her death in 1812 at Fort Manuel in modern Corson County, South Dakota.

■ Fur Trade

Americans had traversed the Missouri, met with tribes, and promoted trade, but the United States struggled to secure what Jefferson had called "commercial intercourse." Ideally, the United States wanted only American goods and merchants on the river. Reality proved otherwise. British traders sifted into the upper Mississippi and Missouri watersheds with ease, erected small cabin-sized "posts," sported the Union Jack without fear of retribution, and won Indian allegiance through commerce.

Various St. Louis traders, anxious to exploit the fruits of Lewis and Clark's efforts, departed the city in the spring of 1807. Chief among them was Spaniard Manuel Lisa who with forty-two rough trappers belabored their heavy keelboat up the Missouri and Yellowstone to the mouth of the Bighorn River where Lisa honored his own effort by erecting a blockhouse he christened Fort Manuel. The Spaniard hired fur trappers under contracts that said each man was "obliged to Hunt, and trap the Beaver of the Missouri the best that he can . . . ."[36] Trappers got five traps, one horse, ten pounds of powder, twenty pounds of lead plus other supplies; in return, they had to report back to Fort Manuel by June 15 and kept profits from half their furs. Lisa also hired John Colter, late of the Lewis and Clark expedition, as a guide. From Fort Manuel, Colter reconnoitered on his own, discovering what became Yellowstone Park ("Colter's Hell") in the process.

American access suffered a serious blow in September 1807, when Nathaniel Pryor, one of Lewis and Clark's sergeants, commanded a small party escorting Sheheke back to his Mandan home. Accompanying them, Pierre Chouteau, Jr., led a modest group of traders. Near Grand River, Arikara stopped them, most likely because of antagonism that Americans had caused Too ne's death the previous year. In a short but vicious battle, Arikara killed three traders and wounded a like number of Pryor's soldiers. Survivors retreated to St. Louis. The Arikara had effectively challenged American power to travel and trade, alarming the new governor of Louisiana, Meriwether Lewis. In a short year, many natives changed their views about Yankees, giving Jefferson's friendship medals and other tokens to enemies in a hope that bad luck would transfer with them.

When Lisa returned to St. Louis in 1808, realizing what would now be a half million dollars in profits from his winter efforts, it became obvious that only large, well-equipped parties could succeed. In February 1809, Lisa spearheaded formation of what became the Missouri Fur Company; its supporters included William Clark, August and Pierre

Chouteau, Pierre Menard, and Andrew Henry. Until 1813 the Missouri Fur Company dominated American trade and travel through South Dakota, Lisa himself probably the most frequent visitor. Within months after its formation, the firm dispatched a huge force of nearly 180 men and nine boats to trade with the Mandan and push beyond to the Crow. They muscled Sheheke back to his people, but the Arikara remained an unpredictable obstacle along their portion of the river.

Andrew Henry extended Missouri Fur Company efforts into Blackfeet country early in 1810. Still smarting from Lewis's killing of two warriors in 1806, the tribe brooked no trapping in their territory and repeatedly attacked Henry's post at Three Forks. By July, surviving traders withdrew to Fort Manuel. Against this backdrop, a new player in the fur trade appeared—John Jacob Astor's American Fur Company. With grandiose plans to build a fort on the Pacific coast and link it to St. Louis through a string of other posts, Astor dispatched parties to bring his dream to fruition. Thirty-three traders left New York City by ship, bound around Cape Horn for the Columbia River. A larger, overland force assembled in St. Louis and awaited spring 1811.[37]

Wilson Price Hunt, one of Astor's partners but inexperienced on the frontier, headed the overland Astorians. Hunt's keelboats left St. Louis in March 1811, intent on retracing Lewis and Clark's route. As they poled and rowed toward Grand River in July, however, word reached them of Andrew Henry's debacle with Blackfeet at Three Forks. Hunt abandoned initial plans and purchased 118 horses from the Arikara and Cheyenne, seventy-six animals to carry trade goods alone. The party struck out along the Grand, angled through western South Dakota, past the Black Hills, into Wyoming, and finally to the Snake River, which they followed to the Columbia and Fort Astoria—half-finished when they arrived in early 1812. Alas, Astor's plan failed that same year with the start of war between the United States and Britain.

Hudson's Bay Company and the North West Company competed as viciously with each other as they did cooperatively against American fur trading interests. In truth, prior to 1815, these two companies *were* the fur trade west of the Great Lakes. Lisa and Astor proved nuisances, at best. The War of 1812 gave both British companies and government opportunity to win Missouri River tribe allegiances and drive out American upstarts altogether. Instrumental in this effort was Robert Dickson, partner of James Aird from whom Lewis and Clark got news, tobacco, and flour near the Big Sioux River in 1806. Dickson married a Yanktonai woman and established himself on Lake Traverse. He used family ties, trading experience, and ample government-supplied goods to win military support for the British from some Yanktons and a few upper Mississippi bands. He tried to coax other Sioux in his direction, but without success.

Americans turned to Manuel Lisa during the war. He worked equally hard shepherding most Missouri River tribes into the American camp or neutrality. After the Treaty of Ghent ended hostilities, Lisa assembled forty-three Missouri River tribal leaders at Portage des Sioux near St. Louis to reaffirm American control along the waterway. Dickson, and the British generally, confined official trading efforts north of the forty-ninth parallel as it marked the United States-Canada border east of the Rocky Mountains. Dakota fur trade from 1815 forward became an American business only—big business, profitable business.

Fur trade meant several things. First, the European-native interchange began a full century before the United States formed. Wags often remarked that "HBC" stamped on something meant "Here Before Christ," not "Hudson's Bay Company." Early efforts in the Dakotas relied primarily on native men to hunt fur-bearing animals (primarily beaver) and for their wives to process pelts that could then be traded for European manufactured goods: muskets, iron kettles, knives, beads, and the like. HBC also employed brigades of French-Canadian trappers dispatched to an area in the fall so they could methodically exploit it during winter, when pelts were thickest and most valuable. North West Company, Lisa's Missouri Fur Company, and later American interests employed or catered to free trappers—individuals who may have traveled collectively but then fanned out on their own initiative, bringing furs of their labors back to a central point for transport to Quebec or St. Louis. Some preferred more solitude and entrepreneurial freedom, traveling and working entirely on their own, rendezvousing annually at a fort or meeting place to sell furs and re-supply for the next season. In the beaver trade, free trappers became the *causes célèbres* of the American effort and the source of romantic tales, both true and tall.

Likewise, a "fur trading post" took many forms. Some made imposing statements on the landscape, like Fort Pierre: "an immense square," in Eugene de Girardin's words, "formed by four walls in the form of palisades five meters high and two hundred long,. . . protected on the north, on the east, and on the southeast by three bastions armed with cannon."[38] The majority assumed more modest proportions: often, just crude cabins used to gather furs for trans-shipment or as winter residences for free trappers. Through company records, historians have identified perhaps one hundred such posts in South Dakota—most clustered along the Missouri, but scattered literally everywhere inside the state's borders. Taken together, they symbolize the extent to which fur traders opened the region to European and American influence.

Beaver alone did not make the fur trade. Companies and trappers attempted to be opportunistic and, thus, profitable. Ledger books and bills of lading included game of every description: deer, elk and antelope hides; muskrat, mink, otter, and ermine; swans and whooping cranes (feathers for ladies' hats); plus buffalo—tongues and hides. Beaver, however, drove the trade before the War of 1812 and dominated it for two decades thereafter, primarily because men's fashion glorified the felt hat, made from

Fort Pierre and surrounding area, looking east across the Missouri River, as painted by Karl Bodmer in 1833.
Courtesy South Dakota State Historical Society–State Archives.

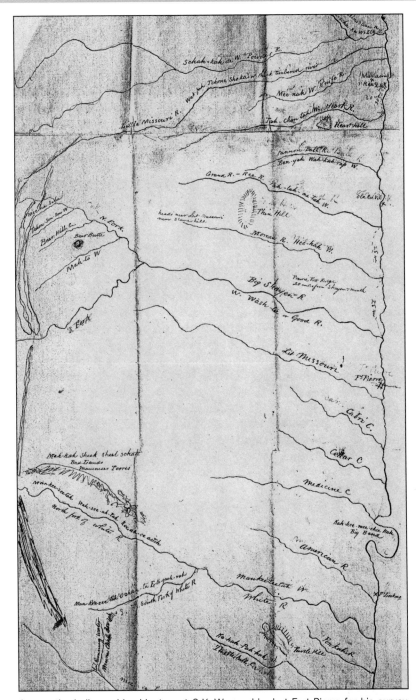

Among the Indian guides Lieutenant G.K. Warren hired at Fort Pierre for his survey expedition of 1855 was Michael DeSomet, who drew this map of the Missouri River and its western tributaries. Michael (also known as Joseph) DeSomet claimed to be the son of Meriwether Lewis.[39] *Courtesy G.K. Warren Papers, New York State Library.*

soft-napped, close-trimmed beaver. By the 1830s, over-trapping seriously depleted the supply of beaver. William Clark, who had seen beaver in abundance between 1804 and 1806, remarked in 1830 on "a very perceptible decrease of the furred animals." At the same moment, fashion turned from beaver to silk hats. Prime pelts brought nearly six dollars a pound in 1830; a decade later, their value fell to $2.62. Raccoon-tail hats, like Davy Crocket wore, became the rage in Europe after 1840, resulting in millions of the skins leaving American ports for the next twenty years. Fur trade depended on urban Europe and America, both as markets for pelts and as sources of many manufactured items used to trade for them.

Manuel Lisa died in 1820. His Missouri Fur Company pioneered big-business trading on the Missouri after Lewis and Clark and lingered, in name but not profitability, for another decade. Two other firms rose to take its place: General William A. Ashley's Rocky Mountain Fur Company, formed in 1822, and the Western Department of John Jacob Astor's American Fur Company, which opened a St. Louis branch the same year. Andrew Henry joined the former corporation and during its twenty-year history, the firm opened the central and northern Rockies to fur trade and provided the era's most romantic images.

Ashley chose not to trade in South Dakota with Teton Sioux, although he did open a small house called Fort Brasseau at the mouth of the White River. He set his sites on mountains. On March 22, 1822, the general ran an ad in the St. Louis *Missouri Republican* soliciting one hundred "enterprising young men" to sign on with the Rocky Mountain Fur Company and trap the Upper Missouri. He assembled an extraordinary party with names on the roster that became stars in the frontiersmen pantheon: part African-American James P. Beckwourth, who eventually married a Crow woman and became a tribal chief; Hugh Glass, remembered for being mauled by a grizzly, then abandoned by friends only to sustain himself on berries and carrion as he crawled one hundred miles across South Dakota into the care of friendly Indians; Jim Bridger, known as "Old Gabe" all over the Rocky Mountains; and Bible-reading Jedediah Strong Smith, who did not drink, smoke, or swear, and who discovered South Pass and the Great Salt Lake and explored the Sierras. Ashley's magic worked in 1822, when his enterprising men established a post at the mouth of the Yellowstone and had an extremely profitable season.

When Ashley led an 1823 party up the Missouri to extend his successes in two packed keelboats named *Rocky Mountains* and *Yellowstone Packet*, Arikara attacked it near the mouth of the Grand River, killing fourteen and wounding a dozen. Ashley asked the government for help. Colonel Henry Leavenworth jumped at the opportunity to demonstrate American military power now based at Fort Atkinson, near Council Bluffs. Joshua Pilcher and forty Missouri Fur Company employees quickly attached themselves to Leavenworth's 220 soldiers. Pilcher, official agent to the Sioux, then convinced several hundred Teton to join the expedition against their traditional enemies. Overawed, Arikara asked to negotiate, doing so successfully until they escaped under cover of darkness. Frustrated fur trappers and Sioux burned the village. Leavenworth returned to Fort Atkinson, satisfied he had once and for all put an end to Arikara harassment.

Henry salvaged Rocky Mountain Fur Company efforts late that same summer, taking eighty men overland, generally paralleling the 1811 Astorian route. Expedition member James Clyman described the lower Teton as "dry roling County" and Cheyenne River bad lands as "this pile of ashes." When he arrived at the Black Hills, Clyman rejoiced: it felt "cool and refreshing so different from the hot dusty planes we have been so long passing over."[40] Also, in 1823, the company moved other trappers into the beaver-rich

Green River Valley, forged what became the Overland Trail, and forever abandoned fur trade in South Dakota.

In its stead arose the rendezvous system, a rowdy, highly profitable trading scheme. For a week or two in July or August, free trappers met St. Louis merchants at a pre-determined mountain valley in the central Rockies. These "mountain men" sold furs, re-supplied for the next trapping season, and debauched themselves. Merchants enjoyed profits in excess of 2,000 percent; trappers enjoyed everything they could. Ashley retired with a fortune by 1826, and, as late as 1832, 168 packs of furs came out of the rendezvous—worth over $1,780,000 today. The bubble burst quickly. Rocky Mountain Fur Company ceased operations in 1836; the last rendezvous, under American Fur Company aegis, took place in 1840.

The American Fur Company remained focused on the Missouri. John Jacob Astor patiently rebuilt his trading power after the War of 1812 fiasco. Eventually, he controlled the upper Great Lakes out of a post at Mackinac and expanded to St. Louis in 1822 with his Western Department. There he combined politics and business, worked with existing St. Louis trading families like the Chouteaus, and built a base. At the same time Ashley looked west, Astor focused north. In 1827 he formed the Western Department under the management of Bernard, Pratte and Company.

Also active in the field was the small, but aggressive Columbia Fur Company, an economic haven for former North West Company employees Joseph Renville, Kenneth McKenzie, and William Laidlow. With their headquarters at Dickson's old Lake Traverse site, they nurtured trade between the Mississippi and Missouri, with a string of posts at the mouths of the Big Sioux, James, and Bad rivers. Renville and associates focused on buffalo hides, not beaver. The change to buffalo elevated Sioux economic fortunes. Men on horseback killed all the buffalo they could; women on the ground found that their work had increased dramatically to process proliferating hides.

Transporting heavy buffalo skins down the Missouri in canoes and mackinaws proved profitable; moreover, the popularity of the warm robes began to grow in Europe and the East. Astor did not want to bother with this competition and simply bought out Columbia Fur in July 1827. In a smart business move, the American Fur Company absorbed its former competitor, infrastructure and all, renaming it the Upper Missouri River Outfit for the Western Department. The UMRO took control of all trade above the Big Sioux. Equally brilliant, one of the Outfit's first moves was to establish Fort Union at the junction of the Missouri and Yellowstone—a trading point Lewis and Clark, Manuel Lisa, and William Ashley recognized as pivotal.

Profit, not principle, drove Astor. He looked for efficiencies and other means to improve his bottom line. Liquor proved lucrative for trade and valuable to lubricate negotiations with natives. Despite official government prohibitions on alcohol in the fur trade, American Fur Company posts defiantly used it and rarely paid any penalty. The company's Pierre Chouteau, Jr., received credit for the greatest technological innovation in Missouri River trade—introduction of the steamboat. In 1831 he used the *Yellowstone* to bring trade goods up to Fort Tecumseh, then returned furs, hides, and 10,000 pounds of buffalo tongue to St. Louis. With carrying capacity greater than any flotilla of bateaux or keelboats, the "Fire Boat that Walked on the Water" impressed Indians, revolutionized river transportation, and maximized profits.

Chouteau, himself, went up the Missouri on the 1832 boat and christened a new namesake fort erected to replace Tecumseh—Fort Pierre. The *Yellowstone* made it all the way to Fort Union that year. That post at the Yellowstone, and Fort Pierre near the Bad, served as American Fur Company bases. From Fort Union, Astor successfully extended trade into Blackfeet domain by the early 1830s and went on to compete with Hudson's Bay Company along fringes of the Oregon country. It all came down the Missouri through South Dakota. For a while, Fort Pierre receipts equaled those of its upriver counterpart; but by 1840 Fort Union surpassed the South Dakota post in importance.

Astor, himself, foresaw the pending decline in fur trading. In 1834 he gave up control of the American Fur Company and focused his business acumen on New York real estate. Pratte, Chouteau and Company, later Pierre Chouteau, Jr. and Company, took over Missouri trade. Their river boats continued to ply the Big Muddy into the early 1860s when Montana gold seekers replaced fur traders on their decks. On April 14, 1855, Chouteau sold Fort Pierre to the U.S. Army, an appropriate date to say the fur trade era ended in South Dakota.

Before the story of exploration in South Dakota closed, one other expedition took place. Under Chouteau family sponsorship, French-born naturalist Joseph N. Nicollet examined Mississippi headwaters in 1836 and 1837. In 1838 the government commissioned him to map geological and topographical features between the upper Mississippi and Missouri. Nicollet ascended the Mississippi, then moved west, eventually visiting the pipestone quarry and Coteau des Prairies. A young second lieutenant named John C. Frémont accompanied the Frenchman and charted a series of lakes in South Dakota's northeast corner: Benton, named after his future father-in-law and powerful Senator Thomas Hart Benton; Preston, after South Carolina Senator William Campbell Preston; Poinsett, to honor friend and benefactor Joel Poinsett, who first imported the poinsettia from Mexico; and Abert, to curry the favor of his superior Colonel J. J. Abert. Alas, this name later became corrupted to Lake Albert.

Nicollet returned to the region in 1839, this time ascending the Missouri to Fort Pierre on the annual June steamboat. July found him exploring the James up to Devils Lake. From there he mapped east to the Red River, followed it to Big Stone Lake, where Nicollet again explored the Coteau before exiting overland to Fort Snelling, and back to St. Louis. The United States got detailed maps of the region; John C. Frémont got exploring experience he put to good use elsewhere in the West.[41]

In retrospect, fur traders finished what explorers began, expanding European understanding of and influence in the entire South Dakota landscape. To make a profit, trapper/traders quite literally decimated fur-bearing animal populations. Native Americans, too, saw reward in the fur and hide trade but, in the process, lost economic control of the land and became dependent on manufactured goods—the "commercial intercourse" President Jefferson sought to promote. As fur traders abandoned the region, farmers and ranchers replaced them—a new generation undertaking different explorations on how to earn livings from the land and its resources.

Chapter 5
Missouri Valley Culture

The Missouri Valley Culture, which originated in the fur trade, grew in response to the creation of six U.S. Indian Agency jurisdictions and thrived mainly on business opportunities made available by the presence of tribal groups and U.S. Army installations as well as the development of transportation services. Geographically, within the boundaries of present-day South Dakota, this valley culture took shape in three phases that produced three distinctive sectors of settlement. The first phase entailed urbanization at scattered locations of fur trade with the Yankton Sioux between the confluences of the Missouri with the Big Sioux and Niobrara rivers. After the establishment of Fort Vermillion in 1827 to house an inventory of manufactured trade goods near the center of Yankton tribal land, this and additional communities took shape to provide lodging and other services for travelers who entered Sioux Country along the Missouri River Valley. From the outset, their stability was assured not only because of the peaceable disposition of Yankton people, but also because of a federal presence following the establishment of the regional Upper Missouri Agency jurisdiction in 1819 and effective federal management mandated by Congress in the Fur Trade Act of 1824. Every urban community in the lower sector of the valley evolved on or near the site of a former fur trade station except Springfield, which appeared on high ground between Bon Homme and Running Water.

Terms in the Yankton Treaty of 1858 brought dramatic change across the lower sector of the Missouri valley in present-day South Dakota. They transformed the ancestral claim of the tribe on 11,155,890 acres in what is today known as East River, South Dakota, into public domain owned by the United States government; formally extended land rights to existing members of the valley culture; and mandated the detachment of the ceded area from administrative and commercial controls created by the Fur Trade Act of 1824. Specifically, Article 7 authorized grants of land free of charge on the ceded territory to influential valley residents with Native American wives as well as to tribal mixed-bloods. Zephier Rencontre, Charles Picotte, Paul Dorian, and others received titles to sites along the north bank of the Missouri River. Rencontre selected 640 acres that soon contained the town of Bon Homme, for example, and Picotte acquired 640 acres that became the city of Yankton. Elsewhere, Dorian received 320 acres, as did others with the names Reulo, Bedand, Traverse, and LeCount—all previously associated with the fur trade. Article 7 also stated that "all other persons (other than Indians, or mixed-bloods) who are now residing within said ceded country, by authority of law, shall have the privilege of entering one hundred and sixty acres thereof, to include each of their residences and improvements, at a rate of one dollar and twenty-five cents per acre."[1] Thus, Article 7 authorized gifts of land to individuals who had been instrumental in treaty negotiations, and it guaranteed pre-emption rights for non-Indians to purchase land they previously occupied during the fur trade era. In effect, Article 7 assured the eligibility of non-Indians for the use of terms already included in the federal Pre-emption Act of 1841.

Article 6 offered treaty benefits to mixed-blood families of fur trade origin whose members were registered on the tribal roll but chose to live off the reservation rec-

Chronology

1819 – Upper Missouri Agency founded as a regional federal jurisdiction

1824 – Fur Trade Act called for designation of trade locations and federal administration equivalent to territorial government

1827 – Fort Vermillion founded to maintain an inventory for trade with Yankton Sioux and accommodate travelers
– Fort Tecumseh (Fort Pierre after 1831) maintained upstream from Bad River for trade above Crow Creek along the Missouri River and among Lakota tribes

1856 – Fort Randall founded upstream from natural feature called "The Tower" and a crossing on the Missouri River

1858 – Yankton Treaty of Washington, DC, called for the cession of tribal land, establishment of reservation, reduction of Upper Missouri Agency jurisdiction, and federal recognition of Missouri Valley Culture

1859 – Yankton (Greenwood) Agency founded in the "Mile Square" at lower edge of Yankton Reservation
– White Swan village appeared above Fort Randall near Andy's Point

1861 – Tackett Station and Andrus appeared on lower Chouteau Creek as Yankton Reservation border communities
– Territory of Dakota founded with Yankton as capital

1862 – Union, Clay, Yankton, and Bon Homme founded (east to west) as original counties in Dakota Territory
– Vermillion became Clay County seat and Bon Homme founded as Bon Homme County seat

1866 – Lower Yanktonais with Two Kettles gathered on Crow Creek Reservation while Lower Brûlés settled along lower White River
– Oacoma took root as Lower Brûlé Reservation border community and Fort Sully founded in Peoria Bottom upstream from Pierre

ognized in the 1858 treaty. Article 10 indicated that no "white person" could trade with Yanktons, except a federal employee or someone duly licensed (by the U.S. Agent in charge with approval from the U.S. Interior Department) to trade with Yankton people. Together, Articles 6, 7, and 10 in the treaty terminated commercial relationships of the past while they reserved special rights for all of those previously affiliated with the fur trade across most of the East River ceded area, which contemporary observers called the "Yankton Triangle," between the Big Sioux and Missouri rivers. Federal supervision of trade with Yanktons remained in place, but the treaty abandoned all other commercial restrictions on the Yankton Triangle except a prohibition on the sale or trade of intoxicating beverages among federally recognized Indian people or on federally recognized Indian land.

The second phase inspired settlement in a middle sector of the valley at locations between lower Chouteau Creek and Bijou Hills in response to several changes in federal management. During the year 1856, General William Harney founded Fort Randall near the center of the middle sector, on the west bank of a narrow known as Tower Reach in the Missouri River Valley, where a natural elevation called "The Tower" marked a shallow river crossing used in the past by tribal travelers on a trail that brought them from the present-day Sioux Falls area by way of Firesteel Creek (Mitchell) to Seven Mile Creek directly below The Tower. Although personnel at Fort Randall relied on steamboat transportation from March to August, the fort's managers opened an all-season Military Road from Sioux City along the east side of the river northward beyond the Fort Randall area. To this crossroad of regional travel, Harney brought nearly 1,000 men, who fast became valley culture customers with reliable salaries to spend. The U.S. Interior Department recognized the superintendent of farming at the fort as a liaison in its formal relationship with Lower Brûlés until 1866, when they gathered upstream on a reservation of their own near the mouth of the White River.

In 1858, terms in the Yanktons' treaty extended federal recognition to a reservation on tribal ancestral land across the Missouri River from Fort Randall that extended eastward to Chouteau Creek. It contained an estimated 400,000 acres (later expanded and surveyed to include about 430,000 acres) to accommodate approximately 2,200 tribal members. At the lower edge on the Missouri River, federal officials reserved a "Mile Square" for the establishment of the Yankton Agency (later named Greenwood). In return for the cession of the Yankton Triangle, the tribe received a $1.6 million annuity fund plus the promise of material support and various services. As a result, tribal members had money to spend, and agency personnel contributed a cash flow from salaries ranging between about $100 and $1,000 per year. The enlargement of the population of valley residents to exploit opportunities at the borders of the new Yankton Reservation was inevitable.

Chronology (cont'd)

1868 – Whetstone, Fort Bennett (Cheyenne River), and Fort Yates (Standing Rock) agency jurisdictions authorized on Missouri River
 – Upper Missouri Agency jurisdiction disappeared
 – Fort Laramie Treaty recognized Great Sioux Reservation
1870 – Springfield platted as Missouri River Valley town
 – Harney City appeared across Missouri River from Whetstone Agency
1874 – Running Water founded, soon became a railhead and Missouri River ferry station
1877 – City of Fort Pierre appeared at mouth of Bad River
1879 – Charles Mix County superimposed on Yankton Reservation
 – Wheeler founded as Charles Mix County seat

Another agency jurisdiction appeared in the middle sector because the establishment of the agency at Greenwood had initiated the dissolution of the regional Upper Missouri Agency jurisdiction, founded in 1819, by its subdivision into smaller agency jurisdictions until the regional unit disappeared in 1868. Along the Missouri River, new jurisdictions included the Crow Creek (founded at Fort Thompson, in 1866); the Lower Brûlé (1866); the Fort Bennett (Cheyenne River, 1868); the Fort Yates (Standing Rock, 1868); and the Whetstone (in the middle sector at the mouth of Whetstone Creek a short distance above Fort Randall, 1868).

As well in 1868, terms in the Fort Laramie Treaty extended a maximum array of treaty benefits to enrolled residents of these five jurisdictions (as well as to those soon gathered at the Spotted Tail and Red Cloud agencies situated to the west). Therefore, during the period 1856-1868, valley culture groups that gathered in the middle sector had easy access to cash flows from a major military fort and two Indian agencies, which together accommodated more than 5,000 people who received annuity payments or salaries from the United States government.

The third phase in the evolution of the Missouri Valley Culture produced settlements in an upper sector from Oacoma on the lower White River to Winona on the east side of the Missouri River above the present South Dakota-North Dakota border. The initial lure was the appearance of new agency jurisdictions at Crow Creek, Lower Brûlé, Cheyenne River, and Standing Rock during the 1860s, as mentioned above. Further incentive for the gathering of valley population was business related to transportation into the Black Hills because of the gold rush during the 1870s.

Across all three sectors of valley culture, an aggregate population engaged in a variety of occupations with little regard for legal restraint. Some valley residents managed

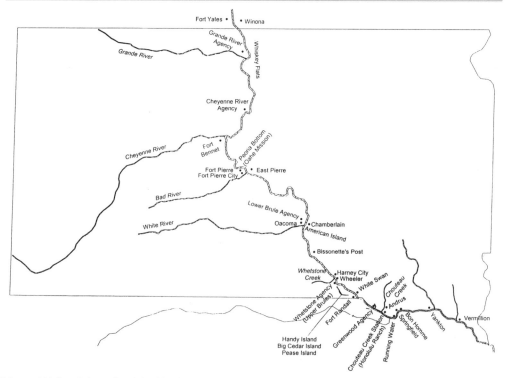

Missouri Valley Culture flourished in the decades between exploration and permanent settlement. *Courtesy Herbert T. Hoover.*

country stores, lodging facilities, restaurants, farms and ranches, and wood yards that provided fuel for steamboats, giving rise to what some call "Steamboat Society." Some of them were judges, sheriffs, or territorial legislators. Some were livestock rustlers, gamblers, prostitutes, and middlemen in the theft or illegal purchase of tribal annuity supplies. Many were men of French or mixed-blood heritage who arrived during the fur trade era, married (by common law or tribal ceremonies) tribal women, and fathered families that later gained importance in the modern tribes that took shape on new reservations. No census exists to suggest the size of the valley culture population, but ample evidence demonstrates its significance to the history of the state.

Few residents strayed far from the river valley. Their best business opportunities were those with members of tribes who drew benefits from treaty or statutory annuities delivered at agency headquarters, with burgeoning traffic on steamboats along the river, with steady traffic on roads that ran close to the river, and eventually with commercial interests that approached the river by cargo wagons and railroads. As a result of the disparate character of the valley population, its changing nature, and the covert disposition of some of its occupations, no single body of literature has appeared to trace its unique history.

The best profile emerges in a description of budding urban communities and service centers scattered along the Missouri River Valley from Fort Vermillion to the North Dakota boundary. Their examination contains ample information about nearly all groups in the culture except two, who are recognized but not described adequately below because of a paucity of information about their activities. Woodcutters (sometimes called "wood hawks") earned their livelihood by gathering driftwood or cutting trees, reducing trunks and branches to sizes useful to fire the boilers on steamboats, and stacking them in cords or wood yards at fairly close intervals of about ten miles each on sites convenient to crews on the steamers. Because captains understood the necessity of dutiful payment in cash or in goods, in order to avoid a boycott as retaliation for the theft of fuel, woodcutters were not necessarily present when the steamers took on fuel. Through the early decades of steamboat travel, a single cutter might have maintained cords of wood scattered along the shoreline for many miles. Ranges of operations and even identities of the cutters did not always appear in public records, except when cutters were charged with illegal activities. One infraction was that of taking wood from tribal property without payment. Ordinarily, a cutter accused of theft retreated from the shoreline to gather driftwood on islands separated from the shore by chutes or sloughs, where islands were included in the navigable water controlled by the U.S. Army Corps of Engineers; or the cutter took a tribal member as a wife. Another infraction was the sale of whiskey in federally recognized Indian Country, which clearly violated federal prohibition laws enforced as early as 1832. One woodcutter accused of such violations was Louis ("Red") Archambault, who operated in the vicinity of the Fort Thompson Agency. For legal access to wood along the shoreline, he, like some others, married into a tribe. For the charge of selling whiskey, there was no alternative to flight from arrest by federal or tribal police.

The primary occupation of Missouri Valley woodcutters, needless to say, was that of maintaining a supply of wood to fuel the engines of steamboats, which provided the most effective transportation services for the northern Great Plains until their gradual replacement by overland traffic on cargo wagons, stagecoaches, and railroads. Into the twentieth century, steamboats continued to haul some cargo with passengers until diesel engines replaced steam power. Their captains faced many obstacles on the Missouri River. During most years, one obstacle was a restriction on transportation from March to August, when the channel was not deep enough to carry the boats. Another was the problem of snags and shifting sand bars that delayed their progress and often destroyed their boats. Yet the most critical hazard was a shortage of fuel, which only the woodcutters could supply.

The only clear public records of woodcutters' locations appeared in the *Map of the Missouri River* commissioned by acts of Congress on June 18, 1878, and March 3, 1879, and created by personnel in the Corps of Engineers during the period 1879-1881. A detailed map of the river valley in the lower section between Sioux City and Niobrara included massive stands of oak and cottonwood trees and marked the locations of six wood yards along the river's edge over a distance of about fifty miles, as the crow flies, at average intervals of approximately ten miles each: (1) Walter's Wood Yard was close to Maanin's Mill, approximately one mile below Elk (Dixon's) Point; (2) Wiscinan's Wood yard was about four miles above; (3) an unnamed wood yard that existed between the City of Vermillion and the Clay/Yankton County Line; (4) Lober's Wood Yard was approximately seven miles above the City of Yankton; (5) Hughes' Wood Yard was about two miles above Ackley's Mill and approximately two miles below Bon Homme Island (Bonhomme Island); (6) Dodson's Wood Yard was some two miles above the City of Bon Homme. Obviously, by 1881, the wood yard and lumber-milling businesses were closely intertwined. Branches, slabs, and driftwood fueled the boilers of the steamboats.

In return, the cutters could demand payment in cash or in merchandise, for which they found increasing use. Without much concern about federal laws and policies, the cutters were principal distributors of whiskey and guns with ammunition. Doubtless, the forty-one different kinds of firearms accompanied by an ample supply of ammunition that destroyed the Seventh Cavalry of George Custer on the Little Bighorn River came from various sources, as did other materials of war used by the Sioux through several decades of resistance. Among the most likely suppliers were the woodcutters in Missouri Valley Culture.

The other mobile group in valley culture difficult to trace is that of women, whose activities seldom appeared in documents except when they were under attack as prostitutes. Oral traditions suggest two characteristics. One is that prostitutes comprised a mobile population whose members remained in the business only for as long as it took them to find husbands or some other means of escape. Perhaps partly because they searched for spouses, and partly because their customers might have preferred variety, there existed an assumption that an individual prostitute should work in no Missouri valley community for more than about two weeks at a time. Steamboat captains tended to transport the women from place to place free of charge.

The other characteristic suggested by the paucity of information is that many prostitutes were white but others were of mixed or tribal heritage caught in desperate circumstances. Whatever their ethnic origins, they should be remembered more for their contributions to cultural developments than for violations of either Christian or tribal moral codes. Some provided entertainment for men at the Missouri Valley stations described below, but evidently a substantial percentage of the women lived in cabins with traders and U.S. Army officers or met enlisted men at isolated places—for example, at the French ovens where army cooks baked bread across the river from Fort Randall. When evaluated according to any moral standard, the women were no more culpable than were the men who purchased their favors. As participants in the shaping of South Dakota history, these women merit recognition as a group essential to the evolution of regional culture.

■ First Phase: Settlements Along the Lower Valley

The activities of groups other than woodcutters and mobile women are more distinct in records and literature about urban and service centers that evolved along the Missouri River. Because many of them originated in the fur trade, most of these groups occupied former locations of trade. Along the river, moving upstream across South Dakota, the first was Fort Vermillion, founded in 1827 east of present Lake Burbank on land owned by the *ospaye* (band) of the Yankton leader Tatanka Witko, known by non-Indians as Mad Bull I, and all but abandoned by the time Mad Bull and his group withdrew because of the Yankton land cession in 1858.[2] Through most of that period, Fort Vermillion was an urban center that maintained inventories, equipment, and facilities to serve travelers of various kinds. The managers offered sleeping accommodations in log cabins, sold food and supplies, and arranged guides for those who wished to travel overland.

Fort Vermillion existed, however, mainly to house a substantial inventory for trade across land claimed by Yankton tribal hunters. Included among its prominent traders was the Frenchman Henri Ange, who lived nearby with a tribal spouse. He was important partly because he was one of few merchants with college training and, as a result, was wholly literate in more than one language and became notably influential in intercultural affairs. His name appeared as "Chief Henri" in records about some Mormons who relied on his assistance when they attempted a settlement adjacent to the fort during their exodus in 1846. Ange's name appeared in Roman Catholic mission records, too, because he served as a host for Father Augustin Ravoux, from Mendota, during the first formal Catholic training endeavor in present-day South Dakota.

Another prominent merchant often affiliated with Fort Vermillion was Theophile Bruguier, a Frenchman from St. Louis who married all the daughters of Chief War Eagle.[3]

Most of the time, Bruguier lived near the mouth of the Big Sioux River, but he left mixed-blood descendants as far up the Missouri as Fort Peck. Others who drew supplies from Fort Vermillion to trade with Yankton Sioux included William Dickson, a Yanktonai mixed-blood with a post near the present-day border between Clay and Yankton counties; Pierre Hurtubise, a Frenchmen who evidently traded within the present city limits of Yankton; Zephier Rencontre, a Frenchman who traded on Bonhomme Island; and Colin Campbell, a merchant of British heritage who manned a trading place near the present town of Running Water.

While Fort Vermillion attracted attention as a federally designated location for trade, it also served as a federal annuity station during the fur trade era. Here, agents distributed goods as annuities required by treaty terms to "Missouri River Santees"—who were exiled Wahpekute Dakotas, including the legendary Inkpaduta.

That such a place should vanish late in the 1850s is easy enough to explain. Three decades of trade devastated the populations of most species of animals in the area owned and occupied by Yankton Sioux. Mad Bull's constituency withdrew from the Fort Vermillion area during the summer of 1859 to settle on a reservation west of Chouteau Creek.

The Frenchman Zephier Rencontre (front row, center), who had married a Yankton Sioux woman, established a trading station on Bonhomme Island. For his efforts on behalf of the Yankton Treaty of 1858, he was rewarded by the U.S. government with 640 acres of land. Other Yankton Treaty participants include (top row, left to right) Medicine Crow, Charles Picotte, Louis Dewitt, and (lower row) Struck by the Ree and the Pretty Boy. *Courtesy* Bon Homme County History, *Hoover et al.*

Because the fort existed on a flood plain of the Missouri River, many of its former occupants were forced onto higher ground during every overflow, but most of them did not leave the area. After the establishment of Dakota Territory in 1861, they remained to engage in business along the Sioux City-to-Fort Randall Military Road and to found communities that gave rise to the town of Burbank, in the valley nearby, and to the larger commercial city of Vermillion, where the Vermillion River entered the valley farther upstream. Although both Burbank and Vermillion mainly grew as railroad stations and service centers for agricultural settlement, both gave abiding expression to Missouri Valley Culture, as well. Vermillion flourished at first as the location of the territorial land office and county seat for Clay County, and it grew rapidly after the establishment of the University of South Dakota within its city limits in 1882.

No noteworthy Missouri Valley station took shape upstream between the mouth of the Vermillion and the lower James River area because of frequent overflows and sometimes catastrophic floods along the Missouri River. The Great Flood of 1881, caused by an ice jam at Vermillion about forty feet deep that extended all across the valley, drove residents with their livestock to high ground and moved the channel of the river from the Dakota Territory to the Nebraska side of the valley. Mainly due to the threat of ice jams and floods, the next significant valley station upstream evolved near the mouth of the James River on high ground abandoned in 1859 by the *ospaye* of the Yanktons' primary spokesman Struck by the Ree or "Old Strike." From appearances, ancestors of this Native American group had occupied the site and surrounding area when they moved from Mille Lacs in the eighteenth century. Thus they had asserted a claim of protracted use and recent occupancy before non-Indians arrived. To initiate trade from St. Louis, the senior Pierre Chouteau appeared near the mouth of the James a short time after the Louisiana Purchase. Following the establishment of Fort Vermillion in 1827, the lower James River area contained commercial stations manned during the heyday of trade by William Dickson and Pierre Hurtubise among others. After the death of War Eagle, through most of the 1850s, it was the center of tribal diplomatic affairs because it belonged to the *ospaye* of Struck by the Ree. After he led his group of Yanktons westward along the valley in 1859, Charles Picotte claimed the site but sold it. Quickly, after 1861, the city of Yankton came into place not only as a territorial capital, but also as a steamboat depot and railroad station, as the political center of Dakota Territory, as the location of the Congregational Yankton College, and as the location of the territorial insane asylum as well as the center of the territorial Catholic diocese. Accordingly, Yankton emerged as the most important community in the lower sector of Missouri Valley Culture.

The next community appeared about twenty miles upstream on the section of land adjacent to Bonhomme Island, donated by terms in the 1859 treaty to Zephier Rencontre. Its location had attracted the attention of Meriwether Lewis and William Clark as they made their way upstream in 1804. Indeed, Clark drew a map that contained "Bon Homme Island" adjacent to the river channel, which he perceived to contain "ancient fortifications"—evidently natural formations of sand created by floods. Although oral tradition in the area has created an assumption that this place took its name from some "good man" (Bon Homme) who occupied it after Lewis and Clark arrived, an alternative and more plausible explanation was the use of the prominent family name "Bonhomme," which has been used to identify various sites and institutions in and around St. Louis. In historical times, there existed no substantial Indian village close by; the nearest one accommodated the Yankton *ospaye* of the leader Mato Sabi Ceya, known by whites as Smutty Bear, which was a few miles above the future city of Yankton on the north bank of the Missouri.

Yet Bonhomme Island was a place of obvious utility during the fur trade era—a way station for traffic on the river and an obvious location for a woodcutter. Scattered information in print suggests that Zephier Rencontre was a non-Indian born in the present state of Missouri during the year 1800, who went to work in the network of merchants controlled by St. Louis trading magnate Pierre Chouteau, Jr., and set up a trading station at Bonhomme Island. In 1837 he married a Yankton woman whose name was written as Sulrado. For his service during the negotiations of the Yanktons' treaty, Rencontre gained title to a section of land adjacent to the island on the north bank of the Missouri. Soon, he sold most of it and spent some time with his mixed-blood family on the Yankton Reservation, but he retained a homesite for his family at the upper edge of his land grant, where he lived most of the time until his death in 1879.[4]

U.S. Indian Agent/Delegate to Congress Walter Burleigh and future Territorial Governor Andrew Faulk purchased most of the section from Rencontre and laid out the townsite of Bon Homme, which became the county seat for Bon Homme County when it was organized in 1862. For approximately two decades, this was a bustling urban center replete with stores, hotels, saloons, churches, and a school—until erosion along the north bank of the Missouri, coupled with agricultural settlement inland, forced the removal of the county seat to Tyndall in 1885. Bon Homme was accessible to steamboat traffic on the river and to overland traffic on the Sioux City-to-Fort Randall Military Road. George Custer rested here with his troops as he made his way up the river valley toward Fort Abraham Lincoln. The bodies of several troopers who died of disease were buried close to a nearby creek, to conceal the possibility of a disease epidemic. Later their bodies were moved to the Bon Homme Cemetery, where the graves have been maintained to honor these men for U.S. Army service. The cemetery that contains the bodies of Custer's troopers is located at the west edge, and the Bon Homme Hutterite Colony is situated at the east edge, of the Bon Homme city site.

A short distance upstream was a more stable site on a natural shelf well above the flood plain, where a man named Ogden Marsh platted the town of Springfield in 1870. It grew as an urban center not only because of its advantageous location on the Missouri River, but also because of its proximity to the Fort Randall Military Road. As a feature in valley culture, Springfield was especially important as a location of "river watchers," who could observe changes in water levels that signaled ice jams or their release upstream and send messages of alarm by telegraph to communities downstream. Beginning in 1873, Springfield became the location of an Episcopal Indian boarding school, initially named St. Mary's, which provided markets and offered jobs while it directly linked Springfield to the Santee Reservation on the opposite side of the river. Springfield also served as an agricultural service center, and its boundaries contained the campus of a higher educational institution named Southern State College.

A short distance upstream from Springfield was a smaller but important valley urban center that took the name Running Water (from the Niobrara River, the "river that runs"). Because it existed on a low shelf close to the water line, surely it was a place of brief respite for Jean Baptist Truteau, Lewis and Clark, and many others. During the 1830s, one of Chouteau's employees, Colin Campbell, operated a seasonal trading place at this location. After the 1858 Yankton tribal land cession, evidently the first non-Indian to claim the site was Catherine Roy, who passed her title along to a Henry Brooks. A settlement took root in 1874, and Running Water flourished as a railroad station with a roundhouse on the Chicago, Milwaukee and St. Paul Railroad a short distance from a busy ferry across the river to Niobrara, Nebraska. Thus, Running Water survived as a feature in valley culture for its service in transportation as well as retail merchandise distribution.

■ Second Phase: Settlements from Chouteau Creek to Bijou Hills

As a result of natural obstacles, another valley station did not take shape between Running Water and the small estuary of Chouteau Creek, where shallow-draft steamboats could land passengers and cargo at the southwest corner of Bon Homme County. Approximately half a mile up the creek, there appeared a hotel with a livery barn, variously known as Tackett Station, Chouteau Creek Station, Trumbo Station, and, colorfully, William Skakel's Honolulu Ranch. Upstream a short distance from the Tackett Station on Chouteau Creek, another community of business enterprises appeared along the Fort Randall Military Road named Andrus. Together, these two counted as the only off-reservation valley culture installations between Running Water and Fort Randall.

Tackett Station and Andrus were important, too, as the first places in valley culture to flourish because of their location at the edge of a U.S. Indian Agency jurisdiction.

Located on Choteau Creek, near the Missouri River, the town of Andrus developed into a commercial center, with a hotel, mill, post office, and burial ground, as a result of its proximity to the Yankton Reservation. *Courtesy Bon Homme County History, Hoover et al.*

Because Chouteau Creek formed the eastern boundary of the Yankton Sioux Reservation, Tackett Station and Andrus emerged as reservation border communities supported to a large degree by expenditures of tribal annuity funds or unauthorized exchanges of annuity goods. Yankton men could slip across the creek into Bon Homme County. At Tackett's station they could gamble, find feminine companionship, and acquire whiskey, which the managers stored in a room beneath the front yard, created as a cache accessible only through a tunnel from the basement of the hotel. At Andrus, they could purchase food and dry goods if not alcoholic beverages. Both Tackett Station and Andrus served as rest stops for Yanktons when they crossed the river by ferry at Running Water to visit the Santee Reservation or to harvest natural tobacco along the lower Niobrara River.

Residents of Andrus and the surrounding non-Indian rural community thrived as a commercial network that sold some annuity supplies to the Yankton Agency—especially fresh beef for distribution every two weeks on issue days. Andrus contained a store, livery barn, and hotel. While Walter Burleigh was in charge as the Yanktons' agent, evidently Andrus provided space for the covert storage of materials he stole from agency supplies through the use of unseemly accounting tactics and purchasing procedures. It survived until the early years of the twentieth century, when inland towns on the railway rendered it obsolete.

Tackett Station, downstream from Andrus on Chouteau Creek, provided swift and efficient justice for non-Indians who were arrested in the western townships of Bon Homme County. George Tackett was the Woodbury County Sheriff at Sioux City before he moved over in 1861 to accept an appointment by Dakota Territorial

Choteau Creek Station, also know as Tackett Station, provided meals and lodging for Missouri River travelers. *Courtesy Bon Homme County History, Hoover et al.*

Governor William Jayne as Justice of the Peace to establish law and order along the eastern edge of the Yankton Reservation. Evidently, Tackett's judicial proceedings took place on the grounds or in the lobby of his hotel. According to local legend, Tackett hanged offenders from a nearby cottonwood tree, on which he carved a notch after every execution, and buried their remains around the grounds without grave markers.

His hotel and grounds served also to accommodate a stagecoach station, livery barn, post office, country store, saloon, gambling facility, and lodging place where prostitutes were available in numbered rooms upstairs. In an adjacent gaming area on the second floor of the hotel, whiskey sold for one dollar per shot—legally to whites, illegally to Indians. By 1872 three of eight stage lines that operated on the Fort Randall Military Road made daily stops. As did men from the Yankton Tribe, soldiers from Fort Randall came down for recreation at a distance from official surveillance.

Ownership changed when Tackett sold out in the 1880s to George and Caroline Trumbo, who in turn sold out to William Skakel and Thomas Hardwick in 1894. By that time, a race track near the hotel drew additional customers and created a demand for space in the livery barn. Like Andrus, Skakel's Ranch finally closed early in the twentieth century due to the appearance of inland towns—Avon, Wagner, and others with railway transportation.

Upstream, the next off-reservation valley station was Fort Randall, founded by General Harney in 1856 to accommodate about 1,000 U.S. Army troopers. A few miles downstream at the "Mile Square," a section of land mainly on the north bank but extending into the Missouri River, the Yankton Agency appeared in 1859 and grew into the largest settlement in the area. In many ways, it served the entire society that appeared on or near the river—as a steamboat docking place, a Missouri River ferry station, a principal stop on the Fort Randall Military Road, a crossroad for overland travel, and a commercial center with shops, churches, schools, and a hotel. Yet it stood apart from the valley culture as the headquarters of an Indian agency and place of service to the Yankton Tribe where federal regulations prohibited gambling, prostitution, or the sale of spirituous beverages. Two congressional investigations, which forced the removal of Walter Burleigh as U.S. Agent, revealed theft and fraud in reservation management

The Episcopal Church established its first headquarters at Yankton Mission, Greenwood, which included (left to right) the Rectory, Cathedral of the Holy Fellowship, and St. Paul's School. *Center for Western Studies.*

during the 1860s. Unauthorized activities largely disappeared during the 1870s, however, when Presbyterian and Episcopal mission stations were established and the Episcopal Reverend John Gassman took over as the U.S. Agent and all but eliminated waste and corruption.

Fort Randall was a federal installation, formally maintained to house federal troops and to prevent illegal activities until it closed in 1896, but it also served the interests of area residents. Along the so-called Fort Randall Narrow (Tower Reach) in the Missouri, federal troops maintained one of the best docking facilities on the river. The military compound extended down to The Tower (the natural formation visible on the skyline that served as a geographical marker for both overland and river travel), below which there existed one of the best crossing places on the Upper Missouri River. The store at the fort was accessible to people of the area. Military personnel operated French ovens as a bakery across the Missouri from the fort, where they established social relations among tribal women and fathered mixed-blood families. The fort provided job opportunities as well as a market for area residents and protection through a succession of wars between non-Indians and the Sioux.

White Swan Village, on the east side of the Missouri River, at the upper end of the Fort Randall Narrow, grew into a substantial community as the permanent location of a Yankton tribal *ospaye* named after its principal leader Maga Ska, known by non-Indians as White Swan. Its recorded occupation originated in a station founded nearby in about the year 1849. During the 1850s, it was known as Handy's Landing or Andy's Point, which contained a wood yard, store, and saloon. The name changed to White Swan Village when the *ospaye* of Maga Ska arrived in 1859. (The facilities at Andy's Point moved and gave rise to the Lake Andes settlement, which became the Charles Mix County seat in 1916.) White Swan Village served as a commercial and service center from the founding of the Yankton Reservation beyond the death of Maga Ska in 1898 until its location was inundated by the reservoir named Lake Francis Case. During the 1860s, White Swan Village contained a commercial station for the North Western Fur Company. Subsequently, it included both Roman Catholic and Episcopal missions plus accommodations for visiting federal personnel. Because the village existed within the legal boundaries of the reservation, it, like the Yankton Agency Mile Square, was of limited use as a station of the valley culture.

As points of access to tribal members, Steamboat Society members occupied, gathered wood, and sold whiskey on islands nearby known by the names of Pease, Handy, and Big Cedar. Seasonal occupants enjoyed easy access not only to Yanktons at the northwest corner of their reservation, but also to Indians assembled around the Whetstone Agency at the mouth of Whetstone Creek on the west side of the Missouri River. The peculiar Whetstone Agency existed during the years 1868-1878 as a federal connection with a heterogeneous society that declined to join Sinte Gleska (Spotted Tail) on the jurisdiction recognized to accommodate most Upper Brûlés, at a considerable distance west of the Missouri. Spotted Tail would not move closer than about sixty miles because he wished to avoid easy access to his constituents by corrupting influences in Missouri Valley Culture.

A gathering of an immigrant population along the east side of the river upstream from White Swan Village preceded the arrival of Maga Ska and his *ospaye* by more than a decade. During the 1840s, Amiable Gallineau, a woodcutter, took up residence and remained until he sold out to General Charles T. Campbell in 1867. From appearances, Gallineau took as his wife a member of the Brûlé Tribe, for after 1867 he moved to the Spotted Tail (Rosebud) Agency jurisdiction.

In 1849 Pierre Peliscien arrived and took up residence along Platte Creek, where he engaged in farming. As stated, during the same year, Handy founded a business establishment that remained in operation until he withdrew after the arrival of Maga Ska.

In 1851 Felice Fallas, who immigrated from France, settled about six miles inland from the Missouri River, in the vicinity of Sully (Hamilton) Island, where he built four log cabins to accommodate his four tribal wives with their families. Fallas acquired some wealth by the possession of a federal contract to supply horses and cattle for forts along the Missouri. During the years 1864-1865, he served in the territorial legislature before he moved with his wives upstream to the new Lower Brûlé Reservation, where he died in 1909.

At some time early in the 1850s, Joseph LaRoche settled in the LaRoche Bottom near LaRoche (Colombe) Island. He made his living as a member of the valley culture until he moved upstream to the Lower Brûlé Reservation where he founded an influential family of mixed heritage.

In about the year 1855, Narcisse Drapeau arrived in the area, where he raised a family that included daughters Maria and Susan, who married Jack Sully and John Kinkaid, respectively. In 1856, General William Harney stimulated growth in the valley culture when he brought his U.S. Army unit to found Fort Randall, downstream in the narrow below Andy's Point.

In 1857 F. David Pease settled at Pease Creek. He exploited opportunities to gain some wealth and later served in the territorial legislature. During the same year, Cuthbert DuCharme founded a trading post approximately fifteen miles above Fort Randall, on the east side of the river about two miles inland from the future location of Wheeler. Better known as Papineau (meaning Pap Water, or whiskey), he ran a "whiskey ranch" and trading post frequented by steamboat crewmen, cowboys, drifters, outlaws, and federal troopers. Because his business establishment was located on the Military Road that ran along the east side of the Missouri River, it accommodated a steady stream of travelers and military units, including those led by Alfred Sully and George Custer. Papineau married Theresa Latina LeCompte, who, during the period 1863-1871, bore him five children. In 1880, after Theresa died, Papineau moved to Gregory County west of the river. In 1903 he died at the insane asylum at Yankton, where he might have gone as an aging pauper or as a person with mental disease.

In 1859 Lizziam and Louis Archambeau, mentioned above, arrived and married into the Yankton Tribe. As members of the valley culture with tribal membership acquired through marriages, they were advantageously connected to commercial opportunities while they established a powerful family of mixed heritage on the Yankton Reservation.

In 1859, as indicated, Maga Ska arrived with his *ospaye* to found White Swan Village. Except for the Yankton Agency at Mile Square, downstream, White Swan Village was the only center of a Yankton community that took shape at water's edge along the Missouri River. It accommodated the northernmost society among the three upper *ospayes* in the tribe.

In 1860 Colin LaMonte, a mixed-blood who came to the Fort Pierre area in 1842, where he married Fannie LaGrant, moved down to White Swan Village and established a school for off-reservation youngsters. LaMonte participated in the founding of an unorganized county government for the river valley society in 1862. As its Register of Deeds and clerk, he exerted influence sufficient to inspire the colloquial name "LaMonte's County" for the extra-legal government, which disappeared when the area was annexed to the Yankton Reservation as an executive (presidential) addition in 1875. At about the same time, Charles Hedges and Joseph Hamilton operated the North Western Fur

Company station at White Swan. Through the period 1862-1875, these men, Foster Wheeler, John B. S. Todd, Papineau, and several others located along the Missouri River, controlled politics in the "homemade" and extra-legal LaMonte's County—most of them as registered Democrats, some of them as members of the territorial legislature, and Todd a former delegate to Congress.

Thus, by the end of the 1860s, there existed a steadily growing population with political influence and highly advantageous commercial opportunities available because of steamboat traffic at the Fort Randall military installation and on the Yankton Reservation. As well, they had access to federal benefits that accrued to Lower Brûlés, because their federal liaison was the superintendent of farming at Fort Randall until they occupied a reservation along the north bank of the White River in 1866.

In 1868, when the regional Upper Missouri Agency jurisdiction disappeared due to the establishment of three smaller jurisdictions along the river, the Whetstone Agency compound appeared upstream from Fort Randall on the west side. It came into place to accommodate a variety of people who declined to settle some sixty miles to the west with the Upper Brûlé leader Spotted Tail. Included were Swift Bear's Upper Brûlés; Big Mouth's Oglala following; a group called Loafers, who were in fact energetic farmers; Wazhazhes, who were of Siouan but not of Sioux heritage; and non-Indians, at least fifty among more than seventy later included on the first consolidated Rosebud Agency roll. Because all of those attached to the Whetstone Agency were eligible for federal benefits accrued through terms in the 1868 Fort Laramie Treaty, their presence provided irresistible incentive for an enlargement of the Missouri Valley Culture nearby, along the east bank and on the islands of the Missouri River. An almost inevitable result was the appearance of a bustling settlement directly across the river from the Whetstone Agency docking facility.

In 1870 this settlement appeared as "a roadhouse across the river from the Whetstone Agency" that soon attracted an assembly of valley culture people and took the name of Harney City. The founders were William McKay and Lewis Obashaw, whose roadhouse gained a reputation as the "Sodom and Gamorrah of the West," where prostitutes gathered following their eviction from the territorial capital at Yankton to become "the first white women to live in the area." Before long, "horse thieves" frequented the saloons and used Harney City as the headquarters for a "vigilante committee" dedicated mainly to the protection of lawlessness. Jack Sully, who became the Sheriff of LaMonte's County in 1872, headed a group of rustlers called the "Pony Boys," which included William McKay, John Kinkaid, William Todd Randall, and several others. While Sully controlled law enforcement, McKay gained election to the territorial legislature, where he appeared for a time under guard during his trial for a murder at Snake Creek, which inevitably ended in acquittal for a lack of evidence. Harney City lost its best pool of customers in 1878, when the Whetstone Agency closed and people on its roll transferred to the Spotted Tail Agency some sixty miles to the west. The brothels and whiskey business remained in operation for at least a year before Episcopal reformer William Welsh purchased the place and closed it down. Jack Sully and John Kinkaid gained tribal connections when they married the Yankton Sioux mixed-blood daughters of Narcisse Drapeau and moved their rustling operation westward to the vicinity of Burke. The brothels and whiskey trade moved to a new location nearby, downstream on the east side of the Missouri River.[5]

By 1879 a new community grew into the town of Wheeler, named after county Judge Foster Wheeler. Although several locations occupied by members of Missouri Valley Culture—Pease, Handy, and Big Cedar islands; and Harney City—all served the general interests of river traffic. Evidently a primary reason for their occupation by valley residents was opportunity at the Whetstone Agency, which closed in 1878. Previously, the location of Wheeler attracted attention as the place of a roadhouse operated by James Bordeaux, who gained immediate power and protection when he married two daughters of the Whetstone Agency "Corn Band Brûlé" leader Swift Bear. Wheeler survived as a steamboat docking place because, in 1879, it became the seat for the new Charles Mix County superimposed on the Yankton Reservation. The town retained this benefit until county offices moved to Lake Andes in 1916. Thereafter, it retained the character of a rural commercial station resulting from business from river traffic and the installation of the Wheeler Bridge during the 1920s. The bridge disappeared early in the 1950s, when the U.S. Army Corps of Engineers moved it to Chamberlain in preparation for the creation of the reservoir named Lake Francis Case. Soon thereafter, the site of Wheeler disappeared as the result of the creation of the lake.

Upstream, the post established by Louis "Bijou" Bissonnette, which accommodated Upper Missouri Sub-agent Manuel Lisa in 1812, had been abandoned for the absence of a resident Indian population in the area. However, a man named Proteau, reportedly married to an African-American woman, ran a roadhouse in the Bijou Hills area during the years 1873-1875. Its brief existence suggests some presence of Missouri Valley Culture between Charles Mix County and the mouth of the White River, upstream. In the absence of a substantial population of immigrants in the area, the roadhouse installed by Proteau must have existed to supply wood for steamboats and to accommodate travelers on the Military Road along the east bank of the Missouri River.

■ Third Phase: Settlements from Bijou Hills to North Dakota

Upstream from Bijou Hills, the next place of Missouri valley settlement was Oacoma, near the mouth of the White River. It came into existence close to a former location of fur trade on the Missouri River island named Cedar at present-day Chamberlain, in 1800, but this facility was destroyed by fire in 1810. Fur traders returned in 1819 and, after that, seasonal traders (including Colin Campbell) and woodcutters appeared. After 1889, Cedar Island became a city park for Chamberlain under the new name of American Island.

Chamberlain had no history directly connected to Missouri Valley Culture. Local legend indicates an origin on the east bank of the Missouri River in the name Makah Tipi, for a house made of mud and occupied by a hermit. The town of Chamberlain did not appear until 1880, when it took its name from an official of the Chicago, Milwaukee, and St. Paul Railroad Company as trains approached the Missouri in need of a railroad station.

Earlier in the year 1866, when for the first time federal officials formally recognized Lower Brûlés as a discrete modern tribe of Lakota people separate from Upper Brûlés, a settlement began to take shape on the west side of the river. Previously, the federal connection with Lower Brûlés had been the superintendent of agriculture at Fort Randall, but circumstances changed. In 1863, federal employees escorted approximately 1,200 Santee refugees from the Minnesota Dakota War into the area, founded Fort Thompson Agency to accommodate them, and established the Crow Creek Reservation at a place that long had been recognized as an unoccupied ancestral boundary area between the Yanktons downstream and Lower Yanktonais upstream. After approximately 200 Santees had perished, and many had joined the Yankton Tribe, in 1866 federal officials created the new Santee Reservation for survivors in Nebraska. Quickly, a group of Lower Yanktonais, with some Lakota Two Kettles, occupied the vacated Crow Creek Reservation on the east side of the Missouri. Lower Brûlés assembled on the west side along the lower White River. Federal officials created a sub-agency under the Fort Thompson Agency as their federal connection and established headquarters for Lower Brûlés on the slope behind present-day Al's Oasis, where they remained until 1894.

Missouri Valley Culture spawned a new settlement at Oacoma, which after the 1868 Fort Laramie Treaty became a part of the Great Sioux Reservation controlled by all laws and policies that governed activities on federally protected Indian land. Steadily, thereafter, both agency officials and tribal leaders complained because "Lower Brûlés found ready access to alcoholic beverages close to their original agency, situated a mile or so above the mouth of White River across the Missouri from Chamberlain." Here "grew a neighboring settlement of approximately one hundred people that soon would evolve into the town of Oacoma." It became "notorious as a resort for gamblers and cut throats of the worst character," an agency spokesman complained to the U.S. Commissioner of Indian Affairs. Merchants at the Oacoma community maintained "six saloons and gambling rooms" where "day after day and night after night" young Lower Brûlé men were "found in debauchery without resistance to" the "temptation into which they are thrown." In order to remove the temptation as well as to improve administrative efficiency, federal officials finally, in 1894, relocated the Lower Brûlé Agency upstream to a place across the river from Fort Thompson, where whiskey merchants fell under the watchful gaze of both agency personnel and Benedictines at the Catholic Stephan Indian School.[6]

A profile of vice similar to that described above in Oacoma appeared in an evaluation of a new Missouri Valley Culture station upstream in the City of Fort Pierre. Soon after the congressional agreement of February 24, 1877, it sprang up quickly at the mouth of the Bad River, within the boundaries of the Great Sioux Reservation, at the place where Fort LaFramboise had appeared in 1817, never having been abandoned by fur traders and valley residents. By 1880 the city contained 118 buildings with a resident census of 294 and a transient population of approximately 600, because Fort Pierre became the eastern terminus of the Black Hills Wagon Road. A federal inspector complained that "during the summer Houses of Prostitution and Dance Halls were in existence and operation." He went on to say that "East Pierre immediately opposite and across the Missouri River is assuming considerable proportions, the Ice being of sufficient thickness persons are crossing hourly." He reported that "liquors of all kinds are sold publicly in Large and Small quantities," and added, "it is reasonable to conclude that at least quite a considerable quantity of liquor finds its way here, and will ever so continue as long as the two places [Fort Pierre and East Pierre] exist."[7]

Both the size and the population of Fort Pierre represented its importance at the east end of the wagon road to Deadwood, whose mining activities otherwise were accessible only along wagon roads from Bismarck and Laramie. A "Bull Whacker's Union" took shape at Fort Pierre to represent as many as sixty men who managed oxen on wagons that carried cargo to Deadwood. Mainly because of this service, the U.S. Secretary of the Interior extended authorization for the existence of Fort Pierre, which took shape within the boundaries of the Great Sioux Reservation in an area to which Lakota tribes that formed the Cheyenne River Tribe held ancestral claim. The wagon road was essential to Black Hills development because it linked the area first to steamboat traffic and, after the arrival of the Dakota Central Railroad on the east bank of the Missouri, to rail transportation.

Inevitably, members of the newly recognized Cheyenne River Tribe drifted into Fort Pierre. They also had access from the area of their Fort Bennett (later renamed the Cheyenne River) Agency to Peoria Bottom, on the east bank of the Missouri River a short distance away, and at Whiskey Island close to the fort. Upstream, whiskey traders camped along Whiskey Flats on the east side of the Missouri with easy access to Indians from the Standing Rock Agency at Fort Yates. The latter group of whiskey traders drew supplies from the town of Winona, in present-day North Dakota, which maintained eight to ten saloons where Indians could exchange clothing for liquor, and from which traders could carry supplies of whiskey on the ice or by ferry boat to the Standing Rock Reservation.[8]

Peoria Bottom took its name from General Alfred Sully's steamer named *Peoria*, which hauled supplies that he used during the establishment and operation of two forts named after himself. Sully founded the first fort downstream in 1863 and the second upstream from Pierre in 1866.[9] Like Fort Randall, downstream, these two military installations existed as communities that brought economic benefit as well as protection at a critical time. Markets for supplies and jobs were available to valley residents as well as revenue derived from expenditures by personnel from the forts. The men spent their salaries on recreation. Officers reportedly engaged the services of personal servants and women from the valley culture.

Scattered from Fort Vermillion to Winona, an undetermined number that assembled along the Missouri River comprised a thriving population through territorial years. Most of its activities are portrayed adequately above, except those that involved the management of railheads and wagon depots, which linked East River to West River through the territorial period. In aggregate, valley residents counted as the second group of immigrant non-Indians (after fur traders) to occupy South Dakota. They were scattered at advantageous places to welcome and serve the third group, composed of farmers, ranchers, and people involved with extractive industries.

Chapter 6
Native Americans in Dakota Territory

The vast majority of tribal members called Sioux in the United States were residents of Dakota Territory, where, as non-citizen Indians, they possessed no political power except in their own tribes. Together they had held an ancestral claim to all the land, which they had defended for seasonal use when their place of common residence was the vicinity of Mille Lacs in eastern Minnesota, beginning long before non-Indians arrived. They had moved out of the Mille Lacs area to scatter as full-time occupants of prehistoric Sioux Country during the last half of the eighteenth century. As hunters and trappers, they had participated in the fur trade. Many of their families blended with whites in Missouri Valley Culture either through intermarriage or common interest. Yet, as a distinctive, non-enfranchised culture in a composite of ancestral political entities, most of the Sioux lived apart from immigrant white territorials with concerns about intercultural relationships in the future.

Non-Indians had similar cause for ambivalence regarding the presence of such a large and powerful federation of tribes. By their presence, the Sioux were responsible for the most stable and profitable business opportunities available in the territory. As indicated in a previous chapter, their agency jurisdictions offered both full-time and part-time jobs, countless local service contracts, steady regional transportation contracts, and seemingly insatiable markets for food items and manufactured goods. In addition, they were responsible for the founding of both federal and mission schools built and staffed mainly by non-Indians. The Sioux gave cause for a steady presence of the U.S. Army, whose personnel sustained demands for supplies, services, and transportation through territorial years. Had the tribes been removed—as were tribes removed from Texas, for example—Dakota Territory would have been an economic wasteland. Because of their presence, it was an environment of reliable economic opportunity, and the Sioux paid most of the costs. A majority of expenditures (except for the U.S. Army) came as annuity distributions, educational costs, and various "civilization" efforts authorized by treaties and congressional agreements (statutes), which delegated authority to Interior Department officials to pay most of the costs using tribal funds derived from land sales. In other words, Sioux people exchanged landed capital for funds deposited in the U.S. Treasury, ordinarily drawing five percent annual interest per year. The same treaties and statutes that arranged the transfer of land ordered expenditures from tribal funds, delegating power over allocations to secretaries of the interior. Accordingly, the Sioux more than paid their own way at the expense of ancestral landed capital, and white territorials were their main beneficiaries.

This was ironic because most of the tribes reacted to non-Indian intrusions and land losses by armed confrontations that lasted nearly half a century and caused a continuum of "Indian scares" among white territorials. Nearly all of the fighting occurred outside the boundaries of Dakota Territory, but resulting disturbances took place within. Santees came as refugees to Crow Creek in 1863 and remained until their removal to Nebraska in 1866. Occasional clashes of arms took place during General Alfred Sully's two punitive expeditions up the Missouri River and, later, at Slim Buttes. Then came the death of

Chronology

1823 – Arikara War

1847 – Federal troops occupy Fort Kearney

1849 – Federal troops occupy Fort Laramie

1851 – Mendota and Traverse des Sioux treaties with Dakota tribes in Minnesota Territory open some 20 million acres to non-Indian settlement

– Fort Laramie Treaty opens Platte River basin to westward travel and recognizes tribal ancestral claims to surrounding area

1854 – Grattan Affair brings death to a U.S. Army unit and initiates Sioux wars in defense of land and culture

1855 – General Harney retaliates at the Battle of Ash Hollow

1856 – General Harney founds Fort Randall for permanent U.S. Army occupation (in place until 1896)

1857 – Spirit Lake Massacre in Iowa exposes weakness in non-Indian defense

1859 – Yankton U.S. Indian Agency founded according to terms in 1858 Treaty of Washington, D.C.

1862 – Dakota War

1863 – First Dakota Cavalry appears

– Yankton and Renville scouts separate tribal refugees from non-Indian settlements

– 38 Dakotas hanged at Mankato, Minnesota

1863-66 – Minnesota Santees banished to Fort Thompson U.S. Indian Agency jurisdiction on Crow Creek Reservation in Dakota Territory

1866 – Fetterman Massacre forces closing of the Bozeman Trail to Montana

– Fort Thompson Agency accommodates Lower Yanktonais and Lower Brûlés

1867 – Federal Peace Commission appears

– Fort Sisseton and Fort Totten U.S. Indian Agency jurisdictions founded by terms in Fort Wadsworth Treaty

Sitting Bull, and the tragedy at Wounded Knee, a year after the founding of the State of South Dakota.

Although most of the military confrontations took place beyond territorial borders, each one somehow directly affected territorial life.[1] A brief review of the confrontations suggests that their timing was a governing factor in territorial history.

In the region, excluding affrays related to the War of 1812, the only clash of arms involving non-Indians during the first half of the nineteenth century was the Arikara War of 1823, during which federal and Sioux troops joined together to attack the Caddoan Rees. Thereafter, federal troops withdrew due to a lack of need for their presence during the fur trade era until streams of settlers approached Sioux Country from the east. As a reaction, federal troops returned to occupy a new Fort Phil Kearney along the Platte River in 1847 and took over Fort Laramie, after its purchase from the American Fur Company, in 1849.

In 1851 teams of federal negotiators fashioned three treaties to accommodate and protect streams of immigrant settlers. Federal representatives designed, and the U.S. Senate with the president approved, terms in two treaties, negotiated at Mendota and Traverse des Sioux in Minnesota, by which four ancestral Dakota tribes surrendered rights of occupancy on about ten million acres and rights of use on an additional ten million acres in exchange for promises of annuity payments and a small reservation along the upper Minnesota River Valley. Mainly Santees assembled around the Lower Agency, and mainly Sissetons and Wahpetons gathered around the Upper Agency. Their removal to this small reservation by 1854 opened millions of acres for settlement in Minnesota by non-Indians—largely Norwegians, Swedes, Germans, and Irish.

In 1851 federal negotiators also invited all except Yanktonais and Assiniboine Sioux—all Lakota, Yankton, and neighboring tribes—to send representatives to Fort

Laramie, where they agreed to allow non-Indian travel up the Platte River basin in Nebraska unmolested in return for annuities, as though they were charging a toll. On the one side of the Platte, "gentiles" traveled along the Oregon Trail. On the other side, Latter Day Saints moved west along the Mormon Trail.

A party of Saints precipitated a confrontation that should be classified as the inadvertent Grattan Affair of 1854—the beginning of Sioux military resistance. The succession of Sioux wars gained both national and international attention not only because of interest in the Sioux, but also because they included all manner of military confrontation. There were "battles," conflicts carried on by traditional rules of combat acceptable to soldiers on both sides; "massacres," tactical assaults designed to carry battles into the desecration of human remains, as a scare tactic as well as an act of defiance; "affairs," spontaneous, unintended eruptions that took place when military discipline broke down and many died as a result; and "incidents," unintentional eruptions quickly brought under control. Most evidence indicates that the initial confrontation of arms along the Platte River in 1854 was an unintentional "affair." A party of Mormons left a lame cow untethered at Fort Laramie. Some Brûlés, accompanied by a Minneconjou who appeared to collect annuities, killed it for food. The Mormons complained. Lieutenant J. L. Grattan sallied forth to arrest the Minneconjou accused of putting the cow out of its misery. A spontaneous military affair, which ended in the death of the lieutenant and his entire U.S. Army unit, motivated the Brûlés to raid other groups of non-Indians headed west on the Oregon and Mormon trails.

Chronology (cont'd)
1868 – Fort Laramie Treaty recognizes some 60 million acres west of Missouri River as the Great Sioux Reservation
– Fort Bennett (Cheyenne River) U.S. Indian Agency jurisdiction founded
– Fort Yates (Standing Rock) U.S. Indian Agency jurisdiction founded
– Upper Missouri U.S. Indian Agency jurisdiction closes
1869-78 – 325 Flandreau Santees renounce tribal membership and settle as homesteaders along Big Sioux River Valley
1873 – Gold rush into the Black Hills
1876 – Great Sioux War of Sitting Bull ends in annihilation of Seventh Cavalry
1877 – Lakotas and Yanktonais gather on new U.S. Indian Agency jurisdictions
– Sitting Bull leads Lakotas and Yanktonais into Canadian exile
– Congress illegally seizes the Black Hills area, reducing the Great Sioux Reservation to 21,735,846 acres
1878 – Spotted Tail (Rosebud) U.S. Indian Agency jurisdiction founded
– Red Cloud (Pine Ridge) U.S. Indian Agency jurisdiction founded
1887 – Dawes Severalty Act set model for land allotment to tribal members
1889 – Congress further reduces the Great Sioux Reservation by terms of the Sioux Agreement of 1889
1890 – Sitting Bull assassinated on Standing Rock Reservation
– at least 340 tribal members die at Wounded Knee on Pine Ridge Reservation
1903 – Incident at Lightning Creek brings Sioux wars to a close

General William Harney appeared in 1855 with approximately 1,000 men to assert the sovereignty of the United States government. After a victory in the Battle of Ash Hollow, in 1856, he led his troops up the Missouri River to Fort Pierre before he withdrew to the historic Tower on the Missouri and established Fort Randall.

In 1857 the Spirit Lake Massacre in northwestern Iowa, led by the Wahpekute Inkpaduta, aroused fear by all non-Indians who lived close to the Dakotas' reservation in Minnesota. This, followed by Inkpaduta's terrorizing of settlers near Jackson, Minnesota, had two effects. It aroused fear among settlers, but it also emboldened the

Minnesota Sioux. When a territorial force failed to track down Inkpaduta, his open defiance of whites foretold weakness in the non-Indians' disposition to react if other Dakotas took a similar course of action.

The Dakota War of 1862 put their defiance into practice through the months of August, September, and October. Although short-lived, it was a bloody confrontation of extremes that included battles, massacres, affairs, and incidents. As many as 25,000 whites fled out of fear, most of them never to return. An estimated 490 of those who remained perished, while, doubtless an underestimate, seventy-one tribal members died and 277 were taken prisoner. Non-Indians of Minnesota demanded that federal officials restore peace, equalize the casualty score, and banish all of the Sioux from Minnesota.

To restore peace, Abraham Lincoln's staff excused four units from Civil War duty—including the First Dakota Cavalry in the territory. General Henry Hastings Sibley and General Alfred Sully led forces in a pincer movement into Dakota Territory to seek out members of Little Crow's so-called war party of Santees. (Taoyatiduta is one of six phonetic spellings of Little Crow's tribal name.) Sully founded the Yankton Scouts and other officials established the Renville Scouts to keep the races apart in eastern Dakota Territory. Meanwhile, the Northern Iowa Brigade prevented the spread of hostilities south of the Minnesota border.

To equalize the casualty score, Minnesotans demanded retribution in blood. For this purpose, at four locations Sibley organized military tribunals that put 307 Dakotas on trial and called for their execution. Abraham Lincoln reduced the list to thirty-nine. Local officials cut the number to thirty-eight and these, plus three others, were executed for "war crimes"—an unprecedented feature of post-war conduct in the United States.

To banish some Sioux from Minnesota, Congress confiscated their land. Approximately 2,500 Indians entered Canadian exile, many never to return. Federal officials cleared Minnesota of other Dakotas, moving some 1,200 to the Crow Creek Reservation in Dakota Territory. Only about seventy Dakotas managed to escape forced removal from the state.

After the war of 1862, the restoration of peace seemed futile. Red Cloud's War came as a reaction of Lakotas against the Bozeman Trail between the Platte River basin and Bozeman, Montana, by way of eastern Wyoming—clearly in violation of the 1851 Fort

Low-profile Great Plains tipis, such as these of the Yankton Sioux, housed the tribes of South Dakota until the founding of U.S. agencies. *Courtesy Herbert T. Hoover.*

Laramie Treaty. The resulting massacre of Captain William Judd Fetterman and eighty in his troop on December 21, 1866, sounded an alarm in Washington, D.C. Members of Congress authorized the Peace Commission in 1867, whose members capitulated, in effect, with terms in the Fort Laramie Treaty of 1868. This most famous of all treaties—perhaps in the entire history of Indian treaty making by the United States government—recognized some sixty million acres west of the Missouri River as the Great Sioux Reservation and assured the Lakota, Yanktonai, and other Indian occupants that it would remain inviolate until three-fourths of the adult males in the signatory tribes gave permission for outsiders to enter.

Gold prospectors violated this provision over the next five years and federal officials allowed it to happen, under orders from President Ulysses Grant. The consequence was the Great Sioux War of Sitting Bull, whose forces challenged and all but wiped out more than 350 under the command of George Armstrong Custer, including his entire Seventh Cavalry unit. For the third time, a unit in the U.S. Army was defeated by Sioux troops, and not once had federal forces been victorious against them.

In 1877 three developments indicated submission by Lakotas and Yanktonais, however, mainly because they could not withstand a buildup in U.S. Army troops supported by the Industrial Revolution and modern transportation systems. The vast majority of Lakotas and Yanktonais came to the agencies, surrendered their arms and ponies, and accepted agency life. Sitting Bull led 2,000 or more into Canada, where he remained until 1881. Congress seized the Black Hills and surrounding area—reducing more than sixty million acres in the Great Sioux Reservation to only 21,735,846 acres—in violation of the 1868 Fort Laramie Treaty realizing that the Sioux no longer could resist. This became the basis for the Black Hills Case against the United States, which remains unsettled. In 2001, at the 124th anniversary of the 1877 Agreement, federal officials held $544 million in a special account, which the tribes refused to accept unless the settlement included at least the return of federal land remaining in the area seized by Congress in 1877.

Soon thereafter, federal officials appeared to negotiate for the surrender of additional acres within the great reservation—especially a corridor from Chamberlain to Rapid City—as direct access to the central Black Hills. After initial failures, they secured the required number of signatures from voting members of the tribes—4,463 of 5,678 eligible to vote—albeit by intimidation and threats about loss of benefits due the tribes under terms in treaties and congressional statutes. The Sioux Agreement, approved March 2, 1889, brought into federal control 9,053,855 additional acres, leaving only 12,681,991 on the Great Sioux Reservation.

Bloodletting did not end. At sunrise on December 15, 1890, Sitting Bull, some of his followers, and several tribal policemen—all Indians—died at the Grand River on the Standing Rock Reservation. On December 29, 1890, many more perished at Wounded Knee on the Pine Ridge Reservation under fire from a new Seventh Cavalry in a tragedy that has been interpreted as a massacre by some, and as an affair by others. The body count of tribal members by federal officials at 153 later was revised by tribal elders to indicate either 340 or 370 deceased—in either instance including 100 or more with arms ready to fight.

An equitable interpretation of the 1868 Fort Laramie Treaty led some Oglalas to believe that they retained rights to hunt in eastern Wyoming until they were attacked by local policemen at Lightning Creek, in 1903. This has been called the "last bloodletting" in a variety of confrontations that had lasted forty-nine years.

This sequence of stands against unwanted intrusions—formally by all Sioux tribes except the Yankton, whose leaders decided against war—brought benefit to Native Americans of South Dakota. It preserved approximately ten percent of the ancestral Sioux Country as a place to nurture and preserve cultural traditions underground—compared to only about 3.5 percent by the aggregate of tribes across the Great Plains. The protracted stand that included three obvious victories over the United States without a loss in the field of battle evoked a sense of pride, which gained expression in numerous legal claims against the United States. At the same time, for peoples of tribal and non-Indian heritage alike, protracted war left bitterness in its wake as a negative consequence, which has lasted as a cause for intercultural suspicion in South Dakota.

As residents of Dakota Territory, all of the Sioux were gravely affected by intercultural relations damaged through the wars and, at the same time, in many ways reminded the Sioux that the only means of escape from the hazards of life on the U.S. Agency jurisdictions was to apply for individual citizenship in the United States. Until they became citizens, as individuals the Sioux lived much like non-contiguous territorials of the twentieth century, with a legal status on the island empire as "people of nationality," called "Nationals," without rights as citizens until they could be accrued through special acts of Congress. The change of status came to members of the Indian population in Dakota Territory, and subsequently in the State of South Dakota, only by a renunciation of tribal membership, or through the individual acquisition of fee-simple title to landed property, until the National Indian Citizenship Act of 1924 made all Native Americans into citizens of the United States.

The first of these avenues to citizenship applied exclusively to Flandreau Santees, who claimed a right extended to Santees by terms in the 1868 Fort Laramie Treaty. Approximately 325 moved from the Nebraska Santee Reservation during the period of 1869-1878 and remained in Dakota Territory. Their family heads appeared at territorial headquarters in Yankton formally to renounce tribal affiliations, traveled over to the federal land office at Vermillion to claim tracts of land according to terms in the Homestead Act of 1862, and settled along the upper Big Sioux River Valley as "Flandreau Santees," federally recognized as "citizens" to be treated "as though they were white." Legally, this status continued until, as a group, they were federally recognized as the Flandreau Santee Tribe in 1935 and took possession of a reservation purchased and recognized by Congress in 1936. Previously, beginning in 1874, Flandreau Santees accrued some benefits through three Indian agencies, followed by the Flandreau Boarding School, as federal gratuities. Legally, however, they were classified and treated "as whites" who through the settlement process had become citizen Indians in this extraordinary way.

As individuals, other members of Sioux tribes became citizens of the United States only through an acceptance of land allotments, like homesteads, followed by the acquisition of title in fee simple. In theory at least, this status brought the burden of taxation on personal property with the privilege of the franchise, but no taxation on their personal allotments as long as the allotments remained under federal protection. Unlike the Flandreau Santees prior to the year 1935, all other Sioux with fee patents to land were dual citizens because they retained their citizenship in the modern tribes to which they belonged.

These modern tribes were, in every instance, different from the ancestral tribes previously recognized as "domestic dependent nations." Every one of the modern tribes accrued advantages along with disadvantages as peoples enrolled at federal agencies, beginning with the Yankton Agency, which came into place during the summer of 1859. Except for individuals who drifted away, all Yanktons were enrolled at the Yankton

Along the Missouri, round-log cabins replaced Great Plains tipis. This one, with a lean-to added, remained in use on the Crow Creek Reservation until the 1970s. *Courtesy Herbert T. Hoover.*

Agency. As a modern tribe, however, the Yankton Tribe became heterogeneous by the addition of as many as two hundred Santee refugees from Crow Creek during the period of 1863-1866. Thereafter, the general council of voting adults in the tribe could embrace others as new enrolled members. Their reservation, federally recognized in 1858 before they began to assemble on it during the summer of 1859, accommodated the entire Yankton Tribe plus an addition of about ten percent who were Santees.

Next in order of federal recognition came two modern domestic dependent nations of Sisseton and Wahpeton heritage through an extraordinary sequence of events. The vast majority of members in the ancestral tribes of Sissetons and Wahpetons had remained aloof from the Dakota War of 1862, primarily carried on by a faction of Mdewakanton and Wahpekute Dakotas known to outsiders as the "War Party," led by Little Crow. After the war, some of the Sissetons and Wahpetons went on trial for "war crimes" or suffered other consequences for participation. After their spokesmen became signatories in the Treaty of Fort Wadsworth in 1867, all but a few in each of the two ancestral tribes were divided into composite groups of Sissetons and Wahpetons who were joined at the Fort Sisseton Agency jurisdiction in present South Dakota, and at the Fort Totten Agency jurisdiction in North Dakota.

No documentation exists to demonstrate precisely how, as individuals or as families, these two jurisdictional groups took shape. Previous reports suggest ancestral divisions—as South and North Sissetons, and as East and West Wahpetons. South Sissetons and East Wahpetons had experienced the greatest exposure to whites, while North Sissetons and West Wahpetons had experienced lesser exposure to non-Indians during the fur trade era. Although all four sub-divisions had been attached to the Upper Agency jurisdiction of Minnesota during the years 1854-1862, they existed as two distinctive groups.

After 1867, those with most prior exposure to non-Indians tended to gather as Sissetons and Wahpetons on the Fort Sisseton Agency jurisdiction, while those with lesser exposure settled with some Cut Head Yanktonais on the Fort Totten Agency jurisdiction. Those at the Fort Sisseton Agency tended to accommodate federal policies as they lived under a Congregationalist Quaker Policy agency staff, while those on the Fort Totten Agency jurisdiction clung more tenaciously to traditions as they lived under a Roman Catholic Quaker Policy agency staff. Early in the 1870s, Congress arranged the acquisition of "surplus" land while it defined boundaries for two reservations: at Lake Traverse, the Fort Sisseton, and at Devils Lake, the Fort Totten. Both groups of Dakotas that assembled as modern tribes rejected all suggestions of a merger with Santee Dakotas. Independently, both groups formed tribal rolls to include both Sissetons and Wahpetons at Lake Traverse, and both Sissetons and Wahpetons with some Cut Head Yanktonais at Devils Lake.

The other modern tribes of Sioux came into place as peoples enrolled at new agency jurisdictions, without reservations defined by federal officials. One reason was the continuation of Sioux wars, during which tribal forces defeated U.S. Army units three times and never lost a battle; hence, the freedom of tribal members to gather and enroll was little encumbered because the U.S. Army lacked the power to "herd" them onto agency jurisdictions. Another reason was the principle of enrollment, recognized by the U.S. government, which acknowledged the authority of the general council of voting adults in every modern tribe to control official standards of enrollment. Yet another reason was that circumstances did not allow a clear definition of reservation boundaries until the Sioux Agreement of 1889.

Accordingly, agency jurisdictional groups emerged as modern tribes to include populations marginally under the control of circumstances and general councils on locations where members chose to gather on ancestral lands. Along the Missouri River, the first two (after the Yankton) came into place by recognition from the Edmunds Commission. When Santees moved down to Nebraska from their (roughly defined) Crow Creek Reservation in 1866, some Lower Yanktonais came down to claim the Fort Thompson Agency jurisdiction area on ancestral Yanktonai land. A group of Two Kettle Lakotas joined them in the Big Bend area, and these two groups created the modern Crow Creek Tribe, whose membership changed significantly only when, in about 1880, Drifting Goose moved over from the James River Valley with his Lower Yanktonais. The reservation did not gain a clear definition until the Agreement of 1889.

On the opposite side of the Missouri River, the Edmunds Commission became the first to recognize Lower Brûlés as a discrete group in one modern tribe. Approximately 1,000 lived under sub-agency status linked to the Fort Thompson Agency until 1894, when Lower Brûlés acquired an agency of their own. The Agreement of 1889 defined their reservation boundaries. About a decade later, Congress recognized that 442 had moved to the Rosebud jurisdiction. On their behalf, federal officials arranged the sale of Lower Brûlé reservation land for funds to compensate the Rosebud Tribe. This left approximately 550 members on the roll at Lower Brûlé—smallest among federally recognized tribes that originated in territorial times.

After federal recognition of Crow Creek and Lower Brûlé jurisdictional tribes in 1866, federal recognition of two jurisdictional groups comprising most of the Saone Lakotas came next. General William Harney appeared to assist J. R. Hanson in closing the Upper Missouri Agency jurisdiction in 1868 while creating two new agency jurisdictions—the Fort Bennett at the Cheyenne River (later named Cheyenne River Agency), and at the Grand River (later named Standing Rock Agency). At the Cheyenne River Agency, four ancestral groups of Lakotas gathered over the ensuing decade or so—Minneconjous, Sans Arcs, Two Kettles, and some Blackfoot Sioux. At the Standing Rock Agency, the rest of the Blackfoot Sioux, the Hunkpapas, and a combination of Lower and Upper Yanktonais settled. These two agency jurisdictional tribes existed on the Great Sioux Reservation without specific reservations of their own until they were defined by terms in the 1889 Sioux Agreement.

This agreement also defined reservations for the two southern, or Teton, Lakota jurisdictional groups. Each of them had begun to take shape through connections with federal officials along the Missouri River during the 1860s and moved about until Congress forced permanent locations by an act of 1876. The modern Rosebud Tribe, recognized by Congress in 1878, was by far the most heterogeneous and unique, for it merged the inter-ethnic Whetstone Agency society into the Spotted Tail Agency group. The first annuity roll contained a head count that registered 3,361 Upper Brûlés (43.9 percent); 1,322 Loafers (17.2 percent); 1,881 Wazhazhes (non-Sioux but Siouan, 24.5 percent); 323 Two Kettles (4.2 percent); 331 Saones (other than Two Kettles, 4.3 percent); and 448 "mixed," including 77 or more Caucasians (5.9 percent).

The group at Pine Ridge Agency, also located and recognized by 1878, was mainly Oglala, but it did not include the entire ancestral tribe. Big Mouth had taken some Oglalas to the Whetstone Agency, and they were absorbed into the Rosebud Tribe. After Wounded Knee in 1890, Oglalas added to their tribal roll more than 800 non-Oglalas who were arrested by federal troops as prisoners of war. Accordingly, Oglalas had lost a fairly small fraction of their ancestral population but added about ten percent of non-Oglala heritage.

Thus, all of the modern tribes of Sioux were in place on congressionally defined reservations prior to the formal replacement of territorial status by the creation of the State of South Dakota in 1889. Only the Flandreau Santees lived without federal recognition as a tribe with rights and privileges accrued exclusively by members of federally recognized "domestic dependent nations." All of the other tribes in the state were affected by the land allotment model established by the Dawes Severalty Act of 1887.

Hewn-log cabins appeared on Lakota reservations, such as this one on Pine Ridge, during the establishment of the allotments in the late nineteenth century. In summer, families continued to live in tipis or Sibley Army tents and, in winter, moved to cabins. These three lodging types coexisted into the twentieth century until they were replaced by frame houses. *Courtesy Herbert T. Hoover.*

Chapter 7
Territorial Politics and Politicians

The Territory of Dakota brought political organization to a region well known because of an extraordinary amount of international attention evoked by sighting reports and journals prepared during the fur trade era and by the importance of the fur trade itself. The territory took shape near the geographical center of Sioux Country, whose Native American claimants have exceeded other tribes or federations in the United States in imaginative appeal, especially during the Sioux wars. Dakota Territory came into being through the machinations of peculiar "squatter governments" without any legal justification for their existence. Subsequently, the territory gained added attention because of the Black Hills gold rush and its settlement by a succession of white immigrations for the purpose of agricultural development and livestock production.[1]

At the time of its establishment, Dakota Territory contained a substantial number of Native Americans with a small and disparate population of resident citizens—at least 25,000 non-citizen Indians and no more than 1,000 non-Indian citizens. In the imperial system of the United States, the land contained by territorial boundaries had moved from territory to territory for administrative purposes since the purchase of Louisiana Territory from France in 1803, and, after 1821, the land had been divided by the Missouri River into "East River" and "West River" segments. One catalyst for the creation of a new territory was the loss of federal administrative services for East River in 1858, after Minnesota became a state. Another was the Yanktons' treaty of 1858, by which the United States government acquired title to most of East River, including the coveted Yankton Triangle between the Big Sioux and Missouri rivers.

The first U.S. Agent for the Yanktons, Alexander Redfield, who took charge during the summer of 1859, might have been the first official who represented the regional Upper Missouri Agency jurisdiction to write a plausible recommendation for its dissolution, thereby initiating a gradual process that continued until J. R. Hanson closed the regional agency in 1868. Redfield's call for administrative change came at a critical time in both regional and national history. A succession of battles and wars between non-Indians and the Sioux was underway on the northern Great Plains. Because the United States was on the verge of a civil war, national partisan affairs dramatically changed. Southern Democrats long had stubbornly opposed any frontier political development that might enlarge the free-state component in the United States to the disadvantage of their slave-state culture. In 1860, the secession of southern Democrats became an obvious probability when their party divided in the presidential election and allowed a victory by Abraham Lincoln with about forty percent of the popular vote. His anti-slave Republican Party, formed as recently as 1856, could enlarge its political influence if Congress and the new president organized a territory. Lincoln appointed a staff, and territorials elected a Republican delegate to Congress. To steal at least some of the Republicans' political thunder as southerners withdrew from national politics, Democrats in the lame-duck Congress and outgoing Democratic President James Buchanan approved territorial organization.

This unique combination of circumstances made the creation of the territory almost inevitable, even though no more than about 1,000 bona fide citizens lived within its boundaries and the Sioux obviously intended to defend their ancestral claims. Their probable resistance and the remote location of the territory on the northern Great Plains foretold a prolonged territorial experience.

Governors of Dakota Territory		
William Jayne	(R)	1861-1863
Newton Edmunds	(R)	1863-1866
Andrew J. Faulk	(R)	1866-1869
John A. Burbank	(R)	1869-1874
John L. Pennington	(R)	1874-1878
William A. Howard	(R)	1878-1880
Nehemiah G. Ordway	(R)	1880-1884
Gilbert A. Pierce	(R)	1884-1887
Louis K. Church	(D)	1887-1889
Arthur C. Mellette	(R)	1889

The historic plan for territorial organization and change to statehood was simple enough, as written into the Northwest Ordinance of 1787, with marginal amendments. Organized territorialism existed to serve as a political maturation process in preparation for statehood. It called for the appointments of a territorial governor, a secretary, at least three judges, and various lesser officials to serve until a suitable constituency was in place. After the assembly of at least 5,000 voters (free males), they were free to organize precincts, establish a bi-cameral legislature, and elect a delegate to the U.S. House of Representatives in Congress, where the one elected could speak, write bills, manipulate patronage, and engage in other political activities but not vote on legislation. Then, Congress could grant statehood in response to a petition representing 60,000 or more citizens after they submitted a suitable state constitution. This historic plan faltered in Dakota Territory. Only by padding a citizen census could territorials claim many more than 1,000 when they founded a legislature and elected their first delegate to Congress. When, belatedly, statehood came to South Dakota (with three other states through an omnibus act of Congress) during the autumn of 1889, however, its population approached 350,000. Two major obstacles had caused delay. One was a contest of Democratic against Republican partisans in national politics. The other was the requisite reduction of ancestral Sioux Country on the Great Sioux Reservation into smaller reservations clearly defined by Congress, which did not occur until the spring of 1889, when the last among eight reservation jurisdictions officially came into being.

Except for these two obstacles, citizens in the southern half of Dakota Territory should have been eligible for statehood no later than 1875. By that time, their population was large enough. Their political development lacked only a suitable constitution, whose preparation had been encumbered by unsettled political conditions.

In practical application, the historic model of territorial life called for the presidential appointments of a governor, a secretary, three federal judges, a marshal, and an attorney, and their approval by the U.S. Senate. Citizens elected members to a bi-cameral legislature and chose a delegate to Congress. Territorial officials were responsible for law and order; public land management; the creation of local governments, including counties, townships, and school districts; and the allocation of funds to support the operation of governmental functions. Until 1878, the governor served as ex-officio Superintendent of Indian Affairs. Governors also asserted their influence in the appointment of a surveyor general and other officials to prepare land for distribution among citizens and a superintendent of public instruction. In the absence of civil-service protection until 1882, public employees were at the mercy of presidential appointees. Few constraints existed to monitor or control self-serving activities or even fraud among presidential appointees in charge of tribal affairs until their activities became extreme—as in the instances of Walter Burleigh and Henry Livingston.

Although territorial politics gave expression to a burgeoning population of enfranchised residents, all except those already on the scene in Missouri Valley Culture were new arrivals. More than one-third of the non-Indian population came as immigrants from abroad with little knowledge of the political traditions of the United States, and most of the others came from central states with limited education or political experience. As a result, the number of new arrivals who surfaced as politicians was relatively small. Most of them came from middle or eastern states with some prior experience and formal education, and they faced limited competition as candidates for appointment to territorial administrative positions, or as candidates for election to territorial offices. For the latter group, the coveted prize was the office of Delegate to Congress, which afforded not only the power of patronage, but also primary influence in the arrangement of lucrative federal contracts for supplies, construction, and transportation services. A lesser but beneficial office was that of membership in the territorial legislature. Most legislators served without leaving much trace in public records of individual political achievement. The most influential politicians among them left their imprints in the honorific names of territorial counties or county seats, as did some of the judges who served in the territorial courts. The identities of many others are known by recognition of the offices they held or roles they played before their names appeared as the names of territorial counties.

From the outset, territorial politics gave expression to exaggerated machinations among politicians because of unusual circumstances in East River. The first aspiring politicians initiated their activities as speculators nearly five years before Congress authorized the creation of Dakota Territory, when East River remained a part of the Upper Missouri Agency jurisdiction administered by rules established in the Fur Trade Act of 1824 and most of East River in present-day South Dakota still belonged to the Yankton Tribe. Well in advance of the land cession by Yanktons in their 1858 treaty, two groups endeavored to found extralegal "squatter governments" in an effort to gain

Chronology

1856 – Fort Randall founded on the Missouri River
– Ezra Millard leads the Western Town Company to Sioux Falls area
1857 – Samuel Medary sends Dakota Land Company to Sioux Falls area
1858 – Yankton Tribe cedes most of East River to U.S. government and retains reservation across the Missouri River from Fort Randall
1861 – Territory of Dakota founded with City of Yankton as capital
– William Jayne appointed territorial governor
– John B. S. Todd elected delegate to Congress
– Walter Burleigh appointed U.S. Agent for Yankton Tribe
– Christ Church Episcopal founded at Yankton, its first political caucus center
1862 – Union, Clay, Yankton, and Bon Homme counties organized
1862-63 – Dakota Sioux refugees from 1862 Minnesota War evoke fear among and inspire organization of First Dakota Cavalry
1863 – Newton Edmunds appointed territorial governor
1864 – Walter Burleigh elected delegate to Congress
1865-66 – Newton Edmunds Peace Commission (Northwest Indian Commission) negotiates treaties (never ratified) recognizing Lower Brûlés as tribal entity and establish diplomatic framework for Fort Laramie Treaty
1866 – Andrew Faulk appointed territorial governor
1867 – Lincoln County organized
1868 – Minnehaha County organized
– S. L. Spink elected delegate to Congress
– Fort Laramie Treaty recognizes the Great Sioux Reservation west of the Missouri River
– Joseph Ward organizes Congregational Church activities and establishes a second political caucus center

Chronology (cont'd)

1869 – John Burbank appointed territorial governor

– U.S. Quaker Policy assigns and empowers Christian denominations at U.S. Indian Agency jurisdictions

– William H. H. Beadle appointed territorial Surveyor General

1870 – Moses K. Armstrong elected delegate to Congress

– Henry Livingston appointed U.S. Agent at Fort Thompson for Crow Creek and Lower Brûlé tribes

1871 – Brookings, Hanson, Hutchinson, and Turner counties organized

1872 – Joseph Ward founds Congregational Yankton Academy

1873 – Lake and Moody counties organized

1874 – Davison County organized

– John L. Pennington appointed territorial governor

– Jefferson Kidder elected delegate to Congress

1875 – Brule County organized

1876 – Martin Marty arrives as Catholic Abbot for Benedictine St. Meinrad Abbey in Indiana

1877 – Custer, Lawrence, and Pennington counties organized

– Under Sioux Agreement, Congress seizes the Black Hills area, reduces the Great Sioux Reservation, and nullifies miners' claims and governments

1878 – Codington, Deuel, Grant, Hamlin, and McCook counties organized

– Granville Bennett elected delegate to Congress

– William Howard appointed territorial governor

1879 – Thanksgiving Day dinner in Yankton is prophetic statehood caucus

– territorial penitentiary founded at Sioux Falls

– territorial insane asylum founded at Yankton

– Charles Mix, Kingsbury, and Spink counties organized

economic as well as political advantages. In October 1856, Ezra Millard and D. M. Mills represented the Western Town Company of Dubuque in an attempt to gain a foothold near the falls of the Big Sioux River (present-day Sioux Falls), and, during the year 1857, this effort brought a small but permanent population into place. In 1857, too, a competing group of Minnesotans formed the Dakota Land Company, which received a charter from the Minnesota territorial legislature with authority to issue as many as 2,000 shares of stock.

The Dakota Land Company served as a speculative vehicle for members of the lame-duck territorial government of Minnesota, led by Governor Samuel Medary and supported by legislators and friends at St. Paul. Their immediate goals were to purchase land (soon to be ceded by the Yankton Tribe through terms in its 1858 treaty) in the Sioux Falls area and to establish a railhead before the trains moved in. As preparation, Governor Medary and his political cohorts gained authority to create four new counties in southwestern Minnesota Territory, and they planned to acquire land in those counties before the Minnesota territorial government disappeared, then to work beyond the southwestern border of the new State of Minnesota to create a squatter government, from which they would petition for territorial recognition in Washington, D.C.

The Western and Dakota companies were on a collision course for a time but, as the Minnesotans prepared for statehood, they joined forces. Medary's group understood that, in the area between the Minnesota border and the Missouri River, after Minnesota statehood there would exist no organized government. To fill this void, the consolidated group of investors created Big Sioux County and Midway County around "Sioux Falls City." Its members formed a squatter government—with a governor and a legislature—which was extralegal, even though it took shape according to a national frontier tradition reaching back to the State of Franklin in Tennessee during the 1780s. Confident in probable success because of this tradition, squatter government officials quickly adopted laws from the Territory of Minnesota for use in the area surrounding the falls of the Big Sioux River, as they initiated an effort to gain recognition from Congress and the president.

Alpheus G. Fuller, who had no prior connection to the Big Sioux Valley area, represented the region before Congress, where he was allowed a temporary seat as a quasi-delegate. His petition for formal recognition as a delegate to Congress failed because the member who still served as a delegate from Minnesota Territory argued that he represented the area in question. Fuller's appeal for recognition of the squatter government failed, as well, to a large degree because of opposition from southern delegations. Congressmen resolved that they would receive no official delegate from Dakota until someone appeared who represented a new territorial government with federal recognition.

As additional preparation in Big Sioux and Midway counties, a legitimate electorate comprising fewer than twenty-five men agreed to parcel out offices among members of the Dakota Land Company and the Western Town Company. Legend suggests that the small electorate formed groups of three or four members each to move around the countryside near Sioux Falls for the purpose of forming precincts. Every few miles, each small group would stop first to take a drink of whiskey then to create a voting place. Subsequently, in each precinct, every man cast several ballots by entering the names of relatives and friends who lived far away. A combination of legitimate and mythical voters created a second squatter legislature, which met to select a candidate for governor, pass laws, and send another delegate to Washington, D.C. This time the group chose the Democrat Jefferson P. Kidder, a recent arrival from St. Paul, who claimed a margin of victory of 1,938 affirmative against only 147 negative votes from

Chronology (cont'd)

1880 – Beadle, Hughes, and Miner counties organized

– Nehemiah Ordway appointed territorial governor

– Richard Pettigrew elected delegate to Congress

1881 – Brown, Clark, and Day counties organized

1882 – Congregational Yankton College opens first territorial higher educational course work

– statehood constitutional convention at Canton

– Aurora, Douglas, and Hand counties organized

1883 – Butte, Campbell, Edmunds, Fall River, Faulk, Hyde, Jerauld, McPherson, Potter, Roberts, Sanborn, Sully, and Walworth counties organized

– Nehemiah Ordway moves territorial capital from Yankton to Bismarck

– statehood constitutional convention at Huron

– statehood constitutional convention at Sioux Falls

1884 – Gilbert Pierce appointed territorial governor

1885 – Buffalo and Marshall counties organized

– statehood constitutional convention at Sioux Falls

1887 – Dawes Severalty Act set model for land allotment to individual tribal members

1888 – Louis Church appointed territorial governor

1889 – Meade County organized

– Omnibus Statehood Act signed into law

– Arthur Mellette appointed last territorial governor

– final statehood constitutional convention at Sioux Falls

– Arthur Mellette elected first South Dakota state governor

– State of South Dakota proclaimed by president

an electorate that included no more than a few dozen enfranchised constituents.

Kidder's problem was not one of exposure for electoral fraud, but of competition from John B. S. Todd at Yankton, where Todd headed a competing group that planned to turn its budding community into the territorial capital and elect him as the delegate to Congress. Like all other aspiring politicians, Todd was an immigrant, born in Kentucky, but he had developed valuable connections through a protracted military career and recent commercial activity on the Yankton Triangle. After graduation from the U.S. Military Academy, he accompanied General Winfield Scott during the Seminole War in Florida, helped to settle eastern tribes in Indian Territory (Oklahoma), and served with the force led by Scott that invaded Vera Cruz during the Mexican War. Thereafter, as a U.S. Army captain, Todd had various military assignments at frontier posts that, in 1855, led to his participation with General William Harney's retaliation against some Lakota Sioux for the Grattan Affair at the Blue Water fight.

Todd remained with Harney's command as it moved into Lakota country, but at Fort Pierre he resigned his commission and, soon thereafter, in

The first U.S. Delegate to Congress from Dakota Territory, John B. S. Todd, was a leading force in the negotiations that produced the Yankton Treaty of 1858, which opened up the vast region between the Big Sioux and Missouri rivers to settlement. *Courtesy South Dakota State Historical Society–State Archives.*

1856, became a trader at the newly established Fort Randall. This led to his partnership with Daniel Marsh Frost and the founding of their commercial establishment at Sioux City—the gateway to the Yankton Triangle. Quickly, Frost and Todd created several trading posts between the Big Sioux and Missouri rivers, the main one along the lower James River.

Soon, Todd joined Zephier Rencontre and Charles Picotte in a successful effort to persuade Yankton tribal leaders to sell all of the Yankton Triangle to the United States government except a reservation west of Chouteau Creek. Todd was no Johnny-come-lately. He was a well-connected resident when, during January 1861, he and Frost drafted a petition and gathered signatures to propose that Congress approve the establishment of Dakota Territory and place its capital near their main trading post at the lower James River on the land vacated by the *ospaye* (band) of Struck by the Ree during the summer of 1859. Appropriately, the new town took the name of Yankton, after the tribe that had claimed the site long before non-Indians arrived and used it as a diplomatic center during the 1850s.

Politically, it made no sense for both Kidder and Todd to run as Democrats for the office of delegate. In fact, there existed no organized political parties in the area. (The territorial Republican Party was organized in 1866 and the Democratic Party in 1868.) Evidently, Todd declared his candidacy as a Democrat because another candidate was a Republican. Although most residents of Yankton called themselves Republicans, a majority supported Todd, for several reasons. He had developed a following through his commercial business. He had political connections in Washington, D.C., through his previous military service and role in the negotiation of the Yanktons' 1858 treaty. Moreover, he was a cousin of Mary Todd, the wife of Abraham Lincoln.

In a political showdown, a larger constituency at Yankton had an advantage over the smaller constituency at Sioux Falls, but a third constituency in the area around Pembina, along the Red River near the Canadian border, might hold a balance of power in a territorial election. Suddenly, word arrived that Lincoln had won election. Republicans were about to take control of Congress. Realizing the loss of partisan advantage when the change came, Democrats at Sioux Falls made an appeal to the lame-duck Congress, but the territorial committee chairman declined to act. As a response, Todd carried his memorial to Congress from Yankton, bearing 478 signatures, on a request to make Yankton the territorial capital while he worked to discredit Kidder's preposterous claim to represent a large constituency. Democrats in Congress eagerly endorsed a bill to establish the Territory of Dakota. The U.S. Senate approved it on February 26, 1861, the House of Representatives agreed on March 2, and outgoing Democratic President James Buchanan signed the bill into law a short time before he relinquished the White House to Abraham Lincoln.

Todd won election to Congress for a short term that would end at the general election in 1862. Meanwhile, political machinations continued in the territory. At a time when unencumbered political spoilsmanship dominated frontier politics, Abraham Lincoln used U.S. Indian Agency as well as territorial appointments to satisfy political debts claimed by partisan supporters and personal friends. On the northern Great Plains, the political plum was the office of territorial governor, which went to Lincoln's personal physician from Illinois, William Jayne. He was not a bad administrator, when he paid attention to his office, but as a politician he was inept enough to be hoodwinked by another physician, Walter Burleigh, whom Lincoln installed in the office of U.S. Agent for the Yankton Tribe.

A questionable but useful tale recorded much later by a storyteller named Zack Sutley seems best to explain how one of the nation's more revered presidents bungled his job and facilitated unconscionable corruption in the Indian Field Service.[2] After Lincoln won election to the presidency, according to Sutley, Burleigh appeared to collect a political debt. He had stumped western Pennsylvania for Lincoln while his father-in-law, "Squire Andrew" Faulk, worked from his office as a county treasurer in Armstrong County as Lincoln's Republican advocate in the critical electoral State of Pennsylvania. Allegedly, Burleigh wanted payment by appointment as minister to the Court of St. James. Instead, Lincoln offered to make Burleigh the Republican replacement of Alexander Redfield, an experienced and able U.S. agent on the new Yankton Reservation, but he was a Democrat who had received his appointment from outgoing President James Buchanan. Burleigh complained that the salary of an agent could not support his family in the manner to which it had grown accustomed; he (with his family) would have to "starve or steal." To this Lincoln allegedly replied, "Dr. Burleigh, if I am

A U.S. Indian Agent and second U.S. Delegate to Congress from Dakota Territory, Walter A. Burleigh was a participant in the corrupt Yankton Indian Ring.
Courtesy Bon Homme County History, *Hoover et al.*

any judge of human nature, you won't starve." As a cover story, a congressional biography later noted that Burleigh "declined a foreign mission tendered by President Lincoln in 1861."

In any event, this set a tone that further blemished territorial politics. Burleigh came from a distinguished family with legitimate medical credentials and strong administrative skills but, from appearances, no integrity or conscience. Quickly, he put together a classic "Indian Ring," which included himself as the agent, Faulk as the licensed trader on the agency jurisdiction, and Jayne as the ex-officio Superintendent of Indian Affairs with a tendency to approve Burleigh's administrative tactics and expenditures—which evidently Jayne did out of trust and not because of personal dishonesty. This combination of forces led twice to investigations by the U.S. Senate, which proved Burleigh's corrupt activities while he worked as the Yanktons' agent and forced his removal from the Indian Field Service.[3] Instead of paying for unconscionable management and theft at the Yankton Agency, in 1864 Burleigh parlayed his political connections in the territory into a victory in the race for U.S. Delegate to Congress as the replacement for John B. S. Todd, the Democrat, who had won election in 1861 and reelection in 1862. Burleigh gained the office of U.S. Delegate in 1864, surrendered control of the Yankton Agency to Patrick Henry Conger on May 1, 1865, and won reelection in 1866 as he gained political influence in the Republican faction led by President Andrew Johnson, Abraham Lincoln's successor.

Through his influence with the new president, Burleigh settled a matter that had antagonized him. Jayne's replacement as territorial governor in 1863 was Newton Edmunds, whose allies in Washington, D.C., were congressional Republicans and opponents of Johnson's faction in the party. Clearly, Edmunds proved himself to be the most proficient and accomplished of governors in the history of the territory, but his term in office lasted only until 1866 because of Burleigh. Edmunds' principal offense against Burleigh was his refusal to encumber senatorial investigations into Burleigh's corrupt administration at the Yankton Agency. Once he gained the advantage of partisan influence in Washington, D.C., Burleigh persuaded President Johnson and a combination of "Presidential Republicans" and Democrats in Congress to remove Edmunds from office and appoint Andrew Faulk, Burleigh's father-in-law and partner in theft at the Yankton Agency, as the third territorial governor.

Previously, from their opening session, territorial legislators at Yankton represented extralegal, competing factions without stable leadership in a tainted political environment. They were charged with a responsibility to legislate, initially in two private buildings and a saloon. They borrowed models of legislation from eastern states as they muddled through procedures to approve legal codes; organize counties and municipalities; authorize support for elementary education, as soon as funds became available; and settle the matter of where territorial headquarters would be. Through sleight of hand in reporting voter preferences, the people of Yankton prevailed over those at Bon Homme and Vermillion. Thus, legislators were obligated to compensate competing populations, and they did so with approval for the establishment of a territorial prison at Bon Homme and the territorial land office plus a two-township federal land-grant university at Vermillion. Bon Homme residents never claimed this benefit, for, by the time the penitentiary gained funding for establishment in 1881, Bon Homme was in decline. The county seat was transferred inland to Tyndall in 1885, and the penitentiary opened in burgeoning Sioux Falls in 1882. Vermillion residents enjoyed an initial benefit by the location of the federal land office in their town, but they had to wait until 1881 for a land grant and until the fall of 1882 for the opening of the university.

Yanktonians prevailed not only because of the location of the territorial capital in their city, but for other reasons, as well. Traffic at the steamboat landing, a stop on the Fort Randall Military Road, and later a railway station assured commercial activity. Almost immediately, in 1861, influential families from various Protestant denominational backgrounds gathered to found Christ Church Episcopal, whose members became as much a political caucus as a religious group.[4] Through their efforts, plus those of a new Congregational caucus that took shape after 1872, the territorial Asylum for the Insane gained funding in 1879 for establishment at the north edge of Yankton. In 1881 the newly appointed Catholic Bishop of Dakota Territory, Martin Marty, created the headquarters for his diocese at Yankton. During the autumn of 1882, Congregationalists opened Yankton College as the first center of Christian higher education in present South Dakota. Clearly, the center of power was Yankton until 1883, when the territorial capital moved to Bismarck.

Highlights in the administrations of ten territorial governors adequately portray their most pressing problems, exemplary achievements, and obvious deficiencies. Along with obligations and responsibilities imposed by the office of governor until the reorganization of the regional Indian Field Service in 1878, every governor carried some burden of responsibility for service as the ex-officio U.S. Superintendent of Indian Affairs across the jurisdiction of the territory.

Evidently, William Jayne (1861-1863) never intended to settle into the office of governor. Quickly, he demonstrated dissatisfaction with frontier administrative duties when he became a candidate for the office of congressional delegate in 1862, with hope of defeating Todd, the incumbent, but he lost in a contested election. Jayne struggled with executive duties for another year, sharing a responsibility with the legislature to install a judicial system and organize local governments.

Together in 1862, they authorized the organization of four counties to accommodate needs in the most populous part of the Yankton Triangle. At its apex, between the Missouri and Big Sioux rivers, Union County (named for the Civil War cause) had no population center until Elk Point emerged as a county seat. Along the Missouri River, they identified boundaries for three other counties that generally corresponded to previous activities in Missouri Valley Culture. Clay County (named after the famous congressman from Kentucky) shared a boundary with Union County, close to the site of the abandoned Fort Vermillion, and extended westward to the approximate location of Dickson's Post during the fur trade era. The town of Vermillion, about midway between these boundaries, evolved as the county seat. Yankton County (named for the tribe) extended westward from the Clay County line. At a location near the trading place of Pierre Hurtubise and the *ospaye* center of Struck by the Ree, the town of Yankton became the county seat. Bon Homme County (named after the island claimed by Zephier Rencontre) had its eastern boundary a short distance east of Rencontre's section of land and extended westward to Chouteau Creek, the eastern border of the Yankton Reservation.[5] After Rencontre sold most of his land to Burleigh and Faulk for the platting of a town, it took the name of Bon Homme and served as a county seat until it was later replaced by Tyndall. All four counties flourished as organized political additions to the riverside culture that had evolved over the preceding decades.

As Superintendent of Indian Affairs, Jayne should be remembered for two involvements. He was a key player in the destructive Indian Ring created by Walter Burleigh, Andrew Faulk, and their families at the Yankton Agency—however inadvertent Jayne's role might have been. More admirably, he shared a responsibility for defense through one of the bloodiest wars in the history of Indian-white relations. During the period

August-October 1862, the Minnesota Dakota War placed all communities of territorial citizens at risk—Vermillion, Yankton, Bon Homme, Sioux Falls, and even Pembina at the Canadian border. Following a fierce battle at New Ulm, and the Dakotas' siege at Fort Ridgely, the army of General Henry Hastings Sibley forced the army of Little Crow westward into Dakota Territory. More than the war, its aftermath presented a crisis in Jayne's jurisdiction which lasted into that of Newton Edmunds. Jayne was the territorial official in charge during the establishment of the First Dakota Cavalry—the forerunner to the South Dakota National Guard—for the defense of citizens in and around Vermillion, Yankton, and Bon Homme. Each gained security by the appearance of a resident militia and, for the entire Yankton Triangle, by the availability of patrols. Jayne merited credit, too, for the establishment of Fort Brule between Vermillion and the Big Sioux River to protect the sparse population scattered across Union County.

Otherwise, Jayne did little to distinguish himself before he resigned in the erroneous belief that he had won election to Congress and turned territorial administration over to his successor, Newton Edmunds (1863-1866). Born in New York and educated in Michigan, Edmunds gained his initial opportunity in the territory when Lincoln appointed his brother, James Edmunds, to the office of U.S. Commissioner of Public Lands, and James arranged for Newton's appointment as Chief Clerk at the Surveyor General's office in Dakota Territory. He arrived during July 1861, brought his family along, and remained. After his political career ended, he became a banker and principal founder of the Yankton National Bank in 1891 and lived in Yankton until his death in 1908.

While in service as a clerk, Edmunds worked and traveled with the governor. When Jayne ran against Todd for the office of Delegate to Congress in 1862, an initial report on ballots indicated that Jayne was the winner, and he resigned as governor in preparation to take the delegate seat in the U.S. House of Representatives. Todd challenged the count of votes and, through some machinations, retained the seat for a full term. Jayne moved away. In the meantime, President Lincoln appointed John Fox Potter of Wisconsin as his replacement, but Potter declined the appointment. Territorial Republicans preferred Newton Edmunds to Justice Philemon Bliss, a Democrat who wanted the office, because they believed Bliss to be a Confederate sympathsizer. The president sent a notice of appointment to Edmunds in October 1863.

Until Burleigh persuaded President Andrew Johnson to remove Newton Edmunds, the second territorial governor served with obvious integrity and considerable distinction. He replaced confusion with order in government while he assigned priority to Indian-white relations. Within a month of his appointment, Edmunds wrote Indian Commissioner William Dole that "the office of superintendent of Indian affairs" has been "virtually ignored by my predecessor" and, as a result, Indian agents were prone to "habits of carelessness and negligence" while "the Indians of this superintendency have greatly been the sufferers."[6]

When Edmunds took office, the most immediate need was for attention to trouble during the aftermath of the Minnesota Dakota War of 1862. One aspect pertained to reports about conditions on the new Crow Creek Reservation, created during the summer of 1863 upstream from the Yankton Reservation to accommodate approximately 1,200 Santee exiles who had not taken up arms against non-Indians. Although the U.S. Agent in charge at the new Fort Thompson Agency was most culpable for the deaths of at least 200 people before federal officials moved the survivors down to the Santee Reservation in Nebraska, this debacle took place on Edmunds' watch as Superintendent of Indian Affairs, and it must have weighed heavily on his mind.

Perhaps he failed to intervene on behalf of these Santees because he was distracted by concern about other refugees—many of them former members of Little Crow's "War Party"—who scattered across the East River area while some made their way into permanent Canadian exile. This situation required a military perimeter that would prevent the return of angry Santee soldiers to Minnesota and, at the same time, provide other Dakotas with places for surrender without fear of punishment or death at the hands of angry whites and federal troops.

As Superintendent for Indian Affairs, Edmunds was involved but must have been relieved to discover that he could rely on two special units. While General Sully moved up the Missouri River with a substantial military force, he commissioned a scouting unit in his army to patrol from Fort Randall through Bon Homme to Yankton, and from the territorial capital up the James River to the approximate location of the Grove of Oaks (present Mellette). Because of these Yankton scouts (all members of the Yankton Tribe), the post-war atmosphere along the Missouri River was relatively calm. No more than a few deaths could be linked to the Dakotas' war.

A second military unit—best known as the Renville Scouts—met the Yankton Scouts at the vicinity of the Grove of Oaks and created a scouting line through Fort Wadsworth (Sisseton) to Fort Abercrombie. Originally formed by Major Joseph Brown, then taken over by Gabriel Renville, these scouts remained on duty for as long as there was a need; the last of them withdrew from the scouting line in 1886.

During Edmunds' tenure, too, at the West River side of Dakota Territory, Red Cloud's War evolved. President Johnson removed him from the office of governor on August 4, 1866, about four-and-a-half months before the Fetterman Massacre, on December 21. This famous military confrontation represented previous, ever-increasing resentment by Yanktonai and Lakota Sioux, as well as by some neighboring tribes, about the Bozeman Trail, which extended northward from the Nebraska Platte River drainage basin into Montana. Because Wyoming was a part of Dakota Territory during the period 1864-1868, and Edmunds was governor and superintendent for Indian affairs, events leading to the Fetterman Massacre took place on his watch within his territorial jurisdiction.

Trouble with Indian-white relations across the territory provided ample incentive for Edmunds to engage in diplomatic efforts. Since the Fort Laramie Treaty of 1851, the only formal negotiations between a federal official and Lakotas and Yanktonais had been those in the 1850s of General William Harney, whose tentative agreements had been ignored in Washington, D.C. Edmunds might best be remembered for his travel up the Missouri River as the head of the so-called Edmunds Commission in 1865-1866, formally named the Northwest Indian Commission. Although Edmunds' "treaties" never were ratified by the U.S. Senate, they both initiated talks and resulted in some extraordinary consequences. The Edmunds Commission extended the first federal recognition to Lower Brûlés, as members of a discrete tribe, and in general terms identified an area more clearly defined as their reservation in 1889. The efforts of Edmunds and his commission to encourage peace preceded activities of the congressional Peace Commission of 1867, which ended in the negotiation of the Fort Laramie Treaty of 1868, and doubtless paved the way for this important diplomatic settlement.

Indian affairs dominated the administrative agenda of Edmunds, but he found time for other matters. In his three annual addresses before the territorial legislature, he emphasized control over the integrity of territorial elections, elementary education, road improvements, and a commission to stimulate non-Indian settlement. Had Abraham Lincoln not been assassinated, or had Andrew Johnson not been persuaded by Walter Burleigh to fire Edmunds, he might have improved territorial life in many ways; and he might have hastened the coming of statehood, which was an item on his gubernatorial agenda.

On August 4, 1866, he relinquished the office to his successor, Andrew Faulk (1866-1869), Walter Burleigh's father-in-law and Indian Ring partner in fraud at the Yankton Agency. Professor Schell barely mentioned his term as governor, making space for only one reference to a single page in the index of his *History of South Dakota*. In fairness to Faulk, the northern Great Plains was devastated by drought and grasshopper plagues through the middle sixties, and territorial affairs were in upheaval because of the Fetterman Massacre and its aftermath in Red Cloud's War. Credit is due Andrew Faulk and an otherwise undistinguished legislature for the creation of two counties on the east side of the Yankton Triangle. The most consequential was Minnehaha in 1868 (named with a Sioux term that translated "water that laughs"), for which Sioux Falls served as a county seat. The other was Lincoln County in 1867 (named after the assassinated president) to fill the space between Minnehaha and Union counties. Local legend suggests that, for the want of a better idea, residents selected Canton as the name for the county seat (after Canton in China, because it existed on the opposite side of the globe). Later in 1883, Faulk gained honorific recognition by the use of his name in Faulk County and the county seat at Faulkton.

John Burbank (1869-1874) held the office of governor during half a decade of changes that might have inspired a more capable governor to a sterling record of accomplishment. As did Jayne, Burbank allowed and, in ways, facilitated political machinations; left the territory soon after the end of his term and never returned; and was a product of careless presidential patronage.

Indeed, the inauguration of Ulysses Grant in 1869 precipitated a flurry of spoilsmanship that became legendary in presidential history. For Dakota Territory, evidently Grant appointed Burbank because he was the brother-in-law of U.S. Senator Oliver Morton of Indiana, a personal friend of the new president and a force in congressional politics. There were others. Former Vice-president Hannibal Hamlin arranged the appointment of his son-in-law, George Batchelder, as secretary for the territory. For political reasons, William H. H. Beadle appeared as surveyor general. The election of Grant indirectly contributed to the defeat of S. L. Spink, who had won election in 1868 as Burleigh's replacement in the office of Delegate to Congress. Because of an opposing faction in the territorial legislature as well as in the general constituency, Spink then lost the office of delegate to Moses K. Armstrong, a Democrat.

Burbank exacerbated political problems in the territory. He ignored his responsibility as governor through excessive periods of absence from Yankton. He exercised the power of patronage for opportunities to invest in land, and he became identified with the Dakota Southern Railroad as a member of its board of directors. Some 1,200 petitioned for his removal from the governorship, but in 1873 Grant renewed his appointment. Political contention at Yankton, which was rife during his tenure, was a cause for the murder of territorial secretary Edwin S. McCook during a brawl in a tavern.

Fraud and scandal finally forced Burbank's resignation on January 1, 1874, and his disappearance "marked the close of a distinct political period" in the territory, wrote Professor Herbert Schell in *History of South Dakota*. He might have added that the tenure of Burbank, disruptive as it was, served in many ways as a general watershed in the territorial era of South Dakota history.

A favorable product of President Grant's political spoilsmanship in the territory was William H. H. Beadle, an unexciting but honest and capable public official whose tenure should linger in the collective memory of South Dakotans because of his contributions to the survey of land and to the preservation of a substantial "school fund" and the remaining "school lands." Beadle's influence as the Surveyor General for the territory matched that of even the most resourceful governor, for no issue was more essential than the survey of land. Evidently, staff at the office of Surveyor General, established on July 1, 1861, had kept pace with gradual settlement but, as immigration grew during the years 1867-1869, the demand for surveys required an accelerated effort. Patiently, meticulously, Beadle hired and trained surveyors to work with compass and Gunter's chain (twenty-six feet long, making eighty lengths per mile) in hand across irregular terrain to mark the boundaries of ranges, townships, and sections of land according to terms written in the federal Ordinance of 1785.

The same federal law included a provision for the donation of a section of public land in every township to support elementary education, which attracted Beadle's special attention. When Congress applied terms in the ordinance to Dakota Territory, its members committed not one but two sections per township as "school lands" to support public, pre-college education through sale or rent. In states to the east, officials had sold their school lands to speculators at the prevailing rates of $1.25 to $2.50 per acre to create a school fund. After Governor William Howard asked Beadle to serve as a private secretary in 1878, then to take the office of Superintendent of Public Instruction, Beadle stood firm against pressure from speculators to insist that no acre of school land should sell for less than $10 per acre. Subsequently, Beadle managed to get this minimum price written into state law and, as a result, earned abiding recognition as a special advocate of education. He remained a resident of the state until his death in 1915. His name continued in public view at the state Beadle College in Madison until it changed to Dakota State College in 1969.[7]

While Beadle initiated his exemplary work on the survey of territorial land, another official appointed by members of Grant's administration, whose activities should have been carefully observed by Governor Burbank, brought discredit to all who officially were involved with Indian-white relations. Dr. Henry Livingston came to Fort Thompson on the Crow Creek Reservation as a contract physician in 1868, where evidently he did his job with health-care delivery. Through the influence of Episcopal leaders during

The Indian rings that both Henry F. Livingston and Walter A. Burleigh set up as U.S. Indian Agents involved the supplying of beef to reservation residents, as seen in this photo depicting "Beef Issue Day" near Crow Creek. *Center for Western Studies.*

applications of Grant's Quaker Policy, he received appointment as agent for the consolidated jurisdiction of Crow Creek and Lower Brûlé in October 1870. For a time, some officials boasted that he was the senior and the best among agents along the Missouri River.

Covertly, however, he built an Indian Ring and, in 1875, divided the Fort Thompson administrative unit into separate Crow Creek and White River jurisdictions, evidently to facilitate administrative corruption. The first agent on the Lower Brûlé side of the river, Thomas A. Reilly, was the son of an Episcopal clergyman at the Carlisle Indian School in Pennsylvania who gained appointment through influence by Dakota Episcopal Bishop William Hare. Reilly lasted for only a year because he was "not a congenial spirit to the ring." In his place, Livingston sent his clerk, Henry E. Gregory, a political appointee and son of the late Admiral Gregory, a former trader, the former Ponca Indian Agent, and a former transportation operative on the Missouri River. Henry Gregory and Livingston acted in concert at opposite sides of the Missouri until 1877, when John H. Hammond appeared as Indian Inspector and charged them with fraud, which had been uncovered by First Infantry Captain William Dougherty.[8] The Secretary of the Interior ordered generals William Sherman and Alfred Terry to detail Dougherty as Acting Agent in Gregory's place. Dougherty and a newsmen uncovered so many types of fraud that Indian Commissioner Ezra Hayt called Livingston the most fraudulent agent in the history of the Indian Field Service.

Dougherty warned the Indian commissioner that "no conviction can be obtained in Yankton [at the territorial court] on any of the charges prepared against Livingston and his associates, no matter what evidence may be brought. The effect of the last trials has been to convict him in the views of that part of the public not directly connected with him by relationship or interest, as conclusively as if found guilty by a jury."

Dougherty was correct in his assessment of the situation for, as he predicated, in the spring of 1880 notice came to the Indian Office: "Livingston acquitted." As indicated above, Christ Church Episcopal at Yankton evolved from the outset as a community caucus of influential people, and Doctor Livingston married Ann Elizabeth Hoyt, a daughter of Reverend Melancthon Hoyt, the venerable founder of Christ Church. Leaders in this vestry included Newton Edmunds, territorial governor, 1863-1866; Downer Bramble, general store owner; Henry Clay Ash, owner of the Ash Hotel; George Kingsbury, lawyer and journalist; and Moses Armstrong, author and Delegate to Congress, 1870-1874. During the 1870s, Governor John Pennington became a member sufficiently active to serve Christ Church as the doorkeeper, usher, and superintendent for the Sunday School. Most fervent of Episcopal leaders, however, was former governor and banker Newton Edmunds. Not only was Livingston married to the daughter of the founder of the church, as a member he served as one of its wardens, as well. Official investigations clearly indicated a record number of fraudulent activities at the agency, but Livingston's acquittal by a federal territorial court in the city of Christ Church was inevitable.[9] As governors, both Burbank and Pennington were culpable for their failure to notice what was going on at Fort Thompson during Livingston's tenure as agent.

To balance against the unfortunate selection of Livingston as an Indian agent, there was Beadle in charge of territorial land survey. This finally gained appropriate attention throughout the administration of Governor Burbank because of the initial flurry of agricultural settlement, beginning about the year 1867, which elevated the citizen population to 11,776 by the 1870 census. Thereafter, for many years, the most important developments evolved beyond the influence of territorial politicians. The gold rush into the Black Hills gained momentum in violation of the 1868 Fort Laramie Treaty.

Political influence in the appointment of U.S. Indian agents shifted from politicians to Christian mission societies, who placed candidates in nomination according to terms in the federal Quaker Policy from 1869 to 1883. The rush of immigrants onto the Yankton Triangle came abruptly to a halt in 1873 because of two developments beyond political control. One was the Panic of 1873, which precipitated a national depression that lasted for nearly half a decade. The other was a severe drought, coupled with a succession of grasshopper plagues, that lasted for several years.

Burbank and his legislature contributed little to territorial management. They did respond to East River immigration during the years 1869-1873, however, by the addition of seven new counties: in 1871, Brookings (named for Judge Wilmot Brookings), Hanson (for Joseph R. Hanson, territorial legislator), Hutchinson (for John Hutchinson, territorial secretary), and Turner (for John Turner, territorial legislator); in 1873, Lake (for lakes in the vicinity) and Moody (for Gideon Moody, territorial legislator); and in 1874, Davison (for Henry Davison, county pioneer).

When Burbank resigned as governor, his replacement was John L. Pennington (1874-1878). He endeavored to avoid any political contention or the appearance of any conflict of interest, perhaps because he had stood his ground as a Unionist in North Carolina during the Civil War and had been involved with Radical Reconstruction techniques in Alabama. Nevertheless, his was a turbulent term in office that ended in a denial of his request for reappointment. One problem was unsettled conditions related to the Great Sioux War of 1876. Another was political controversy between East River and West River residents, which Pennington precipitated through officious intrusion into local politics west of the Missouri River.

The root of the latter problem was the addition of nine new counties by the governor and his legislature: in 1875, Brule (named for the Lakota Tribe); in 1877, Custer (for George Armstrong Custer), Lawrence (for John Lawrence, territorial legislator), and Pennington (for the governor); and in 1878, Codington (for G. S. Codington, territorial legislator), Deuel (for Jacob Deuel, pioneer and legislator), Grant (for Ulysses Grant), Hamlin (for Vice President Hannibal Hamlin), and McCook (for Edwin McCook, territorial secretary). Pennington's problem evolved from the establishment of the three in West River—Custer, Lawrence, and Pennington—and their micromanagement, which technically he could justify.

During Pennington's term in office, miners scattered across the Black Hills in search of placer gold and established extralegal governments in new communities. The only federal interference in their activities came from regulations that controlled mining claims, which prohibited sales of spirituous beverages on Indian land, and which pertained to crimes punishable in territorial courts. In anticipation of the congressional Sioux Agreement approved on February 28, 1877, by which Congress removed the Black Hills from the Great Sioux Reservation and placed them in the public domain, the legislature at Yankton created codes to govern mining activities and to manage the behavior of miners and their extralegal political associations. Because the 1877 agreement nullified the operation of extralegal miners' governments by placing the hills under federal supervision, Pennington asserted his authority to appoint commissioners and other officials for the three new counties, which he accomplished by selecting many officials who previously had not been residents of the Black Hills. Suddenly, outsiders seized control of local governments, designated locations for county seats without regard for local preferences, and called for territorial judicial intercession into miners' claim-jumping conflicts. To make matters worse, most of the outsiders with appointments from Yankton were Republicans, but most of the miners were Democrats.

Miners reacted in two ways. One was to hold a special election on November 15 by which mining constituencies selected Deadwood, Rapid City, and Custer as county seats. The other was a movement to secede from the Territory of Dakota. Incentive came not only from Democratic partisanship and resentment about the imposition of Pennington's appointees into local politics, but also because of indecision by federal judges regarding whether mining claims and other property rights registered on Indian land prior to the Sioux Agreement of 1877 were legal. West River federal district Judge Granville Bennett ruled to validate claims on properties established prior to February 28, 1877, based on his erroneous interpretation of the 1868 Fort Laramie Treaty. The territorial supreme court properly reversed his decision, however, in recognition that claims to properties registered before February 28, 1877, had been illegal. In the 1868 treaty, Congress had recognized the ancestral claim of Indians and assured no intrusions without consent from three-fourths of the adult males (voting populations) in the signatory tribes. Accordingly, claims to the properties acquired by miners before February 28, 1877, were null and void.

In anticipation of government imposed by outsiders that would challenge prior claims to properties, during the summer of 1876 miners initiated a movement to secede. By the end of the year, Congress considered but did not accept a bill to create a new Territory of the Black Hills. After the arrival of Pennington's appointees and a confrontation with them about county seats, miners used confusion regarding the location of the Wyoming boundary, established in 1868, to perpetuate their separatist movement.

Deadwood Democrats spearheaded a second effort that in the summer of 1877 brought before Congress a petition to create a new Territory of Lincoln, made up of the Black Hills and eastern portions of Wyoming and Montana. It would span four degrees of latitude west of the Missouri River plus one degree in Montana. Back in Washington, D.C., there was talk about possible investment by the financier Jay Gould and recognition of sponsorship by political forces from Nebraska and Colorado. Known as Senate Bill 144, this proposal never came up for a vote, but it inspired a sequence of new developments that affected the final disposition of Dakota Territory.

U.S. Delegate to Congress Jefferson Kidder (1874-1878) reacted with stern opposition and made a proposal to divide Dakota Territory on a line east-to-west along the forty-sixth parallel—the future boundary between the states of South and North Dakota. When members of Congress declined to embrace Kidder's proposal, another call arrived for a division of the territory at the one-hundreth meridian, which residents at the budding town of Bismarck embraced with hope of acquiring territorial headquarters and political power.

After competing factions defended their proposals for political change, the importance of Black Hills Democrats in territorial politics became apparent when the Republican Jefferson Kidder sought a third term as delegate in 1878. Black Hills Democrats preferred Judge Granville Bennett, who had misinterpreted the 1868 Fort Laramie Treaty in their favor. A Republican faction in East River supported Gideon Moody as a replacement for Kidder. Due to the division of Republican votes and support from Black Hills Democrats, Judge Bennett won election to Congress. This shift of political power was, in the opinion of historian Herbert Schell, a "forecast" for the "political pattern of the next decade."

The final territorial decade began at Yankton in 1879 when Congregational Reverend Stewart Sheldon (widely recognized author of the allegory *In His Steps*) invited an elite group of guests for Thanksgiving Day dinner, which turned into a political caucus with an agenda that included plans for statehood. Among the guests were General Hugh

Campbell, the territorial U.S. attorney and a force in the statehood movement who advocated the establishment of a state government in advance of a congressional enabling act; Congregational Reverend Joseph Ward, Sheldon's brother-in-law, who agreed with Campbell; General Beadle, who brought the protection of school lands as public capital into the discussion; and Honorable Edward Wilcox. This unofficial caucus started a movement that led to the first formal discussion of a state constitution at Canton in 1882.

Although Reverend Sheldon was the Thanksgiving Day host, Reverend Ward was the facilitator of political action. He had come to Yankton in 1868 to serve the Congregational Church, recently organized in the city. His biographer, Thomas Gasque, wrote of Ward: "In government he held no elective office, but through personal influence, speaking, and writing Ward was one of Dakota's most articulate spokesmen for responsible leadership as territorials worked their way toward statehood."[10] Ward was educated at Brown University and invited by the American Home Missionary Society to serve the denomination at Yankton. John B. S. Todd donated a lot for the Congregational Church, where Ward attracted physicians, lawyers, U.S. Army generals, merchants, and people involved with Indian agencies. He characterized them as "Norwegians, Germans, Danes, Jews, Indians & Africans" from families in which wives attended to religious matters and men discussed secular affairs. Reverend Sheldon was in charge of an outreach effort to organize new congregations on the Yankton Triangle—by 1876, a total of fourteen with ten ministers. In 1872, Ward founded Yankton Academy, which gave rise to Yankton College in 1882—the first to offer college classes in present-day South Dakota. Ward traveled widely as a fund-raiser. Through all of his activities, he sustained political connections while he engaged in the establishment of Statehood Clubs. The Thanksgiving Day dinner of 1879 might be perceived as the establishment of Ward's Congregational political caucus.

The best presentation of the movement it spawned is William Farber's biography of the last territorial governor, Arthur Mellette.[11] Governors who served between the terms of Pennington and Mellette had limited influence in the statehood movement, or even in territorial life, except the one who arranged the transfer of the territorial capital from Yankton to Bismarck in 1883. William Howard (1878-1880) was an honest, constructive, seasoned administrator well remembered for bringing calm after turbulence generated in territorial politics during the administration of Pennington. Evidently, Howard relied for support from both the Episcopal caucus and the Congregational caucus, whose ranking members all shared an interest in the economy of Indian affairs, even though Episcopalians were in a position to control the lion's share of benefits. Although they competed with each other on the Indian agency jurisdictions, Episcopalians and Calvinists all thrived on the agency economies and learned to set aside their differences to share an ecclesiastical war against the "Romanists," who became active competitors by 1876 as a result of the arrival of Martin Marty, at that time the Abbot from St. Meinrad, Indiana.

By the time Howard arrived in Yankton, all U.S. Indian agencies in the territory were in place. Their staff leaders dealt directly with the U.S. Commissioner of Indian Affairs, without the involvement of territorial governors. The Quaker Policy installed in 1869 drew the Episcopal Christ Church caucus to the center of agency affairs because, until 1883, Episcopalians gained the privilege of nominating agents (hence, influencing the selection of all staff members) at all of the Sioux agencies within territorial boundaries except Lake Traverse (assigned to Congregational missionaries), Standing Rock (to Catholics), and Fort Totten (to Catholics). (Indians at Flandreau remained a community of detribalized Santees.) This privilege brought enormous economic benefits to Episcopal caucus leaders and their friends at Yankton. By far, the best full-time jobs in the territory existed at Indian agency jurisdictions, with annual salaries ranging from that of the agent at $1,200 down to about $150 per year. In addition, at every agency jurisdiction there existed many "irregular" or part-time jobs. At a large jurisdiction like that at Pine Ridge or Rosebud, as many as thirty were employed full-time, and dozens had access to part-time employment.

Too, with constraints imposed only by approval from the Interior Department, Indian agents controlled lucrative building contracts, service contracts monopolized by local non-Indians, transportation contracts, and markets. Annuities, distributed across agency jurisdictions once or twice every month, called for the purchase of fresh meat, numerous food items, cloth goods, finished clothing, household wares, garden tools, and farm machinery—for more than 20,000 tribal members eligible for annuity benefits. Although the national Episcopal mission society nominated most of the agents, Episcopal political caucus members at Yankton linked to Bishop William Hare made the choices.

Dr. Henry Livingston, obviously one of the choices made by Christ Church caucus members, set an all-time record for fraud in the Indian Field Service. In fairness to the denomination, most of its nominees made amends for this error. Episcopal Reverend John Gassman followed Burleigh's corrupt regime as agent on the Yankton Reservation during the 1870s, then he cleaned up after Livingston as the agent at Fort Thompson in the 1880s. In the main, the Quaker Policy was successful in bringing at least a modicum of integrity to the Indian Field Service while Episcopalians were in charge. Yet, inevitably, their involvement gave the Christ Church caucus at Yankton direct access to the most reliable and lucrative economic opportunities in the territory, and the Congregational caucus controlled opportunities at Lake Traverse, while the two groups shared some benefits at jurisdictions assigned to Episcopalians. While the Quaker Policy lasted, neither group of Protestants gained a foothold at Standing Rock or Fort Totten, where Catholics were in control.

Governor Howard arrived at a time when a burgeoning economy—based mainly on these opportunities at Indian agencies, U.S. Army installations, and the gold rush—flourished as the Great Dakota Boom of immigrant settlement got underway. Because of an illness, which ended Howard's term in his death on April 10, 1880, territorial secretary George Hand ran the governor's office most of the time. To accommodate economic and population expansion, Howard's administration led by Hand and the legislators added six new counties in two years: in 1879, Charles Mix (named for a former U.S. Commissioner of Indian Affairs); Kingsbury (for George Kingsbury and T. A. Kingsbury, a territorial legislator); and Spink (for the territorial delegate to Congress); and in 1880, Beadle (for the surveyor and educator); Hughes (for Alexander Hughes, territorial legislator), and Miner (for Nelson and Ephraim Miner, territorial legislators).

As well in 1879, Governor Howard and Secretary Hand were the ones responsible for founding the territorial penitentiary at Sioux Falls and the territorial insane asylum at Yankton—both of them costly but lucrative assets for the economies of the two cities. Unfortunately, in 1879, too, Howard was linked to Hand in shouldering criticism from Secretary of the Interior Carl Schurz resulting from the acquittal of Dr. Livingston, despite obvious fraud in his administration at the Fort Thompson Agency. Hand was related to Livingston by marriage, and both were fixtures in the Episcopal caucus at Yankton. Evidently, Howard and Hand stood beside this local oligarchy to provide a jury that would vote acquittal, and both endured political punishment, as a result.

Had not Hand been so closely linked to the Livingston trial, Secretary Schurz might have prevailed on President Rutherford Hayes to offer the governorship to Hand at Howard's death. Instead, Hayes appointed Nehemiah Ordway (1880-1884) of New Hampshire.

As Ordway arrived, Richard Pettigrew made his political debut.[13] This native of Vermont came by way of Wisconsin to Dakota Territory in 1869, entered a claim on 160 acres near Sioux Falls, and became a resident of the city in 1870. He worked as a land surveyor while he practiced law and served in the territorial legislature during the 1870s. He won the office of Delegate to Congress in 1880 as the anti-Yankton establishment candidate from Sioux Falls, where he had railed against the "Yankton Ring" of politicians gathered in the Episcopal and Congregational caucuses. As a delegate, he challenged Governor Ordway's attempt to control patronage and gained a political advantage from Ordway's clouded reputation for the governor's link to the Credit Mobilier scandal, when he had been the sergeant-at-arms in the U.S. House of Representatives.

Pettigrew targeted Ordway's effort to dominate appointments to postmasterships, especially, which the U.S. Post Office Department created

An opponent of the Yankton Ring, Richard F. Pettigrew became a U.S. Delegate to Congress in 1880, challenged Governor Nehemiah G. Ordway's attempt to control patronage, and was a principal proponent of statehood. He became the state's first U.S. Senator, serving for two terms. *Center for Western Studies.*

while Ordway's administration and legislators installed nineteen new counties: in 1881, Brown (named for Alfred Brown, territorial legislator), Clark (for Newton Clark, territorial legislator), and Day (for Merrit Day, territorial legislator); in 1882, Aurora (for the Roman goddess of dawn), Douglas (for Stephan A. Douglas of Illinois), and Hand (for George Hand, territorial secretary); and in 1883, Butte (for buttes in the area), Campbell (for Norman Campbell, territorial legislator), Edmunds (for Newton Edmunds, territorial governor), Fall River (for the river by this name), Faulk (for Andrew Faulk, territorial governor), Hyde (for James Hyde, territorial legislator), Jerauld (for H. A. Jerauld, territorial legislator), McPherson (for James McPherson, Civil War general), Potter (for Joel Potter, territorial legislator), Roberts (for S. G. Roberts, territorial legislator), Sanborn (for George Sanborn, railroad official), Sully (for Alfred Sully, U.S. Army general who founded forts nearby), and Walworth (for Walworth County, Wisconsin). Pettigrew reacted against Ordway's infringements on patronage privileges, ordinarily claimed by delegates to Congress, to discredit the governor in his party. In 1883, Ordway responded by arranging the removal of the territorial capital from Yankton to Bismarck, where he could court favor among constituents above forty-six degrees and also profit from his land investments in the Bismarck area.

Pettigrew redoubled his effort as the champion of statehood south of forty-six degrees, ironically, while he gained strength from support by the Yankton Ring—especially Gideon Moody, William Beadle, and George Kingsbury—whose members shared Pettigrew's resentment of Ordway. At Huron, in 1883, this group endorsed U.S. Attorney Hugh Campbell's disposition for a "we are a state doctrine" to force the issue of statehood south of forty-six degrees. In June 1884, the Yankton Ring arranged an indictment and trial of Ordway for malfeasance in office, which Ordway escaped with the argument that as governor he could not be tried before a territorial court. An outraged majority south of forty-six degrees demanded his removal, however, and soon he was replaced by Gilbert Pierce.

Through his confrontation with Ordway, Pettigrew, as delegate to Congress, stole Hugh Campbell's place as a leader in the "home rule" movement. He then returned to the territorial legislature in 1885, where he joined a majority in demanding statehood. After a Democratic majority in Congress refused, Pettigrew led Moody, Campbell, and others successfully to claim credit for statehood in 1889. Pettigrew then parlayed this image of leadership into election to the U.S. Senate, to which he won reelection in 1895. Failure in business endeavors, as well as recognition of political change among Dakotans, caused his withdrawal from the regular Republican Party to join Silver Republicans, then Fusionists, and then Progressive Republicans. Although

Arthur Mellette was the principal architect of the South Dakota Constitution, last territorial governor, and first governor of the new State of South Dakota. *Courtesy South Dakota State Historical Society–State Archives.*

Pettigrew left a record of political manipulation and self-serving endeavors, his political life stood as a harbinger of change for a majority of South Dakotans. Most retained their affiliation as Republicans, but they favored reform as they drifted, like Pettigrew, through Populism and Fusionism into Progressive Republicanism.

During Pettigrew's rise to power in territorial politics, the nineteen counties added during Ordway's tenure completed the profile of local government for East River and added Butte and Fall River counties to flank the Black Hills. Gilbert Pierce (1884-1887) became an interim Republican governor remembered for little except adding the counties of Buffalo (1885, named for the vanishing bison) and Marshall (1885, for Marshall Vincent, pioneering settler). His term ended when Grover Cleveland won election to the presidency and replaced him—after some delay, out of deference for the new civil service system. As the only Democratic governor in the history of the territory, Cleveland appointed Louis Church (1888), who accomplished little beyond the addition of Meade County (1889, named for General George Meade). He came from New York, initially for his appointment to the territorial supreme court, and occupied the office of governor because he was a close friend of President Cleveland. He was fairly popular until he declared his support for the notion of turning Dakota Territory into a single state. The majority at the south end—especially those in the central counties—tried to impeach him.

The fate of Governor Church was determined, however, by the election of Benjamin Harrison in 1888, replacing President Cleveland. Quickly, a lame-duck Congress passed the Omnibus Statehood Act—to create the states of South Dakota, North Dakota, Montana, and Washington—and Cleveland signed it into law on February 22, 1889. Gracefully, Church submitted his resignation to President Harrison on March 9, and, within two weeks, Harrison extended appointment to Arthur Mellette to bring territorial administration to a close. Accordingly, Mellette served as territorial governor until November 2, 1889, when Harrison proclaimed the existence of South Dakota and North Dakota as states. By then, South Dakotans had elected Mellette as the first governor of their state.

The appointment of Arthur Mellette (1889) in the spring as territorial governor and his election in the fall as governor of the state were appropriate rewards for his work over the previous decade. The statehood issue overshadowed all others. Campbell, Pettigrew, Ward, and several others played key roles in the statehood movement, but Mellette was the lynchpin.

Historian Herbert Schell in his general history and political scientist William Farber in his biography of Mellette have addressed the statehood movement. The Great Dakota Boom not only enlarged the population, but also changed the partisan character of Dakota Territory. In 1880 approximately eighty percent of its citizen population was Republican. By 1889 the Democratic Party grew while Populism evolved through the Farmers Alliance, which first appeared in 1881. Across the territory, the vast majority lived south of forty-six degrees, where most voters favored the creation of South Dakota; those living north of forty-six degrees feared a perpetual territorial status if South Dakota alone became a state. Obviously, the sparse population in the northern part of the territory could embrace the solution written into the Omnibus Statehood Act of 1889.

Working within these developments, the movement toward statehood was complicated only by the need for suitable management of political forces, and Mellette emerged as the principal coordinator. From the 1879 Thanksgiving Day dinner at the home of Reverend Sheldon came a "we are a state" or "home rule" determinist movement that led to the first convention at Canton on June 21, 1882. Delegates chose a committee to draft a bill for presentation to the territorial legislature to authorize a constitutional convention. This evoked strong opposition in the northern constituencies out of fear that counties in the south could gain statehood and those in the north would not. To court favor in the north, Governor Ordway responded to the group from Canton with a veto, which evoked a general outcry and the formation of the Dakota Citizens' League. A petition from sympathetic legislators drew no response in Congress, but the league pressed for a second convention, which met at Huron during June 1883. Delegates agreed to a third convention, at Sioux Falls, where a written constitution began to take shape.

The chairman at Sioux Falls was Arthur Mellette, who at that point in time was an untested leader. After some Civil War duty, he finished an LL.B. degree at the University of Indiana and came to Dakota Territory to find a climate likely to restore health to his ailing wife. In 1879 President Hayes appointed Mellette to the office of Register of Public Lands at Springfield. In 1880 he moved to Watertown to get close to settlement patterns in the Great Dakota Boom. Public respect grew out of recognition for his efficiency in the land office, his success as an attorney, and his insight into real estate investment. The community chose him to represent the Watertown area at the Sioux Falls constitutional convention.

As chairman, he left his mark on the document—especially its length. Mellette argued that "the more there is in a constitution the better for the people" because the legislative process was fickle. This attitude took the label "Dakota Plan," limiting legislative power as protection for popular prerogatives. Public reaction to the draft constitution—12,366 in favor and 6,814 opposed—indicated strong endorsement.

Territorial legislators authorized a fourth convention on September 8, 1885, at Sioux Falls. Delegates made changes and gained endorsements from 25,226 in favor, with only

6,535 opposed. This document called for the election of state officials in the hope that Congress would recognize a new state that already was in place.

At a Republican Party meeting in Huron on October 21, 1885, Mellette again presided, accepting nomination for the extralegal office of governor, and he won election. In Congress, however, a Democratic majority resisted for fear about the election of two Republican U.S. senators. After Cleveland lost to Harrison in 1888, lame-duck Democrats passed and placed into law the Omnibus Statehood Act of 1889 to create four new states.

Congressional requirements for particular changes in the South Dakota constitution made another constitutional convention necessary, on July 4, 1889. A referendum revealed 70,131 in favor and only 3,267 opposed to the final document. At an election on October 1, recently appointed Territorial Governor Mellette gained election as legal governor for the State of South Dakota. On November 2, statehood came through a shuffle of admission documents that determined the order—North Dakota as the thirty-ninth and South Dakota as the fortieth state in the Union. Mellette was ready to organize a government for the State of South Dakota.

Chapter 8
Yankee and European Settlement

Following the settlement of the Missouri River Valley in the first half of the nineteenth century, Yankee land speculators arrived in Dakota Territory to claim the most promising townsites, but they were quickly followed by European immigrants who were seeking the quantity and quality of farmland they had been unable to acquire in their native countries. By the end of the nineteenth century, the initial Yankee settlers were outnumbered by several foreign ethnic groups, the largest being Germans followed by Norwegians and Swedes. But a variety of other foreign groups also came, some to establish discrete colonies thereby lending their ethnic flavor to an area despite their small number in the overall population. The state census of 1885 reported that foreign-born immigrants comprised thirty-one percent of the total population. Immigrants constituted the largest portion of the population in 1890 after which their number continued to increase for the next twenty years while their proportion declined.[1] After 1890 the foreign-born immigrants were increasingly outnumbered in the total population by their children and grandchildren.

■ Pull and Push Factors of Immigration

For the most part, the frontier settlement process was a mass movement of people from areas that were land poor and people rich to a place that was land rich and people poor. This movement did not happen without significant encouragement and stimulation. The United States government played a significant role through its removal of Native American inhabitants by treaty and military force. Equally important was the federal government's liberal policies for the disposal of the public domain contained in the Pre-emption Act of 1841, Homestead Act of 1862, and Timber Culture Acts of 1873 and 1878. A special aspect of the Homestead Act was the provision that Union veterans of the Civil War could count their service time toward fulfillment of the five-year residency requirement. This prompted a large number of veterans, many of whom were foreign-born, to homestead in Dakota Territory.

In addition many other parties, motivated by self-interest, promoted immigration to southern Dakota as soon as the government removed Native American title to the land. Townsite speculators and businessmen, farmland speculators, loan companies, territorial politicians, railroad companies, and even steamship lines all stimulated this movement of people to southern Dakota in the latter half of the nineteenth century and early twentieth. And transportation technology also played a crucial role in facilitating the flow of settlers to the region. Settlement began at a slow pace with riverboats and covered wagons, but it was the coming of railroads that produced the mass movement that historians have described as the "Dakota Boom."[2]

These so-called "pull factors" were not the only elements that caused this great migration from Europe to America in the last half of the nineteenth century and early years of the twentieth. "Push factors" were equally important to the process. Europe experienced a significant population increase in the nineteenth century that put pressure on the limited available land in what was still an agricultural society and economy. Demographers attribute this population explosion to better food and vaccination against diseases like smallpox. The birth rate did not increase. Rather, it was that the death rate declined, especially among the young. As a result there were too many people to live off the available land. The options were to stay and starve, to relocate to an early industrial city or to emigrate to a foreign land. Those who possessed or acquired the means to emigrate often did so because the United States promised them the possibility of continuing their conservative rural life-style based on land ownership. There were other factors, too, that encouraged people to leave the "Old Country." Some left to escape religious persecution or required military service. Others sought freedom from an oppressive social and political system. All hoped that they might find a better future for themselves and their children than they expected at home.

Early immigrants from European countries usually had some assets they could sell to finance their travel to America. These were small land owners who sold out their meager holdings to buy the required tickets and other needed supplies. It was these early immigrants who became part of the "pull" from America as they wrote letters back home that described America in such terms as to encourage more to come. As time passed, these "America Letters" contained money and tickets. Family members and village friends came, worked to repay their passage, and then moved on to the frontier where land could be easily acquired. By the end of the Civil War, Dakota Territory was the edge of the frontier where land was most easily available. In 1878 good economic times returned to America, and a rainy cycle

Chronology

1841 – Pre-emption Act passed
1860-80 – Yankees dominate Dakotas
1862 – Homestead Act passed
 – Dakota War
1866 – Minnehaha County settlement begins
1868 – Swedes move to Dakotas
1869 – Czechs move to Dakotas
1870 – Small stable population of African Americans in Sioux Falls
1871 – Sioux Falls founded for second time
1872 – Czech town of Tabor founded
 – start of Germans from Russia immigration
1873 – Dakota Southern Railroad founded
1874 – German newspaper *Dakota Freie Presse* begins
1875 – Public Reading Room opens in Sioux Falls
1878 – Dakota Boom begins, heavy railroad infiltration
1880 – Third of population from the Northeast, then Norway; Dutch enter Dakotas
1882 – Peak of Norwegian immigration, peak of Danish immigration, Kuipers colony (Dutch) settle in Platte
1889 – South Dakota becomes a state
 – Lutheran Normal School founded
1892 – Sons of Norway founded
1899 – *Bygdelag* movement begins
1910 – German immigration begins, as well as other ethnic groups
1918 – Augustana College moves to Sioux Falls, merges with Lutheran Normal School

came to Dakota while grasshoppers did not. As a consequence, railroads rapidly penetrated Dakota creating the basis for a massive movement of immigrants into the territory from abroad and from other parts of the United States. The Dakota Boom of 1878-1887 occurred when a high-point of foreign immigration coincided with Dakota being the edge of the farming frontier.

The famous Harvard historian Oscar Handlin once wrote that the history of the United States is the history of immigration, for all Americans have their antecedents somewhere else, even, according to archaeologists, Native Americans.[3] In South Dakota, where the frontier experience is relatively recent, individuals, communities, and even sections of the state still reflect or acknowledge their immigrant, ethnic heritage.

▪ Yankees

Germans, Norwegians, Swedes, Germans from Russia, Bohemians, Danes, English, Irish, and others have all made their contributions to the history of the state. But it is appropriate to begin this settlement narrative with a group of immigrants, often over-looked or taken for granted, who were perhaps more important than all the others in shaping the cultural patterns and institutions of this region. These are the immigrants from the northeastern section of this country, from New England, New York, and Pennsylvania. The term "Yankee" was used to describe these people, chiefly of English heritage, who had fled the rocky soils and crowded cities of the Northeast to seek their future and fortune on the ever-retreating frontier of the Great Northwest, or what we today call the Midwest.

The historical literature of South Dakota has not generally identified the Yankees as a separate ethnic group in the same way it has Norwegians, Czechs, Germans, and Swedes. The very early writings about Dakota done in the nineteenth century to promote settlement speak of Yankees. An example is G. A. Batchelder's *A Sketch of the History and Resources of Dakota Territory,* printed at Yankton in 1870 and used by the Secretary of Immigration for Dakota Territory to attract settlers from New England. Another is Moses K. Armstrong's *The Early Empire Builders of the Great West,* printed in St. Paul in 1901, which is the history of Yankee enterprise on the early Dakota frontier. But, for the most part, the role of the Yankees in South Dakota's history is not group oriented; it is instead focused on the efforts of individuals. It is only when one begins noting that most of these individuals came from the northeastern states that you realize that the history of early Dakota is the history of Yankees.

The prominence of Yankees in shaping early Dakota is perhaps most evident when one reads the biographical sketches of early residents in old county histories like *The History of Minnehaha County,* written in 1899 by Dana Reed Bailey, himself a typical Yankee empire builder born in Vermont. Although Bailey's *History* also includes biographical sketches of a number of Norwegians, Germans, and other ethnic representatives, the vast majority of those included were born in the Northeast or were only one generation removed from the Northeast. Modern histories tend to take for granted the common Yankee heritage of the founding fathers of Dakota. Herbert Schell's 1961 *History of South Dakota*, for instance, sums up the social and cultural aspects of South Dakota by focusing on the "state's rich Old World Heritage," virtually ignoring the collective identity of the American-born settlers. Indeed, one will look in vain for a scholarly account of the activities of the Yankees as an ethnic group in South Dakota history.[4]

But to understand the present-day political, economic, social, and institutional characteristics of South Dakota culture, one must look to the early role of the Yankees in this state's history. They set the patterns on the Dakota frontier that resulted in the essential transplanting of New England's political, economic, and social values and ways of doing things. Yankees brought notions of equality before the law, democratic processes, the virtue of hard work, the importance of schools and churches, proper social behavior, and organization to Dakota, where they were nourished, took root, and grew strong. This Yankee heritage has been influenced by the ocean of foreign immigrants that surged into Dakota in the nineteenth century, but the basic structure remains Yankee. As a result, even though South Dakotans may speak of themselves as being Norwegians, Swedes, or Germans and celebrate a foreign ethnic heritage, they are all in their everyday lives really Yankees.

This region is fortunate to have a Yankee heritage, for the Northeast possessed the most energetic and dynamic society of nineteenth-century America. It was in the

Northeast that egalitarianism was most strongly expressed. There, too, the tradition of participatory democracy was strongest, growing out of the Puritan device of the town meeting. The Northeast was also the center of nineteenth-century intellectual life in this country; it was the originator of our public school system and the home of the nation's leading writers, historians, preachers, artists, and architects. As a result, most of the Yankees who came to Dakota Territory were well educated, many having college degrees.

The Yankees who came to the Dakota frontier in the middle decades of the nineteenth century came because of the opportunities they saw here for making their fortunes and futures. They came not to create a new civilization, but to re-establish the one they had known in the Northeast. And they succeeded. It was an imperial enterprise, and they founded a new empire on the Dakota frontier, making it in a very real sense a cultural and economic colony of the Northeast. Moses K. Armstrong, South Dakota's first historian, confirmed this when he titled his history of the early days in Dakota *The Early Empire Builders of the Great West*.

■ Yankees in Yankton and Sioux Falls

The extent of our cultural indebtedness to the Yankee colonizers or empire builders can be seen in the history of practically every city and town in eastern South Dakota, but it is perhaps best illustrated in the history of two towns, Yankton and Sioux Falls. These were the first towns established in southeastern Dakota, selected as prime townsites because of their water assets: the Missouri River, in the first case, and the falls of the Big Sioux River, in the other. Yankton and Sioux Falls both aspired to become the capital city of the territory, both succeeded in acquiring railroad connections early in their existence, both established institutions of higher education, and most importantly, both were founded and shaped by ambitious, well-educated, and energetic Yankees with dreams of making their townsite the largest and most successful city in the region.

Sioux Falls was initially founded by two townsite companies, the Western Town Company, from Dubuque, Iowa, and the Dakota Land Company, from St. Paul, Minnesota. The personnel of both companies were thoroughly Yankee. Most of the Western Town Company's investors had been born or raised in Pennsylvania, New Hampshire, Maine, and Vermont and had settled in Dubuque during the 1840s and early 1850s when eastern Iowa was the edge of the western frontier. The Dakota Land Company people, too, originated in the northeastern states and had come to the Minnesota frontier at about the same time. Governor Samuel Medary, a stockholder in the Dakota Land Company, was born in Montgomery County, Pennsylvania, and most of the other stockholders were also Yankees.

Two individuals from other Yankee states provided the initial leadership in the founding of Yankton, but they were the exception rather than the rule in terms of the origins of the town's early inhabitants. The federal census of 1860 reveals a clear domination of Yankees among the early residents. Captain John Blair Todd was a native of Kentucky, and Henry Ash, who opened the first hotel, was born in Maryland, but D. M. Frost, Todd's partner, was from New York, while Downer Bramble and Joseph R. Hanson, two of the most prominent Fifty-niners, and most of the others are listed in the census as born in New York, Connecticut, New Hampshire, Vermont, and Pennsylvania. There were a few foreign-born persons in Yankton in 1860 but most of them had been raised and educated in the Northeast.[5]

The men who were responsible for creating these two cities out of the vacant prairie of eastern Dakota are memorialized by the buildings, place names, and institutions and by the tone, spirit, and very existence of the communities themselves. That the vast majority of these city builders were Yankees becomes obvious when one studies the federal census schedules for 1860, 1870, and 1880. In 1860, for example, twenty-two of the thirty-eight inhabitants of Sioux Falls were born in the northeastern states and another nine were Yankees one generation removed from the Northeast.[6] The same Yankee dominance was apparent in Yankton in 1860.[7] In 1872 a promotional history of Dakota estimated that Yankees composed half the population of Yankton County while another quarter was Scandinavian and the remainder Bohemians, Germans, and Irish.[8] The population of Minnehaha County in 1872 was estimated to be about half Yankee and half Scandinavian.[9] Eight years later, the federal census of 1880 revealed that nearly one third of the heads of households in Sioux Falls indicated their fathers had been born in the Northeast while the second largest percent had fathers born in Norway.[10]

Yankees were not only the earliest settlers in Yankton, Sioux Falls, and most other Dakota towns; they also dominated the main-street business and professional life of these communities. At the outset of settlement, there were few foreign-born business-men or artisans in most Dakota communities, but Yankee businessmen often hired for-eign-born clerks to make their immigrant customers feel more at ease. The 1870 federal census listed three merchants and one clerk in Sioux Falls—all born in New York. In the same year all the professional and business men in Yankton were Yankees except Charles Eisman, who was born in Prussia. Even as late as 1880, over three-quarters of the main-street leaders in Sioux Falls were Yankees, while Norwegians with five percent were the next largest ethnic group represented.[11]

If the Sioux Falls and Yankton examples are typical, and it appears that they are, the Yankees who established new communities in southern Dakota Territory were young, most in their twenties and early thirties. Two of the leading figures in the early history of Yankton were Joseph R. Hanson and Downer Bramble. Hanson, born in Pennsylvania, was twenty-four years old when he arrived in Yankton in 1859, and Bramble, from Vermont, was just two years older. Moses K. Armstrong, surveyor and early historian, was twenty-five when he came to Yankton the same year.[12] W. W. Brookings came to Sioux Falls in 1857 from Maine at the age of twenty-seven, and Henry Masters, elected governor of Dakota Territory by the squatter legislature in 1858, was only twenty at the time.[13] Later, in 1870, when Sioux Falls had been re-established, its leading citizens were again young men. Dr. Josiah L. Phillips, from Maine, and after whom Phillips Avenue is named, was one of the old men on the scene at thirty-five, as was C. K. Howard from New York at thirty-four. Richard Pettigrew, twenty-one years old, from Vermont, fresh out of law school and already in the real estate business, listed himself on the census as a farmer.[14] Even as late as 1880, the population of Sioux Falls was noticeably young. An analysis of the federal census of that year reveals that three-quarters of the heads of households were between seventeen and thirty-nine years of age and that nearly forty percent were in their twenties. Less than eight percent were fifty or older.[15]

Biographical sketches and census records also indicate that these young Yankee empire builders were well educated. An amazing number of these frontiersmen were college graduates. Yankton could boast of ninety college-bred residents at an early point in its existence.[16] While not all the college men were attorneys, many were, and legal counsel was abundant in both Sioux Falls and Yankton. W. W. Brookings and Dr. Josiah L. Phillips were both graduates of Bowdoin College in Maine, Jefferson P. Kidder held a Masters of Arts degree from the University of Vermont, and Peter P. Wintermute, who opened a bank in Yankton in 1861, was a civil engineer. Each community had a number of clergy, and they were perhaps the best educated of all. The Reverend Eliza T. Wilkes,

With his brother Fred W. Pettigrew, shown here surveying near Green Grass Creek on the Cheyenne River Reservation in the late 1890s, Richard F. Pettigrew secured contracts from the federal government to survey the public domain in Dakota Territory. *Center for Western Studies.*

founder of All Souls Unitarian Church in Sioux Falls, graduated from the State University of Iowa, and the Reverend Joseph Ward, who came to pastor the Congregational Church in Yankton in 1868, was a Brown University graduate.[17]

Most of these Yankee adventurers did not move directly from the Northeast to the Dakota frontier. Richard F. Pettigrew, whose family moved to Wisconsin from Vermont when he was six years old, is an example of the many who moved at a young age to Ohio, Illinois, Wisconsin, Iowa, or some other midwestern state. Biographical sketches also indicate that others left the Northeast when they reached their majority and worked for elder brothers who had migrated west before them. Downer Bramble and Joseph R. Hanson of Yankton are but two examples of this. Many moved westward from one frontier to another as adults, and some moved even further west after spending a few years in Dakota. Artemas Gale, early real estate developer, and the architect Charles Booth both spent some time in St. Paul before coming to Sioux Falls. This westward migration is evident from the census, which notes the birth place of children. Melancthon Hoyt of Yankton, for example, was born in Connecticut, but his children were born in Michigan and Wisconsin.[18]

Despite the rough frontier environment, these young, well-educated, and energetic Yankee town promoters and their wives created a cultural atmosphere reminiscent of the Northeast. Mrs. S. W. Ingham, wife of a minister in Yankton, wrote of the "tone and refinement and culture" that pervaded the town's society in the 1870s. Isolated from outside cultural influences, the early residents provided their own social activities, which included dancing, debating societies, and dramatic presentations. At Yankton the young men organized the Literary and Debating Club of Yankton, which conducted weekly debates on the current topics of the day.[19] A host of fraternal orders and social action organizations were transplanted to these communities at an early date, and they flourished. The first meeting of the Masonic Lodge in Sioux Falls occurred in a grain bin at the back of C. K. Howard's store in 1872. In the same year, the ladies of Sioux Falls organized a temperance society, and three years later Mrs. Artemas Gale opened the first Public Reading Room as an alternative to the many saloons in downtown Sioux Falls. In 1879 a group of Yankee ladies in Sioux Falls began the Ladies' History Club.[20]

One could spend a long time recounting the political events of Yankton and Sioux Falls, for politics was a form of entertainment and excitement to Yankees accustomed to the highly organized social structure of long-settled areas of the country. They played politics with gusto, guile, and, occasionally, even with physical violence. Indeed, they played the political game like their future depended upon winning, as it often did. But the political process and institutions these Yankees established in Dakota bore a striking resemblance to those in Wisconsin, Illinois, Ohio, and the states of the Northeast. Yankees dominated the territorial legislative sessions and any territorial offices they could get their hands on. And these Yankees introduced the foreign-born immigrants to this American political system and encouraged them to participate.

Finally, these Yankee empire builders established the essential elements of the civilized society they had known back East: churches to sustain the spirit and schools to transmit the New England culture to their own children and those of the sea of immigrants that threatened to overwhelm them. In Sioux Falls the first churches to be organized were the Episcopal and Congregational, while in Yankton the Congregational and Methodist were the earliest. These Yankee churches were soon followed by others. In the summer of 1870, the year Sioux Falls was founded for the second time, Mrs. Hattie Phillips and Mrs. Ella Coats organized the Pioneer Union Sunday School in Sioux Falls. Both these women had Yankee parents, and Dana Bailey records in his *History of Minnehaha County* that after Mrs. Phillips arrived on the scene "social matters began to have a standing in the community."[21]

Sioux Falls was only two years old in 1873 when it organized a public school district and constructed its first school building. A list of those who served on school boards and contributed money to establish private schools is like a roll call of prominent Yankee residents in the two communities. Of the fourteen teachers listed in the 1880 federal census for Sioux Falls, all but one were either born in the Northeast or had Yankee-born parents.[22]

There are many proud descendants of these early Yankee empire builders who are part of virtually every community in South Dakota today. They are, however, no longer a majority of the population. Many merged through marriage into the foreign immigrant groups that came to dominate the region in the last two decades of the nineteenth century. It is also true that many of these Yankees left Dakota in the years between 1886 and 1900. Southern Dakota experienced one of the worst of its periodic droughts in the second half of the 1880s, and it was during these periods and again after the Panic of 1893 that a large number of Yankee settlers left Dakota. While foreign-born immigrants often had few options except to tough it out in those difficult years, Yankees more often had the money, contacts, and information that allowed them to relocate to more favorable places. Moreover, many of these Yankees had never intended to settle permanently in Dakota. Once they had proved up their homestead claims or established a business, they were often ready to sell out to newly arriving migrants and to move on. The consequence of this set of circumstances was that, in just a few years, the proportion of the foreign-born in South Dakota increased dramatically while that of American-born, especially those born in New England and New York, declined.[23]

■ Yankee Founders Seek Immigrants

While a number of Yankee adventurers were busy gaining possession of potential townsites in southern Dakota prior to 1864, the immigration tide had not yet arrived. Therefore, territorial officials and townsite speculators were all delighted to learn during the winter of 1863-1864 that several "homestead associations" were forming in the

Northeast with the goal of organizing large-scale migration to southern Dakota. One formed at Syracuse and another near Ypsilanti, Michigan. Both were a response to the Homestead Act that Congress approved in 1862 and took effect on January 1, 1863. The New York group numbered nearly five-hundred persons, and it was the first organized migration to Dakota Territory. Members boarded a special train in April 1864 and traveled to Marshalltown, Iowa, where they were to outfit themselves for the remaining travel to Yankton. By the time they reached Dakota Territory, the New York colony had given up its intention of founding a discrete village, and members took up individual claims in a variety of locations, though most located in or near Yankton. There is no record of the Michigan association actually undertaking migration to Dakota Territory.[24]

The arrival of the New York group sparked considerable envy from other Dakota townsites as well as those in Nebraska. The success of townsites and the prosperity of townsite speculators depended on attracting settlers and, thus, there was great competition. Dakota promoters bemoaned the efforts of communities in Minnesota and Iowa to dissuade immigrants from continuing their travel to Dakota. Railroads, with massive government land grants to support rail-line construction, also used their considerable resources to persuade immigrants to settle on their land where they would become rail customers. Finally, the Dakota War of 1862 and the inability of the army to provide security to settlers during the Civil War meant that actual settlers were few prior to 1866.

The 1900 federal census reported that there were slightly more than 400,000 inhabitants in South Dakota and revealed that over sixty percent consisted of the foreign-born and their children. While Yankees initially were the dominate element in the settlement of southeastern Dakota in the wake of the Civil War, they were soon outnumbered by foreign-born immigrants. The high proportion of foreign-born in the state's population at the end of the settlement period indicates the importance of immigration from Europe, mainly from northwestern Europe, to the settlement of South Dakota. The remainder of this chapter will review briefly the history of the various ethnic groups that emigrated from Europe to pursue a better future for themselves and their children in what became the State of South Dakota than they expected to achieve in their native land. These immigrant groups put their mark upon the culture of the state while also trying to maintain their unique ethnic heritage.[25]

■ Norwegians

Organized Norwegian emigration to the United States had begun in 1825, but did not pick up momentum until the 1840s. According to the 1900 federal census, Norwegians comprised the largest foreign-born ethnic group in South Dakota. Accustomed to an environment that included lots of wood and water and little good land, Norwegians generally followed the watercourses in seeking land in the American Midwest. Most Norwegians had first settled in northern Illinois and Wisconsin and by the early 1850s had sought out government land in southeastern Minnesota and northwestern Iowa. But by the late 1860s desirable government land in those two territories was becoming scarce, and the mainstream of Norwegian land-seekers passed over the treeless prairies of southwestern Minnesota and northwestern Iowa to take up claims in the wooded Missouri and Big Sioux river valleys in southeastern Dakota. A small number of Norwegian immigrants had ventured into southeastern Dakota as early as 1858, but the Indian threat in subsequent years had kept those numbers small. In Dakota, too, Norwegian settlers tended to follow the streams where wood and water were available. Only after these areas were taken, did they venture out onto the prairies.

With little or no timber with which to construct a house or outbuildings, early homesteaders on the prairie, such as these near Arlington, in Kingsbury County, in 1884, cut sod into strips and stacked them up to build walls. Settlers secured poles to form rafters over which they laid boards, prairie grass, and sod. These roofs were seldom waterproof, and dirt floors turned to mud when it rained. *Center for Western Studies.*

Dakota Territory was basically settled in two intense periods of immigration separated by five years of drought and grasshopper infestations. The first of these periods, running from 1866 to 1873, witnessed the initial major coming of Norwegian immigrants to southeastern Dakota. Norway in the 1860s experienced several successive years of crop failure due to bad weather, which encouraged emigration, especially when news of the Homestead Act reached rural districts. In addition to passage of the Homestead Act, the sixties also saw the end of Indian hostilities that had earlier discouraged prospective settlers from seeking land in Dakota Territory. As a result of these factors, the federal census of 1870 recorded 14,181 white people in Dakota Territory with five-sixths of them residing in the Missouri Valley. This number included 1,284 Norwegians who had settled in the lower Big Sioux Valley and along the Missouri River Valley in Union, Clay, and Yankton counties. Then came the Panic of 1873, the grasshoppers, and little rain. By 1874 immigration slowed to a trickle and many left for areas further east where rain was more dependable.[26]

The period of 1878 to 1887 is generally known as the "Dakota Boom." In the first year of the boom the amount of land filed upon in what became South Dakota leaped from 163,739 acres in 1877 to 941,800 acres a year later. The peak year of the boom was 1883 when nearly five-and-one-half-million acres were taken up. During the ten years of the "Boom," homesteaders and speculators filed on more than twenty-four-million acres of land in southern Dakota Territory. While the population of southern Dakota had increased to 81,781 by 1880, the land rush of the 1880s ballooned the population to 328,808 by the next federal census in 1890.[27]

It was during the Dakota Boom that the peak year of Norwegian emigration occurred. In 1882 more than twenty-nine thousand Norwegians left their homeland for America, and a large percentage came to Dakota Territory. Travel to Dakota became easier and faster after 1873 when railroads began to penetrate into Dakota Territory. In that year, the first of these railroads, the Dakota Southern, was completed from Sioux City to Yankton, but the panic of later that year and the drought conditions of subsequent years postponed further rail construction until 1878. But, in that year, railroad construction into southern Dakota began in earnest. Various companies competed in founding towns and dominating the areas that surrounded them. The result was an influx of Norwegian immigrants into the tier of counties along the eastern edge of what in 1889 became the State of South Dakota. By the 1900 census, the heaviest concentration of Norwegians was in the Big Sioux Valley, from where it begins in Deuel County south to where the Big Sioux empties into the Missouri River. The single greatest concentration was in Minnehaha County where, by 1900, there were over 6,500 Norwegians. Norwegian settlements north of Deuel County were smaller, and settlements west of the Big Sioux and James rivers were scattered.[28]

Few of these Norwegian immigrants came directly to Dakota from Norway. Most had stopped in some of the older Norwegian settlements in Wisconsin, southeastern Minnesota, and northeastern Iowa to raise some money by working in the forests, mines, or railroad construction. Many who came to Dakota in the 1870s and 1880s were the offspring of earlier immigrants who now sought their own farms or business opportunities. More than a few had moved several times before and after landing in southern Dakota. The census schedules illustrate the pilgrimages of these immigrants by noting the states in which children were born. The pattern of an eldest child born in Norway, another one in Illinois, a third in Minnesota or Wisconsin, and the youngest in Dakota was not uncommon.[29]

Canton, in Lincoln County, became the center for a large area of Norwegians that reached into the bordering parts of Turner and Union counties. By 1886 a resident writing to the Norwegian language newspaper *Amerika* claimed that half of Lincoln County's population was Norwegian. Three years earlier, the Norwegian Augustana Synod had moved its college across the river from Beloit, Iowa, to Canton, where it remained until a church merger in 1917 led to its moving again, this time to Sioux Falls, where it merged with the Lutheran Normal School.

In Minnehaha County, just to the north of Lincoln, the Norwegian presence was even greater. The beginning of this settlement came in 1866 when John Thompson and John Fosmo Nelson filed on land north of Sioux Falls and encouraged fellow countrymen back in Goodhue County, Minnesota, to join them. By 1870 there were sixty-eight Norwegians in Minnehaha County, and they were the foundation of the 2,302 Norwegians in the county when the 1880 federal census took place. At that point Norwegians constituted about a quarter of the total population of Minnehaha County. Norwegian immigrants continued to enter the county in large numbers during the 1880s, and by 1900 their percentage of the county's population had risen to nearly thirty-seven percent.[30]

Continuing northward, the Lake Hendricks area in Brookings County was the next largest focus of Norwegian immigration. The nucleus of this Norwegian settlement was established in 1873 when a number of families from Houston County, Minnesota, and Allamakee and Winneshiek counties, in Iowa, assembled near Mabel, Minnesota, intent on homesteading in southern Dakota Territory. Most of these settlers were from the Trondelag region in Norway. O. E. Rölvaag based much of his novel *Giants in the Earth* on the experience of his father-in-law, Andrew Berdahl, a member of this party, who, along with a few others, took up claims just north of Sioux Falls. By 1880 there were

1,643 Norwegians in Brookings County, and by the end of the century that number had more than doubled. Brookings was the center of this Norwegian community.[31]

Marking the upper end of the Big Sioux Valley, the northernmost concentration of Norwegian settlement occurred in southern Deuel County. Here, too, the earliest settlers came from Houston and Fillmore counties in Minnesota and Winneshiek County in Iowa. By 1880 there were nearly nine hundred Norwegians in Deuel County, and this number grew rapidly during the following decade. By 1900 the federal census counted more than 2,700 Norwegians in the county. While Norwegians also settled in the counties of extreme northeastern South Dakota, they did so in smaller numbers than the areas farther south.[32]

Few Norwegians ventured into western Dakota Territory in the early years. By 1887 there were about one hundred in Rapid City, but the Norwegian community in the Black Hills remained small compared to the numbers in the eastern portion of the territory.[33] Early in the twentieth century, Norwegians homesteaded in several of the counties west of the Missouri River, including Harding County where they comprised nearly one-third of the foreign-born in 1920. [34]

While most Norwegian immigrants in Dakota Territory were bent on acquiring land of their own to farm, a surprising number of them also settled in the newfound towns and villages. Indeed, Norwegian immigrants were present in many Dakota frontier towns from the outset, and they played an important role in the life and growth of these communities. Sioux Falls offers an example of a phenomena that appears to be typical of many urban communities in Dakota, especially those surrounded by large concentrations of Norwegian homesteaders. According to the 1880 federal census, thirty-five percent, or 382, of the 1,062 independent adults in Sioux Falls were foreign-born. Norwegians comprised the largest foreign-born element in the community representing nearly one third, or 110, of the 382. This was slightly more than ten percent of the total independent adult population. Unique among the five foreign-born ethnic groups in Sioux Falls, the Norwegians were engaged in every occupation category and were particularly well represented in the merchant community.

Almost from the outset of its permanent establishment in 1871, the Yankee founders of Sioux Falls were joined by foreign immigrants including several Norwegians. Soon-to-be brothers-in-law Andrew Thompson and Chris Solie arrived in the fall of 1871, acquired a lot on Phillips Avenue, constructed a building, and were soon in the grocery and dry-goods business. In 1872 Andrew Peterson arrived to open a furniture store, and A. T. Fleetwood (born in Norway) started a tobacco shop. The next year, 1873, C. O. Nattestad joined the growing Sioux Falls business community opening a general merchandise store on Main Avenue. By 1873 the young town had grown to nearly six hundred residents. Despite the discouraging conditions of the mid-1870s, Norwegians continued to open businesses in Sioux Falls. In 1874 Edwin Larson, Nels S. Johnson, John Henjum, and Esten Thompson settled in Sioux Falls. Larson opened a hardware store, Johnson a painting business, and Henjum a grocery store. Esten Thompson, brother to Andrew Thompson, apparently worked in his brother's dry-goods store. Knut Thompson came in 1875 to open a hotel and sell agricultural implements, the next year Ditteff Tharaldson, a shoe maker and veteran of the Civil War, arrived to open a boot and shoe store, and L. O. Johnson began a tailor shop. Throughout the remainder of the decade, and the next one as well, more Norwegian immigrants joined the Sioux Falls business community. In addition, Yankee merchants found it prudent to employ Norwegian-speaking clerks to make their Norwegian customers feel welcome.[35]

By 1887, two years before the southern portion of Dakota Territory became the State of South Dakota, the Dakota Boom had ended. The abundant rains of the early years of the decade, which had encouraged settlers to stretch the farming frontier beyond its natural limits, had succumbed to a series of drought years. The best land, and too much poor land, had already been claimed in southern Dakota, and Norwegian immigrant land-seekers turned to Montana and other western states instead. By 1889 the Norwegian element in South Dakota (foreign-born and those of foreign-born parents) numbered 51,455 or 12.8 percent of the state's total population.[36]

Some settlers were more adept at sod construction than others. This soddy has a board eave and window. Rabbits, prairie chickens, and other small game were an important part of the early settlers' diet. *Center for Western Studies.*

Norwegians very early became involved in politics and entered public office. They served on village councils, as postmasters, and as county officials. Ole Swenson, for example, left the operation of his hardware business to a partner when he won election to the first of two terms as Minnehaha County Treasurer in 1886. Knut Thompson was elected to the Sioux Falls Township Board from 1880 to 1883 and sold his hotel and implement business in 1891 to become deputy county auditor. Norwegians were elected to the state legislature, and nearly half of the governors, after statehood was attained in 1889, were Norwegian, the first being Andrew E. Lee, born in Norway and elected governor of the state in 1897.[37]

The Norwegian element in South Dakota, like most ethnic groups, was torn between a desire to become American and prosper, on the one hand, and to retain their ethnic heritage, on the other. Early plans to establish Norwegian schools gave way to the practicality of tax-supported public schools, while Norwegian summer schools persisted in some communities for several decades. In 1889 the Norwegian Synod of the Lutheran Church established a normal school in Sioux Falls to train teachers for both public and Norwegian schools. Augustana College, founded by the Lutheran Augustana Synod, joined the normal school in 1918 following the merger of the two sponsoring synods. Norwegian history and culture remained an important element of Augustana's academic program until after World War I when the college sought to shed its identity as a Norwegian college and establish a reputation as a liberal arts institution of higher education. English had replaced Norwegian in about half of the Norwegian Lutheran Churches by the mid-twenties and in nearly all of them by the outbreak of World War II.[38]

Norwegian-Americans have sought to retain their ethnicity through a variety of means. In 1892 a fraternal insurance and cultural organization, the Sons of Norway, was established, and Norwegians in several South Dakota communities organized local lodges. More than a century later, there continue to be Sons of Norway lodges in Rapid City, Sioux Falls, Canton, Yankton, Madison, Brookings, Huron, and Aberdeen devoted to keeping the Norwegian ethnic heritage alive. The *Bygdelag* movement began in 1899 as a series of organizations of people whose ancestors came from specific areas in Norway. Many of these groups have continued to be active as Norwegian-Americans have taken an interest in discovering their Norwegian roots. The Norse Federation, headquartered in Oslo, has a chapter in South Dakota with the mission of keeping the connection with Norway alive. In the 1890s, Norwegian male choruses began to be organized in several Norwegian communities to preserve a tradition of Norwegian choral music. By the outset of the twenty-first century, three such singing organizations continue active in Canton and Sioux Falls. Every two years they take part in a "Sanger Fest" that includes nearly a dozen Norwegian male choruses from across the Upper Midwest.[39]

Norwegian-language newspapers were for decades the major vehicle for Norwegian and Norwegian-American literature. Several South Dakota towns had Norwegian-language newspapers, though their life-spans were often short. Sioux Falls had two or three Norwegian-language newspapers during the late nineteenth and early decades of the twentieth century. However, the wartime bias against hyphenated Americanism of World War I and the declining number of South Dakotans able to read Norwegian caused the ultimate demise of this element of Norwegian ethnic culture by the late 1920s. Declining readership also ended a rather active publishing of Norwegian-language novels and religious literature.[40]

The appearance of Alex Haley's book *Roots* and the celebration in 1975 of the 150th anniversary of the first organized emigration of Norwegians to America reinvigorated an interest in heritage among many descendants of Norwegian immigrants in South Dakota and across the nation. Bygdelags became more active and several South Dakota communities established annual events to celebrate and preserve their Norwegian heritage. The Nordland Fest in Sioux Falls and lutefisk or torsk suppers are examples. The Center for Western Studies at Augustana College has established an exhibit of a typical nineteenth-century Norwegian peasant home interior and displays other immigration items.

■ Swedes

More Swedes emigrated to America than did Norwegians, but fewer of them settled in southern Dakota. The 1900 federal census reported that nearly twenty thousand residents of South Dakota had been born in Norway compared to fewer than nine thousand born in Sweden. Still, the Swedish presence in South Dakota has remained visible because of its concentration in an area extending from central Clay County to the southwestern corner of Lincoln County. This area, earlier known as Swedefield, and now more commonly referred to as Dalesburg, began when several settlers arrived from Sweden in 1868. Within the next half-dozen years, over two hundred settlers and their families came to Clay County to secure homesteads. They took up land on the east side of the Vermillion River in northeastern Clay County while Norwegians settled on the west side. During the difficult times of the mid-1870s, a few families left the settlement, but most stayed and were later joined by other countrymen. The immigrants established their claims along the eastern tributaries of the Vermillion, such as Erickson Creek, Baptist Creek, Garfield Creek, and Ash Creek. When land near water and wood was taken, later-comers spilled out into the open prairie between them. It was evident that two low-lying areas close to the Vermillion, Cabbage Flats and Vermillion Bottom, were poorly drained, and the Swedes generally bypassed them.[41]

The Clay County Swedes came from a variety of provinces in Sweden, though the largest number came from the Bothnian Coast, Upper Dalarna, and Ostergotland. The name Dalesburg apparently derived from the large number of settlers who had come from the province of Dalarna. According to historian Robert C. Ostergren, some of these families came directly to Clay County because they were among the first to emigrate from their district. Others, from districts that had already sent emigrants to the American Midwest, stopped off for varying periods of time at these older Swedish settlements to earn some money and learn more about what to expect on the frontier. As one might expect, families from the same home district tended to cluster together in the Dalesburg settlement. This allowed old associations and district dialects to continue and thereby create a more comfortable environment.[42]

The settlement also had religious distinctions. The state Lutheran Church in Sweden had discouraged emigration, and its clergy were part of a dominant privileged class. Not surprisingly, an initial attempt in 1869 to organize a church in the Dalesburg settlement ended in failure because of theological disagreement. But two years later the Dalesburg Lutheran Church was established in the center of the settlement. Later in the same year, a dissident group founded the Dalesburg Baptist Church two miles north of the Lutheran. A third group founded a Mission Covenant Church three years later at Komstad in the northern part of the settlement. These churches have long served as important vehicles for retaining the Swedish character of the Dalesburg community. A major element of the community's effort to retain its Swedish heritage is the Mid-Summer's Festival that occurs each June and features a maypole dance, music, and Swedish foods.[43]

■ Danes

Fewer Danes than either Norwegians or Swedes emigrated to America, and an even smaller number of Danes than Swedes settled in South Dakota. Still, a total of more than 370,000 Danes emigrated to the United States, with a quarter million going between 1850 and 1930. The high point of Danish emigration was the year 1882 when over eleven thousand Danes left for America. Fewer Danes settled in southern Dakota Territory than in Minnesota, Iowa, and Wisconsin, and they tended to settle near Norwegian communities or generally scatter among the general population. The largest and most distinctly Danish settlement in southern Dakota Territory was founded in Turner County in the vicinity of Swan Lake. Daneville, later changed to Viborg, was the settlement's commercial center. The 1900 federal census counted only a few more than five thousand people in South Dakota who had been born in Denmark.[44]

The Danish settlement in southern Dakota began when Peter Larsen Christiansen arrived in 1864 and settled in the vicinity of Swan Lake, Turner County. The federal census of 1870 counted 115 Danes in Dakota, and all but eleven of them lived in this settlement, which extended into nearby parts of Clay and Yankton counties. A decade later the census listed 401 Danes in Turner County and more than one hundred each in Yankton and Clay counties. First called Swan Lake and then Daneville, the community's townsite changed its name again when the railroad arrived in 1893. The name Viborg (pronounced with a long "i" rather than long "e" as in Denmark) reflects the Danish ethnic dominance, for it comes from an ancient town in northern Denmark.[45]

While the Turner County community remains the largest Danish settlement in South Dakota, Danes did establish smaller ones in Hamlin and Kingsbury counties. The social center of the Hamlin settlement was Maple Grove, later changed to Denmark, sited on the bank of Lake Thisted where Peter Christensen built a store prior to 1879. Most of the settlers here came from the Thy district of northwestern Jutland, and they named the lake Thisted in memory of the chief town of their home district in Denmark. In the early 1880s, immigrants from Jutland, Funen, and Seeland settled further west in Kingsbury County. The earliest to settle here was Thomas Sorensen who homesteaded three miles east of Erwin in 1881. Danish immigrants managed to acquire land in the 1890s when hard times forced eastern landowners to dispose of land they had held for speculation.[46]

As was true among the other Scandinavian groups, American religious denominations had significant success in attracting Danish immigrants in South Dakota. While all Danes were nominal members of the state Lutheran Church in Denmark, in America the Methodists, Baptists, and Adventists all courted them. It seems that churches even played a role in the development of new Danish settlements. The Baptists and Lutherans were especially active in such work. As a result, in the eighties and nineties, small Danish concentrations were established in places like Dell Rapids, Millard, Pukwana, Beresford, Conde, Colman, and Ethan. The Baptists organized their first congregations at Lodi in 1872 and at Swan Lake a year later. In 1875 both Adventists and Lutherans organized congregations at Swan Lake.

Lutherans competed with the American denominations and with the pietistic free-free Lutherans, and struggled with internal theological disputes. The internal dissension caused a split among the regular Danish Lutherans into Inner Mission and Grundtvigian congregations, which caused some serious social tensions within the Danish communities. Despite the theological divisions, the churches were the main social institutions of the Danish communities.[47]

Lutheran congregations were most involved in keeping the Danish culture alive. Unlike the American denominations, the Lutherans used the liturgy and language of Denmark in their worship services. Moreover, it was generally the Lutheran clergy who provided leadership in maintaining the Danish language and culture through organizing Danish Sunday and vacation school programs. However, when opposition to the Masonic Lodge became a theological issue in the Lutheran Church in the 1880s and 1890s, it was the Lutheran clergy who discouraged parishioners from joining the Danish Brotherhood, a fraternal mutual-aid society that also sought to preserve Danish culture. Only after this issue had abated were local lodges established in various Danish communities in South Dakota.[48] Despite these efforts, by the final decades of the twentieth century, few descendants of Danish immigrants in South Dakota spoke or read the Danish language. Still, pride in their Danish heritage remains strong. Each July Viborg hosts Danish Days to celebrate the community's Danish heritage, and in 2004 the Daneville Heritage Association opened a museum in Viborg devoted to the area's Danish immigrant roots.

■ Czechs

In June 1868 a group of Czechs in Chicago formed a Czech Agricultural Society to establish Czech settlements in the West. Membership cost one dollar, and the society's advertisements in various Czech areas of the eastern part of the United States soon yielded four thousand members. The membership fees financed expeditions to locate an appropriate site for the settlement. Initial inspections in Kansas and northern Nebraska proved discouraging until a society representative, Frank Bem, stopping over in Sioux City, encountered a man from Yankton. He told Bem there was plenty of good land available at Yankton in Dakota Territory. Following a quick visit to Yankton to confirm the report, Bem returned to Chicago with the good news. However, other members of the society refused to accept the new destination, and the Czech Agricultural Society broke up. The result was a much smaller initial migration of Czech settlers to Dakota Territory than otherwise might have been the case. Most of the early settlers came from other parts of the United States, especially from the Chicago area, rather than directly from Europe. These and later Czech immigrants were usually small farm owners (*sedlák*) in

In 1904 the Rosebud Reservation was opened to homesteaders, the last government land lottery in the U.S. More than 100,000 would-be homesteaders came to six registration towns, including Gregory, on October 1 to register so that they would be in the drawing for the 4,000 available homesteads. *Center for Western Studies.*

their homeland and had sold their land to finance their relocation to America. This is likely why George Kingsbury, in his *History of Dakota Territory,* wrote that "as a class they [Czechs] were well provided with money, and some of them were reputed to be quite wealthy."[49]

The first Czechs came to southeastern Dakota Territory in 1869 and settled around Lakeport, seven to ten miles west of Yankton, and further west into Bon Homme County. By 1872 settlers decided to establish a Czech town. Purchasing a pre-emption quarter section in the spring of that year, they laid out the streets and blocks of what became the town of Tabor. The town grew slowly until the arrival of the railroad sparked a building boom. Since its founding, Tabor has remained the mother town of the Czech population in South Dakota. As late as the 1920s, nearly all the businesses in Tabor were owned by Czechs. Other smaller communities were founded later in the century as the flow of Czech immigrants moved ever westward. They took up land in Charles Mix, Douglas, Brule, and Buffalo counties, and still later across the Missouri in Gregory and Tripp counties. The 1900 federal census reported 2,320 South Dakotans born in Bohemia. In 1930 those of Czech extraction constituted nearly two percent of the state's total population.[50]

Much like the Scandinavians, Czechs had been nominal members of a state church in their native land. In this case the state church was Roman Catholic, and many Czech immigrants regarded it as part of the Hapsburg Empire's oppressive administration that they had left behind. Consequently, many Czechs became "Freethinkers" who were opposed to the Catholic and all other organized churches. This made them strong supporters of the American concept of the separation of church and state.[51] In Dakota these freethinkers, nearly equal in number to those who continued as practicing Catholics, regarded Omaha as their intellectual center. Since most of the Czech settlers in Dakota were farmers, it is not surprising that half or more of the freethinkers lived on the land rather than in the towns.

As a result of this religious division among Czech immigrants, Czech cultural heritage was not tied exclusively to the church. Like other immigrant groups, Czechs formed fraternal organizations as mutual-aid societies and to preserve their ethnic heritage. The most important of these in South Dakota was the Western Bohemian Fraternal Association, organized in Omaha in 1897. Membership was open to those of Czech or "mixed extraction" and was intended to "provide mutual opportunity for improvement, to furnish members relief in sickness and accident, to insure lives of members and children, to support Czech patriotic undertakings, especially schools and Sokol organizations and to establish Czech libraries. . . ."[52] Sokols, which originated in Prague and were sponsored by the fraternal lodges and Catholic congregations, focused on gymnastics as a vehicle to perpetuate the Czech culture, especially among the young.[53]

By 1917 the assimilation of the younger generations of Czechs in South Dakota was well underway. They had learned English in school, Americanized their names, and begun inter-marrying with other ethnic groups. World War I, which emphasized one hundred percent Americanism and suspected the patriotism of hyphenated Americans, was especially hard on Czech efforts to maintain the Czech language and culture. Fresh infusions of the culture by newly arriving immigrants sharply declined after Congress enacted restrictive immigration laws in the 1920s. The state's last Czech-language newspaper, the *Tabor Independent*, ceased publication in 1952. Only Tabor, the center for Czech culture in South Dakota, celebrates its heritage with an annual Czech Days festival each summer.[54]

■ Germans

By 1910 persons of German extraction had come to outnumber all other ethnic groups in South Dakota. The federal census of that year revealed that forty percent of the foreign born in South Dakota was German. While certain elements, such as the Germans from Russia, Mennonites, and Hutterites, have stamped their cultural imprint on specific areas of the state, broadly defined, Germans are more widely dispersed throughout the state than any other immigrant group. Indeed, Historian Anton Richter has noted that although the Germans from Germany outnumber the Germans from Russia, they are so spread out that they are not the ethnic majority in any South Dakota county.[55] Despite being so widely dispersed, by 1940 nearly seventeen percent of the state's population was either German-born or of German extraction.[56]

Germans arrived in the state in a generally steady stream regardless of the economic or environmental conditions of the time. Many were the offspring of earlier German immigrants in Michigan, Missouri, Wisconsin, and Minnesota and, thus, came to the state with some resources and an American education. Others came directly from Germany, Austria, and Switzerland often having spent a short time in these older German settlements before continuing to southern Dakota.[57] A concentration of East Frieslanders occurred in Lincoln and Turner counties in the 1880s, and Germans who came directly from Germany developed some compact settlments in Codington and Brown counties. *Schwarzmeerdeutschen* or Black Sea Germans came later, in the early years of the twentieth century, to settle in the counties of Edmunds, McPherson, Walworth, and Campbell along the northern border of the state.

The earliest German immigrants to Dakota Territory came from Russia rather than Germany. Their story is an interesting one, for although they had been in Russia for several generations prior to immigrating to the United States, they had kept their German cultural identity intact. Beginning in 1763 the German-born Russian Empress Catherine the Great had invited German farmers to come to Russia to develop Russian agriculture on the empire's vast undeveloped steppe. As encouragement, Catherine had granted these German farmers almost total autonomy within Russia. They established compact colonies where they had their own churches, schools, and local governments and were lightly taxed. Moreover, since many were pacifists, Catherine also exempted them from military service. All this allowed these Germans to maintain their language and culture for more than a century. In 1871, however, Czar Alexander II began withdrawing

This homesteading family, possibly Germans from Russia, proudly displays its most valuable possessions, especially its horses (ca. 1890). Such a photo assured relatives that the family was doing well on its frontier claim. Most homesteaders employed oxen in the early period because they were cheaper and hardier than horses. *Center for Western Studies.*

Catherine's concessions prompting many to seek a new location where they could continue their ethnic identity.[58]

While all were ethnic Germans, there were religious distinctions among those who came to Dakota Territory from Russia. Nearly all came from the area of Russia near the Black Sea where they had lived in colonies defined by a common religious belief. Some were Lutheran while others were Catholic, Mennonite or Hutterite. Delegations from the Russian colonies traveled to the United States in 1872-73 seeking land and the same privileges they had earlier enjoyed in Russia. Despite the United States government's refusal to grant such special privileges, beginning in 1873, several thousand Germans from Russia immigrated to Dakota.[59]

The first Germans from Russia, who came to Dakota in the spring of 1873, were of the Mennonite faith, but Lutherans and Catholics soon followed. In all, about 500 adult German-Russians arrived in southeastern Dakota in the first year. Unable to acquire sufficient government or railroad land to re-establish compact village agriculture, as they had known in Russia, they bought up land from private landowners in Yankton, Hutchinson, and Turner counties. Historian George Kingsbury, in his *History of Dakota Territory,* notes that these immigrants possessed substantial monetary resources that allowed them to purchase large amounts of land. The initial Mennonites settled near Yankton while Lutheran and Catholic Germans from Russia settled northwest of Yankton later in the same decade. By the end of the 1870s, the influx of Germans from Russia had expanded up the James River Valley to the Tyndall, Menno, and Freeman areas. These Germans from Russia were accustomed to farming on the semi-arid, treeless steppes of southern Russia and introduced new varieties of wheat that were well adapted to the Dakota environment.[60]

The German-Russian Mennonites and Hutterites held similar religious convictions but also had significant theological differences. Mennonites were followers of the seventeenth-century Friesian clergyman Menno Simons. A dissenter Anabaptist, Menno Simons added the doctrines of nonjuring and nonresistance to the Baptist creed, (i.e., a refusal to take oaths and to engage in violence and war). In these beliefs Hutterites were theologically similar to Mennonites. The chief difference was that Hutterites, followers of the sixteenth-century Tyrolean reformer Jacob Huter, believed in the early Christian practice of communal living as described in the second chapter of the New Testament book of Acts. Menno Simons won many converts in the Netherlands and adjacent Germany. The established Catholic, Calvinist, and Lutheran churches of Germany and Switzerland, however, persecuted the non-conformist Mennonites and Hutterites. Lutherans, Catholics, and Calvinists were also persecuted if they refused to conform to the religion of the local German prince. As a result, many German Mennonites, Hutterites, Lutherans, Calvinists, and Catholics responded to the invitation of the Russian empress and, in the 1760s, emigrated to the Black Sea and Caspian Sea areas of southern Russia.[61]

This distinction between Mennonites and Hutterites became obvious in the Dakota setting where Mennonites settled on separately owned homesteads while Hutterites established communal colonies. Forty Hutterite families came to Dakota in 1874 and established a communal colony in Bon Homme County. Later that year, another Hutterite group developed the Wolf Creek Colony in Hutchinson County. A third colony at Elm Spring began in 1877. All subsequent Hutterite communities in the state developed from these three initial colonies. Hutterite colonies in Dakota closely replicated the exclusive German villages in southern Russia. All property is owned in common and German is the everyday language; they have their own teachers and schools and there is a prescribed dress code. Although their agricultural machines and practices, as well as transportation vehicles, are modern, Hutterites retain many traditional ways of doing things. As a result, the Hutterites, more than any other ethnic group in the state, have maintained their separate cultural identity.[62]

Hutterites prospered in Dakota until 1917 when the United States entered World War I. Their religious doctrine of nonresistance and nonviolence forbade Hutterites to serve in the military or take part in any activity that contributed to the war effort. In the hysteria of wartime, state and federal authorities did not tolerate these religious convictions, and several young Hutterite men were sentenced to long prison terms for refusing to support the war effort. As a result of this persecution, which must have been reminiscent of their reason for leaving Russia forty years earlier, all but one of the fifteen colonies (the Bon Homme colony) emigrated to Canada prior to the war's end. The repeal of state laws banning the incorporation of communal societies during the Great Depression had by 1950 encouraged seven colonies to return to the state. By 2004 the Hutterite population in South Dakota had grown to 6,000 persons living in fifty-three colonies.[63]

The non-communal Mennonites, on the other hand, have assimilated into the larger English-speaking society of the state. Without exclusive domination of local institutions, Mennonites soon found assimilation unavoidable. Local government, business, and tax-supported schools all required knowledge of the English language, and interaction with non-Mennonites was a daily occurrence. Mennonites are most numerous in the Freeman area, and it is there that the greatest efforts were made to retain the German ethnic heritage. Mennonites organized the Freeman Junior College in 1900 to train teachers for schools where Mennonites dominated the school population and for the Hutterite colony schools. As a result of such efforts, the Bethesda Mennonite Church near Freeman continued to worship exclusively in German until 1938 when it moved to add an English-language service. By about 1950, however, attendance at the German-language service was such that the service was discontinued. Freeman Junior College closed in 1986, but Freeman Academy, a middle and secondary school of the Mennonite Church, continues to operate. An academy fund-raising event, the annual Schmeckfest, celebrates the German food heritage of the German-Mennonite community.[64]

As with virtually all other sizeable ethnic groups that immigrated to South Dakota, Germans supported a vigorous German-language press in the state. At one time or another, twenty-five German-language newspapers served the state's large German-speaking population. Newspapers in the immigrants' native tongue played a critical role in both assimilating them into the American culture and in helping maintain contact with their ethnic heritage. These newspapers communicated news from the "Old Country" from other German communities in the United States, and brought German and German-American literature to their German-language readers.

But newspapers also conveyed news about American politics, government, and history. In this way German-language newspapers helped first-generation immigrants retain an element of familiarity while at the same time easing their immergence into the unfamiliar American culture. Succeeding generations, having learned English in the public schools and being less interested in news from Germany, were inclined to read the more readily accessible English-language press. By 1917 there were four German-only and one German-English newspapers in the state. The German newspaper that persisted longest in the state was the *Dakota Freie Presse*, which began in Yankton in 1874 and ceased publication in 1950. Its long existence was due to its becoming the chief communication vehicle of the Germans from Russia throughout the United States, Canada, and, after a certain point, even of those who had remained in Russia. During World War I, the editors of all foreign-language newspapers were required to submit to the local postmaster an English translation of all articles about the war. This put great pressure on German-language newspapers. Violations resulted in the closure of the *Deutcher Herold* in Sioux Falls and the imprisonment of its editor and the eventual relocation of the *Freie Presse* to Minnesota. By 1928 all German-language newspapers had ceased publication in South Dakota.[65]

While Germans have remained proud of an ethnic heritage that included great authors, poets, composers, artists, philosophers, and religious leaders, the two world wars, which pitted the United States against Germany, long made it difficult for German-Americans to celebrate that heritage. Wartime patriotic propaganda portrayed Germans as barbaric, immoral, and a threat to western civilization. And Hitler's pogroms against Jews, Gypsies, homosexuals, and the handicapped raised questions about the core of German culture. But, with the establishment of West Germany as a democratic republic and as an American ally in the postwar period, it became easier for German-Americans to celebrate again their immigrant heritage. As a consequence, towns and cities with a large German ethnic presence have created annual October Fests to boost community spirit and celebrate this ethnic heritage.

■ Dutch

The Dutch were somewhat later than other ethnic groups in arriving in southern Dakota Territory. Few Hollanders had arrived prior to 1880, but that changed during the subsequent decades. By 1910 the federal census counted 5,285 South Dakota residents who were born in the Netherlands. Though fewer in number than the Scandinavians, Germans, and Germans from Russia, the Dutch have retained a visible presence in certain parts of the state. This is particularly the case in Douglas and Charles Mix counties where two Dutch colonies, first planted during the 1880s, became a magnet area for subsequent immigrants. The story of Dutch immigration to southern Dakota has two parts: a movement of individual families from adjacent parts of Minnesota and Iowa into the eastern counties of southern Dakota, and the organized establishment of the two Dutch colonies in the southern part of the territory. Although a large portion of these Hollanders was second generation, moving westward from older Dutch settlements in Michigan, Minnesota, and Iowa, others came directly from the Netherlands. All were seeking fertile, affordable land that would provide their families with a better future.[66]

Large-scale Dutch settlement in northwestern Iowa in the 1870s spilled over into southeastern Dakota Territory in the 1880s. The stream of immigrants from the Netherlands, earlier immigrant Dutch coming from other parts of the United States, and the younger generation of those who had acquired land in northwestern Iowa pushed across the Big Sioux River and took up land in Lincoln, Minnehaha, and Turner counties. Soon the movement had advanced up the Big Sioux Valley to Brookings, Hamlin, Deuel, and Grant counties. The early and mid-1880s was a period of abundant rain that encouraged land-seeking immigrants to settle in Dakota. For the rest of the century, even after less favorable weather patterns and economic conditions pevailed, there continued to be a steady movement of Dutch settlers into southeastern Dakota from the adjacent settlements in Minnesota and Iowa. The continued availability of land at cheaper prices was the main attraction.[67]

The Dutch colony established in Douglas County in 1882 was a well-organized project that originated in Orange City, Iowa, in 1881-82. This was to be a "daughter" colony of the one at Orange City, and the organizers sent two teams of men to determine a suitable location in southern Dakota Territory. In January 1882 the organizers decided to lay claim to the four western townships of Douglas County, and by April the first party of settlers had arrived at the site about twenty-five miles south of Plankinton. The inflow of Dutch settlers was so large and rapid that within two years all the land in these four townships had been taken. Not surprisingly, the first town, founded in 1882, was initially named New Orange. But in 1884, to honor Senator Benjamin Harrison of Indiana, who introduced a bill to divide Dakota Territory into two parts and admit the southern portion as a state, the name was changed to Harrison. Despite its prestigious name, Harrison never secured a railroad connection and lost out to Armour and Corsica, which did. Other towns founded in the next year or so included New Holland and Emden. By 1900 there were 235 families attending Dutch Reformed or Christian Reformed churches in the area.[68]

At nearly the same time, a second Dutch colony was taking shape in neighboring Charles Mix County. But, unlike the one in Douglas County, this colony had its origins in the Netherlands and was inspired by the Dutch "Moses," Albert Kuipers. Kuipers, a well-known farm innovator in the Netherlands, became interested in helping some of the struggling farmers in his district emigrate to America. In 1881 he sent his son Hendrik to the United States to find a site for a projected mass emigration. After exploring many areas from New Jersey to Iowa, young Kuipers reached southern Dakota and decided that Charles Mix County would be an ideal site for the colony. Hendrik and his father then began publicizing their colonizing project, and in April 1882 they, along with about two hundred families, left the Netherlands for America with Dakota Territory as their ultimate destination. Unfortunately, when they arrived in New York, immigration and land agents from other parts of the country scared the colonists with stories of wild Indians, rattlesnakes, and other dangers in Dakota. As a result the group broke up, with some going off to various places while only about thirty families continued on to Charles Mix County. The senior Kuipers had preceded the main party in order to claim land along

Platte Creek for the colony's location. The initial group of families arrived at the site on May 16, 1882, and quickly began to plough and plant. The Kuipers continued promoting the colony, and the group was soon enlarged by the arrival of countrymen from other parts of the United States and from the Netherlands. Within three years the colony consisted of about two hundred families. The primary town was Platte, but the colonists founded other towns that more clearly reflected their Dutch origins. Seven miles southeast of Platte, the colony founded the town of Overijsel, soon renamed Edgerton, and almost an equal distance southwest of Platte they founded Friesland.[69]

At the outset, the Dutch settlers were generally too poor to build a church or to hire a preacher. But religion was important to them, and people met in homes to listen to someone read a sermon from a book, to pray, and to sing favorite hymns. At a remarkably early point, however, these struggling settlers organized congregations, secured ministers, and built churches, even though the churches were usually small and occasionally made of sod. Furnishings were crude, but the theology, governance, and form of worship were a replication of what the worshippers had known in the "Old Country." The local *kerkraad,* or consistory, composed of the minister and several elders and deacons, watched over the congregation to make sure orthodoxy was maintained and members did not fall into worldliness. In the eyes of the *kerkraad,* Dutchness was part of the orthodoxy that was to be maintained. By 1895 there were eighteen Dutch congregations in South Dakota.[70]

The Dutch language was the vehicle of Dutchness, whether in the church worship service and catechism classes, the newspapers, on the street in Dutch communities, or in the immigrant homes. Dutch was the exclusive language of the Dutch Reformed and Christian Reformed churches until World War I rendered anything sounding German suspect. As in most other ethnic groups, the conversion to English in the Dutch churches was gradual and reflected a general decline in fluency among the second and third generations. By the end of World War II, Dutch was no longer used regularly as the language of church worship in Dutch communities. Although a few of the Dutch communities in Dakota had their own newspaper, none survived for long. Instead, the Dutch-language newspaper to which most Dakota Dutch subscribed was the *De Volksvriend,* published in Orange City, Iowa, until 1951. Public schools, the ever-increasing mass media, and greater travel all combined to assimilate the Dutch, like most other ethnic groups, into the greater American culture.[71]

Despite the virtual disappearance of the Dutch language within the Dutch communities of South Dakota, Dutchness has not entirely disappeared. There is a great pride in this ethnic heritage that is reflected in many ways. Certainly, the centrality of the Dutch Reformed and Christian Reformed churches is an important element of this heritage, as are the traits of industriousness and tenacity that were so important to the initial generation of Dutch immigrants.

■ Other Immigrants

In addition to the larger immigrant groups already discussed, several other European ethnic groups settled in Dakota Territory, and even though their numbers were small their presence has been visible. These include the English-speaking immigrants from the British Isles—the English, Irish, Scots, and Welsh—and those from Canada. Finally, a few Icelanders, Finlanders, and Jews from Russia also came to Dakota, some to stay while others left after a short time.

English

Professor Charles Green in his article entitled "The Administration of the Public Domain in South Dakota" writes, "The year 1883 saw several colonies of English and Scotch located in Yankton County."[72] But little else has been written about the English who immigrated to Dakota Territory. Federal census reports reveal that in 1890 there were 5,113 foreign-born English in the state, that this number declined to less than 4,000 during the 1890s, and declined by an additional 1,000 by 1920. Of those foreign-born English still in the state in 1930, more than half had come prior to the turn of the century. By 1930 foreign-born English were most concentrated in the central counties of Spink, Beadle, Sanborn, Jerauld, Hand, Hyde, Hughes, Davidson, and Hanson and in Butte, Lawrence, Pennington and Fall River counties in the far western part of the state. In none of these counties, however, did the foreign-born English constitute more than five percent of the total population. Unlike other nationalities, the English-speaking immigrants were largely urban in their settlement.[73]

Irish

Ireland sent more of its people to America than any other country, most of them emigrating in the two decades prior to the American Civil War. They fled hunger and poverty and were generally too poor to make it further than the large coastal cities of the American eastern seaboard. By the end of the Civil War, the Irish had spread across the Midwest facing bias in the job market and generally being relegated to menial jobs. Still, some Irish did manage to join the homesteaders on the American frontier.

As early as 1870, there were nearly nine hundred foreign-born Irish in all of Dakota Territory with most of them located in Clay, Yankton, and Union counties. Thirty years later, the 1900 census counted only about 3,300 foreign-born Irish in South Dakota. Unlike most other ethnic groups in the state, the Irish did not form concentrated settlements but were spread widely throughout the state. Minnehaha County in 1910 had the largest number of Irish but the total was less than two hundred.[74]

Some of the earliest Irish to enter Dakota Territory were members of the U. S. Army. Following the Civil War, the Irish constituted the largest foreign-born element among the troops sent to Dakota to pacify the Indians. The wages paid by railroad companies building lines into Dakota Territory also attracted a number of Irish, many of whom stayed. But the early promoters of Dakota Territory wanted homesteaders, and in 1869 one of the territory's immigration agents, John Pope Hodnett, undertook the goal of attracting to Dakota the many Irish who resided in eastern cities. He focused on the Irish community in Chicago, and, by the time he lost his position as agent, he had formed an Irish Emigration Society in the windy city. Without his leadership, however, the society disintegrated. While a number of Irish did immigrate to Dakota in the subsequent decade, Hodnett's dream of an Irish colony never materialized.[75]

Generally impoverished, the vast majority of Irish immigrants in America ended up in urban centers rather than on the land. In Dakota, however, a goodly portion of the Irish managed to acquire farms. By 1930 Irish constituted more than two percent of the population in only Lake, Union, Hanson, Lyman, Haakon, and Fall River counties. In none of them were they more than five percent of the population. Due to their scattered nature, there is no town in the state that reflects their culture. The major public expression of Irish culture tends to be an annual Saint Patrick's Day celebration in some of the state's larger urban centers. They are also a major element in the Catholic Church in South Dakota.

Scots

The 1870 federal census counted seventy-seven Scots in the territory, with the largest number residing in Union County. The quarry industry in the Sioux Falls area attracted a number of Scot stonecutters in the 1880s when that business boomed for a time. This and other work opportunities increased the number of foreign-born Scots in South Dakota to nearly sixteen hundred by 1890, but they have never constituted a large ethnic group within the state. Indeed, their presence is notable largely because Scotland town and Scotland township in Day County identify the Scots' place of concentration. It was in the extreme southwestern corner of Day County, at the foot of the coteau in Scotland and Oak Gulch townships, that the largest number of Scots settled in the state.[76]

A smaller concentration of Scots located at Lead in the Black Hills. These generally had immigrated to Dakota from other parts of the United States, but they remained proud of their cultural heritage. There were enough Scots in the Lead area for them to have an active Clan Stewart chapter of the Order of Scottish Clans and to maintain a bagpipe and drum troupe. In religion the Scots were Presbyterian and were an active element in the organization of that church in Lead.[77] By 1920 the number of foreign-born Scots in South Dakota had declined to fewer than one thousand.[78]

Welsh

Thanks to William D. Davies, a Welshman who toured Welsh settlements in America in 1890-91 and wrote a description of them in the Welsh language, we know something about the Welsh who settled in Dakota Territory. From Davies' account it appears that most of the Welsh who came to Dakota were from the neighboring states of Wisconsin, Minnesota, and Iowa rather than directly from Wales. A number of Welsh stonecutters found employment in the booming quartzite quarry business around Sioux Falls in the 1880s. The main body of Welsh homesteaders came to Dakota in the period 1870 to 1890. The high point, as revealed by the federal census, was 1890 when there were nearly seven hundred foreign-born Welsh in South Dakota. Ten years later that number had declined to fewer than 550.[79]

The first Welsh to arrive in Dakota came due to the efforts of William E. Powell, a Welsh poet who was an immigrant agent for the Milwaukee Road. Powell had traveled to Dakota in 1882 and was inspired to promote Welsh settlement there by the splendid crops and conditions he had observed. Powell advertised his Dakota project broadly in the United States and led some three hundred Welsh from neighboring states to Edmunds County in the spring of 1883. These were recent immigrants and the offspring of earlier immigrants who found land unavailable in the older Welsh settlements. All were attracted by Powell's description of Dakota, as having fertile and inexpensive land. Many of the initial settlers were single men, but they soon secured wives in the older midwestern Welsh settlements. When Davies visited Powell in Edmunds County in 1891, it was the largest Welsh community in the state. Davies also visited smaller Welsh communities in Aurora, Miner, Lake, Marshall, Brown, and Moody counties during his tour of the state.[80]

The Welsh in Edmunds County were encouraged during the first couple of years by abundant crops due to favorable weather. Unfortunately, after 1885 a series of dry years, coupled with significant grasshopper infestations and occasional prairie fires, caused some to leave the state. Still, as the census of 1890 confirms, not all were discouraged enough to leave, and their descendants continue to live in the area around Ipswich.[81]

Finlanders

In 1910 the federal census counted 1,381 foreign-born Finns in South Dakota. Most of the Finns who came to Dakota came from industrial mining areas in Minnesota, Wisconsin, and especially Michigan. One element of the Finnish immigrants established agricultural communities in the East River part of the state. The concentration of Finns at Lake Norden, in Hamlin County, and in Savo Township, in Brown County, is sufficient to keep the Finnish heritage visible in those communities.[82]

The other element of Finns in the state settled in the northern Black Hills, especially in the Lead area. Finns had become involved in mining in Michigan and were the largest Scandinavian element in the Lead mining district. Some who came from Finnish settlements in Minnesota engaged in dairy farming. While they were relatively few in number, the Finns brought their custom of the sauna to the northern hills, and it became their ethnic symbol. In religion and even food preferences, notably lutefisk, they shared in the larger Scandinavian culture of the area.[83]

In 1930 foreign-born Finns constituted somewhere between five and ten percent of the population in Harding, Lawrence, and Hamlin counties and between two and five percent in Butte and Brown counties.[84]

Jews from Russia—Am Olam

In the early 1880s a group of well-educated, secularized Russian Jews, disappointed in their hopes of achieving civil equality in Czarist Russia, chose to leave for America. These were not the Jewish immigrants of a slightly later period who settled largely in American cities. They were young, idealistic Jewish intelligentsia who turned to a Rousseauian concept of seeking simple self-sufficiency by living close to the land and working with their hands.

Am Olam, meaning the "Eternal People," was a movement founded by two Jewish teachers in Odessa in 1881 in response to the great anti-Jewish pogrom of that year. The object of the organization was to establish communal agricultural colonies in the United States. Chapters of Am Olam were soon organized in several other towns, including Kiev, Minsk, and Vilna. The first group of twenty-five families left for America in the late summer of 1881 headed for Louisiana to establish an agricultural colony of Russian Jews in America. A disastrous first year, caused by the weather and unhealthy environment, prompted the group to relocate to southern Dakota in 1882.[85]

The site the group selected for its colony in Dakota was about twenty-five miles southwest of Mitchell. The colony was named Cremieux in honor of the French Jewish philanthropist Adolphe Cremieux. The nucleus of the colony was the twelve families that had initially settled in Louisiana, but the number was soon doubled by the arrival of other families. The Cremieux colony was a corporation with a constitution. Members owned their own land, but there was a common colony treasury, permanent property belonged to the collective, and a two-thirds vote was required for major commercial decisions. It was a blending of private ownership and socialism.[86]

These were well-educated non-farming people who were ill prepared for surviving on the Dakota frontier. The colony enjoyed an active social and intellectual life, but the lack of farming knowledge in the end doomed the colony to failure. Weather, insects, and poor judgment had by 1885 caused the colony to begin unraveling. Some sold out seeking to salvage as much of their investment as possible, while others gave up their property to creditors. Several took jobs in area towns or took up whatever occupations they could find.[87]

A second Am Olam attempt to establish an agricultural colony in Dakota Territory fared no better than Cremieux. Initiated in the fall of 1882 about three miles northwest of Cremieux, this new colony, named Bethlehem Yehudah, began with optimism for success. They expected that the colony would prove "to the enemies of our people, that Jews are capable of farming." This colony consisted mainly of unmarried men and was more socialistic in its organization and operation. Despite rigorous discipline and hard work, the same factors of weather, insects, drought, and lack of farming experience brought an end to the colony after only a year-and-a-half of existence. The common property was divided up in the hope of stimulating greater success, but by 1885 Bethlehem Yehudah and Cremieux were both abandoned. Since the colonists were secular, non-practicing Jews, most probably blended into the wider urban culture of the state or left the territory.[88]

■ Taking the Land

When the Lewis and Clark expedition of 1804-06 explored what would become South Dakota, neither its members nor anyone else could have foreseen that this vast prairie-plains region would be populated and converted to farms within a century's time. Yet that is what happened. A combination of circumstances pulling from this side of the Atlantic and pushing from the other, together with new steam-driven transportation technology, made the nineteenth century one of mass migration to the plentiful land of trans-Appalachian America. This rush of New England farmers and entrepreneurs and European peasants quickly overflowed the Old Northwest, leaped the Mississippi River into Minnesota and Iowa, and on the eve of the Civil War breached Dakota Territory. Less than thirty years later, southern Dakota east of the Missouri River had been converted from buffalo-grazing prairie to farms, villages, and cities.

The settlement of the trans-Missouri portion of the state, larger and physically unlike that east of the Missouri River, had a different development. The counties comprising the Black Hills were organized in the 1870s as part of the gold rush era, but the remainder of West River Dakota remained the Great Sioux Reservation until 1889-90. At that time the federal government convinced the tribes to relinquish large portions of their reservation land. When these lands were opened to white settlers around the turn of the century, a new stream of homesteaders came to claim land and establish farms. Early in this period rainfall was plentiful in this arid part of the state. This atypical weather encouraged migrants from the older parts of the state, from adjacent states, and from abroad to establish farms in this West River country. Unfortunately for these hardy pioneers, the wet cycle ended in 1911 causing many to abandon the area. The population of this part of the state has never been large, and the foreign-born have constituted a smaller portion of the population here than in the eastern part.

While the founding of towns was an important part of South Dakota's settlement story, it is primarily a story of land-taking. Yankees came from the rocky hills of New England and immigrants arrived from northern Europe and Scandinavia, all intent on acquiring what they could not acquire at home: good farm land. They came as individuals, families, and members of colonizing groups. Those who did not speak English tended to settle in or near other settlers who spoke their own language. In some of these ethnic enclaves, it was possible for the immigrant generation to live out their lives without ever learning more than a few words of English. And it was in these rural ethnic communities that the old country heritage was preserved longest. Still, the assimilation process was too strong for any but the Hutterites to resist for more than a generation or two. In this sense the Yankees won the cultural struggle that transformed these immigrant peoples into English-speaking Americans.

Chapter 9
African Americans

■ Adventurers and River Men

When the Lewis and Clark Expedition crossed Dakota on its long trek to the Pacific Ocean, it was accompanied by York, William Clark's personal slave and boyhood companion.[1] Reports of this American black man aroused great curiosity among the Indians of the interior. On the "moccasin grapevine," there had always been tales of the occasional shadowy "black white man" who appeared with Spaniards or Frenchmen, or who had been seen by trading Indians, working in the lead mines below St. Louis or as servants on the trading post itself.[2] Indeed, York's presence, together with that of the Indian woman and her infant, served as a disarming influence as the expedition met assorted tribes.

Born in Virginia, York is described by those who encountered him as "a remarkably stout, strong Negro, black as a bear." Over the course of the expedition, he earned the respect of his colleagues as a productive, valued member of the party. He was a powerful swimmer, a skilled hunter, and a courageous companion. He seems also to have been an intelligent, good-humored man, willing, up to a point, to become the object of invasive personal curiosity for Indians who wished to examine this strange human being more closely. At the request of his master, Clark, he even performed for their hosts with displays of physical strength or dancing exhibitions. York's contribution to the expedition's success undoubtedly gave him the confidence, on their return, to press Clark for his freedom. Recently published letters from William Clark to his brother Jonathan suggest that Clark, a slave owner by practice and cultural inclination, was extremely unwilling to free this slave. During the years between the end of the expedition and York's manumission, the two were frequently at odds. Eventually, York received his freedom and established a business hauling freight between Nashville, Tennessee, and Richmond, Virginia. Scholars differ about the circumstances of his death, but the most commonly accepted version is that he died of cholera en route to St. Louis sometime before 1832.

With York began the first of numerous separate waves of African Americans who, over a period of two hundred years, experienced the land that one of their number, Oscar Micheaux, called the Great Northwest.[3] Most merely passed through the area, seeking their fortunes elsewhere. Many of the earliest worked in the rich fur industry. Fur company ledgers identify a number of these men by name and trade and provide tantalizing clues to lives mainly undocumented. Two of the most famous and best documented who traveled extensively in Dakota Territory were the mountain men Edward Rose and Jim Beckwourth. Both worked in the fur trade and both had Indian as well as African ancestry. As well, both had long, colorful histories with both Indians and whites, and both were regarded with suspicion by their white bosses, although there was grudging agreement that they were, indeed, competent men, worthy of the excellent salaries they earned. Both were adopted into Indian tribes and spent long months living with them, where they were highly respected and held leadership positions.[4]

Other African Americans appearing in the trading company rosters include Francoise Duchouquette, who, with Ed Rose, accompanied the St. Louis-to-Astoria overland expedition that left St. Louis in 1810; Baptiste Pointsable, the mixed-race son of the black frontiersman who founded Chicago; and Cadet Chavalier, a "free mulatto" who worked in the fur trade from 1802 to 1812 when he lost his life traveling with Manuel Lisa on the Upper Missouri River.[5]

By the mid-1820s Pierre Chouteau's family firm dominated the commercial activities in the Upper Missouri Basin. Peltries obtained upcountry were transported down river in keelboats or bullboats, often crewed by African Americans. These were dangerous, backbreaking trips with frequent casualties. On one trip, in March 1829, a keelboat loaded with passengers and some four hundred peltries bound for St. Louis, under the command of Francois G. Chouteau, met its demise because of a drunken black pilot. Baptiste Datchurut, a free black man who sometimes worked as an interpreter, was married to an Indian woman and was a good pilot when sober. On this voyage, however, a combination of his impairment, high water, and a strong southern wind drove the boat onto the rocks near Prime's Ferry. Three men drowned, but Chouteau was able to get ashore and commandeer a flatboat that saved the passengers. The damaged boat dangled precariously over the boiling river, an entire season's furs now submerged and presumed lost—until the quick thinking and personal bravery of the African cook, Joseph Lulu, saved it. Lulu dived into the water some thirty-seven times, each time bringing up a pack of furs. His bravery earned him his freedom, and he continued his career as a fireman on a Mississippi steamboat.[6]

By the 1830s regular steamboat service up the Missouri to Fort Union and beyond created opportunities for adventure, business, and the spread of Christianity. The trading posts and forts established by the fur monopolies became tiny urban centers in a huge, unforgiving wilderness. They employed a great variety of individuals and traded with the Indians and the scattering of non-Indians, living, working, or passing through. These people came in all races and varieties, including African Americans—free or slave. Most stayed a while before moving on. Some, like Isaiah Dorman, who was probably a runaway from Louisiana, lived quietly with his Indian wife and two sons, avoiding white contact and working as a trapper and woodchopper. He was a competent man of many skills. When word of freedom reached the wilderness, he turned up at the military forts where he obtained several contracts to serve as an interpreter or mail carrier. He served honorably in these positions for a number of years, making a good living for his family. An old friend of Sitting Bull and other Sioux, he was the only African American in Custer's ill-fated march on the Little Bighorn—perhaps drawn to that service in hopes of seeing his old Indian friends again. After the battle, he perished in the arms of Sitting Bull.[7]

A second wave of African Americans to South Dakota was a direct result of expanding river transportation. Slaves and free blacks worked on the great inland riverboats with their cutting-edge steam technology. In the heady days immediately after Emancipation in 1865, some found work on the forts along the Upper Missouri. Stretching along the Missouri River from Fort Randall on the south to Fort Union on the north, these military forts maintained order between the white settlers on the east and the Great Sioux Nation on the west. Of the ninety-four African Americans identified in the Dakota Territory census of 1870, more than two-thirds were working on these forts. They worked as laborers, body servants, cooks, woodcutters, and general factotums, performing a variety of duties as civilian employees. Many were quite young, suggesting that they took advantage of an opportunity to see new country and perhaps save some money while tasting freedom and having a bit of an adventure. Although nearly every fort employed one or more of these workers, the largest number were employed at Fort Sully on the east bank of the Missouri near the present town of Onida. Interestingly, most did not choose to make this a career. The 1880 census shows a turnover of nearly one-hundred percent at all locations, and by the end of that decade, the forts were gradually closing down.[8]

As frontier steamboat trade gained importance, there were increased opportunities for African American workers on the Missouri runs. They held many jobs, including cook, roustabout, fireman, and pilot.[9] River ports from St. Louis to Bismarck became second homes to these men and women. When they tired of life on the river, they often settled permanently in these ports, buying property and creating a core of old, stable black communities along the river route. Others chose to get as far away from the river as possible. Some became the first black settlers in and around the tiny settlement of Sioux Falls.

■ Early Urban African American Settlements

The first of the Dakota Territory river towns to develop an important black colony was probably Yankton, followed closely by Bismarck in present-day North Dakota. For many black workers, these settlements began as way stations, offering temporary housing along the levee for a few days or during the off-season and a chance to look over the prospects for a more permanent residence. In the chaotic pre-Civil War era, white territorial lawmakers throughout the west had seriously debated whether to allow the African Americans even to settle, much less buy property, vote, or have access to equal educational opportunities. Fortunately, the Dakota territorial legislature, after heated debate, tabled the issue. When they took it up again, cooler heads prevailed and no restrictions regarding race became law.[10] This guarantee of equal access surely was a factor considered by potential black settlers.

By 1870 there were small, stable black settlements in Yankton and Sioux Falls, launching a new wave of African American settlement. In Yankton, especially, many newcomers were small businessmen or skilled craftsmen from the South or the more populated eastern states. In a new country where everything had to be built from the ground up, hard-working, diverse laborers with talent and skills were welcome and immediately found work. By 1883 there were enough African Americans in town to establish a small African American Methodist Episcopal (AME) congregation on a choice city lot they had purchased on Cedar Street. They called their new church Allen Chapel in honor of Richard Allen, who had founded the black denomination. Among the earliest members of the congregation were Henry Robinson, who owned his own barbershop, and John B. Shaw, the successful proprietor of the City Restaurant on Third Street between Cedar and Broadway. Shaw was greatly respected and served a term as local constable. Another restaurateur was C. T. Chapman, whose daughter, Katie, attended Wilberforce University, married George Tillman, one of the early pastors of Allen Chapel, and became a successful writer and pastor's wife, serving mainly in Iowa. Amos Lewis was a master plasterer whose work still exists in some of the town's oldest houses. LeRoy Kinney, a veteran of the Union Army and a former riverboat engineer, became a building engineer in town and was a charter member of the local Grand Army of the Republic (GAR) chapter. Some of his descendants still live in the area.[11]

About the same time, a smaller black community was emerging in Sioux Falls, although among African Americans there is an oral tradition that some found the town less congenial. Local historian David Kemp has identified a tombstone in the Minnehaha

Cemetery as that of "Alice Clark, A Colored Girl," buried there in 1878. The *History of Minnehaha County* identifies Dr. Richard Lamb and family as the first permanent black settlers. Lamb, born in Newcastle, Indiana, in 1832, was trained as a physician and might have been Dakota Territory's first black professional. With his wife, Agnes, a Minnesota native, and year-old daughter, Nora, and newborn son, Jesse, he arrived in time for the 1880 census, which records their presence. Eleven other black residents are listed in that census, including two barbers, at least one farmer, and two black women who appear to be married to white men.

Dr. Lamb was not able to make a living as a physician, although in 1885 he was listed as a member of the South Dakota Medical Association. He supplemented his income by operating a barber shop at 130 N. Phillips Avenue. The Lambs were able, however, to make a successful life in Sioux Falls and were joined before 1900 by other enterprising entrepreneurs who carved out niches for African Americans as barbers and hairdressers.[12]

After 1900 the African American community grew rapidly. Many newcomers joined barber and beauty businesses. A popular barbershop was operated by Wilbert Wright, at 115 N. Phillips Avenue, near the Cataract Hotel. It served the town's leading citizens and offered regular employment to newcomers, some of whom eventually established their own shops. Louise and Harvey Mitchell, both experienced in that industry, arrived in 1906 and became community leaders. For many years, Mrs. Mitchell owned and operated the beauty shop at Shriver Johnson's, the town's leading dry-goods store. Eventually, the couple opened the California School of Beauty, which trained many young hairdressers, including a number of black women, in the art of cosmetology. The community soon became strong enough to support two Baptist congregations.[13]

Two African American urban settlements resulted from railroad expansion across the state. Although the Mitchell community was never large, the Bentleys, Coopers, Walkers, Brookses, and Williams families formed a close-knit community.[14] In Huron, to the north, with its important railroad hub and agricultural trading center, the African American community was large enough early in the century to support Bethel AME Church and provide a good livelihood for twenty or so families who enjoyed the town's egalitarian atmosphere.[15]

■ Treasure Seekers and Buffalo Soldiers

In 1874 the United States government sent General Custer on an expedition to the Black Hills to determine the extent of its gold deposits. The expedition departed from Fort Lincoln near Bismarck. The only woman in the party was the redoubtable Sarah Campbell. She was an African American woman hired by the sutler, John Cook, a civilian trader who sold amenities to the soldiers—whiskey, specialty foods, and other provisions. Ms. Campbell, familiarly known as Aunt Sally, was an elderly warm-hearted, dignified woman of considerable skill, culinary and otherwise, who more than carried her weight during the long, difficult trek. A colorful personality, she attracted the attention of reporter William Curtis, traveling with the expedition. He published a long interview with her during which she identified herself as "the first white woman that ever saw the Black Hills" and characterized her as "having been up and down the Missouri ever since its muddy water was broken by a paddle wheel, and having accumulated quite a little property, had settled down in Bismarck to ease and luxury." Ms. Campbell loved the Hills and succumbed to gold fever along with the rest of the expedition, staking her claim and later returning to the Hills, where she lived out her life, a beloved and colorful figure.[16]

The Custer Expedition opened the Hills to an influx of gold seekers, including African Americans, some of whom did well at mining for gold. Others did better at mining the gold miners. Among those who successfully mined the gold were Anderson Daniels, formerly of Yankton, who struck it rich in Lead City when he discovered gold in a vein that ran under his house.[17] Five African American hopefuls had the last laugh on a local joker who sent them to mine a claim that he knew had no water and believed was worthless. Using ingenuity and persistence, they managed to bring in enough water to recover the gold, which eventually amounted to over $75,000.[18] Others prospected with less success in the gold fields, but more success in building lifelong friendships with their neighbors.

Those who did very well at "mining the miners" included Lucretia Marchbanks, whose kitchen was considered the finest in the West. A dignified spinster, she was deeply respected for her fine character and her charitable good works.[19] The census records of 1880 show more than two hundred African Americans residing in gold country, especially in and around Deadwood. They worked at a surprising variety of occupations besides the handful of placer miners. Occupations include barbers, restaurateurs, woodcutters, porters, housekeepers, liquor dealers, cooks, bakers, boardinghouse proprietors, laundry workers, teamsters, prostitutes, farmers, and hotel keepers.[20]

For many years, the territorial frontier had been garrisoned by units of the U.S. Army, stationed at forts up and down the Missouri River. Until 1880 these troops had always been white, and their presence had become a fact of life for settlers in the area. That year, however, the 25th Infantry (Colored), which had spent ten boring years on the hot, dusty plains of West Texas, was rotated into Dakota Territory. Their work in Dakota would be similar to that performed in Texas: scouting, providing guard and escort duty,

Battalion of the 25th Infantry on parade, Fort Randall, Dakota Territory. Although battalions of the 25th were on duty in Dakota Territory through 1888, they were stationed at Fort Randall only from 1880 to 1882, after which they were transferred to Fort Snelling, Minnesota. *Courtesy National Archives.*

stringing miles of telegraph wires, and building roads. From a home base at Fort Randall, where the majority were stationed, other units were ordered to Fort Hale, up river from Fort Randall, and Fort Meade, southeast of the village of Sturgis on the northern edge of the Black Hills. In nearly every respect, their service in the territory was exemplary, and their fine sports teams and regimental bands lent enthusiasm to many local events. Some veterans chose to stay in the area after their enlistment expired, forming a nucleus of African American families with deep roots in Dakota.[21]

While the black troops were at Fort Meade, there were a series of unfortunate incidents involving the soldiers and a number of unscrupulous businessmen, some of whom were also black. Like all soldiers far from home, the newcomers found the heady nightlife of the goldfield towns irresistible. Abe Hill, a black saloonkeeper, together with others of his ilk, both white and black, were quick to take advantage of the situation. A well-documented combination of too little constructive policing and too much temptation created an unsavory atmosphere that led to several well-publicized and unpleasant incidents involving a few black soldiers and a few locals before the military was able to reassert its authority over its members and restore order.[22] To their credit, the 25th served out their time in Dakota Territory, acquitting themselves honorably, before moving to their next station in Montana in 1888.

■ Homesteaders, Ranchers, and Cowboys

One of the first and most successful homesteaders was Norval Blair of Illinois.[23] Born in slavery in Tennessee, circa 1829, and emancipated only with the end of the Civil War, he had done so well on his Grundy County, Illinois, farm by 1870 that his less prosperous white neighbors were beginning to resent him. That year's census showed that his small farm and personal property were worth $4,000, a considerable sum in that era. He had been fortunate in his marriage to a half-Cherokee woman, Mary Elizabeth Bagby, and their seven children were fine young adults. They were a close-knit family that demonstrated considerable economic teamwork. Still, by the early 1880s, their presence in the county was becoming uncomfortable and they began looking for a new opportunity. In 1884, with a tidy sum set back for the investment, Blair sent his two oldest sons, Benjamin P. Blair and Patrick Henry Blair, ages thirty-four and twenty-eight, respectively, to Dakota Territory to scout out prospects in Fairbank Township, Sully County, Dakota Territory. Located on the banks of the Missouri River at a likely spot for a new bridge, Fairbank Township was in the middle of a huge land boom. The Blairs were pleased to find a new, large hotel, post office, grocery store, two newspapers, a racetrack, skating rink, and the foundation laid for Fairbank University. Other investors found the Blairs personable, well educated, and apparently well heeled and welcomed them into the little community. Before sending for the rest of the family, the Blair brothers closed the deal on a choice piece of land with an excellent water supply on the northwest quarter of Section 1-115-80, just outside of town. Although the town of Fairbank never amounted to much and the railroad bridge was never built, the Blairs prospered. While the neighbors struggled along in shanties, they lived comfortably in a "fine house." The seeds and livestock from Illinois did well on the arid plains, and their fine Morgan foundation stock became the base for a string of outstanding racehorses that eventually enjoyed considerable reputation throughout the Midwest.

For more than twenty years, the Blairs lived quietly in Sully County. Ben Blair became a leader in South Dakota's scattered black community, and in 1906 he became involved with a group in Yankton interested in the national movement to create "colored colonies" of farmers throughout the Midwest. Sully County had plenty of land available and the Blairs were excellent role models. Ben Blair's sister, Mary Elizabeth (Betty), became interested in the settlement opportunities and joined forces with the King Real Estate Company of Iowa. She was a canny, successful saleswoman and over the next several years was able to close land deals with several like-minded, upwardly mobile former slave families who moved to Sully County. Among the most prominent and most successful was the John McGruder family, from northern Missouri, who arrived with a large string of livestock and a prairie steamer that was used to break the tough prairie ground.

By 1910 Fairbank Township boasted twenty-one households, eight of which were black, and, of the nineteen households in neighboring Pearl Township, four were black. Another black family resided in Troy Township, immediately to the north. Most of the families came from Iowa or northern Missouri, and most had enough financial resources to get settled. Many of the households consisted of older couples with no children, but there were, that year, a dozen youngsters under eighteen, including a couple of grandchildren and nieces. Over the next twenty years, the Sully County Colored Colony survived and even prospered, despite the punishing droughts and over-speculation that gripped the northern Great Plains. Although families came and went, the colony remained in existence until the late 1920s, when the combination of dust bowl and depression worked its worst. In the early twenty-first century, only the remnants of the McGruder clan remain on the family land, proud of their pioneer heritage.

South of Sully County on the Rosebud Reservation was the homestead of South Dakota's most famous African American homesteader, Oscar Micheaux. An ambitious young bachelor from southern Illinois, he learned of opportunities on the Rosebud when it opened for settlement while he was working as a Pullman porter and scouting a likely location in which to build his agricultural empire. In 1904 he purchased a relinquishment in Gregory County and later married and joined the boom that accompanied the open-ing of Tripp County. Micheaux was a successful farmer, well respected in the area, for some eight years before drought, over-speculation, and a nasty divorce wiped him out. He was an ardent booster of the Rosebud, writing and preaching to African Americans about South Dakota opportunities. In 1913 he self-published a book about his experiences in Gregory County, *The Conquest: The Story of a Negro Pioneer*, and followed that memoir with six other books written over the course of some thirty-five years. Writing led him to the infant motion picture business, where Micheaux eventually became the most prolific and successful of the independent African American motion picture producers. Over a film career spanning more than thirty years, he created and released some forty black-cast films for black audiences.[24] Still, a part of his heart remained with his beloved "Great Northwest," and he returned to that experience numerous times as themes for his films and one of his last books, a novel entitled *The Wind from Nowhere*.

Micheaux, a man with a considerable ego, enjoyed casting himself as the only Negro farmer west of Omaha. Whether he actually had contact

Oscar Micheaux is seen here shortly after he abandoned homesteading and embarked on his career as a writer and independent filmmaker. *Courtesy South Dakota State Historical Society–State Archives.*

with the thriving Blair colony to the north and other successful black farmers elsewhere in the state will probably never be known. Among those who were contemporary with the Blairs, McGruders, and Micheaux were the Blakey brothers who came to Yankton in 1904 at the behest of one of the state's great all-time boosters. Tom Douglas, of Yankton, was a former slave who sometimes went by a former slave name, Christopher Columbus Yancy. He was a widely traveled opportunist with a few years of education, courtesy of one of his masters. He had considerable drive and, like Micheaux, saw South Dakota as a great place to build new lives. For some years he traveled in the mid-South, promoting the area in struggling African American settlements. Douglas, married to a German woman and the father of five strapping sons, owned land, ran a restaurant that sometimes doubled as a gambling hall, and was rumored to have an interest in a local house of ill repute. He was a huge man who carried himself well and commanded a grudging respect from white community leaders. When he brought the Blakey brothers to Yankton from northern Missouri, he provided them with temporary housing in some "shacks" he owned, and sent them out to work for a local farmer. Henry and Isaac Blakey were so taken with the area and the friendly acceptance of the people that they eventually purchased eighty acres along the river bottom and began a prosperous truck-gardening business. Later, other members of the family joined them, forming the nucleus of a new black community that endured well into the late twentieth century.[25]

In Mellette County, the large McAllister family, formerly of Kansas City, Missouri, raised Black Angus on several large adjoining spreads and enjoyed excellent acceptance in and around the community of Belvidere.[26] Further to the west, Robert Bailey, a former Buffalo Soldier, and his good friend, Ed Barnett, settled on adjoining ranch spreads outside of Edgemont, where they raised large families and became respected members of the community. A son, Bertis Bailey, was the only African American serviceman from South Dakota to give his life in World War II. He died on a battlefield in Italy. Another son, William, one of the last of the clan, had a long, colorful career in the military, as a hobo, and as a businessman and nightclub owner in the Reno of the 1940s, before returning to the home place, which he shared with a sister until their deaths in the late 1990s. They are buried in the Edgemont Cemetery.

Among the other black farmers or ranchers who settled and remained in the Black Hills area were the Wards, near Custer, Kate Reynolds, of Deadwood, and the Kerchervals, who had come to the Black Hills as part of General Custer's entourage.[27] Rapid City's African American population was proportionately quite small in the early days. However, old-timers fondly remembered the large Graves family who arrived from Iowa in 1886. Mr. Graves and five of his children performed with a traveling troupe known as the Woods and Roberts Show, calling themselves the Graves Family Band. A son, Frank Graves, attended Rapid City High School where he won the match footrace championship the year the family moved to town. Later, Frank and his brothers Hance and Charles were members of a local volunteer fire department and were teammates on the Central City Hose Running Team.[28]

■ The Hard Years—1920s-1960s

The era following World War I was an especially difficult time for blacks. Although the racial climate for African Americans in South Dakota in the early years seems to have been relatively benign, the ugly, discriminatory Jim Crow customs that had begun in the South had spread throughout the land. Driven by the economic competition of an increasingly technological era, the post-war years were distinguished by a series of bloody race riots in large cities and increasing suspicion and estrangement elsewhere.

In South Dakota, although the schools were never segregated, de facto segregation in housing, jobs, and public accommodations became the rule. Often, the discrimination was subtle, but it was well understood by those on the receiving end. African Americans, Indians, and other people of color well knew which restaurants, barber shops, or hotels would not serve them, which neighborhoods were closed to them, and which jobs were considered suitable only for white people. When white people did, on occasion, discuss these customs, it was often with embarrassment and discomfort. Leonard "Bud" Williams, who grew up in Mitchell and, after retiring from the army, served as the city's mayor, described a typical response in a 1976 interview with Robert Eggers as, "You know, I'm not prejudiced myself, but if I did thus-and-so, why, then this would cause me to lose my business and people would say this and this and this."[29] For many years, white people ignored the situation, believing that it was not their problem. People of color went along with the game, especially after the state's brief flirtation with the Ku Klux Klan in the early 1920s.

On a national level, the Klan had been revived in the wake of World War I. Its rhetoric was couched in the then-popular language of patriotism and nativism. In an era when fraternal lodges were important recreational outlets for families, it presented itself as an affordable alternative to old-line secret fraternal organizations. Although it was a serious threat to African Americans in many parts of the nation, the rhetoric and violence in South Dakota was directed at rising Protestant fears about an influx of Catholics, mainly from eastern Europe. Klaverns sprang up in Beresford, Sioux Falls, Canton, Elk Point, Oldham, Redfield, Deadwood, Rapid City, Pierre, Huron, Yankton, and other population centers.[30] To the credit of white South Dakotans, many people of good will who had joined the Klan terminated their membership as soon as they realized its true agenda.

Meantime, however, South Dakota's black population was greatly concerned. Many maintained close ties with family and friends in other parts of the country where the Klan was a clear and present danger. These concerns prompted the organization of a state National Association for the Advancement of Colored People (NAACP) chapter

The Sioux Falls chapter of the Ku Klux Klan gathers in Woodlawn Cemetery. In addition to hating African Americans, the KKK was fiercely anti-Catholic and anti-Semitic. *Center for Western Studies.*

in 1920.[31] Although African Americans might not have been the Klan's primary target, blacks worried that their rallies were often conducted at locations close to black neighborhoods. Arthur Hayes grew up in Yankton in the 1920s. At that time, the town had a very large Catholic population and one of the largest black populations in the state. He remembered that the Klan "used to meet in an open field about two blocks from our house, and between that field and our house was a cornfield . . . and in the summertime they would be out there night after night, burning their crosses . . . and we kids were scared of them, but we'd crawl out in the field as close to them as we could, and lay there quiet as mice, watching . . . listening. . . ."[32] The Great Depression eventually turned the state's attention from the Klan, and by the end of the decade the organization was of little significance anywhere in the state.

Times had been hard on the plains for many years before the national disaster of the stock market crash of 1929, but in its wake South Dakotans suffered extreme adversity. Inevitably, people of color suffered the most. Sara Bernson and Robert Eggers write that the 1930 census reported that only 308 out of 645 African Americans who claimed South Dakota residence held jobs, and 118 of the ones working held jobs classed as "Domestic and Personal Service." None were working in the professions, and the remaining 171 who had jobs were doing unskilled work in manufacturing, transportation, and communications. Those who remained on the farms were plagued by drought and grasshoppers that nearly destroyed the Sully County Colored Colony. By 1940, only eighteen people remained in the colony.[33] Some moved out of the state. Other landowners were forced to become tenant farmers. George Day, proudly descended from the original colonists, moved his family to a rented farm near Huron. The loss of their Sully County farm remains a painful memory for his son, Melvin Day. As a man approaching his seventieth birthday, he bitterly recounted the terrible hurt and anger his family felt when white bankers of Onida County found money to save the lands of local white farmers arguably no more successful than they. Somehow, there were no funds to help the black farmers of the Sully County Colored Colony.[34]

Young men from the Yankton community migrated to jobs in Sioux City or Omaha. Young Hazel Warren, daughter of one of the longest established black families in Huron, gave up her dream of attending university and voice training and opted instead for a short course at Mrs. Mitchell's California School of Beauty and part-time classes at Huron College.[35] Mrs. Mitchell trained so many black women in cosmetology that, by 1940, six percent of the total African American work force in the state was working in the field.[36]

The Great Depression brought out the best in the statewide black community. Those who had resources helped those who did not, and mem-

A pioneer in the fields of beauty culture, shops, and schools, Louise Mitchell, who came to Sioux Falls in 1908, was the first African American on the YWCA Board of Directors and the Community Chest Board. *From* South Dakota Negro Yearbook, 1902.

bers of the younger generation were helped to complete their education and find work. Some worked with the Civilian Conservation Corps and other government programs. To combat the persistent discrimination by white hotels in Sioux Falls, the Mitchell family spearheaded the opening of the Booker T. Washington Service Center in 1930. This all-purpose social and community center provided lodging and work for students like the Coakley boys who were struggling to finish high school. The center also provided hotel services for black travelers, including prominent entertainers denied access to the city's white-owned hotels.

One of the most unique efforts at community building was the tradition of the South Dakota Annual Picnic. Organized in 1930 by Louise Mitchell, Harvey Bentley, and Pastor M. W. Withers, of Sioux Falls, the project was joined by leaders of Yankton, Huron, and Mitchell's African American communities and soon became an annual event. Since most of the population was east of the Missouri River, the picnic sites were rotated among Sioux Falls, Yankton, and Huron. Always held on the first Sunday in July and often attended by one hundred or more South Dakota African Americans, the celebration featured down-home cooking, games, and cultural enrichment activities that often included a speaker from outside the state. In addition to providing important social and cultural opportunities, the picnics offered an opportunity for networking, especially during hard times when people needed to pull together to ensure everyone's survival. The picnics continued for more than thirty years, first under the chairmanship of Harvey Bentley for twenty-five years, and then under the leadership of Ted Blakey.[37]

The agony of the Great Depression and the boom of World War II created a temporary decline in the state's black population as old families went elsewhere to seek better opportunities. More than thirty young men from black South Dakota served in the military, and Leonard "Bud" Williams found in his army service a career that would change his life. Others who remained in the state during the war found opportunities to fill business niches vacated by drafted businessmen and went on to create prosperous, long-lasting enterprises.

The Rose Room Club was a social spot for the African American community of Sioux Falls. *Courtesy Upper Midwest Black History Museum Collection.*

The declining population was offset by the massive mobilization of national resources during World War II, when airports and colleges became training bases for young men desperately needed for the war effort. In South Dakota, Sioux Falls and Rapid City were targeted as large-scale training bases. Of the two, Rapid City had the most difficulty coping with the influx of a large contingent of African American airmen. In Sioux Falls, the careful structure built by the Mitchells, Bentleys, and local pastors, and supported by an NAACP chapter with both black and white members, was able to provide the necessary social services from which black servicemen were customarily excluded. St. John's Baptist Church became the black USO, and, when it was outgrown, a local businessman and NAACP member, Benjamin Margulies, donated the use of one of his properties rent free. A coalition of black and white community leaders came together to begin to think about the town's restrictive customs and to plan for ways to overcome them. This made the post-war and subsequent civil rights changes easier for the town to manage.[38]

In Rapid City no such mechanism existed. Relations between the white community and the sizable communities of Lakota people had always been contentious and bitter. The arrival of many black servicemen added to an already difficult situation. Problems arose from the outset over issues of off-base housing for dependents and access to public accommodations, including restaurants, bars, and hotels. The post-war upgrading of the training base to a new Ellsworth Air Force Base coincided with the executive order that desegregated the military. It poured federal money, federal contractors, and servicemen, including black servicemen, into the area. The 1940 population of 13,884 ballooned to 25,310 just ten years later, and by 1960 it had grown to 42,399. Change was slow, agonizing, and sometimes nationally embarrassing as the latest racial incident was trumpeted in the *New York Times* and other national media.[39]

As the federal government's influence was brought to bear on old Jim Crow customs and laws, especially where federal dollars were being spent, South Dakotans gradually acknowledged their own prejudices. Among the issues dealt with were the long-standing problems of exclusion and discrimination with respect to public accommodations, housing, and jobs. In 1962 the South Dakota Advisory Committee to the U.S. Commission on Civil Rights announced a series of open meetings in Rapid City to try to work out the issues between the town and the airbase. The governor and the legislature took its findings very seriously. Shortly after the committee adjourned, South Dakota became the twenty-ninth state to adopt a policy of non-discrimination because of race or color, and took its first steps into a world that would never be quite the same again.[40]

Post-World War II federal dollars also came into the state to build the great dams on the Missouri River. This work offered employment to many, including people of color. Ted Blakey, who rose to prominence in the state as an independent businessman in Yankton, got his start when he was hired for a good job on the Gavin's Point Dam.

The 1960s brought a new sense of inclusion for the state's African Americans. There had always been a few fine high school and college athletes like Cleveland Abbott, whose athletic accomplishments at Watertown High School and South Dakota State University were legendary, leading to a sterling career as coach and professor at Tuskegee Institute. However, as the state's colleges and universities welcomed students of color, a variety of gifted athletes attained recognition. Sports fans were treated to performances by superb African American athletes who fit in well with the local home boys.[41]

During this era, the American Legion Boys State saw three black governors. Several high schools and colleges elected African Americans as homecoming royalty, and black students from all over found that they could receive an excellent and affordable education at any of the state's colleges and universities. A few liked the area, married local spouses, and stayed.[42]

Other newcomers were older. One who became a state leader was William P. Mahone, retired undertaker and Pullman porter, who married Hazel Warren, a successful businesswoman in her own right, and settled in Huron. Mahone became active in the American Legion, eventually serving as commander. He also worked with the local group that brought the town's senior citizens center into being, and was part of the inter-racial committee that included Dr. Arnett Matchett, a Sioux Falls veterinarian with the U.S. Department of Agriculture, Ted Blakey, Maurice Coakley, and Ben Hamilton that helped to repeal the state's outdated poll tax. On January 23, 1974, South Dakota became the thirty-eighth state to ratify the national amendment, which became law just five days later.[43]

Sidney and Corrine Milburn, recent graduates of Tuskegee Institute, were looking for a small town outside the South where they could set up a veterinary practice. In 1957, after considerable thought, they chose Elk Point, where Mrs. Milburn taught in the high school and Doc opened an animal clinic.[44] They became active members of their church and community. Later, Dr. Corrine Milburn served as assistant dean of the Department of Education at the University of South Dakota. This couple found that the "Great Northwest" worked just fine for them, as it had for Oscar Micheaux.

Leonard "Bud" Williams retired from the army with the rank of Lieutenant Colonel and returned with his wife to his hometown of Mitchell. Williams had been the state's first African American Eagle Scout, and on his return he plunged back into the volunteer work he had always loved, including scouting, American Legion, and Young Men's Christian Association (YMCA). He served for a time as director of the town's YMCA and later as coordinator of student affairs for the Mitchell Area Vocational Technical Institute. Subsequently, he entered local politics and served several terms as a popular mayor.

Sam Boykin is the state's other African American mayor. After finishing a military career at Ellsworth Air Force Base, he made his retirement home in the small town of Box Elder, where he was active in community affairs and, ultimately, was elected mayor.

■ New Era—A New Century

Many changes affecting African Americans have come to South Dakota in the last thirty years. The expanding job market in the state's cities has encouraged urbanites from all over to find in the heartland a possible respite from crime, overcrowding, and confusion. In the mid-1970s, Sioux Falls recruited the prestigious Earth Resources Observation Systems (EROS) Data Center, a branch of the U.S. Geological Survey, Department of the Interior, which created some six hundred high-tech jobs for government and contractor employees, including well-qualified professional and technical people of color. In the early 1980s, Yankton College, facing bankruptcy, was purchased by the U.S. Bureau of Prisons as a minimum security facility, bringing both staff and prisoners of African American extraction to the town. Non-government employers came as well, notably Citibank's Sioux Falls credit-card facility. Medical facilities expanded in Rapid City, Yankton, and Sioux Falls, and their staffs include a growing cadre of health professionals and physicians of color.

Recently, a wave of brand-new "African Americans" has come to South Dakota with the arrival in Sioux Falls of African immigrants from Sudan, Ethiopia, Mozambique, and Somalia. These newcomers are already bringing their special flavor to the town with the opening of businesses unique to their several cultures.[45] Elsewhere in the state, there is a new awareness of South Dakota's black history. The annual Oscar Micheaux festival, begun in Gregory in 1995 to honor the black filmmaker, has become an intimate, prestigious film festival drawing filmmakers and scholars from across the country each August. At least two black artists, Joyce Jefferson and sculptor Porter Williams, portray various historical figures from South Dakota's black history at events throughout the state. In tiny Roslyn, black entrepreneur and motivational speaker Lawrence Diggs, sometimes known as "The Vinegar Man," operates his vinegar museum. In Deadwood's old Chinese quarter, where African Americans also lived, archaeologists and scholars are reconstructing in considerable detail the lives of the early pioneers of color. Consideration is also being given to establishing a South Dakota Black History Trail.

The 2000 census showed a black population in South Dakota of 5,100. In a state whose total population is only 756,600, this is a significant percentage. The state's multicultural base can be expected to expand in coming years to include more people of color from many parts of the world.

Chapter 10
Cities and Towns

The urban history of South Dakota began when Native American tribes established villages along the rivers and streams of the state long before Europeans discovered the western hemisphere. Most, if not all, of these urban sites were abandoned or converted to white settlements beginning in the 1850s when town-founding was a speculative enterprise of individual entrepreneurs, townsite companies, and expanding railroads. Transportation and agricultural technology have played crucial roles in the urban history of South Dakota by generally reducing the number of towns needed to serve the state's population. But the booster spirit of town leaders has also been a determining element in the success of many towns in the state. All of these factors will undoubtedly continue to play important roles in shaping the history of South Dakota's urban centers.

The language of townsite founders on the American frontier, according to historian Daniel Boorstin, was "The language of anticipation."[1] The founders of towns on the Dakota frontier followed the formula that had been invented on the earlier frontiers of Ohio, Indiana, and Tennessee and been perfected as the frontier had moved ever westward across the Upper Midwest. The men who founded these new towns understood, writes Boorstin, that "Rewards went to the organizer, the persuader, the discoverer of opportunities, the projector, the risk-taker, the man able to attach himself quickly and profitably to some group until its promise was tested."[2] In addition, these newly termed "businessmen" of nineteenth-century American society believed in the natural connection between public and private prosperity. And most of these frontier urbanizers came from the American Northeast or were one generation and one jump west from there. As noted in Chapter 8, they were "Yankees," and they understood how government worked and, even more importantly, they understood how to make government work for their own benefit.

There was a geographical dimension to the founding of towns, or at least to the sites where they were planted. Before the coming of the railroad, sites on navigable rivers, and especially at the junction of two rivers, held greatest promise. Often these had been the sites of Indian towns or where fur traders had established their trading posts because water made the transportation of goods and people fastest and easiest. Steamboats needed lots of wood to stoke their boilers, and in some instances steamboat landings naturally evolved into townsites. Smaller streams, too, offered good opportunities for townsites, if waterpower could be developed for local industry. And, of course, the discovery of valuable minerals led to the creation of supportive towns, though their future usually depended on the continuation of profitable mineral production.

The railroad and the steam engine overcame the tyranny of geography in the locating of frontier towns. Railroads were more direct and dependable than rivers and steamboats, and they were cheaper to construct than canals. Steam engines, more dependable and portable than waterpower, freed frontier industry from being confined to river or stream-side townsites. Navigable rivers like the Missouri gave towns founded along its banks initial success over rival inland towns. But it was the railroad that evened the playing field. A rail line could be built virtually to any location and carry bulky agricul-

Chronology

1841 – Pre-emption Act passes, giving squatters purchasing rights to land they improve

1850s – Native American settlements converted to townsites or abandoned

1856 – Sioux Falls townsite founded by Western Town Company (Iowa)

1857 – Big Sioux County formed

1858 – Yankton Sioux cede land for Sioux Falls

1861 – Yankton appointed first capital, Dakota awarded territorial status

1862 – Dakota War

1864 – Renewed settlement along Missouri River

1865 – Fort Dakota established at Sioux Falls

1869 – Colony of Bohemian families established near Yankton and Bon Homme

1871 – Sioux Falls City established

1873 – Germans from Russia immigrate to Dakota

– Panic of 1873 causes an economic crash

1874 – Custer leads expedition to the Black Hills for gold

1876 – Battle of Little Bighorn, Teton Dakotas cede Black Hills

1878-87 – Dakota Boom

1879 – Deadwood burns, rebuilding begins immediately

1881 – Penitentiary awarded to Sioux Falls, railroads enter the city

1883 – Sioux Falls becomes first town in Dakota to adopt new lighting technology

1888 – Cleveland signs bill opening Great Sioux Reservation, reducing reservation to five smaller reservations

1891 – Hostilities end in last Indian war

1901 – Sioux Falls power companies spark debate over public utilities

1908 – First electric trolley built in Sioux Falls

1910 – Severe drought causes towns in central Dakota to fold

1920 – Automobiles open Black Hills to tourism

1927 – Gutzon Borglum begins carving Mt. Rushmore

---

tural and manufactured goods cheaply and dependably, even when rivers were frozen or flooded.

Indeed, railroads created towns and caused entire towns to move. Single-track rail lines needed sidings every eight to ten miles to allow trains running in both directions to pass one another. Railroad companies laid out townsites at these sidings to encourage the homesteaders who would become their customers. These were the railroad towns where farmers could sell their crops and buy their needs without having to travel long distances by wagon over primitive roads. Towns founded prior to the coming of the railroad either obtained a railroad connection or died. In many cases, towns by-passed by the railroad packed up and moved to the railroad. In this life-and-death effort to obtain a railroad, townsite promoters induced railroads to build to their location by offering free right-of-ways and depot grounds and liberal grants of money. Indeed, railroads often demanded such inducements before agreeing to build their line to a town.

An individual, group of individuals (a townsite company), or the railroad (or its officials) might initiate the founding of a town on the Dakota frontier, but, when the founders were joined by other businessmen, there was a clear understanding that their individual successes were tied to the success of the town as a whole. Every new town had the possibility of a bright future, and local boosters liberally employed the language of anticipation to attract the people who would make their real estate more valuable and their businesses successful. But if a community lost its promise of success, people quickly moved on to another community that offered a new chance for the illusive success they sought.

In the same way, but on a larger scale, the businessmen of all the towns in Dakota understood that the prosperity of their communities was tied to the success of the territory as a whole. While towns competed with one another for railroads, residents, and the business of the countryside, as residents of Dakota Territory they all also competed with neighboring states and territories for settlers and the largess of the federal government. Initially, there was the frantic effort to obtain from Congress official territorial status. When Minnesota was admitted to the Union as a state in 1858 with its current western boundary, the portion of the former Minnesota territory beyond that boundary was left without organized government. Efforts to gain territorial status for Dakota began almost immediately, for much was at stake. Government gave legitimacy to the land-taking and townsite enterprise, provided authority to make and enforce laws and to settle disputes. It also provided jobs and access to federal funds.

Government was any territory's earliest and most lucrative industry. While all aspiring townsites could unite in seeking territorial status, they competed vigorously to become the territorial capital, for that designation would virtually guarantee a town's future. Yankton won the initial designation as capital when Congress finally granted Dakota territorial status in 1861. To keep the losers content with their lesser status, the territorial legislature distributed territorial institutions among other principal townsites. Vermillion received the federal land office and university while the territorial prison was promised to Bon Homme. When funding for construction of a penitentiary was finally available in 1881, Bon Homme was in decline, and Sioux Falls, with its dramatic growth and rising political importance, secured the institution.

If having the capital was a boon to a city's anticipated success, the same was true, on a lesser scale, for a town that gained the designation of county seat. South Dakota history is replete with stories of how battles to become the county seat were won and lost. Being the county seat meant jobs and money, for people in the entire county had to come to the courthouse town to conduct legal business. Being the county seat did not guarantee a town's future, but it certainly could be an important contributing factor.

In the nineteenth century, Americans who had money to invest typically invested in western land or frontier industries rather than the stock market. There was money to be made in western land, not so much in farming it as in buying and selling it. The federal

As the capital of Dakota Territory from 1861 to 1883, Yankton enjoyed an early advantage. Moreover, its location on the Missouri River afforded Yankton commerce even before the railroad reached it in 1873. Townsites not on the Missouri River, like Sioux Falls, Brookings, and Canton, languished until serviced by railroads in the late 1870s and after. *Courtesy Yankton County Historical Society.*

159

government, beginning with the Land Ordinance of 1785, devised a system for the disposal of western land that generally favored the large investor. After it was surveyed into townships and sections, the government auctioned off land to the highest bidders with the minimum price being $1.25 per acre. Wealthy investors bought up large tracts of western land and held it to sell at a profit to actual settlers. To avoid these middleman speculators, many settlers went to where land was not yet surveyed and squatted on government land. The drawback to squatting was that these settlers usually were outbid for their claim when it finally came up for auction and thereby lost their investment in clearing the land and in any buildings they had constructed. With no organized government yet established in the area, squatters organized claim clubs or squatter governments to provide a semblance of local law and order and to protect their claims against more wealthy bidders.

This situation finally caused Congress to pass a temporary pre-emption act in 1830, which was refined and made permanent in 1841. This law gave squatters first right to purchase their claim to 160 acres at the minimum price of $1.25 an acre, providing they had built a house and lived on the land for at least six months. This was a boon to actual settlers whose aim was to farm the land. However, it also opened the door to a whole new group of transient land speculators. Using a variety of ruses to convince federal land office officials that they had satisfied the technical requirements of pre-emption, these smaller-scale speculators simply acquired their claims at the minimum price with the intention of reselling it for a profit.

Speculators also used the pre-emption act to acquire prospective townsites. If money could be made selling farmland by the acre, selling land by the town lot could make much more. When entrepreneurs learned of a likely townsite on the yet-unsurveyed frontier, they often formed a company to claim the site and promote the town's development. Men were hired, supplies purchased, and transportation arranged to send an expedition out to claim the promising site. To be the first to claim the townsite meant being out ahead of the line of settlement. It might take years before a townsite attracted the settlers required to produce a return to the company's investors. This was an expensive and risky undertaking, and townsite companies represented the pooling of the investment capital required to give townsite speculation the possibility of success. Farmland was bought and sold by the acre, but townsite land was bought by the acre and sold by the lot (usually 25 or 30 feet by 120 or 140 feet for commercial lots and 50 or 60 feet by 120 or 140 feet for residential). With about two-and-one-half acres in a standard city block, the investment cost of just the land, at the pre-emption price of $1.25 an acre, was less than $3.15. Even doubling that cost by allowing for streets, the cost of the land was minimal and the potential for profit great. If a promising townsite could be acquired through pre-emption and town lots could be sold at fifty to two hundred and fifty dollars or more, the townsite company investors could reap a good return on their investment. Still, there were lots of risks involved in townsite speculation, and not all townsites were financially successful.

The first site in Dakota that attracted the interest of townsite speculators was the falls of the Big Sioux River. Waterpower offered the potential of industry and enhanced the site's potential to evolve into a successful town. There has been some controversy over how townsite speculators learned of this geographical feature, which made the site such a prime location for a town. The *History of Southeastern Dakota,* written in 1881, is the oldest published source, which explains why a group of men in Dubuque, Iowa, organized the Western Town Company to claim a townsite at the falls of the Big Sioux River. W. W. Brookings, the author of the section, which covers the origins of

This 1882 drawing of Sioux Falls appeared in the December 7, 1882, issue of the *Sioux Falls Pantagraph* and shows a town that had grown from six hundred residents to nearly 5,000 within the previous five years. Note the falls and the newly completed six-story Queen Bee Mill at the extreme lower right (and in the inset). The city thought it had a bright future in industry and in serving the rapidly developing countryside around it. Residential developers had laid out a number of blocks and planted trees around them in anticipation of home builders who would want shade trees as soon as possible. *Center for Western Studies.*

the Western Town Company, was a member and official of the company when it laid claim to 320 acres surrounding the falls in 1857. He writes that it was Joseph Nicollet's description of the falls in the account of his explorations in western Minnesota in 1839 that inspired the company's formation.[3] Later historians, like Dana Bailey in his 1899 *History of Minnehaha County* and George W. Kingsbury in his 1915 *History of Dakota Territory,* adopted that explanation.[4] The problem is that Nicollet never reached the falls of the Big Sioux River, and his book does not include a description or even an indication that there was such a place. Other writers ascribe the discovery to Captain Joseph Allen who, with a detachment of cavalry, camped at the falls on September 13, 1844, while exploring the Big Sioux River. The probable truth is that Jacob Ferris used Captain Allen's report when he published his *History of the States and Territories of the Great West* in 1856. Company records confirm that it was the Ferris publication that inspired Dr. J. M. Staples of Dubuque to organize the Western Town Company.[5]

By October 1856, the hastily organized Western Town Company had hired two men, Ezra Millard and D. M. Mills, both of Sioux City, Iowa, and instructed them to find the falls and claim for the company 320 acres of the land surrounding them. The two men found the falls, but almost immediately were confronted by Indians who sternly commanded them to leave. Faced with this hostile reception, the two men beat a hasty retreat to Sioux City. Six weeks later, however, Mills returned, reinforced by several more company men, and claimed the land for the company. After building a log cabin on the island at the head of the falls, the group retreated to Sioux City for the winter.[6] Four representatives of the Western Town Company returned to the falls in May 1857 to protect and improve the townsite. This turned out to be a prudent move, for a few days after arriving at the falls a delegation representing the Dakota Land Company, a St. Paul, Minnesota, townsite group, also arrived to claim the site. Discovering that they were too late to acquire the prime site that included the falls, the St. Paul company claimed 320 acres further upstream along the river.[7]

The Dakota Land Company investors had a larger vision than just developing townsites. They were intent on founding a town that would become the capital of a Dakota Territory, which they expected to be made from the western portion of Minnesota Territory. Most of the company's stockholders were members of the Minnesota legislature, and during the winter of 1856-57 they had defined the western border of the imminent state of Minnesota so as to leave the Big Sioux River and the falls outside the boundary of the new state. They were all members of the Democratic Party, and with Buchanan, a Democratic president in the White House, they expected to have a new territory organized and a townsite they owned designated as the territorial capital. The Dakota Land Company representatives had left St. Paul in May 1857 planning to claim several prime townsites along the Big Sioux River. They struck the river first near present-day Brookings and laid claim to a townsite they named Medary after the then governor of Minnesota. Further south on the river, they claimed a site they named Flandreau after Judge Charles E. Flandreau of St. Paul. They were, of course, disappointed to discover that they had come too late to claim the main falls of the Big Sioux. They named their second-best site Sioux Falls City.[8]

The claims of both townsite companies at the falls of the Big Sioux were confined to the eastern bank of the river, for a treaty with the Yankton Sioux had not yet opened the area between the Big Sioux and the Missouri rivers to white settlement. There was much anticipation of such a treaty, especially by those who believed the eastern bank of the Missouri River beyond the Big Sioux offered many excellent townsite possibilities. Two men who understood the potential of the Missouri River sites were D. M. Frost and John B. S. Todd. Both had come to Dakota as army officers, but Frost resigned his commission in 1853 to go into the fur trading business, and Todd did the same two years later and became Frost's partner. Their business headquarters was a store in Sioux City, but Todd, as the sutler at Fort Randall, directed the company's activities in the area east of the Missouri River.[9]

In 1857 the Interior Department had sent A. S. H. White, an attaché of the Indian Bureau, out to convince the Yankton tribe that it should cede to the federal government the land between the Missouri and Big Sioux Rivers. White had failed in his assignment, but later that year the department asked Todd to take up the task. Todd hired as interpreter Charles F. Picotte, a white-educated Indian whom it was said "Had great influence with the Indians." The two men began negotiations with tribal elders. They early on won the support of the principal chief Struck by the Ree, usually referred to as "Old Strike." Other chiefs were not so easily convinced. Thus, Todd led a large party of Yankton chiefs and interested whites to Washington, where the chiefs would meet "The Great White Father" and be persuaded to sign a treaty of cession. The chiefs arrived in the middle of February, but it took two months before all the chiefs agreed to sign the cession treaty on April 19, 1858.[10]

In February 1858, while Todd and the chiefs were in Washington, Frost at Sioux City organized the Upper Missouri Land Company. This new organization was a townsite company, consisting of the members of Todd, Frost & Company and a number of prominent Sioux City men. These townsite speculators, anticipating the terms of the land cession treaty then being negotiated in the nation's capital, expected to establish towns at each of the Frost, Todd & Company trading post sites west of the Big Sioux River.[11]

When the treaty-making party arrived back in Dakota in May, it reported the terms of the treaty. For about seven cents per acre, the Yankton chiefs had ceded to the federal government more than eleven million acres of land. The tribe was to retain a 400,000-acre reservation in what became Charles Mix County, and they were given one year in which to move their villages out of the ceded area and onto the reservation. During that year, there were to be no white settlers allowed into the ceded area with one major exception. The treaty specifically allowed Frost, Todd & Company the right to purchase, for $1.25 an acre, a quarter section of land at each of their trading post sites. Frost, Todd & Company selected a quarter section fronting on the Missouri, the site of Chief "Old Strike's" village, as the townsite of Yankton and chose similar sites on the James, Vermillion, and Big Sioux rivers. These claims included the future towns of Elk Point, Vermillion, and Bon Homme. By this process, Frost, Todd & Company evolved from a fur trading company into a townsite company, an evolution they and their Sioux City investors had apparently envisioned from the outset.[12]

By 1858 two separate groups of Dakota land speculators, those at Sioux Falls and those on the Missouri River, were eager to have Congress create Dakota Territory and designate their town as the territorial capital. Territorial status was crucial to the success of townsite speculators, for until there was legal government and a land office to record deeds, the flow of settlers to Dakota would be minimal. Genuine settlers, the customers for towns and their merchants, were crucial to making town property valuable and townsites successful.

The townsite speculators at Sioux Falls were the first to launch a movement to gain territorial status from Congress. Through the influence of the Dakota Land Company, the Minnesota legislature in 1857 created Big Sioux County, consisting of the area later defined by the Dakota legislature as Minnehaha and Medway counties. Governor Alexander Ramsay of Minnesota Territory appointed officials for these two counties from among the representatives of the two townsite companies residing at Sioux Falls. When Minnesota received statehood in May of 1858, Big Sioux County was purposefully left outside the new state's western border as the starting point for a new territory. The Dakota Land Company had intended that Medary would become the capital of the new Dakota Territory. But in the early summer of 1858 Yanktonais Sioux, who refused to recognize the Traverse des Sioux Treaty of 1851, forced company men to abandon the Medary and Flandreau townsites and burned all the buildings they had erected. Dakota Land Company representatives took the Indian threats seriously, for the memory of the Spirit Lake massacre of the previous year was still fresh in their minds. Despite the danger, the people at Sioux Falls, which now included one woman, decided to stay and defend their claims. They constructed a fort of sod which they defended until help arrived later in the summer. As a consequence of these developments, the Dakota Land Company transferred its territorial capital ambitions from the abandoned Medary to its claim at Sioux Falls City.[13]

By October 1858 the townsite promoters at Sioux Falls were no longer part of Minnesota, and consequently they created a squatter legislature to establish temporary government pending the creation of Dakota Territory. This legislature adopted the laws of Minnesota Territory and elected a governor and other officials. Most importantly, Alpheus G. Fuller was elected to carry a petition to Congress for the creation of Dakota Territory. With a Democrat, James Buchanan, as president and a Democratic majority in both houses of Congress, the Dakota Land Company investors, all Minnesota Democrats, expected their petition would be granted. They also expected that Sioux Falls would be designated as the territorial capital, and that many of them would be appointed to territorial offices.[14]

Confidence was running so high that S. J. Albright of St. Paul brought a printing press to Sioux Falls in the fall of 1858 and began publishing the *Dakota Democrat*, the first newspaper to be printed in Dakota. His goal in starting the newspaper was to be on the scene when Dakota became a territory and Sioux Falls was made its capital. His eye was on the contract to do the public printing, which would assure him a regular and substantial income.[15] The Dakota Land Company had encouraged Albright to come to Sioux Falls, for every hopeful townsite needed a newspaper with which to boost the town. It already had the other crucial element, a hotel dubbed the Dubuque House, which the Western Town Company had erected of stone in the fall of 1857.

Fuller arrived in Washington in the spring of 1859 only to discover that the territorial delegate from Minnesota, W. W. Kingsbury, had not yet vacated his seat in the House of Representatives. Kingsbury argued successfully that, until his term expired in March 1860, he still represented Big Sioux County and other portions of Minnesota Territory that had been excluded from the new state. Congress at this time was dividing over the slavery question, and southern members of Congress opposed the creation of additional anti-slavery states or territories. Thus, the politics of slavery frustrated the hopes and expectations of the Dakota Land Company.[16]

In 1859 the group at Sioux Falls convened another squatter legislature, which elected W. W. Brookings governor, former Governor Henry Masters having died. Voters chose Jefferson P. Kidder, a recent arrival from St. Paul, over Fuller as delegate to Congress. In the election for territorial delegate to Congress, over a thousand votes were canvassed in Medway County, even though Indians had emptied the county of white settlers the previous year. Indeed, a total of over five hundred votes were supposedly cast in the Sioux Falls settlement when only twenty-five settlers were actually known to be there. Imaginary voters were also counted for Vermillion, Rock, and Pembina counties. This creative voter turnout was designed to convince Congress that Dakota had the population required to deserve territorial status.[17]

The Dakota Land Company not only created fictitious voters, in 1859 it also advertised in the *Dakota Democrat* that it had established a number of anticipated towns: Renshaw near Lake Preston, Medary on the Big Sioux near present-day Brookings, Flandreau fifteen miles south of Medary, Sioux Falls City, described as "The recognized capital of the territory," Eminija at the mouth of the Split Rock River, "The more practicable head of navigation for large steamers [on the Big Sioux]," and Commerce City, halfway between Sioux Falls City and the Missouri, possessing "Coal and timber plenty." The company also had the audacity to announce that it had laid claim to all the best townsites along the Missouri River from the mouth of the Big Sioux westward to old Fort Lookout.[18]

In November 1859 Frost and Todd organized an initiative to achieve territorial status for Dakota with their principal townsite, Yankton, the hoped-for capital. Todd went to Washington in the winter of 1859-60 carrying a petition for territorial status with the signatures of what he claimed were 428 actual settlers. His presence doomed Kidder's hopes for quick congressional recognition. Indeed, Congress refused to consider either petition. Todd continued his lobbying efforts in Washington during 1860 without success, so in January 1861 Yankton organized another mass convention to promote the movement for territorial recognition. The signatures of 478 supposed settlers were on a new petition that was forwarded to Todd in Washington. By the time this petition arrived in the national capital, the situation in Congress had been changed by the withdrawal of senators and congressmen from seceded southern states. Todd, as a cousin to the wife of President-elect Lincoln, was able to use his new influence to get congressional passage of a bill "To provide a temporary government for the Territory of Dakota and to create the office of surveyor general therein." President Buchanan signed the bill into law on March 2, two days before leaving office. With Lincoln in the Executive Mansion and Republicans in control of Congress, the patronage of administrative and judicial appointments in the new territory went to Republicans. Lincoln rewarded his Springfield friend and supporter Dr. William Jayne by appointing him governor of the new territory, and Jayne chose Yankton as his capital city.

The townsite speculators at Sioux Falls, having been tied to the losing political party in the 1860 election, had lost the coveted prize of territorial capital and all that would have meant for the potential of their townsite. But even worse was to come in 1862 when the Dakota War in Minnesota spilled into southeastern Dakota and caused the abandonment of Sioux Falls. Nearly every other prospective townsite in the territory except Yankton was at least temporarily abandoned. Women and children were sent east to the security of families in longer settled areas while the men stayed in Dakota to protect their claims the best they could. Preoccupied with its desperate effort to subdue the southern rebellion and preserve the union, the federal government was unable to spare army troops to provide Dakota settlers protection from hostile natives. The year 1864 also witnessed the first experience of drought and grasshopper problems in Dakota. All of these factors resulted in few settlers venturing into Dakota until after the South surrendered. Only then could the army spare soldiers to garrison forts and give settlers in Dakota Territory a sense of security against Indian attacks.[19]

With the ending of the Civil War in April 1865, land and townsite speculators renewed their interest in Dakota's future. But for these speculators to realize their hopes and ambitions it was essential to attract settlers to the territory. In 1862 the Republican-dominated Congress had encouraged the westward movement of settlement by enacting a homestead act that went into effect on January 1, 1863. This new piece of federal land policy offered a quarter section of public land to any adult citizen (or person making a declaration to become a citizen) who paid a small filing fee, built a house, and lived on the land for a minimum of five years. The earliest instance of renewed settlement in Dakota came in the spring of 1864 when sixty families, members of the "Free Homestead Association" of Syracuse, New York, settled along the Missouri Valley. Some of these settlers founded the town of Lincoln which later was renamed Meckling.[20] The decade of the 1860s generally favored the portion of Dakota along the Missouri River. The valley itself was attractive to prospective farmers and experienced a steady inflow of settlers, including numerous Norwegians. Yankton was especially successful in this period because of its role as a supply point for the Indian reservation and the army garrisons. The discovery of gold in Montana also stimulated river traffic, and Yankton and other riverboat towns like Vermillion benefited. Yankton also benefited from its role as territorial capital and county seat. By 1870 it was an incorporated city with about 1,200 residents and possessing several hotels, two churches, a public school, and two newspapers. Yankton was the most successful townsite in the territory.[21]

In 1870 there were few actual towns in Dakota Territory, and nearly all of them were in the Missouri Valley. The first real town west of Sioux City was Elk Point, the county seat of Union County. Claiming a population of around five hundred, Elk Point even boasted a weekly newspaper. Fifteen miles further west a traveler would come to Vermillion on the bank of the Missouri River. Vermillion had an early advantage over most competitors. It was the county seat of Clay County, the site of a U. S. Land Office, the location of the First Judicial District, and a busy river port. It could boast of a population of about six hundred, with two hotels, a newspaper, a sawmill, a number of stores, and several lawyers and doctors. Crossing the Vermillion River by the government bridge and traveling eight miles west, one came to the town of Lincoln. C. N. Taylor, a member of the New York colony that had come to Dakota in 1864, had founded this town (renamed Meckling when the railroad came through) that centered on the hotel that he and his wife kept for travelers. Besides the Taylor hotel, Lincoln possessed a sawmill, blacksmith shop, a schoolhouse, and one store. Sixteen miles further west there was Yankton, territorial capital, county seat of Yankton County, and an incorporated city of 1,200 residents. Twenty miles more brought one to Bon Homme, county seat of Bon Homme County, consisting of two stores, a hotel, a schoolhouse, a blacksmith shop and a scattering of residences. Springfield, eight miles west of Bon Homme and only recently established in 1870, had the promise of success due to the presence of a federal land office, a store, and a small hotel. Springfield also benefited from being across the Missouri River from the new Santee Indian Agency and Reservation in Nebraska. Beyond Springfield there were only military installations.[22]

During the late 1860s settlers came in greatest numbers via Sioux City into the adjacent Union and Clay counties. An exception to this general trend was a colony of five hundred Bohemian families from Illinois that settled near Yankton and Bon Homme in 1869 giving those two towns a major economic boost. The construction of the Sioux City and Pacific Railroad to Sioux City in 1868 had increased the flow of land-seekers into southeastern Dakota. Thus, as the decade neared its end, the flow of homesteaders had moved further up the Big Sioux, Vermillion, and James river valleys, while a smaller stream of settlers had come across southern Minnesota by wagon to take up land in Minnehaha and Lincoln counties. In 1868 the site of the old Dakota Land Company's projected Commerce City, twenty miles south of Sioux Falls, became Canton when a post office was opened there, and it was named county seat of Lincoln County. By 1870 Canton had several stores, two hotels, a schoolhouse, and a population of over one hundred. Its name originated in the belief that the site was on the opposite side of the world from Canton, China. Other trading posts and post office locations, like Eden in Lincoln County and Granville and Mapleton in Minnehaha, Curtis in Clay County, and White Swan and Harney City near Fort Randall, ultimately failed to develop into full-fledged towns. By 1870 few settlers had taken up land north of Minnehaha County, and no mail route existed north of Sioux Falls in the Big Sioux Valley. The federal census of that year counted about ten thousand white people in what would become South Dakota, and most of these settlers had arrived after 1867.[23]

In contrast to the success of towns along the Missouri River, Sioux Falls, the townsite abandoned in 1862, had still not been re-established by 1870. By this time the two townsite companies that had first claimed the townsite at the falls of the Big Sioux River in 1857 had dissolved in financial failure. Only a few former members, still hopeful that their dreams of a town might materialize, remained at the site. Petitions to Congress for military protection in the Big Sioux Valley had finally resulted in the army's establishment of Fort Dakota at the falls in June 1865. This apparent protection against hostile Indians had encouraged settlers to enter the area beginning in 1866. With the Indian threat in the area now minimal, the townsite hopefuls soon sought Fort Dakota's removal so they could re-launch their settlement at the falls. Not just the fort itself blocked their ambitions. The fort was surrounded by a military reservation seven miles wide and ten miles long that was closed to all civilian settlement. In May of 1869, when the army abandoned Fort Dakota, two former townsite company representatives, W. W. Brookings and J. L. Phillips, sought to re-establish their earlier pre-emption claims to quarter sections of land at the falls. Prior to the abandonment of the site in 1862, Brookings had patented his claim and Phillips had filed on but not yet proved up his. These claims and others that had been made prior to 1862 were essentially extinguished when the government created the military reservation in 1865. Since the government's usual policy was to auction off surplus military reservations, the hopes of Brookings and Phillips to recover their claims looked dim.

Luckily for Brookings and Phillips, a young college student from Wisconsin named Richard F. Pettigrew stopped at the falls in June of 1869 on his way to join a government survey party. During his brief stop, he met Phillips, undoubtedly heard the story of the lost townsite claims, and saw the location's potential as a townsite. He marked off a claim to a quarter section of land in what later became part of Sioux Falls and went off on his summer surveying job. The next March Pettigrew returned to Sioux Falls to build a sod house and plow a few acres in fulfillment of pre-emption requirements. He was discouraged to learn, however, that a bill had been introduced in Congress to dispose of the Sioux Falls military reservation at auction, and that a group of land speculators in Maine intended to bid on the entire reservation. If Congress approved this piece of legislation, Pettigrew and the others at Sioux Falls would lose their claims to the townsite.[24]

Fortunately, Pettigrew's classmate at the University of Wisconsin had been Edward Carpenter, brother to the U.S. Senator from Wisconsin, Matthew Carpenter. It was through this connection that Pettigrew saved the townsite dreams of Brookings, Phillips, and himself. He also saved the pre-emption claims of a number of others who had settled on the abandoned Fort Dakota reservation. In the summer of 1870 Pettigrew drew up a petition that everyone at the falls—about twelve in all—signed. The twelve actual signatures on the petition were then fortified with nearly two-dozen anticipated arrivals bringing the total to thirty-four. Pettigrew sent the petition and a map to his friend Ed Carpenter asking him to get his brother, the senator, to introduce a bill opening the Fort Dakota military reservation for settlement under the normal land laws (i.e., pre-emption and homestead). He argued that there were already a number of settlers on the land and that the townsite had been acquired by occupation before the reservation had been established. Carpenter introduced a bill that Congress approved in the winter of 1870-71. Nye Phillips, another settler at the falls, used his influence with territorial delegate S. L. Spink to get support for the bill in the House. As a result Brookings, J. L. Phillips, Nye Phillips, and Pettigrew gained possession of the Sioux Falls townsite. Initially the town consisted of just the abandoned buildings of Fort Dakota that J. L. Phillips had bought for practically nothing. Since the buildings were on Phillips' claim, no one had bid against him. That winter J. L. Phillips laid out the first nine blocks of the anticipated town, and in the spring of 1871 Pettigrew hired some Norwegian settlers to saw up lumber with which he erected the town's first new building. C. K. Howard, who had operated the fort sutler store, bought the old post hospital building on what became Phillips Avenue, enlarged it, and opened a store. In June Harry Corson arrived with his family and began construction of the new town's first real hotel, the Cataract. Before the end of the year, several businesses had been added to the town including Joe Dupries' Central House and William Van Eps's store. In the same year W. F. Kiter launched the *Sioux Falls Pantagraph*, and Sioux Falls seemed finally to have a future.[25]

The late sixties and early years of the seventies witnessed a variety of foreign ethnic groups that took up land in fairly concentrated colonies. Late in the 1860s a large number of Scandinavians had settled in Union, Clay, and Yankton counties. A majority of these Scandinavians were Norwegians, and by the early seventies they had moved up the Big Sioux Valley into Lincoln County as well. Norwegians had also settled in significant numbers north of Sioux Falls after 1866, making it possible to found Dell City (later Dell

Rapids) in 1871 and to organize Brookings County the next year. In 1868 Swedish settlers began coming, and ultimately a large portion of central and eastern Clay County took on a definite Swedish character. At about the same time a number of Danes colonized near Swan Lake in Turner County with Daneville, later renamed Viborg, as its business and social center. As mentioned earlier, a large colonizing party of Bohemians arrived in Yankton County in 1869 and gradually expanded their settlement area into Bon Homme County. Tabor, the trading center for this immigrant community, was begun in 1871.[26]

Germans from Russia migrated to Dakota in 1873, settling in Bon Homme, Hutchinson, Turner, and Yankton counties. In the eighteenth century Czarina Catherine the Great had invited Germans to settle in Russia to increase agricultural production, and had given these people special privileges such as ethnic autonomy and exemption from military service. In 1871 the Czar revoked these special privileges and sought to Russianize these ethnic Germans causing many of them to emigrate to the United States and Canada. Among these immigrants from Russia were Mennonites who settled mainly in Hutchinson and Turner counties with their main focus the town of Freeman. The Chicago, Milwaukee and St. Paul Railroad came through in 1879 and at its siding began a town. Legend has it that the railroad company, intending to name this community Menno, to reflect its ethnic-religious majority, put up the Freeman sign on the depot and never corrected its mistake.[27]

The decade of the 1870s began with much promise and with the anticipation that railroads would soon connect Dakota with the East, making the flow of settlers into Dakota even greater and more rapid. But only the Missouri towns of Elk Point, Vermillion, and Yankton had acquired a rail connection when the Panic of 1873 hit the nation and suspended all further railroad construction. Railroad companies were so badly affected by the panic and the depression that followed that a rail-line completed that year from Winona, Minnesota, to Lake Kampeska was abandoned for several years. The depression also dashed the hopes of the fledgling townsite at Sioux Falls for acquiring a railroad in 1873. Natural disaster followed economic during the mid-1870s as southeastern Dakota experienced another drought cycle and severe grasshopper infestations. A series of failed crops forced many homesteaders to abandon their claims and leave the territory. The effects of this combination of dire conditions was evident in Sioux Falls where the population of about six hundred in 1876 was virtually unchanged from three years ear-

Originally founded on the banks of the Missouri and Vermillion rivers, Vermillion today, home of the University of South Dakota, is located high on the Missouri bluffs, safe from the floods that inundated the town in 1881. *Center for Western Studies.*

lier. By 1877 the nation's economy had recovered, rain had come again to Dakota, and the grasshoppers had not. The stage was set for the so-called "Dakota Boom" of the late 1870s and first half-dozen years of the 1880s.

Neither drought, grasshoppers, nor economic depression prevented a population boom in the western part of the state in the mid-1870s. It was the confirmation in 1874 of the existence of gold in the Black Hills that ultimately brought a hoard of miners to the area and resulted in the creation of a number of new towns. General George Armstrong Custer led a thousand-person expedition through the Black Hills in the summer of 1874. Ostensibly, the expedition was to locate possible sites for military posts and roads, but the real objective was to verify long-existing rumors that there was gold in the Hills. Custer's expedition included a miner and five newspaper correspondents. The miners found gold along streams in the middle portion of the Hills, and the newspapers announced the discovery to the entire nation. During the next two years the army fought a losing battle to keep gold-seekers out of the Hills that were within the Great Sioux Reservation established by the Laramie Treaty in 1868. The Dakota Indians adamantly resisted pressure to cede the Black Hills to the federal government. Unwilling to engage the Indians in war over the Custer expedition's cursory gold findings, a second military expedition of a more scientific nature entered the Hills in 1875. Walter P. Jenney, a professional mineralogist and geologist, led this so-called Jenney Expedition. The expedition, which included prospectors and miners and spent more than four months exploring the southern Hills for gold and other minerals, confirmed the existence of extensive mineral wealth. Finding it impossible to keep miners out of the gold country, the federal government moved ahead with its efforts to obtain title to the Black Hills. A military campaign to force the Indians to agree to a treaty of cession and to relocate them on designated reservations took place in 1876 and included the famous Battle of the Little Bighorn where the Indians annihilated Custer's command. In the end the Teton Dakota were forced to sign a treaty in October 1876 giving up their claims to the Black Hills and allowing the creation of three wagon roads across their reservation so as to connect the Missouri River with the Hills.[28]

Gold seekers did not wait for the government to conclude a treaty of cession with the Teton Dakota. By March 1876 an estimated ten thousand miners were already in the Hills. The "towns" of Hill City and Custer had been founded, with Custer already having some six thousand residents. These mining camps of hastily constructed, temporary buildings and tents were nearly abandoned when news arrived of major gold discoveries in the northern Hills. Deadwood City was established in April 1876 at the junction of Deadwood and Whitewood creeks, and Lead City was laid out at about the same time. In May the town of Spearfish, began as the lush Spearfish Valley, attracted a growing number of ranchers. By the end of 1876 an estimated twenty thousand people inhabited the northern Hills. Congress finally ratified the Black Hills Treaty in February 1877, legitimizing the white invasion that had already occurred. A few months later, when the gold rush had probably peaked, it was estimated the Hills population had reached nearly twenty-five thousand.[29]

Deadwood came to epitomize the wild, roaring mining town. It was the center of the northern mining district and grew in a frantic effort to keep up with the demands and needs of the exploding number of miners and prospectors. With lumber in short supply and store goods coming by freight wagon either from the Missouri River or from some point like Cheyenne on the Union Pacific line, the cost of doing business was high. Hotel, restaurant, saloon, and gambling house operators and store keepers charged high prices, and miners without other options paid with their hard-earned gold dust. These

Deadwood was a roaring mining town when this photo was taken in 1876. Crude placer mining produced more than a million dollars of gold during the months of June and July drawing thousands of fortune seekers and creating virtually overnight the town depicted here. *Center for Western Studies.*

merchants and the whole army of people engaged in the transportation network required to support the miner's needs undoubtedly fared better than the majority of miners. As long as there was gold to be found, Deadwood was essential. When the entire town burned to the ground in December 1879, it was quickly rebuilt. R. F. Pettigrew, who was in Deadwood when it burned, recalled that, by eleven o'clock the morning after the fire, they were already rebuilding. Johnny Manning's saloon, he later recalled, was "In full blast as the liquor warehouse had been saved." Pettigrew also remembered seeing "George Hearst and Jack Gillmer, both drunk, playing poker on a rough board laid on two barrels, with the sky for a roof, and the ashes of Deadwood for a floor."[30]

The townsite destined to become the largest and most successful in the Black Hills was not a mining camp. In February 1876 a group of disappointed gold seekers turned to townsite speculation and laid out a town in the Rapid valley. As the eastern gateway to the interior mining regions, Rapid City fed off the traffic of gold seekers and the supplying of miners and mining camps. Ten years after its founding, Rapid City assured its future by acquiring a rail connection to the Union Pacific transcontinental line at Chadron, Nebraska.[31]

Founded in 1876 to supply miners working the gold fields in the Black Hills, Rapid City needed a railroad connection, which it secured in 1886, before it could grow into South Dakota's second largest city. *Center for Western Studies.*

The Dakota Boom phenomenon of 1878-1887 was most evident on the countryside of Dakota Territory where settlers laid claim to millions of acres of land each year. In 1884 alone over eleven million acres of claims were filed, and not until 1888 did the annual amount of land filed on slip below two million acres. As a result, the population of Dakota Territory grew during the decade of the 1880s from slightly over 136,000 non-native residents at its outset to a combined total of more than 511,000 for the two new states of North and South Dakota at its end. The boom gave new life to townsite speculation as a host of new towns were founded and existing ones either prospered or died. Sioux Falls is an example of a town that prospered during this decade, growing from a mere six hundred residents in 1876 to 2,164 in 1880 and to slightly more than ten thousand by the decade's end.[32]

The Dakota Boom period resulted in the settlement of virtually all the productive land between the western border of Minnesota and the Missouri River. This new surge of land-seekers was far larger than that prior to 1873, and its momentum was greater mainly due to the role played by railroads. In the sixties the most successful townsites had been those along the eastern shore of the Missouri River. River transportation had given the Missouri valley west of Sioux City great advantages over inland rivals like Sioux Falls. Moreover, the advantage of the extreme southeastern region was enhanced when the railroad reached Sioux City in 1868, making it the most convenient jumping-off point for settlers seeking homesteads in Dakota Territory.

It was the rapid and widespread construction of railroads after 1877 that leveled the competitive field between river and inland townsites. For instance, it was no longer crucial for the territorial capital to be a river town. In 1883 several non-river towns were candidates for becoming the capital city even though, Bismarck, river town with a railroad, ultimately gained the prize due to its central location. Faster, more direct, and freed

Sioux Falls received its first railroad connection on July 30, 1878, when construction gangs completed a line from Worthington to Sioux Falls. Towns by-passed by the railroad stagnated or died, and their residents often moved their few buildings to the more fortunate townsites with rail lines. Here an Illinois Central crew is grading the roadbed for the town's fourth rail line, as it built toward Sioux Falls in 1887. *Center for Western Studies.*

from seasonal floods and ice, the railroad was favored over the river steamboat. Having a railroad became better than being a river port, and townsite promoters worked hard to make sure their town acquired a rail connection. The success of in-land towns and the personal prosperity of their promoters were at stake. The experience of Yankton and Sioux Falls during the Dakota Boom period illustrates this fact.

When the townsite at Sioux Falls was finally re-established in 1871, Yankton was already an incorporated town of over 1,200 residents. Moreover, two year later Yankton enhanced its river port advantages by acquiring a rail connection. In 1876 the population of Sioux Falls had been stagnant at about six hundred for the prior three years, and still had no railroad. But, when the federal census was taken in June of 1880, Sioux Falls had suddenly become the third largest town in Dakota with 2,164 residents, and ten years later it was the largest city in the state with a population of 10,171, nearly three times greater than Yankton, the next largest town in the territory. Since that time no city in South Dakota has seriously challenged Sioux Falls' standing as the largest city in the state.[33]

The success of Sioux Falls was due not to its water power but to its becoming a transportation center. Unsatisfied with the single railroad that it first acquired in 1878, the merchant community worked for and paid the heavy costs of attracting more. By 1881 Sioux Falls had acquired three railroads, and by 1888 it had gained two more. As a result Sioux Falls became the wholesale supply and market center for the growing population of the surrounding region. It provided the needs of smaller towns either directly or indirectly through this network of railroads. A growing number of warehouses and factories supported this network supplying goods to the stores in surrounding towns. These smaller towns and their merchants prospered because poor roads and the slow mode of horse-drawn transportation gave them a virtual monopoly on the business of the farm population that surrounded each of them. Small-town residents who wished a greater retail selection took the train to Sioux Falls. The same was true for other regions of the state, but on a smaller scale. Of the seven largest cities in South Dakota in 1890, only two, Yankton and Pierre, were located on the Missouri River, and both also had railroad service. Four others, Sioux Falls, Aberdeen (Hub City), Huron and Watertown, were strictly rail centers, and Lead was home to the giant Homestake Gold Mine.

Beginning in 1878 railroads in Minnesota and Iowa undertook almost frenzied efforts to be the first to tap Dakota Territory. Railroad construction quickly swept through settled areas and plunged into the vast, unpeopled prairies beyond. The result was the

Unable to arrive at a consensus as to the location of the state capital when statehood was achieved in 1889, South Dakotans chose Pierre by popular vote. Graced by one of America's most impressive capitol buildings, Pierre sits on the east side of the Missouri River, across from Fort Pierre, the capital of the fur trade in the early nineteenth century. *Center for Western Studies.*

172

creation of a host of towns along the new rail lines and a flood of immigrants to take up claims on the countryside. Indeed, between 1878 and 1889, 285 towns were established in Dakota, and nearly all of them were along railroads. The railroad train replaced the wagon train in transporting settlers onto the land. Settlers aboard railroad cars flowed into southern Dakota like streams of water following a gully after a hard rain. The railroads built sidings at eight-to-ten-mile intervals to allow trains to pass on the single main track, and towns sprang up over night at each one. For instance, when the Milwaukee Road built west from Milbank, the towns of Webster, Bristol, Andover, and Groton popped up at siding sites. From its terminus at Canby, Minnesota, the Chicago and North Western built westward across the Dakota border in the summer of 1878, reaching Volga by the fall of 1879 and the next spring plotting Huron as a construction camp and division point. In 1878 the Winona and St. Peter division of the Chicago and North Western revived the line it had built to Lake Kampeska and abandoned in 1873. Watertown, its terminus, was quickly populated, and a few years later the line was extended to Redfield. In 1879 the Chicago, Milwaukee and St. Paul entered Dakota by crossing the Big Sioux River at Canton.[34]

The bulk of railroad construction in Dakota occurred in the early 1880s, and these new lines gave birth to a host of new towns. When the Chicago and North Western completed a line from Volga to Pierre in 1880, the Milwaukee Road hurriedly built from Marion to reach the Missouri River at Chamberlain. These extensions and others built in 1880 created the towns of Mitchell, Plankinton, and about twenty others. Aberdeen was established in 1881 when the site was reached by an extension of the Milwaukee Road from Ortonville, Minnesota. And when the Chicago and North Western built a line from Centerville to Yankton late in 1885, it created the towns of Volin and Wakonda. Between 1878 and 1889, a total of 227 towns were either laid out by a railroad or managed to acquire one.[35]

Named after the president (Alexander Mitchell) of the Chicago, Milwaukee and St. Paul Railroad, the town of Mitchell was founded in 1880. Its role as a railroad division point led to rapid growth. Near Mitchell, known for its Corn Palace, is the state's only National Archaeological Landmark, the Mitchell Prehistoric Indian Village. *Center for Western Studies.*

Originally called Kampeska, Watertown was founded in 1871 following the completion of a line of the Winona and St. Peter Railroad. *Center for Western Studies.*

Little railroad construction occurred between 1886 and 1900 largely as a result of poor economic times. But when better times returned at the beginning of the new century, a small number of new lines were constructed to reach unserved areas. One example is the Lake Sinai area of Brookings County where farmers, as late as 1907, were desperate for more convenient rail service. By agreeing to pay for the right-of-way, they were able to get the Dakota Central Railroad Company in Sioux Falls to build a line to Watertown passing through their area. This new rail line gave birth to the town of Sinai in 1907, one of the last new towns to be founded east of the Missouri River.[36] In 1906 the Milwaukee extended its line from Aberdeen and Ipswich and crossed the Missouri River creating the towns of Mobridge, McIntosh, and Lemmon before its line turned north into present-day North Dakota and continued to the West Coast.[37]

Railroads could destroy towns as well as create them, and they often gave shape to those they created. Firesteel, Palisades, and Evarts are three examples of townsites that were abandoned when the railroad passed them by in favor of Mitchell, Garretson, and Mobridge, respectively. Such towns often moved lock, stock, and barrel to the nearest rail siding. And because they created new towns, the railroads also named them. Consequently, even though a community might have a definite ethnic character, its name seldom reflected the fact. Instead, towns were usually named for railroad officials or their friends and relatives.[38] Towns founded by railroads were typically laid out as so-called T-towns, with the main business street perpendicular to the rail line and a public

Called the "Hub City," for its network of rail lines extending out like spokes on a wheel, Aberdeen became a regional center for agricultural and manufacturing businesses. *Center for Western Studies.*

building, a school or courthouse, at the far end. Few towns in South Dakota reflect the older town square pattern with the business streets surrounding the courthouse or town hall.

When the Dakota Boom began in 1877, the Great Sioux Reservation, lying west of the Missouri River, divided into two parts the portion of Dakota Territory that was to become the state of South Dakota in 1889. Dakotans regarded this as a great impediment to the full development of the territory, and efforts began almost from the signing of the Black Hills Treaty of 1876 to reduce further the Great Sioux Reservation. Railroad lines were built first to Bismarck and later to Pierre and Chamberlain, but from there overland traffic to the Black Hills had to cover the approximately two hundred miles via slow and hazardous freight wagons and stage coaches. The other route to the Black Hills was to take the Union Pacific to Cheyenne and go the rest of the way by stage or wagon. Both routes were slow, hazardous, and expensive. The obvious solution was to extend to the Hills the rail lines that had reached Pierre and Chamberlain but were blocked by the Great Sioux Reservation. Land speculators and homesteaders also lusted for the Indian land west of the Missouri.[39]

On May 1, 1888, President Cleveland signed the Sioux Reservation Opening Bill. This legislation reduced the Great Sioux Reservation to five smaller reservations: the Rosebud, Lower Brûlé, Cheyenne River, Pine Ridge, and Standing Rock. The rationale for the bill was to divide and separate the Sioux tribes so they could not unite for an attack upon the whites, though the desire for more Indian land was clearly the main motivation. It took nearly two years before the government managed to secure the Indian signatures required before the bill could become law. The legislation proposed to open about eleven million acres of Indian land to white settlers in a wide corridor linking the Missouri River with the Black Hills. By January of 1890, large numbers of "boomers" had gathered at Chamberlain, Pierre, and other points along the east bank of the Missouri River anticipating President Harrison's signing of the final bill on February 10. The land rush that followed, the federal government's poor fulfillment of previous treaty obligations, and the so-called "Messiah craze" combined to spark the last Indian war in the United States. Hostilities finally ended on January 16, 1891. Over the next twenty-one years, portions of these newly created reservations were also opened to white settlers.[40]

Though opened to settlement, in the various partitions of the reservations that took place between 1890 and 1911, few towns founded in the area between the Missouri River and the Black Hills experienced significant growth. Geography and climate were the main factors in the minimal urbanization of this part of the state. An average annual rainfall of thirteen to eighteen inches is not conducive to the more intensive agriculture of the eastern part of the state. Consequently, the large-scale cattle and wheat ranches and sparse population that came to typify this area did not require or encourage the existence of many urban centers. The great depression of the 1890s also discouraged settlement in the area and delayed the construction of railroad lines through it until after the turn of the century. The Chicago, Milwaukee and St. Paul did not extend its line from Chamberlain to Rapid City until 1907, while the Chicago and North Western hurried to complete its line to Rapid City in the same year.[41]

Several towns were created along the rail lines when they were built to Rapid City in the new century. The most successful of these towns, Kennebec, Kadoka, and Murdo, sprang up at long-time cattle ranching sites when the Chicago, Milwaukee and St. Paul built its line to Rapid City in 1906-07. At the same time the Chicago and North Western Railroad founded a string of towns when it built west from Pierre, but only Philip, which became the county seat of Haakon County, experienced much real growth. Faith blossomed as a railhead for the Chicago, Milwaukee and St. Paul branch line in Meade County and Winner enjoyed the same status in Tripp.

Initially, a large number of homesteaders took up claims in this area west of the Missouri, and the population of hopeful farmers gave some promise to these trans-Missouri railroad towns. Unfortunately, the climate, especially the severe drought of 1910-1911, eventually persuaded many of these farmers to abandon their claims and to seek better prospects elsewhere. As a result many towns struggled just to survive, while others, such as Lucerne and Powell, disappeared entirely. By 1911 the homesteading and the open-range ranching eras had both ended, and those West River residents who persisted had adapted to the realities of the region.[42]

As soon as towns were founded, their boosters worked to attract businesses, industry, educational facilities, and people. In its December 16, 1887, issue, the *Sioux Falls Argus Leader* advertised a "Meeting to Advertise Sioux Falls." "Sioux Falls is just on a turning point between a town and a city," said the notice, and "Now is the time to boom the city." Booming the town also involved giving the town the appearance of a successful urban community. Even sidewalks were an issue. The April 16, 1880, issue of the *Yankton Gazette* noted an item from the *Sioux Falls Times* that stated, "It can scarcely be expected that the moral tone of our town will reach the highest standard so long as the continual incentive of profanity exists in the rickety condition of our sidewalks." Streets needed grading and surfacing, and residents soon demanded safe and dependable public water supplies.

Having secured one or more rail connections, community boosters were quick to adopt new innovations that could further enhance their own and their town's success. Town boosters were especially keen to acquire the new technologies of gas and electric street lighting. A "Great white way" of street lights made towns safer and also brought them prestige. To have an electric streetcar system was even more prestigious, and small towns that could not afford to build one sometimes drew one into postcard photos of their main street. Reality dictated, however, that only those towns large enough to make installation of a gas or electric generating plant profitable were likely to enjoy gas or electric lights. Initially, coal gasification plants, an older technology than electric generation, produced gas for street lighting. At the outset flour mills often undertook the generation of electricity by simply expanding the use of their waterpower. Sioux Falls, Beresford, Bowdle, Springfield, Tyndall, and Vermillion were among the South Dakota towns for which this was true. Towns without waterpower turned to steam power for electric generation, a source more dependable but also more expensive. At the outset the primary use of gas and electric lighting was for streets and factories. For factories, artificial light extended working hours by overcoming the seasonal change in daylight that had defined working hours.[43]

Sioux Falls was the first town in Dakota to adopt new lighting technologies when its city council in 1883 gave J. H. Miller, Jr., a franchise to operate a coal gasification plant in order to supply gas for street lighting. Miller's company, later called the Sioux Falls Gas Company, supplied gaslights for downtown streets until its franchise expired in 1906. By that date alternating electric power had proven superior to gas for street lighting, and the gas company focused on home heating and cooking as its primary market. Gas produced a flickering light in contrast to the steady glare of electric lights, and the open flame of gaslights was a fire danger in many applications.[44]

The gas company's monopoly on street lighting in Sioux Falls was short-lived. In 1884 three local businessmen pooled $75,000 to install an electric plant that would provide arc lights for Sioux Falls' streets. Arc lighting, an electric light technology older than incandescent, produced light by an electric spark jumping between two carbon rods. This worked reasonably well for exterior, but not for interior, lighting. Much public debate surrounded the city council's decisions on which lighting system to adopt, and how much they were willing to pay for better street lighting. In the end the council reached a compromise that gave some business to both the gas and electric lighting companies. Interestingly, it was the concern for better security at the South Dakota Penitentiary that moved the city to expand the use of electricity and adopt Edison's incandescent light system. In May of 1887 penitentiary officials, after visiting prison facilities in Minnesota, Illinois, and Iowa, recommended that Sioux Falls adopt an incandescent system as soon as possible. Before the end of the month George Wheeler, one of the owners of the Cascade Mill, had been east and purchased an Edison direct-current electric generator. The mill owners designed the plant so the mill's waterpower could run the dynamo, but, from the outset, steam power was used to maintain electrical output during dry periods when waterpower was inadequate [45]

The debate between public and private ownership of public utilities that occurred across the nation and in other towns in South Dakota was very heated and prolonged in Sioux Falls. In 1901 the city council decided to install its own electric generating plant to provide street lighting while the privately owned Cascade Mill plant sold power to commercial and residential users. Almost from the outset there was controversy over the municipal power plant. Some residents wanted the municipal plant to supply all electric power to the town, but private companies countered by offering to provide power cheaper than the city's plant. There was strong sentiment in favor of public ownership of both electric power and water systems, but in the end a private company won a virtual monopoly on providing electric power to the city. The rapidly expanding demand for electric power quickly made both the municipal and early private power plants inadequate. This was especially true when an electric trolley company secured a franchise to operate in the city in 1907. Despite strong protests from those favoring public utilities, a proposal from a newly created Sioux Falls Light and Power Company, based on its plan to harness the power of the main falls, proved too attractive to reject. In 1907 the city gave a three-year contract to the new company to provide electric streetlights, and the company undertook construction of a hydroelectric plant just north of the vacant Queen Bee Mill. The company had purchased the Cascade Mill plant, and it used that source of electric power to fulfill its contract even after the new plant was ready in July 1908. By 1916 the high cost of electricity from the Light and Power Company reopened the debate over municipal versus private ownership of electric power production. The city again began to generate electricity to light city streets and forced the private company to reduce its rates. The municipal power plant was expanded through the early 1920s, but after 1923 voters rejected further indebtedness to enlarge the municipal plant. By the 1950s the city was able to purchase electric power from the Bureau of Reclamation's hydroelectric plants on the Missouri River for less than its plant could produce it, and the city closed down its own generators for good.[46]

Sioux Falls may have been the first Dakota town to adopt electricity for lighting its streets, but other towns were just as eager to boast of this new technology. Aberdeen and Rapid City streets were lighted by electric arc lights beginning in 1886, as were Huron's about the same time, Mitchell's in 1890, and Webster's in 1901. While these were mainly steam-driven systems, towns like Huron, Redfield, and Yankton initially utilized the water power of their artesian wells to power generators in the 1880s. Every Dakota town of reasonable size and ambition worked to secure electric street lighting in the 1880s and early 1890s. The depression of the mid-1890s postponed its arrival in most other towns until the new century. Until 1910 electrification was almost entirely urban and public in its application. The homes of wealthy urbanites had been electrified earlier, but only after 1910 did electricity begin to invade private middle-class residences.[47]

Electricity was first used to light the main streets of towns, but after 1900 it expanded rapidly into industry with electric motors replacing the huge coal-burning steam engines that had dominated the scene since before the Civil War. For instance, in 1911 when the United Flour Milling Company of Minneapolis reopened the giant Queen Bee Mill, which had stood idle in Sioux Falls for thirty years, electric motors rather than waterpower ran its machines. After 1910 most businesses and residences in cities and small towns entered the electric age and were transformed by it. Most Dakota farms, however, had to wait until after World War II to become electified. Streetlights were extended to residential neighborhoods, and by the 1920s electric appliances gradually began to invade middle-class homes. In towns electricity brought such things as Saturday-night shopping, illuminated advertising, refrigerated locker plants, and movie theaters. Electricity had overcome the tyranny of sunlight in defining when people worked, shopped, and played.[48]

Most Dakota towns prior to World War II were similar in their form and function. They were trade centers for the rural populations that surrounded them. Farmers were partly self-sufficient, but they were also dependent on their cash crop to purchase the things they could not produce themselves. They hauled their grain or livestock to the nearest railroad where they sold it for the cash they needed to buy their store-bought necessities. Towns had a basic set of specialized stores that usually included a hardware store, jewelry store, meat market, bank, saloon, and general store. But it was the general store, typically selling groceries, dry goods, clothing, and notions, that was essential to both the town and the countryside. Because most of its farmer customers received their major income at harvest time or when livestock was sold, the country general store extended them credit (without interest) during the rest of the year. As a result patrons were loyal to their country store, and each store, if there were more than one in a town, had its own clientele. During the year farm wives went to town once a week or less to do their "trading" at the general store. They brought to the store home-churned butter, eggs, vegetables, and fruits for which the merchant would give them credit against the groceries or other items they purchased. Some of this country produce was sold to local town customers, but the excess was typically shipped by rail to the larger cities. Until World War II or shortly thereafter, most general stores were not self-serve. Customers brought their list of wants to a clerk who filled the order, or a town customer phoned in an order and the store delivered it. Town customers were expected to pay their bill once a week, while farmers typically settled their accounts with the storeowner once a year when they sold their crop.[49]

The second new technology that had a profound impact on urban South Dakota was the internal combustion engine-powered automobile and truck. Aside from the steam-powered railroad, overland travel prior to 1900 was little changed from the Roman era. If no railroad were available, people walked, rode horses, or hauled goods in horse- or ox-drawn wagons. Travel was slow and most roads were only slightly improved trails leading from farms to the nearest market town. This situation was the basis for small-town success in most rural areas. Farmers hauled their crops to the nearest rail market, and they bought their needs from the nearest stores. The automobile changed all that.

Meredith Willson summed it up in his musical *The Music Man* when he had a traveling salesman say that the automobile had made everything different: "It's the Model-T Ford made the people want to go, want to get, . . . twenty-two miles to the county

seat. . . . Nobody wants to patronize a little-bitty two-by-four kind of store anymore."
Automobiles, initially the hobby of the well-to-do, quickly became regarded as a necessity, especially by rural residents. There seem to be no reliable statistics on when the first
automobiles came to South Dakota, but by 1903 there were enough in Sioux Falls so that
city government passed the first automobile-related law. It limited the speed of "[a]ny
vehicle commonly known as a motorcycle [or] automobile" operating on city streets or
alleys to seven miles per hour, "[e]xcept when turning corners, when the speed must not
exceed four miles per hour." Violators faced a fine of not less than $5.00 nor more than
$50.00.[50] By 1913 more than 14,000 automobiles had been licensed in the state, and the
number had exploded to over 154,000 twelve years later.[51]

Automobiles became nearly ubiquitous among farmers immediately after World War
I when wartime prosperity and Henry Ford's inexpensive Model-T made them affordable. By 1930, 86.5 percent of South Dakota farms had one or more automobiles as compared to the national average of fifty-eight percent. Nearly twenty percent of the state's
farms had one or more trucks.[52] The growing number of motorized vehicles created
pressure on local and state governments to improve roads and led to the enactment of a
tax on gasoline to fund road construction and maintenance. Cars and trucks initially only
replaced the horse-drawn vehicle in making travel to the nearest town or railroad depot
easier and faster. Before long, however, the automobile and truck, along wth improved
roads, allowed farmers to by-pass local small-town merchants and rail service in favor
of a larger urban. Greater competition in larger towns usually provided better prices for
crops and livestock and better selection and lower prices for store merchandise. Country
stores and non-railroad-served small towns were the most vulnerable to this new pattern
and began to disappear. Between 1911 and 1956, about 230 of these South Dakota small
towns were abandoned while many more struggled to survive. Farm produce and freight
traffic declined at small-town depots as trucks provided faster and more flexible service,
and railroads began to abandon one small-town depot after another. Motorized power
on farms also began to expand in the post-World War I period, and this gradually led to
farm consolidation and a decline in the number of people on the countryside.[53]

The automobile also altered the urban landscape. Garages and gasoline stations
rapidly appeared to serve the new motor vehicles, and livery stables gradually disappeared. The electric trolley, built in 1908 to connect the growing residential areas with
the downtown in Sioux Falls, was gradually augmented by jitney buses after 1920 and
discontinued altogether in 1929. Automobile owners demanded smoother streets, and
the old cobblestones were replaced with concrete or covered with asphalt. Traffic signals
were installed, and police departments became motorized. Backyard barns with their
smelly, fly-infested manure piles were converted into garages or replaced altogether.
The automobile even seemed to improve the environment, as it gradually eliminated
horse manure and pools of urine from city streets. Motorized taxis and buses replaced
horse-drawn hacks and omnibuses, and new buildings were constructed to house the
growing number of automobile agencies. Wagon makers, harness makers, and farriers
were gradually displaced. Indeed, an entire industry devoted to horse-drawn transportation eventually disappeared. Not that horses disappeared from the landscape overnight.
They continued to be important on many farms through the end of World War II when
farmers, using their wartime earnings, finally replaced them with tractors. Perhaps the
last use of horses in the urban setting was on milk-delivery wagons, where a trained
horse learned the stops and freed the deliveryman to carry the milk from the wagon to
the doorstep.

In addition to water and rail transportation, the automobile had a profound influence on the growth–and demise–of towns and cities. In this photo, the town of Gregory, located at some distance from urban centers, has a number of cars parked down the middle of its main street. *Center for Western Studies.*

The automobile also brought the tourist industry to the state, especially to the Black Hills. The tourist business, enhanced by liberal divorce laws, had existed prior to the automobile, where the railroad could make a natural site accessible. This had been the case for Hot Springs, where its warm mineral waters attracted well-to-do vacationers who would spend time at one of several luxury hotels. Railroad access meant that these wealthy patrons, who usually stayed for a week or more taking the waters, enjoyed a rather exclusive club-like atmosphere. The advent of the automobile brought an end to this type of vacation and clientele. The wealthy set now took up the automobile and measured the success of a vacation by the number of miles traveled.[54] By the 1920s the automobile was no longer a toy of the rich, and Americans were taking to the highways, such as they were, in large numbers. The Black Hills soon became a popular vacation destination. Over the years towns in the Hills developed an entire infrastructure of hotels/motels, restaurants, and attractions to serve the tourist traffic. The gradual improvement of highways across the state encouraged this traffic, and a new set of boosters, like Ted and Dorothy Hustead of Wall Drug fame, successfully cultivated the tourist business. Gutzon Borglum created the greatest attraction of all when he carved the four presidents on Mount Rushmore between 1927 and 1941. Tourists, including motorcyclists, were the new gold to be mined, and they brought prosperity to Rapid City, Lead, Hill City, Deadwood, and Sturgis. More recently, gambling casinos have become an added attraction, especially for Deadwood.

All the consequences of the internal combustion engine, which had such negative effects on small towns, were part of a general population movement to the larger cities of the state during the twentieth century. Of 377 South Dakota towns that existed in 1911, only 148, or thirty-nine percent, were still in existence in 1956.[55] On the other hand, Sioux Falls, the state's largest city, grew by over ten thousand residents between 1910 and 1920 and continued steady growth through the outbreak of World War II. After 1940 the city more than tripled to an estimated 130,000 in 2003. Rapid City, the state's second largest city, also experienced steady growth prior to World War II. The location of Ellsworth Air Base near Rapid City and the booming tourist trade after the war are the major factors in the city's impressive increase to over 60,000 residents by 2003. Other cities having populations of more than 10,000 in 2002 are (in descending order) Aberdeen, Watertown, Mitchell, Brookings, Pierre, Yankton, and Huron. On the opposite end of the spectrum, the 2000 census revealed that half the state's towns had lost population during the previous decade, and it listed seventy-four South Dakota towns having fewer than one hundred residents, thirty of which had fewer than fifty residents.[56]

The founding of towns in Dakota Territory was an integral part of the settling process. Homesteading farmers needed towns, and the towns needed the farm population. Townsite founding was a speculative enterprise. Townsites could produce revenue for their founders, whether individuals, townsite companies, or railroads, only if people came and bought lots on which to build businesses and homes. People came to townsites if they believed that the town offered a promise of commercial success of some kind. Boosters worked hard to promote the success of their town, for their personal prosperity was at stake. Before the advent of the automobile and good roads, a town needed a railroad connection to the outside world if it were to prosper. As farmers acquired faster and easier transportation and roads improved, farmers gradually by-passed the local small town for a larger one where merchants with better buying power and greater competition charged lower prices and offered more selection. Better farm-to-market transportation also reduced the need for many small-town railroad depots. With the development of paved highways and large trucks, railroad branch lines gradually lost customers and were abandoned as unprofitable. The declining number of farms and rural residents after 1900 compounded these trends, as more people moved to the larger towns and cities in search of better employment opportunities. Some small towns have become bedroom communities for those who choose to commute to their jobs in a nearby city. Others have worked with varying degrees of success to attract industries and thereby keep their populations, but many South Dakota towns continue to slide toward oblivion. The changing proportion of South Dakotans living in urban centers (the census uses this term for towns of 2,500 or more residents) and rural areas tells the story. In 1900 only ten percent of South Dakotans lived in an urban center, but by 1930 that percent had doubled and it had doubled again by 1960. The 1990 federal census reported that half of the state's residents lived in an urban area, and that percentage has continued to increase. South Dakota remains rural compared to the nation as a whole, which the 2000 census reported as being three-quarters urban.[57]

Chapter 11
Small Towns: Image and Reality

An essay by John E. Miller

> You know you're in a small town—
> When Third Street is on the Edge of Town
> When you write a check on the wrong bank and it covers for you
> When the undertaker supplements his income with a furniture store
> When you miss a Sunday at church and receive a get-well card
> When a 55-year-old farmer is still referred to as "Young Johnson"
> When someone asks how you feel and listens to what you say
> When the nicest house in town has a beauty shop on the back porch
> When you dial a wrong number and talk for 15 minutes anyway
> When you speak to each dog you pass by name, and he wags at you
> When everyone's seed cap has a seed corn emblem on it
> When you don't use your turn signal because everyone knows where you
>   are going[1]

South Dakota has been labeled many things—the "Sunshine State," the "Mount Rushmore State," the "Land of Infinite Variety," "Land of the Dakotahs," the state of "Great Faces Great Places," fly-over territory, agricultural paradise, Siouxland, KELO-land, among others. Whatever else it may be, it is a state that is defined by its small towns, and there, more than anywhere else, is where its identity is to be found. More than is true in most other places, the experience of its residents and the quality of their lives are determined by the small towns that most of them inhabit or are connected to while living on their outlying farms.

"The country town is one of the great American institutions," Thorstein Veblen, the great American economist and social critic who grew up on a farm in southeastern Minnesota, once wrote, "perhaps the greatest, in the sense that it has had and continues to have a greater part than any other in shaping public sentiment and giving character to American culture."[2] The image of small towns in the eyes of Americans remains a highly ambivalent one, however. Ever since Sinclair Lewis burst on the literary scene in 1920 with *Main Street*, a highly acerbic portrait of a small midwestern community based heavily upon his still-tender memories of growing up in Sauk Centre, Minnesota, urban dwellers have been inclined to view small towns with suspicion and condescension. Scores of books, poems, plays, and movies lambasting the dullness, narrowness, priggishness, and backwardness of small towns have reinforced the notion that the "village virus" rules in them, stunting lives and paralyzing efforts to bring about change.

At the same time, while three-quarters of the population now lives in metropolitan areas, when questioned by pollsters about where they would prefer to live, the largest number of respondents identify the small town as their ideal. The sense of friendliness, stability, cohesiveness, and helpfulness that large numbers of people associate with villages and small towns manifests itself in the popularity achieved by plays like Thornton

Wilder's *Our Town*, movies like Frank Capra's *You Can't Take it With You*, musicals like Meredith Willson's *The Music Man*, and books like Garrison Keillor's *Lake Wobegon Days*. Generally viewed as a nostalgist who pictures rural Midwestern life through rose-colored glasses, Keillor, in his writings and radio monologues, reminds us of just how multifaceted small-town residents are. He recognizes both the bright side and the dark side of the small-town milieu. There, life is lived on a human scale where people matter; they look out for and feel responsible for each other. The same impulses that lead them to care for and be concerned about one another, however, can, when carried too far or in the wrong direction, be transformed into meddling and into unwanted efforts to control other people's behavior. What Sinclair Lewis classified as the "village virus" Keillor encapsulated in his fictional manifesto "95 Theses 95," a catalogue of the narrow-minded and mean-spirited tendencies that too many small-town dwellers exhibit. These foibles range the gamut from "endless boring talk about weather, regularity, back problems, and whether something happened in 1938 or 1939" to malicious gossip, "a monster of greed," bigotry, conformity, obsessive guilt, and hypocrisy.[3]

South Dakotans take no less ambivalent an approach to their small towns. What sets them apart from most of the rest of the country, however, is how many of them remain content to live in small towns and rural areas. It was not until 1990 that the Census Bureau classified the majority of South Dakotans as living in urban places of 2,500 or more (nationally, the balance tipped in 1920). Still, a large part of those classified as urban dwellers actually lived in small towns. In 2000, Sioux Falls (123,975) and Rapid City (59,607) accounted for 24.3 percent of the state's population. The third largest place was Aberdeen, with a population of 24,658, placing it definitely in the small-town category. South Dakota contained only nine towns with populations of more than 10,000, another five between 5,000 and 9,999, and eleven between 2,500 and 4,999. For the past century or so, after the dust settled in the wake of original white occupation during and after the Great Dakota Boom, there have been approximately 300 towns large enough to be incorporated in the state. Even Sioux Falls and Rapid City started out as small towns, and, in the minds of urbanites from Boston to Los Angeles, they, too, continue to evince many of the characteristics associated with small-town life.

The positive attitudes that people harbor toward small-town life in South Dakota manifest themselves in many ways. Tom Brokaw, who grew up in Bristol, Igloo, Pickstown, and Yankton, exited the state in 1962 after graduating from the University of South Dakota, "hungry for bright lights, big cities, big ideas, and exotic places well beyond the conventions and constraints of my small-town childhood," as he described it in his memoir, *A Long Way from Home*, "but forty years later I still call South Dakota home." The longtime NBC news anchorman expressed his ambivalence in observing, "I don't want to move back, but in a way I never want to leave. I am nourished by every visit." Quoting Kathleen Norris's *Dakota: A Spiritual Geography*, he noted the contradictions and tensions in the culture "'between hospitality and insularity, change and inertia, stability and instability, possibility and limitation, between hope and despair, between open hearts and closed minds.'"[4]

Like these and other perceptive observers, the late University of South Dakota English professor John R. Milton also took note of the central importance that contradiction and paradox play in small-town culture. "Extremes," he observed in his bicentennial history of South Dakota, is perhaps "the key word for Dakota."[5] The most obvious extremes in many minds are those of temperature and weather. Also prominent is the geographical division separating East River from West River, which expresses itself in the split between feed caps and cowboy hats, shotguns and rifles, black coffee drinkers and those who take cream and sugar with their coffee, short grass and tall grass country, Minnesota Vikings fans and Denver Broncos rooters, Democrats and Republicans.[6] The contrasts between the regions are not absolute, only relative; nevertheless, they are real. Beyond geography, South Dakota harbors racial divisions among Native Americans, those of European ancestry, and immigrants from other places. Religion, politics, economic status, family relationships, levels of ambition, and openness to change constitute other fault lines separating groups of people.

We can consider the nature of South Dakota's small towns by examining them along several dimensions that illustrate the kinds of tensions and contradictions that make them so interesting and often so unpredictable. First of all, how do South Dakotans perceive their small towns—in basically positive or negative terms? Beyond that, we can evaluate them as being typical or unique and place them along spectrums linking aspiration and accommodation, conflict and consensus, individual and community, and, finally, change and continuity.

When South Dakotans are queried directly about how they view their small towns, their answers tend to be glowing. Respondents emphasize the neighborliness, helpfulness, kindness, and general niceness of people. Folks, they say, look out for their neighbors. They care for you, assist you in times of need or trouble, and, in daily affairs, are pleasant and hospitable. Stock newspaper stories relate how farmers join together to care for their neighbors' cattle or gather in the harvest when they are struck down by illness or, worse, die. Or they might cooperate to paint an elderly person's house, drive a friend to dialysis treatments, or hold a benefit supper for a family whose house burns down.

For small-town residents, there are many things to be appreciative of—something that is impressed upon the young as part of the socialization process. An elementary school student won a "Pride in Huron" essay contest sponsored by the local Chamber of Commerce with the following entry: "I'm proud of Huron because we have excellent schools, beautiful parks, enjoyable swimming pools, a fine library and an art center. It is

A general store, like McDonald's, in the small town of Carter, provided a range of goods, from fresh apples to canned beans, as well as a warm stove, the newspaper, and conversation. *Center for Western Studies.*

a clean city. We have a big mall. We have great Girl Scout leaders. Our moms and dads have excellent jobs. We have fine dentists. We have a nifty hospital. We have wonderful police. We have great coaches for soccer and other sports. We have a dandy little fire department. We have excellent doctors. We have great churches. The swimming pools are clean. The library is enjoyable too. We have great businesses, nice teachers, very, very, very pleasing principals, and no one who steals."[7] Her descriptions echo lists reproduced by scores of towns during the early 1900s describing the attractive businesses and community assets that were used to advertise themselves and to attempt to induce people to settle in them. They often sported several hotels, livery stables, groceries, hardware stores, furniture stores, and other businesses, as well as an opera house, library, fine city hall, an excellent school, majestic churches, and so on and so forth.

What makes South Dakota small towns livable and attractive to people, in addition to business and industry, is their quality of life, reflected in the personal interactions of its residents and the strong sense of community that exists. From this perspective, social capital trumps financial capital. On a variety of measures, South Dakota ranks at or near the top when it comes to social capital, which refers to the connections that bind people together, the social networks that foster communication and activity beneficial to community, and the standards of reciprocity and trust that undergird expectations people have of each other. In *Bowling Alone: The Collapse and Revival of American Community*, political scientist Robert Putnam, of Harvard University, identified the two Dakotas as the states ranking highest on a social capital index that he and his co-workers formulated. It matters that South Dakota's population lives mainly in small towns, because "virtually all forms of altruism—volunteerism, community projects, philanthropy, directions for strangers, aid for the afflicted, and so on—are demonstrably more common in small towns," Putnam observed. "Store clerks in small towns are more likely to return overpayment than their urban counterparts. People in small towns are more likely to assist a 'wrong number' phone caller than urban dwellers. Cheating on taxes, employment forms, insurance claims, and bank loan applications are three times more likely to be condoned in cities than in small towns. Car dealers in small towns perform far fewer unnecessary repairs than big-city dealerships."[8]

Further evidence that high rates of social capital exist in South Dakota's small towns was provided in the Social Capital Community Benchmark Survey, designed by Professor Putnam and his associates, which queried 30,000 people and rated forty communities or regions scattered across twenty-nine states on a numerical scale. The results of that study, published in 2001, showed South Dakota ranking first in five of the eleven categories assessed (social trust, interracial trust, civic leadership, giving and volunteering, and faith-based engagement), while it finished fourth in conventional politics and fifth in associational involvement.[9] Here was comparative statistical support for what most South Dakotans intuitively feel—that their small towns are friendly, helpful, cooperative, and pleasant places in which to live. Anecdotal evidence for the attractiveness of small-town life crops up frequently in newspaper stories, such as one published in 1995 about Californians Ken and Vicky Russell, who, with their sons Bryan, six, and Chris, two, moved to Arlington after the community's development corporation ran an ad in the Los Angeles *Times* in the wake of a January 1994 earthquake. It invited Californians tired of living on the fault zone to check Arlington out. Trading his job as an aerospace engineer and reserve Navy helicopter pilot for a pottery business that he started up in collaboration with his wife, Ken told a newspaper reporter, "I'm having a blast every day." He said he was impressed with a community "where the people are honest and friendly, where there's trust. Those things are much more important than having a theme park next door." Vicky was fitting in well, too. "You guys know how to enjoy life," she said, referring to the variety of social activities available in Arlington. "You throw surprise birthday parties for each other. I'm on a bowling team."[10] Bowling was not a solitary activity in Arlington, as it increasingly appeared to be elsewhere in the country.

A nontraditional student of mine, who had spent three decades on Capitol Hill in Washington, D.C., working in various positions in Congress, and his wife retired to Brookings, where she had family connections. Friends of theirs were surprised, even appalled. "You'll be back in six months with your tail between your legs," one of them predicted. They found it hard to understand why he would want to move to such a God-forsaken place or believe that he could possibly feel comfortable there. But all he could talk about when I first met him was how much he enjoyed living in Brookings. People were friendly, welcoming him easily into their coffee groups. There were no traffic jams; the air was clean. He often left the doors unlocked. Crime was a minor problem. What was there not to like?

In fact, there is much not to like about South Dakota's small towns, if one looks for it. Not all is sweetness and light. There is a dark side that complements the brighter side of life in small towns. Any reader of Sinclair Lewis, Sherwood Anderson, or Garrison Keillor could tell you that. People living in small towns are constitutionally no different from their counterparts anywhere else. They can be mean, stingy, selfish, self-centered, and predatory, as well as kind, considerate, generous, helpful, and thoughtful. As any competent psychologist or amateur cracker barrel philosopher could tell you, they can be all of these at the same time; they are capable of being one or the other depending on the circumstances, and they often change over time. Small towns may provide more opportunities for cooperative action and living life on a human scale, but that does not prevent people in them from often acting in anti-social ways.

Lying, cheating, malicious gossip, racism, skullduggery, spousal abuse, child neglect, vandalism, even murder—these types of behaviors are not unknown, nor even uncommon, in small towns and rural areas. South of Madison in August 2000, vandals broke into a rural Lutheran church, breaking windows, smashing light fixtures, and carving obscenities into the ceiling, causing $20,000 to $40,000 worth of damage. "It was just such a shock," said the congregation's vice president. "Everyone was just totally devastated."[11] Mostly, the dark side of people's behavior finds expression in lack of thoughtfulness and consideration, in petty slights and humiliations, and in smugness and hypocrisy. Another nontraditional student, who had lived with her husband in several different communities in South Dakota while their children were growing up, responded with the following to an assignment asking students to write about their home towns (names of towns have been deleted):

> In town #1, I was isolated and never met anyone beside my husband's boss. My impressions of the town are that it is a dirty, unfriendly, little town and I can't imagine why anyone would want to live there. . . .
> In town #2, both of our children were in elementary school. People there were somewhat friendly, but a little reserved. I had a ready-made place in the community, so I did not feel as much an outsider as my children did. I only learned that they never felt a part of the school community because they had not been born in the area after we had moved. My son started first grade and spent several years there and never felt he fit into the community. He once told me, "We were the only ones in school who didn't have cousins going to school." . . . My children were in high school when we lived in town #3. It is also a dirty little town. There

is a huge gap between the haves and the have-nots. I had a woman in church try to help me out by telling me which groups I should associate with. Unfortunately, on our income, I could not afford to participate in the endless charity events the "elite" women of the community were involved in . . . . Town #4 is more of a bedroom community than town #3 and therefore has more "outsiders" moving in. I also have a ready-made place here. The people in town have been very friendly. However, since I don't have children in the school system, I'm not involved in any disputes about the school. I would not want to live here if my children were still in high school. The main reason is that if you are not in sports, there are few options for extracurricular activities. The entire town is sports crazy. There is a small group interested in music and almost no one at the school promoting debate or drama.

The ambivalence attached to South Dakota's small towns takes many forms. Just as they can be evaluated positively or negatively, with many colorations in between, so they can be thought of as being highly typical or in some way unique. Interestingly, town residents like to be regarded as both—average Americans, on the one hand, and somehow special, on the other. Richard Nixon's first vice president, Spiro Agnew, once made the mistake of saying that after you've seen one slum, you've seen them all. Slightly paraphrasing that, one might say that after you've seen one small town, you've seen them all. Physical appearance, first of all, comes to mind. Most South Dakota towns east of the Missouri River got their starts during the Great Dakota Boom in the early 1880s, and eighty percent of them were railroad towns, most of them being platted by subsidiaries of the railroad companies.[12] Surveyors took a cookie-cutter approach to the task, repeating the same preconceived plan over and over again. Most South Dakota towns were laid out in the shape of a "T," with main street perpendicular to the railroad tracks.[13] Lots with twenty-five-foot frontages were universal, although the depths and heights of the buildings varied considerably. Predictably, as time went by, false-front wooden buildings often gave way to more substantial brick buildings; wooden sidewalks were replaced by concrete ones; high schools, city halls, opera houses, movie theaters, and filling stations appeared; streets got paved; parks, swimming pools, athletic facilities, and golf courses sprouted; and telephone and electric lines, water towers, sewers, and other public utilities were installed.

Never identical in appearance, towns varied considerably in size. Yet a certain sameness existed about them, partly because they were responding to similar demands for services and amenities, partly because most of them were located along railroads, and partly because the state's topography generally was flat or slightly undulating, which allowed for simple site planning by town builders. That most towns got their start during the thirty-year period from 1880 to 1910 was a contributing factor. Black Hills mining towns—products of the 1870s—and other West River locations demonstrated more variety. The major factor accounting for the degree of sameness that existed in the appearance of South Dakota communities was the primary economic function served by most of them—that of agricultural service center. Towns fulfilled a number of different functions from the beginning, operating as river towns, mining towns, service towns around military forts or Indian reservations, county seat or government towns, university and college towns, industrial towns, and, more recently, retirement centers or bedroom communities for nearby cities. Industry never became the large force in the state that it did elsewhere in the United States, and what industry did emerge was grafted onto the normal span of activities that occur in a primarily agricultural community.

The structure of towns in South Dakota reflects their origins in the pre-automobile era. In recent years, American life has been transformed by cars and other transportation improvements; the computer, Internet, and other innovations in communications; the rise of two-income households and changes in family life; demographic trends; and evolution in education, religion, consumption, and lifestyles. Larger towns and those enjoying an upward population curve (the two are mostly the same) exhibit many of the same kinds of developments: convenience stores and quick-stops, franchise restaurants and fast-food places, computer and video stores, and strip malls and shopping centers. For towns struggling with population losses, sameness comes in the form of boarded-up stores and vacant lots; abandoned houses, schools, and churches; old buildings transformed into historical museums; and a general unkemptness. Thus, the observation by many onlookers, especially visitors, is that the towns all look alike.

The stories people tell about themselves also tend to conform to set patterns. Small-town histories reflect a narrative stance familiar to everyone acquainted with the genre. Heavy emphasis on the early pioneers is common in local histories along with a listing of firsts—the first appearance of the railroad, the first election, the first old settlers' picnic, along with the first buildings, businesses, schools, churches, opera houses, and other developments. Special mention goes to town founders, businessmen, mayors, politicians, philanthropists, school superintendents, and other prominent leaders. The story focuses upon individual lives, rather than upon broad social forces and processes, and admiration for these individuals often blends into hagiography and mythology. Weather disasters, floods, blizzards, fires, and murders all provide grist for the mill. Pride in the community shines through in descriptions of civic buildings, churches, schools, parks, and monuments. Some towns were honored by visits of famous people, such as Theodore Roosevelt, Carry Nation, or Charles Lindbergh, and these stories always enter into the historical account. When outside companies are hired to stage historical pageants for anniversary celebrations, the prefabricated quality of such programs is immediately apparent, for these organizations rely upon standard scripts, which only require filling in relevant local dates, names, and events to round out the story.[14]

Even vital and growing towns found it hard to escape the notion that they were dull and boring places, when compared with their cousins in metropolitan America. Sinclair Lewis's observation in his preface to *Main Street* that fictional Gopher Prairie's main-street was "the continuation of Main Streets everywhere. That the story would be the same in Ohio or Montana, in Kansas or Kentucky or Illinois" was in keeping with many people's notion that all small towns are alike.[15] Well aware of the prevalence of such attitudes and wishing to compete successfully with their neighbor for consumers' dollars, small towns endeavored to distinguish themselves. Ironically, even in their search for uniqueness, they often utilized similar approaches.

Many South Dakota towns became known for the types of people who resided in them or for physical landmarks, products, celebrations, former residents, or special events in their history. Viborg was notable for its Danish population, Dalesburg for its Swedes, and Onida for the black colony that once resided there. Freeman staged its Schmeckfest, Tabor its Czech Days, and Sturgis its Rally and Races. Canistota boasted of the Ortman Clinic; Epiphany drew people from nearly every state of the Union and from some foreign countries to receive treatment from Dr. William Kroeger, who was also a Catholic priest; and countless others journeyed to Hot Springs, Midland, and other springs and spas to benefit from their healing waters. Huron advertised itself as "Convention City" and home of the State Fair, Forestburg as "Watermelon Capital of Dakota," Clark as "South Dakota's Potato Capital," Redfield as "Pheasant Capital of the

The Czech settlement of Tabor was well established when this photo was taken in 1910. Aside from a single two-story brick business building, wooden one-story, false-front business buildings dominated its main street. *Center for Western Studies.*

World," and Brookings as "Someplace Special." Canton had a ski hill; Mitchell, its Corn Palace; Keystone, Mount Rushmore; and Custer, Crazy Horse Monument. Wall Drug Store emerged as the ultimate gimmick, becoming better known than the town whose name it incorporated.

Faulkton took pride in being the home of Congressman John Pickler and his suffragist wife, Alice, Sioux Falls that of Richard Pettigrew, Standing Rock that of Sitting Bull, De Smet that of Laura Ingalls Wilder, and Huron that of Gladys Pyle. Edgemont, the site of an ordinance depot during World War II, almost became a garbage dump in the 1980s. Milbank, the birthplace of American Legion baseball, also opened a granite quarry, which provided the stone for the Franklin Delano Roosevelt Memorial in Washington, D.C., and a coal-fired electricity plant. Pickstown was a new town, built to house workers constructing the Fort Randall Dam; Pollock was an old town, lifted lock, stock, and barrel to a new site above Lake Oahe, which submerged its old location under its waters. Deadwood and Flandreau became known for their gambling casinos, Oldham for its Potato Festival, Carthage for its straw-bale museum, Roslyn for its vinegar museum, and Lake Norden for the South Dakota Amateur Baseball Hall of Fame.

Whatever conferred notability on small towns, all of them, in fact, were more alike than different from each other. A continuing tension existed between townspeople's aspirations to succeed and grow, on the one hand, and the necessity for them to accommodate themselves to reality and to the constraints that faced them, on the other. During the heady early days of settlement, many towns aspired to greatness, boasting that they would become a "Little Chicago," a "New Denver," or something else grand. They could hardly be faulted for their ambition, for without such high expectations residents might not have ventured out onto the prairies in the first place. But South Dakotans, like their fellow Americans, were nothing if not pragmatic, and they gradually found it necessary to adjust their goals and expectations, bringing them into conformity with the actual opportunities that were available.

Between 1906 and 1911, Charles L. Hyde, Pierre's optimistic and indefatigable real estate mogul, erected several office buildings and the St. Charles Hotel along Capitol

Avenue and the Grand Opera House on Pierre Street, looking down the bluff toward the Missouri River. The ultimate "go-getter" and town booster, Hyde predicted that the up-and-coming capital city would someday grow to 100,000 people, rivaling Omaha and Denver for precedence on the plains. In December 1911, however, he was convicted of real estate fraud and sentenced to a $1,500 fine and a fifteen-month jail term, only to be pardoned by President William Howard Taft one day before the rotund Republican left office.[16] Hyde may have technically violated South Dakota's laws on advertising and real estate transactions, but his greater sin—if it deserves to be called that—was that of overexuberance. He refused to accept the idea that people could not make a windfall on land speculation or that projected rail and streetcar lines, which existed only in the fertile minds of their promoters, would not be built.

Hyde was not alone in this respect. The booster spirit was infectious on the frontier—and necessary. No town could hope to grow, or even survive, if its main-street storeowners and professionals did not vigorously promote the merits of their particular burgs over against their rivals. Inevitably, struggling communities found themselves caught between the urge to cooperate with their neighbors for mutual benefit and the compulsion to compete with them for customers. Every little town hoped to attract residents by improving its appearance; adding amenities such as water systems, sewer systems, telephone lines, electricity, and paved streets; and establishing thriving schools, churches, and civic organizations. The preeminent booster in most towns was the local newspaper editor, who kept up a running commentary in his editorials and columns, registering improvements and progress and constantly urging the citizenry to pull their weight and try a little harder. Local commercial clubs, set up to promote business and advertise the town, were ubiquitous, although enthusiasm and energy waxed and waned over time. By the 1920s, these groups were often replaced by Chambers of Commerce and Jaycee affiliates of their national organizations. Meanwhile, Lions, Kiwanis, and Rotary chapters began to capture membership from the old fraternal orders, such as the Masons, Woodmen, and Odd Fellows. Around that time, also, high school athletic teams became more prominent and better organized, adopting mascots and team names and establishing athletic conferences for competition with other schools. Increasingly, sports became the focus of town pride and inter-town rivalry, becoming a sort of glue that helped to hold a community together and give it identity.

During horse-and-buggy days, farmers generally did their business at the nearest railhead. Storekeepers and elevator managers worked energetically to solicit the business of those living more or less equidistant between towns. No one explained the

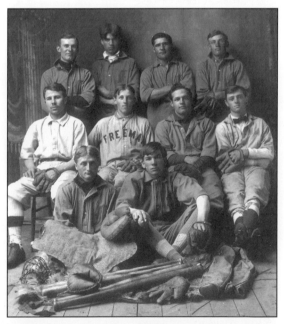

Members of the Freeman baseball team take time out from a game to document their role in providing this town of Germans from Russia with an important source of community pride. *Center for Western Studies.*

dynamics of small-town economies better than Thorstein Veblen. In his 1923 essay on the subject, he noted the central importance of real estate speculation, boosterism, and salesmanship in the life of small towns. In businesses' competition for customers, there were always more traders than conditions warranted. This encouraged collusion to prop up prices and to prevent profit margins from falling too far, which would have driven them all out of business. Main-street businessmen operated on the tacit assumption that they possessed a virtual monopoly on trade within their surrounding market areas, although it was never complete or indisputable. Charging what the traffic would bear, businessmen kept prices up as near they could to the practicable maximum. "And the townsmen are vigilant," Veblen shrewdly observed, "in taking due precautions that this virtual monopoly shall not be broken in upon." The two outside threats to this monopoly were rival country towns and the mail-order warehouses. Protest against the mail-order companies was loud and continual from small-town businessmen and newspaper editors during the early 1900s.[17]

From his vantage point in the early 1920s, Veblen understood that changes already beginning to transform American society would also revolutionize the setup that small-town businessmen were desperately trying to preserve. These changes included, first and foremost, improvements in transportation and communication that allowed both farmers and townspeople to travel beyond the closest market town to shop in larger communities having bigger—and cheaper—stocks of goods to sell, thus undercutting the monopoly that the village storekeepers had depended upon. Beyond that, there were modifications in wholesale distribution, the rise of chain stores, increased expenditures on advertising, and greater dependence upon distant sources of credit, which swept control away from local businessmen.[18] All of this remained a somewhat vague threat at the time Veblen was writing, but during the next half century, along with shifts in agriculture leading to much larger farm sizes and reduction in family fertility resulting in smaller families, the rural/small-town economy was transformed. This left most towns in South Dakota and the surrounding region grasping desperately to survive, let alone trying to become a little Chicago or new Denver.

The primary script for most towns in South Dakota for the past three-quarters of a century has been one of trying to manage change, being resourceful, facing up to new challenges and realities, and working to accommodate themselves to the new realities. Maintaining courage and morale grows more and more difficult as population declines; businesses, churches, and schools shut their doors; and young people depart for bigger places in search of jobs. The old booster spirit remains, however, in attenuated form. Without it—without hopes and dreams and a practical vision of the future—the possibilities for the health, and even survival, of these communities are meager. Hope is gleaned where it can be found. For instance, the 2000 census figures showed only half of the state's small towns losing population during the nineties, an improvement from the previous decade, when three-fourths had been in that category. South Dakotans, therefore, need to maintain a healthy balance between aspiration and accommodation.

Another continuing tension lies between conflict and consensus. Always, there is an effort to portray the population as pulling together, working cooperatively to promote the benefit of the entire community and not just individuals' personal welfare. By many standards, more consensus exists in small towns than in larger places. As noted above, South Dakotans rank high on scales of civic mindedness, social connectedness, philanthropy, volunteerism, and religiosity, while they register lower on measures of criminal activity, income disparity, and inter-racial conflict.[19] With relatively low percentages of blacks, Hispanics, Jews, Muslims, and other racial, ethnic, and religious minorities,

South Dakotans manifest a higher degree of racial and social homogeneity than is true elsewhere. The most notable exception lies in the large population of Native Americans, which constituted 8.3 percent of the population in the 2000 census and which is heavily concentrated on nine reservations, mostly in the West River part of the state. Continuing incidents of violence and discrimination and persistent expressions of racial discrimination and intolerance mar what is a clear record of improved race relations during the past several decades.

Continued tension between Indians and non-Indians, not surprisingly, is not the only thing that undermines consensus in the state. Students of history understand that conflict constitutes an elemental aspect of any culture. Alongside battles and depredations that drove Indians and whites apart during the frontier period, towns contested among themselves for primacy, a process most visibly revealed in the frequency of county seat contests. Many of these confrontations were colorful, some violent. One of the most memorable county seat battles in American history was the "Spink County War," pitting Ashton against Redfield, the latter prevailing in the contest.[20] Carrying the conflict to a higher level, Huron and Pierre engaged in a bitter fight for the location of the new state capital when South Dakota entered the Union in 1889.[21] The following year, an Independent party emerged, predecessor to the Populists, establishing a tradition of agrarian protest in the state, which manifested itself in subsequent decades in the Farm Holiday movement of the 1930s, the National Farmers Organization and American Agriculture Movement in the 1950s and 1970s, and a variety of other agitations and protests over time. Partisan political rivalries, labor union militancy, antiwar protests, debates over issues ranging from the income tax to abortion—all of these have added color and spice to South Dakota history. World War I unleashed a riot of anti-German fanaticism in the state. Persecution was so rife that all but one of its Hutterite colonies moved to Canada (only to return during the Great Depression). The Ku Klux Klan reared its ugly head during the 1920s. Anti-Catholicism was prevalent for many decades in a state where upwards of a third of the population was Roman Catholic. McCarthyism swelled in the 1950s, and debates over animal rights, environmentalism, water resources, daylight savings time, video lottery, taxation, and school consolidation split many communities and families. Needless to say, South Dakotans cannot easily portray themselves simply as "one big, happy family."

Yet, more than in most other states, South Dakotans have ways of moderating their conflicts and living peaceably together despite their differences and disagreements. South Dakota "niceness" is real, even if it does not always rule in particular situations. The high degree of church-going, healthy presence of service clubs and volunteer organizations, informal acceptance of responsibility for taking care of neighbors and members of the community, and traditions of civic duty and community-mindedness all serve to mask differences and lead to higher levels of community cohesion. Beginning in the 1920s, Young Citizens Leagues sprang up in almost every school in the state, training students in citizenship, democratic procedure, and volunteerism. Long gone, they have been replaced of late in many schools by character-education programs because teachers, principals, and parents recognize that living in a toxic popular culture requires aggressive intervention to counteract the pressures and seductions that encourage selfishness, thoughtlessness, and deviancy in young people.

This leads to another perennial conflict—that of the individual against community. South Dakotans are examples, par excellence, of the truth that individuals attain the highest degree of freedom only within the context of strong and supportive communities. Individual and community are not logically separate, but rather conjoined. Nevertheless, the suspicion persists that only if community norms and injunctions are relaxed or discarded altogether can individuals enjoy the highest degree of freedom. Thus, from the beginning, South Dakotans, like people elsewhere, have had to confront and try to work out the dilemma of individual and community.

The frontier experience bred individualism, and South Dakota provided its share of gritty exemplars, from Sitting Bull to Charles ("Pa") Ingalls, who bounced around the midwestern frontier constantly in search of "elbow room," to Oscar Micheaux, the black homesteader noted earlier who, after pioneering in Gregory County, went on to a storied career as a creative novelist and movie-maker long before blacks had carved out a niche in those fields. Prominent South Dakotans who grew up in small towns, from George McGovern to Dona Brown, from E. O. Lawrence to Niels Hansen, and from Al Neuharth to Julie Gerberding, have made their marks in many fields, demonstrating the success that can be won by individuals exhibiting ambition, drive, and creativity.

Community, however, was no less of a goal and a value in small towns than individualism. Success derives as much from the support a person receives from the surrounding institutional matrix as from one's inner drive and ability. Church, school, family, and neighborhood all contribute to healthy personal growth and development. What struck such critics of small towns as Sinclair Lewis and H. L. Mencken as being stifling and retrograde, others, holding perhaps a more balanced viewpoint, understood as healthy and uplifting. Maintaining an appropriate balance between individual and community in small-town culture remains an enduring challenge.

Finally, the admixture of change and continuity always makes for interesting results. The transformations that Laura Ingalls Wilder witnessed in her life, from horse-and-buggy days in De Smet to penicillin, television, jet planes, and earth satellites in small-town Missouri, where she lived most of her life, were remarkable. History, in one of its definitions, is the record of change over time. It emphasizes discontinuities, turning points, cycles, and social evolution. History, however, is no less the record of continuity—a story of permanence, tradition, and stability. A person who lived in or visited one of South Dakota's small towns during the 1880s, 1920s, or 1950s would discover much today that is familiar and recognizable. Many of the original houses and buildings that go back more than a century still stand, although a large number of them have been modified and expanded over the years, or torn down. Downtown streets are still there, though now they are paved and extend out into what used to be cornfields. Many of the same institutions and social organizations still operate, though often in different fashion and with different results. The changes that have occurred, obviously, are profound; no one's life remains unaffected by the process. But in South Dakota's small towns, perhaps as much as anywhere else, historical memory and tradition die hard. There are people in their nineties living in the houses they were born in, third- and fourth-generation businessmen carrying on at what their great-grandmothers and grandfathers started, churches still singing the same hymns they sang a hundred years ago. Schools continue to teach history, geography, and literature; ballplayers still sling the old hummer in there; paraders still march proudly on the Fourth of July; gardeners still dust their potatoes in summer. In change there is continuity, and vice versa.

Chapter 12
Politics Since Statehood

The achievement of statehood for South Dakota in 1889 was cause for special rejoicing among its almost 330,000 residents because they had waited longer than most of their counterparts elsewhere to escape what they considered to be a "colonial" status. It had been twenty-eight long years since Dakota Territory had been established just before the outbreak of the Civil War, and almost three decades of carpetbag rule had left many of the territory's residents increasingly disgruntled. To have to endure rule by political appointees who were relatives or friends of prominent eastern politicians in the governor's office and other high positions was bad enough; making it worse was that few of the interlopers had any ties to the area before arriving there, and several of them were corrupt political hacks whose only purpose was to aggrandize themselves through holding office. Territorial government rested lightly enough on the citizenry, however, and little permanent damage was done by the temporary carpetbag officials. More important, a distinctive political tradition emerged between 1861 and 1889 that became the foundation for political changes that occurred during the 1890s and early 1900s.[1]

Consisting largely of agricultural homesteaders and townbuilders from New England, the Upper Midwest, and countries in Northern and Western Europe, residents of Dakota Territory manifested many of the same political tendencies found in the places from which they had come. Heavily Scandinavian and German in ethnic background, Dakotans exhibited a strong strain of civic mindedness and voted heavily Republican. Dakota Territory, in a real sense, became a means of implementing the nationalist policy of the nascent Republican Party. Patronage politics, by its very nature, invited incompetence and rascality, and territorial government, as a result, was not of very high quality. From the beginning, Democrats found themselves in a minority position, and it would take many decades before genuine two-party competition emerged in what became South Dakota. As was true elsewhere, the citizenry looked first to local government, only secondly to the territory (and later the state), and finally to the federal government for solutions to their problems. A fierce tradition of independence and self-reliance was manifest from the outset. Township government took firm root early on and maintained its influence far past the time when it had withered in other states.[2] Dakota residents were not inclined to place their politicians on a pedestal. During the territorial period, a two-house legislature was elected by the voters to enact laws that were administered by appointed officials. They knew their elected leaders, expected them to be responsive to their needs and interests, and were ready to discard them when they felt they were not doing their duty.

■ Rise of Populism

South Dakota's admission to the Union in 1889 during a period of severe economic distress and rising agrarian protest made the state's first decade of political experience one of the most interesting periods in its history. The 1890s witnessed the rise of Populism, one of the United States' most significant political movements, on the northern Great Plains, and South Dakota was in the forefront of it. Involvement with

Governors of South Dakota

Arthur C. Mellette	(R)	1889-1893
Charles H. Sheldon	(R)	1893-1987
Andrew E. Lee	Fusion	1897-1901
Charles N. Herreid	(R)	1901-1905
Samuel H. Elrod	(R)	1905-1907
Coe I. Crawford	(R)	1907-1909
Robert S. Vessey	(R)	1909-1913
Frank M. Byrne	(R)	1913-1917
Peter Norbeck	(R)	1917-1921
William H. McMaster	(R)	1921-1925
Carl Gunderson	(R)	1925-1927
William J. Bulow	(D)	1927-1931
Warren E. Green	(R)	1931-1933
Thomas M. Berry	(D)	1933-1937
Leslie Jensen	(R)	1937-1939
Harlan J. Bushfield	(R)	1939-1943
Merrell Q. Sharpe	(R)	1943-1947
George T. Mickelson	(R)	1947-1951
Sigurd Anderson	(R)	1951-1955
Joseph J. Foss	(R)	1955-1959
Ralph Herseth	(D)	1959-1961
Archie Gubbrud	(R)	1961-1965
Nils A. Boe	(R)	1965-1969
Frank L. Farrar	(R)	1969-1971
Richard F. Kneip	(D)	1971-1978
Harvey L. Wollman	(D)	1978-1979
William J. Janklow	(R)	1979-1987
George S. Mickelson	(R)	1987-1993
Walter Dale Miller	(R)	1993-1995
William J. Janklow	(R)	1995-2003
Michael Rounds	(R)	2003-

Populism established a tradition of agrarian radicalism in the state that had reverberations during the Progressive Era of the early 1900s, the Farm Holiday protests and New Deal experiments of the 1930s, the reorganization of the Democratic Party during the 1950s, and assorted farm protest activities at various other times. Populism's reign in the state, however, was brief, a reminder of the continuing strength of conservative ideas and organization in the state. South Dakota's political history can be written in terms of a dialectic between Populist/Progressive (or liberal) leanings, on the one hand, and traditional (or conservative) ones on the other.

The conditions setting the stage for the rise of Populism had become increasingly apparent by the spring of 1890. Farmers were suffering from drought conditions and reduced crop yields, while commodity prices continued drifting downward. Farmers, weighed down by heavy debt loads, pointed accusing fingers at eastern banking interests in control of interest rates. Dependent upon the railroad to ship their products out of the state, as well as to import agricultural machinery and consumer goods, agrarians complained of high and discriminatory rates and resented political pressures from corporate interests that prevented effective governmental regulation. "Wall Street" became a term of opprobrium and a symbol of the monopolistic practices of eastern bankers and managers of the "trusts," who prospered while farmers were suffering.

Farmers had played only a minor role in the statehood movement of the 1880s, in part because most of them perceived little benefit in it for them. Their suspicion that South Dakota's Republican-dominated political machinery had little to offer them seemed to be confirmed by the early actions of the new state legislature when it failed to move in 1890 on agrarian demands for remedial legislation and rejected the candidates that were put forward by them for a U.S. Senate seat. Two high-ranking Republican power brokers, Sioux Falls lawyer Richard Pettigrew and Deadwood judge Gideon Moody, received the nod over Farmers' Alliance candidates Alonzo Wardall and A. J. Edgerton. Worse, in the eyes of the farm group, the latter soon obtained a federal judgeship, apparent confirmation of their suspicion that Edgerton had betrayed them by entering into a "corrupt bargain" with the Republican machine by playing down his candidacy in return for a political job.

A territorial Farmers' Alliance had been established in 1885 to promote farm coop-eratives and advance the farmers' cause. At first, it had rejected partisan political action, preferring to back political candidates regardless of party who supported their view-point. President Henry L. Loucks, a farmer from Deuel County, had originally opposed third-party action, but now he changed his mind. At a joint convention of the Farmers' Alliance and the Knights of Labor in Huron on June 6, 1890, the assembled delegates voted 413 to 83 to combine forces and form an Independent Party. Their platform called for a variety of political and economic reforms, including the Australian ballot, a federal income tax, government ownership of the railroads, the abolition of national banks, and the free and unlimited coinage of silver. Preceding Kansas by a matter of days in estab-lishing a farmer-oriented third party, South Dakota could lay claim to being the birth-place of the Populist (or People's) Party, which was organized nationally in Cincinnati the following May.[3]

In Loucks, the South Dakota group possessed a far-sighted and eloquent spokesman who provided a high quality of leadership. The Canadian-born farmer was a tireless and effective advocate of the cooperative principle and improved education for farmers. His capturing of thirty-two percent of the vote as Independent gubernatorial candidate in 1890 launched the new party on a high note, establishing instant credibility and stimu-lating high hopes for its future. Incumbent Republican Governor Arthur Mellette won re-election with forty-four percent of the vote, but saw his total reduced by 20,000 from the previous election. The Democratic candidate trailed with twenty-four percent, based on 5,000 fewer votes than his predecessor had received in 1889.

Just as encouraging, the Independents elected nearly seventy members to the state legislature, gaining virtual parity with the Republicans. In the long, drawn-out balloting to choose a U.S. senator to succeed Gideon Moody, who had drawn the two-year term at the time of statehood, the Independents benefited from a deal of their own in which seventeen Democrats switched over to their candidate, James H. Kyle, of Aberdeen, on the fortieth ballot, while three Independents in the Illinois Senate gave their votes to the Democratic senatorial candidate there.[4] Nevertheless, little else was gained during the legislative session, as conservative lawmakers blocked all efforts to implement the Independent platform.

The following year, South Dakotans influenced national politics by selecting Loucks to preside over the first nominating convention of the new Populist Party in Omaha. The historic platform adopted there established an agenda for political reform in the United States for the next quarter-century. Senator Kyle, a Congregational minister who had first attracted attention for a rousing oration that appealed to disgruntled farmers at a Fourth of July gathering in Aberdeen in 1890, obtained 275 votes for the presidential nomination, but the nod went to General James B. Weaver, a former three-term con-gressman from Iowa, who received 995 votes. That November, Populist gubernatorial candidate A. E. Van Osdel received thirty-two percent of the vote, equaling the percent-age the party had received in 1890. Meanwhile, their legislative representation shrank to seventeen, and their only victory in the third legislative session was passage of a bill requiring the popular election of railroad commissioners.

It has been said that for farm groups to do well (politically) they must fail (economi-cally). Evidence for this observation seemed abundant in the years following 1893, for with the financial panic of that year and the worldwide depression that accompanied it, agricultural protest blossomed. In its wake, the Populist Party achieved its greatest suc-cesses. In 1894 the Populist gubernatorial candidate picked up thirty-six percent of the vote, and the party put twenty-four reformers in the legislature. Once again, the legislative session that followed failed to enact any important reform legislation. In surrounding states and in other regions where the Populists were active, momentum continued to build, however, and by 1896 a single issue had interjected itself on the political scene, rendering everything else secondary. That was the question of the currency and specifically the proposal for "free silver," or the free and unlimited coinage of silver at the ratio of sixteen to one. Agrarians and other debtors found themselves in an untenable position, attempting to pay off loans in a deflationary situation, where the money they paid back was worth more than the money they had originally borrowed. In addition, farmers were of the opinion that expanding the currency supply would tend to drive up farm prices, which during the nineties were sinking to ever-lower levels. A bushel of wheat worth $1.10 in 1881 was down below sixty cents in 1892. Corn, bringing sixty-three cents a bushel in 1881, was down to twenty-eight cents in 1890.

Recognizing the appeal of inflation, former Nebraska Congressman William Jennings Bryan dramatically captured the Democratic nomination in 1896 largely on the basis of his eloquent "Cross of Gold" speech strongly endorsing free silver at the party's Chicago convention. Populists perceived an opportunity in merging their fortunes with the Democrats, and at their national convention that year they chose the "Boy Orator of the Platte" as their nominee (although opting for their own candidate for the vice presidency). Many members of the party objected to the move as one of political expediency that would obscure and perhaps scuttle any chances of enacting the other elements of their program, but the lure of victory in combination with the Democrats was too strong and carried the day. Bryan ran an innovative whistle-stop campaign that summer and fall, traveling 18,000 miles by rail to every section of the country, delivering 600 speeches and providing a model for later presidential candidates. He received thunderous ovations in appearances in Sioux Falls and Aberdeen and carried the state by 183 votes, while losing to Ohio Governor William McKinley nationally, fifty-one percent to forty-seven percent.

South Dakota's Populists joined their national counterparts in fusing with the Democrats in quest of victory that year. Actually, it was a three-way combination, the third component consisting of free silverites from the Republican Party, most prominently Senator Pettigrew, who walked out on the Republicans and declared his allegiance to Populism. Andrew E. Lee, a successful farmer and businessman from Vermillion, whose views on free silver and monopolies and reform-minded administration as mayor of that town had attracted considerable attention, received the gubernatorial nomination. The Democrats, in turn, called off their state convention and endorsed the Populist slate of candidates. The Fusion ticket was boosted by the revelation of a major financial scandal in the Republican administration, in which state Treasurer W. W. Taylor ran off with $367,000 of the state's money, temporarily hiding out in South America before returning to face the music, which turned out to be a relatively light two-year jail term.[5] Lee's margin of victory in the 1896 election was only slightly larger than Bryan's—319 votes out of 82,000 cast. The Fusionists also obtained a majority of about a dozen in the state legislature and captured both congressional seats as well as several other state offices.

Having won power through jettisoning their independent electoral status, the Populists quickly discovered that office-holding by itself did not necessarily bring desired results. The first clue to their weakness came in their failure to dislodge James H. Kyle from his seat in the U.S. Senate. During six years in Washington he had drifted more and more into the Republican orbit, and now he managed to win re-election with the votes of the Republican minority in the legislature combined with thirteen disaffected fusionists.[6]

The most important piece of legislation passed during the 1897 legislative session was the Palmer-Wheeler Act, granting the state railroad commission the power to set maximum rates for railroads. The law, however, was later rendered meaningless by court decisions that culminated in a case before the South Dakota Supreme Court in 1901 declaring it unconstitutional. The most important accomplishment of the Populists while they were in office was the passage by the legislature of a constitutional amendment, subsequently ratified by the electorate, creating the initiative and referendum. South Dakota thereby became the first state in the Union to enable the general public to initiate legislation through the petition process and to have laws referred to them for approval or disapproval on the general ballot.[7] It was a prime example of "returning power to the people," a central slogan of the Populists in their quest for making democracy real.

Governor Lee squeezed back into office in 1898, again by a little more than 300 votes, but now the Populists were reduced to less than forty members in the legislature and accomplished little. Attention in the state turned to the aftermath of the war in Cuba and subsequent use of South Dakota men in military uniform in an effort to put down an insurrection in the Philippines after America's acquisition of that territory from Spain. As new supplies of gold were being discovered in Alaska and South Africa, the national money shortage abated, and the return of better weather and improved farm prices further reduced agrarian discontent. Senator Kyle continued to associate himself with Republicans in Congress, Henry Loucks announced his return to the GOP, and Senator Pettigrew drifted over to the Democrats and later to the Socialists, losing his seat in the Senate as a result of the election of 1900. By the time the last national convention of the Populists was held in Sioux Falls that year, interest in the party was pretty much dormant, and in South Dakota it quickly was reduced to mere historical interest.

During their short period of activity and success, however, the Populist Party established a significant political legacy in South Dakota. Beyond introducing the initiative and referendum and providing a foundation for further governmental regulation, they established a tradition of radical protest and a reform agenda that would play a central role in political debate for a generation. Progressivism, while differing from Populism in many ways, was an extension of it in its attacks on monopoly power, its criticism of the excesses of capitalist development, and its reliance upon governmental power to seek to ameliorate social and economic problems. Populism also established a style of leadership that appealed directly to the populace and encouraged unpredictability and maverick tendencies.

The question of who the Populists were has intrigued many historians, and South Dakota Populism has received considerable attention.[8] Farmers, and especially wheat farmers of Scandinavian, German, and, to a lesser degree, Czech, descent, voted disproportionately for Populist candidates.[9] The most anti-Populist counties were heavily German-Russian in background. Somewhat surprisingly, the strength of Populism increased with increasing wealth but dropped off in the very richest counties.[10] Populists were primarily rural in orientation, while town residents were much less attracted to their banner, although some of the movement's most important leaders resided in towns.

While neither in the state nor in the nation as a whole did the Populist Party succeed in their goal of welding together an effective farmer-labor coalition, there was some degree of labor support, and several other reform-minded groups provided additional support. Up through the early 1890s, the Knights of Labor remained an important presence among artisans and wage-laborers in the state, and they provided significant ballast for the organization. Watertown newspaper editor Sylvester J. Conklin and Catholic priest Robert W. Haire of Aberdeen were specially prominent leaders in the Knights.[11] In addition, there were prohibitionists, advocates of Henry George's single tax, and socialists involved in the movement.[12] Women seem to have played a significant role, given especially that they were not allowed to vote except in school elections.[13]

It appears from a study of Brown County Populists that the party in South Dakota resembled versions in other states in the sense of being a "movement culture," to use a term coined by historian Lawrence Goodwyn. More than simply a political faction or party, Populism enlisted its followers in a highly emotional cause, gathering them together for speeches, rallies, barbecues, camp meetings, and street marches. In a real sense, Populists sought to restore a sense of community as well as address social and economic problems that were facing them.[14] In their social attitudes and values, Populists differed little from the general populace. While they sometimes castigated eastern and international bankers and sometimes included the word "Jew" in their diatribes, they were not necessarily any more anti-Semitic than their neighbors, nor were they measurably more provincial, narrow-minded, or paranoid than others.[15]

While generally "leftist" or "radical" in orientation, the Populists established a style of political campaigning and recruiting that continued to persist in South Dakota for many decades and, to some degree, up to the present time. The sense of community and camaraderie continues to prevail in South Dakota's small towns and its rural environs, in a state where, as late as the 2000 census, only three towns counted as many as 25,000 people. In that context, politics, of necessity, remained heavily personal and local, and politicians got to know their constituents and "press the flesh" in ways that became increasingly uncommon elsewhere in the decades after World War II.

The decline of Populism after the turn of the century did not signal the death of the reform spirit in South Dakota. Rather, the impulse was absorbed by and transformed into something new by the Progressive Movement, which emerged during the early 1900s. Concerned about many of the same kinds of issues that had motivated the earlier protest group, Progressives searched for practical solutions to the problems of industrial monopoly, labor conditions, machine politics, consumer protection, and massive changes that accompanied a rapidly industrializing, urbanizing society and the technological innovations that spawned it. As Kansas journalist William Allen White put it, Progressive politicians during the early 1900s "caught the Populists in swimming and stole all of their clothing except the frayed underdrawers of free silver."[16] As one of the most heavily rural states in the Union, South Dakota had its own special needs and interests.

■ Progressivism: Phase I

Progressivism resembled Populism in its desire to ameliorate social and economic problems; its confidence that practical solutions to these problems were discoverable; its concern for the working classes, farmers, and underprivileged elements in society; and its reliance upon governmental intervention to bring about needed improvements. It differed from its predecessor in being more broadly based, adopting a more moderate tone, exerting greater power and influence, and accomplishing more substantial results. Emerging to influence in the state somewhat later than the national progressive movement and carrying on somewhat longer, South Dakota Progressives played a dominant role in state politics between 1906 and 1924. All five governors holding office during the period identified with the group. While spirited contests continued within the Republican Party between the progressive wing and the more conservative (or stalwart) wing, the former held sway most of the time. While Democrats were also influenced by progressive doctrines during the period, they remained a secondary factor in state politics. For all practical purposes, control of the state was determined by contests between the Progressives and the Stalwarts within the Republican Party, first in the nominating conventions and, after 1908, in primary elections. The general election in November merely confirmed choices that had been made earlier within the Republican primary.

Progressives were more middle class in orientation than the Populists had been, but as an agricultural state, South Dakota had a much more agrarian flavor to its brand of Progressivism than did many other states. Most of the major leadership and much of the energy and initiative of the Progressive Movement in the state emerged along main-street among lawyers, businessmen, ministers, educators, and others who joined it. Any political movement able successfully to embody so many different interests—farmers, laborers, small businessmen, professionals, clergy, educators, women, and others—for such a long period of time displayed both considerable adaptability and practicality, as well as vagueness and expediency. But at its heart Progressivism was idealistic and visionary, moved by a conception of what a better society could be and by high ethical and often religiously motivated impulses.

Progressivism emerged nationally during the 1890s as municipal reform groups coalesced to elect reform-minded mayors to root out corruption and address pressing social and economic problems. The Midwest became a focal point of the movement after 1900. The year 1904 witnessed the election of several Progressive governors—Robert M. La Follette in Wisconsin, Albert B. Cummins in Iowa, and John A. Johnson in Minnesota.[17] That was also the year that Huron lawyer Coe I. Crawford launched his Progressive bid for the governorship in South Dakota, losing on the first try while setting the stage for victory two years later. Crawford and a rapidly expanding coterie of Progressive politicians took as their models two men especially: La Follette of Wisconsin and President Theodore Roosevelt. Both the governor and the president visited and spoke in the state, worked with the Progressive leadership there, vied for their

Before he became governor in 1907, launching the Progessive Movement in South Dakota, Coe I. Crawford (right) practiced law in Huron with his partner, Charles E. DeLand (left), shown here in their law office in 1897. *Courtesy South Dakota State Historical Society–State Archives.*

support while competing with each other for the presidential nomination in 1912, and provided inspirational examples for their followers. Even before Crawford launched his gubernatorial bid, making Progressivism a visible entity in the state, Progressivism was bubbling up at the grass roots, spilling over from surrounding states and being energized by what was happening elsewhere in the country.[18]

Crawford, who for six years had served as chief legal counsel for the Chicago and North Western Railroad at its state headquarters in Huron, was motivated by three factors in December 1903 when he dramatically announced his resignation from the railroad and his decision to run for governor. It was, first of all, a principled decision. Having observed at first hand corporate abuses of power and improper political influence, especially in the form of the liberal dispensation of railroad passes, he had become sick and tired of it all. Personal ambition was also a factor, as Crawford resented being passed over for a U.S. Senate position in 1903, after the yeoman service he had provided to the Republican Party in a variety of positions. Third, he had become alienated from the Republican political machine in control of the state, whose leader, Alfred B. Kittredge, had received the nod for the Senate seat from that group, of which Crawford had previously been an integral part. When the Huron attorney spoke about "machine politics," he knew whereof he spoke. Like La Follette and a number of other Progressives around the country, he had undergone a political "conversion" experience, and now he was battling for the "forces of light" against those of "darkness."

The first battle in 1904 ended in failure, but Crawford took his loss that year in the Republican convention to incumbent Governor Samuel H. Elrod, of Clark, with good grace and campaigned for the ticket in November. Working with fellow Huronite Richard O. Richards, a wealthy businessman and the driving force behind the formation of the Republican State Primary League, Crawford successfully captured the gubernatorial nomination two years later, easily defeating his Democratic opponent in the fall election. The first thing on his agenda in the 1907 legislature was passage of a direct primary law, making South Dakota one of the early states to enact this method, designed to make the political system operate more democratically. Other legislation banning railroad passes, requiring lobbyists to register with the state, prohibiting corporations from making political contributions, setting maximum railroad passenger rates, establishing a pure food and drug commission and a telephone commission, dispensing free textbooks to public schools, and raising tax assessments on corporate property rendered the 1907 legislative session the most productive one in state history in terms of significant legislation passed. Requiring bona fide residence in the state of one year before one could obtain a divorce also ended Sioux Falls' reputation as a "divorce mill."

Crawford, who deserves credit for launching the Progressive Movement in South Dakota, spent only a single two-year term in the statehouse before narrowly unseating his nemesis Alfred B. Kittredge and going on to the U.S. Senate, which had been his primary ambition all along. His successors, former Progressive state Senators Robert S. Vessey and Frank M. Byrne, carried on the Progressive tradition in the governor's chair for the next eight years, though not without considerable opposition from the stalwart faction in the state. Vessey, a general merchandise proprietor and rancher from Wessington Springs and a devout Methodist layman, took special interest in promoting temperance and moral legislation, reflective of the strong religious impulse within Progressivism. As governor, he signed laws prohibiting drinking and gambling on passenger trains, banning profanity, and ending the dispensing of free liquor on election day. He was the first state governor officially to proclaim the observance of Mother's Day, helping make it a popular day of recognition of the family. The most controversial issue during the four years in office of his successor, Frank M. Byrne, a businessman and land dealer from Faulkton, was the establishment of a tax commission, which moved to equalize assessment on real and personal property. He also made the first of many efforts to reorganize the executive branch along more efficient lines and worked for the establishment of a highway commission to help plan and construct more adequate roadways for an increasingly automobile-oriented populace. Under these two governors, the Progressive spirit stayed afloat, but the pace of activity slowed until the ascendancy of Peter Norbeck.

■ Progressivism: Phase II

Peter Norbeck may well have been the most successful governor in South Dakota history in terms of leadership, legislation enacted, cooperation with the legislature, and influence on the general public. A hugely successful well-driller from Redfield,

Norbeck, who spoke with a thick Norwegian accent and maintained his plebian ways despite his personal wealth, had a way of winning over people, especially in one-on-one conversations. Pushed into politics by those around him, he was a highly popular choice for the governorship in 1916 after completing three terms in the state senate and one term as lieutenant governor. Rivalry within the Republican Party between Progressives and Stalwarts had peaked in 1912 when the former, using tricky and underhanded methods, had managed to get Theodore Roosevelt designated as the recipient of Republican electoral votes, despite the fact that incumbent President William Howard Taft had fairly won the Republican presidential nomination at the Republican national convention that year. Two years later, a Democrat, Edwin S. Johnson, had managed narrowly to win the open U.S. Senate seat after Coe I. Crawford's loss to Stalwart Congressman Charles H. Burke, further embittering factional rivalry within the Republican Party. The Progressives were often less than harmonious among themselves for reasons ranging from doubts about Crawford's true commitment to Progressive principles (his first major act as a senator had been to vote for the unpopular Payne-Aldridge Tariff, backed by President Taft) to controversies caused by Richard O. Richards' strident promotion of his own personal version of a new primary election law, which was considered too extreme by many Progressives.[19]

Norbeck's election in 1916 reunified the Progressive faction and poised it for its greatest successes. While America's entry into World War I the following year set the stage for Progressivism's national demise, the movement remained a vital presence in South Dakota for another eight years under Norbeck and his successor, William H. McMaster. Besides providing a charismatic leader for the faction and accumulating a record of legislative achievement that ranked with any other governor in the state's history, Norbeck cobbled together a personal organization that provided the basis for continued Progressive competitiveness until his death, as a U.S. senator, in 1936. His personal, business, and political contacts around the state were numerous, and he was able to call on scores of people for political support and assistance.

Norbeck's prime asset as a campaigner was the farm vote, and his first priority in the 1917 legislative session was a rural credits law, allowing farmers to borrow money from the state at lower interest rates than they could obtain in the open market. The legislation was highly popular with the group it assisted, but the guidelines provided in the law were too lenient and administration of it was too lax, which, along with the drastic decline of commodity prices during

Peter Norbeck, possibly South Dakota's most successful governor, reunified the Progressive faction and provided leadership in such areas as state hail insurance for farmers, development of Custer State Park, and woman suffrage in advance of federal legislation. In this photo, taken in 1927, with Clyde James (on muleback) at the Custer State Park Game Lodge, Norbeck was serving as U.S. Senator. *Courtesy South Dakota State Historical Society–State Archives.*

the early 1920s, led to a meltdown of the system by 1925 and its final demise two years later. Before the bad debts were paid and the program finally liquidated, it had cost the state $57 million, a prime example of how good intentions could lead the Progressives to make bad policy.[20] Other legislation passed during the session was less controversial but in many cases also of long-term significance, including a workmen's compensation act, mother's pensions, statewide prohibition, the creation of an industrial commission and a new, reorganized highway department, and proposed constitutional amendments allowing for state hail insurance, a state-owned coal mine, and the construction of a cement plant, grain elevators, flour mills, packing houses, and hydroelectric projects.

Following passage of these constitutional amendments, at Governor Norbeck's urging the 1919 legislature went on to establish a hail insurance plan, cement plant, and coal mine, while the other "state socialism" projects were dropped. The governor's interest in conservation also found expression in the creation of a state park board to administer development of Custer State Park. Norbeck got involved personally in locating and designing some of the scenic roadways that made the park such a successful tourist attraction in later years. In this and other ways, South Dakota Progressivism allied itself to the national Progressive Movement; both sought to make life better for ordinary people, regulate corporate activities and working conditions, protect consumer interests, promote conservation, and place government in the service of public goals. Seeking to "make democracy real" was its central motive. Writer and editor Henry Croly explained it this way: "Using Hamiltonian means to achieve Jeffersonian ends." By this he meant using the power of the state to promote the interests of ordinary people. Not all of the programs inaugurated by the Progressives panned out. Rural credits went bust; the coal mine and hail insurance were discontinued in the 1930s. Overall, however, what the Progressives initiated became a permanent part of the political landscape, although many specifics underwent modification with time.

Two other political challenges tested the mettle of Governor Norbeck: the rise of the Nonpartisan League and United States participation in the war in Europe. Just like the Populists and other reform-oriented groups before them, Progressives had a tendency to fight among themselves and to form splinter groups. By their very nature they were dissatisfied with the status quo and shied away from predictability and convention. Internal feuding was frequent, but in the fall of 1916 Progressives faced a powerful new rival for factional leadership, as Nonpartisan League (NPL) organizers streamed across the border from North Dakota, having emerged there the year before. The brainchild of former Socialist organizer A. C. Townley, the NPL appealed to the same kinds of people that the Progressives did, especially farmers, and advocated the same kinds of programs, except that they tended to be bolder and more radical than their South Dakota counterparts.

Governor Norbeck could have tried to ally with them and build a broader coalition, but he viewed the group as a rival to his leadership and was determined to stop them in their tracks. Their quick success in selling sixteen-dollar, two-year memberships highlighted the problem. Although the NPL's claim of having signed up 20,000 members in the state by March 1917 was no doubt an exaggeration, the political threat it posed was genuine. Norbeck's strategy for defusing the League was notably successful.[21] First, he contrasted his own record of success in the legislature with the NPL's failure in North Dakota (their major legislative victories would come later). Second, the governor argued that his own programs adequately addressed the problems identified by the North Dakotans. In part, he would have pushed his ideas anyway; in part, no doubt, he backed advanced proposals because of the new threat posed from the outside. As he put it in a letter to Governor Henry Allen of Kansas, "I believe the best way to meet the League proposition is to give the farmers every reasonable thing they ask for and refuse to go along with them on the impractical."[22] Finally, Norbeck portrayed the NPL as too radical and, as the war proceeded, disloyal. The strategy worked effectively in 1918, as he won re-election with a twenty-seven point margin over his nearest competitor.

That year, the NPL candidate received 25,118 votes to Norbeck's 51,175, as the Democratic nominee trailed with 17,858 votes. Unlike the situation in North Dakota, where the NPL played an increasingly important role within the Republican Party, and Minnesota, where the Farmer-Labor Party won elections as an independent entity during the twenties and thirties before melding into the Democratic Farmer-Labor Party in the 1940s, the Nonpartisan League in South Dakota had only a fleeting and marginal impact. The progressive impulse there exerted its effect within the Republican Party and remained a moderating influence on political activity rather than a radical one.

Governor Norbeck also played a role in South Dakota's obtaining the vote for women before the Nineteenth Amendment made it a national phenomenon. The process that had brought South Dakota in as a state in 1889 had provided for a referendum on women's suffrage, which resulted in the rejection of the idea by a two-to-one margin when it was held in 1890. For almost three decades, woman suffrage advocates, including a fair sprinkling of men, continued to push the issue, and seven referendums were conducted over the years, the last one in 1918 finally yielding victory for the movement. The two most powerful and heavily organized groups attempting to block it during that period were the liquor industry and German-Americans. More surprisingly, significant opposition came from women themselves, who were supported in the teens by the Society Opposed to the Further Extension of Suffrage to Women. Success was finally achieved after the reorganization of the suffrage groups in 1911 in the South Dakota Universal Franchise League. Under the leadership of Mary Shields Pyle of Huron, the League organized meetings and rallies, published a newsletter, distributed literature, and got out the vote. The victory came in 1918 when voters approved a constitutional amendment promoted by Governor Norbeck linking voting for women to the withdrawal of voting privileges from alien immigrants. Many South Dakotans did not want to allow voting privileges to German immigrants who had not been naturalized while the country was fighting Germany in World War I. This marriage of convenience worked as planned, and South Dakota women obtained the vote two years before many of their compatriots in other states.[23]

World War I saw state government turn its attention to maintaining security and encouraging support for the war effort. Laws were passed prohibiting criminal syndicalism, making labor compulsory for idle and unemployed persons, restricting foreign language use, and inculcating patriotism in public schools. A state Council of Defense was set up to coordinate county and local councils in their efforts to sell war bonds, foster loyalty and patriotism, conserve fuel and food, and assist local draft boards. Groups and individuals perceived as disloyal or critical of the war effort were arrested or informally persecuted for their offenses. Political Progressivism failed to prevent this growing spirit of intolerance.

Afterwards, people wished to forget about the war and to concentrate on their own personal affairs. Politics in the twenties in South Dakota, as elsewhere in the United States, focused more on economic security and business expansion, discarding the reformist zeal that had characterized it for a decade and a half. Until mid-decade, however, the state's last Progressive governor, Yankton banker William H. McMaster, worked to keep the Progressive spirit alive. His energies were primarily directed toward implementing legislation passed during his predecessor's term—administering the rural credits program and initiating the state-owned enterprises authorized by the 1919 legislature. His most dramatic gesture during his two terms in office was to initiate the "governor's gas war," challenging monopolistic pricing practices of the big oil companies. When gasoline shot up to twenty-six cents a gallon, he instructed the Highway Department to sell it for sixteen cents, just two cents above cost. The oil companies howled in protest, but most of the public viewed the action as a legitimate way to reign in excessive corporate power.

The desire to assist ordinary citizens against trusts and corporations and to make the political system more democratic lay at the heart of Progressivism and remains its lasting legacy. Characterized by a dualistic mindset, pitting "good" against "evil" and "us" against "them," Progressivism resembled Populism in establishing a style of thinking that inclined people to be skeptical of large institutional power, demand fairness and equal treatment for people of all walks of life, and look to government for solutions to practical problems. After McMaster, the state, somewhat later than the rest of the country, fell under the spell of orthodox Republicanism during the late 1920s. By then, a pattern had been set for continuing debate and conflict between the progressive and conservative wings within the Republican Party. Eventually, the progressive impulse found a more congenial home inside the Democratic Party.

■ Conservatism in the Saddle

The election in 1924 of Carl Gunderson, a farmer from Aurora County, marked the return of orthodox Republicanism to the governor's office. An able administrator and possessed of the common touch, he had the misfortune of occupying the position when the financial breakdown of the Bank Depositor's Guaranty Law and Rural Credits Program first became apparent. The 1925 session of the legislature repealed the former, as private investors were eventually stuck with $39 million in worthless certificates issued by the program, and it launched an investigation of the latter, leading to the conviction for embezzlement of its treasurer, Pierre banker A. W. Ewert, who was sentenced to an eleven-year jail term. The loan program collapsed under the weight of agricultural depression and loose lending policies. In attempting to pin the blame for the financial debacle on his Progressive predecessors, Governor Gunderson exacerbated growing tensions between the progressive and conservative wings of the party. These divisions were further fueled by the governor's lack of enthusiasm for Norbeck's park and conservation projects, his abortive efforts to reduce the number of state teacher training institutions, his appointments policy, and the difficulties of trying to increase expenditures to meet state needs while simultaneously maintaining economy in government. The growing economic distress of farmers, as South Dakota experienced an agricultural depression before the Great Depression showed its face, added to voter discontent.

Internal conflicts within the Republican Party created an opening in 1926 for the election of the first Democratic governor in the state's history. Beresford attorney William J. Bulow, who had lost to Gunderson by more than a two-to-one margin two years earlier, defeated him by 13,000 votes on the second round, while Republicans held onto all the other state offices and retained an overwhelming 110-to-37 margin in the legislature. The conservative Democrat made the best of what was essentially a personal victory by working harmoniously with the legislature and avoiding partisan politics during his tenure in office, then moved up to the U.S. Senate after his second gubernatorial term. For all practical purposes, he might as well have been a Republican.

While the late twenties were years of treading water in state politics, the thirties initiated an era of political fireworks and significant change. That was not immediately apparent in 1930, when Hamlin County farmer Warren E. Green was elevated to the governorship. He had been chosen as the nominee by the Republican state convention after finishing last in a group of five candidates in the primary. (Election law provided for this selection process when no candidate received at least thirty-five percent of the vote.) Interestingly, the leading vote-getter in the primary was Gladys Pyle, of Huron, the first woman to serve in the legislature and then, as secretary of state, the first to occupy a constitutional office. She later served for a brief time as a U.S. senator, appointed to fill a vacancy after Senator Norbeck's death in 1936.

◼ Challenge of the Great Depression

Green had the misfortune of holding office just as the Great Depression set in with a vengeance in 1931 and 1932. Well-intentioned and determined, he suffered from the same problems that his Republican counterpart in the White House, Herbert Hoover, did—lack of imagination and unwillingness to experiment. Admittedly, there was not much that one state could have done to counteract the overwhelming impact of the economic slide following the stock market crash, but Green's single-minded devotion to fiscal economy and his unwillingness to modify the state's tax laws foreordained failure. Compounding the Republican's woes was the third major financial scandal in the state's brief history—the conviction and sentencing to a seven-year jail term of state Superintendent of Banking Fred R. Smith for embezzlement.

The impact of the Depression, following upon a decade of depressed agricultural conditions, was overwhelming. Farm foreclosures in a state that counted 83,000 farms at its peak during the early 1930s amounted to 34,419 between 1921 and 1934. During that same period, more than seventy percent of all state banks failed. In addition, as drought conditions descended on the Great Plains, the first huge dust storms hit South Dakota in 1931. By late 1934, with thirty-nine percent of the population on public relief, South Dakota ranked first in the nation in that category, and by the end of the decade its 7.2 percent population decline also was the biggest of any state. Extraordinary leadership and creativity were called for under the circumstances. What Governor Green offered, in addition to budget cuts, was symbolism. As the Farmers' Holiday movement—which organized farm boycotts in an attempt to boost farm prices—spread into southeastern South Dakota from across the border in Iowa in the summer of 1932, Green expressed sympathy for the farmers' cause but refused to provide any substantial aid.[24] He organized a meeting of governors and farm leaders from fifteen agricultural states in Sioux City in September to discuss the agricultural problem, but its only result was a tepid set of resolutions calling on the federal government to address the issue.

By then, it was obvious that voters were ready for a change. All over the country, the "outs" replaced the "ins" in 1932, and South Dakota was no exception. Along with Governor Green, who lost to Belvidere rancher Tom Berry by more than 50,000 votes, the entire Republican state ticket lost decisively, with one exception—Senator Peter Norbeck, whose vast personal popularity enabled him to weather the storm. New York Governor Franklin Delano Roosevelt became the second Democrat to obtain South Dakota's electoral votes, capturing an impressive 63.5 percent of the popular vote. The partisan breakdown in the legislature approximately reversed itself—from a 31-to-14 Republican advantage to one of 29-to-16 for the Democrats in the state Senate and, similarly, from 79-to-24 in favor of the Republicans in the House of Representatives to 70-to-33 in favor of the Democrats.

Top-heavy majorities in the legislature and control of the constitutional offices did not insure smooth going for the Democrats, however. Having never before exercised power like this, they were inexperienced at governing, and the nature of the economic crisis facing them posed overwhelming challenges. Nationally, the "Roosevelt Revolution" as embodied in the New Deal effected a major political realignment, transforming a generation-long Republican majority into Democratic domination. In South Dakota, however, Democratic rule lasted only four years; by 1936 Republicans were returning to office, and by 1938 the transition was complete. While other states in the region began to move in the direction of genuine two-party competition, that process was delayed for several decades in South Dakota, as Republicans resumed their traditional control of state politics during the forties and fifties.

That Democrats were not united in their approach to governing became apparent from the outset during the 1933 legislative session. Governor Berry, whose campaign symbol had been an axe, was determined to slash the budget wherever he could in order to maintain the fiscal integrity of the state. Beyond that, he professed solidarity with Roosevelt and the New Deal, but his main interest in that regard was to obtain as many federal dollars as he could for South Dakota. He never was an enthusiatic New Dealer and remained committed to traditional Jeffersonian principles of small and frugal government at the state level. That insured that there would be a clash between him and the farm-oriented Progressives in the party, led by Emil Loriks in the Senate and Oscar Fosheim in the House along with Lieutenant Governor Hans Ustrud, who had imbibed deeply the La Follette tradition of advanced Progressivism while working as a school teacher in Dane County, Wisconsin.

The more progressive (or liberal) branch of the South Dakota Democratic Party agreed wholeheartedly with Governor Berry in his wish to reduce governmental costs and went a step further, trumping his proposal to cut approximately $2 million out of the biennial budget of $8 million by finding another $500,000 that could be chipped away. Where they departed from him was on his unwillingness to legislate a mortgage moratorium, similar to those being passed in other states, and on his tax policy. Both sides were intent on taking some of the burden off property taxpayers, especially farmers, but while the governor favored a gross income tax—in effect, a transaction or general sales tax—the progressive legislators demanded a net income tax, which would have been more progressive in orientation and more beneficial to farmers. They also objected to his call for a sales tax, because of its regressive nature, and disagreed with his desire to abolish primary elections and with some of his proposals to dismantle government agencies that had been set up during previous Progressive administrations, including the Railroad Commission, state hail insurance fund, and state coal mine.

In 1933 the governor won some of the battles, primarily for his gross income tax law, while the farm progressives also won some, most importantly a tax delinquency law, to extend payment on delinquent taxes for ten years, and a one-year mortgage moratorium. The second time around, in 1935, the progressive forces succeeded in replacing the governor's gross income tax with a version of their net income tax, but as a revenue-producing measure it proved to be highly ineffective, never bringing in more than $1 million a year. The gross income tax had garnered almost $3 million during its second year of operation, and a new sales tax, imposed in 1935, raised similar amounts during the rest of the decade.[25] More controversially, Loriks and Fosheim acquired the title of the "Gold Dust Twins" for their successful effort to impose an ore tax on mining interests in the Black Hills, primarily on the Homestake Mine, whose stock price had shot up from a pre-Depression level of $50 a share to $430 after the Roosevelt administration devalued the dollar, which effectively raised the price of gold from $21 to $35 an ounce.[26] A four-percent gross tax on unrefined ore passed during the 1935 session was upped to six percent two years later.

Democrats around the country benefited from the popularity of President Roosevelt's leadership and engaging personality, and millions of voters appreciated the efforts of the New Deal to right economic wrongs in the form of relief programs, Social Security, farm subsidies, and other actions. The president's periodic "fireside chats" over the radio helped transform presidential communication with the public and won over many former Republicans and new voters. While all of this helped Roosevelt carry South Dakota for a second time in 1936 (his proportion of the South Dakota vote declined from 63.5 percent in 1932 to 54 percent in 1936, while his fraction of the national vote escalated from 57.4 percent to 60.8 percent), his efforts to transform the state Democratic Party into a more liberal entity largely failed, and his hope of making South Dakota a truly competitive two-party state failed altogether. A sign that many Democrats in the state were not in tune with the liberal direction taken by Roosevelt's New Dealers was the defection of Sioux Falls attorney U. S. G. Cherry, who had earlier run unsuccessfully several times for the U.S. Senate on the Democratic ticket, but who now switched party affiliation and began denouncing the president for being unstable and unreliable. Meanwhile, Senator Bulow, who never had been a New Deal enthusiast, remaining fundamentally conservative in outlook, won a second term in 1936, even as Roosevelt was increasingly distancing himself from conservative members of his own party in other states. It is clear that South Dakota Democrats were seriously divided between their conservative and progressive wings, and that the former more than held their own even at the peak of the New Deal's success.

Meanwhile, the progressive coterie within the Republican Party, which had become much weaker over the previous decade, suffered a severe blow with the death of their leader, Senator Norbeck, in December 1936. W. R. Ronald, of the Mitchell *Daily Republic*, who had played a role in developing Roosevelt's farm policy, and S. X. Way, Norbeck's long-time political associate, editor of the Watertown *Public Opinion*, and Republican national committeeman, along with their progressive Republican colleagues, were becoming increasingly isolated within the party, as Roosevelt sought to woo progressive Republicans into the Democratic fold. In 1936 Way took the lead in forming a presidential slate committed to Idaho Senator William E. Borah to run against Governor Alfred M. Landon of Kansas, and Republican gubernatorial candidate Leslie Jensen, a Hot Springs telephone company executive, supported Borah's candidacy, running as a "liberal Republican" during the fall campaign. Even Karl Mundt, a part-time businessman and college professor from Madison who resigned his teaching position to run for the First District Congressional seat, was not afraid to use the "L"-word in his narrowly unsuccessful campaign that year.

If liberalism was on the lips of some Republicans in 1936—a tribute to the powerful appeal of Roosevelt and the New Deal at the time—political breezes in South Dakota were blowing in a different direction. While Democratic Congressman Fred Hildebrandt joined Roosevelt and Bulow in the victory column that year, their margins were reduced from the previous election, and Jensen recaptured the governorship for the Republicans, while Custer newspaper editor Francis Case took the West River House seat. In the legislature, the Democrats hung onto a razor-thin 23-to-22 margin in the senate, while the Republicans comfortably regained control of the house, 66-to-37.[27]

The handwriting appeared to be on the wall for the Democrats, and the 1938 off-year election confirmed it. Just to make sure, the Republicans adopted a strategy that year of painting the major Democratic candidates with the brush of Communism in not too subtle a fashion. It was, in effect, a McCarthy-type campaign twelve years before Senator Joe McCarthy, of Wisconsin, made national headlines with his charges against the Democrats of being soft on Communism.[28] All across the nation that fall liberals stumbled and conservatives reaped the benefits, as the public reacted against President Roosevelt's abortive move to "pack" the Supreme Court with his own nominees, grew nervous about labor conflict, were troubled by the President's failed effort to "purge" the Democratic Party, and worried about foreign conflicts that might suck the country into war. South Dakota Democrats suffered from the political fallout from these developments and also worked under the disadvantage of growing numbers of former Republicans drifting back into their traditional fold.

Perhaps out of frustration with their status of being on the outside looking in after decades of dominating the political scene, Republicans borrowed a technique that would increasingly be used against New Dealers and Democrats—tarring them with the "Communist" label. It was rather far-fetched to try to depict cowboy Tom Berry, who was running for the U.S. Senate, and farmers Emil Loriks (First District Congress) and Oscar Fosheim (governor) as being in any way affiliated with subversive groups, but newspaper editorials, cartoons, and campaign literature did just that. Being friendly to the new Congress of Industrial Organizations or affiliated with the Farmers' Union were reasons given for questioning the Democratic candidates' loyalty. That Congressman Fred Hildebrandt (who lost to Berry in the Democratic senate primary) had once briefly employed on his staff a person who turned out to be a Communist was played up for all it was worth. Republicans did what some of their colleagues in other states did that year: request a formal investigation of subversive activities in the state by the newly formed House Committee on Un-American Activities. "Bear in mind that the Democratic candidates have received the endorsement of the Communists and other subversive groups and ask yourselves why," cautioned an editorial in the *Sioux Falls Argus Leader*. Denying that it was suggesting that Loriks and Fosheim were in fact Communists, the paper went on to state, "Candidates who endorse policies that are communistic in nature should not be surprised when they, in turn, receive the blessings of the Communists."[29] Others were not so circumspect, not hesitating to label the Democratic candidates as Communists.

Karl E. Mundt of Madison, seen here with his wife, Mary, and dog, Cappy, in their Washington, D.C. home, served a total of thirty-four years in the House and Senate and is credited with strengthening federal farm subsidies and bringing the VA Hospital to Sioux Falls and EROS Data Center to South Dakota. *Courtesy Karl E. Mundt Historical and Educational Foundation and Archives.*

The smear campaign did not stimulate a wide swing in voting in 1938. Republican candidates picked up only about three to four percentage points from the previous election. But this was enough to put all of them over the top, placing GOP officials in the governorship and every major state office, both Congressional seats, and the empty U.S. Senate seat. The legislative lineups were radically altered too, with Republican margins growing from a deficit of one to a majority of twenty-five in the Senate and from a twenty-nine vote majority to one of forty-nine in the House of Representatives. The election was a turning point in several ways. In the first place, it established Republican hegemony in the state for the next generation, broken only by the elections of George McGovern to Congress, beginning in 1956, and by Ralph Herseth to the governorship in 1958. More than that, it helped push the Republican Party in a more conservative direction, although progressive or liberal voices could be heard still to some extent during the forties and fifties. After his victory in 1938, Karl Mundt stopped calling himself a liberal and settled comfortably into a conservative, anti-Communist stance that kept him in Congress for the next thirty-four years, the longest tenure of any officeholder in South Dakota history. Before the Depression, South Dakota Republicans had been more progressive in orientation than their counterparts in other states; after World War II, they would be more conservative than the rest of the nation. The Democrats, for their part, found themselves leaderless and without any effective party organization for the next decade and a half. Doomed to be also-rans in campaigns for state office, they saw their representation in the legislature dwindle to miniscule proportions, averaging only four members in the Senate and eight members in the House between 1939 and 1955. Three times during this period the Republicans controlled all thirty-five Senate seats. Thus, while many surrounding states in the region underwent significant political realignment, resulting in more competitive two-party structures after the New Deal revolution, South Dakota reverted to traditional ways, safe in its Republicanism and ensconced in conservatism. Memories of its progressive and even radical orientation during the Populist period and during the first two decades of the twentieth century faded, and the state became one of the three or four most Republican, as well as conservative, states in the union. [30]

■ World War II and the Cold War

America's entry into World War II, which brought much tragedy and heartbreak to South Dakota families, also wrought an economic miracle in the United States, finally ending the Great Depression and launching a thirty-year period of prosperity, surpassing anything the nation had witnessed in the past. The immediate boost to agricultural prices and employment lifted it out of its doldrums and launched it on a path of economic transformation whose results were still being felt at the end of the century. In the process, new political challenges and issues emerged, requiring creative responses and adaptation.

The agricultural economy benefited hugely from war-induced increases in prices and demand and from the rapid adoption of new technologies and methods that came in the wake of the war, but farmers quickly found themselves enmeshed in the same old dilemmas of overproduction and reliance upon federal farm subsidies. South Dakota's small towns, experiencing continued population losses during the conflict resulting from a surge of military enlistments and out-migration of residents flocking to war industries in other states, were briefly encouraged by postwar economic growth and the return of at least some of their veterans. In quick order, however, they found themselves caught on a treadmill of store closings on main-street and continual out-migration of youth, who were looking for better job opportunities in urban areas. The biggest challenge the political system would face during the second half of the twentieth century was what it should do to try to respond to the transformations that were going on in agriculture, to the declining population of small towns, and to the small industrial base that existed to furnish jobs for those who chose to or were forced to leave the farm.

All of this underscored the political challenge of trying to find resources to fund programs that were growing in number and size as a result of changes in society and the economy as well as new governmental responsibilities taken on during the Depression decade. Generally regarded as a poor state, South Dakota saw its per capita income, which had been only sixty-one percent of the national average in 1939, begin to catch up with other states, rising as high as ninety-seven percent in 1951. But continued heavy dependence on agriculture left it prey to the whims of market forces, and in 1965 the figure was back to seventy-five percent, ranking South Dakota thirty-ninth among the states.[31] Economic stringency imposed limits on what state government could do to address the challenges facing it.

The per capita state and local tax burden, while fluctuating yearly, remained below the national average. After having experimented with an income tax during the straightened circumstances of the thirties, the legislature abolished it in 1943, choosing to rely heavily on the more regressive sales tax, which varied between two and three percent over time. During a typical year in the fifties, forty-five percent of state government revenues derived from motor fuel taxes, thirty-three percent from the sales tax, five percent each from taxes on cigarettes and automobile registrations, two percent each from beer sales and inheritance taxes, and one percent from an oleomargarine tax.[32] South Dakota's wide-open spaces helped explain why highway construction and maintenance costs consumed as much as half of the biennial budgets, a considerably larger share than the national average. That left a little less than a quarter for state aid to education, which amounted to about a third less, on a per capita basis, than other states. Public welfare accounted for about one-fifth of the budget and health for about one-twelfth of it.[33] A crazy-quilt conglomeration of state bureaus and agencies added to the burdens placed on the budget.

South Dakota's antiquated tax and budget system left state government officials with very little room to maneuver. Historical tradition, conservative ideology, and an ethic of rugged individualism all fed into the syndrome of frugal expenditures at the state government level. None of this dampened people's enthusiasm for getting their hands on federal funds, however. Like other sparsely populated rural states, South Dakota benefited from funding formulas that typically brought back approximately three dollars in federal expenditures for every tax dollar sent to Washington. Conservative politicians who railed against high taxes and spending were unembarrassed to seek the best deal they could get for the state from the federal government. Thus, regardless of political party or ideology, it became routine for South Dakota's senators and representatives to favor large farm subsidies, military installations, and other expenditures that would benefit citizens of the state.

While former Governor Harlan Bushfield retained many of his isolationist views after he was elevated to the U.S. Senate in 1942, Republican Senator Chan Gurney, who had been elected in the same conservative tide that had lifted Bushfield to the governor's chair in 1938, built up a reputation in Washington as a strong advocate of U.S. defense and foreign aid programs during his two terms in office. In 1940 and 1941, he worked closely with West River Congressman Francis Case to get Rapid City designated one of seven major new air bases being built around the nation. He introduced and helped obtain passage of the landmark National Security Act of 1947, unifying the armed forces, as well as the Selective Service Act of 1948, reinstating the draft. Like his Republican Congressional colleagues, he was also an enthusiastic supporter of farm programs, Missouri River basin development, and rural electrification projects.[34]

Case, who had served in the House since 1937, successfully challenged Gurney in the 1950 senatorial primary, charging that Gurney only reflected the opinion of the military and the Truman administration in formulating defense policy. But until his death of a heart attack in 1962, Senator Case never lost an opportunity to beef up Defense Department spending in South Dakota. Ellsworth Air Force Base became a major prop for the West River economy during the fifties and later, and by the end of the decade intercontinental ballistic missile complexes—first Titans and then Minutemen—were pumping millions of dollars into the region. As a Congressman, Case had fought enthusiastically for Missouri River development, working early on with Colonel Lewis Pick of the Army Corps of Engineers, one of the two key figures in developing the Pick-Sloan Plan of massive earthen dam building on the river, which was approved by Congress in December 1944. As a senator, Case was even more instrumental in shaping the Interstate Highway System, which played an important role in the state's economic growth and development beginning in the 1950s. He liked to characterize himself as "nothing more than a water and road Senator." As ranking minority member on the Public Roads Subcommittee of the Senate Committee on Public Works, he worked closely with the powerful Oklahoma Democrat Robert Kerr to insure that South Dakota would get an extension of Interstate 29 north from Sioux Falls to Fargo. For a while, it had appeared that the north-south route was going to be located along the border in western Minnesota, but Case, along with Karl Mundt, made sure that did not happen.[35]

Karl Mundt, who had entered the House of Representatives two years after Case, was elevated to the Senate two years before him, in 1948, and was re-elected three times. He achieved prominence during that time as a major spokesman for midwestern conservative Republicanism, along with Robert Taft of Ohio, Bourke Hickenlooper of Iowa, Everett Dirksen of Illinois, and others. Having benefited from associating his opponent in 1938 with Communism, Mundt, throughout his career, was connected in the public mind with the anti-Communist crusade. He started to build a national reputation for himself during the forties while working with California Congressman Richard Nixon on the House Un-American Activities Committee, then became known in the fifties for his friendship with Wisconsin Senator Joseph R. McCarthy. For all his conservative credentials, Mundt, who had campaigned as a liberal Republican in 1936 and 1938, never stinted in his efforts to strengthen federal farm subsidies and other governmental programs that were beneficial to South Dakota. In 1955, worried that Republicans were going to be hurt as a result, he warned Vice President Nixon that people in the farm belt did not like Secretary of Agriculture Ezra Taft Benson's free-market farm program, nor did they like the man. The next two cycles of election results confirmed that his concerns were not misplaced.[36]

While traces of isolationism were still detectable in the South Dakota electorate and its political representatives in later years, the experience of World War II largely converted them, as it did the rest of the country, into becoming supporters of an internationalist foreign policy. Republicans and Democrats could find much to quarrel with in the specific application of the foreign policy doctrines that became orthodoxy as the Cold War set in after 1945, but a bipartisan consensus emerged around the assumption that the United States would necessarily play a major role in world affairs. Gone were the days when people could ignore what was happening in Europe, Asia, and the rest of the world. As long as this was the case, South Dakotans were not hesitant to hop on the "gravy train" of federal defense spending.

Mundt's thirty-four years in Congress and Case's twenty-six years there were exceptions to the rule that political office-holding in South Dakota remained a short-term thing. Peter Norbeck's twenty years as governor and senator, likewise, had been exceptional. Tom Berry had learned the hard way in 1936 that the two-term tradition for governors was dangerous to tamper with, a lesson M. Q. Sharpe learned all over again in 1946, when he discovered that the rule applied as much to Republican governors as to Democratic ones. Following four years of Harlan Bushfield, whose draconian cost-cutting approach included job eliminations that reduced departmental costs by twenty-six percent, Sharpe seemed liberal in comparison. With war-generated economic growth feeding state coffers, priorities could be shifted from single-minded focus on balancing the budget to gearing up for war production and coordinating defense facilities and activities in the state. During his term, from 1943 to 1947, Governor Sharpe played a significant role in planning for dam construction on the Missouri River and worked with the legislature to formulate a post-war building and development program.[37]

Seen here with stacks of bills awaiting his signature, Governor George T. Mickelson of Selby is recognized for moving the state forward in the years after World War II with much-needed improvements in highway construction and in the state's human services and educational institutions. *Courtesy South Dakota State Historical Society–State Archives.*

Selby attorney George T. Mickelson rose to Speaker of the House during his three terms in the legislature and served for four years as state attorney general before successfully challenging Governor Sharpe for the nomination in 1946. During the Depression and the war years, the state had neglected construction projects, building improvements, and human services. With treasury receipts rising from $33 million in 1945 to about $77 million in 1954, leaving South Dakota debt-free for the first time in almost four decades, it became possible to begin to address some of the more pressing needs of the state. Much-needed highway building accelerated, and long-delayed construction at the state's charitable and educational institutions commenced.[38] Sigurd Anderson, who, like Mickelson, was a lawyer (from Webster) and had served four years in the attorney general's office, beat out four other candidates for the Republican gubernatorial nomination in 1950 and followed up two years later with the largest margin of any candidate for governor (70.2 percent) until Bill Janklow topped the mark in 1982. The huge Eisenhower landslide of 1952 marked a peak of Republican success during the postwar era. Capturing every major office on the ballot, the GOP also controlled all thirty-five seats in the state Senate and seventy-three of the seventy-five seats in the House of Representatives. Governor Anderson sought to address the problem of school funding and signed a school district reorganization act in 1951, but resistance to consolidation was strong, and South Dakota lagged behind neighboring states on that score for the next two decades.

War hero Joe Foss's election as governor in 1954 reflected the respect and admiration
Americans accorded their veterans during the years
after World War II. Across the United States, men
who had put on the uniform—members of "the
Greatest Generation," in Tom Brokaw's words—
took over positions of authority in business, industry, and politics. Not many had achieved the heroic
stature of Joe Foss, a fighter pilot at Guadalcanal
whose exploits in shooting down twenty-six
Japanese planes earned him the Congressional
Medal of Honor, personally awarded in a visit to
the White House, and a picture on the cover of *Life*
magazine. Back home in Sioux Falls after the war,
he started up a flight service and an auto dealer-
ship; politics was the furthest thing from his mind.
But a group of friends and businessmen persuaded
him to run for the legislature, and, discovering that
he enjoyed the political process, he jumped into the
fray for the governorship in 1950. Narrowly losing
to Sigurd Anderson the first time out, he came back
four years later and won easily. As governor, he left
the details of the day-to-day management of governor to subordinates, focusing his attention especial-

A decorated World War II fighter pilot, Joe
Foss made economic development a theme
of his two terms in office during the 1950s.
*Courtesy South Dakota State Historical Society–State
Archives.*

ly on the need for economic diversification and on the challenge of bringing new jobs
and economic development to the state. Foss's aviation background served him well, as
he became the state's first governor to campaign by plane and spent a great deal of his
time in office flying out of state to woo businesses that might be interested in relocating to South Dakota. His fame as a war hero gave him easy access to businessmen and
industrialists. Never a spellbinder on the speaker's platform, he was best working with
people individually and in small groups. Hoadley Dean, his administrative assistant,
helped schedule his time and plan his efforts. Under him, the state industrial commission
was transformed into the Industrial Development and Expansion Agency (IDEA). Every
governor after him of necessity made economic development a central theme.[39]

■ Revival of the Democrats

Meanwhile, observant onlookers began to notice some interesting developments in
the opposition party. By Foss's second term in office, Democrats had achieved a respectable thirty-six percent of the seats in the House of Representatives and lacked a majority
in the state Senate by only one vote. More unusual, in 1956 they sent to Congress a young
former history and political science professor from Dakota Wesleyan University named
George McGovern, who, like Foss, was a war hero, the recipient of the Distinguished
Flying Cross for piloting a B-24 on thirty-five bombing missions over Europe. Interested
in politics since his days as a high school and college debater, McGovern needed less
persuading than his Republican counterpart to enter the political arena. Nevertheless,
it was a definite gamble on his part when he gave up his teaching position in 1953
to accept an invitation from state Democratic chairman Ward Clark to become full-
time organizer and executive secretary of the party. The Democrats, moribund when he
took on the task, soon began showing signs of life, and in 1954 Ken Holum, a farmer

from Groton who later served as assistant secretary of the Interior during the Kennedy-Johnson years, ran a respectable campaign against Karl Mundt for his seat in the Senate. Two years later, he did much better, losing to Francis Case by less than two percent of the vote, while McGovern surprised political insiders and the general public by winning an 11,000-vote victory over four-term GOP Congressman Harold Lovre.

Most of the credit for the Democratic revival must go to McGovern himself for his tireless and well-conceived organizational efforts to build up the party, but he had a huge ally in the process in the widely unpopular agricultural policies of the Eisenhower administration. Secretary of Agriculture Ezra Taft Benson's concerted drive to reduce agricultural price supports and to get farmers to rely more heavily on the marketplace redounded disastrously for the Republicans, as people in the farm belt were soon labeling him "the worst Secretary of Agriculture in history." An additional boost for the Democrats came from the fallout from Governor Foss's involvement in the question of equalization of taxes at the county level. His advice to the Board of Equalization to "follow the law" in equalizing assessments led many counties to increase their budgets rather than reduce their tax levies in line with increased assessment levels. Along with sending letters of protest to Pierre, voters punished Republican candidates for office in the 1956 fall elections.[40]

Two years later, they startled many observers again by retaining McGovern in his House seat when Governor Foss ran against him, and, more surprisingly, electing Ralph Herseth, a rancher from Houghton, as governor. He was the first Democrat to occupy the office in twenty-two years. Herseth also benefited from the fallout from a bitter fight in the Republican primary contest in 1958. The Democrats enjoyed a five-vote majority in the Senate during Herseth's single term in the statehouse, but, with an eleven-vote deficit in the House and lacking experience at the task of governance, they were unable to accomplish much during their brief day in the sun. In addition to several minor pieces of legislation, including a driver's license law—making South Dakota the last state in the Union to require its citizens to take a test to qualify for driving privileges—the governor's major legacy was the establishment of a bipartisan Citizens' Tax Study Committee, which made an intensive study of the issue under its chairman, former Governor M. Q. Sharpe, and came back with a recommendation to restructure the state's tax system, including consideration of increasing sales taxes and the possibility of instituting individual and corporate income taxes.[41]

McGovern's and Herseth's electoral successes proved short-lived and failed to bring about the permanent realignment in political forces that Ward Clark, Holum, McGovern, and their cohorts had hoped to achieve. The return of better conditions in

Senator and presidential candidate during the Vietnam War years, George McGovern of Mitchell is seen here (at right) with Anson Yeager, editor of the *Argus Leader*. Always a strong proponent of the family farmer, McGovern later became Ambassador, United Nations Food and Agriculture Organization. *Center for Western Studies.*

farm country and the presidential candidacy of Senator John F. Kennedy in 1960 hurt Democratic chances. Herseth lost his campaign for re-election and McGovern failed in his bid to unseat Senator Karl Mundt, both by narrow margins, as Republicans swept the other state offices and gained dominant majorities in the legislature. Kennedy, who obtained only 41.6 percent of the vote in South Dakota while eking out a narrow win nationally over Vice President Richard Nixon, blamed McGovern's loss on his own poor showing in the state, partly because of voter resistance to his Catholicism. Although his brother Robert lobbied strongly for appointing McGovern as Secretary of Agriculture, the president-elect instead named him Food for Peace director, a position that proved much more helpful to the South Dakotan two years later when he returned to South Dakota to challenge successfully for the Senate seat of Francis Case, who died of a heart attack in June 1962.

■ Traditionalism in Turbulent Times

McGovern's presence in the Senate was one of the few encouraging signs on the horizon for South Dakota Democrats during the 1960s, a decade during which the New Frontier and the Great Society reigned in Washington and Democrats enjoyed large majorities in both Houses of Congress. The way McGovern got to the Senate was a further illustration of the weakness of the state party. His margin of victory was so small that it required a recount to declare him a winner by a scant 597 votes, and he benefited considerably from the divisions among Republicans who had to choose among five different aspirants for the nomination in a state convention after Case's death. Six years later, McGovern won re-election by a comfortable margin over former Governor Archie Gubbrud. His brief symbolic bid for the presidency at the Chicago convention in 1968, as he stood in for supporters of the slain Robert Kennedy, probably cut into his vote totals because of backlash against the violence and disruptions accompanying the anti-war protesters who inundated the city that August.

While McGovern's increasingly critical stand against the Vietnam War in the Senate and his presidential candidacy brought increased attention to South Dakota during the sixties, Republicans retained their dominance in the other Congressional positions. Karl Mundt remained a strong voice for orthodox conservatism until a debilitating stroke left him incapacitated in November 1969. In the House, E. Y. Berry, an attorney and publisher from McLaughlin, maintained an equally conservative voting record, and Ben Reifel, a Bureau of Indian Affairs administrator from Aberdeen, took a somewhat more moderate stance. One of the few bright spots for the Democrats during the sixties was the 1964 election, when President Lyndon Johnson rang up the largest percentage of any presidential candidate in American history against arch-conservative Senator Barry Goldwater of Arizona. In the process, Johnson's capturing of South Dakota's electoral votes was only the fourth time a Democrat had ever done that, and Republican majorities in the legislature were reduced to two in the Senate and fifteen in the House of Representatives.[42] By the 1965 and 1967 sessions, however, they were back up to about twenty in the Senate and forty or fifty in the House. The state was back to normal, with real power being contested among groups inside the Republican Party. The Democratic Party buildup that McGovern had achieved during the fifties now mainly remained in the form of his own personal organization for election to office.

For all the turbulence and ferment occurring in American society during the 1960s, politics in South Dakota in many ways continued along familiar paths. Three Republican governors occupied the statehouse—the first two filling out typical four-year terms. The third's inability to win re-election in 1970, however, foretold shifts that would bring some significant change to the system. Archie Gubbrud, a successful farmer and conservationist from Alcester, served five terms in the House of Representatives during the fifties, rising to the speakership before obtaining the gubernatorial nomination in 1960. Elected in part that year by warning against the likelihood of tax increases if his Democratic opponent were elected, Gubbrud was able to increase spending on elementary and secondary education and to authorize building programs for the state's higher education system largely because of healthy economic expansion in the state. His successor was Nils A. Boe, a Sioux Falls attorney who had served four terms in the House of Representatives, including two as speaker, and one term as lieutenant governor. Issues such as school reorganization, legislative and congressional redistricting, and taxation made Boe's tenure somewhat more contentious than usual. Among the innovations introduced while he was in office were a records management center, an inventory control system, property surplus interchanges within state government, a personnel classification system, central data processing, and a state travel pool.[43]

Regardless of which party was in power, the modernization of procedures, such as the ones just mentioned, would have occurred. The fifties and sixties witnessed a considerable number of such changes, similar to ones going on all over the country. In 1967 Governor Boe introduced the first annual budget, replacing the traditional biennial one. Beginning in 1963, the legislature went to annual sessions; with the increasing impact of federal funding, shifts in revenues resulting from economic variations, and other unpredictable factors, it became important to plan on a more limited time schedule. The 1951 legislature had instituted a Legislative Research Council, which assumed increasing significance as relevant and timely information became more and more important in the formulation of government policy. By 1967 the necessity for accelerated school consolidation, something in which South Dakota lagged far behind its neighboring states, had become so compelling that the legislature passed Senate Bill 130 mandating it within three years' time. In 1969, under Governor Frank Farrar, the legislature created a thirteen-member Commission on Constitutional Revision to recommend changes that would streamline and modernize state government.

Farrar, a lawyer and banker from Britton, was the state's youngest attorney general when first elected in 1962 and served three terms in that office before running successfully for governor in 1968. His election at the age of thirty-nine made him the youngest governor in South Dakota history before Bill Janklow and the youngest governor in the United States at the time. Having led all Republican candidates with a 42,000 vote plurality, he ironically witnessed his base rapidly begin to erode once in office, as controversial issues came to the fore. Creative and independent-minded, the Republican governor sometimes antagonized legislators and voters with his brash and outspoken views, such as his statement that George McGovern was "the greatest American of the twentieth century."[44] Farrar initiated state government reorganization, called for substantial increases in state aid to education and higher education funding, and recommended changes in the tax structure to raise needed revenues. During his time in office, momentum built for an income tax, and the Farmers' Union got an initiated measure for a state income tax placed on the ballot in 1970. Introducing a broad program to increase job opportunities and promote tourism and economic development, Governor Farrar said that the 1970s would be a "Decade of Development." Some of his initiatives backfired politically, most importantly a measure he pushed through the legislature to create a Gas and Electric Council. Viewing the law as a direct challenge to their operations, REA co-ops in the state reacted strongly to the measure, leading the battle to get the law repealed, and their influence played strongly in the next election.

■ Genuine Two-Party Competition Arrives

Farrar's sometimes hands-off style of governing and his personal business ventures while in office also proved liabilities in his bid for re-election in 1970. Unfortunately for him and the Republicans, he was facing a very popular and formidable opponent in three-term State Senator Richard Kneip. The Salem milk-equipment salesman ran a "people-to-people" campaign, shaking tens of thousands of hands, relying as much on the force of his personality as on people's agreement with his issue stances. A debilitating stroke suffered by Karl Mundt in November 1969 left him incapacitated and the party organization in disarray. Adding to GOP woes, both of their congressmen in Washington—E. Y. Berry and Ben Reifel—decided to call it quits that year. In the West River district, James Abourezk, who had never held political office, ran a hard-charging campaign, flying around in an airplane and taking advantage of rising antiwar sentiment by using the services of hundreds of college student volunteers. He effectively exploited his opponent Fred Brady's distribution of a small handbook, entitled *This—I Believe*, which proposed "compulsory citizenship training" as a first step toward a "professional service force." To many people, it sounded a little too much like a Hitler youth program.[45] In the

First District contest, former FBI agent Frank Denholm likewise benefited from a weak opponent, giving the Democrats all three major open positions that year, making 1970 the best year for the party since 1934.

In office, Kneip focused on state government reorganization and tax reform. The first was relatively easily accomplished in 1973 after voters approved four completely revised articles of the state constitution, including a plan for executive reorganization, in the 1972 election. The governor largely followed the advice of a Citizens Commission set up to make recommendations in cutting the number of boards, bureaus, and offices from over 160 to 16. Tax revision, always a sticky issue in the state, proved to be a much more difficult problem to address. In the 1970 election Kneip had opposed an initiated law for an income tax put on the ballot by the Farmers Union, one of the main sources of votes for him and other Democratic candidates. Promising to make the tax system fairer and to reduce the burden it placed on property, the governor proposed his own version of an individual and corporate tax in the 1971 legislature and made it his top priority during his first several years in Pierre. He came closest to victory in 1973, when the Democrats enjoyed razor-thin, one-vote

For much of the 1970s, including the turbulent period of the Vietnam War and the occupation of the village of Wounded Knee, Richard Kneip of Salem served as governor, focusing on the reorganization of the executive branch and providing greater access to state services for citizens. In this photo, South Dakota Cowboy Hall of Fame chairman Joe Schomer presents Governor Kneip with the first copy of its magazine *Dakota West*. *Courtesy South Dakota State Historical Society–State Archives.*

majorities in both houses of the legislature. But one Democrat defected in the decisive vote in the Senate that year, and in the years after that the idea of passing an income tax became more and more of a remote possibility in the eyes of the voters and legislators, alike, although a core of supporters remained. Encouraged by a $16 million surplus in the treasury, the last legislative session he presided over finally eliminated the personal property tax, which had become known as the "liar's tax."

Kneip was the first governor to serve more than two terms in office and the first to be elected to a four-year term, after the new executive article to the state constitution was approved by the voters in 1972. Like his predecessors in office, he sought to diversify the state's economy and promote tourism. New Departments of Environmental Protection, Public Safety, Commerce and Consumer Affairs, and Education and Cultural Affairs were launched. A strong Human Rights Act was passed, and Governor Kneip made a concerted effort to foster better communication between the Indian and white communities. With the rise of the American Indian Movement (AIM) during the early 1970s, national attention focused on the state during AIM's 1973 occupation of Wounded Knee, an incident which cost two people their lives. The most explosive political controversy of the Kneip years, however, revolved around higher education, after the Board of Regents attempted to implement a "master plan" for streamlining the system, first, by relocating the engineering school at the South Dakota School of Mines and Technology to South Dakota State University, and then, when that ran into too much resistance, to do it the other way around. SDSU President Hilton Briggs and the community of Brookings rallied their troops in opposition to that, as hundreds of students and town residents descended on Pierre to "Save Our State," and the status quo was retained.[46]

Hardly less controversial, and a more persistent political squabble during the 1970s, was the attempt to pump Missouri River water one hundred miles east to irrigate land in the James River Valley. In passing the Pick-Sloan plan in 1944, Congress had promised South Dakota compensation for the approximately one-half-million acres of land lost when the four big dams were constructed in the state. By the late 1960s plans were finally moving forward to irrigate 190,000 acres in the first phase of implementation. Accepting federal dollars for a program that was billed as beneficial to farmers and conducive to economic growth and development and which provided compensation for obvious losses incurred in the building of the dams appeared to be a "no-brainer" to most of those interested in the project. The coalition of forces behind Oahe—politicians, government officials, main-street businessmen, agricultural representatives, and newspaper editors—seemed unstoppable. This was one issue on which both political parties were in agreement. Everybody from Karl Mundt and Fred Christopherson of the *Argus Leader* to George McGovern and Richard Kneip wanted to see the program go forward. Then doubts appeared. A group called United Family Farmers, led by Beadle county farmers George and Bill Piper, began to raise serious questions about the loss of land that would be incurred in the building of pipes, canals, and reservoirs (about 110,000 acres); the environmental consequences of the program; and its rapidly escalating costs. The Family Farm Act of 1974, sponsored by the South Dakota Farmers Union, protected and continues to protect family farmers against non-farm corporate giants. In 1977 President Jimmy Carter put the Oahe project on his "hit list" of unnecessary water projects, and the Reagan administration later delivered its death warrant. The birth and death of Oahe, in the end, was one of the most unusual, unpredictable, and fascinating stories in South Dakota's political history.[47]

Historical turning points are not always immediately recognizable, and political trends sometimes need time to develop before their consequences can be fully discerned.

The Watergate scandal and the oil crisis of 1973 and the subsequent economic recession seemed to have dealt stunning blows to the national Republican Party, which lost the presidency in 1976, but four years later it came roaring back and put Ronald Reagan in the White House. Important developments were also occurring on the state scene at the time. The 1970s, in retrospect, were significant both for what did and did not change in South Dakota politics. With Democrats occupying the governor's chair for most of the decade (Kneip left office early to take an ambassadorship to Singapore in 1978) and sometimes holding the balance of power in the legislature, the Democratic Party finally established itself as a worthy competitor for dominance at the state level but remained clearly in a secondary position behind the Republicans. The election of 1974 witnessed the emergence of two maverick Republicans on the scene—Larry Pressler of Humboldt, who went to Congress by defeating Frank Denholm, and Bill Janklow of Flandreau, who was elected attorney general over incumbent Kermit Sande, who had appointed Janklow as a special prosecutor to try cases arising out of the incidents instigated in the early seventies by the American Indian Movement. Though both were graduates of the University of South Dakota and its School of Law, they were temperamentally far apart and never had much liking for each other. Four years later, Pressler rose to the U.S. Senate when James Abourezk decided not to run for re-election, and Janklow moved up to the governorship. Meanwhile, Pressler's run for the Senate provided an opening for Tom Daschle, a South Dakota State University graduate and former aide to Senator Abourezk, to capture the East River Congressional seat for the Democrats. Ironically, Daschle, a liberal Democrat, would wind up as a frequent ally and personal friend of the governor, whose political views differed considerably from his.

The rise of these three politicians and the fates that befell them over the following years reflected some profound political trends that were accelerating during the last quarter of the twentieth century. Different as they were in personality and ideology, they all relied heavily on personal contact with their constituents and on their own unique

Tom Daschle of Aberdeen served twenty-six years in the House and Senate, rising to majority leader in the Senate. His legislation emphasized veterans benefits, farm subsidies, and personal contact with constituents, visiting annually each of the state's sixty-six counties. *Courtesy United States Senate.*

styles of campaigning and governing. After the arrival of television in the fifties, more and more attention focused on appearance and personal style, while party organizations played smaller and smaller roles in choosing candidates and running campaigns. It was the personal styles and organizations of candidates such as McGovern, Pressler, Janklow, and Daschle that would increasingly set the tone for politics as the century drew to a close. Campaign costs for major office grew exponentially, as funds from interest groups, especially from organizations outside South Dakota, flowed into the state in ever-larger amounts. McGovern's race for the presidency helped turn national attention to races in the state, and with both national parties looking for vulnerable seats to capture during the presidencies of Reagan, Clinton, and the two Bushes, South Dakota took on increasing prominence as a state into which to pour money. U.S. Senate campaigns now cost millions of dollars, and presidential visits to the state have become common.[48]

■ The Janklow Era

Although it was not apparent at the time, since no governor had served as many as eight years in Pierre before, 1978 ushered in the "Age of Janklow" in South Dakota politics, as the former attorney general began two eight-year terms in office, sandwiched around the terms of George Mickelson and his successor, Walter Dale Miller. A self-admitted former juvenile delinquent, originally from Chicago, who had gone straight when offered the choice at sixteen of entering the Marines or being sent to a juvenile detention facility, Janklow proved to be a highly unconventional but also effective and successful governor. For the better part of a quarter-century, his personality, style of leadership, and unpredictable programmatic approach dominated the political scene in the state. Alternately hailed as an innovator, straight-talker, forceful leader, and effective administrator and damned as a self-absorbed one-man show, dictator, and bully, the governor left few observers neutral about his approach to running the state. He won re-election handily three times, racking up the biggest margin ever for a South Dakota governor in 1982 with 70.9 percent of the vote. When he came back in 1994 to run for a third time, he promised that it would only be for one term, long enough to reduce property taxes, but the lure of power was too great, and by 1998 he returned to run for a fourth time.[49]

The longest serving governor, William Janklow of Flandreau rolled back property taxes, consolidated universities, and promoted economic development, such as persuading Citibank to move its credit-card operations to South Dakota. *Courtesy South Dakota State Historical Society–State Archives.*

The only election he ever lost was in the 1986 senatorial primary to James Abdnor, who had ousted George McGovern in the Reagan tide of 1980. The 1986 contest, undermining Republican Party unity, opened a wedge for Tom Daschle to sneak into the Senate slot with 51.6 percent of the vote (Dachle's first election to the House, eight years earlier, had been by a margin of a mere 139 votes on a recount). Once in the Senate, Daschle made mincemeat of his opponents in his next two re-election races, a reflection of his personal popularity, his strong constituent work, his strong support for the South Dakota farm sector, and his unflagging efforts to stay in touch with the voters who sent him to Washington in the first place. His rapid rise to leadership of the Democrats in the Senate in 1994 focused considerable attention on the state during succeeding years. Not least among his advantages was a personal friendship with Governor Janklow, which defied expectations and frustrated many Republicans.[50] In 2004 Senator Daschle was defeated by former Congressman John Thune.

Meanwhile, Tim Johnson, a Vermillion lawyer and former state representative and senator who took over Daschle's seat in Congress when he went to the U.S. Senate in 1986, moved up to that body himself ten years later, deposing Larry Pressler by a 51-to-49 percent margin. The latter had accumulated a string of impressive electoral victories up until that time, but by 1996 he had grown out of favor with his own party. Johnson, another graduate of the University of South Dakota Law School, won plaudits for his stolid, hard-working style. Hewing to more of a middle-of-the-road line than his Democratic senatorial colleague, he enjoyed the process of making policy more than being on the political trail and earned something of a reputation as a "policy wonk."[51] To outsiders, it was an anomaly for South Dakota to be represented in the Senate by two Democrats while in the governorship and the state legislature Republicans remained solidly entrenched. In this, South Dakota may have been following a pattern replicated in some other states—adhering to an implicit social contract that kept Republicans in charge in the statehouse in order to keep taxes low, while sending Democrats to Congress to, as it were, "bring home the bacon" in the form of federal grants and subsidies. To what extent this formula actually described reality is difficult to assess, but it was so commonly held that there must have been more than a little truth to it.

The challenges and problems facing South Dakota during the last two decades of the twentieth century were similar to those of its neighbors in the region and to other states around the country: increasing demands for social services, growing pressures on its public school system, out-migration of its youth and the decline of its small towns, the transformation of its agricultural economy and the search for well-paying jobs, a regressive tax system that was strained to meet demands placed upon it, the drive to promote tourism and economic growth, and the twin goals of competing with neighboring states while at the same time working with them to promote mutual progress. None of these goals had easy solutions and most of them required tradeoffs of one kind or other. For politicians trying to weave their way through the pitfalls accompanying them, it was a hazardous journey. Leadership of a creative and dynamic sort was needed. In many ways Bill Janklow provided it.

Never one to go the easy or well-trod route, Janklow demonstrated from the beginning of his governorship a willingness to do the unexpected and to confound his critics. Intelligent, intense, and articulate, he was also volatile and displayed strong populist tendencies as governor, even while establishing himself as a solid conservative on fiscal and social issues. Perhaps more than any other South Dakotan who ever occupied the office, he loved being governor and stamped his own identity on the job. A signature quality of his was his propensity to take over personal management of the situation during a crisis, such as the Spencer tornado in 1998, when six people were killed and almost the entire town was wiped out by the twister. No one ever doubted who was in charge while he was in office. He enjoyed doing political battle, and he loved exercising the authority that came along with the office.

Running for office during his first electoral try on the slogan of "Putting the Taxpayer First" and later successfully campaigning to reduce property taxes by thirty percent, Janklow firmly established his identity as a fiscal conservative. That left him free to move down more unpredictable paths, such as temporarily adding an extra penny to the state sales tax to establish a core railroad system in 1980. With the Milwaukee Road verging on bankruptcy, the state purchased over 700 miles of track and later negotiated with the Burlington Northern to operate 480 miles of it in eastern South Dakota. Considered by some to be a socialistic venture, the governor saw it as a practical move and could point to progressive Republican Governor Peter Norbeck's program as precedent for it. He also lured Citibank of New York to transfer its credit card operations to Sioux Falls by getting the legislature to take off restrictions on interest rates and to invite the company to move. No less boldly, he negotiated a deal with Energy Transportation Systems Incorporated (ETSI) officials to sell Missouri River water for a coal-slurry pipeline to transport coal mined in Wyoming to states in the South. Throughout his governorship, Janklow sought to promote economic development and attract jobs to South Dakota, praising the healthy business climate of the state and the qualities of the labor force. As did governors of other states, he promoted tourism and high-tech jobs. A major initiative he was especially proud of was wiring the schools for computer use and the Internet. One of his most controversial actions was obtaining legislative approval for converting one of South Dakota's seven higher education institutions—the campus at Springfield—into a minimum-security prison. The political fallout from the action was intense, and it is hard to imagine any other governor who could have pulled it off—or who would have tried it.[52] In 2002, at the conclusion of his term, Janklow ran successfully for Congress. He resigned less than a year later and was replaced by Democratic Congresswoman Stephanie Herseth.

Much more conventional in approach was the tragically shortened governorship of Brookings attorney George Speaker Mickelson, who was succeeded by Lieutenant Governor Walter Dale Miller when Mickelson's plane, carrying seven other South Dakotans who had been recruiting out-of-state businesses to move to South Dakota, crashed on April 19, 1993, killing all of the plane's occupants. Mickelson had grown up in a political family as the son of South Dakota's eighteenth governor. Educated at the University of South Dakota and its law school, Mickelson served six years in the House of Representatives representing Brookings, rising to the same position his father had once held—Speaker of the House—which also had given him his middle name. Adopting a more consensual leadership style than his predecessor in office, the younger Governor Mickelson did not always obtain the consensus he sought. While Janklow had successfully obtained a temporary increase in the sales tax for his railroad project, Mickelson stimulated dissension in the Republican Party when he obtained a one-year, single-penny sales tax increase to create a loan fund to promote economic development called the REDI Fund. Approximately $40 million was raised for loans to companies that created jobs. Mickelson also advocated for increased state aid to school districts and for extra money to higher education to support research aimed at developing new industries in the state. As part of his economic development program, he elevated the tourism office to a cabinet-level agency. Video lottery was also introduced to help balance the state budget. Although other governors had made attempts in that direction, Mickelson did more than any governor before him to promote better relations between the races. Seizing the opportunity at the time of the state centennial in 1989, he announced a "Year of Reconciliation" and then a "Century of Reconciliation" as ways of promoting dialogue between Indians and whites—initiatives that may remain his most lasting legacy.[53]

Mickelson's successor, Walter Dale Miller, a Meade County rancher and veteran of two decades in the House of Representatives, had less than two years to establish his political identity before facing a challenge from former Governor Bill Janklow in the 1994 Republican primary. His government was primarily a caretaker one, carrying on the initiatives started by his two immediate predecessors.

As South Dakota moved into the twenty-first century, its political tradition was a colorful and somewhat contradictory one. By many standards a heavily Republican and conservative state, South Dakota retained a strong populist and progressive heritage, which was reflected in a variety of its leaders and practices. Though ranking low in taxation, spending, and government services, South Dakota ranked high in the quality of its schools, culture, and social amenities. Political corruption was largely nonexistent, at least by the standards of many other states. Though known for their independence and self-reliance, South Dakotans depended heavily upon federal assistance and were led for much of the last quarter-century by a governor who brooked little objection or dissent. While large numbers of its young people moved out of the state in search of better jobs, those who remained prized South Dakota for its friendliness, strong sense of community, clean environment, and high quality of life. In all aspects of life there are tradeoffs. South Dakota, with a population that still had a considerable way to go to reach a million, remained in many ways a secret. Many people who lived there were content. That translated into a politics that could be characterized as maintaining the status quo. Continuity rather than change remained the rule; consensus rather than conflict was the norm. So long as that remained true, it would continue to receive less attention from outsiders than many of its counterparts.

Chapter 13
Farming: Dependency and Depopulation

Early ninteenth-century reformers argued that the true key to democracy lay in providing public land for the yeoman farmer, who, according to Thomas Jefferson, was the backbone of society. In a letter to James Madison on October 28, 1785, Jefferson wrote, "The small landholders are the most precious part of the state." In his *Notes on the State of Virginia*, Jefferson observed, "I have often thought that if heaven had given me the choice of my position and calling, it should have been on a rich spot of earth, well watered, and near a good market for the productions of the garden. No occupation is so delightful to me as the culture of the earth."

Jefferson would have been pleased with the passage of the Homestead Act on May 20, 1862, for it provided people with little means to venture their lives in the unsettled northern plains. The act stipulated that any twenty-one-year-old adult citizen, or any citizen who had filed a declaration of intent, could claim 160 acres of surveyed public domain. After breaking five acres during the first year and five years' residence on said claim, a sod buster could receive final title to this land upon filing a few papers and paying a registration fee ranging from $26 to $34. Based on the earlier Pre-emption Act of 1841, individuals who possessed adequate capital could purchase 160 acres at $1.25 per acre and after six months' residence exercise the homestead privilege. Eighty million acres in homesteads were given away by Congress. The act caused one of the great population movements in the history of the world. The homesteading boom that occurred in the late 1870s and 1880s developed the southern half of Dakota Territory into a progressive state.

Despite the enticement of the Homestead Act, there had been little settlement of Dakota Territory in the 1860s because of the presence of Indians. Several factors when considered together would soon create an environment in which people dreaming of a farm of their own would move into the territory. The confluence of the following factors influenced the Great Dakota Boom of the 1880s: the rapid industrialization and urbanization in the East and the Old Midwest, improvements in flour milling, extensive railroad construction, new farm technology, a great surge in immigration, and favorable farming conditions in Dakota Territory. The rains came and the grasshoppers left.

Railroad corporations, territorial and state immigration offices, real estate agents, newspapers, and letters from immigrants already living in the United States attracted people primarily from the lower economic stratum of northern Europe to seek farms of their own in Dakota Territory. Railroad executives, sensing an economic advantage, promoted settlement. One executive commented, "A quarter section of land in grain will produce eight car-loads of freight, while a quarter section left in grass will generally produce no traffic for the railroad." Persuasive pamphlets and brochures were distributed with glowing stories of bumper crops and favorable climatic conditions. One of the overblown promotional statements made by Dakota boosters included, "Come to God's country, where the pure north wind impacts vigor to the system and disease is scarcely known; come where you can get land without money and without price. Land that when

Chronology

1862 – Homestead Act

1870s-1880s – Great Dakota Boom

1910-1914 – The "Parity Years"

1920-1940 – Economic depression in rural America

1933-1938 – New Deal farm legislation, beginning with the Agricultural Adjustment Act in 1933

1936 – Rural Electrification Act

1963 – Annual wheat referendum fails

1973 – Agriculture and Consumer Protection Act: Farmers have to depend on market prices for their income

1974 – Family Farm Act

1980s – Continued exodus from the "family farm"

1985 – Conservation Reserve Program (CRP)

1996 – Freedom to Farm Act

you tickle it with the plow . . . laughs with its abundance." After statehood in 1889, the South Dakota Immigration Office was established and among its promotional materials sent overseas was a brochure entitled "Corn is King in South Dakota." Many of those of lesser means who migrated into the region were foreign born and had been residing in Iowa, Illinois, Minnesota, and Wisconsin. The majority of settlers were Scandinavians, Germans from Russia, Dutch, and Bohemians. They would discover that the Great Plains made unique and often onerous demands on its settlers. Farmers settling on the plains required a larger land base, more technological innovation, and larger amounts of capital than did farmers in the eastern United States.

When a land seeker located the available land he desired, he immediately took action to show evidence that the area was occupied. Some homesteaders dug four post holes to indicate the corners of a shack. Others dug a hole a yard or two deep to represent a well. Entrepreneurs in nearby towns often constructed shacks that for a price could be moved quickly to the claim site. Another ingenious tactic was to rent a homestead shack on wheels. It could be rented for about five dollars in order to fulfill proving-up requirements. The typical frame shack, nine-by-twelve feet in size, was constructed of pine boards and covered with tar paper in an attempt to make the crude structure waterproof. Other homesteaders cut sod strips from the prairie, using lumber only for the door, roof, and window frames. Although sod houses tended to be damp, they were relatively comfortable during times of temperature extremes.

The new settlers would have access to improved farm machinery. James Oliver made adjustments to the John Deere plow, making it a more effective instrument in breaking the prairie sod. The plow, with its steel blade and improved mold board, had better wearing and scouring qualities. In turning the virgin prairie into farm land, many sod busters used a team of four oxen, pulling a fourteen-inch plow, to break from one to two acres of the tough, fibrous sod a day. The reaper, first designed and constructed by Cyrus McCormick, became a self-binding reaper as twine replaced wire in the binding attachment. Other technical improvements included the grain drill, the revolving disc harrow, the sulky plow, on which the farmer could ride as he plowed, barbed wire, the windmill, and a threshing machine that separated the wheat and chaff and bagged the grain. Of particular interest to spring wheat farmers in the James River Valley and northern South Dakota was the new technology used in flour mills in Minneapolis. Metallic rollers made it possible to process the hard spring wheat into flour. One of the problems with the Homestead Act was that it did not provide farm families with the several thousand dollars needed to buy much of the new technology. The basic 160-acre farm was not large enough to raise sufficient crops to provide a reasonable return for any significant capital investment.

Harvest scene on J. J. Donovan's 600-acre field of grain, two miles east of Winner. *Center for Western Studies.*

Between 1878 and 1887, almost all of the available land east of the Missouri River was occupied. In what was to become South Dakota two years later, approximately twenty-four million acres had been claimed during the aforementioned years. Within five years, 1880-1885, the population of southeastern South Dakota grew from 81,781 to 248,569. By 1886 the Great Dakota Boom was coming to a conclusion and not all of the people who arrived during the 1880s remained in the area. Free land had been a great temptation, and the Homestead Act had attracted a number of people who were not of pioneering caliber. Because of sweltering summers and snowbound winters, drought, grasshoppers, hailstorms, isolation, and falling grain prices, some would-be farmers yielded to defeatism and left.

Most of the homesteaders, however, remained on the land they had claimed and, in the years to follow, would be joined by a steady flow of compatriots from Europe. Many who remained in South Dakota faced interminable financial difficulties. By 1890 the plains farmer was an angry man. He was not the happy and self-sufficient yeoman and master of his fate envisioned by Jeffersonian idealists. The independent farmer was an illusion. The history of farmers on the northern plains since the 1880s has been one of dependency. For over 130 years, they have been dependent on a favorable climate and ecology and out-of-state economic, political, and social forces. Elwyn B. Robinson, a North Dakota historian, said the Dakotas could be considered as colonial provinces, exploited by the grain trusts in the Twin Cities, railroad magnates, and great banking houses in the East.

Between 1887 and 1894, crop yields were reduced because of a lack of rainfall and periodic incursions of grasshoppers. It became more difficult to pay off mortgages incurred during the Dakota Boom. Regarding the unfavorable climate, one wit observed that a man hit with a rain drop fainted from the shock and had to be revived with two buckets of dust. Despite the uncertain climate, farmers by 1890 were flooding the flour mills and packing houses with grain and cattle. They quickly discovered they were at the mercy of the market and overproduction caused falling prices. Most irritating was exploitation by out-of-state financial and marketing agencies. While commodity prices fell, interest rates and the price of farm machinery remained high. The farmers lacked recourse to adequate credit facilities. Local elevators were usually owned by Minneapolis milling magnates. Under their instruction, local operators engaged in arbitrary methods of grading and weighing the farmer's grain. The quality of the grain was thereby debased and the monetary amount accordingly reduced for each wagon-load brought to the elevator. Particularly galling, railroad corporations were guilty of blatant extortion. The cost of transporting grain to the mills in the Twin Cities was half the value of the product. High freight rates were charged for short hauls. Transit rates were charged to Chicago or Milwaukee even though the grain was usually processed in Minneapolis.

The farmers' response to continued and flagrant exploitation was to enroll in activist farm organizations. The first of these, the Farmers' Alliance, was organized in 1880. One of its subsidiaries, the Northern Farmers' Alliance, issued a charter to a group of Yankton area farmers in February 1881. The alliance received its greatest welcome in the northern area of what would become South Dakota where the price of wheat had dropped as low as eighty cents a bushel in 1884. The continued decline of grain and cattle prices led to the creation of the Dakota Territorial Alliance at Huron in February 1885. Incorporated as a joint-stock company in 1887, the alliance established a cooperative store at Watertown. The store supplied members with binder twine, farm implements, furniture, and coal at an agreeable price. The alliance also provided fire, hail, and life insurance for its members. These pioneer endeavors in cooperative work ended with the economic depression of 1893.

Ignatius Donnelly, a Minnesota congressman, and Henry L. Loucks, who had homesteaded in Deuel County, Dakota Territory, urged alliance members to participate in politics, asserting that "You can do nothing, accomplish nothing, without the ballot box." Rebuffed by the Republican Party, Loucks formed an Independent Party in 1890 and entered the gubernatorial race. Through legislative action, the Independents hoped to achieve the Australian (secret) ballot, equitable tax assessment for farmers, government control of railroads, the free and unlimited coinage of silver to increase inflation, and higher prices for farm products.

When Loucks was rejected at the polls, many South Dakota farmers turned to the Peoples' or Populist Party, first organized in Kansas in 1890. Meeting at Omaha, Nebraska, on July 4, 1892, to nominate candidates for public office, the Populists proposed financial reform. It was the first and most comprehensive plank in their party platform. They called for the free and unlimited coinage of silver and gold at the current legal ratio of sixteen-to-one. If the federal government permitted the free and unlimited coinage of silver at the foregoing ratio, there would be an adequate supply of cheap money to enable rural debtors to ease their financial plight.

Populism enjoyed a brief time in South Dakota's "political sun," from 1896 to 1898. Andrew E. Lee was elected governor and a coalition of Fusionists, Populists, and Democrats dominated briefly the state legislature. The coalition also won both seats in the U.S. House of Representatives, and Senator Richard F. Pettigrew joined their ranks. At the national level, voters rejected the Populist program in 1896 and 1900, and in South Dakota a revived farm economy led to a resurgence of the Republican Party.

A new farm organization, the American Society of Equity, was founded in December 1902. Within four years, the Society had a chapter among wheat growers in South Dakota. When a program to withhold grain from the market failed, the Society of Equity turned to cooperative marketing as a means of controlling their product. The Equity Cooperative Exchange, incorporated in 1911, bought grain at its own country stations or handled it on consignment either for individual shippers or for country elevators. Unable to gain membership in the Minneapolis Grain Exchange, the Equity in 1920 constructed its own grain terminal at St. Paul. The terminal would later be taken over by the Farmers Union Grain Terminal Association (FUGTA).

Although none of the foregoing farm movements ultimately succeeded in easing the farmers' economic distress, their efforts and ideas provided a seedbed for two influential farm organizations of the twentieth century, the South Dakota Farmers Union and the South Dakota Farm Bureau Federation. They would begin to play activist roles with the sudden termination of American agriculture's "golden years" in 1920.

From 1900 to 1920, the economic pressure on South Dakota farmers was temporarily relieved. Increased urbanization, accompanied by rising wages and employment meant that the greater share of farm produce was consumed domestically. Farmers adjusted to market demands through diversification, providing fresh milk, out-of-season fruits and vegetables, cereal grains, and meat. For a short period of time they did not have to worry about the disorganizing effects of world prices. These were the "golden years" for the state's farmers. Market prices and land values rose. The years between 1910 and 1914 became known as the "parity years," when supply and demand stood in effective equilibrium. Parity is a system of regulating the price of farm commodities to provide farmers with the same purchasing power they had in the selected base period, 1910-1914. Thus, rural and urban purchasing power was equal.

Price stability ended with the outbreak of World War I. During the war years, a large number of farmers actually became affluent. Allied demands for foodstuffs and cotton, the requirements of America's armed forces beginning in 1917, and the immediate needs of postwar Europe, 1918-1920, caused the price of crops and agricultural land to soar. The federal government urged intensive planting using such slogans as: "Plow to the fence for national defense"; "If you can't fight, farm"; and "Wheat will win the war." The planting and harvesting of crops was facilitated as draft animals on many farms were replaced by the internal combustion engine, the tractor.

Beginning in 1918, grain was being grown in the more arid sections of the Great Plains, including west of the ninety-eighth meridian in South Dakota. Ignoring the ecological implications of plowing up traditional grass land, farmers engaged in blatant over-cropping. Marginal soil was over-plowed, over-grazed, and denuded. The state's farmers wanted to squeeze maximum productivity out of the land. Across the plains,

A steam-powered tractor breaks the sod on the Rosebud Reservation while a horse-drawn wagon follows behind, showing the coexistence in agriculture of older with newer technologies. *Center for Western Studies.*

wheat production rose to an annual average of approximately 870 million bushels while corn production remained relatively stable. Using the 1910-1914 parity base of 100, farm prices in 1918 stood at 208 and by 1920 at an unprecedented 211, more than double 1915 returns.

Lulled by a false sense of security, many of South Dakota's tillers of the soil pushed out their financial horizons. Land, equipment, and buildings were mortgaged to buy more land and farm machinery. Land prices rose to 160 percent of the pre-war average. Simultaneously, farmers clamored for the expansion of social services by state and county governments, resulting in an ever-mounting tax rate.

While farmers enjoyed their new economic status, there remained dark undercurrents of abuse and exploitation. Along with ranchers, they were still being manipulated by out-of-state corporate grain and railroad interests. The price of wheat and grading and buying conditions were still determined by a corporate oligarchy in Minneapolis. Freight rates remained comparatively high. In 1915 South Dakota farmers paid $24 to ship a car load of hogs one hundred miles. In Minnesota and Iowa, the shipping costs for a similar car load the same distance was $20.48 and $16.15, respectively. Farmers who attempted to pay off mortgages had to contend with banking firms that charged as much interest as the traffic would bear. In many communities, the farmer was almost completely at the mercy of the local banker upon whom he was dependent for operating capital.

The rural prosperity bubble burst suddenly and completely in 1920. The year began with wheat selling for $2.96 per bushel, and within two years the price dropped to ninety-two cents a bushel on the Minneapolis market. Prices plummeted when the government withdrew its support on wheat. Simultaneously, the foreign market collapsed as overseas competitors returned to production. Nations began erecting tariff barriers, prohibiting overseas shipments of grain. New fad diets, promoted via mass advertising, also contributed to reduced urban consumption of farm products. One of the popular cigarette ads during the twenties was "Reach for a Lucky [Strike] instead of a sweet."

As grain and land prices fell, farmers continued to be faced with high mortgage payments incurred during the war years and with tax rates that doubled in the 1920s. Having experienced a higher standard of living during the "golden years," they were caught up in the conspicuous consumption prevalent during the decade. Advertising came of age. Color ads and mail-order catalogs whetted their appetites for the fruits of new technology, such as automobiles, radios, washing machines, and refrigerators. Farm families were trapped in a "scissor crisis," a cost-price squeeze. The prices of manufactured goods rose while farm commodity prices fell. In 1913 a farmer could purchase a suit for twenty-one bushels of wheat; ten years later, the same suit could be acquired for thirty-one bushels of wheat. The farmers' role as a participant in the consumer economy continued to shrink as the decade progressed. With the deteriorating economy, bank failures accelerated. Nine banks in South Dakota closed in 1922, thirty-six in 1923, and, by January 1925, 175 of the state's banks had closed their doors. The federal government attempted to provide temporary relief to rural banks through short-term loans from the Agricultural Credit Corporation, but the loans failed to stem the tide of bank failures.

Farmers responded to their financial shortfall by producing more cereal crops which, given the laws of supply and demand, continued to lower the price. Improved, mechanized machinery made it easier to over-produce grain. The number of acres that could be harvested by a single worker in South Dakota increased from 33.2 in 1920 to 100 by 1929. Land used for crop production increased from 16,441,000 acres in 1924 to 19,003,000 acres in 1929. By placing more acres in production, many farmers cultivated sub-marginal land, endangering the delicate ecological balance. Within a few years, they would be shown the folly of their ways as a prolonged drought, high winds, and an unrelenting sun created the horrendous dust storms of the early 1930s.

The federal government made little effort to help beleaguered farmers. The most important farm legislation proposed in the 1920s was the ill-fated McNary-Haugen Bill. The bill was an effort to protect American producers from foreign competition. It provided for a two-price system, one for the domestic market, another for the world market. Championed by the farm bloc in the U.S. Senate, including Senators Peter Norbeck and William McMaster of South Dakota, enough strength was mobilized to force the measure through both houses of Congress in February 1927 and again in May 1928. In neither instance did the farm bloc have margins large enough to override President Calvin Coolidge's veto. The bill in its final form provided for a federal farm board. The board was authorized to make loans to cooperative associations to assist them in controlling seasonable surpluses in excess of domestic needs. The passage of the Smoot-Hawley Tariff in June 1931 and the resulting paralysis in international trade made it impossible to resurrect the McNary-Haugen plan at a later date.

The Smoot-Hawley Tariff also had a negative impact on the Agricultural Marketing Act, approved by Congress on June 15, 1929. The Marketing Act had established a Federal Farm Board that was authorized to support new and existing farm cooperative marketing associations. Congress appropriated $500 million for a self-sustaining revolving fund. The so-called "stabilizing corporations owned by the cooperative would draw upon the fund to purchase the surplus grain and provide price supports. For the first time in the history of American agriculture, albeit indirectly, the federal government was committed to stabilizing farm prices. During its short existence, the board spent more than $180 million. Two factors, however, contributed to the Farm Board's dilemma. First, the price support program did not succeed because farmers were reluctant to reduce acreage. Secondly, the Smoot-Hawley Tariff raised the tariff on raw agricultural materials from thirty-eight percent to forty-nine percent. It made the sale of commodities overseas almost impossible. When grain prices further declined after the collapse of the stock market on October 29, 1929, the board incurred heavy financial losses, leading to its demise in 1933.

Soon after the collapse of the stock market, when sixteen million shares of stock sold in a single day, commodity prices hit "rock bottom." They fell faster and further than at any other period in the history of American agriculture. Hog prices stood at $11.36 per head in 1931 and at $4.21 in 1933. The market price of a bushel of wheat sank from $1.03 in 1929 to a low of twenty-four cents a bushel in 1932. A person with a wry sense of humor related the story of the champion wrestler who broke his back attempting to lift fifty cents worth of oats.

Plains farmers also had to contend with the vicissitudes of nature and a sub-humid climate. The plowing up of thousands of acres of grassland during World War I and the 1920s led to the infamous "black blizzards" of the 1930s. The drought commenced in July 1930, the second driest ever recorded in the state's history. Summer sun baked the land and any rain that fell did not penetrate the soil. High winds, synonymous with the region, swept over the plains. The wind

SOUTH DAKOTA FARM PRICES 1932-1933	
Wheat	24-28 cents per bushel
Barley	7-10 cents per bushel
Oats	5-10 cents per bushel
Eggs	6-12 cents per dozen
Hogs	2-3 cents per pound, $2.00 per hundredweight
Cattle	5 cents per pound, $5.00 per hundredweight
Milk	10 cents per quart

A massive dust storm, or "black blizzard," descends upon this western South Dakota town at the height of the Dirty Thirties. *Center for Western Studies.*

picked up the parched, dry soil that had nothing to hold it down and darkened the sky with dust.

The dust storms reached their intensity in 1933-34. Hardest hit in South Dakota were counties located between the 98th° and 100th° meridian. R. D. Lusk, editor of the *Evening Huronite,* provided a vivid description of the impact of the "great black blizzard" of November 11, 1933, on the Karnstrum farm in Beadle County. "By mid-morning a gale was blowing, cold and black. By noon it was blacker than night, because one can see through night and this was an opaque black. . . . Inside the house the Karnstrums soaked sheets and towels and stuffed them around window ledges, but these didn't help much. . . . When the wind died and the sunshine shone forth again, it was on a different world. There were no fields, only sand drifting into mounds and eddies that swirled in what was now an autumn breeze. . . . In the farmyard, fences, machinery, and trees were gone, buried. The roofs of sheds stuck out through drifts deeper than a man is tall."[1]

Earl Cronkhite, who farmed near De Smet, said, "The dust was so bad that you couldn't even see across the road. You couldn't see the linoleum [in the house]. The window sills were just drifts of dust. . . . Some of the fences were full of dirt clear to the top." One could walk over the fences without seeing them. A distraught Perkins County resident, Harry Hebner, in a letter published in the *Dakota Farmer* in mid-1935, wrote, "This West River country is not a newly settled country; it is no frontier. It is bankrupt, desolated, poverty stricken, over-populated, over-grazed, semi-desert."[2]

As the drought intensified throughout two-thirds of South Dakota, there was a general feeling of despair and hopelessness among farmers. Lois Phillips Hudson, in *Reapers of the Dust, A Prairie Chronicle,* describes vividly the feelings of the dust's victims: "Dust storms are like that; no matter how many times you clean or how much you scrub and repaint and dig into crevices, you are always finding another niche the dust has found. And in dust is the smell of mortality, of fertility swept away and spring vanished."[3]

Tumbleweeds and thistles blew across prairie and roads until they came to rest against the side of a building or fence line. Farmers sought to keep their herds together by cutting Russian thistles and putting them up for hay. The forces of nature were relentless. The dry conditions provided an excellent environment for grasshoppers to lay their eggs and to multiply. Swarms of grasshoppers made quick work of cornfields, consumed whole gardens, and even devoured the leaves and bark off of trees.

In this hostile economic and natural environment, it was difficult for many South Dakota farmers to "keep body and soul together." The daily lunch for many school

During the Great Depression, wind picked up the topsoil from overly developed land and deposited it against any structure in its path, such as this barn near Gregory. *Center for Western Studies.*

children was egg, lard, mustard, or syrup sandwiches. One farm woman who lived near Montrose commented: "We lived very simply food-wise and got along by buying mostly food staples such as sugar, flour, etc. Some years we couldn't depend much on potatoes and other garden stuff, and fruit trees around, but we had our own milk, cream, and churned our own butter. A couple of years we lost our little chickens in storms, but otherwise we raised our chickens to eat."[4]

Chickens were a large part of farm life in the thirties, not only for the meat, but for the eggs. Farm families ate a lot of eggs. People economized wherever they could. Clothing was often homemade or retailored "hand-me-downs." Holes in the soles of shoes were often covered with cardboard cut to fit inside the shoe. The farm woman recalled that a letter sat on the window sill for several weeks until they obtained the three cents to send it. During the winter months some farmers burned corn or dried cow manure (barnyard lignite) in their stoves. Lorena Hickok, a one-time South Dakota resident and in 1933 a chief investigator for Harry Hopkins, head of the Federal Emergency Relief Administration, visited South Dakota in November 1933. She wrote Hopkins that if President Franklin D. Roosevelt should ever decide to become dictator, "He can label this country out here 'Siberia' and send all the exiles here. . . . A more hopeless place I never saw."[5]

Farmers could no longer be silent about their plight. On May 3, 1932, the Farmers' Holiday Association was formed at Des Moines, Iowa. The primary function of this most aggressive agrarian upheaval of the twentieth century was to withhold farm produce from the market to secure the cost of production. Several South Dakota farmers met at Yankton on July 20 to establish a state Holiday Association, sponsored by the Farmers Union. Emil Loriks, a long-time Farmers Union leader, was named executive secretary of the South Dakota Farmers' Holiday Association.

The strike or withholding action began on August 8, 1932. Violence ensued when pickets attempted to stop non-cooperating farmers from passing through blockades of logs, barrels, old tires, and machine belts containing spikes placed on roads leading into Sioux City, Iowa. On October 5-6, all of the thirteen principal roads entering Sioux Falls were blocked by members of the Minnehaha County Farmers' Holiday Association. They successfully halted grains and livestock headed for the Sioux Falls markets. Roads were also temporarily blocked outside of Watertown and Yankton. In neither instance did the pickets resort to the violence displayed around Sioux City.

The withholding action had two major shortcomings. There was a lack of discipline, as exemplified through the violence near Sioux City and Omaha. Secondly, the economic objective was unsound. The embargo deprived farmers of income needed to feed livestock and families. Keeping marketable animals on the farm meant added costs. Farmers had to market to survive.

The South Dakota Farmers' Holiday Association had greater success in resisting farm foreclosures. Association members gathered at farms where the property was being auctioned off at foreclosure. Through orchestrating the proceedings, the cattle, horses, machinery, and furniture were sold for a penny to ten cents with no competing bids permitted. At the close of the sale, the property was returned to the family victimized by the foreclosure. Overall, the Holiday Association did publicize the farmers' plight.

A more militant farm organization with Marxist affiliation, the United Farmers League (UFL), emerged in northeast South Dakota in the 1920s. The UFL wanted government-sponsored rural credit, direct relief and federal legislation to increase farm prices, and suspension of foreclosures and evictions. Like the Farm Holiday Association, the UFL disappeared from the activist scene in 1936-1937. Politicians were made aware that farmers were being driven to the wall. State governments temporarily stopped foreclosure proceedings through mortgage moratoriums.

At the national level, the Democratic Party, with Franklin D. Roosevelt as its candidate, promised immediate action to ease the farmer's dire situation. In his second Fireside Chat, in May 1933, Roosevelt said his administration would seek "to bring about an increased return to farmers for their major products, seeking at the same time to prevent in the days to come disastrous overproduction which so often in the past has kept farm commodity prices far below a reasonable return." Farm legislation introduced during the first one-hundred days of the New Deal, March to June 1933, diverted attention away from the efforts of the Farmers' Holiday Association. Henry A. Wallace, Secretary of Agriculture, sought an economic balance between urban and rural America, a restoration of parity. Wallace asked, "How are farmers to get equality of bargaining power without help from the government?" He believed commodity prices would improve if the surplus of grain and cattle was reduced. Accordingly, Congress approved the Agricultural Adjustment Act on May 12, 1933. The act incorporated the subsidy principle: in return for voluntarily reducing acreage or crops, farmers were to be granted direct benefit or rental payments. The funds for such payments were to be derived from levies on the processors of specified farm products. The act relieved the credit situation by providing for the refinancing of farm mortgages through Federal Land Banks. Approximately one month later, on June 16, the Farm Credit Act became law. It was designed to facilitate short-term and medium-term credits for agricultural production and marketing, thereby refinancing farm mortgages on long terms at low interest. From May 1933 to July 1938, the Farm Credit Administration loaned $83,378,000 to farmers in South Dakota.

The administration also took more drastic action to reduce the surplus. Certain crops were burned and an estimated six million pigs were killed nationwide in August 1933. In August 1934 the government became the country's largest buyer and distributor of meat. Purchased were drought-menaced animals that could not be fed or watered by their owners. In South Dakota, 915,039 head of cattle from approximately 67,000 farms and ranches, nearly forty-five percent of the state's cattle herds, were purchased by the government for an average of less than ten dollars apiece. Approximately 87,000 of these animals were condemned and destroyed as unfit for human consumption. Although they were not diseased, they were driven into huge prepared pits or dugouts, where they were shot and buried in cattle graveyards. The U.S. Department of Agriculture was criticized for not making this potential source of meat accessible to poverty-stricken families. The last significant piece of farm legislation approved by Congress in 1933, on October 18, was the Commodity Credit Corporation (CCC). The new agency would extend loans to farmers on their crops. The primary purpose was to support farm prices by enabling producers to retain commodities until prices reached reasonable levels. The CCC provided loans of forty-five cents a bushel on properly stored corn. In Hyde County, one of the areas hardest hit by the drought, two-fifths of the receipts of farmers came from production control payments, emergency livestock purchases, or relief grants.

On January 6, 1936, the Agricultural Adjustment Act of 1933 was invalidated by the Supreme Court. Congress responded with the passage of the Soil Conservation and Domestic Allotment Act on February 29. The act enabled the continued restriction of agricultural output, not by contracts with farmers for control of crop production, but by benefit payments to growers who practiced soil conservation in cooperation with the government program. Payments depended upon acreage withdrawn from soil-depleting crops (i.e. corn, wheat, and oats) and turned over to soil-conserving crops.

After it became apparent that the Soil Conservation and Domestic Allotment Act was unable to curb farm surpluses and price declines during the recession of 1936, the Roosevelt administration revived the Agricultural Adjustment Act in modified form. The act empowered the Secretary of Agriculture to fix a marketing quota whenever it was determined that a surplus of any export farm commodity, such as corn or wheat, threatened the price level. The legislation authorized acreage allotments to each grower after two-thirds of the farmers had by referendum expressed their approval of the marketing quota. Lastly, the Commodity Credit Corporation was authorized to make loans to farmers on their surplus crops at a level slightly below parity, for many years ninety percent of parity. Excess crops were to be stored under government auspices in large metal grain bins at the outskirts of rural communities. The farmer would repay the loan and market the surplus during crop failure years when the price was at parity or above. The program stabilized agricultural prices and stored surplus crops without loss to an individual farmer's income. The USDA called the program the ever-normal granary.

Farmers also had recourse to several relief programs available to the general population. The Federal Emergency Relief Administration had $500 million at its disposal to make outright grants to states and municipalities. In turn the latter was expected to

Government Payments to South Dakota Farmers, 1933-1940		
Year	Total Cash Farm Income (Including government payments)	Government Benefit Payments
1933	$ 70,800,000	$ 5,100,000
1934	80,400,000	19,400,000
1935	103,200,000	15,600,000
1936	116,900,000	9,800,000
1937	102,600,000	15,000,000
1938	107,800,000	17,500,000
1939	128,100,000	23,100,000
1940	140,000,000	20,000,000

establish work relief projects for employable individuals. In December 1934 thirty-nine percent of South Dakotans were on relief. Surplus commodities were distributed to the needy who could could pick up boxes of groceries at their county courthouse.

In April 1935 the federal government moved from direct relief via the states and local communities to the establishment of a large-scale national works program, the Works Progress Administration (WPA), for the jobless, who were required to meet a means test to qualify for work relief. Many South Dakota farmers were employed by the WPA during the fall and winter months. Usually, they were employed in road and bridge construction, tasks that involved manual labor. Using their own horses and wagons, they hauled gravel that was placed on the road surface or hitched their teams to scrapers and moved earth to create the roadbed under construction. For working one hundred hours, they received $40 a month. Older sons, in their late teens or early twenties, supplemented the family's income by enrolling in the Civilian Conservation Corps (CCC). They built dams, improved parks, and engaged in forestry work in the Black Hills. Many high school and college youths qualified for National Youth Administration (NYA) employment. The NYA was a type of work-study program whereby enrolled high school students received a monthly stipend of $6 per month and college students $20 per month.

The New Deal did not end the Great Depression but it did help people to survive it. Nevertheless, the farm legislation of the 1930s had lasting impact. Farmers became dependent on the federal government for a variable proportion of their livelihood. The farm subsidy program, albeit with some modifications, remained in effect until 1996. The Freedom to Farm bill of that year, supported by conservative Republicans and urban, liberal Democrats, called for an end to farm subsidies. However, an ensuing farm crisis necessitated further payments to America's farmers. One of the significant negatives associated with the subsidy program was that it overwhelmingly favored large-scale farmers and landowners while providing limited support to farmers tilling small acreages.

After intense heat in June and July 1936, when for thirty-two days the temperature reached or surpassed one hundred degrees, and the average precipitation for the year was 10.88 inches, the rains began to return. The national economy began to revive as the threat of a major war loomed in Europe and East Asia in the late 1930s. The production of armaments for British allies and U.S. armed forces was a primary stimulus for ending the Great Depression.

One cannot overemphasize the importance of farm wives in maintaining the family farm. The wife was usually the only other adult on the farm. Their participation in field work was often a critical factor in staving off failure of the family farm enterprise. In addition to keeping house and working in the kitchen, the garden, and the chicken house, they were involved in field work. They drove reapers, harvesters, and hay wagons and planted seed and dug potatoes. They raised vegetables, fruit, and chickens. Their labor produced milk, butter, and eggs, not only for the kitchen table but for cash or barter at the local grocery store or cream station. Glenda Riley, one of the foremost scholars of women's history, disagrees with literary accounts depicting the loneliness of farm wives. She argues that they participated in many social events, with families and friends, at churches and schools and in nearby towns. There was much card playing and dancing. The early neighborhoods were often small and close knit, held together by a special bond such as kinship and ethnicity.

During the 1930s, there was a significant out-migration of people from South Dakota. Many farmers sold out, and after being hosted at a neighborhood party, they loaded their remaining belongings on a trailer and drove west to find water and survival

Working in partnership with their husbands, women made family farming possible. Today, many farm women find employment in nearby towns as a way to supplement declining farm income. *Center for Western Studies.*

in the Pacific Coast states of California, Oregon, and Washington. There were 84,300 farms in South Dakota in 1931; the 1940 census listed 72,500 farms. The state had 692,849 residents in 1930; the census for 1940 listed 642,961, a decrease of 7.2 percent. Approximately 50,000 people had departed during the traumatic decade, seeking so-called "greener pastures."

As the pall of the Great Depression began to lift from the land, the shadow of the next traumatic event, another general war, gave people little cause for rejoicing. President Roosevelt had asked Congress in 1938 to appropriate $300 million for the defense of the United States. British and French orders for munitions, planes, guns, and tanks also were received by American industry. While these demands for armaments stimulated the American economy, questions about the foreign policy of the United States were debated constantly.

With the Japanese attack on Pearl Harbor on December 7, 1941, the United States entered World War II, declaring war on the fascist powers in Europe and East Asia. Farm production in South Dakota reached a new high during the war years. Rainfall was ample. Between 1940 and 1944 the northern plains received above-average pre-cipitation. The market demand was strong and commodity prices were as high as price controls would permit. In 1940 farmers received sixty-seven cents per bushel of wheat. By 1945 the price per bushel reached $1.53. During the same years, beef cattle per hun-dredweight increased from $6.80 to $10.10.

During World War II, acreage restrictions were lifted and farmers were urged to pro-duce as much food as they could. The government, recognizing that abundant food was essential, gave farm machinery manufacturers some priority for the raw materials neces-sary to produce additional farming equipment. Although seventy-six percent of South Dakota's farmers had tractors in 1945, farmers had to overcome a variety of handicaps in increasing production. There was always the possibility of a fuel shortage, and it was difficult to find repair parts for machinery that was old or worn out. Ingenious ways were discovered to keep machinery operating, and mechanics and blacksmiths were in considerable demand.

There was a shortage of people to operate the machines and to harvest the crops. Thousands of young men were drafted or chose to enlist in the military. Many farmers were lured by higher wages to defense plants in California, Michigan, and Washington. By 1950 there were 5,400 less farms in the state than in 1940. For a while, the Selective Service based agricultural exemptions on essential war units. A percentage was given to each special type of production. Thus, one acre of wheat was one-half percent of a war unit.

Requests for agricultural deferments often created controversy, and there were numerous instances where draft boards, right or wrong, were accused of favoritism. As military preparations were made for the invasion of Western Europe, Selective Service authorities in Washington, D.C., on March 14, 1944, prohibited occupational deferments for men ages eighteen through twenty-five. To counter the growing shortage of farm labor, farmers worked longer hours, and school children, college students, and towns-people were recruited to work in the harvest fields.

The favorable wartime markets enabled many of the state's farmers to recover finan-cially from the Great Depression. Many farmers became free of debt. Others bought farms and tenants became owners. Other farmers were fortunate enough to purchase combines; there were 10,831 combines in the state in 1945. There was a mild recession for a few months in 1946-47, but the American economy quickly recovered and began to expand. A high demand for American farm products, because of the millions of starving people in Europe and Asia and favorable growing conditions at home, favored both pro-duction and marketing. The cash income from crops and livestock, exclusive of federal payments, neared the half-million mark in 1946 for the first time in the state's history. The peak of farm prosperity was reached in 1947, when total cash farm income reached $673,000,000, an average of $7,600 per farm. Prices received by farmers stood at an index of 301, based on the parity level of 100 established in the years immediately prior to World War I. Using the same index, the prices paid by farmers was 230.

Significant changes took place in postwar rural South Dakota. Throughout the 1930s and during the early 1940s, electric utility companies had tended to ignore the farm market in the Dakotas. Farm women continued to be slaves to the washboard and to the coal or wood-burning stove. Cows continued to be milked by hand in the dim light of lanterns. Kerosene lamps, with their sooty chimneys, or gas mantle lamps, provided the only light in most farm homes. A few farmers used wind chargers or gasoline-fueled generators to produce electricity.

The Rural Electrification Administration (REA) changed all of the foregoing. It had been established by Executive Order 7037 on May 11, 1935. The REA's primary goal was to administer a program of generating and distributing electricity in isolated areas excluded from service by the private utilities. The REA became a permanent agency when Congress passed the Rural Electrification Act in May 1936. The act established the REA as a lending agency and gave it authority to lend the entire cost of constructing light and power lines in rural areas on liberal terms of three-percent interest with amorti-zation over a twenty-year period. The legislation gave priority to publicly-owned plants distributing electricity, but it assumed that existing private power companies would use the federal loan program.

Existing power companies did not respond to this opportunity, and it was only through the efforts of farmer-owned electric cooperatives that rural electrification slowly made headway in South Dakota. At the end of 1939, five small electric cooperatives provided power to four percent of the state's farms. It was difficult to build lines because there was no state law giving cooperatives the authority to condemn land. The power of condemnation was rejected in four successive legislative sessions. After the cooperatives threatened to establish public power districts, the opposition ended. On February 26, 1947, Governor George T. Mickelson signed the South Dakota Electric Cooperative Act. The act cleared the way for the construction of transmission lines. By 1950, sixty percent of the farms had electric power. A decade later, ninety-six percent of all the state's farms enjoyed electrical service. Nine-tenths of these farms were serviced by rural electric cooperatives. Power was generated from coal-burning plants and from the main stem dams that were to be completed on the Missouri River, fulfilling the Pick-Sloan Plan. Electric cooperatives decided to build their own transmission lines from these dams. As of 1949, East River Electric provided power for the eastern half of the state. Rushmore Electric did the same for the western half of South Dakota, beginning in 1952.

Electric power, more than anything else, reduced many of the differences between country and city living. It had many uses in agricultural operations as well as in the farm home. Life became easier for rural residents with the use of electric motors to pump water, grind feed, run power milking machines, and cool milk. Farm wives now had refrigerators, washing machines, vacuum cleaners, and electric irons. The entire family enjoyed well-lit homes and radios. After 1953 the television set became a fixture in farm homes, further linking rural areas with urban centers. It was through REA loans for rural telephone systems that most farmers gained access to modern telephone service. Prior to World War II, only 24,821 farms had telephones in South Dakota and many of these were connected to "party lines."

In the postwar era, the production of farm commodities increased dramatically with new or improved technology and modern science. When International Harvester introduced its multi-purpose Farm-All tractor in 1924, the tractor became the primary force for change in American agriculture in terms of production and the size of farms. Within three decades, the efficiency of the tractor was improved with the addition of the hydraulic lift, rubber tires, and the power take-off. With the introduction of the four-wheel-drive tractor in 1957, labor costs per acre, under normal conditions, dropped to new lows. With the advent of the windrower and pickup, combines could harvest and thresh grain in a single operation, enhancing small grain farming in the state. The combine undermined the role of transient labor in the economy of the plains. Farmers now wanted only skilled mechanics and drivers. Farm wives were also pleased as they were freed from cooking for hungry harvest crews. Most hand labor was eliminated with harvesting machines for corn, potatoes, tomatoes, and sugar beets. Improved mechanization meant that the farmer was capable of cropping larger acreages. Production per acre was also increased by using artificial fertilizers and new chemicals to control weeds and the ravages of insect pests and plant diseases. Geneticists developed more productive and disease-resistant varieties of food plants. Better feeds made for meatier cattle and hogs. New antibiotics checked animal diseases.

Improvements in mechanization and biochemistry were not without cost. There were new expenses for gasoline, oil, repairing machinery, seed, fertilizer, herbicides, and insecticides. To meet these expenses, farmers tried to increase production and thereby increase their cash flow. All went well as long as prices remained high. They remained high throughout the Korean War, 1950-53. In 1951 the net farm income for the state's farmers reached $5,141 per farm. Overproduction and declining foreign markets, however, caught farmers, once again, in a cost-price squeeze after hostilities ceased in 1953. Between 1951 and 1956 farm prices declined about twenty-three percent while the price of products the farmer purchased remained basically the same. Those who worked the soil found that their share of national income declined considerably.

The winds of major change were blowing across the prairie and plains of South Dakota. Most alarming was the considerable decrease in rural population and family farms. In addition to low prices and the cost-price squeeze, improved mechanization, and biochemistry, other factors contributed to this decline. Insurance companies sold land, foreclosed in the 1930s, to absentee landlords in towns and cities. Distance was conquered through hard-surfaced roads, the availability of trucks and automobiles, and the beginning of the electronic revolution. With the completion of the interstate highway system, begun in the 1950s, railroad traffic in the state declined as cattle, grain, and fuel were transported by trucks. The introduction of television contributed to the growing awareness of life and opportunities beyond the farm, small towns, and villages.

The exodus from rural South Dakota that began during the Great Depression, when the number of farms declined by thirteen percent, accelerated during the 1940s and 1950s. In 1940 the census listed 72,454 farms in the state. A decade later, the number was down to 66,452 and, by 1961, 16,852 more farms no longer existed, as the census listed only 49,600 farms for that year. Over a span of twenty-one years, South Dakota averaged a loss of approximately 1,088 farms per year. The total population residing on farms in 1961 was 213,000. As the number of farms declined and the average acres per farm increased, the gap between the larger and more prosperous farmers and those who were just getting by widened. This did not bode well for the remaining smaller family farms in the state.

Small-farm advocates had been pleased when President Harry Truman, during the summer of 1948, nominated Charles F. Brannan to be Secretary of Agriculture. Truman believed that a permanent system of price supports for agricultural commodities was needed to avoid extreme variations in farm prices. Brannan, a former administrator of New Deal farm programs, at the president's urging, came up with a plan designed to insure farmers a stable income. The plan emphasized production and abundance. Farmers would produce commodities in a rational manner while consumer prices would be kept at levels where the average person could afford to buy. If the price of a given farm product fell below support levels, the government would make a direct payment to the farmer for the difference between the price he received and the support price.

The Brannan Plan benefited small farmers as it would have excluded from production payments the yields of any one farm over and above a certain limit. The secretary argued that "Price supports are the farmer's equivalent of the laboring man's minimum wage, social security, and collective bargaining arrangements." The Brannan Plan met vigorous opposition in Congress. Large-scale farmers objected to the upper limit on guaranteed income. Conservatives said the plan was too costly and socialistic. The opposition was led by lobbyists from the American Farm Bureau Federation. The Farm Bureau championed free enterprise and individualism, rejecting government intervention. Bureau members wanted the termination of marketing quotas and acreage allotments, less federal spending and stronger control of organized labor. They believed that the threat to family farms by corporate interests was a political myth. Congress rejected the Brannan Plan. Truman said that its opponents lacked humanity; they would surrender the family farm to the absentee landlord or the corporate owner. The fate of the Brannan Plan was a portend of what would happen to pro-small-farm legislation during forthcoming decades.

Many South Dakota farmers journeyed to Kasson, Minnesota, on September 6, 1952, to hear presidential candidates Dwight D. Eisenhower and Adlai Stevenson discuss farm policy. Eisenhower's speech, sometimes called the "golden promise," was filled with ambiguities. At one point in his speech, he said: "I firmly believe that agriculture is entitled to a fair, full share of the national income and it must be a policy of the Government to help agriculture achieve this goal. . . . And a fair share is not merely 90 percent of parity—it is full parity."[7]

These remarks did not concur with the Republican Party's stance in Congress. A two-year guarantee of supports for basics at ninety percent of parity was approved in June 1952 but it had been opposed by Congressional Republicans. In his Kasson address, Eisenhower attacked current farm programs "which make the farmer a political captive." The goal of his administration, he said, "would be programs which do not regiment you, do not put the Federal Government in charge of farms." He disparaged the principle of price supports by stating that "farmers would rather earn their fair share than to have it as a government handout."

Following his election, President Eisenhower appointed Ezra Taft Benson as Secretary of Agriculture. Benson, who had supported Robert Taft for the Republican nomination, was little known to the state's farmers. They soon realized that Benson believed that lower, flexible price supports would discourage production. By 1953 there was enough wheat in storage bins to supply all of the needs of the market for a full year.

The wheat surplus depressed prices, and the government did not have an effective program in place to sell the surplus. Eisenhower said he was willing to give it away through school lunches, disaster relief, and emergency assistance to foreign countries. Over 13,000 small farm advocates, led by spokesmen from the South Dakota Farmers Union, rallied at the Huron arena to insist that they must have parity and price support assurance. In July 1953 Secretary Benson announced marketing quotas on the 1953 wheat crop, noting that the crop would provide a supply forty-eight percent above normal. Current farm law mandated that farmers vote on quotas when the supply of wheat was more than twenty percent above normal. Small-farm advocates mounted a major campaign to get farmers to vote yes on a secret ballot at an election on August 14. A two-thirds vote was required for marketing quotas. Wheat marketed under the quota system would be supported at ninety percent of parity. If farmers voted no, they favored flexible price supports with self-determined controls. South Dakota's farmers voted ninety-eight percent in favor of wheat quotas. On the national level, eighty-seven percent of farmers voted yes. With each ensuing election, the yes vote was less, with more and more farmers from the Old Midwest, a stronghold of the Farm Bureau, voting no. Ten years later, in 1963, a two-thirds vote could not be mustered to support marketing quotas.

With the expiration of the Agricultural Act of 1949 on January 1, 1954, family farmers feared that twenty years of agricultural gains would fall victim to lower parity and sliding price supports. They were right in assuming that ninety percent of parity was vulnerable. President Eisenhower announced a flexible price support program for agriculture. He proposed sliding-scale price supports from ninety to seventy-five percent of parity beginning in 1955. Governor Sigurd Anderson disagreed with his fellow Republican. He favored full parity. Anderson said farmers were entitled to the same subsidies and supports as the rest of the economy. Why, he asked, should farmers be absolutely free competitors in a society that has props for most other economic segments. After much debate, Congress, in mid-August 1954, agreed on a 82.5-to-90 percent level of support for basic crops.

Throughout the 1950s, the difference between farm prices and manufactured products purchased by farmers had reached their widest spread since 1945. The farmers' purchasing power fell to a sixteen-year low on August 15, 1956, as the parity ratio stood at eighty-two percent. Farmers found it difficult to accept a continual increase in retail food prices while the prices paid to farmers for their commodities continued to decrease.

A farm wife took pen in hand and expressed her sentiments regarding Secretary Benson with the following:

> But Ezra sits in his office so bold;
> and "90 percent" he does turn cold.
> Flexible price supports he wants most,
> and of his wonderful policies he does boast.

President Eisenhower, in an effort to reduce the surplus, advocated the reinstatement of an old New Deal program, the Soil Bank. A massive soil conservation program, it enabled farmers to lease their land to the federal government on three-to-ten year contracts, taking land out of production. Otherwise, they could plant wheat or corn and the government would pay them in either cash or kind the value of their product yield. The president wanted the Soil Bank tied to flexible price supports, and he vetoed a Democratic bill that tied the Soil Bank to ninety percent of parity for all crops. He said rigid price supports had created the surplus problem. Eisenhower got his Soil Bank without ninety percent of parity but the surplus of agricultural products continued to mount. Nationwide, 28.6 million acres were removed from production through the Soil Bank program. Many farmers who joined the program never returned to farming. New advances in technology, however, negated the program and there was no decline in production.

The administration also tried to reduce surplus commodities through a domestic food-stamp program and Public Law 480 for countries in need of food but unable to pay for it in hard currency. Farm leaders blamed Benson for the mounting surplus. They said the secretary should have cut production when he took office. Benson did set acreage allotments allowable by law, 55 million acres, in 1956. Senator Karl Mundt warned the administration that "anti-Benson sentiment in the farm belt is something which is just pretty serious. They not only do not like his farm program, but now they do not like the man."

Before the Secretary of Agriculture addressed about 1,000 people at the state corn-picking contest, south of Sioux Falls, on October 10, 1957, five irate South Dakota farmers vented their frustration with the administration's farm policy. They threw eggs, "hen grenades," at Benson. Benson, who called the action "un-American," ducked the barrage and each of the egg throwers was fined $50. Paul Opsahl, president of the South Dakota Farmers Union, issued a press release the following day stating that the state's farmers worked for farm parity through "democratic means" and not violence. He went on to say that "Throwing eggs at a Secretary of Agriculture is not the way South Dakota farm families meet the problems of agriculture."[8]

Farm-state Republicans joined with Democrats to pass a bill in March 1958 that maintained high federal price supports for one year. Eisenhower reluctantly vetoed it while expressing his continued support for Secretary Benson. The Agricultural Act that became law on August 28, 1958, continued the assault on parity. The bill gave farmers a choice between modified price supports and an increase of crop allotments. The price support for some crops was reduced to sixty-five percent of parity.

The irony of the Eisenhower-Benson farm legislation was that none of the measures worked to reduce the surplus. Instead of getting the government out of farming, the federal government in 1961 was more closely involved in agriculture than it had been in 1950, and the amount of money spent to counter a growing surplus had also increased. At the same time, the farmer's purchasing power had fallen and the number of South

Dakota farm families continued to decline. There were 66,452 farms in South Dakota in 1950. Average acreage per farm was 674 acres. Nine years later, the number of farms had decreased to 55,727 while the size of an average farm had increased to 805 acres.

The administration's farm policy, Secretary Benson's personality, and seeming disregard for the family farmer caused many farmers to agree with "The GOP Psalm" that was making the rounds among their union brethren in urban centers. It read:

> Eisenhower is my shepherd, I am in want.
> He leadeth me throughout still factories.
> He restoreth my doubt in the Republican Party.
> He guideth me in the path of unemployment
> For his party's sake.

Farmers hoped that there would be a significant change in agricultural policies when John F. Kennedy was elected president in November 1960. His appointment of Orville Freeman, a Minnesotan and longtime foe of Benson's policies, as Secretary of Agriculture and George McGovern as director of the Food for Peace program were viewed with optimism. Jobless at the time, having lost the senatorial race to Karl Mundt in 1960, McGovern led the surplus disposal program until 1962 when he was elected to the U.S. Senate.

The Food for Peace program, enacted through the efforts of Senator Hubert Humphrey of Minnesota, had limped along during the Eisenhower administration, caught in a political crossfire between the Departments of Agriculture and State. Kennedy established an independent Food for Peace office in the White House. Under McGovern, more food was shipped abroad in eighteen months than Herbert Hoover and his associates shipped in ten years of relief to victims of World War I. The food was either donated, delivered under long-term credit arrangements, or paid for in local currencies.

Freeman took steps to reduce the farm surplus in storage that had increased in value during the Benson years from $2.5 to $9 billion dollars. The domestic distribution of welfare food was expended, wheat and grain acreage were reduced, and farm exports were increased by seventy percent. The domestic program included a revival of food stamps for the needy, more food for the impoverished, and an expanded school lunch and milk distribution program. A Rural Area Development program helped low income farmers to find new jobs and to turn surplus cropland into recreation areas for pleasure and profit.

Defying an amendment to the Agricultural Act of 1961 that opposed the sale of subsidized agricultural commodities to unfriendly nations, President Kennedy arranged the sale of sixty-five million bushels of wheat to the Soviet Union in 1963. He ignored the non-binding declaration of interest and sold the wheat at the world market price. The state's larger and more prosperous farmers, who enjoyed being subsidized to produce crops for storage, opposed the efforts to fit production to consumption. Nevertheless, the administration's use of "supply management" reduced the farm surplus by one million dollars, the first reduction in ten years.

Farmers tilling a limited acreage praised the Food and Agricultural Bill of 1962. It provided for a two-price system designed to keep wheat permanently in line with market needs. The new law required the USDA to support wheat prices between seventy-five and ninety percent of parity of the "fair earning power parity level" if farmers accepted production controls.

The annual wheat referendum to determine whether or not farmers would accept production controls became the ideological battleground for South Dakota's farmers. One side believed that farms should be family size and profitable for farm owners.

They were opposed by farmers who were unhappy with price supports and acreage controls and who favored farming under a *laissez faire* traditional capitalist system. The South Dakota Farmers Union represented the former group, the National Farm Bureau Federation the latter group.

For ten consecutive years the proponents of price supports came out on top. By 1962 supporters of acreage controls were very concerned as each year the percentage of farmers voting "yes" had declined. In 1962, 68.4 percent of the nation's farmers voted "yes," the margin of victory being slightly over the two-thirds votes required to continue quotas. President Kennedy said he regarded the wheat referendum as a test policy for the wheat program. He went on to say that farmers should determine for themselves what role government programs should play in agriculture.

In South Dakota, as early as February 1963, the proponents and opponents of acreage controls began to mobilize their forces. Proponents formed a South Dakota Wheat Committee and a huge rally was held at Aberdeen on April 4. James G. Patton, national president of the Farmers Union warned that a failure to muster a favorable two-thirds vote might mean the "death knell" for further farm programs. Opponents, led by Charles Shuman, president of the National Farm Bureau Federation, launched an all-out assault to do away with price supports. He proclaimed that if you planted crops without restriction you would get full price. The mustering of support for and against took on the aspects of a political campaign with roadside billboards and advertising in every form of media. A large amount of money was invested in the campaign.

In a watershed vote farmers rejected acreage controls. On the national level, there were 597,776 votes opposing price supports and acreage controls and 547,151 votes favoring continuation of the program. Many of the "no" votes came from farmers in the Old Midwest states such as Illinois and Michigan and where Farm Bureau membership was high. In South Dakota, 65.2 percent of voting farmers favored the program; there were 21,771 "yes" votes and 11,616 "no" ballots. Supporters of the program attributed the defeat to a lack of unity among farmers. Strength had been diluted by dividing into three or four farm organizations and dozens of commodity groups.

Following the assassination of President Kennedy in November 1963, farmer-oriented Senator Humphrey, a native of Doland, South Dakota, pleaded with Kennedy's successor, President Lyndon B. Johnson, to draft a new farm bill. Many farmers believed that with no program there would be a precipitous drop in wheat prices. Johnson agreed

The national wheat referendum on price supports and acreage controls in 1963 revealed a widening rift between those who supported family farming and those who favored corporate farming. *Courtesy South Dakota Farmers Union.*

to support a measure that bore considerable similarity to the Congressional Act of 1962. A master politician, Johnson added cotton to the bill to secure Southern votes, and he underscored the importance of food stamps to attract the support of big city Democrats. The House of Representatives narrowly approved the new farm act on April 8, 1964, 211-to-203. The wheat program was voluntary. Small-farm advocates in South Dakota urged farmers to sign up for the program despite its returning about twenty-five cents per bushel less to the producer than the wheat referendum rejected in the prior year. By mid-July 1964 eighty-four percent of the state's wheat acreage was signed up for the program.

Any hopes of maintaining the farm legislation of the Johnson administration was quickly dispelled with the election of Richard M. Nixon in November 1968. The Agricultural Act of 1970, referred to Congress by the new Secretary of Agriculture, Clifford Hardin, proved to be a disaster for farmers tilling a limited acreage. It created a set-aside program that encouraged more acreage planting and lower price support levels. In 1970-71 there were bountiful harvests that flooded the grain market, forcing prices to drop. Farmers resorted to storing their grain, hoping that prices would rise. When parity reached a post-Depression low, the Nixon administration engaged in statistical deception. Hardin announced a change in reporting the parity ratio. A base period of 1967 was substituted for the legislated 1910-1914 period. Through this deceptive maneuver, Hardin set parity at ninety percent as of January 15, 1971. Under the old formula, parity was at sixty-seven percent on December 15, 1970. Champions of the family farmer noted that the old formula was basically sound. It had been continually updated to reflect new technology and the new kinds of expenditures required in farming.

During the 1960s, increased mechanization, resulting in technological unemployment and inadequate farm income, contributed to a further decline in the number of farms in the state. South Dakota, on average, lost between 1,000 and 1,200 farms per year during the decade. Aware South Dakotans witnessed the disappearance of farm families from the land equivalent to a rural county with all of the main-street businesses, schools, and churches that served a thousand families. Census figures indicated that for every six farms that disappeared, one main-street business closed its doors. Another disturbing statistic was that one-third of the farmers worked one hundred days or more off the farm to meet their economic needs.

Secretary Hardin resigned in the fall of 1971, and President Nixon replaced him with Earl Butz, a former dean of agriculture at Purdue University. An indifferent presidential administration and an urban-minded Congress let Butz impress his ideology on agriculture for the next five years. By late 1974 only sixty of the 435 members of Congress had a definite commitment to agriculture. There was no powerful farm bloc as in the 1920s. The continuing decline in rural population had taken its toll.

During his first few months in office, Secretary Butz killed a bill that would have raised price supports on wheat and feed grain by twenty-five percent. He also lowered the dairy support price and undermined farm bargaining bills. The passage of the Agriculture and Consumer Protection Act on August 10, 1973, turned control of agriculture over to the marketplace. Farmers had to depend entirely on market prices for their income. Payments under the new law were made according to "target prices," which established minimum prices. If the market price dropped beneath them, an eligible farmer received a government payment. Payments, if made, were limited to $20,000. For the first two years, Butz set the target price very low, eliminating any payments to farmers. Allotment and parity became obsolete as the law lifted acreage restrictions.

It was Butz's good fortune that a worldwide food shortage began in 1973. Grain reserves fell sharply, and between 1972 and 1981 American exports increased in value from $8 billion to over $44 billion. Over three years, 1972-1974, the price of wheat increased 132 percent, to $4.09 per bushel, and the price of corn rose ninety-two percent. Earl Butz exhorted farmers to plant every available acre, and the number of acres planted to crop increased by twelve percent. In a foolhardy effort to break the market price and to push it below the world price, Butz called in sealed grain. In cleaning out government bins, subsidized U.S. wheat was exported below the minimum set in the 1971 International Wheat Agreement. Dumping on the overseas market caused South Dakota's farmers to soon receive less per bushel than their counterparts in Canada and Australia.

There were other dark clouds on the horizon for the state's farmers. The price of farm commodities had escalated but so had the cost of farming. Once again they became caught up in a cost-price squeeze. Because of war between Israel and the Arab states in 1973, the Arabs cut off oil shipments to most Western countries and Japan in an attempt to compel Israel to withdraw from the war. Farmers faced a serious fuel shortage, and the success of the Arab boycott led to the Organization of Petroleum Exporting Countries (OPEC), which raised the price of a barrel of oil from $3.00 to $11.95. The result was a ground swell of inflation. Economically, farmers lost ground with the rise in fuel and fertilizer prices. From 1970 to 1974, farm production costs increased thirty percent, interest had risen thirty-five percent, and taxes had gone up twenty-five percent. Farm debt at the beginning of 1974 totaled nearly $70 million at a time when the interest rate was over nine percent.

There were no counter-measures or expressions of sympathy coming from the USDA. Butz said that "farmers will just have to take their lumps when market prices tumble." Kenneth Frick, administrator of the Agricultural Stabilization and Conservation Service (ASCS), in a similar vein, said, "Bankruptcies and the unavailability of loans make other farmers more efficient."[9] Butz's political demise came suddenly on October 3, 1976. The government career of the "fair-haired boy" of corporate agriculture was forced to resign after a racist, obscene remark of his became public.

Many of the state's family farmers breathed a sigh of relief when receiving word of Butz's ouster. It was a good news-bad news time. The bad news was a severe drought, particularly in the central part of the state, during the nation's bicentennial year. It was the worst drought to strike the area since 1934. Temperatures in excess of one hundred degrees, accompanied by strong southwesterly winds, eliminated a good portion of the state's corn crop. Although a list of available hay sources was publicized in an effort to preserve foundation livestock herds, many farmers and ranchers were forced to reduce their number of livestock. One-third of South Dakota's farmers experienced a severe economic setback because of the drought, as the state incurred a loss of over $1 billion in farm income. While he remained in office, Secretary Butz turned a "deaf ear" to requests for federal assistance.

President James Carter and his Secretary of Agriculture, Robert Bergland, were champions of the family farmer, but they were unable to stem the tide of surplus production and of farmers leaving the land to seek work in towns and cities. The 1977 Food and Agricultural Act had authorized the Secretary of Agriculture to withhold land from production but he had no power to compel farmers to comply. Bergland could ask for voluntary set asides, and if farmers ignored his request they became ineligible for deficiency payments and loans. Thirteen million acres were taken out of production in 1978 but farmers produced 300 million bushels more of wheat than the year before.

An expected increase in income from exports did not materialize for farmers. Production had outstripped foreign demand, resulting in falling prices. President Carter, by placing an embargo on grain sales to the Russians following the invasion of Afghanistan by the Soviet Union on December 26, 1979, further added to the surplus. At the time, the Soviets had purchased $4.5 billion in grain from the United States but it had not been delivered. In setting loan rates and target prices, the Carter administration did not acknowledge the continued inflationary pressures on farmers. The federal farm program disregarded the continuing increases in production and other inflationary costs that the farmer had to absorb. The USDA's announced loan rate for 1979 was only forty-four percent of parity while the target price was sixty-four percent of parity. In 1981 the farm parity index stood at its lowest level since 1933.

Low commodity prices plus high interest rates contributed to a continuing depopulation of South Dakota. Another 8,500 farms disappeared from the prairie landscape during the 1970s. Acres, however, were not taken out of production; they were incorporated into larger farms. The average farm acreage in 1970, 978 acres, increased to 1,169 acres in 1980. The inflationary impact was obvious. The value per acre of South Dakota farmland had soared from $84 to $292 during the ten-year period.

While South Dakota's family farmers experienced setback after setback because of federal farm policies and unstable world market prices during the 1970s, they achieved some legislative success at home. One state tax that irked them was the personal property tax. In the mid-seventies, farmers made up twenty-five percent of the state's population, but they earned only twenty-four percent of the income in South Dakota. At the same time, they paid forty-two percent of all property taxes and fifty-five percent of personal property taxes, including seventy percent of all taxes paid to support public schools. During the eighth and final year of Richard Kneip's governorship, in 1978, the legislature agreed to repeal the personal property tax or repressive "liar's tax." The tax had developed a bad reputation through minimal validation of self-assessment forms, and it had not been uniformly applied throughout South Dakota.

Citizens who favored family farms launched a full-scale effort to curb corporate farming and its attempt to monopolize the food chain within the state. A survey taken in January 1968 indicated that one acre in twenty-seven in South Dakota was owned by corporations for a total of 1.6 million acres. Meanwhile, the state was losing on average more than one thousand farms per year. Vested interests had defeated any anti-corporate

Number of Farms in South Dakota, 1900-1999[10]			
Year	Number of Farms	Avg. Size of Farm*	Value Per Acre
1900	52,622	362 acres	$ 12
1910	78,000**	335 acres	$ 39
1920	77,200	464 acres	$ 71
1930	83,200	439 acres	$ 35
1940	72,500	545 acres	$ 13
1950	67,100	669 acres	$ 31
1960	58,400	781 acres	$ 51
1970	47,000	978 acres	$ 84
1980	38,500	1,169 acres	$292
1990	35,000	1,268 acres	$291
1999	32,500	1,354 acres	$355

* Total value of land and buildings
** Bureaucrats have a penchant to "round off" larger numbers.

legislation during the legislative sessions of 1971-1973. The key opposition came from the South Dakota Stockgrowers Association and the banking industry. An anti-corporate farm law would not permit banks to farm in South Dakota. Family farm advocates, however, would not be denied and the Family Farm Act was guided through the 1974 legislature by a sympathetic Governor Kneip. The act explicitly prohibited conglomerates or other non-farm corporations from engaging in agriculture within the state. Concerned about foreign investments in rural America, the 1979 legislature voted to limit the purchase of farmland by non-resident aliens to no more than 160 acres.

The changes in technology that led to greater production, increased efficiency, and larger-sized farms had a devastating impact on railroads in South Dakota. The decline in railroad service also coincided with improved roads, the completion of the interstate highway system, and the emergence of large truck transports. From 1965 to 1975, 540 miles of rail service were lost and another 400 miles were pending closure. The Milwaukee Road, which operated over 1,424 miles of the 2,988 miles of railroad track in the state, verged on bankruptcy. The result was that South Dakota had one of the worst rail service and abandonment rates in the nation. Trains could only move at five-to-ten miles per hour on branch lines because of the poor conditions of the roadbed and track.

By 1978 the state was confronted with the wholesale collapse of its railroad system. Fifty-one percent of the system was being abandoned, the largest percentage of any state in the nation. The shortage of rail hoppers and boxcars meant that shipping costs to farmers would increase. It would be difficult for the state's farmers to compete with grain producers located nearer to terminal markets or on good rail systems because the price spread would be too great.

Governor William Janklow brought his proposal for a South Dakota rail authority to the 1980 legislature. Despite opposition from the Farm Bureau and the Stockgrowers Association, the lawmakers agreed to establish and maintain a railroad core system. Funds for the purchase of track and operating costs were secured from an extra penny added to the state's sales tax. The 1981 legislature added a penny to the state's gasoline tax to help fund operation of the state system. Using the $25 million raised through the tax increases, the administration purchased 765 miles of track for immediate use and an additional 219 miles for possible future operation.

Two new farm organizations emerged between 1950 and 1980. Oren Lee Staley, a Missouri farmer, established the National Farmers Organization (NFO) at Corning, Iowa, in 1955. A farm protest movement, the NFO adopted several of the tactics used by the Farm Holiday movement in the early 1930s. The group hoped to pressure state legislatures for favorable farm legislation through withholding actions, collective bargaining and massive public demonstrations. To gain further public attention, NFO members used boycotts, hog shootings, and milk dumpings. Efforts to withhold hogs, cattle, corn, and soybeans from the market in 1962, 1964, and 1967 failed when non-members refused to cooperate with NFO members. The organization was very active in southeastern South Dakota.

In the late 1960s, the National Farmers Organization offered a collective marketing system. Farmers who paid an annual fee agreed to an irrevocable contract through which they turned over control of marketing their products for several years. The NFO, in the 1980s, abandoned its independent stance and moved from competition to cooperation with the South Dakota Farmers Union. In December 1990 the two farm organizations agreed to a joint-marketing agreement allowing Farmers Union members to market livestock through the NFO's eight South Dakota collection points without paying NFO membership dues. The agreement provided additional marketing options for family farmers.

When out-of-state conglomerates proposed to negotiate contracts with South Dakota farmers whereby the corporate firms would supply the hogs, feed, and veterinary services and farmers would provide the buildings and labor, the NFO joined a coalition in May 1997 to revise and strengthen the 1974 Family Farm Act. The coalition formulated Amendment E. The amendment prohibited non-family farms, corporate ownership of agricultural land and livestock or livestock production facilities. Amendment E was approved decisively by the electorate at the general election on November 3, 1998, with 149,470 voters favoring the measure and 105,282 opposed to it. The South Dakota Farm Bureau, the state Sheep Growers Association, several farmers and ranchers, and two electric companies filed a lawsuit against Amendment E. In May 2002 U.S. District Judge Charles Kornmann ruled that Amendment E was unconstitutional, stating that it would hurt interstate trade by unfairly regulating utility corridors. Kornmann's decision was upheld by the U.S. Eighth Circuit Court of Appeals in 2003. The court said that the amendment had discriminatory purposes because its intent was to keep out-of-state companies from operating in South Dakota. Proponents of the amendment, led by Dakota Rural Action, planned to frame new legislation that would be within the bounds of the U.S. Constitution.

Cash flow problems for heavily indebted farmers led to the establishment of the American Agricultural Movement (AAM) in the fall of 1977. Beginning at Springfield, Colorado, the AAM demanded that Congress pass legislation ensuring one-hundred percent of parity for all domestic and foreign used and/or consumer agricultural products. The AAM became best known for its "tractorcades." Farmers drove their tractors to state capitals and paraded before the government buildings. Hoping to capitalize on national publicity, a huge tractorcade entered Washington, D.C., on February 5, 1979. The demonstration gained the attention of the media and the police but did not achieve its goals of higher prices for farmers. Although the South Dakota AAM was established in January 1979, it did not enroll many members in South Dakota. The AAM has been described as being "land rich but cash poor."

The worst farm crisis since the 1930s occurred during the 1980s. It had its roots in the previous decade. Americans had become dependent on foreign oil. The Arab oil embargo in the fall of 1973 and the formation of OPEC had caused oil prices to quadruple and remain high after the embargo was lifted. The radical price increase created runaway inflation in the United States, reaching 14.4 percent in 1979. The inflationary trend coincided with an increased demand for American farm products overseas. By the mid-seventies, one-third of all the farmers' production went to foreign customers. Farmers were urged to plant from fence row to fence row as high prices brought more land into production. During the 1970s, the land cropped in the United States increased from 294 million to 363 million acres. Many farmers borrowed heavily to expand their output. Between 1975 and 1983, the national farm mortgage debt soared to more than $112 billion.

The bubble burst in 1979. The Federal Reserve System, combating inflation, introduced a tight-money policy. Interest rates rose and inflation fell. Farm exports fell as well. They decreased in value by twenty-one percent in 1980-1981. There was no supply management program, and farmers continued to produce for an export market that no longer existed. By the end of 1982 the United States had acquired one of the largest grain surpluses in history. The government began to sell American grain on the world market for less than production costs and subsidized the sales with tax dollars. In 1981-1982 the nation experienced the most severe of nine recessions since World War II.

A positive supply management farm program was not on the agenda of newly elected President Ronald Reagan in January 1981. A four-year farm bill signed by Reagan on December 22, 1981, set a minimum loan rate for wheat at $3.55 per bushel and a target price of $4.05. The law expanded the grain reserve program. At the time, the farm parity level had plunged to fifty-seven percent. The state's farmers once again were caught in a cost-price squeeze. In 1981 farm prices dropped by twelve percent while prices farmers paid for consumer goods rose five to fifteen percent. A Statewide Farm Crisis Committee called for an international Mercy Food Program to avert a total collapse of the agricultural economy. If implemented, the program would reduce the commodity surplus and increase prices. Radical solutions were needed as there was a four-hundred percent increase in farm and ranch bankruptcies in the state in 1982, a result of the high interest rates and low farm prices.

John Block, Reagan's Secretary of Agriculture, attempted to reduce the crop surplus by introducing the "Payment in Kind" (PIK) program in early 1983. Farmers who agreed to withhold land from production would not be paid in money but in corn, sorghum, or wheat from the farmer-owned reserve, grain under loan, or Commodity Credit Corporation stocks. Over eighty percent of South Dakota's wheat, corn, and sorghum farmers enrolled in the program. Farm land taken out of production in the state totaled 3.8 million acres.

The administration removed additional acres from production in 1985 through the Conservation Reserve Program (CRP). At first, more than a half-million acres of South Dakota farmland were idled under CRP. The enrolled land was seeded to permanent grasses and converted into windbreaks or wildlife cover. Many older farmers used the program to reduce their farming operations or to get out of farming by renting their remaining cropland to their rural neighbors. Farmers continued to enroll in the program, and, as of September 2003, South Dakota had slightly over 1.4 million CRP acres.

Meeting in Sioux Falls in early 1985, state leaders of the American Agricultural Movement, the National Farmers Organization, and the Farmers Union called for an immediate moratorium on farm foreclosures and the establishment of a program to restructure farm debt, reducing interest rates to a serviceable level. When President Reagan vetoed an emergency credit bill, more than 8,000 farmers, members of the three organizations, gathered for a Farm Alliance Rally at Pierre on February 12, 1985. After listening to speeches for three hours, the farmers marched to the capitol building. Impressed by the size of the throng, the House of Representatives appropriated the funds necessary to send the 105-member legislative body plus Governor William Janklow to Washington, D.C., to lobby for the restructuring of farm and ranch debt at serviceable interest rates. A radio station in Watertown, KWAT, through its "Give-A-Buck" campaign, raised $20,000 to support the lobbying effort.

The Reagan administration continued to argue that lower market prices would make the United States more competitive in world markets. The expected increase in agricultural exports never materialized, declining by more than thirty-seven percent between 1981 and 1986. In 1986, for the first time in fifteen years, the United States incurred monthly agricultural trade deficits. As President Reagan addressed a large gathering inside the Sioux Falls Arena on September 29, 1986, approximately five hundred farmers and union laborers gathered outside to protest the administration's farm policies. Following his speech, Reagan invited two of the protest leaders to ride with him to the airport. In the ensuing dialogue, the president argued that expanding world markets, not government subsidies, would bring farmers a fair price. He commented that his administration had provided more money for farmers than the five previous administrations. The president was informed of the farmers' credit problems, particularly with the Farmer's Home Administration (FmHA). The FmHA had turned 353 state farmers and ranchers who had already voluntarily liquidated over to a collection agency. The two men told Reagan that the FmHA in South Dakota was not using all of the options available, such as deferring loans and rescheduling payments. The state's farmers did not need more loans; they needed proper service on the ones they already had. There had been over five hundred bankruptcies in South Dakota in 1986 preceding the president's arrival in Sioux Falls.

It was not until March 1993 that President William J. Clinton's Secretary of Agriculture, Mike Espy, took action regarding FmHA loans. He announced the suspension of FmHA foreclosure actions to provide borrowers with the opportunity for a new review of their cases by an independent panel. Espy said borrowers who were in foreclosure but who had not been referred to a court would have thirty days to request that their case be reviewed by an independent review board.

The Reagan administration's continued emphasis on exports, low market prices, and large federal subsidies that flowed primarily to corporate farms and absentee landlords contributed to the further depopulation of rural South Dakota. It was ironic that the United States had a farm program costing more than any other in the country's history while small and medium-sized farm operators were going broke. Rural businesses were selling out and small-town schools were closing. The sale price for the state's farmland in mid-1986 had fallen to early 1970 levels when adjusted for inflation. Approximately 3,500 more farms were lost during the decade. The number of people living on farms and ranches declined from 112,854 in 1980 to 76,170 in 1990, a decline of 32.5 percent.

The last vestiges of the longstanding safety net of federal crop subsidies and regulations crafted by Secretary of Agriculture Henry A. Wallace, six decades earlier, came under assault with the election of the 104th Congress in November 1994. Many of the winning candidates had promised to cut taxes and mandatory spending. The new lawmakers, the great majority representing urban and suburban constituents, were determined to reduce the deficit and gain control over entitlements. Representative Dick Armey (Rep.-Texas), the Majority Leader, was an outspoken critic of traditional farm programs. Throughout 1995, Congress debated the end of traditional subsidies and government control. Opponents of the former practice were determined to move further toward a free-market-based approach to agriculture. Congress finally devised the Freedom to Farm Act, and on April 4, 1996, President Clinton quietly and reluctantly signed the bill, stating that it "fails to provide an adequate safety net for family farmers."

The new farm bill ended government guaranteed prices for corn and other feed grains plus cotton, rice, and wheat. It provided for fixed but declining payments until 2002. A one-time sign-up for payments was scheduled. Payments would total $36 billion over the seven years, accounting for most of the spending of the $47 billion allowed under the new law. Despite opposition from agribusiness corporations and environmentalists from the Atlantic seaboard and Old Midwest states, the Conservation Reserve Program (CRP), which paid farmers to take highly erodible cropland out of production, was retained. The USDA, however, could not enroll more than 36.4 million acres, the current number under contract.

Farm legislation from 1933 to the failure of the annual wheat referendum in 1963 had stressed stability. After that date, policy makers assured South Dakota's farmers that new and expanded foreign markets would keep commodity prices high. Small or

Fundamental shifts in the economics of farming in the late twentieth century led to the abandonment of farms, a reality that the agrarian pioneers of one hundred years earlier could not have envisioned. *Courtesy Lynwood E. Oyos.*

average-sized farm holders faced an uncertain and unstable future because the health of American agriculture would be tied to supply and demand in the global market. The reliance on foreign markets led to disaster in the final years of the twentieth century. Increased foreign competition and a downturn in the economies of the Pacific Rim countries of East Asia caused a drastic decline in commodity prices. In September 1998, based on a statewide average, the cash value of corn fell to $1.46, compared to $3.69 two years earlier. Wheat prices tumbled from $4.30 in 1996 to $2.70 in 1998. A Congress that had rejected traditional subsidies and acreage regulations in 1995-96 was forced to approve a $6 billion emergency aid plan for agriculture in the fall of 1998.

If the agrarian pioneers who in the 1880s envisioned the plains of future South Dakota filled with prosperous farm families were alive today, they would marvel at the acres under production but would be dismayed by the few farms that they would see in motoring across the state from east to west. During the past seven decades, over 50,500 farmsteads have disappeared while the average acreage of the farms that remain tripled from 439 to 1,354 acres. Certainly, improved mechanization and biochemistry enabled agriculture to remain as the state's leading industry, but the economic costs incurred to acquire, operate, or apply this modern technology, coupled with low commodity prices, contributed significantly to the depopulation of rural South Dakota. The daunting challenges placed before family farmers have included the following: adverse weather, periodic cost-prize squeezes, an innate acquisitiveness that led to over-cropping and crop surpluses, political ideology and federal farm policies, the emergence of giant agribusiness firms and food processors, the globalization of agricultural markets accompanied by greater foreign competition, and farm youth lured to urban living, expecting that they will experience a more prosperous and pleasurable way of life.

Thomas Isern, a professor at North Dakota State University, has stated: "The plains have always paid tribute in staples to the metropolitan centers to the east, have cringed culturally to the same centers, [and] have resented the metropolis because of this situation of dependency. . . ."[11] Struggling against this dependency, the state's farmers beginning during the 1930s engaged in direct-action tactics (i.e. the Farm Holiday movement), boycotts, and lobbying at the state and federal levels. In addition, family farmers have attempted to meet the challenges placed before them with programs that were not necessarily dependent on legislative action or favorable domestic or global markets. Beginning in the 1920s, farmers began to engage in cooperative action. The South Dakota Farmers Union, which received its state charter in 1917, had three primary objectives—cooperation, education, and legislation—and encouraged its members to form and patronize cooperatives. Although the Farmers Union did not own any of the state's cooperatives, it facilitated their efforts through two major regional cooperative purchasing and wholesale firms, the Grain Terminal Association (presently Harvest States) and the Farmers Union Central Exchange (currently CENEX). By 1936 the cooperative movement had reached new heights in the state. Cooperative enterprises included grain elevators, livestock markets, insurance, cream stations, mercantile co-ops, service stations, and the bulk delivery of gasoline and oil.

With the continued exodus of farmers and the depopulation of rural communities after World War II, a steady decline in cooperatives occurred. However, a new type of farmer-directed cooperative enterprise began to emerge in the 1980s. To eliminate dependence on middlemen and out-of-state processors, family farmers began slowly to engage in vertical integration. They would not only produce a commodity, they would process and market it. By 1996 South Dakota had two ethanol plants, in Scotland and Aberdeen. Produced from corn, ethanol when blended with gasoline creates a cleaner burning fuel. As the demand for fuels that produce less carbon dioxide has increased, so has the number of ethanol plants in South Dakota. In the early fall of 2003, ten processing plants were operational and others were being considered or under construction.

The South Dakota Soybean Processors plant opened on September 8, 1996, at Volga. This cooperative endeavor produces 1,250 tons of soybean meal and 265 tons of soy oil daily. Another farmer-owned endeavor, a large egg production facility, became operative near Flandreau. Efforts to establish a farmer-rancher-owned meat processing plant have not materialized because an insufficient number of farmers and ranchers have been willing to commit the necessary capital and livestock to the proposed cooperative. Efforts by the four major conglomerates that control the meatpacking industry to create their own form of vertical integration in South Dakota had been stymied through the previously mentioned Family Farm Act (1974) and the contested Amendment E in 1998. In 1999 the state legislature approved Senate Bill 95 which required meatpackers, each day, to report all livestock purchases to federal and state agricultural officials. It also stipulated that a packer purchasing or soliciting livestock for slaughter in South Dakota could not discriminate in prices paid or offered to be paid to sellers of that livestock, unless there were legitimate reasons for price differences. Following a legal action by the American Meat Institute, a federal court struck down the section of the law that required meatpackers to pay the same price for equal-quality livestock. The rest of Senate Bill 95 remained unchanged.

A turkey production and processing plant is on the drawing board and many farmers are pursuing niche markets. Markets of this type include the following: raising buffalo and processing the meat and hides for local markets; establishing aqua farms for production of salmon and other edible fish; large-scale vegetable gardens with the produce being sold directly to urban consumers and grocery stores; and a reinvigoration of the dairy industry in northeast South Dakota.

Farm wives continued to play a pivotal role in the survival of the family farm. During the farm crisis of the 1980s, many of them entered the labor force in nearby towns and cities in disproportionately high numbers. They often spent the day at a job in town and then came home not only to family responsibilities but to "keeping the books" for the farm business. Without non-farm income, many farmers would incur a deficit. Two-income farm households were becoming the norm in South Dakota. In June 2003, a study released by the Center for Rural Affairs, Lyons, Nebraska, said that in Iowa, Kansas, Minnesota, Nebraska, and North and South Dakota, rural workers earned less than half—forty-eight cents on the dollar—of what those employed in the region's big cities earned.

Unless present trends are reversed, the Jeffersonian ideal of the yeoman farmer appears doomed on the northern plains. Roland Leonhardt, a farmer in Kingsbury County, expressed it well when he said, "I can climb up on top of my silo—and it's high—and I can see twenty-five places that have been vacated since I started out there twenty-five years ago. Those twenty-five families would support four merchants in one of these small towns."[12] He went on to list the businesses lost in nearby Oldham, including two grocery stores, a theater, a drugstore, and a barber shop. Since he made that statement in 1968, Oldham and most rural communities have experienced many more business closings on main street.

E. F. Schumacher, in *Small is Beautiful*, questioned the social structure of an agricultural system that obtained its justification from large-scale mechanization and the heavy use of chemicals. Such a system, he argued, lives on irreplaceable capital [the top soil] which it treats as income. Studies confirm that farmers continue to personify the honest, hardworking, and moral ideals associated with a healthy national culture. Farmers are more stable, more religious, happier, and more satisfied with life. All of the foregoing is true but the present reality is that fewer and larger farms and larger processing industries have been the trend over the past five decades. Despite Jefferson's positive view of the small landholder, the majority of the population no longer considers him the most precious part of the state.

Agriculture continues to be the bulwark in South Dakota because of sophisticated technology and biochemistry which makes the remaining farmers more efficient. Many urbanites view farming only through the price they pay for foodstuffs at their local mega-grocery store and are unsympathetic to farmers. Most national politicians now look first to urban areas for their votes. Nationally, farmers make up less than three percent of the population. Politicians count and subsist on numbers. Those farmers who continue to till South Dakota's soil must throw off the shackles of dependency, unite, and invest in their own "seed to shelf" endeavors if there is to be a future for family agriculture in the state.

Chapter 14
Ranching: East to West

Agriculture has been the dominant industry of South Dakota since long before the region achieved statehood in 1889. Growing crops was the main occupation of most of the region's earliest settlers. Over the years, however, the raising of livestock vaulted into the lead as the major producer of agricultural income in the state. This was a natural consequence since, on an acreage basis, most of the state is better suited for grazing than for crops. Cattle ranching, especially, evolved as the primary industry in the state's vast rangelands west of the Missouri River.[1]

The immense herds of buffalo that long roamed the northern Great Plains and sustained the Indian tribes there constituted the original livestock of the region. Estimates of their numbers during the eighteenth and nineteenth centuries range from thirty million to sixty million. The journals of Lewis and Clark's epic journey up and down the Missouri River in 1804-06 contain numerous references to "large herds of buffaloe [sic]" being encountered. On August 29, 1806, while descending the Missouri en route back to its starting point in St. Louis, the expedition saw its single largest herd near the mouth of the White River below present-day Chamberlain.[2]

It was the enormous number of buffalo on the plains of the Upper Missouri that gave birth to the fur trade that flourished there so spectacularly from 1803 to 1850. Traders from both the United States and Canada invaded the buffalo domain of the Upper Missouri River Valley setting up posts along the river to barter with the Indian hunters. Until that period the Indians, most notably the Sioux, made periodic raids on the herds to clothe, feed, and equip their nomadic villages. But the coming of the white hunter and fur trader changed the basis of the buffalo hunts from one of need to that of greed. Thereafter, the whites and Indians alike preyed on the herds constantly and slaughtered them unmercifully for their valuable hides.[3]

Manuel Lisa, founder of the Missouri Fur Company in St. Louis, Missouri, is generally credited with bringing the first domestic livestock into what is now South Dakota. He brought cows and hogs, as well as chickens and cats, with him when he led a two-boat expedition upriver in May of 1812. He established the fur trading post of Fort Manuel on the west bank of the Missouri River just south of the present South Dakota-North Dakota border. In 1817 Lisa boasted of having "large quantities" of horses, horned cattle, and hogs at his trading posts on the Upper Missouri and reported that "not one is touched by an Indian."[4]

There is an abundance of evidence that livestock was also kept at other Missouri River trading posts. Among them was Fort Tecumseh, established in 1822 by the Columbia Fur Company at the mouth of the Bad River downstream from Fort Manuel. This post was rebuilt in 1832 and renamed Fort Pierre. The clerk there noted the deaths of an old bull and a hog in his journal entries for May 24, 1830, and February 19-20, 1831, respectively. A European visitor to Fort Pierre in 1833 reported that the post maintained a 150-head dairy herd for the milk and butter it supplied. Another European visitor to the post eighteen years later noted the presence there of a Devonshire bull kept for breeding purposes.[5]

Chronology

1803 – Fur trade begins in Dakotas

1812 – Domestic livestock brought into Dakotas by Manuel Lisa

1822 – Fort Tecumseh established by Columbia Fur Co., livestock noted in logs

1832 – Fort Tecumseh rebuilt and renamed Fort Pierre

1851 – Buffalo reported scarce, Fort Laramie Treaty defined Sioux lands

1856 – Fort Randall established, encourages settlers and livestock raising

1857 – Warren explores Black Hills and reports Native Americans "herding" buffalo

1859 – Treaty with Yankton Sioux opens land for settlement

1860 – Census reveals a majority of settlers are farmers, as many cattle as people

1861 – Dakota Territory created

1862 – Homestead Act passed—brought settlers and livestock

1865 – Edmunds introduces sheep to Dakota Territory; Herd Law passed, requiring livestock to be fenced in

1868 – Fort Laramie Treaty creates Great Sioux Reservation and cordons off grasslands

1870 – Cattle delivered for reservation use exceeds number in territory

1874 – Custer leads expedition to Black Hills with cattle

1876 – Sioux Wars begin; Deadwood established

1877 – Treaties allow settlers to move into Black Hills with cattle

1880 – Huge numbers of cattle on plains bring high prices on the market

1881 – Herd Law changed to exempt Black Hills ranchers

1886 – Major blizzard kills large number of stock on the open prairie

1887 – Restocking of herds, more purebred strains of cattle introduced

1889 – Reduction in reservation land opens more pasturage to ranchers

---

In 1844 the clerk at Fort Pierre reported an inventory that included thirty oxen, thirty-five cows, twenty-five calves, seventeen yearlings, seven hogs, eleven pigs, two sheep and one buffalo. Livestock was also kept at Fort Vermillion, an American Fur Company post established in 1827 halfway between the Vermillion and James rivers. The clerk there, in 1849, reported having four milk cows, two beeves, five calves and six hogs in his inventory.[6]

The numbers of livestock at both posts were relatively small. Most likely the stock was kept to supplement the diets of the families and employees of the traders rather than for bartering with the Indians. One census reveals that sixty-five persons were living at Fort Tecumseh prior to its becoming Fort Pierre.[7]

Trade with the Native American tribes of the Upper Missouri River declined sharply as the annual kill took an ever-increasing toll on the buffalo herds. In 1831 the clerk at Fort Pierre reported that he could see thousands of buffalo from the fort gate. The following year he wrote that the buffalo had never been more plentiful in the Sioux country. By 1851 Fort Pierre alone was shipping an average of 17,000 buffalo robes a year to company warehouses in St. Louis, Missouri. That was said to be only seventeen percent of the total number annually received there from the Upper Missouri posts.[8] By 1851 however, buffalo were reported to be very scarce in the Fort Pierre region, resulting in much distress among the Indians there.

It was predicted that many of them would starve. The Fort Laramie Treaty of 1851 may have averted that dire prospect. It defined the recognized territory of each of the northern plains tribes, including the Sioux, and promised them $50,000 a year in provisions for a period of fifteen years. In exchange, these Indians permitted the government to build roads and posts, including military forts, within their respective territories.[9]

While the buffalo herds were quickly disappearing in the Missouri River Valley during the early 1850s, they still existed in considerable numbers elsewhere in the immense region defined as Sioux Country in the 1851 treaty. Lieutenant G. K. Warren of the Topographical Engineers, leading a scientific expedition into the Black Hills region in 1857, encountered a large force of Sioux encamped near several herds of buffalo north of the Hills. He reported that the Indians were actually herding the animals. No one was permitted to kill any in the large bands for fear of stampeding the others.[10]

Warren reported that the intention of the Indians was to retain the buffalo near their village until the animal's skins were suitable

Chronology (cont'd)
1892 – Western South Dakota Stockgrowers Association founded (later SDSGA)
1910 – Milwaukee Railroad crosses river and becomes major shipping point for cattle
1925 – State Department of Agriculture created
1934 – Livestock Ownership Area created for West River counties
1949 – Major blizzards kill livestock on open prairie

for robes. Then they would be systematically killed one band at a time. Some of the Indians wanted to attack Warren's party to prevent it from scaring off the buffalo herds, and Warren said their numbers would have ensured their success. So Warren abandoned his explorations in that region. He explained that he had no desire to disturb the buffalo and prevent the Indians from securing their winter stock of meat and skins so essential to their survival.[11]

■ Settlers Arrive

Two major events brought the first settlers and their livestock into the sectors of the future state of South Dakota. One was the establishment of Fort Randall in 1856 on the west bank of the Missouri some 185 river miles downstream from Fort Pierre in what was then Nebraska Territory. The government, which had purchased the old trading post at Fort Pierre for military purposes in 1855, abandoned it after building Fort Randall. The latter post became the first of a series of military establishments built on both sides of the Upper Missouri River when the fur trade era there was virtually ended.[12]

The second development that brought settlers and their livestock into the region was the treaty consummated with the Yankton Sioux in 1858 and ratified by the U.S. Senate on February 17, 1859. It opened about eleven million acres for white settlement in the sector between the Missouri and Big Sioux rivers that was part of Minnesota Territory until 1858. The treaty provided for $1.6 million in annuities to the Yanktons over a period of fifty years and gave them a 400,000-acre reservation on the east bank of the Missouri River in present-day Charles Mix County. Government commitments to supply the Missouri River military posts and Indian agencies with foodstuffs, including fresh beef, created a ready and profitable market for settlers and speculators alike.[13]

By 1859 almost the entire population of what became Dakota Territory in 1861 was located in the southeastern corner of the territory. The federal census of 1860 counted 829 persons in the area between the Missouri River and the western boundary of Minnesota, and the majority of them were identified as farmers. These who came from neighboring Minnesota, Iowa, and Nebraska brought livestock with them as well as their families. The 1860 census also reported almost as many cattle (801 head) for all of Dakota as there were people in the southeastern section.[14]

Hans Myron, who later served in the territorial and state legislatures, was only ten years old when he trailed a small herd of cattle into what is now Clay County in 1859 behind the ox-driven wagon of his Norwegian immigrant parents. Scandinavian families heavily populated the Missouri bottomland between the Vermillion and James rivers just prior to and shortly after the region was encompassed into Dakota Territory in 1861. These early settlers generally combined stock raising with their farming operations and kept a few head of dairy or beef cattle, hogs, and sheep mostly for home consumption.[15]

However, the number of livestock on the small family-sized farms of the new territory rose sharply as the demand for meat grew with the territory. The need for fresh meat in the new settlements, coupled with the government contracts for supplying the military posts and Indian agencies of the region, provided the incentive for expansion of stock-raising activity.

The raising of livestock was reported as highly profitable with the return on investments in it running as high as fifty percent a year. The *Sioux City Register* characterized the resources of the new territory as "eminently agricultural" and predicted that "farming and grazing will pay best."[16]

With the creation of Dakota Territory on March 2, 1861, land companies from St. Paul, Minnesota, Dubuque, and Sioux City, Iowa, and Yankton, especially, competed vigorously in promoting settlement of the region between the Missouri River and the western boundary of Minnesota. Yankton, founded in October 1859 on the east bank of the Missouri across from Nebraska, was the largest settlement in the region and was designated the territorial capital. It was appropriately dubbed the "Mother City" of Dakota and hosted the first session of the territorial legislature in March of 1862.[17]

Thirteen of the twenty-two members of that first legislature listed their occupations as farmers. One of the legislature's first acts was the creation of fourteen counties for southern Dakota and four for the northern part of the territory. All but two of the southern counties were located east of the Missouri. Most of the settlers there lived in the counties of Union, Clay, and Yankton at the time. A "Marks and Brands" law was also enacted at this session. It provided that stockmen could register their brands with the Register of Deeds in their counties for a filing fee of twenty-five cents per brand.[18]

Passage of the Homestead Act on May 20, 1862, by the federal Congress brought a flood of homesteaders to Dakota as it did to other largely unsettled sections of the country. The act was a powerful incentive for homesteaders seeking free land and new opportunities for themselves and their children. Many of those who came to Dakota brought livestock with them, including cattle herds of fifty to one hundred head. But the act's passage was soon followed in August by an event that for a while drove more settlers out of Dakota than were coming into it.[19]

Santee Sioux under Chief Little Crow, frustrated with conditions on their reservation in western Minnesota, attacked and killed settlers and their livestock in Dakota as well as in Minnesota. J. A. Jacobsen, described as a prominent farmer of the Vermillion area, was among the Dakota settlers killed by Indians during this turbulent period. The Union Army was engaged in fighting the Civil War at the time, so the task of responding to the conflict fell largely upon hastily-formed militia units. Abandoning their stock, farmers in both Minnesota and Dakota fled with their families to nearby settlements, where stockades were built for protection. Other frightened farmers left the territory altogether with their families and stock. It was estimated that Dakota lost at least half of its farming population during the conflict.[20]

Settlers gradually returned to their abandoned homesteads after the military restored stability to the territory. The military campaign, which lasted until 1866, gave birth to a number of Army posts along the Missouri River and elsewhere in Dakota. It also culminated in a series of treaties with Indian tribes of the region, which resulted in the establishment of several new agencies along the river. Government contracts for supplying the posts and agencies with fresh meat and other foodstuffs provided additional markets for area farmers and speculators.[21]

Newton Edmunds of Yankton, who became the territory's second governor in 1863 following the resignation of William Jayne, also served as ex-officio superintendent of Indian Affairs for Dakota. In that capacity, he had played a major role in negotiating the treaties that had led to establishment of the Missouri River Indian agencies. Edmunds is also credited with introducing sheep into the territory in 1865, and his success with them inspired others to take up sheep raising too. He reportedly had a flock of 1,700 head by 1867. Also by 1867, every farmer in Clay County reportedly had from fifty to one hundred head of cattle. However, only two cattle brands had been registered in southern Dakota by that time. They were filed by Christopher Maloney and Charles Brazzo in Union County on February 16, 1865.[22]

The early Dakota livestock producers found a profitable market for their animals in the Missouri River steamboat traffic as well as at the military posts and Indian agencies along the river. The steamboat companies would reportedly buy anything the settlers had to sell, including beef, dressed hogs, and poultry, for feeding their passengers. One of the earliest suppliers of beef to Fort Sully, established on the east bank of the Missouri above Pierre in 1863, was Paul Narcelle. He was a French Canadian and former employee of the American Fur Company who had married into the Sioux tribe. He had a herd of four hundred cattle on his ranch on Medicine Creek south of Pierre.[23]

Initially, meat for the forts and agencies in the Upper Missouri Valley was supplied by local farmers and speculators from the neighboring states. But by the late sixties and early seventies Texas Longhorns were being driven north to fill government contracts for supplying these needs. The Texas grasslands had become overstocked with cattle during the Civil War and drought had drastically reduced the carrying capacity of the ranges there. Beef prices dropped so sharply that the Texas cattlemen found it more profitable to drive their cows to the beef-starved north where both demand and prices were higher than at home. Thus began the historic drives of southern Longhorns to northern markets that were to constitute a colorful chapter in the history of the cattle business.[24]

In the early 1860s, when Dakota Territory was still in its infancy, the raising and importation of livestock was principally limited to the region east of the Missouri River and its west bank. However, fur traders and early military explorers had characterized the region farther west to the Black Hills as an immense grasslands ideal for stock raising. Consequently, in its 1865-66 session, the territorial legislature memorialized Congress for funds for a survey to determine the nature of the region's resources. A herd law requiring stockmen to fence their domestic animals and making them responsible for crop damage caused by their animals was also passed at this session. Legislation pertaining to the running-at-large of swine reportedly required the attention of the House for almost half of the session.[25]

Any hopes that the Dakota officials had for opening the West River grasslands for settlement and the white man's livestock were dashed by the Fort Laramie Treaty of 1868. It created the Great Sioux Reservation whose boundaries extended from the Missouri River to the western edge of the Black Hills and from Nebraska to just above the present North Dakota-South Dakota border. This vast region, grasslands except for the Black Hills, was reserved for the "absolute and undisturbed use and occupation" of the Teton, or western, Sioux. White men were prohibited from entering and settling there, and the government committed the army to keeping them out.[26]

Another provision of the treaty promised one pound of meat per day for every Indian over four years of age affected by it. That meant feeding more than 25,000 Sioux of the seven Teton tribes. The Indians agreed to receive their rations on the Missouri River, so a central agency was established for them on Whetstone Creek, eighteen miles above Fort Randall, as the delivery point. It was subsequently discovered that the Red Cloud and Spotted Tail agencies were actually in Nebraska. So they were moved north to new agencies within the Great Sioux Reservation at Pine Ridge and Rosebud, respectively, in 1878.[27]

Creation of the Great Sioux Reservation provided an additional market for the stock growers of eastern Dakota and elsewhere. The federal government purchased between 30,000 and 40,000 head of beef annually to fill its contracts for feeding the Indians of the Upper Missouri during that period. James McDowell of Leavenworth, Kansas, began supplying beef to the Sioux agencies in 1869. Two years later he delivered enough cattle on the hoof, averaging 1,000 pounds each, to add up to 3.4 million pounds for these agencies. He was paid an average price of $2.85 per hundred pounds, live weight, for the meat. Most of the beef for the agencies came from Texas cattle driven to Kansas and Nebraska and sold to speculators who had held the government contracts. H. P. Denham, also of Leavenworth, Kansas, and the Bosler Brothers (Hiram, George, James, and Joseph) of Sioux City, Iowa, were also major suppliers of beef to the Sioux agencies.[28]

By 1870 the number of cattle delivered to the Sioux agencies far exceeded the number held by stock raisers in the eastern part of the territory. The federal census of agriculture that year reported a total of only 4,151 milch cows, 2,125 working oxen, and 6,191 other cattle in all fourteen counties of southern Dakota. Most of the milch cows and other cattle were on farms in Clay, Yankton, and Union counties. The 1870 census also showed only 14,181 persons in all of Dakota, most of them in the southeastern sector where settlement had begun slightly more than a decade earlier. Cattle numbers showed an increase to 56,724 head in the 1880 census.[29]

In March of 1871, an editorial in the *Yankton Press* predicted that Dakota would soon rival Texas in the number of cattle raised and exceed it in superior beef and dairy breeds. It identified twenty-one area citizens whose principal business was stock raising, including former Governor Edmunds, who had left office in 1866. Union County was reported as having the best blooded stock since Charles Wambole, who operated on about two hundred acres along the James River four miles from Yankton, had imported Durham cattle. Neither Dakota Territory nor the two states that were carved from it in 1889 ever came close to matching Texas in cattle numbers. But optimism and boosterism were characteristic of Dakota's early newspapers, and cattle raising did eventually become South Dakota's major source of agricultural income.[30]

Most of southern Dakota's highly coveted grasslands lay within the Great Sioux Reservation that was closed to the whites. But the national financial panic of 1873 set off a series of events that would breach that barrier. One was another memorial from the Dakota Legislature that year urging the government to open the reservation to the whites, particularly the Black Hills region where gold was rumored to exist. The memorial also alleged that the Black Hills were harboring hostile Indians who posed a threat to the territory's settlers.[31]

The government did not want to risk a possible war with the Sioux by breaking the treaty pledge to keep whites out of their reserve simply because of rumors of gold existing there. Desperate for sources of new wealth, however, the government sent an expedition to the Black Hills in the summer of 1874 to determine whether or not gold really could be found there in paying quantities. The expedition was led by Lieutenant

Colonel George A. Custer and spent over a month examining the resources of the previously unexplored interior of the Hills.[32]

Custer, at the head of a column that included 110 wagons and almost 1,000 soldiers and civilians, took along a 300-head beef herd to feed his command during the expedition. They were undoubtedly the first cattle brought into the Black Hills. However, so much wild game was killed on the expedition that Custer returned to Fort Abraham Lincoln on the Missouri River in present-day North Dakota with his beef herd largely intact. In fact, he described the herd as in better condition upon its return than when it had left on the 600-mile round-trip march. He attributed the phenomena to the "rich pasturage" encountered on the expedition.[33]

Although gold had been found in the Hills "in paying quantities" during the expedition, Custer was more effusive in describing the superior grazing provided by the plains surrounding them. "No portion of the United States can boast of richer pasturage," he wrote. Custer considered this resource to be "of greater advantage generally to the farmer and stock raiser than are to be found in the Black Hills." He predicted that the future great wealth of the region would come from agricultural pursuits, but especially stock raising.[34]

Custer's observations about both the gold and the superior grazing resources of the Black Hills region were confirmed by a second expedition sent there the following summer. It was named the Newton-Jenney Expedition for the two geologists who headed it. This expedition, which spent almost five months in the Hills, originated at Fort Laramie, Wyoming, and included a military escort commanded by Colonel Richard I. Dodge. The expedition, like Custer's, also took a beef herd (134 head) along for food. To its surprise, the expedition found the Hills teeming with hopeful prospectors. The trespassers had rushed there despite the 1868 treaty prohibition after reading newspaper accounts of Custer's earlier gold discoveries.[35]

"In ten years the Black Hills will be the home of a numerous and thriving population," Dodge predicted, "the government can't stop it."[36] The government tried, sending troops to escort the unlawful miners out of the Hills. But there were so many of them there that the government finally abandoned the task. Instead, it undertook to negotiate with the Sioux for removing the region from their reservation. That effort would not succeed until the Sioux War, which resulted from the illegal invasion of the Hills, was resolved.[37]

Dodge, like Custer, was also effusive about the stock-raising potential of the Black Hills and the country surrounding them. His journals contain these remarks: "The valleys [in the Hills] are broad and covered with excellent grass. It will be some day the grazing ground of miriads [sic] of cattle. . . . The grass is splendid here. As a grazing country it cannot be surpassed . . . tho' the season may be too short for agriculture, it is a most glori-

George Armstrong Custer's foray of 1874 into the Black Hills found gold, as anticipated, but also rich pasturage. The Newton-Jenney Expedition that followed the next summer predicted that stock raising would be "the great business of the inhabitants." *Courtesy South Dakota State Historical Society–State Archives.*

ous grazing country & will furnish cattle, butter & cheese for a nation. . . . This country will be a magnificent one for sheep . . . there is no finer country for stock raising in the world. . . ."[38]

Walter Jenney and Henry Newton, co-leaders of the expedition, were also impressed with the future economic potential of the region, both in gold and in stock raising. Their report on the findings of the expedition stated, in part: "There is gold enough to thoroughly settle and develop the country, and, after the placers are exhausted, stock raising will be the great business of the inhabitants, who have a world of wealth in the splendid grazing of the region." California Joe Milner, scout for the expedition, put it more succinctly when he said, "there's gold from the grass roots down, but there's more gold from the grass roots up."[39]

Demands for opening the region to white settlement and Native American opposition to them were major factors leading to the Sioux War of 1876-77. Another factor was the large number of Tetons, considered to be the least easily subdued of the Sioux tribes who were off their reservation. The 1868 treaty had given the Tetons hunting rights to unceded lands west of their reservation. Many of them preferred the freedom of the chase that hunting provided to reservation life. Lieutenant General Phil Sheridan, whose military division included Dakota, claimed that the reservation was "the 'last ditch' to the wild Indian, but to get him there he must be forced by the troops."[40]

Custer and his Seventh Cavalry were among the troops sent out to force the Sioux back to their reservation. The regiment paid dearly for its role in precipitating the stampede of prospectors to the Black Hills with its gold discoveries there. Some 263 of its members, including Custer, were killed by the resentful Sioux and their Cheyenne allies at the Battle of the Little Bighorn in Montana in June of 1876. By the following summer, however, additional Army troops rushed to the frontier succeeded in forcing the Indians back to their reservation, and the Sioux War was over.[41]

At this time the Black Hills were already crowded with white trespassers panning its streams for gold and founding support settlements. Custer City, near the original gold discovery site and named for the ill-fated commander of the 1874 expedition, was already one-year old. Five thousand intruders were estimated to be in the Hills at the time. Half of them were said to be crowded around the booming mining center of Deadwood, established in April of 1876. Other younger but equally active settlements were scattered throughout the entire Black Hills. Some of the trespassers paid with their lives for violating the 1868 treaty. The offended Sioux took revenge by attacking parties entering and leaving their forbidden country throughout 1875, 1876, and 1877.[42]

■ Cattle Ranching in the Black Hills

With the coming of the whites to the Black Hills came their cattle. The fast-growing settlements there provided a profitable market for fresh beef, and stockmen from neighboring territories were quick to meet the demand. One of them was M. V. Boughton, a prominent cattleman of Wyoming Territory, who brought a herd of Texas Longhorns to the Custer area in the spring of 1876. He later pastured cattle on Centennial Prairie north of Deadwood, but lost the herd to raiding Indians who also killed his herder.

The Deffenbach brothers, John, Erasmus, and Dan, brought several herds of cattle to the Hills from Wyoming and Nebraska starting in the fall of 1876. The brothers bought the cattle for $15 to $25 per head, pastured them on a ranch they established on the northern edge of the Hills and sold them to Hills butchers for $100 to $125 apiece. John Deffenbach was killed by Indians who intercepted him trailing a herd into the Hills from Wyoming in 1877 and escaped with his stock.[43]

Not until 1877, when Congress coerced the Sioux into relinquishing the most coveted portion of their reservation, did it become safe for the whites and their cattle to remain in the region. The coercion came in the form of congressional refusal to provide funds for support of the Sioux until they agreed to cede their reservation lands between the forks of the Cheyenne and Belle Fourche rivers. That cession included the Black Hills and the superior grasslands around them. More than a century later the U.S. Supreme Court would rule that the Sioux Agreement of February 25, 1877, which opened the newly-ceded reservation land for legal white settlement, had been unlawfully secured. But, by that time, the white man and his cows were firmly entrenched in the region.[44]

The lush meadowlands in the interior of the Hills that elicited so much praise from the early explorers became the site of many of the first ranches in the region. Some of the first prospectors turned to raising or grazing livestock on these small interior ranches when they failed to find gold in paying quantities. Many of them rented out their pastures to the stage and freight companies carrying passengers and supplies in and out of the Hills for grazing of their horse and ox teams. Other disappointed prospectors went into stock raising on a larger scale by establishing ranches along the more open foothills and surrounding plains. These ranches thrived on supplying fresh meat to the mining settlements prior to the arrival of railroads in the late 1880s.[45]

One of the earliest ranches in the interior of the Hills was established by Joe Reynolds in a broad valley ringed by heavily timbered peaks south of present-day Rochford. Reynolds had been among the earliest prospectors to reach the Hills following Custer's gold finds. He had been prospecting in the Colorado gold fields without much success when he joined the rush to the Hills in 1875. He was among the miners ejected from the region by the army that year. But he returned the next year and gave up prospecting to settle on North Castle Creek on what became known as Reynolds Prairie on the road between Custer and Deadwood. He prospered by raising both beef and purebred dairy cattle from foundation stock purchased in Kentucky, Illinois, and Iowa. He also sold hay to freighters and operated a toll road.[46]

Centennial and Spearfish valleys, well-watered, broad, open meadows between the inner and outer rims of the northern Hills, supplied the foodstuffs to the many mining camps in that region. Robert H. Evans, who had come to the Hills with a party of Montana miners in 1875, abandoned prospecting to raise cattle near the town on Spearfish Creek that he helped found the next year. A former Cornish tin miner from England who had also joined the rush to the Black Hills gold fields in the late 1870s was Peter Crago. He too found cattle raising more profitable than prospecting. He established a ranch in Spearfish Valley that produced four generations of cattle industry leaders on the national as well as the state level. The Crago family gradually expanded their registered cattle operations to almost 50,000 acres in three western South Dakota counties.[47]

James Anderson, a Danish immigrant from Yankton, trailed a herd of milk cows to Centennial Valley in 1877 and established a prosperous dairy farm at the base of Elk Mountain. He was soon milking up to one hundred cows a day and keeping the milk fresh from a springhouse where the water remained at forty degrees year around. Anderson died in 1890 after serving from Lawrence County in the first state legislature. His daughter, Christina, married Henry Frawley, who had come to the Hills from Bismarck in 1877 and became a prominent Deadwood attorney. Frawley also acquired and consolidated a number of Centennial Valley ranches, including Anderson's dairy, which continued in operation into the twenty-first century. The Frawley Ranch, whose unique stone buildings have been preserved, became noted as the oldest ranch in the valley in continuous operation by the same family.[48]

Small family-sized ranches dotted the interior meadows and foothill grasslands of the Black Hills region from Edgemont in the south to Belle Fourche in the north during the early years of settlement. Rapid City, established in 1876 on the eastern edge of the Hills, was primarily a hay camp during those years. It thrived by providing feed for the ox teams carrying freight to and from the interior settlements. It became the transportation center of the region in later years. For many years Rapid City also celebrated the importance of the burgeoning cattle industry to the economy of the region by annually hosting "Stockmen's Days." It was usually a boisterous event, with bronc riding on main street, mock stagecoach holdups, and cowboys and Indians reenacting earlier actual conflicts. Quite a number of leading businessmen of the pioneer Black Hills settlements engaged in entrepreneurial enterprises that included stock raising.[49]

A number of former freighters carrying supplies in and out of the Hills in the early years of settlement also later turned to stock raising in the region. Prominent among them were John D. "Jack" Hale and his brother Tom. They gave up freighting from Nebraska to establish the Pleasant Valley Stock Ranch near present-day Tilford in Meade County. Besides cattle, they also had the largest sheep flock in the area and were annually shearing over 2,000 head in the 1890s. Jack Hale, who served in both the territorial and state legislatures, is also credited with driving 1,000 hogs overland from Nebraska to Deadwood in the early 1880s. He was responsible for many of the early laws pertaining to livestock adopted in the legislature.[50]

Hale died in Sturgis in 1928 after his pioneer Pleasant Valley ranch had been sold to the Blair brothers from Missouri, who established the Black Hills Hereford Ranch. It became famous for the numerous champions it exhibited at state and national stock shows. Moreover, two of the Blair brothers and one of their sons continued Hale's tradition of riding herd on bills of importance to the stock raising industry through the state legislature. Family members served both in the Senate and the House, the first elected serving in 1937-38 and the last in 1979-86.[51]

Another former freighter who made a reputation as an outstanding stockman and industry representative in the legislature was Charles Ham, a Canadian, who came to the Hills in 1878. He hauled freight for a mining company for a while. Then, in late 1878, he and Jack Hale purchased 600 hogs at Yankton and Vermillion, shipped them by boat to Fort Pierre and then drove them overland to Deadwood, where they were sold to butchers. With his share of the proceeds Ham purchased some dairy cows in Wisconsin for the ranch he established on Box Elder Creek in Pennington County. He subsequently switched to raising beef cattle on Elk Creek too. Ham served three terms in the state legislature, and two of his sons (Eardley and Ernest) and two of grandsons (Donald and Carl) served there between 1926 and 1990.[52]

Word of the nutritious and hardy native gama and western wheat grasses on the public domain ranges surrounding the Black Hills spread rapidly as the region became familiar to the newcomers. They soon learned that stock could be fattened quickly, cheaply, and largely unattended on the seemingly unlimited open plains. These early arrivals confirmed what Custer, Jenny, and Dodge had written so glowingly of the stock-raising potential of the region. Soon a large number of big cow outfits whose herds ran into the thousands were driving them onto the grasslands surrounding the Hills. Among them were cattle companies that held government contracts for supplying beef to the Rosebud and Pine Ridge Indian agencies on the unceded lands west of the Missouri River. These contractors found that their Longhorns quickly regained the weight lost on the long drives north when they were pastured on the sturdy grasses there prior to being delivered to the agencies.[53]

By 1880 the estimated number of cattle being fattened on the western Dakota grass-lands ranged from 89,800 to 136,000 head. Most of them had been driven up from Texas, Nebraska, and Wyoming and were being herded on the unfenced ranges watered by the Little Missouri, Grand, Moreau, Belle Fourche, and Cheyenne rivers. These cattle were generally two-year-olds who could grow to 1,200 pounds or more within two years of grazing on the western Dakota grasslands. They often brought premium prices when they were shipped to market after being "doubled wintered" in the vast area between the Missouri River and the Black Hills.[54]

■ Stockmen's Organizations

A preliminary gathering of area stockmen in Rapid City in October of 1880 resulted in the organization of the Black Hills Live Stock Association the following Thanksgiving Day. Its purpose was to advance and protect the interests of the growing number of stock-men operating in the area. The twenty-seven charter members elected Frank Stearns as their first president. Stearns had a cattle herd on the Cheyenne River south of Rapid City. He also had the contract for supplying beef to the lone military post in the Black Hills established near the town of Sturgis in the northern Hills two years earlier. Elected secretary was Frank Moulton, whose cattle ranged on Box Elder Creek east of Rapid City and who was sheriff of Pennington County at the time. The territorial secretary at Yankton chartered the organization on December 20, 1880.[55]

The association, described as the first organization of stockmen in the territory, had a short, but eventful, existence. It organized spring and fall roundups of cattle on the Black Hills District ranges in 1881-82. Its members began advertising their brands in Black Hills newspapers in late 1881, and the association offered a $100 reward, later doubled, for information leading to the conviction of cattle thieves. The association boasted of having fifty-two members by January 1, 1882, many of them owning 5,000 or more head of cattle. It also claimed that its members owned seventy-five percent of the estimated 40,000 to 70,000 cattle in the Black Hills District at that time.[56]

Newborn calves were branded in the spring roundups and mature animals driven to the railheads for shipment to eastern markets in the fall roundups. The closest shipping points for western Dakota cattle at the time were Bismarck and Dickinson in the north-ern part of the territory and Pierre on the east bank of the Missouri River in the southern sector. The Northern Pacific tracks had reached Bismarck and Dickinson in 1874 and 1880, respectively. The Chicago and North Western rails were extended to Pierre in 1880. Pioneer Rapid City businessman and stockman Tom Sweeney spent five days observing the first association-organized round-up along the Cheyenne River east of the Hills in the spring of 1882. He described the event as "a regular old-fashioned jolly time" with "much sport" mingled with hard work. Besides cutting out the cattle ranging on the open plains and returning them to the various outfits they represented, Sweeney explained, the cowboys engaged in horse racing and marksmanship contests. He also happily reported that the roundup had found that the stock loss on the open plains had been less than five percent, despite the severity of the previous winter.[57]

The Black Hills newspapers reported roundup activities in 1883 and 1884 too. But the last mention of the Black Hills Live Stock Association appeared in March of 1884, when it was quoted as estimating there were then half a million head of cattle in the district. Ten cattle companies were identified as having between 10,000 and 45,000 head apiece. But no meetings of the association were reported in the area newspapers after 1884. The roundup notices published in the spring of 1885 were inserted by unidentified persons labeled as "The Committee."[58]

Despite the brevity of its existence, the association succeeded in leaving its mark on the 1881 session of the territorial legislature. With the considerable help of member Jack Hale, who was then serving his first term in the House, a number of laws pushed by the association were enacted. One amended the 1862 brand law that gave the county Register of Deeds sole authority to rule on disputed brands. The amended law added the requirement that two stock owners experienced in brands in each county also take part in the decisions. It further provided that brand rejections would require at least two votes from the three-member board.[59]

Other new laws pertaining to livestock promoted by the association were designed more for the benefit of the developing West River cattle industry than for the smaller East River farm operations. For instance, the 1871 herd law was amended to exempt the Black Hills counties from its provisions. The fence law was also changed to put the burden of keeping livestock out of cropland upon the farmer rather than the stockman. Protests from settlers in lower Bear Butte Valley east of Sturgis and others led to an amendment in the latter law four years later. The change made the stockmen responsible for fencing in their herds or being liable for damages caused by them. Hale was praised by the stockgrowers for his legislative efforts on their behalf, but vilified by those opposed to these measures. Nonetheless, Hale was elected to three terms in both the House and Senate and continued to push laws favorable to the western stock growers through the legislature.[60]

■ Independent Operators

Most of the stockmen who pioneered the West River cattle industry were independent operators with herds that seldom exceeded a few thousand head. Smaller herds characterized the ranches within the Black Hills and along its fringes. Most notable among the independents with larger herds were Jesse Driskill, who came up from Texas in 1878 and ranched west of Spearfish, Milton C. Connors, who placed 3,000 head on the upper Belle Fourche River that same year, Henry Weare, who made a fortune in both cattle and sheep before going into the banking business at Spearfish, and the Dickey Brothers, who ran up to 10,000 head on the Grand and Moreau rivers of northwestern Dakota.[61]

In the early 1880s the open ranges surrounding the Hills were also heavily stocked with numerous big herds owned by well-capitalized cattle companies whose stockholders lived in the East or in England and Scotland. Some of these companies, like the Bosler Brothers, the Anglo-American Cattle Company, and the Sheidley Cattle Company, had government contracts for supplying beef to the Pine Ridge and Rosebud Indian agencies. Others, like the Standard, Continental, Western Ranchers, Ltd., Vermont and Cresswell cattle companies, fattened their herds on the western Dakota grasslands for eastern markets. Their brands—101, Hash Knife, VVV, BXB, and Turkey Track, respectively—became legendary in the history of the West River cattle industry.[62]

Coming to the western ranges with the cattle of the big outfits were a number of colorful characters who became legendary in the range country too. One of them was G. E. "Ed" Lemmon who trailed Texas cattle from Nebraska to the Red Cloud and Spotted Tail Indian agencies in 1877 and later became a partner in major sheep and cattle companies in western Dakota. The town of Lemmon, South Dakota, is named for him. Another outstanding figure in the early history of the Dakota cattle business was Sam N. Moses, formerly a stock detective in Wyoming, who performed yeoman service as a West River lawman as well as becoming a prominent rancher. Both Lemmon and

Moses were among the first inductees into the National Cowboy Hall of Fame from South Dakota.[63]

Unlike Lemmon and Moses, who had been working cowboys, John Clay was a different breed of noted cattle industry figures. Clay, a Scottish financier, became famous for his skillful management of a number of large cattle operations, including Western Ranches, Ltd. This firm ran large herds in Wyoming as well as in western Dakota and was one of the most successful of the cattle ventures in the American West financed by Scottish and British stockholders. Clay also started a number of banks in northwestern Dakota and operated a commission house in Chicago. More of a capitalist than a cowman, Clay nevertheless won the respect if not the admiration of the cowboys who rode for the VVV with his canny management decisions.[64]

Cattle placed on the northwestern Dakota ranges in the early 1880s competed for grass with the last of the large buffalo herds seen in the region. The Reverend Thomas L. Riggs, who had founded the Oahe Indian Mission on the east bank of the Missouri near Pierre in 1874, accompanied a group of Indians on a buffalo hunt there in the winter of 1880-81. The party spent three months hunting along the Grand and Moreau rivers and returned to Pierre with the meat and hides of about two thousand buffalo. Reverend Riggs subsequently established the Peoria Bottom Hereford Ranch near his mission church with registered stock imported from Illinois. His motive for going into stock raising was to demonstrate to his Indian charges how cattle ranching could replace the disappearing buffalo as their main source of livelihood. His model ranch became highly successful and continued in operation through several generations of his family.[65]

It was left to two West River ranchers, both former freighters who had married Sioux women, to preserve the buffalo heritage of Dakota as the herds there were nearing extinction. Fred Dupree, a French-Canadian, had freighted to the Hills prior to establishing a ranch on the Cheyenne River. He captured a few buffalo calves during a hunt on the Grand River in 1881. They became the foundation of the herd that was sold after his death to James "Scotty" Philip, who ranched on the Bad River near Fort Pierre.[66]

Philip was among the prospectors the army ejected from the Black Hills in 1875. He freighted from Nebraska to the Hills after their opening to settlement two years later. He married a mixed-blood Sioux woman and ran cattle on her reservation allotment as well as elsewhere in western Dakota. Philip became known as the first "cattle king" to operate along the west bank of the Missouri River after settling on a homestead there. His cattle herds eventually grew to between 15,000 and 20,000 head. Philip also became known as "the man who saved the buffalo" after animals from his herd became the seed stock for the herd placed in Custer State Park in 1914. Philip had secured a lease of 3,500 acres of government land in 1906 for the exclusive purpose of pasturing buffalo and nothing else. Another early inductee into the National Cowboy Hall of Fame from South Dakota, Philip served in the State Senate in 1899-1900.[67]

Two of the most colorful personages to operate sizeable cattle outfits in the northern part of Dakota in the 1880s were Theodore Roosevelt and the Marquis de Morès. Roosevelt, destined to become the twenty-fifth president of the United States, came to Dakota in 1882 to hunt. He became so enamoured of life on the open plains that he acquired ranches in the Little Missouri River country and in the North Dakota Badlands. His managers ran upwards of 3,000 head on the two ranches. Although an absentee owner most of the time, Roosevelt returned to Dakota often enough to join in the semi-annual roundups and to be elected the first president of the Missouri Valley Stock Association in 1884. Of that time and place, Roosevelt wrote, "I regard my experience during those years when I worked and lived with my fellow ranchmen on what was then the frontier as the most important educational asset of my life."[68]

De Morès, a controversial Frenchman married to the daughter of a wealthy New York banker, launched a number of bold enterprises in the Little Missouri Valley of northwestern Dakota starting in 1883. He acquired 45,000 acres of grazing lands there and stocked it with both cattle and sheep numbering in the thousands. He also founded the town of Medora on the east bank of the river, named it for his wife, and built her a luxurious chateau nearby that remains an attraction even today. He also operated a short-lived stage line between Medora and Deadwood. However, his most ambitious project was building or acquiring a number of packing plants and cold storage warehouses and founding a refrigerated railway car company. De Morès, unlike Roosevelt, was not popular in the region, particularly after fencing his lands and bringing sheep into what was then considered strictly cow country. All of de Morès' undertakings in Dakota had brief lives and he left the country in 1886. He was reported to have purchased 15,000 head of cattle during the three years he spent in northwestern Dakota. He also reportedly lost nearly $2 million in his ill-fated ventures there.[69]

De Morès' sheep may have been unwelcome in the Little Missouri Valley, but they proved to be popular in the western sections of Dakota south and north of the Black Hills. In fact, their numbers there jumped from about 85,000 in the early 1880s to over half a million by the end of the decade. Sheep ranches were especially numerous in the Edgemont area of Fall River County and in the region between Belle Fourche and Buffalo in Butte and Harding counties. A Sheep Breeders and Wool Growers Association was organized at Sturgis in May 1884, probably the first of its kind in the territory. The ubiquitous Jack Hale of nearby Tilford was a leading figure in its activities. Hale was also among the thirty-three men who organized the Black Hills Horse Breeders Association in Rapid City on January 9, 1892.[70]

Virtually all ranches in western Dakota, large and small, had horses for herding their livestock, whether cattle or sheep, and for getting around on the ranges where their stock were pastured. With good horses in demand, it did not take long for horse breeders to make their appearance in the region. Sol Star and Seth Bullock, partners at Deadwood in the farm implement business, established the SB Horse Ranch at the juncture of the Redwater and Belle Fourche rivers north of the Hills in the late 1880s. They specialized in raising trotting horses for the buggies and wagons they sold out of Deadwood and Sturgis. Charles Ham, founder of the Farmingdale Land and Cattle Company in eastern Pennington County, brought several carloads of mares to his ranch on Elk Creek in 1886. The horses were shipped by rail from Oregon to Medora and then trailed to Ham's ranch. Ham became secretary of the Black Hills Horse Breeders Association when it was organized in Rapid City.[71]

In the summer of 1885, two Frenchmen—R. Auzias Terenne and M. Marion—arrived in Custer from Paris to establish the Fleur de Lys Horse Ranch near Buffalo Gap in the southeastern sector of Custer County. They brought with them four fullblood stallions, two Percheron and two Arabian, "with the complete pedigree from the French government." They advertised themselves as the "Percheron & Arab Importing and Breeding Company" and boldly announced that these four stallions were intended for serving mares throughout the entire Black Hills. Other prominent horse ranches in the region included those established by Abe and Dave Jones, brothers, and J. P. Gammon north of the Hills. The Jones Brothers, branding JB, started a horse ranch in the Slim Buttes country of Harding County in 1885. Gammon, who had a contract for supplying horses to Fort Meade, did the same on Crow Creek in Butte County in 1888.[72]

Large and small cattle-raising outfits employed cowhands like these sixteen men (and one boy) from the Mulehead Ranch. *Center for Western Studies.*

The early 1880s was a bonanza period for ranchers large and small who placed their stock on the public domain lands of western Dakota where grazing was free and there were no fences. The cattle, sheep, and horses pastured there went largely unattended until roundup time. This situation invited thievery, and stock rustling was a major problem for livestock owners, most of whom lived far from their grazing stock. Especially vulnerable were the "mavericks," unbranded stock, whose ownership was difficult to prove. Cowboys were employed to make periodic checks on the cattle and horse herds and to drive the stock to greener pastures when necessary to prevent overgrazing. Sheepherders, usually well armed, lived with their bands, so rustling was a rarity. Wolves and coyotes were of more concern to them than rustlers.[73]

The hiring of stock detectives to track down rustlers was one of the objectives of the early stockgrower organizations in the region. Stealing stock was considered a serious crime and the penalty for committing the offense was severe. The earliest hanging of horse thieves in the Black Hills took place at Rapid City in the summer of 1877 when two men and a young boy paid with their lives for the crime. Two Central City butchers caught slaughtering cattle stolen from a Spearfish Valley herd that same summer were also summarily hanged. The frontier justice was meted out by a group of unidentified men described as "The Vigilantes." There was a noticeable decline in the number of horse and cattle thefts in the region thereafter.[74]

The pioneer stockmen of western Dakota were fortunate that weather conditions on the northern plains in the early 1880s were generally mild and winter storms limited in scope, so stock losses were minimal. However, all that changed in the winter of 1886-87 when large-scale blizzards began in November and did not let up in intensity until the following March. Sub-zero temperatures that lasted for weeks froze snow on the faces of the livestock, blinding them, and heavy drifts trapped them in gullies where they had sought refuge from the bitter winds. The terrible storms were especially costly to the big outfits that had left thousands of head of cattle unattended on the unprotected plains. Their losses ran as high as ninety percent and put many of them out of business. There had been nearly one million head of cattle valued at $21 million on the Dakota ranges when the storms began and a fraction of that number when they ended. Dorr Clark and Duncan Plumb, whose E-6 herd was pastured on the Grand River in northwestern Dakota, had brought up eleven carloads of Texas cattle the previous August. It was the first shipment of livestock into the region by rail after the railroad had reached Rapid City a month earlier. The E-6 herd numbered 18,000 head going into the winter, but only 1,900 head remained by the time of the spring roundup.[75]

The disastrous winter was a painful lesson for the stockmen. It demonstrated that they could not depend on grass alone for sustaining their stock through the winter. Thereafter, they would provide sufficient hay to supplement the scarce grass available to their herds during the winter months. In addition to the heavy stock losses in 1886-87, the cows that somehow survived that winter produced a calf crop in the spring that was sharply lower than the previous year. "It is criminal carelessness for the Dakota farmer to neglect his stock during the winter months," commented the territorial Commissioner of Immigration. It was a situation that the stockmen had to correct or get out of the business.[76]

There was considerable restocking of the western Dakota ranges in the summer of 1887. However, most of it was done by the smaller ranchers. The big outfits that had suffered such heavy losses the previous winter had either reduced their holdings or pulled out altogether. There was also a distinct improvement in the quality of cattle placed on the western Dakota ranges. Purebred Shorthorn, Hereford, and Angus bulls were exhibited at the Pennington County Fair in the fall of 1887, reflecting their growing popularity with ranchers of the region. George B. McPherson, who had settled on Alkali Creek in what is now Meade County, is credited with bringing the first herd of Herefords to the Black Hills in 1883. He bought them in Menlo, Iowa, shipped them by rail and steamboat to Pierre and then drove them overland to his homestead. When the post office was established there in 1902, it was appropriately named "Hereford." The ranch McPherson founded stayed with Herefords through three generations of his family.[77]

■ New Stockmen's Organizations

Although the Black Hills Live Stock Association had faded from public notice by 1884, separate cattle and horse roundups were organized at Spearfish in the spring of 1887. Fourteen brands were represented in the cattle roundups, where the devastating loss from the previous winter's blizzards became fully known. Annual spring and fall roundups continued into the 1890s under the sponsorship of local stockmen's organizations. In the Black Hills district, these included a new Black Hills Stock Association formed in Custer on August 15, 1883, by ranchers of the Hermosa and Buffalo Gap areas. A Black Hills Stockmen's Mutual Protection Association was formed at Spearfish in August 1889 to combat horse stealing in the region. The group changed its name to Western Dakota Stockmen's Association the following December. Three other stockmen's groups appeared in the Hills in 1891. The largest of them was the Fall River Stockgrowers Association at Hot Springs, which boasted of having 141 members and eleven branch "lodges." The others were the Black Hills Horse Breeders Association, headquartered in Rapid City, and the Black Hills Protective Association, formed by ranchers along Spring Creek in Pennington County.[78]

Outside the Black Hills district, the earliest organization of southern Dakota stockmen was the Brule County Livestock Association. It was formed at Chamberlain on the east bank of the Missouri River on April 28, 1882, for the purpose of "the importation and breeding of fine blooded livestock of all kinds."[79] E. C. Stearns, who had a 2,500-acre ranch four miles south of Chamberlain, was its first president. There had been only 677 head of cattle in all of Brule County in 1880. Five years later, however, the number had jumped to 5,383 head. This county group preceded by two years the formation of the Little Missouri River Stockgrowers Association organized in present-day North Dakota by Theodore Roosevelt and others. The next oldest organization of Dakota cattlemen was the Missouri River Stockmen's Association founded at Fort Pierre on the west bank of the river on December 10, 1891. Its first president was A. D. Marriott, formerly of Omaha, Nebraska, who later became postmaster at Pierre. Marriott owned the HAT outfit that ran cattle in Stanley County and on the Grand River farther north. Scotty Philip was on this association's executive committee. This group offered a $200 reward for information leading to the conviction of rustlers and conducted a roundup in the spring of 1892. It also published its members' brands in the *Sioux Livestock Journal* that had begun publication at Fort Pierre on March 3, 1888. The newspaper also published an edition in Rapid City where the *Northwestern Stockman* was printing the brands of area stockmen too. The latter newspaper started publication there on November 6, 1891.[80]

Two major milestones in the history of Dakota Territory took place in 1889. The first was the reduction of the Great Sioux Reservation by nine million acres and the creation of six smaller reservations within the unceded lands. This event became effective in March and led to the subsequent opening of the ceded West River lands, roughly the area between the White and Cheyenne rivers, to white settlement. It provided a big boost to the livestock industry since most of the ceded area consisted of grasslands ideal for stock raising. The Sioux had consented to the reduction in exchange for $3 million and other benefits, including individual land allotments and the distribution of two milch cows, two mares, and two oxen per family. In addition, the 1889 agreement with the Sioux promised them up to 25,000 head of cows and 1,000 bulls for tribal use. Appeals for opening the reservation to the white man and his cattle had been sounded in the Black Hills as early as March 15, 1882. Representatives of the three Black Hills counties met at the Deadwood courthouse on that date to promote the reduction. They termed the reservation "unequaled in America for its nutritious grasses, sufficient to maintain one million head of stock. The benefits to be derived from this must be obvious to all."[81] The other major event of 1889 was the division of the territory into the separate states of North and South Dakota, effective on November 2. South Dakota joined the union with a population of 328,000. That was slightly lower than the number of cattle (350,937 head) the U.S. Department of Agriculture reported in all of Dakota Territory four years earlier.[82]

Thirteen stockmen met in Rapid City on February 20, 1892, to make preliminary plans for organizing the Western South Dakota Stockgrowers Association. The stated purpose of the new organization was to protect and advance "the livestock interests by consolidating the various associations now in operation." Permanent organization of the new association was effected at another meeting in Rapid City on April 21. H. A. "Lon" Godard of Smithwick, formerly foreman of the Keystone Cattle Company as well as former sheriff of Fall River County, was elected president. Godard had represented Fall River County in the first state legislature in 1889-90 and also in 1891. Fred Holcomb, who ran cattle under five different brands in Meade County, was elected vice president. Frank Stewart, who raised horses as well as cattle on the Cheyenne River east of Buffalo Gap, was elected secretary. Stewart would hold his post until his death thirty-five years later. His daughter Queena succeeded him and served for almost fifteen years.[83]

Scotty Philip represented the Missouri River Stockmen's Association at the Rapid City organizational meeting. He presented a letter from President Marriott endorsing the concept of a single organization to represent the stockmen in the western section of the state. Marriott, Philip, Ed and Narcisse Narcelle, and Louis LaPlant, all stockmen of the Fort Pierre area, were the first members of the Missouri River group to join the western association. The latter organization set annual dues at five dollars, hired Sam Moses as range detective at $125 per month, and established voluntary assessments of two cents per head on cattle for the inspection fund and the same fee on horses for the detective fund. The brand inspections were conducted at stockyards and shipping points. Fifteen first-year members paid assessments on 15,750 head of cattle and 2,295 horses.[84]

From an initial membership of thirteen, the Western South Dakota Stockgrowers Association grew to 133 members during 1893 and to 240 by 1894. It began printing brand books periodically, starting in 1894, that also included the association's bylaws. These provisions placed most of the responsibility for management of the association in the hands of a board of directors elected on an area basis by the members from those areas. Brand inspection and the promotion of legislation favorable to the livestock industry have been the association's main activities since its inception.[85]

The Missouri River Stockmen's Association, although organized earlier than the West River association, did not incorporate until 1894. The western group had received its charter a year earlier. The two groups cooperated in the spring roundup of 1892 working their wagons and riders toward each other from the east and west. Both groups hired brand inspectors and range detectives, with the Missouri River stockmen claiming jurisdiction for the Fort Pierre, Chamberlain, and Forest City shipping points. The eastern association also maintained inspectors on the Lower Brûlé and Crow Creek Indian reservations. In 1906, half of the charter members of the Missouri River group, including Scotty Philip, were also members of the western association.[86]

■ Role of the Railroads

Cattle shipments in the Black Hills region were centered at three points following the arrival of the Fremont, Elkhorn and Missouri Valley Railroad, a branch of the North Western, from Chadron, Nebraska, in Rapid City on July 4, 1886. Buffalo Gap became the shipping point for cattle in the southern Hills. The railroad leased land at Brennan six miles below Rapid City and built stockyards there for watering and penning cattle prior to shipment from the central Hills. James Wood, who had helped organize the fledgling Western South Dakota Stockgrowers Association, shipped out twenty-four carloads of cattle to the Chicago market from there in August. In the following month one hundred carloads of Texas cattle, the first in the region to come by rail, arrived for the northern ranges of John Clay, the Driscoll and Dickey Brothers.[87]

Belle Fourche, at the forks of the Redwater and Belle Fourche rivers, however, became the largest livestock shipping point in South Dakota because of its fortuitous location. It was situated in the northwestern sector of the state where both cattle and sheep raising were thriving industries. It also bordered on the vast stock-producing areas of eastern Wyoming and Montana. The town was established when the Fremont, Elkhorn and Missouri Valley Railroad tracks reached there in 1891. Seth Bullock and Sol Star, partners in the SB Horse Ranch located there, donated the land for the townsite to the railroad. It quickly became a cowboy town as cattle and sheep were driven in from the tri-state ranges for shipment to eastern markets. The railroad built shipping pens and watering holes leading to them and soon was sending out carloads of both cattle and sheep in record numbers.[88]

Evarts and LeBeau, both located on the east bank of the Missouri River north of Pierre, became noted as major shipping points and lively cowboy towns shortly after the turn of the twentieth century. The Milwaukee Railroad established Evarts when it extended its tracks to the river from Glenham and aggressively pursued the cattle trade from the West River ranges. It secured a lease of a strip of land six miles wide and ninety miles long along the northern boundary of the Cheyenne River Indian Reservation in 1901. The railroad built dams about a day's trail drive apart along the length of "the Strip," as the cowboys named it, for watering the herds on their way to the river. At first the cattle were ferried across the Missouri to the railroad's shipping pens at Evarts. In 1903, however, the railroad erected a pontoon bridge for the crossings. The number of carloads of West River cattle shipped to market from Evarts in its first five years of existence totaled 22,000. Moreover, many thousands of carloads of Texas cattle were shipped to Evarts for restocking the western ranges during that period too.[89]

Antoine LeBeau, a French former fur trader, founded LeBeau's original site on Swan Creek as a stage station in 1875. But the community moved downstream a short distance when the Minneapolis and St. Louis Railroad extended its tracks from Watertown to the Missouri River in 1907. The new LeBeau became the shipping point for cattle companies that had obtained large leases of Indian grazing lands on the Cheyenne River and Standing Rock reservations on the west side of the river. Ed Lemmon, as field manager of the Lake, Lemmon & Tomb Cattle Company, branding L7, secured a lease of 865,429 acres on the Standing Rock Reservation in 1902. The tract was enclosed with a three-wire fence, and some 53,000 head of L7 cattle were fattened in what was described as the largest fenced pasture in the world. Murdo MacKenzie and Burton "Cap" Mossman of the Matador and Diamond A outfits, respectively, were also among the holders of big Indian leases who shipped cattle in and out of LeBeau. MacKenzie was to serve as president of the National Livestock Association as well as on the executive committee of the Western South Dakota Stockgrowers Association. Cattle from the reservation leases were ferried across the Missouri on a paddle wheeler named the *Scotty Philip* for the prominent West River rancher so active in the stockgrower organizations of the period. LeBeau's glory days as a major shipping point for West River cattle ended when the Milwaukee Railroad crossed the river at Mobridge and built on to Isabel and Faith in 1910. By 1907, the Chicago and North Western had also pushed its rails westward from Pierre, and the Chicago, Milwaukee and St. Paul Railroad had extended its tracks from Chamberlain to Rapid City. These extensions, coupled with the opening of surplus Indian reservation lands to white settlement between 1904 and 1911, brought a heavy influx of homesteaders into the region. The West River population jumped from 57,579 in 1905 to 137,687 five years later.[90]

■ Political Influences

A Northwestern Stockgrowers Association was formed at Belle Fourche in 1903 with H. M. Behyymer of Aladdin, Wyoming, as president. It was still functioning in 1905 and had lured Sam Moses away from the older Western South Dakota Stockgrowers Association to become its range detective. But the Belle Fourche association faded from public mention after its 1905 convention, and the Missouri River Stockmen's Association did likewise a few years later. The Western South Dakota Stockgrowers

Raising livestock is the state's major source of agricultural income. Here a rancher herds cattle along the Missouri River bluffs near Pierre in the 1960s. *Courtesy Joel Strasser.*

Association dropped "Western" from its title in 1935 to reflect its role as the leading stockgrower organization of the state. It moved its headquarters from Buffalo Gap, where Secretary Frank Stewart lived, to Rapid City in 1937.[91]

The South Dakota Stockgrowers Association (SDSGA), although representing only a small fraction of the cattle owners of the state, has wielded considerable political influence throughout its long history. Don Beaty of Vermillion, who served as a SDSGA director as well as a leading East River cattle feeder, termed it "the most powerful organization in the state." He wrote, "its leadership has been composed of the most rugged individuals of the West who have only cattle interests and objectives at heart. They fight openly, and hard, and are generally successful."[92] George McGovern, when serving South Dakota in the U.S. House of Representatives in 1960, blamed the association for the removal of cattle from the price support bill that he was championing that year.[93]

South Dakota's stockgrowers, like other segments of the agricultural community, have been plagued with fluctuating prices for their products over the years. Low prices for their commodities during periods of rising costs have been particularly harmful to the farmer and rancher alike. But the SDSGA has consistently argued that price supports on cattle are not the solution to the problem. It has also consistently pushed for indirect support of the cattle industry through periodic appeals for larger government purchases of beef for the military, and for school lunch and foreign aid programs. In addition, it has lobbied vigorously against the importation of livestock and meat products in competition with domestic production.[94]

■ Associated Organizations

Although separate organizations, the Last Roundup Club, the Junior Stockgrowers and the South Dakota CowBelles have been closely associated with the SDSGA since their foundings. The Last Roundup Club, composed of members who had participated in the big West River roundup of 1902, was formed during the stockmen's convention at Hot Springs in June 1948. Ex-governor Tom Berry was elected its first president. Its members were guests of the stockgrowers at a reunion breakfast during the annual SDSGA conventions each year. Bert Hall, the club's historian from Kennebec, published the colorful personal remembrances of the old cowboys in a monumental book, *Roundup Years: Old Muddy to the Black Hills*, that is now considered a classic. A commemorative reprint of the book was published by the Black Hills Buckaroos, a riding club, in 2002. Unlike the other two organizations, the membership of the Last Roundup Club diminished each year with the deaths of the old cowboys. The club went out of existence in the 1970s.[95]

The Junior Stockgrowers were also formed during the SDSGA's convention in Hot Springs in 1948. John Sutton, Jr., of Agar was its first president. Its purpose was to prepare its members for active participation in the senior organization when they became adults. Most of the juniors were sons and daughters of members active in the SDSGA. They usually had dances and raffles to fund their activities and tours of area attractions as well as business meetings during the senior organization's annual conventions throughout the state. They also had space for reporting their activities in the SDSGA's monthly magazine, the *South Dakota Stockgrower*, between conventions. A number of the South Dakota Junior presidents were also elected president of the National Juniors. This organization was formed in Nebraska in 1933 and had chapters in nine states by 1948. It operated under the guidance of the American National Livestock Association, of which the SDSGA was an affiliate.[96]

It was in June 1951 that fifty-three women, most of them wives or daughters of SDSGA members, met in Rapid City to organize the South Dakota CowBelles. Mrs. John Sutton of Agar, whose husband was president of the SDSGA at the time, was elected to head the women's organization. The state organization soon had county units throughout most of the state. but it was especially well represented in the West River area. Its state officers also played a prominent role in organizing the American National CowBelles Association in Denver in August 1951. The role of all the CowBelle units was to aggressively promote beef consumption through a wide variety of programs, including sale of beef certificates and assisting at state and national "Beef Cook-Offs." The CowBelles also conducted an annual "Miss South Dakota Stockgrower" competition with the contestants sponsored by the local units. Space was also allotted in the SDSGA's monthly magazine for reporting on the activities of the CowBelles as had been done for the Junior Stockgrowers. In 1973 a number of South Dakota CowBelles journeyed to Detroit, Cleveland, and Philadelphia on an educational mission designed to counter beef boycotts organized by consumer groups in protest to high retail meat prices. They appeared at supermarkets to explain that ranchers were not getting rich at the cattle prices then in effect. The higher retail meat prices were attributed to wage and benefit increases in the packing plant and grocery industries that drove up costs. In 1986 the national organization changed its name from "CowBelles" to "CattleWomen" and the South Dakota units followed suit two years later. Most members of the state units are also members of the national organization. Kay Snyder of the Carcass Cutups at Sturgis, state president in 1989-90, served as national president in 2000.[97]

Addressing the Jubilee of the Stockgrowers Association in 1967, Gov. Nils Boe noted that livestock now represented 71% of the state's cash receipts from agriculture, in excess of $561 million. *Center for Western Studies.*

■ The Legislature and Stockgrowers

Governor Nils Boe, in declaring "South Dakota Stockgrowers Association Week" during the group's Jubilee Anniversary in 1967, commented on the importance of the livestock industry to the state's economy. He noted that the value of livestock and livestock products produced in the state exceeded $561 million at that time, representing seventy-one percent of the state's total farm cash receipts. Further, Governor Boe cited the industry for producing "a disproportionately high number of leaders in every aspect of life in South Dakota, from territorial days to the present."[98]

In addition to the early members of the SDSGA who had served in the territorial legislature, seven of the forty stockmen elected as association presidents between 1892 and 2003 also served terms in the state legislature. Two of the association's members have served as governor of the state. Democrat Tom Berry of Belvidere, whose fifteen years on the association's executive committee included the four years he was governor, was chief executive in 1933-37. Republican Walter D. Miller, a New Underwood rancher and a long time SDSGA member, was governor in 1993-95. Democrat Ralph Herseth of Houghton, governor in 1959-61, was not a SDSGA member, but he was a prominent East River registered commercial Angus breeder. Republican L. R. Houck of Gettysburg, the first of nine SDSGA presidents from the East River, was the state's lieutenant governor in 1955-59. The state's directory of legislators from territorial days to the present lists numerous stockgrowers. They include Democrats and Republicans alike and they came from both sides of the Missouri River.[99]

Governor Berry doubled as South Dakota's state relief director for ten months during the Great Depression and directed the spending of millions of federal aid dollars among the distressed populace. He supported the government's cattle buying program that cost $8 million nationwide in 1934 alone. But he opposed raising the prices that the government was paying for cattle—$6 to $14 per head for cattle over two years old, $5 to $10 for yearlings and two-year-olds and $1 to $5 for calves—in its efforts to help stock raisers survive the depression years. He feared that higher prices would empty the state of cattle that would be needed for rebuilding foundation herds when the depression was over. Another government program of great assistance to stockgrowers during the depression was the Taylor Grazing Act of 1934. It opened over eighty million acres of the nation's public domain land, some of it in South Dakota, for livestock grazing under government supervision.[100]

Legislation of importance to the state's livestock industry has occupied the attention of the lawmakers since territorial days. The State Department of Agriculture, created in

1925, administered the laws pertaining to livestock. However, in 1935, the legislature divorced the State Brand Board and State Livestock Commission, established in 1896 and 1905, respectively, from the Department of Agriculture and made them independent agencies. The latter agency became the Livestock Sanitary Board in 1937 and the South Dakota Animal Industry Board in 1990. The board and its six staff employees have responsibility for carrying out laws pertaining to the prevention, control, and eradication of animal diseases. It is composed of seven members representing the cattle, pork, swine, and sheep industries, livestock feeders, veterinarians, and the marketing industry. The governor appoints the board's seven members for staggered four-year terms and the state veterinarian serves as its executive secretary. The agency licensed a record high of sixty-two registered auction markets in 1960, but the number was down to forty-three in 2003.[101]

In 1934 the legislature created a Livestock Ownership Area to include all of the West River counties and to require brand inspection of all cattle, horses, and mules entering or leaving the area. It also authorized the State Brand Board to contract with a private, non-profit corporation to conduct mandatory brand inspections. In addition, it provided for a per-head inspection fee at a rate determined by the board to cover the costs of the inspections. The contract has gone to the SDSGA ever since with the inspection fee cap gradually increased from the original fifteen cents per head to eighty cents in 2003. The legislature also authorized East River counties to petition into and out of the ownership inspection area by majority vote of the affected stockraisers. Eighteen East River counties gradually voted into the area, but all of them later withdrew from it. In 1969 two-thirds of the state's beef herd and sixty percent of the registered brands in the state were located outside the inspection area.[102]

Statewide brand inspection was proposed in the legislature in 1969, but its defeat was due principally to the opposition of East River feeders and auction markets. The opposition reflected the differing nature of livestock production on each side of the Missouri River. The West River generally, but not entirely, is cow/calf country. There calves are raised to one- or two-year-olds, on grass during the summer and alfalfa in the winter, to weights of 600 to 800 pounds. Then they are sold to feeders for finishing with grain to market weights of about 1,200 pounds before being sent to slaughter. The cow/calf operations extend east of the river north of Pierre to the Huron region too. Elsewhere throughout the East River, the stockmen are generally, but not entirely, feeders or purebred breeders. Every type of cattle operation can be found in certain areas on both sides of the Missouri. The basic conflict between cow/calf operators and feeders is that the former seek to sell their cattle at the highest possible price while the latter seek to buy cattle for fattening at the lowest possible price. "Well bought is half sold," one veteran East River feeder asserted. "No feeder ever lost money if he bought his cattle right."[103]

There has been opposition, too, to the contract for brand inspection awarded exclusively to the SDSGA since 1934. The South Dakota Farmers Union, for instance, considered the contract unconstitutional because it delegated police powers to a private corporation. It sought, unsuccessfully, to have brand inspection returned to the State Department of Agriculture, where the SDSGA claims it had previously been poorly administered. The association defended the contract as a means of protecting cattlemen against livestock thefts at no expense to the state treasury since the inspection fee covers all costs of the program. In 1974 the South Dakota Supreme Court ruled that the Brand Board's contract with the SDSGA was constitutional. It found that the legislature had established sufficient standards and guidelines to permit the delegation of police powers to a non-governmental agency through the supervision of the State Brand Board.[104]

In administering the inspection program, the SDSGA set up a Brand Department to separate its functions from those of the association. It also established a ten-member brand committee to provide association oversight of the program. The department operates under a chief brand inspector, three supervisors, eleven full-time inspectors and 162 part-time inspectors paid on the basis of the number of livestock inspected, plus mileage. The office staff consists of one secretary/assistant. In 2002-03 the department collected $1.1 million in fees on 1.8 million head of cattle and horses inspected. The inspections were conducted at twenty-one South Dakota auction markets, seven of them located in the East River, and at sixteen open markets and locker plants outside the brand area where no inspection fee is collected. The largest single auction market during the May 1, 2002, to May 1, 2003 period was at Fort Pierre, where $156,908 was collected on 261,514 head of livestock inspected.[105]

The State Brand Board, headquartered in Pierre, is composed of five members and a majority of them must reside in the brand area. Not more than three of them can belong to the same political party. The members serve staggered five-year terms and are appointed by the governor from a list of nominees submitted by the state's agricultural organizations. The members periodically negotiate the contract for brand inspections with the SDSGA. Since 1924, the West River association has been granted authority by the Packers and Stockyards Division of the U.S. Department of Agriculture to inspect cattle for ownership at market centers. The State Brand Board's main function, aside from awarding the inspection contract, is brand registration, transfers, and renewals. At latest count, the board had registered 24,101 brands, including 17,405 in the West River, 4,730 in the East River, and 1,966 to out-of-state owners of South Dakota brands.[106]

A mandatory $1 per head check-off on cattle sales for beef research and promotion was approved by seventy-nine percent of the producers participating in a national referendum in 1986. The proposal had failed in referendums held in 1977 and 1980. But approval came in 1986 by making imported as well as domestic cattle subject to the check-off. The check-off raised about $84 million in 2002, and about $10 million of that sum came from imported cattle. Half of the check-off revenue goes to state beef councils for promotional projects. The other half goes to a National Cattlemen's Beef Promotion and Research Board, whose membership is based on the number of cattle in each state. South Dakota had five members on the national board in 2003.[107]

South Dakota's Beef Industry Council (SDBIC), headquartered in Pierre, is responsible for deciding how the state's share of the check-off revenue is spent. The council is composed of representatives of eight South Dakota agricultural organizations—the Beef Breeds Council, Cattlemen's Association, Women's Auxiliary, Stockgrowers Association, CattleWomen, Farm Bureau, Farmers Union, and Livestock Auction Markets Association. The SDBIC collected $2.9 million from the check-off on cattle sold in South Dakota in 2002. It could have retained half that amount for in-state programs designed to increase beef consumption. But, in 2002-03, it chose to send all but about $700,000 of the revenue to the national board in support of its promotional, research, and educational programs that reach a wider market. Pat Adrian of White River has been the Council's executive secretary since 1973, and she also served as president of the national board in 1985-86.[108]

The future of the check-off program was endangered in 2000 when a group of ranchers, the Livestock Marketing Association, and others challenged its constitutionality in U.S. District Court in South Dakota. The challengers opposed the beef advertising campaign of the National Cattlemen's Beef Promotion and Research Board, claiming it promoted imported as well as domestic beef. Judge Charles Kornmann of Aberdeen ruled that the program was unconstitutional because it infringed on the First Amendment. A three-judge panel of the Eighth U.S. Circuit Court of Appeals affirmed his ruling in late 2003. However, the check-off was permitted to continue pending final resolution of the case after further appeals.[109]

A number of breed organizations, mostly affiliates of national organizations, have been active in South Dakota since the turn of the twentieth century. The oldest of them are the state Hereford, Angus, and Shorthorn associations. However, other breed organizations formed in the state after World War II included the Red Angus, Simmental, Gelbvieh, Tarentaise, Maine-Anjou, Salers, Scotch Highland, and Limousin associations. "Black Baldies," a Hereford-Angus cross, is popular with many western South Dakota commercial cow/calf operators.[110]

■ South Dakota Cattlemen's Association

About one hundred livestock feeders formed the Clay County Corn Belt Feeders Association at Wakonda on March 12, 1948. There were also feeder organizations in Yankton, Lincoln, and Union counties at the time. These groups combined to form the South Dakota Corn Belt Livestock Feeders Association at a meeting at Yankton on June 23, 1950. Don Beaty of Vermillion was chosen as its first president. The state organization was renamed the South Dakota Livestock Feeders Association in 1957, the South Dakota Livestock Association in 1978, and the South Dakota Cattlemen's Association in 1987 with headquarters at Kennebec.[111]

Beaty, in his history of the feeder organizations, credited South Dakota State University at Brookings with being a great factor in the development of the state's cattle industry. He cited the livestock research conducted over the years at the university and at the experimental stations established throughout the state as being particularly useful to the industry. "Its county agents," Beaty wrote, "have been invaluable to most of our livestock organizations throughout the state."[112] He also noted the spread of cattle feeding from the southeastern corner of the state to the Sioux Falls, Brookings, Madison, Huron, Mitchell, Platte, and Chamberlain areas.[113]

From the earliest years, women played a vital role in ranching operations. *Center for Western Studies.*

Since it was first established as a feeder's organization in 1948, the SDCA has had thirty presidents, and all but one of them have come from the East River. The lone exception was Merrill Karlen, Jr., of Reliance who headed the organization in 2000-01. However, the SDCA membership includes all types of stockmen—cow/calf operators, feeders, dairy producers, commercial, and registered breeders. Its officers are elected by the membership at large. Its board of directors includes the association's executive committee composed of the officers, plus two members each from its affiliate organizations chosen by the members of those groups. These include the Cattle Feeders, Beef Breeds, and Cow/Calf Councils, the Dairymen's Association of South Dakota, and fifteen designated areas of the state. The SDCA's stated mission is "To advance the interests of South Dakota cattlemen through the representation and promotion of the beef industry." It is on record as supporting brand inspection and the continuation of the Livestock Ownership Area as it exists in the West River. The association is served by a seven-member staff at its headquarters office at Kennebec.[114]

It was on November 28, 1989, during the SDCA's convention in Huron, that a Women's Auxiliary was organized as an affiliate to the men's association. Trudy Olson of Irene, whose husband, Doyle Olson, headed the SDCA at the time, was its first president. Most of the auxiliary members are wives and daughters of the cattlemen's members. Like the South Dakota CowBelles (later CattleWomen), founded in Rapid City thirty-eight years earlier, the SDCA Women's Auxiliary's main mission has been to promote beef consumption, information, and education. The auxiliary functions as a single unit without affiliate local chapters throughout the state. It sells "South Dakota Beef Bucks" (similar to the CowBelles "Beef Certificates") in $5, $10 and $20 denominations and also uses them as contest prizes. It annually selects a "Beef Ambassador" at the State Fair in Huron and also exhibits beef industry promotional material there and at the Sioux Empire Fair in Sioux Falls. The auxiliary members also published the *First Ladies Edition of the Beef Recipe Collection* and in June of 2003 hosted the Region VI meeting of the American National CattleWomen. Their list of activities is long and varied, but can be summarized as comprised of projects that enhance the demand for beef in a state whose economy depends so heavily upon it.[115]

Rural women have been important to the development of South Dakota's livestock industry since its beginnings during territorial days. During frontier times, whether on farms or ranches, women did the gardening, milked the cows, churned the butter, slopped the hogs, and carded the wool while the men were plowing, planting, harvesting, fixing fences, or caring for the stock. In hard times, many women took off-farm/ranch jobs to supplement depressed family incomes. More recently, Linda Hasselstrom of Hermosa became a best-selling author on the joys and tribulations of ranch life along the Cheyenne River east of the Black Hills. Other ranch women became active promoters of beef consumption in support of their family livelihoods through their volunteer work with the projects of the South Dakota CattleWomen or SDCA Women's Auxiliary.[116]

■ Bison Enterprises

There was a resurgence in the raising of bison in South Dakota as well as nationally after World War II, especially among the Native Americans of the state. Some of the tribes have maintained bison herds intermittently since the early 1900s. All of the South Dakota tribes, however, had bison herds by the turn of the twenty-first century, some of them reestablished from an earlier period. They range in size from fifty to over 2,500 head. The Intertribal Bison Cooperative, a non-profit organization representing fifty-one member tribes, including eight in South Dakota, covers a sixteen-state region. The cooperative headquarters is at Rapid City. Its avowed common purpose is "Restoring the American Bison to its rightful range."[117]

"Tribes are restoring bison for cultural, ecological, nutritional and occasionally economic purposes," according to cooperative spokesman Tony Willman. He points out that the social hierarchy of the bison is not unlike that of the Sioux where the elders, especially the tribal matriarchs, teach valuable life lessons to the young and immature. "If you have a couple of trouble makers in the herd and there are no elders to straighten them out, you will be plagued with ongoing troubles." Willman contends this is true in the tribes as well as in the bison herds. "Today bison represent hope to tribes for better health," he adds. "The rate of diabetes, heart disease and obesity on many reservations is catastrophic. These health problems are being directly linked to the modern high fat/cholesterol diets of the past fifty years. Native Americans evolved on a diet that consisted of lean meats and high fiber fruits and vegetables. Many tribes are currently raising buffalo not only for use in cultural events, but they are beginning to make bison meat available to tribal members to help reverse these unfortunate trends associated with modern diets."[118]

Native American bison enterprises received an economic boost in 2003 when Congress appropriated $3 million for the purchase of bison meat specifically from tribes with herds. The meat was purchased for distribution through the government's commodity program on the Indian reservations. Additionally, also in 2003, the U.S. Department of Agriculture designated $1 million to be spent on bison purchases from Indian producers for its Food and Nutrition Services' Emergency Food Assistance Program. These purchases came at a propitious time, as prices had fallen sharply since the boom in bison ranching of the late 1990s. Bison were selling for an average of $2,000 per head then, but had dropped to between $200 to $500 per animal by 2003. A three-year drought in South Dakota had forced bison raisers, as well as cattlemen, to reduce drastically their herds, and the resulting calf crop of both bison and cattle was considerably below normal.[119]

Custer State Park in the Black Hills has maintained a buffalo herd in a 70,000-acre fenced pasture since 1914 when it obtained thirty-six head from the Scotty Philip estate. The herd now ranges in size from 1,500 head in the summer to about 950 during the winter months. The park annually holds roundups that attract large crowds of onlookers prior to selling off the excess animals at a fall auction that is also well attended. At the park's 2003 auction, breeding bulls sold for an average of $515 per head, cows $470, two-year-olds $406, yearling heifers $168, heifer calves $94 and bull calves $58—all considerably lower than in pre-drought years. The owner of the state's largest private bison herd for many years was Roy Houck, president of the South Dakota Stockgrowers Association in 1946-48. He ran a 3,000-head herd on his Standing Butte Ranch on the west bank of the Missouri River some thirty miles north of Fort Pierre, not far from where Scotty Philip had established his pioneer herd. Houck was the first president of the National Buffalo Association when it was organized in 1966. Don Hight of Murdo, another owner of a major bison herd, was elected to the association's five-member board of directors at the organizational meeting. In 1995 the National Buffalo Association merged with the American Bison Association, formed in 1975, to become the National Bison Association. It had over 2,400 members representing all fifty states and sixteen foreign countries in 2003. Its stated mission is to promote the preservation, production, and marketing of bison.[120]

Houck's son, Jerry, also a former SDSGA president, continued the family's extensive cattle and bison operations following Roy's death. He says it is more costly to raise bison than cattle because of the stronger fences, gates, and chutes needed for them. But he adds that bison are better rustlers than cattle, thriving on weeds and coarse forage that cattle will not touch, and they require less winter care if kept in the wild state. "As long as they can move, they are fine," another bison raiser stated. "Grass, water and room is all they need."[121]

In 1996 the Dakota Territory Buffalo Association was formed at Rapid City for the purpose of educating the public on the growing buffalo industry. Although headquartered in Rapid City, the association is not strictly a Dakota organization. Its membership was opened to those outside of what was formerly Dakota Territory, and by 2003 it boasted of having over three hundred members from twenty-four states and three Canadian Provinces. The association conducts the Black Hills Buffalo Classic at Rapid City every winter where buffalo are both exhibited and sold. It also hosts a summer conference every June and educational seminars throughout the year at different locations to promote the buffalo industry. Bison producers in the Black Hills region include Dan O'Brien, award-winning fiction author, who ranches north of Whitewood and markets grass-fed, field-killed bison meat packages on the Internet. The movie actor Kevin Costner opened "Tatanka: The Story of the Bison," a $5 million interpretative center and Indian encampment on the edge of Deadwood in the fall of 2003. It features a seventeen-piece bronze sculpture of bison being driven over a steep cliff by Indian horsemen as was done on the northern plains before the coming of the white man. Native Americans from the Cheyenne River Sioux Reservation tell the epic story of the near disappearance of the buffalo and their resurgence in modern times. They also demonstrate the many uses their ancestors made of the buffalo. The visitor center gives a spectacular view of the plains to the north where immense buffalo herds were last seen in the 1880s.[122]

Bison producers and their organizations stress the healthful qualities of bison meat in their promotional activities. They point out that the nutrient composition of 100 grams of cooked lean bison meat is 2.42 grams of fat, 143 calories and 82 milligrams of cholesterol, lower than most other meats. The National Bison Association reported there were 350,000 bison in the United States in 2003. Only 20,000 head of them were processed for slaughter under federal inspection during 2002. That compares with a national cattle inventory of 9.6 million head that year and a slaughter rate of more than 100,000 per day. Consumers spent an estimated $60.2 billion on beef in 2002. Bison producers believe their product will become more popular as consumers become better informed about its healthful qualities and good taste. "The biggest challenge," as one bison producer put it, "is just getting people to take the first bite."[123]

■ Sheep Raising

Sheep raising in South Dakota, aside from the farm flocks that came with the first settlers into the southeastern part of the state, did not develop extensively until after the Sioux War of 1876-77. Ed Lemmon, the pioneer West River cattleman, described Jakie Mills as "the very first sheepman of importance in the [Black] Hills."[124] Mills ran sheep between Spring and Battle creeks south of Rapid City. Mills' impact on the Black Hills sheep industry was apparently short-lived as there are no further mentions of him in the historical records of the region. In any event, Mills did not leave a mark on the sheep industry of the Black Hills district to match that of John "Jack" Hale, who was a commanding figure on the political scene there as well as a leading sheepman. Lemmon is best remembered as a prominent West River cattleman. However, he and his son, James, both became deeply involved in the West River sheep business too.[125]

Numerous sheep ranches were established in the northwestern corner of the state between 1877 and the opening of the twentieth century. One of them in northern Butte County was operated by William Chiesman and his brother-in-law, Matt Ward. The partners shipped the first carload of wool out of Belle Fourche in June of 1891. A branch of the North Western Railroad had reached Belle Fourche the previous December 28. It built shipping pens and watering facilities on the outskirts of the town and carried 1,315 carloads of cattle from the tri-state ranges to eastern markets within the next thirty days. Soon Belle Fourche became famous as the largest shipping point in the northwest for both cattle and sheep.[126]

There was no trouble between cattlemen and sheep raisers in the northwestern corner of the state bordering on Wyoming and Montana, as there had been farther west. There were stockmen who believed their cattle would not graze or drink where sheep had been pastured. However, Archer Gilfillan, who worked seventeen years as a sheepherder in the Slim Buttes country of Harding County, reported that they soon learned otherwise. In fact, Gilfillan wrote in his book, *Sheep: Life on the South Dakota Range*, that some cattlemen became converted to sheep when prices for them exceeded those for cattle. He considered Harding County ideal for sheep raising as it is fifty by sixty miles in size, its largest town (during Gilfillan's time there) had a population of only one hundred and fifty, and land was so cheap that even persons of modest means could acquire large holdings. "There is an abundance of grass everywhere," Gilfillan wrote, "and enough running water to supply the needs of stock."[127] About sheep herding, bachelor Gilfillan also wrote that anybody who became a sheepherder had to be crazy before becoming one or would be crazy within six months of taking up the profession.[128]

Perhaps the largest sheep raiser in that section of South Dakota was Myron J. Smiley, who in 1904 moved his operations from Wyoming, where the war between cattlemen and sheepmen had turned violent. Smiley, headquartering on a home ranch near Belle Fourche, ran as high as 50,000 head of sheep on ranges in Butte, Meade, Harding, Perkins, Dewey, and Corson counties. He was also instrumental in promoting Belle Fourche as a shipping center for cattle, sheep, and wool. James G. Rogers, who opened a land office at Midland shortly after the Chicago and North Western Railroad reached there in 1906, also engaged in sheep ranching on tracts he had acquired for himself in that area. His sheep bands were never as large as Smiley's. Nonetheless, he was partially credited with developing the sheep industry east of the Black Hills much as Scotty Philip had done for the cattle business. Rogers was the first president of the South Dakota Sheep and Wool Association when it was founded in 1920 with headquarters at Pierre. His land-office business was short-lived, but he continued enlarging his land holdings and sheep operations until his death in 1924. While his sheep numbers did not match those of Smiley, the pair had more in common than their prominence in the business. They also both went broke raising sheep.[129]

Sheep raising, like other segments of the livestock industry, is a risky undertaking. A producer can do everything right while so many things beyond his control—low prices, bad weather, animal diseases, predators, etc.—can go so wrong that he is financially ruined in a single season. That happened to many stockmen during the big blizzard of January 1949 when over 16,000 head of cattle and calves and upwards of 13,000 sheep and lambs perished in the West River region. The state legislature then in session appropriated $100,000 in emergency funds to finance a "hay drop" from Air Force and National Guard planes to feed snowbound livestock that had somehow survived the storm. There was a sharp drop in the calf and lamb crops the following spring as a result of the disastrous blizzard too. Earlier winter storms had been a factor in the financial losses suffered by Smiley and Rogers.[130]

Sheep raising was considered to be a good venture during hard times, though, because it offered two incomes—from the lambs and from the wool. Henry Scheele, an Ipswich native who spent thirty-two years as an area wool buyer, said nearly every farmer had fifteen to fifty head of sheep during the Great Depression of the 1930s. The drought of that period was especially instrumental in farmers in eastern South Dakota and western Minnesota turning to sheep when they failed to get crops. Scheele claims sheep helped that generation of farmers pay for and keep their land. Scheele remembered Otto Wolff of Rapid City and Ray Garrett of Britton as among the biggest sheepmen of his era. Wolff ran between 4,000 and 5,000 head of sheep in the Black Hills and Garrett had close to 8,000 head on his Roberts County farm.[131]

Sheepmen, like other livestock raisers, had state and national organizations representing their interests. Members of the South Dakota Livestock Marketing Association, organized in 1931, were East River feeders and West River rangemen cooperating to move feeder lambs. They sought to cut out commission and yardage charges by moving the lambs directly from the range to the feedlots. The association moved 30,000 lambs, mostly from the northwestern corner of the state, from feedlots in the southeastern counties during the fall of 1933. The South Dakota Sheep and Wool Growers Association that Rogers had helped found in 1920 was reorganized as the Cooperative Wool Growers of South Dakota in 1927. It affiliated with the National Wool Growers Association and moved its headquarters from Pierre to Brookings. In 1938 the South Dakota and Minnesota cooperatives merged to form the North Central Wool Marketing Corporation. Its headquarters was moved from Brookings to Minneapolis in 1945.[132]

Carl Nadasdy, general manager of the Cooperative Wool Growers of South Dakota, also served in that position with the North Central Wool Marketing Corporation. He was the leading figure in both organizations until his retirement in 1971. One of his early actions was the establishment of the *Wool Sack* as the news organ of the South Dakota Wool Growers in 1931. Ed Lemmon, who bought wool for the cooperative, wrote a column for it. Nadasdy also ran about 5,000 sheep in partnership with Lemmon's son, James, on leased Indian land in northwestern South Dakota. The South Dakota Cooperative had warehouses at Aberdeen, Sioux Falls, Huron, Mitchell, and Belle Fourche where it stored the wool after spring shearings. Then it usually shipped the wool directly to eastern mills in late fall or early winter when prices were generally highest. The merged South Dakota and Minnesota Co-Ops that formed the North Central Wool Marketing Corporation grew from 15,193 members producing 6.9 million pounds of wool in 1938 to 20,246 members producing 15.2 million pounds in its peak year of 1942. The corporation obtained prices for its members that usually exceeded those paid to independent producers and was considered to be a highly successful partnership. It was so successful, in fact, that the Iowa Wool Growers joined the corporation in 1955 and the Nebraska Wool Growers two years later to make it the largest organization of its kind in the United States. It was said, "no rural organization has ever accomplished more for its members."[133]

Sheep and lamb numbers in South Dakota peaked in 1943 when the federal government was buying the entire domestic wool clip of the country for the military during World War II. There were 2.4 million head of sheep and lambs on South Dakota farms and ranches that year. Their numbers dropped sharply after the war, nationally as well as in South Dakota, when the government had a surplus of wool in its Commodity Credit Corporation storage facilities. The USDA's Crop and Livestock Reporting Service estimated their numbers to be down to only 380,000 head by January 1, 2003, the lowest count since annual estimates were started in 1920. Sheep, lambs, and wool production in 2001 accounted for only one-half of one percent of the state's total cash receipts from farm and ranch marketings. Yet in 2003 the state was ranked fourth nationally in sheep and lamb numbers.[134]

The northwestern counties lead the state in sheep and lamb numbers. Butte and Harding counties rank first and second, respectively. The southeastern counties are the leading sheep and lamb producers in the East River region with the largest flocks in Yankton and Turner counties. Wool production in the state in 2002 totalled 3.1 million pounds valued at $1.3 million, a drop of only 197,000 in pounds but over $1.5 million in value from 1997. Sheep and lambs were valued at an average price of $97 per head in 2002, compared to $88 the previous year. The decline in the number of sheep raisers in the state reflects the sharp drop in prices for their products during a period of rising costs. Sheep and lamb brought average prices of $37.70 and $93.20 per hundredweight, respectively, in 1997. But they brought only $30 and $79.10, respectively, in 2002.[135]

■ Swine, Hogs, and the Dairy Industry

South Dakota had 1,500 hog operations and an inventory of 1.29 million hogs and pigs at the end of 2002. That was a loss of one hundred hog farms from the previous year, but the inventory of hogs and pigs was virtually unchanged. The industry contributes about seven percent to the state's total cash receipts from farm marketings, including government payments, ranking eleventh nationally. Ten counties in the southeastern sector of the state, led by Hutchinson, Charles Mix, and Minnehaha, in that order, produce nearly two-thirds of the state's entire hog and pig inventory.

In 2002 the largest single group of producers owned from one to one hundred hogs. Only sixty producers owned more than five thousand head. In 2003 the voters of Bon Homme and Hutchinson counties rejected proposals to build large hog confinement farms because of environmental concerns.[136]

In February of 1954 the South Dakota Swine Improvement Association was formed, with headquarters at Huron, to represent the hog producers of the state. Its annual meetings were held at the State Fair while many of their members were exhibiting their hogs and pigs. The organization changed its name to South Dakota Pork Producers Council in November 1967 and affiliated with the National Pork Producers Council to assist in its national objectives. It became a non-profit organization in 1975 with authority to generate income at fairs and trade shows for promotional purposes. Headquarters were then moved to Madison and subsequently to Sioux Falls in 2002. Passage of the Pork Promotion, Research, and Consumer Information Act by Congress in 1985 imposed a mandatory national check-off on hogs and pork products, including those imported, at the point of their sale. The check-off rate was set at forty cents per $100 of value and produced about $40 million a year nationwide and about $1 million in South Dakota. Twenty-eight percent of the check-off income collected in South Dakota was returned to the state in support of projects restricted to industry promotion, research, and educational purposes.[137]

The National Pork Board, composed of representatives from the pork-producing states, was charged with distributing the check-off income under U.S. Department of Agriculture guidelines. South Dakota had two representatives on the board, which functioned independently of the National Pork Producers Council. The state was also represented on the board of directors of the latter organization too. In 2002 the National Pork Producers Council initiated a voluntary ten cents per $100 value additional check-off to finance its legislative and regulatory activities. The South Dakota Pork Producers Council received one half of this non-restricted additional check-off income collected within the state for its programs. Among the programs it supports are 4-H, Ag in the Classroom, South Dakota Master Pork Producers, and South Dakota Swine Breeders, along with scholarships and projects that promote the production, marketing, and consumption of pork. The officers and a sixteen-member executive committee, supported by a three-person staff at Sioux Falls, conducted the council affairs. Eighteen counties were represented in the council's membership, numbering almost one thousand. Local pork groups provided many of its members, with a majority of them coming from the southeastern sector of the state.[138]

By resolution, the council went on record as supporting the Country of Origin Labeling law for meat products, the national mandatory and voluntary check-offs and federal legislation that requires processors of livestock to bargain with producer cooperatives. It was also on record by resolution as opposed to packer concentration and to corporate packers engaging in the feeding of livestock in competition with producers. At the 2001 session, the South Dakota Legislature gave the council a refundable pork check-off plan that goes into effect only if the national program is discontinued.[139]

South Dakota's dairy industry ranked twenty-sixth in the nation in the production of milk and milk products in 2001. It contributed less than five percent to the state's total cash farm receipts that year. The estimated number of milk cows in the state was at an all-time low of 94,000 head in 2003. That compares to the record high of 675,000 head in 1934. One third of the state's milk cows were located in the northeastern counties. Milk production in the state during 2002 totaled 1.4 million pounds. East River farms and almost all West River ranches have horses and/or mules. They numbered 75,000 head by the end of 1998. The raising of Quarter Horses was a popular activity throughout the state, but especially in the West River.[140]

Livestock produces just under half of the state's annual cash farm receipts, but it is the largest single source of that income. Crops produce about thirty-nine percent of the total with the rest coming from government payments of price-supported commodities. Income from the sale of cattle and calves accounts for almost thirty-three percent, with hogs contributing just under seven percent, dairy products about five percent and sheep, lamb, and wool less than one-half of one percent. Miscellaneous livestock sales account for about two-and-a-half percent.[141]

It is a common misconception that the West River is the state's principal cattle region because that is where most of the big acreage ranches are situated. However, since the end of the open range era in the late nineteenth century, there have been far more cattle raised in the East River than west of the Missouri. On January 1, 2003, there were 2.8 million head of cattle on East River farms compared to only 849,000 on West River ranches. There were 21,606 farms averaging 1,026 acres in the forty-two East River counties and 8,271 ranches averaging 3,515 acres in the twenty-two West River counties. Most cattle raised in the East River sector of the state are located on "farms" where crops are also raised. Those in the West River are more apt to be found on "ranches" where few crops besides alfalfa are raised. Of course, there are some exceptions on both sides of the river. Some sizeable cattle operations can be found in the East River, and some West River ranchers raise crops other than alfalfa. In general, however, since statehood the East River has been considered farm country and the West River cow country. In 2002 the largest single number of cattle producers statewide owned between one hundred and five hundred head. Herds in the thousands dominated the western ranges in the late 1890s and early 1900s. But only five hundred producers statewide owned more than one thousand head in 2002.[142]

Livestock operations in South Dakota have come a long way since the first cows, hogs, and sheep came up the Missouri River to the trading posts along its banks prior to the establishment of Dakota Territory. There have been dramatic changes since the first settlers crossed into the territory with their families and stock to settle in the Missouri River Valley prior to South Dakota's becoming a state in 1889. The colorful era of the dusty trail drives, the bawling Longhorns, the open range, and the hard-riding cowboy is long past. However, today livestock continues to be the backbone of the state's leading industry with cattle in the forefront in both the East and West River regions.

Chapter 15
Black Hills in Transition

From the time humans first appeared on the northern Great Plains, they have been attracted to the small outpost of mountains known as the Black Hills. Measuring about one hundred miles north to south and sixty miles east to west, these "hills" rise as much as 4,000 feet above the surrounding land, making them appear as an "Island in the Plains." Four basic geological features give this island some of its unique qualities. At the center is a granite core which contains Harney Peak, the Hills' highest mountain, and the granite spires of the Needles. A limestone plateau surrounds the granite core, and this limestone holds and then releases the water for the Hills' numerous streams. It also contains most of the region's caves and the escarpments that are seen in Spearfish Canyon and elsewhere around the Hills. Around the limestone and at the edge of the Hills are sandstone formations. The sandstone is most notable in the Red Valley and the Hogback that ring the mountains. Finally, igneous intrusions brought some of the most distinctive elements to the area, such as Devils Tower to the west and Bear Butte to the east, and they deposited the precious metals in the northern Black Hills. A Ponderosa pine forest predominates over these geologic features, and when viewed from a distance it gives the Hills a dark coloration and their name as the Black Hills. Many people have appreciated this last feature. For instance, the Sioux call this region the *Paha Sapa*, "Black Hills."

Archaeological evidence indicates that the first arrivals to the area were associated with the Clovis culture, dating from about 11,000 years ago. While little Clovis evidence has been found within the Hills proper, a Clovis mammoth kill site has been located to the east in the White River Badlands. As Paleo-Indian cultures diversified from dependence on mammoths to other animals and plants and a number of cultural variants developed, people began utilizing the area more and more. Western Plains Indians foraged for food around the Black Hills, while people to the east, especially along the Missouri River, adopted a more horticultural and sedentary lifestyle. But these eastern village societies also exploited the resources of the Hills, at least on a seasonal basis. The streams, grass, and wildlife drew people to the Black Hills from all directions, making the region a cultural transition zone where plains people interacted with people from the Missouri River.[1]

■ Sacred Land

The Black Hills also attracted a variety of Native American groups during the more recent historic times. Among historic Indian populations, the Lakota are the most closely associated with the area. They not only lived in and around the Hills when Euro-Americans arrived, but the Lakota also make an earlier claim to the Hills. Some Lakota believe that life began as they emerged from Wind Cave in the southern Black Hills, followed by a migration away from the Hills until their return centuries later. This belief gives them a strong spiritual connection to the Hills. Historic evidence indicates that the Sioux arrived from the east about 1775. They were the last in a succession of Indian peoples who made the Black Hills home. The Kiowa, Crow, and Cheyenne all lived in the region and still have connections to the Hills. For instance, the Kiowa tell stories of

Devils Tower arising from the plains to rescue seven young girls from a bear. The presence of Crow Indians in the northern Black Hills is noted with such place names as Crow Peak and Crow Creek near Spearfish. And the Cheyenne not only have accounts of Devils Tower, but for them Bear Butte is particularly significant. Here their cultural hero, Sweet Medicine, acquired the Cheyenne's sacred arrows, and Bear Butte is still the holiest place in the Cheyenne world. Each of these peoples moved on when pressured by another Indian group, concluding with the Sioux.[2]

When the Lakota arrived, they soon came to dominate not only the Hills but the region around them. By the early 1800s, the Lakota controlled territory from the Missouri River to the Bighorn Mountains. The Black Hills sat at the center of their world, physically, spiritually, and materially. As the Lakota holy man Black Elk related to John G. Neihardt, the Black Hills were "like a big food pack for our people."[3] Here they hunted, fished, and cut lodge poles. The Lakota also have sacred traditions connected with Devils Tower and Bear Butte. For instance, they believe that White Buffalo Calf Woman gave them their sacred Calf Pipe at Bear Butte.[4]

While many native people used the Hills, most of their activity seems to have been either in the southern Black Hills, where the climate is milder, or around the periphery of the Hills. Archaeological digs near Custer and rock art found in southern canyons indicate well over a thousand years of human activity in these areas. Then along the margins of the Hills, Indians found nearly everything they desired: game, water, grass, and protection. They developed a trail around the Hills within the Red Valley, turning it into what was known as the "Race Track." In reality, there was little need to enter the Hills. The mountains and trees made travel difficult, and the Hills had less game than the plains. Some Native accounts call the Hills "bad medicine," in part because of the intense thunder and lightening storms that roll through the mountains during the spring and summer. Indeed, archaeologists have found only scattered native material within the Hills. Yet Indians did

Chronology

1775 – Sioux arrive in Black Hills from the east

1800 – Sioux control region

1811 – Hunt leads expedition north of Hills and describes them

1830 – Oglala Post established at Rapid Creek and Cheyenne River

1851 – Fort Laramie Treaty established

1857 – Warren Expedition encounters Lakota, explores Hills

1865 – Powder River campaign

1866 – Red Cloud's War – Lakota resist encroachment into Hills

1873 – Panic of 1873 leads to financial recession

1874 – Custer leads expedition into Hills

1875 – Black Hills Gold Rush begins

1876 – Battle of Little Bighorn

1877 – A Chinatown develops in Deadwood following the Gold Rush

1878 – Rapid City stabilizes as the county seat

1886 – Elkhorn Railroad reaches Rapid City

1891 – Burlington and Elkhorn railroads race to Deadwood, securing its future

1907 – Improved rail service brings in industry and tourism

1922 – "Days of '76" begins in Deadwood

1927 – Work begins on Mount Rushmore sculpture

1929 – Potato Creek Johnny appears in Deadwood with large gold nugget

1933 – CCC and WPA work camps employ thousands of men of the region

1942 – Ellsworth AFB created for training purposes

1944 – Flood Control Act passed

1948 – Work begins on Crazy Horse Memorial sculpture

1956 – Pactola Dam completed

1972 – Rapid City flood kills 235

1989 – Limited-stakes gaming permitted in Deadwood

2001 – Homestake Mine closes

enter and use the Hills. When Custer led his expedition through the Black Hills in 1874, he encountered a small hunting band on Reynold's Prairie, a high treeless plain in the northern Black Hills, and other evidence of previous Indian activity exists. Although varying in intensity from location to location, there is no doubt that Native peoples used all of the Black Hills.[5]

The 1874 Custer Expedition marked a turning point in the history of the Hills. As Custer left, a tidal wave of American invaders entered, forever changing the area's human dynamics. Yet Custer and his men were not the first Euro-Americans to visit the Hills. That distinction may fall to Francois and Louis-Joseph La Verendrye, brothers from a French-Canadian fur trading family, and two other white men who possibly stood at the base of the Black Hills in early 1743. They had come west looking for the "Western Sea," but instead found mountains. Whether they actually saw the Black Hills remains uncertain. They wrote sparingly in their journals, and their vague comments could apply to most mountain ranges. Two pieces of evidence do exist. The Verendryes left small lead plates along the Cheyenne River and at the mouth of the Bad River on the Missouri in March 1743. While the plates claim the territory for the king of France, their location infers that the adventurers may well have been in or at the Black Hills some time before.[6]

For eighty years after the Verendryes, the Missouri River was the main highway west for explorers and fur traders. Since the Black Hills sit just two hundred miles west of the river, many of these adventurers either heard about the Hills or saw them first hand. Lewis and Clark stayed close to the river in 1804, but they met traders such as Jean Valle who claimed to have gone up the Cheyenne River to the "Black Mountains." Lewis and Clark also met Cheyenne Indians who lived in the area of the Hills. Even though the Corps of Discovery did not come near the Black Hills, their return to St. Louis in 1806 stimulated other traders and explorers to head west, and some of these men encountered the Hills.[7]

A fear of Indian hostilities sometimes convinced fur traders to leave the Missouri River for overland routes to the West. In 1811 Wilson Price Hunt and his sixty-two men bound for the Pacific Northwest left the Missouri for this reason and traveled up the Grand River. Their route took them north of the Black Hills, and Hunt left an account describing the Hills as "an extensive chain, lying about a hundred miles east of the Rocky Mountains."[8] An armed conflict with the Arikara Indians caused two more groups or brigades of fur men to abandon the Missouri River in 1823. Jedediah Smith led one of these parties up the White River to the area of the Black Hills. Smith and his group of twelve men apparently entered the region via Buffalo Gap. As they traveled in the vicinity of Wind Cave, a grizzly bear surprised Smith, and grabbed him by the head. Smith lost an ear before a member of his party dispatched the bear. Some historians place this incident in the Powder River Basin of Wyoming, with Smith's party missing much of the Black Hills. No matter the location, the troop waited ten days for Smith to recover, and during this time fellow adventurer James Clyman investigated the Black Hills. Later he recounted that he saw "putrified" trees on which "putrified" birds sang "putrified" songs.[9]

Beyond these scant encounters, fur traders and trappers seemingly spent little time in the Black Hills. Apparently just one fur trading post was established near the Black Hills. Oglala Post was constructed in 1830 at the confluence of Rapid Creek and the Cheyenne River, but then it was destroyed in an 1832 gunpowder explosion. The Hills apparently did not have enough beaver or streams to attract the large fur brigades that worked the Rocky Mountains. Yet the Black Hills has a French Creek and a couple of Beaver Creeks. These place names indicate a fur trade heritage, albeit a small one.[10]

By the 1830s, however, a number of men were in the West either trading or trapping for furs. Also a number of fur forts had been established. Some were along the Missouri River, such as Fort Pierre. Two hundred miles to the south of the Hills, Fort William, later to become Fort Laramie, was started in 1834. With so much going on in the region, some of these fur adventurers may have continued to work the Black Hills, and they might have found more than furs. In 1887 a Spearfish stonemason named Louis Thoen found a stone on Lookout Mountain inscribed with a message of desperation. It told of seven men who came to the Hills in 1833, and by 1834 they had found all the gold their horses could carry. But the Indians had discovered them, and they all had been killed except the author, Ezra Kind. And he wrote that Indians were hunting him. The authenticity of the Thoen Stone has long been debated. The fact that Thoen was a stonemason raises much suspicion, but a variety of adventurers were in the area, and the 1831 gold discoveries in Georgia had piqued the nation's interest in gold. Actual proof, however, remains elusive.[11]

Despite the occasional problem along the Missouri and the tale of terror that Ezra Kind told, most Indians and fur traders/trappers got along fairly well during the first half of the nineteenth century. Each benefited by having a cordial relation with the other. Relations, however, became strained as the number of people heading west exploded with the California gold rush. Misunderstandings developed along the Platte River Road, and the federal government rapidly saw the need to bring peace to the plains. In 1851 the government invited the plains Indians to attend a council at Fort Laramie. Almost ten thousand Indians came, including Lakota, Cheyenne, and Crow, and out of this came the Fort Laramie Treaty of 1851. In return for annuities and goods, the Indian people promised peace along the trail, granted the right to establish roads and military posts in their territory, and recognized specific boundaries for their lands. For the Lakota this area stretched from the Missouri River in Dakota to the Powder River just east of the Bighorns, with the Black Hills squarely in the middle.[12]

Peace along the trail, however, proved short-lived. Only three years after signing the document, a Lakota brave killed a cow belonging to a wagon troop. The owner demanded the cow back, and Lieutenant J. L. Grattan led twenty-nine men from Fort Laramie to the Indian camp to find the animal or the guilty party. The negotiations grew heated, and someone fired a shot. In the exchange that followed, Grattan and his command were destroyed in what has been called the Grattan Massacre or Grattan Incident. In response, the army wanted retribution, and when General William S. Harney and his command of one thousand left Fort Laramie for Fort Pierre in 1855 to pursue the attack, the Euro-American presence drew closer to the Black Hills.[13]

Traveling with the Harney expedition was Lieutenant Gouverneur Kemble Warren of the Army Corps of Topographical Engineers. Ordered to explore and assess the resources of Western Dakota, Warren found much of the territory unsuitable for settlement, except when he continued his explorations and directly confronted the Black Hills in 1857. In that year Warren, accompanied by Ferdinand V. Hayden and seventeen other men, left Fort Laramie and moved along the western edge of the Hills. Near Inyan Kara, they encountered a large Lakota hunting party, which included Sitting Bull. The Indians informed Warren that they did not want roads, forts, or whites in their territory, and they believed that when one white came, many followed. Without much effort, they convinced Warren to retreat south. Instead of leaving the Hills, however, Warren decided to inspect the Hills from another angle. His party moved around the southern end and up the east side, traveling as far north as Bear Butte before turning south again. In his report, Warren gave the first reasonably accurate account of the Black Hills, which included identifying place names and giving a report of gold. Warren also argued that war with the Lakota was inevitable, and the best place to attack them would be near the Black Hills.[14]

Other army groups followed Warren into the Black Hills area. Only two years later, 1859, another Army Corps of Topographical Engineers troop swung around the Black Hills. In this venture, Captain William Raynolds led about fifteen men from Fort Randall on the Missouri River to near Bear Butte. They then moved along the northern edge of the Hills, and finally on to Powder River country. Raynold's report built on Warren's, with more information about possible roads, and it also talked of gold discoveries. Six years later, as many as two thousand soldiers saw the Black Hills for the first time as the army sent a large expedition into the area during the Powder River campaign of 1865. This campaign began when the plains Indians had erupted in violence following the killing of several hundred peaceful Cheyenne and Arapaho at Sand Creek, Colorado, in 1864. The army meant to subdue the Indians, but the real fighting proved to be near the Bighorn Mountains. Those soldiers who came near the Black Hills only enjoyed the view and speculated about the possibility of gold.[15]

The 1862 and 1863 gold discoveries in Montana piqued many people's interest in the precious metal and made Indian-white relations on the northern plains all the more difficult. John Bozeman developed a short-cut from the Platte River Road to the gold fields, running through the Powder River country and then along the Bighorn Mountains, across territory the Lakota did not want to have invaded. The army made a half-hearted effort to negotiate a settlement, but the talks rapidly broke down. The army then built three forts along the trail, and the conflict on the northern plains intensified as the Lakota resisted the encroachment in what is known as Red Cloud's War. The key event came in December 1866 when the Indians surprised and killed eighty soldiers under Captain Fetterman's command near Fort Phil Kearney on the Bozeman Trail.[16]

The violence on the plains brought a demand for peace from congressmen and reformers in the East. Adding to the urgency for peace was the construction of the transcontinental railroad. As the Union Pacific moved west, the government wanted to ensure a safe corridor, and this could only happen with a general peace on the northern plains. The army invited Indians to Fort Laramie for negotiations in 1867, but with little luck. The army negotiators, led by Generals Sherman, Harney, and Terry, tried again in 1868. This time they drafted the Fort Laramie Treaty of 1868, but to get it approved by enough Lakota they had to have it signed at different times and at different places. Several bands appeared separately at Fort Laramie to sign the document; the noted Jesuit missionary Father De Smet took it up the Missouri River for more signatures; and Red Cloud agreed to it only when he saw the army live up to its terms.[17]

Red Cloud wanted the Bozeman Trail and its forts closed. The treaty did this, and it seemed to offer other advantages for the Sioux. It established the Great Sioux Reservation in western Dakota Territory, including the Black Hills. And no further land cessions could be made unless three-fourths of the adult male members of the tribe agreed. Hunting was allowed in western Nebraska, and the Powder River Country of Wyoming remained opened for the Lakota as "unceded" Indian territory. Other measures included establishing an agency where a physician, school, and mission would be available; and the government made promises to provide education and tools to encourage agriculture. Yet the treaty allowed for the construction of roads or "other works" on reservation land with a promise of compensation for damages.[18]

Historians disagree about the clause that allows for the construction of roads and other works on the reservation. Some argue that the military added those stipulations at a later "rewrite," while others say that the Lakota did not understand the intent of those provisions in the original draft. Nevertheless, the government believed it had the authority to enter the reservation, and in 1874 it sent Lieutenant Colonel George Custer and a command of about one thousand men into the Black Hills, outraging the Lakota. His orders were to find a suitable location for a military post. Officially, Lakota/white violence to the south of the reservation convinced the army that an outpost within the Hills would calm the region. Unofficially, the nation apparently wanted the expedition to find a new gold field. The Panic of 1873 had brought a national recession, and many believed that more gold in circulation would solve the problem. To this end, Custer allowed two prospectors to accompany him.[19]

■ Gold Frontier

Custer's Expedition left Fort Abraham Lincoln, northeast of the Hills on the Missouri River, on July 2, 1874, and spent the next sixty days traveling through the northern plains and the Black Hills. Along with the prospectors, his organization included 110 wagons, 300 cattle, four scientists, three newspaper correspondents, a band, and a photographer, William H. Illingworth. During the trip, Custer climbed Harney Peak, killed a grizzly bear, and camped several nights along French Creek, in the area of present-day Custer. On August 2, while at French Creek the two prospectors, Horatio N. Ross and William T. McKay, found small quantities of gold. While the scientists in the party discounted the importance of the find, many of the soldiers became quite excited, taking time to look for the metal. Soon after the discovery, Custer sent a scout, Charlie Reynolds, to Fort Laramie with a variety of dispatches. Among these were the messages that the newspaper reporters sent out; and beginning on August 11, the New York *Daily Tribune* began broadcasting the news of gold in the Black Hills. Very soon, scores of Americans started wondering about their chances of acquiring some of the new wealth.[20]

As word of gold spread, groups organized to invade the Black Hills. Since the closing of the Black Hills in 1868, promoters from Cheyenne, Yankton, and Sioux City, had talked about sending private gold expeditions to the Hills. In particular, two Sioux City boosters, Charles Collins and Thomas Russell, had organized the Black Hills Mining and Exploring Association in 1872, but without any results. Then with Custer's report in hand they tried again. This time Collins and Russell attempted to recruit one hundred people who were willing to take a chance, but when the troop departed in October 1874 only twenty-six men, one woman, and a boy left for the Black Hills. While sponsored by Collins and Russell, the party took its name from the guide and captain, John Gordon.[21]

According to the terms of the Fort Laramie Treaty of 1868, the government promised to keep unauthorized people out of the reservation. Consequently, the government deemed such groups as the Gordon Party illegal and made efforts to remove them, sending patrols out from Fort Randall. The Gordon Party, however, managed to elude the army patrols and arrived at French Creek, near where Custer had camped, on December 23, 1874. Here they built a stockade for protection and organized a mining district, a necessary step before mining. Arriving in winter, they found life difficult, and some left, with two of the former members making it to Fort Laramie. While several military patrols had tried unsuccessfully to find the Gordon Party, a detachment from Fort Laramie, led by the two former Gordon Party members, located and removed the remaining eighteen gold seekers in April 1875.[22]

These events of early 1875 were just a quiet prelude to the tumult that followed during the rest of the year. During 1875 four different activities demonstrated the early patterns and contradictions of the Black Hills gold rush. In the first place, the removal of the Gordon Party did not subdue the gold rush, and gold seekers continued to enter. Second, the government remained uncertain as to what actual value existed in the Hills, and it sent another party of explorers to verify the area's potential wealth. Third, while Americans rushed in, the army felt obliged to stem the flow, and more military men entered to remove the miners. And fourth, the government foresaw the inevitable outcome and began negotiating with the Lakota for the Hills.

Gold seekers could not easily be kept out. By summer's end of 1875 maybe 1,500 Euro-Americans were wandering the region looking for gold. The majority of these walked or rode from Cheyenne. This Wyoming town had the advantage of rail connections, and the trail to the Hills ran entirely outside of the Great Sioux Reservation. Moreover, Fort Laramie sat about one hundred miles north of Cheyenne, making the first leg of the three hundred-mile journey relatively secure, although the gold seekers needed to keep out of sight of any military patrols. Once in the Hills, the majority went to the original "diggings" on French Creek. They soon discovered that only limited gold existed there, and the quest began for better paying locations. Checking each stream and

Placer mining operation near Deadwood. *Courtesy Adams Museum and House.*

gulch, the prospectors moved north, and by the end of 1875 gold had been located along the streams at Hilyo (Hill City), Sheridan, Pactola, and Deadwood. In this last location, by the end of 1875 perhaps fifty miners were finding gold in some of the richest placer mines in the Black Hills.[23]

While the rush continued, the government appointed scientists Walter P. Jenney and Henry Newton to verify the value of the Black Hills. In part, this was done to determine if the rush would be sustained, and if so, what kind of settlement should be made with the Lakota. They were escorted by Lieutenant Colonel Richard Dodge's command of four hundred soldiers, with California Joe Milner acting as guide. Calamity Jane, disguised in soldier's clothing, joined the party. Despite California Joe's propensity to get lost, and the distraction of Calamity Jane, the explorers moved around the Hills for about four months, beginning in early June. They started in the southern Hills, moving slowly north, eventually reaching the Belle Fourche River. They visited many of the main stream drainages, and in the process they attracted the attention of those already there. Dodge did not threaten to remove them, and indeed Newton and Jenney wanted to find out what the prospectors knew. In fact, the military men provided some protection for the trespassers.[24]

Newton and Jenney did not speak highly of the Black Hills' gold prospects. Colonel Dodge reinforced what they said by declaring that "pan mining will pay nowhere in the Hills." California Joe most cogently reported what they all believed: "there's gold from the grass roots down, but there's more gold from the grass roots up," meaning that agricultural pursuits promised greater rewards. Considering where they went in the Hills, their negative view of potential gold was accurate. They missed the richest diggings on Whitewood and Deadwood Creeks, and they did not test any hard-rock outcroppings. But, as Dodge forecasted, the negative reports did not dampen the enthusiasm Americans had for the Black Hills.[25]

While the Newton-Jenney Expedition moved about the Hills, General Crook entered the region in July to uphold the treaty obligations and remove the miners. While Crook felt that his task was essential, he did not do it because he believed in the sanctity of the treaty. Crook felt the Hills should be removed from Indian territory, but the army needed to eject the trespassers as a gesture of good faith while the negotiations went on. Crook met with the prospectors and convinced several hundred to leave, with the understanding that their claims would be valid once the Hills were legally opened, and that a number of men could remain behind to guard the claims. Once out of the Hills, Crook released the miners if they promised not to return to the area until a treaty had been signed. Naturally, a number of men made such a promise and then promptly made for the Hills again.[26]

While Crook removed trespassers, the federal government took steps to wrest the control of the Black Hills from the Sioux. In September 1875 federal commissioners called a council for the Red Cloud Agency on the White River in Nebraska. In response, about twenty thousand Sioux showed up to hear the negotiators offer to buy the Hills for $6 million. Failing with this, they next proposed to rent the region for $400,000 a year. The Indians counter-offered with demands for a payment of $70 million. In reality, most of the Lakota had no intention of vacating the Black Hills and negotiations collapsed.[27]

With the failure of an agreement, President Grant and other federal officials decided to give in to the inevitable. In violation of the Treaty of 1868, they secretly ordered the federal troops to stop patrolling the Black Hills in November 1875. In other words, the government unofficially opened the gold field to the prospectors. While the government made no announcement of this change in policy, it soon became evident, and more gold seekers flooded in.[28]

Where the government had failed to control the white invaders, it decided instead to control the Lakota. Since the Treaty of 1868, American settlers had complained of Indian attacks, most often committed by Lakota not living around an agency, but residing in the unceded Indian territory of Wyoming. And the violence only multiplied as the whites invaded the Hills. With the number of gold seekers increasing, the government ordered all Indians to report to the agencies by January 31, 1876. If they did not, they would be considered hostile, and the army would treat them as such.[29]

When the end of January passed, the army officials prepared to march against what they saw as recalcitrant Indians. In fact, many Lakota had not got the message, others could not and would not leave their winter camp, and others did not want to go to an agency that they already knew lacked adequate food. Then as spring came, more Sioux left the agencies for the hunting grounds in Wyoming. They joined with the Indians already there, making for a force of about 3,500 warriors to defend their homeland and ward off attack. The army launched its assault from three directions in the spring, with the fight culminating in the Battle of the Little Bighorn and the demise of Custer and much of his command on June 25, 1876.[30]

By the time of Custer's death, the Hills held perhaps as many as fifteen thousand gold seekers, and the news of his defeat sent waves of panic through the miners. They expected the Sioux warriors to sweep down on the Hills and take out their vengeance upon the trespassers. To bring a measure of safety, the towns formed irregular volunteer troops. When tensions started rising in April of 1876, the men living in the town of Custer formed a militia they called the "Custer Minute Men." The death of Custer gave their efforts a new urgency, and other gold camps soon formed militias of their own. Deadwood not only organized a unit, but in an act of bravado, the miners there apparently offered bounties for the heads of Indians. In Spearfish and Rapid City, on the edge of the Hills, the local citizens built stockades.[31]

Despite the efforts to bring some security, death stalked the trails and the region around the Hills in 1876, before and after Little Bighorn. Estimates run as high as one hundred whites killed from Indian attacks in that year, with the most famous incident happening not far from Deadwood. Henry Weston Smith, better known as Preacher Smith, was killed while he was on his way to Crook City. The people of Deadwood still today recall this popular frontier preacher. But, in this frontier environment, not all deaths can be unilaterally blamed on Indians. Many whites came to the Hills to take advantage of the wide-open atmosphere and the lack of law and order. These men could, and did, kill people and then disguise the murders so that Indians would get the blame. During these early years of the Black Hills gold rush, wise prospectors sought security in numbers, and they sought stability in their community, however mobile it may have been.[32]

The events of 1876 convinced Congress that it was time to take the Black Hills from the Sioux. In August Congress voted to cut off food and rations to the Lakota until they agreed to relinquish the region. Commissioners took the imposed settlement to the reservation, and with the threat of starvation a number of Lakota agreed. The number, however, never reached the three-quarters adult male population as prescribed in the Fort Laramie Treaty of 1868. The commissioners were satisfied, however, and Congress ratified what became known as the Black Hills Cession of 1877. The document not only took the Black Hills, but it also closed the unceded lands in Wyoming to Indians and authorized the construction of three roads across the reservation. In return the Indians received 900,000 acres of additional grazing land on the north side of the reservation, and a continuation of the promises made in 1868: education, farm assistance, and support. The illegal taking of the Black Hills still angers many Lakota today.[33]

By the time of the Black Hills Cession, the gold rush had fully developed, and had focused on the richest locations along Deadwood and Whitewood creeks in the northern Hills. In just six miles of creek bed, prospectors found enough gold to make the gold rush worthwhile. Many areas of the West showed small amounts of gold, and these initial discoveries started gold rushes. But small discoveries cannot support a gold rush for long. What kept a gold rush going and made it a success was the discovery of paying locations—where enough gold existed to allow for a good return on labor. Deadwood and Whitewood creeks offered that kind of return. Without these paying locations, it is possible that the Black Hills gold rush would have faded into obscurity and been a footnote in western history.

Prospectors such as Frank Bryant and Alfred Gay first uncovered the wealth of these northern streams in late 1875. They were not alone, however, and these early arrivals knew what they needed to do to protect their finds. All prospectors knew they needed to stake a claim, but to make that claim valid where no governmental authority existed, they had to establish the rules and regulations of a mining district. Four mining districts encompassed the richest areas of the creeks, such as the Lost Mining District and the Deadwood District. The district rules included defining the size of mineral claims, and those in the northern Black Hills were generous. They ran three hundred feet along the creek and extended from rim to rim in the gulch. The mining district also established a miners' court to handle disputes. In many ways, the mining districts brought order and stability to the mineral frontier, and the first arrivals craved this stability because they knew that thousands of other men would be close behind them, wanting their share of the gold. The mining district gave legitimacy to an essentially illegal activity and put in place a common credo of the West: "first in time, first in right."[34]

With such large claims, prospectors rapidly staked out the valuable mineral ground. By early 1876, a few hundred prospectors had staked claim to every foot of placer ground. In placer mining, these men were looking for the loose nuggets, flakes, or specks of gold that collected on bedrock in a stream drainage. The gold seekers needed to dig through tons of unwanted dirt to reach the bedrock and the wanted pay streak. Once uncovered, the valuable dirt could be run through a variety of appliances to recover the gold. These tools included a gold pan, rocker box, sluice box, and a long tom. No matter the piece of equipment, the goal was the same—get the gold out of the dirt. Since gold had the highest specific gravity of anything else in the stream bed, gravity allowed all of these appliances to work. But prospectors often used a little mercury to further ensure their success. Gold amalgamates with mercury, allowing it to be more easily separated from the unwanted material. But mercury was expensive and easily lost if handled incorrectly.[35]

In April 1876 the city of Deadwood was laid out at the confluence of Deadwood and Whitewood creeks, but it was just one of a number of towns that popped up in the area, including Central City, Gayville, Montana City, Elizabethtown, Ingleside, Pluma, and Gold Run. Thousands of men came to these camps, some say as many as ten thousand, but more realistically, perhaps five thousand arrived in the gulch. Some of these came with the hope of making their own big strike, but since they got there a little late, they had to look beyond the Deadwood area. However, no other great placer finds were made. As hope for new discoveries faded, the prospectors tried other avenues to wealth. Some bought claims, some leased them, and others went to work for those who already owned claims. The claims were so large that owners often hired crews to work the ground. For instance, one claim owner regularly employed from sixteen to thirty men. And some

Early Deadwood's main street, laid out in April of 1876. Opportunistic merchants prospered by selling goods at inflated prices to the gold miners. *Courtesy Adams Museum and House.*

who did not get a claim the honest way would "jump" a claim, using either force or legal tricks to separate the claim from its original owner.[36]

Many came to the Hills not to dig in the dirt, but to "mine the miners." Selling goods at premium prices in the gold fields brought many opportunistic merchants to the new town of Deadwood. In fact, the people who became famous in Deadwood for making money did not prosper by panning gold but by selling goods. Seth Bullock and Sol Star came as business partners, arriving on August 1, 1876. They soon opened a hardware store which served as the foundation for a variety of business activities throughout the northern Hills. Other arrivals of 1876 included Jacob Goldberg, who entered the grocery business, and James K. P. Miller, who also started a grocery, along with an exchange bank where the prospectors could bring their gold dust. Over the next few years other famous Deadwood citizens would arrive. W. E. Adams came in 1877 to open a grocery store, the Chinese merchant Fee Lee "Wing Tsue" Wong arrived in 1878, and the liquor dealer Harris Franklin came in 1879. All of these men would ultimately do better than most of the prospectors.

Along with the prospectors and merchants were a number of other people who came for the excitement or saw an opportunity to make some money by participating in the lower forms of entertainment. Saloons, gambling houses, and dance halls stretched up and down Deadwood's developing Main Street, and here a hard-luck prospector could find the card tables, liquor, and ladies to ease his problems. The Gem Theater stood out as perhaps Deadwood's most notorious dance hall, with a combination of entertainment, liquor, and prostitution. Two of Deadwood's most famous early residents came for this type of activity. James Butler "Wild Bill" Hickok came to Deadwood from Cheyenne in June 1876, reportedly to do some gold prospecting. But he spent his time gambling until August 2 when Jack McCall placed a bullet in the back of his head. "Calamity Jane"

Canary also spent time in Deadwood working as a prostitute and hustling drinks from the predominantly male population. Legend sometimes connects Wild Bill and Calamity Jane as close friends or even lovers. But beyond a probable passing acquaintanceship, they did not associate, and Jane moved in and out of Deadwood over the years. She became a permanent resident only in 1903 when she died at the nearby town of Terry, and was buried next to Wild Bill at Mount Moriah cemetery.[37]

Beyond prospectors, merchants, and the infamous, gold-rush Deadwood attracted a very diverse population. While a number of women arrived to work as prostitutes, other women came, most often accompanying their husbands. These women undertook a variety of tasks that brought a more genteel world to Deadwood, such as teaching school. By October 1876 Deadwood had as many as sixty school-age children but no functioning school until the coming January. The gold camp also attracted Chinese. By 1876 the Asians had worked in every gold camp of the West, as well as along the railroads. As soon as the Black Hills boomed, Chinese began arriving, and by 1877 a Chinatown had developed in lower Deadwood. Here a few entered retail business, such as Fee Lee Wong, but most of the two hundred or so Chinese took on tasks in the service industry, such as washing clothes. African Americans also appeared in town, numbering less than one hundred in 1877, and like the Chinese, many of them lived in lower Deadwood in an area known as Elizabethtown. They, too, generally took service jobs. But some African Americans and Chinese did try their hand at panning gold.[38]

The placer gold deposits along Deadwood and Whitewood creeks produced perhaps as much as $1.5 million in 1876, and this increased to $2 million in 1877. But all good prospectors knew that the placer gold in those creek beds had to come from someplace else. They understood that their gold nuggets were once part of a larger vein of gold ore, and that the slow process of erosion had freed the gold from the vein and carried it to the creek. While some prospectors chose to work placer deposits, others went up and down the mountainsides to find the source of the gold. These prospectors were hoping to make the one great find, the mother lode of the mining district.[39]

As the prospectors surveyed Deadwood and Whitewood creeks, they recognized that these streams became barren of gold at particular points. Along Deadwood Creek the gold disappeared just above the mining camp of Central City. As they followed Whitewood Creek, the gold seekers noticed that the trend of gold went up a small creek, Gold Run Creek, that fed into Whitewood Creek. Near the head of Gold Run Gulch a group of miners laid out the camp of Washington, commemorating the nation's centennial. Washington and Central City sat to the southwest of Deadwood and were about one mile apart, separated by some mountains. The trend of the placer gold pointed to these mountains, and in the spring of 1876 a number of prospectors were camped in the area, waiting for the snow to melt before they began exploring the hillsides.

Among those waiting for spring were Fred and Moses Manuel, Hank Harney, and Alex Engh. These four men came to Deadwood Gulch as partners in 1875 and decided to seek out the source of the placer gold. The Manuel brothers arrived in the Hills with a long history of prospecting, having spent time in nearly every gold field of the West. Immediately before coming to the Black Hills, they were working ground in Montana. In early 1876 they found themselves in Bobtail Gulch, a small offshoot of Deadwood Gulch. Here they searched for the ore outcropping. While the winter hindered their efforts, they did manage to stake a small claim in Bobtail Gulch, later called the Golden Terra. Not satisfied with this discovery, the men kept on looking as the weather permitted.[40]

The four partners began searching as the snow started to melt. As Moses later reported: "I saw some quartz in the bottom [of the draw] and water running over it. I took a pick and tried to get some out and found it very solid, but I got some out and took it to camp and pounded it up and panned it and found it very rich. Next day Hank Harney consented to come and located what we called the Homestake, the 9th of April, 1876."[41] The Homestake claim sat above Gold Run Gulch, and its name indicated the men's faith that the claim would pay their way home.

The next day they began working what would become the Black Hills' and North America's greatest gold mine. The original Homestake location was only one of over two hundred claims that prospectors would eventually stake along what became known as the Homestake lode. It was this large ore outcropping that had supplied the placer gold in Whitewood and Deadwood creeks. On the Homestake claim, the Manuel partners promptly dug a discovery shaft, as was required to hold a hard-rock mining claim, and in the process took out a very rich two-hundred-pound chunk of gold ore. They soon recognized the extent of the quartz outcropping and began running an open cut to remove as much ore as possible, starting the Homestake open cut that would eventually become the northern Hills' most famous piece of landscape. The men also staked out an adjoining claim they called the Old Abe.[42]

With the mountainsides attracting so much attention, a number of men decided to lay out another townsite in the gulch below the heaviest mining activity. They named their gold camp Lead City, after the number of ore outcroppings or "leads" found in the area. By 1877 the town included the area around Gold Run Creek, the town of Washington, and the neighboring mountainsides. Although established in the heat of a mineral rush, Lead did not take on the boom attitude of Deadwood. The prospectors that came to the Homestake Lode and Lead knew that it was hard work to get a hard-rock claim to pay. The men lucky enough to have placer claims in Deadwood got their wealth as soon as they dug the gold out of the creek bed. A hard-rock claim required much more work. The ore needed to be mined and then crushed before it released its gold. This operation required time, equipment, and money. Most men working hard-rock claims, such as Fred and Moses Manuel, hoped to work their claims just enough to prove their potential value. They would then sell them at the best possible price and leave the development to moneyed capitalists.[43]

Lead City then did not resemble Deadwood; it did not explode into the rowdy boomtown that its neighbor two miles to the east did. No Wild Bills or Calamity Janes made Lead famous, and the town did not even attract the number of merchants that Deadwood did. In fact, only one prominent merchant emerged in Lead's early years: Peter A. Gushurst. Mr. Gushurst came to Deadwood from Cheyenne in March 1876 and opened the Big Horn grocery. But with the creation of Lead in August 1876, he sold his Deadwood store and moved up the hill, believing a better opportunity existed in that hard-rock town. Besides Gushurst, the history of Lead became completely entwined with the history of the Homestake Mining Company.[44]

The Manuels and their partners worked the Homestake and their other claims for about a year before selling them. They sold the Golden Terra for $35,000 to investors from Cheyenne and Denver and entertained offers for the Homestake and Old Abe claims. In the spring of 1877, L. D. Kellogg appeared in Lead to look over the properties. He offered the miners a bond of $70,000 for the Homestake claim, meaning he had thirty days to come up with the money. Kellogg was not a mining capitalist; however, he was acting on behalf of a group of California investors led by George Hearst. Kellogg's report motivated Hearst to come to the Black Hills, and when he examined the property, he agreed with Kellogg's assessment, and paid the price. In the meantime, the Manuel brothers sold the Old Abe for $45,000 to another investor. These two sales netted the Manuels what all prospectors wanted, a handsome payoff.[45]

Hearst came to the Black Hills with the wealth and experience to craft a great mine. Earlier in his career, he made money in the Mother Lode country of California and then hit it big on the Comstock Lode of Nevada. He went from there to invest in mines in Idaho, Montana, and Utah. But Hearst did not invest alone. He had two partners, Lloyd Tevis, who was president of Wells Fargo Express and Banking Company, and James Ben Ali Haggin, a land speculator in California. In their arrangement, Hearst apparently owned fifty percent of the company, Haggin thirty percent, and Tevis the remaining twenty percent. Certainly, Hearst dominated the organization. He incorporated the Homestake Mining Company in the state of California on November 5, 1877, and then aggressively pursued all neighboring claims, using every method at his disposal, from payment to threats. And he soon brought in the equipment necessary to treat large quantities of ore. In early 1878 an eighty-stamp mill, used to crush the ore to a powder, arrived from San Francisco. With each stamp weighing between eight hundred and one thousand pounds, transporting the equipment by wagon train from the Union Pacific Railroad station in Sidney, Nebraska, represented a major undertaking. While Hearst sought a monopoly on the Homestake lode, other companies did manage to operate on the gold vein, such as the Golden Star, the Highland Chief, and the Father De Smet, at least for a time. But by the end of 1881, Hearst had gained control of most of the Homestake lode.[46]

While several hundred men worked for a variety of companies on the Homestake lode in the late 1870s, many other miners still worked the placers in Deadwood and at other locations around the Hills. Off of the Homestake lode and just north of Central City, another type of ore deposit was located. Here placer gold had recombined with country rock in a type of metamorphic rock. This activity formed deposits of what was known as conglomerate ore. Soon after gold was discovered in Deadwood Creek, a number of mines opened on these deposits, such as the Ismerelda and the Keats. This ore needed to be crushed for treatment, and hundreds of small stamp mills popped up in this area, as well as on the Homestake lode itself.[47]

Away from the Lead/Deadwood area, many prospectors continued to look for the next great placer deposit or another Homestake lode. North of the towns, prospectors repeatedly sought gold in a creek they called False Bottom because they believed that the precious metal was hidden beneath a layer of bedrock. No gold was ever found. To the south and west of Lead, the country rock showed signs of mineralization, and two mining districts were created, the Bald Mountain and Ruby Basin, and the town of Terry was located nearby; but little gold could be recovered. Much further to the west, close to the Wyoming border, prospectors found gold in a series of adjoining gulches, Potato, Bear, and African gulches, but nothing near what they found in Deadwood. Five miles south of Deadwood, miners found some values in Bear Butte Creek, and the town of Galena was established. Again, the prospectors were disappointed in the quantity of gold. The town, however, took its name from silver ore they found, and the miners struggled unsuccessfully for some time to recover the silver. And then sixteen miles south of Lead, Richard B. Hughes and Michael D. Rochford founded Rochford in the center of a new mining district in 1877. But none of these areas came close to equaling the excitement or values coming from Lead and Deadwood.[48]

One of the more unique mining undertakings of 1876 happened at Rockerville, about fifty miles south of Deadwood near the eastern edge of the Hills. Here miners found gold, but they lacked the water necessary to run the placer gravel through their gold rockers (the namesake of the town). In 1878 the Black Hills Placer Mining Company under the direction of Ambrose Bierce built a seventeen-mile flume from Spring Creek near Sheridan to the Rockerville diggings. The company recovered about $500,000 in gold, but the flume cost $300,000 to build and caused an unending amount of annoyance to Ambrose Bierce, who left the Hills and later became a famous author of short stories.[49]

On the edge of the Hills other towns had been organized during the gold rush that did not deal directly in gold. Nine miles northeast of Deadwood was Crook City. It sat where a trail left the plains to begin its hard, uphill haul to Deadwood. Teams, teamsters, and wagon trains began forming up there as soon as the northern Hills exploded in activity, but it soon lost its prominence as other trails opened into Deadwood. One was the Centennial Trail, which left the valley four miles west of Crook City.[50]

Spearfish, on the northern edge of the Hills, and Rapid City on the east provided auxiliary services to the gold-rush communities. A group from Montana founded Spearfish in early 1876, envisioning wealth not from digging gold, but by selling agricultural products to the hungry miners. Soon they diverted water from Spearfish Creek through a series of irrigation ditches, and farms appeared down Spearfish valley. Along Rapid Creek in the central Hills, John Brennan had a similar vision. From time he spent in Denver, Brennan knew the value of gold-rush service centers, and after he came to the Hills in late 1875, and failing at prospecting, he decided to create his own version of Denver in the Black Hills. Brennan and a few associates laid out Rapid City in early 1876, and hoped to sell lots in what they were sure would be the next metropolis of the West. Rapid City initially struggled because of its distance from the big excitement at Deadwood, but by 1878 the town began stabilizing as stagecoaches started stopping there, farmers and ranchers began using the fertile valley land, and placer miners worked Rapid Creek above town; and it became the county seat of Pennington County. Rapid City soon acquired the nickname of "Hay Camp."[51]

Between Spearfish and Rapid City developed Sturgis, another type of auxiliary town. By 1878 army officials and politicians had heard so many calls for protection from Black Hills settlers that they authorized a military post near Bear Butte. As construction began on Fort Meade, entrepreneurs established Sturgis to profit from the military men. The town soon got a reputation for taking soldiers' pay, and it earned the title of "Scooptown." Prostitution, gambling, and alcohol put Sturgis on the map, and it eventually became associated with one of the Black Hills' most famous woman gamblers and madams, Poker Alice Tubbs.[52]

By 1880 about fifteen recognizable towns existed in the Black Hills, serving a variety of functions. Some of these came with the first wave of the gold rush, such as Custer and Hill City, and after five years they survived but did not boom. For instance, Custer had 271 people in 1880. Spearfish and Rapid City started as service centers, and by 1880 they held 170 and 292 people respectively. By far, the locations around the Homestake belt had the greatest concentrations of Black Hills' residents. The census taker found about 16,500 people in the Black Hills region in 1880, and nearly 9,000 of those lived in the Lead/Deadwood/Central City area, or "around the belt." In specific numbers, Lead had 1,437 people and Deadwood 3,777. The remainder lived in Central City, Terraville, or scattered between the towns. Despite a significant population base in the northern Hills, and four years of proven gold production, no railroad companies had built to the Black Hills. The large Hills' population still had to rely on wagons to provide their needs, but travelers could select from a variety of routes.[53]

Certainly, when the rush began, prospectors came to the Hills from all directions, regardless of trails, but soon four improved trails led to and from the area. As previously mentioned, the trail from Cheyenne gathered much of the early business, and in 1876 the Cheyenne and Black Hills Stage Line initiated stagecoach runs. In late 1876 a trail from Sidney, Nebraska, opened as entrepreneurs completed a toll bridge across the North Platte River. Like Cheyenne, Sidney sat on the Union Pacific Railroad and hence had good connections to the east and west. But this trail soon challenged Cheyenne's popularity because it was a little shorter, and because it had a more direct shot to the markets in Lead and Deadwood. The Sidney trail ran up the eastern side of the Hills, and then it had only about nine miles of mountainous terrain before reaching Deadwood. The Cheyenne trail had a more difficult time winding its way through the Hills. The Sidney trail became a particular favorite among freighters who hauled such heavy items as the Homestake stamp mill.[54]

Other routes to the Black Hills did not depend on the Union Pacific railroad. Gold seekers from Minneapolis rode the Northern Pacific to Bismarck and took a trail to Deadwood from there. Freight wagons began using the trail in late 1876, and it was soon recognized as the shortest route to the Hills. This advantage motivated some investors to organize the Northwestern Express, Stage and Transportation Company in the spring of 1877. They aspired to run a stagecoach day and night to cut the trip that took the Cheyenne stage four-and-a-half days down to less than two days. While the stage seldom made it in two days, the Northwestern company kept operating this route until 1880, when a railroad arrived at Pierre and made the Pierre to Deadwood trail the shortest route.[55]

Since 1874, when the Gordon Party left Sioux City, Iowa, promoters in that town wanted a connection to the Hills. But that required a road across the Great Sioux Reservation. Permission for a road came with the Black Hills Cession of 1877. Travelers arrived at Sioux City via a train, took a steamboat to Fort Pierre, and then headed overland to the Hills. When the Chicago and North Western Railroad arrived in Pierre in 1880, the Sioux City connection became unnecessary, and the Northwestern Express company took advantage of the shorter distance and moved its operations from Bismarck

Mountain railroading ca. 1900. The completion of two railroads into Deadwood in 1890 and 1891 revolutionized the economy of the northern Black Hills. *Courtesy Adams Museum and House and Colorado State Historical Society.*

to Pierre. All of these wagon routes became unnecessary, however, when a railroad finally reached the Black Hills in the mid-1880s.[56]

By the time railroads reached the Hills, the gold rush had long been over. In fact, when the census taker came through in 1880, he caught the tail-end of the gold rush. Beginning in 1881, the amount of gold produced in the Black Hills decreased every year for the next six years. Certainly the mines on the Homestake belt kept producing substantial amounts of precious metal. Here consolidation had been Hearst's driving principal, and by 1881 he had acquired controlling interests in at least seven other mining companies that worked along the ore body. While the mines near Lead continued to produce, gold fields elsewhere in the Hills yielded little. The Deadwood placers had played out, and the gold ore found in the Ruby Basin, Bald Mountain, Galena, and Carbonate districts had been labeled as refractory since it would not release its precious metal by using the available recovery methods. Deadwood especially suffered as a fire destroyed the town in 1879, causing many residents to leave. Outside of Lead, economic doldrums threatened most of the Black Hills' communities as the decade of the eighties began.[57]

Many people who had come to the Hills during 1876 were gone by 1880. Of the thousands who sought gold, very few found any, and of those who did, none became prominent in Black Hills society. Either they left with their fortunes, as did the Manuels, or they lost it at the card tables before they could get away. Two types of people found long-term success in the Black Hills: businessmen in Deadwood, such as Seth Bullock and James K. P. Miller, and outside investors such as George Hearst and his partners in California. Those who did not find the riches may have gone home no better off than they arrived. Like many thousands of gold seekers in other gold rushes, they failed in their quest for wealth, but they certainly returned home with experiences, memories, and stories of the last gold frontier that would permanently enrich their lives.

As economic doldrums hit the Black Hills in the 1880s, the businesses of Deadwood should seemingly have been immune to the problems as several hundred miners lived only a few miles away in Lead, Central City, and Terraville. Yet these people did not need to travel to Deadwood to shop since they could go to the company store, the Hearst Mercantile, which the Homestake built in 1879. Here the miners and their families found what they wanted, bought it on credit, and avoided the three-mile trip to Deadwood, especially important since all roads to Deadwood were toll roads.[58]

At this critical juncture in Deadwood's existence, a group of its leading citizens, including Seth Bullock, Sol Star, James K. P. Miller, and Harris Franklin, stepped forward to save their town. In 1881, they organized a Board of Trade with the intent of encouraging enterprise, investment, and development in Deadwood. Their first projects included a twenty-five-page pamphlet advertising the resources of the northern Black Hills, plans to build a free public road from Deadwood to Centennial Prairie, and efforts to gain a railroad connection. By the 1880s all Western towns knew that permanent success came with a railroad, and in 1881 the Homestake began building its logging railroad, called the Black Hills and Fort Pierre. Representatives from the Board of Trade met with Homestake officials to convince them to build into Deadwood. The Homestake managers, however, only had timber on their minds and had no intention of building to Deadwood. Not to be deterred in their quest for progress, the Board of Trade next incorporated a smelter company they called the Deadwood Smelting and Reduction Works, with the hope of building a plant in town. They had heard of successful smelters in Colorado and Omaha and felt that this process could possibly treat the refractory gold ores at Carbonate, Galena, Bald Mountain, and Ruby Basin. And if they could build a successful plant in town, and reawaken these surrounding gold districts, they felt that Deadwood would once again be at the center of Black Hills mining activity.[59]

While some of the Board of Trade's projects succeeded, such as the free road, the rail connections and the smelter became delayed, but Deadwood maintained hope. When the Fremont, Elkhorn and Missouri Valley Railroad (the Elkhorn) began building out of Nebraska and heading for the Black Hills, Franklin and Miller from the Board of Trade met with railroad officials to make sure the Elkhorn would extend its line to Deadwood, but they had little success. The railroad built up the eastern edge of the Black Hills, reaching Rapid City in 1886, and then on to Whitewood in 1887, a town the railroad created. Here the railroad stopped. The rail officials knew they could control the northern Black Hills' business activity from this point, nine miles from Deadwood. They cared little that wagons needed to make the last haul into town.[60]

The Elkhorn's snub caused anguish in Deadwood, but people such as J. K. P. Miller and Harris Franklin would not be deterred. They had originally anticipated the railroad's building into town and had expanded their investments. Franklin bought the Golden Reward mining ground in Ruby Basin, and Miller purchased, with the help of investors known as the Syndicate, Deadwood commercial property. They also helped reinvigorate the Board of Trade's idea to build a smelter in town, except that they changed the process from smelting to a chemical reduction procedure. Nevertheless, when the Elkhorn stopped short of town, these investors went ahead with their planned projects. The Board of Trade built the Deadwood Reduction Works, finishing it in early 1889; Miller and his Syndicate constructed a new business block on Main Street called the Syndicate Block in 1888; and Miller decided to build a short-line railroad between Deadwood and Lead, with extensions to the mining ground beyond, calling it the Deadwood Central; and Franklin worked with the reduction works while developing his own mining ground.[61]

Disaster briefly slowed Deadwood's progress when the Deadwood Reduction Works mysteriously burned to the ground in March 1889, but the promoters decided to rebuild. The setback, however, motivated Miller to build his own ore treatment plant, and he built a small smelter, which soon became known as the Deadwood and Delaware Smelter. Franklin took sole control of the reduction works ruins and soon started the Golden Reward Chlorination plant.[62]

This internal activity brought an image of prosperity to Deadwood, and it soon had a positive effect. In late 1889 the Burlington and Missouri River railroad was building out of Nebraska and heading for the Wyoming coalfields. As it passed the southern edge of the Hills, Deadwood's new-found vitality caught the railroad's attention. In fact, Miller had been meeting with Burlington officials trying to convince them to build to Deadwood. The railroad men saw potential in Deadwood, and from Edgemont, a town they created at the southern tip of the Black Hills, the Burlington began building through the center of the Hills, essentially bisecting the Black Hills south to north, going through Custer and Hill City, in 1890. The Fremont, Elkhorn and Missouri Valley soon realized that it was going to lose its northern Hills' monopoly and started building the nine miles from Whitewood to Deadwood. Essentially, the two railroads were racing to Deadwood, and in December 1890 an Elkhorn train pulled in first. Then in January 1891 a Burlington train arrived. With two outside rail connections, Deadwood suddenly saw its future secured. In fact, Mayor Sol Star pronounced that Deadwood had finally become a "city of permanence."[63]

Indeed a new day had arrived for the entire northern Black Hills. Miller bought mining ground in the Ruby Basin and expanded his Deadwood and Delaware Smelter into a large operation. Franklin similarly increased his Golden Reward holdings and enlarged his chlorination works. New mines opened throughout the Bald Mountain and Ruby Basin Mining districts, and in other areas, such as at Carbonate and Galena. Miller's plan for a rail-line from Deadwood to Lead became a reality, and this short interurban carried miners and their families back and forth between the two towns, particularly helping Deadwood's merchants. In addition, Miller's Deadwood Central, with the assistance of the Burlington, built a narrow-gauge railroad into the remote mining districts, soon followed by the Elkhorn's own narrow-gauge line. With new processing plants and railroads running through the gold fields, the value of Black Hills gold production went from $2.4 million in 1887 to over $4 million in 1893.[64]

The railroad construction reinvigorated Black Hills towns and brought new ones into existence. The Burlington helped the economies of Custer and Hill City, and when the Elkhorn and Burlington both built narrow-gauge lines into the heart of the Ruby Basin mining district, the town of Terry went from having just a few souls in the 1880s to being a mining camp of over a thousand people by the early 1890s. The new town of Belle Fourche sprang up along the Belle Fourche River. When the Elkhorn constructed its branch to Deadwood, it also ran a line from Whitewood to the cattle country just north of the Hills. Most folks in the area assumed that the railroad planned to build to the town of Minnesela along the Redwater River. This town developed in the early 1880s, supporting a flour mill, a newspaper, and a number of businesses, and it became the county seat of Butte County. But the Elkhorn did not build to Minnesela. Instead, it built to the new town of Belle Fourche, a few miles west of Minnesela. Seth Bullock and his partner Sol Star ran the S-B Ranch at this location, and they gave the Elkhorn free access to their land. With the railroad in Belle Fourche by 1891, Minnesela's residents began to move there, and Minnesela ultimately collapsed when the county seat went to the new town in 1894.[65]

The railroads and new gold processing plants helped enrich legitimate businessmen such as Bullock and Franklin. But a number of Black Hills entrepreneurs tried to make money in dishonest ways. Black Hills' pioneer Robert Flormann joined forces with a supposed mining expert named Joseph Taylor in 1883 to publicize the Greenwood mine, eighteen miles southeast of Deadwood, as the next Homestake. By cleverly enriching an ore sample with extra chunks of gold, Flormann and Taylor convinced a Chicago investor to spend at least one hundred thousand dollars on the operation. By early 1885, the scam became apparent as the mine produced only five dollars of gold, setting off a firestorm of publicity and litigation that entertained many in the Black Hills.[66]

A scam in the Harney Peak area caused not only a local stir, but brought international attention to the Black Hills. In 1883 reports of a tin strike at the Etta Mine brought investors from New York and then England, all hoping to cash in on the United States' first and only tin deposit. The Harney Peak Tin Company existed in one form or another for over ten years, and during that time it bought hundreds of mining claims, built a mill, hotel, and offices in Hill City, and spent probably three million dollars of investors' money. When the company finally closed in 1893, it had produced only $1,545 worth of tin, ending a decade of intercontinental debate of whether tin actually existed in the Black Hills.[67]

Such failures did not dampen the real success that came to the operating mines of the Hills, and that prosperity got a further boost when the cyanide process of gold ore treatment made it to the region. When handled properly, cyanide will dissolve the vast majority of gold out of ore and then release it later. This technique was discovered in Scotland in 1885 and then slowly spread around the world, arriving in the Black Hills in 1893. After a decade of experimentation, cyanide came to challenge all other ore processes for supremacy. The cyanide method increased the recovery and reduced the cost of ore processing to the point where companies either replaced their old recovery plants, or added cyanide to their on-going activities. The Golden Reward replaced its chlorination plant in lower Deadwood with a cyanide mill in 1903; the Horseshoe-Mogul Mining Company constructed a large cyanide mill in the Ruby Basin and began treating very low-grade ore in 1903; and the Homestake enhanced its operation by building cyanide plants in 1901 and 1902, one in Central City and one in Lead.[68]

While mining companies experimented with the cyanide process, two Black Hills metallurgists emerged to become nationally recognized. John V. N. Dorr came to the Black Hills in 1894 and began working as a chemist and assayer for a number of companies. In 1901 he formed a partnership and built the Lundberg, Dorr and Wilson mill just below Terry in the Ruby Basin. Here he developed an array of equipment that made the cyanide process more efficient, and over the years, his Dorr Thickeners, Dorr Classifiers, and other inventions became known around the world. Similarly, Charles W. Merrill's fame began in the Black Hills. Merrill came to the region at the invitation of the Homestake in 1899, and he soon built an experimental cyanide annex on one of the existing mills. Success there led to the large cyanide plants in Central City and Lead, but the Homestake gave Merrill another assignment. While the addition of the new cyanide plants brought gold recovery to eighty-eight percent of the reported values, the company and Merrill wanted more. He experimented with the mud-like solution that came out of the cyanide plants known as slime, and in 1906 he built the Slime Plant in Deadwood, which captured gold from the mud, bringing recovery to ninety-four percent. After a decade of working in the Hills, Merrill left with an international reputation, and through his and Dorr's efforts, the Black Hills set the standard for modern cyanide milling practices.[69]

With outside rail connections and prosperity all about, Deadwood and Lead lost their frontier pasts and came to resemble urban centers. Large stone buildings replaced the wooden ones, and brick commercial centers popped up. In Deadwood, such buildings appeared as the Federal Courthouse, finished in 1907, and the Lawrence County Courthouse, completed in 1908. Elsewhere around town, local investors built the grand Franklin Hotel in 1903, and W. E. Adams expanded his business block four times by 1903 as his wholesale grocery business continued to grow. Adams would eventually use the profits from his grocery enterprise to build the Adams Memorial Museum across the street from his business block in 1930. And then in the upscale residential neighborhood of Ingleside, Harris Franklin constructed a Victorian mansion for his family in 1892. W. E. Adams bought the home in 1920, and in 2000 it became the Adams House Museum.[70]

■ Timber Industry

While gold stood out as the most obvious draw to the Hills, the logging and timber industry developed as an important adjunct. Entrepreneurs brought steam-powered sawmills to the Hills with the first gold rush, and other mills soon followed. Each Hills town attracted at least one operation, with most locations having multiple ventures. The sawmills produced lumber for houses, businesses, gold mills, and mining appliances such as sluice boxes. The forest also provided vast quantities of wood to burn. Until outside rail connections arrived in late 1890 and coal became available, wood provided all of the heating and energy needs. A large stamp mill consumed eleven cords of wood every twenty-four hours to create the steam that drove the stamps, and with a half-dozen large mills just on the Homestake belt, trees disappeared rapidly in the northern Hills. At first, only large trees were used, the favorite for construction and for use as mine supports, but then loggers moved through the landscape again, clear-cutting everything. The depletion of usable timber in the Lead area motivated the Homestake to begin constructing its logging railroad, the Black Hills and Fort Pierre, in 1881. It ran south and east toward Nemo looking for more wood.[71]

Initially, the mining companies and loggers took the timber from the public domain at will. The federal government recognized this and in 1878 passed the Free Timber Act that accepted the obvious; it allowed free use of the forest, but it also tried, unsuccessfully, to put some limits on harvesting immature trees. The government took a stronger step toward stopping the waste of timber resources with the passage of the Forest Reserve Act of 1891. This law allowed the president to create a forest reserve where timber harvesting would be regulated. The Black Hills remained outside of the law until 1897 when Grover Cleveland created the Black Hills Forest Reserve, ordering an end to timber harvesting within the public domain. Hills residents were outraged, and those who wanted the wood just violated the law and paid the fines when caught. The Homestake had the largest timber demand and the biggest problem. It needed a solution, and began working with the General Land Office. In 1899 they agreed to what became known as Timber Case No. 1. The Homestake bought thousands of trees in the Nemo area, guaranteeing a stable timber supply. The guidelines that went into Timber Case No. 1 established a national precedent, and the same procedures were applied to sales in other Forest Reserves for years to come.[72]

The Homestake's need for resources did not end at timber or gold; it also had a terrible thirst. Water carried the gold pulp through the gold mills; water created the steam in the power stations; and the growing industrial town of Lead needed water. Hearst not only sought other mining companies for their gold in the early years of the Homestake, but he also wanted their water rights. He waged an ugly fight with the Father De Smet mine over water rights in 1879. The Homestake prevailed then, and it succeeded at gaining control of virtually all of the water in the northern Black Hills by the early twentieth century. From the headwaters of Spearfish Creek, Little Rapid Creek, and Whitewood Creek, the Homestake brought in water for its mine plant and for use in Lead and Deadwood. It then used Whitewood Creek below Lead as its drain, dumping thousands of tons of mill tailings into the stream. And along lower Spearfish Creek, the company built two hydroelectric plants, one in 1911 and another in 1917. To make these work, it diverted large portions of the stream. The Homestake used every resource the Black Hills had to offer.[73]

The cyanide process brought prosperity to the gold towns of the Black Hills. By the second decade of the twentieth century, the value of annual gold production exceeded seven million dollars. Lead stood out as the region's largest and most prosperous town. In 1910 Lead had over 8,000 people, while other communities lagged well behind. Deadwood had almost the same number of people in 1910 as it did in 1880, about 3,700. Rapid City had grown to more than 3,800 by 1910, while Sturgis, Belle Fourche, and Spearfish each had less than 2,000. In the southern Hills, towns such as Custer and Hill City numbered under 1,000. Gold was the economic engine of the Black Hills.[74]

A weakness, however, existed in the industry. The federal government had set the price of gold at $20.67 an ounce in 1879, and there it remained. Despite more efficient processes, Black Hills gold companies felt a pinch as expenses went up. When World War I came, escalating labor costs and inflation took a heavy toll. Some gold producers had to close, such as the Golden Reward, the Black Hills' second largest gold operation. This closure shut down mines in the Ruby Basin and gold mills in lower Deadwood. The

Homestake could persevere because of the vastness of the Homestake lode. Still, gold production fell from its former heights. As World War I came to an end, many residents of Deadwood sought another economic support for their town, and they turned to tourism.[75]

■ Tourism

Tourism had always played a role in the economic makeup of the Black Hills. When George Hearst came to Lead to inspect the value of the Homestake claim, he was essentially a tourist, and area promoters saw such visitors as necessary to the region's continuing prosperity. In 1881 the Deadwood Board of Trade published a twenty-five-page booklet entitled the *Black Hills of Dakota* that promoted the wonders of the Hills while trying to attract new investors. Several years later, the Black Hills Mining Men's Association dramatically eclipsed the earlier effort by producing a large volume called the *Black Hills Illustrated* which discussed area towns and several of the more under-capitalized mining operations, hoping again to attract outside money. The number of visitors such publicity attracted was heavily dependent on the ease of transportation. With stagecoach travel the standard in 1881, the visiting public remained small, but with the arrival of outside rail connections in the late 1880s, the Black Hills became much more accessible.[76]

In the early 1890s a variety of venues opened that attracted tourists. In the southern Black Hills, Fred Evans opened a hotel and spa around the hot mineral waters at Hot Springs as both the Burlington and Elkhorn railroads built into town. In the northern Hills, the Burlington built a branch line down Spearfish Canyon in 1893, exposing its wonderful vistas to the traveling public. And then away from rail connections, Custer enthusiasts contracted for the construction of an artificial lake to attract visitors. Sylvan Lake began holding water in 1892, and in 1895 a sixty-room hotel went up next to it. Because it sat several miles from a rail-line, the Sylvan Lake facility struggled to attract guests. In fact, most early tourists were from the area. Residents of Lead and Deadwood began to enjoy the sights along Spearfish Canyon and saw Hot Springs as a welcome change of pace. Many newlyweds spent time there, and the expression "Hot Springs tonight and Deadwood tomorrow" became common.[77]

Improved rail connections came to the Black Hills in 1907 when the Milwaukee Railroad and the Chicago and North Western crossed the Missouri River and built directly to Rapid City. Prior to this, all rail traffic came out of Nebraska, a rather round-about route. The new rail connections had little practical effect on much of the Black Hills, except they made Rapid City the hub for rail-lines, giving that town an economic boost, and they allowed visitors from the Midwest, particularly Chicago, to come more rapidly to the Hills. The better rail connections meant more outside tourists, and they also made rail rates more affordable for the average American. When the first through-train from Chicago arrived in Deadwood in 1907, the locals celebrated as they had fifteen years before when trains first arrived in town. Both tourists and business people enjoyed the new speed and convenience.[78]

The rail travelers who came to the Hills in the early twentieth century most often came for the mountain scenery and healthy climate. Trains would often deposit the visitors in Rapid City, and then motor coaches would take them to a mountain retreat. But new attractions were soon added to the vacation get-away. In 1903 the federal government acquired Wind Cave and set aside over 10,000 acres around it as a game reserve. Near Wind Cave, the state of South Dakota negotiated a swap of state lands for a block of over 60,000 acres of federal forest land in 1911. Two years later the state legislature,

Rail passengers dressed in their finery visit the Black Hills. With the coming of rail service in the 1890s, the Black Hills became a popular tourist destination. *Center for Western Studies.*

led by Peter Norbeck, made this a game preserve. From this point on, Norbeck worked to make the preserve a key attraction as Custer State Park. In 1914 he personally supervised building a fence around the park. Six years later he promoted federal legislation that added to the preserve another 30,000 acres of federal land, which contained Sylvan Lake and the Needles. And then in 1922 Norbeck helped lay out the highway through the Needles, ensuring visitor accessibility.[79]

As mentioned before, Deadwood's economic slip in the early 1920s motivated residents there to search for other economic supports, and tourism appeared as a viable option. The town had good rail connections, and local promoters worked to open the area for automobile travel. Throughout the 1910s, Lawrence County had turned old wagon roads into improved highways. By 1919 the county bragged of having the best roads in western South Dakota and reported tourists coming from all over the United States. Deadwood recognized that it had an attraction in its Wild West past and decided to exploit it. Beginning in 1922, Deadwood enthusiasts sponsored races and contests on the Fourth of July, and this soon turned into the annual Days of '76. This event combined the lore of Wild Bill and Calamity Jane with the activities of a rodeo. In reality, little in Deadwood's past hearkens back to the cowboy West, but in the 1920s this romantic interpretation of the past was more appealing than the gold frontier.[80]

Over the following decades, Deadwood continued to highlight its frontier past. Some merchants covered the fronts of their brick buildings with log siding, and the famous Old Style bar opened its main-street location in 1938, combining images of cowboys on bucking broncos with gold picks and pans. And Deadwood found a new character to symbolize its past, Potato Creek Johnny Perrett. In 1929 he showed up in town with the largest gold nugget ever found in the Black Hills, weighing 7.75 ounces. Johnny claimed to have found the specimen on Potato Creek, fifteen miles west of Deadwood. Some skeptics, however, argue that Johnny manufactured the large nugget from many small ones. Nevertheless, his nugget, and his authentic prospector look, made him an instant attraction. The Chamber of Commerce hired Johnny to demonstrate gold panning, tell tall tales, and in general make the West come alive. Before he died in 1943, Johnny came to epitomize Deadwood's frontier past.[81]

While Deadwood built on its western past, South Dakota State Historian Doane Robinson envisioned a grander tourist attraction in the southern Black Hills. In 1923 he advanced the idea of carving Wild West figures in the granite spires of the Needles. The next year, Robinson contacted Gutzon Borglum about carving his project. The noted artist was working on a Confederate memorial at Stone Mountain, Georgia, but problems there encouraged him to visit South Dakota. Soon, Borglum expanded the idea from local to national heroes, and he wanted a larger format than the Needles. He identified a granite cropping known as Mount Rushmore as perfect for the undertaking. On this mountain, Borglum envisioned the heads and upper torsos of four presidents, an entablature where the great events of America's past were recorded, and a hall of records that would house significant historical documents. But funding problems allowed only the heads to be finished by the time the project shut down in 1941.[82]

The project might have died a quick death, except for a boost it received in 1927. In that year, South Dakota's congressional delegation, led by Peter Norbeck, convinced President Calvin Coolidge to spend much of his summer in the Black Hills. Norbeck and his associates wanted to show Coolidge South Dakota's agricultural problems first-hand, hoping the president would approve farm legislation, but they also hoped the publicity would be a boon for tourism. While Mr. and Mrs. Coolidge headquartered at the State Game Lodge in Custer State Park, they traveled extensively around the region. One of those trips was to Mount Rushmore, where Coolidge gave a speech and a few drills to Borglum. In his speech, the president essentially promised federal support, and then the sculptor ascended the mountain and drilled the master points for the face of George Washington. As Gilbert Fite comments, "The President's visit . . . was a turning point in the history of Mount Rushmore." It put the monument and the Black Hills in the nation's consciousness.[83]

Congress, however, would not support the carving of Mount Rushmore completely, or without much discussion. Fortunately for the monument's supporters, the Great Depression inspired a new day of federal spending, and as Congress spent millions funding a variety of work projects, it periodically gave money to the Rushmore project. Without the New Deal mentality or generosity, Mount Rushmore may not have advanced beyond the Washington and Jefferson heads.[84]

Just as Mount Rushmore progressed during the Great Depression, parts of the Black Hills witnessed a new day of prosperity during much of the 1930s. This situation stood in stark contrast to that in the rest of South Dakota, where hard times reigned. The federal government took two types of actions which helped the Black Hills. In the first place, the government operated a number of work projects in and around the Hills. The Civilian Conservation Corps (CCC) established eighteen camps in the Black Hills employing nearly 3,000 young men by the end of 1933. These workers built a number of projects that would have a lasting benefit for the Hills' recreation industry, including small reservoirs, roads, and picnic areas. In addition, the CCC thinned tree stands and made other forest improvements to diminish the chance of fire and enhance the

Since its completion by Gutzon Borglum in 1941, the Mount Rushmore sculpture has proven to be the most popular tourist attraction in the Black Hills and in all of South Dakota. *Center for Western Studies.*

forest's health. The Works Progress Administration (WPA) also had a large role in the Black Hills, completing at least nine projects, including Dinosaur Park in Rapid City, which has educated and entertained three generations of young people.[85]

Where the CCC and WPA offered work relief, the Roosevelt administration created hundreds of jobs when it raised the price of gold from $20.67 to $35 an ounce in 1934. Roosevelt's higher price brought a new enthusiasm for the yellow metal. Modern-day prospectors set up placer operations along Black Hills streams, and long-forgotten mines reopened. Most importantly, the Homestake dramatically expanded its operation. During the 1930s, the mining company sank the Ross and Yates shafts, expanded the South Mill, constructed the Kirk Power Plant, and undertook a housing project in Lead. These activities, among others, transformed the look and operation of the Homestake mine plant, and the company used these facilities until the mine ceased operation in 2001.[86]

■ World War II and After

Where federal actions brought a flurry of activity to the Black Hills during the 1930s, the government then squelched that activity in the early 1940s. World War II naturally ended the New Deal programs, but the government also took a step that killed gold mining. In 1942 the War Production Board labeled gold mining as a non-essential industry and ordered its suspension. The board anticipated that the 2,200 miners would move to mining areas that produced strategic metals, such as copper in Butte, Montana. An estimated 1,600 workers did leave Lead as the Homestake and other mines closed, but most went to the Pacific coast and the more lucrative war-manufacturing industry. Some odd jobs remained in Lead. For instance, in 1944 and 1945 the company made hand grenades in its machine shop.[87]

While the war order turned Lead into a virtual ghost town, and Deadwood went into a slump, other places in the Black Hills fared better. Sawmills in such places as Spearfish worked at full capacity supporting the nation's military construction, and some of that construction went on in the Black Hills area. Most notably, the Army Air Corps built a base east of Rapid City in 1942. In a two-ocean war, the Army Air Corps wanted training bases with plenty of flying room removed from the coasts, and West River South Dakota provided that. By mid-1943, over 5,000 military personnel were assigned to the new air base as part of a B-17 training program. When dependents and civilian employees are added in, the economic importance of the facility cannot be underestimated. The operation doubled Rapid City's population. Where the town had not prospered during the 1930s, World War II brought flush times. Elsewhere in the Hills, the War Department turned Fort Meade over to the Veterans Administration in 1944, and German prisoners of war began converting and expanding the facility.[88]

Soon after the war ended, these operations became permanent additions to Rapid City and Sturgis. While the air base seemed on the verge of closing at the end of World War II, the advent of the Cold War brought new life. The recently created U.S. Air Force took control of the airfield in 1948 and continued using it for bombers. For much of the 1950s, the base serviced B-36 Peacemakers, followed by B-52 Stratofortresses. In 1953 President Eisenhower dedicated the base as Ellsworth Air Force Base to honor a fallen base commander, and then in the 1960s, the Air Force placed missiles under the base's command, Titan Missiles in 1962 and Minuteman Missiles shortly after. At Sturgis, the creation of a veterans hospital gave a surplus, out-of-date cavalry post a new lease on life. The facility opened as a neuropsychiatric hospital, but it soon expanded into general medicine and surgery, with a large building complex.[89]

The post-war years were not as kind to Lead and Deadwood as they failed to return to their prewar levels of economic activity. While the Homestake reopened, only one other gold company attempted any mining in the Black Hills after the war, and then with only limited success. From population peaks in 1940, both of these northern Hills towns steadily lost population in the decades that followed. In 1940 Lead had over 7,500 people and Deadwood 4,100; a decade later those numbers dropped to near 6,400 and 3,300 respectively. On the other hand, Sturgis noticed a slight upswing, going from just at 3,000 in 1940 to near 3,500 in 1950. And Rapid City experienced an explosion of growth. The town counted about 13,850 in 1940, and ten years later that went to over 25,300. Rapid City had been the region's largest municipality in 1920, but it had only a few hundred more people than Lead. That changed dramatically with the surge of growth that came in the 1940s. In 1950 Rapid City was four times larger than Lead.[90]

World War II then enlarged the government's position in the Black Hills, but the 1940s also saw the government expand its role in terms of developing water resources. In 1944 Congress passed the Flood Control Act, which authorized the damming of the Upper Missouri River and its tributaries. Working together in what was known as the Pick-Sloan Project, the Army Corps of Engineers and the Bureau of Reclamation began building four dams on the Missouri River and two dams on the Cheyenne River drainage. In fact, the Bureau of Reclamation had long looked at damming rivers in and around the Black Hills. When Congress passed the Newlands Reclamation Act of 1902, which authorized federal participation in big water projects, Orman Dam and the Belle Fourche irrigation district on the Belle Fourche River north of the Black Hills became the state's first project, finished in 1914. The bureau then surveyed Rapid Creek drainage, envisioning projects that could irrigate Rapid Valley and provide water to Rapid City. Only Deerfield dam was built, and only because of the assistance of New Deal programs.[91]

The passage of the Pick-Sloan Project introduced an era of great water projects, and dams that once seemed impractical got the go-ahead. For the Cheyenne River in the southern Black Hills, the Bureau of Reclamation had long talked about a possible irrigation project, and to that end the agency built Angostura Dam in 1949, "hailed as the first completed unit of the Missouri Basin Project." Then the government renewed its search along Rapid Creek and began surveying a site near the town of Pactola in 1948. By this time, the air base and a growing Rapid City needed the water, and construction began on Pactola Dam in 1952, with the project completed in 1956. This large dam, sitting ten miles above Rapid City on Rapid Creek, also seemed to promise security against potential floods. Unfortunately, it provided little help during the 1972 Rapid City flood that killed 235 and destroyed an estimated $100 million in property. The intense storm that caused the flood sat between Rapid City and Pactola, and then the breaking of Canyon Lake Dam, just above Rapid City, resulted in disaster. Nevertheless, Pactola Dam continues to have plenty of water available for Rapid City's use.[92]

With the guarantee of water and the air base's economic stimulus, Rapid City grew dramatically in the 1950s. It added over 17,000 people by the 1960 census, bringing a total population of over 42,000. The city's growth then stabilized over the next few decades. Outside of the federal activity, Rapid City's economy has relied on a number of businesses. It has both agricultural and industrial components, with the industrial aspect most obviously displayed by the cement plant northwest of town. The state of South Dakota built the plant in the early 1920s as a public necessity and operated it for years. The Janklow administration sold the cement plant to private interests. Rapid City also houses the South Dakota School of Mines and Technology, as well as other public and private schools of higher education. But like all Black Hills towns, Rapid City has a large tourist-based economy. The completion of I-90 enhanced the city's position as a transportation center and further designated the town as the gateway to Mount Rushmore. The road from Rapid City to Mount Rushmore has become a mecca for roadside attractions, all hoping to snare tourist dollars.[93]

Two tourist-based activities perhaps stand out as the Hills' most famous. The first is the Reptile Gardens. Opened just south of Rapid City in 1937, it provided the opportunity to see live snakes close-up and encouraged a number of visitors to stop; and in 1965 the Reptile Gardens moved and expanded operations six miles south of Rapid City in Spring Creek valley. Also seen on the road to Mount Rushmore, and in locations around Rapid City, are plants that manufacture Black Hills gold jewelry. The three-color grape leaf style came to the Black Hills with gold-rush pioneers who had produced it elsewhere. The design soon became identified with the Black Hills, and the F. L. Thorpe company of Deadwood billed its creations as the "original Black Hills gold jewelry." The company's success brought competitors, and in 1944 Ivan Landstrom started offering Landstrom's Original Black Hills Gold Creations. Others have followed, such as the Stamper company. The local companies got a boost in the 1980s when a federal judge ruled that for jewelry to be called Black Hills gold, it had to be made in the Black Hills.[94]

Lead and Deadwood had less economic diversity than Rapid City and they struggled from the 1950s to the 1980s. Lead's economy continued to center on gold mining and the great Homestake mine, but with gold fixed at $35 an ounce, profits remained limited, and Lead saw a continual decline in population through these decades. In 1950 Lead held nearly 6,500 people, and this number fell to just over 4,300 by 1980. Through these same years, Deadwood provided services for the miners and others in the northern Black Hills. It had the New York Store, the Montgomery Wards, and a variety of other retail outlets. In addition, it had a variety of watering holes, and prostitution remained active and accepted until 1980. Tourism overwhelmed the everyday commercial activities during the summer, with the nightly arrest of Jack McCall taking precedent over most other business activities. Still, Deadwood declined much as Lead did. It went from nearly 3,300 people in 1950 to just over 2,000 in 1980.[95]

Most other Black Hills towns fell into a similar duality from the 1950s to the 1980s, a primary economic activity and then a claim to some part of the tourist business. Custer, Hill City, and Spearfish all had logging and sawmills as a strong part of their economic mix, with a unique tourist attraction enhancing their appeal during the summer.

Homestake Gold Mine's Yates Shaft and South Mill, Lead, in the 1970s. Established by George Hearst in 1877, the Homestake Mine dominated gold mining in the Black Hills until its closing in 2001. *Courtesy A. J. Wolff.*

Near Custer sits Crazy Horse Memorial. Korczak Ziolkowski began this mountain-carving in 1948 to serve as a focus for a cultural and education complex he planned for Native Americans. At Hill City, Bill Heckman began operating the Black Hills Central or the "1880 Train" tourist railroad in 1957. Then, in 1938 Josef Meier decided to locate his Passion Play, which recounts the last seven days in Christ's life, permanently in Spearfish. Each of these towns now had at least two economic elements to provide some stability during this era, while Keystone, at the foot of Mount Rushmore, had substantial business only during the summer.[96]

Three events happened in the 1980s that brought changes to the northern Black Hills. During the 1970s, the federal government released gold from its fixed price of $35 an ounce and allowed it to float free, and by 1980 gold hit $850. While gold did not stay at this peak, the metal's increased value set off a frenzy of prospecting and mine development. Gold companies explored historic mining districts, and in 1983 Wharf resources opened its first open-pit gold mine in the upper regions of the Bald Mountain mining district, not far from Terry Peak, and others followed. Near the historic towns of Terry, Carbonate, and Galena, mining companies began laying out new operations. Some Black Hills residents became concerned about long-term environmental damage, and initiatives brought the question of mine development before the voters. But Black Hills voters wanted economic development, and the projects were allowed to proceed.[97]

In Lead, Homestake officials similarly looked for ways to benefit from the higher gold prices. They investigated historic gold areas around Lead, did exploration in their current underground workings, and explored areas in the open-cut that had been mined years before. In 1983 Homestake miners began working in the open cut, removing ore that once was deemed too low in gold content to be mined profitably. The project continued until 1998 when the combination of lower gold prices and less readily available ore brought the project to an end.[98]

315

By 1998 all open pit gold mining ended in the Black Hills except at the Wharf. The mines certainly brought some short-term economic benefits to the region, a few hundred extra men found mining jobs, with many coming from out of state. But finding long-term benefits is more problematic. When the mines closed, the miners left, and what remains are new valleys where mountains used to be, and new mountains where valleys used to be. Some observers believe that correctly reclaimed mine sites offer the same potential for enjoyment as the earlier landscapes. Yet problems exist. The Gilt Edge open pit near Galena exposed a highly sulfuric ore that turns to acid when it becomes wet. The operating company went bankrupt, and the Environmental Protection Agency made it a Super Fund site. In 2003 the South Dakota environmental office announced that the state would have to monitor and treat the water in perpetuity. And at all of the sites, the remains of earlier gold operations, either from the 1880s or 1930s, were bulldozed away, removing artifacts that once thrilled Black Hills historians.[99]

Another event from the 1980s did not have the major ramifications of another gold rush, but it certainly had great symbolic importance. In 1984 the Burlington Northern began removing its rail-line that bisected the Hills. Certainly by this time passenger service had been long over, and the amount of freight had diminished to just coal shipments for the Kirk Power Plant. Yet the arrival of railroads in 1890 and 1891 had brought permanence to Deadwood and allowed for the mining boom of the 1890s. The removal of the rail-line indicated that the industrial era of the Black Hills' past was emphatically gone.[100]

The last major event of the 1980s came in 1989 when voters in South Dakota allowed Deadwood to adopt limited-stakes gaming. To do this, community boosters formed the "You Bet" committee, which convinced South Dakotans of Deadwood's near demise. The ease of auto travel allowed shoppers to bypass Deadwood businesses and go to other places, such as Rapid City's Rushmore Mall, and three months of tourism was just not enough to support Deadwood's infrastructure. The burning of Deadwood's Syndicate block in 1987, a grand edifice built in 1888, convinced many across the state that Deadwood was about done. With the understanding that much of the money would go to historic preservation, gambling became law, and Main Street went from hardware, furniture, and clothing stores to gambling halls.[101]

In 2003 little else exists in Deadwood except gaming. And it can be argued that without it Deadwood would die. The northern Black Hills' most consistent economic support, the Homestake gold mine, closed in late 2001, and as people have left the region, many other businesses closed. Deadwood survives because of year-round tourism, gaming, and snow sports in the winter, and the West of Wild Bill in the summer. Moreover, Deadwood promoters anticipate even more tourists wanting the 1876 experience because of a new Home Box Office series called *Deadwood*. It features many of the town's famous and infamous, presenting Deadwood as a "dirty rotten town." It premiered in March 2004.[102]

Not far away in Lead the closing of the Homestake has brought a struggle for survival. As people leave, some folks joke that Deadwood should annex Lead, but the reality is much more complicated. Lead has tried to reinvent itself. The greatest promise comes with a scientific project based around a subatomic particle known as a neutrino. Since 1965 the Homestake mine has hosted a science lab on the 4,850-foot level. The surrounding rock filters out all atomic particles except neutrinos. Some scientists want South Dakota and the National Science Foundation (NSF) to take control of the mine and turn the complex into a neutrino lab. The 2004 South Dakota legislature set up a state agency and provided the funds to get the project moving. People in Lead hope the NSF will take the next step.[103]

Change has come to other Black Hills communities as well. Spearfish has slowly become the service center for the northern Black Hills, replacing Deadwood. It has the Wal-Mart and other major stores, and it has Black Hills State University, attracting students from throughout the region. Hill City and Custer still have tourism and lumber, but more and more people have moved into country estates around the towns to enjoy a quieter and more scenic way of life. Both towns have attracted new upscale shopping options, with Hill City featuring a series of art shops. Rapid City continues to prosper, but residents fear that Ellsworth air base may close. From having missiles, bombers, and air tankers in the 1960s, its mission has been diminished to having only B-1B bombers. Ellsworth has played an important role in Rapid City's development, and local, state, and federal politicians are all arguing its case before Congress and the Department of Defense.[104]

The closing of Ellsworth would take its toll on Rapid City, but it would fit in with what has happened historically within the Black Hills. The region has experienced a number of booms and busts. The gold rush brought the first boom, and then rising and falling fortunes of gold brought a number of booms and busts. The Homestake mine seemingly had a long run of prosperity, but it did go bust during World War II, and then the final bust came in 2001. And the people in Lead are looking for a new way to boom.

Much of what has happened in the Black Hills has been decided elsewhere. The Homestake was controlled from San Francisco, the railroads that entered the region had headquarters in Chicago, and scientists elsewhere will decide about the neutrino lab. Also, the ultimate decision about the future of the air base will be made in Washington. When outside people control an area's economy, that is generally referred to as colonialism, and because of limited local control, boom and bust often follows. Remote investors have little real concern about what happens in places like the Black Hills.

Governor Mike Rounds hopes to bring more local control to South Dakota's economy and to stimulate new events that can bring more tourist dollars to the state. Rounds often refers to the Sturgis Motorcycle Classic as an example of a locally produced success story. Motorcycle enthusiasts began the Sturgis Rally in 1938, featuring a variety of racing events. The event gradually grew until it began exploding in the 1980s with as many as 350,000 riders coming to Sturgis and the Black Hills. But the primary focus shifted from racing to exhibition. People wanted themselves and their motorcycles, preferably Harley-Davidsons, to be seen and heard. Plus, the predominant rider is not a young racer, but an aging baby boomer. Many of the visitors are searching for the excitement of their youth or for a sense of western individualism. Nevertheless, this annual celebration brings more motorcycle riders to the Black Hills in one year than all of the gold miners who ever worked in the Hills. But this event could go bust as well. The very name attached to the generation known as the baby boomers infers that a bust must follow, and the Sturgis promoters well know they need to attract a younger enthusiast. But change happens. From the time Native Americans first visited the area, the Black Hills have supported a number of different economic activities: lodge poles for the Indians, gold for the greedy, and scenery for the bikers. No matter if they have been good or bad, these changes have happened, and Black Hills' communities continue to change.[105]

Chapter 16
Catholic Missions, Churches, and Schools

The origins of the Catholic Church for the area that became the state of South Dakota began arguably with the establishment of the Diocese of Gardar, Greenland, in the year 1124, as a result of a sketchy Vatican awareness of land across the Atlantic Ocean reported by Norse explorers. This diocese exercised no actual authority over North America, as Norse exploration came to a halt, but in theory it encompassed Vineland as a continental station and was administered from Greenland for 250 years.

Centuries later, French explorers, traders, and missionaries again reported North American discoveries, to which the Roman Catholic Church responded with ecclesiastical designations. The northern Great Plains (including variously present-day eastern and western South Dakota) generally fell under the Vicariate and Diocese of Quebec (Archdiocese of Rouen) in 1658; the Diocese of Santiago de Cuba in 1777; the Diocese of Christopher de Havana in 1787; the Diocese of New Orleans in 1793; the Diocese of St. Louis in 1826; the Diocese of Dubuque in 1837; the Diocese of St. Paul in 1850; the Vicariate of Indian Territory in 1851; and the Vicariate of Nebraska in 1859. Finally, the specific Vicariate of Dakota Territory was created in 1879, and its first Vicar Apostolic, Martin Marty, OSB, established Yankton as the see city.

Along with statehood, the Diocese of South Dakota came into place in 1889. Martin Marty remained as the first bishop of the new diocese, moving the see to Sioux Falls. During the reign of South Dakota's second bishop, Thomas O'Gorman, the statewide diocese was subdivided in 1902. The East River Diocese of Sioux Falls remained under the aegis of Bishop O'Gorman, while the West River Diocese of Lead fell under the leadership of its first bishop John Stariha. Although the see city for eastern South Dakota remained in Sioux Falls, the see for western South Dakota was moved from the city of Lead to Rapid City in 1930, where it remains.[1] Today, the two dioceses of South Dakota exist within the Catholic Province of St. Paul, which also includes six dioceses in Minnesota and two in North Dakota.

Because the earliest Catholic efforts in the region were related to the Indian mission field, and because policies and activities were unique in that regard, the relationship between the Catholic Church and Indians must be treated as a theme separate from general South Dakota diocesan histories.

■ Catholic Indian Missions[2]

The history of Catholics in their relationship to the Sioux began sporadically in the seventeenth century; however, consequential features in this history had their inception with the appearance of Belgian Father Pierre Jean De Smet of the Society of Jesus, who arrived at a community of Yanktons in 1839. Over the next decades, he baptized hundreds of Sioux people and arranged catechetical training mainly by priests led by Monsignor Augustin Ravoux from Mendota, Minnesota. Before De Smet died in 1873, he earned a reputation that made his memory the linchpin for a growing body of Dakotas, Nakotas, and Lakotas who would identify themselves, at least nominally, as Catholics by the end of the nineteenth century.

His first visits in Sioux Country and his earliest peacemaking efforts are well remembered in the oral tradition of the Sioux. Traveling from his home base near St. Louis, Missouri, De Smet sought to remove the threat of violence between the Yanktons and the neighboring tribes. About his first visit to the Yanktons, he wrote: "The object of this journey was to afford the benefit of baptism to some children, to give adults some ideas of our holy religion, and to establish a durable and advantageous peace between two nations."[3] Although he was unable to establish a permanent mission in Sioux Country before his death, his legacy was of abiding influence.

The positive tribal memory of De Smet in Sioux Country endured and paved the way for others who followed him. Three years after his death, the Swiss Benedictine Abbot Martin Marty became his successor, arriving from St. Meinrad Abbey, Indiana, during a critical time in 1876—the year of George Custer's demise at the Battle of the Little Bighorn River. Marty was different from De Smet. A new conservatism that swept through Europe after the 1848 revolutions created a reactionary Catholic conservatism that Marty brought with him. In addition, he faced and participated in vigorous, sometimes vicious, interdenominational competition for souls in Sioux Country. Episcopalians, Presbyterians, and Congregationalists vied with Marty for converts as well as for funds allocated by Congress for the education of tribal youngsters, as authorized by the Quaker Policy of 1869. Through this policy, which was part of President Ulysses Grant's Peace Policy, federal officials hoped to reduce corruption in the Indian Field Service, which was a perpetual problem, and to inspire assimilation by the assign-

ment of one Christian mission society to each agency jurisdiction. This assignment empowered the society to nominate a person for service as the Indian Agent, who favored the denomination in his jurisdiction, and to receive federal funds in return for educational services—all in the interest of "civilizing" and "christianizing" Indian people. Marty dispatched Catholic missionaries to several Lakota and Nakota agencies in present South Dakota, as well as to Fort Totten in North Dakota, in spite of this one-church policy. Formal Quaker Policy assignments ended in 1883.

In addition to Protestant-Catholic competition in the mission field, Marty faced the problem of a dramatic change in the cultural environment of the tribes. Whereas De Smet had encountered Native groups as semi-nomadic people scattered across the northern Great Plains, Marty found them in a state of transition in the wake of the Little Bighorn Battle. During his lifetime, they surrendered or lost claim to nearly ninety percent of historic Sioux Country and gathered around twelve U.S. Agency centers. In the process,

Vicar Martin Marty's mission work was based on the belief that a Catholic boarding school system could "civilize" Indian children in a generation. *Courtesy Sacred Heart Monastery Archives.*

Chronology

1839 – Fr. De Smet arrives among the Yankton Sioux

1860 – First Catholic Church built near Vermillion

1879 – Martin Marty becomes Vicar Apostolic of Dakota Territory

1883 – St. Joseph Cathedral replaces St. Michael's in Sioux Falls

1888 – Holy Rosary Mission (later Red Cloud Indian School) opens at Pine Ridge

1889 – Diocese of South Dakota formed; St. Martin's School opens in Sturgis

1897 – Sacred Heart Hospital founded in Yankton

1902 – East River Diocese of Sioux Falls and West River Diocese of Lead (later Rapid City) are formed

1909 – Columbus College founded in Chamberlain, relocated to Sioux Falls in 1921

1913 – Cathedral High School (later O'Gorman) opens in Sioux Falls

1927 – St. Joseph's Indian School opens in Chamberlain

1936 – Mount Marty College founded in Yankton

1950 – Blue Cloud Abbey founded in Marvin

1951 – Presentation College founded in Aberdeen

1996 – Our Lady of Guadelupe parish formed for Hispanic population in Sioux Falls

their fourteen ancestral tribes amalgamated into the modern tribes that since have occupied reservations. Only the ancestral Yankton and Oglala tribes remained intact geographically. Other federally recognized tribes evolved to include fragments or combinations of ancestral tribes melded by circumstance into new domestic, dependent nations.

De Smet had endured difficulty locating or funding an appropriate mission site for wandering Sioux, but Marty faced no such problem, for the wandering tribes had settled on new agency jurisdictions. De Smet had met a hopeful people comfortable in their traditional culture, but Marty faced a frustrated, politically fragmented group, fully aware that its cultural integrity was in jeopardy. De Smet had sought accommodation and understanding among cultural groups, but Marty inherited a mission field governed by federal agencies and the new Bureau of Catholic Indian Missions, formed in 1874 to support aggressive and well-organized Catholic mission efforts.

Marty began his mission work from the "civilization" premise that Sioux people needed to work the land and support themselves. Schools were necessary and should be built and maintained ultimately by the Indian people themselves. His criticisms of federal policies included that these "made people idlers, loafers, and beggars and as long as the military shall control them, it will be impossible to change their position and character."[4]

Marty's missiology developed over the years to emphasize a belief that children schooled in a Christian environment with European underpinnings would become "civilized" within a generation—an ideology shared by other Christian denominations and federal policy-makers. He believed that through a boarding school system children could best be educated in Catholic teachings and its resulting "civilizing" effects. To that end, he called upon his fellow Benedictines at St. Meinrad, Indiana, as well as diocesan clergy to undertake the work of spiritual leaders, builders, and teachers. The evangelization of indigenous peoples represented the highest of all callings. Therefore, recruitment efforts were not difficult in the Catholic Indian mission field, especially when facilitated by federal funding for educational efforts and when problems in Europe caused members of religious orders to seek refuge in the United States.

Marty's first challenge was meeting pastoral needs at the Standing Rock Agency. Earlier, in 1872, Catholics accepted a federal Quaker Policy assignment on the Grand

River (Standing Rock) Agency jurisdiction but hesitated, first, due to the death of Father De Smet and a delay in finding a replacement and, secondly, because of the absence of a coordinating agency belatedly formed as the national Bureau of Catholic Indian Missions in 1874. Funding became available for a permanent Indian school in 1877, to be staffed mainly by Benedictine men and women. Marty also planned construction of a Benedictine abbey and seminary at the Grand River Agency (renamed Standing Rock in 1878). This plan for Grand River was too ambitious, however, given conditions surrounding the Great Sioux War, lack of funding, and paucity of staff.

Subsequently, to deal with confusion following the Great Sioux War, and the return of the famed leader Sitting Bull and other combatants, U.S. Interior Department officials installed James McLaughlin as U.S. Agent at Standing Rock. His appearance in the autumn of 1881 brought stability to the jurisdiction. McLaughlin, a devout Catholic, encouraged Marty and the Benedictines in their efforts. An Indian day school opened in 1883, with twenty-five students, located about twenty-five miles north of the agency. By then, Marty's staff included three priests, three Benedictine brothers, eight Sisters of Charity, and a seminarian.

In addition to the Standing Rock school, Marty had established St. Peter's Parish in 1876, plus several scattered missions close to the largest Indian villages. Before long, he founded the St. Joseph's and St. Mary's Societies, which served as a community of Catholic Indian men and women who gathered periodically to discuss their faith, sing hymns, and pray. Marty also initiated the Annual Indian Congress, a yearly summer encampment that offered opportunities for community recreation and Catholic liturgies. Soon the model of the societies and congresses spread successfully to other Indian missions in southern Dakota.

Marty sought additional staff for the Indian mission field as he expanded operations to other tribal groups. In 1884 he assigned two diocesan priests to initiate the St. Francis Mission at Rosebud Agency. He then invited Jesuits of the German Province, in exile from their homeland, residing in Buffalo, New York, to assume abiding control of this mission. They agreed, arriving in 1885, and began work not only on an Indian boarding school and mission stations, but also ministering to the non-Indian immigrant population that was growing, particularly in the Black Hills. The Sisters of St. Francis of Christian Charity and Penance, from Stella Niagara, New York, worked with the Jesuits as teachers and domestic workers. In 1888 the Jesuits expanded their ministry to the neighboring Pine Ridge Agency, establishing the Holy Rosary Mission and boarding school.

At Yankton City, Marty opened an Industrial School for Indian boys in 1884. In just a few years the school failed, mainly because federal officials withdrew funding for an Indian school located at such a distance from Indian Country. Marty decided to move the school to the north edge of the Crow Creek Agency jurisdiction. As a result, Benedictine men (from St. Meinrad) and Benedictine women (from Maryville, Missouri) appeared at the Crow Creek Agency beginning in 1886, relieving two diocesan priests who struggled to build a mission and school there. The abandoned school building in Yankton City became the property of the Maryville Benedictine sisters for use as a convent, which they named "Sacred Heart." In return, the sisters continued to provide assistance at the new school on Crow Creek (named Immaculate Conception) alongside their brother Benedictines. In 1897 the sisters responded to an epidemic in Yankton by adding a health care apostolate—Sacred Heart Hospital. Following this shift in commitment, they would proceed to found an academy in Yankton in 1922, and Mount Marty College in 1936.

By assignment under the Quaker Policy, the Cheyenne River Agency was under the jurisdiction of the Episcopal Church until 1883. Five years later, a series of itinerant Catholic missionaries attempted to start a mission there. The first Catholic Church appeared in 1892, and by 1911 there were ten Catholic churches in the jurisdiction. Catholic missionaries struggled to serve the needs of the Cheyenne River community, because they were forced to spread their time and energy between Cheyenne River and other agencies. Finally, in 1923 the Priests of the Sacred Heart arrived to assume ministerial responsibilities at Cheyenne River and Lower Brûlé. From the time of their arrival, they hoped to build an Indian school to serve both. In 1927 property became available in Chamberlain, and the Sacred Heart Fathers opened St. Joseph's Indian School, which remains as an effective boarding institution.

Catholic efforts at Sisseton and Flandreau were stifled by competition from Congregational ministers and Episcopalian priests, but Catholics enjoyed belated success on the Yankton Reservation. Episcopalians had received the Yankton Reservation under Quaker Policy assignment, but after the policy dissolved in 1883, itinerant Catholic priests appeared to nurture a Catholic following established by Father De Smet. Finally, in 1921 a Catholic priest was permanently assigned—Father Sylvester Eisenman, whose first priority was the building of an Indian school at a place named Marty. For help, he petitioned the heiress and religious superior, Mother Katherine Drexel, who agreed to send three Sisters of the Blessed Sacrament as teachers. Father Sylvester launched a substantial fund-raising campaign and completed construction of the Marty Indian School, along with three mission farms, in the 1930s. In 1935 he and the Blessed Sacrament Sisters founded a new order of Indian religious women, called the Oblate Sisters of the Blessed Sacrament. Although small in numbers, the Oblate Sisters remain at Marty alone to staff the mission. In 1942 St. Paul's Church at Marty was completed and, viewed as the Queen of the Prairie, displayed a classic design combining Catholic and Indian themes.

After mid-century, the Catholic leadership began to reevaluate its role in the modern world in light of a scriptural and theological renaissance. These reflections, along with other social movements and concerns, would come to fruition as the 1960s' Second Vatican Council. The teachings of the council, and subsequent teachings called post-conciliar, required that Catholic missionaries be trained through the lens of a "New Evangelization." No longer were Catholics to present a "one true faith" approach or attitude. For example, Church teaching on dialogue between Catholics and members of other faiths, called officially "interreligious dialogue," abandoned any suggestion of proselytizing. Rather, respect must be afforded regardless of one's religious belief. "Inculturation," which became a new theological term, encouraged missionaries to embrace as much Native culture as possible, rather than to replace Native elements with Catholic ones. Much of Marty's original missiology was abandoned. These conciliar and post-conciliar teachings, along with secular pressures toward Indian self-determination and the global liberation movements of indigenous peoples, led to dramatic changes in the relationship between the Catholic Church and the Sioux.

As a result, all but one of the Catholic schools on South Dakota Indian reservations were turned over to tribal management during the 1970s. The single exception was Red Cloud (former Holy Rosary) Indian School on the Pine Ridge Reservation, which remains under Jesuit administration at the local parents' request. Elsewhere, the tribes presently receive full funding from Congress to offer education in grades K-12, while Catholic leaders restrict their activities to other pastoral ministries. In addition, in 1999 the Rapid City Diocese established the Inculturation Project Office to address the needs of its Native Catholic population by conducting the nation's first systematic survey of a United States Native population regarding faith issues. The Diocese also oversees an Office of Native Concerns and the Sioux Spiritual Center mentioned below.

Two clerics warrant special identification for their abiding efforts in sustaining and enhancing the relationship between pre- and post-Vatican II Catholics and the state's Native people. In West River, Jesuit Father Richard Jones was awarded the *Lumen Christi* Award in the year 2000 for his forty years of service to the community on the Rosebud Reservation. Benedictine Father Stanislaus Maudlin was inducted into the South Dakota Hall of Fame in 2003 for his more than sixty years of pastoral ministry among the East River tribes.

■ Non-Indian Catholic History: The Dioceses[5]

The general objectives of the diocesan church, in South Dakota or elsewhere, are the founding, staffing, and building of churches to serve local communities (or parishes); the provision of Catholic education; and the creation of health care and social services to match local needs when possible. The origins of this total process in South Dakota preceded the arrival of Bishop Marty.

The first recorded Catholic Mass in present South Dakota was celebrated in 1842 by Monsignor Augustin Ravoux, a diocesan priest who founded the first parish at Mendota. Soon, the cleric appeared at Fort Vermillion and, at De Smet's request, celebrated Mass at budding communities along the Missouri River. The first Catholic church in southern Dakota appeared in 1860, after August Bruyer donated ten acres of land for a church and cemetery east of Vermillion. Two years later, the Jefferson congregation took shape, approximately twenty miles away, where a mainly French community was served by itinerant priests from Sioux City, Iowa. The Jefferson church represents the oldest surviving parish in present South Dakota.

Martin Marty became Vicar Apostolic of the Vicariate of Dakota Territory in 1879, expanding his responsibilities to include the non-Indian population, which was growing and underserved, and spread out over 149,112 square miles. His confreres from St. Meinrad Abbey and the few resident diocesan priests would be insufficient in numbers to meet overall territorial needs. Marty began by recruiting and inviting Catholic men and women from Europe and the eastern United States to take up vocations in the territory. Encouraging and retaining Catholic clergy on the non-Indian frontier was (and continues to be) a major challenge. To serve a Catholic population of 14,000 that spanned the Dakotas, he had available thirty-nine active priests in the early years, and only twelve of these were from the United States. (Eight were from Ireland, five from Germany, and one or two each from Belgium, Bohemia, France, Switzerland, Scotland, Holland, and Canada.) Within the first five years, Marty founded eighty-two parishes to serve a growing population of 25,600. Particularly difficult, however, was parish-building in the western part of the territory, where the non-Indian population was small and relatively scattered. Yet it demanded attention because a substantial percentage of the Black Hills miners were Irish Catholics and Democrats who were at odds with the Protestant/Republican majority living east of the Missouri River.

The first resident priest assigned to the Black Hills was Father John Lonergan, who in 1877 established himself briefly in Deadwood. One year later, Father J. M. Toohey, CSC, from South Bend, Indiana, assumed a leadership role in the Black Hills, choosing the city of Lead as his headquarters, rather than the bustling Deadwood, because he believed that Lead was on the rise. This choice would affect subsequent decisions that led to the creation of a new West River diocese centered at Lead.

In 1880, in the northern sector of southern Dakota, Father Robert W. Haire from Flint, Michigan, distinguished himself, becoming quite famous in the annals of South Dakota history. He established churches in Groton, Redfield, Huron, Zell, Aberdeen, Columbia, and other locations quickly and effectively. Before the end of the decade, however, the prolific priest's zeal would lead him into open dispute with Marty over Haire's public pro-prohibition stance, which was contrary to Catholic teachings. Also an avid and outspoken supporter of Populism, Haire would be relieved of his priestly duties from 1890 to 1902 as a result.

Responding to early needs for Catholic education, in 1878 religious women from several orders arrived in southern Dakota. For example, the Holy Cross Sisters of Notre Dame came from Indiana to establish a school (and a makeshift hospital) in the Black Hills. After three separate, failed attempts at this, the sisters permanently returned to Indiana in 1897. Another group, the Sisters of Mercy from Omaha, Nebraska, came to Yankton City to build a convent and school there. Unfortunately, they were plagued by indebtedness and an amorous scandal that caused Marty to send them back to Omaha. The last of the Mercy sisters left in 1886. One year later, their Yankton properties were transferred to Benedictine Sisters from Maryville, Missouri, who remain there at present. At about the same time, Father Haire invited the Irish Presentation Sisters to Aberdeen. Previously, beginning with their arrival in 1880, brief attempts at ministry in Wheeler and Deadwood had caused them to relocate in Fargo. The sisters began their Aberdeen educational apostolate in 1886 and opened Presentation Academy in 1888. That same year, five sisters came to southern Dakota to open West River schools from the Benedictine Convent of St. Nicholas de Flue in Melchtal, Switzerland. After a brief stay with the Yankton Benedictines to learn the English language, they arrived in Sturgis to begin their abiding apostolates in the Black Hills.

In 1889, with statehood, came the separation of North and South Dakota. Marty then became the first Bishop of the new Diocese of South Dakota with Sioux Falls as the new see city. A decade earlier, thirty Sioux Falls Catholics had raised $1,100 to build a small church on the site of the present Cathedral. This original church, St. Michael's, burned in 1881, and the small community met for services in Van Epp Hall. Two years

In 1897 the Benedictine Sisters founded Sacred Heart Hospital in Yankton, one of four hospitals established by the Catholic Church between 1897 and 1901. This photo, taken in 1960, shows the hospital, Sacred Heart Monastery, and Mount Marty College. A new hospital replaced the original and is today known as Avera Sacred Heart Hospital. *Courtesy Sacred Heart Monastery Archives.*

later, a new St. Michael's replaced the lost church, which would evolve into the present St. Joseph's Cathedral, mentioned below.

Bishop Marty's new South Dakota jurisdiction included 30,000 Catholics, and more than 77,000 square miles. To facilitate administration, he divided the diocese into four deaneries: Aberdeen, Mitchell, Sioux Falls, and Lead. Each of these was led by a Dean (who had special authority delegated to him by the Bishop) with twelve pastors in support.

Providing Catholic education in the late nineteenth century was a mandate. In a total of ten Councils of Baltimore, held between 1829 and 1884, the American Catholic Church issued a series of regulations decreeing that schools should be erected in all parishes, and that priests who were negligent in that regard should be removed. On the frontier, these regulations presented an overwhelming challenge. To indicate how challenging the task has been, more than fifty groups of religious women have attempted educational (and other) apostolates in South Dakota over the last century.[6]

To serve the see city, Marty invited a group of Ursuline Sisters from Malone, New York, to begin a diocesan school. Not long after their arrival in 1890, however, the five sisters entered into a dispute with a parish priest, because they extended hospitality to prospective divorcees at a time when Sioux Falls was reputed to be the "divorce capital of the West." As a result, the sisters closed their St. Rosa's Academy in 1898, returning to New York. It would be left to the second Bishop of South Dakota, Thomas O'Gorman, to recruit the Sisters of the Dominican Order of the Most Holy Rosary from Sinsinawa Mound, Wisconsin, to assume this frontier educational apostolate. They arrived seven years later to teach in parochial schools, initiating their abiding contribution to education in South Dakota.

When the new Bishop O'Gorman arrived in South Dakota, there were fourteen parochial schools and one hospital in his diocese to serve 30,000 Catholics. In response to health care needs that increased dramatically after statehood, with his encouragement between 1897 and 1901 four hospitals were established: Sacred Heart Hospital in Yankton, founded by the Yankton Benedictine Sisters in 1897; St. Joseph's Hospital in Deadwood, founded by the Sturgis Benedictine Sisters in 1898; St. Mary's Hospital in Pierre, established by the Yankton Benedictine Sisters in 1899; and St. Luke's Hospital in Aberdeen, founded by the Aberdeen Presentation Sisters in 1901. The Presentation Sisters would later staff St. Joseph's Hospital in Mitchell in 1906, and McKennan Hospital in Sioux Falls in 1911.

After 1902 the South Dakota Diocese ceased to exist. The state was divided along geographical, cultural, and economic lines. At about that time, there were 150 priests, 208 churches, twenty-eight parochial schools, and five hospitals in the statewide diocese serving a Catholic population of approximately 68,000. In addition, the state also boasted twenty-five Catholic academies, most of them east of the Missouri River. Accordingly, by the time the statewide diocese divided in 1902, there existed suitable distributions of parishes served by scattered academies and rudimentary hospitals to serve non-Indian Catholics on both sides of the Missouri River.

■ Diocese of Lead/Rapid City (West River)[7]

The first Bishop of the new Diocese of Lead, headquartered in the Black Hills, was John Stariha. He had available to him nine diocesan and eight regular priests; four Catholic schools; and two makeshift hospitals to serve the pastoral needs of 9,000 Catholics spanning more than 40,000 square miles. Lead's St. Patrick's Church, a small frame building, became St. Patrick's Cathedral. By 1910 the Lead diocesan Catholic population had grown to 18,000, with eighteen priests to serve Indian as well as non-Indian Catholics, both on and off reservations. In addition to Indian schools, mentioned above, the diocese needed to increase the number of Catholic schools for the off-reservation communities. As a result, in 1889 the Sturgis Benedictine Sisters opened St. Martin's School at Sturgis, which in 1914 became an academic high school. Furthermore, these sisters staffed two small health-care facilities in Deadwood and Hot Springs, and three parochial schools by 1916, when the second Bishop of Lead, John Lawler, arrived. That same year, Bishop Lawler invited the Sisters of Charity of the Blessed Virgin Mary, from Dubuque, Iowa, to assist in staffing Catholic schools. They arrived and, by 1917, the sisters were teaching in schools at Lead and Rapid City.

In 1925 the Catholic population of the settlement era in West River had peaked at 38,672, according to the state census. To meet health-care needs, Benedictines opened St. John's Hospital in Rapid City in 1926 and, ten years later, Our Lady of Grace Hospital in Gregory. Because Rapid City's population had escalated due to its accessibility, Bishop Lawler moved the see city from Lead to Rapid City in 1930, and St. Mary's Immaculate Conception Church became the Cathedral of the Immaculate Conception. In 1962 a new Cathedral of Our Lady of Perpetual Help was constructed.

By mid-century, West River's population had dwindled for a variety of reasons, including the decline in mining operations, the devastation of drought and depression, and the simple fact that the land could not sustain the population. Low enrollments in Catholic schools caused a shift in the educational apostolates. In 1961 the diocese opened a new elementary school in Rapid City, Perpetual Help Grade School. In 1983 this school coalesced into St. Elizabeth Ann Seton, which was an inter-parish pre-school-eighth grade diocesan school. Additionally, in 1991 the Benedictines announced they were closing St. Martin's Academy, which had moved from Sturgis to Rapid City in 1962. The diocese responded by assuming direct responsibility for Catholic secondary education and in 1995 opened St. Thomas More High School.

By 2002 the Rapid City Diocese served a Catholic population of 29,940 (a reduction of twenty-three percent since 1925), of which about twenty-seven percent were Indians. These communities were served by ninety-seven parishes, thirty-two missions, and four pastoral centers. The diocese sponsored three schools: the Red Cloud Indian School on the Pine Ridge Reservation (2002 enrollment—419); St. Elizabeth Ann Seton (2002 enrollment—480); and St. Thomas More High School (2002 enrollment—180). No Catholic hospitals remained in the diocese. A Catholic influence remained in a regional management system because St. John's Hospital merged with a community hospital to form Rapid City Regional Hospital in 1975. The diocese funded thirteen special centers for social services, a licensed home for abandoned and abused children in Manderson, and a shelter for abused women and runaway children in Eagle Butte. Together, these centers served 1,696 persons in 2002. In addition, a staff assigned to the Office of Native Concerns acted as liaison between the Native community and the diocese, and the Sioux Spiritual Center evolved as a diocesan house of prayer for Lakota people.

Although in 1902 the West River Diocese had served far fewer parishioners than the one in East River, it had thrived to meet the needs of a distinctive culture west of the Missouri River. Religious and diocesan leaders provided essential services for most Catholic Indians in the state. The Diocese of Rapid City existed as the most remote frontier extension of the Province of St. Paul.

■ Diocese of Sioux Falls (East River)[8]

In 1902 Bishop O'Gorman inherited the larger portion of the state's Catholic population, estimated at 59,000 and growing, served by about 130 priests. By 1939 the Catholic population had risen to nearly 71,000 served by 156 priests. Unlike the West River problem of decline, the Catholic population in East River continued to rise.

The new Bishop O'Gorman initiated the process of building a cathedral in the see city of Sioux Falls. In 1915 the small St. Michael's pro-cathedral was moved from its foundation to the north side of the same block and construction began on St. Joseph's Cathedral. The new and present cathedral was dedicated in 1919. The Bishop also recognized a need for a second parish in the see city. In 1917, to accommodate a growing population, he created the parish of St. Therese, which served Catholics from rural communities eastward and across the Minnesota border. This parish gave rise to the present Our Lady of Guadelupe in 1996, the only Spanish-speaking parish in the state created to serve a growing community of Hispanic immigrants.

Bishop O'Gorman, like his predecessor, faced the need for Catholic education as mandated by the Councils of Baltimore. In 1902 he invited the Sisters of St. Francis of Assisi to staff St. Mary's parochial school in Salem and, a few years later, in Parkston. In 1905 the Dominican Sisters, who earlier had replaced the Ursuline Sisters, opened St. Michael's elementary school to serve the one thousand Catholics in Sioux Falls, and in 1913 Cathedral High School, which in 1961 would evolve into O'Gorman High School. In 1921 the School Sisters of Notre Dame, from Mankato, Minnesota, also arrived to staff parochial schools.

Beyond the mandate for primary and secondary Catholic education, Bishop O'Gorman recognized a need for an institution of higher learning, as well as a seminary to train local men for the priesthood. In 1909 he purchased property in Chamberlain from federal officials, who had operated a substantial Indian boarding school there, at a reasonable price with the proviso that the plant would always be used for educational purposes. His goal was to establish a Catholic college with a seminary attached. In appreciation for the work of South Dakota's Knights of Columbus, he named the new school Columbus College, and invited the Clerics of the Viatorians to administer it.[9]

The new Columbus College conferred its first baccalaureate degrees in 1914, but the school was plagued by low enrollment. In 1921 Columbus College moved to Sioux Falls in order to reach a larger market, to no avail. Its managers continued to struggle in spite of its new location, attempting various programming, from a school for girls to a

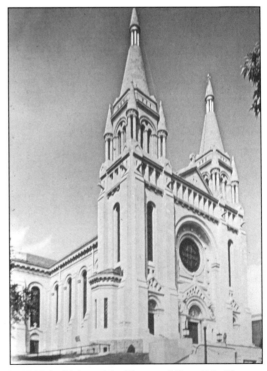

In 1915 the bishop of the Diocese of Sioux Falls, Thomas O'Gorman, initiated the construction of the imposing St. Joseph's Cathedral. Designed by Emmanuel Louis Masqueray, the structure was dedicated in 1919. *Center for Western Studies.*

Responding to the need for an institution of higher learning in his diocese, Bishop O'Gorman established Columbus College in Chamberlain. Low enrollments led to the institution's being moved to Sioux Falls in 1921, where it underwent bankruptcy. In 1944 it was purchased by the federal government and converted into a Veterans Administration hospital in 1948. *Center for Western Studies.*

seminary, but underwent bankruptcy during the Great Depression. Finally on May 1, 1944, federal officials purchased the Sioux Falls property and in 1948 converted it into a regional Veterans Administration Hospital Center. The Chamberlain property remained with the Viatorians, now called St. Viator Normal School, which served as a novitiate for the Order until the Fathers of the Sacred Heart purchased the plant in 1927 to found St. Joseph's Indian School—which remains in operation.

Responding to the continued, unfulfilled need for Catholic higher education, Benedictine Sisters opened Yankton's Mount Marty College in 1936, and Presentation Sisters opened Aberdeen's Presentation College in 1951. Most Catholics continued to attend state colleges, however. As a result, in 1948 Newman Centers opened in each college town to bring the Catholic campus community together with special programs and services.

To meet growing health care needs, in 1920 the Daughters of St. Mary of Providence arrived in South Dakota to staff Milbank's St. Bernard's Providence Hospital. In 1934, Sisters of the Divine Savior staffed Tekakwitha Hospital at Sisseton, and the Yankton Benedictines opened a facility in Parkston. In 1943 the Catholic community in Hoven invited the Bernardine Sisters of the Third Order of St. Francis to staff their hospital. These sisters withdrew and were replaced by the Canadian sisterhood of St. Elizabeth of the Third Order of St. Francis, who also withdrew. The Hoven hospital would remain, staffed by lay professionals. In 1947 the Bernardines staffed St. Ann's Hospital in Watertown and, one year later, the Yankton Benedictines established St. Michael's Hospital in Tyndall. The Benedictine Community in Watertown (the Mother of God Priory founded in 1966) would take over St. Ann's Hospital from the Bernardines in

1973. By 1975 East River included twelve Catholic hospitals, three
of which (Tyndall, Gettysburg, and
Hoven) were community hospitals
owned by municipalities but staffed
by Catholic professionals. By the end
of the century, as indicated in another
chapter, all of the Catholic health care
facilities merged into the management
system named Avera.

In 1950 the St. Meinrad Benedictine
monks, who had worked in the diocese since the arrival of Martin Marty,
belatedly took action for detachment
from distant St. Meinrad and established a South Dakota monastery,
which evolved as Blue Cloud Abbey,
at Marvin, in the northeast corner of
the state. In 2002 Blue Cloud Abbey
offered the only Retreat Center in East
River with a capacity to accommodate
large groups.

In the 1960s the Catholic Church
was in the midst of a profound process
of reevaluation that came to fruition
as the Second Vatican Council. The
teachings of the council introduced
sweeping changes within the Catholic
community: new instructions on the liturgy; the role of the hierarchy, religious
orders, and laypersons in the modern
world; enhanced ecumenical efforts;

Serving at Blue Cloud Abbey, founded by Benedictine
monks at Marvin in 1950, Father Stanislaus Maudlin was
recognized by the state Hall of Fame for his over sixty
years of pastoral ministry among the East River tribes.
Courtesy Blue Cloud Abbey.

the goals of education; the empowerment of parishes; greater scholarship in biblical
exegesis; and more instructions were published after 1962. English replaced the Latin
language, guitars competed with church organs, lay lectors read from Holy Scripture,
congregational singing replaced silence, and the Friday abstinence was abrogated. In
addition, access to members of religious orders—so fundamental years ago—to provide
basic education, health care, and other services dramatically declined after mid-century.
Religious communities suffered decreased vocations, and those who remained tended to
serve the interests of higher education rather than other pastoral ministries. As a result,
the increased dependence on lay professionals changed the Catholic landscape in Sioux
Falls and elsewhere.

The Catholic population in East River continued to grow as the diocese entered the
twenty-first century. In 1987 there were 110,632 Catholics. By 2001 the number rose to
exceed 125,000. The demographics related to this increase, however, have changed over
the years resulting from increased urbanization and the decline of rural populations.

The Catholic East River Community of the new century contained five unique socio-
economic units: a burgeoning urban population in Sioux Falls, which reflected an increasing international composition; local farmers; livestock ranchers; shrinking small towns

and cities; and Native communities on four Indian reservations. To meet these diverse needs, the Sioux Falls Diocese was divided administratively into eight Deaneries—Aberdeen/Mobridge, Milbank/Groton, Watertown, Pierre/Huron, Brookings/Madison, Mitchell, Sioux Falls, and Yankton—subdivided further into 151 parishes. The diocese was the largest provider of private education in the state of South Dakota at two colleges serving approximately 2,000 students, three high schools serving more than 1,000 students, and twenty-two elementary schools serving nearly 5,000 students, while employing more than 300 teachers. Four Newman Centers operated in Brookings, Madison, Vermillion, and Watertown. Catholic health care ministries included nine hospitals/health care facilities located in Sioux Falls, Aberdeen, Gettysburg, Milbank, Mitchell, Parkston, Pierre, Tyndall, and Yankton along with nine Homes for the Aged. The diocese sponsored a variety of special social service centers in seventeen cities and towns, and housed seven monasteries/religious communities.

In 2001 the aggregate Catholic population of South Dakota exceeded 156,000. Only the ten Lutheran denominations, which together report more than 160,000 faithful, are competitive in Christian membership. Other large Christian churches (for example, the South Dakota United Methodist Church, the United Church of Christ, the South Dakota Episcopal Church, the American Baptist Conference, and the Mennonite Church) represent an additional 62,000 registered parishioners collectively. With the inclusion of smaller denominations, it would appear that Herbert Schell's 1960 estimate that 63.4 percent of South Dakota's citizens were registered members of a Christian congregation was still appropriate in 2002.[10] In addition, South Dakota society also includes Jewish and Islamic communities.

The overall contribution of the Catholic Church in South Dakota is visible in its sustained influence and ministry among Native communities. The enduring provision of education and health care for more than a century is a tangible and current example of Catholic contributions to the state. From the first Diocese of Gardar to the two dioceses in the state at present, the history of the Catholic Church in South Dakota has been long and richly varied.

Chapter 17
Protestant Faith and Learning

Dakota Territory appeared to offer something for everyone willing to meet the onerous demands placed upon them. For the hunter and trapper there were furs and hides to be secured. For the trader there were dollars to be made in dealing with the forenamed hunters and trappers and with the Indians who resided on the banks of the Territory's major waterways. For the settler there would be 160 acres of land. For the missionary there was another opportunity to adhere to Christ's command: "Go therefore and make disciples of all nations, baptizing them in the name of the Father and of the Son and of the Holy Spirit" (Matthew 28:19).

The field appeared ripe for the harvest for those first Protestant missionaries who came from New England or with New England antecedents. Among the Christian denominations sending missionaries to the frontier were the Presbyterians and Congregationalists, operating jointly under the American Board of Commissioners for Foreign Missions and the Protestant Episcopal Church. In 1835 Reverend Thomas S. Williamson, M.D., his wife, and family arrived on July 8 at Lac qui Parle, a trading post on the Upper Minnesota River, to establish a mission station. Two years later, they were joined by Reverend Stephen Return Riggs and his wife Mary. On April 19, 1839, Riggs became the first missionary to set foot in Dakota Territory. After a fifteen-day journey, he and his small company of men reached Fort Pierre, where he delivered the first sermon ever given in what became South Dakota. He did not attempt to organize a church. His son, Thomas L. Riggs, returned to the same locale thirty-three years later and founded the first Protestant mission in the Fort Pierre area.

Upon his return to Lac qui Parle, Stephen Riggs and Williamson, who had mastered the Dakota language in two years, began an over-two-decade project to translate the Bible into Dakota. With the assistance of a linguist, Reverend Samuel W. Pond, they also compiled a grammar and dictionary in that tongue. The Dakota-English dictionary gave the Dakota words and their English equivalents. The Riggs family also became associated with the Sisseton mission.

The Protestant Episcopal Church became involved in missionary work during the presidency of Ulysses S. Grant. In his inaugural address (1869), he asked Congress to establish a Peace Policy with the Indians. Grant said, "The proper treatment of the original occupants of this land—the Indians—is one deserving of careful study. I will favor any course toward them which tends to their civilization and ultimate citizenship." Congress approved the Peace Policy in April 1869 and proceeded to establish a Board of Indian Commissioners. William Welsh, a philanthropist and Episcopalian with an interest in Dakota Indians, was named chairman of the Board. In mid-July 1870, Congress, in implementing the Peace Policy, mandated that religious groups would nominate Indian agents. In turn, the Episcopal Church created the Indian Commission of the Domestic Commission of the Board of Missions. Five Dakota agencies were among the seven agencies assigned to the newly created Episcopalian Indian Commission.

In 1873 William Hobart Hare was named bishop of the Jurisdiction of Niobrara, a separate missionary district for the area west of the Missouri River, bounded on the south by the State of Nebraska and on the north by forty-six degrees north latitude. The thirty-five year old Hare arrived in Dakota Territory in April 1873 to begin his work. In addition to the agencies in the Niobrara, Bishop Hare was responsible for the Yankton and Crow Creek reservations east of the Missouri River and the Santee Reservation in Nebraska. In her history of the Episcopal Church in South Dakota, Virginia Driving Hawk Sneve wrote that the Indians sometimes called Hare Zitkana Duzahan (Swift Bird) because of his rapid movement from agency to agency. In his travels, he carried only the bare necessities, having learned that ". . . much luggage is a weariness to the flesh."[1]

Three years after he arrived, a new administration in Washington, D.C., that of Rutherford B. Hayes, stated that church representatives were becoming too paternalistic. The Indian Service criticized the missionary policy that Indians be first Christianized and then educated. It was Hare's belief that the Indians must be self-supporting Christians, and he carried out his philosophy through the establishment of boarding schools to teach children and through them their parents. A primary goal was to develop native clergy, believing that they could effectively evangelize fellow Indians.[2] Ten years after his arrival in Dakota Territory, Hare was asked to include among his responsibilities the care and nurturing of white people. They were swarming into the territory as a result of the Dakota Boom. In 1883, the same year that the Quaker Policy went out of existence as a federal policy, Hare was appointed Bishop of South Dakota with responsibility for both the Indians and whites.

Indians sometimes called Episcopal Bishop William Hobart Hare Zitkana Duzahan (Swift Bird) because of his rapid movement from agency to agency following his arrival in Dakota Territory in 1873. *Center for Western Studies.*

■ Establishing Denominational Roots

Two events in 1868 were to cause the major influx of settlers into Dakota Territory. The railroad was extended from Denison, Iowa, to Sioux City, and intermittent warfare between Indians and whites in the eastern part of the territory ended with the Treaty of 1868. Sioux City became the gateway to farmland and commercial opportunities to the west. Throughout history, civilization and settlement have usually advanced along major waterways and this was true in Dakota Territory. From Sioux City, white settlers moved up the Big Sioux, Missouri, and James river valleys. Yankee merchants established themselves in the valley towns of Elk Point, Vermillion and Yankton. Some were members of the eastern establishment, and they became the Territory's politicians, educators, and cultural advocates. Dakota Territory also attracted immigrants from Europe who were seeking farmland. The French became prevalent in the Jefferson area, Norwegians and Swedes in Clay County, and Germans from Russia in the James River Valley. Missionaries accompanied these settlers, bringing the Gospel to a community's residents and to isolated homesteads in the countryside.

These Protestant missionaries were often called circuit riders as they were known to serve up to a dozen congregations. They were dedicated and hardy men. Traveling by foot, horseback, sleigh, or buggy, they had to contend with blizzards, cold rains, mud, and mosquitoes. The grass in many areas stood from six- to ten-feet tall. Reverend L. P. Dotson, a Baptist missionary, who arrived in Dakota Territory in May 1864, reported that in traveling through the James River Valley he went for miles through grass when it was higher than his head when standing up in his carriage. He used a compass as a sight point on the river when entering this grassland. The Norwegian missionary Reverend Gunder Graven first traveled by foot between settlements. Often he became chilled from tramping through slush and water. Eventually, he was given a pony and he sat upon a sack of hay in lieu of a saddle. Having no reins, he converted his suspenders into reins. Missionaries in the southeastern part of the territory found that traveling in mud was as difficult as in snow. The wheels of a buggy would become larger and larger, until the circuit rider had to stop, get out his knife and cut the gumbo from the rims.

One of the first circuit riders to arrive in Dakota Territory was Charles D. Martin, a thirty-eight-year-old Presbyterian lay preacher from New Hampshire. One account has him preaching at a worship service in a little store located on the levee in Yankton in

> **Chronology**
>
> **1835** – Protestant mission post established at Lac qui Parle
> **1860s** – Decade of the Circuit Riders and the establishment of the first immigrant congregations
> **1873** – Bishop Hare arrives in Dakota Territory
> **1878-1883** – Gen. William H. H. Beadle serves as Supt. of Public Instruction for Dakota Territory
> **1881** – Joseph Ward establishes the first four-year, private "Yankee" college (Yankton College)
> **1882** – The University of South Dakota holds its first classes
> **1884** – The first four-year, private "immigrant" college is established (Augustana College)
> **1912** – Organization of the Young Citizens League (YCL)
> **1935** – Legislation approved that provides specific state appropriation for school purposes
> **1965** – The first of four vocational-technical institutes established
> **1968** – Richard Gibb appointed Commissioner of Higher Education
> **1984** – Yankton College closes

February 1859. Doane Robinson said Martin's pulpit was an upturned whiskey barrel, the most available article at hand for the purpose. Martin's sermon text was "Who so despiseth the Word shall be destroyed; but he that feareth the commandment shall be rewarded" (Proverbs 13:11). In August 1860, he erected the first church structure in Dakota on the bottom land at Vermillion. The walls were constructed of logs, and dirt dug up near the building covered the roof. Fifty dollars was sent from the national Presbyterian office to defray building costs. In addition to worship services, the building housed a Sabbath school. Public school classes were also taught there until the summer of 1862.

A Methodist circuit rider, Reverend Septimus Watson Ingham, in two years traveled 7,700 miles, the first year almost all on horseback or on foot. The second year he sometimes used a buggy. In his traveling ministry, he performed the first wedding ever held above the James River in Bon Homme County. At the Fort Randall chapel, in June 1861, he baptized the female child of Captain J. B. S. Todd. His counterpart in the Black Hills was the Reverend Henry Weston "Preacher" Smith. Smith carried with him a Bible, a collection of Wesleyan hymns, and an English translation of *Evidences of Christianity*. This devout Methodist accepted the challenge of ministering to the miners, business entrepreneurs, saloon-goers, and residents of the brothels in gold-crazed Deadwood. Smith's preaching career was cut short on August 20, 1876, as he attempted to walk to

Crook City to hold services. Only a few miles from Deadwood, he was shot, allegedly by an Indian from ambush.

Worship services took place in a variety of locales with the arrival of the circuit rider. Quite often in the countryside they were held in a settler's home. At John Thomson's home, north of Sioux Falls, worshippers gathered in the cellar of his little sod house on August 11, 1868. Here they joined in prayers, sermon, and song. They sang old Lutheran hymns that many had committed to memory in childhood. The following day they organized the Nidaros congregation. German Lutherans in northern South Dakota often held services out-of-doors at someone's homestead. Plank benches were improvised for the women, and the men sat on wagon tongues. Many brought their dinners because they had to drive several miles. The settler hosting the service would alert his neighbors by setting a small pile of dry hay on fire. A quantity of wet hay over the flaming hay made smoke that could be seen for miles. In river towns, worship services were held in stores, boarding houses, and even in a railroad boxcar.

The circuit-riding missionaries, with a heritage of over-optimism, often founded churches that did not survive. Among the so-called Eastern or Yankee denominations, the first church to survive was Christ Church in Yankton. Founded by Reverend Melancthon Hoyt in 1861, it was called by Episcopalians the "Mother Church of the Dakotas." In the summer of 1864, Reverend L. P. Judson organized a Baptist church at Yankton, but the First Baptist Church, Vermillion, founded in December 1870, is the Baptist church that has had a continuous history. The preceding year, in July 1869, a Swedish Baptist church was begun at Big Springs, Union County.

Elk Point became the center of Methodist work in the lower (Big) Sioux and Missouri valleys. A Methodist church was founded there in January 1867. Following an eastern frontier tradition, area Methodists held a camp meeting between September 11 and 14, 1868. Meetings were held in the shade of overhanging trees. A stand was erected for the ministers and a crude altar was constructed in front of it. Tents for campers were arranged in rows nearby. In the Black Hills, a formal Methodist Society was organized at Deadwood in the fall of 1877 under Reverend James Williams. A church erected in 1881 was swept away in the flood of Whitewood Creek in 1883.

On April 6, 1868, under the guidance of Reverend E. W. Cook, the Congregationalists founded a church in Yankton, the second denomination to be officially organized in the territorial capital. A renowned person in Dakota Territory, Reverend Joseph Ward became the pastor of the congregation. Well educated, he advanced the cause of education and culture in this frontier town of about four hundred people. Ward played a pivotal role in the establishment of Yankton College and his congregation supported the college financially. The Congregationalists brought with them their New England Puritan heritage, and they influenced the social consciousness of churches in the Dakotas. They championed the prohibition of liquor and promoted laws that allowed divorce only on the grounds of adultery.

The oldest continuing Presbyterian church was established in Dell City (Dell Rapids) on August 18, 1872. Services were first held in private residences, and one of the congregation's members, R. S. Alexander, added a room to his house to accommodate his fellow worshippers. Presbyterians called the Dell Rapids church "our Dakota first born." The formal establishment of old-line denominations was dependent on outside aid. National Mission Boards, with funds received from Eastern donors, provided the money for the materials needed to build the first churches. Townsite companies gave free lots to all churches; and lumber yards, based on trust, were willing to sell lumber for new churches on a promise that funds would be forthcoming.

The first African Americans to settle in Dakota Territory were ex-slaves who served as menial laborers on steamboats plying the Missouri River. Yankton was a major port of call, and a number of the former slaves, with their families, determined to make the community their home. Two of the more influential members among these new residents, J. B. Shaw and William McIntyre, encouraged other African Americans to join them. Beginning in 1885, several individuals and family units from Eufaula, Alabama, began arriving in Yankton by train. An African Methodist Episcopal congregation (AME) was formed, and on November 11, 1887, a brick AME church was dedicated in Yankton.

Within two decades, from 1870 to 1890, the dominant Yankee Protestant heritage, exemplified by Joseph Ward and William Hobart Hare, was replaced by European immigrant churches that added an international and cultural tradition lacking until then in the Dakota experience. When South Dakota achieved statehood, the largest denominations were Catholic and Lutheran.

The immigrants from Europe, who began pouring into Dakota Territory in the late 1860s, had two primary goals, insuring their survival through the acquisition of farm land and founding a church. Ole E. Rölvaag, a Norwegian immigrant author, wrote in *The Third Life of Per Smevik*, "For the early pioneers, there was no force other than the church which could draw mind and thought away from the struggle for survival."[3]

In late July 1859, at St. James, Nebraska, two Norwegian men constructed a raft for crossing the Missouri River into Dakota Territory. They had migrated from Wisconsin and were waiting for the Territory to be opened for settlement. In December 1857, tribal chiefs of the Yankton Dakotans had agreed to a treaty that ceded to the U.S. government the land north of the Missouri River between the (Big) Sioux and James rivers. The treaty took effect on July 10, 1859. The Norwegians, seeking land of their own, had heard rumors of the rich Missouri River bottomlands in Dakota. Following their exploratory trip, they moved their families to the Meckling area and staked out their 160-acre homestead sites. By 1890 Scandinavians—Norwegians, Swedes and Danes—were the largest ethnic group in South Dakota.

Rölvaag, in *The Third Life of Per Smevik*, indicated what happened next. He wrote, "It is impossible for one who hasn't seen it to imagine how the church has followed in the footsteps of the pioneer, followed him through struggle and suffering into the wilderness, into the forest, and out over the endless prairie. . . ." The organization of immigrant churches usually took place in a settler's home. Robert Ostergren has noted that "doctrinal difference and schism" caused the establishment of more than one church in an area—especially among the Norwegians—who "were greatly inclined toward schismatic activity."[4] At one time in the latter part of the nineteenth century there were at least seven Norwegian Lutheran church bodies.

As with the Yankee denominations, Scandinavian Lutherans first established congregations near the river systems in southeastern South Dakota. In 1863-64 Norwegian congregations were formally established from Brule Creek (near Elk Point) in Union County to Vangen (near Mission Hill) in eastern Yankton County. Swedes settled in northern Clay County and founded Dalesburg Lutheran Church on January 3, 1871. Close by, near Viborg, the Danes established Swan Lake Lutheran church on March 8, 1875. The Finns, who arrived at different times in the territory, were in the Black Hills for the 1876 gold rush, but an Apostolic Lutheran church did not come into being until 1889 in Lead. Apostolic Lutheran churches were established at Lake Norden in 1882 and in Savo Township, Brown County, in 1884.

German immigrants arriving in the Dakota Territory in the early 1870s also came out of denominational backgrounds. Many of them migrated from Russia and not the newly created German Empire. Between 1763, when Catherine II of Russia issued her first manifesto, to her Supreme Edict in 1786, thousands of Germans went to Russia. These documents were masterpieces of immigration propaganda. To attract foreign settlers, she made generous promises, including free transportation to Russia, freedom to settle anywhere in the country, generous allotments of free land to those who chose agriculture, freedom from taxes for five to thirty years, freedom to practice their religion, and freedom from military service. All of these privileges were to be applicable to their descendants. German Lutherans, Catholics, Reformed, Mennonites, and Hutterites settled in the area north of the Black Sea and toward the mouth of the Volga River. Because of their farming skills and hard work, the area became known as the "bread basket" of Russia.

German Congregationalists migrated from the Odessa region, arriving in the United States in 1872. They departed Russia as would most Germans because Czar Alexander II (1855-1881) revoked the privileges given by Catherine II. The Congregationalists journeyed to Yankton and then took up homesteads south of Scotland and near Parkston. Others would ultimately settle in northern South Dakota in Edmunds, McPherson, and Campbell counties. The first German Congregational church in the territory was organized January 9, 1884, near Scotland.

The very conservative Reformed Germans had left their native homes in the German states and settled on the Russian steppes. They were Calvinists and Trinitarians and very opposed to liberal attitudes. They would tenaciously cling to the German language through World War I. The first Reformed church was established at Yankton in September 1915. The Reformed element reluctantly merged with the Evangelical church in 1940.

The Evangelicals came out of Lutheran and Reformed traditions. They were affected by Pietistic and rationalistic thought. The Prussian King, Frederick William II (1797-1840), decreed that the Lutheran and Reformed elements were to work together in one united body called the Evangelical church. German Evangelicals came to the United States in the early 1880s. The Salem congregation at Tulare was organized in 1882. The Evangelical and Reformed denominations decided to merge with the Congregational Christian Church in 1957. The merger was consummated in 1963.

When King Frederick William II ordered a merger of the Lutheran and Reformed churches in 1817, confessional-minded "Old Lutherans" opposed the merger. They left Saxony and migrated to the United States in 1838, settling in Missouri. A brilliant theologian, Carl F. Walther, organized the Missouri Synod in 1847, a synod with a conservative theology. The first of these German Lutherans moving into the Dakota Territory in the 1870s were served in part by *Reiseprediger* (traveling missionaries). Reverend John F. Doescher, commissioned to serve in Dakota Territory, preached his first sermon at Heilbronn, the first Missouri Synod congregation in Dakota Territory, organized in 1876. Peace Lutheran church at Alcester began in 1874, but it was not formally organized until 1878.

Two men, John Diefendorfer and George Grossman, broke with Walther's conservative theology, moved to Iowa in 1853, and established a seminary at Dubuque. The following year, they organized the German Evangelical Synod of Iowa. In 1881 Scotland became the center for its parish work. St. John's Church at Dimock was organized in 1883. A separate Dakota District of the Iowa Synod was organized in 1890. The Iowa Synod represented confessional middle-of-the-road Lutheranism. It differed from the Missouri Synod in allowing theological development based on historical and Scriptural studies.

The construction of railroad lines in northern South Dakota brought more settlers to that region of the state. Hamlin Garland, in *A Son of the Middle Border*, underscored the importance of the railroad in settling the Territory. He wrote: "The epoch of the canvas-covered wagon had passed. The era of the locomotive, the day of the chartered car had arrived. Free land was receding at railroad speed, the borderline could be overtaken only by steam, and every man was in haste to arrive."[5]

The Chicago, Milwaukee and St. Paul Railroad brought many Lutheran Black Sea Germans into north-central South Dakota. The first train arrived at Eureka on July 27, 1888. Located at the end of the tracks for a number of years, Eureka became a boom town. Having twenty or more elevators in operation, the town became known as a major wheat-shipping center. The Iowa Synod established an academy, later a college, at Eureka in 1910. Eureka College closed in June 1933 because of the Great Depression.

Other Germans who went to southern Russia at the invitation of Catherine II in the eighteenth century were the Hutterites and Mennonites. When Catherine's grandson, Alexander II, revoked their special privileges, including exemption from military service, they decided to leave Russia. They sent out an advance party of twelve men to America to seek a suitable place for relocation. The head delegate, Reverend Paul Tschetter, directed those waiting a decision in Russia to the Dakota Territory. In 1874 the first group of Hutterites arrived in Yankton aboard a Dakota and Southern train. This first group, the Hutterdorf Colony, was a communal group. They established their new colony west of Yankton along the Missouri River and became known as the Bon Homme Colony. Other communal groups established the Wolf Creek and Elm Spring colonies.

Of the approximately 1,300 Hutterites who arrived in Dakota between 1874 and 1879, about one-third continued their communal way of life. The other two-thirds homesteaded on private farms, joined Mennonite churches, and were known as *Prairie Leut*, the Prairie People. They had wanted to settle in one area, but this was impossible near Yankton as the only available claims were scattered throughout the area. Thus, many of them moved north to unclaimed land in Hutchinson and Turner counties, with Freeman becoming a primary site for commercial activity. Over the decades, they have deliberately kept a low profile, desiring to avoid persecution because of their belief in adherence to the Beatitudes found in Christ's Sermon on the Mount. During World War I, because of their pacifist views and adherence to the German language, colony Hutterites were objects of scorn and hostile acts. They sought refuge in Canada, and by 1934 only the Bon Homme Colony remained in South Dakota. In 1935 the state legislature passed a law permitting communal societies to incorporate, and as of 1936 colonies began to return gradually from Canada.

Another German Lutheran element that entered Dakota Territory were members of the Wisconsin Evangelical Lutheran Synod (WELS). The original Wisconsin Synod was formed at Granville, Wisconsin, on May 27, 1850. The synod emphasized firm confessional Lutheranism in doctrine and practice. In 1869 the Wisconsin Synod ratified fellowship with the Missouri Synod. The most conservative of Lutheran church bodies, the Wisconsin Synod broke fellowship with the Missourians in 1961. It was not until the early 1930s that the Wisconsin Synod basically ceased being a German-speaking synod. The Dakota-Montana District was formed on June 25, 1920. Congregational strength was located primarily in northeast and north-central South Dakota.

Many of the Dutch settlers, who began arriving in Dakota Territory in 1882, came from older Dutch communities in Michigan, Wisconsin, and Iowa. After most of the land in northwest Iowa had been taken up, the Dutch looked to the west for homestead claims. A group in Orange City, Iowa, wanting to establish a "daughter" colony, sent "locators" into Dakota Territory to determine sites where concentrated settlements could be made. The plan was to lay claim to a large block of land. The first of these settlements were in Douglas and Charles Mix counties. Another colony was established south of Plankinton in Aurora County. Platte, founded in 1883, Friesland, and New Orange (Harrison) became community centers. Bon Homme and Minnehaha were other counties with a significant number of Dutch settlers.

Missionary work was promoted by the Domestic Board of the Reformed Church of America. One of the early missionaries was Reverend Fred Zwemer who moved about the southeastern part of the Territory in a buggy pulled by two ponies. Before pastors arrived, worshippers met in homes on Sunday to pray and to listen to a sermon by one of the more literate men. Congregations were soon organized, and ministers, well steeped in the Calvinist tradition, arrived to assume leadership. Conservative agricultural people, hidebound by tradition, the settlers were strict Calvinists in their belief and customs. There would be no desecration of the Sabbath as businesses must not be open nor should there be inter-league baseball. Women were not allowed to hold official positions in the church. By 1894 there were eighteen Reformed or Christian Reformed congregations in South Dakota. The majority of them had their own church buildings.

Jews from Germany and Eastern Europe also began settling in Dakota Territory in the mid-1870s. Several arrived in the Black Hills shortly after the discovery of gold. Some came as miners, others as peddlers, and others who would become successful businessmen in Custer, Deadwood and Lead. By the 1880s, they were conducting religious services in homes or rented halls. A member of the Deadwood Jewish community, an immigrant from Germany, brought with him a Torah (a scroll of the five books of Moses) that had traveled across Dakota Territory by covered wagon and was called "the covered wagon Torah." Ultimately, it was passed on to Mt. Zion congregation in Sioux Falls.

Members of the Judaic faith also settled in several locations in the eastern part of the territory during the 1870s. Aberdeen, Yankton, Rapid City, and Sioux Falls were chosen destinations. Russian Jews, victims of the pogroms of 1881, founded two short-lived agricultural colonies in Davison County. The first Reform Jews to settle in Sioux Falls, primarily German in origin, arrived in the early 1880s. For a while, Reform and Orthodox Jews, who came to the United States from Eastern Europe at the beginning of the twentieth century, worshipped together in a synagogue located on North Minnesota Avenue. Differences in ritual and observances caused them to separate in 1916. The Reform element, Mt. Zion congregation, purchased a building at fourteenth and Duluth Avenue in 1919, and Mt. Zion temple became their permanent site of worship. The Orthodox Jews, the Sons of Israel congregation, moved into a synagogue built in 1934. Faced with declining membership, the synagogue was sold in 1973.

■ Prairie Churches

A former rural sociologist at South Dakota State University, John P. Johnson, who specialized in immigrant studies, said that the "churches represent the most evident embodiment of the immigrant heritage." He estimated that immigrants founded about one-half of all churches in South Dakota. Church architecture exemplified their European heritage. In the countryside, aside from the elevator, the church was the dominant structure. The typical rural church was rectangular in shape. Many of them had narrow, white, clapboard siding with a steeple above the entry or narthex. The steeple of many churches contained a bell; the bell rope dangled down into the entry. The windows often featured a gothic arch and wealthier congregations had stained-glass windows. Stained-glass windows were customary in the stone- or brick-veneer churches of the old-line denominations having their roots in the Old Midwest or New England. Elements of Victorian architecture were often found in these churches.

The interior décor of immigrant churches reflected their European heritage. The churches featured ornately carved white altars, a large altar painting, decorated wood-work, and foreign language inscriptions. There was a throne-like pastor's chair, and off to one side were several steps leading up to the elevated pulpit where the pastor could look down and over the congregation while delivering his sermon. On one wall there was an attendance and hymn board. Accompaniment for liturgical chanting and the sing-ing of hymns was provided by a piano or pump organ.

The church basement served many purposes. In assessing the cultural contributions of the immigrants, John R. Milton writes that they put all their energies into settling the land and, thus, had little time to cultivate the arts. Their major contributions to culture, he declared, were confined to religious values and native foods.[6] If food was available, the settlers were hearty eaters. Women brought potluck dinners to the church base-ment—hot dishes, salads, and desserts. The basement was used for fund-raising dinners and bazaars at which folk crafts and baked goods were sold. Sunday school was usu-ally conducted in the basement. Rooms or teaching spaces were created by attaching strong wire to the walls and hanging curtains or blankets over the wire. Confirmation classes, usually held on Saturdays, were conducted by the pastor in the church or at the parsonage. Children and adults alike looked forward to the annual Christmas program presented by the Sunday school children. Dressed in bathrobes, shawls, or white dish towels draped over their heads, and the shepherds carrying canes to represent shepherd staffs, the youngsters presented the Nativity account while the old carols "Hark! The Herald Angels Sing," "O' Little Town of Bethlehem," and "Silent Night" were sung. At the close of the program, brown paper bags of treats were distributed. The bags usually contained unshelled peanuts, hard-striped candy, one or two chocolate creams, a large red apple, and sometimes an orange. During the Great Depression, it might be the only orange that children would see during the year.

Pastors often had a three- or four-point parish. They traveled many miles, often in adverse winter weather, conducting worship services. As late as the 1930s, when autos and gravel roads were available, the pastor, following the service, would scurry to his car and drive rapidly the eight to twelve miles to his next ministerial obligation. Pastoral pay was meager. Many were provided with a parsonage, with the congregation paying for the heating fuel and upkeep of the structure. The pastor's wages were often supple-mented by congregational members bringing him staples—meat, bread, eggs, milk, butter and home-canned fruits and vegetables.

Women were the primary fund-raisers for the church. They raised money through their adeptness with knitting needles, crochet hooks, and quilt tying, and the use of foot-powered sewing machines. Women's auxiliaries, or ladies aids, through bazaars and bake sales placed their saleable items on display, and the profits were used to pay the pastor, maintain and repair the church, and purchase equipment and supplies. During the Great Depression, the women held afternoon coffees at which one could enjoy home-baked pie or cookies and coffee for twenty-five cents.

Despite women's vital role in maintaining the church and worship services, the conservative nature of late nineteenth-century immigrants quashed women's efforts to fulfill non-domestic roles. At business meetings of the congregation only the men were permitted to vote. Women did not hold any of the leadership offices. South Dakota's recently adopted constitution stipulated that the question of woman suffrage would be

Trinity Lutheran Church (Moe Parish) near Hudson, South Dakota, is an example of a rural immigrant church. After the original church (built in 1875) was destroyed by fire, the current structure was built in 1895. *Courtesy Lynwood E. Oyos.*

on the ballot in the first state election on November 4, 1890. South Dakota's male voters rejected enfranchisement for women by a two-to-one margin, 45,802 to 22,072. The churches had been silent or openly opposed to woman suffrage. Calling the churches a male, theocratic tyranny, the suffragettes, prior to the election, had criticized churches for denying the right to participate in the ministry and offices of the church.

The suffragettes failed to recognize how deeply rooted ethnicity and tradition were in immigrant churches. The church was a defense against rapid change. When believers settled in Dakota Territory, they went where their countrymen were settling. By settling in homogeneous communities, with the church as the focal point of their values, these European transplants satisfied their need of belonging. Robert Ostergren states that immigrant churches also served a territorial function. They created ethnic boundaries which separated their members from other groups and denominations. There were limitations on travel by horse-drawn conveyances, Ostergren calls it "team-haul spacing"; thus, the church became the center of group activities, whether for worship, church school, meetings, box socials, picnics, or bazaars.[7] After worship services, members gathered to catch up on neighborhood news and to discuss the weather and crops. For decades, the church played a vital role in preserving localized cultural unity, handing down heritage, language, and a value system to succeeding generations.

In addition to stressing Scripture and morality, pastors warned their flocks not to associate closely with outside groups. There was very little ethnic intermarriage well into the twentieth century. Pastors encouraged endogamy, or marriage within one's own cultural group. They had exclusive ideas on marriage outside of the community. Young male homesteaders often married young women from older settlements to the east in Illinois, Iowa, Minnesota, and Wisconsin. A young woman who came from the home parish in northern Europe to assist a homesteader's wife with her domestic responsibilities soon caught the eye of the neighborhood's males.

The pastors and congregations of immigrant churches maintained their native language as long as possible. The service and church documents continued to be in German, Norwegian, Dutch, and other European languages. Church schools instructed their young people in the old language. With the entry of the United States into World War I, the use of foreign languages became an emotionally charged issue. American nationalism hastened the transition to the use of English. In addition, the churches had to Americanize or lose younger generations. The movement toward English built momentum during the 1920s, but remnants of ethnic identity persisted into the 1940s. As an example, it was not until 1946 that Lutherans dropped Norwegian from the Norwegian Evangelical Lutheran Church of America and became the ELC, the Evangelical Lutheran Church.

From being bastions of ethnicity and conservatism, many of the Protestant denominations in South Dakota became much more inclusive and liberal in thought and practice. There were significant mergers and agreements for full communion with denominations that once were shunned or considered competitors. The several Scandinavian Lutheran synods and the former German American Lutheran Church (ALC) merged into the Evangelical Lutheran Church in America (ELCA). The ELCA established full communion agreements with the Presbyterian, Moravian Brethren, and Episcopal churches. As indicated earlier, the Congregational, Evangelical, and Reformed synods merged into the United Church of Christ (UCC).

The prairie-plains became over churched; South Dakota ended up with too many churches, more than members could support. The early settlers had been overly optimistic and were spurred on by denominational rivalry to form more congregations than were actually needed. Since the 1940s, modern technology, a succession of economic setbacks for family farmers, and the lure of urban living have caused the depopulation of rural South Dakota. The loss of family farms and the abandonment of commerce in the rural town led to the demise of many rural churches. The smaller and weaker congregations went first. In many existing rural congregations, the majority of worshippers were middle-aged or elderly. There is a scarcity of young people. They have sought employment and pleasure in urban areas.

At the end of the twentieth century many congregations did not have the funds to support a pastor, and there was a shortage of young pastors in rural areas. The fore-mentioned full communion agreements came into play, and a Presbyterian minister might preside over a Lutheran worship service or a Lutheran pastor at Presbyterian worship services. Time and mortality will cause many white, clapboard churches, whose spires have loomed over the prairie, to be vacated. Some of these churches will be placed on flatbed trucks, steeples removed, and hauled to historical or tourist sites. Others will have their interiors cleared of worship artifacts to become granaries. Others will stand vacant and gradually deteriorate because of natural forces or vandals. The church, whether on the prairie or in a small town, was more than a place bringing spiritual refreshment to the worshippers; it was the glue that held much of the community together. The church was the place that provided meaning, identity, and belonging.

■ Strengthening the Faith Through Education

During the 1880s, the pioneer church bodies began to establish academies and colleges. The denominations that originated in the northeastern section of the United States had a strong belief in educational opportunities. Through education, the faith could be promoted and cultural values transmitted to future generations. Emphasis was placed on educational programs for the ministry and classroom teachers. Immigrants also viewed

Assigned the task of promoting Christian education in Dakota Territory, Reverend Joseph Ward as a Congregational minister in Yankton played a major role in territorial politics. *Courtesy South Dakota State Historical Society–State Archives.*

academies as the first step toward giving their children the opportunity to rise above the level of learning of their parents.

Prior to his arrival in Yankton in September 1869, the Reverend Joseph Ward was ordered to "see to it that the cause of Christian education be vigorously carried out in the great Northwest." Given his ancestry and training, he took this charge seriously. Ward was impressive in stature as well as in accomplishments. Ephraim Miner, a founder of the Congregational church in Yankton, provided the following description of Ward: "He was something over six feet in height, broad shouldered, well proportioned, plainly but well dressed, and looking as if he might be a traveling man or a young lawyer, or doctor, or possibly a young preacher. At all events he looked like a man who could do things."[8]

Ward first established Yankton Academy. The building constructed for the academy was given to the city in 1876, and it became Yankton High School, the first public high school in Dakota Territory. By this time, Ward was formulating plans for a four-year Christian college to be known as Pilgrim College. In the deliberations that followed, the name was changed to Yankton College and the school was incorporated on August 30, 1881. When classes began in the fall of 1882, it was the first institution of higher learning in Dakota Territory.[9]

The Congregationalists also opened several short-lived academies, including Ward Academy near Platte in 1892,[10] Spearfish, 1880-82, Plankinton, 1885-87, and another near Strool in the 1890s. The academy opened at Redfield in 1885 became a college, and in 1916 a seminary. Its latter role was to educate young German men for the ministry. In 1928, because of financial hardship, it was relocated to Yankton and merged with Yankton College. Lack of funds and students plagued all of the foregoing institutions. Yankton College was the last to close its doors. The school began to experience serious financial problems in the mid-1970s and the last classes were held in 1984. In 1988 the school was offered to the federal government for conversion into a minimum security prison.

Ward's educational efforts were quickly emulated by other denominations and by the public sector. By 1890 South Dakota had twelve colleges and universities. Given the state's population, it was obvious that there were too many institutions of higher learning. Without serious consideration of adequate future income and student numbers, overbuilding occurred. The "too many" syndrome was caused by over-optimism associated with the Dakota Boom, denominational competition, fervent lobbying by civic boosters, and a hearty welcome, including financial support, from main-street merchants.

On September 16, 1883, the Presbyterians opened Presbyterian University of Southern Dakota at Pierre, enrolling thirty students. The school's name was changed to Pierre University the following year. Eastern money, a gift from Mrs. C. H. McCormick,

Chicago, funded the school's first building, McCormick Hall. Two other schools were established by the Presbyterian Church in 1885, Scotland Academy and Groton Collegiate Institute. The Groton venture lasted three years. Pierre University, in 1898, found itself short of funds and students, and it was merged with Scotland Academy and moved to Huron. Huron's civic leaders offered a hotel building, debt free and taxes paid, for a campus. Huron College opened on September 20, 1898. Toward the end of the twentieth century, still plagued by debt and enrollment problems, the Presbyterian Church sold the school. With a name change to Huron University, it became a secular institution. Emphasis was shifted from the liberal arts to training for specific occupations. The school's financial woes continued, and in the spring of 2001 the Cheyenne River Lakota Tribe bought Huron University. Renamed Si Tanka University, the school had campuses in Huron and Eagle Butte.

At the Baptist convention at Lake Madison in 1881, the subject of a proposed Dakota Collegiate Institute arose. A committee was formed and bids were solicited from various communities for money and land. Sioux Falls made the best offer—$3,000 in cash and forty acres of land valued at $3,000. On September 18, 1883, Dakota Collegiate Institute officially opened. While construction of the first building was underway, classes were held in the basement of the Baptist church. With the completion of the building in 1885, the school was reorganized and renamed Sioux Falls University at the bequest of an influential local booster. Reverend E. B. Meredith, pastor of the Baptist church, resigned that position to become the school's first president. Determined to "sink or swim with the college," Meredith served not only as president but as a teacher and financial agent. In 1899 the school's board of directors renamed the institution Sioux Falls College. Almost a hundred years later, the school's name was changed to the University of Sioux Falls.

The North American Baptist (Conference) Seminary established its campus in Sioux Falls in 1949. The Seminary had been founded at Rochester, New York, in 1858. It is the only professional graduate school of theology in South Dakota.

When the Methodist Episcopal Church began to consider a college in Dakota Territory, residents of Huron, Mitchell, and Ordway competed to have the school located in their community. Aggressive community boosters and land developers in Mitchell were successful in convincing the Methodist leadership that Mitchell should be the home of Dakota University. The school, chartered in 1883, opened in 1885 and was officially accepted by the Methodist Episcopal Conference in 1886.

The first forty students lived and studied in Merrill Memorial Hall. Construction of the building had not been completed when the students arrived. Three years later, in 1888, the building was destroyed by fire. With survival at stake, the community's business leaders organized a fund drive and raised $39,000 to liquidate the school's debt. Dakota University also had a preparatory department, or academy, to prepare students for college-level courses. The school was renamed Dakota Wesleyan University in 1904, and three years later the academy was made a separate entity. The secondary education curriculum was discontinued in 1926. The Free Methodist Church established the Wessington Springs Seminary and Junior College in 1886. In 1923 the Seminary was dropped from the school's title. The junior college was an accredited institution until 1964 when college courses were terminated. The school continued as an academy until the spring of 1968.

The other Yankee denomination, the Protestant Episcopal Church, concentrated on Indian missions, operating parochial schools in various communities. After William Hobart Hare was named Bishop of South Dakota, he selected Sioux Falls as the new site for his headquarters. When he announced plans for a school for girls, Sioux Falls offered him land and $10,000 if Hare could match the amount. He did and the All Saints School for Girls opened in September 1885, primarily, but not exclusively, for the daughters of missionaries under his jurisdiction. With the assistance of Helen Peabody, the principal, he formulated the curriculum and employed the teachers.

The Norwegian Lutherans were the first of the immigrant denominations to establish a four-year college in Dakota Territory. Prior to its arrival in 1884, and after its arrival, Augustana College, in its early years, had a contentious history, torn between forces of disunity and unity. On June 5, 1860, representatives of Norwegian and Swedish Lutheran congregations gathered near Clinton, Wisconsin, to found the Scandinavian Evangelical Lutheran Augustana Synod. In the same year, the new synod established Augustana Seminary in Chicago, Illinois. When the school officially opened for classes on September 1, it had two departments, theological and preparatory.

Influenced by land speculators and railroad officials who gave schools and colleges land and a commission on land sales if an educational institution moved to a proposed new townsite, Augustana Seminary moved to Paxton, Illinois, in 1863. Six years later, the Norwegians and Swedes parted ways and the Norwegians established a seminary and academy at Marshall, Wisconsin. The school experienced financial woes at Marshall, and church leaders decided that if the school was to have a future it would have to move westward along with the migration of Norwegians into Iowa, Minnesota, and the Dakota Territory.

James Wahl, Canton, the well-traveled Commissioner of Immigration, was a leading proponent of the school's westward movement. In 1881, under his leadership, Augustana was located at Beloit, Iowa, in the midst of the thousands of Norwegian immigrants settling on the northern plains. Three years later, in 1884, the school was moved to Canton and housed in a three-story wooden structure originally intended to be a hotel. The merger of three Norwegian synods in 1890 led to the seminary's being moved to Minneapolis and all preparatory and college courses being offered on the Canton campus. During the prior year, a Lutheran Normal School had been established in Sioux Falls. One of the city's leading citizens, R. F. Pettigrew, donated four acres of land in southwest Sioux Falls for the school. Local boosters guaranteed $8,000 toward construction of the school's first building, Old Main.

Following a major merger of synods in 1917, which brought ninety percent of all Norwegian Lutherans into one synod, the Norwegian Lutheran Church of America (NLCA), the normal school was merged with the college and the college was moved to Sioux Falls. A bitter verbal struggle between boosters in Canton and Sioux Falls took place over the move; Canton residents believed the college had been stolen from them. With the move to Sioux Falls, the so-called "College on Wheels" reached its final destination. Augustana became a true liberal arts institution during the 1920s. The liberal arts have remained the core for the school's various professional and vocational programs.

In 1919 frustrated Cantonites received permission to establish a "four year Normal course of High School grade" until such time as the Normal Department at Augustana College in Sioux Falls would be transferred to Canton. When the school opened in 1920, it was promoted as a six-year normal school. During the mid-1920s, the NLCA recognized the Canton school as an academy, placing it and the college under one administration. In 1931 Augustana Academy was completely separated from the college and operated successfully until financial problems caused its closure in 1971.

German Lutherans opened two academic institutions in South Dakota. The Dakota District of the Evangelical Synod of Iowa decided at a District meeting, May 5-10, 1909, to establish a college at Eureka. In mid-September 1910, the first school year opened, with ninety-one students enrolled. They ranged from fourteen to twenty-four years of age. The school had three courses of study—preparatory, commercial, and a normal course. The school's founders emphasized the need for bilingual training. While being provided with religious instruction, the students would become proficient in English and German.

By 1917 maintenance of the institution had become a financial burden for the Dakota District, and support of the college was assumed by the General Synod. The school became truly a college in the fall of 1927. The preparatory classes were dropped and two years of junior college were added. The college was reaching new heights when the national economy collapsed. Lacking finances and students, the college held its final commencement ceremonies on June 7, 1933. Eureka College was merged with St. Paul-Luther College.

The Dakota-Montana District of the Wisconsin Synod was organized in June 1920. The new district covered a vast expanse of territory, and church officials believed that it was necessary to establish a residential Christian academy in the midst of this territory. Thus, Northwestern Lutheran Academy at Mobridge was opened on September 5, 1929. The academy was to provide a general Christian education on the high-school level and was to be a "feeder" to synodical colleges. The twenty-two students enrolled in the first ninth-grade class came from fourteen different communities. Nationwide, residential high schools suffered declining enrollments in the 1960s, causing their closure. After fifty years of operation in Mobridge, the Wisconsin Synod decided to close Northwestern Lutheran Academy on August 15, 1979.

Seeing the need for teachers, the Mennonites chartered a college at Freeman on December 4, 1900. In September 1903 it offered courses at the academy level, accompanied by teacher training. The school supplied teachers to operate an elementary school system that was almost entirely Mennonite. In the ensuing years, while maintaining the academy, accredited in 1922, Freeman Junior College offered its first courses in 1918. The college was accredited in 1929. In May 1968 college courses were dropped but the academy continued its academic program.

■ Beadle and Public School Lands

Visitors to the nation's Capitol can view statues of two Dakotans, Reverend Joseph Ward and General William Henry Harrison Beadle. Both men made major contributions to territorial politics and to education. Ward, as has been noted, founded the first private academy and college in Dakota Territory. He was allied with General Beadle in promoting public education, and he was a major supporter of Beadle's effort to prevent the sale of public school lands at lower prices.

Beadle, born in Indiana and a graduate of the University of Michigan, was appointed Surveyor General of the United States for the Territory of Dakota by President Ulysses S. Grant in 1869. Nine years later, he agreed to serve as superintendent of public instruction for the territorial governor, William Howard. It was in this capacity that Beadle made a lasting contribution to education in South Dakota. The Land Ordinance of 1785 had created the specifications for a standard township—six linear miles on each side, creating a thirty-six-square-mile township. The government further specified that Section 16 in each township should be sold or rented to create a fund that would support public education. At a later date, Section 36 was also designated for this purpose. As a surveyor, Beadle was very familiar with the law. In his *Autobiography*, he wrote, "The schools and this endowment were live issues in my mind on the first day I saw Dakota."[11] He knew

Serving as Superintendent of Public Instruction for Dakota Territory, General William H. H. Beadle created a permanent fund to support public education from the sale of land in Sections 16 and 36 in each township. *Courtesy Dakota State University Archives.*

that in states east of the Mississippi River, public-school land was being sold for $1.25 to $2.50 per acre. Beadle determined that that would not occur in Dakota Territory, stating that "no school lands should ever be sold for less than their appraised value, and never for less than ten dollars an acre."[12] Governor Howard was a strong supporter of the idea. At the time, land was cheap and ten dollars seemed an excessive amount. In the drafting of the state's constitution, in which Beadle played a role, the ten dollar minimum was written into the proposed draft and it was part of the document ratified in 1889. The interest accumulating in a permanent fund was to be divided among the school districts in proportion to the number of children of school age. In the early days of statehood, people believed that revenue accrued from school lands would provide almost all the funds needed for public education. By 1896 the permanent school fund had grown to more than $2 million. George W. Kingsbury, a Yankton newspaper editor, said that it was not far distant when proceeds from the school lands would be so large that taxation for school purposes would be reduced to a small sum. When South Dakotans celebrated the state's centennial in 1989, there was over $62 million in the permanent fund. Kingsbury and other low-tax adherents were wrong. In the twentieth century, the operational costs for public schools continued to increase and the permanent fund became less important. The major part of funding for public education would come from local sources, primarily the general property tax.

General Beadle also advanced federal legislation to set aside two townships, seventy-two sections in Dakota Territory and four other western territories to fund professional universities. Although he resigned as superintendent of education in 1883, he remained involved in education for the remainder of his life.

Prior to statehood, two types of public school districts were authorized by the territorial legislature, common and independent. The latter districts were not approved until 1887 when the legislature permitted public schools with towns and cities to organize independently of common school districts. The state's first governor, Arthur Mellette, believed that the two-district system contributed to inequalities of opportunity. He was sensitive to the lack of educational facilities in the country schools. In his message to the legislature in 1893, he said, "The failure to secure benefits for the rural schools in every degree equal to those in the more densely populated communities is the acknowledged weakness of the public school system."[13]

■ One-Room Country Schoolhouses

Despite Mellette's misgivings, the common school districts or one-room country schoolhouses played a significant role in educating the state's young people well into the twentieth century. Unlike the immigrant churches that emphasized ethnicity and denominational diversity, the one-room rural schools became the true melting pots of late nineteenth-century and early twentieth-century America. It was in these schools that many pupils, ranging in age from six to twenty, struggled to learn English. In many cases, only the teacher could speak English. In this one-room environment, young Germans sat side by side with Scandinavian youths and freely mingled in playground activities during recess and the noon hour. They were co-actors in the annual school Christmas programs, and they were to be allies in spelling bees and arithmetic contests. Early schoolhouses were seldom locked and they became the social center for the entire community. Settlers were brought together for celebrations, literary societies, parties, plays, and square dances. Ethnic intermarriage did not occur in the rural areas until the emergence of public schools. One cannot overestimate the role of these schools in social change.

Public school classes in the territory were held in sod houses, log cabins with dirt floors, and in the homes of settlers until sufficient tax money could be raised for constructing a school building. By 1870 lumber for this purpose was being transported from Iowa and Minnesota using wagons and draft animals. Like many rural churches, the school buildings were rectangular in shape, consisting of one room and an entryway. Some of the buildings had a cupola above the entry which housed a bell and a flag staff. Again, as with the churches, construction included clapboard siding that was painted white.

Usually, country schoolhouses were located within walking distance of the homesteads in a particular area. The schools were built on parcels of land, approximately one

The Eggers one-room school in Minnehaha County, east of Renner, was opened in 1909 with Kate Jennings as the teacher for ten students. It was closed in 1957 when only four students were enrolled. The school has been moved to the Augustana College Heritage Park. *Courtesy Eleanor Eggers Emmel.*

acre in size, donated by a landowner. If the school should close, the land would revert back to the landowner. School districts were numbered but they were often named for the farmer who owned the land; in many instances, the teacher received bed and board at the landowner's home.

The interior of the school included student desks with traditional ink wells, a teacher's desk and chair, slate blackboards, a pot-bellied stove, a kerosene lamp with a reflector mounted on wall brackets, a rack containing a pull-down map or maps, a water pail and dipper, wash basin, and a coal bucket. Students viewed pictures of Presidents Washington and Lincoln hung on the wall behind the teacher's desk. Outside buildings included a shed used to store coal or wood, a privy, and often a barn to house the horses of the teacher and older children who rode or drove buggies to school.

Following World War I, many school districts replaced the first generation of rural school buildings. New construction included a larger classroom, more windows, an entry and a cloakroom. Many of the newly constructed schools had basements where students could play during recess and the noon hour. The furnace and its fuel were located in the basement, and heat was brought up through floor registers into the classroom. Twentieth-century schools also had indoor chemical toilets for use during the winter months.

Many of the first teachers in the common school districts had come from the eastern United States. In a short period of time, thereafter, the instructors in most rural schools were the daughters and sons of townspeople and homesteaders. They were poorly educated and poorly paid. During the last two decades of the nineteenth century, it is estimated that less than thirty percent of them had four years of education beyond the eighth grade. They received their training at required teachers' institutes at the county courthouse with the county superintendent of schools presiding. The institutes were one to four weeks in length. Institute curriculums included the latest teaching methods, model classroom situations, and suggestions regarding discipline and busy work for students whose class was not in session at a given time. Other training was available through three- to-six-week sessions of summer school at a nearby normal school.

The county superintendent of schools determined whether applicants should receive teaching certificates, using three criteria in the evaluation—moral character, learning, and ability to teach. Applicants had to be of very low quality not to be certified because of the constant shortage of teachers in the common school districts. There were decided changes after statehood with an on-going broadening of requirements as well as uniform examinations and a system of graded certificates.

Although requirements for certification were minimal, there were many excellent, committed teachers in the late nineteenth century who more than earned their meager pay. In 1881 male teachers received $27.50 per month and their female counterparts $25.20 a month. The pay scale was little improved five decades later. In 1937-38, in the final years of the Great Depression, the average annual salary was $864 or $96 per month. Teachers were also required to do custodial and maintenance work. They cleaned the school and brought in the wood and coal, sometimes with assistance from older students. They built the fire in the stove in the morning, banked it at night, and carried out the ashes. Students often lent a hand in washing the blackboard and pounding the chalk dust out of the erasers on an outside wall of the school building. The country school teacher faced dismissal if he or she did not lead an exemplary life. Thus, they were to abstain from drinking alcoholic beverages, chewing or smoking tobacco, and cursing. The school day began with the pledge of allegiance to the flag and the singing of songs from the *Golden Song Book*. Then the teacher faced the reality of a crowded daily class schedule. A typical schedule for first through fifth grades in 1896 follows:

Time Begins	Min. Long	Classes	Grade of Readers
9:00	10	General Exercises	
9:10	10	1st Reader	
9:20	15	2nd Reader	
9:35	15	3rd Reader	
9:50	20	4th Reader	
10:10	20	5th Reader	
10:30	15	Recess	
10:45	10	Number Class	1st Reader and 1st half 2nd
10:55	20	Elementary Arithmetic	2nd half 2nd Reader and half 3rd
11:15	20	Complete Arithmetic	4th and 5th Readers
11:35	10	Language Class	2nd and 3rd Readers
11:45	15	Physiology	5th Readers
12:00	60	Noon Hour	
1:00	15	1st Reader and Language	
1:15	10	2nd Reader	
1:25	15	Elementary Grammar	4th Grammar
1:40	15	Higher Grammar	5th Reader
1:55	10	Hygiene	4th Reader
2:05	10	Oral Geography	2nd and 3rd Readers
2:15	15	Elem. Geography	4th Reader
2:30	15	Recess	
2:45	20	Complete Geography	5th Reader
3:05	15	Writing	3rd, 4th and 5th Readers
3:20	15	Primary History	4th Reader
3:35	15	Complete History, Civil Government	5th Reader
3:50	10	Spelling Classes	4th and 5th Readers

Among the textbooks used in the foregoing classes were McGuffey, and Barnes and Appleton Readers, Barnes' Geography and History, Robinson and Melines arithmetic text, and Read and Kellogg's Grammar.

The Young Citizens League (YCL) played a major role in the rural school after it was organized in 1912 by M. M. Guhin, the Brown County Superintendent of Schools. The YCL pledge emphasized devotion to the United States, a study of its ideals, and a constant interest in the general welfare of the state and nation. The pledge concluded, "I shall strive to do something each day to improve the standards of my school and community, and thereby endeavor to promote better citizenship." The YCL provided training and experience in holding office, serving on committees and preparing and participating in programs. There were county YCL associations and state conventions held at the State Capitol building beginning in 1927. They were held each ensuing year until school reorganization took place. At these meetings the Young Citizens League *Marching Song* was always sung:

First verse:

O, up from ev'ry valley,
And down from ev'ry crest,
We come, thy loyal children,
By all thy favors blest,
To pledge our firm allegiance,
America to thee
The guardians of tomorrow,
By mountain, plain or sea.

Chorus:
We march and we sing; our voices ring;
Young citizens are we;
Leagued in a host whose watchwords are
Youth, courage, loyalty.
Hailing our nation's banner,
Afloat in the sunlit sky,
Which through hopes and fears,
Thru future years,
We will hold evermore on high.

By the mid-1970s, only a few rural schoolhouses, most of them west of the Missouri River, remained. Some of the vacant buildings became township halls, others became granaries or were moved to museum sites. Many sat empty for decades and were eventually razed. The number of rural schoolhouses peaked at 5,011 in 1916. At the end of the twentieth century there were fifty elementary schools enrolling fewer than twenty students. The majority of them were in the remote areas west of the Missouri River. Autos, motorized buses, and improved roads enabled students to travel great distances, contributing to school consolidation.

The rural schoolhouse played a major role in shaping the lives and culture of at least three generations of South Dakotans. Generally, people who attended rural schools believed that with a quality teacher they experienced a unique and excellent learning environment. Younger and older students alike listened to the instructions given and class recitations in the various grades. Hearing what transpired in the different classes reinforced learning for all of the students.

"Town schools" grew apace with the expansion of railroad lines across South Dakota, and school enrollments increased as settlers moved into each newly platted community. Independent school districts, encompassing both elementary and secondary grades, were established in the growing communities. Ultimately, more schools were built than the state was either able or willing to support adequately.[14]

■ The School Problem: Deficits and Demography

As noted earlier, funds derived from the Beadle-initiated school lands fund proved woefully inadequate to support the state's public school system. The bulk of the funding was to come from local mill levies on real property. The plight of the public schools became desperate during the 1930s. Drought, depression, and tax delinquency brought many districts to insolvency. In many districts, teachers remained unpaid for several months. When it became apparent that state aid was needed, the 1935 legislature responded, providing specific appropriations for school purposes.

Changing demographics and the need for greater economy and efficiency motivated the legislature to enact a voluntary school district reorganization measure in 1951. Four years later, in 1955, a law was approved requiring each county board of education to prepare a master plan for school district reorganization in accordance with standards established by the state board of education. Additional legislation required the rural common school districts that had already closed their one-room schools to join an independent district that offered a K-12 curriculum. Remaining rural districts were required to join an independent district in 1969.

Enrollment and financial problems arose as modern farm technology and transportation caused a continuing exodus from rural areas during the latter half of the twentieth century. Small farm operators left the land, farms grew larger, and smaller towns found

The "Cold Lunch" program at a rural school during the 1930s. Note the practical and affordable lunch buckets. *Courtesy Farm Security Administration.*

there was a decreasing demand for the services they offered to farmers in their adjacent area. A declining birthrate, the movement of rural youth to urban centers for employment and a different lifestyle, and an aging population caused a significant movement toward consolidation and/or reorganization of school districts.

Despite the obvious demographic data, many small towns reluctantly gave up their high schools. Schools, along with churches, had been the central foci for residents. Alumni had fond memories of their high-school years. The school building was a community center and a rallying site for the town's athletic teams. The high school played an essential role in enhancing the local economy. Some parents objected to transporting their youngsters long distances to another school, and others feared a tax increase if they were required to support a larger school.

Nevertheless, reorganization and consolidation had taken place, and by 1945 South Dakota had 3,415 common and independent school districts. In August 2003 the number of districts totaled 171, with Cresbard and Bristol proposing to close their high schools and have their students transported to adjacent communities. A state regulation that a high school had to enroll thirty-five students to receive state aid played a significant role in several school boards voting for reorganization.

Independent school districts that remained struggled to maintain balanced budgets as per capita costs for education soared. Several districts had aging school buildings that were constructed in the 1920s and had to be replaced. Federal mandates, many of them directed toward special education, were inadequately funded by the federal government and much of the cost had been absorbed by local school districts. The state legislature, consistently conservative and determined to maintain a balanced budget, had been reluctant to increase adequately per-pupil payments to financially beleaguered school districts. As of 2003 the state expenditure per pupil varied according to enrollment. Fifty-five districts with fewer than 200 students received $4,771 per student; seventy-seven school districts enrolling between 201 and 600 students received between $3,968 and $4,771 per student; the largest forty school districts received the standard amount of $3,968 per pupil. The national average was $5,255 per student.

Local school districts were forced to rely on the regressive real property tax, and with changes in the tax structure this tax was not adequate. In 2002 property tax provided 43.4 percent of school revenue and state aid supplied 15.3 percent. In 1995 an initiated measure that would have limited property taxes to one percent of the assessed value failed on a 49.5 percent to 50.5 percent vote. Governor William Janklow proposed a thirty percent cut in property taxes for homes and farmland over several years. At first, the legislature settled on a twenty percent reduction with a promise to cut the remaining ten percent in ensuing years. At the same time, a "freeze" was placed on real property taxes at the county and local level. The law limited the amount of additional property taxes that could be collected at the local level each year to three percent or the rate of inflation, whichever was lower. School districts, desperate to meet their budgets, were forced to call special elections, requesting an opt-out from the tax freeze. Voters responded favorably in some districts but negatively in others. A positive solution to funding public education in South Dakota had not been brought forward as the state entered the twenty-first century.

■ Public Higher Education

The movement for private colleges was paralleled by the locating of public institutions of higher education during the 1880s. William H. H. Beadle, as superintendent of public instruction, expressed a great interest in the common school districts that were growing in number throughout the territory and in supplying teachers for them. He became an ardent proponent for establishing teacher education at the university and normal school levels. Needless to say, his views were supported by townsite boomers and the Yankee merchants on main street.

The first public institution, the University of South Dakota, became a reality in 1882, two decades after being authorized by the first territorial legislative assembly. Although no money was appropriated, the legislature had stipulated that when the school was established it should be in Vermillion. A second legislative assembly, in the same year, acted to incorporate the University of Dakota, appointing an eighteen-member Board of Regents and even prescribing course offerings.

Heavy snow during the winter of 1880-81 spelled disaster for the settlements along the Missouri and Big Sioux rivers. An early spring melt swept away 118 dwellings in Vermillion on a frightening night in March 1881. Following this devastating blow, civic leaders gathered in April 1881 to make plans for rebuilding the town. At this meeting, the city fathers determined that the university that existed only on paper would become a reality. Clay County was bonded for $10,000 to construct a university building. Prior to its completion, the school opened on October 16, 1882, with thirty-five students attending classes in a room on the second floor of the Clay County courthouse. Dr. Ephraim Epstein, a scholarly medical doctor in Yankton, was the faculty member for the first year. In 1883 the territorial legislature authorized a bond issue of $50,000 for capital improvements and the school was firmly established. During the following year, Beadle proudly announced that the university had a reference library of five hundred volumes for the 116 students enrolled at the Vermillion campus.

There followed a steady stream of community boosters from several towns to lobby the territorial legislature to authorize an institution of higher learning for their particular community. Adhering to the time-honored practice of "pork barrel politics" and overly optimistic because of the Dakota Boom, but with little foresight or consideration of demographics, legislators authorized five additional schools during the 1880s. Included were an agricultural college at Brookings (1881), normal schools at Madison, Spearfish, and Springfield (1881), and the Dakota School of Mines at Rapid City (1885). Ten years after statehood, the legislature, once again, yielded to the clamor of civic boosters, this time from Aberdeen, who believed they, too, were deserving of a public higher education institution. In 1899 compliant legislators created the Industrial Institute of South Dakota. When the legislature added a teacher training program, the school's name was changed to Northern Normal and Industrial School.

The legislature required that a community provide, at a minimum, twenty acres for a campus. Legislators, in turn, appropriated from $7,000 to $20,000 for the first classroom building. These three and four-story structures stood tall on a landscape usually devoid of trees. Old Central on the Brookings campus dominated a treeless hill, and the Central Building at Northern Normal and Industrial stood in the midst of a harvested wheat field with shocked grain standing all around.

Governor Arthur C. Mellette quickly realized the financial difficulties the state faced in funding public higher education. He reaffirmed his support for the state's common and independent school districts, but he questioned how the state was going to maintain the six institutions of higher education lavishly established during the Dakota Boom of the 1880s. In his report to the legislature in 1890, he said, "It is suggested as matter of serious inquiry by the legislature whether these institutions are not being maintained at a cost beyond what is warranted by the resources and needs of the new state. . . . It is suggested that a decided reduction of expenditures for the institutions devoted to higher education might be safely made for the relief of our overburdened taxpayers and still preserve their substantial benefits to the state."[15]

George Kingsbury, the veteran newspaperman from Yankton, provided a more critical assessment of what had transpired and what was transpiring. He wrote that in the locating of the state's higher education institutions, no consideration had been given to the benefits that might result to the state fifty to one hundred years hence. Instead, he wrote, "In reality [they] had been located arbitrarily under the influence of . . . politics, favoritism, a division of spoils, or legislative logrolling or trade. Accordingly, those towns and cities which had failed to secure, during territorial days, such institutions, now become clamorous for such benefits, honors and distinctions."[16]

When the territorial legislature voted to incorporate the University of Dakota (Vermillion) in December 1862, it authorized the appointment of a board of regents for the proposed school. The five schools that followed, at Brookings, Madison, Spearfish, Springfield, and Rapid City, each had its own board of regents. This provincial system of governance came to an end in 1889 as the first South Dakota Legislature placed all public institutions of higher learning under one board of regents.

For decades, the regents considered consolidating programs if not institutions, but discussions had led to no significant action. As the schools matured, they increased in size and became permanently embedded in their respective communities. The colleges and universities became almost untouchable as they were essential in sustaining the local economy. At the recommendation of the regents, the state legislature did authorize name changes in the various institutions. South Dakota State College was renamed South Dakota State University in 1964. Dakota State Normal School, Madison, became Eastern State Normal School in 1921, General Beadle State Teachers College in 1947, and Dakota State College in 1969. Dakota Normal, Spearfish, officially became Black Hills Teachers College in 1941. Springfield Normal was renamed Southern State College and Northern Normal became Northern State College in the early twentieth century. The Dakota School of Mines was renamed the South Dakota School of Mines in 1943.

Upon the urging of Governor William Janklow, the mission of Dakota State College was changed by the state legislature on February 19, 1984. Under its new mission "to provide instruction in computer management, computer information systems, electronic data processing and other related undergraduate and graduate programs" the school thrived. On July 1, 1989, the state legislature gave university status to Dakota State, Black Hills State, and Northern State to better reflect their purpose in the total scheme of the state's higher education system.

A seeming decisive moment occurred after 1968 when a commissioner of higher education was appointed to provide data and research for the regents. In 1970, the commissioner, Richard Gibb, prepared a study entitled *A Master Plan for Public Higher Education in South Dakota*. His master plan concurred with Kingsbury's observation that a primary problem in South Dakota "is that of too many colleges and universities." Gibb tampered with something almost sacred as there was little public support or interest in changing the statewide system. No college community would relinquish that institution that civic boosters had ardently lobbied for and secured in the 1880s and 1890s. Gibb's recommendations that all engineering courses be moved to South Dakota State University and that the School of Mines be made a comprehensive college for western South Dakota with a junior college branch located in Spearfish aroused the ire of residents of the Black Hills. Following a great amount of vocal and print opposition from West River communities, the regents opted to maintain the status quo.

The only significant change involved Southern State College. In the 1970s the school was merged administratively with the University of South Dakota. The state legislature also declared that the University of South Dakota at Springfield should become a vocational-technical college. The school's fate was determined in the 1980s when Governor Janklow recommended to the legislature that the college be closed and transformed into a minimum-security prison. Despite vocal opposition from residents of Springfield and Yankton and several legislators, Southern State College was closed and the buildings renovated to accommodate four hundred inmates.

Although it was obvious that there were too many schools for too few people, the number of post-high school academic and vocational institutions continued to grow. Specific jobs and the training for them had taken precedence over the type of liberal education that was and continued to be an excellent preparation for a well-rounded life as well as quality employment. Beginning in 1965 the first of four vocational-technical institutes was established. They were located at Watertown, Sioux Falls, Mitchell, and Rapid City. The state board of regents gave its approval to a non-traditional student program in Sioux Falls that is staffed by faculty from Dakota State University, South Dakota State University, and the University of South Dakota. This new institution has the potential of becoming a seventh public university campus. Several private schools have entered into the competition in offering training for specific vocations. Located in the state's two largest urban centers are Kilian Community College, Colorado Technical University, and National American University.

■ Current Realities

The optimism of those community boosters and church and educational leaders, including General Beadle, during the 1880s has been tempered by a much different economic and social environment a century later. Changing demographics in South Dakota have created serious problems for organized religious and educational institutions. As the majority of the state's populace continues to settle along the north-south and east-west interstate highway corridors, rural South Dakota will continue to have more congregations and school districts abandoning their sites of worship and learning. Most rural congregations find it difficult to maintain their houses of worship and finance adequately a pastor. Many recent seminary graduates are reluctant to accept a call to a rural parish. The residents, many middle-aged and older, remaining in small towns that are almost totally devoid of main-street merchants will have to search elsewhere for worship services and for learning facilities for the youth who remain.

Many of the schools that remain confront increasing costs and diminishing student numbers. Unless major adjustments are made in the state's current tax structure, all schools, K-12 and higher education, will have to cut programs, reduce faculty numbers and rely to a greater degree on private donors. Despite this rather grim depiction of current realities, one must take into account that the state's residents successfully overcame past crises—the Great Depression, for example—that severely affected faith and learning. Four generations of students have valued an education that enabled them to achieve recognition in the professions, agriculture, business, and community service.

Chapter 18
Literature

■ Frontier Era

For the citizens of a small state in a remote region of America to create things of power and beauty is by some standards a remarkable accomplishment. Whether a sheep herder in Harding County, a cavalry scout in the Black Hills, a country girl from De Smet, or a professor at a college in Sioux Falls, the creative spirits of South Dakotans have continued to seek expression in spite of circumstances.

The first creative writer to bring South Dakota to the attention of the readers of America was Captain Jack Crawford (1847-1917). In 1879 he published a collection of poems called *The Poet Scout,* about fights with Indians, mining, camp meetings, celebrations, and other episodes of life in the Black Hills. He later traveled with Buffalo Bill Cody's Wild West Show and for the rest of his life roamed the United States, lecturing, performing, and reciting extensively in the character of the Poet Scout. His biographer, Paul T. Nolan,[1] cites a January 1917 *New York Times* story on Crawford, reporting that in recent years the Poet Scout "has visited many of the cities of the United States as an entertainer, and has delighted thousands by his verses, his recital of experiences on the frontier, and his stories of service with General Custer." South Dakota artist and historian Richard C. Cropp (1903-1980) once revealed that as a child he was taken by his mother to meet the aged Crawford at his New York home and was appropriately "patted on the head," a treatment not accorded to any other South Dakota artist, it appears.

The first major writer to bring South Dakota to national renown was Hamlin Garland, whose plans to be a pioneer writer were dashed by the harsh climate and the struggles of sodbusting. *Main-Travelled Roads* (1891) was his realistic look at Dakota Territory. He won the Pulitzer Prize for *A Daughter of the Middle Border* (1922). *Courtesy South Dakota State Historical Society– State Archives.*

The first major literary figure to bring substantial national attention to South Dakota was Hamlin Garland (1860-1940), whose *Main-Travelled Roads* (1891) brought together six realistic stories about Dakota Territory and the West. He had spent little time in South Dakota, however, just two weeks in the Aberdeen area in 1881 helping his father and grandfather build a house on their claim, and then a hot summer and frigid winter on his own claim in McPherson County (1883-1884) that ended his plans to be a pioneer farmer. Out of those experiences and a visit he made to his parents' homestead in 1887 he wrote the stories that made up the collection. In nearly all of them, his view of Dakota is pessimistic; life is miserable there, he concluded: "The ugliness, the endless drudgery, and the loneliness of the farmer's lot smote me with stern insistence." In American letters, this was a new view of the West, redeemed from stark pessimism only by Garland's eye for prairie scenery and his sympathy for the lot of women on the farming frontier.

Another well-known American writer of fiction also spent a relatively short time in South Dakota and also included in his writing something of life there. L. Frank Baum (1856-1919) spent more time in South Dakota than did Hamlin Garland—nearly three years in fact—and seems to have incorporated into his best-known work, *The Wonderful Wizard of Oz* (1900), such ingredients as the tornado that carries Dorothy away to Oz, the drought that plagues her Uncle Henry and Aunt Em and that appears to be the essence of the Witch of the West (only the water with which Dorothy douses her can control her), and so on. In actuality, Baum was in Kansas, where he decided to locate Dorothy's fictional farm home, for only a few days. The connection of South Dakota to the Oz stories, however, seems not to have been

L. Frank Baum wrote *The Wonderful Wizard of Oz* (1900) in part out of his South Dakota experiences. *Courtesy Dr. Robert A. Baum.*

made by readers until recently. In the century that has passed since its publication, *The Wonderful Wizard of Oz* has sold more than seven million copies, and the film version, with Judy Garland as Dorothy, has been seen "by more people than any other theatrical production in the history of mankind."[2] Baum's reputation as a writer of fantasy stories for children is firmly fixed. As a writer of editorials and columns for the *Aberdeen Saturday Pioneer*, which he edited from January 1890 to March 1891, his irony was often heavy-handed, ridiculing whites and Indians alike. In one editorial, much as Jonathan Swift castigates the English for their mistreatment of the Irish in "A Modest Proposal" (1729), Baum advocates eliminating the Indians altogether since white people have "wronged them for centuries" and had better follow up with "one more wrong." Despite the irony, many readers today find his position troublesome.

The novelists who have described the settlement era in South Dakota with such power that their depictions of the farming frontier have been permanently fixed in the American consciousness are Ole E. Rölvaag (1876-1931) and Laura Ingalls Wilder (1867-1957). The works of both have been standards in American classrooms for decades. Wilder's nine Little House novels for children so convincingly portrayed life in the American prairie West that the books have not only continued in print from the appearance of the first, *Little House in the Big Woods* in 1932, but a television series based on Wilder's *Little House on the Prairie* ran from 1974 to 1983 on NBC. Its popularity reached around the globe, as exemplified by a Radio Japan *Magazine* program that found it noteworthy that one Japanese viewer was so moved by the rural life portrayed in the series that he left his secure corporate job to start up farming on a few acres of Japanese soil. Wilder's writings are assigned additional consideration in the special section below given over to women writers of South Dakota.

The earlier of the two writers, O. E. Rölvaag, immigrated to South Dakota in 1896, well after the settlement of the eastern half of the state had taken place. He came alone, a mature man with high ideals and a burning desire to find a career to match his dreams.

As he wrote in his diary (translated by his wife, Jennie Berdahl), quoting the Norse writer Bjornstjerne Bjornson, "Someday, I believe, I shall reach the goal, far, far beyond the high mountains."[3]

From the time of his arrival until his graduation from Augustana College in 1901, Rölvaag lived in South Dakota, first working as a hired hand on the Sivert Eidem farm near Elk Point until 1898, then in Canton as a student in the Augustana College preparatory and parochial course, where he learned English and excelled in his studies. After four more years of study at St. Olaf College, Northfield, Minnesota, Rölvaag completed a year of graduate work at the University of Oslo, returning to St. Olaf in 1906 to teach Norwegian. For the next seventeen years he taught there, wrote five novels, three of them set in South Dakota—*Amerika Breve* (Letters from America), 1912; *Paa Glemte Veie* (On Forgotten Paths), 1914, and *To Tullinger* (Two Fools), 1920. In 1923 he began what would prove to be his masterpiece and an American classic, *Giants in the Earth*, writing out the first half in two months in his cabin in northern Minnesota.

First published in Norway in two parts in 1924 and 1925, the novel gained—as his biographer Einar Haugen concisely expresses it—"wide critical and popular acclaim."[4] In Oslo, Rölvaag told an American friend that when the novel would be translated into English and published in America, he would become famous. His prediction came true in 1927, when *Giants in the Earth: A Saga of the Prairie* appeared in one volume, translated by novelist Lincoln Colcord and the author, and was immediately successful across America.

What drew readers then and continues to captivate them today were two overriding themes—one romantic and one tragic. On the one hand, South Dakota is pictured as a vast and fertile land, part of the great central grasslands of America, where hard work, ingenuity, and persistence can wring from the land a living and even a kingdom. By the end of the novel Per Hansa tames the prairie and founds his kingdom, but his wife Beret, on the other hand, clings to her Norwegian roots, afraid of losing her identity in an alien land where terrible storms raged winter and summer and grasshoppers devoured their crops. Even worse, the Christian values from their homeland were dangerously threatened in this wild land. Beret sees it clearly: "This desolation out here called forth all that

Giants in the Earth (1927) is arguably the most authentic and powerful depiction of immigrant life on the sod-house frontier. Pictured is the author, Ole Rölvaag, with his wife Jennie and children in 1922, near the Minnesota north-woods cabin where he wrote the first half of the novel. *Courtesy the Rölvaag family.*

was evil in human nature. . . . What would become of the children who had to grow up in such an atmosphere? . . . her soul shuddered."

Peder Victorious (1929) and *Their Fathers' God* (1931), the two novels that follow *Giants in the Earth*, continue the story of Beret the traditionalist, trying to preserve the heritage of language, custom, and faith that she believes are rapidly disappearing in her community. It is a challenge that continues to face immigrants, from whatever background, and Rölvaag's profound wrestle with the issue in *Giants* is one explanation for the extravagant success of this novel about South Dakota. When it appeared, reviewers ranked Rölvaag with the greatest of American writers; the poet and biographer Carl Sandburg, himself the son of immigrants, labeled it one of the most important American novels of all time.

■ Sioux Indian Writers

At the time of Rölvaag's arrival in Elk Point, in 1896, there was only the beginning of a literary tradition in South Dakota. American Indian literature, the oral stories of the Sioux people in what is now South Dakota, had yet to be collected and translated and made available to a reading audience; and it would be half a dozen years before the Dakota Sioux Indian Charles Eastman would begin to publish the tales of his boyhood and youth for American readers. In her essay about the authors who reflect in one way or another this oldest tradition of oral literature in South Dakota, Janette K. Murray[5] (in *An Illustrated History of the Arts in South Dakota*, 1989) divides Sioux writing into three periods: Indigenous, Transitional, and Modern. To the first group, she proposes, belong those few tales that are written in the Dakota (Eastern Sioux) or Lakota (Western Sioux) languages. While these tales are not widely known, they remain important records of a culture's ideals, beliefs, and history, many of them with their origins in a time before white contact. Principal among these stories are those that were told in Lakota by George Sword, a member of the Indian police at the Pine Ridge Agency in the 1890s. His stories are the basis for most of the later anthropological works about Sioux life and religion, including *Dakota Texts* by Ella Deloria, the one author who is culturally and linguistically Lakota and writes in her native language.

In the Transitional Period, Murray places the four authors of autobiography who were born between 1858 and 1875 and lived into the late 1930s, and in the case of Black Elk, until 1950. Charles Eastman (1858-1939), the oldest of the group, was born in Redwood Falls, Minnesota, fled with an uncle to Canada after the 1862 Minnesota Dakota War, and returned to the United States with his father ten years later and was placed in the boarding school at Flandreau. He went on to study at Beloit College, Knox College, Dartmouth College (B.S., 1887), and Boston University (M.D., 1890). In his first position, as government physician at Pine Ridge Agency in South Dakota, he treated the survivors of the Wounded Knee Massacre, and there met

A physician of mixed Santee Sioux and white parentage, Charles Eastman attained a national reputation as a writer, speaker, and advocate of Indian rights. *Courtesy South Dakota State Historical Society–State Archives.*

and shortly after married Elaine Goodale, a writer and reformer. With her assistance he began his career as a published author. In two autobiographical books, *Indian Boyhood* (1902) and *From Deep Woods to Civilization* (1916) he tells about growing up in a traditional Sioux Indian society and of pursuing an education in white society. Eastman had a long and productive career supporting Indian rights and correcting misapprehensions that whites had about Indians.

The first Indian woman writer from South Dakota to gain renown as an author was Gertrude Simmons (1875-1938), born on the Yankton reservation to a Yankton mother and a white father. While a child of eight she rejected her white name and took the name Zitkala Ša (Red Bird). Her autobiographical essays show her to be, as Murray observes, "a very willful woman, who both embraced and rejected her Indian heritage." Her writings are discussed below in the section on women writers in South Dakota.

Two Sioux Indian writers had short careers with Buffalo Bill Cody's Wild West Show. A Rosebud Reservation Sioux, Luther Standing Bear (1863-1939), was a member of the show during a tour of England. He wrote about his childhood and youth in two books of collections—*My Indian Boyhood* and *Land of the Spotted Eagle*. Murray considers that it is somewhat ironic that on the one hand Standing Bear wrote to dispel myths about Indian life and on the other he contributed to the myth-making Hollywood Western by his work with Buffalo Bill and later in the movie industry. Nicholas Black Elk (1863-1950), who also traveled for a time with Buffalo Bill, has written the most influential biographical work about Sioux Indian life, *Black Elk Speaks*, as recorded and edited by Nebraska poet John Neihardt. The book was given a new life in the 1960s when a reprinting became widely popular. Its portrayal of the destruction during Black

Elk's lifetime of a great Indian society on the northern plains caught the attention of many Americans in that era of the Vietnam conflict, especially young people, some of whom felt themselves betrayed by their government.

Among the Sioux Indian writers of legends and tales Murray places Luther Standing Bear (*Stories of the Sioux*, 1934), Zitkala Ša (*Old Indian Legends*, 1901), James La Point (*Legends of the Dakota*, 1976), Charles Eastman (*Old Indian Days*, 1907; and *The Soul of the Indian*, 1911), and—perhaps most important—linguist Ella Deloria (1888-1971), whose *Dakota Texts* (1932) represents her life work as a recorder and editor of Lakota tales. Murray calls her "the greatest scholar and linguist to study and document the complexity and expressiveness of the Lakota language in the traditional legends, stories, and tales." The sixty-four tales in *Dakota Texts*, both in Lakota and in English translation, range widely in subject matter and treatment, from stories that come from a very remote past with a number of mythological personages,

Black Elk's reminiscence about Sioux Indian life, as recorded and edited by John Neihardt, has become widely popular. *Courtesy South Dakota State Historical Society–State Archives.*

to stories of the recent past in which the supernatural plays a part, to stories from the Pine Ridge and Rosebud reservations that Deloria obtained herself.

In the Modern Period of Sioux Indian literature from the 1970s to the present can be placed a number of writers, many of them still at work, who represent a range of genres and subject matter. Not much fiction or poetry has been written by the Sioux themselves, and so a novelist like Virginia Driving Hawk Sneve and a poet like Lydia Whirlwind Soldier represent new literary traditions in the making. Autobiographies have continued to appear, however, including *Lame Deer: Seeker of Visions* (1972), by Lame Deer, as told to Richard Erdoes. It is the story of a contrary or *Heyoka* on the Rosebud Reservation whose life is led in an eccentric way as a vision requires him to do. In 1979 the late Reverend Thomas Mails published *Fools Crow*, the life story of the last of the traditional Lakota chiefs. Among the events recounted by Fools Crow are several of recent date, including the occupation of Wounded Knee in 1973 by members of AIM, the American Indian Movement, to protest certain government policies and practices. Also considered by Murray to belong to this period is Tim Giago, editor of the *Lakota Journal* and winner of the H. L. Mencken award for his journalistic writing. In *The Aboriginal Sin: Reflections on the Holy Rosary Indian Mission School* (1978) Giago revisits his largely unpleasant experiences in a Pine Ridge Reservation boarding school.

Of the writers of fiction and poetry there are five who stand out. Linguist Ella Deloria, whose most important work was collecting and editing the stories of others as well as tales in oral tradition, wrote out a novel in the 1940s and 1950s that remained unpublished until 1988. *Water Lily*, the story of a Lakota girl held captive by a band other than her own, was intended by Deloria to make Indian people understandable to whites. The work of Elizabeth Cook-Lynn, a Crow Creek Reservation Sioux and retired professor of English and Indian studies, is considered at length in the section below about women authors. Her widely admired 1996 book *Why I Can't Read Wallace Stegner and Other Essays* includes her declaration that the plains Indians will persist, will "continue to multiply and prosper" in spite of the assumptions of the many non-Indians who believe that assimilation is the preferred alternative to the reservation system. Dr. Cook-Lynn was a National Endowment for the Humanities fellow at Stanford, received the Literary Contribution Award from the Mountain Plains Library Association, and was cited for the Gustavus Meyers Award for her defense of human rights in *Why I Can't Read Wallace Stegner*. Her writings have appeared in many anthologies and periodicals, including *Prairie Schooner, South Dakota Review*, and *Wicazo Sa Review*, of which she is a founding editor. Virginia Driving Hawk Sneve is the state's best-known writer of children's stories about Indian people. Her career is also examined below in the special section on women authors.

A late addition to the growing tradition of creative writing by Sioux Indian people is Lydia Whirlwind Soldier, a Sicangu Lakota from the Rosebud Reservation. Her single book of verse, *Memory Songs* (1999), consists of thirty-two poems that celebrate the traditions and culture of her people, the *Lakol wicoun*, or Lakota way of being. One reviewer said of the poems, "They offer a world view that is every bit as profound and powerful as that found in the works of our famous and much-revered 'great' poets."[6] Poet and artist Allison Hedge Coke, who has lived in many places in Canada and the United States, most recently in Rapid City and now in Sioux Falls, is of mixed racial background—Huron, Tsalagi, French Canadian, and Portuguese. Her book of poetry *Dog Road Woman* received an American Book Award from the Before Columbus Foundation, and her memoir *Rock, Ghost, Willow, Deer* was published by the University of Nebraska

Press in 2004. For her extensive writing and editing, in 2003 Hedge Coke won the Sioux Falls Mayor's Award for Literary Excellence.

■ Settlement to Mid-Twentieth Century

Throughout the first half of the twentieth century a number of novelists wrote about aspects of life in South Dakota, many of them doing their important work after leaving the state. Oscar Micheaux, the African American writer who lived near Gregory from 1905 to 1915, wrote two novels about his homesteading career, *The Conquest: The Story of a Negro Pioneer* (1913) and *The Homesteader* (1917). Both express the optimism of most settlers about the future of South Dakota. As Micheaux writes about the grassland there, "I gazed over the miles of it lying like a mighty carpet; I could seem to feel the magnitude of the development and industry that would someday replace this state of wildness." Micheaux successfully marketed his own novels in Sioux City, Iowa, and after leaving South Dakota, made a film of *The Homesteader* that led to a life-long career as a maker of films for black audiences.

William Otis Lillibridge (1878-1909) achieved national fame with his Western books *Ben Blair, Plainsman* (1905) and *Where the Trail Divides* (1907), both national best sellers. Lillibridge is the only important early novelist to have been born and reared in the state and to have written all of his work there. At the opposite extreme is Stewart Edward White, who spent only a short time in South Dakota. His novel *The Westerners* (1910) launched his long career as a writer of fiction. This story of the invasion of the Black Hills in 1875 by gold seekers was the successor to an earlier work, *The Claim Jumpers* (1910), set in the mining camps near Keystone.

Two novelists wrote about life in central South Dakota: J. Hyatt Downing grew up in Blunt and wrote his first novel, *A Prayer for Tomorrow* (1938), after leaving the state. Its message is clear, that it is futile to try to grow crops in such an arid region and that much of the state should never have been plowed up. Another rural South Dakotan, Arvid Shulenberger, wrote *Roads from the Fort* (1954), an adventure story set in the Fort Randall area in 1857. Two young soldiers from the fort experience at first hand the dangers of living among competing bands of warlike Sioux Indians.

A contemporary of Downing and Shulenberger was Herbert Krause, a novelist who lived and wrote most of his work in South Dakota but whose three novels have Minnesota settings. Shortly after coming to head the English Department at Augustana College in Sioux Falls, Krause saw his first novel, *Wind Without Rain* (1939), become a best seller and prize winner. Two other novels, *The Thresher* (1946) and *The Oxcart Trail* (1954) added to Krause's reputation as a novelist of merit. His

Novelist Herbert Krause contributed essays, reviews, and poems to the literature of South Dakota, as well as a co-edited account of George Armstrong Custer's expedition into the Black Hills in 1874. *Center for Western Studies.*

contributions to the literature of South Dakota are essays, reviews, and a handful of poems that deal with the natural history of our region, and two books that are important contributions to the literature of the state: *Prelude to Glory: A Newspaper Accounting of Custer's 1874 Expedition to the Black Hills,* edited with Gary D. Olson (1974), and an unpublished play, *Crazy Horse: A Drama of the Plains Indians and the Black Hills* (1960), about the most successful—and the most mysterious—of all the Sioux Indian war leaders.

In the field of humorous writing, South Dakota can claim three notable journalists and a sheep herder. The journalists belong to the very early days of newspapering in South Dakota, and one of them—L. Frank Baum—has only recently been rediscovered in an edition of *Our Landlady* by Nancy Koupal. Baum's satiric essays appeared regularly in the *Saturday Pioneer* in Aberdeen during the fourteen months that he owned and edited the newspaper. Fred Hayden Carruth also left what is now South Dakota after a short stint of writing humor columns for the *Estelline Bell* and the *Dakota Bell.* In 1888 he won a spot on the *New York Tribune* as a humor columnist and in 1905 began a thirty-four year career with the *Woman's Home Companion.* His popular boys' book, *Track's End* (1911), set in Estelline, remained in print for over half a century. At the other end of the state, Kennett Harris ran the Hot Springs *Hatchett* for many years and published in national magazines a number of short stories with Black Hills settings. In 1920 his collection *Meet Mr. Stegg* was published, and a serialized novel followed in 1921 in the *Saturday Evening Post,* a comic treatment of life in the Hills after the gold rush.

The master of rural humor in South Dakota remains Archer B. Gilfillan, a sheep herder in Harding County, South Dakota, for seventeen years, whose autobiographical *Sheep* (1929) became a best seller for a short time. Although Gilfillan went on to publish two more books, made up of his newspaper columns—*A Shepherd's Holiday* (1936) and *A Goat's Eye View of the Black Hills* (1953)—*Sheep* remains his masterwork of comic insight into the ways of sheep, and of humans. Gilfillan's tale of old Three Toes, however, the killer wolf, shows him at his serious best, telling a tale that has become a classic in American literature.

■ Reaching an American Reading Public

The face that South Dakota has presented to the world over the decades since settlement began has been largely determined by the literary works that are most widely read and studied. Rölvaag and Wilder have remained in print and accessible for most of the twentieth century and into the twenty-first. A few of the state's writers have had national success—with a South Dakota work or two popular for a time—including Lillibridge, Garland, Black Elk, and most recently Frederick Manfred. The poetry and drama of the state, however, are little known in the larger world of letters. As to poetry, for the most part a very private literary genre, much has been written, some has appeared in print, but poetry has not sold well and continues to be little read. Consequently, poetry lovers are pleased when a poet or a book of poetry receives attention. In South Dakota the position of Poet Laureate helps to do just that. Four writers have been designated Poets Laureate for the state. The first such award was given in 1937 to Charles Badger Clark, Jr. (1883-1957), by Governor Leslie Jensen. It was a suitable recognition for the "cowboy poet" who had once been summoned to a visit with President Calvin Coolidge, on vacation in the Black Hills in 1927. Clark began writing cowboy poems in 1906 while working as a ranch hand in Arizona Territory. He returned to South Dakota in 1910, published his first book, *Sun and Saddle Leather* in 1915, and followed it with four more books during his

A writer who mined material from the Black Hills, Badger Clark was named the first state Poet Laureate in 1937 by Governor Leslie Jensen. *Courtesy South Dakota State Historical Society–State Archives.*

lifetime. A sixth collection of his verse, garnered from the State Poetry Society publication *Pasque Petals* and other periodicals, was published as *Boots and Bylines* in 1978.

Clark was followed by Adeline Jenney (1874-1973), succeeding him the year after his death. Jenney edited *Pasque Petals* for thirty-four years, seeing 310 of her poems published in its pages. She was followed for a brief time by Mabel Frederick. The next state Poet Laureate, Audrae Visser (1919-2002), was given that title in June 1974 by Governor Richard Kneip. She began publishing in *Pasque Petals* in 1940 and produced eight books of poems, most of them from the pages of that publication. In 2002 a new Poet Laureate was appointed by Governor William Janklow, upon the recommendation of the South Dakota Poetry Society, David Allan Evans, a professor of English at South Dakota State University in Brookings. Beginning with *Among Athletes* (1971), Evans has published six books of his verse, the most recent being *The Bull Rider's Advice* (2003), a brilliant selection from four of his previous books and with twenty-seven new poems. Early in his career Evans won an NEA Creative Writing Fellowship (1976), the first to be awarded in South Dakota. Evans' verses have appeared in many anthologies and magazines, including the *Norton Book of Sports*, *Esquire*, *Saturday Review*, the *New York Times*, and *Prairie Schooner*. He is considered to be one of America's best-known poets writing about sports.

The role of the South Dakota Poetry Society has been a significant one ever since its founding in 1927. Its publication, *Pasque Petals*, is known as the country's longest-lived poetry magazine. Two other magazines have been especially instrumental in publishing works by South Dakotans and about South Dakota. *South Dakota Magazine*, begun in 1984 by Bernie and Myrna Hunhoff, a bi-monthly that includes book reviews and occasional fiction and poetry; and *South Dakota Review*, begun in 1963 by writer John R. Milton, a quarterly journal of poetry, essays, and short fiction that has attained national prominence. Milton's hope, expressed in an editorial in the first issue, was that "the next renaissance in American letters will occur in the West." Milton has himself contributed to that renaissance, through his editing, his reviews, his literary criticism, and his historical writing.

In the forty years that have passed since John R. Milton's vision of a literary renaissance for South Dakota, the one fiction writer who has set out on a large scale to treat of the diversity of life experiences in this northern plains state has been Frederick Manfred (1912-1994), creator of the term "Siouxland" to name his home territory and author of five novels that are set in whole or in part in South Dakota. More than any other writer, Manfred has brought South Dakota to the attention of an American reading public. *Conquering Horse* (1959) treats of Indian life in the pre-contact era, depicting the coming of age of a Sioux chief at a time when his people are at war with the Pawnees to the south. In *Lord Grizzly* (1954) Manfred follows the adventures of mountain-man Hugh Glass in 1823-24, a hunter with General William Ashley's expedition up the Missouri River. In *Scarlet Plume* (1964) he finds his subject matter in the Sioux Indian war in Minnesota in 1862, with some of the action set in what is now South Dakota, and two years later he published *King of Spades*, a story of gold-rush days in Deadwood and the last of the five novels in the series that Manfred named the Buckskin Man Tales. Two novels not in the Tales group have dealt with events in South Dakota in the twentieth century: *The Golden Bowl* (1944) a story of the Dust Bowl in South Dakota, reminiscent of *Grapes of Wrath*; and *Of Lizards and Angels* (1992), subtitled by Manfred "A Saga of Siouxland," about that region drained by the Big Sioux River that encompasses the connecting corners of South Dakota, Minnesota, and Iowa. Several of Manfred's novels have been national best sellers, and one—*Lord Grizzly*—narrowly missed receiving the National Book Award for 1954. In February 1975 his reputation as a careful researcher as well as a novelist of great narrative strength reached a high point when his Buckskin Man Tales were praised by a *New York Times* reviewer, who wrote, likening Manfred to the Greek epic poet Homer: "Not many novelists can match Manfred's powers as a story teller. . . . The whole world is alive for him. . . ."[7]

In recent years, other South Dakota writers whose work has achieved regional and national attention and who might be recognized as contributing to a literary renaissance for the state are playwrights Craig Volk, whose *Sundancers* was selected by Edward Albee for the Festival of New American One-Acts; Wayne Knutson, whose *Ola Rue* was sponsored by the state Centennial Commission and chosen by the South Dakota Arts Council for a three-year project throughout the state; and Ronald Robinson, the most productive playwright in the state as well as a novelist of accomplishment. Two of his musical comedies, *What Ever Happened to Radio?* (1970) and *Aces and Eights* (1989), and his drama *Nation Invisible* (1991) have South Dakota locations. So does his picaresque novel *Thunder Dreamer*, which received the New York Public Library "Fiction for Young Readers" recognition in 1997, and his novel *Diamond Trump* (2000), which takes as its climactic event the 1936 New Year's Eve Powder-house blast in Sioux Falls.

A novelist of epic accomplishment, Frederick Manfred was for a time the writer in residence at the University of South Dakota and a writing teacher at Augustana College. *Lord Grizzly* stands out as his most successful novel with a South Dakota setting.
Center for Western Studies.

One of Frederick Manfred's students in the writing program at the University of South Dakota was Pete Dexter, the only novelist from the state to win a National Book Award (for *Paris Trout* in 1988). While he has written only one novel with a South Dakota setting—*Deadwood* (1986)—Dexter has gone on to a long and successful career as a writer of suspense and mystery stories. As a self-proclaimed South Dakotan, Dexter credits his University of South Dakota writing professors—Dorothy Selz, John R. Milton, and Frederick Manfred—with giving him some of the tools needed by a writer, among them a dedication to accuracy. Of the writing of *Deadwood*, he avers that he spent weeks on researching the language of the times and read everything he could find about Calamity Jane, Wild Bill Hickok, and actor-manager Jack Langrishe. Dexter, who has also won the Pen Center USA West Award, writes regularly for major magazines and for filmmakers.

Although a handful of widely read South Dakota novelists have contributed substantially to the impression of South Dakota held by readers throughout America, there are also novelists who are not well known abroad but whose fictional presentations of life in the state ring true and have the power to engage the reader in the lives of their characters. Such a list must include Douglas Unger's *Leaving the Land* (1984), the story of the death throes of a family farm and winner of a Society of Midland Authors Award for fiction in 1995. Michael Doane's first novel, *The Legends of Jesse Dark* (1984), reprinted by Ballantine Books in 1990, is the story of a counter-culture outlaw in contemporary South Dakota. Doane's latest novel, *Bullet Heart* (1995), sets forth a clash of cultures over the ancient remains of a Sioux Indian girl. Like Dexter a student of Manfred, Dan O'Brien published *Spirit of the Hills* in 1988, a picture of aspects of contemporary life in the Black Hills, including drug dealers, Indian activists, and a host of environmental concerns. The novel was reprinted by Random House in 1989. Because he now writes as a South Dakotan but has set his series of detective novels in nearby Omaha, Nebraska, William R. Reynolds merits inclusion in this chapter. His first novel, *The Nebraska Quotient* (1984), was nominated for a Shamus Award. In 1996 *The Naked Eye* (1990) was featured by the Book-of-the-Month Club, and *Money Trouble* was reprinted by Ballantine Books.[8] Also deserving of mention is author Kent Meyers, whose most recent novel, *The Work of Wolves* (2004), was included on the *Christian Science Monitor's* list of the best novels of 2004, won the Mountain and Plains Bookseller's Association Award, and received the 2005 "One Book South Dakota" designation by the South Dakota Humanities Council. His collection of essays, *The Witness of Combines* (1998), won a Minnesota Book Award and a Friends of American Writers Award. Struck by the human capacity to endure, Meyers, who teaches at Black Hills State University, writes eloquently of isolation in the midst of community, but also the possibility of belonging. Two other books, *The River Warren* (1998) and *Light in the Crossing* (1999), were *New York Times* Notable Books.

It may be that creative writing programs in the colleges and universities of South Dakota will continue to contribute to the development of able young poets, playwrights, and fiction writers. The South Dakota Arts Council has modest programs as well to encourage creative writing, and publications like the *South Dakota Review*, *South Dakota Magazine*, and *Pasque Petals* offer opportunities to publish in-state. If the careers of the writers who over the past century have written in and about South Dakota are an indication of what the future holds, the work of telling the stories of South Dakota people will continue to be solitary work, and the writers of those stories will publish at home and abroad, sometimes in unlikely places, and there will often be surprises in the results that come from their pens—and from their computers.

Chapter 19
Women Writers

An essay by Ruth Ann Alexander

Although women began writing about life in South Dakota in 1890, they were regarded as scribbling amateurs and never won much acclaim. Except for historical scholarship, today they are virtually forgotten. Yet more than a century later, South Dakota has produced women writers who have been recognized as accomplished literary professionals and artists. Much has changed in women's lives over the years to make their success possible, but every generation has produced women who attempted to tell their stories and who have found inspiration in the state and its people. The state's dramatic landscape of prairies, plains, and mountains; its colorful history of conflict, adventure, and hardship; its changeable climate of harsh winters and blistering summers; the mingling of its diverse cultures; the variety and monotony of life on its farms, ranches, reservations, and in its small towns and cities have all found expression in the work of late twentieth-century women writers.

Women writers in South Dakota can be grouped in time over four generations. The first generation published from statehood in 1889 through World War I when many middle-class women were just beginning to emerge from the confines of home and children to which nineteenth-century American culture confined them. These first writers were largely Anglo-Americans who either visited the Dakota frontier or spent some years in the state experiencing some of the rigors of pioneer life. The freedom and independence that young girls had on a Dakota ranch or farm inspired them to create heroines who exhibited those traits. Yet the early writers looked down upon the Dakota frontier as inferior socially and culturally to the East, where they intended to make permanent homes.

Two very early works, Mary Locke's *In Far Dakota* (1890) and Mary E. Q. Brush's *Sarah Dakota* (1894) reveal an enthusiasm for all things English. In the former work, the narrator/mother has come to visit her three children in Dakota Territory. She deplores the lack of manners and social graces in the frontier community and the malevolent influence that gambling, drinking, and easy morality have on her son. She does not want him to marry a local girl, however attractive and lively she is, and longs for the influence of a proper English girl. The latter book describes a ranch near the Missouri River as a kind of English country estate, with the importation of a class system. Norwegian and French Canadian employees are seen as decidedly inferior to the British owners, and an Indian as downright savage. The rancher/father appears to resemble an English country squire. He envisions something better for his tomboy daughter and sends her east to be "tamed."

Novels by Stella Gilman and Eleanor Gates appear slightly more credible, although they also conclude that the Dakota frontier is no place for a young woman. Gilman's *That Dakota Girl* (1900) is set on a Big Sioux Valley ranch where the heroine with the improbable name of Nitelle M'Jarrow grows up. Although very accomplished for the time, since she claims an "Iowa school education" that provides her with the ability to speak "boarding school French," she is decidedly western. She is perpetually on horseback, "sitting in her saddle as if she were in a rocking chair." In addition, she has a sunburned face, and whistles, shoots, hunts, fishes, plays practical jokes, and is outrageously independent in her behavior. Ultimately, although she loves life on the ranch, she marries the rich Easterner rather than the local cowboy.

Eleanor Gates' *Biography of a Prairie Girl* (1902) and *The Plow Woman* (1906) are based upon slightly more real experience of South Dakota life. She spent ten years of her childhood on a South Dakota farm on the Vermillion River. However, during the Indian troubles of the late 1880s the family moved to California, where Eleanor eventually attended Stanford and the University of California. She married a playwright in 1901, moved to New York, and became a journalist. Her famous novel *Poor Little Rich Girl* (1912) was made into a movie starring Mary Pickford. Gates qualifies as a professional writer, although her South Dakota tales never achieved much fame and she had only a slight connection with the state after she left it. Nonetheless, her two stories can claim a readability that the earlier works do not achieve.

The "little girl" (never named) in *Biography of a Prairie Girl* describes many activities that dominate much regional literature: school events, a wedding, Christmas celebrations, pets, and hours spent herding cattle on the prairie. After the novel was published, Gates claimed that she remembered every day on the prairie, where she rode her pony with skill and learned to recognize wild flowers and antelope.[1] Her mother, however, did not want her to spend her life "hoeing and herding and working . . . in the kitchen with nothing to brighten your days." Yet there's nothing in her two books about Dakota life that indicates she found the experience bleak, drab, and dreary.

Several years after *Biography of a Prairie Girl* was published, Gates returned to the state to gather material for her second novel about the country she knew as a child. The result was *The Plow Woman*, in which she creates a fictional pioneer heroine without the crutch of autobiography and with greater maturity and insight. Dallas Lancaster is a more fully conceived character than the "little girl." She takes care of her crippled father's land near the Missouri River and cares for her frail sister. We see her working in a slouch hat, wiping her face on the sleeve of her jersey, hitching her skirt through her waistband to "cool her ankles," and plowing in a red flannel petticoat. She is a genuine western heroine with an unfashionable "sun-browned face" on which there is a "look of deep content."

Probably the most significant writer of the first generation was Kate Boyles Bingham. She was born in Yankton, the daughter of a prominent family, and she spent most of her adult life in the state. Kate graduated from normal college and taught school in Yankton, during which time she began to write. Eventually, with her brother Virgil, she published a series of western novels based upon authentic South Dakota events. Her brother furnished plot lines and much factual material, but she did most of the writing.[2] Her influence on the novels is clearly visible in the creation of strong, independent female characters, reflecting Kate's own feminist sentiments. Even after she married and lived in Chamberlain, she was active in the community and a strong advocate of woman suffrage.

The first novel of the brother and sister combination, *Langford of the Three Bars* (1907), was a best seller for a time. Although the story is based upon the activities and murder of the outlaw Jack Sully in the Chamberlain area and involves his trial, the story is really a western love story. Kate gave the role of court reporter in the novel to the fictional Louise Dale. This was a job that Virgil Boyles had held, but Kate gave the story a decidedly feminist slant. The real heroine in the tale, however, is the fictional Mary Williston, the rancher's daughter. When her home is attacked by the outlaws, she defends her father, firing shot for shot with her attackers. She is sickened by the fact that she has killed a man, but that does not prevent her from firing again. She takes care of the horses on the ranch and acts as her father's "son." After some obstacles in the course of true love, Langford, the cowboy hero, wins her hand in marriage.

The Homesteaders, which followed in 1906, deals with the conflict between sod busters and the cattle ranchers who want to drive them off the land so that they can have unfenced grazing for their cattle. The story also introduces an Indian woman, Rosebud, a young Lakota from the nearby Lower Brûlé reservation. She has returned from an Eastern boarding school, the fate of so many Indian children from reservations during these years, and finds that she fits into neither culture. Kate Boyles demonstrated her growing awareness of problems facing the native people when Rosebud proclaims: "I thought I would learn to be white. I learned—almost. I learned this

Kate Bingham, with her brother Virgil, is significant as the creator of strong western heroines, like Bonibel in *Daughter of the Badlands* (1922). *Courtesy Literature of South Dakota, by O.W. Coursey (Educator Supply, 1917).*

much . . . that I might learn to read and write, comb my hair according to the mode, wear abominable stiff corset things, sing and dance and play the piano and embroider . . . but that I never could be white. . . . I beat my heart out until it was all bruised and bleeding with sorrow at first, then with rage, because you had lied to me, you know, and then because I would not be a dog of a half-breed to fawn upon the white man."

Kate Boyles Bingham's interest in the Native American people and their relations with whites was apparent in her next novel as well. *The Spirit Trail* (1910) is set in 1874-75 during Custer's incursion into the Black Hills which led to the Battle of the Little Bighorn in 1876. It is a story in which the historic figure of Bishop William Hobart Hare, the "White Robe" in the story, exerts a kind of unseen presence in the book without actually appearing as a character. Kate was a great admirer of Bishop Hare and was active in the Episcopal Church both in her hometown of Yankton and in Chamberlain, where she lived after she married John Bingham.[3]

The plot of the novel is complex, based roughly on the illegal whiskey trade on the reservation that led to the trial of Dr. Henry F. Livingston, Crow Creek Indian agent, in 1876. Under Grant's Peace Policy of 1869, the Church appointed the Indian agent, and Bishop Hare defended Livingston, who was eventually acquitted.[4] In Bingham's rendering of the incident, fictional characters play a large role. Katharine Mendenhall is the daughter of an army officer at Big Bend on the Missouri River and has come from the East to teach Indian children. She makes friends with White Flower, a native woman from the reservation, and she learns much about native life. The third character is Hugh Hunt, the missionary priest who discusses Indian policy with Katharine as well as his admiration for "White Robe." Hunt is presumably modeled upon the legendary Heckaliah Burt, who served as an Episcopal missionary on the Crow Creek Reservation for several decades.

The theme of the divergent story lines in this novel is the need for better understanding of Native American culture by the white people who serve them and greater integrity of agents and government officials in fulfilling treaty obligations. These ideas are voiced by Hunt in his discussions with Katharine. His ideas are assimilationist, but he does not regard native people as "savages," and he is critical of white treachery and the lust for gold that led to Custer's expedition into the Black Hills. He says, "We must live with them man to man, friend to friend, brother to brother; then only the miracle is accomplished and we will live together as one people."

The central theme in Kate Boyles Bingham's final novel, *Daughter of the Badlands* (1922), focuses upon both a western heroine and the tension between whites and Indians. The heroine, Bonibel Sherwood, is of mixed blood, and she is also intelligent, athletic, and independent. Her father is a white rancher and her mother a Dakota woman. Bonibel is sent east to school, where a potential suitor is dismayed to learn of her heritage. She returns to the ranch and remains loyal to her mother. The young man follows her west and pursues her through a whole series of adventures, including a roundup, a shoot-out, and several chases. A true western heroine, Bonibel excels in western skills, wins a horse race, and teaches in an Indian school. She finally agrees to marry her Eastern admirer when he takes up land himself and becomes a rancher, a genuine triumph. Such an ending reverses the conclusion of Owen Wister's classic western tale, *The Virginian*, where the cowboy wins the heart of the eastern schoolteacher.

Another writer during this period did not describe the usual details of pioneer life in her epistolary novel but dealt with a problem in modern society that was gaining prominence at the turn of the century. The West has always been seen as a place to cut ties to the past and make a new start. Throughout territorial days, South Dakota maintained very relaxed legal requirements for severing the marriage bond. By the time of statehood, Sioux Falls advertised in national magazines that it had only a ninety-day residency in order to obtain a divorce. The city was soon the divorce capital of the world, with many Easterners coming by train and leaving immediately after the decree was issued.[5]

The point of view of one such traveler is detailed in Jane Burr's epistolary novel *Letters of a Dakota Divorcee* (1909). The first half of the book has the brazen flamboyance that the title evoked at the turn of the century. The writer dedicates her book to her "Sioux Falls Friends," but the letters are full of criticism of the city she is visiting. She found it hopelessly provincial and dull, the food unappetizing, the company boring, and the social life non-existent. She is shunned by other women at church because she is a divorcee, but she scoffs at their narrow-minded views. She yearns for the sophistication of New York: "I long so to flash my calcium on a Fifth Avenue stroller that I would flirt with God if I met him," she writes. Eventually she meets a rich man, also from the East and seeking a divorce. Without benefit of clergy, as soon as they get their decrees, the two run off to what they believe will be idyllic bliss in the Black Hills. The tone of the letters shifts sharply toward the sentimental in the second part of the book. She bears a child but her joy is short-lived. Her lover is killed in a mountain road accident. In a complete turnabout, she returns to New York and is finally, but unconvincingly, reunited with her first husband. Although obviously not a great novel, *Letters of a Dakota Divorcee* presents a picture of life in South Dakota that is quite different from that of other women writers.

The second generation of writers did not follow the Burr model but wrote primarily about the pioneer or rural experience of living in South Dakota. By the nineteen-twenties, homesteading days were over and electricity, automobiles, and telephones had changed life in much of the nation. Yet the period between the two World Wars was difficult for many South Dakota residents. Farm foreclosures, drought, dust bowl, and depression sapped the optimism of some, and World War II meant privation and sacrifice. Some people left the state for California or elsewhere to begin a new life. In fact, some women who wrote about South Dakota did not reside in the state. A number recalled their childhood years and based stories upon the experiences they remembered. Others were inspired by mere visits to the state. Some followed traditional careers for women—as teachers and librarians. Some did not write their stories until late in life, but they had more professional experience as journalists and writers than the first generation. Although not strong feminists, they nonetheless cherished an image of the independent and free young woman who was nurtured on Dakota plains and prairies and was capable of leading others and achieving something in life.

Several wrote for young readers, an audience that has appealed to South Dakota female authors to the present day. One of the earliest was Marian Hurd McNealy. Although she is not well known today, she wrote a number of children's books after she was fifty years old. She was born and lived most of her life in Iowa, but for two years she and her husband homesteaded near Dallas, South Dakota, which is the setting for her story *The Jumping Off Place* (1929). The central characters in the story are Dick and Becky Linville, teenage orphans who have inherited a claim from an uncle and decide to move to South Dakota to prove up on it.

The story is told from the point of view of Becky, the eldest and the leader, whose grit and determination keeps the family alive, fed, and together on their "jumping off place."

The writings of Laura Ingalls Wilder have helped to fix in the American consciousness her depiction of the settlement era in the state. Pictured (at center) with Pa and Ma and her sisters. *Courtesy South Dakota State Historical Society–State Archives.*

She struggles with claim jumpers, thieving neighbors, backbreaking work, drought, and loneliness. When she realizes the family cannot survive the winter on their food supply, she gets a job teaching country school. This provides her with a dramatic opportunity to keep the children alive and safe in a blizzard until they can be rescued—an incident that occurs in other stories of the region.[6]

The best-known South Dakota woman writer of books for young readers for this period is, of course, Laura Ingalls Wilder. She also wrote them late in her life, long after she had left South Dakota for Mansfield, Missouri. In her "Little House" series of books, made famous by the inauthentic television series based upon them, four deal with her South Dakota experience and were written during the 1930s and 1940s: *By the Shores of Silver Lake* (1939), *The Long Winter* (1940), *Little Town on the Prairie* (1941), and *These Happy Golden Years* (1943). They recount the Ingalls family's adventures in and around De Smet during its early settlement from Laura's twelfth year in 1879 through her school teaching and marriage. The young Laura depicted in *By the Shores of Silver Lake* loves the open prairie, explores the wonders of the birds and flowers near the Big Slough, goes out to the railroad camp with her father, longs to follow the road even farther west on her pony, and faces down a wolf in the winter prairie night. Her mother Caroline cautions her about her "tomboy" ways and lectures her about the proper manners of a "lady." Although the character Laura suggests the independent, pioneer heroine, the stories themselves actually celebrate the happy, loving family life that persists through physical hardships of a cold, snowy winter, the financial privations and sacrifices demanded by providing an education for a blind sister, and the difficulties of teaching in a country school. Pa is a central figure in Laura's life in all of these books.

Laura's real-life daughter Rose Wilder, who assisted her mother in getting the books published, wrote her own story of homesteading in 1938, called *Let the Hurricane Roar*. It is based on an interpretation of her grandmother's life, very different from her mother's portrait of the older woman. The characters, Caroline and Charles, are partners in a joint enterprise. Caroline carries her share of the load, holding down the claim alone when Charles goes east to find work after the grasshoppers have eaten them out. She stays alone in the dugout with her baby throughout the winter months, maintaining her home and conquering her fears. She kills a half-frozen cow and butchers it for meat. She fights off a wolf. She emerges triumphantly after her ordeal as the self-reliant, capable pioneer heroine, certainly the central figure in the story.

The fact that Rose's own life was unconventional for the time may have contributed to this interpretation. She worked variously as a telegraph operator, a real estate agent, a journalist for the *San Francisco Bulletin*, and a Red Cross worker in Europe following World War I. She divorced her husband, became staunchly conservative in politics, espousing industrial capitalism and idolizing Henry Ford and Herbert Hoover. She worked for the latter's election in 1932. Shortly before her death she became a correspondent for the Vietnam War. Yet, in spite of her own adventures, she glorified women's domestic role, championed women's folk art, and certainly encouraged her mother to emphasize the happy family life of the Ingalls in the "Little House" books.[7]

Another writer of this period is Frances Gilchrist Wood, whose *Turkey Red* (1932) recounts the story of Janet and Allen Craig, who stake a claim near Blunt, South Dakota. Unlike the work of Wilder and Lane, whose extensive quotidian detail gives readers the sense of being there, Gilchrist is sometimes rhapsodic, often digressive, and always sentimental. The most interesting section of the book is a sort of "turnabout" in which Janet and Allen switch roles. In order to keep the family alive, Janet holds down the claim while Allen uses his team to haul freight from Huron and runs a printing press to publish a local paper. When he hurts his hand and can no longer drive the team or run the press, Janet takes over his work while he looks after the baby and home. He thinks his usual work is too difficult for her to handle since she is used to the "ease" of domestic life and is surprised when she seems almost glad to go! "You would be too if you lived here all alone a million miles from everywhere and never saw anyone in a thousand years!" she tells him angrily. Allen does indeed learn the problems of caring for a baby as well as chickens and a garden, carrying water from the well, scrubbing clothes, cooking food and cleaning. Janet, on the other hand, enjoys her trip. Thereafter, Janet helps in getting out the paper as well as looking after her child and home.

Not all the stories of this generation are about married women. One of the best stories about single homesteaders is Eudora Kohl's *Land of the Burnt Thigh* (1938).[8] Although she based the work on her own experiences, Kohl did not regard herself as a "pioneer," nor did she consider her book an autobiography. The central characters are the Ammons sisters, Edith and Ida Mary, who take up an abandoned claim thirty miles from Pierre and almost immediately decide to return to their home state of Illinois. But they do not. They are interested in their neighbors, who come to visit their very first day, and in the wildlife nearby—prairie dogs, coyotes, wolves, sheep, and cattle. They are soon fully engaged in the life of the area. They not only stay on the homestead but take up a second claim when Lower Brûlé reservation land is opened for settlement. In addition, they print a newspaper and run a post office.

The book is a rollicking, gutsy tale of their adventures. Life was hard but enjoyable, with an impressive number of other single women homesteaders to share their experience. They believe in what they are doing—that settling the plains is an important cooperative enterprise among people, business, and the railroads. The newspaper, they think, is its voice. The most surprising aspect of the women's lives is the sociability. The homesteaders exchange visits and have informal gatherings. They share meals, sleigh rides, and songs. They believed it took great courage and resourcefulness, but in spite of the hardships, Kohl concludes, the settlers "made merry."

One writer of this period did not write about homesteading but focused on life in one of the little towns that dotted the prairie, often on a railroad or waterway. Lucile Fargo's first work, *Prairie Girl* (1937), chronicled life in Rocky Rim from the point of view of a young girl growing up in it. Rocky Rim is Dell Rapids, in which Fargo spent most of her childhood in the 1880s and 1890s before she went to college and the family moved to Washington state. Ultimately, Fargo became a distinguished librarian and did not turn to writing stories about her childhood until late in life. Some return visits to South Dakota stimulated her desire to write about her adventures growing up in this pioneer environment.

Fargo makes no secret of her feminist views, and Prairie, the heroine in both of Fargo's books, is independent and adventuresome. She works in her father's hardware store, explores the Big Sioux River with her young friend Wells, helps her father build their home with its wonderful "tower" room, where Prairie forms a secret club of girls, goes to school, and finally settles on the career of a school teacher. She later keeps the children in her school alive in a blizzard until they can be rescued. But she also becomes an outspoken feminist, even debating the issue of women's rights with her friend Wells. Her views are strengthened when she visits the Women's Building of the Chicago World's Fair of 1893.

Fargo's second book, *Prairie Chautauqua* (1943), recounts Prairie's adventures of bicycling to Lake Madison from Dell Rapids to spend two weeks camping at the summer Chautauqua there. This is an interesting picture of a primary summer activity in many small midwestern towns at the end of the nineteenth century and the beginning of the twentieth. Here, her adventures swimming and boating with young students from the "agricultural college" at Brookings intermingle with a description of the entertainment program and educational activities of Chautauqua. The book also provided an engaging description of camping in those days.

Other writers tried their hands at writing stories about South Dakota, sometimes after only a brief visit to the state. Ethel Houston is a case in point. After a visit to the Black Hills she wrote a novel about a cowgirl, *Blithe Baldwin* (1933). The heroine is rebellious and independent, giving up a college education to work on a dude ranch, but she is too successful to be entirely credible. Elizabeth Nicol Hutton's *No Man's Child* (1930) is a sentimental story of redemption but which also depicts the Indian in an unattractive light. Sarah Comstock's *Speak to the Earth* (1927) is set in the Badlands and also involves the redemption of a man, this time by a sort of earth-mother heroine. In Mary Gates' *Out of This Nettle* (1937), the orphan heroine is redeemed when she runs away to the Badlands, disguises herself as a boy, and succeeds as a ranch hand. Although the story is sentimental and strains belief, Gretchen McCowan and Florence Stebbins Gleason describe the adventure of a young girl who explores Deadwood in its lusty early days of gold mining in *All the Days Were Antonia's* (1939). None of these books is particularly memorable, but they reveal the potency of western scenes upon women writers' imaginations.

Noticeably absent among the works of the first two generations of South Dakota women writers are novels by Native American writers or women from ethnic backgrounds other than Anglo-American. The former had been residing in South Dakota for a much longer period of time, but they did not turn naturally to the novel, a European

Yankton Sioux writer Zitkala Ša began publishing stories of her life on and off the reservation in the *Atlantic Monthly* in 1900. She is seen here, standing right of center, at the Santee Normal Training School. *Center for Western Studies.*

374

literary invention. Instead, they relied on an oral tradition of stories and legends. Zitkala Ša (Gertrude Simmons Bonnin), a Yankton Dakota woman, is one writer whose work appeared briefly in the early part of the twentieth century. As a child, she was sent away to boarding school in Indiana and acquired a college education at Earlham College. She worked for the Indian Service and later married a man who also worked for the Indian Service. In 1900 in the *Atlantic Monthly* Zitkala Ša published stories of her happy childhood on the reservation, the misery of her first days at boarding school, and experiences in teaching. These were followed for a few years by stories in other periodicals, which were collected and published in 1921 under the title *American Indian Stories* and reissued with an introduction by Dexter Fisher by the University of Nebraska Press in 1985. She is probably better known by readers in the last decades of the twentieth century than in her own day.

Marie McLaughlin, Dakota wife of the Indian Agent on the Standing Rock reservation, used her family knowledge to write *Myths and Legends of the Sioux,* which was published in Bismarck, North Dakota, in 1916. Indian women did not depart from their native oral traditions until much later in the twentieth century.

Not until the middle of the twentieth century and the third generation of South Dakota women writers did the work of descendants of Scandinavian and German pioneers begin to appear for the reading public. Following World War II in the late 1940s and 1950s, a new generation of women writers appeared who had no direct experience with the early days of settlement. The automobile, radio, and television made dramatic changes in the lives of rural South Dakotans. Women went to high school and college, participated in 4-H events, served in the armed forces, and held jobs outside the home, at least until they married. Yet the inspiration of pioneer life continued to prove powerful for writers with Scandinavian or German heritage.

Borghild Dahl was one such writer. She used her Norwegian heritage and the immigrant experience in novels she wrote after blindness prevented her from continuing to teach at Augustana College in Sioux Falls in 1941. A second-generation Norwegian, she was born in 1890 in Minneapolis, where her parents had settled after emigrating from Norway. Fiercely ambitious for education, she graduated from the University of Minnesota and did graduate work at both Oslo and Columbia Universities. Her disability led to her first and best-known book, *I Wanted To See* (1944), which was used by returning servicemen from World War II who had lost their vision. Her next book, *Karen* (1947), has both a South Dakota prairie setting and the Norwegian immigrant experience.

The central figure in this novel is a classic pioneer heroine. Coming with her sister from Norway to Iowa and unable to speak English, Karen finds work as a cook and maid before she meets the man she will marry, Arne, another immigrant. They move to a homestead in Dakota Territory. Karen recognizes that Arne is not strong willed and resourceful enough to survive on the prairie, so she takes over leadership of the enterprise. She bakes bread for single male settlers in town in exchange for supplies for the homestead; she learns how to use a gun and kills a wolf while she is alone on the claim; she measures and cuts the wood for their barn; she encourages Arne to play his violin at local dances to keep him satisfied with the hard life; she organizes the Norwegian women in the area to start a church; she even studies English in her spare time. By the time her son is born she is confident and mature—a successful pioneer, a virtual superwoman.

Dahl's later work deals again with pioneer experience but is set in Minneapolis and small-town Minnesota. However, two books by other South Dakota writers follow the narrative plan of *Karen* in recounting the pilgrimage from homeland in Norway or Denmark to the South Dakota prairies. Inga Hansen Dickerson's *Trina* (1956) and Doris Stensland's *Haul the Water, Haul the Wood* (1977) are both fictional works based on stories of their families. Neither woman is a professional writer, but both are devoted to their subjects. The stories show weaknesses in character development and narrative structure but are tributes to their foremothers. Dickerson writes of her mother, who homesteaded near Yankton, and Stensland writes of her great grandmother, who homesteaded in Lincoln County. Both of these women thrive on the hard work and the demands of life on the prairie in the last three decades of the nineteenth century. They show great courage and endurance in facing the challenges of grasshoppers, illness, loneliness, wild animals, hungry Indians, droughts, and blizzards. They take pride in the homes they create, the churches they build, the distressed neighbors they assist, the butter they churn, the food and clothing they produce. They have unshakable faith in God and hard work.

While Scandinavian writers celebrated the opportunity, independence, and accomplishment that awaited them on the new land, settlers with a Yankee background sometimes found such ethnic diversity threatening. Many Anglo-Americans from eastern states migrated to the small towns along the railroads to establish businesses that served surrounding farmers. The novel *The Land They Possessed* (1956) by Mary Worthy Breneman deals with such participants in early South Dakota history. The "writer" of this tale is a mother/daughter combination who created it together out of the mother's memories of her childhood and young adulthood.

Mary Worthy Thurston came to Dakota Territory with her parents in the 1880s, grew up on homesteads in north-central South Dakota, and became a teacher in Eureka before she married and left the state. The central character Michal is loosely patterned after the young Thurston, although Michal's romance with Karl Gross is pure fiction. The characters John and Mavis Ward are based upon Mary's parents Joseph and Martha Worthy. Muriel Breneman, Thurston's daughter by the man she married, never lived in South Dakota, but assisted her mother in the writing and publication of the book. These writers drew upon the family history as well as the history of the town of Eureka for the story. Mary's father (Muriel's grandfather) actually ran a store in Ipswich but lived on a farm some seventeen miles from town.

The story revolves around the Ward family, who arrive in 1885 during the Great Dakota Boom, hoping to make it rich. John Ward is a speculator who hires help to manage the farm; he loves horses and pedigreed dogs, and when South Dakota fails to live up to expectations, moves his family farther west to Montana to seek a fortune there. His wife Mavis hates the prairie and fears it, much like Beret in Ole Rölvaag's *Giants in the Earth*. She maintains a home that is an oasis of eastern gentility in the empty wilderness—with hired help, Spode china, kid gloves, and fashionable clothes. She longs for trees and neighbors and is delighted when the family finally moves into town (Eureka) where they live in the back of a store.

Furthermore, she looks down on the Germans from Russia, recent immigrants to the area who came by trainload to the Dakota plains and prairies in the last decades of the nineteenth century and who would help turn Eureka into the wheat capital of the world by 1893. Mavis cautions her daughter Michal about association with them. To her and to other Anglo-Americans they appeared very foreign—with their tall astrakhan hats, colorful sashes, boots, sheepskin coats, feather beds, and bags of seed wheat.

On the other hand, her daughter Michal, age nine when the story opens, loves the prairie from the beginning. For her, as for Mary Worthy Thurston, it was a place of beauty. She flees to it—to a pigweed patch, a buffalo wallow, a slough, the top of a hill—when she is troubled or uncertain and needs privacy. Descriptive passages in the book marvelously evoke the sights, smells, and sounds of the birds, grass, and wild flowers of the northern prairie. Unlike her mother, Michal is fascinated by the Germans from Russia. She is curious about the dugouts they live in, the food they eat, the clothes they wear, and she shares their passion for the land itself.

Michal's story does not include the usual school and rural activities of a young girl in earlier frontier novels. She grows and questions her social world, challenging her parents' disdain for the "Rooshans" (as the Germans from Russia were called by the other settlers) and challenging the minister at church about God after the death of her beloved Uncle Fred. But it is her romance with Karl Gross from one of the "foreign" families that creates the major conflict in the book. Her parents, of course, strongly disapprove, and Michal herself is uncertain for a while. She finds Karl physically and personally compelling—proud, arrogant, demanding, independent. He has the energy, the optimism, and the love of the land that will make him a successful farmer. She shares his passion and his dream for the future it promises. Yet she does not want to be dominated by him any more than she wanted to be dominated by her family. Eventually, Michal chooses to embrace the "foreign" culture. She and Karl elope, entering a marriage that promises to be enduring yet tempestuous.

Another third-generation writer sets her story in more modern times but portrays her pioneer heroine fighting battles like women on the frontier many decades earlier. Verna Moxley's *Wind 'til Sundown* (1954) relates the struggles of her heroine, Anne Holland, who moves with her family from Michigan to an abandoned homestead in West River country. Automobiles, electricity, and telephones exist, but are of little use to Anne in the trackless plains where her family settles. She experiences the same hardships of earlier pioneer women—loneliness, brutally hard work, droughts, blizzards, and always the wind. At first she is terrified of isolation on the empty land and wants to leave, but through determination and will she conquers her fears—driving their old car through gumbo, finally getting a well dug, and getting to know her distant neighbors. Like pioneer heroines before her, she triumphs.

Marian Castle's *Deborah* (1946) confirmed the value of the pioneer experience in post-World War II America. Although born in Iowa, the writer taught school for a number of years in South Dakota and knew it well. The novel spans three generations, beginning on a homestead in the 1890s near the imaginary town of Black Willow, South Dakota. Deborah is the seventeen-year-old daughter who wants the education, culture, and sophistication of the East and can hardly wait to leave the farm for the big world. She goes away to college, teaches in a small South Dakota town, marries the superintendent, who dies suddenly and leaves her to fend for herself with three young children. She marries again—this time for financial security. She confuses wealth and social position in town with the culture and education she sought.

All of her dreams come to nothing. Her son is killed in World War I. She loses her two daughters to the high life of the twenties in Chicago—bootleg liquor, smoking, falling in love with men who do not intend to marry them. In the economic disaster at the end of the twenties, her second husband dies and she is left with the care of the illegitimate child of her daughter, who dies in childbirth. The only thing she has left is the South Dakota farm to which she and her granddaughter Linda return in the depths of the depression. Deborah finds a certain satisfaction in the privation and challenge of making the farm productive again. It requires hard work, ingenuity and resourcefulness, but they are up to the challenge. Both Linda and Deborah survive a dust storm and feel a kinship with their pioneer women foremothers and that they can meet future challenges. The image of the pioneer heroine lived even in the middle of the twentieth century.

One writer of considerable eminence belongs in this group by age, but her reputation grew substantially after her death In 1971. A member of the distinguished Deloria family that produced Yankton leaders, Episcopal priests, lawyers, and writers, Ella Deloria more than lived up to the family reputation and is now regarded as a notable South Dakotan. When interest in Native American culture blossomed in the 1970s, her books *Dakota Texts* (1932) and *Speaking of Indians* (1944) were reprinted. Her unpublished novel *Waterlily* has circulated widely since the University of Nebraska Press published it in 1988. All have been used in college literature and Indian studies classes. She is listed in Radcliffe's *Notable American Women*, Janette Murray has written a doctoral dissertation on her work, and an Ella Deloria Research Project is underway in Chamberlain, directed by Agnes Picotte.

Through such works as *Dakota Texts* and *Speaking of Indians*, Ella Deloria sought to make her Indian culture familiar to Americans. *Courtesy Dakota Indian Foundation.*

Born on the Standing Rock Reservation, Ella eventually studied at the University of Chicago, Oberlin College, and Columbia University. However, she never forgot her native heritage and was a "good relative." At various times, she sacrificed her own interest and her career to care for her brother Vine, her sister Susan, and her mother. She taught school on the Standing Rock Reservation and at Haskell Indian Institute, but she was also comfortable in the company of such notable anthropologists as Dr. Franz Boas, Dr. Ruth Benedict, and Margaret Mead at Columbia University. It was there that she was encouraged to study the culture and language of her own people. Professionally, her anthropological work was recognized with the publication of *Dakota Texts*, native stories she gathered from Standing Rock, Pine Ridge, and Rosebud reservations.

Ella Deloria wanted to make native culture familiar to Americans. Her second book, *Speaking of Indians*, attempts to explain the history, language, and culture of native people, including their kinship system, traditional religious practices, and reservation life, to white people who knew so little about them. Written during World War II, the book does not harshly criticize government or church policies that attempted to obliterate native culture. Deloria does comment that Americans do not distinguish between tribes, and that the government and churches fail to credit native people with leadership potential but "presuppose a static mind on racial lines." Her novel *Waterlily* creates a tribal love story before the arrival of white people in which the daily life of Dakota people is convincingly described.

In the last three decades of the twentieth century, a number of women writers became increasingly professional and began to receive critical recognition. Many of the fourth generation were teachers of literature in higher education at least part of the time, and they had much more popular encouragement to write stories, poetry, and essays and were taken more seriously than their literary predecessors. In the early seventies, the South Dakota Committee on the Humanities (later the South Dakota Humanities Council) gave a great boost to reading, discussing, and writing about South Dakota subjects. It sponsored seminars, conferences, and programs, and funded literary projects all over the state, using scholars from the colleges and universities. Later, it established reading groups across the state which sometimes read and discussed local authors. The council also reprinted some out-of-print books by South Dakota authors. Also important was the South Dakota Arts Council, which funded Poets in the Schools so there was greater recognition of the reading and writing of poetry.

Both the Indian Rights Movement and the Women's Movement of the seventies and eighties focused attention on Native American literature and on the professional and literary achievements of women writers. Writing programs and conferences at the University of South Dakota, South Dakota State University, and Augustana College gave additional impetus to both native and women writers. One example is the Writer's Retreat at Oak Lake Field Station, coordinated by Charles Woodard of South Dakota State University and sometimes assisted by writer Elizabeth Cook-Lynn. Writers read and discussed their work, learning from and encouraging each other. All of these efforts have led to a number of local writers who have found inspiration in South Dakota's natural environment, history, diversity of cultures, and way of life.

Further encouragement of women writers has come from the publication of *Pasque Petals,* the South Dakota poetry magazine that began life in 1926 under the direction of the South Dakota Poetry Society. Although the magazine was first edited by Badger Clark, these titles were soon taken over by women. Adeline Jenney became editor in 1936 and Poet Laureate in 1958. She was followed by Mabel Frederick, and in 1974 by Audrae Visser of Elkton, who also became editor of *Pasque Petals* in 1998. The organization gave great encouragement to local writers by publishing their work in the magazine and in occasional anthologies. In addition, they sponsored poetry contests among high school and college students, and organized conferences of state poetry societies. Of course, some women writers who are better known for their published fiction and nonfiction have also written poetry: Nancy Veglahn, Linda Hasselstrom, Kathleen Norris, and Elizabeth Cook-Lynn.

Many women writers have turned to South Dakota history for subject matter. Helen Rezatto wrote short sketches based on specific historic events before she published *Mount Mariah: the Story of Deadwood's Boot Hill* (1980). The slogan "Kill a man— start a cemetery" gave her the inspiration to explore the notorious history of Deadwood and who exactly was buried on Boot Hill. Sally Roesch Wagner, an Aberdeen native who also explored the early woman suffrage movement of that city, edited a whole series of books based on the Pioneer Daughters Collection in the South Dakota State Historical Society State Archives. *Daughters of Dakota* (1989-94) in six volumes, include stories of ethnic pioneer women (Germans from Russia, Germans, Scandinavians, Native Americans, and Anglo-Americans) as well as stories of Black Hills women. Somewhat hastily put together, the series does reveal much information about the lives of pioneer women, the subject that has fascinated so many South Dakota women writers over the century. Renée Sansom Flood's *Lost Bird of Wounded Knee* (1995) recounts the life of the living baby found after the massacre at Wounded Knee in 1890. She also has contributed to increased publication of Native American materials with her printing of photographs and brief discussions of former Yankton Sioux leaders in *Remember Your Relatives* (1985).

Writing for young readers continued to appeal to the fourth generation as it did earlier in the century. Outstanding among these is Nancy Veglahn of Sioux Falls and formerly a member of the faculty at South Dakota State University. She has written extensively for young readers, both fiction and non-fiction, particularly biographies. Especially relevant to South Dakota is her skill in fictionalizing the history of South Dakota for young readers. In addition to writing *South Dakota* (1975), one volume in a series on the states, she wrote *Follow the Golden Goose* (1976), a fictional tale set in the Black Hills during the Gold Rush, and *The Buffalo King, the Story of Scotty Philip* (1978). Nancy Veglahn writes well, incorporating accurate factual material gracefully into the narrative and creating plausible, if imaginary, dialogue of historic figures.

Another writer for the young reader is Pamela Smith Hill. Although a native of Missouri, Hill earned a master's degree at the University of South Dakota. She became interested in geology in the Badlands after writing a magazine story about *tyrannosaurus rex*. She learned about the competition among geologists known as the Great Bones War of the late nineteenth century, traveled extensively in South Dakota, and wrote the novel *Ghost Horses* (1996). Set in the Badlands, the novel has a feminist heroine, a young girl who is a true pioneer, but who finds adventure and excitement in searching for dinosaur bones. In order to participate in the scientific project, she masquerades as a boy, is eventually discovered, but ultimately triumphs. The narrative line is familiar to readers of South Dakota novels for young women, but the setting and background are created from a somewhat unusual chapter in South Dakota's history.

Honored with a National Humanities Medal, Virginia Driving Hawk Sneve appeals to both Native American and white readers. *Center for Western Studies.*

In the last three decades there have been four writers who have achieved a body of publication and substantial recognition that suggest real artistic achievement. The first of these is Virginia Driving Hawk Sneve, who has more than three decades of accomplishment to her credit. She has received numerous honors, including an honorary doctorate from Dakota Wesleyan University, a Distinguished Alumni Award from South Dakota State University, and a National Humanities Medal from President Bill Clinton. She has written some twenty books, numerous articles and essays, short stories, poems, and television programs. They cover a wide range of subjects but most of them deal with her Native American heritage.

Born on the Rosebud Reservation, Virginia Driving Hawk spent many childhood summers with her maternal and paternal grandmothers, imbibing traditional stories, history, and points of view from them. This provided her with a rich store of native material. In addition, her immersion in academic study of Euro-American history and literature has enabled her to address the inadequacies she found in that curriculum in failing to discuss and understand Dakota culture. As a result, she has written persuasively and accurately to fill that gap, appealing to both native and white cultures. Although a teacher or counselor most of her professional life, she began to write soon after graduation, beginning with a novel *Betrayed* (1974), set in Minnesota and Dakota Territory, which attempted to tell the truth about the Dakota War of 1862. She is best known, perhaps, for her children's books *High Elk's Treasure* (1972), *When the Thunders Spoke* (1974), and *The Chichi Hoohoo Bogeyman* (1975), all of which have been reprinted by the University of Nebraska Press. She has written an official history of the Episcopal Church's mission to the Indians, *That They May Have Life: The Episcopal Church in South Dakota, 1859-1976* (1977), and a family memoir, *Completing the Circle* (1995), that is particularly insightful in describing the lives of women during their transition from traditional hunting and gathering tribes to reservation life. Like her predecessors Zitkala Ša and Ella Deloria, Virginia Driving Hawk Sneve has tried to help Americans understand native people and culture through her writing.

Linda Hasselstrom is a fourth generation South Dakota women writer who has focused on the land—specifically the family ranch near Hermosa where cattle have ranged since the early days of settlement on the grassland prairies and plains east of the Black Hills. In fact, she describes her mother's and father's forebears, who migrated from Scandinavia to this arid country to carve cattle ranches out of what appeared to be inhospitable terrain. She is passionate about her connection with the land—identifying the wildflowers and grasses that thrive among its limestone outcrops, the host of birds who nest upon it and fly above it, and the wild animals that inhabit it. In addition, she loves cattle ranching. She vividly recounts pulling calves from too-small cows, driving a herd from one pasture to another, riding her horse to check fences, losing animals to blizzards, fire, and lightning, and trucking cows to an unpredictable market. The reader shares the experience and cannot miss Hasselstrom's gusto and enthusiasm for ranching as well as her passion for the land.

In most of her writing, Hasselstrom has a narrative line—her personal life as it relates to her family's South Dakota ranch. In a sense her writing is an extended memoir. This writer/teacher/editor/rancher is the main character in her works—all are written in first person. Some of her books are compilations of earlier essays: *Windbreak: A Woman Rancher on the Northern Plains* (1987); *Going Over East: Reflections of a Woman Rancher* (1987); *Feels Like Far* (1999), and *Between Earth and Sky* (2003). Each one recounts periods of her life and is structured around a central theme: the seasons, the ten fences she has to open to get to the summer pasture, the metaphor of grass, or the spiraling image of a high-flying hawk. Hasselstrom's deftness with concrete and vivid detail lends itself to poetry, which she also has published, notably *Bones* (1993). She makes the reader feel, see, smell, and hear the wind blowing across the plains or the cattle that bawl and run when they are herded into a new pasture.

The life she recounts in her narratives has been beset by troubles. Although born in Texas, her real life began when, with her mother and a new father, she moved to a South Dakota ranch and was given her first horse, Rebel. She claimed he was the most perfect love affair she ever had. As she wrote in *Going Over East*, "Others ended in heartbreak or marriage or both. He never betrayed me." Although she later earned a degree in English at the University of South Dakota, married a divorced man with three children, attended graduate school at the University of Missouri with him, taught at a college, edited a magazine of the arts, divorced, married again, and was soon widowed, the ranch is the center of her life. After her beloved second husband died, she had difficulties with her father over the future of the ranch. However traumatic her personal life, she returns to the ranch for comfort and inspiration and incorporates both her pain and her joy into her writing.

Linda Hasselstrom has won numerous honors for her work. She has been named Author of the Year by South Dakota's Hall of Fame and she won the 1989 Governor's Award for Distinctive Achievement in the Arts and the 1990 Western America Award, presented by the Center for Western Studies. Some of her work has been reviewed by the *New York Times*. She has also been active in the environmental movement to protect the land she loves so much. Through workshops, editing, and publication of the magazine *Sunday Clothes* from 1972 to 1976, she encouraged other South Dakota writers.

Kathleen Norris's connection with the plains has followed a totally different path from that of Linda Hasselstrom. Yet both found spiritual sustenance by living on them. Norris belongs only partly to South Dakota. Born in Washington, D.C., as a child she knew the state in summers when she spent time in her grandmother's house in Lemmon. By the time she arrived to live in that house in 1974, she was married to poet David Dwyer and had already lived among young literati in New York. During her high school years she lived in Hawaii; she graduated from Bennington College in Vermont; and she had published some poetry of her own. Yet she exploded on South Dakota's literary scene with the publication of *Dakota: A Spiritual Geography* when it was glowingly reviewed on the front page of the *New York Times Book Review* in 1993 and became a best seller. In this important book, she describes how she found her own soul by living in a very small town on the plains. The plains "have been essential not only for my growth as a writer, they have formed me spiritually. I would say they have made me a human being," she wrote.

The book is actually a collection of essays and poems, some of which appeared in earlier publications. She found that the isolation, far from stifling her imagination and sensibility, allowed her spiritual life to flourish. She said the silence of the plains reminded her of a monastery. Her reading of Thomas Merton and desert fathers led her to the belief that the silence and solitude she experienced on the plains was a kind of "literary desert," but she felt greater peace and serenity than she had ever known before. Though not a Catholic convert, nor even a true believer, she became an oblate of a Benedictine community and increasingly interested in spirituality. She identifies with the farmers and likes the hard, concrete language of the "unschooled." But she also writes of the economic problems of farms and small towns, of potential environmental degradation of the land, of its harsh climate (there are intermittent "weather reports" in the book), of narrow-minded, small-town citizens who cannot relate their lives to larger issues in the world. "Combatting inertia in a town like Lemmon can seem like raising the dead," she comments. Yet the book is primarily a journey into herself, which she believes has been possible only because she has been transformed by the stark and lonely beauty of the plains. In the words of a monk whom she quotes, it is there that she can be "alone with the Alone."

The prose work Kathleen Norris has written since *Dakota* has continued her spiritual journey, but has not dealt so specifically with South Dakota. *The Cloister Walk* (1996) recounts her year spent as an oblate at St. John's Abbey in Minnesota, and *Amazing Grace* (1998) is an exploration through language of her growing faith. She has published some poetry which reflects her South Dakota experience, such as *Little Girls in Church* (1995). Even though her reputation extends far beyond the state, Kathleen Norris remains a significant South Dakota literary figure we can claim as one of our own.

One other writer who has achieved distinction requires some further discussion. Elizabeth Cook-Lynn is another strong voice from and for the Native American people in South Dakota. She claims she writes for the cultural survival of her people and is more militant in tone than Virginia Driving Hawk Sneve, Ella Deloria, or Zitkala Ša. Born in1930 at Fort Thompson and a member of the Crow Creek Reservation, she claims distinguished ancestry of tribal leaders and linguists. She has been a university teacher and writer, and since her retirement in 1990 she lives in Rapid City. Her recent writing has been political in character, such as *Anti-Indianism in Modern America, a Voice from Tatakeya's Earth* (2001), but even her early stories and poems cry out over the cruelties and injustices of treatment of Native American people in the United States.

Her novel *From the River's Edge* (1991) deals with a man, John Tatakeya, who loses some of his land in the 1960s to the great power dams on the Missouri River and finds himself in a court of law over his horses which have been stolen. The story is fiction but based on historical events involving real people like Smutty Bear and Struck by the Ree. After a lengthy court trial which tests all of John's loyalty and faith in the government, he at last comes to an understanding of his real permanence when he sits by the Missouri River. He has been changed just as the government dams have changed the course of the river, but they both will endure.

The Power of Horses and Other Stories (1990) provides glimpses of native people who live and work in the white man's world but who continue to carry their culture with them. They do not forget their stories; they continue to identify with the land and songs of their ancestors that still sing in their hearts. "Loss of the Sky" tells of the sorrow of a father whose son fell in France during World War I and was buried there. The old man sits on the earth he loved and weeps because the bones of his son will never mingle with the bones of his grandfathers. As Cook-Lynn writes, the "soul of the tribe continued in the imagination to be inherent in *maka*, the earth." In her stories, Elizabeth Cook-Lynn powerfully expresses the grief of a displaced people and the injustices they have suffered.

Women writers continue to provide significant voices in expressing feelings and thoughts about life in South Dakota. Even in the twenty-first century, the state's geography, people, history, and culture continue to inspire them. The writers of the fourth generation are more professional and certainly better educated than some of the early writers. They have more opportunities to learn, write, and publish than women did at the end of the nineteenth century. Yet they still draw upon the solid tradition established by the generations of writers before them. May future South Dakota women writers have as much to say and the capacity to say it as well as those who have gone before them.

Chapter 20
Visual Arts

> Far as we aim our signs to reach,
> Far as we often make them reach,
> Across the soul-from-soul abyss,
> There is an aeon-limit set
> Beyond which they are doomed to miss.
> Two souls may be too widely met.
> That sad-with-distance river beach
> With mortal longing may beseech;
> It cannot speak as far as this.
> —Robert Frost, "A Missive Missile"[1]

Frost wrote "A Missive Missile" in response to an archeologist who had sent him a prehistoric artifact. The poem is a plaintive admission of the limitation of communication between cultures while at the same time suggesting the power of art to stir us in ways beyond words. Art is a matter, Frost implied, of the way people see things. When the Lakota looked at the spruce-covered slopes, the crags, and the park-like meadows of the *Paha Sapa*—the Black Hills—the vistas inspired awe and reverence; the European-Americans looked at the same vistas and saw economic opportunity—trees equalled lumber, mountains meant ore, meadows translated into pasture or building sites, the beauty suggested tourism and settlement. This example of cultural division is emblematic of the diversity affecting the arts in South Dakota, for the way people look at nature reflects the way they look at art.

In this account, culture is understood to be a matter not just of race, nationality, or religion, but rather as a complex interplay of factors including economic class, education, gender, and age, all of which affect personal taste. "Cream rises," is the old-fashioned way of saying that the best things make themselves known; but in this homogenized age, people who seek the best may find themselves sorting through what at times seems a bewildering array. It is as little helpful to embrace all art equally as it is to exclude some kinds of art on the basis of immature taste. A start may be to acknowledge that what unifies the best art in the state is what connects it to the best art everywhere—a desire to penetrate beyond the superficial, to reach toward something not yet fully perceived.

If this history were to include only those artists who were born in South Dakota, spent their lives here, and contributed significantly to the visual art of the state, the account would be abbreviated indeed. Fortunately, there is a tradition of claiming as historic South Dakota figures those who spent only a brief but significant time in the state (Wild Bill Hickok, George Armstrong Custer), prominent figures who roamed the plains beyond state boundaries (Crazy Horse, Sitting Bull), and the native-born who left the state to find fame and fortune elsewhere (Tom Brokaw, Al Neuharth, Sparky Anderson); this tradition may be applied as well to the visual arts. On the other hand, visual art in South Dakota has grown to be a crowded field, and no brief history such as this one can hope to catalog all of its contributors; instead, salient points in the development of visual arts in the state will be touched upon—the ancient artifacts and petroglyphs which influenced later Lakota-Dakota art, the Euro-American nineteenth-century documentarians and the Wild West iconographers who followed them, the mountain-monument-makers and other public artists, the illustrators and illuminators, the printmakers and the money-makers, the abstract artists and the concrete.

■ Ancient Art: The Missive Dismissal

Like Robert Frost, archeologists have long recognized both the appeal and the opaqueness of prehistoric American art. Etienne B. Renaud, in his report on "The Pictographs and the Petroglyphs of the High Western Plains," notes the attraction of laymen to the art and the artifacts under his purview: "Indian pictographs have a great power of fascination for all ages. Young and old, cultured and illiterate, all are immediately interested at the simple mention of Indian pictographs. There is a queer attraction in those strange signs and primitive pictures. What can be the cause of this quickened attention, of this almost magic spell, which so many more significant archaeological facts do not succeed in awakening among most people?"[2]

Renaud attributes the fascination in pictographs to adults watching children attempting to draw familiar things: "But, this feeling may come from our erroneous conception that art is the flower of civilization, while, in fact, it reached a high degree of perfection in the midst of extremely barbaric conditions. We must remember the splendid mural painting of Font-de-Gaume in France, of Altamira in Spain, and of several other caves of Western Europe, as well as the astonishing Bushman paintings of South Africa, together with the marvelous carving and engraving on bone, horn, and ivory of Upper Paleolithic times, to understand the remarkable artistic sense, the power of observation and adaptation, the unbelievable manual skill of the savage Cro-Magnon hunter and other races, white and black, living in a stone age culture, yet truly great artists just as some of our Indians have been or still are."[3] Renaud's patronizing diction aside, his assessment of the artistic qualities of so-called "primitive" works is a valid one.

Like Frost, however, Renaud is chary of attempts to interpret the meaning of ancient pictographs: "they are human manifestations, sometimes attempts at esthetic representations, and a challenge to our mind to decipher."[4] People often think of petroglyphs as "Indian writing," apparently in analogy to Egyptian hieroglyphics, but while highly speculative meanings have been assigned to these works from time to time, no scientific evidence supports the idea that they have "meaning" the way conventional writing does. They seem best regarded as sacred art rather than as declarative inscription.

For over 10,000 years human beings have existed in what is now South Dakota, and almost all cultures have left behind reminders of their existence. Whatever else their art may tell us, the main inference remains: "We were here." Clovis spearheads, used to hunt mammoth; exquisitely fashioned Folsom flint points; stone axes and bison-bone hoes of the agricultural tribes—all suggest a complex prehistory of migration and occupation. Petroglyphs and pictographs are fascinating to us because they resemble what we most readily identify as art, although the people who made them would likely make no such distinction, just as contemporary Indians do not distinguish between the created objects of their cultures.

The petroglyphs examined by Renaud were in the southwestern corner of the state near Edgemont, at Red Canyon and Coal Creek. He classified the petroglyphs at these sites as pecked (chipped out of the surface), incised (scratched into the surface), or painted. The figures, mostly outlines but occasionally filled in, apparently represented human figures (shown often with arms raised, but whether in supplication, surrender, or praise, no one knows) and animal shapes (predominantly elk or deer with prodigious racks), along with various symbolic motifs. Other petrolyphs and pictographs, often dating between 3,000 and 5,000 years old, have been found elsewhere in the state since Renaud's time. The style of all suggest ties to modern Lakota-Dakota art.

■ Late Prehistoric and Historic Art

While the Lakota-Dakota were the dominant Indians in Dakota Territory in historic times and while their cultural appurtenances are what many people think of today as essentially Indian, many cultures preceded them and coexisted with them. One thing that seems obvious to even the casual observer, however, is that the paleolithic petroglyphs have a similarity to Lakota-Dakota pictographs found in winter-counts. Moreover, as Arthur Amiotte points out in his praiseworthy treatise on Sioux art in *An Illustrated History of the Arts in South Dakota*, the conventions of pictographic accounts—the deliberate two-dimensional lines, the flat areas of fill, an undifferentiated background, and the general lack of three-dimensional shading or perspective—became "the very foundation of modern Indian painting."[5]

Amiotte points out, however, that the scope of Indian art goes beyond pictographs to include decorative quillwork, beadwork, pottery, sculpture, and all the other imaginative works constituting a unified cultural vision, and that the Sioux as a whole value no one category over another.[6] In this chapter, the emphasis will remain on the inheritors of the pictographic tradition, but this emphasis is not meant to diminish the contributions of those working in other traditional media. It should be noted as well that motifs found in such alternative media as shield design have strongly influenced modern artists such as Oscar Howe. Amiotte includes a more complete treatment of the quill and bead workers, the pipestone carvers, and other branches of Lakota art in his section in the *Illustrated History*.

Amos Bad Heart Bull (1869-1913), a cousin of Crazy Horse, is often cited by Amiotte and other Indian art historians as among the most influential late-traditional artists. His pictographic ledger history of the Sioux inspired many later artists.[7] The pictographs found in winter-counts and in Bad Heart Bull's work are mnemonic, meant as reminders of events, and this commemorative aspect likewise influenced later artists.

Oscar Howe (1915-1983) emerged in the twentieth century as the preeminent schooled artist to combine traditional conventions with European influences in an expression of plains Indian culture. Pivotal in his artistic development were the three years he spent at the Studio of the Santa Fe Indian School in the mid-1930s. The variation of the Art Deco style taught there incorporated many of the elements which came to be associated with Indian art.[8] Howe returned to South Dakota to teach at the Pierre Indian School through the early forties, before serving in World War II. In the 1950s, growing steadily in skill and reputation, Howe developed a style calling upon traditional pictographic and shield design, giving his compositions powerful dynamics with geometric shapes and radiating lines that suggested the mysticism and spirituality of his native culture.[9] This instantly identifiable style won him increasing acclaim nationally and internationally. His academic work at Dakota Wesleyan University, in his summer workshops, and at the University of South Dakota helped to produce a new generation of Indian artists.

One of the most notable of those touched by Howe's ideas is Arthur Amiotte (b. 1942), who moved from works reminiscent of the Howe style to work reflecting both a broadening interest and a determination to commemorate personal, familial, and cultural high points. Although Amoitte is knowledgeable of the European traditions, his obvious preference is a Lakota-Dakota world view which includes reverence toward higher powers, the kinship of all creatures, and the cyclic movement of life. Much of his later work has dealt with the clash between Sioux culture and the European-American world experienced by his ancestors in the late nineteenth and early twentieth centuries. As teacher, art historian, and artist, Amiotte has been instrumental in fashioning the sensibilities of the more recent generation of Indian artists.

Other artists in the Howe tradition include Herman Red Elk (1918-1985), Donald Montileaux (b. 1948), and Robert "Bobby" Penn (1947-1999), all of whom studied with Howe, but each of whom developed a style of his own. Of the three, Penn studied longest with Howe, not only in workshops but also as a work-study assistant at the University of South Dakota. Penn's work at first tended to be more abstract than the work of other artists in the tradition, and Lakota-Dakota influences more subtle, but later he accumulated a considerable body of more straightfor-

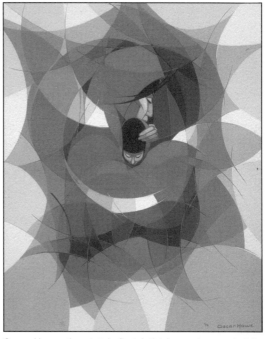

Oscar Howe, the state's first Artist Laureate, created for himself and for Indian artists who followed him a whole new vocabulary for art reflecting the Lakota-Dakota culture. His work, based in part on winter-count and ledger art of his ancestors, refined and abstracted the essentials geometrically to produce an instantly recognizable style, as seen here in *Sioux Mother and Child* (1972) © Adelheid Howe. *Center for Western Studies.*

ward portrayals of traditional subjects. His premature death choked off one of the most notable talents to emerge from the Howe inheritance. Red Elk came to art late in life as part of therapy to treat tuberculosis; Howe's influence seems less important in his work than the influence of traditional plains Indian modes. Montileaux, on the other hand, continued to produce work highly reminiscent of Howe's.

Painters like Robert Freeman claim connections to Oscar Howe, as well, but the connections are more tenuous. While Freeman's mother was a Yanktonai Sioux, he was born on the Rincon Reservation in California. Freeman often visits South Dakota, but his career was built and remains strongest in California and the Southwest. Oglala Lakota printmaker and painter Roger Broer also maintains ties to South Dakota while living and working mostly in Washington state. His work, widely exhibited and collected, is characterized by what he calls a "no holds barred" approach, using unusual techniques to achieve unique effects. Donald Ruleaux, born in Martin in 1931, has taught at the Oscar Howe Summer Workshop at the University of South Dakota and has maintained a reputation as artist and educator. The university offers a touring exhibition of his work. Colleen Cutschall (b. 1951), an Oglala Lakota from Pine Ridge, cites Oscar Howe as an early influence. Essentially a painter, Cutschall, also known as Sister Wolf, has expanded into many other media, always preserving a strong traditional flavor. A powerful example is *Spirit Warriors*, the Little Bighorn Aboriginal Monument, dedicated in

2003. Sculpted in bronze, it replicates pictographic drawings, like stained glass leading without the glass. Cutschall teaches at Brandon University, Manitoba, Canada.

Constraints of space prevent a complete listing of all the later Native American artists making names for themselves in South Dakota. Shows specializing in Indian art, such as the annual Northern Plains Tribal Arts Show in Sioux Falls, demonstrate the great store of talent available in the field, the variety of media employed, and the range of expression achieved. The growing multitude of collectors has made Indian art a highly commercial specialty, as well. Popular artists such as Joanne Bird, of Brookings, have made something of an industry out of the sale of beguiling images with Indian themes. Bird's splashy, painterly style, derived from impressionism, has become virtually a trademark, and her work is welcomed in galleries.

The commercial dimension of Indian art offers a problem for younger artists of whole or partial Indian heritage, a problem not faced by those of wholly European descent. An artist with even a small fraction of Indian inheritance might be swayed by circumstances to capitalize on that facet to the exclusion of all else, despite an inclination toward more eclectic expression. If the Indian spirit wells up from the heart, of course, the point is moot. Talented Native American artists such as Sioux Falls painter James Starkey, Oglala abstractionist Gerald Cournoyer, and the twins Edwin and Edward Two Eagles, inspired by traditional themes and techniques, offer ample evidence of the power of ancient impulses combined with contemporary sensibilities. Starkey's work grows out of a knowledge of ledger art, combined with street-smarts of an urban Indian. Cournoyer's abstract work, which has been more widely exhibited, shows the influence of academic training in its sophisticated expression of a Lakota world-view. The Two Eagles are working out their own means of expressing the sense of mysticism inherent in the Lakota-Dakota culture. With luck, these and other young Indian artists will avoid the pitfalls and temptations of the commercial Indian art world and maintain their integrity.

■ Catlin and Bodmer

From earliest contact European curiosity about the aboriginal inhabitants of the Americas encouraged explorers and adventurers to profit from their experiences in books, lectures, illustrations, and frequently in exhibits of human beings. The Euro-American artists who traveled in South Dakota in the early nineteenth century, most notably George Catlin and Karl Bodmer, were relative latecomers to the industry, but offered the opportunity of documenting ways of life already mightily changed by contact with white culture and in the process of even more violent transition. The works of Catlin and Bodmer would seem to fall somewhere between the fanciful, romantically exaggerated peaks and valleys of Alfred Bierstadt and the exacting portraits of birds and mammals by John James Audubon.

Pennsylvania-born George Catlin (1796-1872) was an investigator, an artist, and a showman. His interest in the Indians of the plains was spurred by the realization that the native cultures were being transformed by the encroachment of European civilization. While his artwork was less elegant than that of contemporaries, he provided a valuable record of lives that were to be changed even more rapidly than he might have guessed. He has been called the father of the Wild West show because of his collection and exhibition of tribal garb and paraphernalia and because he included in his touring shows even tribal members themselves. He was not above dressing friends and relatives in the Indian regalia that he had collected to make portraits of them that might be mistaken for the images of true Native Americans.[10] The possible shortcomings of his art are more than made up for by his accomplishments, however. Catlin's trip along the Missouri in 1832, including his passage through what is now South Dakota, produced valuable records of personages, landscapes, and ways of life that in less than a decade were to be altered irretrievably. Smallpox ravaged the Missouri River cultures, and the advance guard of Euro-American traders, soldiers, and settlers would soon transform the riverbanks themselves.

Swiss-born Karl Bodmer (1809-1893) was a better artist than Catlin but perhaps less dedicated to documenting Indian customs and mores. For Bodmer, the record he preserved was less a calling than a commission, since he had been employed to accompany the German naturalist Maximilian, Prince of Wied-Neuwied, on a trek through the American West. Following Catlin's 1832 route just a year later, the expedition brought Bodmer to many of the same locales. He cast an objective eye on the people and on the scenery, avoiding both Bierstadt's romanticism and Catlin's cataloging. Well-practiced in animal and human anatomy, Bodmer portrayed people, horses, and wildlife more convincingly than had Catlin, and with a more refined sense of composition. The Maximilian journey was short compared to Catlin's, however, and Bodmer's part in it merely an episode in a career that positioned him essentially as a landscape and wildlife artist. Most of Bodmer's expedition work is now with the Joslyn Art Museum in Omaha, Nebraska.

■ Wild West Iconographers

The likes of Catlin, Bodmer, Bierstadt, and Audubon pointed the way for generations of artists who found the subject matter of the northern plains both intriguing and lucrative. Some, like Charles M. Russell, salted their romanticism with authenticity that grew out of an intimate acquaintance with the people and traditions of the open range. Other painters, like Frederic Remington, peppered their observations of Western life with vivid imagination. These universal spices—authenticity and imagination—were passed along to the artists who have dished up a savory Wild West for an insatiable public into the twenty-first century.

No one of the reputation and popularity of Russell or Remington and dealing primarily with western subject matter—cowboys, Indians, western events, western landscapes—has emerged in South Dakota, although scores have aspired to that distinction. The names listed below are meant to be representative rather than exhaustive and are not ranked by anything other than rough chronology.

Rose Mary Goodson was born in St. Louis in 1917 but spent several years in South Dakota, where she began to draw and paint South Dakota themes and to publish books on such subjects as touring the state and exploring the Black Hills and the Badlands. Jim Savage (1932-1985) was one of the preeminent woodcarvers in the Western mode. Born near Sioux Falls, Savage started carving in 1967 and quickly built up a regional and national reputation. He came to specialize in Western figures and Indian portraits, and his popularity contributed greatly toward the recognition by the public of Western art as a mode of some influence in the state. An exhibit made up of his original carving shop and works including carvings, paintings, and metal pieces is on permanent display in the Center for Western Studies in Sioux Falls. Mick Harrison is a prime representative of the Russell spirit of authenticity. He has lived in the western region of South Dakota and knows post-open-range ranching thoroughly. Widely collected and published, Harrison has received the Artist of the Year designation both by the South Dakota Hall of Fame and by the Center for Western Studies.

Although Ron Backer's recreations of historical events almost escape the parameters of western art, he has devoted enough paintings to such subjects as the Lewis and

Clark expedition, western expansion, and pioneer days to qualify. He is clearly of the Remington imagination school. He is well represented in galleries and in 1996 was selected "Artist of the Year" by the South Dakota Hall of Fame.

Brenda Buckner is so thoroughly absorbed in her ranching subjects, most often horses, that she omits background in her drawings and paintings. Raised on a wheat farm in South Dakota, she is regarded as a specialist in equine subjects and the contemporary ranching scene. She works most often in pencil (both colored and graphite).

Other Western artists fill special niches. A resident of Hermosa, South Dakota, Nancyjane Huehl is noted for her deft landscapes of the northern plains. Tony Chytka is another specialist, not only in subject matter (rodeo events), but also in medium (cast bronze sculpture). His life-size bronze of rodeo star Casey Tibbs may be found at the Tibbs Museum in Pierre. Black Hills artist Cat Deuter, twice chosen South Dakota Artist of the Year, is known for her renderings of Lakota Sioux children and other Western subjects. Kathy Sigle, of Spearfish, renders wildlife and other Western subjects mostly in watercolor. She has been the artist-in-residence at Custer State Park several times. Landscape specialist James Van Nuys was born in Whittier, California, but has spent much of his life in South Dakota rendering exacting oil paintings of the Black Hills, the Badlands, and ranching and farming country. Steve Roselles, born in South Dakota and living in the Black Hills, is unusual among Western artists (who often use sketches or photographs as sources for studio paintings) in that he works completely in the outdoors, or in the fancy French term *en plein air*. He prefers the palette knife to brushwork, and the resulting landscapes have a solid, crisp aspect.

The wildlife artists, following the Audubon tradition, constitute a separate subgroup sharing a common goal: the precise and accurate depiction of the animals and birds to be found in the West. Waterfowl-stamp and and other wildlife painting competitions resulting in significant cash prizes and publicity, had created a subculture assuring that every pin-feather and every hair will be accounted for and that skeletal and muscular structure will be rendered with caliper-close accuracy. The result is art too painstaking to be labeled photographic; the detail and clarity is actually closer to the surreal tradition. Minnesota-born Roger Preuss is regarded as the standard-bearer for wildlife artists in South Dakota and beyond. His depictions of animals native to South Dakota for the *South Dakota Conservation Digest* in the 1960s and 1970s set perfectionist benchmarks for those who followed. A large collection of Preuss originals is in the Center for Western Studies.

South Dakota wildlife artists include Mark Anderson, who won the Federal Duck Stamp competition for 2005-06, Russ Duerksen, and Rosemary Millette, all of Sioux Falls; Joshua Spies and John Wilson, Federal Duck Stamp winner for 1981-82, of Watertown; and Adam Oswald, of Brandon, along with many others. All of those named may be found on Web sites offering original art and prints.

◼ Man-Mountain Makers

The art for which South Dakota is best known is Gutzon Borglum's presidential portraits at Mount Rushmore. Born in Idaho territory in 1867, the son of a Mormon of Danish descent, Borglum became a sculptor after his brother Solon gained some fame in the field and after exposure to the work of Auguste Rodin. His first mountain-carving was done at Stone Mountain in Georgia, eventually abandoned, to be refashioned by other hands.

Mount Rushmore was conceived as a tourist attraction by South Dakota historian Doane Robinson, and after first being proposed as a tribute to regional heroes, was cannily repositioned as a national super-monument. While the selection of presidents to be represented seems obvious enough, some critics suggest that a theme of western expansion and Manifest Destiny was one goal. As Tim Giago has pointed out, none of the presidents represented was considered particularly friendly by Indians.[11] In addition, many of the Lakota-Dakota tradition, who consider the Black Hills to be sacred, might regard the work as desecration. Nevertheless, the attraction of the carvings to tourists and the iconic status they achieved seems far beyond even Robinson's and Borglum's inflated expectations. The patriotic overtones of the work and its status as a symbol of everything American has defused most possible criticism. Objects that have achieved such mythic proportions are clearly beyond the scope of aesthetics, ethics, or politics.

In 1939 a group of Lakota leaders summoned by Henry Standing Bear proposed Crazy Horse as a fitting hero to challenge the *wasicu* (white) leaders honored at Rushmore and Korczak Ziolkowski, who worked with Borglum at Rushmore, as the man to fashion the Lakota colossus. Largely self-taught, Ziolkowski established his reputation as a sculptor with a bust of Ignacy Paderewski that won first prize at the 1939 World's Fair in New

Gutzon Borglum designed and supervised the carving of the famous "Shrine of Democracy" at Mount Rushmore. He set a standard for grandiosity that only Korczak Ziolkowski, with his Crazy Horse Monument, has attempted to match or surpass. *Courtesy South Dakota State Historical Society– State Archives.*

York. After serving in World War II, the sculptor returned to South Dakota in 1947 to undertake the epic task that was to consume the rest of his life. He conceived the monument as the warrior astride a horse, fully modeled and free-standing, as opposed to the high relief faces at Rushmore or the low-relief carving at Stone Mountain, and nearly nine times higher than the Borglum work.[12] The Ziolkowskis—including wife Ruth, five sons and five daughters—had not only to blast the mountain, but to build and rebuild roads, living quarters, and tourist facilities, dig wells, string wires for electricity, and in short do everything needed to sustain the viability of the project over a period exceeding fifty years, with Ruth taking over direction of the work following her husband's death in 1982, at age 74. At that time considerable imagination was still required of tourists to envision the completed work. In the ensuing years, much of the face has emerged and observers are encouraged to believe that the work may actually be accomplished in the not-so-distant future.

While many of the criticisms raised about Rushmore apply to the Crazy Horse monument—ameliorated to a great extent by the nearly universal acceptance of the warrior as a man worthy of such an exhibition of praise—such achievement easily withstands efforts at belittlement. There is nothing little about the Crazy Horse Memorial, and its development seems to have taken on the force of nature rather than art.

■ Public Artists

Despite the incomparable nature of the man-mountain projects in the Black Hills, they have cast little or no shadow on South Dakota's other public artists—sculptors, muralists, architects, and liturgical artists. The inherent qualities of the public arts, however—that they are openly exhibited—has drawn criticism from those factions who may disagree with the modes, concepts, placement, or moral and political implications involved. While much of this criticism in South Dakota comes across as parochial, it is derived from the earnest belief that public art is the public's business.

The protracted furor over the exhibition of a bronze replica (executed by Felix de Weldon) of Michangelo's statue of David—a gift in 1971 from Sioux Falls' favorite son, inventor and businessman Thomas Fawick—is emblematic of concern expressed about many other public artworks in the state. Some Sioux Falls residents protested the replica's location, its nudity, and its very existence, although the furor has abated more recently. A companion piece, a de Weldon replica of Michelangelo's fully draped Moses, also a gift from Fawick, escaped criticism. It is located on the campus of Augustana College. The difficulty, perhaps, is that public art conceived as Michelangelo conceived it, as an expression of the ideals of the people as a whole, is possible only in a society where there is general agreement upon those ideals. In the diverse and pluralistic mix that is contemporary South Dakota, perhaps no general agreement can be reached.

James Earle Fraser with a clay maquette of *End of the Trail* (ca. 1910). Fraser grew to early manhood in Mitchell, where he learned extraordinary sympathy for Native Americans. His most replicated work was undoubtedly the 1913 buffalo-head nickel, which also featured one of the most famous composite portraits of an American Indian. *Courtesy National Cowboy and Western Heritage Museum.*

The criticism fomented by public art in the state is nevertheless remarkable. It has extended to the placement of a statue of World War II ace and late Governor Joe Foss (by Blaine Gibson of the Disney organization) in the Sioux Falls airport named for him; to a monumental modern work *Hoe Down* by sculptor Guy Dill, commissioned by the federal government for placement outside the Federal Building in Huron; to the concrete lodgepole I-90 rest stops designed by Sioux Falls architect Ward Whitwam; and to a proposed mural by a young Ethiopian-American artist, Eyob Mergia, for the Multi-Cultural Center in Sioux Falls, to cite just a few examples. Given the risk of public protest, the wonder is that there is so much public art in the state. Sculpture alone accounts for some notable pieces. James Earle Fraser (1878-1953), the designer of the 1913 buffalo nickel and one of the most famous Western bronzes ever cast, *End of the Trail*, was born in Winona, Minnesota, but was reared from the age of three in Mitchell. He was one of the most successful sculptors of his time, and his work is still widely exhibited. In South Dakota it is included in collections at Dakota Wesleyan and at the Middle Border Museum (life-sized Lewis and Clark sculptures).

The bust of Abraham Lincoln by Gilbert P. Risvold (1881-1938), located in the Lincoln Memorial Library at South Dakota State University, the artist's alma mater, is only one of the sculptures that helped win the Baltic native national acclaim. The *Mother Sherrard Memorial* in the capitol building in Pierre is another of Risvold's better-known works. His success as an artist inspired a later Baltic native, Palmer Eide. Eide's twenty-one symbolic relief panels in Indiana limestone on the exterior of Sioux Falls' City Hall, designed by Harold Spitznagel and completed in 1936, followed the Art Deco style of the building and established Eide as a public artist of note. Like many sculptors, Eide's artistic accomplishment ranged across media, mode, and subject matter. Some of his most noted church commissions include an aluminum Christ for the First Lutheran Church Chapel in Sioux Falls; an exterior mural at Our Savior's Lutheran, Sioux Falls, and a wood

Particularly noted for his church commissions, Palmer Eide specialized in public art. *Center for Western Studies.*

Christus at Augustana's Chapel of Reconciliation. Other public art includes *The Muse of Music* outside the Humanities Building at Augustana, which he completed following his retirement in 1971 with the aid of his long-time friend and colleague, Ogden Dalrymple, an accomplished artist in his own right.[13]

Four bronzes representing the qualities that helped forge the state of South Dakota—*Wisdom, Vision, Courage, and Integrity*—by sculptor Dale Claude Lamphere, of Sturgis, occupy each corner alcove of the rotunda of the capitol in Pierre. They were dedicated in the South Dakota Centennial year of 1989. Lamphere is nationally recognized and widely exhibited. Most of his public works—including such religious pieces as a bronze of Mary and two angels for the Basilica of the Shrine of the Immaculate Conception in Washington, D.C., or *The Immaculate Heart of Mary, Queen of Peace* at the Trinity Heights development in Sioux City, Iowa, and such secular works as *The Spirit of Dakota* at the Crossroads Convention Center in Huron—are in conventional style, but Lamphere has worked in more abstract contemporary modes as well.[14] He has over forty public works to his credit in a career spanning over a quarter-century. An exhibit of Lamphere's works in various materials was shown in 2003-04 at the South Dakota Art Museum in Brookings.

Rapid City has undertaken a long-term project entitled *City of Presidents* which will place life-sized sculptures of United States chief executives at street corners all over the town. The project is expected by be completed in the year 2011. Included among the artists commissioned for the task are Edward Hlavka, James Michael Maher, Sherri

Treeby, Lee Leuning, and John Lopez, all South Dakota artists. The *Rapid City Journal* reports, not surprisingly, that the project "generated controversy, especially in the arts community, when the presidential statues first started showing up. Objections arose over numerous aspects of the project, including its artistic merit and the city review process that allowed the use of public space for it."[15] Lee Leuning, along with Sherri Treeby, is also responsible for the multi-figure *Warriors of World War II* on the grounds of the capitol.

Several projects deserve brief mention: Among many other public sculptures in Rapid City is the concrete *Rapid Trout*, designed in the mid-1990s by Martin Wanserski as a tribute to fishing in the Black Hills. *Fighting Stallions*, enlarged in bronze from a 1935 mahogany carving by the late Korczak Ziolkowski, was chosen in 1994 for instal-lation near the capitol as a memorial to Governor George S. Mickelson and others who died in a plane crash in Iowa in 1993. *Tatanka—the Story of the Bison*, a complex, multi-part bronzework by Peggy Detmers of Hill City, was commissioned by Kevin Costner (Academy Award-winning director and star of *Dances with Wolves*) for his proposed Dunbar resort near Deadwood. The work features three mounted warriors and fourteen bison. Detmers is native to eastern South Dakota and specializes in bronzes and two-dimensional art of wildlife. Steve Thomas' early work *Sea Dream* is near the historic site of Fort Sod, across from Fawick Park and the statue of David in Sioux Falls. Thomas, a graduate of Augustana College, now teaches at the school.

Christiane Martens, a native of Germany noted for her striking abstract metal sculp-ture, is represented in Sioux Falls by her *Centripeton* at Spitznagel Partners and by *Homage to Victor Vasarely* (the Hungarian abstract painter recognized as the father of op-art) on the Augustana College campus. Both pieces have been repainted, in the case of *Homage*, because of vandalism, and so do not completely represent Martens' original intention. Martens taught for four years at Augustana and later at South Dakota State University. Her work, including such monumental pieces as the stainless steel *Denali* on the campus of the University of Alaska in Fairbanks and *Molecular Reflection* at the Benali Gallery in Illinois, has since achieved worldwide attention.[16] She currently teaches at the University of Illinois at Champaign-Urbana.

Other work deserves at least passing mention: a geometric piece titled *Isosceles*, one of several by metal-worker Harry Klessen in Sioux Falls, may be found at Eighth Street Railroad Center. John Peters' multi-tiered mobile, a four-dimensional (given its con-stantly changing aspect) panorama of South Dakota skies, hills, grasslands, and waters, hangs in the Minnehaha County Courthouse. Peters is on the art faculty at Augustana. Wanserski's bust of William Shakespeare is found in the Shakespeare Garden at the University of South Dakota. Wanserski is associate professor in the Department of Art at the university. Porter Williams is represented by two public works in Sioux Falls, a bronze head of civic leader Kenny Anderson at the Kenny Anderson Community Center, and *Petrograph*, a monumental quartzite wall construction at Sherman Park, depicting a mounted Sioux hunter and five bison. It was designed in part by James Starkey.

Not all sculptors produce public works, of course. Some, like Carol Hepper (b. 1953) concentrate on more intimate venues and more fragile materials that would not stand up to, say, a South Dakota winter. Having grown up on a ranch in a South Dakota reserva-tion, Hepper developed an appreciation for natural materials like animal hides, bones, willow branches, and fish skins that might be used as creatively as Native Americans used them. Her work was included in the Solomon R. Guggenheim Museum's 1983 exhibition "New Perspectives in American Art" in New York City, and in 1984 she won the South Dakota Governor's Award in the arts.[17] She currently makes her home in the Catskill Mountains and in New York City.

Dick A. Termes (b. 1941) is another South Dakota artist who defies categories. He is mentioned here because his most noted work is three-dimensional, which is the quality that usually designates sculpture, but he also incorporates painting; the results are dubbed "Termespheres" and seem a cross between the mobiles of Alexander Calder and the eye-tricking graphics of M. C. Escher, whose influence, along with Buckminster Fuller's, Termes readily acknowledges.[18] Termes received the Governor's Award for Distinction in Creative Achievement in 1999 and a South Dakota Museum of Art Artistic Achievement Citation in 1986. He makes his home in the Black Hills.

Muralists are as plentiful as sculptors in South Dakota. Arts councils throughout the state have sponsored mural projects, amateur and self-taught painters have found walls to paint, and professional artists frequently win mural commissions. Fairly typical of interior murals in public buildings are the sixteen murals in the Old Courthouse Museum in Sioux Falls; they were painted by Norwegian immigrant

Dick A. Termes, shown here with his "Termespheres," is the creator of an unusual art form, part painting and part sculpture, rendered in six-point perspective on globes. He has received the Governor's Award and the South Dakota Museum Citation for his imaginative work. *Photo © Paul Horsted/dakotaphoto.com*

Ole Running in 1915 and represent scenes in and around Sioux Falls. Restoration of the paintings, dimmed by time and damaged in some cases by moisture, is in progress at this writing. Edwin Johnson's murals in the Spitznagel-designed Sioux Falls City Hall are in a style influenced by noted Mexican muralist Diego Rivera and by Johnson's teacher, Merlin Pollock, and in a manner prescribed by the Works Progress Administration at the time of their creation in the 1930s.[19] Although not known primarily as a muralist, Oscar Howe designed a number of murals for the Corn Palace in Mitchell in his early career. Similarly, Robert Penn, one of Howe's protegés, did murals for the W. H. Over Museum in Vermillion, as well as for a number of other commissions around the country. Steve Troy of Huron, a photographer as well as a muralist, has graced walls in his hometown with several scenes of historical and patriotic subjects, including a depiction of "The Great Race," run round trip from Huron to De Smet and back in 1913. Sioux Falls muralist David Sieh is represented by interior murals in stores in Sioux Falls, the dioramas of the Delbridge Museum, several *coup d'oeil* residential murals, and a monumental railroad mural in Huron.

Bernard Preston Thomas (b. 1918) of Sheridan, Wyoming, has produced undoubtedly the largest mural in South Dakota, the *Cyclorama* at the Dahl Fine Arts Center in Rapid City. The painting, 180 feet long, also lays claim to being the largest historical

Robert Aldern has established a reputation as one of the foremost liturgical artists in the U.S. His liturgical style, marked by strong verticals and abstractions of the figure, stands in contrast to his landscapes, strongly horizontal in composition and reduced to essentials. *Courtesy Robert Aldern.*

mural in the country. It illustrates over two hundred years of United States history.[20] Thomas' murals are found in numerous other venues in Wyoming and Montana.

Robert Aldern (b. 1929) is a public artist through and through. Aldern's work has graced not only churches and chapels, but also such secular places as the rest stop in Chamberlain. The vertical parallels of much of Aldern's liturgical work, combined with the stylized, elongated figures, are distinctive elements of his work. His liturgical and religious compositions, often on vertical strips of hardwood, may be found at sites nationwide, and, among many other places in Sioux Falls, at the Augustana College Chapel of Reconciliation, at Our Savior's Lutheran Church, and at the Good Samaritan national headquarters.

Architecture is one of the most basic public arts. Even private dwellings exhibit a public face and are characterized according to distinctive styles. Arthur R. Huseboe's thorough treatment of the subject in *An Illustrated History of the Arts in South Dakota*, from which the following notes are drawn, is recommended for a more detailed account. Wallace L. Dow was thirty-six years old when he came to South Dakota in 1880. Before long his distinctive and indelible mark was evident in public buildings throughout the region. Thoroughly schooled in the popular styles of the day—Venetian Gothic and Richardsonian Romanesque—Dow also is noted for his use of the pinkish Sioux quartz-ite abundant in the area. His masterworks include the old Minnehaha Courthouse in Sioux Falls (1890), Pettigrew House (later to become the museum), Lincoln County Courthouse in Canton (1889-1899), First Baptist Church in Sioux Falls (1885), Dakota School for the Deaf in Sioux Falls (1885), All Saints School (1885), Territorial Penitentiary in Sioux Falls (1882-1884), and several commercial blocks in downtown Sioux Falls.[21] It was not until the middle of the twentieth century that Dow's dominance began to wane with a new wave of construction of more modern style.

What Dow was to Sioux Falls and the surrounding area, F. C. W. Kuehn was to Huron and central South Dakota. Beginning near the turn of the twentieth century, Kuehn came to be credited with over five hundred buildings in the region by 1969. He worked on smaller structures until 1915, when he designed the First Presbyterian Church in Huron, which was distinguished by a prominent central dome. Just as Dow was heavily influenced by the popular styles of his day, Kuehn embraced such styles as Classical Revival, which became popular in America about 1900. Other churches designed by Kuehn were the Huron Methodist Episcopal church in the Prairie School style, the Methodist Church in Geddes, and the American Lutheran Church in Huron, in Gothic style.[22]

It was Harold Spitznagel (1894-1975) who contributed most to the turnaround from traditional to modern styles of architecture, especially in eastern South Dakota. The Sioux Falls City Hall (1937) was one of Spitznagel's first triumphs, and the Art Deco building set the precedent of working closely with other artists to incorporate elements into the finished work. Spitznagel and later Spitznagel Partners, continued the practice of teaming with other visual artists. The Spitznagel Partners style was characterized by directness, simplicity, and functionalism, a step away from Spitznagel's more individual and innovative early work. Among Spitznagel credits are the Northwest Security Bank in Sioux Falls (1949), Tuve Hall at Augustana College (1950), Our Savior's Lutheran Church in Sioux Falls (1957), First Congregational Church in Rapid City (1958), and Sylvan Lodge (1936-37) in the Black Hills.[23]

Contemporary architects in South Dakota are too numerous for a complete listing here, but mention might be made of Koch Hazard Baltzer, responsible for the monumental refurbishing of the Washington Pavilion of Arts and Science in Sioux Falls and for the prize-winning design of the Center for Western Studies Fantle Building on the Augustana campus. Like the Spitznagel firm before it, Koch Hazard Baltzer has undertaken active support of the visual arts in Sioux Falls, particularly with exhibitions in its gallery of prominent and promising regional artists.

Likewise, there is not room here to undertake a listing of all the architectural landmarks in South Dakota, but the mention of some salient buildings seems obligatory. Certainly the State Capitol Building in Pierre (1910) cannot be overlooked. The large neo-classical building was constructed to the specifications of C. E. Bell of Bell and Detweiler in Minneapolis. Likewise inescapable is the Mitchell Corn Palace, the most recent of four such tourist attractions, with the latest incarnation (1920-22) designed by theater architects Rapp and Rapp. The lodgepole rest stops designed by Ward Whitwam, so prominent to tourists traversing the state, also deserve mention.

■ Illustrators and Illuminators

The term "illustrator" is sometimes used with pejorative overtones by those who think that it designates one whose work, since it does not originate solely with the artist, is therefore inferior; but more enlightened artists and critics realize that all artists are in the trade of showing what discursive language sometimes falteringly attempts to explain. Some artists might be happier with the label "illuminator," which in all of its connotations more fully expresses what they are about.

Harvey Dunn (1884-1952) was not only an illustrator, of course, but illustration was the means by which he won public recognition. After instruction at the Chicago Art Institute, he persuaded artist and teacher Howard Pyle to take him on as a student at Pyle's school in Wilmington, Delaware. Dunn illustrated stories for many publications, but perhaps for the *Saturday Evening Post* most often. Following his service as war artist in France during the Great War, he started to make increasingly more frequent visits back to South Dakota. By the late 1930s he was devoting more and more time to non-illustrative painting, with particular emphasis on subjects drawn from the prairie. Some of that

later work, including such paintings as *The Prairie is My Garden*, have attained the status of pop-culture icons. Dunn's gift of some forty-two of his prairie paintings to South Dakota State University in 1950 formed the nucleus of what was to grow to ninety works currently in the Dunn collection at the South Dakota Art Museum.[24]

Charles W. Hargens (1893-1996) was born just after the end of the classic open-range period, but his early years in his native Hot Springs and the Black Hills introduced him to authentic ranching experience. His background served him well as an illustrator for the *Saturday Evening Post* and for books such as the Zane Grey series published by Lippencott. He did

Harvey Dunn in his Tenafly, New Jersey, studio, in the 1940s. Dunn grew up in Dakota Territory and went on to become a major illustrator of his time. His prairie paintings form the nucleus of the South Dakota Art Museum in Brookings. *Courtesy South Dakota Art Museum.*

cover work for many magazines and often ranged beyond strictly western themes. In 1982 he was awarded an honorary Doctor of Fine Arts degree by Dakota Wesleyan University.[25]

Paul Goble's interest in the American Indian seems unusual in one born and raised in England, but this interest eventually led him to residency in Rapid City and a distinguished career as artist and author, mostly dealing with Indian subjects. He has written and illustrated some twenty-nine books and has shown his work in museums and galleries across the country. His original paintings and limited edition prints are eagerly sought by collectors.

Given the vast range shown by Aberdeen artist Mark McGinnis, it may seem surprising to find him under the category of illustrator, yet illustration is what he has been up to more and more. In McGinnis' case, the term "illuminator" seems definitely more appropriate. His subject matter is drawn from religion in the largest sense. Among works enriched by his art are *Elders of the Faiths, Lakota and Dakota Animal Wisdom Stories, Elders of the Benedictines, Designs of Faith, Buddhist Animal Wisdom Stories*, and Rabindranath Tagore's *Gitanjali* poems. In *Designs of Faith* he attempted the formidable task of producing a canvas representing each of the world's major religions. Besides his publications, McGinnis, who teaches at Northern State University in Aberdeen, has had over seventy one-person shows. McGinnis' work as a whole suggests an attempt at the synthesis of faith, learning, justice, and understanding.

■ Printmakers and Moneymakers

Fine art prints—true lithographs (that is, those printed using a stone), engravings, etchings, and serigraphs or silkscreen prints, among others—are limited to editions ranging in number from one or two up to a few hundred. Commercial prints—accomplished by offset lithography and computerized inkjet printers, among other methods—are capable of endless reproduction. A recent edition of a Terry Redlin offset lithograph, for example, was given a "limited edition" number of 29,500. True lithograph prints require a time-consuming, painstaking process which, because of numerous variables involved, often results in each print's being slightly different from the next. Most important of all is this distinction: a fine art limited-edition print is an original work of art because the stone image or plate is simply a tool in its creation; a commercial print is an infinitely replicable copy of an original. All of this goes to explain why fine art printers usually must subsidize their income by taking positions as teachers while commercial printmakers can make million-dollar donations to charities, build shrines to their own talent, and have public schools named after them.

Although it was with printmaking that Carl Grupp of Augustana College made his first and greatest impression on the national and international art world, Grupp is equally at home dealing with media ranging from watercolor and oils to pencil and ink drawing. A man of capacious interests, Grupp has explored virtually every print mode, but is particularly skilled as a lithographer. In many prints he seems to be working out a personal allegory of the soul. Among his recent work is a monumental series on the biblical parables for the Gloria Dei Church in Sioux Falls. Grupp's wit is evident in such works as his "fabulous fossil" series, which creates the fossil remains of animals never before imagined (such as the "Deinoshopper" and the "Levisaurus"), and in the self-portraits such as the one called *Training the Pet* in which he is shown as a medieval juggler putting a goldfish through a hoop. Beneath the levity, however, lies a profound self-examination, an appreciation of the tragedies as well as the comedies of humanity. A major retrospective of his work was held at the South Dakota Art Museum in 2004.

Often the subject of his own work, as seen here in *Grupp*, either with self-critical intensity or disguised as a juggler or a clown, Carl Grupp has established an enduring reputation as printmaker, draughtsman, and painter. His style is marked by grace, playfulness, and sometimes the grotesque. *Courtesy Carl Grupp.*

Lloyd Menard has been at the University of South Dakota almost as long as Carl Grupp has been at Augustana. A tireless promoter of the art of printmaking, Menard has served the cause not only as a teacher but as the owner and operator of Frogman's Press and Gallery in Beresford. The showings there are eagerly awaited by art-lovers across the region. Frogman's Press is also the site for workshops that have brought printmakers together to share techniques and insights. In his large paper works, often resembling tapestries or Oriental rugs, Menard "fills every chink with ore" in the form of distinctive patterns and images. His work is marked by humor, color, and wild imagination. He often augments the two-dimensional patterns of the work with three-dimensional patterns pressed into the paper.

Kansas native Ken Grizzell specializes in abstract serigraphs or silk-screen prints. Now emeritus professor of art at the University of South Dakota, Grizzell is largely self-taught as a screen printer but clearly fascinated with the technical possibilities of the medium. Like other artists who employ the technique, Grizzell cannot resist experimenting with the inherent elements of printing and overprinting color. The results is often a dazzling and enigmatic pattern or composition, such as his representative *Heidi Hates Red Triangles*. His work has been widely shown.

While South Dakota's most popular artist and money-maker is known for his commercial lithographs, Terry Redlin is really a painter rather than a printmaker. His appeal to sentiment makes him a favorite in galleries across the country. Redlin's landscapes are typically backlit, either by natural sources—a setting sun, stars, or moon—or by man-made lights, thus earning the adjective most used to describe them—"glowing." What is portrayed serves as a kind of emotional bookmark for the viewer's own fond memories of what the poets used to call "yore," a comfortable, uncomplicated past that exudes warmth and love. What is being sold here, as the old advertising phrase has it, is "the sizzle, not the steak." The "sizzle" in this case is an unspecific nostalgia. The resulting product is eminently marketable, and those seeking nostalgia can buy Redlin in prices to suit almost any pocketbook, from unframed paper editions for under one hundred dollars to deluxe canvas lithographs ranging up to a few thousand dollars. Originals, which might be considered priceless, since they are the potential source of unlimited income, are on view at the Redlin Art Center at Watertown, the artist's hometown.

Jon Crane, often mentioned in the same breath with Redlin, differs in having a long art lineage (both his great-grandfather and great-great-grandfather having been popular painters), in working in watercolors rather than oils or acrylics, and in reproducing his work mostly using the ink-jet (giclée) process rather than offset photolithography. Moreover, the locales Crane paints are actual places rather than constructs of his imagination. Crane lives and works mostly in the Black Hills, but his subjects range across rural settings. The sentiment derives more from implications of such subjects as old elevators or farm places, fueled by the knowledge that the family farm way of life has passed into history along with the open range, than from any extraneous or forced elements. The tints of his washes reproduce well using the computerized ink-jet printing and archival inks on watercolor paper.

■ Abstract to Concrete

Many people who say they do not understand or like abstract art often use abstractions every day in their language and thought, enjoy the most abstract of all arts—music—without complaint, and are stirred by abstract symbols such as the Stars and Stripes. Physical scientists, who are most insistent upon hard evidence, have in the last century seen the once solid and mechanistic universe dissolve into ambiguities and apparent contradictions of relativity, quantum mechanics, and most recently, string theory (which in some interpretations includes the possibility of alternate universes). Even one of the most concrete of the arts, photography, has moved from being a reliable record of facts to being one of the media most easily maneuvered by digital means and the one most often put to the use of propaganda by advertising and ideology. All these facts support the legitimacy of abstract art in South Dakota.

University of South Dakota art professor Jeff Freeman has established himself as one of the state's finest abstract artists with paintings and mixed-media works that defy categorization. His more conventionally framed oils and mixed-media paintings in the "Changing Monument" series arrange imagined shapes assembled out of a catalog of recognizable forms, often traditionally modeled and shaded, into pleasing designs. Freeman's strategy is to place before the viewer a scene which bears a resemblance to actual objects translated into an unfamiliar visual language. The three-dimensional pieces in the "New Lost Cryptic" series most resemble paintings artfully deconstructed and frozen in the process of tumbling off the wall and onto the floor or leaping up to reassemble themselves. With numerous solo shows and a solid presence in the collections of museums (including the Joslyn in Omaha) and private corporations, Freeman may be reckoned perhaps the region's foremost worker in abstract modes.

Tom Shields, originally of Texas, has become one of the most intriguing abstract expressionists in South Dakota during the years he has been on the art faculty at Augustana College. His colorful, fluid oil compositions resemble curtains opening upon the collective unconscious. Wavering lines suggestive of seaweed and crustacean shapes are reminders of a youth spent near the Gulf of Mexico, while later, lighter works are clearly more reflective of the Dakota plains. His more objective drawings of trees are so exacting as to reach toward unreferenced form, almost as though to say inside-out or outside-in approaches lead to the same end. More than most other artists in the state, Shields' work seems to bear strong comparison to musical forms, the realm of pure beauty, where color and form and emotion are one.

In an inspired 2003 exhibition at the South Dakota Art Museum, Shields' work was paired with the ceramics of Mary Selvig, whose vessels are throbbing with life and often rent with pain. Selvig builds her works from coils of clay, then stamps and incises them, fires them in sawdust, and further stains and manipulates them until they attain organic shapes and almost mystic significance. As with Shields, Selvig's pieces have a sensual quality contrasting with the primitive geometries with which they are marked and which extend beyond humanity and beyond nature to some yearned-for abode. Selvig, also of Sioux Falls, was the recipient of a McKnight Artist Residency Award in 2000-01. Sioux Falls ceramicists Gerry and Julie Punt, often linked with Selvig, are among other ceramicists in the state whose work rises to the level of high art. Julie Punt's innovative slab and glaze techniques have come to complement strongly the more traditional forms of her partner.

A cooler kind of abstraction is represented in the work of Tim Steele, professor of art and design at South Dakota State University. His encrusted collages, nearly hidden by layers of thick wax and opaque inks, are more easily overlooked than the work of artists who grab viewers with bright colors. Anyone who takes the time to probe the apparently simple compositions of horizons and flags, however, is rewarded with what seem artifacts or specimens embedded in the work, shapes which raise questions about what really is being portrayed: Who or what has left claw marks on these horizons, what battles have these flags been through, and where have they led? Like cool jazz, Steele's self-absorbed work risks either antagonism or casual dismissal, but it also offers pleasure for those willing to accept it on its own terms.

A former South Dakota State University professor, Signe Stuart, working in mixed media, is still associated with the state although living and working elsewhere. Her work has been widely exhibited.

The skulls and rainbows of Jay Olson (1943-2000) might not have become known to a wider audience if he were not recognized by other artists as among the state's best painters. Olson, who taught for Sioux Falls College (later the University of Sioux Falls), shunned the usual means of gaining notice—self-promotion, grantsmanship, marketing—yet his work was recognized as superior by academics such as Robert Aldern, Carl Grupp, and John Day. One of his major motifs was the human skull, in a series sometimes known as "My Self-Portrait is Your Self-Portrait," symbolizing mortality with both morbid humor and ironic sensuousness. Another series featuring the rainbow offers the fragile symbol of hope set against the darkness of the storm. His paintings are in collections at the South Dakota Art Museum, University of Illinois, Augustana College, and University of Sioux Falls, among other regional and national institutions, and in private collections.

Eyob Mergia's abstract acrylics and murals were unveiled to the Sioux Falls art community at the start of the new millennium. Although a prime example of the new cultural transfusions affecting recent South Dakota art, Mergia represents as well the way more earthbound art education provides the basis for flights of abstraction. His thorough grounding in realistic tradition at the Ethiopian Fine Arts Institute in Addis Ababa was augmented by his own investigations into the European traditions of Cubism and Expressionism. Further training at Augustana College after his arrival in this country in 1997 proved his ability in a wide range of modes. His series on the 9/ll disaster employs both scenes familiar from televised accounts and imaginative projections into the horror of the catastrophe. Similarly, his triptych *The Form and Sound of the Falls* offers not only a recognizable view of the falls of the Big Sioux River, but also a daring attempt to convey the feel of spray and the music of crashing water. Although Mergia's sojourn in South Dakota may prove to be short, it will leave a mark against which future emerging artists will be measured.

Jim Pollock is yet another South Dakota painter whose work is a bridge between the abstract and the concrete. A native of Pollock (named after his great-grandfather), and a graduate of South Dakota State University, Pollock first emerged as an artist after his assignment to the U.S. Army's Vietnam Combat Art Program. Working in media ranging from traditional to computer-generated, Pollock has compiled an impressive list of exhibitions and other credits. His style varies widely, sometimes drawing on the abstract styles reminiscent of artists of the early twentieth-century Bauhaus school, characterized by strong lines and bold colors, sometimes resembling ancient cave paintings, and sometimes straightforward renderings of landscapes and objects. He was named Artist of the Year in 1980 by the South Dakota Hall of Fame.[26]

Perhaps the broadest category of art in the state (and therefore the one least compassable in a short treatment) is objective art not falling under one of the more specialized groupings outlined above. Even limiting the range to artists with academic background does not help much in reducing the sheer volume of work. What is offered here is meant to be a small sampling.

Charles Greener (1870-1935) was born in Wisconsin and came with his parents to Dakota Territory in 1883, eventually settling in Faulkton. Trained in art programs in Grand Forks, North Dakota, in Cincinnati, Ohio, and in Minneapolis, Minnesota, Greener became one of the most authentic of the prairie painters, drawing heavily on his experience and knowledge of the Great Plains reflecting the flat horizons and the workaday world of farming. The South Dakota Art Museum has many of his works.[27]

Also collected at the South Dakota Art Museum are several pieces by Greener's contemporary, Ada Caldwell (1869-1937), the teacher who helped to guide Harvey Dunn's career. Caldwell was born in Ohio and came with her family to Nebraska, where she attended the University at Lincoln and taught at Yankton College for a year and at South Dakota State College of Agriculture and Mechanic Arts (later SDSU) from the turn of the century until near her death.[28] Her distinctive impasto oil landscapes display a sure hand.

Milton Kudlacek was influential not only in his large canvases exploring sun-blanched landscapes of the plains, but also in his long career as a teacher at Dakota Wesleyan University. An Augustana College graduate, Kudlacek developed a style that was easily recognizable for its broad swaths of pale tones and an economical line describing perfectly the seedy buildings, animals, and machines that are a part of his West River vistas.

Among the many painters Kudlacek taught was Mel Spinar, who like Kudlacek was of Bohemian background. Spinar delves more thoroughly into his European heritage in his art than did Kudlacek, however; his series of oils on Bohemian Women from West River has travelled widely to display the scenes garnered from his immigrant family's past. Spinar holds an M.A. and an M.F.A. from the University of Iowa and is on the faculty of South Dakota State University.

The two painters of the Pantura Studios of Sioux Falls call themselves the only classically trained painters in South Dakota. The work of Hans-Peter Szameit and Sanna Tomac is more like that of the old masters of the Renaissance than like anything that has been produced since the middle of the nineteenth century. Szameit tries, for example, not to show such contemporary props as tennis shoes in his oils, averring that what he and Tomac wish to achieve is a timeless quality.[29] Art changed a century and a half ago in part because the invention of photography challenged the role of painting as a recorder of reality; in a 2003 show at the Washington Pavilion Arts Center, however, Szameit and Tomac were linked with photographer Rod Evans, and viewers were dared to sort the paintings from the photographs. Szameit and Tomac both attended the Florence School of Art and subsequently worked with Norwegian neo-classicist Odd Nerdrum.

Photography's reputation as a straightforward record of reality is belied by distortions that were built into the technology from the start. Relatively small changes in focus, framing, exposure time, development of negatives, and printing could result in radically different images. Digital photography is subject to even greater manipulation. What is seen in the final image is not necessarily what was there. While the public has come to realize the degree to which photographic images may be distorted and therefore has lost confidence in the medium's unimpeachable adherence to reality, its reputation as a genuine artistic medium has grown. Even photographers such as Ansel Adams, recognized as a great chronicler of nature, have spent hours in the darkroom burning and dodging prints to achieve that sense of verisimilitude. The growing evidence that realistic painters such as Jan Vermeer might have used the *camera obscura* in order to achieve their effects further adds to the blurring of the distinction between painting and photography.

Nevertheless, the speed with which a photographic image could be captured, along with the apparent objectivity of the image doomed the documentary role of painting in the late nineteenth century. When William H. Illingworth accompanied the Custer expedition into the Black Hills in 1874, his views of the park-like valleys gave substantiation to the more florid descriptions of correspondents. Photographers in the state ever since have been valued for their ability to show South Dakota as it was. Just two years after the appearance of Illingworth's photographs, Silas Melander set up his photographic gallery (significantly called the Black Hills Art Gallery) in Deadwood Gulch. Melander provided an invaluable record of the development of the Black Hills from the beauty of its peaks to the ugliness of boomtown construction and destruction, with forests decimated for building materials; tents, shanties, and commercial buildings strewn across what had been pleasant meadows, and later the buildings and trees both charred by fire; and slopes scarred by miners in search of gold. Melander was just one of many photographers roaming the West in that era. The John C. H. Grabill collection provides a exhaustive index of picturesque sites in the southwestern corner of the state during the 1880s and 1890s, when tourism was first developing. Most of Grabill's images are available online.

Of the hundreds of photographers who flourished in South Dakota during the twentieth century, some stand out from the rest, but selection still seems highly arbitrary. This treatment will content itself with major representatives of the the first and second halves of the century, along with a few of the most salient contemporary photographers.

Levon West was born very close to the turn of the century, in fact, on February 3, 1900, in Centerville. After serving in the Great War, West worked his way through the University of Minnesota and originally studied etching, watercolor, and photography. During the Great Depression, he settled on photography as the most lucrative of the media and established a solid career as a photographic illustrator for magazines such as the *Saturday Evening Post*, *Rodeo*, and *Dude Ranching*. However, writing under the pseudonym Ivan Dmitri, West made an eloquent pitch for photography as one of the fine arts in a 1954 essay in *Saturday Review* and saw the realization of his vision in the exhibition called "Photography in the Fine Arts" at the Metropolitan Museum in 1959. He died in 1968.[32]

Joel Strasser, who was born in Fairview, worked as a reconnaissance photographer for the U.S. Air Force and got further instruction at Augustana College and at the Progressive School of Photography, New Haven, Connecticut. A substantial boost was given to his career when he was helped by Harold Spitznagel to become an architectural photographer. In those assignments Strasser tried to limit his shooting to those views that best captured the spirit of the structure. One result was that Strasser learned to shoot on a much-reduced negative-to-print ratio, a practice that ran counter to that of photographers who shoot many rolls to get one print. Another result was that relatively little manipulation of the image was required in the printing process. Strasser's justly famed photographic studies are available in books such as *Buy Me, Where My Heart Is, South Dakota 100, Newton Hills*, and *Love of the Land*.[33]

A photographer who goes to great lengths to shape images to his artistic will is John Banasiak, who teaches at the University of South Dakota. His work is also set apart by its subject matter, which is dominated by night shots of cemeteries. A 2003 exhibition at the university was entitled "Book Hill Chronicles." He cites Edgar Lee Masters' *Spoon River Anthology* as an artistic precedent. Starting with graveyard images on litho film, he alters the image physically by drawing, scratching, and rubbing it before producing the final positive print. The results are both eerie and witty. Other exhibitions have resulted from Banasiak's trips to China and Nicaragua.[34]

Among many other photographers in the state Greg Latza of Sioux Falls stands out for his productivity. While not pretending to be anything other than a commercial photographer, Latza has set himself up as a successor to the likes of Joel Strasser with a best-selling series of books exploring life in the state: *Hometown, S.D., Back on the Farm*, and *The Missouri*.[35] Another younger photographer, John Sundby, formerly a photographer for the *Rapid City Journal*, contributed to the collection of Black Hills and Badlands scenes called *God's Country* and is among many sharpshooters who have been featured in *South Dakota Magazine*.

■ Conclusion: The Multi-cultural Mix and How Art Means

Faced with the competition of the camera, artists of the nineteenth century either adapted the lessons of photography to their own work or sought other paradigms.

Painters like Edgar Degas and Eduoard Manet learned from photography to concentrate on the world around them rather than to rely upon classical and religious themes, and their work often has the feeling of snapshots, catching subjects "in the act." Degas even used the camera to help create his studies and was fascinated with how shifts in the point of view—what we think of as camera angles—could change the perception of the subject. His *Frieze of Dancers*, for example, shows four subjects in almost the same pose captured from four different angles. Others, such as Claude Monet and George Seurat, concentrated the technicalities of light and color which photography relied upon and became skilled in "painting with light," turning themselves into cameras, so to speak. However, the greatest break from traditional art was to come from those who, inspired by the art of other cultures—African masks and Oriental paintings, for example—attempted to fashion entirely new ways of seeing: the Fauves, the Cubists, the Expressionists. The art of other cultures resounds with modern artists who choose to evoke emotional responses, to beseech rather than to speak, to show rather than to tell.

Ample evidence of the multi-cultural heritage of South Dakota art is afforded in this account; just a look at the names of artists gives some idea of the nationalities represented. Sliced other ways, the multi-cultural pie includes religious art, African American art, feminist art, regional art, academic art, and many other categories and subcategories. Such diversity is a blessing in that it encourages a critical eclecticism among both artists and art patrons.

One cultural division that is not so benign is the one between art and the art market. The way people look at art today is roughly similar to the way they looked at the Black Hills 150 years ago: either with reverence or with avarice. Artists who chase after the best-selling mode run the risk of betraying their own talents. The best art allows us to see things in a different way, to notice truths that we have overlooked, or to seek beauty in places we have never thought to look before. The market encourages repetition, imitation, and the repackaging of clichés; truly original art often languishes while minor variations on the current mode become all the rage. Adding to the danger from the standpoint of the art patron is the distrust many people grow to have of their own tastes in the presence of astounding abundance; many find it easier to follow the crowds rather than to pick and choose on their own.

In what could be a response to Robert Frost's "A Missive Missile," the poet Archibald MacLeish declared: "A poem should not mean/ But be."[36] To put it another way, if the sole purpose of art is to convey a message, then art is redundant. "There is a worm in this rose" is a message, but William Blake's poem "The Sick Rose" is another thing entirely, and his illustration for the poem is something else again. The poetry and the visual art are closer to each other than either is to the message. Although each contains the message, both go far beyond it. Art touches us in ways that are indirect, even covert. The visual arts of South Dakota, therefore, are best judged not as communication but as communion. The ancient "mortal longing" to make a mark stirs our recognition even when words fail. Eugene Delacroix gets at the heart of the matter: "To be understood a writer has to explain almost everything. In a painting, a mysterious bridge seems to exist between its painted subjects and the spectator's spirit."[37]

Chapter 21
Performing Arts

In South Dakota the musical and dramatic arts have played a crucial role in the lives of its people from the exploration and settlement eras right up to the present. The explorers, traders, and trappers who ventured first into the land of the Sioux, Arikara, and Mandan Indians brought their own music with them. When they traveled up the Missouri River in 1804, the Lewis and Clark Corps of Discovery could boast of musicians like Pierre Cruzatte who could play the violin and the jew's-harp and lead the men in singing voyageur songs and the songs of the Mississippi boatmen. The men on the expedition entertained themselves as well, and on occasion entertained the Indians with their dancing, as they did among the Mandans in North Dakota. There they were treated in turn to the music and dancing of the Indian men and women. When the cavalry traveled through, as General George Armstrong Custer did in 1873 and after, there was military music for marching and for entertaining wherever the opportunity arose.

Non-Indian travelers in the northern plains had from earliest times been fascinated by the music and dance of the Sioux and other Indian people whom they met there. Although a number of white anthropologists have written on the subject of traditional Sioux music and dance, says Arthur Amiotte, "the Sioux themselves have not yet produced a scholar who can enlighten us from the perspective of the performer, composer, and dancer as to the tribally defined aesthetics."[1] Amiotte, himself a Lakota Sioux, recommends the summation of scholar Lynn Huenemann, who points out that song and dance for the Sioux are not art for art's sake, as with European and American music, but are central to Lakota and Dakota Sioux culture: music and dance are valued because of what they are good for, because they are "received from, and useful for, contact with the spirits of the universe, or for healing, honoring, blessing, or empowering individuals."[2] A new book by R. D. Theisz, *Sharing the Gift of Lakota Song*,[3] is valuable as a resource for teachers wishing to introduce Indian music and traditions into the curriculum. Music today in Sioux society, while undergoing changes of various kinds, continues to play an important part in the lives of young people and adults.

Throughout the settlement era, from the later 1860s and into the 1880s, the pioneers from the East brought the songbooks and hymnals that were popular in America, and the Scandinavian and German communities and other groups in what is now South Dakota entertained themselves with music and songs, both secular and sacred, brought along from Europe. The honor of having the first frontier band is claimed by Dalesburg,[4] and the first organ to appear in what is now South Dakota came by steamboat to the Cheyenne River Mission, where it was played by the wife of the Reverend Thomas L. Riggs.[5]

■ Early Yankton and Deadwood

As the settlements in the state grew into villages and towns, concert halls and theaters began to arise, first in the east, then among the mining communities in the Black Hills, and finally all across the Dakota frontier. In two towns, east and west, Yankton on the Missouri River and Deadwood in the northern Hills, the performing arts had their earliest flourishing. John C. Koch observes in his thesis[6] that before the first professional entertainment, Professor LeDon's "Wonderful Panorama," came to Yankton in February 1867, there had been Fourth of July and Christmas dances, among many entertainments organized by the townspeople. In early 1869 a series of scenes presented by Yankton citizens and directed by professional actor Mr. Stevenson, says Koch, were the stimulus for many later theatrical endeavors. The construction of three performance halls—Stone's Hall in 1869, the Yankton Opera House in 1878, and Turner Hall in 1881—permitted amateur productions as well as professional to be housed in capacious facilities.

By steamboat and railroad, professional companies of actors and musicians came to Yankton. A sampling from Mr. Koch's thesis of three decades of musical and dramatic entertainment underscores the fact that the citizens of Yankton enjoyed quantity and variety. In Stone's Hall there were plays like *Rip Van Winkle* and *Uncle Tom's Cabin*, "dances by Sioux chieftains," bell ringers, violinists, and the "Boston Philharmonic Ladies Band and Orchestra." The Yankton Opera House was the home of a local company of singers, comedians, and musicians, including Felix Vinatieri, formerly General Custer's bandmaster. The first professional opera company to come to town performed in Turner Hall, and the August 1886 production of *The Mikado* by the Andrews Opera Company was praised by the *Daily Press and Dakotan* as "the happiest evening's manifestation" since the opening of the hall. For the next two decades, until the hall closed, the musical and dramatic fare available to Yanktonians was remarkably varied, ranging from operettas to variety shows to legitimate theater like Henrik Ibsen's *A Doll's House* in November 1899. On Friday, February 19, 1897, the Electric Novelty Company of St. Paul brought to the hall Edison's Vitascope motion-picture machine, a foretaste of the technological revolution that would dominate the performing arts in the state throughout the next century.

In the western part of the state the performing arts had a heyday in the mining town of Deadwood and soon after in neighboring Lead City. Only two summers after Custer's Seventh Cavalry musicians played the first band music ever heard in the Black Hills, concerts and dances were underway, the first theater had been built, and the classics of the nineteenth-century American theater repertory were being staged. As Lawrence Stine concludes,[7] among the hordes of gold seekers in the Hills were enough trained musicians and enough men and women with cultured tastes to populate the dances, stage shows, and elegant balls there. Deadwood's isolation—there was no railroad until 1886 to bring in touring theatrical and musical companies—made possible a unique flourishing of professional theater. On July 22, 1876, actor-director Jack Langrishe opened the first theater in western South Dakota with a performance of the melodrama *Lillian's Last Love; or, The Banker's Daughter*. Between October 1877 and the last show in September 1879, his company presented over 150 productions in repertory, including a performance of *Othello*; in the role of Desdemona was Augusta Chambers, direct from a role in Buffalo Bill Cody's *Red Right Hand* in New York City.

Many other theatrical companies followed Langrishe's lead. With the coming of the railroad in 1886, the Black Hills were opened to a flood of traveling entertainers. For many years Deadwood was the central point for the organizing of these tours, and an opera house in nearby Lead City, opened in 1878, was the venue for shows by the Langrishe company and touring repertory companies. In his "History of Lead, South Dakota, 1876-1900," Joseph H. Cash reviews the musical and dramatic entertainment available during that era, concluding that its rich variety was owing (as it was in neighboring Deadwood) to the diversity of the nationalities who came to work in the mines:

the English and Italian brass bands, Scottish bagpipe and drum troupes, and Slavonian music and dance.[8]

■ Early Enterprises in Music and Theater

Throughout the settlement era in all regions of the state, the performing arts grew as the villages and towns grew. As in Yankton and Deadwood, the people entertained themselves with music, dance, and stage plays, but when the railroad arrived, it brought to every community of any size a wide variety of entertainments, a cross section of what Americans were seeing and hearing in halls and theaters from New York City to San Francisco and all the points between.

In the six decades or so, from the beginning of the touring company era in the late 1870s to its ending in the late 1930s, there are a number of instances of facilities and ensembles that deserve to be noted in a historical sketch of the arts in the state. Examples of facilities that affected greatly the performing arts in their communities are the opera houses in Dell Rapids, Spearfish, and Lead, the Corn Palace in Mitchell, the Grain Palace in Aberdeen, the Matthews Opera House in Spearfish, and the Homestake Opera House in Lead.

Following the devastating fire of 1888 that destroyed much of the Dell Rapids business district, two local businessmen—J. A. Cooley and M. R. Kenefick—decided that their new store would include an upstairs opera house. In her master's thesis about the first fifteen years of operation,[9] Gerry A. Perrin points out that the opera house began a new era for live drama and music in Dell Rapids, with professional touring companies providing most of the productions until 1903, when the facility joined a theatrical circuit. In the century that has passed, the little theater has been often used for musical and dramatic entertainments. Opera houses in Spearfish (1906) and in Lead (1914) have served their communities well. The former, the Matthews Opera House, continues today as a venue for drama and music and serves as well as the home of the Spearfish Center for the Arts and Humanities. The Lead Opera House, built at the instigation of Mrs. Phoebe Hearst and lavishly decorated, was the home of a wide range of dramatic and musical entertainments until destroyed by fire on April 2, 1984.

At Aberdeen and at Mitchell were built two notable examples of the many distinctive "grain palaces" scattered across South Dakota. The enormous Interstate Grain Palace in Aberdeen was completed in time for the harvest festival in 1893; the Corn Palace in Mitchell also was intended to tout the state's agricultural products. The first of four Corn Palaces was built there in 1892; the latest was completed in 1921 and remains a centerpiece in Mitchell's community life. The most entertaining story about the Corn Palace is that told of John Philip Sousa. The famous band master is reported to have been so unimpressed by the little town when he arrived on a rainy day in 1904 that he refused to detrain until $7,000 in cash was delivered to him. He was pleased enough with his payment—and the audience's subsequent reception—that he returned to conduct his band there three years later.

Among the musical ensembles that date from the frontier era and are worthy of note are the Lennox Band, formed in 1883 by eight young businessmen, and the Bower Family Band. The Lennox ensemble, which claimed to be "the best in Southeastern Dakota territory," took pride in being recognized during the state's centennial in 1989 for its 106 years of existence. The most unusual band in the state was the Bower Family Band, famous throughout the Black Hills in the later nineteenth century for its musical versatility. As Laura Bower Van Nuys reports in her book,[10] the group had its unofficial beginning in Vermillion in 1882 when two of the sons of Calvin and Keziah Bower

The Bower Family, famous across the state and the subject of a Walt Disney film, *The One and Only Original Family Band* (1968). *Courtesy South Dakota State Historical Society–State Archives.*

joined the town band. Soon their younger sisters joined in, and the ensemble's debut at Christmas 1884 was praised by the Vermillion *Republican*: "This little band . . . all play upon brass instruments with a melody and precision in time that completely took the audience by storm. . . ." The family moved to the Black Hills the following year, playing on new instruments that Father Bower purchased by mortgaging his cattle. In 1968 a Disney feature film starring Buddy Ebsen and Walter Brennan was released, *The One and Only Genuine Original Family Band*, a posthumous tribute to the talented Bowers.

■ Higher Education Steps In

From their earliest years of existence, the colleges and universities that sprang up across the state included music and drama to some degree in their curricula. However, the most notable of their achievements are in the long and productive careers of a handful of faculty leaders in the performing arts and in the creation of agencies that have taken on a life of their own and have become indispensable to South Dakota's cultural life. In the former group were the members of the Yankton College Faculty Trio, the leading ensemble within the remarkable Yankton College Conservatory: Lewis Hamvas, piano; Leona Marek, cello; and J. Laiten Weed, violin. Besides providing instruction in strings, the group served as a valuable musical resource for the state, performing with orchestras like the Lewis and Clark Symphonette and the South Dakota Symphony.

At the University of South Dakota, where the first classroom study of a play was not until 1887, dramatic performances were long in coming.[11] In 1901 the sophomore class was permitted to present *The Wreck of Stebbins Pride* and *A Case of Suspension* in the university chapel; and the music department presented the operetta *The Chimes of Normandy* in the Vermillion opera house. Over the years thereafter music and theater flourished at the university, and from the efforts of faculty in both departments unique programs have developed that have continued until the present. In 1946 a professor there began what has come to be one of the the the most long-lived theatrical enterprises in the state, the Black Hills Playhouse. Begun by Dr. Warren Lee as a private enterprise, it quickly became associated with the university and continued that relationship over the next half century. Its present managing artistic director, Jan Swank, is an associate professor whose salary is paid by the university. The playhouse has served as a training school for actors, directors, and designers; and it has been the home of the longest-running legitimate play in the state's history, *The Legend of Devil's Gulch* (written by Lee). By 1960 the 100,000th customer had attended the playhouse, and in 1971 a single offering, *Fiddler on the Roof*, set a total attendance record of 17,632. A typical season offers a mixture of musical comedy, romance, and tragedy, as in the summer of 2004 when *The Playboy of the Western World*, *The Philadelphia Story*, *The King & I*, *Once Upon a Mattress*, and *Who's Afraid of Virginia Woolf?* anchored the season.

Twenty-seven years after the beginning of the Black Hills Playhouse, Dr. Arne Larson began another musical organization that is now an indispensable part of South Dakota's cultural heritage. In 1966 he accepted a position as professor of music at the university and brought with him from Brookings his collection of 2,000 musical instruments. In 1973 the Shrine to Music Museum (now named the National Music Museum) was founded, dedicated to assembling and preserving musical instruments from around the world, and—as the museum's informational video says—dedicated to the "study of the history of musical instruments." By 2003 the collection of Western and non-Western instruments had grown to more than 10,500.[12] Moreover, the museum, now directed by Larson's son Dr. Andre Larson, has added musical and educational programs. In

Dr. Arne Larson began the collection of instruments that today has become the National Music Museum.
Courtesy National Music Museum.

the fall of 2003, the museum in cooperation with the South Dakota Symphony and the Washington Pavilion of Arts and Science jointly sponsored an innovative program, "Beethoven & Berlioz," that brought seventy rare instruments to the Pavilion's Everist Gallery for public viewing, and followed the opening reception with musical events including a concert by the university's Rawlins Piano Trio, a piano recital, three South Dakota Symphony concerts featuring the music of Beethoven and Berlioz, and a recital by the Brentano String Quartet.

South Dakota State University may be said to have followed the lead of the University of South Dakota in the forming of a summer theater. It was begun in 1970 at the invitation of the Prairie Historical Society at Madison, and so that season, the plays already planned for presentation at the university were performed in the Oldham Opera House, which had been moved to Prairie Village near Madison. The success of *Bus Stop* and *Barefoot in the Park* led the theater staff to plan four plays for the following summer. By 1980 the Prairie Repertory Theatre, Inc., had been proven to be a financial success, and the pattern of offering four plays each summer season has been continued to the present.

At Sioux Falls College, now the University of Sioux Falls, Professor William Lee Bright established for his school and for Sioux Falls an enviable record as a conductor of vocal ensembles. During his thirty-four years of service on the faculty, he was dean of the music department, began the a cappella choir, and directed a wide range of vocal groups in the city. His greatest success was as the founding conductor of the American Legion Chorus. In less than two years, the newly formed group won the choral competition at the 1949 national convention. During the eighteen years that Professor Bright directed the chorus, it won eleven national championships, a record that has never been eclipsed.

Over the years since Augustana College's relocation to Sioux Falls in 1918, there has been strong faculty leadership in music and theater. In 1921 Professor Carl R. Youngdahl organized an a capella concert choir that continues to perform today, and the next year a college orchestra was begun that would grow into today's South Dakota Symphony. Professor Earl Mundt became director of the college theater in 1950 and over the next three decades not only staged six or seven plays each year in the Little Theatre, but he launched a long series of efforts to found public theaters for popular entertainment.

While the performing arts have flourished in the state's liberal arts universities and colleges, the example of the South Dakota School of Mines and Technology can show the value of the teaching of music in an unlikely setting. When Professor Jim Feiszli arrived at Mines in 1983 to teach music appreciation, he found the Singing Engineers and a jazz band and little else to channel the musical talents of the students.[13] Now Professor Feiszli can look back on two decades of success in organizing bands, choirs, and other singing groups, and in convincing future engineers and scientists that they did indeed have talent and that the study and performance of music could help to prepare them for their careers.

■ Civic Associations: Chautauqua to Community Concerts

While colleges and universities in South Dakota have made music and theater important aspects of their curricula and have produced professors of note and museums, theatrical enterprises, and orchestras that have become essential elements of the state's cultural life, two non-academic enterprises—Chautauqua and the civic concerts movement—have from their earliest years provided South Dakota with a consistent fare of performing arts, richly varied and readily accessible to most of the state's residents. These are the Chautauqua programs of the early twentieth century and those beginning in the 1970s, and—most notably—the civic concerts programs in the state's two largest cities, Rapid City and Sioux Falls.

The earlier of the two Chautauquas came into the state by railroad, a program of lectures, music, and drama brought to the communities across all of America that had little access to the arts. In South Dakota the most popular and long-lasting of the programs was held at Lake Madison. It came there in 1891, founded by the Reverend C. E. Hagar and a stock company. As W. Cory Christenson points out,[14] the first week-long program—attracting 5,000 visitors a day—featured the Ladies Band, the Madison Knights of Pythias Band, and the Ladies Quartet. Subsequent programs over the next four decades included, for example, great speakers like William Jennings Bryan, town bands from all across eastern South Dakota, the Dunbar Male Quartette (from all-black Fisk University), and elocutionist Gay Zenda MacLaren, from Howard, South Dakota,

411

billed as "The Girl with the Camera Mind," who could, after a dozen viewings, recite whole plays. At least fourteen other communities in the state had Chautauquas until the program came to an end nationally in 1932.

A new and much different style of Chautauqua program has appeared on the scene to educate and entertain South Dakota audiences. Created by the North Dakota Humanities Council in the mid-1970s and brought to South Dakota for the first time in 1981 by the South Dakota Committee on the Humanities, the out-of-doors summer program has been designed to bring audiences together with scholars who act out the roles of historical characters. Over the years the programs have varied widely, in many instances presenting on stage individuals who are connected in some way to South Dakota, from Father Pierre Jean De Smet, for example, and Meriwether Lewis, to Elizabeth Custer and L. Frank Baum.

Just when the original Chautauqua program was coming to an end in America, so was the phenomenon of touring companies of actors and musicians trundling about the country by rail and setting up in every community with a suitable hall. A comment by Harry P. Harrison about the demise of Chautauqua applies to the end of railroad touring shows as well: They "died in 1932 under the hit-and-run wheels of a Model-A Ford on its way to the movies on a new paved road. Radio swept [them] into the ditch and the subsequent depression gave . . . the *coup de grace*."[15]

In South Dakota, community concerts programs sprang up to fill some of the void. The Sioux Falls and Rapid City programs were the most successful and ambitious, with the Sioux Falls committee, organized in November 1930, also the longest-lived. Begun first as Civic Music, the Sioux Falls organization has been able to bring to the city an astonishing array of soloists and ensembles of national and international repute. Following a five-year hiatus in 1932-37, during which time Coliseum manager Fred Beecher brought George Gershwin to perform his *Rhapsody in Blue*, Civic Music presented to Sioux Falls audiences such well-known entertainers as black contralto Marian Anderson, the Don Cossack Chorus, the Minneapolis Symphony, pianist Arthur Rubinstein, violinist Isaac Stern, Agnes DeMille Ballet Theatre, and tenor Jan Peerce. Following a change in affiliation in 1959 from Civic Concert Service to Columbia Artists, the name was changed to Community Concerts, and the pattern of sponsoring renowned artists continued unabated. The practice of bringing major symphony orchestras continued until the mid-1970s, when travel costs became prohibitive and the South Dakota Symphony began offering more concerts. Since the opening of the Washington Pavilion of Arts and Science in 1999, the newly renamed Sioux Falls Concerts Association has enjoyed a home in the Great Hall there as well as the challenge of coordinating its entertainment offerings with those of the Pavilion's management. In 2003-04, the offerings included a ballet ensemble and music by a piano trio, a soprano, a brass ensemble, and the Butch Thompson Jazz trio.

The Rapid City Concert Association had a later beginning than its Sioux Falls counterpart, in 1937-38, but it has been able to offer an identical level of nationally and internationally known entertainers. Among them have been opera greats Marilyn Horne, Leontyne Price, Jess Thomas (Hot Springs heldentenor), and Jerome Hines, Arthur Rubinstein, Robert Shaw Chorale, National Ballet of Canada, Minnesota Orchestra, Utah Symphony Orchestra, Glenn Miller Orchestra, and flamenco dancer José Greco. Concerts were first held in the 1,400-seat auditorium of the Rapid City High School, and since 1976 in the 1,774-seat theater of the magnificent Rushmore Plaza Civic Center. Adjacent to the theater is an arena that seats 11,000 and offers the Rapid City community and the citizens of the Black Hills area a splendid venue for popular entertainments.

■ The Electronic Revolution

The electronic age of entertainment in South Dakota, including movies, radio, television—and increasingly computers—had its beginnings with Projectoscope programs on the Chautauqua circuit from 1892 and on, with a presentation using Edison's Vitascope by the Electric Novelty Company in Turner Hall, Yankton, on February 19, 1897, and with the Orthoscope motion-picture projector installed at the Sioux Falls Orpheum Theatre in 1913. In Aberdeen, a town whose film-going has been studied by historian Arthur R. Buntin, the early movies and live vaudeville coexisted for a time, each supporting the other in attracting audiences.[16] The partnership soon dissolved as filmmaking became more sophisticated. The reception given by Aberdeen theater-goers was no doubt typical of the audiences across the state when 13,000 attended D. W. Griffith's *Birth of a Nation* in 1915. In 1928 the first all-talking movie, *Lights of New York*, was shown in South Dakota, and a decade later the introduction of color film was the final innovation in modern filmmaking. Multi-million dollar blockbusters like *Gone with the Wind* in 1939 set standards for movie makers that have persisted into the twenty-first century, right up to that most famous made-in-South Dakota film *Dances with Wolves* (1990).

More revolutionary even than the movies in the cultural life of South Dakotans was the coming of radio to the state. It was a surprise to everyone, especially to those living in the most remote counties, because it was free and available everywhere. As Reynold Wik observes in his study of radio in South Dakota, "Many of the 'old timers' today insist that the first radio provided a greater thrill than the arrival of television. . . . Rural people often drove miles for a chance to hear a radio for the first time."[17] Beginning in 1920 with the first broadcasts in America, radio stations grew rapidly in numbers and range. In South Dakota, WNAX in Yankton soon after its beginnings in 1927 emerged as dominant because of its powerful signal and popular programming. From *Station Book*, the booklet issued in 1929 by the Gurney Seed and Nursery Company, owners of the station, we discover how much live music the station offered to its listeners. Unlike today's commercial radio stations, which offer little live music, WNAX in the early years filled the airwaves with the sounds of musical groups like Lawrence Welk's Novelty Band, Gurney's Hawaiians (including Frances Kia the Singing Hula Girl), and Gurney's Concert Orchestra—which in 1928 received the Grand Gold Plaque from *Radio Digest* as America's most popular radio orchestra. And there were a number of soloists—among them George B. German, the Cowboy Ballad Singer; Roy L. Eastman, "Harmonica Dutch"; and Happy Jack O'Malley on violin—as well as poetry reading, comedy and novelty acts, and musical competitions. In the decades since, competition increased from small local stations, national networks grew in influence, and locally created live music and live radio drama were gradually pushed aside by recordings and network programming until there was virtually none, except on public radio stations.

WNAX radio launched the career of musician Lawrence Welk. *Courtesy Institute for Regional Studies, North Dakota State University.*

Three colleges have been responsible for the beginnings of public radio in the state—the University of South Dakota, South Dakota State University, and the School of Mines and Technology. All three began experiments with radio before the First World War and all were broadcasting by 1923. According to Adrian E. Dalen's history,[18] the most influential of the college stations has been KUSD. Student Ernest O. Lawrence, who would win the Nobel Prize in 1939 for inventing the cyclotron, originated the idea of an amateur station in 1919 and went on the air with voice and music programming on May 20, 1922. Regular broadcasts followed with live and recorded music playing an important part in each day's programming. The other university- and college-based stations have followed suit, and are today woven into a network of FM and AM stations that blanket South Dakota with their own programming as well as that of Minnesota Public Radio and other public networks.

The younger sibling of radio in the state is television. Like radio, it was "free as air" throughout most of its existence in South Dakota, beaming its signals to every part of the state and serving increasingly to entice people to indulge in its varied offerings and away from live performances by the state's own creative musicians and performers. Yet television now offers its viewers a range of esthetic and intellectual experiences that were unimagined when KELO, the first station to broadcast in the state, signed on the air in Sioux Falls on May 19, 1953. In 1955 KELO-TV president Joe Floyd added a satellite station and began to broadcast from Garden City in order to reach Watertown, Huron, and Aberdeen; and other commercial stations have been added throughout the state, so that network television can be viewed by nearly all of the state's 700,000-plus citizens.

Some idea of what the future holds in store for viewers statewide can be gotten by reviewing the lineup of the cable channels currently offered by Midcontinent Communications in Sioux Falls: more than fifty channels devoted largely or exclusively to recently released movies and some older films; a slightly smaller group of sound-only channels that feature classical, semi-classical, and popular music of all sorts; and—the largest number of channels—news, information, sports events, religious programs, and foreign language programs and commentary, more than 250 different channels in all.[19]

The good news is that viewers in the state are able to choose what to watch and what to leave alone. For those who seek opportunities to enjoy the best of the performance arts, there is South Dakota Public TV, a latecomer to the entertainment scene. Beginning at the University of South Dakota with closed-circuit programs in 1957, KUSD television moved to broadcasting a low-powered signal in 1961. In 1965 the legislature created a board of directors to promote educational television in the state. On August 29, 1967, KUSD-TV began broadcasting from a tower near Beresford, reaching as far as Sioux Falls to the north and Sioux City to the southeast. In 1968 KESD in Brookings went on the air and KBHE began serving the Rapid City area. Five more stations were added by 1978 to complete the South Dakota Public Television Network; and now a new delivery system for the arts was in place, served by microwave, and committed to programs of high quality. In his master's thesis,[20] Patrick Rioux points out the arts orientation of the first quarter-century of broadcasting, including programs about the plays of Shakespeare and home-grown programs such as John Milton's series of interviews with eight western American writers, among them Frederick Manfred, Frank Waters, Max Evans, and Vardis Fisher. The chapter on public television in *An Illustrated History of the Arts in South Dakota* presents dozens of examples of programs that feature the cultural arts, in particular the performing arts. During one two-year period, for example (1978-79) one program alone, *Mosaic*, offered nearly thirty half-hour programs on the arts: represented in the category of performing arts were guitarist Chris Johnson, the Black Hills

Playhouse, the Dakota String Quartet, the Rapid City Children's Theatre, oboist Jeffrey Kull, the University of South Dakota Brass Choir, and guitarist Alicia Zerrudo.

The pattern of presenting the best in locally produced arts has continued right up to the present. On the last Sunday of 2003, for example, one could tune in to a public television program about artist Dick Termes; visit great museums for thirty minutes, spend an hour with the Lawrence Welk Orchestra; and view John Galsworthy's *The Forsyte Saga*. All in all, it would have been a well-spent evening.

■ Dramatic Arts

The 1930s were a watershed decade for the performing arts in the state, a time that saw the demise of Chautauqua and of the touring troupes of entertainers that poured into the state wherever the railroad would take them. The decade saw the spectacular introduction of radio into the lives of South Dakotans, the rapid introduction of movies, the rise of community-based concerts programs like the Rapid City Concert Association and Community Concerts in Sioux Falls, and the growing role of colleges and universities as leaders in the teaching of the performing arts and, on occasion, the creating and sustaining of new arts organizations to serve the public, like the Black Hills Playhouse, the National Music Museum, and the South Dakota Symphony. Throughout these years when new forms of the performing arts were replacing the old, community theater all across South Dakota continued to survive and even to flourish. Wherever there is acting talent and an appreciative audience, theaters arise. As has been seen in this section of the *History* in the examples of Yankton and Deadwood during the settlement era in the state, live theater plays a significant role in the cultural lives of South Dakotans. In the two largest towns in the state—Sioux Falls and Rapid City—community theaters have offered amateur productions for most of the twentieth century. The antecedents of the Sioux Empire Community Playhouse were a number of theaters that were given over largely to imported entertainment. In 1879, according to historian Lester R. Kremer, the town's first footlights were to be found in the Emerson Building on north Phillips.[21] Other theaters followed—Germania Hall (1881), the Booth Grand Opera House (1886), the New Theatre (1898), and the Orpheum Theatre (1913). The latter served as the home of the town's first organized theatrical company, in operation from 1925 to 1927. In the latter year, the Orpheum was turned into a movie theater. When the Sioux Falls Community Theatre was formed in 1945, its first home was the YMCA's small theater, but in 1954 the organization was able to acquire the Orpheum and return it once again to its intended use, the presenting of live theater. In the fifty years since, the Community Playhouse has offered a varied fare to audiences and to amateur actors. The city's purchase of the building and new management may soon lead to a new era in community theater in Sioux Falls. Reorganized in late 2003, the newly named Sioux Empire Community Theatre opened the season in the Orpheum with *The Nerd*, followed by *The Diary of Anne Frank*.

In the meantime, an energetic effort has been launched to establish a children's theater company in Sioux Falls. In an article about the founder, Nancy Halverson,[22] Jennifer Dumke reviews the three years of plays for children that have been performed by student and adult actors, beginning in 2001 with *Wiley and the Hairy Man* and *Steal Away Home*. The company's productions are intended to combine arts and education, says Halverson. Her goal is "to create a community of artists to provide quality professional theater for young people and their families." The musical production *The Quiltmaker's Gift* had its Midwest premiere on the main stage of the Edith Mortenson Theatre at Augustana College in February 2004.

A new dimension has been added to the performing arts in the eastern half of the state by the opening of the Washington Pavilion of Arts and Science. With a performance hall seating nearly 1,850, a small theater seating 290, and a smaller "Cinedome Theater" of 170 seats for touring films, the Pavilion has had an impact on the Sioux Falls community comparable to that the Rushmore Plaza Civic Center had on Rapid City after its opening in 1976. Approved by the voters in 1993, the Pavilion—a radical remodeling of the old Washington High School building downtown, closed in 1992—was opened on June 1, 1999, to an admiring public. Designed by Koch Hazard Baltzer Architects, the $31 million multi-purpose facility has been a magnet for audiences in the region, offering non-stop entertainment ranging from symphony orchestras (the Pavilion opened with a performance by the New York Philharmonic Orchestra and has become home for the South Dakota Symphony), to rock music, Broadway-style productions of all sorts and, recently, to a performance by the Guthrie Theater of Minneapolis of a production of Shakespeare's *Othello* (in January 2004), a prominent part of a national touring program sponsored by the National Endowment for the Arts, the largest such enterprise in the NEA's history.

From the very first, the Pavilion management has hosted touring entertainers throughout the year and has presented its own seasons of varied entertainment. For its fifth season, in 2003-04, the Pavilion offered the following: Kathy Mattea—folk, pop, and country singer; Opera Verdi Europa—U.S. premiere of *Rigoletto*; *Kiss Me, Kate*, musical comedy; Brentano String Quartet; "Flight," Dayton Contemporary Dance Company; the Guthrie's *Othello*; *Seussical the Musical*, based on the Dr. Seuss stories; Newport Jazz Festival, Fiftieth Anniversary tour; *Fosse*, by Gwen Verdon and Ann Reinking; BalletNY; "Dreamcatcher" by Diavolo dance company; Moscow Chamber Orchestra; Pucci: Spat, athletic dancing; The Kennedy Center's production of *The Adventures of*

Former South Dakota Symphony conductor Henry Charles Smith stands in the Great Hall of the Washington Pavilion of Arts and Science, which has added rich variety to musical and dramatic offerings in the Sioux Falls area. *Courtesy South Dakota Symphony.*

Tom Sawyer; *Frogz* by Imago Theatre; and a number of films in the Cinedome Theater.[23] The variety and quality of such programs is impressive. That city will be twice blessed that can in the future also enjoy the creations of its own talented citizens in symphonic music and community theater.

The story of community theater in Rapid City is somewhat briefer than that in Sioux Falls. Richard Sethney's history[24] traces the earliest beginnings of today's Group Theatre to the late 1930s and the efforts by the local American Association of University Women to produce children's plays. A Rapid City Theater Group followed and in turn was supplanted in 1946 by the Rapid City Theatre Guild and in 1953 by the Rapid City Civic Theatre, which continued successfully until its demise in 1959. After a nine-year hiatus, a new organization was formed, the Group Theatre, and in 1974 installed in the newly opened Dahl Fine Arts Center. By 2003-04 the successor to the Group Theatre, the Black Hills Community Theatre, was offering a full season of theatrical productions and educational outreach activities.

A number of other notable dramatic enterprises deserve mention. The Black Hills Passion Play, America's own Oberammergau, has been performed near Spearfish nearly every summer since 1938, and until his retirement in 1991 always by German-born Josef Meier. Presented in a 6,000-seat amphitheater, the play reconstructs the seven last days of Christ, climaxed with the "Glorious Ascension." In Yankton, the Lewis & Clark Theatre Company now performs plays throughout the year, having begun as a summer theater in 1962 at the instigation of the Yankton County Historical Society. Notable productions by the playhouse have been an original musical, *Hangin'* (1976), written by Floyd McClain for the national bicentennial, and the presentation each year of a children's play, a practice that began in 1965. The closest thing to a successful professional drama company in recent years was the Dakota Theatre Caravan. Begun in May 1977 at Yankton College by six actors—led by Doug Paterson—the Caravan was an attempt to find grant support and ticket sales enough to create and perform original drama on a full-time basis. In the first season, their original show, *Dakota Roads*, was one of the most popular to be sponsored by the South Dakota Arts Council (SDAC). Three more original plays were created—*Dusting off the '30s*, *Welcome Home*, and *In the Heart of the Hills*—but uncertain funding led to a cessation of touring activities after only six years. For two decades, beginning with *The Song of Norway* in 1957, the Sioux Valley Hospital Auxiliary presented a musical in Sioux Falls as a fund-raising activity. Relying on guest conductors and volunteers from the community, the auxiliary put on stage a wide range of popular American musicals—including *Oklahoma*, *The Merry Widow*, *Grease*, and *Camelot*. On a much smaller scale are two examples of long-standing small-town theaters in eastern South Dakota. The Olde Towne Theatre Company in Worthing was begun in the early 1980s and presents mostly classics of contemporary American theater. The Mighty Corson Art Players is the older of the two companies, having connections to the Corson Dramatic Club which performed in the 1930s and 1940s. A story by Don Lane in *South Dakota Magazine* for March/April 2004 notes that a highlight in the company's long career was a presentation of the 1934 play *Sod*, performed at Mount Rushmore for the state's centennial in 1989.

Mention should be made as well of South Dakota filmmakers, who—in a state where many obstacles face those who would produce movies—have nevertheless made noteworthy contributions. Charles and Jane Nauman have produced principally documentaries but also full-length features such as the prize-winning *Johnny Vik* (1977, about an American Indian veteran) and another prize winner, *Lakota Quillwork* (1985), which includes a song by Nellie Two Bulls about the legendary quillworker Double

Barbara Schock won an Oscar for directing *My Mother Dreams the Satan's Disciples in New York*. Courtesy Al Schock.

Woman. Next in length of years in the state is Cottonwood Productions of Wakonda, owned by Douglas and Judi Sharples. The company has specialized in documentary films. Beginning in 1980, Unity Productions began turning out award-winning documentaries, one of them the acclaimed *Letters from America*, a half-hour program about the life and times of Norwegian-American novelist O. E. Rölvaag.

Two films of particular interest to South Dakotans are *Dances with Wolves* (1990), directed by Kevin Costner and set in South Dakota, and *My Mother Dreams the Satan's Disciples in New York* (1999), directed by Sioux Falls native Barbara Schock. Both were Academy Award winners, the Costner film about a Yankee officer among the Lakota winning as best feature film of the year and Schock winning an Oscar as director of a live-action short film. While set principally in New York City, its opening scenes take place in rural South Dakota, and Schock includes cameo appearances by her brother Steve and father Al Schock.

■ Musical Arts

In the second half of the twentieth century, two orchestras, east and west, have been the "flagship" ensembles for orchestral music in the state. The older of the two, the South Dakota Symphony Orchestra, had its beginning in November 1922, when a small group of string players, led by violinist Isa J. Duncan, began practicing for the Christmas program at Augustana College. A bass viol and "the usual brass instruments" were to be added later, wrote the reporter in the campus newspaper. The orchestra grew as a largely student organization under the direction of Professors Marie Toohey and Richard J. Guderyahn. In 1952, after working toward that goal throughout his career at the college, Guderyahn convinced his board to rename the ensemble the Augustana Town and Gown Symphony Orchestra. Under his successor, Maestro Leo Kucinski, the orchestra became independent of the college in 1966 and assumed the name the Sioux Falls Symphony Orchestra. Its final name change took place when in 1985 the organization applied to Governor William Janklow and received the designation the "South Dakota Symphony Orchestra."

Highlights in the symphony's more than eight decades of existence include its first performance of a premiere (Joseph Anton Dvorak's *The Black Hills Suite*, February 26, 1929); the largest audience at a regularly scheduled concert (2,200 persons at Mendelssohn's *Elija* in 1962), two concerts by pianist Van Cliburn in the fall of 1970 that tripled the season's attendance; a fiftieth-anniversary celebration in 1972, featuring a South Dakota native, heldentenor Jess Thomas; the addition of a string quartet (1978) and a wind quintet (1982) of full-time musicians, an increase in the number of concerts offered each season from four in 1966-67 to fifteen in 2003-04, plus eleven special concerts, including a run-out concert in Watertown. A series of outstanding conductors has succeeded Maestro Kucinski: Dr. George Trautwein, James MacInnes, Emanuel Vardi, Kenneth Klein, Henry Charles Smith, Susan Haig, and Delta David Gier, an assistant conductor for the New York Philharmonic and for the Metropolitan Opera, selected for the 2004-05 season as music director and conductor.

In the west, the Black Hills Symphony Orchestra has served the people of that region with a full offering of symphonic music and guest artists. Founded about 1930, the "Civic orchestra" of Rapid City grew under the direction of conductors Alex Schneider (1937-42), who was also the high-school band and

Internationally renowned cellist Yo-Yo Ma soloed with the South Dakota Symphony in 1999 to open its first season in the Washington Pavilion of Arts and Science. *Courtesy South Dakota Symphony.*

orchestra director; Vernon Malone in the 1940s, and Arnold Rudd from 1952 to 1972. In 1972 Jack Knowles took over as conductor and music director, positions that he has held right to the present. His years on the podium have been marked by a succession of significant musical accomplishments: in 1974 a performance of *The Black Hills Suite* by Tabor native Joseph Anton Dvorak; in 1977 the first concert season in the new Rushmore Civic Center; in 1979 the establishment of the Young Artist concert competition; in 1983 the awarding to Maestro Knowles of the Rapid City Arts Council Award, "Distinction in Creative Achievement in the Arts"; in 1988 the Rapid City orchestra assumed the name "Black Hills Symphony Orchestra" in conjunction with its affiliation with the Black Hills Chamber Music Society; the 1988-89 five-concert season marked the South Dakota Centennial with a recognition of state composers Paul Royer and Robert Marek; in 2003-04 the orchestra crowned its season under Knowles' baton with a performance of Verdi's *Manzoni Requiem*, with a full orchestra of ninety players, a professional quartet of vocalists, and a chorus of two hundred, composed of the Dakota Choral Union and the concert choirs of Black Hills State University and Chadron State College.[25] In an interview in *South Dakota Magazine*, violinist Curtis Peacock, formerly conductor of the Wyoming Symphony Orchestra, praised the teaching skills of Knowles' staff and the orchestra's reliance on local talent: "Rapid City can be proud the symphony's ability to go with excellence developed here."[26]

Affiliation with the Black Hills Chamber Music Society has strengthened the programs of both organizations. Begun in 1964, the Society invited Maestro Joseph Dellicarri, of New York, to become the director of a summer festival. He has been followed by conductors Robert Marek, Dale Warland, Steve Parker, and James MacInnes. Highlights over the years have included the importation of the University of Wisconsin Pro Arte String Quartet for a series of concerts, production of a number of operas, and creative programming that has included the St. Paul Chamber Orchestra, local soloists like soprano Johanna Meier, dinner-theater evenings, the formation of a chamber chorus, and commissioned works. For 2003-04, the society presented its own chamber orchestra; an Austin, Texas, instrumental trio; the "J. Laiten Weed Honors Orchestra" of high-school string players, a Colorado ensemble playing traditional Celtic and Irish music, and a piano-violin duo from the University of South Dakota.

These three musical organizations together have existed in South Dakota for a total of 196 years—the South Dakota Symphony for eighty-two years, the Black Hills Symphony for nearly seventy-four, and the Black Hills Chamber Music Society for forty years. Not very many musical organizations can claim such long and productive life spans. The Sioux Falls Municipal Band is the oldest of the city bands in the state, having been created in 1919 and continuing until today with a full program of summer concerts. The conductors with the longest tenures have been Russ Henegar, a former trumpet player with John Philip Sousa, who conducted the band from 1935 to 1963, and Leland Lillehaug, who was chosen in 1964 and held the post until 1987. Lillehaug's innovations over the years included admitting women as players, offering theme concerts throughout each season, and performing at nursing homes, on college campuses, and elsewhere throughout the city, as well as in the parks. In recent years, the conductor has been Christopher Hill, also the principal clarinetist with the South Dakota Symphony and a member of the Dakota Wind Quintet.

Among the vocal ensembles in the state whose existence has been of unusual length are the Grieg Male Chorus, formed in Canton in 1892 and continuing to perform primarily Norwegian music as a means to "preserve a fond recollection for our Fatherland"[27]; and the Faulk County Chorus, founded in 1921 in rural north-central South Dakota as a feature of the Faulk County Sunday School Convention. In 1929 *Musical America* reviewed the chorus's production of Handel's *Messiah*: The Rockingham Legion Hall, wrote the reviewer, was filled and "the adjacent sidewalks were packed with people who had driven in from surrounding farms and towns to enjoy this musical feast. . . ." Since 1968 Jim Wagner has been the conductor, and the ensemble now prepares an Easter cantata each spring, performing in recent years in the United Methodist Church in Faulkton.

As Robert Marek observes, an authoritative book about the musical life and the musicians of South Dakota has yet to be written.[28] Composers living in the state at the time of Marek's essay include Floyd A. McClain (Yankton College), Lewis Hamvas (Yankton College), George B. Whaley (Yankton College), Stephen Yarbrough (University of South Dakota), Paul Royer (South Dakota State University), Merritt Johnson (Northern State University), Walter May (Augustana College), Robert Marek (University of South Dakota), and John Cacavas (writer of movie music). Composers of note writing before 1984 include Achilles LaGuardia (conductor at Fort Sully in 1886), E. W. Grabill (University of South Dakota), Marjorie E. Dudley (University of South Dakota), Joseph Dvorak (Tabor), Clarence Loomis (born in Sioux Falls), Edwin Mike Hoffman (South Dakota homesteader in 1911-13), Decort Hammitt (composer of the state song), and Lloyd Norlin (composer of movie music). Among the many composers and solo performers, both vocal and instrumental, who have had lengthy careers are a number who have had notable success and deserve special notice in a historical review such as this: Felix Vinatieri was a remarkably versatile musician during territorial days as a bandmaster at Fort Sully, a community band director in Yankton, and later as General George Custer's bandmaster for three years, 1873-76. As James R. Gay concludes in his study,[29] following his discharge and until his death in 1891, Vinatieri traveled widely, performing with circus bands, and composed an impressive body of music, capped by his masterpiece, an opera titled *The American Volunteer*. Arriving in 1910, Norwegian immigrant Jarle Foss became a state champion fiddler as a young man, competed in state and regional contests throughout his long career, performing at the Smithsonian Folk Festival in Washington, D.C., in 1975 and on Garrison Keillor's radio show "A Prairie Home Companion" in 1982.

Three operatic singers from the state have earned national recognition during their careers. The oldest of the three is Myrtle Stolt Kaponin, who began her studies in music at Dakota Wesleyan University and went on in the 1930s to leading roles with the Chicago City Opera and the Hippodrome Opera Company of New York. Hot Springs native Jess Thomas came late to a career in opera, going from a counselor's position in an Oregon high school to winning the San Francisco Opera auditions in 1957. In Germany he established himself as a Wagnerian tenor, opening the new Berlin Opera House in 1961. In 1962 he made his Metropolitan Opera debut, and in 1972—at a time when he was acclaimed as the first American to reign as the leading Wagnerian tenor in the world—Thomas appeared with the South Dakota Symphony to help celebrate its fiftieth anniversary. As the daughter of Josef Meier, famed for his portrayals of Christ in the Black Hills Passion Play, Johanna Meier has established a reputation for herself in performances in America and throughout the world, including appearing with the New York City Opera, the Metropolitan Opera, the Lyric Opera Company of Chicago, and the Black Hills Symphony, where she has sung with her husband tenor Guido Della Vecchia.

In recent years an organization, Friends of Opera, has been formed in Sioux Falls to highlight opera singers from South Dakota. The first program, presented in the spring of 2003, featured Louis Otey and Carla Connors, the former a native of Flandreau who has sung at the Spoleto Festival in South Carolina and with the Metropolitan Opera, and the latter a Vermillion native who has performed with the New York City Opera Company on its national tour and has sung with more than a dozen symphony orchestras in the United States and abroad. It its spring 2004 showcase, the Friends of Opera featured Connors again and two male vocalists with South Dakota connections. Erich Parce spent his childhood in De Smet and Watertown and now performs dramatic and comic roles with opera companies throughout North America and Europe. Scott Piper, currently a resident of Vermillion, has sung with opera companies across America and with the Compania Lirica National in Costa Rica. In its program for the 2004 showcase the Friends of Opera also saluted other South Dakota opera singers of note: tenor Jess Thomas (Hot Springs), soprano Johanna Meier (Spearfish), tenor White Eagle (Rosebud), mezzo-soprano Stacey Rishoi (Watertown), soprano Lindsey Larson (Sioux Falls), baritone Stanford Felix (Flandreau), baritone Monty Barnard (Sioux Falls), and soprano Kristi Vensand (Brookings).

This review of the musical arts that have flourished in South Dakota has made extensive use of Arthur Huseboe's *An Illustrated History of the Arts in South Dakota* and for recent years of reports published by the South Dakota Arts Council (SDAC) and its partner organization South Dakotans for the Arts. When Herbert Schell wrote his history of the state over forty years ago, the resources available to him allowed for only a brief chapter on "Social and Cultural Aspects of South Dakota Life." Today the information available to historians about the musical and dramatic arts in the state is astonishing by comparison. A recent report in *Arts Alive: South Dakota* (Autumn, 2003), published by South Dakotans for the Arts, announces the awards given by the SDAC to non-profit organizations, schools, and individuals who have applied for aid for the 2003-04 year. A selection from the listing of those organizations receiving grants of $1,000 or more suggests the variety and quality of the performing arts in the state:

In Custer—the Black Hills Playhouse; Deadwood—Adams Museum and House, to present three plays; Flandreau—Crystal Theatre; Freeman—Swiss Choral Society; Gregory—Oscar Micheaux Film Festival; Hill City Arts Council; Onida—High Plains Arts Council; Piedmont—Stagebarn Elementary; Pierre—Capital City Children's Chorus, Short Grass Arts Council, and Pierre Players; Rapid City—Backroom Productions (songwriting workshop), Black Hills Chamber Music Society, Dakota Choral Union, Rapid City Recreation Department/Rapid City Children's Chorus, Storybook Island Theatre Company, Black Hills Community Theatre, Black Hills Symphony Orchestra, and Children's Theatre Company of South Dakota; Sioux Falls—South Dakota Dance Network, South Dakota Friends of Traditional Music, Sioux Falls Jazz and Blues Society (summer Jazzfest and concert series), South Dakota Symphony, Comfort Theatre Company, and Dakota District Pipes and Drums; Sisseton—Sisseton Arts Council (theater residencies); Spearfish Center for the Arts and Humanities (theater at the Matthews Opera House); Vermillion—USD Community Orchestra, South Dakota Public Broadcasting ("South Dakota Originals," local performers), National Music Museum, and Discovery Mime Theatre; Volga—Jazz Portraits (touring performers); Wagner—Morning Star Community Theatre/Yankton Sioux Tribe; Wakonda—Poker Alice Band; Watertown—Town Players; Worthing—Olde Towne Dinner Theatre; Yankton—Yankton Children's Choir, Yankton Parks and Recreation Department (summer musical), and Lewis & Clark Theatre Company.

This selection of recipients does not include dozens more organizations whose SDAC awards are smaller than $1,000. Nor does it include—and should—the notice of awards to three individuals whose projects are related to preserving elements of Native American traditional arts in South Dakota: Alfreda Beartrack (Lower Brûlé), a video of Lakota oral traditions; Dallas Chief Eagle (Martin), Native American dancing; and Kevin Locke (Wakpala), dance programs. Even the entire list of awards, as announced in the Autumn 2003 *Arts Alive* newspaper, does not represent the complete picture of the performance arts activities that characterize South Dakota in the twenty-first century. But the work of the South Dakota Arts Council, now more active than ever before, since its founding in 1966, is touching the lives of virtually every South Dakotan and, by means of its alliances and partnerships with individual artists and arts organizations of every stripe, has given those grant recipients new energy for the task and joy of contributing to this value-added society on the South Dakota prairie-plains.

Chapter 22
Health Care

A major source of jobs and revenue that flourished through the final quarter of the twentieth century and that helped to buffer a decline in the rural economy comprised two health-care delivery systems. The two had evolved through the history of South Dakota: one for Native Americans, the other mainly for non-Indians. Each has existed with unique features because of the legal separation of the two societies and, as a result, different sources of funding and strategies of management. Each one was fashioned to accommodate the needs of the majority in a separate group of South Dakotans. Each matured with both salutary characteristics and deficiencies that have evoked complaints from the patients. During the year 2000, the most visible system in use by federally recognized Indians existed as a network of "Service Units" funded by Congress, but substantial groups in all of the tribes also relied on traditional healing assistance. As citizens of the United States, tribal members were eligible for public assistance in non-Indian programs, as well, and veterans among them had access to free or inexpensive health care in the Veterans Administration medical network. The prevailing system in use by other South Dakotans existed in four networks of facilities, but many continued to rely on alternative procedures for healing.

■ Native American Health Care

Federal involvement with the health of tribal members living in present-day South Dakota originated with the establishment of Dakota Agency in the year 1820. The Agency's headquarters were located on a site adjacent to Fort Snelling, near the confluence of the Minnesota and Mississippi rivers, but its jurisdiction extended from the Mississippi to the Missouri River. U.S. Agent Lawrence Talliaferro could arrange access to a U.S. Army physician at Fort Snelling, and he possessed the authority at least to order the vaccination of tribal members. Although from the outset of the 1820s Talliaferro and other federal employees who managed the Upper Missouri Agency were expected to deal with disease epidemics, their range of responsibility did not become clear until 1832, when a treaty with the Winnebago Tribe set a precedent in national Indian policy. By its terms, federal officials promised to provide the services of a physician to the tribe as partial payment for rights and properties ceded to the U.S. government. Thereafter, this arrangement became the basis of a trust responsibility for all tribes or jurisdictional groups with federal recognition as domestic dependent nations.

Its application in Sioux Country became evident during the 1840s, when employees on the list of staff members at the Dakota Agency were identified by the title of physician. On a roster for the year 1849, for example, a Dr. Martin served at Fort Snelling for the salary of $240; and a Dr. Thomas Williamson, a medical missionary at Little Crow's Village, received $260 per year. Although they lived and worked within the Territory of Minnesota, their responsibility extended into present South Dakota, where many Dakota Sissetons and some Wahpetons lived or frequently traveled to hunt and gather food.

In 1854 two new jurisdictions along the upper Minnesota River replaced the Dakota Agency. Dr. Asa Daniels joined one staff at Lower Agency, and Dr. Jared Daniels the other at Upper Agency. Thereafter, Asa attended to the needs of Santees and Jared to the

423

Chronology

Native American Health Care

1820 – U.S. Dakota Indian Agency and Fort Snelling personnel assume obligations to control disease epidemics as far west as Missouri River

1832 – Treaty with Winnebago Tribe sets precedent to provide services of a physician to a tribe as partial payment for rights and properties ceded to the U.S. government, thus making health care a trust responsibility for federally recognized tribes

1840s – Physicians join U.S. Agency staff rosters and draw salaries to serve Dakota tribes

1854 – Physicians join Upper and Lower Sioux Agency staff and in 1859 evaluate tribal health-care techniques

1902 – Asylum for Insane Indians founded at Canton

1905 – *Waldron v. United States*, et al. recognizes legal equality between mixed-blood and full-blood Native Americans in federally recognized tribes

1917 – Rosebud Indian Hospital first in full operation on a Sioux reservation

1918 – Federal "quarter-blood" quantum becomes minimum tribal biological heritage to qualify for health care at federal expense

1921 – Snyder Act clearly establishes health care as trust responsibility of U.S. government for eligible members of federally recognized tribes

1924 – Creation of Health Division within Bureau of Indian Affairs establishes modern "Indian Health Service" (IHS) – Nurse Corps appears on medical staff rosters at agency jurisdictions

1926 – Commissioned Corps of medical doctors appears in the IHS

1935 – Kiowa School of Nursing initiates exclusive professional training programs for tribal members

1936 – Yankton Reservation IHS Hospital exemplifies use of New Deal funds to open hospitals on most large reservations

needs of Sissetons and Wahpetons. In 1859 they both answered a circular addressed to all Field Service personnel containing instructions to provide information regarding the medical uses of plants by Indians. Asa reported twenty "medicinal plants" used "for the cure of diseases." He and Jared supplied both their popular and scientific names and described their medicinal values. Although the two physicians had a vague perception about how the plants were prescribed, they believed them to be administered "by passing through a course of conjuration by a 'medicine man.'" In this way, they acknowledged both the use of a natural apothecary and the practice of medicine by spiritual leaders who doubled as herbalists and faith healers. Thereafter, traditional specialists in all of the tribes and white physicians employed at agencies were about equally suspicious and disdainful in their perceptions of each other as they competed for acceptance among tribes of Sioux.

Although at every new agency jurisdiction there existed resistance to non-Indian health-care techniques, nearly every jurisdictional roster called for the employment of a physician at a salary second in size only to that of the agent in charge. Where agents failed to attract licensed physicians, U.S. Army doctors occasionally appeared to deal with severe health-care needs. Missionaries practiced medicine, too, some of them without prior training or licensure. In Sioux Country, one of these was the Episcopal Father Joseph Cook, at the Yankton Agency. Another was the Catholic Father Francis Craft, who moved about among Lakotas west of the Missouri River. Neither of them was a licensed physician, but both men held clinics and performed some surgical procedures if formally trained physicians were not available.

Through the 1880s, when only the Yankton and Lake Traverse reservations in present-day South Dakota were clearly defined, and the enrollment rosters at most of the other agency jurisdictions remained unsettled, the advancement of health care seemed to be a matter of low priority. Mainly, agency personnel focused their attention on the installation of educational institutions, formal preparations for the allotment of land, and appointments of agency policemen and judges. The only obvious improvement in medical services came through the establishment of boarding schools on reservations, which included health care among mandatory responsibilities—at the federal Yankton Reservation Boarding School, for example, founded in 1882.

During the 1890s, several changes both improved the quality and enlarged the range of medical services available to tribal members. One was the inclusion of the Indian Field Service in the U.S. Civil Service system, beginning in the year 1895, which for the first time required that all regular (full-time) federal employees (except tribal members) qualify for Indian Field Service jobs by passing examinations. A second was the appearance of the first U.S. Field Matrons, whose general responsibilities were similar to those of modern social workers, which included attention to personal hygiene, nutrition, and rudimentary nursing care. A third change was the construction and operation of substantial boarding schools—some on but others off the reservations of the northern Great Plains—where federal regulations required the availability of an infirmary and the services of matrons at each school as well as either contract or resident physicians.

During the first two decades of the twentieth century, federal officials accumulated additional responsibilities through several developments. One was a new educational policy that called for the enrollment of tribal youngsters at integrated district schools, for which federal officials paid tuition costs and screened tribal members to prevent the spread of particular diseases. Indian students could not share classrooms with whites unless they passed yearly medical examinations that revealed they were not affected by tuberculosis, venereal diseases, or other communicable maladies.

Chronology (con't)
Native American Health Care

1938 – Sioux Sanitarium opened at Rapid City to control tuberculosis
1950 – Physicians and dentists invited to accomplish compulsory military obligations with service in the U.S. Public Health Service (PHS)
1955 – Indian health care transferred from Bureau of Indian Affairs to PHS, which allows physicians and dentists to fulfill compulsory military obligations with service on Indian reservations
1959 – Indian Sanitation and Facilities Act allows PHS-tribal cooperation for improvement of sanitation on reservations
1972 – End of compulsory military duty in the U.S. leads citizen physicians and dentists to flee from reservation environments, forcing IHS and tribal officials to enlist other medical personnel
 – Congress allocates special funds for urban, off-reservation Indian health care
1975 – Indian Self Determination and Education Assistance Act allows tribal officials an option to staff, manage, and operate IHS facilities
1976 – Indian Health Care Improvement Act clarifies federal trust responsibility outlined in 1921 Snyder Act, reinforced tribal self determination, and emphasized a federal obligation for urban, off-reservation health care
1986 – *McNabb v. Heckler* rules that state and county governments share responsibility for Indian health care with IHS
1988 – IHS becomes a separate agency of U.S. Public Health Service, restoring independence lost since 1955
1993 – *Lincoln, et al. v. Vigil, et al.* describes the size of the IHS aggregate staff and number of Native Americans who receive benefit of health care as trust responsibility under authority from Snyder Act and Indian Health Care Improvement Act
1997 – Northern Great Plains Indian Health Service Aberdeen Area Office publishes report on 16 service units to care for 104,500 tribal members scattered across the region

The Buy Indian Act of 1910 called for tribal involvement, inasmuch as it allowed the preferential consideration of Indians in applications for jobs as well as in the award of contracts supported by tribal or federal funds allocated for the benefit of Indian peoples. Terms in this statute assured some employment as well as business-contract preference in health-care delivery, at the discretion of the Secretary of the Interior, and with direct involvement assured an opportunity to judge the quality of medical care. Later, on two occasions, the principle of "Indian preference" gained reinforcement. The Indian Reorganization (Wheeler-Howard) Act of 1934 included a section that made affirmative action for members of federally recognized tribes a principle in statutory law. Executive Order no. 11246 issued by Lyndon Johnson in the 1960s applied the congressional mandate to all but required Indian preference.

Other changes early in the twentieth century included the opening and operation of the Asylum for Insane Indians at Canton in eastern South Dakota, beginning in 1902; and the construction of the first reservation hospital in Sioux Country, at Rosebud, which became fully operational by the year 1917. Thereafter, Congress funded the construction of additional physical plants created exclusively for the delivery of health care in the tribes.

In 1918 federal officials established a "quarter-blood rule" to determine eligibility for health care as well as education and other aspects of federal trust responsibility for federally recognized tribes. This controversial restriction was a solution to a point of confusion in federal Indian policy that had caused trouble in Sioux agency administration for nearly a century. After an unsuccessful attempt to segregate "half breeds" on separate reservations (like the Canadian Métis) during the 1830s, federal officials accepted enrollment decisions from general councils of tribal adults and intervened only when tribal politics seemed to cause inequities. Some modern tribes, such as the Rosebud, enrolled many Caucasians married to Indians as well as an ever-increasing number of progeny born to tribal and white parents. Reactions from traditionalist factions in the tribes as well as from federal officials in charge of trust responsibilities led to the case *Waldron v. United States, et al.* (1905), which for the first time ordered the legal equality of mixed-bloods and full-bloods in tribal enrollments. Thereafter, increasing numbers of immigrant whites (mainly men) married into the tribes and, as family heads, claimed all federal benefits except land allotments. As a solution in 1918, federal officials chose the arbitrary quarter-blood rule. Subsequently, except under extraordinary circumstances, medical care became available free of charge only among those members who could prove a quarter or more Indian biological heritage. Theoretically, this rule has remained in place, although federal employees have used discretionary power in its application, and since the implementation of the Indian Self Determination and Education Assistance Act in 1975, described below, tribal officials have enjoyed some freedom in the modification of the quarter-blood regulation.

■ The Snyder Act

All of the developments described above served as backdrop for the Snyder Act of 1921, a benchmark, which contained the first clear congressional order to provide health-care services for all federally recognized Indians who possessed a quarter Native American heritage or more.[1] Specifically, this prevailing statute granted authority to "expend such moneys as Congress may from time to time appropriate, for the benefit, care, and assistance of the Indians throughout the United States," of a quarter-blood Indian heritage or more, for the "relief of distress and conservation of health." It also called for "the suppression of traffic in intoxicating liquor and deleterious drugs."

Yankton Public Health Hospital opened in 1936 at Wagner and today accommodates outpatients from the Yankton, Santee, and Northern Ponca Tribe. *Courtesy Herbert T. Hoover.*

With the Synder Act in place, several organizational changes affected the tribes on the northern Great Plains during the 1920s. One was the creation of the Health Division within the U.S. Office (Bureau) of Indian Affairs in 1924, which marked the formal beginning of the modern Indian Health Service (IHS). A second was the addition of a federally licensed nurse corps to medical staff rosters at agency jurisdictions, which became active in 1924. Elinor Gregg, who served at the Rosebud Indian Hospital and the Pine Ridge Indian Hospital, later wrote about resulting changes in nursing care.[2] A third was the assignment of medical doctors as a Commissioned Corps to positions in the Indian Health Service, beginning in 1926.

Several improvements affected health care during the 1930s. The one of greatest significance was the use of various New Deal program budgets to supplement special congressional allocations for the construction of Indian Health Service hospitals on most of the large reservations. The one opened on the Yankton Reservation during the year 1936 was fairly typical. Congress provided a special appropriation for the purchase of materials. New Deal administrators employed construction personnel by the use of Works Progress Administration (WPA) funds. This facility accommodated both inpatients and outpatients until 1990 when, during a reorganization of reservation health service accommodations, inpatient facilities were eliminated and services were restricted to trauma and outpatient care at an expanded facility called the Yankton Service Unit.

In 1935 a new Kiowa School of Nursing represented the beginning of professional participation by groups of tribal members in the Indian medical service. Through a segregated, nine-month course of study, tribal members gained credentials for practical-nursing employment.

For Sioux Country in 1938, Indian Health Service personnel used a former federal boarding school compound in Rapid City to open the Sioux Sanitarium. It responded to a critical need for the control of tuberculosis until the mid-1960s, when other methods of treatment rendered the sanitarium obsolete. Thereafter, "Sioux San" became the center for urban Indian health care described below as the Rapid City Service Unit.[3]

427

■ Post World War II

Distractions by World War II and changes in federal Indian policies after the war prevented any additional improvements until mid-century. Beginning in 1950, physicians and dentists were invited to serve their compulsory terms of military service in the Public Health Service. In 1952 a shortage of funds caused personnel in the Bureau of Indian Affairs to close some Indian health facilities, but at the same time they enlarged support for contract health services through state or local non-Indian hospitals. In 1955 responsibilities for the Indian Health Service transferred from the Bureau of Indian Affairs to the U.S. Public Health Service, within the U.S. Department of Health and Human Services. This change brought physicians and dentists seeking escape from service in the Armed Forces to Indian reservations for limited terms of service with benefits of federal employment. The conscription inducement served as a steady recruitment device until the abandonment of compulsory military service in 1972. The Indian Sanitation and Facilities Act of 1959 authorized funding to support sanitation facilities and services for Indians, allowing cooperative agreements between the Public Health Service and the Indian tribes to provide sanitation facilities.[4]

Federal reservation programs implemented during the 1960s had limited effect on health-care delivery, but a succession of developments brought substantial changes during the 1970s. As indicated above, mandatory military service by physicians and dentists, which had lured them into the Indian Health Service since 1955, ended in 1972. Since then, managers of reservation hospitals have been forced either to recruit immigrants from abroad with medical credentials or to rely on part-time contract physicians and dentists. In 1972, as well, Congress began to allocate funds specifically for use in the support of health care among all eligible Indians who lived off the reservations in urban communities. This concession accommodated hundreds of thousands of tribal members until Congress sharply reduced allocations for urban Indian health care during the last decade of the twentieth century. At about the same time, Congress began to fund the construction or operation of medical facilities given over to tribal officials for management—one noteworthy example being a new hospital on the Omaha Reservation in Nebraska. This concession represented a recent trend in reservation management that gained legislative expression through the Indian Self Determination and Education Assistance Act of 1975, which offered all federally recognized tribes contracts with

Standing Rock Public Health Service Unit hospital at Fort Yates (1980). *Courtesy Herbert T. Hoover.*

funds to staff, manage, and operate Indian Health Service as well as various Bureau of Indian Affairs programs in their communities. In its effect, this act brought reservation health-care allocations into reservation economies while it invited tribal officials to participate in decisions previously under the control of Indian hospital managers—for example, informal but effective insistence upon the availability of health care for tribal reservation residents of less than a quarter Indian heritage.

In 1976 the Indian Health Care Improvement Act reinforced the principle of self-determination while it clarified the federal health-care responsibility outlined in the Snyder Act of 1921.[5] The goal was "to implement the Federal responsibility for the care and education of the Indian people by improving the services and facilities of Federal Indian health programs," which is "required by the Federal Government's historical and unique legal relationship with, and resulting responsibility to, the American Indian people." The 1976 act reiterated federal assurance for preference extended to Indians and tribal firms during the use of congressional allocations for the Fiscal Year 1978 to support Indian Health Service hospitals, health centers, and health stations. Specifically, it also emphasized a trust responsibility for the eligible "urban Indian population." The Improvement Act of 1976 even called for a study to determine feasibility in the establishment of a school of medicine to train Indians for health-care delivery service. In 1980, an amendment to the 1976 act further explained the goal of federal responsibility as one to elevate the status of health among Native Americans and Alaska Natives.

By 1980 the importance of the Buy Indian Act, the affirmative action section of the Wheeler-Howard Act, and Executive Order No. 11246 issued by President Johnson, became obvious. Rarely did the Indian Health Service employ non-Indians unless they possessed skills or credentials that tribal members could not supply. Seldom thereafter did a non-Indian gain appointment to a managerial position. Through various applications of mandatory Indian preference, the entire service fell increasingly under the control of federally recognized tribal members.

In 1986 a U.S. District Court decision in Montana—*McNabb v. Heckler*—ruled that although the Indian Health Service was the primary provider, state or county governmental personnel held responsibilities as additional providers who could not escape a responsibility for health care among Indians. Neither the Synder Act nor any historical development related to Indian welfare relieved the governments of states or counties whose boundaries contained reservations of responsibility for the well being of tribal members, who like non-Indians were citizens of the United States. While ruling on a case that entailed litigation against the Indian Health Service and a county government for the payment of medical bills for a child born prematurely, the judge determined that this mutual obligation was clear, and he cited the Synder Act of 1921 and the Indian Health Care Improvement Act of 1976 to show that the "federal trust responsibility" extended beyond activities on land under federal trust protection. Together, the two acts of Congress, coupled with the historical trust responsibility, evoked an order from his court for the payment of these medical bills by a county as well as the Indian Health Service. On appeal, justices ruled that Congress did not intend that the federal government would be exclusively responsible for Indian health care; it was an obligation incumbent upon every level of government.

On January 4, 1988, the Indian Health Service became a separate agency of the U.S. Public Health Service. In its effect, this change restored some of the independence that had been lost when in 1955 Indian health had become a subdivision of the Public Health Service.

■ Contemporary Issues

In 1993 the majority opinion in the case *Lincoln, et al., v. Vigil, et al.* summarized historical trends and provided some revealing data to indicate steady increases in the size and the cost of this historical trust responsibility.[6] Justice Souter wrote for the Supreme Court of the United States to reverse a judgment from a Court of Appeals and remanded it for corrections consistent with Supreme Court opinion. "The Indian Health Service" counted as "an agency within the Public Health Service of the Department of Health and Human Services." In 1993 it employed "roughly 12,000 people" and operated "more than 500 health-care facilities in the Continental United States and Alaska" to provide "health care for some 1.5 million American Indians and Alaska Native people." It received yearly lump-sum appropriations from Congress and expended funds "under authority of" the Snyder Act of 1921 and the Indian Health Care Improvement Act of 1976 to provide health care for Indians as a "special trust relationship" responsibility. Litigation for this case came from a group that protested after the Indian Health Service closed a program for children in the Southwest and allocated funds for a similar program nationwide, an action that Souter regarded as one in keeping with "agency discretion . . . traditionally regarded" as correct during the use of lump-sum appropriations. He recognized the Snyder Act of 1921 as a source of historical authority for the Bureau of Indian Affairs to "expend such monies as Congress may from time to time appropriate" for the care of Indians; and the Improvement Act of 1976 as recent authority to use congressional allocations for mental-health care as well as "therapeutic and residential treatment centers." As a consequence, although some tribes controlled the management and operation of medical centers, Souter's decision made clear the discretionary power of the Indian Health Service during the use of congressional lump-sum allocations for Indian health care. Accordingly, there were limits on tribal prerogatives in health-care delivery.

By 1996 the Indian Health Service had grown to include approximately 14,000 employees to implement a proposed annual budget of $2.4 billion. This amount could meet the cost of contract physician care as well as responsibilities for treatments of life-threatening diseases, medical emergencies, and various elective procedures.

The continuum of changes described above clearly indicates that since the approval of the Snyder Act in 1921 the trust responsibility of the U.S. government for health care among federally recognized Native Americans never has been in jeopardy. Congress has recognized an obligation to provide health care for all federally recognized Indians who could prove a quarter-blood Indian heritage or more. Most of the managers have allowed treatment for some patients of lesser Indian blood quantums, especially since 1975, when tribal officials gained managerial prerogatives.

All along, members of nine federally recognized tribes in South Dakota have been included as residents of the northern Great Plains Indian Health Service Aberdeen Area Office jurisdiction. In 1997 Aberdeen Area Office personnel sustained sixteen service units to accommodate seventeen federally recognized tribes scattered across a region approximately 600 miles wide and 625 miles long. The annual cost to Congress for the care of 104,500 eligible Indians was approximately $2 million. For use by the eleven tribes of Sioux in this region, Aberdeen Area Office personnel operated six hospitals, eleven "health centers," and numerous "health locations" to meet the needs of 79,616 individuals.[7]

Indian Health Service personnel sustained most of these facilities within the boundaries of South Dakota. The Rapid City Service Unit (situated on forty-two acres previously occupied by the federal Rapid City Indian Boarding School and the Sioux

Sanatorium) offered health services to an urban population of 7,500 or more enrolled in various tribes. North of Rapid City, the Cheyenne River Service Unit provided care for 7,739 tribal members in a hospital and four health locations at Cherry Creek, Red Scaffold, Swiftbird, and White Horse. South of Rapid City, the Pine Ridge Service Unit accommodated 20,672 at the largest hospital in the Aberdeen Area plus health locations at Manderson and Allen.

East of Pine Ridge, the Rosebud Service Unit operated to serve 12,190 in a hospital facility as well as in health locations at Norris, Horse Creek, Antelope (Mission), and St. Francis. East of Rosebud, the Yankton Service Unit occupied the hospital opened at Wagner in 1936, which had been converted in 1990, and in 1997 (and subsequent years) received only outpatients from a resident population of 4,641 enrolled in the Yankton Tribe and coordinated services or contracts extended to the Santee and Northern Ponca tribes in Nebraska.

In 1975 the Rosebud Public Health Service Unit ambulance represented ready access to health-care delivery both on and off the reservation. *Courtesy Herbert T. Hoover.*

Upstream from the Yankton Reservation along the Missouri River on the east bank, the Crow Creek Service Unit accommodated 4,641 outpatients and included an outreach clinic at the Pierre Indian Learning Center. On the west bank, the Lower Brûlé Service Unit served 1,781 outpatients. Upstream on the west bank, the Standing Rock Service Unit accommodated 8,763 in a hospital at Fort Yates, a health center at McLaughlin, and health locations at Cannonball, Bull Head, and Wakpala.

At the northeast corner of the state, the Sisseton-Wahpeton Service Unit in the town of Sisseton included a small hospital for a population of 5,326 as well as a health center at the Circle of Nations Tribal Boarding School (the former federal Indian Boarding School) near Wahpeton, North Dakota. South of Sisseton, the Flandreau Santee Sioux Service Unit occupied a facility on the campus of the Flandreau Indian Boarding School for use by approximately three hundred outpatients from the Flandreau Santee Sioux Tribe.

During recent years, several advantages have been obvious in this Indian Health Service network. One has been a stability lacking in the medical facilities available to most rural South Dakotans. Because the trust responsibility for Indian health is rooted in legal precedents, crystallized in the Snyder Act, and reinforced by the Indian Health Care Improvement Act, only a modification of the responsibility or reductions of funding by Congress could diminish the extent or quality of health care at Rapid City and on the reservations of South Dakota. Another advantage has been the existence of health locations at remote places, where medical specialists frequently have appeared to perform examinations, offer immunizations, and order the transfer of patients to major medical centers at federal expense. Yet another advantage has been the financial benefit accrued in tribal economies through the application of the Indian Self Determination Act of 1975. Finally, the beneficiaries of this system have enjoyed the only fully socialized system of health care available in the United States (except the ones available to U.S. military personnel and veterans.)

Several complaints have been consistent among eligible Native Americans. Since the end of compulsory military service in 1972, Indian Health Service managers have struggled to attract physicians, dentists, and paramedical personnel. Mainly, they have had to rely on immigrants from abroad with credentials of varied quality or on retired citizen personnel through part-time contracts. As a result, physicians, dentists, and paramedical personnel have come and gone because of a problem with adjustment to reservation culture, or because of limited salaries and inadequate equipment.

Beneficiaries have complained, too, about long hours in waiting rooms and an absence of suitable patient-to-doctor relationships. In this regard, the reservation experience has been similar to that of all citizens who have sought health care at hospitals managed by the Armed Forces of the United States and the Veterans Administration, or to those who have been forced into Health Management Organizations (HMOs).

More insidious even than the shortage and frequent turnover of medical personnel and some inevitable inconvenience for patents has been a restriction or decline in federal funding coupled with the contract of management under the guise of "tribal self-determination." During an interview in the summer of 2003, Ramona O'Connor, a respected Yankton tribal elder employed by the Yankton Service Unit at Wagner, voiced some opinions. With insight enhanced by the possession of one master's degree in social work from Portland University and another in public health from the University of Minnesota, she discussed problems and consequences of contract funding that inevitably curtailed health-care delivery. One result was the termination of inpatient service during the construction of a new clinic in 1989. Tribal members "thought they were getting a new hospital" to replace the original facility constructed in 1936, "but what they were getting was an ambulatory clinic . . . . We should have demanded to keep our inpatient" service and now "we can't get it back unless we go to Congress again and lobby for it."

Chances for success in the lobbying effort would be slight because of self-determination for the tribes that "contract" for funds to provide the delivery of services. In O'Connor's opinion, this seemed less a benefit than a means by which Congress "seems to be pushing toward not" fulfilling the "treaty obligation" guaranteed in the Snyder Act of 1921. "They say, 'here, take it, you run it.' Once you contract, you are going to be limited to the amount of dollars you are given. You can't go to Congress, which we can under the IHS, and say we are short" and need additional funds to offer medical care to the end of a fiscal year.

O'Connor explained that, in the absence of inpatent care, the service unit could refer a person "to another facility like Sacred Heart [Hospital in Yankton] or the Community Hospital in Wagner, or in Sioux Falls." However, tribal members "can't be referred unless they are in Priority-1 category, which means risk of life or death. . . . You have to wait until you become Priority-1."

Nevertheless, O'Connor added: "without it [the service unit], what would you do? We are grateful for the fact that we can get medication here [free of charge] from the service unit pharmacy. . . . If we didn't have a turnover in the doctors, most people would feel satisfied. The negative is that we don't have inpatient, and we have some deficit in dollars."

Longtime tribal chairman Stephen Cournoyer, Jr., disagreed: "I don't think it is a very good system. . . . They bury their mistakes. . . . When you have people that need to be referred out to see specialists, you can't send them out because we don't have that kind of money available to send anybody unless they're deathly sick and dying. . . . What I would like to do" is "something similar to what the small community hospitals have done. I would hire something like Avera [Health management, discussed below] to administer what we have. We always say that we don't have enough money to serve the needs of our people. But we pay way too much money out in administration cost."

Although the former chairman's suggestion was plausible, if implemented it would nullify the economic benefit extended to a tribe through contract funding in self-determination. Nevertheless, tribal elder Stephen Cournoyer, Sr., agreed with his son's appraisal and added: "Once the government brought our own people in to run our programs, the effectiveness, I found, we started losing. Those Indian people . . . got good jobs. They didn't have to really know anything. Our health care deteriorated. It is not the pattern that there isn't enough money to get things done. It is just that people don't know how to manage. . . . Rather than push every dollar they have to be spent on the health care of the people, they are trying to sock that away because they get their bonuses for doing a 'good job.'"

Rose Mary Rouse, another Yankton elder, complained that when she called about medication an IHS worker replied: "Well, you have to come to see a doctor. We don't have time today. You have to wait until next week." Yet she recounted an experience with confusion about medication that left her unconscious. Because she was a Priority-1 emergency case, IHS personnel summoned a helicopter that flew her to Sioux Valley Hospital in Sioux Falls, where she recovered. Like most others in the tribe who voiced opinions during the summer of 2003, Rouse expressed some resentment about callous treatment by IHS personnel and because non-tribal observers viewed free health care as just another welfare entitlement instead of a federal trust responsibility founded in treaties and perpetuated by congressional statutes in return for the relinquishment of land in the past. Bitterly she exclaimed: "Some of them still believe that we get a check every month" from the government because of tribal membership. In her case, two checks arrived every month: one from the Social Security Service, the other as a veterans' benefit due her deceased husband.[8]

Despite some pejorative remarks by outsiders and the obvious disadvantages, the health-care delivery system available to federally recognized Indians has been far more stable than the disjointed delivery system available to non-Indians in South Dakota. Obviously, it has been affordable, inasmuch as it evolved as a trust responsibility funded entirely through allocations by Congress.

A part of this benefit since the 1970s has been the availability of federal funding for long-term care facilities on or near most reservations in South Dakota. (To this date, only the Rosebud Reservation has had a full-service, long-term care facility operated exclusively for use by tribal members.) An integrated facility at Wagner on the Yankton Reservation close to tribal housing units seems exemplary. It is staffed by credentialed medical personnel and receives state and federal payments for the care of persons with limited means. Free of charge to elders and other disabled tribal members, it competes in quality of environment with any long-term care facility available to non-Indians in the state at a cost of approximately $40,000 a year per individual non-Indian occupant.

In addition to health care provided by the U.S. government, tribal members have retained the freedom to seek help from the alternative, traditional health-care delivery system recognized as early as 1859 by Asa and Jared Daniels on the Dakota reservations. A substantial body of literature, written mainly by ethnologists and federal employees, clearly indicates that cultural imperialism never destroyed traditional health care across Sioux Country. Steadily in the face of criticism and economic discrimination, tribal members who embraced ancestral ways continued to use "medicinal plants," as the Daniels brothers indicated, together with the services of "medicine men" and women who doubled as herbalists and faith healers in the belief system represented by the Sacred Pipe. Since 1902, as well, some tribal members in South Dakota have found relief through the use of peyote as a medicine administered by "roadmen" during prayer meetings of the Native American Church. Since the founding of reservations, only social and economic pressure from federal employees and missionaries, and never the federal law, encumbered the uses of these two traditional health-care systems. During the civil rights era of the 1960s, they began to surface into public view. During the Native American Renaissance period of the 1970s, they began to flourish. Through the last quarter of the twentieth century, members of federally recognized tribes have had as much freedom in the use of alternative, traditional medicines administered by medicine men with medicine women, or by roadmen of the Native American Church, as they have enjoyed in the use of the congressionally funded Indian Health Service System.

■ Non-Indian Health Care

No similar centralized network of facilities and services has evolved for use by non-Indians mainly because there has existed no single network or source of support equivalent to the Indian Health Service system founded and sustained by Congress. As a consequence, no equivalent body of literature or collection of records has existed to describe a disjointed legacy of medical care that has frustrated most South Dakotans since the establishment of their territory in 1861. Its history must be pieced together from oral traditions, snippets of printed information, medical biographies, and institutional chronicles or advertisements.[9]

During territorial years an accumulation of some 350,000 citizens was forced to rely on the services of "country doctors," who used metaphysical procedures and treated maladies with patent medicines and other intoxicating analgesics. Most communities had no access to adequately trained physicians. Nowhere in the present state of South Dakota did there exist a facility that might have passed inspection as a legitimate hospital.

Publicly funded services were restricted to those provided for particular groups of residents who could not care for themselves. Territorial officials responded to urgent needs mainly in the care of the "insane"—a term that could encompass disorders ranging from depression and alcoholism to homicidal tendencies. Through the period 1873-79, territorial officials contracted for "insane care" at institutions in Minnesota. When the managers of these neighboring institutions rejected new applications because of overcrowded conditions, Governor William Howard ordered the relocation of two unoccupied "immigrant houses" to a site approximately two miles north of territorial headquarters. In 1879 territorial legislators funded an asylum for "the insane," which has remained in operation with public funding as a state institution to the present.

The only other publicly funded facilities to appear during territorial years were "poor farms" in the counties created to look after physically disabled or demented elders who had no families to care for them. The one in Bon Homme County was typical.

County commissioners assumed a responsibility for "the poor" and "the paupers" as early as 1872, when they began to fund the costs of food, boarding arrangements, and coffins. After the removal of county headquarters from Bon Homme to Tyndall in 1885, the commissioners developed a plan that led to the founding of a "County Poor Farm" in 1888. The following year, in Albion Township they purchased a site, contracted the breaking of ninety acres of farmland, and approved the construction of a two-story home. In 1890 they hired a manager, ordered construction of farm buildings, added a cistern, and received the first residents. Thereafter, managers contracted the services of country doctors, marketed crops from the farm, founded a cemetery, and struggled with a paltry budget. They transferred residents who were too confused or deranged for survival in this environment to the Insane Asylum at Yankton. Although other residents at the poor farm endured the onus of "pauperism" implied by public care, they continued to assemble at the farm until it was rendered obsolete through the implementation of the Social Security Act of 1935. County officials closed the poor farm in 1939, about the time that private hospitals came into place with rooms available for the care of elders, many of whom were eligible for Old Age Assistance (OAA) funding from the Social Security revolving account.

Previously, medical care for others in rural communities was available mainly through house calls by country doctors, who struggled to find accommodations for patients in need of hospitalization. Characteristically, at Tyndall in Bon Homme County in 1892, Dr. S. G. Berry opened a private hospital at a second-floor location and kept it in operation for nearly forty years. Not until 1948 did St. Michael's Hospital open as a ten-bed facility, which by 1965 grew to include twenty-five beds for acute care plus nine rooms for elders' nursing care.[10]

At Vermillion in Clay County, a more demanding community that included uni-

Chronology

Non-Indian Health Care

1879 – Asylum for the Insane founded at Yankton

1888 – Bon Homme County Poor Farm founded, exemplified local health care at taxpayers' expense, rendered obsolete by federal funds authorized in the 1935 Social Security Act

1895 – Benedictine Sisters at Yankton add health-care apostolate to community responsibilities

1897 – Benedictine Sisters found Sacred Heart Hospital at Yankton

1900 – Presentation Sisters at Aberdeen add health-care apostolate to community responsibilities

1901 – Presentation Sisters found St. Luke's Hospital at Aberdeen

1907 – University of South Dakota opens 2-year medical school at Vermillion, which changed to a 4-year, M.D.–granting school in 1975

1910 – Rapid City Hospital founded as private facility, changed to Methodist Deaconess Hospital in 1911, and to Black Hills General Hospital in 1939, renamed Bennett Clarkson Memorial Hospital in 1954

1915 – Ortman Clinic of chiropractic care founded at Canistota

1917 – State law requires formal training for nurses and the governor appoints first State Board of Nursing

1926 – Catholic St. John's Hospital founded at Rapid City, changed to St. John's McNamara Hospital in 1928

1926 – South Dakota Hospital Association founded

1935 – Social Security System founded, including an Old Age Assistance (OAA) component to support health care for elders

1948 – Veterans Administration Hospital opens at Sioux Falls

1965 – Federal Medicare extends health care to all elders and creates economic stability in health-care delivery systems

Chronology (con't)

Native American Health Care

1973 – Rapid City Regional Hospital founded through merger of Catholic St. John's McNamara Hospital with public Bennett Clarkson Memorial Hospital

1981 – North Central Heart Institute opens at Sioux Falls, later adds a hospital

1998 – Catholic Benedictine Sisters at Yankton and Presentation Sisters at Aberdeen form "partnerships" with the managerial network of Avera Health, merge in 2000 to include seven Catholic institutions plus numerous other facilities and services across East River, South Dakota

– Sioux Valley Hospitals and Health System takes shape and soon acquires Central Plains Clinic organization to become an effective competitor of Avera Health network across East River, South Dakota

versity personnel had an experience that differed from the one at Tyndall mainly in timing. In 1902 two physicians converted an abandoned hotel into a hospital, but it failed. In 1919 two trained nurses opened St. Catherine's Hospital, which provided services until 1935. Meanwhile, in 1923 Dr. W. H. Stansbury opened a private facility to accommodate his medical practice. Finally, in 1935 Vermillion city officials teamed with a local association to open Dakota Hospital, which contained forty-two beds for use in acute care. This facility remained almost unchanged until the last quarter of the twentieth century, when its managers added a long-term care unit, then negotiated a contract with Sioux Valley at Sioux Falls for its management, renovation, and expansion as a satellite "partnership" equipped with modern technology, referral services, and a helicopter pad.

The Bon Homme and Clay county experiences represented conditions that prevailed in communities across the state except where unique circumstances at urban centers inspired greater efforts. At Yankton, the key to greater success was the arrival of Benedictine Sisters (historically known as Nuns for a cloistered lifestyle) dedicated mainly to teaching and parish work yet inspired by a tradition of care for the sick and needy. In 1895 they added a medical apostolate to their responsibilities and converted some local facilities into a hospital to serve a growing urban population and the surrounding agricultural communities. In 1897 the Mother Superior sent sisters away for training as nurses while she formally opened the Sacred Heart Hospital for business.[11]

At Aberdeen, the key to similar success was the arrival of Presentation Sisters, who also appeared mainly for the purpose of teaching and parish work but honored a charge to extend health-care services among the poor. A diphtheria epidemic in 1900 inspired them to care for patients in an old church. By the time the epidemic passed in 1901, they had founded St. Luke's Hospital.[12]

Both religious orders expanded their hospital systems. To Sacred Heart, the Benedictines added St. Mary's at Pierre, St. Barnabas at Parkston, and Mother Grace Home at Gregory as well as other facilities in a neighboring state. The Presentation Sisters added St. Joseph Hospital at Mitchell and McKennan Hospital at Sioux Falls and other facilities in a neighboring state. Thus through the addition of medical apostolates, the two religious orders became aggressive pioneers in health care for South Dakotans. By design at the outset, the Benedictine Sisters worked mainly to serve Roman Catholics of German or Czech heritage, while the Presentation Sisters purported mainly to serve Catholics of Irish heritage. Elders among them have recalled that Protestants seldom appeared for health care until they were forced by circumstances—an influenza epidemic in 1918 and hard times during the 1930s. By the outset of World War II, both the Benedictine and Presentation medical systems gained acceptance as primary networks of health care for Protestants and Catholics alike.

Presentation Sisters' St. Luke's Hospital in Aberdeen. *Courtesy Herbert T. Hoover.*

Both have also served as laboratories for the development of modern, scientific strategies in health-care delivery. Either or both might be credited for a state law passed in 1917 to require formal training for nurses, and soon thereafter for inspiring Governor Peter Norbeck to appoint the first State Board of Nursing. Both orders established training programs for nurses, which evolved as hospital-based practicum experiences that required minimal training in classrooms and greater individual experience with hospital service in all departments. Three-year programs led to the award of graduation with Registered Nurse (RN) credentials. One- or two-year programs led to the award of Licensed Practical Nurse (LPN) registration. With rare exceptions, the graduates were women. Few aspired to earn baccalaureate or graduate degrees until after mid-century, when the two religious orders founded degree programs affiliated with their respective colleges—Mount Marty College in Yankton and Presentation College in Aberdeen.

Although the development of nursing programs remained their primary contributions through the 1920s, members of the two religious orders also turned their attention to other specialties. Both concentrated on the professionalization of pharmacy, laboratory technology, x-ray training, and anesthesiology.

The work of Benedictine and Presentation Sisters best represented improvement in the delivery of health care across the state, but these two groups of Catholic religious women were not alone in the endeavor. Elsewhere, similar efforts were in progress at local hospitals, whose history is elusive because they came into place in the absence of central leadership. Early in the twentieth century, characteristically in towns and cities across the state, one or two local physicians helped to arrange the opening of make-shift hospital facilities—in most instances at homes donated by the heirs of local estates or provided by local physicians and nurses. Hospital personnel had no formal access to participation in statewide improvement until the organization of the South Dakota Hospital Association in 1926. Gradually, thereafter, facilities improved in a way similar to the evolution of Dakota Hospital at Vermillion, described above.

Some four hundred miles from Vermillion at the west end of the state, two hospitals opened at Rapid City. Their appearance came after some delay. Following the Black Hills gold rush early in the 1870s, and the creation of Pennington County in 1877, slowly Rapid City emerged as a small commercial center because of the absence of access through Lakota land to the east until 1889, when the Sioux Agreement created the desired corridor to Chamberlain on the Missouri River. Thereafter, Rapid City became a crossroad, but its growth was delayed because of a limited population of ranchers around it and the scattering of people engaged in extractive industries across the Black Hills. Inevitably, however, it was destined to become the commercial hub and service center for West River.

As a response to its growth, in 1910 Dr. William Robinson opened the private Rapid City Hospital at his home to replace makeshift accommodations in hotel rooms or at other private homes.[13] In 1911 Methodists took it over, gave it the name Methodist Deaconess Hospital and, by 1923, expanded the bed capacity from twenty-five to fifty. Soon the managers hired an instructor to provide training for nurses. Thus, the Methodists kept pace with health-service improvements in evidence at other northern Great Plains facilities while they initiated improvements that led to the establishment of the Rapid City Regional Hospital in 1973.

Rapid City Regional Hospital, incorporated in 1973 following the merger of two older hospitals, St. John's McNamara and Bennett-Clarkson, represents the consolidation of health care in western South Dakota. *Courtesy Rapid City Regional Hospital.*

The Regional Hospital chronicle does not include any mention of a problem that, in retrospect, might seem an embarrassment. In South Dakota, the Roman Catholic population has been second in size only to the aggregate Lutheran population. West River Catholics must have been no more at ease in a hospital owned by Methodists than East River Protestants were at Benedictine and Presentation hospitals. As a remedy in 1926, Benedictine Sisters founded St. John's Hospital in Rapid City and, in 1928, added a nurses' training program. The same year, they opened a new facility that contained seventy-five beds and changed the name to St. John's McNamara Hospital in recognition of a sponsor.

St. John's McNamara provided an environment as vital to Catholics as it might have seemed objectionable to Protestants. A photograph portrayed the Catholic "Most Reverend John Lawler," the former Bishop of Lead then first Bishop of Rapid City Diocese (1930) who sanctioned the Benedictine establishment, as an officious clergyman adorned with vestments that represented the religious monarchy to which he belonged. Dangling from a cord around his neck was a cross that was larger than his hand. Benedictine Sisters wore habits that among Protestants might have conjured images of demons and witches. A crucifix in every hospital room and the smell of incense wafting from the chapel would have calmed the apprehensions of mainly Catholic patients but might have frightened almost any Protestant who by chance happened to be admitted.

During the 1930s, Catholics might have suspected that misguided Protestants received their proper punishment—for heretical behavior. Methodists struggled to make ends meet though the Great Depression. Finally, in 1939 they surrendered their hospital to community ownership and management under the new name, Black Hills General Hospital.

Meanwhile, through hard times, Catholics managed to expand St. John's McNamara. During the 1940s, it further grew to include 106 beds as well as departments of obstetrics and pharmacy and a central service (for supply sterilization procedures and supply distribution). They modernized laundry, sanitation, and heating facilities.

After the war, Black Hills General Hospital flourished with community support to embrace techniques recommended by physicians and nurses who returned from wartime service with new ideas about health care. In particular, the staff at the hospital added a medical records librarian, a dietician, and an anesthesiologist. By 1954 General Hospital occupied a new building under the name Bennett Clarkson Memorial Hospital, in honor of two donors, and offered 125 beds for inpatient use.

St. John's McNamara kept pace in the competition. In 1953 its Catholic supporters provided funds for a new wing, which brought the bed capacity to 155 and included obstetric, surgery, pediatric, and pharmacy departments.

Prior to the Second Vatican Council of the early 1960s, perhaps conflicting philosophies regarding health care as well as the social-religious separation of Catholics and Protestants would have prevented a merger of two hospitals burdened by costly duplications of facilities, departments, and services. At Catholic hospitals, for example, abortions were forbidden, as was counsel about contraception or any other process that challenged the teachings of the church.

The Rapid City Regional Hospital chronicle contains no mention of the Catholic/ Protestant separation, or of changing attitudes regarding ecumenism in the wake of the Second Vatican Council. Appropriately, it makes references to rising costs and declining birthrates in the 1960s as principal reasons for signs of a merger. First came the consolidation of obstetrical services at the Bennett Clarkson facility. St. John's McNamara retained its pediatric department and added a costly building to accommodate its school of nursing.

In the 1970s several factors contributed to an agreement about a complete merger. Staff members at the two hospitals were forced into cooperative efforts after the Rapid City Flood of 1972, when they shared a responsibility for some five hundred patients. Soon, spiraling operational costs stimulated a discussion about terms of a merger. In 1973 the result was the incorporation of the Rapid City Regional Hospital licensed to contain 280 beds and sustain eighty physicians on its staff. Incorporation led to construction. In 1979 a new hospital opened on Fairmont Boulevard. Through the 1980s, it grew to include additions. In 1985 its administrators employed a professional management service, which negotiated the first outreach network connection at the thirty-bed Hans P. Peterson Memorial Hospital and a nursing home at Philip that became Philip Health Services managed by Regional Hospital in 1987. In 1987, too, the network grew by a management agreement with the sixteen-bed Custer Community Hospital, which changed to a lease agreement in 1993. Through the ensuing decade, the Regional Hospital network expanded to include 1,400 people involved with the delivery of health care, 401 beds at the central facility, and sixty-six beds in affiliated hospitals plus facilities to accommodate elders.

The Regional Hospital chronicle (refined by a listing entitled "Network Services History") accounts for expansion and improvements every year. In 1987 new procedures of cardiac care and chemical dependency treatment improved capacities in delivery. In 1988 and 1989 Regional Hospital administrators took over the management of the Five Counties Hospital and Nursing Home at Lemmon, on the north, and established an affiliation with the community hospital at Martin, on the south edge of West River, South Dakota. In 1989 they installed associate and baccalaureate nursing programs at Rapid City, improved air ambulance service, and initiated new medical procedures; in 1990 physician-to-rural community services; in 1991 more new procedures; and in 1992 a family practice residency program and a plan to accommodate future medical specialty needs. In 1993 Regional Hospital administrators signed management or lease agreements with Northern Hills General Hospital in Deadwood (listed as "controlled" but as a separate corporation since 1995), Custer Community Hospital (leased since 1993), and Community Memorial Hospital at Crawford, Nebraska (no longer in the network). In 1994 they signed a management agreement with Weston County Hospital and Nursing Home in Newcastle, Wyoming. In 1995 they established an affiliation with the Massa Berry Clinic at Sturgis (now listed as "owned") while they changed the relationship with Northern Hills General Hospital at Deadwood into a "controlled" affiliate and reported program achievements at the central hospital. In 1996 a management services organization invited "physicians to partner" with Regional Hospital management expertise, while administrators contracted to manage the Wall Clinic east of Rapid City. During the year 2001, Regional Hospital administrators gained relationships with the Black Hills Medical Center at Deadwood and Spearfish (listed as "owned") and the Colonial Manor Nursing Home at Custer (listed as a "leased" facility).

By 2001 Rapid City Regional Hospital administration included an official with the title Director of Networking, to whom administrators at "managed, owned or leased" facilities must report. "Employees remain employees of the local facility and are governed by their own Board of Directors," just as employees at the hospital in Rapid City were governed by the Regional Hospital Board of Directors. Its spokespersons described "methods and services" throughout the network as "clinic management, physician locum tenens, outreach clinics, continuing medical education programs, telemedicine, group purchasing, long-range planning, data processing, budgeting and cost reporting, public relations and marketing, and physician recruitment."

The Regional Hospital chronicle does not mention an added element in its service network. Both referrals from the Indian Health Service Rapid City Unit and tribal recipients of federal urban health-care support have been profitable affiliations that have contributed to the success of the network. The chronicle raises the issue of spiraling costs in health-care operations, and the corresponding need for efficiency, which were factors that inspired both the merger by incorporation in 1973 and the initiation of the network by a contract to manage the hospital and nursing home at Philip in 1985.

Overall, the chronicle provides a suitable model to represent periodic changes in the delivery of health care across South Dakota. The only anomalous feature in the Rapid City experience has been competition followed by a merger of Catholic and non-Catholic systems into a central unit that has spread its influence through a single managerial/merger network across one of two cultural regions within the state. Several other features in the West River profile stand out. One is the segregation of non-Indian health care. Nowhere in the chronicle is there any mention of a formal connection to the Indian Health Service, or even to referrals from Sioux San Indian Hospital or federally funded urban Indian health income, even though federal health service personnel vividly recall this relationship. A second is spiraling costs because of progress in physician and paraprofessional specialization and professionalization. By implication, a third is the accumulation of an aggregate annual income large enough to sustain the growth in the Regional Hospital network of facilities. The chronicle does not explore influences that have produced medical professionalism and specialization.

Across the state, the latter changes have been products of numerous national influences but, within the state, none has been more important than the training of physicians to deal with patients, which must be traced to its origin at the University of South Dakota in Vermillion. Here as elsewhere on the Great Plains, a visit by the scientist Abraham Flexner persuaded regents of higher education as well as university personnel to open a two-year medical school in 1907 for the purpose of changing a metaphysical process into the scientific practice of medicine. Thereafter, students earned baccalaureate degrees in the physical sciences while they enrolled to complete two years of classroom training then transferred to medical schools outside the state to finish requirements for their medical degrees.

Needless to say, the attraction of a faculty at the University of South Dakota and the presence of a two-year medical school inspired "Flexnerian" professionalization. Yet strategies in health care for non-Indian South Dakotans did not dramatically change before mid-century. World War II inspired a national frenzy of desire for specialization, which meant an almost excessive commitment among physicians to acquire advanced training in various medical specialties. For acute care, this change was a harbinger for improvement. To the value of family practice, it was an obvious threat, with which South Dakotans struggled through the last half of the twentieth century.

From appearances, politicians and medical personnel gave little attention to the possibility of change in the training of physicians within the state before the end of the 1960s. Since World War II, graduates of the two-year program at Vermillion had continued to move away for the completion of requirements for the degree Doctor of Medicine (M.D.). Some recipients of the M.D. degree remained out of state at medical centers to acquire advanced training in various specialties. A limited percentage returned to serve the needs of South Dakotans.

By the end of the sixties, two problems inspired consideration for the expansion of training at Vermillion into a four-year, degree-granting program. One was hesitation by most of those who graduated outside the state ever to return—especially for medical practice in rural communities. Another was concern about quality in the two-year program expressed by curriculum evaluators from the American Medical Association.

Early in the 1970s, politicians, medical personnel, and citizen groups debated relative merits in several possible solutions. One was to close the two-year school at Vermillion and seek state legislative funding for the education of physicians outside the state. A second was a formal arrangement with the University of Minnesota, which would allow greater emphasis in the program at Minneapolis but certification for graduation from the University of South Dakota—a proposal that gained little support in Minneapolis. A third possibility was the transformation of the University of South Dakota Medical School into a four-year, degree-granting institution.

American Medical Association evaluators extended their approval for the latter solution in return for a commitment to emphasize family practice, with an expectation that graduates would remain in the state for work in rural communities if not on Indian reservations. The conversion of the program began in 1974, when the state legislature approved the beginning of four-year instruction in 1975. Three years later, legislators agreed to subsidize medical students who specialized in family practice. Through the first eleven years, the four-year program produced 256 graduates, of which about fifty-one percent remained in the state. In this number, only sixty-one percent established practices at communities with fewer than 40,000 residents, and only ten percent at communities with fewer than 3,000 people. Obviously, the establishment of the degree-granting program had not solved the need for family practitioners in the communities of all South Dakotans who paid taxes in support of the operation of an expensive school to produce physicians.

Some graduates of the University of South Dakota Medical School helped to satisfy this need with dedication to rural medical practice. An exemplary family practitioner named Roscoe Dean grew up at the remote town of Wessington Springs in the Missouri hills south of Pierre. During the 1940s, he finished the two-year medical program at

Vermillion, graduated from the University of Minnesota Medical School, and trained and passed examinations to gain a specialty in surgery at a hospital in St. Paul. Dr. Dean returned to Wessington Springs, where he sustained a career at a private clinic and a makeshift hospital while he worked as a contract physician on the Crow Creek Indian Reservation. To his biographer, he explained why few followed his example. All but a small percentage of graduates would not endure long hours, accept low pay for their services, make house calls, and practice medicine in inadequate facilities. Obviously, some solution other than the graduation of physicians at Vermillion was essential.[14]

The best was the one that evolved from the 1970s to license nurse practitioners and physician assistants for work in rural communities. Belatedly, in 1994 the state legislature initiated an offer of scholarships for the training of these paraprofessional practition-ers and then added a program to attract physicians to family practice. The appearance of these three types together in small towns and rural communities required an adjustment among the users of health-care services. At a clinic in Beresford, for example, a patient encountered business cards bearing the names of nurse practitioners and physician assistants as well as the name of a person with the M.D. degree, who saw patients only one day a week. Which of these appeared in a treatment room depended on his or her availability on the day when the patient came for treatment. This circumstance alone was enough to erode the patient-doctor relationship.

More dramatic still, from the viewpoint of patients, was the appearance of strange logos in waiting rooms. These indicated that a local hospital or clinic had been taken over by some larger entity in a South Dakota urban center. Among patients, the sense that health-care delivery had turned into a game of chance was inevitable. Confidence grew at the sight of modern ground-transportation by ambulance and air-transportation from helicopter pads. Yet obvious uncertainty regarding who might provide health care, and where this would be accomplished, reinforced the sense that the days of a patient-to-doctor relationship had passed.

With their medical service in a state of flux, non-Indian South Dakotans, like tribal members, were forced to accept care from almost any practitioners they might attract. Some found "doctors" who practiced medicine without legitimate credentials, who immigrated due to the suspension of licensure elsewhere, or who came from abroad with credentials that were suspect. Because of this problem, belatedly in 1987 the state legislature required that an applicant for licensure pass an examination before gaining reciprocal certification from outside the state. Although this requirement has been help-ful, patients have been forced to evaluate the probable competence of medical personnel without much basis for their judgments.

Understandably, under these conditions, alternative medical practices have gained increasing acceptance. Fundamentalists in nearly all Christian denominations—like traditionalists among Native Americans—have turned increasingly to faith healing. One manifestation has been confidence in the value of "prayer lists" publicized at Christian sanctuaries, as in the days of pioneering settlement. Another has been the uses of anoint-ment with oil or the laying on of hands by clergy in hospital rooms as well as in sanctu-aries and private homes. Like tribal traditionalists, non-Indian Christian fundamentalists in search of alternative healing methods never have relinquished belief in the interven-tion of spiritual forces. Many rely on both systems, evidently with an assumption that personnel in clinics and hospitals need some assistance from a higher power.

Along the streets of every city in the state are signs bearing the names of chiroprac-tors, many of whom advertise their alternative methods in newspaper and television advertisements. More prominent than these scattered practitioners in the health-care delivery systems of South Dakota are the ones at Canistota.

The Ortman Clinic is a veritable institution, founded in 1915 by Amon Ortman when he first "provided chiropractic care for friends, relatives and neighbors using his farmhouse" as his "original clinic."[15] Since 1915, more than three million patients have appeared, seeking help from "a hands on approach." The Ortmans distinguish theirs from other chiropractic procedures for its application "to a patient in a sitting position. It involves a method that utilizes deep thumb pressure to the patients' "problem area" with a strategy that "conforms to basic principles of chiropractic healing." It is "effective, inexpensive, and in many cases" the "results are seen very quickly." Blood tests and urinalysis seem to be available, and "the clinic also has state of the art x-ray facilities and physiotherapy modalities such as traction, diathermy, ultrasound, and microcurrent stimulation" for use during treatments.

Publicity indicates that Amon Ortman founded this clinic "by chance or providential assignment" to develop "an art, yes, a clinical science of 'healing' by a technique and singular method of 'touching' and 'hands on.'" This strategy originated in an immigrant family of Germans with "beliefs similar to the Mennonite faith." The Ortmans entered Dakota Territory in 1874. Their Anabaptist origin explains why in the "year 2000 the Amish continue to be a significant percentage of the patient clientele." Amish have come from fourteen states—from as far away as Pennsylvania and South Carolina. For use by these as well as other patients Canistota contains seven motels and hotels.

Although the Ortmans have trained to practice medicine by the Northwestern College of Chiropractic in Chicago, their literature makes clear the point that their delivery system originated in Amon's submission to "a higher calling" and a pledge to develop and use a "God-given ability." On average every year, close to 2,000 Amish appear because their beliefs in a "natural health . . . blend with chiropractic principles." Openly, the Ortmans advertise such a blend of chiropractic treatment with faith healing.

Few clinics or hospitals in South Dakota have been open for business since 1915. Few could claim the treatment of some three million patients in the past. Doubtless no M.D. in the state could match a boast on a plaque that Dr. Herb Ortman became a "world record holder treating 429 patients in a single day." Dr. Ervin Ortman, author of the text *A Touching Story*, holds credentials that refute any accusation that he might be a huckster. He was educated at the University of Minnesota, St. Norbert's College in Wisconsin, and the National College of Chiropractic in Chicago. He is an active elder in the United Methodist Church, a moderate fixture in the spectrum of Protestant denominations, recently regarded as the United Church of Canistota due to a merger of Methodists and Presbyterians because of limited memberships and availability of pastors.

In many instances, the search for practitioners whose services cost less than those of physicians with M.D. degrees in the networks of medical clinics and hospitals might have been driven by economic need. Rising costs because of improvements in diagnostic procedures, changing expectations about the incomes of medical personnel, and increasing costs of hospitalization, coupled with needs for long-term care, assisted-living care, and retirement facilities for elder citizens without families willing to look after them, have turned health-care delivery into a maze of expensive industries. Although in theory the oath of physicians requires service to rich and poor alike, in reality some combination of insurance carriers has become a necessity for most non-Indians seeking health care. A recent debate in Congress about the need for a "patients' bill of rights" represents this dilemma as a national problem for some forty million without medical insurance, about 75,000 of whom lived in South Dakota during the year 2003. Gone are the days when a needy patient might pay for services with chickens and vegetables or even spread payments for health care over months or years without fear of a legal action, even foreclosure on a home. Gone are the days when a person indebted to the system for care could reach anyone interested in listening to his or her financial concerns. Even the Benedictine and Presentation religious orders have retreated into a disposition that vaguely resembles the apostolate that brought them into the medical business more than a century ago.

In other words, the payment of medical bills has become a mandatory responsibility of patients when they present themselves for treatment by the networks of clinics and hospitals, because health-care delivery personnel have grown accustomed to demanding evidence of responsibility for prompt payment in cash. This expectation took root because of the inclusion of an Old Age Assistance (OAA) component in the Social Security system established in 1935. It matured because of the entry of insurance companies into the process of funding during the 1950s. The expectation of prompt payment with some perks sharply grew after the introduction of federal Medicare in 1965. The anticipation of prompt and full payment for medical services became a way of life, like an entitlement, with the addition of HMOs during the 1980s. Impoverished as well as middle- and upper-economic class patients were expected to present some combination of resources along with co-payment, if necessary, to assure the payment of all medical bills in full. Delay in payments resulted in the destruction of credit ratings, at the least, and in the impoverishment of families, at the extreme.

■ Movement Toward Consolidation

Economic expectations among health-care providers inspired consolidation. In West River, the prevailing but not exclusive network has been the Regional Hospital at Rapid City, described above. In East River, two competing managerial networks have appeared. One bears the name of "Avera Health." Its role in the medical business might be likened to that of a financial holding company in a network of participating corporations. During September 2000, its literature indicated no process of evolution from hospital experience into the management of a medical network including "23 hospitals, 15 long-term care facilities, 12 assisted living complexes, 13 senior apartment complexes and 35 clinics with 31 additional satellite locations." In occupational detachment from health care itself, it controlled all of these as well as "home care agencies"; and "medical supply companies at several locations," a euphemism for a monopoly in the pricing and sale of equipment and supplies across the network. With business contracts in hand, its managers asserted authority to provide "quality assurance, legal, group purchasing and other support services" at facilities owned by various communities and other institutions. Avera managers used the term "partners" to portray their relationship with the owners of facilities in which Avera Health had little if any financial investment while assuming managerial control over a significant portion of the most profitable growth industry on the northern Great Plains.

Network managers established their central office at Sioux Falls to deal with the owners of the participating facilities, who gained representation on an "Avera Health Board of Directors" divided into several committees with responsibilities for general policies and profit expenditures. Accordingly, owners of the facilities were in a position to exercise some influence, but administration remained under the exclusive control of Avera's managers. Some of its facilities were located in Minnesota, Iowa, Nebraska, and North Dakota, but most of them were scattered across eastern and central South Dakota—and a few of them west of the Missouri River.

By far the largest and most visible component in this network was the aggregate of facilities worth hundreds of millions of dollars owned and previously managed by the Catholic Benedictine Sisters of Yankton and the Presentation Sisters of Aberdeen who, as individuals, lived under the "vow of poverty." In 1998 each group of religious women formed a "partnership" with Avera. In the year 2000 the two groups merged for the purpose of "jointly sponsoring Avera and its seven Catholic institutions."[16]

In the year 2003 University of South Dakota student Megan Kotz investigated the origin of Avera, as a classroom project, and from personal interviews learned about several causes. Benedictines and Presentations were running themselves and each other out of business in a large degree because of administrative ignorance. They agreed to a "partnership" and the addition of independent facilities under professional management. The two groups reportedly chose the name Avera because Avera rhymed with Sarah, which meant "to be well." Its logo contained a cross to represent Catholicism plus two uplifted, open hands to represent the two orders of religious as symbols, like doves, of hope. Under the title "Avera Health: Is It Just a Brand Name?" Kotz summarized Avera literature and quoted a spokesman who said his organization had no plan for expansion. It was boxed in by competition within East River, South Dakota, and surrounding provincial monopolies centered at Rapid City, Omaha, Fargo, and Rochester.

A brochure bearing the Avera logo briefly addressed "common values" it shared with the two religious orders, but it also recognized a more compelling reality. "At a moment in history when religious vocations have declined, and when health care often seems more a business than a ministry," the two religious orders formed a managerial relationship with Avera, which claimed its "ministry" to be "ecumenical, serving the health needs of all" in the interests of "all religious traditions."

During the autumn of 2000, an administrative official employed by the Benedictines, who wished to remain anonymous, clarified the rhetoric with candid explanations about the circumstance of the two religious orders. Aging Benedictine and Presentation Sisters discovered their inability to manage modern hospitals at a profit and formed a "partnership" with a corporation, which they created to take over the management of medical facilities at risk because of weak and ineffective administration. The two orders of religious retained ownership of their facilities and land, and enjoyed representation on Avera's Board of Directors, but they surrendered all control over both the employment of staff and the day-to-day administration of facilities. More than a desire to dedicate themselves to religious "ministries," it was their recognition of an inability to keep pace with the demands of medical trends yet turn a profit that forced them to surrender control over their own medical properties.

The text above describes the origins of these properties. With some changes in names, they blended with scattered facilities previously operated by others who were at risk of losing them. Avera Health literature listed elements in its administrative network by alphabetical order of place names. The city of Aberdeen included St. Luke's Hospital; Mother Joseph Manor Retirement Community, providing long-term care, assisted living, and senior apartments; United Clinic, with satellites in Bowdle and Ipswich; and Northeastern Mental Health Center, with satellites in Mobridge, Redfield, and Webster. Britton contained the Marshall County Healthcare Center, which included its hospital, an assisted-living facility, and a clinic. Burke featured the Community Memorial Hospital plus the Burke Clinic with a satellite in Naper. Corsica contained the Corsica Medical Clinic, and Colton the Kannan Clinic. Dell Rapids retained the Dell

Rapids Medical Clinic, with satellites in Colman and Garretson. Eureka contained the Eureka Community Health Services, including its hospital and an assisted living facility. Flandreau listed the Flandreau Municipal Hospital, and the Flandreau Municipal Clinic with a satellite in Elkton. Garretson had the Palisade Manor Nursing Home, which included long-term care accommodations and senior apartments. Gregory was the location of the Rosebud Family Clinic, with a South Dakota satellite in Fairfax. Howard had the St. Joseph Clinic, and Irene the Sunset Manor to provide long-term care and senior apartments. Milbank contained the Milbank Medical Center with a satellite in Wilmot. Miller featured the Hand County Memorial Hospital, which included an assisted-living facility. Mitchell had the Queen of Peace Hospital, and the Brady Health and Rehab Center, which included long-term care, assisted living, and senior apartments. Mobridge listed the Family Practice Clinic and a satellite station in McLaughlin. Parkston had the St. Benedict Health Center, which included the hospital, long-term care facility, and assisted living; and the Dakota Family Practice with satellite stations in Lake Andes and Tripp. Platte listed the Platte Health Center, which included a hospital and provided long-term care, senior apartments, a clinic, and a clinical satellite in Geddes. Salem had the Salem Family Medical Clinic, and Scotland the Landmann-Jungman Memorial Hospital and Senior Apartments.

Sioux Falls contained the largest number of Avera facilities. Among them were the McKennan Hospital; the Prince of Peace Retirement Community, including long-term care, assisted living, and senior apartments; the Cancer Institute; the Regional Perinatal Center; the Children's Acute Care Clinic; the Gastroenterology Clinic; the Gutnik Clinic; and the Midwest Psychiatric Medicine facility.

Wakonda had the Wakonda Heritage Manor, which included long-term care, assisted living, and senior apartment facilities. Wessington Springs listed the Weskota Memorial Medical Center. Hot Springs retained its hospital. Winner had the Schramm Medical Clinic.

Yankton, like Aberdeen, retained a number of facilities second only to those managed by Avera in Sioux Falls. Included were Sacred Heart Hospital; Sister James Nursing Home to provide long-term care; Sacred Heart Majestic Bluffs, with long-term care, assisted living, and senior apartments; and Sacred Heart Clinic with South Dakota satellites at Irene and Wakonda.

Some features in the network are obvious. Except for facilities at Winner, McLaughlin, and Flandreau, none existed on or near the reservations of Native Americans, inasmuch as the federally recognized tribes of South Dakota have been served by the Indian Health Service. Doubtless a half a dozen or more hospitals located in small towns would have closed without administrative intercession by Avera. Because of its network, many clinics survived and sustained satellite stations in small towns plus various facilities designed for the care of elders. Obviously, Avera managers reacted to local needs as well as to economic opportunities in a large degree because of a growing population of senior citizens.

In East River, the only alternative network substantial enough to compete with Avera Health in the burgeoning medical business has been another with headquarters in Sioux Falls, the Sioux Valley Hospitals and Health System—best known simply as Sioux Valley. It achieved approximate equality in influence as the competitor of Avera late in the 1990s by the acquisition of the Central Plains Clinic organization. The Central Plains had emerged during the previous decade as an extensive network of clinics owned and operated by physicians as a means of controlling decisions and delivering care in varied specialties without interference from administrators. It grew to include facilities

Sioux Valley Hospitals and Health System includes over 130 facilities across the state. *Courtesy Gary D. Olson.*

as far west as the Medical Arts Clinic in Rapid City, generated as much as $100 million per year in revenue, yet accumulated a debt of some $20 million. Its owners defended their autonomy for the freedom of choice during referrals—in East River between Sioux Valley and McKennan at Sioux Falls; and in West River between the Rapid City Regional Hospital and others in neighboring towns. Central Plains owners succumbed to the pressure of indebtedness, however, and sold out to Sioux Valley. This transaction not only brought relative equality of size to the networks in the state of Avera Health and Sioux Valley, but it also gave Sioux Valley an advantage in referrals—especially to the disadvantage of Avera McKennan situated nearby.

Local managers at some of the former components in the defunct Central Plains network reacted out of concern about autonomy, insisting on the right to buy back their own facilities from Sioux Valley. This became a decision by majorities of physicians at the Medical Arts Clinic in Rapid City, for example, and at the Brown Clinic in Watertown. Both groups preferred to recover local ownership and, with it, a freedom to engage in competitive referral decisions. At Watertown, too, public discussion included fear about the loss of "second opinion" opportunities for patients, because Sioux Valley already owned the Barton Clinic and Mallard Point Surgical Center and managed business affairs for the local Prairie Lakes Hospital, although it belonged to the community. In both Rapid City and Watertown, resistance to the Sioux Valley network brought into public discussion fears about the surrender of decisions regarding business hours and equipment purchases, and opposition based on resistance to the loss of a rural-medical environment. One Watertown physician remarked that "we're concerned about rural health. . . . There are decisions that need to be made here for our patients' best interests." By implication, he brought to light the previous surrender of power by local physicians to professional administrators at Sioux Falls, whose primary responsibilities were those related to efficiency and economy across the network.[17]

Soon the network centered at Sioux Valley in Sioux Falls contained 136 facilities (compared to 129 at Avera Health), including similar types. Among them, seventy-nine were located in East River and five in West River, South Dakota, and fifty-two were situated in neighboring states. Sioux Valley represented itself as "a non-profit, commu-nity-owned facility" that evolved from a (former Lutheran) "surgical hospital" into "an integrated health system" designed to consolidate former "cottage industry" facilities under one administrative umbrella to contain "hospitals, clinics, home health agencies and insurance companies" within a single network.[18] In the title of its advertisement, the inclusion of the clever colloquial phrase "building a better mousetrap" must conjure an image among prospective patients as a representation of an intention to lure them away from the other East River competitor, Avera. Evidently as a network, Sioux Valley has a profile similar to that of the Rapid City Regional Hospital. It is very different from the model fashioned like a holding company at Avera Health. Sioux Valley has acquired the Dakota Hospital in Vermillion, for example, and has assumed control over local clinics.

Yet it has two anomalous developments in its past. It bought out the Central Plains Clinic network of local facilities by absorbing a debt of some $20 million, as indicated above. Its administrators seem to have arranged various relationships with local "cottage industries" of health care. Included in the entire network are twenty-five hospitals, sixty-seven clinics, sixteen nursing homes, eighteen assisted-living facilities, twenty-seven home health locations, and fifteen pharmacies. In addition, there are twelve undefined "Prairie Crossing locations." Within the boundaries of South Dakota, in an alphabeti-cal order by facility locations, a map identifies the following: Aberdeen*, Beresford, Brookings, Burke*, Canton, Centerville, Chamberlain, Clark, Clear Lake, Dell Rapids*, Elk Point, Freeman, Hartford, Huron, Kennebec, Lake Norden, Madison, Mitchell*, Montrose, Parker, Sioux Falls*, Vermillion, Viborg, Watertown, Webster*, and Winner*. (Locations marked by the asterisk include facilities owned or managed by both Sioux Valley and Avera.)[19]

Salutary features in the networks are undeniable, but some negative character-istics are equally obvious. Both rural and urban South Dakotans have little sense of a personal relationship with health-care delivery personnel and little sense about an individual determination of who controls the care of their health or even where this might be accomplished. As compensation for "cottage industry" advantages for patients, they find in Avera and Sioux Valley as at Regional Hospital impersonal but scientific improvements in diagnostic and treatment procedures. The three networks also facilitate easy access to larger facilities beyond the borders of South Dakota. On Interstate 90, the renowned Mayo Clinic with ample hospital space exists at Rochester, Minnesota, no more than 240 miles east from Sioux Falls, and about 600 miles from Rapid City. Because of distance, many West River referrals also are directed to Denver.

In addition to the three networks of medical facilities that operate in the private sector, there exists a fourth centered at Sioux Falls that stands out for service in health-care delivery across the region. The Veterans Administration (VA) Hospital operates in a physical plant established as the Catholic Columbus College and Seminary in 1921. The bishop acknowledged its bankruptcy, during the Great Depression, before federal offi-cials seized the facility in 1943 as an infirmary to cope with an epidemic on a military base at the airport nearby. Evidently, the office of the bishop expressed no opposition when federal officials converted the facility into a veterans processing center in 1946, then into a veterans hospital in 1948.

At the outset of the twenty-first century, magnificent architecture and regional ser-vice make this VA facility into a star feature among some 1,300 VA medical facilities that comprise the largest managed-care system in the country, if not in the world: 162 hospitals, 850 clinics, 137 nursing homes, and extraneous stations designated for peri-odic medical examinations. Public Law 104-262, passed by Congress in October 1996, created a Uniform Benefits Package that is portable across the national network for every veteran after approval for VA health-care enrollment. Included are preventive services, primary health care, diagnosis and treatment, surgery, mental health and substance abuse treatment, home health care, respite or hospice care, emergency care, and drugs or pharmaceuticals prescribed by a VA physician. Through case-by-case authorization, some enrollees may also gain support for nursing-home care, non-VA hospitalization, dental work, homeless programs, adult day care, and counseling. At the Sioux Falls facility, VA enrollees find a social atmosphere which is more compatible than any that exists at private facilities, and accommodation for disability needs.

The national Veterans Administration network dwarfs the Indian Health Service system. Its annual cost to Congress for the year 2003 grew to approximately $23.9 billion to serve about 7 million of some 26.4 million potentially eligible veterans. The budget for the Sioux Falls VA Medical Center alone was $73 million. Because for two decades following an analysis in 1980, the veteran population across the country declined by eight percent due to the deaths of World War II and Korean War veterans, Congress invited all veterans to participate by the act of 1996. Soon successive military commitments in the Middle East added to those in Western Europe, and the Far East changed the profile of veterans' demographics, however, and evoked the new Department of Veterans Affairs Network Policy V23-CMO-006, dated November 23, 2002, for use through the year 2003. This invited co-management care by the VA and private doctor/providers. For all services as well as prescriptions, it imposed a means test. Category 8 veterans, with annual incomes in excess of $37,650 if married or several thousand dollars less if single, paid $7 per prescription and about $35 per doctor visit. Because of an increase in prospective veteran rosters, the VA suspended new enrollments while some enrollees waited more than six months for appointments. Federal administrators called for higher fees from veterans plus an annual enrollment fee, but military commitments abroad suggested expansion in the system under pressure from more than twenty-six million veterans and rising expectations among men and women on military duty around the world.

As citizens of the United States, all veterans enrolled in the tribes of South Dakota who are eligible for care at Indian Health Service facilities also are eligible for treatment at the VA center in Sioux Falls, and they enjoy some other special benefits. In East River at Flandreau, VA physicians appear to conduct examinations. In West River, the VA operates small hospitals at Hot Springs and Fort Meade as well as clinics at Rapid City, Pierre, Winner, and Eagle Butte and examination services at McLaughlin and Rosebud. During August 2003, editor Tim Giago wrote in the *Lakota Journal* that at least the hospital in Hot Springs "fills up with Indian veterans in the wintertime." When "winter comes and the jobs dry up" on the reservations, "veterans turn themselves in to VA facilities near the reservations."

One other facility that stands out for its excellence is the North Central Heart Institute and Hospital, founded in 1985 near the junction of I-229 with Louise Avenue on the south side of Sioux Falls. In a new facility, cardiac patients find well-trained cardiologists, nurses, and paramedical personnel using state-of-the-art equipment in a quiet and friendly atmosphere free from the bedlam that exists in most hospital environments. This new facility with a satellite in Aberdeen provides an essential service to people across the northern Great Plains region.

Changes accomplished near the end of the twentieth century mean South Dakotans no longer endure unique hardships with health care because of living in a western state. Enrolled tribal members have available two managed systems operated entirely at federal expense: Indian Health Service facilities in Rapid City and on all reservations, which supply prescription medications as well as inpatient or outpatient and referral services free of charge; and Veterans Administration facilities, which are open to all who have served in the Armed Forces of the United States. In addition, as citizens of the United States, all tribal members are eligible for Medicare and Medicaid assistance as well as state and local health assistance, as indicated by the case *McNabb v. Heckler*, and many who are gainfully employed carry private health-care coverage. An extraordinary variety of opportunities, mainly secured by a federal trust responsibility, leaves no enrolled tribal member in South Dakota without access to health care and prescription medications free of charge. This fact tempers complaints that Congress invests less in the IHS system than the average U.S. citizen spends on health care, because all tribal members are U.S. citizens, as well.

Approximately ten percent of South Dakota's population (75,000, all of them non-Indians or non-enrolled Indians) live without private insurance or guaranteed public support. The remaining eighty percent (excluding about ten percent enrolled in the tribes) must somehow pay for the costs of medical care and drugs. Among these people, many belong to a group of approximately 23,000 eligible for help from the Veterans Administration. In an aging population, a steadily increasing percentage qualifies for Medicare and Medicaid support. The rest are on their own to seek treatment mainly from three management systems: Rapid City Regional, Avera, and Sioux Valley. All three management systems are as impersonal and financially demanding as distant corporations, and all contribute to a decline in patient-to-doctor relationships.

Yet all three management systems, coupled with the Veterans Administration and the Indian Health System networks, place state-of-the-art health care within the reach of the entire population of some 754,000 South Dakotans. By the outset of the twenty-first century, no hint of frontier medical treatment could be detected at any except the most remote locations in sparsely populated counties of West River.

Rising costs placed more than half of the population at some financial risk, but the cost translated into an essential element in the economy of the state, which has been at risk because of a decline in the economies of agriculture. During the year 2003 in Sioux Falls, health-care industries sustained 9,000 jobs and more than twenty percent of the economy for an urban population of approximately 125,000. Statewide, health-care businesses provided at least 40,000 jobs and stimulated economic growth in both local and tribal economies. Increasing access to care and even rising costs represented a redistribution of funds, most of which remained in the state to buttress a changing economy.

Chapter 23
Communications

From *Columbian Centinel*, Boston, Massachusetts., on Wednesday, November 2, 1806:
By the last Mails:
　　Maryland. Baltimore, Oct. 29, 1806.
　　A LETTER from St. Louis (Upper Louisiana), dated Sept 23, 1806, announces the arrival of Captains Lewis and Clark, from their expedition into the interior.—They went to the Pacific Ocean; have brought some of the natives and curiosities of the countries through which they passed, and only lost one man. . . .[1]

The datelines at the beginning of this report reveal much about the state of communication in the early nineteenth century. What seems in retrospect momentous news took over a month to get from St. Louis to Baltimore; another week was required for the message to reach Boston and to be printed and distributed. As official postal history shows, the Post Office Department had changed little since Colonial times, except for the purchase of coaches to haul mail along officially designated post roads. Navigable waterways were not qualified as post roads until 1823.[2] The printing press, meanwhile, was not much advanced over Gutenberg's day.

The change that came in that century—and was to continue at an accelerated pace through the twentieth century—is dramatized by a comparison of the treatment given the Lewis and Clark Expedition to the news generated by the exploration of the Black Hills by George Armstrong Custer in 1874. Custer's expedition, officially to search for a site for a fort, was accompanied by a photographer and by a clutch of reporters who sent lengthy reports on the progress of the expedition by way of courier, train mail, and telegraph.

By the time South Dakota became a state, four main elements of modern communication had been established: increasingly broader distribution (initiated by more efficient printing methods), efficient mail service (initiated by the growth of railroads), virtually instantaneous telecommunication (initiated by the telegraph and telephone), realistic visual representation (initiated by photography), and data storage (initiated by telegraph and sound recording). The innovations yet to come were to be extensions and consolidations of these pioneering technologies.

This chronology of communication technology and its effects will demonstrate that, despite South Dakota's supposed geographical isolation and its undeniably low population, the state has been the beneficiary of most of the significant developments in communication and the surprising source of some of the most important innovations.

■ 1800-1889

Mail service between the coasts began in 1847, but the route was tortuous: a letter posted in New York would travel by steamship to Chagres on the Atlantic Coast of Panama, by mule and canoe through the rain forests to Panama City on the Pacific side of the isthmus, and by steamship again to San Francisco. A one-ounce letter sent by that route, a journey of several weeks, would cost eighty cents to mail.[3] Heroic efforts to accelerate mail service across the West during the mid-nineteenth century were exem-

Chronology

1836 – First mail contracts with railroads

1847 – Coast-to-coast mail service exists through Panama Canal

1870 – Steam printing press first used in Yankton

1878 – First telephone exchange in Deadwood

1886 – Linotype process invented

1890 – Color process printing developed

1902 – Rural Free Delivery made permanent

1912 – Much of South Dakota connected by telephone service

1914 – Mail delivered by automobile

1920 – Airmail instituted

1922 – First radio broadcasts in state from USD and SDSM

1936 – Turing Machine invented (early computer)

1939 – Television debuts at New York World's Fair

1940 – Radio takes off with war reports; regional talent takes off

1953 – KELO begins broadcasting

1955 – KELO begins live broadcasts across coverage area

1956 – *Pollock Pioneer* is first newspaper in South Dakota to use offset lithography

1969 – Internet begins first practical use in academic community

1972 – Electronic mail (e-mail) begins in academic and military communities

1976 – Apple markets first personal computers

1981 – IBM markets personal computers; *Indian Country Today* begins

1982 – *USA Today* becomes first national newspaper (run by South Dakota native Neuharth)

1996 – Telecommunications Act passed (anti-monopoly aspects, created mega-mergers)

plified by the eighteen months of pony-express service from St. Joseph, Missouri, to Sacramento, California—a romantic effort in communication by means of amplification of primitive concepts. What was required was entirely new means of conveying information, a requirement answered by the almost simultaneous development of railroads and telegraph systems, supplemented by the development of photography and telephony and by new printing methods.

Rail and Wire

The first mail contract was awarded to railroads in 1836, and railroads designated officially as post roads in 1838. In the 1860s mail cars facilitated the sorting of mail on the run.[4] Delivery was speeded even for "whistle stops" by the use of the L. F. Ward's catcher system, which allowed mailbags to be transferred to and from the mail car by means of mechanical arms without the train's stopping or even slowing down.[5]

Telegraph lines generally followed the tracks. Operators were typically housed in the depots, and station agents used the telegraph to account for rail traffic. At the time of the Custer Expedition, there were no rail lines crossing the Missouri River in Dakota Territory. The dispatches of correspondents accompanying the expedition and the reports of Custer himself were sent by courier to Fort Abraham Lincoln, across the river from Bismarck, or to Fort Laramie, Wyoming, with access to transcontinental mail and telegraph service.

The longer expedition pieces were rambling missives intended more to describe "the way it was" than to convey news. A (perhaps intentionally) ludicrous example of the round-about nature of these letters, collected by Herbert Krause and Gary Olson in *Prelude to Glory*, comes in the penultimate paragraph of a long piece by the correspondent of *St. Paul Press* dated August 2 and printed August 15: "Oh! I forgot to say gold has been discovered." That letter was undoubtedly meant to be delivered by mail, that is, via horseback courier and the railroad. In a much shorter piece (six short paragraphs) labeled "Special Dispatch" and datelined "CUSTER'S VALLEY, AUG. 2, via FORT LARAMIE, AUG. 8," the same correspondent provides pithy news of the death of two soldiers, the injury of two others in accidents, and this conclusion: "Gold and Silver are found in quantities that will pay. . . . From indications this is the Eldorado of America."[7] The shorter report, written at nearly the same time as the longer one, was delivered by courier to Fort Laramie together with the longer piece, but was presumably sent by wire to the newspaper, since the piece was printed the next day, August 9. Comparable examples are seen in other expedition correspondence.

Telegraph wires at that time consisted of a single strand of iron wire which handled both incoming and outgoing traffic. Messages flowed along this conduit one at a time, sometimes causing backlogs. The most sensational news of the expedition, the discovery of gold, was dispatched from Custer's camp on August 2, and was sent via Laramie. However, the *Tribune* did not print it until August 14 (albeit with seven decks of headlines, starting with "Gold!"). The *Tribune* was scooped by five days by the *Press*, as noted above. The *Chicago Inter-Ocean* lagged behind until August 27, with a shorter report datelined August 7, a twenty-day delay.[8]

The *Bismarck Tribune* redeemed itself and the reputation of the telegraph two years later when it scooped the nation on the battle of Little Bighorn. Clement A. Lounsberry, the publisher of the *Tribune*, met the steamboat *Far West,* which bore word of the massacre. He commandeered the telegraph at the railroad depot, and started to write a report about Custer's last battle, keeping the line open at times by having the telegraph operators send passages of the *New Testament*. The story, published in the *New York Herald*, ran to 50,000 words and cost $3,000 to send.[9]

Whatever the shortcomings of wire transmission or railroad mail in the Custer Expedition, they were faster than the boats, coaches, and horseback couriers that preceded them. It was clear by the time of statehood that these innovations foreshadowed a new age of rapid communication.

Boomers

The accelerating settlement of Dakota Territory during the 1870s and 1880s exemplified the extraordinary interdependence of railroads, telegraph lines, newspapers, and homesteading.

The Homestead Act of 1863 gave a great boost to the newspaper trade in Dakota by furnishing a monetary incentive. Homesteaders had to publish "proving up" notices at the cost of about five or six dollars each. Publishers saw that if they could promote a region sufficiently, they might earn a decent living. There was only one railroad line in what was to become South Dakota. The Dakota Southern Railroad had been established over sixty-one miles of track from Sioux City to Yankton in 1873. Yankton won the distinction of becoming the first capital of the enormous territory of Dakota, and the Yankton *Weekly Dakotian* (later *Press and Dakotaian* and still later *Daily Dakotan*) became the official government paper.[10]

The first railroad from Minnesota into what was to become South Dakota was to the little town of Gary, on the eastern border. The *Gary Interstate* was begun in 1878 as a branch of the Chicago and North Western pushed into the territory.[11] The paper profited from the homesteading notices and from access to outside news available from mail and telegraph at the depot; in turn the paper became a vehicle to promote the growth of the surrounding area as settlers sent copies to friends and relatives back East, augmenting already heavy promotion by the railroads; and growth provided incentive for the railroad to move even further west. This cycle repeated itself again and again during the late 1870s and early 1880s as the railroads crept across the eastern prairie. Sioux Falls, the hub of a half-dozen railroad lines, fulfilled the promise that had lain fallow since the printing press of its first newspaper, the *Dakota Democrat*, was dumped into the Sioux River during a Santee Sioux raid in 1862. In the 1870s the *Argus*, the *Daily Press*, the *Leader*, the *Pantagraph*, and the *Times*, among others, flared into existence.[12] Within a month after the first Chicago and North Western train arrived in Pierre in 1880, that city had two new papers, the *Signal* and the *Dakota Journal*, and both began to campaign for the transfer of the capital to that town.[13]

Given the obvious power of the rail lines to make or break a town, it is not surprising that the railroads often exacted a high price for routing decisions. The first railroad to extend from Minnesota into Sioux Falls, the St. Paul and Sioux City, was lured with the promise of thirty-five thousand dollars in cash and fifteen thousand worth of right-of-way and depot property.[14] Many railroads were already raking in incentives from the federal government in land grants, outright cash subsidies, and guaranteed low-interest loans.

Telephones and Sound Recording

The development of telephone service came mostly in the last decade of the territorial period and was not widespread enough to have a significant effect before the 1890s, but it was apparent to almost everyone what it could mean for personal and public communication. In 1876, the year of Custer's total defeat at Little Bighorn, Alexander Bell was still attempting to prove that his invention was not a hoax. But with some refinement, the first telephones were ready to go into service the following year. In a crucial decision, the first Bell Telephone Company adopted the policy of leasing the equipment rather than selling it. The policy practically guaranteed greater profits in the long run and remained in effect over a hundred years. American Bell's legal action against Western Union and the dozens of other companies that sought to elbow in on the telephone business secured it an edge that eventually became a monopoly.

South Dakota's first telephone exchange was established in Deadwood in 1878.[15] Other exchanges in the state followed, mostly in larger towns. In 1886 a company called the Dakota Central Telephone Lines was organized to provide service using a process different from Bell's. By 1887 the company had built exchanges in Aberdeen, Groton, Columbia, and Watertown, along with toll lines between those towns. Pressure and threats from American Bell were sufficient to drive many other independents to extinction, but Dakota Central survived to become what Doane Robinson called the "largest business proposition in South Dakota, organized exclusively by South Dakota men and conducted with South Dakota capital. . . ."[16]

As early as 1877, with Edison's famous "Mary had a little lamb" recitation, sound recording was demonstrated as a possibility, although its application in the world of communication was slow to develop. Both cylinder and disc recordings were acoustic in the beginning, that is to say, engraved by the strength of sound waves alone, rather than electronically amplified, and the machines were powered by hand, by treadle, by weights (like a grandfather clock) or by a wind-up mechanism; Edison's electric motor was waiting in the wings. By 1889 the Columbia Phonograph Company, eventually to mutate into the Columbia Broadcasting System, had been organized, and a major contributor to communications revolution was taking its first baby steps.[17] A century later, the ability to record and store data—using technology growing out of the first recording devices—became a central element in computer development.

Photography

Undoubtedly the most objective views captured on the Custer Expedition were those of its photographer, William H. Illingworth. His stereoscopic prints of the peaks and valleys in the Black Hills speak more authoritatively than poetic prose of the vistas encountered by the expedition. The photographs were distributed at the time primarily by photographic reproduction rather than by newspaper. The process of reproducing photographs in newspapers by means of halftones had been invented in 1865 and put into use in the 1870s, but did not gain wide currency until the next century. The process was essential to mass distribution of photographs, since much of the realism of a photograph depended upon gradation of tone, formerly impossible in letterpress printing. The halftone broke gray areas in a photograph into patterns of small black dots which were blended by the eye back into gray.

For the duration of the Dakota Territory, the papers, both weeklies and dailies, were in effect devoid of photographs. Readers had to settle for word-pictures, and writers were happy to oblige.

Press Innovation

Gradual improvements were made on the presses making them lighter and more easily operated: iron frames replaced heavy wooden ones, rollers or "brayers" replaced ink-soaked leather daubs for inking the type, levers replaced screws, and rotary motion gradually replaced the up-down motion for imprinting type on paper, making possible steam-powered presses. However, printing a newspaper remained highly labor-intensive through most of the nineteenth century, especially for small weeklies. Type was still set by hand, letter by letter, in flat beds, and, after being used for printing, the type was just as meticulously taken apart, sorted, and returned to the type case, both steps occupying hours. The steam-powered press, first used in Dakota Territory by the *Yankton Press* in 1870,[18] was out of the reach of many small publishers until later in the century. Someone with a farm background viewing such a contraption in operation would likely be reminded of an early farm machine—a thresher or a reaper—and, as with those farm implements, the first mechanized presses did not eliminate the tedium, but merely reduced it.

Stereotype allowed small papers to fill whole pages at a time with "boiler-plate," pre-cast blocks of type from subscription sources that furnished articles and illustrations with little or no element of timeliness. The stereotype process, an eighteenth-century innovation, involved pressing set type into soft material such as *papier maché* in order to create a matrix which could then be used to cast hot metal into blocks of type. Those metal blocks could be duplicated indefinitely. The term "boiler-plate" came to be extended to pre-printed pages, as well. Whole pages of commercial notices, consisting largely of patent medicine ads, were sold to newspaper publishers grateful for not having to set additional type to fill their pages.[20]

Quick-Draw Journalism

Stereotype in the figurative sense flourished during this era, although the call for objectivity had been made as early as the colonial period, based on the principle that unencumbered information was one requirement of a democracy. The idea was virtually swept away in the high emotions that arose before, during, and after the Revolutionary War (and in every war since). However, James Gordon Bennett made this declaration in 1835 at the founding of his *New York Herald*: "We shall support no party, be the organ of no faction or coterie, and care nothing for any election or any candidate from President down to a constable. . . . We shall endeavor to record facts on every public and proper subject, stripped of verbiage and coloring, with comments when suitable, just, independent, fearless, and good tempered. . . ."[21]

In the years between 1835 and 1874 the Civil War—including its run-up and its aftermath—once again whisked away impartiality with the contrary winds of public debate; the doctrine of Manifest Destiny was enunciated (most memorably by John L. O'Sullivan in 1839); and Indian wars fed virulent racism. Many papers in Dakota and in the country at large were openly partisan, split along lines created during the struggle over the abolition of slavery, with nameplates or "flags" that proclaimed their bias— *Republican, Democrat,* or *Independent.* Robert Karolevitz counts nineteen *Democrats,* eighteen *Republicans,* and sixteen *Independents* among the papers begun in Dakota, not to mention the less specific banners of advocacy: *Booster; Leader;* and, most simply, *Advocate.*[22] A temperance paper in Sioux Falls was initially called the *Gatling Gun,* presumably to dramatize the Women's Christian Temperance Union war on alcohol.[23] Other papers announced their slants with proclamations in their mastheads such as the one in the *Chicago Inter-Ocean:* "Republican in everything, independent in nothing."[24] In late summer of 1874, near the end of the Custer Expedition, Aris B. Donaldson of the *St. Paul Pioneer* posed the following hypothetical question: "One question, shall the grand and beautiful Eden just discovered 'well-watered as the garden of the Lord,' rich for horticulture, agriculture, and mining, be longer left as only an occasional hunting ground for the most obstinately depraved nomad that bears the 'human form divine,' and that too, when thousands through whose veins thrills the noble Anglo-Saxon, Scandinavian, and German blood demand it for their homes?"[25]

Almost all of the Custer correspondents warned of the possibility of bloody battles with the tribes at the outset of the expedition, and some were still playing upon such fears at its end, even though actual contacts with Indians were few and insignificant during the trek itself. The fears were stirred by what they were really promoting—illegal breaking and entering: breaking of the Fort Laramie Treaty and entering the Black Hills region to grab its wealth.

The Black Hills gold rush marked the start of the territory's Wild West era, for journalists as well as for the miners, cattlemen, and other settlers. Charles Collins, the editor of the *Sioux City Times* declared immediately after the return of the expedition that the Hills contained not only gold, but quicksilver, which might also be mined profitably.[26] He organized the first illegal incursion of miners into the area and capitalized on it by establishing the *Black Hills Champion* in 1877. He bragged that he had started 113 newspapers, including one in every new territory except Montana; he started another paper near Chamberlain, for which he claimed an outrageous potential circulation of 125,000; and he advocated an Irish takeover of Canada.[27] If shooting from the lip were the equivalent of careless gunplay, Collins would be the Jack McCall of the Dakota press.

Collins was not alone among newspapermen in making bold pronouncements. Ed Barker of Vermillion's *Dakota Republican* managed to call one victim a liar thirty-one times in a half-column story. The editor of the *Dakota Herald* at Yankton termed the territorial secretary, General Edwin Stanton McCook, an "ignorant, vainglorious, drunken lout, who is an eyesore to our people and a depression upon the good morals of this community."[28]

If the vitriol were limited to editorials, the partisanship and carelessness with the truth would not have been so notable, but writers of the territorial era had not mastered the knack of assuming an objective persona even in ordinary news stories. Most scribblers of the time—following the lead of such other frontier writers as Mark Twain, Bret Harte, Artemus Ward, and Ben Nye—cultivated individual styles marked by wry comment and an arch, sardonic manner.

No issue incited newspapers more than the removal of the territorial capital from Yankton to Bismarck. Territorial Governor Nehemiah G. Ordway sided with those who wanted to move the capital—including officials of the Northern Pacific—and rallied support by putting pressure on newspapers who had contracted with the territorial government. The *Yankton Press and Dakotan* bristled at the governor's moves. When Ordway traveled to the new capital in August of 1883, the *Press and Dakotan* reported the trip in this way: "Governor Ordway and his wife left Yankton yesterday for Bismarck and it is understood that he is to settle down. . . . As he has never had a home since he came to Dakota, this disposition to . . . stay somewhere will lead people to believe that he proposes to abandon the profession of a tramp."[29]

Even the issue of statehood aroused controversy, mostly on behalf of railroad executives who apparently favored territorial law over what state laws might bring. The railroads feared state regulation and taxation in the same way the early settlers feared Indian attacks. Again Ordway sided with the railroads against statehood.[30] Little wonder then that state historian Doane Robinson records the following about Ordway: "It was the prevailing opinion that he was a man of some ability, thoroughly unscrupulous. For months leading newspapers had opened their editorial paragraphs with the exclamation, 'Ordway must go!' and when the welcome news came that his successor was appointed they exclaimed: 'Thank God; Ordway has gone!'"[31]

William Randolph Hearst

Having achieved statehood, South Dakota was poised for larger leaps in communication. Many journalists who started in territorial days would go on to notable achievement in the decades following, but one of the state's most oblique contributions to journalism was also to be one of the most far-reaching.

The entrepreneur George Hearst managed to acquire controlling interest in the Black Hills' richest mine, Homestake, in Lead. Profits from the mine were poured into other investments, including the struggling *San Francisco Examiner*. His son, William Randolph Hearst, took over the paper in 1887. That, of course, was the beginning of an empire which embraced publishing, motion pictures, and politics, and which produced the most sensational journalism ever before seen. W. R. Hearst's influence continued to be felt into the twenty-first century.

■ 1890-1920

The first three decades of South Dakota statehood saw notable advances in print technology, the coming of the automobile and the airplane, and the advent of motion pictures. The technological achievements, substantial in themselves, contributed to changes in communication and in society—the rise of advertising; the struggle between sensationalism and objectivity; shifting attitudes toward race; and new political currents.

Revolutions in Print

Mark Twain bought a Remington typewriter in 1873 for $125 and used it briefly for letters. A year later his secretary typed the last half of *The Adventures of Tom Sawyer* from his manuscript, something he considered a first for an author.[32] The first typewriter, invented by Christopher L. Sholes, was obviously inspired by the piano-forte. The innovation was in arranging the type in such a way that each letter would strike in exactly the same spot while another mechanism moved the platen to the right the space of one letter and in using a lever to shift the position of the platen so the type would produce a capital letter. All typewriters for the next hundred years used variations of that system.[33]

Samuel Clemens' enthusiasm for the typewriter had been stirred in part by his having been a type compositor in his newspapering days and realizing how tiresome and time-consuming the job was. The same knowledge led to his heavy investment in the Paige Compositor typesetting machine, a venture that brought the author to the brink of financial ruin.[34]

Paige was scooped by Ottmar Mergenthaler's Linotype. Mergenthaler's process, invented in 1886, cast whole lines of type, justifying as it went, in molten-type metal molded in brass matrices, an idea inspired by stereotype.[35]

The typewriter was important enough for writers, but the Linotype was earth-shaking in newspaper and book publishing. It cut composition time to a fraction of that of hand-set type. The first Linotype in South Dakota was put into use at the *Deadwood Pioneer* in 1900, and other papers soon followed suit, using either Mergenthaler's machine or some other mechanical typesetter based on similar principles.[36]

It was the stereotype idea that made possible the first high-speed rotary press, as well as the Linotype. While early powered cylinder presses used rotary motion to imprint type, the type itself was still on flatbeds. With flexible stereotype matrices, a curved stereotype could be cast in typemetal and the curved plate placed on the rotary press. Inventor Richard Hoe contributed several improvements to the concept during the nineteenth century. Continuous roll newsprint, made almost entirely of wood pulp rather than cloth rags, was added to the formula, and the first Hoe "web" press was created. Hoe later completed the formula by designing a "rotary perfecting web press," which allowed both sides of the paper to be printed in one run.[37]

Experimentation with the teletype began in the early 1900s and eventually produced two solutions, one using a paper tape on which to type the letters (used in stock tickers and by the Western Union for messages—with the tape cut and pasted onto a form for the receiving customer), another printing on a continuous roll of paper that could be cut and read as regular copy.[38] The Associated Press first used early Teletype technology in 1914, simplifying matters for newspaper editors who formerly had to employ an operator to send and decode Morse code.[39] By the mid-1920s the familiar continuous roll machine was in use. Variations of that machine were in newsrooms until the 1960s and were adapted for printed computer output after that. The Associated Press was widely subscribed to during the early decades of South Dakota statehood, and the larger dailies in the state were able to include considerable news of the nation and of the world without maintaining New York, Washington, or foreign bureaus.

Photojournalism made rapid gains toward the end of the nineteenth century as publishers invested in the halftone process. Hearst papers and others like them used photographs, along with larger display type for headlines and dramatic multi-column layouts that "sorted" the news according to headline and story size—to pump up circulation. The cumbersome equipment used by Illingworth on the Custer Expedition was by then all but extinct; George Eastman was even marketing his famous box camera, which could be used by anyone who could aim a lens and press a button and which recorded images on rolled celluloid film. The value of readers "seeing for themselves" the faces and events in the news added to the appeal of newspapers dependent upon large, low-cost circulation to support the advertising rates that sustained their operation.

With the coming of color presses in the 1890s, the last element of modern print journalism fell into place. Hearst capitalized on color technology with the use of color cartoons, most notably by Richard Outcault, who created the "Yellow Kid," a bald, gap-toothed urchin in a yellow nightshirt. Outcault was hired away from Joseph Pulitzer's *New York World*, with which Hearst waged a constant battle. This cartoon war not only increased circulation for both papers, but also helped paint sensational newspapering ever after with a colored brush—"yellow journalism."[40]

South Dakota's small weeklies and dailies adopted the new technologies slowly and in piecemeal. Linotype, since it addressed a huge need, was most widely welcomed, and presses powered by steam and later electricity became standard after 1900.[41] Rotary presses seemed an unnecessary and extravagant expense for most country newspapers, however; and even the state's larger publications clung to older technology. The photo-engraving process, for example, was simply too costly to be used widely by most papers and was reserved for standard shots of public buildings and for head-and-shoulder portraits of key citizens and officials. Color was infrequent and true four-color photographs far in the future.

Advertising versus Circulation

In the late 1890s the New York papers—the *World*, the *Journal*, and the *Times*—all sold for one cent per copy. Even with circulations in the hundreds of thousands, newspaper sales could not come close to paying for the cost of newspaper production. However, the greater the circulation, the more newspapers could charge for advertising, because advertisers naturally wanted to get word of their products to as many readers as possible. With advertising money, in turn, newspapers could afford better writers, editors, technicians, and technology. This cycle was expressed memorably, if redundantly, by Gardner Cowles Sr., publisher of the *Des Moines Register and Tribune*, in a mantra delivered at intervals to his staff: "We must have more circulation to get more advertising to make a better paper to have more circulation to get more advertising. . . ."[42]

South Dakota newspapers were also dependent on advertising. Smaller county and village papers were limited by small populations, however, and either maintained a fairly constant size and scope or faded away. In larger population centers the dynamic of circulation and advertising applied, spurring financial growth and technological advances.

Prejudice, Panic, and Populism

Racial tension and hard times prevalent in the first decade of South Dakota statehood gave rise to strong stances, with newspapers leading the way.

L. Frank Baum, later to become author of the the beloved classic *The Wonderful Wizard of Oz*, as editor of the *Aberdeen Pioneer* called attention to the plight of the Indians by advocating their extermination on at least two occasions. An example: "Having wronged them for centuries we had better, in order to protect our civilization, follow it up by one more wrong and wipe these untamed and untamable creatures from the face of the earth."[43] Baum's case is extraordinary only in that a decade later he became the creator of an almost universally cherished book that has been interpreted as a parable of Populism.[44]

The first years of statehood brought drought, failing crops, panic, and fears of business failure. The *Sioux Falls Argus Leader,* establishing itself as the leading journal in a city full of newspapers, put an optimistic interpretation on events, promoting the city's assets at every opportunity. Editors Joseph Tomlinson, Jr., and Charles M. Day were not above dosing the populace with a panacea compounded of boosterism and disdain—disdain for Indians, for the negativism of "kickers and croakers," for homeless drifters, and for immigrants of nationalities other than English, German, or Scandinavian. During that decade populism made headway, a curious blend of farmers and laborers who saw the out-of-state corporate interests as an enemy, with special enmity reserved for the heavily subsidized railroads, whose high rates reduced or eliminated farm profits; those who felt the gold standard was foolish and largely responsible for the Panic of 1893;

and those simply dismayed at the havoc wreaked by financial depression. Dynamic Senator Richard Pettigrew, seemingly omnipresent in the doings of the age, went from Republican entrepreneur to Populist-sympathizer to Socialist. In contrast, the *Argus Leader* went in the opposite direction, switching its loyalty to the Republican McKinley in the 1896 election, and never looking back.[45]

Countering conservative views was the bold liberalism emanating from editorials written by Frederick Knowles at the other end of the state. Knowles moved from one newspaper venture to another in the Black Hills, always maintaining the most flamboyant style and radical views. In the *Lantern*, one of three papers Knowles started in Deadwood, he professed, "I sincerely believe in the teachings of the Great Socialist, Jesus."[46] Like most Populists, Knowles was champion of small farmers and of laborers, often bemoaning the treatment of the poor at the hands of the wealthy. In one editorial he put the blame for the death of a local girl in a botched abortion on a society that "steps in and cries 'shame' and causes the mother to kill both herself and the baby."[47] Knowles rode the crest of the Populist wave into Congress during the 1896 election, in which the Populist candidate for governor, Andrew W. Lee, also won, but the elation was short-lived. Knowles lasted only one term; Lee, who managed two terms, was blocked by a Republican legislature in his efforts to regulate railroads and to make other reforms.[48] One clear Populist accomplishment, however, was the institution of the initiative and referendum, the first adoption of the concept in the country and the brainchild of a Populist Catholic priest, Father Robert W. Haire of Aberdeen. Governor Lee hailed initiative and referendum as an expression of direct democracy.[49]

Perhaps the most complicating factor in the coverage of state and national politics at the end of the century was the Spanish-American War, often seen as the fruit of the New York newspaper rivalry between Pulitzer and Hearst. Hearst was said to have responded to the artist Frederic Remington, who had written to complain of the lack of subject-matter in Cuba, "You furnish the pictures, I'll furnish the war." Hearst denied that he used those words, but he did not seem embarrassed by the implication that he helped to ignite the flames of conflict.[50] Governor Lee did much to see that the state had a contingent of soldiers in the war.[51] Pettigrew, seeming more and more a contrarian, was one of few voices raised in the state opposing the war as imperialistic.[52] The South Dakota troops were forced to sit out the Cuban conflict, but saw considerable action in the Philippines in the extension of the war. At last dealing with the guerrilla insurrection became so unpopular in the South Dakota press that Lee demanded, and got, the return of the South Dakota contingent.

By the turn of the century, with the rising flow of the economy, the Populist tide was at ebb, and both Lee and Pettigrew were out of office. Nevertheless, the spirit of Populism seems to have haunted South Dakota politics ever since. In the new century, some of the principles of populism found their way into the platforms of Progressive Republicans such as Coe Crawford, Robert Vessey, and Peter Norbeck. Newspapers in the state had new alignments to consider, siding with Progressive Republicans or the conservative Stalwarts, along with traditional Democrats and Independents. By that time, however, political opinion was increasingly confined to the editorial pages.

The coming of journalism education might be credited for some of the changes in the treatment of news and opinion. Through most of the nineteenth century, reporters and printers for the most part "learned by doing" under what was essentially an apprentice system. In the early twentieth century journalism education was introduced in midwestern colleges and universities. In 1908 the first journalism course was taught at South Dakota State College. Colleges and universities around the state and nation adopted journalism courses and degrees and encouraged professional standards of writing and editing, although a general liberal arts curriculum was still recognized as desirable. The study of libel law, ethics, and efficient writing produced graduates who entered the field and gradually changed the practices of earlier publications.

The Second Wave

The second big land boom came in the early years of the twentieth century when the government opened for settlement reservation lands which had not been claimed by Indians under the Dawes Act of 1887. With thousands of settlers competing for relatively few homesteads, a lottery system was devised to determine who won the right to buy the land at very low prices—four dollars an acre or less. As with the earlier land boom, the railroads were instrumental in settlement, but this time they were following as much as they were leading. Newspapers boomed along with West River settlement. According to Robert Karolevitz, one crusading newspaperman, Edward L. Senn, dominated the scene. Starting with a small sheet, the *Pioneer*, in Lyman County, Senn went on to start papers all across western South Dakota, eventually becoming known as "the final-proof king" as he garnered income from the publication of homestead notices. Everywhere he went, Senn served new settlers and campaigned against outlawry, prostitution, and gambling, sometimes standing up to threats and physical assaults. As the railroads pushed across the western grasslands, Senn established an estimated twenty-five papers along the Milwaukee and North Western routes. No reliable final tally of his papers is available, but Karolevitz counts fifty papers possibly originated by Senn.[53]

Newsprint was not the only communications medium to benefit from West River boom times. Among the settlers on the Rosebud agency near Gregory was a young black man who worked hard, kept to himself, and gradually accrued more property. His name was Oscar Micheaux, to be known by the end of the century as a major contributor to motion pictures.

Motion Pictures and Racism

The most spectacular addition to communication technology in the early twentieth century had been evolving for decades, from the motion studies of photographer Eadweard Muybridge, initiated by curiosity as to whether a horse ever had all feet in the air while running (answer: yes), to the film cameras and projectors of pioneers like the Lumiere brothers and Mélies in France and Edison in the United States. The Lumieres, Auguste and Louis, specialized in real-life studies depicting trains arriving in a station or factory workers arriving at a plant. Mélies, who was a professional magician, used the invention for elaborate illusions such as making things appear or vanish or seem ghostly (using double exposure). His *A Trip to the Moon* (1902) was one of the first narrative films. Edison's *Great Train Robbery*, made a year later, introduced American audiences to the excitement of narrative cinema and incidentally introduced one of the most enduring of American film modes, the Western. But it was David W. Griffith, in *Birth of a Nation* (1915), who created a sensation with strong melodramatic content and use (and sometimes the invention) of film conventions. The work was not just entertainment, either; it sent a message, neither subtle nor gentle, which inflamed viewers for years to come and stirred racial hatreds that survive to this day. In one scene of the groundbreaking epic, a young girl is forced to leap to her death when cornered on a cliff by a renegade black man bent on assault. In another, an innocent family of whites huddles in a cabin beset by black troops; the males hold the butts of rifles over the heads of women, to keep them, if need be, from "the fate worse than death." The besieged whites are rescued, of course, by the white-robed knights of the Ku Klux Klan, galloping through the night to the accompaniment of Wagner's *Ride of the Valkyries*, in the orchestral score designated for use with the silent film.[54]

Evidence of the influence of the film as propaganda is in the resurgence of the KKK—its hate now extended to Roman Catholics, anarchists, foreigners, and Jews—not only in the South, but also in the Midwest and West. In the 1920s there were klaverns in all regions of South Dakota, with particularly strong concentrations in the southeast, at Canton and Beresford, and in the Black Hills. Crowds estimated in the tens of thousands attended KKK rallies in the Black Hills.[55] The Klan was active in Sioux Falls, as well; members were photographed in the white robes meant to instill fear in minorities.[56] Part of the irony of *Birth of a Nation* is that it would not have been so bad if it had not also been so good; the epic is endlessly analyzed by film scholars for its pioneering technique.

Oscar Micheaux, traveling back and forth across the country as a Pullman porter, came to have a special affection for the expansive spaces of the upper Great Plains. When the land lotteries opened up after the turn of the century, he entered and finally won the chance to purchase property in Gregory County. The homesteading experience became central in his life, mined again and again in his creative work. He wrote his first novel, *The Conquest*, in 1913, published it himself, successfully marketed it, and followed it with others. Offered the chance in 1918 to have his third book, *The Homesteader*, produced as a movie, Micheaux decided to reject the offer, to set up his own production company, and to do the film himself, using studios in Illinois and locations in South Dakota, near Winner. He followed that venture with three other movies in rapid succession, all released before 1920. One of them, *Within Our Gates*, was clearly conceived as a refutation of *Birth of a Nation*, using strong melodramatic situations to portray black characters as intelligent, hardworking, and victims of the bigoted whites. His work was enormously popular with black audiences, and his skills as a director and producer are recognized widely within the film community. Supremely self-confident, he continued to write and produce films for thirty more years. In all, he published seven novels and produced some forty-four feature-length films.[57]

RFD, Party Lines, Phonographs, and Airmail

After Rural Free Delivery (RFD) was instituted on a permanent basis by the U.S. Postal Service in 1902, farmers were connected to the rest of the world as never before. Among unanticipated consequences were mail-order shopping and better roads. Parcel post service was initiated in 1913, and subsequently mail-order companies such as Sears, Roebuck and Co. and Montgomery Ward and Co. capitalized on the rural market, producing the "wish books" famous in rural lore. Even before that, RFD services encouraged road building, since the Post Office would not approve of rural delivery if roads were inadequate. Rural mail delivery requirements pressured counties to produce grades, culverts, and other improvements. With the coming of delivery by automobile (1914) even higher standards of road building and maintenance were demanded. Governor Peter Norbeck contributed to the cause in 1919 by working for a state highway system.[58]

Rural telephone lines developed slowly but steadily, producing by 1912 a total of 32,000 companies across the nation involved in rural phone service, most often on party lines with up to twenty subscribers per line. Because many existing urban phone companies were reluctant to extend services to farmers, cooperative telephone companies were organized to fill the gap. Typical was the Roberts County Farmer's Cooperative, begun in 1907.[59] By 1920 telephone service had been extended to 44,000 farmers in South Dakota.[60]

An unexpected advantage to remote newspapers was the so-called "Pony" service provided by the Associated Press, which offered newspapers without telegraph lines the option of having stories dictated to their offices over the phone.[61]

In the recording industry discs had won out over cylinders as the preferred format for musical performance, but cylinder-format Dictaphones were put to use for office communication in 1907 (Schoenherr). A less well known application for recording was in high-speed telegraph transmission. In 1915 a Telefunken wire recorder, used to send messages to Germany, was seized by the U.S. Navy.[62]

The influence of air travel on South Dakota communication was less direct than for rural mail delivery, automobiles, or rural telephone service. Airmail was not officially instituted until 1918, initially making use of the planes and pilots of the Army Signal Corps. By late 1920 a transcontinental air service was in place, saving almost a full day over train delivery.[63] Although the air route cut south of the state, it could be accessed by train service to Omaha.

Women, Minorities, and War

Newspapering for years was essentially a man's game, and a rough one at that. Male compositors were famous for their hard-drinking, tobacco-chewing ways. In a letter written to her future husband, newspaperman Joseph Gossage, Alice Bower said she could hardly believe that he did not drink: "Drinking and chewing have been the greatest trouble with which I have had to contend since I became a printer and it will be four years next Saturday since I first took up the stick."[64] The stick she writes of taking up is, of course, the type stick, used in the hand-composition of type. Alice Gossage was born Bower, the family of *The Family Band* fame, but at age sixteen she announced to her father her intention of making a career in newspapering. Despite her father's objections, she and a friend began the time-honored trade of typesetting at the *Vermillion Standard*, and she worked her way up to occasional reporting. She married Joseph Gossage in June of 1882, and the two started working together on the paper that was to become the *Daily Rapid City Journal*. As her husband's health foundered, Alice became the real power behind the paper, stamping it with her own crusading zeal for charitable works, temperance, and women's suffrage. In her columns and editing Alice challenged local officials, insisting, for example, that juvenile offenders not be named in order to give them a chance to rehabilitate. Her tough-love style prevailed at the *Journal* into the 1920s.[65]

Gradually, women became familiar figures in newspapers across South Dakota, working primarily on the technical side at first, as hand typesetters and later as Linotype operators, then working up to reporting and editing. There were many couples, as well, who followed in the footsteps of Joe and Alice Gossage, establishing husband-wife teams that ran newspapers. Many women wrote popular columns. Eventually old bars against newspaperwomen dropped away, and women came to make an equal claim on the profession.[66]

Editor Alice Gossage crusaded for temperance, women's suffrage, and charitable works in the *Daily Rapid City Journal*. *Courtesy* Rapid City Journal.

Indians in the state were only sparsely represented in the newspaper business. Boys on the Pine Ridge Reservation were trained in presswork in the years after statehood, but no papers expressly by or for Indians emerged, as had been the case with the Cherokee Nation in Oklahoma.[67]

Foreign-language newspapers had been relatively plentiful in the state from early times. Papers catering to Scandinavian, Dutch, and German settlers included the *Vesterheimen* at Flandreau, the *Folkebladet* and the *Dakota Deutsche Zeitung* in Sioux Falls, the *Dakota Freie Presse* and the *Dakota Post* at Yankton, the *Dakota Volksblatt* at Parkston, the *Newe Deutsche Presse* in Aberdeen, and *De Nederlandsche Dakotan* at New Holland. German-language papers were particularly popular up to World War I.[68]

South Dakota responded to the war with Germany by turning against the Germans in their midst, and newspapers were not spared. The Espionage Act of 1917 authorized the denial of mailing privileges to any publication considered seditious or treasonable. Raids in Aberdeen and arrests in Sioux Falls led to the snuffing out of most German language papers. By the early 1920s, only one remained.[69]

■ 1921-1950

The changes taking place following the first world war were so extreme as to mark each decade with its own special brand: the Roaring Twenties, the Dirty Thirties, and the Warring Forties. There was one communications medium that tied them all together, however, and quickly mounted to its Golden Age in those three decades before being bested by the advent of television. South Dakota boasted its own pioneers in the new medium of radio, and was affected in ways peculiar to the region.

The Wireless Voice

Radio telephony got a stuttering start in South Dakota during the 1920s. In 1922 WEAJ, later to become KUSD, began broadcasting from the University of South Dakota in Vermillion and WCAT began broadcasting from the School of Mines in Rapid City. Most experts believe these two academic stations virtually tied for the distinction of becoming the first in the state. The *Argus Leader* began WFAT in Sioux Falls later in the same year almost simultaneously with the beginning of on-again, off-again operation of WNAX in Yankton.[70] By November the market and weather reports were being broadcast nightly.[71] A year later the WFAT equipment was sold to Columbus College in Sioux Falls, a Catholic institution. The school continued intermittent broadcasting until 1926, when the equipment and the license were transferred to new owners. The WNAX license was purchased by Gurney Seed and Nursery Company in 1926, as well. With these purchases, the groundwork was laid for South Dakota broadcasting legends.

Much of the popularity of WNAX early on came from a large staff of entertainers like George B. German, "Happy Jack" O'Malley, Lawrence Welk and his Honolulu Fruit Gum Orchestra, and the aggregate of musicians on the "Saturday Night Missouri Valley Barn Dance." The station's investment in musical talent derived from the fact that pre-electronic musical recordings were unsuitable for broadcast. Rural listeners liked WNAX reports of weather, news, and markets. Chan Gurney became the chief announcer at WNAX, and the exposure eventually landed him a U.S. Senate seat.[72] His father, Deloss Butler Gurney, also took his turn at the microphone, delivering the equivalent of newspaper editorials.[73] Since batteries could be used for radio reception, even the most remote rural farm or ranch could pick up the station's signals before the coming of rural electrification. Letters and telegrams poured into the station expressing gratitude.

Programming on the Sioux Falls station KSOO at first was not much different from what WNAX offered, although with perhaps less emphasis on farm matters.[74] In addition to news, weather, and sports scores, occasional live local sports events were aired.[75] KSOO, by then under the management of Morton Henkin, faced difficulties WNAX avoided: because of low wattage and static generated by electric trolleys and other sources in the city, the KSOO signal was often difficult to pick up even in town.[76] Increases in power to 250, 500, and then to 2,500 watts, along with some frequency shifts mandated by the newly-created Federal Radio Commission (FRC), helped to solve technical problems and to boost listenership.[77]

During the Depression years of the 1930s radio came into its own. It was "free," for one thing, paid for by advertising. Moreover, the medium seemed capable of projecting personalities in such a way that the audience came to feel as though the disembodied voices were like friends or neighbors. Franklin D. Roosevelt capitalized on his distinctive delivery in defeating Herbert Hoover—whose no-nonsense monotone was no match. Roosevelt went on to ease the country through hard times and threats of world conflict with his "fireside chats." Entertainers became beloved celebrities, Will Rogers, for example, by way of his radio broadcasts, along with his motion pictures and newspaper columns.

The negative potential of the medium became apparent in the 1930s with the insidious broadcasts of Father Charles E. Coughlin and Huey Long. Coughlin, who championed a radical monetary policy, was a Roosevelt supporter early on, but by 1936 he was calling the president "the great betrayer and liar" and "Franklin Double-Crossing Roosevelt."[78] Coughlin seemed in the end to espouse the anti-semitic ideas being sown by Hitler and Mussolini. Huey Long, who built up his political base in Louisiana with down-home demagoguery, brought his "share-the-wealth" ideas to the nation by way of the radio networks; these ideas included limiting income to one million dollars per person per year and using the surplus to give each poor family, among other things, a radio.[79]

During the Great Depression, WNAX-owner Deloss Butler Gurney positioned himself as a champion of the farmer, opposing oleomargarine and beating the drum for low-cost gasoline, going so far as to start his own Fair Price gasoline outlets.[80] In the mid-1930s the station built a new transmitter, boosted its power to 5,000 watts, and became affiliated with the Columbia Broadcasting System. By the end of the decade, however, the Gurneys had relinquished ownership.[81]

Verl Thomson, off and on at KSOO since WFAT days, started a "man-on-the-street" broadcast in the late 1930s; "Granada Radio Theater" (highlights of films); and "The World Parade," in which he dramatized news events.[82] Among the many musicians featured on the station during this time was accordionist Myron Floren.[83] KSOO acquired a license for a new station, KELO, in 1936 in order to serve nighttime listeners. In 1937 the stations became affiliated with the National Broadcasting Company, with KSOO broadcasting network shows during the day and KELO using the network's evening programming.[84] Live programming decreased and better sound recording encouraged the use of records and transcriptions.

The war years of the 1940s saw in many ways the culmination of the radio medium. War reports from overseas brought World War II into South Dakota homes. Newscasters such as Edward R. Murrow, William Shirer, and Eric Sevareid delivered reports via shortwave on military and political maneuvering.

The late 1930s and the 1940s brought to prominence outstanding regional talent, as well. Ray Loftesness, for example, began his Holiday Inn broadcasts of Christmas music

Wynn Speece was one of the most recognizable voices on radio in South Dakota. For generations she was "The Neighbor Lady" on pioneer station WNAX in Yankton. From 1941 on, she brought companionship and household hints to listeners across a wide area of the northern plains. *Courtesy Wynn Speece.*

for KSOO. Loftesness was a musicologist as well as a mellow-voiced announcer, and he interspersed recorded carols and popular songs with entertaining stories of the origins of the music he played. Wynn Speece started her long career as "The Neighbor Lady" on WNAX in 1941. The show featured a mixture of recipes, ad-libbed chat, and household hints. Her following grew to include fans in South Dakota, Nebraska, and parts of Iowa, Minnesota, North Dakota, Kansas, Missouri, and even Canada.[85] Dave Dedrick and others getting a start in radio during the 1940s would go on to became pioneers in television.

In 1943 the Federal Communications Commission (FCC), which had replaced the FRC in 1934, ruled that one owner could not have two radio stations in the same community. The Henkins sold KELO, which eventually moved into separate quarters and went on to launch empires of its own.

The importance of radio communications by the time of World War II was brought home when Sioux Falls became the site for a training school for radiomen of the Army Air Corps (later the Air Force). Trainees virtually doubled the populations of the city during the war.

After the war, Frequency Modulation (FM), offering low interference and high fidelity at the expense of signal range, elicited great interest, and some postwar receivers included FM capability. Anyone buying such a set in South Dakota, however, would find little or nothing to listen to on the FM band. There were no FM broadcasters in the state by the end of the decade. In fact, there were relatively few AM (Amplitude Modulation) stations in the state. On the listener level, the growth of radio was staggering: some 2.5 million radio sets in the U.S. by 1924. Ten years later radio sets were found in half the homes in the country.[86] By the late 1940s, radio receivers were all but ubiquitous, found in farm houses and barns; city living rooms, kitchens, and bedrooms; carried in portable form to parks and beaches; and a permanent fixture in automobiles.

The Competition

Earlier media were challenged by the rise of radio but survived by drawing on their own inherent appeal augmented by new technology. Newspapers could not match broadcasting's instantaneous reports, even with wire services, but they could offer more complete coverage, including halftone photography and wire photos. Motion pictures had a whole arsenal of innovations to rival radio's appeal: documentaries and newsreels, Technicolor, sound, and, at the movie-house level, special promotions. Sound recording was increasingly important in radio broadcasting, and with the coming of tape recording and high fidelity long-playing records, made live entertainment on radio all but extinct.

Newspapers relaxed in time and accepted the inevitable. They published radio program schedules and reported on the rival medium. For a time the *Argus Leader* ran a radio column called "Listenin' In," written by F. H. Wulff, with items, often congratulatory, about the growth of local and regional stations.[87] Gradually, it dawned on editors that while radio triumphed in the speed of reporting, it was no rival at all in the thoroughness of coverage. Any report over a few sentences long began to sound tedious on radio; newspaper accounts could delve into details and explanations. In a newspaper, moreover, with its smorgasbord approach to news, readers could pick and choose which sections and stories to taste and which to devour whole, whereas radio's linear reporting left sorting, ranking, and emphasis in the hands of the editor or announcer. Even in areas where radio seemed to have a clear advantage—sports play-by-play, for example—newspapers were not completely cut out. Fans would listen to the game and then read the story the next day in the *Argus* or the *Journal* to examine statistics and other details that on radio seemed ephemeral.

Timeliness was not a big issue with weeklies: readers subscribed in order to find the news that they could not read or hear anywhere else and that affected them more directly, and they did not much care if the news was a few days old. The dailies acknowledged radio rivalry and met it with broader coverage, new technology, and an involvement in the great issues of the day. The news staffs of radio stations were puny compared to those built by daily newspapers, and as time progressed, smaller stations relied more and more on wire services while their news announcers, often doubling as disc jockeys, did little more than "rip and read." Advertisers were drawn to radio for its novelty and persuasiveness, but some found the time they bought on radio tenuous compared to their black-and-white newspaper displays. These shortcomings in radio news and advertising left a considerable opening for daily papers.

The Dust Bowl years found South Dakota newspapers deeply involved. The *Yankton Press and Dakotan* drew vivid word-pictures of the "black blizzards" that swept over the area.[88] W. R. Ronald, editor of the Mitchell *Evening Republican*, was so stirred by the difficulties of farmers that he shifted his allegiance to progressives Franklin D. Roosevelt and then-Senator Peter Norbeck. After Roosevelt's election and a surprising win by state Democrats, Ronald took the hacksaw to his paper's nameplate and made it the *Republic*.[89] Robert D. Lusk wrote lucidly of South Dakota's dust-bowl farmers not only in his own paper, the *Huronite* (later the *Huron Daily Plainsman*), but also in articles in national magazines. He promoted irrigation, the development of Missouri River water projects, the reclamation of dust bowl acres, and plague- and drought-resistant crops.[90] Many old-line Republican papers, of course, were at odds with Democratic Governor Tom Berry for his proposed relief legislation.

One thing that radio could not do was to show pictures to go along with the words, and newspapers stepped up their use of photographs to take advantage of that fact. Many of the technological advances had to do with sending pictures by wire, via either telegraph or telephone. After years of experimentation and sending photos by rail freight and airmail, the Associated Press adapted an AT&T process; the tag "AP Wirephoto" began to appear under cuts in newspapers across the country. The technology, going back to "recording telegraph" systems in the nineteenth century, employed a cylinder onto which a photograph was fastened, a photo-electric cell to scan the photograph as the cylinder rotated, and a similar cylinder on the receiving end to record the result. During the war years, the system made possible the appearance in South Dakota dailies of battle photos taken only hours before. Joe Rosenthal's famous shot of the raising of the flag on Iwo Jima, for example, was flown to Guam, sent by radio to San Francisco, and transmitted as an AP Wirephoto to newspapers countrywide. Only seventeen-and-a-half hours transpired between the event and the publication of the photograph.[91]

As for newspaper writing during the war, the sympathetic coverage of Ernie Pyle equalled or surpassed anything heard on radio, providing not so much an overview of the war as an "underview"—war as it looked from the perspective of the GIs who fought it. As a climax to war coverage came William Laurence's eye-witness account of the dropping of the atomic bomb on Nagasaki. Although Laurence was a science correspondent for the *New York Times*, his story was released by the War Department for publication across the county.

Despite editorial excellence and new print technology, the depression was hard on newspaper advertising. Some papers resorted to barter for advertising or circulation promotions. The war years that followed were, if anything, even worse for the newspaper publishing business, plagued as it was by a shortage of newsprint and short on personnel because of enlistments and the draft. Some South Dakota papers closed down for the duration of the war and others closed down permanently. Following the war, however, as servicemen returned, many bought or revived newspapers.[92]

As a communications medium, motion pictures offered two alternatives to radio broadcasting: documentaries and newsreels. Robert Flaherty initiated the documentary form in *Nanook of the North* in 1922, reviving an interest in "things as they are" that the Lumiere brothers had exploited at the very birth of cinema. The genius of Flaherty's approach was to string the shots together in something approaching a narrative form. His influence survives in the thousands of movie and television documentaries produced since. One such was Robert D. Lusk's *RFD '38*, produced in South Dakota as a complement to Lusk's *Saturday Evening Post* story "Life and Death of 470 Acres."[93]

Newsreels, which had been around since early in the silent era, came into their own with the talkies. Fox Movietone News, the first to use sound-on-film rather than sound discs synchronized with film, led the way in eliminating intrusive title cards. Much newsreel footage was simply shot silent, with sound dubbed in later, resulting in the voice-over narrations and the banal martial accompaniments that became clichés. News of the Day, Paramount, Hearst Metronone, RKO-Pathé, The March of Time, and Universal, along with Fox, produced ten- to fifteen-minute reels at the rate of one or two a week to be shown with short subjects, cartoons, and previews (or trailers) as a prelude to the feature motion picture.[94] Gritty black and white shots of breadlines, striking workers, whirling dust storms, and migrating refugees from the the Dust Bowl, interspersed with chin-up portraits of President Roosevelt, added up to a national memory of what the 1930s were like. Newsreel coverage of World War II stirred great interest, even though filtered through voluntary or involuntary censorship. The coverage often seemed to aspire to be upbeat, tasteful, and devoid of gore—the opposite of war itself. More objective coverage frequently suffered from being distant from the heat of action and the pain and death involved.

Amateur filmmakers contributed considerably to non-fiction movies. In contrast to the grim newsreels of the time, the artless clips assembled by amateur movie-maker Ivan Besse of Britton, in 1938 and 1939 provide a considerably brighter view of small-town life at the end of the decade. The citizens of Britton are shown smiling, self-conscious, coy, trying to hide from the prying lens, going about their daily business, going to school, or staging parades. Besse used the reels to lure local patrons into his Strand Theatre in Britton, but the films were recovered late in the century, proclaimed a lost treasure, shown nationwide on television, and even made available on the Internet.[95] The color-film images of World War II come largely from amateurs, as well.

Sound-recording technology advanced by giant steps almost equal to radio in the three decades after 1920, owing in part to the close relationship of the two media.

Records went from shellac to vinyl, from 78 rpm to 45 and then to 33.5; input went from sound-powered to ribbon microphones; phonographs went from wind-up to electric; and most significant of all, transcription went from stylus engraving to magnetic tape.

An American Army signalman, John T. Mullin, revolutionized both radio and the recording industry. Mullin was stationed in England when he became curious about how German radio stations managed to broadcast symphonies and other long classical works day and night without a break. The secret, as Mullin found out after war's end, was magnetic tape. He brought tape and some German electronic components back to the states, made some improvements, and demonstrated the product for the Ampex company and for a singer named Harry Lillis, "Bing" Crosby.[96]

Crosby was a great fan of recording innovation, owing his close-up crooning style to the sensitive ribbon microphones that emerged in the mid-1920s. The relaxed atmosphere of the recording and movie studios, where mistakes could be fixed, suited his casual demeanor, but his live radio shows, popular as they were, gave him a bad case of nerves. Sixteen-inch transcription discs at 33.5 rpm were available, but editing them required several generations of recording and re-recording on disc, with the end product often of dismally low quality. Crosby jumped at the chance to use magnetic tape to transcribe his show and to finance further development.[97] Thus was born the state-of-the-art Ampex recording machines, the 3M magnetic tape business (then under the chairmanship of South Dakota native William McKnight), videotape (first manufactured by Crosby Enterprises, Inc.), and high-fidelity, long-playing recording. Subsequently on radio networks, musical, comedy and dramatic shows were almost all pre-recorded on tape, leaving newscasters, sportscasters, and disc jockeys as the most common live programming. Magnetic tape was eventually one of the first choices for storing and recalling computer output.

■ 1950-1980

Just as radio dominated the previous three decades, television dominated the three after 1950. In South Dakota that domination was engineered primarily by one station, KELO-TV, and by one man, Joseph L. Floyd. The impact of television staggered every other medium. Perhaps the most profound upset came in newspaper journalism—offset printing and computer composition rendered the Gutenberg technology obsolete while competition with television mandated new approaches to writing, editing, and layout.

The Tube

While still a Mormon schoolboy in Idaho, Philo T. Farnsworth had conceived a way of scanning an image electronically. He eventually held more than one hundred patents related to television and won a patent battle with media behemoth RCA in the 1930s, but he did not become known for his achievement until much later.[98] Television was a sensation at the World's Fair in New York in 1939. Shortly after the fair RCA (after grudgingly agreeing to a license with Farnsworth) and other companies started producing television sets, and the first television stations were built. The war effort slowed commercial development of television, but postwar growth was nothing less than astounding. Sales of television receivers grew by five hundred percent between 1945 and 1948; the number of television stations grew from nine to forty-eight. The first news programming, such as John Cameron Swazey's weekly *Camel Newsreel Theater*, was introduced.[99]

The growth of television corresponded with the rise to prominence of Wisconsin Senator Joseph McCarthy, whose anti-communist crusade, drawing on the Cold War anxiety, at first went nearly unchallenged by the press. Gradually, journalists began to realize that it was not enough simply to report what he said without background information. By the time he was brought down by the reporting of Edward R. Murrow, among others, the concept of what constituted objective had been forever changed.

Between 1950 and 1951, TV sets in the U.S. grew to one and a half million, ten times the number of the year before.[100] As television growth took place on the east or west coasts, however, the hinterland became noticeably impatient. Since the range of TV transmission was severely limited compared to radio, many of those who purchased sets in the Midwest could see only snowy images or snow. Television was most feasible in urban areas where dense population made the medium a paying proposition; viewership was the equivalent of circulation for newspapers: both determined advertising revenue. That left sparsely populated states like South Dakota scant hope for getting in on the boom any time soon.

Enter Joe Floyd. Joseph L. Floyd moved from Minneapolis to Sioux Falls in 1933 to manage the Granada Theater, adding the Hollywood Theater later in the decade. During the war years he created a promotion called *G.I. Blind Date*, an incipient version of *The Dating Game*, as a way of getting airmen from the Sioux Falls training base to come to his theaters. Floyd took the idea to New York, where it ran on the NBC radio network for four years with Arlene Francis as host. In 1952 Floyd, by then the head of a subsidiary of the Welworth Theater chain called Midcontinent Broadcasting Co., bought KELO radio from Sam Fantle, Jr., along with the television license that came with it.[101]

After an outlay of a quarter million dollars to build an antenna, Floyd did not have enough money to pay for even one camera. However, after twenty-five years in the film business, he was able to jury-rig a cinematic solution to make possible local programming. Local news shows and advertising were shot on film, the film developed quickly through an arrangement with Harold's Photography, the raw film edited by a staff left over from the closing of the RKO distribution center in Sioux Falls, and the edited film rushed to the transmitter (by Floyd's son) for broadcast. Floyd called the process "live film," predating the familiar "recorded live" by years.[102]

Joe Floyd, once publicized as "a helluva salesman," brought television to the state with KELO-TV and created a media empire that came to include Midcontinent Communications, a television and computer cable provider. *Courtesy South Dakota State Historical Society–State Archives.*

KELO-TV began regular programming on May 23, 1953. Both shows and advertising spots were done without scripts or teleprompters.[103] Doing a weather show on film was especially tricky, since it was filmed hours before it was shown. The problem was solved by filming the weatherman pointing to various towns on a map. When the film was broadcast, Dave Dedrick would announce the temperature and conditions for each locale, synchronizing his reports with the pointer.[104] The rest of the programming was on film, as well, kinescopes of popular national programs like *The Colgate Hour*, or other specially purchased programs. The next hurdle was arranging to broadcast network shows live.

Floyd was aided in that effort, as well as in his dealing with New York advertising firms, by a promotion campaign that became famous in the industry. A photo of Floyd with a cigar clamped in his teeth ran in trade papers along with this pronouncement: "I'm Joe Floyd. I consider myself a helluva salesman. I believe I could go door to door and sell any bloomin' product ever made." Floyd later professed not to like the ad, but it opened doors.[105] In 1954 "interconnection," the rebroadcast of signals from other stations, made possible the live broadcast of network programming.[106] By 1955 the station could afford a camera, and local programming went live, with film reserved for some advertising and for remote news events. The same year Dave Dedrick's *Captain 11* went on the air for the first time. It was eventually to establish a record as the longest continuously run children's program. Other personalities—sportscaster Jim Burt and newscasters Murray Stewart, Doug Hill, Leo Hartig, and Steve Hemmingsen—became familiar faces throughout the KELO coverage area.[107]

Things were not going well for the Sioux Falls station. High wind brought the KELO tower down in September 1957. A temporary tower was erected in time for the World Series, but the collapse was the first of many that plagued the station over the years. One, a year-old 2,000-foot giant, was brought down after being struck by an airliner in 1968. A winter storm brought its replacement down in 1975.[108]

In 1957 KELO expanded into the center of the state, paying half the cost of a new station at Reliance (KPLO) and later taking over the station and tower altogether. Midcontinent also acquired KDLO in Florence, and eventually KCLO in Rapid City. These acquisitions brought new viewers in low-population areas and at the same time helped the stations dominate the market. By 1958 KOTA-TV in Rapid City was the only competition to the Midcontinent stations in the state, although licenses had been acquired at Aberdeen and Mitchell. KSOO-TV was in the building stage in Sioux Falls, as well, along with KRSD-TV in Rapid City.[109]

If there was any doubt remaining about the efficacy of television as a communications medium, that doubt was erased during the 1960s. Coverage of the assassination of President John F. Kennedy in 1963 seared visual images into the national consciousness. The Vietnam conflict was the first war covered by the medium, and the stark images and reports appearing on evening news programs have been credited with much of the antiwar sentiment growing on the home front. The country was polarized as it had not been since the Civil War. Coverage of the killing of Martin Luther King and Robert Kennedy stunned a nation already reeling from foreign and domestic violence. Live broadcast of the landing of Americans on the moon in 1969 offered some respite from a decade of troubling news.

At the same time, people started to become aware of the potential for distortion of events rendered by the television camera. Point the camera in one direction and you see a peaceful city street with people going about their business; point it in another direction and you see peace-marchers chanting and carrying signs condemning the war. Increasingly suspicious, some went so far as to claim the moon landing had been staged in a television studio. At the same time, satellite technology was starting to make possible speed-of-light global communication. Of the estimated two hundred million television sets in the world in 1968, some seventy-eight million were in America.[110]

The Watergate hearings in the 1970s, followed by President Richard M. Nixon's resignation, were given saturation television coverage. The practice of many television newscasts of counting the days Americans had been held hostage in Iran crippled President Jimmy Carter's reelection efforts.

In South Dakota, television helped to dramatize the AIM movement in the 1970s by broadcasting protests at Wounded Knee and the Custer Courthouse. AIM spokesmen Dennis Banks and Russell Means came to prominence in television interviews. So did a brash attorney general by the name of William Janklow; by the end of the decade he was governor. Increasingly people seemed to think that if it were not on television, it did not matter.

All the Rest

Radio, meanwhile, saw the de-emphasis on network programming and the rise of the local disc jockey. The rock 'n' roll revolution produced new radio formats: top-forty, oldies, soft rock, hard rock, and later talk radio. Motion pictures, now competing with "free" television entertainment, fought for a share of the entertainment dollar with more and more color, with wide-screen processes and, for a short while, with three-dimensional techniques. With the exception of rail mail service, now virtually eliminated from the communications mix, all media managed to survive in altered form, but newspapers constituted a special case.

The newspapers might have had an easier time of it if the technological foundations of the business were not being shaken at the same time. Letterpress printing, going back to the time of Gutenberg, was succumbing to a new printing process with a mile-long name—offset photolithography; and new cold-type composition and layout, eventually to be computerized, was replacing the hot lead techniques of Linotype and cast rotary plates. Offset photolithography—"offset" for short—was derived from lithography which employed a flat surface (originally a stone, or *lithos*, marked with grease pencil) instead of raised letters. Certain substances such as grease and water repel each other, so on a surface dampened with water only those marked areas would retain printer's ink. A paper pressed upon that surface would be imprinted with the marked design in reverse. The new process employed a metal sheet, the image was created by a photographic process, the plate was bent onto a cylinder, inked, and transferred, or "offset," onto a rubber roller that in turn imprinted the paper. The process did not reverse the image. Moreover, it did not require cases full of type or any kind of cast type whatsoever.

The adoption of offset ran counter to the adoption of Linotype half a century before. Smaller presses, such as those used for job printing or small weeklies, tended to adopt the process first, while large papers with heavy investments in web letterpress machines were slower to change over. Later on, the introduction of computerized typography and layout encouraged the move to offset. Robert Karolevitz picks the *Pollock Pioneer* as the first paper in the state to be published on offset presses in 1956, followed in 1960 by the *De Smet News*, the *Onida Watchman*, and the *Lemmon Tribune*. The first web (i.e., continuous roll, as opposed to sheet-fed) offset press in the state was installed by the *Madison Daily Leader* in 1963.[111] By 1980 composition rooms, which had once been noisy, dirty, and rich with the smell of printer's ink and hot lead, were quiet and genteel, the compositors busy with razor knives and rubber cement at first and later staring at computer screens. Newsrooms were similarly tamed, the clatter of typewriters replaced by the muffled click of computer keyboards.

What seemed at the time an audacious publishing experiment turned out to be an omen of things to come for newspapers in both the state and the nation. In 1952 Allen H. Neuharth, using skills he had honed as editor of the University of South Dakota *Volante*, and his friend Phil Porter, former USD student-body president, modestly promoted their brainchild, *SoDak Sports*, as "The COMPLETE weekly Sports Paper for ALL South Dakota." The peach color was lifted from the playbook of Cowles' *Des Moines Register*, which had made "reach for the peach," a byword among Iowa sports fans. When the *Argus Leader* gave the "Fisherman of the Year" award to someone who had caught a fifteen-pound Northern Pike, Neuharth pointed out that his paper and two others had reported a twenty-pound catch. "It's embarrassments like that that will cause the *Argus* to return to its former and rightful role as a South Dakota regional newspaper and leave the business of statewide reporting and statewide awards to a statewide publication like *SoDak Sports*," Neuharth gibed. Such taunting didn't help when, hamstrung by slow advertising sales, Neuharth went to the editor of the *Argus*, Fred C. Christopherson, looking for someone to take over the paper. "He just laughed at us," Neuharth says. With the venture deep in the red in 1954, *SoDak Sports* called for a "time out." The publishers promised to come back after a month, but Porter went to Rapid City and Neuharth headed south to Florida.[112] Still, there was some potency in the implied prophecy: "We'll be back."

One of journalism's greatest innovators, Allen H. Neuharth began his media career with *SoDak Sports*. His brainchild *USA Today* set the pace for a newspaper revolution leading to terser stories, more colorful layouts, and presentation geared to capture the short attention spans of television watchers. He has continued to promote excellence in journalism through The Freedom Forum and the Al Neuharth Media Center at USD. *Courtesy University of South Dakota Archives and Special Collections.*

SoDak Sports wasn't the only paper to go under during those years. In 1950 the directory of the South Dakota newspapers listed 181 papers, most of them weeklies. By 1980 the number was down to 158, a loss of twenty-three papers.

Many of the local and regional papers were being gobbled up by chains. Karolevitz notes that the decline started back in 1928 when the *Aberdeen American News* was acquired by the Ridder group. Seaton Publishing consolidated the *Lead Daily Call* and the *Daily Deadwood Pioneer-Times* in 1946. The acquisition of the *Argus Leader* by the Speidel syndicate in 1963, however, heralded an accelerating trend. Stauffer Communications followed in 1971 with the purchase of the *Brookings Daily Register*, and again in 1979 by buying the *Yankton Daily Press and Dakotan*. Freedom Newspapers acquired the *Huron Daily Plainsman* in 1980. In the midst all this wheeling and dealing, Speidel had been merged with the Gannett chain. And among the list of executives at Gannett—the president of the firm, in fact—was a name familiar to many in South Dakota, Allen H. Neuharth. In what must have been a bittersweet irony, Neuharth was now in charge of the *Argus Leader*.[113]

■ 1980-2000

By 1980 the computer had become a familiar tool in large business settings. The coming of the personal computer, however, along with the creation of the Internet, released the power of the cyber-world into the realm of personal communication. Other media might well have shrivelled away, if only in trepidation at the versatility of the beast. Instead, they made use of it. By the end of the century all the media seemed alive and well and ready to take on unforeseen roles in the future.

The Universal Machine

In 1936 a twenty-four-year-old English mathematician by the name of Alan Turing was exploring in abstract a machine that could carry out instructions given to it in order to accomplish some particular task—call it a Turing Machine. From there he moved to the idea of a machine that, incorporating mathematics and logic, could interpret and carry out any number of tasks, a machine that embodied in it the possibility of infinite numbers of other machines—a Universal Turing Machine. Today one might associate a Turing machine with a program and the Universal Turing Machine with a computer capable of embodying and carrying out infinite programs. Working on breaking German codes during World War II, Turing began to see how electronics might make his dream machine possible.[114]

Although certainly not as central as Turing, a South Dakotan by the name of Eugene Myron Amdahl exemplifies the work done in the United States in applying the computer to practical purposes. Born in Flandreau and a graduate of Augustana Academy, Amdahl earned a B.S. from South Dakota State University in 1948 and a Ph.D. in theoretical physics from the University of Wisconsin in 1952. After attaining his graduate degree, he worked for IBM, where, among other accomplishments, he was in charge of the architecture of the IBM System/360, a computer widely used in business applications. He left IBM in 1970 and founded Amdahl Corporation, which became one of IBM's major competitors, capturing a significant share of the mainframe market. He went on to establish other companies involved in the production of computer chips, central processing units (CPUs), and components compatible with IBM products.[115]

Much of the future of computers lay in self-contained desk models. The first IBM PC came onto the market in 1981 with sixteen kilobytes of user memory. In choosing a disc-operating system (DOS), the corporation turned to Bill Gates of Microsoft. Gates, in turn, went to Seattle Computer Products, which already had a DOS, and bought it for $50,000. With adaptations, that system became MS-DOS. Not designing its own DOS may have been a big mistake for IBM; it certainly was good luck for Gates, who was able to parlay the dominance of his version, used also in IBM-compatible equipment made by other manufacturers, into a fortune.

Apple computers, using different architectures and operating systems, had evolved through several generations from Apple I in 1976 through Lisa in 1983. Designed and marketed by Steven Wosniak and Steve Jobs, the machine had respectable sales, especially to schools. A breakthrough came in 1984 with the introduction of the first Macintosh. The graphical user interface, the first in the business, made possible the icons and graphic effects that later were to becomes familiar. The machine was small, with monitor and computer boards combined in one unit, had a speedy processor, and used a mouse, at that time a novelty. The point-and-click procedures were, as the jargon had it, "intuitive," and appealed to those who did not need the business-oriented programs for which the IBM was designed.

The real impetus for the use of the computer for communications was the Internet, first conceived at the Massachusetts Institute of Technology in 1962. After much experimentation in the academic community dealing with the transfer of data, the first net that approached the original concept was achieved in 1969. By 1972 electronic mail was introduced as a major application. Soon there grew up "networks of networks" which required the adoption of protocols, gateways, and routers. One of the overriding principles of the Internet resulted from the involvement of the Rand Corporation, which had been working on the problem of communication following a nuclear attack. The solution was to assure that the net was not to be controlled or managed from a central location;

that way, if one part of the net were destroyed, it could still function; in short, anarchy was built in. For politicians who would like somehow to regulate the Internet—on financial, ideological, or moral grounds—this lack of central control was to become a major hindrance.

The authorized history of Gateway, Inc., says the company was started in a farmhouse in Iowa with a $10,000 loan backed by Ted Waitt's grandmother. With the head office located in North Sioux City, South Dakota, the company built its market with humorous and inventive ads run in *PC World* and other computer magazines. The black-and-white spotted-cow shipping boxes captured national attention in 1991, and two years later the corporation went public and attained the status of a Fortune 500 company.[116] According to Rob Swenson of the *Argus Leader*, Waitt credited South Dakota's lack of an income tax and low property costs for some of the company's early success.[117] A branch office was opened in Sioux Falls, but as the company's fortune swelled in the 1990s, along with those of thousands of other computer-related firms, Gateway apparently started having greater difficulty in luring talented computer personnel to the cold and windy clime. Things were to become colder and windier in the new millennium, both for the company and for those who had pinned on it their hopes of continued economic benefits for the state.

Meanwhile, Internet service providers (ISPs), both homegrown and national, allowed virtually every computer owner in the state to "get connected." Some of the larger firms, such as America Online, powered by deep pockets and aggressive marketing, came into dominance when connections were limited to telephone lines. The demand for faster connections—Digital Subscriber Lines (DSL), broadband, and wireless—left openings for regional companies to expand. Cable television providers such as Midcontinent Communications, which had grown out of Joe Floyd's KELO-land empire, discovered particular advantages to the TV cable system already installed in thousands of homes; those same cables could be used to connect home computers to the Internet at lightning speeds. The MidcoNet online site chronicles the evolution of the firm from motion picture theaters to television to television cable to Internet provider to regional communications giant. Under the guidance of Floyd's son Joe H. Floyd, who had run film out to the transmitter in the early days of KELO-TV, Midcontinent sold the KELO broadcasting interests to Young Broadcasting, Inc., and established its first cable modem in 1996, eventually providing cable television, Internet services, and long-distance telephone service for customers in North Dakota, South Dakota, and northern Nebraska. Midco Media became the parent firm of Midcontinent Communications.[118]

Governor William Janklow was among those who saw great opportunities opening up as a result of the computer revolution. He nudged the state legislature into action on his cyber version of "no child left behind," which succeeded in wiring public schools across the state into local networks. According to a speech reported by the *Education Technology News*, Janklow hoped computer-aided education would help give the state's young people an edge in an increasingly computer-dominated world. He persuaded Cisco Systems to cooperate with the academic networking. The governor counted the gains in computer education a major accomplishment of his second administration.[119]

Dakota State University in Madison became, according to its mission statement, "an institution specializing in programs in computer management, computer information systems, and other related undergraduate and graduate programs."[120] However, nearly every university and college in the state instituted computer training; computers had become too important to ignore.

Convergence of the Media

One indication that the rise of computer communication differed from earlier media booms was the near absence of competition. Almost all earlier media wanted to make use of the new technology, not to take it on. Computerized word-processing and layout, data processing, Internet sites, computer automation, e-mail, digital photography, computer animation, and digital recording were welcomed by newspapers, radio stations, the postal service, and motion picture studios. The recording industry was the exception, and even it was conflicted. The industry had been revolutionized by the coming of digital recording and wanted to use the Internet to sell records, but worried about the sharing of MP3 music files. It was here, and in other fields concerned with intellectual property rights, that the free-for-all nature of Internet butted heads with capitalism. Passing laws against theft may be easy, but enforcing them might be a challenge—too many cyberthieves, not enough cybercops.

Among the myriad changes in communication during this period was one of particular interest to South Dakotans because it involved a native son. A national newspaper, *USA Today*, was launched in 1982 with great fanfare as something new under the sun. Still, there was something vaguely familiar to South Dakotans about the mission of the new journal; it sounded like a paraphrase of a slogan for another paper launched by Al Neuharth decades before—*SoDak Sports*—except that this time the mission was even broader: "The COMPLETE daily newspaper for ALL of the United States." Established papers—the *New York Times*, the *Wall Street Journal*, and the *Washington Post*—had expanded coverage and circulation in an attempt to appeal to readers across the country. According to Peter Prichard, however, Neuharth was convinced that none of those earlier efforts amounted to a true national newspaper. The model he had in mind was along the lines of the national papers already in operation in Australia, England, and Japan—each with circulations measured in the millions.[121] Armed with the experience of the successful start-up of *Today*—"Florida's Space Age Newspaper"—and of being in charge of a large publishing chain, Neuharth marshaled the considerable resources of Gannett in studying the feasibility of a national paper. The studies took place in an unassuming cottage in Florida, with security comparable to top-secret government projects. By 1981 the paper moved to the prototype stage in Washington, D.C., where the tactical problems were smoothed out. The launch in 1982 was the culmination of three years of preparation and millions of dollars in investment.

The new paper attracted attention and criticism for its terse reporting, its colorful photography and graphics, and its ambitious agenda. Among those who preferred the traditional expansive approach to news, *USA Today* became known as the "MacPaper," a derogatory reference to fast-food chains.

On the business side, the paper was leaking like a rusty bucket. In contrast to the sleek technology used for publication, the business offices were hampered by outmoded computers and inefficient practices. Advertisers were slow to climb aboard, many subscribers rebelled at slow or non-existent delivery, and a high return rate from newsstand sales crippled profits. The outflow decreased gradually, however, and by 1987 circulation had grown to over 1.5 million, readership surpassed that of the *Wall Street Journal*, and the paper finally broke into the black.[122] Under the editorship of Peter Prichard (1988-94), *USA Today* surpassed the two-million mark in circulation.

Another sign of *USA Today*'s success was the flattery of imitation. Papers across the country copied elements of the paper's front-page layout, its lavish use of color photos, and its large color graphics intended to explain complex issues. Even the "Gray Lady," the *New York Times*, acceded to more interesting layout and to the efficacy of graphics.

One of the paper's most copied features was the large, colored weather map that dominated a full page of weather information.

The heart of *USA Today*'s technological achievement was centralized editing and composition combined with decentralized publishing. Pages made up in Washington were transmitted by satellite to presses around the country and issued in uniform format. Although hundreds of professionals contributed to the success of the process, Al Neuharth was decidedly in charge, directing, demanding, and approving at every stage.

The benefits of the Neuharth connection to South Dakota are many and varied. The Al Neuharth Media Center on the University of South Dakota campus, a renovation of the "New Armory" funded by the Freedom Forum, houses all campus media; conference facilities for the Freedom Forum; campus offices for the Freedom Forum and other journalism organizations; the USD Department of Contemporary Media and Journalism; South Dakota Public Broadcasting; and the Native American Journalists Association. The Freedom Forum sponsors the annual Al Neuharth Award for Excellence in Journalism, which has honored such journalism notables as Walter Cronkite, Helen Thomas, Judy Woodruff, Larry King, and South Dakota native and USD alumnus Tom Brokaw. The Freedom Forum also has ambitious programs nationwide, including the Newseum, an interactive exploration of news to be housed in Washington, D.C., and a bundle of services, scholarships, and projects furthering First Amendment rights.[123]

The Freedom Forum's support of Native American journalism is indicative of the relatively recent advance of Indian media. There have been eloquent Indian writers in South Dakota and elsewhere, not the least among them Zitkala Ša (Gertrude Simmons Bonnin) who was born on the Yankton reservation in 1876 and went on to become a teacher and a writer credited with books and with articles in such magazines as *Atlantic Monthly* and *Harper's Monthly*.[124] But Indian newspapers were few, with none at all in South Dakota until 1981.

Over a hundred years after newspapermen with the Custer Expedition were calling the Indian, among kinder things, an "obstinately depraved nomad" and urging a land grab in the Black Hills on the basis of the racial superiority of Northern Europeans, there appeared a weekly called *Indian Country Today*, Indian-owned and edited, to try to set the record straight. Tim Giago (Nanwica Kciji) started the paper after a two-year apprenticeship with the *Rapid City Journal* as columnist and reporter. He sold *Indian Country Today* in 1998 and later started another paper, the *Lakota Journal*. Giago was outspoken in his editorials, in his syndicated columns, and in his books about misapprehensions about Indians. He campaigned for Indian religious rights, against the use of Indian names and mascots for sports teams, and for a clear look at the complicated dynamics of Indian life in South Dakota and in America at large. Overall, he demanded respect for Indian views, and won nationwide recognition for his efforts, including appearances on national media (Oprah Winfrey's TV show and others), a Nieman Fellowship at Harvard University, and many awards, including the H. L. Mencken Award for Journalism (returned after revelations about Mencken's anti-semitism).[125]

Giago's candid style made some people wince, as when during a celebration at the Mount Rushmore Memorial he criticized its builders: "Not only did they desecrate our sacred land, they also memorialized four presidents who committed acts of atrocity against our people."[126] The American Indian Movement did not escape his criticism, either, and AIM spokesmen have reciprocated in kind. No one person speaks for the Lakota people or for Indians as a whole, any more than one person speaks for Anglos or for blacks or for Chicanos. However, Giago has gone far in countering the casual prejudice and misunderstanding prevalent among non-Indians. He was instrumental

The founder of *Indian Country Today* and *Lakota Journal*, Tim Giago campaigned in his newspapers for Indian rights. *Courtesy Tim Giago.*

in bringing about reconciliation efforts under Governor George Mickelson and in establishing Native American Day in South Dakota in lieu of Columbus Day.

In radio communications, station KILI at Pine Ridge is Indian-controlled, but KINI at Mission is operated by the Catholic Church, with which many Indian traditionalists such as Giago have serious quarrels. An Indian presence in the media has been increasing, helped by public broadcasting's regular programs of Indian news and documentary specials and by education initiatives such as Freedom Forum's Chips Quinn Scholars. Thanks to such programs, writers with Indian background have been placed in newsrooms around the state.

Of the communications developments in the 1990s with South Dakota connections, perhaps the most far-reaching was the Telecommunications Act of 1996, the passage of which was led by South Dakota Senator Larry Pressler. One of the most salient differences separating broadcast media from newspaper publishing was the long-held understanding that broadcasting required regulation. The airwaves belonged to the public, the reasoning went, so the airwaves should be used to benefit the public. Federal Radio Commission (FRC) licensing required stations to devote a certain amount of their air-time to public-service programming. The argument for newspapers was that, because of the first amendment guarantee of the freedom of the press, they should not be regulated. When it was seen how powerful the broadcasting media could be in providing news and shaping public opinion, the FCC, replacing the FRC in 1934 with broader powers covering all telecommunications, kept one owner from controlling more than one station in a broadcast area and worked for "universal service," spreading modern communication to people in all geographical regions.

AT&T escaped monopoly regulation because of its official designation as a "natural monopoly." That monopoly was challenged by would-be long-distance carriers in the later 1940s and again in the 1970s; finally, in 1982, the courts ordered AT&T to split up the regional Bell Operating Companies—the one serving South Dakota, for example, becoming U.S. West—and to allow carriers such as MCI and Sprint to compete for AT&T's long-distance services. Since long-distance rates dropped drastically thereafter, the lesson seemed to be that competition was a good thing.

By 1996 the growth of computer communication led to a rethinking of telecommunications regulations, and the result was the first comprehensive revamping of telecommunications law since 1934. The legislation effectively wiped out most prior regulatory restrictions, both federal and state, on telephone services, cable television, ownership of radio and television stations, and telecommunication competition. It did retain, however, the power to censor obscene and violent programming on television and computer networks. Pressler, who introduced the legislation, felt justified in crowing after its passage: "Thanks to my bill, the communications industry will see an explosion in new investment and development. Who are the winners? The consumers. There will be more services and new products at lower costs. All of this economic activity will mean new jobs. Competition is the key for this development. My bill unlocked the regulatory hand-cuffs restricting the communications industry. . . ."[127]

President Clinton signed the bill willingly, citing its anti-monopoly aspects. Almost immediately, however, the ACLU and other groups began court challenges of censorship provisions. Pressler's reelection efforts in that same year possibly foreshadowed things to come. His opponent, Tim Johnson, who had voted against the bill in Congress, won the election after alleging, among other things, that the Telecommunications Act had already resulted in higher telephone rates.

Senator John McCain of Arizona was an early opponent of the bill, suspicious of the effectiveness of universal service provisions and of its supporters' anti-monopoly claims: "The 1996 Telecommunication Act has failed miserably and has left us with results that are the exact opposite of what was intended. Rather than promoting competition in the industry, the Act has led to a flood of megamergers."[128]

When in 2003 the FCC under Michael Powell proposed further deregulation of media ownership as allowed by the bill, McCain went even further. The act "should have been called the 'leave no lobbyist behind act,'" McCain said. He proposed that "stringent, but reasonable, limits on media ownership may very well be appropriate."[129]

McCain's wrath was exercised over the trend toward ever-larger corporate ownership of media, mergers such as produced AOL Time-Warner (with the AOL lopped off when America Online showed signs of losing ground to other Internet providers). According to its own online summary, the Time Warner empire includes AOL, Time Warner Books, Home Box Office (HBO), New Line Cinema (which produced, among many other films, the hugely successful *Lord of the Rings* series), Time Warner Cable (serving over eleven million customers); Turner Broadcasting (CNN, TBS, TNT, Cartoon Network, Turner Classic Movies), Warner Bros. Entertainment (the *Harry Potter* series, among many other movies), Warner Music Group (including both recording—more than 1,000 artists—and music-publishing), and Time, Inc. (*Time, Sports Illustrated, People, Entertainment Weekly, Fortune, Money*, and more than 120 other magazines with a total readership over three hundred million).[130]

All of the major television networks available in South Dakota are parts of corporate titans, according to the Center for Public Integrity and the corporations' own sources. Fox Broadcasting is owned by Australia-based News Corp., with Rupert Murdoch as CEO, with two hundred affiliates, and boasting ownership of 20th Century Fox, DirecTV, the *London Times*, the *New York Post*, the publishing firm of HarperCollins, *TV Guide* magazine, along with satellite service in Europe, thirty-five Fox TV stations, two radio subsidiaries, plus all those newspapers Murdock owned in Australia prior to acquiring U.S. outlets.[131]

NBC is part of the General Electric Corp., manufacturer of home appliances and aircraft engines, which also has CNBC, MSNBC (in conjunction with Microsoft), A&E Television Networks (controlling interest), American Movie Classics, Bravo, Telemundo, Paxson Communications, Inc., fourteen TV stations, and two hundred affiliates. ABC is owned by the Walt Disney Co., which also has ESPN (controlling interest), five film studios (including Miramax and Touchstone), two record companies, three printing companies, four magazines, ten television stations, sixty-nine radio stations, 226 television affiliates, 4,600 radio affiliates, and the Walt Disney theme parks in the U.S. and abroad.[132] CBS, with some 190 TV affiliates, was sold by Westinghouse in 1999 to Viacom Corporation, which according to its own count also controls MTV, Nickelodeon, VH1, BET, Paramount Communications, Viacom Outdoor, Infinity, UPN, Spike TV, TV Land, CMT: Country Music Television, Comedy Central, Showtime, Blockbuster,

Tom Brokaw, along with Mary Hart of *Entertainment Tonight*, has been the most visible media person from South Dakota on the national scene. The sole anchor on NBC Nightly News from 1983 to 2004, Brokaw also contributed to several specials, was a guest on talk shows and in movies, and won numerous awards for his work in television journalism. His best-selling book *The Greatest Generation* was a treatment of the World War II era. *Courtesy University of South Dakota Archives and Special Collections.*

and Simon & Schuster.[133] The Center for Public Integrity adds Blockbuster Video (controlling interest), sixty-two television subsidiaries, and 186 radio subsidiaries to the Viacom total.[134] The annual revenue of each of these conglomerates is in the tens of billions of dollars.

After the 1996 deregulation, Clear Channel Communications, based in San Antonio, Texas, started adding to its already significant holdings in the radio market, and now has some 1,200 radio stations in the U.S.[135] Complaints about this company were central in the efforts to block further FCC deregulation in 2003. The company often centralizes programming via satellite transmission, so the same programs are heard on many of its stations. The company has been criticized by the music companies for its playlist policies, and by others for its indifference to local programming. Still, the chain flourishes. The Clear Channel stations in Aberdeen had over half of the market share in that area in 2002.[136]

The degree to which media ownership affects news and public service programming is debatable. Most news organizations in networks and newspapers have a tradition of independence that is honored by the conglomerates that own them. William Randolph Hearst, however, undeniably put his stamp on the content of his newspapers. And few would deny that Fox News reflects the conservative views of Rupert Murdoch. Given the lack of motivation for giant conglomerates to endorse liberal views, the prevalence of the perception of a "liberal media" is difficult to explain.

The advantages that conglomerates have are mostly financial. In advertising products from other arms of their operations, they can promote, say, books and movies from their publishing and cinema holdings by way of their media branches and simply transfer advertising charges, if any, from one pocket to another. Conflict-of-interest statements are routinely made by news organizations in reporting on parent organizations; there are no similar compunctions on the business side.

Local affiliates maintain independence, especially in the traditional networks, but pressure to broadcast certain network shows at certain times is still felt, and local programming often has to be placed in off-hour gaps in the network schedule. Prime-time evening programming is especially sacred to the networks.

It hardly needs to be observed that the media conglomerates wield enormous lobbying clout. Considering that a good share of their billions are made from election advertising, for example, some doubt must be allowed when considering the chances of reforms which would reduce election spending.

■ The New Millennium—and Beyond

The United States approached the new millennium with jitters induced largely by the computer boom. "Y2K" became shorthand for the myriad calamities forecast for initiation after New Year's Eve 1999, many of them involving fears of a complete breakdown in computer systems resulting from the inability of older computers to register '00 as 2000 rather than as 1900. New Year's Day 2000 arrived, therefore, amid collective sighs of relief when the changeover proved largely uneventful.

That Y2K fears may have been misdirected became obvious on September 11, 2001, when the country was plunged into paroxysms of mourning. The U.S. subsequently faced a new enemy, one peculiarly abstract, called "terrorism." Because of blanket media coverage, the catastrophes in New York, Pennsylvania, and Washington, D.C., impacted the national psyche with extraordinary strength. South Dakotans watched the twin towers fall at the same instant as the rest of the country, and with the same gut-wrenching effect. That is the moment, perhaps, that the new millennium really began.

Where We Are—Where We're Going

In 2003 the South Dakota Newspaper Association represented 137 weeklies and dailies across the state, excluding some college publications. According to Band Radio. com, there were 139 radio stations in the state.[137] TVRadio World lists twenty-six television stations.[138]

Almost all media outlets also have Web sites. When one combines traditional media with computer access to thousands of Web sites, the sources of information and opinion in the state are almost overwhelming. According to one media study, Americans overall spend about seven-and-three-quarters hours a day with media, about three-and-a-quarter hours each on television and radio, about thirty minutes each with newspapers and the Internet, and twenty minutes or less with magazines.[139]

Telephone communications in the new millennium are especially interesting and particularly hard to pin down with reliable statistics. Casual observation suggests many more people are using cell phones. They even figured prominently in the tragedy of 9/11, particularly in the calls made from the airliner before it plowed into the ground in Pennsylvania. The growth in cell phone use has spurred debates over cell phone etiquette and the prevalence of cell phones as a cause of car accidents, but few conclusions can be drawn. Anecdotal evidence would confirm that driving with a cell phone pressed to the ear is dangerous. On the other hand, in 1997 a woman stranded in her car in a South Dakota blizzard used her cell phone to summon aid,[140] and an Augustana College student who was being stalked while driving on I-29 used her phone to summon authorities, who caught and convicted the offender.[141] Cell phones seem to be replacing regular phone service for some customers, but one drawback is that the cell phone customer is charged for incoming calls. Another drawback is that cell phone service is not always available, especially in rural areas. Great swaths of South Dakota are inaccessible via any wireless provider, but satellite technology could change that.

Meanwhile, business telephone service has become more and more automated, often resulting in frustrating efforts to reach a "live person." Fax is still preferred by some businesses for instances in which hard copy is needed—orders and legal or quasi-legal documents, for example; however, most computers can process Fax transmissions, and e-mail easily wins out for more casual communication.

With all the new communication technology, are people more informed? Polls are more adapted to finding out what people believe than what they know. In September 2003 polls showed sixty-nine percent of the American people believed that Saddam Hussein conspired with Osama bin Laden to bring about the 9/11 attacks.[142] This was after widespread media reporting on the complete lack of evidence for such claims. Results such as this suggest that emotions negate facts in highly charged issues. In the free-for-all of media, emotional support may be found for the most outrageous opinions. White-supremacist sites abound on the Internet, for example; and many radio talk shows encourage ideological extremes. Contradictory propaganda and persuasive advertising, abundant in all media, seems to have led to apathy, confusion, or unjustified certainty on major issues. For all the election campaigning on television in the general election of 2002, for example, just seventy-one percent of eligible voters turned out in South Dakota and fifteen percent of those of voting age did not bother to register; yet those figures are considered good compared to the country as a whole.[143]

The immediate future for communications in South Dakota seems evident, although the record of previous predictions urges caution. One thing fairly safe to say is that communication will increase. The FCC has plans to extend wireless access to the Internet to rural areas across the country. There will be more wireless phones and more communications via satellite. Newspapers and news magazines will lose ground as people turn more and more to Web sites where the very same stories may be found at no charge. There will be even greater consolidation of the media, more advertising, more miniaturization of electronic media. Technologically, there seems no end in sight, and judging from history South Dakotans will be prominently involved in the changes to come.

In the 1967 film *Cool Hand Luke*, one of the characters, a work-camp captain, had a line that became a catchword, "What we've got here is a failure to communicate."[144] The captain, of course, equated communication with submission to authority; neither he nor anyone else in the film really understood the main character's plea for justice. Some time ago it became apparent that an overabundance of information might actually result in less, rather than greater understanding. In such a situation the danger is that people will either believe anything or nothing at all, will become either sheep or cynics. Technology alone cannot help people to avoid those extremes; it cannot inoculate people against virulent propaganda; it cannot help people to make wise decisions in their own lives or in the voting booths. Complicated issues are ill-served by abbreviated summaries; entertaining trivialities detract from the essentials. The real challenge for South Dakota and for the nation is to sort through the information and opinion that is pressing in from all sides. Lacking that, there will be a real failure to communicate.

Chapter 24
Transportation and Tourism

◼ Transportation

South Dakota's landscape of infinite variety is at once a challenge to traverse and an attraction to admire. Travel and tourism weave together much of the state's history. That said, markets and technology also figure importantly into the discussion. If humans want buffalo on the hoof, pipe-quality calumet, beaver pelts, precious metals, grain, good fishing, or sight-seeing entertainment, they create a market for that resource. The most efficient means of getting to it depends on technology—walk or ride, and riding is a complicated story.

On foot, South Dakota's size and scope are intimidating. Barefoot or with hide-covered feet, prehistoric peoples drifted here in pursuit of game far more nimble than they. Historic tribes came to the region in like manner—treading moccasin-worn paths, carrying possessions themselves or with the aid of dogs using twin pole sledges called travois. First Europeans also walked into South Dakota, like Pierre Le Seuer's voyageurs probing the Big Sioux Valley in the 1680s.

In 1680 Pueblo Indians temporarily expelled Spaniards from what is now New Mexico. The date is important for Dakota Indians, because their southwestern counterparts suddenly controlled new technology—abundant horses to breed and trade. These animals greatly modified how Indians traveled; indeed, they made prairie life functionally more pleasant. Tribes ranged farther faster, enjoyed increased efficiency hunting buffalo, accumulated and transported more abundant possessions.[1] Some tribes named the horse "ten dogs" indicating the magnitude by which this animal improved travois carrying capacity. Paths became trails, cut deeper with passing hooves. When Pierre Verendrye visited Mandans in 1738-39, his party traveled on foot; when his sons returned in 1742, they got horses from the Arikara.

Rivers cut their own routes into South Dakota's landscape in a pattern resembling a leaf—the Missouri as a central stem. South Dakota tribes often saw rivers as obstacles to cross, rather than avenues to travel. Natives built what Europeans called "bull boats"—bowl-shaped craft made of supple willow branches with a bull buffalo hide stretched over them. William Clark likened these "skin canoes" to basins.[2] Expedition members built two bull boats in 1806: seven feet, three inches in diameter, sixteen inches deep, with capacity for eight men and equipment. Relatively easy for a single person to carry and stable in water, the saucer shape made bull boats challenging to maneuver. Arikara deserve credit for the first manufactured boats in South Dakota. Sioux, pushed out of Minnesota (where they used canoes), walked west. Lacking Minnesota birch bark, they did not build such craft for Missouri use.

A second canoe type, more popular with Europeans than Indians, was the dugout—a hollowed tree trunk tapered on both ends. Lewis and Clark Expedition members made six of them during the winter of 1804-05 (it took five months) and fifteen altogether (men crafted one in two days once they learned how). Thirty or forty feet long, dugouts carried four men and a couple of tons of cargo. Their excessive weight made them difficult to portage around the Missouri's Great Falls. In 1806 most of the party floated down the Missouri through South Dakota in dugouts en route to St. Louis.

Three non-native vessel types dominated early Missouri River traffic: pirogues, bateaux, and keelboats. Pirogue design varied: little more than canoes in simplest form, but always with keels. Lewis and Clark used two pirogues, thirty-five and forty-one feet long, equipped with oars, rudders and square sales, capable of carrying eight or nine tons. Flat-bottomed, keelless and "wide in proportion to their length," French bateaux (also known as "mackinaws") proved popular with St. Louis-based traders. Most measured thirty to forty feet long, eight feet wide, with six oars for rowing. More mobile than pirogues, mackinaws navigated tricky Missouri currents and sand bars with relative ease. Jacques d'Eglise probably used bateaux when he ascended the Missouri in 1790. Trappers also built them upriver out of crudely sawed planks to float down furs or hides—a single mackinaw held thirty packs of buffalo robes, for example.

Lewis and Clark's Pittsburgh-built keelboat became the largest vessel on the Missouri to date in 1804: fifty-five feet long, eight feet wide, with a stern cabin and a hinged twenty-two-foot tall mast. Loaded, the boat carried twenty-seven men (who could row, pole, or sail it), twelve tons of supplies, and drew less than four feet of water—not much, but a draft deep enough to make the Missouri difficult going in many places. It went only as far as the Mandan villages, returning to St. Louis in 1805. Keelboat capacity made it popular with fur traders between 1806 and 1831, but they paid for cargo volume in the labor of forcing the craft upstream—usually a mere dozen miles per day.

In 1831 American Fur Company's Pierre Chouteau, Jr., applied steam technology to the fur trade.[3] The company's 130-foot-long, 144-ton, side-wheel *Yellowstone* left

Chronology

1680 – Dakota acquire horses for faster and easier travel

1742 – Verendrye purchases horses from Arikara

1790 – Bateaux are used for transporting goods up and down river

1804 – Lewis and Clark make dugout canoes for river travel

1806 – Lewis and Clark build "bull boats" for river travel

1811 – Start of South Dakota tourism

1831 – Steam power is applied to river travel with the *Yellowstone*

1832 – Fort Pierre becomes docking point on river

1856 – Congress approves surveying of Fort Ridgely-South Pass Wagon Road

1867 – Col. Sawyer surveys Niobrara-Virginia City Road

1875 – Stagecoaches run between Cheyenne and Custer

1880 – Chicago and North Western Railroad reaches Pierre

1885 – Pierre has first horse-drawn street cars

1886 – Chicago and North Western Railroad reaches Rapid City via Nebraska

1893 – Panic spreads financial and economic disaster

1897 – Rural Free Delivery of mail instituted

1899 – Oldsmobile has first production car

1903 – Wind Cave National Park founded

1908 – First automobile ad in *Dakota Farmer*

1911 – Railroads peak with 4,420 miles of track

1918 – First highway in South Dakota opens

1925 – Work on Mount Rushmore begins

1926 – Permanent bridge over Missouri River

1929 – Commercial aviation in Huron

1941 – Mount Rushmore completed

1956 – Interstate Highway Act

1989 – Deadwood legalizes gambling

St. Louis and snaked up to Fort Tecumseh with seasonal trade goods. It returned with the year's collection of fur. This highly profitable trip generated another effort in 1832, when the *Yellowstone* stopped at a new post Chouteau named after himself—Fort Pierre—then continued all the way to Fort Union. Thereafter, the American Fur Company used river-

Riverboat traffic on the Missouri boomed with the discovery of gold in Montana. *Center for Western Studies.*

boats annually. They impressed natives as a "Fire Boat that Walked on the Water" and company officials with their profitability.

South Dakota served riverboats more as an avenue than destination. American Fur Company boats usually docked only at Fort Pierre between 1831 and 1855. River traffic boomed in the 1860s, however, with the discovery of gold in Montana that lured paddle wheelers 2,300 miles upriver to Fort Benton. In the peak year—1867—thirty-eight boats came through South Dakota. Many steamers stopped briefly at Vermillion, Yankton, Fort Pierre, and more frequently along riverbanks where crews cut wood to feed steam boilers or purchased ready-cut cords from "wood hawks," who earned a good living in anticipation of passing boats. Military traffic, material for Indian treaty allotments, and gold-field supplies provided more profitability than selling stuff to the mere 13,000 people residing in South Dakota.

Called "spoonbill bow mountain boats," these stern or side wheelers averaged two hundred feet long, thirty-five feet wide, and needed no more than forty-two inches of water when fully loaded—four hundred tons or forty times the capacity of a single keelboat. Steamers generally made only one trip per year since it took forty or sixty days to reach Fort Union or Fort Benton. A new boat cost about $15,000, but paid for itself in a single season because of high freight rates: $6-8 per hundredweight to Fort Union and as much as $15 to Fort Benton. Typical results: $24,000 in clear profits for the *Luella*; $42,594 for the *Ida Stockdale*.

The Missouri's capricious sand and snags took a toll. Lucky boats survived four seasons. Of 295 steamers lost on the Upper Missouri between 1833 and 1897, 193 hit snags; ice took another twenty-six; boiler explosions destroyed only six. For all their romanticism, steamboats constituted only a stage in the technological evolution of transportation. Another application of steam power—railroads—cut into Missouri riverboat traffic even as it boomed. Rails reached Sioux City in 1868. Most important for upriver trade, the Northern Pacific extended to Bismarck in 1872. *F.Y. Batchelor* was the last riverboat to Fort Benton, in 1890. Freight shipments anywhere above Sioux City stopped altogether in 1934, but a few boats operated during 1940s-1950s' dam construction.

Just as South Dakota was "along the way" for riverboats, interest in early "freighting" roads had the same justification. In 1856 Congress approved money to survey the

Fort Ridgely-South Pass Wagon Road to California.[4] It came to naught. In March of 1865 Congressional attention focused on three roads to Montana's gold fields. Funding challenges and "Indian problems" frustrated them all, although Colonel James Sawyer did get the Niobrara-Virginia City road surveyed, and between 1867-69 there was enough money to improve a route connecting Sioux City and Fort Randall with real bridges over the Big Sioux, Vermillion, and James. This road made it easier for southeast Dakota farmers to transport supplies and produce; it also put some of them to work for much-needed cash. By 1870 Congress abandoned all South Dakota wagon road construction.

Gold in Dakota Territory itself stimulated a genuine spate of heavy freighting.[5] Nothing came easily to the Black Hills in 1875. The Sioux Treaty permitted only three routes through Indian land. Bismarck (Northern Pacific), or Sidney, Nebraska, and Cheyenne, Wyoming (Union Pacific) had the nearest railway connections. Fort Pierre constituted closest riverboat access. Spotted Tail Express and Stage Company got coaches running between Cheyenne and Custer in March 1875. The Cheyenne and Black Hills Stage, Mail and Express Line started thereafter then gave way to the well-known Utah/Montana staging firm Gilmer and Salisbury. Their semi-weekly schedule (the trip took five days) soon extended to Deadwood. Gilmer and Salisbury transported most heavy milling machinery that arrived in the Hills during the first ten years. Likewise, the majority of Black Hills gold bullion found its way out via Cheyenne. Tales of outlaws and stagecoach robberies romanticized frontier travel, but did not prove a serious problem.

Dakota farmers and merchants took quick advantage of their proximity to the Hills. Fort Pierre became the favored jumping-off point for companies like Fred T. Evans Transportation, or Yanktonites Bramble and Miner's Merchants Transportation Company: riverboats to Fort Pierre, freight wagons to the Hills. By the late 1870s hundreds of men and thousands of animals kept a busy schedule. Mail tended to come by stage from Bismarck—in point of fact, the closest railroad. Northwestern Express and Transportation Company built seventeen stage stations for trips that took only three days.

Circumstances changed in 1880 when the Chicago and North Western Railroad reached Pierre. Northwestern Express dropped Bismarck immediately, and soon most Cheyenne freighters opted to work out of the South Dakota city. The Pierre-Deadwood stage line used Concord coaches, famous for their rocking leather springs. Fare between the two cities for the thirty-six-hour ride was $20.30, entitling the traveler to one hundred pounds of baggage. But freighting enjoyed only six more years of prosperity. In 1886 the Chicago and North Western reached Rapid City via Nebraska and goods came to the Black Hills in railroad cars, not behind teams of mules and oxen.

Clearly railroads had dynamic impacts on Dakota life.[6] Track cross-hatched the face of South Dakota; communities and farms filled in empty spaces. Politicians and public exuberantly welcomed railroads, often with financial incentives; but in quick reversal, the same folks then cursed them as heartless, domineering big businesses. Make no mistake, railroad companies intended to operate at a profit—extended track with every intention of making money; set freight and passenger rates with a positive bottom line in mind; abandoned lines as quickly as practical in the face of losses. In the years between laying track and tearing it up, they provided essential service.

In the fall of 1866 Yankton businessmen figured if a railroad extended to the Dakota capital, they could secure all transshipping business for riverboat traffic. They helped form the Dakota and Northwestern Railroad, got a charter from the territorial legislature, surveyed a route to Yankton, and prepared to apply for a federal land grant. Both the

In 1911, the peak year, South Dakota had 4,420 miles of railroad track. *Center for Western Studies.*

Union and Northern Pacific received generous land grants to help pay for their construction; Dakota and Northwestern officials suggested Congress continue their largess. No such luck. The proposal died in Congress in June 1870.

Discouraged, but undaunted, Yankton boosters incorporated the Dakota Southern Railroad. In lieu of a federal land grant, supporters proposed bond issues which required approval from the legislature, just recently adjourned. Pressing ahead, they finagled a special session, which authorized counties and townships to issue railway bonds. Delighted, Yankton businessmen used stock subscriptions to provide some revenue, payable in cash, land, or "sweat equity" from settlers along the proposed route who used their own teams to build roadbed. Yankton and Union county voters ultimately approved bond issues to fund construction, but Clay County's electorate proved more realistic. If a railroad ran between Elk Point and Yankton, as proposed, it would certainly pass through Clay County. Ninety-two percent of the voters saw no reason to pay for it. Nevertheless, Vermillion merchants donated $4,000 for a depot. As a quiet aside, Gary actually became the first South Dakota town with rail service when the Chicago and North Western extended track there in 1872, pressing on to Lake Kampeska the year after.

In February 1873 train service began between Sioux City and Yankton amid great rejoicing and high hopes. On the bright side, Yankton became a bit player in the Black Hills freighting business between 1875 and 1880. Generally, however, expectations went unrealized. Northern Pacific rails reached Bismarck months earlier, diverting Montana riverboat traffic. A national depression also commenced five years of economic gloom, effectively stifling railroad construction everywhere.

The sound of recovery after 1878 became the Great Dakota Boom. Ringing hammers of gandydancers laying track added to the economic symphony. Two railroads accounted for most South Dakota construction: Chicago and North Western ("the Northwestern"), Chicago, Milwaukee and St. Paul ("the Milwaukee Road"). Together, they laid three quarters of the state's track, but they did nothing together. Fierce competition drove both lines across South Dakota and into a frenzy of East River branch line construction. In time, rails probed West River ranching country, but only as solitary fingers through dirt and grass.

Demand for eastern South Dakota land sparked the boom, railroads fed it. The Northwestern moved first in 1878 out of Tracy, Minnesota. Eager settlers anticipated the railroad's arrival, staking land claims progressively westward. The Chicago and North Western accommodated settlement with stations every six to ten miles—approximately the distance a farmer could travel in a day bringing crops to market and supplies back home. In the decade after 1878, 285 South Dakota towns appeared; 142 railroad-sponsored, often in a "T" pattern, where Main Street abutted railroad track: "Along the Line in Dakota have been laid out a number of Towns in which are needed the Merchant, Mechanic, and Laborer."[7]

Northwestern crews surveyed their route in 1878 and built it the next two years, laying track to the Missouri River with towns strung along it like beads. Huron, at the James River crossing, became its hub. A new end-of-track city on the Missouri's east bank—Pierre—instantly became *the* Black Hills shipping point. Trains brought people and goods to Pierre, a ferry took them across where wagons and stage coaches served Deadwood, Lead, and Rapid City.

Also interested in securing Black Hills traffic, and promoting farms in "rich prairies," Milwaukee Road President Alexander Mitchell pushed track into South Dakota at Canton in 1879, then angled northwest across the James River at a new town named in his honor. Mitchell, like Huron, became a railroad division headquarters. In 1880 the Milwaukee reached the Missouri, where it created yet another town—Chamberlain—at best a second cousin to Pierre vis-a-vis Black Hills freighting.

The Milwaukee Road paralleled the Northwestern north as well as south. From Ortonville, it extended past Big Stone Lake during the summer of 1880, platting Milbank and other towns as it went. In January 1881 Aberdeen began attracting settlers. Within two years, the Milwaukee connected Yankton and Aberdeen. Before the Panic of 1893 railroads tied together all of eastern South Dakota. Homesteaders filled in "the great wheat, corn and cattle country"—nearly twenty-four million acres settled and a population mushroomed from 13,000 in 1870 to more than 328,000 by 1890.

Railroads also fed the rise of a new city which overtook Yankton as the state's metropolis. Between 1878 and 1888, no less than five different lines reached Sioux Falls. Water power and transportation access soon made it an economic hub. Street railways developed as an adjunct to urbanization. Sioux Falls had extensive lines, in time, but Pierre took the honor of South Dakota's first urban transportation system with a horse car line in 1885. Before long Sioux Falls, Mitchell, Rapid City, and Lead/Deadwood had street cars. Big cities electrified lines by the turn of the century, and Sioux Falls held on to trolleys until 1929, when buses replaced them.[8]

Black Hills railroading constituted its own little island. The Homestake mine operated a twelve-mile timber-hauling narrow gauge in 1881, but it connected to nothing. Northwestern track extended from Nebraska to Rapid City in 1886 and Deadwood by 1890; Chicago, Burlington and Quincy (also out of Nebraska) came in 1890. But from the east, track did not extend beyond the Missouri. Two conditions prevented this. The Sioux Treaty of 1876 reserved most West River land for natives. Closed to white settlement, devoid of gold, this land lacked markets, so railroads had no enticement to serve it. Only in the new century did lines bridge the river and cross the land.

Both the Northwestern and the Milwaukee went west in 1906. Allotment of Indian lands opened vast acreage to white settlement after 1904. Both companies built temporary bridges across the Big Muddy in 1905 with permanent ones and completed track to the Black Hills by 1907. Milwaukee officials indulged in grander aspirations—a line to the Pacific. With that in mind, they crossed the Missouri at Mobridge in 1906, heading west through Lemmon. The Milwaukee also branched into cattle country as far as Faith; similarly, the Northwestern reached north out of Nebraska to Dallas and Winner. Generally, West River populations remained sparse and agricultural receipts minimal, so neither railroad built a lattice work of track as they had East River. South Dakota also never benefited from a true transcontinental railroad, like the Union Pacific, Northern Pacific, or Great Northern. The Milwaukee Road's extension proved ill-advised—the Panama Canal opened within a year of its completion, changing Pacific coast trade and transcontinental railroad profitability.

Initial enthusiasm for railroads often diminished or evaporated altogether. Companies charged more to make short hauls and handle "less than carload" shipments than they did for multi-car through trains to Milwaukee or Chicago. On the one hand, stock holders, corporate leaders, and local employees did not see themselves as eleemosynary agents. On the other, individual farmers, small-town merchants, and residents suffered declining incomes from economic conditions beyond their control and wanted help—reduced rates. Farmers' Alliance, Populist, and Progressive politicians jumped on reform bandwagons. Like every western state, public demand for rate and service regulation flowered enthusiastically in South Dakota, usually to wither under interstate economic realities and federal pronouncements.

At its 1911 peak, South Dakota had 4,420 miles of track; after that date, abandonment set in—no one has laid a mile of new track since 1948. Companies tried to revitalize passenger traffic after World War II, with crack trains like Milwaukee's Olympian-Hiawatha and Arrow or the Northwestern's Dakota 400. Streamlined diesels replaced steam, but rail passenger service dwindled, then ceased all together in the 1960s. In 1980, as the Milwaukee tottered toward bankruptcy, South Dakota took a bold step and purchased railroad right-of-way to preserve bulk grain shipping capacity. This arrangement shook out over the next twenty years; South Dakota preserved about 1,800 miles of track operating under the aegis of eight different railroads. Dakota, Minnesota and Eastern owns 586 miles, primarily the old east-west Northwestern route; Burlington Northern/Santa Fe has slightly less, including the former Milwaukee line through Aberdeen. Other companies operate smaller segments.

New technology rolled into South Dakota on rubber wheels in the twentieth century and put an end to steel-rail domination.[9] Wagon, stage, and farm-to-market roads predated automobiles, of course, most often connecting the shortest distance between two points, allowing for rivers and coulees. But as homesteaders took up surveyed land, sections lines became logical road paths. Most evident in the flat terrain of eastern South Dakota, roads run east/west or north/south every mile—time and volume widened and paved some; others remain dirt.

National demand for better roads came first not from farmers, but bicyclists. The League of American Wheelmen began a Good Roads Movement in 1897. Better mail service interested farmers. That same year, Dakota County, Minnesota, first experimented with Rural Free Delivery. Bicycle riders and mail carriers wanted better roads and when the next technological improvement came along, car and truck owners joined the chorus.

By 1910 there were 4,962 automobiles in South Dakota. *Center for Western Studies.*

Ransom Olds' curved-dash Oldsmobile became the first production car in 1899. By 1903 Henry Ford perfected his first model while Milwaukee entrepreneurs William Harley and Arthur Davidson started making motorcycles. Who brought the initial automobile into South Dakota is a good question: some rich man's toy rather than serious transportation. In 1905, however, Redfield businessman Peter Norbeck completed a trip from the Missouri to the Black Hills demonstrating the feasibility of auto travel and the miserable condition of state roads.

On June 1, 1908, the first automobile advertisement appeared in the *Dakota Farmer*: "The Car for Country Roads." When a basic buggy cost $50, the "Rambler's" $1,350 to $2,400 price tag made it an extravagance beyond the reach of most farmers. But Model 41 came with four seats and a removable back section, leaving a flat surface to carry "farm implements and produce." South Dakota got serious about the new technology in 1910 when it counted 4,962 autos, and more serious two years later when federal dollars became available for road construction. So in 1913 legislators created a State Highway Commission, and in 1916 voters passed a "good roads" constitutional amendment. By 1918 the first eleven miles of federally funded highway opened between Watertown and Kranzburg at a cost of nearly $45,000. In 1920, 112,589 cars, 7,806 trucks (most farmer-owned), and 777 motorcycles spread out on ever-improving roads.

Auto aficionados did not wait for state or federal funding to promote travel. In 1912 enthusiasts surveyed and planned a route from Chicago to the Black Hills and Yellowstone Park; the "Black and Yellow Trail," roughly followed present U.S. 14 with alternate black/yellow/black stripes on fence posts, barn corners and telephone poles to mark the route. When the first state highway map appeared in 1922, it identified this and seven other trans-state routes: Yellowstone Trail (Big Stone City to Lemmon); Custer Battlefield Highway (Sioux Falls to Spearfish); Black Hills Sioux Trail (Sioux City, Hot

Springs, and Lead); King of Trails (Sioux City to Big Stone City); Meridian Highway (Yankton to Sisseton); and the Sunshine Highway (Yankton to Frederick). "Why drive around South Dakota on your way to points farther west?" the Highway Commission asked rhetorically.[10] That same year, the state decided to tax gasoline sales at the rate of one cent per gallon to pay for roads, and to develop a numbering system.

Like railroads, it took highways several decades to bridge the Missouri. In 1923 the legislature approved five spans across the Big Muddy, replacing twelve different ferry locations. As early as 1890 entrepreneurs had tried seasonal pontoon bridges, floating wooden structures at the river's mercy, but not until 1926 did permanent steel trestles span the Missouri. The state boasted 5,000 miles of highway that year; half graveled, a few concrete. Oiled roads came in 1931 and so did the first state highway patrol officers—two of them.

Roads got better, vehicles more plentiful, and travel times shorter with every improvement. Pressure grew for a system of multi-lane federal highways connecting states and major population areas. Under President Dwight D. Eisenhower, the Interstate Highway System won congressional funding in 1956. Initial plans called only for a route linking Sioux Falls and Rapid City—Interstate 90. South Dakota Senator Karl Mundt and Minnesota's Hubert Humphrey, who had been born in South Dakota, wrestled a bit and the South Dakota senator prevailed, with Interstate 29 the result. Senator Francis Case, also a proponent of Interstate 29, tried to get a bend or branch in Interstate 90 to reach Pierre, but died before his bill passed Congress; hence, South Dakota, like Nevada and Alaska, has a state capital without interstate access. The state has 678 miles of interstate, 83,000 total miles of highways, roads, and streets, with 772,000 autos and trucks plus 32,600 motorcycles licensed to travel them.[11]

The good news of South Dakota highway modernization has been a century of improved access to markets. The bad news has been the death of small towns. Railroad-built towns ten miles apart were convenient for 1880s horse-drawn transit. Highway transportation facilitated farther travel. Interstates made bigger cities, malls, and Wal-Marts 150 miles away reachable in a few hours. Small towns withered as improved technology changed the face of South Dakota once again.

Airplanes shrank distance and travel time even more.[12] The Wright brothers got off the ground aeronautically the same year Henry Ford and Harley-Davidson did likewise with their vehicles. Before World War I "daring young fliers" captivated audiences at fairs and picnics; after 1919 aviators barnstormed around the country as "gypsy" fliers. Aberdeen built the state's first commercial airport in 1920, and by decade's end seven cities had followed suit. Charles Lindbergh's 1927 cross-country tour stoked interest. Commercial aviation came within South Dakota in 1929 when Rapid City Air Lines connected to Huron. United Airlines brought interstate service in 1932 with its "Watertown Extension"—Stinson tri-motors out of Omaha.

World War II temporarily ended private flying, but the Army built a number of training facilities, the most notable near Rapid City, which became Ellsworth Air Force Base. In 1935 South Dakota's Aeronautics Commission came into being, but growth really jumped after 1945 when federal money improved airports. Veteran pilots returned to the air and new pilots imported military experience. South Dakotan Clyde W. Ice discovered in the late 1930s that he could apply insecticides by air; crop dusting became a reality after 1946. The South Dakota Farmers and Ranchers Association's "Flying Farmers" built many private landing strips beginning in the 1950s. State residents owned one thousand airplanes by the twenty-first century and improved public airports increased to seventy-three. Only seven provided commercial service, however, and that number is declining. As railroads discovered, it is more profitable to serve urban centers.

■ Tourism

Getting people to South Dakota challenged geography ever since fur trappers and traders struggled up the Missouri. Some came to work at fur posts, on homesteaded land, or in mines. Others just visited the "Sunshine State," the "Land of Infinite Variety," or "Great Faces, Great Places." "Tour-ist" entered the English language only in 1780—somebody who visits a place for pleasure; by choice, not assignment; and to spend money, not make it. Identifying South Dakota's first tourist becomes no easier than finding the first native to put a bullboat on the Missouri or the first automobile driver. Nominations might include John Evans, an adventurer who visited Mandan villages in 1795-96 looking for Welsh-speaking Indians. But Evans also drew pay and actually traded a bit, so the trip cannot be termed pure pleasure.

The best year to date the start of South Dakota tourism is 1811. That spring, two British botanists, John Bradbury and Thomas Nuttall, departed St. Louis with Wilson Hunt's Astorians, set on obtaining specimens of plant and animal life for the Liverpool Botanical Society.[13] Three weeks later, Pennsylvanian Henry M. Brackenridge left hot on their trail with a party under Manuel Lisa. Brackenridge had no other reason for travel than "the mere gratification, of . . . an idle curiosity."[14] Near Big Bend, the two expeditions connected, then traveled together to the Mandan villages. Brackenridge reveled in the countryside, "delightful prairie, the grass short, of deep blue, and intermixed with a great variety of beautiful flowers." Bradbury identified more than one hundred new plants, but focused on little else, "his attention arrested by a plant or flower." French-Canadian boatmen found merriment in botanist behavior. *"Ou `est le foul?"* "Where is the fool?" boatmen jested. *"Il est ufries ramasser des raciness."* "He is gathering roots."

Brackenridge and Bradbury quickly tired of Sioux threats and jumped at the chance to return to St. Louis in July when Lisa sent back two boats. Nuttall stayed until summer's end, making detailed observations, not only about plant and animal life but also about Mandans themselves. Published accounts by all three tourists are rich sources on South Dakota flora, fauna, and people.

Rich also describes Prince Paul of Wurttemberg. Then, as now, it cost money to be a tourist. Prince Paul made three trips to the American West between 1823 and 1850. The twenty-year-old royal scion met Jean Baptiste Charbonneau ("Pomp"), two year's his junior, in 1823, and the two wandered overland into the middle of South Dakota, spending time along the White River and at Joshua Pilcher's fur post about where Chamberlain is today. The prince's friendship with Sacagawea's son lasted beyond the trip; he took Jean Baptiste to Europe for six years, where the American learned several languages and traveled as a tourist himself. Prince Paul and Pomp returned to the U.S. in 1830, once more exploring the Upper Missouri. We know little about that trip and not much more about a third excursion in 1850.[15]

Artist George Catlin visited South Dakota in 1832, when Pierre Chouteau, Jr. invited him to ride the *Yellowstone* on its second Missouri ascent. Catlin spent two weeks at Fort Pierre, from which he ventured daily among Teton Sioux camped in the vicinity. Catlin reboarded the *Yellowstone* to Fort Union and back—his summer's worth of sketches and painting provided glimpses of actual Teton life, culture and leaders, plus a portrait of Fort Pierre itself.[16]

Another artist, twenty-three-year-old Swiss-born Karl Bodmer, booked passage on the 1833 American Fur Company boat. Under the sponsorship of German Prince Maximilian of Wied-Neuwied, Bodmer made illustrations for the Prince's *Travels in the Interior of North America*.[17] The travels lasted from 1832 through 1834, stopped at Fort Pierre, and extended all the way into what are now Montana and Wyoming. Most notably, Bodmer wintered at Fort Clark, 1833-34. His paintings of Mandan for the prince's book are extensive and sensitive.

South Dakota, specifically Big Stone Lake and the Coteau des Prairies, held little fascination for English geologist George W. Featherstonhaugh and his 1835 *Canoe voyage up the Minnay Sotor*. Better known and more enamored of the prairie, John James Audubon visited the Upper Missouri in 1843, while preparing *Quadrupeds of North America*. Like predecessor artists, Audubon rode a fur company steamboat to Fort Union, stopping at Fort Pierre. He brought assistants, including a taxidermist, and their little party ventured well into the Yellowstone River headwaters. As they traveled, Audubon sketched, everyone killed quadrupeds, and the taxidermist preserved them. Like William Clark, the artist expressed amazement over jackrabbits. His spring and fall stops at Fort Pierre showed up in his extensive journals, revealing he had not, by the way, abandoned entirely his interest in resident or migrating birds.[18]

Eugene de Girardin joined the list of visiting artists in 1849.[19] The Frenchman became fascinated with the American West, traveled to St. Louis, which was then bustling with California gold seekers, and attached himself to a party of geologists going up the Missouri. He booked passage on the fur company's *Iowa,* sharing space with three geologists, a botanist, two army officers, "a young German prince with his staff," and two Blackfeet women—wives of fur company officials. Girardin disembarked at Fort Pierre with its "charming landscape" surrounded by hundreds of Sioux tipis, "some dazzling white, others striped and covered with fantastic and primitive paintings." A couple days later, two of the geologists, Girardin, mule-skinners and guides, set out to visit the breathtakingly beautiful White River badlands: "at intervals on a soil white as snow rise embattled chateaus of brick red pyramids with their sharp-pointed summits topped with shapeless masses which seem to rock in the wind, a pillar of a hundred meters rises in the midst of this chaos of ruins like a gigantic light-house." He found the "Black Mountains" equally captivating, and walked amazed among "thick beds of petrified bones." The party collected rock samples and fossils before returning to Fort Pierre. At the end of July they headed off again, this time through the Little Missouri country to Fort Union. Back in France, his "Tour of the World" appeared in a travel magazine.

Fort Pierre *was* South Dakota from the 1830s through the 1850s. Many who visited the area took advantage of American Fur Company steamboats and that meant a Fort Pierre stop. Girardin's cabin mates illustrated the cross section of "tour-ists." Add missionaries, "poor adventurers," and nameless others who came to see the country or work in it; almost everyone stopped at the fur post and had a look around.

From the Civil War forward, South Dakota busied itself with the processes of separating Indians from their land, finding gold, land "booming," statehood, and surviving idiosyncratic business cycles. Visitors came and went, generally lost among the hubbub of those who came and stayed. By the end of the 1890s, residents began to see profit in attracting more folks as pure sightseers. "Wonderful Windcave Improvement Company" touted an underground "frostwork" of rock crystals.[20] Mitchell residents built a structure (common at agricultural festivals) covered with corn and produce in 1892. Local businessmen decided it attracted enough extra traffic to warrant doing it again the following year, and the year after that, and on for more than a century as the "Corn Palace."[21]

Federal officials saw the benefit in preserving South Dakota's geological beauty in 1903 when they created the nation's first subterranean park—Wind Cave. Five years later, they added Jewel Cave National Monument. South Dakotans, like businessman-turned-politician Peter Norbeck, envisioned additional Black Hills possibilities. In 1912 the state created a forest and game preserve in Custer County, adding buffalo two years later, and finally making it South Dakota's first official park in 1921. Then followed the challenges of promoting it. Black Hills commercial clubs published color brochures; the first state highway map clearly showed everyone how to get there.[22]

"Tourists soon get fed up on scenery unless it has something of special interest . . . to make it impressive," state historian Doane Robinson declared in 1923, suggesting some-one carve something in granite somewhere in the Black Hills. How about a "notable Sioux such as Red Cloud" on one of the pinnacles in the Needles area, he proposed to sculptor Lorado Taft.[23] When Taft declined, Robinson turned to Gutzon Borglum, then working on Confederate sculptures at Stone Mountain, Georgia. The idea caught fire with Borglum, who visited the Hills in 1924, dropped Stone Mountain, and selected

Gutzon Borglum designed and executed the sixty-foot-high images of four U.S. presidents on Mount Rushmore. *Courtesy South Dakota Tourism.*

Mount Rushmore as a good site for carving. Other South Dakotans fanned the flames and by October 1925, the spot became a national monument. Three years later, now-Senator Peter Norbeck convinced President Calvin Coolidge to spend his summer vacation in the Black Hills, dedicate the pro-posed sculpture, and serve as a model tourist. Borglum began the expensive work of carving sixty-foot-high images of Washington, Jefferson, Theodore Roosevelt, and Lincoln; a project not completed until after his death in 1941. Thereafter, Mount Rushmore became the keystone in state travel and tourism efforts and source of the state's official nickname.

Badlands National Monument added to area attractions in 1929.[24] In 1946 another sculptor, Korczak Ziolkowski, saw potential on Thunderhead Mountain for an addi-tional carving. Envisioned grandiosely 563 feet high and 641 feet long, the Crazy Horse monument is well underway at the start of a new century, under family direction after Ziolkowski's death in 1982.[25] It certainly meets Doane Robinson's vision of something "impressive" and a "notable Sioux."

The 1945 state legislature expanded the South Dakota State Park system adding Hartford Beach, Lake Herman, and Oakwood Lakes. Today twelve state parks, plus more than 340 other areas, marinas, and prairies attract nearly nine million visitors annually. At more than 73,000 acres, Custer State Park is one of the nation's largest and still the state's most popular.[26]

What else would attract people to South Dakota? Hunting. Residents decimated wild game as they settled. When the *Volga Tribune* looked at waterfowl hunting in 1884, it noted that "sportsmen are amusing themselves by slaughtering them at wholesale." By 1900 most native game birds had disappeared and efforts to introduce others fal-tered. The State Game Department got serious in 1911 importing forty-eight Chinese ring-necked pheasant pairs to Redfield. The next year they added another two hundred pairs. The state spent $20,000 on the effort, but it paid off handsomely. In 1919 a limited season took place for residents, and five years later pheasant hunting opened to non-residents as well.[27] Later still, the ring-necked became the state bird and South Dakota the only polity to extensively promote the killing and eating of an official symbol. Combined federal, state, and sportsmen efforts renewed migratory waterfowl hunting along the central flyway, and also encouraged non-game birds. Perhaps the most interesting effort provides nesting boxes for American Kestrels on the back of select interstate highway signs near Sioux Falls and Brookings—"they are beautiful little birds and eat grasshoppers."[28]

Fishing and water recreation go hand-in-hand on state lakes and waterways, but became big business along the Missouri after World War II with construction of large Pick-Sloan project dams. Controlling and using Missouri River water occupied public attention off and on since early settlement. Only federal involvement coming out of New Deal spending made possible six multi-purpose dams (one each in Montana and North Dakota, four in South Dakota) to provide irrigation, electricity generation, flood control and recreation. Pierre's Oahe dam is the state's largest and with Big Bend, Fort Randall, and Gavin's Point, supports in-state and out-of-state tourism, simultaneously submerging most of the state's historic river course.[29]

History took an interesting recreational turn in 1989, when the "Deadwood, You Bet" campaign authorized limited stakes gambling in the old mining city. Within a decade, ninety gambling halls lined Deadwood streets. Another eight scattered themselves on state reservations. Deadwood gambling draws a million-and-a-half people to slot machines, blackjack and poker tables each year—a third from outside the state. Casino taxes support Lawrence County, but also state-wide tourism and historic preservation.[30]

The Black Hills and surrounding areas represent South Dakota's primary tourist draw. Over half of the $624 million dollars that tourism generates annually is spent in four Black Hills counties. Thirty thousand people are employed in related industries statewide, again, most in the Hills. Mount Rushmore sees approximately two million visitors a year; the Badlands, one million.[31] But neither site is the most-visited South Dakota attraction. Sioux Falls' Empire Mall (180 stores) pulls in fourteen million people each year; half of them qualify as out-of-town tourists.[32]

■ Museums

Tourists visiting South Dakota will find a wealth of museums that present aspects of the state's history, led by the renowned National Music Museum—discussed elsewhere in this book—and by the Museum of the State Historical Society at the Cultural Heritage Center in Pierre. The latter is the flagship organization for South Dakota. Its mission, to preserve "the written and artifactual" records of the state's heritage, is carried out by means of expertly designed museum displays. Of particular importance is the museum's collection of 1,339 Native American objects, focusing on the Sioux Indians of the state.[33] Among the most often visited museums that are listed in the *Directory* of the Association of South Dakota Museums, Inc., are the following:

The South Dakota Art Museum in Brookings, opened in May 1970 as a home for the prairie paintings of Harvey Dunn, holds collections of Native American tribal art as well as work of South Dakota and foreign provenance. A special feature is a permanent exhibit of Marghab linens from the Portuguese islands of Madeira. Also located in Brookings is the Agricultural Heritage Museum, housing an extensive collection of farm

The Cultural Heritage Center in Pierre is the flagship institution of museums in the state. *Courtesy South Dakota State Historical Society–State Archives.*

equipment and household furnishings. The collections feature, among many examples of rare farm tractors, a 1915 J. I. Case Steam Traction Engine. Restored in 1982-83, the tractor has been ranked by the J. I. Case Company as one of the three finest restorations in the country. Founded in 1883, the W. H. Over Museum is named after an early curator, who promoted it as a study collection in the natural sciences at the University of South Dakota in Vermillion. Begun by the state geological survey as a collection of biological and fossil specimens, the museum has since grown to become "the state's largest collection, representing both its natural and cultural history."

The Journey Museum in Rapid City unites five historic and prehistoric collections under one roof: the Museum of Geology, the Archaeological Research Center, the Sioux Indian Museum, the Minnelusa Pioneer Museum, and the Duhamel Collection of traditional Sioux artifacts. The Journey's offerings are complemented by the collection of art at the Dahl Fine Arts Center in Rapid City. At nearby Ellsworth Air Force Base, visitors are able to trace the history of the base and review significant South Dakota aviation events and personnel.

The Adams Museum and House, Inc., in Deadwood offers a variety of displays and holds an extensive archive of photos and other information relating to Deadwood and the Black Hills. Beginning in 2002, the museum has provided background information for the popular HBO series *Deadwood,* written by award-winning TV writer David Milch. The High Plains Heritage Museum at nearby Spearfish features western art and artifacts, including the original Spearfish-to-Deadwood stagecoach. Located at the Crazy Horse Monument in the southern Black Hills, the Indian Museum of North America contains an extensive collection of Native American art and artifacts. Its special feature is the large collection of sculptures by founder Korczak Ziolkowski.

In Sioux Falls, the newly opened Washington Pavilion of Arts and Science offers six galleries of changing exhibits in the Visual Arts Center; the Kirby Science Discovery Center offers dozens of permanent educational exhibits and many traveling exhibits. Also in Sioux Falls, the Siouxland Heritage Museums, founded in 1926, are housed in the historic Minnehaha County Courthouse (designed by Wallace Dow and completed in 1890) and the Richard F. Pettigrew House. Special features include regularly changing displays, the Ole Running murals, and a unique 1908 Fawick Flyer automobile, given to the museums by Augustana College.

The Center for Western Studies at Augustana is one of the state's most versatile historical agencies. Its public programs include a history conference, art shows, and autograph parties; its archives hold cultural and religious institution records; its publications include the official geography of the state, a comprehensive history of South Dakota, and histories of the Sioux Sun Dance, of agriculture, of the EROS Data Center, of the arts in the state, and of the Lewis and Clark Expedition. Art and artifact collections include Scandinavian rosemaled furniture, plains Indian artifacts, and art by world-renowned Norman Rockwell and state laureate Oscar Howe. The Center's collections of art are complemented by those of the Eide-Dalrymple Gallery, also on the campus.

In Aberdeen, the Dacotah Prairie Museum offers many permanent and changing exhibits. Of special interest are the Hatterscheidt Wildlife Gallery, the Education Art Gallery, and the Lamont Gallery of local and regional art. At Sisseton, the Nicollet Tower highlights the career of explorer Joseph Nicollet; the Stavig House Museum holds Scandinavian photos and letters; and the Tekakwitha Fine Arts Center features Dakota Sioux visual art. The Prehistoric Indian Village Museum and Archeodome in Mitchell offers a unique opportunity to visit a 1,000-year-old plains Indian village site. Located north of the historic Corn Palace, the museum also provides occasional programs that permit visitors to participate in the scientific excavation work. A few miles south of the Archeodome is the Friends of the Middle Border Museum, begun in 1939 by Leland Case. The museum includes among its founders such notables as John Dewey, Gutzon Borglum, Badger Clark, and Hamlin Garland. Its holdings feature Indian artifacts and examples of the work of Charles Hargens, James Earle Fraser (designer of the buffalo-head nickel), Oscar Howe, and Harvey Dunn.

The Dakota Territorial Museum in Yankton features collections relating to the history of Yankton and Dakota Territory. Its current emphasis is the Lewis and Clark Expedition through displays and programs that "Re-live the Adventure" on the Lewis and Clark Trail. The South Dakota Hall of Fame in Chamberlain exists to honor citizens of the state who have contributed to its development and heritage. Special features are biographies of the more than four hundred honorees and exhibits and artifacts relating to their accomplishments. The Akta Lakota Museum, also in Chamberlain, opened in 1991 on the campus of St. Joseph's Indian School. It presents life on the plains in four stages—pre-contact Indian life, the arrival of the Euro-Americans, the government's involvement with the Sioux, and the present successes of the Sioux in preserving their traditions and heritage. Complementing the artifact collection at Akta Lakota are the archives of the Sicangu Heritage Center at Mission, a Lakota museum affiliated with Sinte Gleska University, and the Beuchel Memorial Lakota Museum at St. Francis, featuring historic photos and botanical specimens.

Around the state are smaller efforts—Victorian mansions, little houses on the prairie, train depots, forts, harvest and historic festivals, passion plays, summer theaters, rodeos, and waterfalls. There has been free ice water at Hustead's Wall Drug since 1931, bikers in Sturgis beginning in 1938 thanks to the Jackpine Gypsies Motorcycle Club, five-cent coffee and fresh pie at Al's Oasis in Oacoma, panoramic views of the mapmaker's beloved Coteau des Prairie from the Joseph N. Nicollet tower, and personal pleasure at all the private little corners of splendor and solitude that attract resident and visitor to pause and enjoy.

Dwindling populations in rural western counties reflect an emptying of the Great Plains in recent decades. An area larger than Germany and France combined stretches from the Canadian border into Texas and officially qualifies as "frontier" with fewer than six residents per square mile. Some see new potential for eco-tourism in a "buffalo commons," but chambers of commerce are reticent to extol the virtues of wide-open space when it means declines in population, small farms/ranches, and business.

South Dakota's natural beauty in prairie vistas, Black Hills grandeur, and badlands ruggedness will continue to charm resident and visitor alike. Man-made attractions of "special interest" add to the allure. There is a market for what South Dakota has and people will find their ways to enjoy it.

Chapter 25
Tiyospaye: A Traditional Sioux Family Today

An essay by Virginia Driving Hawk Sneve

My family does not all reside in South Dakota. We are spread over the United States from California to Massachusetts, from Minnesota to Arizona, and states in between, and we live on and off reservations. If location is a determinate, we are not a traditional family, or *tiyospaye*.

Tiyospaye the word has come to be synonymous with "extended family" and describes the social organization of tribal members related by blood, marriage, or adoption. *Tiyospaye* is what has become known as the traditional family.

Thousands of anthropologists, archaeologists, sociologists, historians, economists, and others have studied, researched, written, and reported about American Indians ever since the first European contact. These scholars probably know more about the topic of *tiyospaye* than I do. I will write only of what I know from my heritage from the Lakota, Nakota, and Dakota branches of what has become known as the Sioux. But I must also include of the influence of French, Scots, and English men who cohabited with my Indian grandmothers. Additional current information comes from relatives on and off reservations and studies of twentieth-century researchers.

My great-great-great-great grandmother Hazzodowin would have been among the Santee Dakota who in 1660 met the French explorer and fur trader Pierre Esprit Radisson.[1] She grew up in the era of fur trade and the Indians' first contact with whites. My Lakota ancestress was Skanskanwin, a Minneconjou Lakota. She lived in that brief and glorious era before the white man: the time of the horse. The Santee never fully made the transition to the plains culture before they left Minnesota in the 1860s.[2] Female descendants of this woman married a man of the Yankton or Nakota tribe whose home range was between the Dakotas and Lakotas.

The Minneconjous, whose name indicates that they had once planted crops by water, willingly gave up the life of the woodlands for a new culture of dreams and songs that would come to be the stereotypical images of all American Indians. Yet the customs of courtship, child rearing, and family structure for the Dakota, Nakota, and Lakota remained the same in many ways.

A young woman was wooed by a warrior who serenaded her with his flute until she allowed him to stand close within the shelter of her blanket. He brought horses, which the girl's father accepted, and the couple was wed.

After marriage, women kept their names and each of their children were given individual names. The woman was called *mitawicu* (my wife) by her husband and she called him *mihigna* (my husband). They openly showed their affection in the daily act of braiding each other's hair.[3] When the couple had children, their household was one of many that made up *tiyospaye*.

There may have been more than one wife in the lodge, for in a warrior society there were always more women than men, and the practice of polygamy ensured that all women could marry and have children. Often the second wife would be a sister of the first. If his brother died, a man would marry his sister-in-law. The more wives a man had, the more skins could be tanned for the comfort of the lodge, and the fewer an individual wife's duties.

There was a strict division of labor with the men doing the hunting and fishing and the women nearly all of the other work. Santee men did help with the making of maple sugar and harvesting of wild rice. But neither male nor female thought one's duties of less worth than the other's. The male provided for and protected his family and *tiyospaye*, and his prowess in battle and the hunt brought esteem to his family.[4]

It was the men who killed the game and then gave the kill to the women of the lodge. They then skinned, butchered, cooked, and served the meat, dried the surplus for later use, and tanned the hides.

A woman cared for her lodge, and its contents were hers, as were the children, whom she treasured. Rarely was she apart from her baby, who was either carried on the mother's back or securely placed in a cradle board within view. It was the duty of an older sister or brother to watch over the younger ones.[5] When the man was not away hunting or waging war, he was a father who took time to play with and sing to his young children.

Proper behavior was expected of each member of a *tiyospaye*, and children learned how to act by watching adults interact with their relatives. They learned to love and respect their parents and, in turn, were treasured by them. They also loved their grandparents and enjoyed being with them because they knew that *Unci* (Grandmother) was more indulgent than *Ina* (Mother). Elderly relatives were cared for by adult children or grandchildren.

Men hunted together and the women shared their labors. All adults watched over the children, on whom the tribe's survival depended. Grandparents, uncles, and aunts (considered also to be fathers and mothers) showered attention upon the babies. They assisted in the care and training of all the children.

Skanskanwin was *Ina* to her sister's children, and the same relationship was true of brothers: not uncle, but *Ate* (Father) to his brother's offspring. The children were not first cousins, but considered as brothers and sisters. All other relatives of the same age were cousins. There were no orphans in Lakota life. If the natural parents died, relatives took the children in as their own.

SANTEE BIRTH-ORDER NAMES[6]

	Male	Female
First	Chaske	Winona
Second	Hepan	Hapan
Third	Hepi	Hapistinna
Fourth	Catan	Wanske
Fifth	Hake	Wehake

Children each had individual names, as did the adults, since there were no surnames among the tribes. The Santee custom of giving children birth-order names has survived to modern times. These names were (often still are) used by family in addition to the individual name by which a child was known within the village.

At the age of about five or six, a boy spent his days with other boys and adult males. In games of hunting and fighting he began to learn his male role. At the same age, girls spent time with females and played with dolls and miniature tipis to begin learning how to be a wife and mother.

Brothers and sisters had great respect for each other which carried over into adult lives. A girl's first pair of moccasins was made for her brother. He brought trophies from his hunts and battles. Later he kept an eye on his sister's suitors, and even after she was wed, she could count on his protection.

But the greatest devotion after parent to child was that of sister with sister and brother with brother. Sisters not only considered each other's children as their own but supported each other in all things. The brothers' loyalty was more intense because they relied on each other in times of extreme danger, such as during the hunt or in battle.

This sense of loyalty extended beyond immediate family to the whole *tiyospaye* and individuals within it. The *tiyospaye* gave affection and security to individuals. Single families lived near each other and worked together in cooperative *tiyospaye* units. But a man could not marry within his own unit, so the *tiyospaye* joined with another band in large annual tribal gatherings for council or ceremony, as well as for trade, games, visiting, and courtship.

And so it was for Skanskanwin, Hazzodowin, and their children until it all changed with the coming of the white men, fur traders who took Indian women as wives. It was French, Spanish, and Anglo-Saxon traders who came to barter trade goods for hides and furs, and one of the first things they did was to obtain an Indian wife. Sometimes these men had a wife in each of the tribes with which they dealt, or married sisters, or had several wives in one tribe. These liaisons were a mixed blessing, bringing many new and useful goods to the tribes but also products, customs, and diseases that proved disastrous to the Indians. The children of these liaisons had mixed blood and grew up experiencing a blend of customs and values.[7]

The marriages of white men and Indian women occurred in my family. Some of these traders followed tribal ways and had more than one wife. Because these men had married Indian women, they and other white men were considered members of the tribe, were entitled to all annuities and rations, and later were allotted land.[8]

Indian women cared for their white husbands as they would have done for Indian ones. They were a liaison with the white world through their husbands, who often served as interpreters and tribal advocates. The white men benefited in acquiring an extended family with tribal affiliation to ensure their economic success.[9]

French men adopted Lakota languages and customs and were often called "French Indians." Anglo-Saxon traders were most likely to retain their cultural identities, and their Indian wives became bilingual and had to adapt to their husbands' lifestyles. These men were known as "squaw men," which, along with "French Indians," was a derogatory label given by white society, which generally thought of Indian women as fiendishly immoral snares who entrapped civilized men.[10]

My grandmothers and other Indian women who were the first of their tribes to cohabit with white men brought honor to their families and tribes by doing so. But they soon found that their lives were filled with drudgery if there were no "sister-wife" to share the household and conjugal duties. A single wife gave birth more frequently and over a longer period of time and, as a result, suffered more in childbirth.[11]

By the 1850s all tribes were distrustful of the whites, and a woman who married a white was lowered in status and frequently lived apart from her family. If she were physically abused, there were no brothers to protect her, no family to shelter her if she ran away. In the early fur trade years, such women were welcomed back into the family circle, but later she became an outcast because her former alliance was considered shameful. The most difficult aspect for these women to accept was that all the goods in the house were the property of the man, and so she lost control of her home and children.[12]

With the advent of the fur trade, these changes led to the deterioration of the female's status as Indian husbands began bartering the pelts their wives had tanned for guns and whiskey. Later at Fort Laramie, the Indian relatives of women married to traders became dependent on trade goods and whiskey, no longer hunting to supply food, clothing, or shelter. These Indians, called "Fort Indians" or *waglukhe*, became known in written history as the "Loafer band," among the Brûlé. Others still living the nomadic life scorned these "hang-around-the-fort" Indians and those who had already moved to reservations.[13]

Fort Laramie, best known as the site of treaty negotiations, is infamous for the alcohol-related abuse of women that occurred there. As Indian men became addicted to alcohol, fathers, brothers, and husbands traded their daughters, sisters, and wives for whiskey.[14] The military presence in the West resulted in large numbers of fatherless half-breed children born as the result of the alcohol trade or prostitution during and after military engagements.[15]

A worse tragedy occurred when Indian women began drinking. The secure structure of family and *tiyospaye* disintegrated. Although I know of no studies to support my suspicions, I believe that children born to drinking mothers suffered from what we now know as fetal alcohol syndrome. These children became dysfunctional adults who could not care for their own children. Fortunately, the non-drinkers in *tiyospaye* still cared for all children.

The bands that held out against moving to the forts and reservations were known as "hostiles," which referred not only to their military resistance but also the attitude they had against any kind of white influence. They retained, as far as they could under increasingly difficult circumstances, the traditional *tiyospaye* customs and values.

But more change came with Christianity. The early missionaries insisted that converts repudiate the most basic elements of their culture. An Indian man was destined to be a warrior and hunter. To refuse to fight or hunt and agree to plow the land was a sign of weakness.[16] Indian women more easily made the conversion to Christianity than did the men. Their roles as wife and mother did not change. However, white civilization's mores, imposed on the Indians through Christianity, further lowered the status of Indian women. Male Christian converts could have only one wife. The other wife or wives and children were set aside. Some women found refuge in *tiyospaye*, where a brother or another relative gave her and her children a home. But others were not so fortunate. Now the Indians were expected to farm, but barely eked out an existence and remained on government rations to survive. Single set-aside mothers and their children were too often a burden that these new farmers could not support.[17]

As noted earlier, there had always been more women than men in the warrior societies, but the practice of polygamy ensured that all women could marry and have children. Now, in the early reservation days, there were still not enough men to go around, and the unmarried women and set-aside wives came to be considered in the same light as white society viewed unwed women—as objects of pity and scorn.

Grandparents, now more than ever, became the caregivers of children of set-aside mothers. Grandparents had always had a vital role in child rearing. They often relieved busy parents by watching over young children. In some families, grandparents would take a child into their home to be raised as their own. Such a child knew and loved his natural parents and was considered to be especially loved by them if they permitted the grandparents to take the child.[18] This custom did not change.

But Christian Indian men who individually could not care for single women and their children, or the elderly with no children, could collectively do so. In 1873 an

Moved by a concern over the growing cultural division between traditional and modern lifestyles, three young Native American men founded the Brotherhood of Christian Unity in 1873. The brotherhood, seen here at its annual meeting at Crow Creek Agency in 1890, taught tribal men to farm, manage money, adjust to town life, and attract industry to the reservations. *Center for Western Studies.*

interdenominational group, *Wojo Okolakiciye* ("The Planting Society," later called the Brotherhood of Christian Unity), was organized for the purpose of aiding the people no matter their denominational connection:

1. We Indians, before the coming of the whiteman, knew what was good, but not what was very good. We knew what was bad, but not what was very bad. The whiteman has brought us the very good and the very bad . . . we clearly see that before the coming of our Lord, strangely, we were more united than we are now . . . . Therefore, through this brotherhood club, let us try to stay together. . . .

2. Let us look on the chain of Indian life, try to spot the weakest link, concentrate upon that with what resources we may have in material, energy, and wisdom, for the temporal welfare of our Indian people. . . . [19]

But more change would come, for wherever Christians went, so did education. In order to obtain converts, the missionaries had first to educate the Indians, not only in religion but in language, which was needed for the transference of ideas and values.[20]

Up until now, Indian children had learned by precept and example, with the spoken word reinforcing this learning. They had to pay attention to what was said, and in so doing develop memory skills which were vital to a culture without a written language. The moral code and virtues of a tribe were not presented through lecture but through example of adult and peer behavior. These examples were reinforced by stories, usually told by grandparents.[21]

When children were disobedient, they were reminded that all that they did or said reflected on the whole family. Children behaved properly so that they might never bring shame or disgrace upon the family. Rarely were children physically punished for fear that a child's spirit would be harmed. In the early days of the reservation, these child-rearing practices still prevailed until children were taken from their homes to attend boarding school.[22]

In Dakota Territory, Episcopal and Presbyterian boarding schools were the first to be established. These schools were in agencies near the students' homes. They were given "school clothes" to wear and their hair was cut, but they learned to read and write in Dakota/Lakota before they learned English. They could don their "Indian" clothes when they went home in the summer. They often did not return until their parents thought it was time to do so, not when the alien calendar said it was. Thus the term "Indian time" came into being.[23] Children educated in this way remained all of their lives proud of being able to read and write in their native language. They often became leaders in their reservation churches and were ordained or became missionaries to their own or other tribes.

The government and Roman Catholic boarding school experience was harsher. Children, often as young as five and six years old, were taken to school wearing comfortable buckskin garments and moccasins; these were burned and exchanged for wool trousers, skirts, and hard shoes. Their hair was cut and all were forbidden to speak to one another in their native language. They stayed in school until their education was completed in their early teens. They spoke only English and many forgot their Indian customs and languages.[24] These children returned to the reservation confused and alienated from their families. If they readapted to traditional customs and relearned the language, they were scornfully described by whites as "going back to the blanket." Others returned home to families that were highly suspicious of the educated child.[25]

Missionary and government teachers assumed that the Indian identity would be absorbed into the general white society and that their schools were instruments of assimilation. For some children, this happened; others adapted white civilization to traditional ways, and *tiyospaye* continued.

Young Native American women were taught domestic skills in addition to such academic subjects as reading, writing, arithmetic, and geography at St. Mary's Boarding School, operated by the Episcopal Church. *Center for Western Studies.*

When I was a child growing up on the Rosebud reservation in the 1930s and 1940s, Lakota families still adhered to pre-reservation family structure. The first home I remember was in Mission, South Dakota, a two-room house next to the home of my grandparents, Robert and Flora Driving Hawk. My great-grandparents lived across the road, down towards the creek lived an aunt and uncle, and nearby were other kin. This was *tiyospaye*, and the whole community cherished children who learned to honor and respect all of their relatives, but especially the elders.

That environment survived into the 1970s, as Delphine Red Shirt wrote in her book *Bead on an Anthill*: "I grew up among many children—brothers, sisters, cousins, and friends. We were sacred as children. Never physically punished, never yelled at. We watched, listened to adults, and learned how to behave. Children learned to listen, obey and respect others."[26]

Individuals were valued and protected simply because they were related to the group. The sources of this security were multiple—biological family, kinship, and tribal. If one failed, security was still provided by the others. It was a system that offered unconditional and unsolicited affection. The reservation was a wonderful place to be a child despite the poverty of reservation economy.

Today on reservations the community still has a strong sense of obligation to care for all children and particularly for the children of relatives. Young children receive stable support and care from adults with grandparents still practicing traditional roles.[27]

By the 1930s Indians were traveling off of the reservations to summer jobs picking potatoes or other migrant labor opportunities. During World War II large numbers of young men and women served in the armed services. Others worked at the Black Hills Army Ordnance Depot in the Igloo, near Edgemont, and some found employment at military installations in Rapid City and Sioux Falls.[28]

After the war many Indians who returned to the reservation did not resume life in the isolated communities of subsistence farming and low wages—if a job were available at all. Many moved to towns bordering reservations and to South Dakota's larger cities where there was employment.[29] Families also moved to Sioux Falls to be near a father, brother, or son who was serving a sentence in the state penitentiary. Again change came as family moved away from the closeness of *tiyospaye* in reservation communities.

During the war years, for the first time in Indian families, both parents were employed and children were often left unsupervised, without the presence of grandparents, aunts, or others. Children had to make decisions and choices without adult guidance. After the war, they found it difficult to accept the resumption of parental direction.[30]

But related families tended to find housing or camp sites near each other when they moved to off-reservation towns. In Rapid City Indian families camped near Sioux San and along Rapid Creek, which ran all through the city. During the winter off-season for tourism, motels offered weekly rentals to Indian families, but they had to vacate before Memorial Day. This group often moved between reservation and town as seasonal migrants.

Sometimes children were left with reservation grandparents. A low-income housing area was developed in North Rapid called "Sioux Addition," also known as Lakota Homes, although it was open to all races.[31]

I worked for ten years in the Rapid City School District and found that *tiyospaye* was still supporting children. I had contact with counselors and relatives in Sioux Falls, Yankton, and Aberdeen who found this to be also true in their city schools. Aunts, cousins, siblings, and grandparents still made sure that a young child was loved even in the most dysfunctional and impoverished families. Indian children in their early teens, on and off of reservations, tend to develop an intense loyalty to friends that often includes gang membership, which supplants family. Parents and grandparents have a difficult time maintaining discipline. But when a child gets in trouble at school or with the law *tiyospaye* support is there.

This support is vital to the success of individuals moving away from the reservation whether to school or employment. A relative willingly provides a security net while the newcomer finds a place in the community. Persons who leave a place where being an Indian is not unusual will move to an area where they can disappear in a white community without the help of relatives or friends.[32]

My ninety-year-old mother in California maintains a close connection with relatives across the nation through phone calls and e-mail. She visits relatives and they her at least once a year. Recently, she was delighted to find descendants of an uncle, her mother's brother, whose daughter had seemed to vanish into a non-Indian world. But one of his granddaughters, living in California, began searching for her roots. After discovering the relationship, she wrote, "My sister and nieces are very interested in our family. We always thought that there were so few of us, but now we have all of these relatives—we are rich in family." [33]

She has found *tiyospaye*.

Chapter 26
Modern Tribes

The circumstances of American Indians in South Dakota society during the twentieth century represent only one component in a larger history of imperialism. For more than half a millennium, indigenous peoples in every continental environment have been the victims of conquerors and colonizers. On most locations, original inhabitants simply disappeared, were enslaved, or were absorbed into new, dominant societies. Across the British Empire in North America and Australia, however, indigenous peoples were allowed to retain political identities and legal claims to ancestral land. The United States government inherited these extraordinary British imperial practices and gave them expression in South Dakota.

Throughout the twentieth century, perceptions more than circumstances of nine federally recognized tribes in the state controlled Indian-white relations. In 2001 Minnesota Red Lake Chippewa educator Lee Cook spoke for Native Americans here and elsewhere across the United States when he said that "Indian tribes and nations have made more economic strides in the past 25 years than in the previous 150 years."[1] During an interview in 2003, Michael Scarmon, a non-Indian native of South Dakota who has served the Yankton Tribe as both legal counsel at trial and tribal judge, challenged a contrary point of view: "Majoritarian culture seems to believe—it is mythology—that these Indians are living on some handout. 'They are getting a good deal,' whereas it is just the opposite. White people around Indians are making out like bandits."[2] Literally boxcar loads of documents preserved in federal archives reveal that immigrant non-Indians have relied on tribal and related federal opportunities since the settlement era in Dakota Territory, which would have been an economic wasteland had the tribes not been present. At the outset of the twenty-first century, obvious improvements in the condition of Wagner, where Scarmon presided as a judge, indicated that non-Indians have shared in the eco-

Contemporary Sioux Indians continue to maintain ancestral ceremonies. The Dakota wacipi, representing the dance component in the larger powwow, is frequently in use in all seasons. Here Medicine Man Bill Scheigman, in headdress, dances in the USD Old Armory. *Courtesy Herbert T. Hoover.*

507

Chronology

1779-1871 – Period for negotiation of treaties to govern relationships between federally recognized tribes and the U.S., whose terms abide as factors in tribal-to-federal relationships

1789 – U.S. Constitution delegates to Congress alone authority for dealing "with the Indian tribes"

1797 – For the first time, Congress recognizes tribal ancestral land as a legal possession known as "Indian Country"

1832 – The federal case *Worcester v. Georgia* classifies federally recognized tribes as "domestic dependent nations"

1849 – U.S. Department of the Interior established with responsibilities including management of federal-to-tribal affairs

1871 – Special congressional statutes called "Agreements" replaces treaties to govern relationships between federal recognized tribes and the government

1875 – Congress orders "Indian preference" (affirmative action) among Sioux tribes for the first time

1877 – Illegally, Congress seizes the Black Hills and surrounding area, creating legal basis for the modern Black Hills Case against the United States

1887 – Dawes Severalty Act set model for land allotment to individual tribal members

1889 – Tribes of Sioux in South Dakota retains ownership of nearly 14 million acres (about 28 percent of the land in the state)

1905 – *Waldron v. United States, et al.* recognizes legal equality of mixed-blood and full-blood tribal members regarding eligibility for federal benefits

1910 – Buy Indian Act allows involvement of tribal members in reservation business activities without competitive bidding procedures

1918 – Indian quarter-blood quantum rule established as a general minimum requirement regarding access to some federal benefits

nomic progress of the past twenty-five years described by Cook.

Nevertheless, a prevailing view generated by a majority of non-Indians gained expression in the University of South Dakota student newspaper during the autumn of the year 2000 under the title "Reasons for separate Native American reservations gone; benefits should end."[3] Its young adult author believed that Indian reservations came into place in the state as "huge tracts of land allocated [given] to the tribes" by the U.S. government; that "once we [non-Indian citizens] started giving handouts" to Indian residents of reservations "it became nearly impossible to stop"; that Congress spent "thousands of federal dollars" as "tuition assistance" for tribal members [by implication, the ones enrolled in colleges and universities during the year 2000]; and that "the most impractical, illogical and imbecilic idea (which is nonetheless still being considered) calls for the return of the *entire* Black Hills area to tribal control." The author advised that "We should erase every law that gives and takes anything from anyone based on race," promptly "abolish the reservations," and "declare everyone citizens with all the rights and duties that are implied."

The author of this article not only parroted perceptions handed down through several generations of non-Indian South Dakotans, but he also articulated the greatest threat to the perpetuation of tribal cultures in segregated reservation environments for future generations of Indians, who tend to believe that current trust responsibility benefits will be with them as "treaty rights for as long as grass grows and water flows." Properly, during an interview in the summer of 2003, longtime Yankton Tribal Chairman Stephen Cournoyer, Jr., remarked, "Our people deserve what was promised in the treaties. They gave up millions of acres of land. We didn't, but our ancestors did with hopes that the health, education, and welfare of our people will be taken care of." He added, "If we had control of what they gave up, we could probably take care of ourselves, but we don't. We are reliant on the federal government" to sustain its commitment to the compensation for land surrendered by tribes in the past.

For the Sioux, like other federally recognized tribes across the United States, the term "for as long as grass grows and water flows" never appeared in a treaty, and the notion of perpetual benefits is seldom implied. The treaty approved by Yanktons in 1858 created an annuity system to last for fifty years and contained no indication of perpetual benefits. Yankton Tribal Judge Scarmon acknowledged the resulting risk during his interview: Indian tribes "have an adversarial relationship with the government" that pays the costs of trust responsibility benefits. "There could be a one-line act of Congress to do away with the whole reservation and tribal system. 'Indian tribes no longer exist'" as legal entities "is all they [members of Congress] would have to say. They [Indians] are citizens of the United States. Congress has the power." To the question of whether this might happen, he replied: "I don't know why it hasn't happened. I don't know who supports the tribes. I don't know what it is," but "it gives me some hope that there is some substance to most Americans. Somehow the majority in Congress has never come down on that side."[4]

Chronology (cont'd)

1921 – Synder Act provides health care for federally recognized Indians as a "trust responsibility" of the U.S. government

1934 – Indian Reorganization (Wheeler-Howard) Act encourages the survival of tribalism and includes statutory mandate regarding "Indian preference" (affirmative action) as national benefit for federally recognized Indians

1934 – U.S. Indian Office Circular 2970 extends legal protection for Indian cultural freedoms, including language and religion

1937 – Housing Act affirms general authority for housing as a federal "trust responsibility," later enlarged by other housing acts in 1974, 1988, and 1996

1975 – Indian Self Determination and Education Assistance Act surrenders trust responsibility funds to federally recognized tribal governments for management and inevitable profit

1975 – *Decoteau v. District County Court* disestablishes (destroys) the outer boundary of Lake Traverse Reservation, reducing tribal jurisdiction to less than 15 percent of original acreage

Shown in this photo (1913) of a Yankton allotment are a prefabricated "issued house," provided to encourage allottees to live on individual farm sites, a tipi, a barn, and a horse-drawn "BIA wagon." *Courtesy Herbert T. Hoover.*

Both former Chairman Cournoyer and Judge Scarmon demonstrated accurate grasps of history in their remarks. Trust responsibility benefits earned by tribes through the surrender of land ought to survive. Congress has the power, however, to terminate them. "Some substance to most Americans" has prevented this in the past, but the perpetuation of federal recognition for about 570 tribes comprising approximately 2.5 million members in the United States by Congress in the future depends on a realistic public understanding of the history of Indian-white relations, which becomes more faint in the national society with every passing generation.

One reason is that most non-Indians misunderstood the tribe-to-government land-transfer process as it took place. Europeans who occupied most of the land contained by the boundaries of the state settled with a belief that the U.S. government had supervised the successful conquest of its previous occupants, then gave some of the land back for occupancy by surviving native groups, and offered most of the acreage as public domain for settlement by immigrants under terms written into federal land laws. At the same time, Congress initiated payments to reservation groups. In addition, Congress extended benefits unavailable to immigrants and their descendants. According to many non-Indians in South Dakota, Native Americans not only failed to acknowledge the generosity of Congress, but they also wished to recover ownership of the magnificent Black Hills and surrounding area, which they lost during their wars against the United States late in the nineteenth century.

Inevitably, this flawed perception about the circumstances and expectations of tribal members concludes that the time has arrived for Indians to acknowledge the conquest of their ancestors and, like descendants of European immigrants, accept the rights and perform the duties incumbent upon all patriotic citizens of the United States. Most non-Indian advocates of this viewpoint appeared to be sympathetic about the lingering hazards of reservation life, which they attributed to an addictive reliance on federal generosity. If the descendants of immigrants could support themselves through individual effort under inhospitable natural conditions on the northern Great Plains, it seemed reasonable to expect that Indians could fend for themselves, as well.

Characteristically, tribal residents of reservations in South Dakota formulated a response based on an equally simplistic perception. Their ancestors claimed rights of ownership and occupancy on the northern Great Plains long before non-Indians arrived. Valiantly, tribal armies defended their claims through a succession of victories over the military forces of non-Indians and received rights in treaties "for as long as grass grows and water flows." As a response, Congress defined boundaries surrounding reservations, funded the buildup of U.S. Army units, herded Indians like cattle into segregated confinement, and approved unrestrictive promises written into treaties, most of which were "broken" by federal officials. At the same time, illegally the government "took our land" for purposes of exploitation and settlement. Federal employees and missionaries participated in unconscionable efforts to destroy the cultural underpinnings of tribal societies. The right to retain ancestral land on reservations and receive benefits in perpetuity represented only partial payment for the callous mistreatment of tribal ancestors in the past. This tribal response concludes: Any additional compensation—such as the return of land in the Black Hills—should accrue as further compensation for broken treaties and the unconscionable loss of land occupied by European Americans during the settlement era.

For more than a century, non-Indians and tribal members nurtured these conflicting perceptions, with some variations, while they learned to maintain social distances from

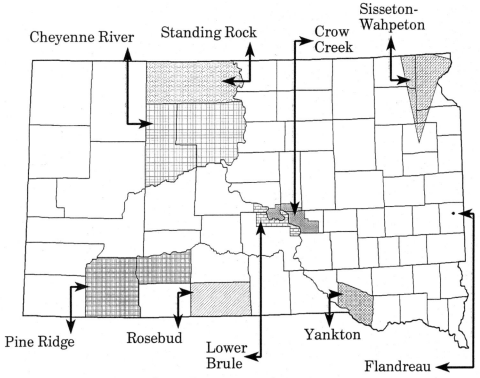

South Dakota Indian Reservations

There are nine federally recognized Native American reservations in South Dakota, constituting approximately 4.7 million acres, or six percent of the land. *Courtesy Herbert T. Hoover.*

each other. For example, at Winner in Rosebud Country, Indians lived mainly along the north side and whites along the south side of the highway. At Wagner in Yankton County, Indians dined in one restaurant and whites in another. Out on the reservations, Indians affiliated with one set of religious and cultural activities and Caucasians with another. Publicity inspired by the Civil Rights Movement of the 1960s, the appearance of the American Indian Movement, and the militant occupation of Wounded Knee in 1973 provoked suspicion and fear. Nervous co-existence gave way to abrasive interaction and occasional confrontation.

Finally, after nearly a century of statehood, during the 1980s George Mickelson became the first South Dakota governor to issue a formal call for "reconciliation" between tribal and non-Indian adversaries through dialogue, but his well-intentioned effort was futile. Public discussion was destined to fail in the absence of accurate historical information, beginning with a proper identification of cause for intercultural friction, which the young Caucasian author at the University of South Dakota misconstrued this way: "It may be true that one of my ancestors lied to one of yours," he wrote to tribal members. "After all, the pioneers, explorers, homesteaders and other government representatives did enough blundering around in the frontier to appall anyone who reads history. However, I can't be convinced that that still matters now. If I, personally, haven't passed someone a blanket full of small pox, how can I possibly owe him or her anything?" His question represented an attitude common among non-Indian South Dakotans. His statement identified all immigrating forces as "government representatives" in interethnic relationships.

Defensive rhetoric of this kind only exacerbated tension and circumvented the central issue. Throughout the history of the United States, responsibility for any abiding inequity in Indian-white relations must be attributed to action or neglect by the elected representatives of enfranchised citizens in Congress. If over time the majority of its members erred in their relationships with federally recognized tribes, such as those in South Dakota, Congress alone must accept the blame and atone for its own mistakes.

If, as the student suggested, the atonement process is complete and the time has arrived to "abolish the reservations" and terminate the special "benefits" promised to the tribes in the past, there could exist only two or three legal means of effecting change. One is a dramatic rejection of policies formulated by Congress in the past by the current members of Congress, as Judge Scarmon warned, which surely would lead to protracted litigation in federal courts. Another is the addition of an amendment to the Constitution of the United States through prescribed procedures—by three-fourths of all state legislatures or special constitutional conventions called for the purpose of amendment—which seems implausible even after a protracted national debate. Yet either legal avenue continues to loom as a threat to the abiding federal recognition of tribes and corresponding trust responsibility benefits.[5]

In the absence of a defining change in the legal status of tribes, reconciliation in Indian-white relations can be accomplished only through a mutual replacement of myths with an understanding of historical realities that created the relationships of federally recognized tribes with their non-Indian neighbors and produced their segregated existence under protection by policies applicable across the United States. One reality is that the circumstances of nine modern tribes in South Dakota are similar to those of other federally recognized tribes scattered across the country and cannot be changed by state or local governmental action. Through individual choice, enrolled members of the tribes in South Dakota may dwell in relative isolation on federally protected reservation land and continue to claim special benefits. The legal principles that protect them originated in the British colonial treatment of native peoples and gained expression after the American Revolution in the Indian policies of the U.S. government. One policy was a disposition to treat some but not all native groups or tribes as separate political entities, which the Second Continental Congress perpetuated by a treaty with Delaware Indians in 1779. Steadily, this federal relationship evolved through a treaty-making process until 1871, when Congress substituted unilaterally rescindable action through federal statutes sometimes called congressional "Agreements" with the tribes. Because Article I, Section 8, in the U.S. Constitution delegated authority for dealing "with the Indian tribes" to Congress alone, since 1789 its members have controlled all official standards for government-to-government relationships with federally recognized tribes and have been obligated to deal with terms in treaties and agreements approved by their predecessors in the past.

Their predecessors also perpetuated the British recognition of ancestral land as "Indian Country," under federal protection, beginning with a statute approved in 1797.[6] Accordingly, each of the nine reservations in South Dakota came into place as a component in "Sioux Country" under federal protection. Eight of the reservations gained geographical definitions by terms in treaties and congressional agreements, not as gifts extended by Congress, but as areas retained on ancestral land by the tribes. Only the Flandreau Santee Reservation came into place as a gift, which Congress extended because of the extraordinary circumstance of this particular group. Acts of Congress had confiscated the ancestral land of Santees and ordered their expulsion from Minnesota following their war against non-Indians in 1862. After establishing the Santee Reservation in Nebraska, Congress purchased small reservations for Flandreau Santees in South Dakota as well as for five other groups of Santees who returned to Minnesota, placed reservations under federal protection, and offered them for use by the scattered groups of Santees.

Thus, non-Indians should understand that the circumstances of nine federally recognized tribes in South Dakota and the legal condition of their reservation land must be perceived as products of a unique legal feature in Anglo-American heritage. Retrospectively, tribal members should realize that the option to live in isolation on reservations under federal protection with special benefits is a special privilege extended to an infinitesimal percentage of peoples whose ancestors occupied the Western Hemisphere when Columbus arrived in 1492. At a distance in South Dakota, the circumstances of all who live south of the border of the United States must be taken into account—the vast majority being descendants of those who confronted the imperial forces of Spain and Portugal. All early modern European imperial forces represented the selfish interests of evolving European nations, but those dispatched by Spain and Portugal were the worst in their treatment of Indian peoples. Not only did they intend to exploit natural resources at the expense of natives who already claimed the Western Hemisphere, they also represented feudalistic monarchies that refused either to recognize native tribes as political entities or to classify the land they occupied as ancestral properties of the tribes. As a result, colonizing Spaniards and Portuguese treated natives as individual subjects of European kings and queens without collective rights or tribal properties, who, as subjects, lived on conquered territory claimed by the Crown. Every native subject was on his own, or her own, to survive in colonial society on services extended by colonizers or support provided by non-recognized native social groups to which they belonged. For individual Native Americans, the most obvious difference in the experiences of those colonized by Spaniards and Portuguese was that Portuguese brought with them slavery as it then affected captured Africans, while Spaniards used the European institution called the *encomienda* and several other strategies to enforce the obedience and demand the labor of individual Native Americans called to service as groups of royal subjects.

Spanish and Portuguese feudalistic assumptions regarding Native American circumstances were handed down through revolutions to the modern nations of Latin America. The impacts of governmental dispositions south of the border of the United States are excruciatingly portrayed in two powerful video film productions. *The Mission* (issued in 1986) exposes the consequences of both Spanish and Portuguese policies, which in this instance led to the slaughter of countless Guarani Indians in Paraguay during the colonial period 1750-1770. *Romero* (1989) reveals the murder of a Roman Catholic Archbishop in El Salvador during the year 1980 and leaves no doubt in the mind of a viewer about why at least 80,000 Salvadoran Mayan Indians have died in this tiny republic since that time. These films make it clear why annually in recent years hundreds of thousands with mainly American Indian heritage in Latin America have fled across the border into the United States.

In the United States they have joined other Hispanic Americans—approximately thirty-seven million at the 2000 census—most of whom trace their principal ancestries to Indian tribes and with the term *mestizo* acknowledge Spanish or other European heritage, as well. In the film *The Mexican Americans* (2000), credible spokespersons claim Native American heritages in this largest of national ethnic groups and explain how its members have survived through the preservation of tribal traditions.

Many of them live in South Dakota. During the summer of 2003, Colombian native Catholic Father Luis Mesa reported approximately 8,000 best known as "Hispanics" or "Mexicans" in the state—about half legal and half illegal immigrants. As the parish priest for the Hispanic Our Lady of Guadalupe Parish in Sioux Falls, founded in 1996, Father Luis registered approximately half of the South Dakota Hispanic population as 360 families. Most of the 8,000 lived in East River. The vast majority came from Mexico (fifty percent), Guatemala (twenty percent), Oscar Romero's El Salvador (ten percent), and others from elsewhere in Central America, Venezuela, Colombia, and Puerto Rico. By cultural affiliation as well as biological heritage, according to U.S. standards, nearly all were American Indians in exile who added about one percent to the ten percent of the state population claiming enrollment in federally recognized tribes.[7] The primary difference in historical circumstance for the one percent comprising Hispanics was that none could claim any federal trust responsibility benefits or the right to occupy federally protected reservation land. Nevertheless, they live in the state with a right to be recognized as persons of Native American heritage.[8]

The misfortune of the Hispanic one percent illustrates the fundamental difference between the historic experience of native tribes in Latin America and those in the United States (and Canada). Although British colonial forces might have differed little from Latin American colonial forces in the callous management of Indian-white relations, they represented different suppositions about the legal treatment of native peoples. For reasons that cannot adequately be explained, British colonial forces brought to the Western Hemisphere an assumption that at least the most viable tribal societies should be recognized as political entities which merited government-to-government relationships with colonizing forces, in some instances through the use of treaties. Tribal ancestral lands should be recognized and protected by colonizing forces as Indian Country until particular areas were formally acquired for use by Anglo Americans.

Transferred through the era of the American Revolution as congressional policies, these assumptions abided in national legacies, as described above, which must be respected as do any assumptions regarding the benefits of citizenship. If legacies that accrue to the benefit of federally recognized tribes should be whisked away, so could the privilege to vote, for example, or easy access to legal remedies, or other benefits of citizenship held in common between Indians and non-Indians.

After the pivotal years 1779 (recognition of a tribe by treaty) and 1797 (recognition of Indian Country by Congress), hundreds of treaties and laws approved by Congress set legal parameters for the perpetuation of tribal recognition and protection for Indian Country from intrusions by territorial, state, local, or foreign governments. During the year 1996, according to a report by the Bureau of Indian Affairs, Congress recognized 569 tribes whose aggregate membership grew by the year 2000 census to approximately 2.5 million. All nine reservation societies comprising about ten percent of the population in South Dakota were included with assurances about federal recognition and protection as tribes as well as the designation of areas on their reservations classified as non-taxable Sioux Country under federal trust protection.

Throughout national history, constitutional authority to control Indian affairs has been in Congress, but there has existed a constitutional link between congressional and executive authority, because Article 2 in the constitution authorized the President of the United States to engage in the negotiation of treaties, required the signature of the president on all treaties and congressional statutes, and charged the president with a responsibility to "take care that the laws shall be faithfully executed." From the implementation of constitutional government in 1789 to the year 1849, presidents delegated their authority for the management of Indian Affairs to the U.S. Department of War and, since 1849, to the U.S. Department of the Interior—specifically to the U.S. Secretary of the Interior. Accordingly, since 1849, policies derived from treaties and congressional statutes have been supervised by the Secretary of the Interior and managed by federal employees in the U.S. Indian Field Service and other agencies of the U.S. government. Their executive policies bear evidence of details in federal commitments that must be treated as elements in national heritage.

Added to congressionally approved treaties and statutes as well as executive policies have been "case law" precedents determined by federal courts through an extra-constitutional function assumed by federal judges to engage in the constitutional "judicial review" of congressional legislation and administrative policies. The most memorable expression of this judicial prerogative regarding American Indians was the classification of federally recognized tribes as "domestic dependent nations" by Chief Justice John Marshall in the case *Worcester v. Georgia* (1832). As domestic nations, federally recognized tribes have claimed the liberty to seek tribal justice through litigation in the appellate court system of the United States. Since Congress and the president approved the Indian Citizenship Act of 1924, all tribal members also have been "citizens with all the rights and duties that are implied," as the University of South Dakota student put it, including the right to seek justice in the courts and the duty to pay all taxes levied, among citizens, except on Indian land under federal trust protection and profits derived on federally protected land.

Stability in the link between individual tribal members and their biological ancestors has been complicated by two factors. One has been the freedom of an individual to move formal enrollment from one tribe to another, which results in eligibility to claim benefits initiated by treaties in the tribe of current enrollment and in the surrender of benefits accrued through biological heritage. The other has been the fragmentation of ancestral tribes. Soon after treaty making ended in 1871, the ties of all Sioux people in South Dakota to fourteen ancestral tribes became muddled because of confusion related to wars in the nineteenth century—albeit during wars in which tribal forces never lost

a significant battle west of the Minnesota border and defended the retention of ancestral land through victories in battle and terms in treaties and congressional agreements.
Federal recognition changed to define modern tribes as fragmented or mixed societies that assembled on agency jurisdictions—described in a previous chapter—which
evolved into modern tribes on federally recognized reservations established and sustained mainly not by treaties but by acts of Congress. Eight were in place by the time
of statehood in 1889. Detribalized Flandreau Santees received only educational and
health-care benefits at the Flandreau Indian Boarding School until 1936, when 325 in
the group voted almost unanimously for federal recognition as a tribe and received it
with a reservation provided by Congress. Benefits previously accrued by ancestral tribes
through treaties and congressional statutes transferred to nine heterogeneous groups
assembled as modern tribes on federally protected reservations—not either as gifts or
as treaty rights accrued by all members of any one tribe but as justifiable benefits recognized by acts of Congress. Because of these two complicating factors added to a
federal rule that an individual is eligible for benefits of only the tribe in which he or she
is enrolled (except under special circumstances recognized by Congress), an individual
Indian might be denied some benefits provided through biological heritage.

Despite some confusion about benefits that differ in value from tribe to tribe, on their
reservations after statehood the nine heterogeneous societies in South Dakota retained
claim to more than ten percent of their ancestral land (compared to 3.5 percent by thirty-
seven Great Plains tribes overall). The Yankton Reservation created by a treaty in 1858
contained approximately 430,000 acres, and the Lake Traverse Reservation occupied
by Sissctons and Wahpetons following their Fort Wadsworth Treaty of 1867 an estimated 918,779 acres. The Pine Ridge, Rosebud, Cheyenne River, Standing Rock, Lower
Brûlé, and Crow Creek reservations contained an aggregate later determined to include
12,681,911 acres, when Congress defined their boundaries in 1889. The Flandreau
Santee Reservation created by Congress during the 1930s comprised 2,721 acres. Thus,
the nine reservations in South Dakota came into place with an aggregate land mass
estimated at 14,033,411 acres—approximately 28.4 percent of the land contained by
boundaries that defined South Dakota at the time of statehood in 1889.[9]

In return for the previous relinquishment of about 71.6 percent of the land in the
state and ancestral rights to lands on the perimeter, plus reservation areas sold as "surplus land" following the allotment of tribal land to individual Indians after 1889 under
the Dawes Severalty Act, the modern tribes of Sioux received, as a quid pro quo, two
considerations required mainly by congressional acts called agreements. One was the
creation of tribal funds in the U.S. Treasury (for all except the Flandreau Santee Sioux
Tribe), which Interior Department personnel distributed in either cash or treasury vouchers for use in retail purchases, or in annuity goods, wages, and services related to survival
in reservation life. Understandably, non-Indians mistook distributions in cash or treasury
vouchers with goods at tribal expense as gratuitous benefits—"handouts"—because
Interior Department employees managed distributions at the local level for more than
seventy years without a proper explanation. Nearly all of these funds acquired by the
surrender of land were gone by the end of the 1920s.[10]

The other consideration was the assumption and gradual refinement of a "trust
responsibility" by the U.S. government to provide additional benefits—without terminal dates. Tribal members perceived them as benefits in perpetuity, but Congress never
committed itself to "forever" terms in treaties or statutes that directly affected ancestors
of modern tribal members in South Dakota. Yet despite frequent variations in federal
Indian policies, Congress has sustained its commitment to all of these benefits—as a

part of the land-relinquishment quid pro quo often called "treaty rights" by tribal members—through which modern tribes of Sioux might survive under inhospitable natural conditions on the northern Great Plains.

■ Eight Tribal Benefits

Theoretically, some of the benefits remain available to all federally recognized Indians across the United States, due to the loss of land in the past, but some of them accrue according to the geographical location of a tribe and/or the residence of tribal members on reservation land under federal trust protection. Because of geographical location and historical circumstance, the nine reservation societies in South Dakota have received the maximum consideration from eight special benefits extended to federally recognized Indian tribes with land under federal trust protection:

(1) For tribal members in Sioux Country, non-Indian health-care delivery can be traced back to the year 1820, as explained in a previous chapter. Although restricted in application by the "quarter-blood rule" of 1918, it has evolved through terms in the Snyder Act of 1921 and the Indian Health Care Improvement Act of 1976 plus the case *McNabb v. Heckler* in 1986 to offer treatment and medications free of charge to all tribal members who qualify. As a previous chapter indicates, the Indian Health Service is controversial. When managed under tribal self-determination contracts, Congress is able to diminish services offered to enrolled Indians by the reduction of funds. In theory, tribal members are restricted to the use of Indian Health Service facilities at their places of enrollment but, in reality, as individuals they are accepted at most IHS stations regardless of the locations of their tribes. Despite its own legislation to include urban Indians, Congress has denied this benefit with a paucity of funds. Nevertheless, most federally recognized tribal members enjoy the privilege of access to health care and medications free of charge, and many receive long-term care support at public expense.

Numerous tribal members in the state have access to alternative health-care management systems, as well, at public expense. Those who have served in the Armed Forces of the United States may receive similar services in the massive Veterans Administration management system, at little if any cost, and cannot be denied at any of some 1,300 facilities scattered across the country. As citizens, tribal members are eligible for Medicare and Medicaid and senior citizens' long-term care support. As the case *McNabb v. Heckler* clearly indicates, those without means may use the IHS yet also rely on state and county support. No other group of citizens has access to a greater variety of health-care services at little if any cost. Inconveniences common to those who rely on management systems evoke complaints, but no federally recognized tribal member enrolled in South Dakota is at risk because of an absence or the cost of health-care delivery services. At least in the near future this system seems secure because the health-care trust responsibility benefit enjoyed by tribal members in the state originated in a treaty and received benchmark assurance accrued from the congressional Snyder Act of 1921. By individual choice, tribal members may seek care through ancestral methods, as well, offered by medicine men and women or roadmen in the Native American Church.

(2) Freedom from taxation on remaining Indian land under federal protection, or on business profits derived from protected land, has been responsible for the success of many tribal enterprises. For example, a tribe engaged in farming and ranching has been eligible to receive federal agricultural subsidies as a "legal person" yet has escaped the taxation of agricultural profits produced on trust land. Similarly, a tribe has escaped taxation on profits derived from hunting and fishing industries centered on federally protected land. Most advantageous of all, tribes operating high-stakes casinos on eight

of the nine reservations in South Dakota under terms in the National Indian Gaming Regulatory Act of 1988 have not paid taxes on casino earnings except by the voluntary entry of a tribe into a compact with the government of the state.

Two issues regarding federal trust lands and the taxation of profits derived from them have caused conflicts for tribes with state and local governments. Most of the land under federal trust protection includes acreages that tribes never have relinquished or that its members never have changed to fee simple subject to taxation. There is ample precedent to allow the recovery of fee land by tribes and its return to tax-free status, but the change has been allowed only to accommodate special circumstances—for example, trust land on the Flandreau Santee Sioux Reservation. Recently those tribes with casino or other business profits have purchased lands, but they have had little success gaining their return to trust, tax-free status because of opposition by state and local officials to prevent a corresponding loss of tax revenue. With authority delegated by Congress, Interior Department personnel may order a return to trust status through complicated procedures that almost inevitably fail.

The other issue is the extent of tax exemption, which mainly has applied to real estate levies, agricultural profits, and casino receipts. At issue have been such items as fees for auto licensure and the taxation of automobile and truck fuel sold by a tribe on trust land to an enrolled Indian, which in either instance has contributed to road construction and maintenance in the past. A recent decision by the Supreme Court of South Dakota determined that no state tax could apply to the purchase of fuel by tribal members. Issues such as the sales of hunting licenses within tribal boundaries have not been satisfactorily resolved. Nevertheless, a valued trust responsibility benefit that has in most instances been available to tribes has been the exclusion of trust lands and profits derived from them from taxation. (This benefit has not affected the imposition of income and excise taxes on individual tribal members.)

(3) "Indian Preference" (as affirmative action in individual employment), ordered by Congress in 1875 and implemented by agency personnel in Sioux Country as early as 1879, was strengthened by an article in the Indian Reorganization (Wheeler-Howard) Act of 1934, and has provided preferential access to federal or tribal employment. Congressional incentive for the offer of this special benefit represented the goal of economic self-sufficiency for federally recognized Indians, who remain the only national citizens whose affirmative action opportunities are required by law (instead of administrative policy). In the Indian Field Service, at Indian Health Service units, and at reservation schools, the employment of a tribal member with suitable qualifications is nearly required. In some instances, unqualified applicants have had access to training at federal expense. Beyond reservation boundaries, too, federally recognized Indians have enjoyed this preference, mandated by law, in employment funded by Congress. *Lakota Journal* newspaper issues in the year 2003 contained many affirmative action announcements. For example, applicants for positions at the Little Wound School at Kyle were required to prove "tribal enrollment to claim Indian preference" in employment, and "Indian preference will apply" for applicants seeking jobs at a distant Paiute police department in Oregon.

(4) A similar advantage of "Indian Preference" in business opportunities has been assured under terms in the Buy Indian Act of 1910 corroborated in provisions of Public Law 93-638 as well as in tribal ordinances. This benefit has allowed tribal members access to reservation business opportunities funded by tribal or federal funds without competitive bidding procedures. The advantage originated in an effort to involve tribal members in business contracts offered to build reservation facilities. It abides

in housing, school, hospital, road, or other construction at federal or tribal expense. *Lakota Journal* issues in the year 2003 contained many Buy Indian announcements. For instance, "the successful bidder" on a construction contract at Standing Rock "must provide Indian preference" assurances for "subcontractors and in its employment and training." A Rosebud water and sewer contract was "subject to Indian preference but bids" were "invited from non-Indian" contractors. A $1 million contract announcement at Pine Ridge indicated that "Indian preference will apply."

(5) Education at federal expense for reservation residents in grades K-12 originated as an elementary education commitment during the treaty-making era, and it has continued in lieu of taxation on tribal land to support education at public schools. In recent decades, self-determination policies and laws have allowed tribes to take over mission and federal schools and sustain their operation at federal expense. This benefit has assured access to pre-college education and, since about the year 1970, Congress has provided some funding for tribally operated colleges. As well, Congress has carried on its commitments to the Johnson-O'Malley Act of 1934. This law authorized federal expenditures on behalf of Indians mainly in education and health care in lieu of taxable land. For example, *Lakota Journal* issues in 2003 carried an announcement for the Oglala Sioux Tribe Johnson O'Malley Program to pay educational assistance for "members of a federally recognized tribe" with a "minimum one-quarter degree Indian blood" at South Dakota public district schools in Bennett County, Hot Springs, Kadoka, Wall, Rapid City, and Shannon County; and in Nebraska public district schools at Alliance, Chadron, Crawford, Rushville, and Scotts Bluff. Clearly, at least the pre-college educational commitment of the federal government remains as undiminished as the one provided in health care.

(6) Tribalism, as a business, originated in nineteenth-century reservation land management and agency jobs, gained stability through the Indian Reorganization Act of 1934, acquired momentum from Great Society funds allocated to assist poverty-stricken citizens during the 1960s and 1970s, and crystallized under terms in the Indian Self Determination and Education Assistance Act of 1975. Through terms in the 1975 law, a tribal government could acquire congressional funding to provide services previously

A modern school on the Standing Rock Reservation represented improvement in federally funded K-12 educational environments by the 1980s. *Courtesy Herbert T. Hoover.*

delivered by the Bureau of Indian Affairs or other federal agencies. In recent decades, Congress also has contributed to the salaries of elected and appointed tribal officials as well as administrative costs of housing developments and other services. Obviously, growing attachment to tribalism represents economic as well as cultural interest.

In a report issued during the year 1996, Crow Creek tribal member and political candidate Gerald Lytle provided an example of the importance of the economy linked to tribal government on his reservation. From approximately 1,500 members in residence, the executive council employed 240 persons in twenty-three divisions of tribal government, most with support from federal allocations. In addition, seventy-five worked at the tribal casino. Because of Indian Preference, twenty-six others worked for the Bureau of Indian Affairs on the reservation, eighteen as paramedical personnel at the Indian Health Service Unit; and twelve for the U.S. Postal Service, the U.S. Army Corps of Engineers, and private service industries. Some remained unemployed but, because the executive council controlled eighty percent of the jobs with federal support, a large percentage of the adult population drew incomes from the tribe itself.[11]

During his interview in the summer of 2003, former Yankton Tribal Chairman Cournoyer provided a more recent example of job opportunities on his reservation that similarly illustrated the importance of government contracts under terms of the 1975 Self Determination Act. Approximately one hundred worked at the tribal school in Marty, about forty-five were employed by the Indian Health Service Unit, twenty-two at the Bureau of Indian Affairs, and perhaps twenty-five on housing construction and improvement. These opportunities plus jobs at the tribal casino sharply reduced unemployment. Indeed, in his opinion "all the people that would work are working." Many of those unemployed were idle because they refused to accept manual labor.

(7) Suitable housing for reservation residents originated in an obligation of agency officials during the nineteenth century, gained stability as a part of the trust responsibility through the application of the federal Housing Act of 1937, and has improved because of increased federal support through special Indian housing acts in 1974 and

Sixteen federally sponsored communal colonies accommodated families in greatest distress during the Depression. *Courtesy Herbert T. Hoover.*

1988, and the block-grant housing act of 1996. Late in the twentieth century, this commitment provided tens of millions of dollars in annual congressional allocations for the Sioux reservations in South Dakota alone. In Sioux Country since the 1960s, this has become a cornerstone in the economy of federally recognized tribes with reservation land under federal protection. In recent years, tribal "housing authorities" have managed congressional block grants and issued contracts for all housing constructed or improved at federal expense.[12] Uses of these grants have been supervised very little except by the requirement for occasional reports and assurances that congressionally funded houses will be constructed and maintained only on land classified as reservation acreage. The block grants authorized by the 1996 housing act have been substantial. Reports in the *Lakota Journal* for the year 2003 indicated $9,915,277 for the Pine Ridge, for example, $5,639,345 for the Cheyenne River Reservation, and so on.

Housing block grants sustained Indian preference employment and construction on every reservation. In addition, congressional support for special projects were substantial for the year 2003. An omnibus appropriations act of Congress reported in the *Lakota Journal* supplied $56.4 million for similar special projects to benefit Native Americans in South Dakota. Because most federal allocations were delivered as grants under contracts, the nine tribes flourished as business enterprises on all of the reservations that enlivened political participation at every election of a new executive council and discussion at every general council meeting of eligible voters in the tribes.

(8) The administrative U.S. Indian Office Circular 2970 (1934) and the congressional Freedom of Religion Act (1978) reversed previous acculturative efforts and assured legal protection for all Native American religious and other cultural activities. Federally recognized tribal members stand alone among citizens afforded explicit cultural protection only implied for others in amendments to the Constitution of the United States.

Not because of laws as much as through federal administrative policies that gained expression in social and economic pressures, late nineteenth- and early twentieth-century agency and mission personnel endeavored to suppress vital elements in traditional culture. The *tiospaye*, an ancestral extended-family system that defined both political and social structures, as described by Virginia Driving Hawk Sneve in her essay, gave way to the organization of reservation administrative (farm) districts. A traditional belief system, which provided access to the supreme being *Wakantanka Tunkasila* through the Sacred Pipe, all but vanished from public view because federal and mission personnel

Following concealment through two generations, ancestral ceremonies and teachings have emerged into open use. Native American Church Roadman Asa Primeaux, with staff and gourd, authorized this photo of a ceremony to honor his son during winter in the 1970s. *Courtesy Herbert T. Hoover.*

endeavored to replace it with Christian denominational religious services and alternative community activities. The ancestral language in several dialects, which federal and mission educators tried to suppress among youngsters in schools, continued to bond tribal members in isolated locations across the reservations occupied by Sioux. After two generations of preservation mainly "underground," these and other cultural elements surfaced almost unscathed during the Native American Renaissance of the 1960s and 1970s. In reservation environments under federal protection since 1934, tribal members have preserved them as defining characteristics in tribal heritage.

■ Tribal Enrollment Issues

The lure of federal trust responsibility benefits and the appeal of a cultural renaissance revived general interest in tribal affiliations during the 1960s and have been primary causes for burgeoning tribal memberships since the 1970s. As a domestic dependent nation, every federally recognized modern tribe across the United States has controlled its own rules of enrollment—ranging from a faint trace to a quarter-Indian blood quantum. Thus, the survival of modern tribes represents not only ethnic tenacity, but also a desire by enrolled tribal members to claim as many trust responsibility benefits as possible in a reservation environment. Because each domestic nation controls its own standards of enrollment, and individual members may transfer enrollment from tribe to tribe according to those standards, memberships in the Sioux tribes of South Dakota may change from day to day. Total enrollment in the Pine Ridge tribe has grown to the largest number for a tribe in South Dakota while the aggregate membership in modern Sioux tribes across the state has increased to approach three times the original estimate of 32,000 Sioux in fourteen ancestral tribes at the outset of the eighteenth century. On average, approximately half of the enrolled members in the burgeoning roll of a tribe has fulfilled requirements for classification as reservation residents eligible for all of the eight trust responsibility benefits listed above.

Because congressional allocations are restricted by annual appropriation parameters, and under terms in the Indian Self Determination Act have been parceled out in specific increments through contracts and grants for tribal use, members of the general councils of voting adults in the tribes have grown increasingly reluctant to accept additions to membership rolls. On many occasions, Yankton tribal members have rejected petitions to reduce the minimum enrollment requirement of one-quarter Indian (half of which must be Yankton heritage) by replacing this requirement with one of only proving descent from someone whose name appeared on the 1921 annuity roll, regardless of blood quantum.

Speaking in favor of such a change has been the Yankton tribal member Ron Joseph, a successful, self-employed, off-reservation resident in the city of Beresford whose spouse is non-Indian. Their five children miss enrollment under the quarter-blood standard by a small fraction of Indian blood quantum. As a result, the younger Josephs were denied the trust responsibility benefits listed above even though they live their lives as Native Americans. Among opponents of a blood-quantum requirement reduction in enrollment procedures was Ramona O'Connor, a Yankton traditionalist, who expressed a belief that a quarter-blood quantum Indian should stand as a minimum demonstration of heritage to justify formal enrollment.[13] In agreement with O'Connor during the summer of 2003, Yankton traditionalist and educator Lana Gravatt voiced concern about the loss of commitments to traditional ways on the reservation with the existing enrollment requirement. She believed that a change to accept a lesser degree of heritage would gravely diminish the cultural meaning of tribalism.

In some instances, tribal enrollment committees have gone beyond resistance to new enrollments by examining existing roles in an attempt to remove some of the names. According to a series of articles in the *Sioux Falls Argus Leader* during the year 2000, in a purging effort Flandreau Santee Sioux enrollment officials endeavored to strike the name of Mona Miyasato. She had been born on the Lower Brûlé Reservation in 1943 but adopted at eight months of age on the Flandreau Reservation by Alex Wakeman—a member of the celebrated family of Little Crow. With legal assistance, she avoided removal from the tribal roll and remarked, "[if disenrolled] I won't have a country. . . . I won't be eligible for Indian Health services. All the tribal benefits won't be there. No Indian preference. . . . I will become an orphan again."

The question of membership through the tradition of adoption, under discussion in the Miyasato case, never has been resolved, but the issue of mixed biological heritage has been clearly defined. During the nineteenth century, federal officials recognized authority in tribal councils of voting adults to determine who could enroll in a tribe and receive federal benefits, regardless of Indian blood quantum and, in many instances, the enrollment of whites married into a tribe. Officials did not interfere unless the Secretary of the Interior believed that a denial for enrollment was unjustified, or that an addition included someone who should not share benefits reserved for tribal members. During the initial allotment of tribal land into individual plots through the last two decades of the nineteenth century, federal officials denied the inclusion of non-Indians on allotment rolls, and both voting adults and federal officials questioned the inclusion of some people who claimed mixed racial extraction. To settle the matter, the federal decision *Waldron v. United States, et al.* (1905) recognized the legal equality of mixed-bloods with full-bloods enrolled in tribes across the United States.

Into the twentieth century, federal officials continued to question whether non-Indians married into the tribes or progeny of little Indian blood quantum should be eligible for particular benefits delivered through the federal trust responsibility—especially education and health care. As a response, beginning in 1918 the quarter-blood quantum of Indian descent became a general standard, which agency personnel could adjust to accommodate individual circumstances. With limited variation, this remained a rule until the implementation of the Indian Self Determination and Education Assistance Act of 1975. Although the quarter-blood quantum standard remained in place, after a tribe took over an educational facility, gained influence in health-care delivery, or took charge of housing development, federal employees found it necessary to allow informal adjustments in applications of the quarter-blood rule.[14] Nevertheless, most of the tribes in South Dakota have written into their constitutions, bylaws, and ordinances some manifestation of the quarter-blood Indian minimum for membership by enrollment.

Since 1975 both federal and tribal officials have become vigilant about the exclusion of tribal members who could not qualify as reservation residents but, instead, were classified as either relocated or urban-enrolled Indians. Ordinarily in health-care delivery, for example, non-resident tribal members have received treatment at the Indian Health Service units on their respective reservations, but they have been denied federal support for off-reservation treatment and hospitalization, or for referrals to acquire medical treatments and procedures off the reservations. The only exception in South Dakota has been health-care delivery service at the Sioux San IHS Unit in Rapid City, operated mainly for an intertribal society in the Rapid City area. As a result, many enrolled members classified as non-residents of the reservation groups have complained about exclusion from such benefits as housing, Indian Preference in business contract applications, and some health-care services even though they have been eligible for other benefits accrued through the federal trust responsibility.[15]

Uncertainty about eligibility for trust responsibility benefits has been exacerbated, too, by periodic changes in congressional commitments to the benefits during the twentieth century. As a general rule for tribes in the state, steadily through the period 1910-30 Congress curtailed its spending while federal administrators shifted the burden of fiscal responsibility to the use of tribal land-sale funds, which nearly vanished by the outset of the Great Depression. From 1933 to 1942, federal New Deal programs, jobs, and gratuities improved reservation facilities, stimulated new industries, and prevented starvation. From 1942 to 1960, federal officials attempted a gradual withdrawal from trust responsibilities by the reduction of reservation populations through urban relocation efforts. After 1960, Great Society programs, followed by self-determination initiatives, restored federal spending for all trust responsibility benefits mainly to accommodate the needs of reservation residents.

Inevitably, tribal enrollments waxed and waned according to varying congressional commitments to trust responsibility benefits. During the 1920s, when tribal funds were nearly depleted and federal officials arranged national citizenship for Indians in preparation for eventual withdrawal from trust responsibilities, many tribal members left the reservations and some neglected to enroll their children. Through the years 1932 to 1942, interest in tribal governments grew while tribal enrollments increased because many relocated Indians returned to the reservations in response to federal New Deal spending and, in most instances, to the reorganization of tribal governments under terms in the Wheeler-Howard Act of 1934. Through the years 1942 to 1960 interest faded and tribal enrollments declined because of reductions in federal support. Since 1960 the influence of tribal governance like that of cultural attachments has undergone a renaissance, and steadily tribal enrollments have escalated to record numbers.

Through recent decades, both the councils of voting adults and the officials they have elected to manage tribal affairs have become acutely aware of the eight special benefits listed above, which have been refined as federal trust responsibilities by means of growth in tribal spending prerogatives as well as tribal enrollments. Under terms in constitutions and bylaws approved by the U.S. Secretary of the Interior, the nine tribal societies have held elections. Their officials have maintained legislative, executive, and judicial functions of government with reliance on maximum assistance through federal trust responsibility benefits. In addition, they have become defensive about intrusions into their prerogatives by state and local governmental officials and aggressive in the pursuit of means through which to enhance the influences and opportunities of their tribes.

■ Tribal Distinctions

During the twentieth century, through periods of change in federal assistance and tribal memberships, three developments distinguished the nine tribes of South Dakota from each other and significantly affected their relationships with non-Indians. One was a dramatic reduction in reservation acreages owned by the tribes or by their respective members, mainly through sales of individual allotments. At the middle of the twentieth century, the society enrolled at Pine Ridge retained nearly fifty-five percent of its original reservation acreage, but the one enrolled on the Yankton Reservation retained only about eight percent, and each of the others except at Flandreau retained some percentage between these two extremes. Overall, across the nine reservations, non-Indians had gained ownership of more than half of the land.[16] The erosion of acreage continued. As indicated above, when South Dakota became a state in 1889, the Sioux tribes owned slightly in excess of fourteen million acres—more than twenty-eight percent of the acreage. A century later, the nine reservations contained an aggregate of land owned or used by tribes of about 4.7 million acres—approximately six percent of the acreage in the state.[17]

A second development has been the evolution of fairly stable tribal governments, each controlled by terms in written constitutions and bylaws approved by the U.S. Secretary of the Interior. The one at Lake Traverse lapsed from 1892 to the 1930s, then quickly revived and gained approval as a Wheeler-Howard government. The one on the Yankton Reservation operated according to terms in a constitution and bylaws approved in 1891; then in a constitution and bylaws approved in 1932, with amendments, as guidelines for a non-Wheeler-Howard government. The one at Flandreau came into existence as a Wheeler-Howard government in 1936 to govern tribal affairs on a new reservation provided by Congress. All of the others represented uninterrupted tribal governance modified and enhanced by terms in the Wheeler-Howard Act of 1934.[18]

A third development has been a growing propensity among federally recognized tribes to seek justice in federal courts. This process originated in 1863, when Congress authorized tribal litigation against the U.S. government in the U.S. Court of Claims (created in 1855), and it gained easy application after the establishment of the Indian Claims Commission in 1946. Through the last half of the twentieth century, across the United States as well as in South Dakota, tribes have increased litigation either in the U.S. Court of Claims or in U.S. District Courts followed by appellate activities sometimes ending in the Supreme Court of the United States. Claims court litigation often produced financial compensation for unconscionable federal management or deficient payments in the past, most of which was distributed among tribal members as belated quid pro quo payments by the United States government, which non-Indians mistakenly tended to perceive as a continuation of gratuitous "handouts." Other litigation resulted from allegations of infringements on tribal jurisdictional rights by state and local governmental officials.

Most internal affairs in the tribes have evoked interest among non-Indian South Dakotans only when they exposed flaws in tribal management useful as grist for the mills of criticism. During the year 2000, for instance, journalists reported indictments at Pine Ridge. Accusations against tribal officials included the use of self-determination contracts to manipulate general assistance funds for personal benefit. Allegedly without the payment of rental fees, tribal officials drawing substantial salaries occupied low-cost housing funded by Congress to shelter the poor. Primary causes for irregularities have been limited supervision of federally funded programs and excessive spoilsmanship in the tribal political process plus frequent changes in personnel elected or appointed to manage tribal affairs. In the absence of a stable bureaucracy on any reservation similar to the federal civil service, members of families without political influence have voiced justifiable complaints. During an interview in the summer of 2003, the seventy-three-year-old Yankton widow Rose Mary Rouse was critical of internal discrimination in housing assignments, about elders not receiving any payments from casino profits, about the payments of salaries to relatives of politicians who allowed their relations to be absent from work for successive days without reductions in salaries, and about the creation of jobs for friends and relatives who sat in offices without job responsibilities.[19]

Non-Indians have focused even greater attention on issues that directly affected the interests of the entire population of the state. One that often has evoked controversy was the matter of tribal jurisdiction within reservation boundaries, especially as it pertained to the exercise of tribal prerogatives relating to the authority of tribal police, social service prerogatives, wildlife management, and environmental concerns. Several times, controversies pertaining to tribal jurisdiction led to litigation in federal courts. Cross-deputization between tribal and county sheriff's forces sometimes alleviated tension but never resolved the question of how simultaneously to enforce state, county, municipal, tribal, and federal laws on a single reservation containing a "checker-board" of acreages formed by federally protected tribal properties interspersed with fee simple tribal and fee simple non-Indian lands. This became the central issue in the cases *Yankton Sioux Tribe v. Southern Missouri Waste Management District and State of South Dakota* (1996), and *South Dakota v. Yankton Sioux Tribe, et al.* (1998), wherein South Dakota officials claimed rights to govern environmental management and charged deficiencies in tribal policing efforts.

A second issue has been the defense of reservation boundaries, which have been at risk among tribes that surrendered large portions of their original reservation acreages. In the case *Decoteau v. District County Court* (1975), federal judges disestablished the entire outer boundary of the Lake Traverse Reservation, diminishing the area under tribal jurisdiction to only scattered acreages owned by the tribe and its members—less than fifteen percent of the original reservation acreage. For jurisdictional purposes, the tribe surrendered the remaining acreage to Roberts County and the State of South Dakota. Rationale used by judges for disestablishment was the argument that at the time of a surplus land sale in 1891 this reservation was "terminated." By implication, the judges' conclusion embraced an ill-founded assumption (evidently based on erroneous information provided by witnesses) that a previous generation of Sissetons and Wahpetons had desired the disestablishment of the reservation boundaries. As further evidence to justify the disestablishment of the reservation in 1975, the judges took note that within the original boundaries only about 3,000 resident Indians retained some fifteen percent of the original acreage and approximately 30,000 non-Indians owned the rest of the land.

In the case *Rosebud Sioux Tribe v. Kneip* (1977), federal judges similarly used contemporary head counts of tribal members and non-Indians as rationale to order a reduction of the outer boundary of the reservation, for jurisdictional purposes. Although Rosebud tribal members retained ownership of allotment and heirship lands in Gregory, Tripp, and Mellette counties, judges reduced the jurisdictional authority of the tribe to only the Indian land contained by boundaries surrounding Todd County.

In a succession of cases—*Yankton Sioux Tribe v. Southern Missouri Waste Management District and State of South Dakota* (1996), *South Dakota v. Yankton Sioux Tribe, et al.* (1998), and *1998 WL 23206 (U.S.)*—judges inexplicably abandoned a previous guarantee by Congress that 1858 treaty terms including reservation boundaries would remain in place. In the last of these cases, they ordered the disestablishment of the entire outer boundary, for jurisdictional purposes. This left only 36,111 of the about 430,000 original acres under tribal jurisdiction, and denied tribal authority along roadways, as well.

A third issue of general interest to non-Indians has been the prospect of reservation geographical expansion and the recovery of federal protection for land under tribal control. A prime example was a parcel of land purchased by the Lower Brûlé Tribe in the Oacoma area, where its sub-agency existed until 1894. Federal officials have been reluctant to restore trust status to land previously removed from federal protection out of fear of a precedent that might cause trouble in the future, and due to a corresponding reduction of the taxable state and local land base. An article entitled "Bush rescinds Clinton rule to restore lost Indian Lands" explained that "actions by the federal government in the late nineteenth and early twentieth century removed about two-thirds of tribal land from their reservations"—a fairly accurate assessment that includes both "surplus land" sales after allotment and individual or heirship sales of allotments changed from "trust" to "fee patent" land—ranging between a loss of about forty-five percent on the Pine Ridge and nearly ninety-two percent on the Yankton Reservation. The statement that "the Bush administration has rescinded a Clinton-era rule that would have made it easier" for tribes to "restore lost land" fails to recognize that, constitutionally, Congress must be involved with approval.

In another context, the article clarified the meaning of "restore lost land" with the phrase "land-into-trust requests." This process met resistance by "municipalities and state attorneys general and governors who complained that, since the tribes wouldn't have to pay taxes on the land, it could erode their tax base." In addition, there was concern that "tribes could build casinos and low-income housing on the land" returned to trust status. Ron Allen, vice president of the National Congress of American Indians (NCAI), thought that resistance came, too, from people who are "afraid of Indian power" and "don't trust tribes."[20]

The lack of trust came from more than a century of uneasy co-existence, but the fear of Indian power was a response of recent origin. It was little related either to a faint memory of nineteenth-century wars or the militant demonstrations of American Indian Movement members during the 1970s. Instead, fear came from a continuous reminder of tribal economic power by the advertisement of tribally operated casinos. From the appearance of the reservation gaming industry, first in bingo halls that produced little revenue, then in high-stakes casinos that generated substantial economic returns, most non-Indian observers were not prepared to reconcile a new image of economic success with the historical perception of tribal reliance on federal support.

Indeed, images of tribes and their activities that took root in the nineteenth century remained a perplexing problem into the twenty-first century. Rouse discussed the problem of paying taxes and utilities costs and emphasized that "we pay just like the white man. I don't know why they [non-Indians] are so down on us. Some of them still believe that we get a check every month from the government." Her grand-son-in-law, a white man, asked, "How much money do you get every month?" She replied, "I get a VA check and my husband's social security. He said, 'Oh, I though you got it from the government.' I said, 'The government never gave me a dime yet'" that she has not earned like any citizen or did not have coming as a "treaty right."

Unfortunately, the mistaken impression that tribal members have lived as parasites at the expense of tax-paying citizens has been perpetuated by journalists and academicians posturing as do-gooders. Journalists have reported that Shannon County, which contains the Pine Ridge Reservation, long has been one of the most poverty-stricken counties in the United States. Young academicians have endeavored to establish credentials in their professions with profiles of Indians as down-trodden and abused peoples in texts implying that they were shiftless and beggarly parasites. Among the most unconscionable texts issued in recent years was *Lakota Culture, World Economy*, printed by the University of Nebraska Press in the year 2000. Kathleen Pickering, a doctoral candidate in anthropology at the University of Wisconsin, claimed to have interviewed about 250 residents of the Pine Ridge Reservation but refused to name her sources or to make their taped interviews available. She used the explanation that tribal members would not speak in the presence of tape recorders or reveal their identities. This came as a surprise to academicians at the University of South Dakota who have gathered more than 5,000 interviews on audiotapes, several of them cited in this chapter, and have not been refused formal interviews by more than a dozen prospective interviewees in thirty-five years. The academicians were further perplexed to read Pickering's implied conclusion that Pine Ridge residents all remained in economic bondage. In her condescending text, Pickering failed to point out that non-Indian residents of Shannon County shared with tribal members inevitable hardships of life on the Great Plains or that most residents of the reservation lived under far better circumstances than her text implied. Evidently, she searched to find the most poverty-stricken ten percent of the reservation population. She might have found at least ten percent of the non-Indian, Hispanic, or other residents in Rapid City and Sioux Falls living under no better conditions.

Representing a far more reliable tribal viewpoint, NCAI Vice President Allen acknowledged that "reservation gambling has been the economic engine for many tribes over the past decade," and that some tribal leaders called for publicity about profits with hopes of putting "to rest the perception that Indian Country is a drag on the economy." Allen called for caution, however, because "fewer than half of the . . . recognized Indian tribes have opted for bingo halls or Nevada-style casinos." Moreover, in excess of "half of all Indian gaming revenues are generated by the operations of only eight tribes," which included the Foxwoods Resort Casino of the Mashantucket Pequot Tribe in Connecticut and the gaming operation of the Prior [Spirit] Lake Tribe of Mdewakanton Dakotas near Minneapolis.

None of the nine tribes in South Dakota have earned substantial revenues from gaming, due to an absence of large populations of prospective gamblers in the state, but gaming has created an image of economic progress that all tribes have achieved since the 1970s. As indicated above, Red Lake Chippewa educator Cook expressed the opinion that "Indian tribes and nations have made more economic strides in the past twenty-five years than in the previous 150 years." As reasons, he explained: "Government anti-poverty programs of the 1960s and 1970s set the stage for tribal self-governance" that gained momentum through the implementation of 1975 Indian Self Determination and Education Assistance Act funding, which "prepared them for the coming of gaming enterprises." Although tribes in South Dakota have not grown rich from gaming, it has been responsible for visible improvements across reservation areas in better lodging accommodations and restaurants, and in the replacement of battered "reservation cars" with new automobiles.[21] By the outset of the twenty-first century, most reservation communities reflected a middle-class lifestyle at least equal to that of most neighboring non-Indian communities.

Because of visible improvements in reservation economies, sympathy based on poverty conditions so obvious in the past has been replaced by growing resentment about special benefits extended to tribes by the U.S. government. Legitimate reconciliation of abiding consequence must include the education of all citizens in the state regarding the origin and perpetuation of these benefits as a federal trust responsibility.

Tribal members must have ready access to the same information for several reasons. One is to acquire a clear definition of each special benefit, an understanding of how it evolved, and a perception of its limitations. Rouse voiced a fairly typical perception: "The government made all the promises to us. . . . They should give us what we need. . . . We don't have to pay taxes. We don't have to go to hospital" at personal expense, "pay for our electricity, all of that, in a treaty." This is an exaggerated view of trust responsibility benefits.

With more reliable information, tribal members could transfer attention from popular myths to historical realities. No treaty even implied "for as long as grass grows." All terms in treaties between the U.S. government and the tribes of Sioux were not "broken." The charge that "white people took" the ancestral land of the Sioux without compensation can be demonstrated in only two post-war circumstances. The first came after the 1862 war in Minnesota. Congress took actions to compensate by funding per capita distributions in cash during the period 1908-18; by purchasing land for use by a total of seven groups of Santees removed from Minnesota, including the Flandreau Santees; and by classifying land on all seven reservations (six of them still in use in Nebraska, Minnesota, and South Dakota) under federal protection. The other anomalous circumstance was the illegal seizure of the Black Hills area by Congress in 1877. In response to a recommendation by the U.S. Court of Claims in 1979, Congress ordered a cash payment. The Black Hills Case has yet to be settled because the tribes declined to accept a cash settlement without the return of some of the land.

Blame for provable inequities in Indian-white relations must be assigned primarily to Congress, whose past performance has not been as unconscionable as mythmakers insist. Careful documentary research easily proves that, through the transfer of land ownership, modern tribes earned all of the payments and trust responsibility benefits they received from the U.S. government through the twentieth century. Accordingly, archival research disproves the accusation that reservation societies ever have imposed an unjustifiable "drag on the economy" of taxpayers through unearned benefits provided by federal, state, and local governments. Both sacrifice by tribes in the surrender of landed capital and congressional performance have been far more responsible than popular mythmakers are prone to admit.

As a result of the transfer of ancestral Indian land, non-Indian descendants of immigrants have enjoyed benefits comparable to trust responsibilities extended to tribal members. Some immigrants appeared to improve advantageous circumstances elsewhere or to satisfy a yearning for adventuresome experiences, but the vast majority appeared to escape agonizing if not catastrophic circumstances in Western Europe. Tribal members relinquished, and federal employees surveyed, land that Congress offered under reasonable terms in either general or special land laws. Late in the nineteenth century, the West in the United States was one of few places in the world where individuals and families could gain access to land and a new life, and in no place in the West was access more advantageous than in South Dakota.

Mutual recognition by tribal members and non-Indians in South Dakota that the two groups share inherited benefits must replace reciprocal false accusations based on myths in order to allow sensible dialogue about more critical issues that stand out among others with the onset of the twenty-first century. One that has caused abiding aggravation in Indian-white relations for several generations was the Black Hills Case—grandfather of all claims by Native American tribes against the U.S. government. Stripped of legal jargon and conflicting myths, facts in this case are simple. Congress and the president approved terms in the 1868 Fort Laramie Treaty that promised no encroachment on more than sixty million acres west of the Missouri River until at least three-fourths of all voting adult males in signatory tribes extend approval. After illegal encroachment by gold prospectors and the Battle of the Little Bighorn, unilaterally with the Sioux Agreement of 1877 Congress seized more than thirty-eight million acres in a corridor extending westward from the river that included the Black Hills. In 1887 tribes initiated litigation for payment, which the U.S. Court of Claims rejected more than once but in 1979 approved and recommended a cash settlement. Congress responded with an offer to pay more than $100 million and the Supreme Court of the United States approved the settlement. Tribes agreed to accept the money only if Congress also ordered the return of some land. In the absence of a compromise settlement, South Dakotans have expressed various perceptions about how much land might be involved—estimated between approximately 1.3 million acres remaining in federal ownership and "the *entire* Black Hills Area," as the USD student understood the matter. While adversaries continued to exchange views, the congressional offer with accrued interest has grown to some $600 million in the U.S. Treasury. No plausible solution has been in the offing. A resolution is essential to an abiding improvement of Indian-white relations in South Dakota.

No presentation could better portray the historical confrontation over the Black Hills than the video documentary film entitled *In the Light of Reverence: Protecting America's Sacred Lands* (2001). It features a clash in fundamental values between non-Indians and tribal traditionalists in three regions of the American West: Lakotas in the Black Hills, Hopis in the Southwest, and non-federally recognized Wintu Native Americans in California. On these regional locations, tribal members confront economic developments and react with efforts to defend ancestral philosophy, religious practice, and spirituality. The opening segment (some twenty-five minutes) is about the Black Hills in general, and one defining feature in particular, which evokes discussions among film participants regarding fundamental differences in philosophical values and cultural behavior.

The main object under discussion is the protrusion at the west edge of the Black Hills known to non-Indians as Devils Tower but to Native Americans as *Mato Tipila*, which narrators translate to mean Lodge of the Bear. In spiritual imagery, the bear is a powerful force with a capacity to instill physical as well as spiritual healing. This assertion leads to a broader perception that, in the opinions of tribal traditionalists, all of "the Black Hills are sacred." Reverence is expressed by Lakotas through the use of the Sacred Pipe. Non-Indians insist that they enjoy "spiritual experiences" as well as economic and recreational benefits from uses of the land. Tribal members find most of these ways to be either forms of desecration or damage beyond repair. U.S. Park Service personnel endeavor to straddle primary points of contention to discover some compromise that could accommodate all uses of this place on public land by tribal traditionalists and non-Indians alike. A film narrator asserts the interesting observation that federal employees allow mountain climbers to drive spikes and scale walls at Devils Tower at all times except one brief period reserved for Native Americans every year. Yet they prohibit driving spikes and climbing on Mount Rushmore at any time because the damage or desecration of this national icon is against the federal law.

Conflicting philosophical dispositions are clear. Johnson Holy Rock, an elder and former chairman in the Oglala Lakota Tribe, displays a dignified demeanor as he recognizes the economic interests of non-Indians. Yet he summarizes the meaning of the *Mato Tipila* and surrounding area in the phrase, "The Black Hills was the center of life." Lakotas came with reverence to restore their health, and to fast in the quest for divine guidance. In a reference to mountain climbers, bluntly he asks, "Don't they have any respect for anything?"

The writer Vine Deloria, Jr., emphasizes that at "sacred places Indians should have time of their own." As an Indian, "you cannot go on public land and pray" on cue. The *Mato Tipila* is one of hundreds of sacred sites that "energize" and facilitate revelations "to adjust to the rest of the world." The use of this particular place grew out of a lot of experience that proved its value. Deloria represents only Protestant Christians when he expresses their temporal disposition to believe that "God works in history, in events, and not in people or places," while Indians like Roman Catholics worship through spatial practices. Another attorney misses the mark when he presumes to speak for all non-Indians: "Religion is something you do in a church" erected for that purpose. "It is not something done in nature," but at a convenient location created by parishioners for religious uses.

One mountain climber insists that the Devils Tower is "my church," as well. Another insists that "This is federal land, not private property, managed by Park Service personnel" for recreational purposes. Another says that while climbing Devils Tower he is "fully engaged with nature," which to him is a religious experience. Yet another says, "I definitely have a religious experience," when climbing, "but I don't see it as a church." A Wyoming rancher, located nearby, exclaims, "Our culture is as important as Indian culture. . . . Our family history goes back seven generations" to a time when there were no resident Indians. The tribal response is, we have "always been there," but "you don't visually see an Indian going to a place to pray."

Members of a University of South Dakota history film class expressed viewpoints in formal film reviews that ranged between reverence for tribal religious philosophies and forthright antagonism. One of them, a student with an academic performance clearly in the upper ten percent of the class, challenged values espoused by the film *In the Light of Reverence* while she bluntly portrayed the cultural gulf that separates non-Indians from tribal traditionalists in the state: "The Lakota are struggling to keep people off the Land that they may go to their places of worship" like Devils Tower "without having people come just for recreation. . . . The only thing I liked about this film was the beauty of the land. . . . Native Americans talked about the sacredness of the land," but "I do not think that land is sacred. It is as if they worship the Land." But "they shouldn't be calling up the spirits of the land. They should be calling upon the One who created the Land." We all "must worship Him," the student added, "I believe that our forefathers were Christians, not in a religious way but in the Biblical way. They knew that Jesus Christ was the only way," for he said, "I am the Way, I am the Truth, I am the Life. That doesn't leave any room for argument." In this student's opinion, "the Native American God is not the God of the Bible" who "sent his Son Jesus and also he sent the Bible."

Simultaneously, a similar confrontation and public debate took place regarding the North Point of the White Swan area of the Yankton Reservation, upstream from the Fort Randall Dam on the Missouri River at the east side of Lake Francis Case. In a belated attempt to compensate South Dakotans for taking land and intangible resources for the development of the Missouri River Valley under terms in the Flood Control Act of 1944, in the year 1999 Congress granted the return of "taking areas" along the lakes—mainly to tribes on the west and to the State of South Dakota on the east shores of the lakes. Included in properties returned to the state was a U.S. Army Corps of Engineers recreation area near White Swan. In an effort to expand and improve it, South Dakota officials ordered excavations on the North Point location.

Earth-moving equipment dug up human remains. Yankton tribal members responded in protest. Funerary items indicated that at least some of the remains were those of Native Americans. Federal district judge Lawrence Piersol ordered a suspension of excavation. Because the White Swan area was a place occupied by non-Indians and members of several tribes during the nineteenth century, as indicated in a previous chapter about Missouri Valley Culture, none ever could be certain about the identification of the North Point remains. As a result, the confrontation might end in no satisfactory conclusion. Tribal concerns extended beyond a mere respect for the dead into philosophical perceptions of afterlife and relationships between the living and their deceased ancestors.

In 2003 another cultural confrontation quickly evolved when groups of non-Indians in West River, South Dakota, arranged the opening of a firing range near Fort Meade. Their effort was wholly defensible as an effort to provide training and experience for a growing body of citizens with guns, but the proposed location aroused many tribes, whose attorneys initiated litigation at the federal district court in Rapid City. Tribal dispositions were explicit and simple. Five miles from the proposed firing range stood Bear Butte, an ancestral place of spiritual importance to many tribes turned into a South Dakota State Park in 1965. Like the National Park facility at Devils Tower, Bear Butte was open to the general public. Tribal members who have used it as a fasting place have been antagonized and, yet, have found ways of compromising with curious tourists, but they vigorously reacted against the sound of fire arms five miles away.

Questions regarding the possibility of finding places free from noise for religious activities, and about what kinds of noise might be acceptable, seemed to suggest no answers amenable to members of the two opposing groups. In addition, because Bear Butte has been used every year by many on spirit quests, this case involved whether or under what conditions spirits would come to the persons fasting—an issue that brought into the discussion the most important religious site for Native Americans on the northern Great Plains. At the Pipestone National Monument, in Minnesota, since the year 1972 tribal members have appeared to fast in lodges with noisy tourists following a trail no more than two hundred feet away, and with sounds of trucks on the highways and noises of the city of Pipestone fewer than five miles away. The central issue at Pipestone and Bear Butte pertained to the tolerance displayed by spirits as well as to preferences expressed by tribal members on spirit quests—matters that federal judges cannot reconcile with facts of a type that ordinarily appear in documents and testimonies before federal courts.

The Lodge of the Bear, Bear Butte, Pipestone, and White Swan North Point illustrate change in the nature of conflicts between non-Indians and tribal groups in South Dakota. Mainly outsiders such as Kathleen Pickering perpetuate myths about massive abject poverty on all reservations, where—in fact—at least half of the enrolled members of the nine tribes live voluntarily and have access to eight trust responsibility benefits earned by the surrender of land in the past. Since the 1960s, economies, living conditions, and public services have improved. At the vast majority of housing sites, a visitor can identify circumstances that must be classified as some level of middle-class existence—in many instances in beautiful natural environments. At the outset of the twenty-first century, annual infusions of federal support coupled with tribal profits on the nine reservations in South Dakota could provide a middle-class lifestyle for all reservation residents, if political leaders on the reservations provided equitable distributions of jobs and benefits.

Observers from outside the state relish the publication of a problem with alcoholism and illegal drug abuse. Judge Scarmon, with graduate education and university teaching experience in substance-abuse education, indicated that the percentage of people plagued by the abuse of alcohol and drug consumption on reservations is about the same as it is for the entire population of South Dakota. Approximately twenty percent are affected in almost any group. About half of those affected find relief in sobriety.

As Chippewa educator Cook pointed out, tribes have made material progress over the past twenty-five years. No longer should the retention of voluntary reservation residence be perceived as oppressive containment but, instead, as a method of ancestral cultural and philosophical preservation. Improvements in Indian-white relations must stem from mutual respect for the right of tribal members to choose where they wish to live as well as to claim benefits due them in order to sustain a respectable existence. Attempts at intercultural reconciliation during the twenty-first century should feature solutions to cultural misunderstandings represented in the Black Hills Case, the Lodge of the Bear,

A Yankton tribal alcohol/drug control center opened during the 1970s at Lake Andes. Chemical abuse is no greater in reservation communities than in most non-Indian societies. *Courtesy Herbert T. Hoover.*

Bear Butte, and White Swan North Point. Descendants of original occupants constitute about ten percent of the population of a state where all residents share privileges of occupancy and experience limited distress comparable to that of the entire population during the territorial settlement era.

Moreover, tribal and non-Indian South Dakotans share freedoms, benefits, and opportunities denied most peoples on other continents. Evidence exists in the recent arrival of some 8,000 Native Americans from Latin America, and in the gathering of increasing numbers of refugees from around the world. By the outset of the twenty-first century, Sioux Falls has acquired the character of an international city with a burgeoning aggregate population seeking refuge and the privilege of incorporation into the peaceful cultural environment that the descendants of the ancestral Sioux tribes and original immigrant settlers had come to take for granted.

Chapter 27
South Dakota in the Twenty-first Century

■ Return of the Frontier

No essay is more famous in the history of the American West than Frederick Jackson Turner's "The Significance of the Frontier in American History."[1] Turner's hypothesis was that the frontier had made America the nation it was. Borrowing from the 1890 Census Bureau report, Turner claimed the frontier no longer existed.[2] When Turner published his essay in 1893, South Dakota had been a state for only four years, and many Dakotans had spent the 1880s working to transform the frontier into homesteads. The result of all this was an end to "the first period of American history."[3] At the time of Turner's essay, no self-respecting South Dakotan would have seen the state as standing outside the mainstream of American development. After all, if the frontier was, as Turner argued, "the meeting point between savagery and civilization," then South Dakotans had just experienced the transformation firsthand. They had transformed the rugged prairies and plains into farms and ranches.[4] They were, in 1893, the primary actors in the story of American history.

Often forgotten today is that when Turner first articulated his thesis it carried a particular resonance in places like the Dakotas, and not just because it made the region's pioneers the focus of America's great story. What readers of Turner's essay would have immediately caught was his division of urban and rural America. The "progressive period" of American history had just begun when Turner wrote his essay. At the time, Progressives perceived the urban environment as where poverty, alienation, and chaos resided. South Dakota, with its farms, ranches, and recently opened lands represented opportunity, wealth, and familiarity. The South Dakota settler embodied Thomas Jefferson's yeoman ideal. Turner's articulation of American history not only placed Dakotans within the dominant framework of American history, it also suggested their future on the plains was likely to be more advantageous than the future of those stuck in America's cities. The residents of those enclaves were doomed to wage labor and likely to experience the same problems Europe's cities did. The recently deceased frontier offered an alternative to the "fears and doubts arising from the image [of] the inner city."[5]

When Turner retired from academia in 1924, his "frontier thesis" had become the standard model for interpreting American history.[6] Under this model, America had experienced four successive stages of frontier development. First had come the Indian trader; then came the rancher; the miner followed; and finally the farmer arrived on the scene. As the preceding chapters make clear, this structural framework dovetailed closely with South Dakota's Euro-American development. While mining and ranching arrived at roughly the same time in western Dakota, many South Dakotans could feel a connectedness to Turner's historical narrative.

The frontier had, according to Turner, promoted America's "composite nationality" and "industrial independence" from Europe. It had promoted the "evolution of American political institutions." This description fit South Dakota well. The Scandinavians who had settled eastern Dakota had given way to new Western European immigrants who settled West River Dakota. The key to understanding how the frontier was settled was land—cheap land. As Turner wrote, "the competition of the unexhausted, cheap, and easily tilled prairie lands compelled the farmer either to go west . . ." or "turn to intensive farming and to manufacture."[7] South Dakotans, looking around, saw land being settled and towns springing up along the railroad lines. While it was true that America had become an industrial and urban nation, and South Dakota was still predominately agricultural, the mining enterprises in the Black Hills suggested South Dakota's history paralleled that of the nation.[8]

Undoubtedly, Turner and his supporters would be surprised to find that not only has the frontier returned to South Dakota in the twenty-first century, so too has wilderness.[9] Turner's suggestion that the frontier process ultimately led "into the complexity of city life" and greater settlement densities seems unfilled in South Dakota.[10] Indeed, many South Dakota counties have fewer people living in them in 2005 than they did when Turner retired. Today it is harder to see South Dakota as fitting into the mainstream paradigm of American history. The frontier's return to South Dakota has left many residents wondering about their future and romanticizing their past. At the beginning of the twenty-first century, many Dakotans wonder where their state fits in the larger panorama of American history. Is the story of South Dakota one of success or failure?

No matter where one places the state within the larger picture of American history, the return of the frontier is at the center of the appraisal. One way the frontier's reappearance makes its presence felt is in contemporary South Dakota literature. The frontier's reappearance is due, at least in part, to changes in modern agriculture. Whether farming or ranching, the size of the operation is increasing. Contemporary South Dakota writers such as Linda Hasselstrom and Ann Daum have documented this change in very personal family stories about the end of their family ranches.[11] Other memoirs, such as Lawrence Brown's *Buffalo Commons: Memoirs* document the rise and fall of entire communities tied almost exclusively to agricultural production.[12] Kathleen Norris documented the struggles of Perkins County in her *Dakota: A Spiritual Geography*. At the heart of these narratives is the debate about corporate farming, survival of the family farm, and return of the frontier. What all these writings share is a sense of loss. Collectively, these writers suggest a longing for what was.

"Blank maps invite speculation and exploration," so begins Chapter Four. What makes South Dakota different from most places, and a reason for South Dakotans' nostalgia, is that the blank spaces are returning. While South Dakota's population grew over the last two decades, its growth has been uneven. The 1990 census reported fifty-two of the state's sixty-seven counties as losing people. The 2000 census showed a slowing of this trend, but thirty-one counties continued to lose population.[13] While the 2000 census shows the state's population as 8.5 percent higher than a decade earlier, the figure is misleading. The former director of the state's census project argued the state effectively lost 10,000 people because so many eighteen- to thirty-four-year olds left the state.[14] Growth focused on the edge of the state: along the I-29 corridor in the east and Rapid City and its environs in the west.

Politicians lament the "brain-drain" they see in the central part of the state. Yet it is important to understand that the return of the frontier is nothing new to South Dakota. Before statehood occurred, "almost all the entire [white] population of what became Dakota Territory in 1861 was located in the southeastern corner of the territory."[15] This is part of the I-29 corridor. The population trends documented in the 1990 and 2000 censuses remind us that South Dakota's demographic situation is not new. Perhaps we ought to look at what is happening as a historical correction. This does not make it any easier for the people who are currently relocating, or trying to hang on. It does, however, allow one to understand that the current movement of people to the edges of South Dakota fits a historical pattern.

One way to see the frontier's impact is to take a drive along the state's highways and interstates. Out-of-state visitors are more likely to catch it than long-time residents. What visitors notice (while residents ignore it) is the distance between towns of substantial size. These visitors, unfamiliar with South Dakota's history and the changes occurring in modern agriculture, assume South Dakota's sparse density pattern and small hamlets are the historic norm. Many wonder why anyone stays in the small towns, farms, and ranches they pass. While visitors have heard of the values and quality of life associated with small-town living, they balance these values against the things they do not see: movie theaters, a variety of restaurants, and other modern "conveniences." These observations prick South Dakotans' pride and makes them defensive.[16]

What these visitors do not understand are two things. First, the people remaining on the farms and ranches are there by choice. They are the "winners" in South Dakota's settlement. These families have survived the homesteading boom, the Dust Bowl, the Pick-Sloan projects of mid-twentieth century, the Farm Crisis of the 1970s and 1980s, the rise of corporate farming, and the drought of 2003. They have been smart enough to avoid debt burdens that forced their neighbors off the land. Those left on the land are the successful farmers and ranchers who provide distant markets with their food. They arc, as one visitor discovered, very attuned to international affairs. After all, much of the food grown and raised in South Dakota is geared for foreign markets.[17] The merchants who remain in South Dakota's small towns are those who have, so far at least, withstood the Wal-Mart onslaught, or the rise of the Empire Mall in Sioux Falls.

The second thing visitors miss as they drive through South Dakota is this: South Dakota has not always been so desolate. The demographic and economic contours of South Dakota today are very different than they were sixty years ago. The emergence of the frontier marks a reversal of demography dating back to the Middle Missouri Village Period (800-1600). For the first time in historic memory, portions of the state are emptying out their human inhabitants. Rural South Dakota is producing more food than ever, yet the exodus begun in the 1930s continues. Thirty-two of the state's sixty-six counties lost population between 1990 and 2000.[18] Where are these people going? Most likely they are moving to the borders of the state—to either the I-29 corridor or to the Black Hills.[19]

■ Growing Diversity

The result is a demographic reconfiguration of the state's population. This reconfiguration is the result of changes in agriculture and the economic diversification in cities such as Sioux Falls and Rapid City. The result of these changes is a paradox. South Dakota is more heterogeneous, richer, and more economically diverse than at any time since statehood. At the same time, there is a growing sense of pessimism about the future of the state among significant sections of the population. The return of the frontier fosters this pessimism because it represents failure, at least in the minds of many.

What we have, then, are really two distinct experiences in post-1980s South Dakota. Its largest cities (with the notable exception of Aberdeen), are experiencing growth—political, economic, and demographic. The 1980s and especially the 1990s were years of opportunity. In some cases they were also years of prosperity. At the same time, many portions of the state experienced real struggles. The farm crisis of the early 1980s, declining farm income for those who survived, changes in federal subsidy policy (a sign of the farm block's decline at the national level),[20] the rise of corporate farming, and the continued out-migration of its people have transformed most of our agricultural counties. Perhaps the historic division between East River and West River needs to be reconfigured in South Dakota. Today, the real divisions are between urban and rural counties; between those counties with some diversification of the economy and those still dependent almost exclusively on agriculture. One reason for a rethinking of our historic divisions: the 2000 census reports more urban residents than rural.[21]

While it is impossible to predict South Dakota's future, an examination of current trends suggests that South Dakota today fits more closely within the larger movement of American history than many understand. At the same time, the changing nature of agriculture and the large number of rural counties still reliant on it give South Dakota a set of issues that are location specific. For example, how does one balance agricultural productivity with the cultural sustainability of our small towns?[22] Put another way, is something lost when small-agricultural towns disappear? Many people, and not just those involved, would say, "yes."[23]

It is the return of the frontier, and in some cases the wilderness, that creates the anxiety associated with South Dakota's present and future. South Dakotans illustrate this anxiety by how they market their state. At the beginning of the twenty-first century, most residents conceive of their state in nineteenth-century terms: agricultural, homogeneous, a land of opportunity. Tourist officials emphasized South Dakota's past when they promoted visiting the South Dakota of *Dances with Wolves,* or the new Home Box Office show *Deadwood.* Officials promote Lewis and Clark, or the homes of Laura Ingalls Wilder in De Smet. They promote the "historic Deadwood" of Wild Bill Hickok and Calamity Jane. All these events date back to the nineteenth century. While some man-made twentieth-century edifices are now marketed—Wall Drug, Mount Rushmore, or the Corn Palace—they are promoted as places to stop and visit on your way to somewhere else.[24] In a state where politicians worry about the "brain-drain" of the young, the demise of the small town, or the implications of world trade, South Dakotans remain committed to re-imagining their past.

The state's premier historical journal, *South Dakota History*, emphasizes South Dakota's earlier history. Contemporary issues in South Dakota worthy of academic inquiry—the farm crises of the 1980s; the rise of white-collar industry in Sioux Falls; the rise (and fall?) of the computer company Gateway, or the impact of agricultural centralization—have been left largely unaddressed. A perusal of the journal over the last twenty years shows only five articles focused on South Dakota history post-1960.[25] The result is an effective silencing of South Dakota's history for the post-World War II period. As South Dakotans enter the twenty-first century, then, they do so with a sense of longing and a desire to recapture the "good old days."[26] As Chapter Fifteen noted, these recreations are often wrong. Some of the facades of Deadwood, for example, are not historically accurate. They do, however, reinforce the notion of a cowboy past, and the glorious days of yesteryear.

Given the lack of interest in South Dakota's recent history, then, what is most important about the state's history over the last twenty years? Is it the farm crisis of the late 1970s and early 1980s? Is it the continued decline in the number of farms in South Dakota? Is it the growth of Sioux Falls and its diversified economy? Is it the creation of Gateway, and the company's subsequent roller-coaster existence? Or is the history of South Dakota best understood by the dominant role William Janklow played in state politics? Is it the controversy surrounding the "Buffalo Commons" hypothesis? Is it the increasing importance of tourism to South Dakota's economy? Or is it something else? How one answers the questions about South Dakota's past is likely to influence how one views the state's future too. In looking at the past, then, one determines the parameters of where South Dakota is going.

One possible reason for South Dakotan's nostalgia for yesteryear might be that the issues listed above involve change, and change is never easy. For agriculture, corporate farms and ranches, growing political pressure to reduce price supports, the vertical integration of agriculture, and the concentration of agribusinesses have made the last twenty-five years different from anything seen before. For timber interests, increasing environmental pressures, the rise of tourism, and changing views of how forests ought to be managed have challenged the industry's staying power. In mining, an earlier decision to allow gold prices to float on the international market set off new mining activity. By 1998 this new gold rush was over, and the miners found themselves looking for other employment opportunities. Many are hoping that Homestake Mine will be converted into a national science laboratory. This lab would focus on neutrino research, and supporters hope it will be Lead's economic salvation. Federal funds for the project are not yet secure, but at least there is the possibility of a new enterprise. Even where the economy has been diversified, in Sioux Falls, Mitchell, and Rapid City, for example, increased size means expanding demands on city services, schools, and social services. The growth of suburbs means a reorienting of spacial and personal relationships. Add to this mix a growing heterogeneity of the population, and some long-time residents often find themselves looking backwards.

Answering the question of what is most important about South Dakota's recent history is not likely to involve questions of cultural transformation. The reason for this is simple and oft repeated: South Dakota's population is homogenous and its economy still driven by agriculture. One wag claimed this is one of the few areas where "what passes for ethnic conflict here has to be imported from a Europe of hundreds of years ago."[27] This is no longer true. The Great Plains as a whole are becoming less "white" and the driving economic force may no longer be agriculture, but medicine or a service sector enterprise. This is true in both rural and urban South Dakota. The problem is that South Dakotans continue to see the state as ethnically homogenous. In reality, ethnic heterogeneity is one of the key developments in post-1980 South Dakota history.

In Sioux Falls and its environs, the fastest growing region of the state, minorities now comprise ten percent of the population. This figure represents a tripling of Sioux Falls' minority population over the last twenty years, and this rate of growth is unlikely to slow in the foreseeable future.[28] Currently, students in the Sioux Falls School District speak forty-five different languages.[29] One school, Whittier Middle School, has twenty-five percent of its student body speaking at home a language other than English.[30] Just how quickly Sioux Falls has changed is illustrated by two distinct episodes. In September 1990 an executive memo within the John Morrell & Company surfaced. Written the previous October, the memo suggested, "Morrell would need to integrate Mexican-Americans slowly" into the company's plant in Sioux Falls.[31] The memo suggested Hispanics would make up a significant portion of the company's future workforce. Given its appearance after a very divisive strike at the plant, the memo created a temporary tempest. Fourteen years later, Washington High School in Sioux Falls, the high school closest to John Morrell & Company, celebrates ethnic awareness days. On these days, minority groups from the community introduce other students to the food, clothing, culture, and dress of their homeland.[32]

Kamall Muthukrishnan and daughter and friend prepare for a prayer service at the Siouxland India Cultural Association in Elk Point. In Sioux Falls and environs the minority population has tripled during the past twenty years. *Courtesy* Argus Leader, *photo by Christopher Gannon.*

While it might be easier to see this trend in cities, it is also happening in the countryside. Here, Dakotans of European descent are moving into town, dying, or leaving the state. South Dakota's Indian reservations, on the other hand, are growing in population and prosperity. Seven counties in West River South Dakota have, according to the 2000 census, a significant portion of children under the age of seventeen. Five of the these counties have a connection to one of South Dakota's Indian reservations; the two other counties, Lawrence and Pennington, have cities Sturgis and Rapid City, respectively, which are growing. Other counties are not so lucky in retaining population. Harding County, in northwestern South Dakota, has less than five percent of its residents under the age of four. Its neighbor, Perkins County, has 5.8 percent of its population under four. While this might seem acceptable, the figures get worse if one looks at the under-eighteen ratio. Just under forty-one percent of Corson County's population is under eighteen years old, while Perkins County is just over twenty-four percent.[33] Corson County is home to the Standing Rock Indian Reservation. The long-term implication of this demographic trend is a growing Native American population and a declining Caucasian base.

This trend is not unique to the northwestern portion of South Dakota. Demographically, South Dakota is becoming less "European descendant," and more Native American. McPherson and Shannon counties illustrate this trend. In 1950 Shannon County had half the population density of McPherson. It is different today. McPherson County averages 2.6 to Shannon's 5.95 residents per square mile. Unofficially, Shannon County is much more densely populated since it was one of the "under counted" counties in the 2000 census.[34] What is happening in Shannon County is not unique. The state's Indian population increased twenty-three percent between 1990 and 2000.[35] Native Americans are now 8.25 percent of the state's total population, third highest percent in the nation.[36] The result of this is the return of an Indian presence within the state and outside the reservation. The election of 2002 showed the growing political muscle of Indian voters within the state. Rural South Dakota, then, is becoming less white, just as are South Dakota's cities.

Not only is rural South Dakota becoming less European, it is now the Indian community that is driving the economy of many portions of the state. What is clearly missing from our current understanding of South Dakota history is the growing importance of Native American enterprises to the regional economy. While Indian gaming has caught the attention of many, as Chapter Twenty-six makes clear, the diversity of South Dakota's Indian economy is growing. The growing economic power of Indian entrepreneurs and tribes has begun to challenge traditional assumptions. An example of this was when Lower Brûlé Reservation leaders attempted to purchase land and enlarge the reservation. County and state officials immediately challenged the tribe's efforts. Officials worried about the increased tax-burden such a purchase would create. Catering to their traditional constituents, politicians immediately challenged the tribe's efforts, and, at the time of this writing, negotiations are ongoing to determine whether the Lower Brûlé Reservation can be enlarged.[37] The episode's outcome is not what makes the tribe's effort so important. Rather, it is important because it foreshadows the future. Just over a century after the Dawes Act reduced tribal land holdings in South Dakota by more than half,[38] South Dakota's Indian people are beginning to reacquire land that was once theirs. Their actions, occurring within the context of "white flight," suggests the future of South Dakota may not lie with descendants of South Dakota's first European settlers.

Some scholars see the growing Indian population, and the "influx of Latinos to many Great Plains areas" as offsetting "some of the aging and decline in the native [European descendant] population."[39] What makes the Latino infusion so interesting is that in South Dakota Latinos are not trying to make a living off the land per se. While many are employed in tertiary aspects of agriculture, there are no "farmers of Hispanic descent listed" on the agricultural census of 1997 and 2002.[40] For the first time in nearly one-hundred and forty years, most immigrants coming to South Dakota are not trying to establish an economic foothold in the state by farming.[41]

For South Dakota, the growing importance of minority workers in the tertiary aspects of agriculture has profound importance. Sioux Falls, for example, saw an increase in its minority population, partially as a result of increasing numbers of Hispanic and Sudanese workers laboring for John Morrell & Company. Sioux Falls was not alone in this experience. Worthington, Minnesota, saw its minority population rise from six percent of the total population in 1990 to twenty-three percent in 2000.[42] In April 2004 the city of Huron announced the addition of a 750-1,000-employee turkey processing plant. Many South Dakotans assume that these potential jobs will help stem the tide of out-migration. This is possible, but if history is any guide, many, if not most, of these jobs will be taken by non-Caucasians. Most workers at the plant will be either Hispanic or Asian because many locals will be unwilling to do the work a processing plant requires. Huron's efforts suggest that the future of South Dakota will no longer be Indian and/or white. It will also include Asians and Hispanics in ever greater numbers.

The growing importance of Indians and non-Caucasians to South Dakota suggests the state is undergoing a cultural transformation. This transformation, however, is often missed because South Dakota is perceived by its residents and outsiders as being outside the mainstream of American development since World War II. Unlike the Midwest, South Dakota never developed an industrial capacity; unlike the Southwest, the state did not experience a population explosion after World War II; and unlike the Northeast, this state's education problems are not overcrowding, but too few students. The list could go on, but the idea that South Dakota stands outside the traditional means of interpreting America's history needs to be revised.

In many ways, South Dakota fits mainstream developments within American society as a whole. Besides its growing heterogeneity, South Dakota is becoming more urban than rural. According to the 2000 census, 51.2 percent of state residents live in an urban environment.[43] Like Silicon Valley, South Dakota found that long-term growth does not always accompany computer firms, such as the PC maker Gateway. Gateway's rise and fall has left thousands of South Dakotans either unemployed or wondering when they will be laid off.[44] Education, at all levels, is underfunded in South Dakota, as it is elsewhere. Finally, South Dakotans are coming to terms with generational mobility: their children are more likely to move than they were. These issues suggest South Dakota's recent history does fit within a larger framework for interpreting America's recent history.

■ Competing Paradigms

When South Dakotans, or others, attempt either to fit or exclude South Dakota from the larger story of American history they are, whether they realize it or not, placing South Dakota within competing paradigms of how they understand the history of both America and the Midwest. For the last quarter century, the story of South Dakota has fit into one of two general paradigms. The first paradigm is the story of improvement. With respect to schools, economy, tourism, or race relations, South Dakotans are better off than they were twenty-five years ago. This "progressive" view suggests South Dakota is "happier, richer, freer, better" than before. This is the story of South Dakota and the good life. It is the story that census officials suggest in their demographic profiles of South Dakota, released in May 2002.[45] In this scenario, the late Governor George Mickelson's "century of reconciliation" showed how the blessings of the present could be used to begin reconciling the tangled relationships of the past.

The second paradigm emerges from the impression that South Dakota is growing "sadder, poorer, less free, worse" as the years go by. These South Dakotans want vibrant small towns, filled classrooms, and family farms for as far as the eye can see. They want what their parents had. A resident of Lemmon articulated this second paradigm when she told Kathleen Norris, "We don't need change, what we need is to turn back the clock to the way things were twenty years ago."[46] The economic promise of the Dakotas remains unfulfilled. After all, "no previous frontier had been settled with such breathtaking speed and amid so much hope and optimism as Dakota."[47] In this paradigm, South Dakotans long for an imagined, supposedly better, past.

These two paradigms are antithetical to each other. Howard Lamar, one of America's leading frontier historians, noted the inherit contradiction when he wrote, "the settlers of nineteenth-century Dakota saw themselves in a main-line American tradition of growth and success right down to the drought years of the late 1880s and early 1890s. . . . But there is also a counter theme: the tradition of the failure of the dream, of being defeated on occasion."[48] Whether the glass is seen as half-full or half-empty depends on one's perspective. What the continued existence of the paradigms suggests is that the history of South Dakota is anything but simple, and in the last twenty years it has become perhaps more complex.

The modern root of these two paradigms is found in the human history of South Dakota. This is true whether one examines the Native American occupation period,

ing mechanization and economies of scale account for much of the change documented over

South Dakota's territorial phase, early statehood, the Great Depression, or the post-World War II period. The preceding chapters have shown how climate, physical topography, or economic opportunity have lured humans into the region; these factors have also driven them out. South Dakota's landscape has acted as a pump rather than a sponge when it comes to history. During good climatic or economic conditions, people move into the state. When times are tough, people leave. This is true for most regions. Thinking of South Dakota's land as a pump, rather than a sponge, allows one to see that not all places continue to grow in population, and not all regions require the emergence of an urban environment.[49]

Visitors to South Dakota instinctively articulate this connection between competing paradigms when they comment on the distance between cities of any significant size in the state. South Dakota has only nine cities with populations greater than 10,000 residents. Only two of these cities have populations larger than 25,000 inhabitants. One of these cities, Sioux Falls, with a population of 123,975, is now home to more than sixteen percent of the state's entire population. Pierre, the state capital, has 13,876 residents according to the 2000 census. Some counties, Perkins and Harding, for example, have more antelope than people in them.[50]

The context, then, of South Dakota's paradigms is that the state is producing more goods and more food, yet it is losing its rural population, its agricultural way of life, and its ability to provide an adequate living for a significant portion of its population. For South Dakotans, the loss of small towns and small farms means more than just economic and demographic change. Many see the values learned on the farm as essential to their being. As one writer noted, "people genuflect in the direction of values they believe are taught by the family farm." How long will South Dakota's "traditional values" last if the family farm disappears?[51] In 2005, then, the paradigms center around the changing nature of agriculture, just as in the nineteenth century.

Complicating the paradigms is the way South Dakotans see themselves. South Dakotans like to think that the state's rural nature made them what we are, and that it is worth saving. Most South Dakotans would agree with the scholar who wrote, "Rurality has come to connote stability and worthy simplicity; it has become our collective past."[52] As the preceding chapters make clear, stability, whether economic or demographic, does not characterize South Dakota. Whether it was drought, dust, dam construction, or mechanization, the South Dakota farmer has led neither a stable nor a simple life. In 1990 the total number of American farms was only one-third of what it had been at its peak sixty years before.[53] The last ten years have seen an even further decline in numbers. South Dakota witnessed a decline of 4.4 percent in the number of farmers between 1997 and 2002. While dust and grasshoppers account for the farm exodus of the 1930s, mechanization and economies of scale account for much of the change documented over the last twenty-five years. The government noted these trends and their effects in the late 1990s.[54]

■ Changing Nature of Agriculture

It would not have surprised John Wesley Powell that South Dakotans are struggling to succeed in the current economic system.[55] At the time of statehood, Powell was the director of the federal geological surveys, and he recognized the handicaps South Dakota's unique geography presented farmers and ranchers. In 1878 Powell argued against opening South Dakota up to homesteading under the original 1862 act. He argued that much more land was required to make a living in the region. Powell suggested "at least 2,560 acres" as the minimum amount of land a homesteader would need for any pasture enterprise. He also admitted that some areas "must be much larger" for successful homesteading.[56] Congressmen ignored his recommendation, and not even the enlargement of the homestead acreage from 320 to 640 acres was enough.[57] In this sense, the drive to enlarge farm size fits what planners envisioned in the nineteenth century. Interestingly, as late as 1974, the average size farm or ranch in the region was still not as large as Powell suggested in 1878.[58]

In South Dakota, the debate about farm size crystalizes two distinct elements of the South Dakota story. Elsewhere, in California, Florida, or Illinois, for example, when farmers stop farming, the land often becomes a suburb or a new town. Elsewhere, the loss of farmland represents the appearance of more people. In South Dakota, that is not happening. Only in Minnehaha and Pennington Counties do we see suburbs encroaching on farmland. For most of the state, when a farm family moves off the land it means something different. It means depopulation, but not declining agricultural output. While this trend poses difficult questions for South Dakota, it is important to recognize that the trend also fits a worldwide pattern: fewer people are farming throughout the world.

From China to South Africa, from France to Mexico, millions of rural citizens are moving from the countryside to urban areas. Genetically modified crops, such as rice in China, allow fewer people to produce more food. In 1980, for example, 68.7 percent of China's workers were employed in some aspect of agricultural production. By 1998, the last year data was reported for China, that number had dropped to 47.5 percent.[59] Historically, one of the factors that best correlated per-capita income for a population was the percentage of people farming.[60] It still is, but for how much longer? The United States has less than two percent of its population engaged in farming; the poorest nations of the world have more than half of their populations living on farms. Western Europe, which has ten percent of its population engaged in farming, maintains that number by government subsidies. For example, the French government sees sustaining farmers as a "quality of life," not a financial, issue. Rural society produces intangible benefits for the French nation, and these benefits trump cheaper food prices. That is not necessarily the case in the United States, and that is why South Dakota farmers found themselves confronting more than just economic problems at the end of the twentieth century.

The farm crisis of the late 1970s and 1980s shared an eerie similarity with the crisis of the 1930s. At the time of the Great Depression, the government found itself trying to understand what had caused the problems so prevalent in South Dakota during the early 1930s. The causes government researchers listed for the farmers' plight in the 1930s were exactly the same ones listed for the rural crisis of the 1970s and 1980s. What were these issues? "The tractor, combine and other power machinery enabled an individual to plant and harvest a much larger acreage than before. At the same time the cost of buying and maintaining this expensive equipment obliged him to secure a cash crop."[61] This was the very situation in which farmers in South Dakota found themselves during the 1970s and 1980s. It was the basis of a 1998 government report on the state of the family farm.

This U.S. Department of Agriculture report, entitled *A Time to Act*, was the government's most systematic examination of family farming since *A Time to Choose*, nearly twenty years earlier. Focusing on small producers, those with gross revenues under $250,000, the report detailed the changes that had occurred in agriculture in the 1980s and 1990s.[62] The report began by noting, "it is evident that this warning [*A Time to Choose*'s summary] was not heeded, but instead, policy choices made since then perpetuated the structural bias toward greater concentration of assets and wealth in fewer and larger farms and fewer and larger agribusiness firms."[63] The report noted that between

1979 and 1998, 300,000 farmers had gone out of business. Farmers now received "13 percent less for every consumer dollar" spent. The report also cataloged the growing problem of market concentration, a trend that helped continue the human exodus from South Dakota farms and ranches during the 1980s and 1990s.

In 1980 four firms controlled thirty-six percent of the beef slaughter industry. Eighteen years later the four firms controlled "over eighty percent of the beef market."[64] The concentration of market share had resulted in "the emergence of two food streams shaping the structure of agriculture."[65] The two food streams were "contract production" that infringed "upon the competitiveness of the open cash market," and a "direct marketing stream." In the case of beef, contract production cut the ranchers' share of the retail beef dollar from "64 percent in 1979 to 49 percent in 1997." In February 2004 a federal judge in Alabama found the Tyson Company guilty of manipulating beef contracts. Tyson, it seems, had contracts which allowed it to stay out of the beef business when beef prices rose and only enter the market when prices dropped below a certain level. Although Tyson appealed the case, and a different judge threw out the verdict, the case illustrated how agribusiness conglomerates used contract production to squeeze first-level producers.[66] First-level producers are those who actually produce the commodity in question.

The "direct marketing stream" referred to in *A Time to Act* focused on making "smallness" an attribute. To overcome the economies of scale prevalent in ranching and farming, the report encouraged the creation of cooperatives and "adding value to raw commodities." The key, the report said, was to keep more dollars "within the local and regional economies" instead of sending the commodities elsewhere.[67] This is easier said than done. Nevertheless, the creation of ten ethanol cooperatives and the building of a mozzarella cheese factory in Lake Norton, a soybean processing facility in Volga, and a planned turkey processing plant in Huron, whose capacity will exceed the number of turkeys produced in the state each year, suggest efforts at tapping into the "direct marketing stream." The problem with this segment of the agricultural economy is that "vertical coordination and integration" have produced new demands on cooperative ventures. There is "fragmented marketing" to overcome, and cooperatives will have to "take deliberate steps to refocus" the movement toward family farms. Further complicating these efforts are that "new start-up co-ops need professional assistance when they are least able to pay for it."[68] Farmers and ranchers are caught in a vicious cycle: they do not have the money to enlarge their market share without professional assistance, but they cannot pay for the professional assistance unless they increase their market share.

As *A Time to Act* suggested, the family farm underwent profound changes in the 1980s and 1990s. Most of these changes have been missed by the larger American public because only two percent of the nation's population is engaged in farming. Since most Americans live in urban areas, they have no real direct connection with agriculture. In a way, Robert Kennedy's 1968 comment to South Dakota farmers portended the future of agricultural policy on American politics. When asked what he would do for the farmers, Kennedy responded by saying that he had nine kids, and they ate cereal every morning for breakfast. While the response drew a laugh from the audience, it suggested that national politicians were unaware of what was happening "down on the farm."[69]

Even if politicians wanted to help rural communities survive, there are certain trends that do not bode well for South Dakota's small communities. Economic efficiencies in agriculture mean fewer farmers are necessary. In 1965 it took 6.1 worker hours to produce a harvest of 7.1 bushels of corn per acre. Twenty years later it took only 3.1 worker hours to produce 109.3 bushels of corn per acre. Wheat and soybeans show similar, though far less spectacular, results. Wheat took 2.9 worker hours to produce 25.9 bushels. In 1985 the figures were 2.5 worker hours to produce 37.1 bushels of wheat. Soybeans went from 4.8 worker hours for 24.2 bushels per acre to 3.2 hours for 30.7 bushels.[70]

The trend is obvious—fewer people are needed to work the farm. It also means fewer merchants, service-sector workers, and teachers are needed for South Dakota communities. Yet even those who survive on the farm or ranch are not necessarily making more money; after all, farming and ranching are "boom or bust" enterprises.[71] South Dakota farmers are probably similar to Great Plains farmers as a whole in thinking themselves fortunate to have "three profitable years out of five."[72] As a result, only about one-half of all farm families earn their livelihoods solely from agriculture.[73] One South Dakota rancher commented that among the things needed to ranch in western South Dakota today was a "good wife with a full-time job at the courthouse."[74] Not surprisingly, while farm productivity has risen, real income in rural South Dakota has not. South Dakota is not alone in this development. Today, the poorest counties of the nation are found on the Great Plains, not in America's urban centers.

Stagnating incomes on South Dakota's farms have helped shape another trend in South Dakota—the two-income family. State promoters talk about how South Dakotans are more likely to attend church and experience less crime than those in other regions of the nation and that farmers "still personify the honest, hardworking and moral ideals associated with a healthy national culture."[75] The goal of this promotion is to show South Dakota as a bastion of traditional "family values." Left unsaid is the fact that Sioux Falls has the highest percentage of working mothers in the nation. Seventy-two percent of all mothers of below or at school-age children work. The trend is not unique to Sioux Falls; farm women "appear to have increased their participation in the labor force in the 1980s," too.[76]

While either men or women could seek off-farm employment, women are more likely to do so. One-third of these women sought employment in nursing or education.[77] Not surprisingly, the most likely candidates to seek off-farm employment were those families who "bore higher debt loads," and these were often the newest farmers.[78] As opportunities for off-farm employment shrink, fewer families may be able to survive on the farm. A June 2003 study noted that rural workers in South Dakota already "earned less than half—48 cents on the dollar—of what those employed in the region's big cities earned."[79] The future of farming, then, is a continued decline in the number of farmers, fewer off-farm opportunities for those struggling to stay on the farm, and the gradual shrinking of South Dakota's small towns.

At the same time women are seeking off-farm employment, more of them are taking control of more farms. While the number of Caucasian farmers declined 5.1 percent between 1997 and 2002 in South Dakota, the number of female farmers increased by 16.1 percent over the same time period.[80] According to the USDA 2002 Census of Agriculture, there are now 2,184 female farmers, and nearly 90 percent of their enterprises are classified as "family or individual" farm. They account for 14.5 percent of all farmers in the state, but it is impossible to know who these women are ethnically.[81] Nevertheless, commentators have identified two primary reasons for the increasing percentage of female agriculturalists: changes in inheritance practices and farming's being less physically demanding than before. These women farmers face the same issues as their male counterparts, and if trends do not reverse themselves, many of these operators will have to seek additional employment off the farm. Perhaps, the creation of home-based businesses offers some alternative for both men and women.

The 2000 census reported that South Dakota ranked first in the nation in home-based businesses.[82] Many of these businesses begin as a means to supplement family incomes. Most of these businesses are not Internet enterprises, and while they may account for South Dakota's low unemployment rate, they have not significantly increased the per-capita income of South Dakotans. Indeed, the economic condition of many small communities has led some to wonder if "the frontier Plains will become the next Appalachia?"[83] For South Dakotans, the debate of the 1980s and 1990s has forced them to confront the fact that a new vision of South Dakota is needed. The question is what will that vision look like and how will the costs be paid?

What all of this means is that transition is the order of the day in South Dakota. The motorist traveling the South Dakota interstate sees farms and a few towns and thinks this is what the state, or perhaps the nation, was like forty years ago. It is not. What the motorist does not understand is that the empty spaces are the result of trends begun sixty and seventy years ago. They represent both the promise of scientific agriculture and problems of farming/ranching on the high plains. One Harding County rancher commented on the situation: "Used to be you could make a living with 150 cows out here; now it takes 600 or more just to get by . . . . The big just get bigger, and everyone else leaves. We can't all live in the city, but it looks like most of us will wind up there."[84] In an age when "bigger" connotes "better," South Dakotans wonder about the cost of such developments.

Like all Americans, South Dakotans have grown up with the Jeffersonian myth of the yeoman farmer, which has been transformed into the myth of the modern family farm. Farmers and ranchers, we are told, are "better people because they lived on the land." They are more independent, more democratic, more "wedded to liberty" than others because of their close connection to the land.[85] We have idealized farmers. What Americans do not understand about Jefferson's support for the yeoman was that it had nothing to do with farming, and everything to do with economics. Jefferson championed the yeoman farmer because this person was the only individual in America not in debt to someone else. Southern plantation owners and northern merchants were both heavily

The future success of South Dakota's agriculture-based economy relies heavily on developing new technologies. *Courtesy South Dakota Tourism.*

indebted to British merchants and factors. The yeoman was free. Jefferson championed the yeoman because the yeoman was the only person "self-sufficient" in economic terms. That is not the case today.

Today, the federal government simply assumes a priori that the family farmer is losing money.[86] These farmers represent some of the most heavily leveraged households in the nation, with "over 80 percent of a farmer's gross sales" being absorbed "by farming expenses."[87] Moreover, Jefferson's championing of the yeoman occurred at a time when "old assumptions about a politically active elite and a deferential, compliant electorate" were in force.[88] Jefferson's support of the agriculturalist represented an attempt to create a new political reality in America.[89] That is not the case now. Today, farmers are politically important in only a few states—South Dakota being one of those. Their political influence at the national level has declined. Only thirteen states have a rural majority. These states represent fifty-nine electoral votes, or only five more than the state of California alone.[90] If Jefferson tried to create a national party today, it is doubtful he would begin by championing the family farmer.

The economic problems associated with late twentieth-century farming helped fuel the psychology of farming's dilemma. South Dakotans were forced to confront the changes modern agriculture had produced in their communities. South Dakotans could no longer view farming and the small towns it supported as "operating under dictates distinct from those governing industrial capitalism."[91] As Chapter Thirteen makes clear, this is (and was) not the case. Farmers and ranchers are integrated into the economic trends at both the national and international levels. The appearance in 2004 of BSE (Bovine Spongiform Encephalopathy), better known as "mad cow disease," illustrates both of these connections. Dietary trends such as the "Atkins diet" had, between 2000 and 2003, increased the profitability of South Dakota's beef exports. The appearance of a confirmed case of BSE in the nation led Japan and Korea, two of South Dakota's primary beef export markets, to ban the importation of American beef. As Chapter Fourteen shows, beef production accounts for the single largest area of agricultural income in the state. While the cow with BSE apparently came from Canada, Japanese and Korean consumers were not willing to rescind their beef ban immediately. They did not have to, and this is where the psychological impact came into play.

Twenty years ago, the United States was one of the few nations capable of exporting grains and meat. Today, that is not the case. Argentina and Brazil are challenging America's hold on soybean production. In the case of beef production, Australia immediately announced it would increase its beef production by twenty-five percent to replace the American beef banned by Japan and Korea. Brazil also reported increases. Its beef exports to Asia jumped thirteen percent in January 2004.[92] While it is, at the time of this writing, too early to tell for sure, there is no guarantee South Dakota ranchers will recover the market share lost by the outbreak of mad cow disease. While America can still outproduce the rest of the world agriculturally, it no longer maintains a monopoly over export production. Just as the American industry lost market share to Asian and European companies in the 1970s and 1980s, American agricultural producers lost market share in the 1990s and early 2000s. One hundred years ago, agricultural production gave way to industrial production. What, if anything, can take the place of agriculture in South Dakota's economy?

This is an important question for South Dakota because the industrialization of agriculture has reduced farm incomes. Whereas farmers received twenty-one percent of the income generated by the agricultural sector in 1910, that figure had dropped to five percent by 1990.[93] In the Great Plains, "only 10 cents of the consumer dollar spent on cereal and bakery products are returned to the producers" who grew the grain.[94] While farmers and ranchers are producing more food, they are receiving proportionally less for it. An example of this is the dairy industry. Dairy producers received $1.06 less per hundred weight of milk in 1997 than they had in 1981. The price of milk consumers paid, however, had risen ninety cents per gallon. Indeed, retailers were using dairy products to "cover losses on other retail products."[95] While agricultural concentration has been good for tertiary producers and retailers, it has not benefited South Dakota farmers and ranchers. If rural South Dakota is to recover economically, socially, and psychologically, then additional types of business opportunities need to be found.

The economic trends of agriculture are not unique to South Dakota, but the state does have an added burden. Most of its counties are still classified as "farm dependent" economies. This means the counties "derive 20 percent or more of their earned income from farming." These counties are most likely to have a higher percent of 18-34-year olds leave the county than any other type of county in the nation. They are also losing people and jobs faster than elsewhere.[96] It is the loss of people, particularly young people, that has captured the imagination of state politicians. Ignoring the 1930s and 1970s, when out-migration was even higher, politicians talk about reversing the "brain-drain" among the young. What is unsaid, at least by politicians, is that "farm dependent" counties "have a poverty rate 60 percent greater than that of metro counties."[97] Like the urban ghetto, "farm dependent" counties are pockets of hidden poverty. Children, even if they wanted to stay in the area, could not plan on improving their economic condition. There were no jobs for them.[98]

For those who remain in the central portions of the state, then, the trends are not good. Excluding the Indian reservations, South Dakota's rural population is getting older, farm and/or ranch size is increasing, and income is falling. While the roads remain, fewer people need to use them. As a result, the frontier has returned to South Dakota. In 1930 no county in South Dakota qualified as a frontier county. In 1950 seven counties qualified for "frontier" status. A frontier county is one which has fewer than six residents per square mile. In 1950 these frontier counties all lay in western South Dakota. Today, only two of the twenty-two West River counties are officially not frontier counties, and 42.1 percent of South Dakota qualifies as frontier. East River South Dakota is becoming depopulated also.

The Frontier Education Center excludes only twelve South Dakota counties from its frontier category analysis. Thirty-four East River counties contain some portion of territory that qualifies for "frontier" status. Making matters worse, eight counties have already passed into "wilderness" status. This means there are fewer than two people per square mile, or fewer people living in the region than during the pre-Columbian period.[99] The problem is so severe that in March 2003, U.S. Senator Tim Johnson co-sponsored "A New Homestead Act" designed to attract new residents and businesses for "rural areas suffering from high out-migration."[100] It is too early to determine if a new homestead act will reverse the flow of humans out of central South Dakota.

The continued depopulation of most South Dakota counties carries important implications for the state as a whole. Is it feasible to provide health care services in a traditional manner when a hospital or clinic may serve fewer than one thousand people? Can a rural health-care system be economically viable when medicaid reimbursements are smaller for rural hospitals than urban ones?[101] Depopulation also impacts education. South Dakota leads the nation in the percentage of schools in rural areas. Seventy-seven percent of South Dakota's schools are found in rural areas.[102] Typical school consolidation is not an option in many parts of the state, and in those places where it might be an

Long a tradition in farm country, the auction is a way for one farmer to recoup a portion of the substantial investment in equipment necessary for operational efficiency and for another farmer to acquire the same equipment at reduced cost. *Courtesy Joel Strasser.*

option, school consolidation has stalled.[103] What will happen if a school fails to meet the standards federally mandated by "No Child Left Behind"? Sending students to another school may not be feasible. There are often no other schools to which to send them. No wonder South Dakotans are ambivalent about the future. All the while, vacant farm and ranch houses continue to appear, and the emptying of the land continues.[104] South Dakota has forty-nine counties with home vacancy rates exceeding ten percent. Potter County had a home vacancy rate of nearly thirty-five percent.[105] It was this winnowing out of South Dakota's population that evoked a controversial proposal from the East for what to do with the region.

That there should be controversy about the future in South Dakota during the 1980s and 1990s surprised some. In 1981 Joel Garreau's *The Nine Nations of North America* suggested the region "was most at peace with itself. It is the nation that works best."[106] It was also, he pointed out, a region which understood how interdependent the world had become. South Dakota, and other "breadbasket" states understood how their economic livelihood depended on events overseas. While residents on either coast might see the region as quaint and perhaps even culturally backwards, South Dakota's agricultural productivity meant the region did not "feel obligated to leap at an increase in low-paying jobs" or embrace "the boom-town syndrome" of other regions.[107] This type of attitude changed in 1987 when an interesting article appeared in the academic journal *Planning*.

■ Buffalo Commons

Written by Frank and Deborah Popper, "The Great Plains from Dust to Dust" shattered the apparent peace about which Garreau wrote. So important is their article, no contemporary account of South Dakota and its future can ignore it.[108] While the Poppers were not the first to suggest that fundamental changes were coming, or even should come, to the plains, the Poppers and their analysis became lightening rods for discussions about the future of western Dakota.[109] Sixteen years later scholars still debate the implications of the Poppers' findings.[110]

The Poppers' thesis suggested demographic trends boded ill for the state. An aging population, the flight of young people to other regions, and the increasing scale of agriculture meant significant portions of South Dakota would eventually be abandoned. The authors suggested the result of this abandonment would be the restoration of the plains "to their pre-white condition" of the nineteenth century.[111] In the years since the Poppers first presented their findings, South Dakota, indeed all northern plains states, have seen portions of the Popper hypothesis born out.

More than anything, the Poppers articulated the one thing many rural families did not want to admit: farming was no longer profitable. Declining farm income helped explain the demise of small-town businesses. As towns saw people move away and businesses close their doors, they faced a difficult decision. They could either raise taxes or get by with fewer services. Most towns choose fewer services. When this happens, the Poppers argued, "the quality of life also declines."[112] Add to this a nation already burdened by agricultural surpluses, and the future did not look bright. The question was what was to be done.

For some, the Poppers suggested tourism and recreation might be an answer, although it would not stem the loss of people from the region. For others, there was no hope. "We believe . . . much of the plains will inexorably suffer near-total desertion over the next generation." This would happen, the Poppers predicted, rapidly in parts of "Montana, New Mexico, South Dakota, and Texas, especially those away from the interstates." Therefore, the Poppers suggested the federal government "recognize its [the plains'] unsuitability for agriculture" and re-establish the native grasses of the region.[113] The idea was to create a national reserve that recreated the plains as they existed in the nineteenth century.

To say this proposal met with a cold reception in the plains states is an understatement. The Poppers, perhaps unwittingly, had opened a deep wound in South Dakotans dating back to the Great Depression.[114] This is one reason why locals reacted with tremendous hostility to the Poppers personally. On one speaking engagement, Frank Popper needed the local sheriff department to intervene when an irate farmer seemed unwilling to keep the conversation civil. Another speaking engagement was cancelled because of death threats.[115] One opponent of the thesis put it this way, "Frank Popper represents Europe, the East, Harvard, federal interference—everything the good people of the Plains want to get away from. . . . We will fight the Poppers, all the way."[116] This type of attitude has not changed the general trends observed by the Poppers in 1987. Nor does it recognize that the "Buffalo Commons" proposal is a new twist on an old proposal. The federal government felt the same way earlier.[117]

During the Great Depression the Roosevelt administration initiated a study of the Great Plains. The resulting report, *The Future of the Great Plains*, suggested western South Dakota was overpopulated and that agriculture had reached its natural limit. The report suggested the federal government begin thinking about strategies designed to reduce the number of ranchers and farmers. Toward this end, the federal government began buying up abandoned farm holdings in 1937. This initial round of purchases resulted in 7.3 million acres being transformed into "national grasslands."[118] Three such grasslands are found in South Dakota—Grand River, Buffalo Gap, and Fort Pierre—and occupy 866,391 acres.[119] Located west of the Missouri River, in the region proposed by the researchers of *The Future of the Great Plains*, these grasslands are overseen by the

U.S. Forest Service, and over the decades West River ranchers were able to run livestock on this land for a fee. The Poppers were simply updating a trend the government recognized as inevitable fifty years earlier.

So why had the "Buffalo Commons" not occurred by 1987? One answer lay in the damming of the Missouri River as a result of the Pick-Sloan project. The dams created by Pick-Sloan in the 1940s and 1950s provided jobs to many people who otherwise would have been forced off the land earlier. Employment in construction or as contract suppliers kept many in the area after farming was no longer an option. Another reason rests with the Cold War, in response to which the federal government built hundreds of silos for the Titan Missile in western South Dakota. The work provided others with economic opportunities. As the Cold War wound down in the late 1980s, some Dakotans blamed the government for their situation. "The wages paid were so high that ranch hands, sons, fathers—many of the able-bodied men—went to work there while it was under construction." With their economic expectations raised, Linda Hasselstrom wrote, "some of them would no longer accept the wages ranchers could afford to pay, and left the area. Others, reluctant to give up the extra cash, took second jobs in town or urged their wives to do so. Their lives became oriented toward making more money."[120] Her assessment seems rather unfair. She is condemning those who desire more than the farmers and ranchers of the area can provide. Perhaps another way to view it is that the Cold War and Pick-Sloan project kept people in South Dakota during the post-World War II period longer than they otherwise would have stayed.

Perhaps Hasselstrom is reacting to the notion that those who stayed on the land are afraid of change. There is an impression, albeit an unfair one, that those who remain are "behind the times" or "not too smart."[121] Garreau attacked this attitude in *The Nine Nations of North America*, but it continues to persist. What critics such as Harold Ross of the *New Yorker* failed to recognize is that those on the farm and ranch are often ahead of the learning curve. Farmers used Global Positioning Systems (GPS) for their planting grids long before the devices made their way into automobiles. Also, walkie-talkies served farmer and home long before the ubiquitous cell phone appeared on the scene. On more than one farm a call went out via walkie-talkie to have a spouse run into town for a replacement part or other suddenly necessary item. Many farmers and ranchers charted their crop and animal requirements on computers before most urban households had them.

Some urbanites think of ranchers, farmers, and even small-town business people as uneducated. Why else, they wonder, would these people remain where they are? That may have been the situation in the past, but it is not today. Today's successful farmers and ranchers are likely college educated. In the mid-1980s, members of the relatively small Lutheran congregation in Hope, South Dakota, boasted an eighty-five percent college-educated congregation.[122] While the parishioners of Hope Church might be tied to the land economically, they are not interested in "high culture" and entertainment. The Internet, as the radio did before it, allows Hope parishioners to access the Berlin Philharmonic; they can order tickets for the South Dakota Symphony, or buy a CD of hula music. They might sample a Van Gogh exhibit on the World Wide Web. One reason those farming, ranching, and doing business in small towns can stay is that the world has become smaller. Good roads have reduced the amount of time it takes to get to the big city. The Internet (and radio and television) brings the world closer to those who remain on South Dakota's farms and ranches. Isolation, while still an issue, is not the factor it once was in South Dakota.

When these farmers and ranchers visit Sioux Falls or travel to Omaha or Minneapolis for an art exhibition, they take the very roads often blamed for the demise of the small towns from which they come. This, then, is the paradox of modern South Dakota: while more of the outside world is available, via the Internet or our highways, our local communities continue to shrink.

Some might question the importance of the family farm or the small town's demise. After all, fewer than two percent of rural Americans live on farms, and urbanization is the trend around the world.[123] From China to Mexico, people are leaving the countryside for the promise of a better life in the city. This transformation has not produced mass starvation or even a declining standard of living. Indeed, America has benefited. Urbanization in China and Latin America means greater export opportunities for those who remain on the land. The last decades of the twentieth century witnessed tremendous agricultural export growth. By the early 1980s wheat farmers in the United States accounted for eighteen percent of the world's exports of wheat. At the same time, Saudi Arabia accounted for only fourteen percent of the world's production of oil.[124] Why, one might ask, should we worry about the depopulation of South Dakota's hinterland when it does not entail the loss of food production? Those who are left on the farm have opportunities their parents did not. Besides, we are told the future is in the service and post-industrial economies.

Those who promote the new economy are following in the linear direction of history promoted by Turner and his "The Significance of the Frontier" essay. Turner talked about "stages of Frontier Advance" in the same manner that economists talk about evolving economies. Agriculture gave way to industrialization; this, in turn, gave way to the service economy. In this scenario, agriculture, implicitly important, is reduced to invisibility. We are not concerned with the producers of the food. They are neither the apex of the agricultural economy nor the dominant voting sector at the national level. As long as sufficient food is produced, then the agricultural community is ignored. Answering this question centers around the importance of "place" and "community."

Depopulation of the Great Plains threatens the survival of the family farm and the communities dependent upon its existence. In 1950 seven counties in South Dakota with frontier status (less than six residents per square mile) were located east of the state capital; today that number has grown to seventeen. *Courtesy Joel Strasser.*

In recent years, organizations such as the Miner County Community Revitalization and the Rural Learning Center have sprung up.[125] These agencies are attempting to help small towns recognize that there are alternatives to withering away. While it is too early to tell whether they will be successful, or if success will be geographically specific, these agencies have brought an energy to the question of what community and place mean for towns such as Howard, Wessington Springs, and others. These entities are getting communities to ask questions about their future. Will a community become a bedroom community to a larger hub? How does a community become a bedroom community? Will townspeople redirect some of their purchasing power to local communities, or will they continue to shop in Rapid City, Sioux Falls, or even out of state?[126] Will a community opt-out of the state property tax freeze to improve schools? Will schools consolidate to marshal resources? Indeed, the question of school funding has become one of the most divisive issues in the state and helps explain the problems confronting South Dakota today.

In the mid-1990s South Dakota Governor William Janklow convinced the state legislature to wire elementary and high schools for Internet access. Ostensibly, distance learning programs and electronic resources would allow schools to overcome the limitations of local libraries and create an informed student. South Dakota received high marks from outside observers for the effort. Still many schools continue to see declining enrollments.

Distance matters, and given South Dakota's great size, school consolidation is not as easy as many outsiders would think. While small school size might warrant the closing of a school elsewhere, the problem of having students on a bus two, three, or perhaps four hours a day, particularly with South Dakota's winters, creates much larger problems. Ironically, despite being more connected to the outside world than ever before, students and residents of many small towns feel more isolated than before. As Elvin Hatch, in his *Biography of a Small Town*, points out, school affairs are often the "chief focus of community interest" in small towns, and "school events" play "a major role in the locality's organized social life." By the late twentieth century, schools, not churches, "had become the center of the community."[127] The question of school consolidation and the Internet, then, is not just a question of money; it is a question of local identity.

Proponents of the Internet as a means of stemming the tide of out-migration have forgotten important lessons from the 1920s, and again the 1960s. In the 1920s radio gave South Dakotans access to the larger United States.[128] One scholar who has looked at radio's impact on South Dakota is Paula M. Nelson. She concluded, "the impact of the radio on rural life in general, and west river country in particular, over the long run was ambiguous."[129] The radio reminded listeners of the disjuncture between their current existence and that of life in the larger city. Television gave listeners an actual image of what existed outside of South Dakota. While the image often lied, it still enticed.

This is true of the Internet, but with a difference. The Internet can be multifaceted; one can interact with the World Wide Web in a way that one cannot with radio or television. South Dakotans can now participate in the larger world without giving up their vistas and way of life, or leaving home. Students can visit the pyramids, see a Picasso exhibit, and explore the early history of Jamestown, Virginia. Nevertheless, the Internet reminds students about opportunities they cannot imagine. They hear about salaries paid and opportunities for advancement. The question for many is, why stay? More precisely, where should I move? The answer is often Rapid City or Sioux Falls. It is in these cities that much of South Dakota's story has begun to unfold since 1980.

■ The Urban Experience

South Dakota's major cities no longer serve as mere hubs to the agricultural hinterland—as they did from the 1850s through the 1930s. Now, these cities are integrated more fully into the national economy. Sioux Falls, with its credit-card operations, medical facilities, growing technology sector, and historic ties to meat-packing, has truly diversified its economic base. Rapid City, benefiting from its growing tourism trade, proximity to Ellsworth Air Force Base, and the home of South Dakota School of Mines and Technology, is no longer just a ranch town. While other cities—Brookings, Mitchell, Pierre, Aberdeen, and Huron—still serve as hubs to agricultural enterprises, they too are beginning to diversify their economies.

As the rural communities of South Dakota struggle to deal with increasing isolation, limited economic opportunities, and their place in the emerging "global economy," trends suggest an ironic development. While South Dakota is getting more "vacant," it is also becoming more "urban." South Dakotans are living increasingly in metropolitan areas, locally important hubs, or small towns. They are not living on farms. In 1990, excluding the cities of Sturgis and Rapid City, 115,002 people lived in western South Dakota. Of these people, only 14,693 lived on farms.[130] Despite the Internet, the lure of the land, or some other siren, South Dakota, like the rest of the nation, is becoming more urban.

This, too, is difficult for many South Dakotans. After all, the Euro-Americans who usurped control of the region from its indigenous inhabitants had "uprooted their families . . . to farm."[131] They had chosen to circumvent the industrializing tendencies of the nation at the time. Now, in a post-industrial economy, these children of farmers and ranchers are entering the very world their forebears had rejected a century earlier. While the farm may produce the goods that many of the locally important hubs turn into something new, the economic engine driving South Dakota since the 1980s is the urban economy.

Writing about the transformation of South Dakota cities over the last two decades is challenging. Very few works on individual cities exist,[132] and no work exists on the growth of South Dakota industry relative to agriculture. Of the books that do exist, most are jingoistic boosterisms rather than historical analyses. Many of these books do not try to connect the growth or decline of a particular town with larger trends. Instead, they list the number of residents, the growth of this business or that enterprise. A quick perusal of some of these works would lead one to think that no one ever left South Dakota and the depression never happened. Despite this lack of scholarly attention, few deny that urban South Dakota emerged as the driving engine of the economy in the post-1980 period.

What allows South Dakota's larger towns to enjoy greater economic growth than the rest of the state is the automobile, and in the case of Rapid City and Sioux Falls, substantial airports. This is nothing new. As early as the 1920s small-town merchants complained about the locals going to other towns to do their shopping. In the 1990s this lament became a little more vocal. Marvis Hogen, a Kadoka businessman, ends his *Fifty Years on Main Street* with a section entitled "Sermon Time." The sermon begins with a criticism of his fellow Kadoka residents: ". . . there are few of your needs that you can't get in Kadoka, IF YOU WANTED TO. That's the key phrase: 'IF YOU WANTED TO.' If every resident of a small town would try their hometown merchants first, the Main Streets would look different than they do today."[133] Still, a quick look at the demographic changes occurring at the county level shows the importance of access to interstates. The twenty-two counties along the state's two interstates saw an average population growth

The appearance across South Dakota of large retail stores, owned by out-of-state corporations and selling products made overseas, has sparked controversy in many communities, such as Aberdeen, Rapid City, and Sioux Falls, pictured here. *Courtesy Gary D. Olson.*

of 13.3 percent. The forty-four non-interstate counties saw their population grow by only 1.5 percent. The automobile is influencing where growth occurs.[134]

The crux of this dilemma is money. In their hearts, residents know that driving to Sioux Falls, Rapid City, Aberdeen, or worse, out of state, means their local store is going to have difficulty surviving. Yet knowing what their cash balance is, their heads tell them it is worth a trip to Wal-Mart or K-Mart for the purchases they have to make. When money is tight, the farther a dollar stretches, the better. Mike Schommer, owner of Oelrichs General Store, demonstrated that he understood the situation when he said, "we had a pretty good business until the Wal-Mart moved into Chadron. . . . There's not much for loyalties anymore, but if it was me, I don't know how loyal I'd be either."[135] The question is, then, what does the future hold for South Dakota? Or, more precisely, what do the trends of South Dakota history suggest for the state?

Working against South Dakota, whatever it decides to do, is its weather. Americans prefer warm climates to cold ones. Low taxes do not necessarily overcome locale. Most companies do not "locate in regions and cities in response to exogenously given characteristics."[136] That is, most companies do not simply pack up and move to a new location because officials ask them to, or offer them tax incentives. Some do, of course, and several Minnesota companies have moved to South Dakota because of a favorable tax structure. Other issues are involved: quality education, affordable housing, and cultural amenities. Instead, companies are more likely to move a portion of one existing operation, as Citigroup did when it moved its credit-card enterprise to Sioux Falls in 1981. This means that many towns should begin to rethink their proposals for survival; as Gilbert C. Fite commented, "many Great Plains towns have promoted the idea of attracting industry to reverse their economic stagnation. However, this is mostly a false hope and no amount of promotion and ballyhoo will change the situation."[137] If South Dakota is going to reverse the trend of out-migration, it is likely going to have to do so internally.

In this effort, it is the largest cities of South Dakota that are going to have to take the lead. Officially, forty percent of the state's population resides in its nine largest towns not including the bedroom communities surrounding Sioux Falls and Rapid City. These towns offer the most diverse economic base in the state and so have been able to withstand the economic downturn of rural South Dakota better than most.

Access to airports and interstates will help Rapid City and Sioux Falls continue to grow. The proximity of such towns as Brookings, Vermillion, Mitchell, Hill City, and Custer to these major hubs will likely help them too. For other towns, the future is not so bright. One of the stories of South Dakota is the rise and fall of many such towns. Chapter Fifteen mentions the fate of Mennesela, originally the county seat of Butte County. When the Elkhorn railroad built its spur to Belle Fourche and not Mennesela, the latter town "ultimately collapsed" and Belle Fourche emerged as the county seat. Sioux Falls ultimately beat out Dell Rapids for domination of Minnehaha County because of the political maneuvering of R. F. Pettigrew and railroad developments. While Dell Rapids is currently thriving as a bedroom community of Sioux Falls, it is not the dominant player in Minnehaha County affairs many assumed it would be when founded. There are many towns that share a fate in between Mennesela and Dell Rapids. The point is that throughout the history of South Dakota, towns have risen and fallen as a direct result of access to the most recent transportation developments. This pattern is not likely to disappear in the future.

Rapid City's growth is a post-World War II phenomenon. While World War II hurt Lead and Deadwood, Rapid City residents did not face the same curtailment of business enterprises. Moreover, the creation of an Army Air Corps base east of the city helped stimulate the city's growth. After the war, governmental decisions relating to the Cold War helped solidify Rapid City's future. Ellsworth Air Force Base, dedicated in 1953, and the placement of Titan and Minutemen Missiles in West River silos beginning in 1962 meant the injection of cash into the West River economy. Much of this money flowed into Rapid City. By 1950 Rapid City was clearly the dominant West River urban entity.[138]

The Cold War, however, is over. Still, Rapid City, Pennington County, state officials, and South Dakota's congressional delegation continue to work to make Ellsworth Air Force Base attractive to national officials. Fearing Ellsworth would be a target of the federal government's Base Realignment and Closure Commission, officials reconfigured interstate off-ramps, reserved sections of land for base expansion, and created a task-force designed to keep Ellsworth operational. This forward-thinking approach shows how important Ellsworth Air Force Base is to Rapid City and the surrounding region economically. What these officials could not plan for is the changing nature of military combat. While the B-1 Bomber's role in traditional nation-against-nation struggles remains obvious, its role, and the role of traditional bombers as a whole, is not so clear when it comes to fighting terrorism or localized conflicts such as those in Bosnia or Kosovo. In this sense, then, Rapid City shares something with its smaller, more rural neighbors. Part of its future is tied to government policy decisions. Like the farmer struggling to survive after the "Freedom to Farm" bill attempted to end the traditional subsidy program, Rapid City will suffer from Ellsworth's closing.

Like Sioux Falls, Rapid City enjoys success because of its economic diversification. Tied to agriculture, military strategy, such industrial enterprises as its cement plant, and tourism, Rapid City is not dependent on any single enterprise. While its growth may be slow and steady, rather than the boom-and-bust cycle of earlier times, Rapid City's future looks promising. The increasing medical services offered in the community are an example of its bright future.

A town with a very different story than Rapid City's is North Sioux City. The initial home to Gateway, North Sioux City illustrates the dilemma of any town tied to a single enterprise. In the mid-1990s, Gateway employed over 6,000 workers in this town on the Iowa-South Dakota border. The city experienced a construction boom, and the future seemed limitless. Ten years later, Gateway is closing its computer manufacturing in the city.[139] Employment at the firm has shrunk by more than sixty-six percent, and North Sioux City is facing declining home prices and a shrinking service sector. What gives North Sioux City an opportunity to survive is its proximity to Sioux Falls and Sioux City. North Sioux City's geographic location may be the key to its future development.

■ Promise of Opportunity

In 1893, when Frederick Jackson Turner suggested that the frontier had ended, South Dakotans could see themselves as part of a larger process. Today, the return of the frontier has made the descendants of those first pioneers nervous. Nevertheless, a review of the last twenty years suggests that South Dakotans continue to fit within the larger story of American history. In 2005 South Dakotans are primarily an urban constituency; centralization in agribusiness fits within the larger trend of corporate consolidation. The state's population is becoming more heterogeneous. True, "white flight" has a different connotation in South Dakota than in Chicago or Boston; still, the result is the same—a growing minority presence for the county in question. Interestingly, the counties that face this situation are also the ones most impacted by No Child Left Behind legislation. South Dakota's rural schools cannot meet the national norms required for teacher certification. Just like their urban counterparts, South Dakota school districts find themselves challenged to prove they are meeting the needs of their students.

The uncertainty of the future, particularly economic uncertainty, ties South Dakotans to their predecessors. What lured first the Native Americans and then the immigrants was the promise of opportunity. That promise remains, although it is most likely to be found in the state's urban environs. The past, sold to tourists and residents today in the form of nostalgia, was not nearly as bright as we might like to believe; and the future is not nearly as dim as some would have us believe.

Notes

Chapter 3: Native Peoples, *Herbert T. Hoover (pgs. 40-46)*

[1] Nomenclature in use for the identification of ethnic groups changed during the civil rights period in national history; for example, *Hispanic American* became *Chicano* but, since the 1970s, the term *Hispanic American* has returned to general use and some Latinos prefer *Mexican American*. In some cultural environments, *American Indian* was replaced by *Native American* but, for various reasons, both terms remain in use. *American Indian* has been the term of choice in public records, including the national census reports down to the present and, accordingly, must be used for access to public records. *Indian Country* is a legal term that has no synonym and that identifies tribal land under federal protection against taxation or foreclosure. Across South Dakota, *Indian* is the term mainly in use within reservation societies, with pride, while *Native American* sometimes is used to placate outsiders and urban Indians, even though some tribal members regard *Native American* as condescending if not pejorative. In the tribal press—the *Lakota Journal*, for example—*American Indian* and *Native American* are used as synonyms without any explanation. For all of these reasons, the term *Indian* will appear most often in texts about the history of Indian-white relations, but the term *Native American* will be used, as well, with the assumption that readers will understand that neither should be regarded as a term of condescension or derogation. Similarly, as the text below indicates, the term *Sioux* is used because it has no synonym that includes all of the original fourteen tribes in the federation, and the term *Sioux* appears in tribal documents; for example, in a tribal constitution to identify the elected Yankton Sioux Business and Claims Committee.

[2] The best general source for information about prehistoric South Dakotans is Larry J. Zimmerman, *Peoples of Prehistoric South Dakota* (Lincoln: University of Nebraska Press, 1985). Greater detail exists in unpublished manuscripts prepared for use in archaeological field work by Richard Fox, Jr., and preserved in his files at the University of South Dakota.

Chapter 4: Exploration and the Fur Trade, *Rex Meyers (pgs. 47-68)*

[1] David J. Weber, *The Spanish Frontier in North America* (New Haven: Yale University Press, 1992), provides an excellent overview of Spanish interests.

[2] A.P. Nasatir, ed., *Before Lewis and Clark: Documents Illustrating the History of the Missouri, 1785-1804,* 2 vols., Vol. 1 (St. Louis: St. Louis Historical Documents Foundation, 1952), 1-3, has an insightful discussion of geographic claims in the region.

[3] Nasatir, 1: 3.

[4] Louis Hennepin, *A Description of Louisiana,* John Gilmary Shea, trans., (New York: John G. Shea, 1880; reprint., Ann Arbor, University Microfilms, 1996), 344.

[5] Louis Armand de Lom d'Arce Lahontan, *New Voyages to North America,* Reuben Gold Thwaites, ed., 2 vols. (Chicago, 1905; reprint, New York: Burt Franklin, 1970), 179-97, 214.

[6] Nasatir, 1: 6.

[7] Frank Norall, *Bourgmont: Explorer of the Missouri, 1698-1725* (Lincoln: University of Nebraska Press, 1988), 105-11.

[8] A number of sources are helpful in understanding the actions and motivations of the senior Verendrye and his sons. Donald Jackson, *Thomas Jefferson and the Stony Mountains* (Urbana: University of Illinois Press, 1981); Nasatir, 1: 33-34; Charles E. DeLand, "The Verendrye Expeditions and Discoveries," in *South Dakota Historical Collections* 7 (Pierre: State Historical Society, 1914): 99-322.

[9] Translation from the Latin by Dr. Daniel Taylor, Lawrence University, Appleton, WI.

[10] Discussion of events involving the first plate appear in various state newspapers; among them the *Sioux Falls Argus Leader,* July 21, 1995, October 10, 1995, October 15, 1995.

[11] M. Le Page du Pratz, *The History of Louisiana,* Joseph G. Tregle, Jr., ed. (Baton Rouge: Louisiana State University Press, 1975).

[12] Jackson, 6, 8.

[13] John Parker, *The Journals of Jonathan Carver and Related Documents, 1766-1770* (St. Paul: Minnesota Historical Society Press, 1976), 193.

[14] Parker, 136-39.

[15] Jackson, 34-36.

[16] Warren L. Cook, *Flood Tide of Empire: Spain and the Pacific Northwest, 1543-1819* (New Haven: Yale University Press, 1973), 446. Julian P. Boyd, ed., *The Papers of Thomas Jefferson,* Vol. 15 (Princeton: Princeton University Press, 1958), 610.

[17] Jackson, 45-48. Stephan E. Watrous, ed., *John Ledyard's Journey Through Russia and Siberia, 1787-1788* (Madison: University of Wisconsin Press, 1966).

[18] Nasatir, 1: 119-27.

[19] Abraham P. Nasatir, *Borderland in Retreat: From Spanish Louisiana to the Far Southwest* (Albuquerque: University of New Mexico Press, 1976), 73.

[20] Nasatir, *Borderland,* 71.

[21] Nasatir, *Borderland,* 75.

[22] Nasatir, *Borderland,* 77;*Before,* 1: 217-29. Cook, 435.

[23] Details of the Truteau expedition are in Nasatir's two works, *Before,* 1: 88-90, 243-53, and *Borderland,* 78-79, as well as Cook, 436-37.

[24] Cook, 437.

[25] Nasatir, *Borderlands,* 79-81.

[26] David Williams, "John Evans' Strange Journey; Part 1, The Welsh Indians," *American Historical Review,* 54 (January 1949): 277-95; "John Evans' Strange Journey; Part 2, Following the Trail," *American Historical Review,* 54 (April 1949): 508-29. These two articles contain details and assessment of Evans' expedition.

[27] Nasatir, *Before,* 2: 410-14.

[28] Williams, 1: 278.

[29] Nasatir, *Before,* 1: 341-45; Cook, 437.

[30] Gary E. Moulton, ed., *The Journals of the Lewis and Clark Expedition*, 13 vols. (Lincoln: University of Nebraska Press), Vol. 2 (1986), 253, and Vol. 3 (1987), 100-03.

[31] Derek Hayes, *First Crossing: Alexander Mackenzie, His Expedition Across North America, and the Opening of the Continent* (Vancouver, B.C.: Douglas & McIntyre, Ltd., 2001).

[32] Donald Jackson's *Thomas Jefferson and the Stony Mountains* provides an excellent overview of Jefferson's on-going interest in the Missouri River region.

[33] Jefferson's instructions to Michaux appear in Donald Jackson, ed., *Letters of the Lewis and Clark Expedition* (Urbana: University of Illinois Press, 1962), 669-72. See also Henry Savage, Jr., and Elizabeth J. Savage, *Andre and Francois Andre Michaux* (Charlottesville: University Press of Virginia, 1986).

[34] One could reasonably argue that the Lewis and Clark Expedition began with Jefferson's hiring of Meriwether Lewis. Not only did members of that 1804-1806 expedition write more than members of any other western exploration party, more has been written about them. Only a true aficionado should make an effort to read everything. For purposes of the discussion that follows, three sources are sufficient to note: Donald Jackson's two works, cited above, and Gary Moulton's thirteen volume edition of the journals themselves. The last work is thoroughly indexed, superbly documented, and illuminated with extensive footnotes. All quotes from, as well as data and details about, the Lewis and Clark journals, come from Moulton's editions.

[35] http://monticello.org/jefferson/lewisandclark/congress_letter.html; Internet; accessed February 28, 2005.

[36] Richard Edward Oglesby, *Manuel Lisa and the Opening of the Missouri Fur Trade* (Norman: University of Oklahoma Press, 1963).

[37] Ray Allen Billington and Martin Ridge, *Westward Expansion: A History of the American Frontier* (New York: Macmillan Publishing Company, 1982), in their chapter "The Traders' Frontier, 1776-1840," have an excellent overview of western fur trade, including what is now South Dakota. The general history of the trade that follows comes from this chapter.

[38] E. de Girardin, *Le Tour du Monde, 1864.* http://projectgirardin.free.fr/pages/BADLANDS2-5.html; Internet; accessed August 20, 2003.

[39] Upper Missouri River trapper and guide Joseph DeSomet (Lewis) appears in the Fort Pierre records of the 1830s and 1840s, the Warren Expedition journals of the 1850s (as Michael), the Yankton Agency census for 1860, and the South Dakota Episcopal Church mission registers of the 1870s. See Harry F. Thompson, "Meriwether Lewis and His Son: The Claim of Joseph DeSomet Lewis and the Problem of History," *North Dakota History* 67 (Winter 2000): 24-37. Reprinted in David Kvernes, ed., *The Lewis and Clark Expedition: Then and Now* (Sioux Falls, SD: Center for Western Studies, 2004): 97-115.

[40] James Clyman, *James Clyman, Frontiersman, 1792-1881,* Charles L. Camp, ed. (San Francisco: California Historical Society, 1928), 17.

[41] Edmund C. Bray and Martha Coleman Bray, eds. and trans., *Joseph N. Nicollet on the Plains and Prairie* (St. Paul: Minnesota Historical Society Press, 1976).

Chapter 5: Missouri Valley Culture, *Herbert T. Hoover (pgs. 69-85)*

[1] *Administrative Procedure Act, Statutes at Large,* 11: 743 ff.

[2] Yankton elders have advised the use of *ospaye* to identify a tribal sub-division with its own political leadership and historic land claim. This definition distinguished an *ospaye* from a *tiospaye* (also spelled *tiyospaye*), which was a biological extended family. Although most public records use the word band as a synonym of *ospaye*, the term band is confusing because it also has been used to identify military units and other groups of Native Americans. *Ospaye* clearly identifies a political subdivision represented in the general council but recognized as "a company separated from the main body" known as the general council of a tribe. See Reverend Eugene Buechel, S. J., *Lakota-English Dictionary* (Pine Ridge, SD: Red Cloud Indian School, 1970).

[3] War Eagle was an extraordinary Mdewakanton Dakota who probably grew up in Wisconsin, served as a Mississippi River steamboat docking pilot, and became fluent in English and French languages as well as in Dakota dialect. For reasons unknown, he moved west to the confluence of the Big Sioux with the Missouri River in the company of his wife, Mazakirawin (Laughs at Iron Woman). He might have been the signatory for the Yankton Tribe recognized as Wambdi Okicize during treaty negotiations concluded in 1837, which earned him the award of a medallion issued by President Martin Van Buren. Although he was of Dakota heritage, Yanktons enlisted his services as their regional diplomat (called Head Chief by non-Indians) from the death of his predecessor, Little Dish, until War Eagle died in 1851 at his village, which soon gave rise to Sioux City. War Eagle's diplomatic successor was Padaniapapi (Struck by the Ree), a Yankton *ospaye* leader until he died in 1888. A plethora of records indicates that Mad Bull I, War Eagle, and Struck by the Ree stood out among tribal leaders for their unwavering and abiding support of the Missouri Valley Culture.

[4] Detailed information about the histories of valley culture settlements named Bon Homme, Springfield, and Running Water is available in Herbert T. Hoover, Carol Goss Hoover, and Elizabeth A Simmons, eds. *Bon Homme County History* (Freeman, SD: Pine Hill Press, 1994).

[5] Quotations and some detailed information in this description of the middle sector of Missouri Valley Culture between White Swan Village and Bijou Hills come from Jim Nelson, "Western Charles Mix County," *Dakota West,* Winter 1978, 17-22. This useful article gathered information from a variety of published sources, most of it folklore or oral tradition. Yet it gave plausible substance to a profile of valley culture in the White Swan-Bijou Hills area. Information used to create contexts and explication comes mainly from documents in the National Archives, Record Group 75.

[6] Hoover, "Whiskey Trade," 17-18.

[7] Ibid., 18.

[8] Ibid.

[9] Harold H. Schuler, *Fort Sully: Guns at Sunset* (Vermillion: University of South Dakota Press, 1992) thoroughly describes the histories of the two forts Sully.

Chapter 6: Native Americans in Dakota Territory, *Herbert T. Hoover (pgs. 86-94)*

[1] Two fairly detailed descriptions have appeared in other publications by Herbert T. Hoover and Carol Goss Hoover. The first is "Sioux Wars," *Encyclopedia of the American West* (New York: Macmillan, 1996), 1466-71. The second is "The Sioux Wars, 1854-1903," *Sioux Country: A History of Indian-white Relations* (Sioux Falls, SD: Center for Western Studies, 2000), 51-62.

Chapter 7: Territorial Politics and Politicians, *Herbert T. Hoover (pgs. 95-116)*

[1] South Dakotans (with North Dakotans) are fortunate for their membership in one of few state groups whose entire territorial political experience has been portrayed in book form by a distinguished scholar. A specialist in Western America, Yale University Professor of History Howard Lamar worked through documents at the National Archives to create a reliable analysis of the territorial experience the way it existed before territorialism changed in the non-contiguous imperial environment of the twentieth century. South Dakotans also can read an analysis of territorial life in the 1860s, when most resident citizens occupied only six counties in the southeastern quadrant of the state, written by University of South Dakota Professor of History Herbert Schell, a leader among pioneering state historians in the West. They have available, too, a useful source book comprising contemporary insights by George Kingsbury, a territorial journalist. At least seven other publications merit classification as general works about Dakota Territory, as well. Howard R. Lamar, *Dakota Territory, 1861-1889: A Study of Frontier Politics* (New Haven: Yale University Press, 1956) and Herbert S. Schell, *History of South Dakota* (Lincoln: University of Nebraska Press, 1975).

[2] Zachary Taylor Sutley, *The Last Frontier* (New York: Macmillan Company, 1930), 77.

[3] A summary statement about corruption in Burleigh's Indian Ring at the Yankton Agency is available in Special U.S. Agent Alexander Johnston to Indian Commissioner D. N. Cooley, July 16, 1866, M234, roll 250, National Archives.

[4] Reverend Melancthon Hoyt founded the first territorial parish at Yankton. Its role as a political center as well as an Episcopal institution in the history of Yankton is described by Eric Schultz, "Inside Christ Church, Episcopal, 1861-1976" (M.A. thesis, University of South Dakota, 2001).

[5] No literature explains how Bon Homme Island received its name before Meriwether Lewis and William Clark ascended the Missouri River in 1804, but scattered documents exist to suggest a plausible explanation. A Métis culture Web site records the name of Jean Baptiste Bonhomme, whose daughter Marguerite married Joseph Berthiaume at Detroit. This information suggests how the family name of Bonhomme reached St. Louis, where it marked an avenue and various institutions as well as a place across the lower Missouri River from St. Charles, which served as a commercial center near St. Louis vital to trade up the Missouri River during the fur trade era. Thus Bonhomme, across the river from St. Charles (renamed Chesterfield and platted in 1813), was a name accessible to pioneering traders. The Spanish governor at this site during the 1790s was Zenon Truteau, and the first trader to winter over in a cabin along the Missouri River upstream from present-day Omaha was Jean Baptiste Truteau, in 1794, who wrote the first description of tribal culture in the vicinity of this cabin. Because he passed by Bon Homme Island on the way to his cabin site along the Fort Randall narrow, it seems reasonable to conclude that the trader Truteau might have assigned the name Bonhomme to the island, similarly identified by Lewis and Clark as Bon Homme Island. If this assumption is true, the term came from the family name Bonhomme and not from Bon Homme (literally translated a "good man") as residents of Bon Homme County have supposed since it was founded by territorial officials in 1862.

[6] The best biographical profile of Edmunds is John E. Rau's "Political Leadership in Dakota Territory: Newton Edmunds as Governor, Peace Commissioner, and Elder Statesman," in *South Dakota Leaders: From Pierre Chouteau, Jr., to Oscar Howe,* Herbert T. Hoover and Larry J. Zimmerman, eds. (Vermillion: University of South Dakota Press, 1989), 15-27. Historian Rau accepted an invitation to prepare a biography of Edmunds for inclusion in this state centennial volume from a group of scholars that selected approximately fifty subjects worthy of commemoration. All agreed that the only territorial governors whose service merited inclusion were Newton Edmunds and Arthur Mellette.

[7] General Beadle's autobiography and two published biographies supplied information for an interpretive biography by Thomas Gasque, "Territorial Surveyor General, Protector of School Lands, Educator: William Henry Harrison Beadle," in Hoover and Zimmerman, 153-61.

[8] A recitation of fraudulent activities uncovered by William Dougherty appeared in his report: Captain W. Dougherty, Crow Creek Agency, to Assistant Adjutant General, Headquarters Fort Snelling, December 10, 1881, Letters Received by the U. S. Office of Indian Affairs for 1882, 270, National Archives.

[9] George W. Kingsbury, *History of Dakota Territory,* 5 vols. (Chicago: S. J. Clarke Publishing Company, 1915) 2: 1042-51, contains a belated rebuttal against Dougherty's report, accusing Hammond and Dougherty of inflating their charges against Livingston in reports to newsmen before the trial to "throw dust in the eyes of the public." Kingsbury argued that Livingston's accusers covered their own irregularities as well as fraud in the Indian Field Service that led to the removal of Ezra Hayt from the office of Indian Commissioner. Kingsbury failed to bring up the Christ Church connection, or that Lucius Kingsbury sat as a juror during Livingston's trial. George Kingsbury could not have known that bad conditions on the Crow

Creek and Lower Brûlé reservations for decades to follow validated Dougherty's charges of mismanagement and fraud. Careful students of historical evidence all are likely to conclude that the conduct of Livingston and his group at Fort Thompson included fraud as well as mismanagement, but they might reach different conclusions regarding which territorial politicians threw the most "dust in their eyes."

[10] Thomas J. Gasque, "Church, School, and State Affairs in Dakota Territory: Joseph Ward, Congregational Church Leader," in Hoover and Zimmerman, 143-51.

[11] William O. Farber, "From Territorial Status to Statehood: Arthur Calvin Mellette," in Hoover and Zimmerman, 163-83.

[12] Kenneth Hendrickson, Jr., condensed detailed information from his University of Oklahoma doctoral dissertation about the life of Pettigrew into a succinct political biography, "The Populist-Progressive Era: Richard Franklin Pettigrew, Andrew E. Lee, and Coe I. Crawford," in Hoover and Zimmerman, 185-205.

Chapter 8: Yankee and European Settlement, *Gary D. Olson (pgs. 117-142)*

[1] John P. Johansen, *Immigrants and Their Children in South Dakota,* Department of Rural Sociology, Bulletin 302 (Brookings, SD: South Dakota State University, 1936): 31.

[2] Herbert S. Schell, *History of South Dakota* (Lincoln: University of Nebraska Press, 1961), 168-74 passim.

[3] Oscar Handlin, *The Uprooted: The Epic Story of the Great Migration* (Boston: Little, Brown, 1951), 3.

[4] Schell, 387. One of the few modern studies even to refer to Yankees as a group in South Dakota history is Douglas Chittick, "A Recipe for Nationality Stew," in *Dakota Panorama,* ed. J. Leonard Jennewein and Jan Boorman (Sioux Falls: Dakota Territory Centennial Commission, 1961), 96-97.

[5] U.S. Census Office, *Population Schedules of the Eighth Census of the United States for Dakota Territory,* Washington, D.C., 1860.

[6] *Eighth Census,* 1860.

[7] *Eighth Census,* 1860.

[8] John Brennan, *The Condition and Resources of Southern Dakota: Prospective Trade and Travel of the Dakota Southern Railroad* (Sioux City, IA: Daily Journal Printing & Bindery, 1872), 28.

[9] Ibid., and George A. Batchelder, "A Sketch of the History and Resources of Dakota Territory," *South Dakota Historical Collections* 14 (Pierre: State Historical Society, 1928): 45.

[10] U.S. Census Office, *Population Schedules of the Tenth Census of the United States for Dakota Territory,* Washington, D.C., 1880.

[11] U.S. Census Office, *Population Schedules of the Ninth Census of the United States for Dakota Territory,* Washington, D.C., 1870, and *Tenth Census,* 1880.

[12] *Ninth Census,* 1870.

[13] *Eighth Census,* 1860.

[14] *Ninth Census,* 1870.

[15] *Tenth Census,* 1880.

[16] M. Claudia Duratschek, "The Capital is a River Town," in Jennewein and Boorman, 210.

[17] Dana R. Bailey, *History of Minnehaha County, South Dakota* (Sioux Falls, SD: Brown & Saenger, 1899), 468, 591, 663; Robert F. Karolevitz, *Yankton: A Pioneer Past* (Aberdeen, SD: North Plains Press, 1972), 51, 53.

[18] *Ninth Census,* 1870; George W. Kingsbury, *History of Dakota Territory,* 5 vols. (Chicago: S. J. Clarke Publishing Co., 1915), 4: 12, 315; Bailey, 437, 452, 537.

[19] Duratschek, 210, 218-19.

[20] Bailey, 402-30 passim.

[21] Ibid., 33, 333-58 passim; Duratschek, 212.

[22] Bailey, 185-89 passim and 321-22; *Tenth Census,* 1880.

[23] S.S. Visher, *Geography of South Dakota* (Vermillion: University of South Dakota Press, 1918), 155; Chittick, "A Recipe for Nationality Stew," 96-97.

[24] Kingsbury, 1: 331-35.

[25] Robert C. Ostergren, "European Settlement and Ethnicity Patterns on the Agricultural Frontiers of South Dakota," *South Dakota History* 13 (Spring/Summer 1983): 49-50.

[26] Ibid., 133-34.

[27] Schell, 158-59.

[28] Carleton C. Qualey, *Norwegian Settlement in the United States* (Northfield, MN: Norwegian-American Historical Assoc., 1938), 140-47 passim.

[29] A good survey of this subject can be found in Gabriel B. Ravndal, "The Scandinavian Pioneers of South Dakota," *South Dakota Historical Collections* 12 (Pierre: State Historical Society, 1924): 296-330.

[30] Qualey, *Norwegian Settlement in the United States*, 143.

[31] Ibid., 145.

[32] Ibid., 146-47.

[33] Ibid., 148.

[34] Myrle G. Hanson, "A History of Harding County, South Dakota, to 1925," *South Dakota Historical Collections* 21 (Pierre: State Historical Society, 1942): 546.

[35] Ravndal, 326-27; *History of Southeastern Dakota, Its Settlement, and Growth* (Sioux City, IA: Western Publishing Company, 1881), 28, 96, 314, 317, 472.

[36] Qualey, 134.

[37] Lynwood E. Oyos, ed., *Over a Century of Leadership: South Dakota Territorial and State Governors* (Sioux Falls, SD: Center for Western Studies, 1997), 66.

[38] Odd S. Lovoll, *The Promise Fulfilled: A Portrait of Norwegian Americans Today* (Minneapolis: University of Minnesota Press, 1998), 96.

[39] Ibid., 211-14; Odd S. Lovoll, *A Folk Epic: The Bygdelag in America* (Boston: Twayne Publishers, 1975), 72-80 passim.

[40] Orm Overland, *The Western Home: A Literary History of Norwegian America* (Northfield, MN: Norwegian-American Historical Association, 1996), passim.

[41] Robert C. Ostergren, "Migration Patterns to a Swedish Settlement," in *Ethnicity on the Great Plains,* ed. Federick C. Luebke (Lincoln: University of Nebraska Press, 1980), 74-76.

[42] Ibid., 84-88.

[43] Ibid., 76-78; August Peterson, *History of the Swedes Who Settled in Clay County, South Dakota, and Their Biographies* (Privately published by the Swedish Pioneer & Historical Society of Clay County, SD, 1947), 4-5.

[44] Thomas P. Christensen, "The Danes in South Dakota," *South Dakota Historical Collections* 14 (Pierre: State Historical Society, 1928): 540-42.

[45] Ibid., 541.

[46] Ibid., 542.

[47] Ibid., 545-48.

[48] Ibid., 547-48.

[49] Kingsbury, 1:531; Joseph A. Dvorak, *History of the Czechs in the State of South Dakota* (Tabor, SD: Czech Heritage Preservation Society, Inc., 1980), 21-24; Marilee Richards, ed., "Life Anew for Czech Immigrants: The Letters of Marie and Vavrin Stritecky," *South Dakota History* 11 (Fall/Winter 1981): 255.

[50] Dvorak, 25, 39-44; U.S. Bureau of the Census, *Special Reports: Supplementary Analysis and Derivative Tables, Twelfth Census of the U.S. 1900* (Washington, D.C.: Government Printing Office, 1906), 857; Schell, 381.

[51] Ibid., 265.

[52] *Souvenir of Czechoslovak Day Festival in the State of South Dakota* (Gregory, SD: Western Bohemian Fraternal Association, 1936), 5.

[53] Richards, 260-61.

[54] Rex C. Myers, "An Immigrant Heritage: South Dakota's Foreign-Born in the Era of Assimilation," *South Dakota History* 19 (Summer 1989): 148; Richards, 263-64.

[55] Anthony H. Richter, "'Gebt ihr den Vorzug': The German-Language Press of North and South Dakota," *South Dakota History* 10 (Summer 1980): 195.

[56] Schell, 380.

[57] Ostergren, "European Settlement," 66-68.

[58] Anthony H. Richter, "A Heritage of Faith: Religion and the German Settlers of South Dakota," *South Dakota History* 21 (Summer 1991): 155-56.

[59] Ibid.; Myers, 148; Kingsbury, 1: 711-12.

[60] Ostergren, "European Settlement," 71; Myers, 147; Richter, "A Heritage of Faith," 169; Kingsbury, 1: 714.

[61] Ibid., 705-07; Richter, "A Heritage of Faith," 169.

[62] Ibid., 169-70; Myers, 146.

[63] Richter, "A Heritage of Faith," 171-72; Steve Young, "Colony Mixes Tradition, Technology," *Sioux Falls Argus Leader*, November 17, 2003.

[64] Richter, "A Heritage of Faith," 169; Freeman, SD, Web home page, 2004.

[65] Richter, "'Gebt ihr den Vorzug,'" 192-203 passim.

[66] The best and most complete account of Dutch settlement in South Dakota is Gerald DeJong, "The Coming of the Dutch to the Dakotas," *South Dakota History* 5 (Winter 1974): 20-34 passim.

[67] Ibid., 25-27.

[68] Ibid., 29-30, 38.

[69] Ibid., 46-47.

[70] Ibid., 48-49.

[71] Ibid., 49-50.

[72] Charles Green, "The Administration of the Public Domain in South Dakota," *South Dakota Historical Collections* 20 (Pierre: State Historical Society, 1940): 120.

[73] John P. Johansen, "Immigrant Settlements and Social Organization in South Dakota," Dept. of Rural Sociology Bulletin 313 (Brookings, SD: South Dakota State University, 1937): 38, 49.

[74] Ibid., 7; U.S. Bureau of the Census, *Supplementary Analysis and Derivative Tables, Twelfth Census of the U.S.*, 856.

[75] Myers, 144; Louis M. McDermott, "The Primary Role of the Military on the Dakota Frontier," *South Dakota History* 2 (Winter 1971): 2; William H. Russell, "Promoters and Promotion Literature of Dakota Territory," *South Dakota Historical Collections* 10 (Pierre: State Historical Society, 1952): 437; Green, 151.

[76] J. Olson Anders, "The Making of a Typical Prairie County: Day County, South Dakota, 1881-1906," *South Dakota Historical Collections* 36 (Pierre: State Historical Society, 1972): 534.

[77] Joseph H. Cash, "History of Lead, South Dakota: 1876-1900," *South Dakota Historical Collections* 34 (Pierre: State Historical Society, 1968): 118-19.

[78] Johansen, 9.

[79] Phillips G. Davies, ed., "Touring the Welsh Settlements of South Dakota, 1891," *South Dakota History* 10 (Summer 1980): 223-24.

[80] Ibid., 225-26.

[81] Ibid., 226-27.

[82] Ostergren, "European Settlement," 73.

[83] Cash, 123.

[84] Johansen, 18.

[85] Violet and Orlando J. Goering, "Jewish Farmers in South Dakota—the Am Olam," *South Dakota History* 12 (Winter 1982): 232-37.

[86] Ibid., 238-40.

[87] Ibid., 241-44.

[88] Ibid., 245-46.

Chapter 9: African Americans, Betti C. VanEpps-Taylor (pgs. 143-156)

[1] The story of York is taken from the many sources dealing with his presence on the expedition. See *Original Journals of the Lews and Clark Expedition, 1804-1806*, Reuben Gold Thwaites, ed., 8 vols. (reprint 1904-1905; New York: Antiquarian Press, 1959), 1: 185. His presence is briefly noted in most of the current studies of the Lewis and Clark Expedition. W. Sherman Savage discusses him in "The Negro in the History of the Pacific Northwest," *Journal of Negro History* 13 (1928); and in his later book, *Blacks in the West*, (Greenwich, CT: Praeger Publishing Company, 1976), 4-6, 13, 25. John M. Carroll, who edited *The Black Military Experience in the American West* (New York: Liveright Publishing Corporation, 1971), devotes a chapter to York. Two important studies provide new primary source documentation and will contribute to a greater understanding of this man and his world: *Dear Brother . . . Letters of William Clark to Jonathan Clark*, edited and with an introduction by James J. Holmberg (New Haven, CT: The Filson Historical

Society and Yale University Press, 2002), and Robert B. Betts, *In Search of York: The Slave Who Went to the Pacific with Lewis and Clark* (Boulder: Colorado Associated University Press, 1985; revised, 2000).

[2] Monroe Lee Billington and Roger D. Hardaway, *African Americans on the Western Frontier* (Boulder: University Press of Colorado, 1998), introduction, 1-2. See also Lorenzo J. Greene, Gary R. Kremer, and Antonio F. Holland, *Missouri's Black Heritage* (Columbia: University of Missouri Press, 1989), 8-17.

[3] Oscar Micheaux, *The Conquest: The Story of a Negro Pioneer* (Lincoln, NE: Woodruff Press, 1913; reprinted by University of Nebraska, Bison Books, 1994).

[4] Beckwourth and Rose are both discussed in detail by Kenneth Wiggins Porter in *The Negro on the American Frontier* (New York: Arno Press and *The New York Times*, 1971), 125-26. Beckwourth also dictated his own autobiography, *The Life and Adventures of James P. Beckwourth as Told to Thomas D. Bonner*, first published in 1856, but reissued in 1972 by the University of Nebraska Press, Lincoln, NE. This reprint is introduced with notes and an epilogue by Delmont R. Oswald, of Brigham Young University, and attempts with meticulous notes to cross check and validate issues which have been open to question over the years. Ed Rose is also discussed in detail by Hiram Chittenden in *The American Fur Trade in the Far West* (New York, 1902, and Stanford, CA: Academic Reprints, 1954), including an account of his participation in the ill-fated Ashley Expedition in South Dakota in 1823, 263-67, 686-88.

[5] Porter, 125-26.

[6] Stanley Vestal, *The Missouri* (Lincoln: University of Nebraska Press, 1945), 101-02.

[7] John W. Ravage, *Black Pioneers: Images of the Black Experience on the North American Frontier* (Salt Lake City: University of Utah Press, 1997), 75-78.

[8] U.S. Census Office, *Population Schedules of the Ninth Census of the United States for Dakota Territory,* Washington, D.C., 1870.

[9] There are several excellent references that describe life on the steamboats and in the process discuss the experiences of African Americans who did this work. See William E. Lass, *A History of Steamboating on the Upper Missouri* (Lincoln: University of Nebraska Press, 1962) and Hiram Chittenden, *The History of Early Steamboat Navigation on the Missouri River* (New York, 1902, and Minneapolis, MN: Ross & Haines, Inc., 1962).

[10] Sara Bernson, "A Black History of South Dakota" (M.A. thesis, University of South Dakota, 1977), 3.

[11] Willard B. Gatewood, Jr., "Kate D. Chapman Reports on 'The Yankton Colored People, 1889,'" *South Dakota History* 7 (Winter 1976): 28-35.

[12] David Kemp, "African American Residents of Early Sioux Falls," paper presented at Thirty-third Annual Dakota Conference, May 24-25, 2001, in Sioux Falls.

[13] Sara Bernson and Robert Eggers, *Black People in South Dakota History* (Yankton, SD: Yankton Chamber of Commerce, 1976), 19, 24-25. See also Georgia Lee, interviewed by Freda Hosen, 1976, notes from recorded interview, South Dakota Oral History Center, University of South Dakota, Vermillion, SD, Tape 1185.

[14] Leonard "Bud" Williams, interview by Robert Eggers, June 17, 1976, transcription of recorded interview, South Dakota Oral History Center, University of South Dakota, Vermillion, SD, Tape 1692.

[15] Polks' Sioux Falls City Directories (Kansas City, MO: R. L. Polk & Co.) for 1905, 1907, 1908, 1913, and 1916. Hazel Mahone, interview by Robert Eggers, June 17, 1976, transcription of recorded interview, South Dakota Oral History Center, University of South Dakota, Vermillion, SD, Tape 1695; G. Melvin Day, telephone interviews by author, 1996-2003.

[16] Jessie Y. Sundstrom, "Black Women in the Black Hills," *Sixth Annual West River History Conference Proceedings* (Keystone, SD: Keystone Area Historical Society, 1998): 166-77. See also Helen Rezatto, *Tales of the Black Hills* (Aberdeen, SD: North Plains Press, 1983), 184-88.

[17] *Black Hills Daily*, April 2, 1878.

[18] This story has been retold in several different places: Federal Writers' Project, *South Dakota Place Names* (Vermillion, SD: University of South Dakota, 1941), 427-28, 488; Watson Parker, *Gold in the Black Hills* (Norman, OK: University of Oklahoma Press, 1966), 100.

[19] Todd Guenther, "Lucretia Marchbanks: A Black Woman in the Black Hills," *South Dakota History* 31 (Spring 2001): 1-25.

[20] U.S. Census Office, *Population Schedules of the Tenth Census of the United States for Dakota Territory,* 1880.

[21] Thomas Newgaard, William C. Sherman, and John Guerrero, *African Americans in North Dakota* (Bismarck, ND: University of Mary Press, 1994), 54-60.

[22] For a detailed account of these incidents, refer to Thomas R. Buecker, "Confrontation at Sturgis: An Episode in Civil-Military Race Relations, 1885," *South Dakota History* 14 (Fall 1984): 238-61.

[23] The most contemporary account of the early Sully County Colored Colony was the result of work done by the Sully County Old Settlers' Association in *The History of Sully County* in 1939. Edited by two of the "old settlers," Bessie B. Lumley and Mrs. B.M. Lister, and published by the Association and the Onida *Watchman*, it relied on memories of the early days of the colony. See also the Illinois Census Records for 1870 and the South Dakota Census Records for 1880, 1900, and 1910.

[24] Micheaux, *The Conquest*. For other accounts of his homesteading experience, see *The Homesteader* (Sioux City, IA: Western Book and Supply, 1917) and *The Wind from Nowhere* (New York: Micheaux Book and Supply Company, 1941). For more information about Oscar Micheaux's life, see Betti C. VanEpps-Taylor, *Oscar Micheaux: Dakota Homesteader, Author, Pioneer Film Maker*, (Rapid City, SD: Dakota West Books, 1999).

[25] Ted Blakey, "Early Black Residents," *Yankton County History* (Dallas, TX: Curtis Media Corp. and Yankton County Historical Society, 1986), 46-49, 348-49. Blakey tells of his own family and about Tom Douglas. See also Ted Blakey and Lovie Kinney Blakey, interviewed by Sara Bernson, June 1, 1976, South Dakota Oral History Center, University of South Dakota, Vermillion, SD, Tape 1718 and 1719. For additional information about the Yankton black community of this era, see Ellen Tobin, "Black History," *Yankton County History*, 46.

[26] Jan Rasmussen, interviewed by Betti VanEpps-Taylor, April 13, 2002. Rasmussen is the daughter of a McAllister neighbor who provided details supplied by Derrill Glynn, another neighbor, who eventually bought some of the McAllister land when they returned to Missouri in the 1950s.

[27] William Bailey, interviewed by Sara Bernson, June 27, 1976, South Dakota Oral History Center, University of South Dakota, Vermillion, SD, Tape 1717; See also Ravage, 103-06.

[28] Joyce Jefferson and Lilah Pengra, "Anonymous No More, A Teacher's Guide" (Rapid City, SD: It's About Time Committee and The Journey Museum, 2000), 66-67.

[29] Leonard "Bud" Williams, interviewed by Sara Bernson, June 17, 1976.

[30] Kenneth R. Stewart, "The Ku Klux Klan in South Dakota," *Selected Papers of the First Nine Dakota History Conferences, 1969-1977,* Herbert W. Blakely, ed. (Madison, SD: South Dakota State College, 1981), 344.

[31] Bernson and Eggers, 20.

[32] Arthur Hayes, interviewed by Sara Bernson, May 18, 1976, South Dakota Oral History Center, University of South Dakota, Vermillion, SD, Tape 1717.

[33] Bernson and Eggers, 17-18.

[34] G. Melvin Day, interviewed by Betti VanEpps-Taylor, October 3, 2003.

[35] Mahone, interview.

[36] Bernson and Eggers, 19.

[37] Interviews with Ted Blakey, Leonard Smith, Ernest Hayes, Melvin Day; see also *Yankton County History*, 49; Bernson and Eggers, 22.

[38] Bernson and Eggers, 27-30.

[39] Bernson and Eggers, 34.

[40] Bernson and Eggers, 34-35.

[41] Bernson and Eggers, 37-40.

[42] Ibid.

[43] Mahone, interview.

[44] Yosiya Niyo, "Doc Milburn's Prescription," *Reader's Digest,* April 1999, 25-30.

[45] Jerry Wilson, "Home At Last," *South Dakota Magazine*, May-June 2002, 40-44.

Chapter 10: Cities and Towns, *Gary D. Olson* (pgs. 157-181)
[1] Daniel J. Boorstin, *The Americans: The National Experience* (New York: Random House, 1965), 296.

[2] Ibid.

[3] *History of Southeastern Dakota, Its Settlement and Growth* (Sioux City, IA: Western Publishing Company, 1881), 41.

[4] Dana R. Bailey, *History of Minnehaha County, South Dakota* (Sioux Falls, SD: Brown & Saenger, 1899), 10; George W. Kingsbury, *History of Dakota Territory*, 5 vols. (Chicago: S. J. Clarke Publishing Company, 1915), 1: 97.

[5] Jacob Ferris, *The States and Territories of the Great West* (New York: Miller, Orton & Mulligan, 1856), 260; Stock Holder's Report of the Western Town Company for 1857, Old Courthouse Museum, Sioux Falls, SD. Captain James Allen's Report is reprinted in C. Stanley Stevenson, ed., "Expeditions into Dakota," *South Dakota Historical Collections* 9 (Pierre: State Historical Society, 1918), 363-64.

[6] *History of Southeastern Dakota*, 41-42; Dana Bailey in his 1899 *History of Minnehaha County* disputes the account of Indians forcing Millard and Mills to retreat from the falls upon their first visit in October 1856. It is evident, however, that he mistakenly believed there had been only the one visit in the fall of 1856, when there had actually been two. The writer of the *History of Southeastern Dakota* in 1881 clearly relates that Millard and Mills encountered Indians on their first visit but spent some time at the site six weeks later when they marked off the company's claim and built a log cabin. Bailey, 10.

[7] *History of Southeastern Dakota*, 42-43.

[8] Ibid., 41-43.

[9] Herbert S. Schell, *History of South Dakota* (Lincoln, University of Nebraska Press, 1968), 70.

[10] *History of Southeastern Dakota*, 16-17; Kingsbury, 1: 117-18; Schell, 70.

[11] Kingsbury, 1: 120.

[12] Ibid., 119-20.

[13] Ibid., 100-01; *History of Southeastern Dakota*, 48; Schell, 72-74.

[14] *History of Southeastern Dakota*, 48-49.

[15] Kingsbury, 1:104.

[16] Ibid., 102.

[17] Ibid.

[18] Ibid., 103-04.

[19] Moses K. Armstrong, *History and Resources of Dakota, Montana and Idaho* (Yankton, SD: G. W. Kingsbury, 1866), 46, as reprinted in *South Dakota Historical Collections* 15 (Pierre: State Historical Society, 1928), 10-70.

[20] Kingsbury, 1: 331-33.

[21] Ibid., 537.

[22] Ibid., 537-38.

[23] Kingsbury, 1: 530, 539.

[24] Richard F. Pettigrew Papers (microfilm edition), reel 35, frames 813-14.

[25] Richard F. Pettigrew, "Scroll of Time," *Sunshine State Magazine*, April 1926, 60-61; *History of Southeastern Dakota*, 55; Bailey, 33.

[26] Schell, 115-17.

[27] Ibid.; Freeman Centennial Steering Committee, comp., *Freeman Facts-Freeman Fiction* (Freeman, SD: Pine Hill Press, 1979), 6-10; *History of Southeastern Dakota*, 55.

[28] Schell, 129-39.

[29] Ibid., 140-41.

[30] Watson Parker, *Deadwood, The Golden Years* (Lincoln: University of Nebraska Press, 1981), 3-15; Richard F. Pettigrew, "Pettigrew Visits the Black Hills," *Sunshine State Magazine*, March 1926, 39-40.

[31] Schell, 142.

[32] Ibid., 158-60.

[33] U.S. Census Bureau, *Population Schedules of the Ninth Census of the United States for Dakota Territory*, Washington, D.C., 1870, *Tenth Census of the United States for Dakota Territory*, Washington, D.C., 1880; and *Eleventh Census of the United States for South Dakota*, Washington, D.C., 1890.

[34] Ibid., 161, 164-65; Kingsbury, 2: 1015-18; James F. Hamburg, "Railroads and the Settlement of South Dakota During the Great Dakota Boom, 1878-1887," *South Dakota History* 5 (Spring 1975): 169-75; Green, 136.

[35] Hamburg, 170-72.

[36] H.C. Halvorson, *The First Fifty Years in Lake Sinai Township* (Brookings, SD, 1956), 52-53.

37 Schell, 252.

38 Hamburg, 174-76.

39 Kingsbury, 2: 1233-34.

40 Ibid., 1280-92. Kingsbury provides an extensive description of the government's process in securing the opening of the Great Sioux Reservation; See also Schell, 254-57.

41 Ibid., 253.

42 Ibid., 256-63; Linda Hasselstrom, *Roadside History of South Dakota* (Missoula: Mountain Press Publishing Company, 1994), 234, 238-40.

43 Schell, 370.

44 Bailey, 391-93.

45 George W. Hall, "Lights for Sioux Falls," Unpublished South Dakota Writers' Project, 17-18.

46 Reuben Bragstad, *Sioux Falls in Retrospect* (Sioux Falls, SD: Privately Printed, 1967), 141-56.

47 Bill Beck, *Light Across the Prairies* (Eden Prairie, MN: Viking Press, Inc., 1989), 15-20; Ross P. Korsgaard, "A History of Rapid City, South Dakota During Territorial Days," *South Dakota Historical Collections* 38 (Pierre: State Historical Society, 1976): 544; David Nye, *Electrifying America: Social Meanings of a New Technology, 1880-1940* (Cambridge: MIT Press, 1990), 382.

48 Ibid.

49 For a fine description of small-town general stores, see Robert A. Mittelstaedt, ed., "The General Store Era, Memoirs of Arthur and Harold Mittelstaedt," *South Dakota History* 9 (Winter 1978): 36-60.

50 Bragstad, 168.

51 *South Dakota Historical Collections* 9 (Pierre: State Historical Society, 1918): 30; Ibid., (1926), 561.

52 Arthur G. Horton, comp. and ed., *An Economic and Social Survey of Sioux Falls* (Sioux Falls, SD: privately published, 1938), 48.

53 Schell, 362-63.

54 Suzanne Julin, "South Dakota Spa: A History of the Hot Springs Health Resort 1882-1915," *South Dakota Historical Collections* 41 (Pierre: State Historical Society, 1982): 248-65.

55 Schell, 363.

56 Ibid., 356; U.S. Census Bureau, *Census 2000*, Washington, D.C., 2000.

57 Ibid.

Chapter 11: Small Towns: Image and Reality, *John E. Miller* (pgs. 182-193)

1 "Thank God—For Small Towns!" *Dakota West,* March 1984, 27.

2 Thorstein Veblen, "The Country Town," in *Absentee Ownership and Business Enterprise in Recent Times: The Case of America* (New York: Augustus M. Kelley, 1923, reprint 1964), 142-65, quotation at 142.

3 Garrison Keillor, *Lake Wobegon Days* (New York: Viking, 1985), 251-74.

4 Tom Brokaw, *A Long Way from Home: Growing Up in the American Heartland* (New York: Random House, 2002), 3, 7, 21; Kathleen Norris, *Dakota: A Spiritual Geography* (New York: Ticknor & Fields, 1993), 7.

5 John R. Milton, *South Dakota: A Bicentennial History* (New York: W.W. Norton, 1977), 185.

6 See James D. McLaird, "From Bib Overalls to Cowboy Boots: East River/West River Differences in South Dakota," *South Dakota History* 19 (Winter 1989): 456-57.

7 *Huron Daily Plainsman*, June 13, 1990.

8 Robert D. Putnam, *Bowling Alone: The Collapse and Revival of American Community* (New York: Simon & Schuster, 2000), 292, 298, 310-11, quotation on 138.

9 Randy Hascall, "Survey Finds Character in Country," *Sioux Falls Argus Leader,* August 4, 2001.

10 Molly Miron, "Thank You, South Dakota," *Brookings Register*, November 23, 1995.

11 Kathy Gustafson, "Madison Church Vandalized Early Sunday Morning," *Sioux Falls Argus Leader*, August 29, 2000.

12 James F. Hamburg, *The Influence of Railroads upon the Processes and Patterns of Settlement in South Dakota* (New York: Arno Press, 1981).

[13] On the layouts of plains towns, see John C. Hudson, *Plains Country Towns* (Minneapolis: University of Minnesota Press, 1985); John E. Miller, "Place and Community in the 'Little Town on the Prairie': De Smet in 1983," *South Dakota History* 16 (Winter 1986): 351-72.

[14] John E. Miller, *Looking for History on Highway 14* (Pierre: South Dakota State Historical Society Press, 1993, reprint, 2001), 29-32.

[15] Sinclair Lewis, *Main Street* (New York: Harcourt, Brace, 1920), preface.

[16] Miller, *Looking for History on Highway 14*, 140, 146-53.

[17] Veblen, "The Country Town," 146-48, quotation at 147.

[18] Ibid., 154.

[19] Putnam; Hascall; Steven Barrett, "South Dakotans Rank High on Trust," *Huron Daily Plainsman*, August 5, 2001.

[20] Herbert S. Schell, *History of South Dakota*, 3d. ed. (Lincoln: University of Nebraska Press, 1975), 204; James A. Schellenberg, *Conflict Between Communities: American County Seat Wars* (New York: Paragon House, 1987), 66-69.

[21] John Elmer Dalton, *A History of the Location of the State Capital in South Dakota*, Government Research Bureau Report 14 (Vermillion: University of South Dakota, 1945).

Chapter 12: Politics Since Statehood, *John E. Miller (pgs. 194-224)*

[1] The classic work on Dakota Territory and perhaps the best study of any territory's political system is Howard R. Lamar, *Dakota Territory, 1861-1889: A Study of Frontier Politics* (New Haven: Yale University Press, 1956).

[2] On the special place of township government in South Dakota history, see J. P. Hendrickson, "Grass-roots Government: South Dakota's Enduring Townships," *South Dakota History* 24 (Spring 1994): 19-42.

[3] Herbert S. Schell, *History of South Dakota*, 3d. ed. (Lincoln: University of Nebraska Press, 1975), 227.

[4] Kenneth E. Hendrickson, "Some Political Aspects of the Populist Movement in South Dakota," *North Dakota History* 34 (Winter 1967): 84-85.

[5] C. Perry Armin, "A State Treasurer Defaults: The Taylor Case of 1895," *South Dakota History* 15 (Fall 1985): 177-99.

[6] Kenneth E. Hendrickson, 89.

[7] H. Roger Grant, "Origins of a Progressive Reform: The Initiative and Referendum Movement in South Dakota," *South Dakota History* 3 (Fall 1973): 390-407.

[8] See the bibliographical comments on the subject in William C. Pratt, "South Dakota Populism and Its Historians," *South Dakota History* 22 (Winter 1992): 309-29, and Terrence J. Lindell, "South Dakota Populism" (M.A. thesis, University of Nebraska, 1982), 1-12.

[9] Lindell, 217, 225-41.

[10] Michael Paul Rogin, *The Intellectuals and McCarthy: The Radical Specter* (Cambridge, MA: M.I.T. Press, 1967), 140.

[11] Erling N. Sannes, "Knowledge Is Power: The Knights of Labor in South Dakota," *South Dakota History* 22 (Winter 1992): 400-30.

[12] Pratt, 309.

[13] Little work has been done on this phase of the movement, Ibid., 322.

[14] Daryl Webb, "'Just Principles Never Die': Brown County Populists, 1890-1900," *South Dakota History* 22 (Winter 1992): 366-99; Lawrence Goodwyn, *Democratic Promise: The Populist Movement in America* (New York: Oxford University Press, 1976).

[15] Norman Pollack, "The Myth of Populist Anti-Semitism," *American Historical Review* 68 (October 1962): 76-80, and *The Populist Response to Industrial America: Midwestern Populist Thought* (Cambridge: Harvard University Press, 1962).

[16] Quoted in Russel B. Nye, *Midwestern Progressive Politics: A Historical Study of Its Origins and Development, 1870-1950* (East Lansing: Michigan State College Press, 1951), 125.

[17] Nye, 206-32.

[18] C. Perry Armin, "Coe I. Crawford and the Progressive Movement in South Dakota," *South Dakota Historical Collections* 32 (Pierre: State Historical Society, 1964): 79.

[19] Richmond L. Clow, "In Search of the People's Voice: Richard Olsen Richards and Progressive Reform," *South Dakota History* 10 (Winter 1978): 39-58.

[20] Gilbert C. Fite, "South Dakota's Rural Credit System," *Agricultural History* 21 (October 1947): 247.

[21] Gilbert C. Fite, "Peter Norbeck and the Defeat of the Non-Partisan League in South Dakota," *Mississippi Valley Historical Review* 33 (September 1946): 217-36.

[22] Quoted in Gilbert C. Fite, *Peter Norbeck: Prairie Statesman* (Columbia: University of Missouri, 1948), 69.

[23] Patricia O'Keefe Easton, "Woman Suffrage in South Dakota: The Final Decade, 1911-1920," *South Dakota History* 13 (Fall 1983): 206-26.

[24] While radical by South Dakota standards, the Farmers' Holiday movement in the state was more restrained and conservative in its actions than were most of the units in surrounding states. See John E. Miller, "Restrained, Respectable Radicals: The South Dakota Farm Holiday," *Agricultural History* 59 (July 1985): 429-47.

[25] Matthew Cecil, "Democratic Party Politics and the South Dakota Income Tax, 1933-1942," *South Dakota History* 26 (Summer/Fall 1996): 156, 163.

[26] Joseph V. Ryan, "Tom Berry," in *Over a Century of Leadership: South Dakota Territorial and State Governors, 1861-1987,* ed. Lynwood E. Oyos (Sioux Falls, SD: Center for Western Studies, 1987), 130.

[27] John E. Miller, "The Failure to Realign: The 1936 Election in South Dakota," *Journal of the West* 41 (Fall 2002): 22-29. See also Philip A. Grant, Jr., "Presidential Politics in South Dakota," *South Dakota History* 22 (Fall 1992): 261-75.

[28] For the following section, see John E. Miller, "McCarthyism before McCarthy: The 1938 Election in South Dakota," *Heritage of the Great Plains* 15 (Summer 1982): 1-21.

[29] *Sioux Falls Argus Leader*, October 28, 1938. See also editorials on October 15, 16, 20, 22, 26, 31, 1938.

[30] On South Dakota's persisting Republican tendencies, see Alan L. Clem, *Government By the People? South Dakota Politics in the Last Third of the Twentieth Century* (Rapid City, SD: Chiesman Foundation for Democracy, Inc., 2002), 13. John Gunther, in *Inside U.S.A.* (New York: Harper & Brothers, 1947), 247, characterized South Dakota as "extremely conservative" and "almost as Republican as, say, Alabama is Democratic." The state's high ranking among Republican states after World War II is noted in Fred W. Zuercher, "A Measure of Party Strength in the Fifty States," *Public Affairs* 32 (Vermillion, SD: Governmental Research Bureau, February 15, 1968).

[31] *Sioux Falls Argus Leader*, Sept. 7, 1952, April 25, 1966.

[32] *Sioux Falls Argus Leader*, August 7, 1958.

[33] *Sioux Falls Argus Leader*, March 31, 1955.

[34] "Chan Gurney," in Larry Pressler, *U.S. Senators from the Prairie* (Vermillion: Dakota Press, 1982), 114-16.

[35] Richard R. Chenoweth, "Francis Case: A Political Biography," *South Dakota Historical Collections* 39 (Pierre: State Historical Society, 1978): 321-28, 382, 417-18, quotation at 407; Loren Carlson, "The Republican Majority: Francis Higbee Case and Karl E. Mundt," in Herbert T. Hoover and Larry J. Zimmerman, eds. *South Dakota Leaders: From Pierre Chouteau, Jr., to Oscar Howe* (Vermillion: University of South Dakota Press, 1989), 293-302.

[36] Scott Heidepriem, *A Fair Change for a Free People: Biography of Senator Karl Mundt* (Madison, SD: Karl E. Mundt Historical and Educational Foundation, 1988), 22-28, 105-27, 131-40.

[37] Charles W. Gardner, "Harlan John Bushfield," and Harry A. Robinson, "Merrill Quentin Sharpe," in Oyos, 139-46.

[38] Ellsworth Karrigan, "George T. Mickelson," in Oyos, 149-52.

[39] Bob Lee, "Joseph Jacob Foss," in Oyos, 161-67; Joe Foss, with Donna Wild Foss, *A Proud American: The Autobiography of Joe Foss* (New York: Pocket Books, 1992), 198-231.

[40] Robert Sam Anson, *McGovern: A Biography* (New York: Holt, Rinehart and Winston, 1972), 66-98; George S. McGovern, *Grassroots: The Autobiography of George McGovern* (New York: Random House, 1977), 52-83.

[41] Robert Thompson, "Ralph E. Herseth," in Oyos, 169-72.

[42] Alan L. Clem, "The 1964 Election: Has South Dakota Become a Two-Party State?," *Public Affairs* 20 (Vermillion, SD: Governmental Research Bureau, February 15, 1963).

[43] William O. Farber, "Archie M. Gubbrud," and Alice Kundert and Sid I. Davison, "Nils A. Boe," in Oyos, 175-89.

[44] Quoted in Bob Lee, "Frank L. Farrar," in Oyos, 192.

[45] James G. Abourezk, *Advise and Dissent: Memoirs of South Dakota and the U.S. Senate* (Chicago: Lawrence Hill Books, 1989), 79-89.

[46] Daniel B. Garry, "Richard F. Kneip," in Oyos, 199-205.

[47] Peter Carrels, *Uphill Against Water: The Great Dakota Water War* (Lincoln: University of Nebraska Press, 1999).

[48] On presidential visits to South Dakota, see Harold H. Schuler, "Patriotic Pageantry: Presidential Visits to South Dakota," *South Dakota History* 30 (Winter 2000): 339-90.

[49] "Janklow says he would serve only one term," *Sioux Falls Argus Leader*, May 29, 1994.

[50] "Tom Daschle," *1995 Current Biography Yearbook*, 111-15.

[51] "Zeal for policy propels Johnson's Senate push," *Sioux Falls Argus Leader*, October 6, 2002.

[52] James Soyer, "William Janklow," in Oyos, 212-16; Peter Harriman, "Janklow runs on dynamic, controversial past," *Sioux Falls Argus Leader*, September 29, 2002; Kurt Andersen, "The Triumphs of a Prairie Populist," *Time*, August 22, 1983, 19.

[53] Chet Brokaw, "Fallen governor left enduring legacy," *Pierre Capital Journal*, April 7, 2003.

Chapter 13: Farming: Dependency and Depopulation, *Lynwood E. Oyos (pgs. 225-254)*

[1] R. D. Lusk, "Life and Death of 470 Acres," *Saturday Evening Post*, August 13, 1938.

[2] *Dakota Farmer*, July 6, 1935, 255.

[3] Lois Phillip Hudson, *Reapers of the Dust, A Prairie Chronicle* (Boston: Little, Brown and Co., 1964), 3.

[4] Deborah Jorgensen, "Defeats and Successes of South Dakota Farmers in the Depression Era," Augustana College, interview with Mrs. J. S. Jorgensen, Madison, SD, August 8, 1979, 26.

[5] Richard Lowitt and Maurine Brady, eds., *One Third of a Nation: Lorena Hickok Reports on the Great Depression* (Urbana: University of Illinois Press, 1981), 83.

[6] *Statistical Abstracts of the United States, 1935-1940*.

[7] *National Farmers Union Newsletter*, vol. 1, no. 11, September 17, 1954.

[8] Opsahl Apology, October 11, 1957, Box 6, File 39, Opsahl-Haugland, et al., 1936-1958, Emil Loriks Papers, Center for Western Studies, Sioux Falls, SD.

[9] *South Dakota Union Farmer*, March 1974.

[10] *100 Years of South Dakota Agriculture, 1900-1999*, (Sioux Falls, SD: South Dakota Agriculture Statistics Service, 2000).

[11] Thomas D. Isern, "The Comedy of the Commons; or, My Life on the Post-Colonial Plains," *South Dakota History* 33 (Spring 2003): 70.

[12] *Minneapolis Tribune*, April 1968.

Chapter 14: Ranching: East to West, *Bob Lee (pgs. 255-287)*

[1] Bob Lee and Dick Williams, *Last Grass Frontier: The South Dakota Stock Grower Heritage* [Vol. 1.] (Sturgis, SD: Black Hills Publishers, Inc., 1964), 1:13; Hazel Adele Pulling, "History of the Range Cattle Industry of Dakota," *South Dakota Historical Collections* 20 (Pierre: State Historical Society, 1940): 469; *South Dakota Agriculture 2003*, Bulletin 61 (Sioux Falls: South Dakota Agricultural Statistics Service, June 2003): 36, 51.

[2] James H. Shaw, "How Many Bison Populated Western Rangelands?," *Rangelands Magazine*, October 1995, 4; Laurie Winn Carlson, *Cattle: An Informal Social History* (Chicago: Ivan R. Dee, Pub., 2001), 276-77. Meriwether Lewis, *The Lewis and Clark Expedition* (Philadelphia and New York: J. B. Lippincott Company, 1961), 3: 789.

[3] Lee and Williams, 1:10; Herbert S. Schell, *South Dakota: Its Beginnings and Growth* (New York: The American Book Company, 1955), 46, 75.

[4] Harold E. Briggs, "Ranching and Stock Raising in the Territory of Dakota," *South Dakota Historical Collections* 14 (Pierre: State Historical Society, 1928): 417; Doane Robinson, "Fort Manuel," *South Dakota*

Historical Collections 12 (Pierre: State Historical Society, 1924): 99; Donald D. Parker, "Early Explorations and Fur Trading in South Dakota," *South Dakota Historical Collections* 20 (Pierre: State Historical Society, 1951): 148; Lee and Williams, 1: 8-9.

[5] Ibid., 9-10.

[6] Herbert T. Hoover, *South Dakota History: A Custom Textbook*, 2nd ed., (Vermillion: University of South Dakota, 2002), 15, 52.

[7] Parker, "Early Explorations and Fur Trading in South Dakota," 111-12.

[8] Harold H. Schuler, *Fort Pierre Chouteau* (Vermillion: University of South Dakota Press, 1990), 21, 115, 126.

[9] Ibid., 131-32; Don C. Clowser, *Dakota Indian Treaties: From Nomad to Reservation* (Deadwood, SD: self-published, 1974), 25-26, 31.

[10] Lieutenant Gouverneur Kemble Warren, *Preliminary Report of Explorations of Nebraska and Dakota in the Years 1855-'56-'57* (Washington, D.C.: Government Printing Office, 1875), quoted by James McLaird and Lesta Turchen in "Exploring the Black Hills, 1855-1875: Reports of the Government Expeditions," *South Dakota History* 3 (Fall 1973): 376.

[11] Ibid., 375-77.

[12] George W. Kingsbury, *History of Dakota Territory*, 5 vols. (Chicago: S. J. Clarke Publishing Co., 1915), 1:137-38, 162; R. F. Karolevitz, *Challenge: The South Dakota Story* (Sioux Falls, SD: Brevet Press, Inc., 1975), 47.

[13] Herbert S. Schell, *Dakota Territory During the Eighteen Sixties,* Governmental Research Bureau, Report 50 (Vermillion, SD: University of South Dakota, 1954), 17, 27, 29, 31; *Population of the United States in 1860* (Washington, 1864), 552.

[14] Lee and Williams, 1:12; Briggs, 2, 417; *Biographical Directory of the South Dakota Legislature, 1889-1989, L-Z,* 2 vols. (Pierre: South Dakota Legislative Research Council, 1989), 2: 792; G. Bie Rayndal, "The Scandinavian Pioneers of South Dakota," *South Dakota Historical Collections* 12 (Pierre: State Historical Society, 1924): 309.

[15] Briggs, 418.

[16] Lee and Williams, 1: 16.

[17] Briggs, 420-21; Carlson, 87; Lee and Williams, 1: 18, 20.

[18] Ibid., 31; Kingsbury, 1: 429-30; Robert Lee, *Fort Meade and the Black Hills* (Lincoln: University of Nebraska Press, 1991), 2.

[19] Francis Paul Prucha, ed., *Documents of United States Indian Policy* (Lincoln: University of Nebraska Press, 1975), 110; Lee and Williams, 1: 22-23.

[20] Ibid.; Prucha, 110; Kingsbury, 1: 526.; Schell, *Dakota Territory in the Eighteen Sixties*, 60; Schell, *History of South Dakota*, 84-85.

[21] Ibid.

[22] Schell, *Dakota Territory in the Eighteen Sixties*, 32; Lee and Williams, 1: 70.

[23] Ibid., 18; Schell, *Dakota Territory in the Eighteen Sixties*, 31.

[24] Ibid.; Lynwood E. Oyos, ed., *Over a Century of Leadership: South Dakota Territorial and State Governors, 1861-1987* (Sioux Falls, SD: Center for Western Studies, 1987), 9; Kingsbury, 1: 213; J. A. Jacobsen, member of the first session of the territorial legislature from Clay County in 1862, was among the settlers killed by Indians during the Dakota War of 1862: Lee and Williams, 1: 70.

[25] Schell, *Dakota Territory in the Eighteen Sixties*, 31; Briggs, 419-420, 422; Lee and Williams, 1: 14.

[26] Briggs, 420-21; Carlson, 87; Lee and Williams, 1: 18, 20.

[27] Ibid., 31; Kingsbury, 1: 429-30; Lee, *Fort Meade and the Black Hills*, 2.

[28] Prucha, *Documents of United States Indian Policy*, 101; Lee and Williams, 1: 22-23.

[29] Ibid.; Prucha, 110; Kingsbury, 1: 526; Schell, *Dakota Territory in the Eighteen Sixties*, 60; Schell, *History of South Dakota*, 91.

[30] Lee and Williams, 1: 24, 27-28; Carlson, 90.

[31] Lee and Williams, 1: 29; Briggs, 435.

[32] Peterson, *Pioneer Footprints* (Belle Fourche, SD: Half Century Club, 1964), 115; Bob Lee, *Bob Lee's Black Hills Notebook*, (Sturgis, SD: Dickson Media, 1999), 48.

[33] *Yankton Press*, March 1, 1873; Lee and Williams, 1: 30; *South Dakota Agriculture 2001,* Bulletin 61 (Sioux Falls, SD: South Dakota Agricultural Statistics Service, June 2001): 35, 84.

[34] U.S. Congress, Senate, Legislative Assembly of Dakota Territory, "Memorial Asking for a Scientific Expedition of that Territory," 42d Congress, 3d session, 1872-73, S. Misc. Doc. 45, 1-3; Legislative Assembly of Dakota, "Memorial in Reference to the Black Hills serving as a retreat for hostile Indians," 42d Congress, 3d session, Misc. Doc. No. 65; Watson Parker, *Gold in the Black Hills* (Norman: University of Oklahoma Press, 1966), 24-25.

[35] George A. Custer, "Opening the Black Hills: Custer's Report," *South Dakota Historical Collections* 7 (Pierre: State Historical Society, 1914): 594.

[36] Wayne R. Kime, ed., *The Black Hills Journals of Colonel Richard Irving Dodge* (Norman: University of Oklahoma Press, 1996), 13, 129, 134.

[37] Ibid., 83, 151-153, 165; Schell, *History of South Dakota*, 132-33.

[38] Kime, 58, 83, 89, 110, 137.

[39] Henry Newton and Walter P. Jenney, *Report on the Geology and Resources of the Black Hills of Dakota with Atlas* (Washington, D.C.: Government Printing Office, 1880), 299-300. See also, "The Scientists' Search for Gold 1875: Walter P. Jenney and Henry Newton," *South Dakota History* 4 (Fall 1974): 404-38; Lee and Williams, 1: 39.

[40] Prucha, 117; Kingsbury, 1: 526.

[41] Charles du Bois, *The Custer Mystery* (El Segundo, CA: Upton & Sons, 1986), 164.

[42] Jessie Y. Sundstrom, *Custer County History to 1976* (Custer, SD: Custer County Historical Society, 1977), 29; Bob Lee, ed. *Gold, Gals, Guns, Guts* (Deadwood, SD: Deadwood-Lead '76 Centennial, Inc., 1976), 22; Parker, *Gold in the Black Hills*, 92, 95; John S. McClintock, *Pioneer Days in the Black Hills: Accurate History and Facts Related By One of the Early Day Pioneers* (reprint, Norman: University of Oklahoma Press, 2000), foreword by Wayne R. Kime, 269-74.

[43] Lee and Williams, 1: 43-48.

[44] Ibid., 47-49; Briggs, 425-26; Clowser, *Dakota Indian Treaties*, 211; Edward Lazarus, *Black Hills White Justice: The Sioux Nation Versus the United States 1775 To the Present* (New York: Harper Collins Publishers, 1991), 381-402.

[45] *The Black Hills Tribune*, [Crook City, DT] August 31, 1876; Lee and Williams, 1: 47.

[46] Lee and Williams, 1: 47.

[47] Ibid., 51-52, 91, 409; Bob Lee, *Last Grass Frontier,* Vol. 2 (Sturgis, SD: Black Hills Publishers, Inc., 1999), 2: 83-84.

[48] Lee and Williams, 1: 63; Molly Frawley, "Henry and Christina (Anderson) Frawley," *Some History of Lawrence County* (Pierre, SD: Lawrence County Historical Society/The State Publishing Co., 1981), 158-59; Vince Coyle, "The Frawley and Anderson Families," *The Society of Black Hills Pioneers* (Deadwood, SD: The Society of Black Hills Pioneers/Dakota Graphics, 2003), 1: 1, 9-14.

[49] David Strain, *Black Hills Hay Camp: Images and Perspectives of Early Rapid City* (Rapid City, SD: Dakota Books and Fenske Printing Co., 1989), 10, 34, 57, 170, 208.

[50] Lee and Williams, 1: 58.

[51] *Biographical Directory of the South Dakota Legislature, 1889-1989, A-K,* 2 vols. (Pierre: South Dakota Legislative Research Council, 1989), 1: 412; Lee and Williams, 1: 58-59, 85, 131; *Echoes Through the Valleys* (Piedmont, SD: Elk Creek Pioneer Society, 1968), 221; Schell, *History of South Dakota*, 243.

[52] Ibid., 58-59; *Biographical Directory of the South Dakota Legislature, 1889-1989, A-K,* 1: 103-04.

[53] Ibid., 419-21; Lee and Williams, 1: 69-70; *Echoes Through the Valleys*, 221.

[54] Lee and Williams, 1: 83, 85, 88, 92.

[55] Ibid., 81, 84.

[56] Ibid., 92.

[57] Elwyn B. Robinson, *History of North Dakota* (Lincoln: University of Nebraska Press, 1966), 195; Briggs, 448-51; *Black Hills Journal*, June 4, 1881; *The Deadwood Pioneer*, April 16, 1882; March 17, 1884; *Black Hills Journal*, April 20, 1882, May 25, 1883, Lee and Williams, 1: 96-99.

[58] Ibid., 85-86, 96-99.

[59] Ibid., 85-88; *Black Hills Journal*, March 5, 1881; *Black Hills Times*, February 11, 1883; James McLaird, "Cowboy Life: Myth and Reality," *South Dakota History* 32 (Fall 2002): 211-12; Briggs, 463-64; Lee and Williams, 1: 85-86.

[60] Ibid., 85-86.

[61] Ibid., 1: 67-72.

[62] Lee and Williams, 1: 103-05; Briggs, 432-433.

[63] Lee and Williams, 1: 63-64, 73-74; Herbert T. Hoover, "North Central Wool Marketing Corporation History, 1950-1988," TMs, Department of History, University of South Dakota, epilogue, 8.

[64] Lee and Williams, 1: 106-07.

[65] Ibid., 103; Thomas L. Riggs, "A Buffalo Hunt," *South Dakota Historical Collections* 5 (Pierre: State Historical Society, 1910): 95-97; "A Pioneer Hereford Ranch," *Farmer and Breeder*, April 1, 1918; "Herefords an Aid in Teaching Indians," *The Hereford Journal*, November 15, 1934, Oahe Mission Collection, UCC Archives, Center for Western Studies, Augustana College, Sioux Falls, SD.

[66] Lee and Williams, 1: 128,159, 186, 229.

[67] Ibid., 128; Bob Lee, "Scotty Philip: Man Who Saved the Buffalo Was True Black Hills Pioneer Too," *Sturgis Tribune*, April 30, 1975; Wayne C. Lee, *Scotty Philip: The Man Who Saved the Buffalo*, (Caldwell, ID: Caxton Printers, Ltd., 1975), 116, 318 fn 5; McLaird, "Cowboy Life and Reality," 195; *Biographical Directory of the South Dakota Legislature, 1889-1989*, 2: 885; Dana Close Jennings, *Buffalo History and Husbandry* (Freeman, SD: Pine Hill Press, 1978), 378.

[68] Lee and Williams, 1: 117; 171; Briggs, 461-63; *Sioux Falls Argus Leader*, September 4, 1910; Bruce Nelson, *Land of the Dacotah* (Minneapolis: University of Minnesota Press, 1947, 2d ed.), 193-94.

[69] Lee and Williams, 1: 114-15, 120, 171, 181; Schell, *History of South Dakota*, 188-90; Nelson, *Land of the Dacotah*, 190-206.

[70] Schell, *History of South Dakota*, 245-46; Lee and Williams, 1: 186.

[71] Lee, *Bob Lee's Black Hills Notebook*, 48; Sundstrom, *History of Custer County to 1976*, 162; Lee and Williams, 1: 56, 161, 181.

[72] Sundstrom, *History of Custer County to 1976*, 162-63; Lee and Williams, 56, 175,

[73] Lee and Williams, 1: 62-63; Schell, *History of South Dakota*, 243.

[74] Lee and Williams, 1: 62-63, 66, 74, 106, 150-51, 155; The Fremont, Elkhorn and Missouri Valley Railroad, a branch of the Chicago and North Western, reached Rapid City on July 4, 1886; Parker, *Gold in the Black Hills*, 180; Archer B. Gilfillan, *Sheep: Life on the South Dakota Range* (Minneapolis: University of Minnesota Press, 1956), originally published in 1929 by Little, Brown and Company, reprinted by Emily Muriel Dean, 21, 40; McClintock, *Pioneer Days in the Black Hills*, 175-77; David F. Strain, *Hay Camp*, 4.

[75] Lee and Williams, 1: 154-56; Robinson, *History of North Dakota*, 190; Schell, *History of South Dakota*, 244-45.

[76] Lee and Williams, 1: 154-56.

[77] Ibid., 157; Schell, *History of South Dakota*, 244-45, 249; *Central Meade County, 1903-1963*, ed. Ella Wahl (Stoneville, SD: Stoneville Steadies Extension Club, 1964), 318.

[78] Lee and Williams, 1: 172-77, 181-87,

[79] Ibid., 172, 185.

[80] Ibid.

[81] Kingsbury, 2: 1283-91; Lee and Williams, 1: 131-32, 165-66, 172; Schell, *History of South Dakota*, 222.

[82] Lee and Williams, 1: 55, 81, 192-93, 274, 297; *Biographical Directory of the South Dakota Legislature, 1889-1989*, 1: 370.

[83] Lee and Williams, 1: 192, 195, 200, 204.

[84] Ibid., 185.

[85] Ibid., 149, 151-52.

[86] Ibid., 209, 211, 234.

[87] Lee, *Bob Lee's Black Hills Notebook*, 48; Petersen, 12, 87.

[88] Lee and Williams, 1: 85, 239, 263, 550-53.

[89] Ray H. Mattison, "Report On Historical Aspects of the Oahe Reservoir Area, Missouri River, South and North Dakota," *South Dakota Historical Collections* 27 (Pierre: State Historical Society, 1954): 79, 80-81.

[90] Ibid., 85, 550-53; Frank P. Donovan, Jr., "A Ghost Town on a Ghost Road," 548-56; Will G. Robinson, *The Wi-Iyohi* (Pierre: State Historical Society, 5(12), March 1, 1952; Petersen, 91-92; Lee and Williams, 1: 23, 229, 231, 237-38, 454.

[91] Ibid., 226, 286.

[92] Don Beaty, *A History of the South Dakota Livestock Feeders Association and the Clay County Livestock Feeders Association from 1948 to 1963* (Vermillion, SD: self-published, 1963), 4.

[93] Lee and Williams, 1: 412.

[94] Ibid., 275, 365-67, 418, 426.

[95] Ibid., 327.

[96] Ibid.

[97] Ibid., 435.

[98] Lee, 2: 39-40.

[99] Oyos, 126, 180; Lee and Williams, 279, 315; *Biographical Directory of the South Dakota Legislature, 1889-1989,* 1 and 2, passim.

[100] Oyos, 120; Lee and Williams, 1: 282-83.

[101] Ibid., 201, 231-32, 283; Dr. Sam Holland, State Veterinarian, interviewed by Bob Lee, October 17, 2003.

[102] Brand Department, South Dakota Stockgrowers Association, Annual Report, 2002-2003, 2-6.

[103] Ibid. I, 97; II, 54; Bob Gadd, Spearfish, former secretary of the State Brand Board, interviewed by Bob Lee, September 17, 2003; Jack McCulloh, former secretary of the South Dakota Stockgrowers Association, interviewed by Bob Lee, October 10, 2003; Beaty, 33-34.

[104] Lee, 2: 11, 79.

[105] Brand Department, South Dakota Stockgrowers Association, Annual Report, 2002-2003, 2-6.

[106] Lee, 2: 11-12; October 30, 2003, interview with Shawn Bowles, State Brand Board, Pierre, SD.

[107] Pat Adrian, secretary of the South Dakota Beef Industry Council, Pierre, SD, interviewed by Bob Lee, October 21, 2003.

[108] Pat Adrian, interviewed by Bob Lee, November 3, 2003; "SDBIC Elects New President," *Rapid City Journal*, October 20, 2003.

[109] Pat Adrian, interviewed by Bob Lee, November 3, 2003.

[110] Eric Iverson, South Dakota Department of Agriculture, interviewed by Bob Lee, October 30, 2003.

[111] Beaty, 5, 7-12, 26.

[112] Ibid., 5.

[113] Ibid., 33.

[114] Tonya Ness, Executive Director, South Dakota Cattlemen's Association, Kennebec, SD, interviewed by Bob Lee, October 22, 2003; Fact Sheet, South Dakota Cattlemen's Association, November 21, 2002; October 22, 2003 letter to author from Tonya Ness.

[115] Susan Kontz, Colman, SD, South Dakota Cattlemen's Auxiliary Activities 2003, November 1, 2003; Delina Nagel, Avon, vice president, South Dakota Cattlemen's Auxiliary, interviewed by Bob Lee, October 31 and November 5, 2003.

[116] W. H. Hamilton, "Dakota: An Autobiography of a Cowman," *South Dakota Historical Collections* 19 (Pierre: State Historical Society, 1938): 506; Linda M. Hasselstrom, *Going Over East* (Golden, CO: Fulcrum, Inc., 1987), passim.

[117] Intertribal Bison Cooperative, Fact Sheet, 1560 Concourse Drive, Rapid City, SD 57703, March 5, 2003; Tony Willman, Intertribal Bison Cooperative, to Bob Lee, March 18 and July 13, 2003.

[118] Tony Willman to Bob Lee, July 13, 2003.

[119] "Bucking for Buffalo," *Rapid City Journal*, July 6 and September 29, 2003.

[120] Jessie Y. Sundstrom, *Pioneers and Custer State Park: A History of Custer State Park and Northcentral Custer County* (Custer, SD: self-published, 1994), 111-12, 213; "Buffalo on the Rebound," *Rapid City Journal*, February 2, 2003, and "Custer State Park Buffalo Auction," July 21, 2003; Lee, 1: 46.

[121] Jennings, *Buffalo History and Husbandry*, iii, 259; Bisoncentral.com [Web site of the National Bison Association].

[122] Jennings, *Buffalo History and Husbandry*, 5, 7, 33; "Raising Buffalo Growing in Popularity," *Rapid City Journal*, July 6, 2003; "History of the Dakota Territory Buffalo Association," Dakota Territory Buffalo Association, P.O. Box 4104, Rapid City, SD, 57709, to author, June 30, 2003.

[123] Bisoncentral.com; "Buffalo on Rebound," *Rapid City Journal*, February 2, 2003; "Costner's Dream About to Unfold," *Deadwood Gaming*, monthly publication of the Deadwood, SD, gaming industry, April 2003; "Bison Industry Tries New Strategy," *Rapid City Journal*, January 26, 2003; "Buffalo on Rebound," February 2, 2003; "Raising Bison Growing in Popularity," July 6, 2003; "Bucking for Bison," April 29, 2003; *South Dakota Agriculture 2003*, Bulletin 63 (South Dakota Crop and Livestock Reporting Service, June 2003): 37.

[124] Herbert T. Hoover and Charles L. Roegiers, "North Central States Sheep and Wool Growers: A History," TMs, Department of History, University of South Dakota, 1988, introduction, 2, 5.

[125] Henry Scheele, interviewed by Herbert T. Hoover, June 29, 1988, South Dakota Oral History Center, University of South Dakota, Vermillion, SD, Tape 2368: 4-5, 6-7, 13, 16, 18, 28; Hoover and Roegiers, epilogue, 20; Lee and Williams, 1: 85-86, 88.

[126] Peterson, *Pioneer Footprints*, 115; Lee, *Bob Lee's Black Hills Notebook*, 48, 136.

[127] Gilfillan, *Sheep*, 3, 15, 17, 271.

[128] Jami Huntsiger, "Pioneering Black Hills Sheepman: Myron John Smiley," in *South Dakota Leaders: From Pierre Chouteau, Jr., to Oscar Howe*, ed. Herbert T. Hoover and Larry J. Zimmerman (Vermillion: University of South Dakota Press, 1989), 261-62, 266-67; Petersen, *Pioneer Footprints*, 165; Hoover and Roegiers, introduction, 8; Herbert T., Karolyn J., and Christopher J. Hoover, "Pioneering Sheepman at Midland: James Galette Rogers" (Vermillion, SD: unpublished manuscript), 5, 8.; Herbert T. Hoover, "Emergence of Collective Wool Marketing: From the South Dakota Sheep and Wool Growers Association to a South Dakota-Minnesota Bi-State Cooperative Wool Marketing System, 1920-1950" (Vermillion, SD: unpublished manuscript), 2.

[129] Lee and Williams, 1: 335-36; Huntsinger, 267.

[130] Henry Scheele, interviewed by Herbert T. Hoover, June 29, 1988, South Dakota Oral History Center, University of South Dakota, Vermillion, SD, Tape 2368: 1, 4, 14, 16.

[131] Hoover, "Emergence of Collective Wool Marketing," 2, 10; Hoover and Roegiers, introduction, 3.

[132] Ibid., 6, 8; Hoover, "Emergence of Collective Wool Marketing," 9, 3, 22-23; Hoover, "North Central Wool Marketing Corporation History, 1950-1988," 3, 9, 24, epilogue, 2-3.

[133] Hoover, "Emergence of Collective Wool Marketing," 18-19; *South Dakota Agriculture 2003*, Bulletin 63 (Sioux Falls, SD: South Dakota Agricultural Statistics Service, June 2003): 36, 57.

[134] *South Dakota Agriculture 2003*, Bulletin 63: 35, 45, 49, 111, 117, 125.

[135] Ibid., 9, 35-36, 41, 50-51, 108, 130; "Hogs Lose in County Elections," *Rapid City Journal*, April 17, 2003; "South Dakota Hog-Farm Numbers Decrease," *Rapid City Journal*, January 3, 2003.

[136] South Dakota Pork Producers Council, Sioux Falls, to Bob Lee, November 7 and 9, 2003. Letters contain a history of the organization, along with its mission statement and list of officers and committees.

[137] Ibid.

[138] Ibid., 2003 South Dakota Pork Producers Council Resolutions Manual, 3-8, 138.

[139] *South Dakota Agriculture 2003*, Bulletin 63: 35-36, 46, 51, 102; Lee and Williams, 2: 85.

[140] *South Dakota Agriculture 2003*, Bulletin 63: 51.

[141] Ibid., 8, 102, 114-36.

Chapter 15: Black Hills in Transition, David A. Wolff (pgs. 288-317)
[1] Edward Raventon, *Island in the Plains: A Black Hills Natural History* (Boulder, CO: Johnson Books, 1994), 32-35; Sven G. Froiland, *Natural History of the Black Hills and Badlands* (Sioux Falls, SD: Center for Western Studies, 1990), 19-25; E. Steve Cassells, *Prehistoric Hunters of the Black Hills* (Boulder, CO: Johnson Publishing Company, 1986), 31-77; E. Steve Cassells, David B. Miller, and Paul V. Miller, *Paha Sapa: Notes on the Cultural Resources of the Black Hills of South Dakota and Wyoming* (Custer, SD: Black Hills National Forest, 1984), 33-34, 48, 88.

[2] Cassells, Miller, and Miller, 109, 111.

[3] John G. Neihardt, *Black Elk Speaks: Being the Life Story of a Holy Man of the Oglala Sioux* (Lincoln: University of Nebraska Press, 1979), 65.

[4] Cassells, Miller, and Miller, 111.

[5] Froiland, 67; Cassells, Miller, and Miller, 113; Donald Jackson, *Custer's Gold: The United States Expedition of 1874* (Lincoln: University of Nebraska Press, 1972), 77-80.

[6] Cassells, Miller, and Miller, 123; Bob Lee, ed., *Gold, Gals, Guns, Guts* (Deadwood, SD: Deadwood-Lead '76 Centennial, Inc., 1976); Bernie Hunhoff, "A Discovery on the Cheyenne," *South Dakota Magazine*, September/October 1995, 30-33.

[7] Ibid., 124.

[8] Hunt quoted in Cassells, Miller, and Miller, 126.

[9] Ibid., 131.

[10] Ibid., 133.

[11] Watson Parker, *Gold in the Black Hills* (Norman: University of Oklahoma Press, 1966), 10-11; Frank Thomson, *The Thoen Stone: A Saga of the Black Hills* (Detroit: The Harlo Press, 1966), 19-104.

[12] Philip Weeks, *Farewell, My Nation: The American Indian and the United States in the Nineteenth Century* (Wheeling, IL: Harlan Davidson, Inc., 1990), 78.

[13] Rex Alan Smith, *The Moon of Popping Trees: The Tragedy at Wounded Knee and the End of the Indian Wars* (Lincoln: University of Nebraska Press, 1975), 18-24.

[14] James D. McLaird and Lesta V. Turchen, "Exploring the Black Hills, 1855-1875: Reports of the Government Expeditions. The Dacota Explorations of Lieutenant Gouverneur Kemble Warren, 1855-1856-1857," *South Dakota History* 3 (Fall 1973): 375-77, 388.

[15] James D. McLaird and Lesta V. Turchen, "Exploring the Black Hills, 1855-1875: Reports of the Government Expeditions. The Explorations of Captain William Franklin Raynolds, 1859-1860," *South Dakota History* 4 (Winter 1973): 18-49; Parker, *Gold in the Black Hills*, 17-18.

[16] Edward Lazarus, *Black Hills, White Justice: The Sioux Nation Versus the United States, 1775 to the Present* (Lincoln: University of Nebraska Press, 1991), 35-37; Smith, *Moon of Popping Trees*, 41-43.

[17] Lazarus, 45-51; Cassells, Miller, and Miller, 157.

[18] Lazarus, 48-49; Cassells, Miller, and Miller, 153-56; The full text of the treaty can be viewed at the Avalon Project at Yale Law School, <http://www.yale.edu/ lawweb/avalon/ntreaty/nt001.htm>.

[19] Cassells, Miller, and Miller, 158; Jackson, *Custer's Gold*, 14, 23-24; John D. McDermott, "The Military Problem and the Black Hills, 1874-1875," *South Dakota History* 31 (Fall/Winter 2001): 191; Francis Paul Prucha, ed., *Documents of United States Indian Policy* (Lincoln: University of Nebraska Press, 1975), 110.

[20] Parker, 26; Ernest Grafe and Paul Horsted, *Exploring with Custer: The 1874 Black Hills Expedition* (Custer, SD: Golden Valley Press, 2002), 4-5.

[21] Parker, 22, 30.

[22] Ibid., 35.

[23] Lazarus, 86; Parker, 54, 78, 80, 82, 91.

[24] Parker, 63-64; Richard Irving Dodge, *The Black Hills* (Minneapolis: Ross & Haines, Inc., 1965), 28, 146; Lesta V. Turchen and James D. McLaird, *The Black Hills Expedition of 1875* (Mitchell, SD: Dakota Wesleyan University Press, 1975), 1-9.

[25] Dodge, *The Black Hills*, 105-08; Parker, 65.

[26] Charles M. Robinson III, *General Crook and the Western Frontier* (Norman: University of Oklahoma Press, 2001), 162; Parker, 67-68.

[27] Robinson, *General Crook*, 162; Lazarus, 80-84; Parker, 127-28.

[28] Lazarus, 83; Parker, 129.

[29] Cassells, Miller, and Miller, 159; Lazarus, 84.

[30] Lazarus, 87-88.

[31] Parker, 76, 131-34.

[32] Ibid., 133-34.

[33] Lazarus, 90-93.

[34] Parker, 91.

[35] Ibid., 91.

[36] Ibid., 92, 94; Watson Parker, *Deadwood: The Golden Years* (Lincoln: University of Nebraska Press, 1981), 17, 32.

[37] Parker, *Gold in the Black Hills*, 154, 164-65; James D. McLaird, "Calamity Jane: The Life and the Legend," *South Dakota History* 24 (Spring 1994): 1-18; Joseph G. Rosa, *They Called Him Wild Bill: The Life and Adventures of James Butler Hickok* (Norman: University of Oklahoma Press, 1964), passim.

[38] Parker, *Deadwood*, 223; Grant K. Anderson, "Deadwood's Chinatown," *South Dakota History* 5 (Summer 1975): 267; *Black Hills Daily Times*, November 3, 1877; "Ethnic Oasis: The Chinese in the Black Hills," *South Dakota History* 33 (Winter 2003): 289-362.

[39] Parker, *Gold in the Black Hills*, 95; Paul T. Allsman, *Reconnaissance of Gold-Mining Districts in the Black Hills, South Dakota*, Bulletin 427 (Washington, D.C.: Government Printing Office, U.S. Department of the Interior, Bureau of Mines, 1940): 8.

[40] William Bronson and T. H. Watkins, *Homestake: The Centennial History of America's Greatest Gold Mine* (San Francisco: Homestake Mining Co., 1977), 24-25.

[41] Bronson and Watkins, 25; Mildred Fielder, *The Treasure of Homestake Gold* (Aberdeen, SD: North Plains Press, 1970), 25.

[42] Fielder, *The Treasure of Homestake Gold*, 27, 31.

[43] Joseph H. Cash, "History of Lead, South Dakota: 1876-1900," *South Dakota Historical Collections* 34 (Pierre: State Historical Society, 1968): 52-53.

[44] Cash, "History of Lead," 74; Mark S. Wolfe, *Boots on Bricks* (Deadwood, SD: Deadwood Historic Preservation Commission, 1996), 29.

[45] Bronson and Watkins, 27; Duane Smith, *Staking a Claim in History: The Evolution of Homestake Mining Company* (Walnut Creek, CA: Homestake Mining Co., 2001), 22-27.

[46] Bronson and Watkins, 27, 29, 31; Fielder, *The Treasure of Homestake Gold*, 109.

[47] Allsman, 22-23.

[48] *Black Hills Daily Pioneer*, May 26, 1877; Watson Parker and Hugh K. Lambert, *Black Hills Ghost Towns* (Chicago: The Swallow Press, Inc., 1974), 98, 164; Mildred Fielder, *Silver is the Fortune* (Aberdeen, SD: North Plains Press, 1978), 109-10.

[49] Parker and Lambert, 166-67; Paul Fatout, *Ambrose Bierce and the Black Hills* (Norman: University of Oklahoma Press, 1956), 24-44.

[50] Parker and Lambert, 73; Irma H. Klock, *All Roads Lead to Deadwood* (Lead, SD: privately published, 1979), 231.

[51] Parker and Lambert, 98; Parker, *Gold in the Black Hills*, 85; Ross P. Korsgaard, "A History of Rapid City, South Dakota, During Territorial Days," *South Dakota Historical Collections* 38 (Pierre: State Historical Society, 1976): 522; David B. Miller, *Gateway to the Hills: An Illustrated History of Rapid City* (Northridge: Windsor Publications, Inc., 1985), 9.

[52] Parker, *Gold in the Black Hills*, 98.

[53] *The Miscellaneous Documents of the House of Representatives, 52nd Congress*, 1st session, vol. 50, part 8 (Washington, D.C.: Government Printing Office, 1895): 312-15.

[54] Klock, 59; Annie D. Tallent, *The Black Hills; or, The Last Hunting Ground of the Dakotahs* (Sioux Falls, SD: Brevet Press, 1974), 138; Agnes Wright Spring, *The Cheyenne and Black Hills Stage Express Route* (Lincoln: University of Nebraska Press, 1967).

[55] Klock, 28, 146-47.

[56] Ibid., 116-31.

[57] Allsman, 8.

[58] Bronson and Watkins, 46; Klock, 227.

[59] *Black Hills Daily Times*, January 30, 1881, April 27, 1881, May 4, 1881, August 1, 1881, November 2, 1881.

[60] *Black Hills Daily Times*, February 7, 1886, February 9, 1886, November 22, 1887.

[61] *Black Hills Daily Times*, February 17, 1888, March 11, 1888; David A. Wolff, "Pyritic Smelting at Deadwood: A Temporary Solution to Refractory Ores," *South Dakota History* 15 (Winter 1985): 318-21.

[62] Wolff, "Pyritic Smelting," 318-19.

[63] *Black Hills Daily Times*, October 29, 1889, January 29, 1891; Mildred Fielder, *Railroads of the Black Hills* (New York: Bonanza Books, 1964), 94, 123.

[64] Wolff, "Pyritic Smelting," 330-35; Fielder, *Railroads of the Black Hills*, 74, 125; Allsman, 8.

[65] Fielder, *Railroads of the Black Hills*, 125-26; David B. Miller, "Seth Bullock: Black Hills Entrepreneur," unpublished paper, 12.

[66] David A. Wolff, "No Matter How You Do It, Fraud is Fraud: Another Look at Black Hills Mining Scandals," *South Dakota History* 33 (Summer 2003): 92-96.

[67] Ibid., 99-105.

[68] Otis E. Young, Jr., *Western Mining* (Norman: University of Oklahoma Press, 1970), 283-84; Richmond L. Clow, *Chasing the Glitter: Black Hills Milling, 1874-1959* (Pierre: South Dakota State Historical Society Press, 2002); "The North Side Tailings Plant Better Known as 'Cyanide No. 2,'" *Sharp Bits* 16 (November 1965): 14; David A. Wolff, "Mining Ground on the Fringe: The Horseshoe-Mogul Mining Company of the Northern Black Hills," *Mining History Journal* (1995): 22-24.

[69] Clow, 13; Bronson and Watkins, 51; David W. Ryder, *The Merrill Story* (San Francisco: The Merrill Co., 1958), 34-50; Carolyn Torma, "Dakota Images," *South Dakota History* 15 (Winter 1985): back cover.

[70] Wolfe, *Boots on Bricks*, 23, 103, 121-23.

[71] Clow, 43; Cassells, Miller, and Miller, 280; Richmond L. Clow, "Timber Users, Timber Savers: Homestake Mining Company and the First Regulated Timber Harvest," *South Dakota History* 22 (Fall 1992): 217; John S. McClintock, *Pioneer Days of the Black Hills* (Norman: University of Oklahoma Press, 2000), 76; Martha Linde, *Sawmills of the Black Hills* (Rapid City, SD: Fenske Printing, Inc., 1984).

[72] Cassells, Miller, and Miller, 282; Clow, "Timber Users, Timber Savers," 230-31.

[73] Fielder, *The Treasure of Homestake Gold*, 82-83; "Our Water Supply," *Sharp Bits* 5 (August 1954): 12-13; "Hydro-Electric Power Plants," *Sharp Bits* 12 (September 1961): 6, 22.

[74] U.S. Bureau of the Census, *Thirteenth Census of the United States Taken in the Year 1910, Population* (Washington, D.C.: Government Printing Office, 1913), 3: 690-91.

[75] Pierre Lassonds, *The Gold Book: The Complete Investment Guide to Precious Metals* (Toronto: Penguin Books, 1992), 23; Allsman, 38-39.

[76] Watson Parker, "Booming the Black Hills," *South Dakota History* 11 (Winter 1980): 43; George P. Baldwin, *The Black Hills Illustrated* (Deadwood, SD: Black Hills Mining Men's Association, 1904); *Black Hills Daily Times*, March 2, 1881.

[77] Cassells, Miller, and Miller, 308-09; Jessie Y. Sundstrom, *Pioneers and Custer State Park* (Custer, SD: Jessie Y. Sundstrom, 1994), 90-91; Hol Wagner, "The Spearfish Combine," *Burlington Bulletin* 34 (May 1998): 58-69.

[78] Fielder, *Railroads of the Black Hills*, 134; Miller, *Gateway to the Hills*, 35.

[79] Cassells, Miller, and Miller, 312, 315-16.

[80] Shebby Lee, "Traveling the Sunshine State: The Growth of Tourism in South Dakota, 1914-1939," *South Dakota History* 19 (Summer 1989): 208-09; "Days of '76 History Celebrated," *Days of '76* (July 2002): 6.

[81] Wolfe, *Boots on Bricks*, 77; Helen Rezatto, *Tales of the Black Hills* (Aberdeen, SD: North Plains Press, 1983), 239-42.

[82] Gilbert C. Fite, *Mount Rushmore* (Norman: University of Oklahoma Press, 1952), passim.

[83] Fite, 75-76; Harold H. Schuler, "Patriotic Pageantry: Presidential Visits to South Dakota," *South Dakota History* 30 (Winter 2000): 355-63.

[84] Fite, 160-61.

[85] Michael L. Dennis, *Federal Relief Construction in South Dakota, 1929-1941* (Pierre: South Dakota State Historic Preservation Office, 1998), 14-21, 43-44.

[86] Fielder, *The Treasure of Homestake Gold*, 294, 324.

[87] Ibid., 330-34.

[88] Miller, *Gateway*, 85; Robert Lee, *Fort Meade and the Black Hills* (Lincoln: University of Nebraska Press, 1991), 226-27.

[89] Miller, *Gateway*, 88, 97; "Remembering the Titans: Missiles Launched Hills into Nuclear Age," *Rapid City Journal*, October 28, 2001; *Battle Mountain Sanitarium, Hot Springs, South Dakota: 1907-1997* (Hot Springs, SD: VA Black Hills Medical Center, 1997), 38-39; Bill Cissell, "Ellsworth Marks Crash Anniversary," *Rapid City Journal*, March 18, 2003.

[90] U.S. Bureau of the Census, *Census of Population: 1950, Number of Inhabitants*, Vol. 1, Part 41 (Washington, D.C.: Government Printing Office, 1952): 41-12, 41-18.

[91] Herbert S. Schell, *History of South Dakota*, 3d. ed., (Lincoln: University of Nebraska, 1975), 304-06; "Project Features of the Belle Fourche Unit: Belle Fourche Dam," www.gp.usbr.gov/sd/bfrpf.htm;

Internet; accessed January 24, 2001; "Construction of the Rapid Valley Unit: Deerfield Dam," www.gp.usbr. gov/sd/ dfrpc.htm; Internet; accessed January 22, 2001.

[92] Tim Velder, "Irrigating the West," *Rapid City Journal*, August 28, 2002; "History of the Development of the Angostura Unit," www.gp.usbr.gov/sd/agrhp1.htm; Internet; accessed January 8, 2001: "Construction of the Rapid Valley Unit: Pactola Dam," www.gp.usbr.gov/sd/ptrpc.htm; Internet; accessed January 22, 2001; Miller, *Gateway*, 98-100.

[93] U.S. Bureau of the Census, *Census of Population, Characteristics of the Population, South Dakota, 1960*, Vol. 1, Part 43 (Washington, D.C.: Government Printing Office, 1961): 43-60; Schell, *History of South Dakota*, 274.

[94] "History of the Reptile Gardens," http://www.reptile-gardens.com/main%20page/history.html; Internet; accessed March 2, 2004; "Black Hills Gold History," http://www.goldoutlet.com/history.html; Internet; accessed February 27, 2004.

[95] U.S. Bureau of the Census, *Census of Population: 1980, Characteristics of the Population, South Dakota*, Vol. 1, Part 43 (Washington, D.C.: Government Printing Office, 1981): 43-14.

[96] "Chronology of Major Events in the Progress at Crazy Horse Memorial," http://www.crazyhorse. org/chronolo.htm; Internet; accessed August 3, 2001; Jeff Terry, "Riding the Black Hills Central," *Railfan & Railroad* (May 2001): 38-40; Paul Higbee and Kathleen Aney, *Spearfish* (Spearfish, SD: Black Hills and Bighorns Project, 2000), 31-33.

[97] Lassonds, *The Gold Book*, 36-37; "Wharf Resources (USA) Inc.," *Black Hills Pioneer*, "Progress Edition," March 2003; Peter Carrels, "There's gold in them 'thar hills," *High Country News*, April 13, 1987, 13.

[98] "Homestake Time Line," http://int.phys.washington.edu.NUSEL/timeline.html; Internet; accessed March 5, 2004.

[99] "Mine Clean-up Moving Forward," *Rapid City Journal*, September 11, 2002.

[100] A. J. Wolff, interviewed by David A. Wolff, January 20, 2004.

[101] "Deadwood by the Numbers," *Rapid City Journal*, May 14, 2003.

[102] Quote from HBO promotion run on the network during March 2004.

[103] "Homestake Bills Signed," *Black Hills Pioneer*, February 12, 2004.

[104] Bill Cissell, "Quality of Life Asset to Base," *Rapid City Journal*, August 31, 2003; *Rapid City Journal*, March 19, 2004.

[105] "A Brief History of the Sturgis Rally," *Black Hills Pioneer*, August 6, 2001.

Chapter 16: Catholic Missions, Churches, and Schools, Carol Goss Hoover *(pgs. 318-330)*

[1] South Dakota Bishops following Martin Marty in the Sioux Falls Diocese: Thomas O'Gorman (1896); Bernard J. Mahoney (1922); William O. Brady (1939); Lambert A. Hoch (1956); Paul V. Dudley (1978); Paul F. Anderson, Auxiliary Bishop, (1982); and Robert J. Carlson, Coadjutor (1994), Bishop (1995). Bishops in the Lead Diocese: John Stariha (1902); Joseph F. Busch (1910); and John J. Lawler (1916). Bishops in the Rapid City Diocese: John J. Lawler (1930); Leo F. Dworschak (1946); William T. McCarty, Coadjutor, (1947), Bishop (1948); Howard J. Dimmerling (1969); Charles J. Chaput (1988); and Blasé J. Cupich (1998).

[2] See Carol Goss Hoover, *Building the Indigenous Church: Tools for Pastoral Ministers in Sioux Country* (doctoral dissertation, Graduate Theological Foundation, 2002).

[3] Hiram Chittenden and Alfred Talbot Richardson, *Life, Letter and Travels of Father Pierre-Jean De Smet, SJ, 1802-1873*, 4 vols. (New York: Francis P. Harper, 1905), 1:185-86.

[4] Abbot Martin Marty, Marty Collection, Bureau of Catholic Indian Missions Records, Marquette University, Milwaukee, Wisconsin, Letter of May 9, 1876, Box 4, Number 6.

[5] Most specific names, dates, and statistics were derived from Sister Mary Claudia Duratschek, *Builders of God's Kingdom: The History of the Catholic Church in South Dakota* (Diocese of Sioux Falls, 1979).

[6] This partial list represents religious orders who worked in West River only: Daughters of Charity of St. Vincent de Paul, St. Louis, MO; Daughters of the Heart of Mary, New York, NY; Benedictine Sisters, Atchison, KS; Benedictine Sisters, Bismarck, ND; Benedictine Sisters, Richardton, ND; Benedictine Sisters, St. Joseph, MN; Benedictine Sisters, Switzerland/Sturgis; Benedictine Sisters, Maryville, MO/Yankton; Congregation of Notre Dame of Montreal; Dominican Sisters, Adrian, MI; Dominican Sisters, Racine, WI; Franciscan Sisters, Chicago, IL; Franciscan Sisters of Blessed Kunegunda, Chicago, IL; Franciscan

Sisters of Little Falls, MN; Handmaids of the Precious Blood, Jemez Springs, NM; Hospital Sisters of the Third Order of St. Francis, Springfield, IL; Notre Dame Sisters, Omaha, NE; Oblate Sisters of the Blessed Sacrament; School Sisters of Notre Dame, Baltimore, MD; School Sisters of Notre Dame, Mankato, MN; School Sisters of Notre Dame, Milwaukee, WI; School Sisters of Notre Dame, St. Louis, MO; School Sisters of St. Francis, Milwaukee, WI; Servants of Mary, Omaha, NE; Sisters of Charity, Cincinnati, OH; Sisters of Charity of Leavenworth, KS; Sisters of Charity of St. Joan Antida, West Allis, WI; Sister of Charity of the Blessed Virgin Mary, Dubuque, IA; Sisters of Charity of the Incarnate Word, Grapevine, TX; Sisters of Christian Charity, Wilmette, IL; Sisters of Divine Providence, Melbourne, KY; Sisters of the Humility of Mary, Cleveland, OH; Sisters of Mercy, San Francisco, CA; Sisters of St. Francis of Penance and Christian Charity, Stella Niagara, NY; Sisters of St. Francis of Perpetual Adoration, Colorado Springs, CO; Sisters of St. Francis of the Holy Family, Dubuque, IA; Sisters of St. Francis of the Immaculate Conception, West Peoria, IL; Sisters of St. Joseph, Concordia, KS; Sisters of St. Joseph of Carondelet, St. Paul, MN; Sisters of the Divine Savior, Milwaukee, WI; Sisters of the Holy Cross, South Bend, IN; Sisters of the Holy Family, Fremont, CA; Sisters of the Presentation of the Blessed Virgin Mary, Fargo/Aberdeen, SD; Sisters of the Presentation of the Blessed Virgin Mary, Dubuque, IA; Sisters of the Presentation of the Blessed Virgin Mary, Fitchburg, MA; Sisters of the Third Order of St. Francis of Penance and Christian Charity, Tiffin, OH; Sister Servants of the Immaculate Heart of Mary, Monroe, MI; Society of the Sacred Heart, St. Louis, MO; Ursuline Nuns of the Congregation of Paris.

[7] See Duratschek; Sister Eleanor Solon, *We Walk By Faith: The Growth of the Catholic Faith in Western South Dakota* (Strasbourg, France: Editions du Signe, 2002); *The Catholic Encyclopedia* (1917) at www. newadvent.org/cathen.

[8] See Duratschek; and Robert Karolevitz, *With Faith, Hope and Tenacity: The First Hundred Years of the Diocese of Sioux Falls* (Mission Hill, SD: Homestead Publishers, 1989).

[9] In 1885, the first southern Dakota branch of the Knights of Columbus was founded in Mitchell. The Knights represent the largest Catholic lay organization in the United States, whose mission includes a full array of charitable works.

[10] Herbert S. Schell, *History of South Dakota*, 3d ed. rev. (Lincoln: University of Nebraska Press, 1975), 390.

Chapter 17: Protestant Faith and Learning, Lynwood E. Oyos (pgs. 331-355)

[1] Virginia Driving Hawk Sneve, *That They May Have Life: The Episcopal Church in South Dakota, 1859-1976* (New York: The Seabury Press, 1977), 116.

[2] Ibid.

[3] O. E. Rölvaag, *The Third Life of Per Smevik* (Minneapolis: Dillon Press, Inc., 1971), 105.

[4] Robert C. Ostergren, "European Settlement and Ethnicity Patterns on the Agricultural Frontiers of South Dakota," *South Dakota History* 13 (Spring/Summer 1983): 75.

[5] Hamlin Garland, *A Son of the Middle Border* (Lincoln: University of Nebraska Press, 1979), 244.

[6] John R. Milton, *South Dakota, A Bicentennial History* (New York: American Association for State and Local History, 1987), 143.

[7] Robert C. Ostergren, "The Immigrant Church as a Symbol of Community and Place in the Upper Midwest," *Great Plains Quarterly* 1 (Fall 1981): 228.

[8] Edward C. Ehrensperger, *History of the United Church of Christ in South Dakota, 1869-1976* (Freeman, SD: Pine Hill Press, 1977), 272.

[9] For a more comprehensive account of the extant colleges and universities introduced in this chapter, see *From Idea to Institution: Higher Education in South Dakota*, ed. Herbert T. Hoover, Ruth Ann Alexander, Patricia M. Peterson, and Larry J. Zimmerman (Vermillion: University of South Dakota Press, 1989).

[10] The town of Academy was incorporated at this site. Joseph Ward died in 1889 from complications related to diabetes.

[11] William H. H. Beadle, *Autobiography of William Henry Harrison Beadle* (Pierre: South Dakota State Historical Society, 1938), 8.

[12] Ibid., 77.

[13] George W. Kingsbury, *History of Dakota Territory and South Dakota*, ed. George Martin Smith, 5 vols. (Chicago: S. J. Clarke Publishing Co., 1915), 3: 829.

[14] During the early 1940s, South Dakota had over 3,000 common school districts in the rural areas and over 300 independent school districts.

[15] Kingsbury, 3: 593.

[16] Ibid., 595.

Chapter 18: Literature, *Arthur R. Huseboe (pgs. 356-366)*

[1] *John Wallace Crawford* (Boston: Twayne, 1981). Much of the present chapter on the literary arts is based on Arthur R. Huseboe, *An Illustrated History of the Arts in South Dakota* (Sioux Falls, SD: Center for Western Studies, 1989).

[2] C. Warren Hollister, *The Wizard of Oz*, by L. Frank Baum, ed. Michael Patrick Hearn (New York: Schocken Books, 1983), 193.

[3] Rölvaag Collection, Center for Western Studies, Augustana College, Sioux Falls, SD.

[4] Einar Haugen, *Ole Edvart Rölvaag* (Boston: Twayne, 1983), Chronology.

[5] "An Overview of Literature by Dakota/Lakota Authors," in Huseboe, 147-59.

[6] George F. Day, *South Dakota History* 31 (Summer 2001): 175-76.

[7] Madison Jones, *New York Times Book Review*, February 16, 1975, 6. A defining characteristic of the western American novel is its concern with achieving historical veracity. For a recent examination of the problem of historical authenticity in the western novel, specifically in Manfred's *Scarlet Plume,* see Harry F. Thompson, "History, Historicity, and the Western American Novel: Frederick Manfred's *Scarlet Plume* and the Dakota War of 1862," *Western American Literature* 37 (Spring 2002): 50-82.

[8] www.exmac.com

Chapter 19: Women Writers, *Ruth Ann Alexander (pgs. 367-383)*

[1] Eleanor Gates Tully to Doane Robinson, November 14, 1902, Robinson Papers, Folder 3, Doane Robinson Papers, South Dakota State Historical Society, Pierre, SD.

[2] O.W. Coursey, *Literature of South Dakota* (Mitchell, SD: Educator Supply Company, 1928), 114.

[3] Reverend Ruth Potter, Deacon, Christ Church, Chamberlain, interviewed by Ruth Ann Alexander, February 14, 1991.

[4] Virginia Driving Hawk Sneve, *That They May Have Life: The Episcopal Church in South Dakota, 1859-1976* (New York: Seabury Press,1977).

[5] Doane Robinson, "Divorce in South Dakota," *South Dakota Historical Collections* 112 (Pierre: State Historical Society, 1924): 268-80.

[6] See Lucile Fargo, *Prairie Girl* (New York: Dodd Mead, 1937), and Rose Wilder Lane, *Home Over Saturday,* (De Smet, SD: Laura Ingalls Wilder Memorial Society, 1974).

[7] William Anderson, "The Literary Apprenticeship of Laura Ingalls Wilder," *South Dakota History* 13 (Winter 1983): passim.

[8] Another example is *Bachelor Bess: The Homesteading Letters of Elizabeth Corey, 1900-1919*, ed. Philip L. Gerber (Iowa City: University of Iowa Press, 1990).

Chapter 20: Visual Arts, *Ron Robinson (pgs. 384-405)*

[1] Robert Frost, *The Complete Poems of Robert Frost* (New York: Holt, Rinehart and Winston, 1968), 436.

[2] Etienne B. Renaud, "Report 8: The Archaeological Survey of the High Western Plains: Pictographs and Petroglyphs of the High Western Plains," *Archaeological Survey of the High Western Plains, Reports 1930-1940* (Denver: University of Denver, 1936): 1; available from http://www.penlib.du.edu/specoll/Renaud/15rpt8cover.html; Internet; accessed October 10, 2003.

[3] Ibid., 2.

[4] Ibid.

[5] Arthur Amiotte, "An Appraisal of Sioux Arts," in Arthur R. Huseboe, *An Illustrated History of the Arts in South Dakota* (Sioux Falls, SD: Center for Western Studies, 1989), 115.

[6] Ibid., 116.

[7] Amos Bad Heart Bull, *A Pictographic History of the Oglala Sioux*, Text, Helen H. Blish (Lincoln: University of Nebraska Press, 1967).

[8] Oscar Howe Biography, South Dakota Art Museum; available from http://www3.sdstate.edu/Administration/SouthDakotaArtMuseum/Collections/Howe/; Internet; accessed October 12, 2003.

[9] Ibid.

[10] See "Theodore Burr Catlin, in Indian Costume, 1838," in *George Catlin and His Indian Gallery*, Renwick Gallery of the Smithsonian American Art Museum; available from http://americanart.si.edu/collections/exhibits/catlin/index.html; Internet; accessed October 15, 2003.

[11] "Tim Giago," Biography Resource Center, Gale Group; available from http://www.nativepubs.com/nativepubs/Apps/bios/0166GiagoTim.asp?pic=none; Internet; accessed November 10, 2003.

[12] Huseboe, 257-58.

[13] Ibid., 256.

[14] Ibid., 261-62.

[15] Dan Daly, "Four more presidents debut downtown," *Rapid City Journal,* October 15, 2003; available from http://www.rapidcityjournal.com/articles/2003/10/15/news/local/news04.txt; Internet; accessed November 17, 2003.

[16] Huseboe, 258-59.

[17] Ibid., 259.

[18] "A Little about Dick Termes," Termespheres.com; available at http://www.termespheres.com/termes.html; Internet; accessed November 22, 2003.

[19] Huseboe, 222.

[20] Dahl Fine Arts Center; available at http://www.rapidweb.com/dahl/; Internet; accessed November 15, 2003.

[21] Huseboe, 214-16.

[22] Ibid., 216-17.

[23] Ibid., 220-23.

[24] "Harvey Dunn Biography," South Dakota Art Museum; available at http://www3.sdstate.edu/Administration/SouthDakotaArtMuseum/Collections/Dunn/; Internet; accessed November 16, 2003.

[25] "Charles Hargens," *Art On the Move*, Bucks County Schools Intermediate Unit 22; available at http://www.bucksiu.org/art/html/bios/hargens.htm; Internet; accessed November 16, 2003.

[26] "Jim Pollack Art," website; available at http://www.iw.net/~jpollock/; Internet; accessed November 17, 2003.

[27] Huseboe, 231.

[28] Ibid., 236-37.

[29] Ronald Robinson, "Pantura Studios: A Space Beyond Time," *etc. Magazine*, November 1, 2002.

[30] David R. Phillips, ed., *The West: An American Experience* (Chicago: Henry Regnery Company, 1973), 114-37 and passim.

[31] "Grabill Photographs," Library of Congress Prints and Photographs Online Collection; available at http://memory.loc.gov/pp/pphome.html; Internet; accessed November 18, 2003.

[32] "Levon West," Meadowlark Gallery, Billings, MT.; available at http://www.meadowlarkgallery.com/WestLevon.htm; Internet; accessed December 1, 2003.

[33] "Joel Strasser: Light and Shadow," Gallery; Ex Machina Books and Art, available at http://www.exmac.com/; Internet; accessed December 1, 2003.

[34] "Art Professor at the U to display Boot Hill Chronicles," University of South Dakota, October 20, 2003; available at http://www.usd.edu/urelations/news/archives/2003/October/October21.html; Internet; accessed December 2, 2003.

[35] "About Us," Peoplescapes Photography; available from http://www.peoplescapes.com/; Internet; accessed December 2, 2003.

[36] Archibald MacLeish, "Ars Poetica," The Academy of American Poets; available from http://www.poets.org/poems/poems.cfm?prmID=985; Internet; accessed December 3, 2003.

[37] Eugene Delacroix, "Communications," Resource of Art Quotations at PaintersKeys.com; available from http://www.painterskeys.com/getquotes.asp?fname=ac&ID=43; Internet; accessed January 8, 2004.

Chapter 21: Performing Arts, *Arthur R. Huseboe (pgs. 406-422)*

[1] Arthur Amiotte, "An Appraisal of Sioux Arts," in Arthur R. Huseboe, *An Illustrated History of the Arts in South Dakota* (Sioux Falls, SD: Center for Western Studies, 1989), 159. Much of the present chapter

on the performing arts is based on this book. A useful bibliography to supplement the Huseboe book is Ron MacIntyre and Rebecca L. Bell, *The Arts in South Dakota: A Selective, Annotated Bibliography* (Sioux Falls, SD: Center for Western Studies, 1988).

[2] Huenemann, "Sioux Music and Dance," in *An Illustrated History of the Arts in South Dakota*, 160.

[3] (Ranchos de Taos, N.M.: Dog Soldier Press, 2003).

[4] Catherine McGovern, "Early Culture in the Sunshine State" (manuscript, 1976).

[5] Lois Abby Cornell, "A New Culture Emerges," in *Dakota Panorama* (Sioux Falls: Dakota Territory Centennial Commission, 1961), 266.

[6] "Yankton Theatre" (Vermillion: University of South Dakota, 1971).

[7] "A History of Theatre and Theatrical Activities in Deadwood, South Dakota, 1876-90" (Ph.D. dissertation, University of Iowa, 1967).

[8] *South Dakota Historical Collections* 25 (Pierre: State Historical Society, 1958).

[9] "A History of the Theatrical and Community Activities in the Early Dell Rapids, South Dakota, Opera House" (master's thesis, South Dakota State University, 1970).

[10] Laura Bower Van Nuys, *The Family Band* (Lincoln: University of Nebraska Press, 1961).

[11] Betty Jean Collins, "The History of Dramatic Art at the University of South Dakota, 1882-1948" (master's thesis, University of South Dakota, 1948).

[12] Andre Larson and Jim Koster, *Beethoven & Berlioz, Paris & Vienna* (Vermillion, SD: National Music Museum, 2003), 4.

[13] "A Duet of Music and Engineering," *South Dakota Tech Magazine*, Fall 2003, 22.

[14] "The Early History of the Lake Madison Chautauqua," (master's thesis, University of South Dakota, 1956).

[15] *Culture Under Canvas* (New York: Hastings House, 1958), 15.

[16] "Movie Time, Aberdeen, South Dakota: 1919-1930," *Northern Social Science Review* (Spring 1980): 30-56, and "Movietime Aberdeen, SD, 1931-1941," *Sixteenth Dakota History Conference*, April 12-14, 1984, (Madison, SD: Dakota State College, 1985): 56-72.

[17] "Radio in the 1920s: A Social Force in South Dakota," *South Dakota History* 11 (Spring 1981): 100.

[18] "A History of KUSD, the University of South Dakota Radio Station" (master's thesis, University of South Dakota, 1949).

[19] "Midcontinent Communications Connections," *Sioux Falls Argus Leader*, February 29, 2004, 3.

[20] "A History of the South Dakota Educational Television Network" (master's thesis, University of South Dakota, 1985).

[21] *Theatre in Spite of Itself* (Sioux Falls, SD: Sioux Falls Independent School District, 1976).

[22] "The Role of a Lifetime," *Sioux Falls Woman*, February/March 2004, 46-49.

[23] Washington Pavilion, "2003-2004 Performance Series," brochure.

[24] "History of Rapid City Community Theatre from 1943 to 1973" (master's thesis, South Dakota State University, 1973).

[25] Black Hills Symphony Orchestra, Black Hills Chamber Music Society, Dakota Choral Union, brochure, 2003.

[26] "Playing Big in Rapid City," *South Dakota Magazine*, March/April 2003, 17.

[27] G. S. Hanson, *The Monthly South Dakotan*, July 1901.

[28] "Contemporary South Dakota Composers," *South Dakota Musician* (Winter/Spring 1985).

[29] "The Wind Music of Felix Vinatieri, Dakota Territory Bandmaster," (Ph.D. dissertation, University of Northern Colorado, 1982).

Chapter 22: Health Care, *Herbert T. Hoover* (pgs. 423-450)

[1] *Administrative Procedure Act, Statutes at Large*, 42: 208 ff., amended in *U.S. Code*, 25: 13 ff.; Indian Health Care Improvement Act of 1976, *Statutes*, 90: 1400 ff.; and *U.S. Code*, 25: 1601 ff.

[2] "Nursing Care for Indians: Yesterday and Today," *Indians at Work* 4 (1936): 13-16.

[3] A clear description of life in this tuberculosis sanitarium is available in Mark St. Pierre, *Madonna Swan: A Lakota Woman's Story* (Norman: University of Oklahoma Press, 1991).

[4] P. L. 86-121, 289, *Statutes*, 37: 267 ff.

[5] *Statutes*, 90: 1400 ff., amended *U.S. Code*, 25: 1601 ff.

[6] *U.S. Supreme Court,* 113: 2024 ff.

[7] *Aberdeen Area Profile: Indian Health Service* (Aberdeen SD: Indian Health Service Office of Planning and Legislation, May 1997).

[8] Electronic copies and transcripts of interviews recorded during the summer 2003 with Yankton tribal members O'Connor, the Cournoyers, and Rouse, quoted above, are available in the Herbert T. Hoover Collection, I. D. Weeks Library, University of South Dakota, Vermillion, SD.

[9] Neyton and Celina Baltodano wrote and privately published *History of South Dakota Medicine* (Sioux Falls: Dakota Printing Company, 1990) as a learning experience soon after they immigrated from Latin America to enter medical practice in Sioux Falls. Factual errors do not reduce value in brief representations of organizational structure, hospital development, physician and nursing care, pharmacy, and dentistry. Their contributions cannot be denied in the absence of any other effort within the medical community to describe the history of health care for use by all South Dakotans.

[10] George W. Mills, *Fifty Years a Country Doctor in Western South Dakota* (Wall, SD: Wall Drug Store, 1971), supplies insight into the problems and contributions of rural physicians before the appearance of modern hospitals and clinics.

[11] The standard general history of this Benedictine order is Sister Mary Claudia Duratschek, *Under the Shadow of His Wings: History of Sacred Heart Convent of Benedictine Sisters* (Aberdeen, SD: North Plains Press, 1971). Greater detail about its commitment to health care is available in Dixie Hausman, "The Benedictine Sisters of the Sacred Heart: An Administrative History of Their Roles in Nursing and Health Care for South Dakota, 1897-1986" (master's thesis, University of South Dakota, 1986). The central theme is the history of training for nurses and its applications in South Dakota Benedictine hospital history, derived from documentary files preserved in the archive of the order at Yankton.

[12] An excellent history of these Presentation Sisters exists in Susan Peterson and Courtney Vaughn-Roberson, *Women of Vision* (Urbana: University of Illinois Press, 1988). Evaluations of both medical and paramedical accomplishments are based on both documents and oral history sources.

[13] Information about the Rapid City Regional Hospital is derived in part from the Regional Hospital Public Relations staff in 2001.

[14] Rodney Mittelstedt, "County Doctor: The Life of Roscoe Dean, M.D." (master's thesis, University of South Dakota, 1993) contains reminiscences by Dean about the life of a country doctor, causes for the withdrawal of physicians from rural medical practice, and circumstances that led to the founding of the four-year medical school at the University of South Dakota.

[15] See "Ortman Clinic: A Tradition in Healthcare" and Ervin Ortman, *A Touching Story* (Canistota, SD: Canistota Clipper, 1985).

[16] Information packet from Avera Health, 3900 West Avera Drive, Sioux Falls, South Dakota 57108-5721.

[17] Competition bordering on confrontation between the Avera Health and Sioux Valley networks and growing concern about their monopolistic tendencies were featured in an article in the *Sioux Falls Argus Leader,* July 19, 2001.

[18] See *Building a Better Mousetrap, Creating a Health System for the Next Century* (Sioux Falls, SD: Sioux Valley Health Systems, 2001).

[19] See "Sioux Valley Organized Healthcare Arrangement Entities" for a list as of 2003.

Chapter 23: Communications, *Ron Robinson (pgs. 451-482)*

[1]In John McClelland, "Lewis and Clark: They were not legends in their own time," *Columbia Magazine,* Summer 1987, Washington State Historical Society [online database]; available at (http://www.wshs.org/lewisandclark/notlegends.htm); Internet; accessed June 25, 2003.

[2]United States Postal Service, Significant dates in postal history, *History of the Postal Service 1775-1993* [online database]; available at http://www.usps.com/history/history/ his1.htm#DATES); Internet; accessed July 15, 2003.

[3]Bruce C. Cooper, "Postal History of the First Transcontinental Railroad," in *Central Pacific Railroad Photographic History Museum* [online database]; available from http://www.cprr.org/Museum/Ephemera/Postal.html; Internet; accessed August 22, 2003.

[4] "The Postal Role in U.S. Development," *History of the Postal Service 1775-1993* [online database] available from http://www.usps.com/history/his2.htm#ROLE; Internet; accessed August 18, 2003.

[5]"Inventions of Wellington," *The History of Wellington, Ohio* [online database]; available from http://www.wellingtonohio.net/history.html; Internet; accessed August 18, 2003.

[6]Herbert Krause and Gary D. Olson, *Prelude to Glory: A Newspaper Accounting of Custer's 1874 Expedition to the Black Hills* (Sioux Falls, SD: Brevet Press, 1974), 92.

[7]Ibid., 93.

[8]Ibid., passim.

[9]Robert F. Karolevitz, *From Quill to Computer: The Story of America's Community Newspapers* (USA.: privately printed, 1985), 74.

[10]Robert F. Karolevitz, *With a Shirt Tail Full of Type: The Story of Newspapering in South Dakota* (Freeman, SD: South Dakota Press Association, 1982), 5-6.

[11]Ibid., 18.

[12]Ibid., 22.

[13]Ibid.

[14]Gary D. Olson and Erik L. Olson, *Sioux Falls, South Dakota: A Pictorial History* (Norfolk, VA: Donning Co., 1985), 24.

[15]Laura Allen, "Deadwood, SD: A Brief History," SDPB.org Webcam Locations [online database]; available at www.sdpb.org/DakotaCast/webcam/deadwood.htm; Internet; accessed July 15, 2003.

[16]Doane Robinson, *History of South Dakota,* 2 vols. (Chicago: B.F. Bowen & Co., 1904), 1: 481.

[17]Steve Schoenherr, "Recording Technology History," *History at University of San Diego* [online database]; available at http://history.sandiego.edu/gen/recording/notes.html 3/04/03; Internet; accessed September 2, 2003.

[18]Robert F. Karolevitz, "*The Press & Dakotan*: A Living History," *History of Yankton, South Dakota* [online database]; available at http://www.yankton.net/stories/091599/bus_pressdak.html; Internet; accessed July 15, 2003.

[20]Karolevitz, *From Quill to Computer*, 66.

[21] In Charlotte D. Jones, "The Penny Press and the Origins of Journalistic Objectivity: the Problem of Authority in Liberal America" (unpublished dissertation, 1985); available at http://etd.lsu.edu:8085/docs/available/etd-1114101-191429/unrestricted/04The sischapter5.pdf; Internet; accessed July 17, 2003.

[22]Karolevitz, *With A Shirt Tail Full of Type*, 37.

[23]Ibid., 53.

[24]Krause, 97.

[25]Ibid., 25.

[26]Ibid., 137.

[27]Karolevitz, *From Quill to Computer*, 72-73.

[28]Ibid., 84.

[29]Robinson, quoted in Lynwood E. Oyos, ed., *Over a Century of Leadership: South Dakota Territorial and State Governors, 1861-1987,* (Sioux Falls, SD: Center for Western Studies, 1987), 39.

[30]Oyos, 38.

[31]Robinson, quoted in Oyos, 35.

[32]Samuel Clemens, "From My Unpublished Autobiography" in *Harper's Weekly,* March 18, 1905, reprinted in *The $30,000 Bequest and Other Stories* (New York: Harper & Brothers, 1906), quoted in *First Writing Machines*, Chapter 1 [online database]; available at http://www.worldwideschool.org/library/books/lit/ marktwain/TheFirstWritingMachines/Chap1.html; Internet; accessed August 2, 2003.

[33]Mitchell Wilson, *American Science and Invention: A Pictorial History* (New York: Bonanza Books, 1954), 253-54.

[34]Karolevitz, *From Quill to Computer*, 99.

[35]Ibid., 100.

[36]Karolevitz, *With a Shirt Tail Full of Type*, 45.

[37]*Encyclopedia Britannica*, Concise [online database]; available at http://concise.britannica.com/ebc/article?eu =392491; Internet; accesed August 20, 2003.

[38]R. A. Nelson, K. M. Lovitt, eds., "History of Teletype Development," October 1963, Teletype Corporation [online database]; available at http://www.thocp.net/hardware/history_of_ teletype_development_.htm; Internet; accessed August 23, 2003.

[39]*History of the AP*, "The Next Fifty Years" [online database]; available at http.//www.ap.org/anniversary/nhistory /next50.html; Internet; accessed August 23, 2003.

[40]Kenneth Stewart and John Tebbel, *Makers of Modern Journalism* (New York: Prentice Hall, 1952), 108-09.

[41]Karolevitz, *With a Shirt Tail Full of Type*, 45.

[42]Stewart and Tebbel, 313.

[43]L. Frank Baum, *Aberdeen Saturday Pioneer*, January 3, 1891.

[44]Henry M. Littlefield, "The Wizard of Oz: Parable on Populism," *American Quarterly* 16 (1964): 47-58.

[45]Wayne Fanebust, *Where the Sioux River Bends: A Newspaper Chronicle* (Sioux Falls, SD: Minnehaha County Historical Society, 1985), 329-44.

[46]Karolevitz, *With a Shirt Tail Full of Type*, 36.

[47]Ibid., 36.

[48]Herbert S. Schell, *History of South Dakota* (Lincoln: University of Nebraska Press, 1968), 239.

[49]Oyos, 68.

[50]Stewart and Tebbel, 111.

[51]Schell, 239.

[52]Fanebust, 382.

[53]Karolevitz, *With a Shirt Tail Full of Type*, 42-43.

[54]Gerald Mast and Bruce F. Kawin, *A Short History of the Movies*, 6th ed. (Boston: Allen and Bacon, 1996), chapters 2-4, passim.

[55]Charles Rambow, "Ku Klux Klan in the 1920s: A Concentration on the Black Hills," *South Dakota History* 3 (Winter 1973): 63-81.

[56]Olson, 124.

[57]Betti C. VanEpps-Taylor, *Oscar Micheaux: Dakota Homesteader, Author, Pioneer Film Maker* (Rapid City, SD: Dakota West Books), chapters 2-8.

[58]Oyos, 100.

[59]Roberts County Telephone Cooperative Association, *Our History* [online database]; available at http.//www.rctca.net/ progress.html; Internet; accessed 29 August 29, 2003.

[60]Lynwood E. Oyos, *The Family Farmers' Advocate: South Dakota Farmers Union, 1914-2000* (Sioux Falls, SD: Center for Western Studies, 2000), 202.

[61]*History of the AP*, "The Next Fifty Years."

[62]Schoenherr.

[63]United States Postal Service.

[64]Karolevitz, *With a Shirt Tale Full of Type*, 52.

[65]Ibid.

[66]Ibid., 53-56.

[67]Ibid., 68.

[68]Ibid., 21, 46.

[69]Ibid., 47.

[70]Dick Neish, "Early Broadcasting in Sioux Falls, South Dakota, 1922-1952," TMs, Siouxland Libraries, Sioux Falls, SD, 1953, appendix 1.

[71]Ibid., 6.

[72]Reynold M. Wik, "Radio in the 1920s: A Social Force in South Dakota," *South Dakota History* 11 (Spring 1981): 98-99.

[73]Robert F. Karolevitz, "Station WNAX: the Beginning Years" in Wynne Speece with M. Jill Karolevitz, *The Best of the Neighbor Lady* (Mission Hill, SD: Dakota Homestead Publishers, 1987), 11.

[74]Neish, 15, 18.

[75]Ibid., 21.

[76]Ibid., 23.

[77]Ibid., 21.

[78]*Social Security Online-History*, "Father Charles E. Coughlin" [online database]; available at http://www.ssa.gov/history/cough.html; Internet; accessed September 8, 2003.

[79]*Social Security Online-History*, "Brief History of Huey Long" [online database]; available at http://www.ssa.gov/history/hlong1.html; Internet; accessed September 8, 2003.

[80]Karolevitz, "Station WNAX: the Beginning Years," 11.

[81]Ibid., 24.

[82]Neish, 24.

[83]Ibid., 23.

[84]Ibid., 31.

[85]Kelly Hertz, "Wynn Speece Leaves Her Mark On Radio History," *Yankton Press and Dakotan*, posted September 14, 1999 on Press & Dakotan-Century Edition [online database]; available at www.yankton.net/stories/091499/bus_0901990005.html; Internet; accessed August 7, 2003.

[86]Irving Fang, *Timeline of Communications History* [online database]; available at http://www.mediahistory.umn.edu/time/; Internet; accessed September 8, 2003.

[87]Neish, 16.

[88]Karolevitz, *With a Shirt Tail Full of Type*, 37.

[89]Ibid., 56.

[90]Ibid., 58.

[91]History of AP Photos, *AP History* [online database]; available at http://www.ap.org/pages/history/photos.htm; Internet; accessed September 9, 2003.

[92]Karolevitz, *With a Shirt Tail Ful of Type*, 61-62.

[93]Ibid., 58.

[94]Mast and Kawin, 205-206.

[95]Amateur films, *Ivan Besse collection: Britton, South Dakota 1938-39* [online database]; available at http://www.archive.org/movies/movieslisting-browse.php?collection=prelinger& cat=Home%20movies; Internet; accessed September 2, 2003.

[96]*John (Jack) T. Mullin (1913-99) Recalls the American Development of the Tape Recorder* [online database]; available at http://www.kcmetro.cc.mo.us/pennvalley/biology/ lewis/crosby/mullin.htm; Internet; accessed September 4, 2003.

[97]Ibid.

[98]Vince Horiuchi, "Mormon Farm Boy: Inventor of Television," *Salt Lake Tribune*, March 20, 2000 [online database]; available at http://www.adherents.com/misc/ philo_farnsworth.html; Internet; accessed September 8, 2003.

[99]Federal Communications Commission-History, *Golden Age, 1930's through 1950's* [online database]; available at http://www.fcc.gov/omd/history/1930-1959.html; Internet; accessed September 9, 2003.

[100]Fang.

[101]Brenda Wade, "'Guy with the cigar' brought TV to SD" in *The Argus Leader South Dakota 99* (Sioux Falls, SD: Ex Machina Publishing Co., 1989), 450-52.

[102]Dave Dedrick, *It Ain't All Cartoons: Memoirs of The Captain* (Huron, SD: East Eagle Co., 1989), 56-57.

[103]Ibid., 58-60.

[104]Ibid., 66-67.

[105]Wade, 250.

[106]KELOLAND.com, *Our History* [online database]; available at http://www.keloland.com/OurHistory/Index.cfm; Internet; accessed September 9, 2003.

[107]Dedrick, 75.

[108]KELOLAND.com, *Our History*.

[109]Jeff Miller, *U.S. and Canadian TV stations as of 1958, Media History* [online database]; available at http://members. aol.com/jeff560/1958tv.html; Internet; accessed September 9, 2003.

[110]Fang.

[111]Karolevitz, *With a Shirt Tail Full of Type*, 64.

[112]Peter Prichard, *The Making of McPaper: The Inside Story of USA Today* (Kansas City, New York: Andrews, McMeel and Parker, 1987), 29-44.

[113]Karolevitz, *With a Shirt Tail Full of Type*, 64.

[114]Andrew Hodges, "Part Three: The Turing Machine," *Alan Turing: A Short Biography* [online database]; available at http://www.turing.org.uk/bio/part3.html; accessed August 23, 2003.

[115]*Eugene Amdahl's Bio* [online database]; available at http://actscorp.com/acts/amdahl.htm; Internet; accessed August 24, 2003.

[116]Gateway Computers, "Company Background," [online database]; available at http://www.gateway.com/about/ news_info/company_background.shtml); Internet; accessed September 9, 2003.

[117]Rob Swenson, "Calif. town wins out over return to S.D.," *Sioux Falls Argus Leader*, May 19, 2002, ArgusLeader.com [online database]; available at http://www.argusleader.com/specialsections/ 2002/gateway/Sundayarticle1.shtml; Internet; accessed September 9, 2003.

[118]MidcoNet.com [online database]; available at http://www.midcocomm.com/ midconet_about.php; Internet; accessed September 9, 2003.

[119]*Education Technology News* [online database]; available from http://www.odedodea.edu/instruction/support/tpo/docs/ 05_01%20BBN.doc; Internet; accessed September 10, 2003.

[120]South Dakota Board of Regents [online database]; available at http://www.sdbor.edu/jobopps/locations/locations. cfm#dsu); Internet; accessed September 10, 2003.

[121]Prichard, 93.

[122]Ibid., 139-57.

[123]FreedomForum.org, *About the Al Neuharth media center* [online database]; available at http://www.freedomforum.org/templates/document.asp?documentID=13147; Internet; accessed September 12, 2003.

[124]Connie Piper, "Zitkala Sa: Keeper and Maker of Myth" [online database]; available at http://www.burwell.k12.ne.us/ piper/ZitkalaSa.html; Internet; accessed September 12, 2003.

[125]*Lakota Journal*, About Lakota Journal [online database]; available at http://www.lakotajournal.com/about.htm; Internet; accessed September 12, 2003.

[126]NativePubs.com, *Biography of Tim Giago* [online database]; available at http://www.nativepubs.com/nativepubs/ Apps/bios/0166GiagoTim; Internet; accessed September 12, 2003.

[127]FCC, Sen. Larry Pressler, "Telecom Reform: It Ain't Over 'Til It's Over," reprinted from *Roll Call*, March 11, 1996 [online database]; available from www.fcc.gov/cgb/dro/comments/99360/5006314191.txt; Internet; accessed September 14, 2003.

[128]Press Release Senate Commerce Committee [online database]; availble at www.senate.gov/~commerce/press/106-57.htm; Internet; accessed September 14, 2003.

[129]Mark Wigfield, "Supporters of FCC Media Rules Admit Likely Senate Defeat," *Dow Jones Newswires*, September 12, 2003 [online database]; available at http://sg.biz.yahoo.com/ 030911/15/3e430.html; Internet; accessed September 14, 2003.

[130]AOL Time Warner [online database]; available at http://www.aoltimewarner.com/corporate_information/index.adp; Internet; accessed September 15, 2003.

[131]Center for Public Integrity [online database]; available at www.openairwaves.org/telecom/analysis/default.aspx? action=org&ID=8028); Internet; accessed September 15, 2003.

[132]Ibid.

[133]Viacom [online database]; available at http://www.viacom.com/thefacts.tin; Internet; accessed September 16, 2003.

[134]Center for Public Integrity.

[135]Ibid.

[136]Ibid.

[137]BandRadio.com [online database] available at http://band radio.com/radio/?mode=state& st&st=SD; Internet; accessed September 20, 2003.

[138]TVRadio World [online database]; available at http:// www.tvradioworld.com/region1/sd/digital_television.asp; Internet; accessed September 20, 2003.

[139]Readership Institute, *Consumers Media and U.S. Newspapers* [online database]; available at http://readership. org/consumers/data/consumersmedianewspapers.pdf; Internet; accessed September 20, 2003.

[140]CNN, "Cell phone signal leads rescuers to stranded woman," January 10, 1997 [online database]; available at http://www.cnn.com/WEATHER/9701/ 10/missing.woman/; Internet; accessed September 20, 2003.

[141]John-John Williams IV, "I-29 stalker to spend 140 more days in jail," *Sioux Falls Argus Leader,* September 19, 2003 [online database] available at http://www.argusleader.com/news/Fridayarticle4.shtml; Internet; accessed September 20, 2003.

[142]Jimmy Moore, "Polls Find Americans Believe Hussein Linked to 9/11, Support War in Iraq," *Talon News*, September 8, 2003 [online database]; available at http://www.gopusa.com/ news/2003/september/0908_hussein_911. shtml; Internet; accessed September 20, 2003.

[143]Registration Voter Turnout Statistics 1988-2002 [online database]; available at www.state.sd.us/sos/ elections/; Internet; accessed September 20, 2003.

[144]Cool Hand Luke [online database]; available at http://www.destgulch.com/movies/luke/; Internet; accessed September 20, 2003.

Chapter 24: Transportation and Tourism, *Rex Myers (pgs. 483-498)*

[1] Robert V. Hine and John Mack Faragher, *The American West* (New Haven: Yale University Press, 2000), discuss the 1680 Pueblo revolt and the impact horses had on plains natives.

[2] The source for all references to the Lewis and Clark Expedition in this section is Gary E. Moulton, ed., *The Journals of the Lewis and Clark Expedition,* 13 vols. (Lincoln:University of Nebraska Press, 1983-2001).

[3] Useful to understand the steamboat era on the Missouri are William A. Lass, *A History of Steamboating on the Upper Missouri River* (Lincoln: University of Nebraska Press, 1962), and Jerome E. Petsche, *The Steamboat Bertrand* (Washington, D.C.: National Park Service, 1974).

[4] For information on federal wagon roads, see W. Turrentine Jackson, *Wagon Roads West: A Study of Federal Road Surveys and Construction in the Trans-Mississippi West, 1846-1869* (New Haven: Yale University Press, 1964).

[5] Herbert S. Schell's *History of South Dakota* (Lincoln: University of Nebraska Press, 1961) has an excellent discussion of freighting in early South Dakota.

[6] Railroads in South Dakota have attracted much attention both for their romantic appeal and their economic impact beginning with the Dakota Boom. All general histories of the state deal with them at length, and each railroad has at least one book devoted to its history. See Rick W. Mills, *Railroading in the Land of Infinite Variety* (Hermosa, SD: Battle Creek Publishing Co., 1990) and Mark Hufstetler and Michael Bedeau, *South Dakota Railroads: An Historic Context* (Pierre: South Dakota State Historic Preservation Office, 1998).

[7] Chicago and North Western advertising flyer, distributed outside South Dakota to encourage immigration. See also Sig Mickelson, *The Northern Pacific Railroad and the Selling of the West: A Nineteenth-century Public Relations Venture* (Sioux Falls, SD: Center for Western Studies, 1993).

[8] Sioux Falls' growth is chronicled in Gary D. Olson and Erik L. Olson, *Sioux Falls, South Dakota: A Pictorial History* (Norfolk, VA: Donning Company, 1985). Mention of Pierre street railways appears in Harold H. Schuler's *A Bridge Apart: History of Early Pierre and Fort Pierre* (Pierre: State Publishing Company, 1987).

[9] Less romanticism attaches to internal combustion transportation than to railroads. John E. Miller's *Looking for History on Highway 14* (Ames: Iowa State University Press, 1993), follows that highway, but broadens the context. R.L. Beatty, *The Truck and Bus Industries in South Dakota,* Business Research Bureau Bulletin 42 (Vermillion: University of South Dakota, 1955), is also helpful.

[10] 1922 South Dakota State Highway map.

[11]Information supplied by author Harold H. Schuler, former assistant to U.S. Senator Francis Case. See also South Dakota Department of Transportation Web site (www.sddot.com).

[12] Airplane travel gets less historic attention than autos, but early developments are well-chronicled in V.E. Montgomery, *South Dakota Aviation,* Business Research Bureau Bulletin 36 (Vermillion: University of South Dakota, 1956).

[13] John Bradbury, *Travels in the Interior of America* (Ann Arbor: University Microfilms, Inc., 1966).

[14] Henry Marie Brackenridge, *Views of Louisiana* (Ann Arbor: University Microfilms, Inc., 1966).

[15] W. G. Bek, trans., "First Journey to North America in the Years 1822 to 1824, by Paul, Prince of Wurttembeg," *South Dakota Historical Collections* 19 (Pierre: State Historical Society, 1938).

[16] George Catlin, *North American Indians* (Edinburgh: J. Grant, 1926).

[17] Bodmer and Maximilian have attracted attention from many scholars and art historians. See Maximilian of Wied-Neuwied, *Travels in the Interior of North America* (New York: Dutton, 1976) and David C. Hunt, et al., *Karl Bodmer's America* (Lincoln: University of Nebraska Press, 1984).

[18] Like Bodmer, Audubon's work remains popular, with reproductions of his bird and animal prints common. See James J. Audubon, *The Narratives and Experiences of John James Audubon,* David Culross Peattie, ed. (Boston: Houghton Mifflin Co., 1940).

[19] Eugene de Girardin, *Le Tour du Monde, 1864;* http://projectgirardin.free.fr/BADLANDS2-5.html; Internet; accessed August 20, 2003.

[20] See the National Park Service Web site: http://www.nps.gov/wica.

[21] The Corn Palace, too, has a Web site: http://www.cornpalace.org.

[22] Edward Raventon, *A Piece of Paradise: A Story of Custer State Park* (Helena, MT: Falcon Press, 1996).

[23] As South Dakota's ultimate tourist destination and license plate decoration, Mount Rushmore has attracted and continues to garner much attention. Start with the Web site http://www.nps.gov/moru. Also useful are Gilbert C. Fite, *Mount Rushmore* (Norman: University of Oklahoma Press, 1952), and Rex Allen Smith, *The Carving of Mount Rushmore* (New York: Abbeville Press, 1985).

[24] Again, the National Park Service provides help: http://www.nps.gov/badl.

[25] Robb DeWall, ed., *Korczak, Storyteller in Stone,* rev. ed. (Crazy Horse, SD: Korczak's Heritage, Inc., 1996).

[26] See the South Dakota State Parks Web site: http://www.sdgfp.info /Parks.

[27] South Dakota Writers Project, Works Progress Administration, *Fifty Million Pheasants* (Pierre: South Dakota Dept. of Game and Fish, 1941).

[28] South Dakota Game, Fish and Parks Dept., Sioux Falls Office.

[29] John R. Ferrell, *Big Dam Era* (Omaha, NE: U.S. Army Corps of Engineers, 1993).

[30] South Dakota Legislative Research Council, *Economic and Fiscal Impacts of the South Dakota Gambling Industry* (Pierre: South Dakota Legislative Research Council, 1998).

[31] South Dakota Department of Tourism, *Report 2001* (Pierre: South Dakota Dept. of Tourism, 2001).

[32] Empire Mall Public Relations Office, 2003.

[33] *Directory of South Dakota Museums and Galleries* (Chamberlain, SD: Association of South Dakota Museums, Inc., 2004). The *Directory* offers "a complete listing of museums, art galleries, interpretive centers, historic sites, zoos, botanical gardens and other cultural facilities," totaling more than 170 entries.

Chapter 25: Tiyospaye: A Traditional Sioux Family Today, *Virginia Driving Hawk Sneve* **(pgs. 499-506)**

[1] Virginia Driving Hawk Sneve, *Completing the Circle* (Lincoln: University of Nebraska Press, 1995), 37.

[2] Ibid., 7, 9.

[3] Ibid., 12.

[4] Ibid., 20.

[5] Ibid., 10.

[6] Ibid., 42.

[7] Ibid., 20.

[8] Ibid., 22.

[9] Ibid., 24.

[10] Ibid.

[11] Ibid.

[12] Ibid., 25.

[13] Ibid.

[14] Ibid.

[15] Ibid.

[16] Virginia Driving Hawk Sneve, *That They May Have Life: The Episcopal Church in South Dakota, 1859-1976* (New York: Seabury Press, 1977), 3.

[17] Sneve, *Completing*, 64.

[18] Ibid., 41.

[19] Sneve, *That They May Have Life*, 15. The name was changed to Brotherhood of Christian Unity (BCU) in 1883.

[20] Ibid., 97.

[21] Virginia Driving Hawk Sneve, "Children of the Circle: Life Experiences of Nineteenth Century Indian Children," in *Growing Up in Siouxland*, ed. Arthur R. Huseboe and Sandra Looney (Sioux Falls, SD: Nordland Heritage Foundation, Augustana College, 1989), 14.

[22] Sneve, "Children," 14, 15.

[23] Ibid., 17.

[24] Ibid.

[25] Ibid.

[26] Delphine Red Shirt, *Bead On an Anthill: A Lakota Childhood* (Lincoln: University of Nebraska Press, 1998), 25.

[27] Kathleen Ann Pickering, *Lakota Culture, World Economy* (Lincoln: University of Nebraska Press, 2000), 12.

[28] Robert A. White, "The Lower-Class 'Culture of Excitement' Among the Contemporary Sioux," *The Modern Sioux: Social Systems and Reservations Culture*, ed. Ethel Nurge (Lincoln: University of Nebraska Press, 1970), 182. See also Robert G. Raymond, *Scouting, Cavorting, and other World War II Memories: A Young Sioux Indian Lad's Memories of World War II* (Billings, MT: Robert G. Raymond, 1994), 14.

[29] White.

[30] Raymond, 158.

[31] White, 183.

[32] Pickering, 29.

[33] Roberta Fitzsimmons, Stockton, California, e-mail to Virginia Driving Hawk Sneve, December 21, 2002.

Chapter 26: Modern Tribes, *Herbert T. Hoover (pgs. 507-533)*

[1] *Sioux Falls Argus Leader*, December 2, 2001.

[2] Michael Scarmon, interviewed by Herbert T. Hoover, July 20, 2003, Herbert T. Hoover Collection, I. D. Weeks Library, University of South Dakota, Vermillion, SD.

[3] *Volante*, October 18, 2000.

[4] Stephen Cournoyer, Jr., interviewed by Herbert T. Hoover, June 17, 2003, Herbert T. Hoover Collection, I. D. Weeks Library, University of South Dakota, Vermillion, SD.

[5] In the case *Lone Wolf vs. Hitchcock* (1903) the Supreme Court of the United States ruled about a confrontation involving Kiowa Indians that when "treaties were entered into between the United States and a tribe of Indians it was never doubted that the power to abrogate existed in Congress." Only when dealing with the Black Hills has Congress taken action to abrogate terms of a treaty pertaining to Sioux Country. On some occasions, such as in the disestablishment of the outer boundaries of the Yankton Reservation, federal judges have exercised this questionable liberty.

[6] *Administrative Procedure Act, Statutes at Large*, 1: 469 ff.

[7] That ten percent of the resident population of South Dakota in the year 2003 was constituted by federally recognized tribes seems to be a plausible estimate, which represents great variations in census figures, Bureau of Indian Affairs statistics, and tribal reports. The latter reports change from day to day and must take into account that on average only about one half of the enrolled members in a tribe live on its reservation. For example in the year 2003, 39,734 were enrolled at Pine Ridge and 20,806 were reservation residents; some 30,000 were enrolled at Rosebud and 14,304 were reservation residents; 7,148 were enrolled at Yankton and about half were reservation residents; 2,355 were enrolled at Lower Brûlé and 1,237 were reservation residents. See *Lakota Journal*, May 16-23, 2003. Among the non-resident members, an estimated 10,000 live in Rapid City and perhaps 3,000 live in Sioux Falls. It seems reasonable to suppose that approximately 75,000 members of the federally recognized tribes actually live in South Dakota.

[8] Father Luis Mesa, Guadalupe Parish, interviewed by Carol Hoover, July 22, 2003.

[9] Original documentation supports information contained in Herbert T. Hoover, "The Sioux Agreement of 1889 and Its Aftermath," *South Dakota History* 19 (Spring 1989): 68.

[10] Although a generic plan for the installation of landed capitalism among tribes appeared in the Dawes Severalty (Allotment) Act of 1887, indicating parcels of 160 acres as the size of non-Indian homesteads, legal authority for allotment across Sioux Country came from treaties and other statutes more than from the Dawes Act itself.

[11] Herbert J. Hoover and Carol Goss Hoover, *Sioux Country: A History of Indian-white Relations* (Sioux Falls, SD: Center for Western Studies, 2000), 134.

[12] James Legg, "A History of Native American Housing Types and Funding on Selected Reservations: Yankton, Rosebud, Pine Ridge, Crow Creek, and Lower Brûlé" (M.A. thesis, University of South Dakota, 1998).

[13] Ramona O'Connor, interviewed by Herbert T. Hoover, June 17, 2003, Herbert T. Hoover Collection, I. D. Weeks Library, University of South Dakota, Vermillion, SD.

[14] Bruce Johnson, interviewed by Herbert T. Hoover, July 28, 1999, Herbert T. Hoover Collection, I. D. Weeks Library, University of South Dakota, Vermillion, SD, explains recent changes. Mr. Johnson worked as an Indian Health Service official in the Aberdeen Area Office of the IHS, 1972-1993.

[15] The article "Urban Indians file suit for benefits and voting rights," *Lakota Journal,* May 17-24, 2002, initiated by Sidney Whitesell of the Standing Rock Sioux Tribe, represented a desire shared by countless tribal members living in non-Indian urban centers.

[16] Hoover, "The Sioux Agreement of 1889 and Its Aftermath," 91-92.

[17] Loren Carlson, *Government of South Dakota* (Vermillion: University of South Dakota, 2002), 8-9.

[18] The Indian Reorganization (Wheeler-Howard) Act of 1934 stands as a legal benchmark that encouraged survival and improvement in tribal constitutional government, terminated the allotment of land, and included Indian Preference as a congressional mandate plus the offer of maximum access to federal economic programs. Acceptance or rejection of this plan was wholly voluntary. To become a full-fledged "Wheeler-Howard tribe," majorities of the members were to cast three votes in Wheeler-Howard elections. The only tribe in South Dakota that rejected the change was the Yankton, which continues to govern under terms in its 1932 constitution and bylaws, substantially revised in 1963 and subsequently changed by constitutional amendments. According to Judge Michael Scarmon, the main deficiency in the Yankton and in other tribal constitutional systems is the absence of formal legal codes to define standards of behavior and opportunity in the tribes.

[19] Rose Mary Rouse, interviewed by Herbert T. Hoover, June 17-18, 2003, Herbert T. Hoover Collection, I. D. Weeks Library, University of South Dakota, Vermillion, SD.

[20] *Lakota Journal*, November 16-22, 2001.

[21] *Sioux Falls Argus Leader*, December 2, 2001.

Chapter 27: South Dakota in the Twenty-first Century, *Michael J. Mullin (pgs. 534-557)*

[1] Frederick Jackson Turner, "The Significance of the Frontier in American History," *Annual Report of the American Historical Association* (Washington, D.C.: Government Printing Office, 1894): 199-227.

[2] Ibid., 199.

[3] Ibid., 227.

[4] Ibid., 200.

[5] David T. Herbert, "Introduction: Geographical Perspectives and Urban Problems," in *Social Problems and the City: Geographical Perspectives,* ed. David T. Herbert and David M. Smith (Oxford: Oxford University Press, 1979), 1.

[6] Richard Etulain, "The Frontier and American Exceptionalism," in *Does the Frontier Experience Make America Exceptional?*, ed. Richard Etulain (Boston, MA: Bedford/St. Martin's, 1999), 9-11.

[7] Turner, 215.

[8] The 1920 U.S. Census reported that America became a more urban than rural nation for the first time. See Paul S. Boyer, et al., *The Enduring Vision: A History of the American People*, 5th ed. (Boston: Houghton Mifflin Company, 2004), 720 and graph 23.2, 713.

[9] Laurent Belsie, "Sioux returning to the Plains," *Christian Science Monitor*, February 20, 2003; for the definition of a "wilderness" or "frontier" county, see http://www.frontierus.org/2000counties0.html.

[10] Turner, 18.

[11] Linda M.Hasselstrom, *Seems Like Far* (New York: Lyons Press, 1999), 212-17; Ann Daum, *The Prairie in Her Eyes* (Minneapolis: Milkweed Editions, 2001), 3-5.

[12] Lawrence Brown, *Buffalo Commons: Memoirs* (Bowman, ND: The Grapevine, 1995), 12.

[13] See http://www.state.sd.us/news/issues/19.pdf; Internet.

[14] James Satterlee made the claim in "Rural prediction: fewer babies," *Sioux Falls Argus Leader*, September 8, 2001; http://www.argusleader.com/census/2000/families06.shtml; Internet. One reason for

Satterlee's pessimism lies in the demographics of the state. Twenty-seven percent of the state's population is under the age of 17, while 35 percent of the population is above 45 years old. Demographically speaking, there are not enough young people to replace those who will die in the future. The state has double the percent of people 65 and older than it does four and under. See http://www.sdgreatprofits.com/SD_Profile/demographics.htm; Internet.

[15] See Chapter 14 in this publication, 255-87.

[16] Joel Garreau, *The Nine Nations of North America* (Boston: Houghton Mifflin Company, 1981), 337-38.

[17] Garreau, 338.

[18] See http:///www.state.sd.us/news/issues/19.pdf, pp. 10-11; Internet.

[19] Counties along the I-29 corridor saw their population grow by 15.8 percent between 1990 and 2000; as a whole, West River counties grew 7.4 percent, but most of that growth was driven by growth in the Black Hills counties and Indian reservation counties. See http:///www.state.sd.us/news/issues/19.pdf, 12-15; Internet.

[20] Keith Mueller, "Toward a Place-Based Rural Policy: the Current U.S. Experience," paper presented at the International Rural Network Conference, Inverness, Scottish Highlands, U.K., June 27, 2003, 21. Talk accessed at http://www.rupri.org/ruralPolicy/presentations/mueller062703.pdf; Internet; accessed April 28, 2004.

[21] See http://www.sdgreatprofits.com/SD_Profile/demographics.htm; Internet; South Dakota has 51.2 percent of its residents living in urban settings and 48.8 percent in rural areas.

[22] Charles J. Bicak raised this question in his "The Rigors of Existence on the Great Plains: The Role of Water," in *Water on the Great Plains: Issues and Politics,* ed. Peter J. Longo and David W. Yoskowitz, (Lubbock, TX: Texas Tech University Press, 2002), 13.

[23] Kim Ode, "Plains culture adds virtues and values to American Identity," Listening to the Land, A Special Report in *Minneapolis Star Tribune*, December 19, 1993, 8.

[24] Shebby Lee, "Traveling the Sunshine State: The Growth of Tourism in South Dakota, 1914-1939," *South Dakota History* 19 (Summer 1989): 194.

[25] This number excludes articles that begin their analysis in the pre-1940 period and continue forward. It also omits the special issue on *The Wizard of Oz*, which contained references to contemporary interpretations of the story, but were focused on the historical placement of the story. A number of articles focus on World War II, and some continue into the 1950s, but only five deal with the post-1960 period as a discrete subject matter. The five articles are Ruth Ann Alexander, "South Dakota Women Stake a Claim: A Feminist Memoir, 1964-1989," *South Dakota History* 19 (Winter 1989): 538-55; James D. McLaird, "From Bib Overalls to Cowboy Boots: East River/West River Differences in South Dakota," *South Dakota History* 19 (Winter 1989): 454-91; Charles L. Garrettson III, "Home of the Politics of Joy: Hubert H. Humphrey in South Dakota," *South Dakota History* 20 (Fall 1990): 165-84; Daryl Webb, "Crusade: George McGovern's Opposition to the Vietnam War," *South Dakota History* 28 (Fall 1998): 161-90; and Akin D. Reinhardt, "Spontaneous Combustion: Prelude to Wounded Knee 1973," *South Dakota History* 29 (Fall 1999): 224-44.

[26] Randell Beck, "Too much nostalgia can stop us from embracing growth," *Sioux Falls Argus Leader*, June 23, 2002, 12B, col. 2.

[27] Garreau, 344; another example of this experience is Harry F. Thompson, et al., eds., *A Common Land, A Diverse People: Ethnic Identity on the Prairie Plains* (Sioux Falls, SD: Nordland Heritage Foundation, 1986), 1-8.

[28] Gary D. Olson and Erik L. Olson. *Sioux Falls, South Dakota: A Pictorial History* (Norfolk, VA: Donning Company, 2003), 200.

[29] Corrine Olson, "Minority populations rise in Sioux Falls, state," *Sioux Falls Argus Leader*, March 11, 2001, 9A.

[30] KELO Television, 5:00 pm news, January 14, 2004.

[31] Brenda Wade Schmidt, "Memo Shows Morrell Plan for Hispanics," *Sioux Falls Argus Leader*, September 5, 1990, 1D, col. 6.

[32] KELO Television, "Good Morning Kelo-Land," February 25, 2004. Segment section on "Asia Day."

[33] This figures comes from a county-by-county analysis of South Dakota provided by the U.S. Census Bureau at http://quickfacts.census.gov/qfd/states/; Internet.

[34] Laurent Belsie, "Sioux returning to the Plains," *Christian Science Monitor*, February 20, 2003, Gale Group, 1.

[35] Terry Woster, "Census finds rural exodus; reservations, cities grow," *Sioux Falls Argus Leader*, March 11, 2001, 1A.

[36] Terry Woster, "Working to amplify Indians' political clout," *Sioux Falls Argus Leader*, July 13, 2001, 1A.

[37] "Settle Tribal Land Issue," *Sioux Falls Argus Leader*, editorials, June 18, 2004.

[38] Joe Starita, *The Dull Knifes of Pine Ridge: A Lakota Odyssey* (New York: Berkeley Books, 1995), 158.

[39] Refugio I. Rochín, "Latinos on the Great Plains: An Overview," *Great Plains Research* 10 (Fall 2000): 245.

[40] Jay Kirschenmann, "Growers become more diverse," *Sioux Falls Argus Leader*, February 17, 2004, 6A. The U.S. Department of Agriculture recommended dividing agricultural production into four levels. The third level, "Tertiary," consists of enterprises that process "raw commodities; including livestock slaughter, canning, milling, etc." For the divisions, see *A Time to Act: A Report of the USDA National Commission on Small Farms* (Washington, D.C.: Government Printing Office, 1998): 48.

[41] In the last two years the State of South Dakota began offering an incentive program to foreign dairy farmers. The state will secure a green card for any foreign farmer who invests $600,000 and employs four people. In the last two years 20 foreign dairy farmers have re-located to South Dakota from Ireland, Holland, and England. See KELO Television, "Got Milk," *Eye on Keloland*, April 23, 2004; transcript at http://www. keloland.com/News/EyeonKELOLAND/ NewsDetail4790.cfm?Id=22,31497; Internet; accessed April 29, 2004 .

[42] Melanie Brandert, "Hispanic boom changes culture of small city," *Sioux Falls Argus Leader*, April 7, 2001; http://www.argusleader.com/census/2000/diversity02.shtml; Internet; accessed April 28, 2004.

[43] South Dakota Governor's Office of Economic Development Web page: http://www.sdgreatprofits. com/ SD_Profile/demographics.htm; Internet.

[44] Sioux Falls has seen Gateway drop from 1,850 to 300 employees, while North Sioux City, where the firm's manufacturing plants are, has dropped from over 6,000 employees in the mid-1990s to under 2,000 today. "Gateway to lay off 300 in South Dakota," *Sioux Falls Argus Leader*, May 13, 2004, 6c, col. 1.

[45] See "Demographic Profiles: South Dakota," http://www.state.sd.us/; Internet; accessed May 14, 2003.

[46] Kathleen Norris, *Dakota: A Spiritual Geography* (Boston: Houghton Mifflin Company, 1993), 64.

[47] Gilbert C. Fite, "The Great Plains: Promises, Problems, and Prospects," in *The Great Plains Environment and Culture,* ed. Brian W. Blouet and Frederick C. Luebke (Lincoln: University of Nebraska Press, 1979), 187.

[48] Howard R. Lamar, "Public Values and Private Dreams: South Dakota's Search for Identity, 1850-1900," *South Dakota History* 8 (Spring 1978): 140-41.

[49] Federal researchers recognized this pump-sponge dichotomy in 1936. See *The Future of the Great Plains* (Washington, D.C.: U.S. Government Printing Office, 1936), 60.

[50] The figures provided come from the U.S. Census data provided online via http://quickfacts.census. gov; Internet, for South Dakota. The comparison between humans and antelopes for Perkins and Harding Counties is implied in Brown, *Buffalo Commons: Memoirs*, 12; and mentioned specifically in Norris, 177.

[51] Garreau, 350.

[52] Brian Page, "Across the Great Divide: Agriculture and Industrial Geography," *Economic Geography* 72 (October 1996): 376.

[53] Daniel B. Suits, "Agriculture," in *The Structure of American Industry*, ed. Walter Adams, 8th ed., (New York: Macmillan Publishing Company, 1990), 1.

[54] See *A Time to Act*, Miscellaneous Publication 1545 (MP-1445): 10-11, "The Structure of Agriculture Today," http://www.reeusda.gov/smallfarm/report.htm; Internet; accessed February 15, 2004.

[55] For a summary of Powell's career, see George P. Merrill, "John Wesley Powell" in *Dictionary of American Biography*, ed. Dumas Malone, 20 vols. (New York: Charles Scribner's Sons, 1928-1936), 15: 146-48.

[56] John Wesley Powell, *Report on the Lands of the Arid Region of the United States, With a More Detailed Account of the Lands of Utah,* ed. Wallace Stegner (Cambridge: Belknap Press of Harvard, 1962), 32. Powell reiterates his call for farms to be of the same size on pages 35 and 40.

[57] *The Future of the Plains* (Washington, D.C.: U.S. Government Printing Office, 1936), 3.

[58] Fite, "The Great Plains: Promises, Problems, and Prospects," 190.

[59] Jennifer Oldstone-Moore to Michael J. Mullin, April 27, 2004. Dr. Oldstone-Moore, a Chinese specialist, obtained the information from the World Bank.

[60] Suits, 1.

[61] *The Future of the Plains,* 4.

[62] The federal government uses gross receipts of $250,000 as its standard measurement for family farms. The reason for this is, as the report states, farms this size are [normally] those "on which day-to-day labor and management are provided by the farmer and/or the farm family that owns the production or owns, leases, the productive assets." *A Time to Act,* 4.

[63] Ibid., 3.

[64] Ibid., 9.

[65] Ibid., 33.

[66] Kyle Winfield, "Tyson to pay $1.28 billion," *Sioux Falls Argus Leader,* February18, 2004, 6C. A federal judge overturned the jury decision in April 2004. See "Tyson beef verdict tossed out," *USA Today,* April 26, 2004, 1B, col. 1.

[67] *A Time to Act,* 34.

[68] Ibid., 43.

[69] South Dakota Public Radio Broadcast, News Report, "Presidential Primaries," February 18, 2004; http:///www.sdpb.org; Internet.

[70] Suits, 29.

[71] Ibid., 12.

[72] Daniel S. Licht, *Ecology and Economics of the Great Plains* (Lincoln: University of Nebraska Press, 1997), 110.

[73] Suits, 2.

[74] Brown, 55.

[75] See Chapter 13 in this publication, 225-54.

[76] Linda Lobao and Katherine Meyer, "Economic Decline, Gender, and Labor Flexibility in Family-Based Enterprises: Midwestern Farming in the 1980s," *Social Forces* 74 (December 1995): 582.

[77] Lobao and Meyer, 585. The figures given for seeking off-farm work are 38% for women and 23% for men.

[78] Ibid., 595.

[79] See Chapter 13 in this publication, 225-54; Center for Rural Affairs, Walthill, NE.

[80] Jay Kirschenmann, "Women take charge of farms," *Sioux Falls Argus Leader,* February 17, 2004.

[81] U.S. Department of Agriculture-State Data, "Women Principal Operators: Selected Farm Characteristics: 2002 and 1997," Table 48.

[82] Denise D. Tucker, "S.D. first in home-businesses," *Sioux Falls Argus Leader,* August 14, 2001.

[83] Laurent Belsie, "The Dwindling heartland: America's new frontier," *The Christian Science Monitor,* February 11, 2003, Gale Group, 1.

[84] Woster, "Census finds rural exodus."

[85] Gilbert C. Fite, "'The Only Thing Worth Working For': Land and Its Meaning for Pioneer Dakotans," *South Dakota History* 15 (Spring/Summer 1985): 4.

[86] Three-quarters of all farms having annual sales of under $50,000 "do not generate enough sales to be commercially viable on their own." Nearly 86 percent of all farmers in the next highest sales class, $51,000-$250,000, have a negative "average return on equity." *A Time to Act,* 10.

[87] Ibid., 15.

[88] Joyce Appleby, *Capitalism and a New Social Order: The Republican Vision of the 1790s* (New York: New York University Press, 1984), 73.

[89] Ibid., 86.

[90] Keith Mueller, "Toward a Place-Based Rural Policy: The Current U.S. Experience," talk given June 27, 2003, Inverness, Scottish Highlands, U.K., 21; http://www.rupri.org/ruralPolicy/presentations/mueller062703.pdf; Internet; accessed April 28, 2004.

[91] Page, 378.

[92] "Brazil sees beef sales to Asia up after US mad cow," *Reuters*; http://www.agriculture.com/worldwide/IDS/2004-02-12T170251Z_01_N12474403_ RTRIDST_0_FOOD-BRAZIL; Internet; accessed February 15, 2004.

[93] *A Time to Act*, 4.

[94] Ibid., 19.

[95] Ibid., 39.

[96] Ibid., 19.

[97] Center for Rural Affairs, "Rural Income Trends," news release, June 24, 2003; http://www.cfra.org/newsroom/newsrelease/Swept%20Away%20release.htm; Internet.

[98] See, for example, Anne Matthews. *Where the Buffalo Roam* (New York: Grove Weidenfeld, 1992), 6.

[99] Licht, 106-07; The U.S. government introduced the "wilderness" designation to the 1980 census. See http://www.frontierus.org; Internet.

[100] Senate Bill 602; Center for Rural Affairs, "Summary of New Homestead Bill," http://www.cfra.org/resources/summary_newhomesteadact.htm; Internet.

[101] See *Extended Stay Primary Care*, June 2000, http://www.frontiersus.org/rep_espc.html; Internet.

[102] "No Rural Child Left Behind: The Importance of Rural Education," Center for Rural Affairs, *Newsletter*, May 2003, 7; http://www.cfra.org/newsletter/2003_05.htm; Internet.

[103] John E. Miller, "Education in South Dakota since World War II: A Statistical Portrait," *South Dakota History* 33 (Spring 2003): 57.

[104] Rob Swenson, "More rural housing goes empty in S.D.," *Sioux Falls Argus Leader*, May 20, 2001; http://www.argusleader.com/census/2000/more02.shtml; Internet; accessed February 12, 2004.

[105] Swenson.

[106] Garreau, 331.

[107] Ibid., 332.

[108] Deborah Epstein Popper and Frank J. Popper, "The Great Plains From Dust to Dust: A daring proposal for dealing with an inevitable disaster," *Planning* 12 (December 1987): 12-18.

[109] Bret Wallach, "The Return of the Prairie," *Landscape*, 28: 3 (1985): 1-6, especially page 3, Wallach's homepage at Oklahoma University; Internet; accessed January 23, 2004.

[110] See, for example, Thomas D. Isern, "The Comedy of the Commons; or, My Life on the Post-Colonial Plains," *South Dakota History* 33 (Spring 2003): 64-79; Mary L. Umberger, "Casting the Buffalo Commons: A Rhetorical Analysis of Print Media Coverage of the Buffalo Commons Proposal for the Great Plains," *Great Plains Quarterly* 22 (Spring 2002): 99-114; Brown.

[111] Popper and Popper, 17.

[112] Ibid., 15.

[113] Ibid., 17.

[114] Paula M. Nelson, *The Prairie Winnows Out Its Own: The West River Country of South Dakota in the Years of the Depression and Dust* (Iowa City, IA: University of Iowa Press, 1996), 189-90, 200.

[115] Matthews, 54; Pete Letheby, "Grasslands, bison indeed may again dominate the Plains," *Denver Post*, August 10, 2003; LexisNexis, accessed February 6, 2004.

[116] Matthews, 74.

[117] Nelson, 163.

[118] Popper and Popper, 14.

[119] The acreage total comes from Licht, 93.

[120] Linda M. Hasselstrom, *Going Over East, Reflections of a Woman Rancher* (Golden, CO: Fulcrum Press, 1987), 93.

[121] Garreau, 337.

[122] Norris, 163-64.

[123] Mueller, 4.

[124] Garreau, 332.

[125] The Miner County Community Revitalization project aims to work "with the towns of Canova, Carthage, Fedora, and Howard. Miner County Community Revitalization seeks to build a stronger local economy, strengthen families, expand financial assets, create quality jobs, and build affordable housing options." See http://www.mccr.net. The Rural Learning Center, led by Dr. James Beddow, is not tied to a single county but tries to help small towns throughout the state identify their strengths, goals, and opportunities. Michael Knutson from Miner County Community Revitalization and Dr. James Beddow presented papers on what their organizations are doing at the Thirty-Sixth Annual Dakota Conference on Northern Plains History, Literature, Art, and Archaeology in Sioux Falls, South Dakota, on April 23, 2004.

[126] See, for example, Marvis Hogen, *Fifty Years on Main Street* (Kadoka, SD: self-published, 1996), 67; for politicians talking about the "brain drain" and policies designed to reverse the out-of-state exodus, see http://www.argusleader.com; Internet.

[127] Elvin Hatch, *Biography of a Small Town* (New York: Columbia University Press, 1979), 164-65.

[128] Reynold M. Wik, "Radio in the 1920s: A Social Force in South Dakota," *South Dakota History* 11 (Spring 1981): 101-02, 107.

[129] Nelson, 114.

[130] Ibid., 202.

[131] Bill Holm, *The Music of Failure* (Marshall, MN: Plains Press, 1985), 65, cited in Robert Bly, "Norwegian Roots on an American Tree," in *A Common Land, A Diverse People: Ethnic Identity on the Prairie Plains,* ed. Harry F. Thompson, et al. (Sioux Falls, SD: Nordland Heritage Foundation, 1986), 22.

[132] Among works on individual cities are Olson and Olson; Harold H. Schuler, *Pierre Since 1910* (Freeman, SD: Pine Hill Press, 1998), and Marvis Hogen.

[133] Hogen, 67. Emphasis in original text.

[134] Figures from http://www.state.sd.us/news/issues/19.pdf; Internet.

[135] Greg Latza, *Hometown South Dakota: Life in Our Small Towns* (Sioux Falls, SD: PeopleScapes Publishing, 2001), 83.

[136] Page, 377.

[137] Fite, "The Great Plains: Promises, Problems, and Prospects," 195.

[138] McLaird calls Sioux Falls and Rapid City the "capitals" of East and West River South Dakota, 457.

[139] Jay Kirschenmann, "Gateway to cut more jobs," *Sioux Falls Argus Leader*, June 11, 2004, 1A.

Selected Readings

Abel, Annie Heloise, ed. *Tabeau's Narrative of Loisel's Expedition to the Upper Missouri*. Translated by Rose Abel Wright. Norman: University of Oklahoma Press, 1939.

Abourezk, James G. *Advise and Dissent: Memoirs of South Dakota and the U.S. Senate*. Chicago: Lawrence Hill Books, 1989.

Adams, Walter, ed. *The Structure of American Industry*, 8th ed. New York: Macmillan Publishing Company, 1990.

Alexander, Ruth Ann. *Patches in a History Quilt: Episcopal Women in the Diocese of South Dakota, 1868-2000*. Sioux Falls: Episcopal Women's Council, 2003.

_____. "South Dakota Women Stake a Claim: A Feminist Memoir, 1964-1989." *South Dakota History* 19 (Winter 1989): 538-55.

Allsman, Paul T. *Reconnaissance of Gold-Mining District in the Black Hills, South Dakota*. Bulletin 427. Washington, D.C.: Government Printing Office, U.S. Department of the Interior, Bureau of Mines, 1940.

Amiotte, Arthur. "An Appraisal of Sioux Arts," in Arthur R. Huseboe, *An Illustrated History of the Arts in South Dakota*. Sioux Falls: Center for Western Studies, 1989, 109-61.

Anders, J. Olson. "The Making of a Typical Prairie County: Day County, South Dakota, 1881-1906." *South Dakota Historical Collections* 36 (Pierre: State Historical Society, 1972): 522-65.

Anderson, Grant K. "Deadwood's Chinatown." *South Dakota History* 5 (Summer 1975): 266-85.

Anderson, Kristen, and Elizabeth B. Scott. *Guide to Historical Repositories in South Dakota*. Rev. ed. Pierre: South Dakota State Records Advisory Board, 2002.

Anderson, William. "The Literary Apprenticeship of Laura Ingalls Wilder." *South Dakota History* 13 (Winter 1983): 285-331.

Anson, Robert Sam. *McGovern: A Biography*. New York: Holt, Rinehart and Winston, 1972.

Argus Leader South Dakota 99. Sioux Falls: Ex Machina Publishing Company, 1989.

Armin, C. Perry. "A State Treasurer Defaults: The Taylor Case of 1895." *South Dakota History* 15 (Fall 1985): 177-99.

_____. "Coe I. Crawford and the Progressive Movement in South Dakota." *South Dakota Historical Collections* 32 (Pierre: State Historical Society, 1964): 23-231.

Armstrong, Moses K. *The Early Empire Builders of the Great West*. St. Paul: E. W. Porter, 1901.

_____. *History and Resources of Dakota, Montana, and Idaho*. Yankton: G.W. Kingsbury, 1866. Reprinted in *South Dakota Historical Collections* 14 (Pierre: State Historical Society, 1928): 9-70.

Bad Heart Bull, Amos. *A Pictographic History of the Oglala Sioux*. Text by Helen H. Bish. Lincoln: University of Nebraska Press, 1967.

Bailey, Dana R. *History of Minnehaha County, South Dakota*. Sioux Falls: Brown & Saenger, 1899.

Baldwin, George P. *The Black Hills Illustrated*. Deadwood: Black Hills Mining Men's Association, 1904.

Baltodano, Neyton, and Celina Baltodano. *History of South Dakota Medicine*. Sioux Falls: Dakota Printing Company, 1990.

Batchelder, George A. "A Sketch of the History and Resources of Dakota Territory." *South Dakota Historical Collections* 14 (Pierre: State Historical Society, 1928): 181-251.

Battle Mountain Sanitarium, Hot Springs, South Dakota: 1907-1997. Hot Springs: VA Black Hills Medical Center, 1997.

Baum, L. Frank. *The Wizard of Oz*. Michael Patrick Hearn, ed. New York: Schocken Books, 1983.

Beadle, William H. H. *Autobiography of William Henry Harrison Beadle*. Pierre: South Dakota State Historical Society, 1938.

Beck, Bill. *Light Across the Prairies*. Eden Prairie: Viking Press, Inc., 1989.

Beckwourth, James P. *The Life and Adventures of James P. Beckwourth as Told to Thomas D. Bonner*. 1856, reprinted. Lincoln: University of Nebraska Press, 1972.

Billington, Monroe Lee, and Roger D. Hardaway. *African Americans on the Western Frontier*. Boulder: University Press of Colorado, 1998.

Bingham, Kate Boyles, and Virgil D. Boyles. *Langford of the Three Bars*. Chicago: A. C. McClurg & Co., 1907.

Blasingame, Ike. *Dakota Cowboy: My Life in the Old Days*. New York: G. P. Putnam's Sons, 1958.

Blouet, Brian W., and Frederick C. Luebke, eds. *The Great Plains Environment and Culture*. Lincoln: University of Nebraska Press, 1979.

Boyer, Paul S., et al. *The Enduring Vision: A History of the American People*, 5th ed. Boston: Houghton Mifflin Company, 2004.

Bradbury, John. *Travels in the Interior of America, in the Years 1809, 1810, and 1811*. Vol. 5 of *Early Western Travels, 1748-1846*. Edited by Reuben Gold Thwaites. Cleveland: Arthur H. Clark Co., 1905.

Bragstad, Reuben. *Sioux Falls in Retrospect*. Sioux Falls: privately printed, 1967.

Brennan, John. *The Condition and Resources of Southern Dakota: Prospective Trade and Travel of the Dakota Southern Railroad*. Sioux City: Daily Journal Printing and Bindery, 1872.

Briggs, Harold E. "Ranching and Stock Raising in the Territory of Dakota." *South Dakota Historical Collections* 14 (Pierre: State Historical Society, 1928): 417-66.

Brokaw, Tom. *A Long Way from Home: Growing up in the American Heartland*. New York: Random House, 2002.

Brokenleg, Martin, and Herbert T. Hoover. *Yanktonai Sioux Water Colors: Cultural Remembrances of John Saul*. Sioux Falls: Center for Western Studies, 1993.

Bronson, William, and T. H. Watkins. *Homestake: The Centennial History of America's Greatest Gold Mine*. San Francisco: Homestake Mining Co., 1977.

Brown, Joseph, ed. *The Sacred Pipe: Black Elk's Account of the Seven Rites of the Oglala Sioux*. Norman: University of Oklahoma Press, 1953.

Brown, Lawrence. *Buffalo Commons: Memoirs*. Bowman: Grapevine, 1995.

Buecker, Thomas R. "Confrontation at Sturgis: An Episode in Civil-Military Race Relations, 1885." *South Dakota History* 14 (Fall 1984): 238-61.

Carlson, Loren. *Government of South Dakota*. Vermillion: University of South Dakota, 2002.

Carrels, Peter. *Uphill Against Water: The Great Dakota Water War*. Lincoln: University of Nebraska Press, 1999.

Carroll, John M., ed. *The Black Military Experience in the American West*. New York: Liveright Publishing Corporation, 1971.

Cash, Joseph H. "History of Lead, South Dakota: 1876-1900." *South Dakota Historical Collections* 34 (Pierre: State Historical Society, 1968): 33-141.

Cassells, E. Steve. *Prehistoric Hunters of the Black Hills*. Boulder: Johnson Publishing Company, 1986.

————, David B. Miller, and Paul V. Miller. *Paha Sapa: Notes on the Cultural Resources of the Black Hills of South Dakota and Wyoming*. Custer: Black Hills National Forest, 1984.

Catlin, George. *North American Indians*. Edinburgh: J. Grant, 1926.

Cecil, Matthew. "Democratic Party Politics and the South Dakota Income Tax, 1933-1942." *South Dakota History* 26 (Summer/Fall 1996): 137-69.

Chapman, William McKissack. *Remember the Wind: A Prairie Memoir*. Philadelphia: J. B. Lippincott Co., 1965.

Chenoweth, Richard R. "Francis Case: A Political Biography." *South Dakota Historical Collections* 39 (Pierre: State Historical Society, 1978): 288-433.

Chittenden, Hiram. *The American Fur Trade of the Far West*. New York, 1902. Reprint. 2 vols. Stanford, CA: Academic Reprints, 1954.

_____, and Alfred Talbot Richardson. *Life, Letter, and Travels of Father Pierre-Jean De Smet, SJ, 1802-1873*. 4 vols. New York: Francis P. Harper, 1905.

Christensen, Thomas P. "The Danes in South Dakota." *South Dakota Historical Collections* 14 (Pierre: State Historical Society, 1928): 539-52.

Clark, Badger. *Sun and Saddle Leather, Including Grass Grown Trails and New Poems*. Boston: Gorham Press, 1922.

Clem, Alan L. "The 1964 Election: Has South Dakota Become a Two-Party State?" *Public Affairs* 20. Vermillion: Governmental Research Bureau, 1963.

_____. *Government by the People? South Dakota Politics in the Last Third of the Twentieth Century*. Rapid City: Chiesman Foundation for Democracy, Inc., 2002.

Clow, Richmond L. *Chasing the Glitter: Black Hills Milling, 1874-1959*. Pierre: South Dakota Historical Society Press, 2002.

_____. "In Search of the People's Voice: Richard Olsen Richards and Progressive Reform." *South Dakota History* 10 (Winter 1978): 39-58.

_____. "Timber Users, Timber Savers: Homestake Mining Company and the First Regulated Timber Harvest." *South Dakota History* 22 (Fall 1992): 213-37.

Clowser, Don C. *Dakota Indian Treaties: The Dakota Indians from Nomad to Reservation*. Deadwood: self-published, 1974.

Collins, Betty Jean. "The History of Dramatic Art and the University of South Dakota, 1882-1948." Master's thesis, University of South Dakota, 1948.

Coursey, O.W. *Literature of South Dakota*. Mitchell: Educator Supply Company, 1928.

Custer, George A. "Opening the Black Hills: Custer's Report." *South Dakota Historical Collections* 7 (Pierre: State Historical Society, 1914): 583-94.

Dalton, John Elmer. *A History of the Location of the State Capital in South Dakota*. Governmental Research Bureau, Report 14. Vermillion: University of South Dakota, 1945.

Daum, Ann. *The Prairie in Her Eyes*. Minneapolis: Milkweed Editions, 2001.

Davies, Phillips G., ed. "Touring the Welsh Settlements of South Dakota, 1891." *South Dakota History* 10 (Summer 1980): 223-40.

Dedrick, Dave. *It Ain't All Cartoons: Memoirs of the Captain*. Huron: East Eagle Co., 1989.

DeJong, Gerald. "The Coming of the Dutch to the Dakotas." *South Dakota History* 5 (Winter 1974): 20-51.

Deloria, Jr., Vine. *Custer Died for Your Sins: An Indian Manifesto*. New York: Macmillan Co., 1969.

_____. *God is Red: A Native View of Religion*. Golden: North American Press, 1992.

Dennis, Michael L. *Federal Relief Construction in South Dakota, 1929-1941*. Pierre: South Dakota State Historic Preservation Office, 1998.

Densmore, Frances. *Teton Sioux Music*. Washington, D.C.: Government Printing Office, 1918.

DeWall, Robb, ed. *Korczak: Storyteller in Stone*. Rev. ed. Crazy Horse: Korczak's Heritage, Inc., 1996.

Dick, Everett N. *The Sod-House Frontier, 1854-1890: A Social History of the Northern Plains from the Creation of Kansas & Nebraska to the Admission of the Dakotas*. Lincoln: Johnsen Publishing Co., 1954.

Directory of South Dakota Museums and Galleries. Chamberlain: Association of South Dakota Museums, Inc., 2004.

Dodge, Richard Irving. *The Black Hills*. Minneapolis: Ross & Haines, Inc., 1965.

Duratschek, M. Claudia. *Builders of God's Kingdom: The History of the Catholic Church in South Dakota*. Sioux Falls: Diocese of Sioux Falls, 1979.

_____. *Under the Shadow of His Wings: History of the Sacred Heart Convent of Benedictine Sisters*. Aberdeen: North Plains Press, 1971.

Dvorak, Joseph A. *History of the Czechs in the State of South Dakota*. Tabor: Czech Heritage Preservation Society, Inc., 1980.

Eastman, Charles A. *From the Deep Woods to Civilization: Chapters in the Autobiography of an Indian*. Boston: Little, Brown & Co., 1916.

Easton, Patricia O'Keefe. "Woman Suffrage in South Dakota: The Final Decade, 1911-1920." *South Dakota History* 13 (Fall 1983): 206-26.

Ehrensperger, Edward C. *History of the United Church of Christ in South Dakota, 1869-1976*. Freeman: Pine Hill Press, 1977.

Erpestad, David, and David Wood. *Building South Dakota: A Historical Survey of the State's Architecture to 1945*. Pierre: South Dakota State Historical Society Press, 1997.

Fanebust, Wayne. *Where the Sioux River Bends: A Newspaper Chronicle*. Sioux Falls: Minnehaha County Historical Society, 1985.

Fargo, Lucille. *Prairie Girl*. New York: Dodd, Mead, 1937.

Fatout, Paul. *Ambrose Bierce and the Black Hills*. Norman: University of Oklahoma Press, 1956.

Feikema, Feike. *The Golden Bowl*. St. Paul: Webb Publishing Co., 1944.

Fielder, Mildred. *Railroads of the Black Hills*. Deadwood: Dakota Graphics, 1993.

_____. *Silver is the Fortune*. Aberdeen: North Plains Press, 1978.

_____. *The Treasure of Homestake Gold*. Aberdeen: North Plains Press, 1970.

Fite, Gilbert C. *Mount Rushmore*. Norman: University of Oklahoma Press, 1952.

_____. "'The Only Thing Worth Working For': Land and Its Meaning for Pioneer Dakotans." *South Dakota History* 15 (Spring/Summer 1985): 2-25.

_____. "Peter Norbeck and the Defeat of the Non-Partisan League in South Dakota." *Mississippi Valley Historical Review* 33 (September 1946): 217-36.

_____. *Peter Norbeck: Prairie Statesman*. Columbia: University of Missouri, 1948.

Foss, Joe, with Donna Wild Foss. *A Proud American: The Autobiography of Joe Foss*. New York: Pocket Books, 1992.

Frawley, Molly. "Henry and Christina (Anderson) Frawley." Lawrence County Historical Society. *Some History of Lawrence County*. Deadwood: Lawrence County Historical Society, 1981, 158-61.

Freeman Centennial Steering Committee, comp. *Freeman Facts - Freeman Fiction*. Freeman: Pine Hill Press, 1979.

Froiland, Sven G. *Natural History of the Black Hills and Badlands*. Sioux Falls: Center for Western Studies, 1990.

Garland, Hamlin. *Main-Travelled Roads*. New York: Harper & Brothers, 1899.

_____. *A Son of the Middle Border*. Lincoln: University of Nebraska Press, 1979.

Garreau, Joel. *The Nine Nations of North America*. Boston: Houghton Mifflin Company, 1981.

Garrettson III, Charles L. "Home of the Politics of Joy: Hubert H. Humphrey in South Dakota." *South Dakota History* 20 (Fall 1990): 165-84.

Gerber, Philip L., ed. *Bachelor Bess: The Homesteading Letters of Elizabeth Corey, 1900-1919*. Iowa City: University of Iowa Press, 1990.

Gilfillan, Archer B. *Sheep: Life on the South Dakota Range*. Boston: Little, Brown & Co., 1929.

Goering, Violet, and Orlando J. Goering. "Jewish Farmers in South Dakota-the Am Olam." *South Dakota History* 12 (Winter 1982): 232-47.

Goertz, Reuben. *Princes, Potentates, and Plain People: The Saga of the Germans from Russia*. Sioux Falls: Center for Western Studies, 1994.

Goodwyn, Lawrence. *Democratic Promise: The Populist Movement in America*. New York: Oxford University Press, 1976.

Grafe, Ernest, and Paul Horsted. *Exploring with Custer: The 1874 Black Hills Expedition*. Custer: Golden Valley Press, 2002.

Grant, H. Roger. "Origins of a Progressive Reform: The Initiative and Referendum Movement in South Dakota." *South Dakota History* 3 (Fall 1973): 390-407.

Grant, Philip A. "Presidential Politics in South Dakota." *South Dakota History* 22 (Fall 1992): 261-75.

Green, Charles. "The Administration of the Public Domain in South Dakota." *South Dakota Historical Collections* 20 (Pierre: State Historical Society, 1940): 7-280.

Greene, Jerome A. *Slim Buttes, 1876: An Episode of the Great Sioux War*. Norman: University of Oklahoma Press, 1982.

Halvorson, H. C. *The First Fifty Years in Lake Sinai Township*. Brookings: n.p., 1956.

Hamburg, James F. *The Influence of Railroads upon the Processes and Patterns of Settlement in South Dakota*. New York: Arno Press, 1981.

_____. "Railroads and the Settlement of South Dakota During the Great Dakota Boom, 1878-1887." *South Dakota History* 5 (Spring 1975): 165-78.

Hamilton, Henry W., and Jean Tyree Hamilton. *The Sioux of the Rosebud: A History in Pictures.* Photographs by John A. Anderson. Norman: University of Oklahoma Press, 1971.

Hamilton, W. H. *Dakota: An Autobiography of a Cowman.* Pierre: South Dakota State Historical Society Press, 1998.

Handlin, Oscar. *The Uprooted: The Epic Story of the Great Migration.* Boston: Little Brown, 1951.

Hanson, Myrle G. "A History of Harding County, South Dakota, to 1925." *South Dakota Historical Collections* 21 (Pierre: State Historical Society, 1942): 515-65.

Hasselstrom, Linda M. *Going Over East: Reflections of a Woman Rancher.* Golden: Fulcrum Press, 1987.

_____. *Seems Like Far.* New York: Lyons Press, 1999.

_____. *Windbreak: A Woman Rancher on the Northern Plains.* Berkeley: Barn Owl Books, 1987.

Hassrick, Royal B. *The Sioux: Life and Customs of a Warrior Society.* Norman: University of Oklahoma Press, 1964.

Heidepriem, Scott. *A Fair Change for a Free People: Biography of Senator Karl Mundt.* Madison: Karl E. Mundt Historical and Educational Foundation, 1988.

Hendrickson, J. P. "Grassroots Government: South Dakota's Enduring Townships." *South Dakota History* 24 (Spring 1994): 19-42.

Hendrickson, Kenneth E. "Some Political Aspects of the Populist Movement in South Dakota." *North Dakota History* 34 (Winter 1967): 77-92.

Higbee, Paul, and Kathleen Aney. *Spearfish.* Spearfish: Black Hills and Bighorns Project, 2000.

History of Southeastern Dakota, Its Settlement and Growth. Sioux City: Western Publishing Company, 1881.

Hogan, Edward P., and Erin Hogan Fouberg. *The Geography of South Dakota.* Rev. ed. Sioux Falls: Center for Western Studies, 1998.

Hogen, Marvis. *Fifty Years on Main Street.* Kadoka: self-published, 1996.

Holm, Bill. *The Music of Failure.* Marshall: Plain Press, 1985.

Hoover, Carol Goss. *Building the Indigenous Church: Tools for Pastoral Ministers in Sioux Country.* Doctoral dissertation, Graduate Theological Foundation, 2002.

Hoover, Herbert T. "The Sioux Agreement of 1889 and Its Aftermath." *South Dakota History* 19 (Spring 1989): 56-94.

_____, and Carol Goss Hoover. *Sioux Country: A History of Indian-white Relations.* Sioux Falls: Center for Western Studies, 2000.

_____, Carol Goss Hoover, and Elizabeth A. Simmons, eds. *Bon Homme County History.* Tyndall, SD: Bon Homme County Historical Society, 1994.

_____, and Charles L. Roegiers. "North Central States Sheep and Wool Growers: A History." TMs, Department of History, University of South Dakota, 1988.

_____, and Larry J. Zimmerman, eds. *South Dakota Leaders: From Pierre Chouteau, Jr., to Oscar Howe.* Vermillion: University of South Dakota Press, 1989.

_____, and Karen P. Zimmerman, comps. *The Sioux and Other Native American Cultures of the Dakotas: An Annotated Bibliography.* Westport: Greenwood Press, 1993.

_____, and Karen P. Zimmerman, comps. *South Dakota History: An Annotated Bibliography.* Westport: Greenwood Press, 1993.

_____, et al., eds. *From Idea to Institution: Higher Education in South Dakota.* Vermillion: University of South Dakota Press, 1989.

Horton, Arthur G., comp. and ed., *An Economic and Social Survey of Sioux Falls.* Sioux Falls: privately published, 1938.

Hudson, John C. *Plains Country Towns.* Minneapolis: University of Minnesota Press, 1985.

Hudson, Lois Phillip. *Reapers of the Dust, A Prairie Chronicle.* Boston: Little, Brown, & Co., 1964.

Hufstetler, Mark, and Michael Bedeau. *South Dakota's Railroads: An Historic Context.* Pierre: South Dakota State Historical Society, 1998.

Hughes, Richard B. *Pioneer Years in the Black Hills*. Edited by Agnes Wright Spring. Glendale: Arthur H. Clark Co., 1957.

Hunhoff, Bernie. "A Discovery on the Cheyenne." *South Dakota Magazine,* September/October 1995, 30-33.

Hunt, David C., et al. *Karl Bodmer's America*. Lincoln: University of Nebraska Press, 1984.

Hurt, Wesley R., and William E. Lass. *Frontier Photographer: Stanley J. Morrow's Dakota Years*. Vermillion: University of South Dakota, 1956.

Huseboe, Arthur R. "From Feikema to Manfred, from the Big Sioux Basin to the Northern Plains." *Great Plains Quarterly* 21 (Fall 2001): 309-19.

_____. *Herbert Krause*. Western Writers Series Number 66. Boise: Boise State University, 1985.

_____. *An Illustrated History of the Arts in South Dakota*. Sioux Falls: Center for Western Studies, 1989.

_____, and William Geyer, eds. *Where the West Begins: Essays on Middle Border and Siouxland Writing in Honor of Herbert Krause*. Sioux Falls: Center for Western Studies, 1978.

Iseminger, Gordon L. T*he Quartzite Border: Surveying and Marking the North Dakota-South Dakota Boundary, 1891-1892*. Sioux Falls: Center for Western Studies, 1988.

Isern, Thomas D. "The Comedy of the Commons; or, My Life on the Post-Colonial Plains." *South Dakota History* 33 (Spring 2003): 64-79.

Jackson, Donald. *Custer's Gold: The United States Cavalry Expedition of 1874*. Lincoln: University of Nebraska Press, 1972.

_____, ed. *Letters of the Lewis and Clark Expedition*. Urbana: University of Illinois Press, 1962.

_____. *Thomas Jefferson and the Stony Mountains*. Urbana: University of Illinois Press, 1981.

Jennewein, J. Leonard, and Jane Boorman, eds. *Dakota Panorama*. Sioux Falls: Dakota Territory Centennial Commission, 1961.

Johansen, John P. "Immigrant Settlements and Social Organization in South Dakota." Department of Rural Sociology, Bulletin 313. Brookings: South Dakota State University, 1937.

_____. *Immigrants and their Children in South Dakota,* Department of Rural Sociology, Bulletin 302. Brookings: South Dakota State University, 1936.

Julin, Suzanne. "South Dakota Spa: A History of the Hot Springs Health Resort, 1882-1915." *South Dakota Historical Collections* 41 (Pierre: State Historical Society, 1982): 193-272.

Karolevitz, Robert F. *From Quill to Computer: The Story of America's Community Newspapers*. USA: privately printed, 1982.

_____. *Where Your Heart Is: The Story of Harvey Dunn, Artist*. Aberdeen: North Plains Press, 1970.

_____. *With a Shirt Tail Full of Type: The Story of Newspapering in South Dakota*. Freeman: South Dakota Press Association, 1982.

_____. *With Faith, Hope, and Tenacity: The First Hundred Years of the Diocese of Sioux Falls*. Mission Hill: Homestead Publishers, 1989.

Kilian, Tom. *Tales of Old Dakota*. Sioux Falls: Pine Hill Press, 2004.

Kingsbury, George W. *History of Dakota Territory*. George Martin Smith. *South Dakota: Its History and Its People*. 5 vols. Chicago: S. J. Clarke Publishing Co., 1915.

Kinyon, Jeanette, and Jean Walz. *The Incredible Gladys Pyle*. Vermillion: Dakota Press, University of South Dakota, 1985.

Klock, Irma H. *All Roads Lead to Deadwood*. Lead: privately published, 1979.

Kohl, Edith Eudora. *Land of the Burnt Thigh*. New York: Funk & Wagnalls Co., 1938.

Korsgaard, Ross P. "A History of Rapid City, South Dakota, During Territorial Days." *South Dakota Historical Collections* 38 (Pierre: State Historical Society, 1976): 515-60.

Koupal, Nancy Tystad, ed. *Baum's Road to Oz: The Dakota Years*. Pierre: South Dakota State Historical Society Press, 2000.

Krause, Herbert. *Poems and Essays*. Edited by Arthur R. Huseboe. Sioux Falls: Center for Western Studies, 1990.

_____. *The Thresher.* Indianapolis: Bobbs-Merrill Co., 1946.

_____, and Gary D. Olson. *Prelude to Glory: A Newspaper Accounting of Custer's 1874 Expedition to the Black Hills*. Sioux Falls: Brevet Press, 1974.

Kvernes, David, ed. *The Lewis and Clark Expedition: Then and Now*. Sioux Falls: Center for Western Studies, 2004.

Lamar, Howard R. *Dakota Territory, 1861-1889: A Study of Frontier Politics*. New Haven: Yale University Press, 1956.

_____. "Public Values and Private Dreams: South Dakota's Search for Identity, 1850-1900." *South Dakota History* 8 (Spring 1978): 117-42.

Lass, William E. *A History of Steamboating on the Upper Missouri River*. Lincoln: University of Nebraska Press, 1962.

Latza, Greg. *Hometown South Dakota: Life in Our Small Town*. Sioux Falls: PeopleScapes Publishing, 2001.

Lawson, Michael L. *Dammed Indians: The Pick-Sloan Plan and the Missouri River Sioux, 1944-1980*. Norman: University of Oklahoma Press, 1982.

Lazarus, Edward. *Black Hills, White Justice: The Sioux Nation Versus the United States, 1775 to the Present*. New York: HarperCollins, 1991.

Lee, Bob. *Last Grass Frontier: The South Dakota Stockgrowers Heritage*. Vol. 2. Sturgis: Black Hills Publishers, 1999.

_____, and Dick Williams. *Last Grass Frontier: The South Dakota Stock Grower Heritage*. [Vol. 1.] Sturgis: Black Hills Publishers, 1964.

Lee, Robert. *Fort Meade and the Black Hills*. Lincoln: University of Nebraska Press, 1991.

Lee, Shebby. "Traveling the Sunshine State: The Growth of Tourism in South Dakota, 1914-1939." *South Dakota History* 19 (Summer 1989): 194-223.

Legg, James. "A History of Native American Housing Types and Funding on Selected Reservations: Yankton, Rosebud, Pine Ridge, Crow Creek, and Lower Brule." M.A. thesis, University of South Dakota, 1998.

Lewis, Sinclair. *Main Street*. New York: Harcourt, Brace and Howe, 1920.

Licht, Daniel S. *Ecology and Economics of the Great Plains*. Lincoln: University of Nebraska Press, 1997.

Linde, Martha. *Sawmills of the Black Hills*. Rapid City: Fenske Printing Inc., 1984.

Lindell, Terrence J. "South Dakota Populism." M.A. thesis, University of Nebraska, 1982.

Littlefield, Henry M. "*The Wizard of Oz*: Parable on Populism." *American Quarterly* 16 (Spring 1964): 47-58.

Lobao, Linda, and Katherine Meyer. "Economic Decline, Gender, and Labor Flexibility in Family-Based Enterprises: Midwestern Farming in the 1980s." *Social Forces* 74 (December 1995): 575-608.

Longo, Peter J., and David W. Yoskowitz, eds. *Water on the Great Plains: Issues and Politics*. Lubbock: Texas Tech University Press, 2002.

Lovoll, Odd S. *A Folk Epic: The Bygdelag in America*. Boston: Twayne Publishers, 1975.

_____. *The Promise Fulfilled: A Portrait of Norwegian Americans Today*. Minneapolis: University of Minnesota Press, 1998.

Lowitt, Richard, and Maurine Brady, eds. *One Third of a Nation: Lorena Hickok Reports on the Great Depression*. Urbana: University of Illinois Press, 1981.

Lusk, R.D. "Life and Death of 470 Acres." *Saturday Evening Post*, 13 August 1938.

MacIntyre, Ron, and Rebecca L. Bell. *The Arts in South Dakota: A Selective, Annotated Bibliography*. Sioux Falls: Center for Western Studies, 1988.

Mails, Thomas E. *Sundancing at Rosebud and Pine Ridge*. Sioux Falls: Center for Western Studies, 1978.

Manfred, Frederick. *Lord Grizzly*. New York: McGraw-Hill Book Co., 1954.

_____. *Scarlet Plume*. New York: Trident Press, 1964.

_____. *The Wind Blows Free*. Sioux Falls: Center for Western Studies, 1979.

Matthews, Anne. *Where the Buffalo Roam*. New York: Grove Weidenfeld, 1992.

Mattison, Ray H. "Report on Historical Aspects of the Oahe Reservoir Area, Missouri River, South and North Dakota." *South Dakota Historical Collections* 27 (Pierre: State Historical Society, 1954): 1-159.

McClintock, John S. *Pioneer Days in the Black Hills: Accurate History and Facts Related by One of the Early Day Pioneers*. Edited by Edward L. Senn. Deadwood: self-published, 1939.

McDermott, John D., comp. *Gold Rush: The Black Hills Story*. Pierre: South Dakota State Historical Society Press, 2002.

_____, "The Military Problem and the Black Hills, 1874-1875." *South Dakota History* 31 (Fall/Winter 2001): 188-210.

McDermott, Louis M. "The Primary Role of the Military on the Dakota Frontier." *South Dakota History* 2 (Winter 1971): 1-22.

McGillycuddy, Julia B. *McGillycuddy, Agent: A Biography of Dr. Valentine T. McGillycuddy*. Stanford University: Stanford University Press, 1941.

McGovern, George S. *Grassroots: The Autobiography of George McGovern*. New York: Random House, 1977.

McIntosh, Elaine Nelson. *The Lewis and Clark Expedition: Food, Nutrition, and Health*. Sioux Falls: Center for Western Studies, 2003.

McLaird, James D. "Calamity Jane: The Life and the Legend." *South Dakota History* 24 (Spring 1994): 1-18.

_____. "Cowboy Life: Myth and Reality." *South Dakota History* 32 (Fall 2002): 181-93.

_____. "From Bib Overalls to Cowboy Boots: East River/West River Difference in South Dakota." *South Dakota History* 19 (Winter 1989): 454-91.

_____, and Lesta V. Turchen. "Exploring the Black Hills, 1855-1875: Reports of the Government Expeditions. The Dacota Explorations of Lieutenant Gouverneur Kemble Warren, 1855-1856-1857." *South Dakota History* 3 (Fall 1973): 359-89.

_____, and Lesta V. Turchen. "Exploring the Black Hills, 1855-1875: Reports of the Government Expeditions. The Explorations of Captain William Franklin Raynolds, 1859-1860." *South Dakota History* 4 (Winter 1973): 18-62.

Meyer, Roy W. *History of the Santee Sioux: United States Indian Policy on Trial*. Lincoln: University of Nebraska Press, 1967.

_____. *The Village Indians of the Upper Missouri: The Mandans, Hidatsas, and Arikaras*. Lincoln: University of Nebraska Press, 1977.

Micheaux, Oscar. *The Conquest: The Story of a Negro Pioneer*. Lincoln: Woodruff Press, 1913.

Mickelson, Sig. *The Northern Pacific Railroad and the Selling of the West: A Nineteenth-Century Public Relations Venture*. Sioux Falls: Center for Western Studies, 1993.

Miller, David B. *Gateway to the Hills: An Illustrated History of Rapid City*. Northridge: Windsor Publications, Inc., 1985.

Miller, John E. *Becoming Laura Ingalls Wilder: The Woman Behind the Legend*. Columbia: University of Missouri Press, 1998.

_____. "Education in South Dakota Since World War II: A Statistical Portrait." *South Dakota History* 33 (Spring 2003): 46-63.

_____. "The Failure to Realign: The 1936 Election in South Dakota." *Journal of the West* 41 (Fall 2002): 22-29.

_____. *Looking for History on Highway 14*. Pierre: South Dakota State Historical Society Press, 2001.

_____. "McCarthyism before McCarthy: The 1938 Election in South Dakota." *Heritage of the Great Plains* 15 (Summer 1982): 1-21.

_____. "Place and Community in the 'Little Town on the Prairie': De Smet in 1983." *South Dakota History* 16 (Winter 1986): 351-72.

_____. "Restrained, Respectable Radicals: The South Dakota Farm Holiday." *Agricultural History* 59 (July 1985): 429-47.

Mills, George W. *Fifty Years a Country Doctor in Western South Dakota*. Wall: Wall Drug Store, 1971.

Mills, Rick W. *Railroading in the Land of Infinite Variety: A History of South Dakota's Railroads*. Hermosa: Battle Creek Pub. Co., 1990.

Milner II, Clyde A., et al., eds. *The Oxford History of the American West*. New York: Oxford University Press, 1994.

Milton, John R. *South Dakota: A Bicentennial History*. New York: W. W. Norton & Company, Inc., 1977.

Mittelstaedt, Robert A., ed. "The General Store Era, Memoirs of Arthur and Harold Mittelstaedt." *South Dakota History* 9 (Winter 1978): 36-60.

Mittelstedt, Rodney. "Country Doctor: The Life of Roscoe Dean, M.D." M.A. thesis, University of South Dakota, 1993.

Monaghan, Jay. *Custer: The Life of General George Armstrong Custer*. Boston: Little, Brown & Co., 1959.

Moulton, Gary E., ed. *The Journals of the Lewis and Clark Expedition*. 13 vols. Lincoln: University of Nebraska Press, 1983-2001.

Myers, Rex C. "Immigrant Heritage: South Dakota's Foreign Born in an Era of Assimilation." *South Dakota History* 19 (Summer 1989): 134-55.

Nasatir, Abraham P. *Before Lewis and Clark: Documents Illustrating the History of the Missouri, 1785-1804*. 2 vols. St. Louis: St. Louis Historical Documents Foundation, 1952.

Neihardt, John G. *Black Elk Speaks, Being the Life Story of a Holy Man of the Oglala Sioux*. New York: William Morrow & Co., 1932.

Nelson, Bruce. *Land of the Dacotah*. Minneapolis: University of Minnesota Press, 1946.

Nelson, Jim. "Western Charles Mix County." *Dakota West,* Winter 1978: 17-22.

Nelson, Paula M. *After the West Was Won: Homesteaders and Town-Builders in Western South Dakota, 1900-1917*. Iowa City: University of Iowa Press, 1986.

_____. *The Prairie Winnows Out Its Own: The West River Country of South Dakota in the Years of the Depression and Dust*. Iowa City: University of Iowa Press, 1996.

Newton, Henry, and Walter P. Jenney. *Report on the Geology and Resources of the Black Hills of Dakota with Atlas*. Washington, D.C.: Government Printing Office, 1880.

Norris, Kathleen. *Dakota: A Spiritual Geography*. New York: Ticknor & Fields, 1993.

Nye, David. *Electrifying America: Social Meanings of a New Technology, 1880-1940*. Cambridge: MIT Press, 1990.

Nye, Russel B. *Midwestern Progressive Politics: A Historical Study of Its Origins and Development, 1870-1950*. East Lansing: Michigan State College Press, 1951.

Olson, Gary D. "A Dakota Boomtown: Sioux Falls, 1877-1880." *Great Plains Quarterly* 24 (Winter 2004): 17-30.

_____, and Erik L. Olson. *Sioux Falls, South Dakota: A Pictorial History*. Norfolk/Virginia Beach: Donning Co., 2004.

Olson, James C. *Red Cloud and the Sioux Problem*. Lincoln: University of Nebraska Press, 1965.

100 Years of South Dakota Agriculture, 1900-1999. Sioux Falls: South Dakota Agriculture Statistics Service, 2000.

Ostergren, Robert C. "European Settlement and Ethnicity Patterns on the Agricultural Frontiers of South Dakota." *South Dakota History* 13 (Spring/Summer 1983): 49-82.

_____. "The Immigrant Church as a Symbol of Community and Place in the Upper Midwest." *Great Plains Quarterly* 1 (Fall 1981): 225-38.

_____. "Prairie Bound: Migration Patterns to a Swedish Settlement on the Dakota Frontier," in Frederick C. Luebke, ed., *Ethnicity on the Great Plains*. Lincoln: University of Nebraska Press, 1980, 73-91.

Overland, Orm. *The Western Home: A Literary History of Norwegian America*. Northfield: Norwegian-American Historical Association, 1996.

Oyos, Lynwood E. *The Family Farmers' Advocate: South Dakota Farmers Union, 1914-2000*. Sioux Falls: Center for Western Studies, 2000.

_____. *Over a Century of Leadership: South Dakota Territorial and State Governors, 1861-1987*. Sioux Falls: Center for Western Studies, 1987.

Page, Brian. "Across the Great Divide: Agriculture and Industrial Geography." *Economic Geography* 72 (October 1996): 376-97.

Parker, Watson. "Booming the Black Hills." *South Dakota History* 11 (Winter 1980): 35-52.

_____. *Deadwood: The Golden Years*. Lincoln: University of Nebraska Press, 1981.

_____. *Gold in the Black Hills*. Norman: University of Oklahoma Press, 1966.

_____, and Hugh K. Lambert. *Black Hills Ghost Towns*. Chicago: Swallow Press, Inc., 1974.

Peterson, August. *History of the Swedes who Settled in Clay County, South Dakota, and Their Biographies*. Clay County: Swedish Pioneer and Historical Society, 1947.

Peterson, Susan, and Courtney Vaughn-Roberson. *Women of Vision: The Presentation Sisters of South Dakota, 1880-1985.* Urbana: University of Illinois Press, 1988.

Pettigrew, Richard F. "Pettigrew Visits the Black Hills." *Sunshine State Magazine,* March 1926.

_____. "Scroll of Time." *Sunshine State Magazine,* April 1926.

Phillips, Charles, and Alan Axelrod, eds. *Encyclopedia of the American West.* New York: Macmillan Reference USA, 1996.

Phillips, David R., ed. *The West: An American Experience.* Chicago: Henry Regnery Company, 1973.

Pickering, Kathleen Ann. *Lakota Culture, World Economy.* Lincoln: University of Nebraska Press, 2000.

Pollack, Norman. "The Myth of Populist Anti-Semitism." *American Historical Review* 68 (October 1962): 76-80.

Popper, Deborah Epstein, and Frank J. Popper. "The Great Plains From Dust to Dust: A Daring Proposal for Dealing with an Inevitable Disaster." *Planning* 12 (December 1987): 12-18.

Powell, John Wesley. *Report on the Lands of the Arid Region of the United States, with a More Detailed Account of the Lands of Utah.* Edited by Wallace Stegner. Cambridge: Belknap Press of Harvard, 1962.

Pratt, William C. "South Dakota Populism and its Historians." *South Dakota History* 22 (Winter 1992): 309-29.

Pressler, Larry. *U.S. Senators from the Prairie.* Vermillion: Dakota Press, 1982.

Prucha, Francis Paul, ed. *Documents of United States Indian Policy.* Lincoln: University of Nebraska Press, 1975.

Pulling, Hazel Adele. "History of the Range Cattle Industry of Dakota." *South Dakota Historical Collections* 20 (Pierre: State Historical Society, 1940): 467-521.

Putnam, Robert D. *Bowling Alone: The Collapse and Revival of American Community.* New York: Simon & Schuster, 2000.

Qualey, Carleton C. *Norwegian Settlement in the United States.* Northfield: Norwegian American Historical Association, 1938.

Rambow, Charles. "Ku Klux Klan in the 1920s: A Concentration on the Black Hills." *South Dakota History* 4 (Winter 1973): 63-81.

Ravage, John W., ed. *Black Pioneers: Images of the Black Experience on the North American Frontier.* Salt Lake City: University of Utah Press, 1997.

Raventon, Edward. *Island in the Plains: A Black Hills Natural History.* Boulder: Johnson Books, 1994.

Ravndal, G. Bie. "The Scandinavian Pioneers of South Dakota." *South Dakota Historical Collections* 12 (Pierre: State Historical Society, 1924): 297-330.

Red Shirt, Delphine. *Bead on an Anthill: A Lakota Childhood.* Lincoln: University of Nebraska Press, 1998.

Reed, Dorinda Riessen. *The Woman Suffrage Movement in South Dakota.* Governmental Research Bureau, Report 41. Vermillion: University of South Dakota, 1958.

Reeves, George S. *A Man from South Dakota.* New York: E. P. Dutton & Co., 1950.

Reinhardt, Akim D. "Spontaneous Combustion: Prelude to Wounded Knee 1973." *South Dakota History* 29 (Fall 1999): 229-44.

Richards, Marilee, ed. "Life Anew for Czech Immigrants: The Letters of Marie and Vavrin Stritecky." *South Dakota History* 11 (Fall/Winter 1981): 253-304.

Richter, Anthony H. "'Gebt ihr den Vorzug': The German Language Press of North and South Dakota." *South Dakota History* 10 (Summer 1980): 189-209.

_____. "A Heritage of Faith: Religion and the German Settlers of South Dakota." *South Dakota History* 21 (Summer 1991): 155-72.

Riggs, Thomas L. "A Buffalo Hunt." *South Dakota Historical Collections* 5 (Pierre: State Historical Society, 1910): 95-97.

Robinson III, Charles M. *General Crook and the Western Frontier.* Norman: University of Oklahoma Press, 2001.

Robinson, Doane. "Divorce in Dakota." *South Dakota Historical Collections* 12 (Pierre: State Historical Society, 1924): 268-80.

_____. *History of South Dakota*, 2 vols. Chicago: B.F. Bowen & Co., 1904.

Robinson, Elwyn B. *History of North Dakota*. Lincoln: University of Nebraska Press, 1966.

Robinson, Ron. *Diamond Trump: Events Surrounding the Great Powder-house Blowup by the Man Who Lit the Fuse*. Sioux Falls: Ex Machina Publishing, 2000.

_____. *Thunder Dreamer*. Vermillion: University of South Dakota Press, 1996.

Rochín, Refugio I. "Latinos on the Great Plains: An Overview." *Great Plains Research* 10 (Fall 2000): 243-52.

Rölvaag, O. E. *Giants in the Earth*. New York: Harper & Bros., 1927.

_____. *The Third Life of Per Smevik*. Minneapolis: Dillon Press, Inc., 1971.

_____. *When the Wind is in the South, and Other Stories*. Edited and translated by Solveig Zempel. Sioux Falls: Center for Western Studies, 1984.

Ronda, James P., and Nancy Tystad Koupal. *Finding Lewis and Clark: Old Trails, New Directions*. Pierre: South Dakota State Historical Society Press, 2004.

Rosa, Joseph G. *They Called Him Wild Bill: The Life and Adventures of James Butler Hickok*. Norman: University of Oklahoma Press, 1964.

Russell, William H. "Promoters and Promotion Literature of Dakota Territory." *South Dakota Historical Collections* 26 (Pierre: State Historical Society, 1952): 435-55.

Ryder, David W. *The Merrill Story*. San Francisco: The Merrill Co., 1958.

Sannes, Erling N. "Knowledge is Power: The Knights of Labor in South Dakota." *South Dakota History* 22 (Winter 1992): 400-30.

Savage, W. Sherman. *Blacks in the West*. Greenwich: Praeger Publishing Company, 1976.

Schell, Herbert S. *Dakota Territory During the Eighteen Sixties*. Governmental Research Bureau, Report 50. Vermillion: University of South Dakota, 1954.

_____. *History of South Dakota*. 4th ed., rev. with a Preface and New Chapters by John E. Miller. Pierre: South Dakota State Historical Society Press, 2004.

Schellenberg, James A. *Conflict Between Communities: American County Seat Wars*. New York: Paragon House, 1987.

Schuler, Harold H. *A Bridge Apart: History of Early Pierre and Fort Pierre*. Pierre: State Publishing Co., 1987.

_____. *Fort Sisseton*. Sioux Falls: Center for Western Studies, 1996.

_____. *Fort Sully: Guns at Sunset*. Vermillion: University of South Dakota Press, 1992.

_____. "Patriotic Pageantry: Presidential Visits to South Dakota." *South Dakota History* 30 (Winter 2000): 339-90.

Shaw, James H. "How Many Bison Populated Western Rangelands?" *Rangelands Magazine,* October 1995, 148-50.

Smith, Duane. *Staking a Claim in History: The Evolution of Homestake Mining Company*. Walnut Creek: Homestake Mining Company, 2001.

Smith, G. Hubert. *The Explorations of the La Verendryes in the Northern Plains, 1738-43*. Edited by W. Raymond Wood. Lincoln: University of Nebraska Press, 1980.

Smith, Rex Alan. *The Carving of Mount Rushmore*. New York: Abbeville Press, 1985.

_____. *The Moon of Popping Trees: The Tragedy at Wounded Knee and the End of the Indian Wars*. Lincoln: University of Nebraska Press, 1975.

Sneen, Donald. *Through Trials and Triumphs: A History of Augustana College*. Sioux Falls: Center for Western Studies, 1985.

Sneve, Virginia Driving Hawk. *Completing the Circle*. Lincoln: University of Nebraska Press, 1995.

_____. *That They May Have Life: The Episcopal Church in South Dakota, 1859-1976*. New York: Seabury Press, 1977.

Solon, Eleanor. *We Walk By Faith: The Growth of the Catholic Faith in Western South Dakota*. Strasbourg, France: Editions du Signe, 2002.

South Dakota Agriculture. Pierre: South Dakota Agricultural Statistics Service, 1919-present.

South Dakota Department of Tourism. *Report 2001*. Pierre: South Dakota Department of Tourism, 2001.

South Dakota Federal Writers' Project, Works Progress Administration, comp. *A South Dakota Guide*. Pierre: South Dakota Guide Commission, 1938.

South Dakota Legislative Research Council, comp. *Biographical Directory of the South Dakota Legislature, 1889-1989*. 2 vols. Pierre: South Dakota Legislative Research Council, 1989.

_____. *Economic and Fiscal Impacts of the South Dakota Gambling Industry*. Pierre: South Dakota Legislative Research Council, 1998.

Spring, Agnes Wright. *The Cheyenne and Black Hills Stage and Express Routes*. Lincoln: University of Nebraska Press, 1967.

St. Pierre, Mark. *Madonna Swan: A Lakota Woman's Story*. Norman: University of Oklahoma Press, 1991.

Starita, Joe. *The Dull Knifes of Pine Ridge: A Lakota Odyssey*. New York: Berkley Books, 1995.

Strain, David F. *Black Hills Hay Camp, Images and Perspectives of Early Rapid City*. Rapid City: Dakota West Books and Fenske Printing, Inc., 1989.

Sunder, John E. *The Fur Trade on the Upper Missouri, 1840-1865*. Norman: University of Oklahoma Press, 1965.

Sundstrom, Jessie Y. *Custer County History to 1976*. Custer: Custer County Historical Society, 1977.

_____. *Pioneers and Custer State Park: A History of Custer State Park and Northcentral Custer County*. Custer: self-published, 1994.

Sutley, Zachary Taylor. *The Last Frontier*. New York: Macmillan Company, 1930.

Tallent, Annie D. *The Black Hills; or, The Last Hunting Ground of the Dakotahs*. Sioux Falls: Brevet Press, 1974.

Thompson, Harry F. "History, Historicity, and the Western American Novel: Frederick Manfred's *Scarlet Plume* and the Dakota War of 1862," *Western American Literature* 37 (Spring 2002): 50-82.

_____. "Meriwether Lewis and His Son: The Claim of Joseph DeSomet Lewis and the Problem of History," *North Dakota History* 60 (Winter 2000): 24- 37. Reprinted in David Kvernes, ed., *The Lewis and Clark Expedition: Then and Now*. Sioux Falls: Center for Western Studies, 2004, 97-115.

_____. et al., eds. *A Common Land, A Diverse People: Ethnic Identity on the Prairie Plains*. Sioux Falls: Nordland Heritage Foundation, 1986.

Thomson, Frank. *The Thoen Stone: A Saga of the Black Hills*. Detroit: The Harlo Press, 1966.

Thwaites, Reuben Gold, ed. *Original Journals of the Lewis and Clark Expedition, 1804-1806*. 8 vols., reprinted 1904-1905. New York: Antiquarian Press, 1959.

Turchen, Lesta V., and James D. McLaird. *The Black Hills Expedition of 1875*. Mitchell: Dakota Wesleyan University Press, 1975.

Turner, Frederick Jackson. "The Significance of the Frontier in American History." *Annual Report of the American Historical Association*. Washington, D.C.: Government Printing Office, 1894, 199-227.

Umberger, Mary L. "Casting the Buffalo Commons: A Rhetorical Analysis of Print Media Coverage of the Buffalo Commons Proposal for the Great Plains." *Great Plains Quarterly* 22 (Spring 2002): 99-114.

Utley, Robert M. *Cavalier in Buckskin: George Armstrong Custer and the Western Military Frontier*. Norman: University of Oklahoma Press, 1988.

_____. *The Indian Frontier of the American West, 1846-1890*. Albuquerque: University of New Mexico Press, 1984.

_____. *The Last Days of the Sioux Nation*. New Haven: Yale University Press, 1963.

VanEpps-Taylor, Betti C. *Oscar Micheaux: Dakota Homesteader, Author, Pioneer Film Maker*. Rapid City: Dakota West Books, 1999.

Van Nuys, Laura Bower. *The Family Band*. Lincoln: University of Nebraska Press, 1961.

Veblen, Thorstein. "The Country Town," in *Absentee Ownership and Business Enterprise in Recent Times: The Case of America*. New York: Augustus M. Kelley, 1923, 142-65.

Wallach, Bret. "The Return of the Prairie." *Landscape* 28: 3 (1985): 1-6.

Watson, Robert P., ed. *George McGovern: A Political Life, A Political Legacy*. Pierre: South Dakota State Historical Society Press, 2004.

Webb, Daryl. "Crusade: George McGovern's Opposition to the Vietnam War." *South Dakota History* 28 (Fall 1998): 161-90.

_____. "'Just Principles Never Die': Brown County Populists, 1890-1900." *South Dakota History* 22 (Winter 1992): 366-99.

Webb, Walter Prescott. *The Great Plains*. Boston: Ginn & Co., 1931.

Weeks, Philip. *Farewell, My Nation: The American Indian and the United States in the Nineteenth Century*. Wheeling, IL: Harlan Davidson, Inc., 1990.

White, Robert A. "The Lower-Class 'Culture of Excitement' Among the Contemporary Sioux," in Ethel Nurge, ed., *The Modern Sioux: Social Systems and Reservation Culture*. Lincoln: University of Nebraska Press, 1970, 175-97.

Wik, Reynold M. "Radio in the 1920s: A Social Force in South Dakota." *South Dakota History* 11 (Spring 1981): 93-109.

Wilder, Laura Ingalls. *By the Shores of Silver Lake*. New York: Harper & Bros., 1939.

_____. *Little Town on the Prairie*. New York: Harper & Bros., 1941.

Wishart, David J., ed. *Encyclopedia of the Great Plains*. Lincoln: University of Nebraska Press, 2004.

Wolfe, Mark S. *Boots on Bricks*. Deadwood: Deadwood Historic Preservation Commission, 1996.

Wolff, David A. "Mining Ground on the Fringe: The Horseshoe-Mogul Mining Company of the Northern Black Hills." *Mining History Journal* (1995): 15-27.

_____. "No Matter How You Do It, Fraud is Fraud: Another Look at Black Hills Mining Scandals." *South Dakota History* 33 (Summer 2003): 91-119.

_____. "Pyritic Smelting at Deadwood: A Temporary Solution to Refractory Ores." *South Dakota History* 15 (Winter 1985): 312-39.

Wyman, Walker D. *Nothing but Prairie and Sky: Life on the Dakota Range in the Early Days*. Norman: University of Oklahoma Press, 1954.

Yeager, Anson. *Anson Yeager's Stories, Vol. 1: Northern Plains Adventures, Vol. 2: Famous Faces and Places*. Sioux Falls: Center for Western Studies, 2001.

Young, Jr., Otis E. *Western Mining*. Norman: University of Oklahoma Press, 1970.

Zhu, Liping, and Rose Estep Fosha. *Ethnic Oasis: The Chinese in the Black Hills*. Pierre: South Dakota State Historical Society Press, 2004.

Zimmerman, Bill. *Airlift to Wounded Knee*. Chicago: Swallow Press, 1976.

Zimmerman, Larry J. *Peoples of Prehistoric South Dakota*. Lincoln: University of Nebraska Press, 1985.

Zuercher, Fred W. "A Measure of Party Strength in the Fifty States." *Public Affairs* 32. Vermillion: Governmental Research Bureau, 1968.

Index

613

Talleyrand, Charles-Maurice de, 57
Talliaferro, Lawrence, 423
Tatanka, 74, 282, 394
Tax Study Committee, 215
Taylor, C. N., 166
Taylor, Joseph, 306
Taylor, W. W., 197
Taylor Grazing Act, 276
Tecumseh, 67, 70, 255-256, 484
Tekakwitha Fine Arts Center, 497
Tekakwitha Hospital, 328
Telecommunication Act of 1996, 452, 478-479
telegraph, 452-454
telephone (telephony), 454, 478-479, 481-482
teletype, 458
television, 193, 221, 239-240, 357, 372, 375, 380, 413-415, 443, 452, 464, 466, 468-473, 475, 477-482, 496, 552-553
temperatures, 24-28, 33-34, 41, 246, 270
Tennessee, 98, 143, 148, 157
Terenne, R. Auzias, 268
Termes, Dick, 395, 415
Terraville, SD, 302, 304
territorial politics, 95-97, 102, 110-111, 114, 342, 345
Terry, Alfred, 108, 292
Terry Peak, 24, 315
Teton River, 38, 54
Teton Sioux (see also Lakota Sioux), 3, 6, 9, 38, 44-45, 50, 53-54, 59, 61, 66, 94, 158, 169, 259-260, 262, 492
Tevis, Lloyd, 301
Texas, 86, 147, 259-260, 262, 265-266, 270, 272-273, 381, 401, 420, 480, 497, 550
Texas Longhorns, 259, 262
Tharaldson, Ditteff, 127
theater, 254, 298, 397, 407-413, 415-418, 422, 465, 470
Theisz, R. D., 406
Thoen, Louis, 291
Thomas, Bernard Preston, 395
Thomas, Helen, 477
Thomas, Jess, 412, 418, 421
Thomas, Steve, 394
Thompson, Andrew, 127
Thompson, Esten, 127
Thompson, Harry F., viii, 65, 560, 582
Thompson, John, 126-127
Thompson, Knut, 127-128
Thompson, Ronelle, viii

Thomson, John, 334
Thomson, Verl, 465
Thorpe, F. L., 314
Three Forks, 51, 63
Thrond, Elizabeth, viii
Thunderhead Mountain, 494
thunderstorms, 25, 28, 31, 38
Thune, John, 222
Thurston, Mary Worthy, 376-377
Tibbs, Casey, 390
Tilford, SD, 264, 268
Tillman, George, 145
Timber Case No. 1, 308
Timber Culture Acts, 117
timber industry, 307-309
Titan Missiles, 212, 313, 479, 551, 556
tiyospaye (tiospaye), 3, 499-502, 504-506, 521
Todd, John Blair Smith, 82, 97, 100, 102, 111, 120, 162, 333
Todd, Mary, 101
Todd County, 30, 33, 510, 526
Tomac, Sanna, 403
Tomlinson, Joseph, 459
Toohey, Marie, 418
Toohey, J.M., 323
Tornado, 25, 222, 357
tourism, 309-312, 492-498
Tower Reach, 70, 80
Town Players, 422
Townley, A. C., 203
towns, 157-181, 182-193
trains, 72-73, 75-77, 83-84, 98, 106, 113, 117-118, 120, 124, 126, 128, 130, 132, 134-135, 137, 139, 146, 148, 157-159, 166, 168, 170-176, 178-181, 187-188, 195-196, 198, 200-201, 207, 212, 223, 225, 227-228, 230, 240, 248, 257, 263, 270, 272-273, 283, 289, 292, 299, 301-306, 308-309, 315-317, 327, 332, 334-335, 337, 344, 350, 370, 372-373, 376, 394-395, 407-408, 411-412, 415, 429, 451-454, 457, 459-461, 463, 484-489, 491-492, 497, 535, 556
transportation, 483-492
trappers, 51, 53, 60-62, 64, 66-68, 86, 144, 290-291, 331, 406, 484, 492
Trautwein, George, 419
Traverse des Sioux, 87, 163
treaties, 48-49, 63, 69-72, 75-76, 82, 84, 86-88, 90-92, 95, 97-98, 100-101, 105, 108,

110, 117, 162-163, 169, 175, 256-262, 289, 291-293, 295-296, 332, 335, 370, 423-424, 432-433, 456, 485-486, 488, 502, 508-509, 511, 513-517, 526-529
Treaty of Fort Wadsworth, 92, 516
Treaty of Ghent, 63
Treaty of Utrecht, 48-49
Treaty of Washington, 70, 87
Treeby, Sherri, 394
tribal benefits, 517-522
tribal distinctions, 524-533
tribal enrollment, 522-524
Trinitarians, 336
Trinity Heights, 393
Trinity Lutheran Church (Moe Parish), 340
Tripp, SD, 27, 32, 132, 176, 446, 526
Tripp County, 26, 28, 149
Troy, Steve, 395
Troy Township, 149
Truman, Harry, 240
Trumbo, Caroline, 79
Trumbo Station, 77
Truteau, Jean Baptist, 53, 60, 62, 77, 492, 561
Tsalagi, 361
Tschetter, Paul, 337
Tubbs, Poker Alice, 302
Turing, Alan, 452, 474
Turkey Creek, 19
Turkey Red, 372
Turkey Ridge, SD, 19
Turkey Track, 266
Turner, Frederick Jackson, 534-535, 557
Turner, John, 109
Turner County, 98, 109, 126, 130, 133-134, 137, 168, 285, 337, 407, 413, 479, 534-535, 552
Turner Hall, 407, 413
Tuskegee Institute, 154-155
Tute, James, 52
Twain, Mark, 456-457
Twenty-fifth Infantry (Colored), 147-148
Twin Cities, 227-228
Two Bulls, Nellie, 417
Two Eagles, Edward, 388
Two Kettle, 44, 46, 70, 83, 93-94
Tyndall, SD, 77, 102-103, 134, 176, 328-330, 435-436
Tyrolean, 135
Tyson Company, 544

U.S. Air Force, 313, 404
U.S. Army, 39, 42, 68-69, 73-74,
77, 79, 81, 83, 86-88, 90, 93,
100, 111-113, 139, 147, 402,
423-424, 511, 520, 531
U.S. Army Corps of Engineers,
39, 73, 83, 212, 313, 520, 531
U.S. Banking, Superintendent
of, 206
U.S. Bureau of Indian Affairs
(BIA), 84, 96, 102-105, 111-
112, 216, 259, 424-425, 427-
430, 509, 515, 520
U.S. Bureau of Prisons, 155
U.S. Civil Service, 114, 425, 525
U.S. Commission on Civil Rights,
154
U.S. Commissioner of Indian
Affairs, 84, 111-112
U.S. Commissioner of Public
Lands, 104
U.S. Constitution, 48, 96, 111,
114-116, 141, 218-219, 249,
339, 346, 508, 512-513, 515,
521, 525
U.S. Court of Claims, 510, 525,
529
U.S. Delegate to Congress, 76,
82, 95-102, 104, 106, 108, 110,
112-114, 164
U.S. Department of Agriculture
(USDA), 155, 235, 243, 246-
247, 251, 257, 271, 276-278,
281, 284-285, 543, 545
U.S. Department of Defense,
212, 317
U.S. Department of Health and
Human Services, 428, 430
U.S. Department of War, 313,
468, 515
U.S. District Court, 278, 429,
532, 525
U.S. Eighth Circuit Court of
Appeals, 249, 279, 430
U.S. Field Matrons, 425
U.S. Forest Service, 551
U.S. Geological Survey, 155, 496
U.S. House of Representatives,
96, 101, 104, 113, 164, 206,
210, 212-214, 216-217, 223-
224, 228, 245, 250, 274
U.S. Indian Affairs,
Superintendent of, 96, 102-
104, 259
U.S. Indian Agency, 43, 46, 69,
77, 79, 87-89, 91, 98, 101,
111-112, 166, 319, 424-425

U.S. Indian Agent, 52, 70, 76, 79-
80, 95, 97-98, 101, 104, 108,
319, 321, 369, 375, 423
U.S. Indian Field Service, 101-
103, 108, 112, 319, 425, 515,
518
U.S. Indian Office Circular, 509-
510, 521
U.S. Interior Department, 70, 86,
112, 162, 321, 516, 518
U.S. Land Office, 75, 91, 102,
115, 159-160, 163, 165-166,
283, 308
U.S. Military Academy, 100
U.S. National Historic Landmark,
58
U.S. Navy, 463
U.S. Park Service, x, 530-531
U.S. Postal Service (see also mail
and post office), 78-79, 113,
148, 166, 373, 451, 462, 476,
520
U.S. Public Health Service, 425,
428-431
U.S. Public Instruction,
Superintendent of, 96, 107,
345-346, 352
U.S. Secretary of Agriculture,
212, 215-216, 234-235, 240-
243, 245-246, 250-251
U.S. Secretary of Immigration for
Dakota Territory, 119
U.S. Selective Service, 211, 238
U.S. Senate, 87, 96, 101-102,
105, 114, 195, 197, 201-202,
205, 208-211, 220-222, 231,
243, 257, 464
U.S. Senator, 106, 113, 167, 196,
202, 206, 548
U.S. Superintendent of Indian
Affairs, 96, 102-104, 259
U.S. Supreme Court, 110, 114,
198, 209, 235, 263, 277, 430,
518, 525, 529
U.S. Treasury, 86, 516, 530
U.S. West, 478
Unger, Douglas, 366
Uniform Benefits Package, 449
Union County, 27, 103-104, 140,
165, 259-260, 334-335, 487
Union Jack, 54, 62
Union Pacific Railroad, 169-170,
175, 292, 301, 303, 486, 489
United Church of Canistota, 443
United Church of Christ (UCC),
330, 341
United Clinic, 445
United Family Farmers, 219

United Farmers League (UFL),
234
United Flour Milling Company of
Minneapolis, 178
United Methodist Church, 330,
420, 443
United States-Canada, 63
Unity Productions, 418
Universal Turing Machine, 452,
474
University of Alaska, 394
University of California, ix, 368
University of Chicago, 378
University of Colorado, iii
University of Illinois, 394, 402
University of Indiana, 115
University of Iowa, 122, 403
University of Michigan, 345
University of Minnesota, 375,
404, 432, 441-443
University of Minnesota Medical
School, 442
University of Missouri, 381
University of Nebraska Press, ix-
x, 361, 375, 378, 381, 527
University of Oslo, 358
University of Sioux Falls, 343,
401-402, 411
University of South Dakota
(USD), vii-xi, xiv, 75, 155,
168, 183, 220, 222-223, 333,
352, 354, 365-366, 379-381,
386-387, 394, 399-400, 402-
404, 409-410, 414-415, 420,
422, 435, 440-441, 445, 452,
464, 472-473, 477, 480, 496,
507-508, 512, 515, 527, 530-
531
University of South Dakota Brass
Choir, 415
University of South Dakota
Community Orchestra, 422
University of South Dakota
Department of Contemporary
Media, 477
University of South Dakota Law
School, 121, 222-223
University of South Dakota
Medical School, 441
University of South Dakota Press,
xi
University of South Dakota
Volante, 472
University of Vermont, 121
University of Wisconsin, ix, 167,
419, 474, 527
University of Wisconsin Pro Arte
String Quartet, 419

Contributors

Ruth Ann Alexander, Ph.D., is professor emeritus of English, South Dakota State University, and the author of *Patches in a History Quilt: Episcopal Women in the Diocese of South Dakota, 1868-2000.*

Vine Deloria, Jr., is professor emeritus of history at the University of Colorado and author of numerous books, including *Custer Died for Your Sins, God Is Red: A Native View of Religion,* and *Power and Place: Indian Education in America.*

Edward P. Hogan, Ph.D., is professor emeritus of geography, South Dakota State University, the State Geographer of South Dakota, and author of *The Geography of South Dakota.*

Carol Goss Hoover, D.Min., teaches at Colorado Technical University and Mount Marty College and is co-author of *Sioux Country: A History of Indian-white Relations.*

Herbert T. Hoover, Ph.D., is professor of history at the University of South Dakota and author and/or co-author of numerous publications, including *To Be an Indian: An Oral History,* and *South Dakota Leaders: From Pierre Chouteau, Jr., to Oscar Howe.*

Arthur R. Huseboe, Ph.D., is executive director of the Center for Western Studies, holder of the NEH Chair in Regional Heritage at Augustana College, and, with Arthur Amiotte, is the author of *An Illustrated History of the Arts in South Dakota.*

Bob Lee is a journalist and author of *Fort Meade and the Black Hills* and *The Black Hills after Custer.*

John E. Miller, Ph.D., is professor emeritus of history at South Dakota State University and author of *Looking for History on Highway 14* and *Becoming Laura Ingalls Wilder: The Woman Behind the Legend.*

Michael J. Mullin, Ph.D., is professor of history at Augustana College and the author of the entry on Francis Parkman for the *Dictionary of Literary Biography.*

Rex C. Myers, Ph.D., teaches at Northwest College and is the author of *Lizzie: The Letters of Elizabeth Chester Fisk, 1864-1893.*

Gary D. Olson, Ph.D., is professor emeritus of history at Augustana College and the author of *Sioux Falls, South Dakota: A Pictorial History.*

Lynwood E. Oyos, Ph.D., is professor emeritus of history at Augustana College and author of *The Family Farmers' Advocate: South Dakota Farmers Union, 1914-2000.*

Ron Robinson, M.F.A., is professor emeritus of English and journalism at Augustana College and the author of the two novels *Thunder Dreamer* and *Diamond Trump.*

Virginia Driving Hawk Sneve, LL.D., of Rapid City, South Dakota, is the author of *Completing the Circle* and *Grandpa Was a Cowboy and an Indian, and Other Stories* and recipient of the National Humanities Medal and the South Dakota Living Indian Treasure Award.

Betti C. VanEpps-Taylor, M.A., of Buhl, Idaho, is the author of *Oscar Micheaux: A Biography.*

Harry F. Thompson, Ph.D., is the director of research collections and publications at the Center for Western Studies, Augustana College, and the principal editor of *A Common Land, A Diverse People: Ethnic Identity on the Prairie Plains.*

David A. Wolff, Ph.D., is associate professor of history at Black Hills State University and author of *Industrializing the Rockies: Growth, Competition, and Turmoil in the Coalfields of Colorado and Wyoming, 1868-1914.*